Marketing

An Introduction

Global Edition

Marketing

An Introduction

Global Edition

GARY ARMSTRONG

University of North Carolina

PHILIP KOTLER

Northwestern University

Boston   Columbus   Indianapolis   New York   San Francisco   Upper Saddle River
Amsterdam   Cape Town   Dubai   London   Madrid   Milan   Munich   Paris   Montreal   Toronto
Delhi   Mexico City   Sao Paulo   Sydney   Hong Kong   Seoul   Singapore   Taipei   Tokyo

Editorial Director: Sally Yagan
Editor in Chief: Eric Svendsen
Executive Editor: Melissa Sabella
Acquisitions Editor, Global Edition: Steven Jackson
Product Development Manager: Ashley Santora
Editorial Project Manager: Kierra Kashickey
Editorial Assistant: Karin Williams
Editorial Assistant, Global Edition: Elizabeth Walne
Director of Marketing: Patrice Lumumba Jones
Senior Marketing Manager: Anne Fahlgren
Marketing Manager, International: Dean Erasmus
Marketing Assistant: Melinda Jensen
Senior Managing Editor: Judy Leale
Senior Production Project Manager: Karalyn Holland
Senior Operations Supervisor: Arnold Vila
Operations Specialist: Ilene Kahn
Design Director: Christy Mahon
Senior Art Director: Janet Slowik
Interior Designer: Karen Quigley
Cover Designer: Jodi Notowitz
Cover Image: © Maksim Toome-Fotolia.com
Manager, Visual Research: Beth Brenzel
Manager, Rights and Permissions: Shannon Barbe
Image Permission Coordinator: Richard Rodrigues
Manager, Cover Visual Research & Permissions: Karen Sanatar
Media Editor: Denise Vaughn
Media Project Manager: Lisa Rinaldi
Full-Service Project Management: S4Carlisle Publishing Services
Composition: S4Carlisle Publishing Services
Printer/Binder: Courier/Kendallville
Cover Printer: Lehigh-Phoenix Color/Hagerstown
Text Font: 9/12 LinoLetter Roman

Credits and acknowledgments borrowed from other sources and reproduced, with permission, in this textbook appear on appropriate page within text (or on page 627).

Microsoft® and Windows® are registered trademarks of the Microsoft Corporation in the U.S.A. and other countries. Screen shots and icons reprinted with permission from the Microsoft Corporation. This book is not sponsored or endorsed by or affiliated with the Microsoft Corporation.

This is a special edition of an established title widely used by colleges and universities throughout the world. Pearson published this exclusive edition for the benefit of students outside the United States and Canada. If you purchased this book within the United States or Canada you should be aware that it has been imported without the approval of the Publisher or the Author.

10 9 8 7 6 5 4 3 2 1

ISBN 10:   0-13-509486-0
ISBN 13: 978-0-13-509486-0

To Kathy, Betty, Mandy, Matt, KC, Keri,
Delaney, Molly, Macy, and Ben; Nancy, Amy, Melissa, and Jessica

About the Authors

As a team, Gary Armstrong and Philip Kotler provide a blend of skills uniquely suited to writing an introductory marketing text. Professor Armstrong is an award-winning teacher of undergraduate business students. Professor Kotler is one of the world's leading authorities on marketing. Together they make the complex world of marketing practical, approachable, and enjoyable.

Gary Armstrong is Crist W. Blackwell Distinguished Professor Emeritus of Undergraduate Education in the Kenan-Flagler Business School at the University of North Carolina at Chapel Hill. He holds undergraduate and masters degrees in business from Wayne State University in Detroit, and he received his Ph.D. in marketing from Northwestern University. Dr. Armstrong has contributed numerous articles to leading business journals. As a consultant and researcher, he has worked with many companies on marketing research, sales management, and marketing strategy.

But Professor Armstrong's first love has always been teaching. His long-held Blackwell Distinguished Professorship is the only permanent endowed professorship for distinguished undergraduate teaching at the University of North Carolina at Chapel Hill. He has been very active in the teaching and administration of Kenan-Flagler's undergraduate program. His administrative posts have included Chair of Marketing, Associate Director of the Undergraduate Business Program, Director of the Business Honors Program, and many others. Through the years, he has worked closely with business student groups and has received several campuswide and Business School teaching awards. He is the only repeat recipient of the school's highly regarded Award for Excellence in Undergraduate Teaching, which he received three times. Most recently, Professor Armstrong received the UNC Board of Governors Award for Excellence in Teaching, the highest teaching honor bestowed by the sixteen-campus University of North Carolina system.

Philip Kotler is S. C. Johnson & Son Distinguished Professor of International Marketing at the Kellogg School of Management, Northwestern University. He received his master's degree at the University of Chicago and his Ph.D. at M.I.T., both in economics. Dr. Kotler is author of *Marketing Management* (Pearson Prentice Hall), now in its thirteenth edition and the world's most widely used marketing textbook in graduate schools of business worldwide. He has authored dozens of other successful books and has written more than 100 articles in leading journals. He is the only three-time winner of the coveted Alpha Kappa Psi award for the best annual article in the *Journal of Marketing*.

Professor Kotler was named the first recipient of two major awards: the *Distinguished Marketing Educator of the Year Award* given by the American Marketing Association and the *Philip Kotler Award for Excellence in Health Care Marketing* presented by the Academy for Health Care Services Marketing. His numerous other major honors include the Sales and Marketing Executives International *Marketing Educator of the Year Award;* The European Association of Marketing Consultants and Trainers *Marketing Excellence Award;* the *Charles Coolidge Parlin Marketing Research Award;* and the *Paul D. Converse Award,* given by the American Marketing Association to honor "outstanding contributions to science in marketing." In a recent *Financial Times* poll of 1,000 senior executives across the world, Professor Kotler was ranked as the fourth "most influential business writer/guru" of the twenty-first century.

Dr. Kotler has served as chairman of the College on Marketing of the Institute of Management Sciences, a director of the American Marketing Association, and a trustee of the Marketing Science Institute. He has consulted with many major U.S. and international companies in the areas of marketing strategy and planning, marketing organization, and international marketing. He has traveled and lectured extensively throughout Europe, Asia, and South America, advising companies and governments about global marketing practices and opportunities.

Brief Contents

Contents

11

5 Understanding Consumer and Business Buyer Behavior 162

6 Customer-Driven Marketing Strategy: Creating Value for Target Customers 200

> ❯ **REST STOP:** Reviewing the Concepts **567**, Navigating the Key Terms **568**, Travel Log **568**, Under the Hood: Marketing Technology **569**, Staying on the Road: Marketing Ethics **569**, Rough Road Ahead: Marketing and the Economy **569**, Travel Budget: Marketing by the Numbers **570**, Drive In: Video Case **570**

Preface

THE TENTH EDITION OF *MARKETING: AN INTRODUCTION!*

ON THE ROAD TO LEARNING MARKETING!

The tenth edition of *Marketing: An Introduction* makes the road to learning and teaching marketing more effective, easier, and more enjoyable than ever. Its streamlined approach strikes a careful balance between depth of coverage and ease of learning. The tenth edition's brand new learning design—with integrative Road Map features at the start and end of each chapter and insightful author comments throughout—enhances understanding. And when combined with mymarketinglab, our online homework and personalized study tool, *Marketing: An Introduction* ensures that you will come to class well prepared and leave class with a richer understanding of basic marketing concepts, strategies, and practices. So fasten your seat belt and let's get rolling!

THE MARKETING JOURNEY: CREATING AND CAPTURING CUSTOMER VALUE

Top marketers all share a common goal: putting the consumer at the heart of marketing. Today's marketing is all about creating customer value and building profitable customer relationships. It starts with understanding consumer needs and wants, deciding which target markets the organization can serve best, and developing a compelling value proposition by which the organization can attract, keep, and grow targeted consumers. If the organization does these things well, it will reap the rewards in terms of market share, profits, and customer equity. In the tenth edition of *Marketing: An Introduction,* you'll see how *customer value*—creating it and capturing it—drives every good marketing strategy.

New in the Tenth Edition

We've thoroughly revised the tenth edition of *Marketing: An Introduction* to reflect the major trends and forces impacting marketing in this era of customer value and relationships. Here are just some of the major changes you'll find in this edition.

- The tenth edition has a **completely new learning design**! The text's more active and integrative presentation includes new in-chapter learning enhancements that help to ease you down the road to learning marketing. The newly designed chapter-opening layout provides a *Road Map* that previews and positions each chapter and its key concepts, outlines chapter objectives and links them by page number to specific chapter sections, and brings important chapter themes to life in an annotated *First Stop* chapter-opening story. Explanatory author comments on major chapter sections and author-annotated figures help to simplify and organize chapter material. End-of-chapter features summarize important concepts and highlight important themes, such as marketing and the economy, technology, ethics, and marketing financial analysis. In all, the new design enhances student understanding and facilitates learning.
- Throughout the tenth edition, you will find important new coverage of the rapidly **changing nature of customer relationships** with companies and brands. Today's marketers aim to create deeper consumer involvement and a sense of community surrounding a brand—to make the brand a meaningful part of consumers'

conversations and their lives. New relationship-building tools include everything from Web sites, blogs, in-person events, and video sharing, to online communities and social networks such as Facebook, YouTube, Twitter, or a company's own social networking sites.

- New coverage in every chapter shows how companies are dealing with **marketing and the turbulent economy** in the aftermath of the recent worldwide economic meltdown. Starting with a major new section in Chapter 1 and continuing with discussions and examples integrated throughout the text, the tenth edition shows how, now more than ever, marketers must focus on creating customer value and sharpening their value propositions to serve the needs of today's more frugal consumers. At the end of each chapter, a new feature—*Rough Road Ahead: Marketing and the Economy*—provides real examples for discussion and learning.

- A revised Chapter 16 pulls marketing together under an important new **sustainable marketing** framework. Additional discussions throughout the tenth edition show how sustainable marketing calls for socially and environmentally responsible actions that meet both the immediate and the future needs of customers, the company, and society as a whole.

- Increasingly, marketing is taking the form of two-way conversations between consumers and brands. The tenth edition contains new material on the exciting trend toward **consumer-generated marketing**, by which marketers invite consumers to play a more active role in providing customer insights (Chapter 4), shaping new products (Chapter 8), developing or passing along brand messages (Chapter 12), interacting in customer communities (Chapters 5, 12, and 14), and other developments.

- This edition provides new and expanded discussions of new **marketing technologies**, from "Web 3.0" in Chapter 1 to neuromarketing in Chapter 5 to RFID in Chapter 10 to the new-age digital marketing and online technologies in Chapters 1, 5, 12, and 14.

- In line with the text's emphasis on **measuring and managing return on marketing**, we've added end-of-chapter financial and quantitative marketing exercises that let you apply analytical thinking to relevant concepts in each chapter and link chapter concepts to the text's innovative *Appendix 2: Marketing by the Numbers*.

- The tenth edition provides refreshed and expanded coverage of the explosive developments in **integrated marketing communications** and **direct and online marketing**. It tells how marketers are incorporating a host of new digital and direct approaches to build and create more targeted, personal, and interactive customer relationships. No other text provides more current or encompassing coverage of these exciting developments.

- A restructured **pricing** chapter (Chapter 9) provides improved coverage of pricing strategies and tactics in an uncertain economy. And a reorganized products, services, and brands chapter (Chapter 7) helps to clarify the role of **services** in today's service economy.

REAL TRAVEL EXPERIENCES: MARKETING AT WORK

Marketing: An Introduction features in-depth, real-world examples and stories that show concepts in action and reveal the drama of modern marketing. In the tenth edition, every chapter contains with a *First Stop* opening vignette and Marketing at Work highlights that provide fresh and relevant insights into real marketing practices. Learn how:

- Web seller Zappos' obsession with creating the very best customer experience has resulted in avidly loyal customers and astronomical growth.
- Upscale discounter Target is shifting its strategy in the aftermath of the recent economic recession, now emphasizing the "pay less" side of its "Expect More. Pay Less." slogan.

- Google innovates at the speed of light—it's part of the company's DNA.
- McDonald's, the quintessentially all-American company, now sells more burgers and fries outside the United States than within.

Beyond these features, each chapter is packed with countless real, relevant, and timely examples that reinforce key concepts. No other text brings marketing to life like the tenth edition of *Marketing: An Introduction*.

MARKETING JOURNAL TRAVEL AIDS

A wealth of chapter-opening, within-chapter, and end-of-chapter learning devices help you to learn, link, and apply major concepts:

- *Chapter-opening Road Maps*. The new, more active and integrative chapter-opening spread in each chapter features a brief *Previewing the Concepts* section that introduces chapter concepts, an *Objective Outline* that outlines chapter contents and learning objectives, and a *First Stop* opening vignette—an engaging, deeply developed, illustrated, and annotated marketing story that introduces the chapter material and sparks student interest.
- *Author comments and figure annotations*. Throughout the chapter, author comments ease and enhance learning by introducing and explaining major chapter sections and figures.
- *Marketing at Work highlights*. Each chapter contains two highlight features that provide an in-depth look at real marketing practices of large and small companies.
- *Rest Stop: Reviewing the Concepts*. A summary at the end of each chapter reviews major chapter concepts and links them to chapter objectives.
- *Navigating the Key Terms*. A helpful listing of chapter key terms by order of appearance with pages numbers facilitates easy reference.
- *Travel Log*. Discussing the Issues and Application Questions help you to keep track of and apply what you've learned in the chapter.
- *Under the Hood: Marketing Technology*. Application exercises at the end of each chapter facilitate discussion of important and emerging marketing technologies in this digital age.
- *Staying on the Road: Marketing Ethics*. Situation descriptions and questions highlight important issues in marketing ethics and social responsibility at the end of each chapter.
- *Rough Road Ahead: Marketing and the Economy*. End-of-chapter situation descriptions provide for discussion of the impact of recent economic trends on consumer and marketing decisions.
- *Travel Budget: Marketing by the Numbers*. An exercise at the end of each chapter lets you apply analytical and financial thinking to relevant chapter concepts and links the chapter to Appendix 2, Marketing by the Numbers.
- *Drive In: Video Case*. Short vignettes with discussion questions appear at the end of every chapter, to be used with the set of mostly new 4- to 7-minute videos that accompany the tenth edition.
- *Marketing Plan*. Appendix 1 contains a sample marketing plan that helps you to apply important marketing planning concepts.
- *Marketing by the Numbers*. An innovative Appendix 2 provides you with a comprehensive introduction to the marketing financial analysis that helps to guide, assess, and support marketing decisions.

More than ever before, the tenth edition of *Marketing: An Introduction* provides an effective and enjoyable total package for moving you down the road to learning marketing!

A Valuable Learning Package

Custom Videos

The video library on DVD (ISBN: 0136102530) contains 18 exciting segments for this edition, including all new videos featuring:

- Monster.com's global expansion
- Zappo's direct marketing
- Radian6's unique social media monitoring software
- Plus Google, ZIBA, Progressive, Crispin Porter + Bogusky and more!

PEARSON
mymarketinglab™

mymarketinglab (www.pearsonglobaleditions.com/mymarketinglab) gives you the opportunity to test yourself on key concepts and skills, track your own progress through the course, and use the personalized study plan activities—all to help you achieve success in the classroom. The MyLab that accompanies Marketing: An Introduction includes:

- **Interactive Company Cases** for class or written discussion. These cases challenge you to apply marketing principles to real companies in real situations.
- **Careers in Marketing** information to help you discover what types of marketing jobs might best suit your specific skills and interests, offers tips on job searches, describes the many different marketing career paths available, and suggests other information resources.

Plus:

- Personalized study plans—Pre- and post-tests with remediation activities directed to help you understand and apply the concepts where you need most help.
- Self-assessments—Prebuilt self-assessment allows you to test yourself.
- Interactive elements—a wealth of hands-on activities and exercises let you experience and learn firsthand. Whether it is with the online e-book where you can search for specific keywords or page numbers, highlight specific sections, enter notes right on the e-book page, and print reading assignments with notes for later review or with other materials.
- iQuizzes—Study anytime, anywhere—iQuizzes work on any color-screen iPod and are comprised of a sequence of quiz sections, specifically created for the iPod screen.

Find out more at **www.pearsonglobaleditions.com/mymarketinglab**

Acknowledgments

No book is the work only of its authors. We greatly appreciate the valuable contributions of several people who helped make this new edition possible. We owe extra special thanks to Keri Jean Miksza for her deep and valuable involvement and advice throughout *every* phase of the project, and to her husband Pete and little daughter Lucy for sharing Keri with us during this project. We thank Andy Norman of Drake University for his skillful development of company cases and video cases, and Lew Brown of the University of North Carolina at Greensboro for his able assistance in helping to prepare selected marketing stories. Thanks also go to Laurie Babin of the University of Louisiana at Monroe for her dedicated efforts in preparing end-of-chapter materials and keeping our Marketing by the Numbers appendix fresh; Michelle Rai of Pacific Union College for updating our Marketing Plan appendix for the tenth edition; and our supplement authors, including Test Item File author Bonnie Flaherty; PowerPoint authors Deborah Utter of Boston University and Karen James of Louisiana State University at Shreveport; and Instructor Manual author Tony Henthorne of University of Nevada Las Vegas.

Many reviewers at other colleges and universities provided valuable comments and suggestions for this and previous editions. We are indebted to the following colleagues for their thoughtful inputs:

Tenth Edition Reviewers

George Bercovitz, York College
Sylvia Clark, St. John's University
Datha Damron-Martinez, Truman State University
Ivan Filby, Greenville College
John Gaskins, Longwood University
Karen Halpern, South Puget Sound Community College
Jan Hardesty, University of Arizona
Hella Elona Johnson, Olympic College
Mark Newman, Hocking College

Vic Piscatello, University of Arizona
William M. Ryan, University of Connecticut
Elliot Schreiber, Drexel University
Robert Simon, University of Nebraska, Lincoln
John Talbott, Indiana University
Rhonda Tenenbaum, Queens College
Tom Voigt, Judson University
Terry Wilson, East Stroudsburg University

Previous Reviewers

Chris Adalikwu, Concordia College
Doug Albertson, University of Portland
Christie Amato, University of North Carolina, Charlotte
Corinne Asher, Henry Ford Community College
Bruce Bailey, Otterbein College
Turina Bakken, Madison Area Technical College
David Bambridge, Warner Southern College
Donald Barnes, Mississippi State University
Susan Baxter, Bethune-Cookman College
David Beck, Delaware Valley College
Colleen Bee, University of San Diego
Kenn Bennett, Irvine Valley College
Carl Bergemann, Arapahoe Community College
Donna Bergenstock, Muhlenberg College
Charles Besio, Southern Methodist University
John Bierer, University of Southern Maine

James Black, University of Maine
Alan Blake, New Hampshire Technical Institute
David Bland, Cape Fear Community College
Ross Blankenship, State Fair Community College
Earl Boatwright, Bowling Green State University
Kimberly Boyer, Washington University
Kevin Bradord, Somerset Community College, Laurel North
Donald Brady, Millersville University
Jenell Bramlage, University of Northwestern Ohio
Frederic Brunel, Boston University
Jeff Bruns, Bacone College
Kendrick Brunson, Liberty University
Derrell Bulls, Texas Woman's University
Gary Bumgarner, Mountain Empire Community College
Dale Cake, Pennsylvania State University
Jacqueline Callery, Robert Morris College

Guadalupe Campos, Borough of Manhattan Community College

Frank Carothers, Somerset Community College

Ray Carpenter, Indian River Community College

Erin Cavusgil, Michigan State University

Larry Chase, Tompkins Cortland Community College

Yun Chu, Frostburg State University

Janet Ciccarelli, Herkimer County Community College

Patricia Clarke, Boston College

Joyce Claterbos, University of Kansas

Gloria Cockerell, Collin County Community College

D. M. Coleman, Miami University of Oxford

Kathleen Conklin, St. John Fisher College

Craig Conrad, Western Illinois University

Scott Cragin, Missouri Southern State University

Martha Cranford, Stanly Community College

Carter Crockett, Westmont College

John Cronin, Western Connecticut State University

Julia Cronin Gilmore, Bellevue University

Stanley Dabrowski, Hudson County Community College

Richard M. Daiely, University of Texas at Arlington

Cynthia Davies, Rosemont College

David Davis, South Dakota State University

Helen Davis, Jefferson Community College

Tamara Dawson, Redlands Community College

Beth Deinert, Southeast Community College

Lola Dial, Robeson Community College

Susan Dik, University of Hawaii

Claudiu Dimofte, Georgetown University

Dennis Dowds, Hudson Valley Community College

John Drea, Western Illinois University

Robert Drevs, University of Notre Dame

Jose Duran, Riverside Community College

Robert Eames, Calvin College

C. R. Echard, Glenville State College

Robert Erffmeyer, University of Wisconsin, Eau Claire

Scott Erickson, Ithaca College

Denis Fiorentino, Fitchburg State College

Harry Fisher, Eureka College

Judy Foxman, Southern Methodist University

Jodi Frank, Harrisburg Area Community College

Douglas Friedman, Pennsylvania State University, Harrisburg

Karen Fritz, Bridgewater College

David Furman, Clayton State University

Jeff Gauer, Gallaudet University

John Gauld, University of Georgia

Paul Gentine, Bethany College

Katie Ghahramani, Johnson County Community College

Gaetan Giannini, Cedar Crest College

John (Jack) Gifford, Miami University of Ohio

Bill Godair, Landmark College

Dennis Goecks, Chemeketa Community College

James Gould, Pace University

Bryan Greenberg, Elizabethtown College

Bob Gregory, Bellevue University

J. D. Griffith, Brigham Young University, Idaho

Alice Griswold, Clarke College

Perry Haan, Tiffin University

Dorothy Harpool, Wichita State University

Tim Hartman, Ohio University

Joseph Hartnett, St. Charles Community College

Tim Heinze, Waynesburg College

James Hess, Ivy Tech Community College

Stacey Hills, Utah State University

Tanawat Hirunyawipada, University of North Texas

David Houghton, Northwest Nazarene University

George Hozier, Fort Lewis College

Doug Hurd, Fort Scott Community College

Mick Jackowski, Metropolitan State College of Denver

Donald Jackson, Ferris State University

Frank Jacobson, Vanguard University of Southern California

Charles Jaeger, Southern Oregon University

James Jarrard, University of Wisconsin, Platteville

Carol Johanek, Washington University

Luke Kachersky, Baruch College

Marlene Kahla, Stephen F. Austin State University

Karl Kampschroeder, St. Mary's University

Faye Kao, University of Wisconsin, Eau Claire

Janice Karlen, LaGuardia Community College

Eric Karson, Villanova University

Erdener Kaynak, Pennsylvania State University

Eileen Kearney, Montgomery County Community College

Philip Kearney, Niagara Community College

Jennifer Keeling Bond, Colorado State University

Wayne Keene, Stephens College

Jeremy Kees, Villanova University

William J. Kehoe, University of Virginia

Dale Kehr, University of Memphis

DeAnna Kempf, Middle Tennessee State University

David Kimball, Elms College

Greg Kitzmiller, Indiana University

Gary Kritz, Seton Hall University

Claudia Kubowicz Malhotra, University of North Carolina, Chapel Hill

Jean Kujawa, Lourdes College

Chris Lachapelle, Mercyhurst College

Curt Laird, University of Charleston

Roger Lali, DePaul University

Jodi Landgaard, Minnesota West Community & Technical College

Felix Lao, Baker College

Robert Lauterborn, University of North Carolina at Chapel Hill

James Lawson, Mississippi State University, Meridian Campus

David Levy, Des Moines Area Community College - West

Frank Lilja, Pine Technical School

Ingrid Lin, Saint Xavier University

Ann Little, High Point University

Karen Loveland, Texas A&M University, Corpus Christi

Marvin Lovett, University of Texas at Brownsville

Dolly Loyd, University of Southern Mississippi

Leslie Lukasik, Skagit Valley College, Whidbey Island

Kerri Lum, Kapiolani Community College

Larry Maes, Davenport University

Igor Makienko, Loyola University of New Orleans

Jennifer Malarski, Lake Superior College

Manuel Mares, Florida National College

Craig Martin, Western Kentucky University

Deanna Martin, Southwest Mississippi Community College

Nora Martin, University of South Carolina

Wendy Martin, Trinity International University

James Mason, Oklahoma State University

Brenda McAleer, University of Maine at Augusta

Chip Miller, Drake University

Jakki Mohr, University of Montana

Ed Mosher, Laramie County Community College

Jay Mulki, Northeastern University

Lewis Myers, St. Edward's University

Elaine Notarantonio, Bryant University

Gail Olmsted, Springfield Technical Community College

Lois Olson, San Diego State University

John O'Malley, New York University

Carol Osborne, University of Southern Florida

Joseph Ouellette, Bryant University

Karen Pafumbo, University of St. Francis

Glenn Perser, Houston Community College

Karen Petersen, Augustana College

Joanna Phillips, Western Kentucky University

Ray Polchow, Zane State University

Sandra Rahman, Framingham State College

Bobby Reynolds, Troy University Campus

Eric Rios, Eastern University

Chin Robinson, Oral Roberts University

Heidi Rottier, Bradley University

June Roux, Delaware Technical & Community College

Patricia A. Ryan, College of the Canyons

Doreen Sams, Georgia College & State University

Nanette Sanders-Cobb, Craven Communtiy College

William Sannwald, San Diego State University

Anshu Saran, University of Texas of the Permian Basin

Diana Scales, Tennessee State University

Fritz Scherz, Morrisville State College

Jeff Schmidt, University of Oklahoma

Kirk Schueler, University of Michigan

Joe Schwartz, Georgia College and State University

Stephen Schwarz, Saint John's University

Biagio Sciacca, Pennsylvania State University

Del Shepard, Simpson College

Scott Sherwood, Metropolitan State College of Denver

Bill Shockley, Bluefield College

Jonathan Silver, Alvernia College

Rob Simon, University of Nebraska, Lincoln

Ruth Smith, St. Anselm's College

Latanya Smith, Edinboro University of Pennsylvania

Gene Steidinger, Loras College

Alex Stein, Goucher College

Peter Stone, Spartanburg Community College

Chad Storlie, Creighton University

J. P. Stratton, Furman University

Karolina Sudwoj-Nogalska, University of Cincinnati

G. Knude Swensen, Dickinson State University

Albert J. Taylor, Coastal Carolina University

Michael Taylor, Marietta College

Surinder Tikoo, State University of New York, New Paltz

Donna Tillman, California State University, Pomona

Lisa Toms, Southern Arkansas University

Patrick Tormey, Iona College

Jessica Town-Gunderson, St. Cloud Technical College

Carrie Trimble, Illinois Wesleyan University

Carolyn Tripp, Western Illinois University

Leo Trudel, University of Maine

Gary Tucker, Oklahoma City Community College

Joseph Turner, College of the Ablemarle

David Urban, Virginia Commonwealth University

Chandu Valluri, St. Mary's University of Minnesota

Brian Vander Schee, University of Pittsburgh–Bradford

Alexia Vanides, University of California, Berkeley

Richard Vaughan, University of St. Francis

Candace Vogelsong, Cecil Community College

Simon Walls, Fort Lewis College

D.J. Wasmer, Saint Mary-of-the-Woods College

Joyce Whitehorn, University of Alaska, Fairbanks

Bob Willis, Rogers State University

Doug Wilson, University of Oregon

Kelly Wolfe, Webber International University

David Wright, Abilene Christian University

Donna Yancey, University of North Alabama

Joan Zielinski, Northwestern University

Gail Zwart, Riverside Community College, Norco Campus

Global Edition Contributors and Reviewers

Mona H. Allouba, School of Business, The American University in Cairo, Egypt

Dr. Jaafar A.M. Almahy, Department of Management & Marketing, College of Business, University of Bahrain, Bahrain

Dr. Melodena Stephens Balakrishnan, Associate Professor, University of Wollongong in Dubai, Dubai

Dr. Yoosuf A. Cader, Associate Professor (Marketing), Zayed University, Abu Dhabi, U.A.E.

Dr. Kenny Teoh Guan Cheng, Universiti Putra Malaysia, Malaysia

Regina Koh Lay Cheng, Temasek Polytechnic University, Singapore

Reena Ng Su Eng, Temasek Polytechnic University, Singapore

Steven Ng Chee Kuen, Temasek Polytechnic University, Singapore

YH Lek, Temasek Polytechnic, Singapore

Alison E. Lloyd, The Hong Kong Polytechnic University, Hong Kong

Sue Lou, Temasek Polytechnic University, Singapore

Aida Nakhla Rizkalla, Ain Shams University, Egypt

Dr. Hamed M. Shamma, School of Business, The American University in Cairo, Egypt

Philip Siow Khing Shing, Temasek Polytechnic University, Singapore

Dr. Arnold Marc Tan Kim Soon, Temasek Polytechnic University, Singapore

Jon and Diane Sutherland

Gary Lin Guo Xin, Temasek Polytechnic University, Singapore

We also owe a great deal to the people at Pearson Prentice Hall who helped develop this book. Executive Editor Melissa Sabella provided fresh ideas and support throughout to revision. Project Manager Kierra Kashickey provided valuable assistance and ably managed many facets of this complex revision project. Janet Slowik developed the tenth edition's exciting new design. We'd also like to thank Karalyn Holland, Anne Fahlgren, Karin Williams, and Judy Leale. We are proud to be associated with the fine professionals at Pearson Prentice Hall. We also owe a mighty debt of gratitude to Project Editor Lynn Steines and the fine team at S4Carlisle Publishing Services.

Finally, we owe many thanks to our families for all of their support and encouragement—Kathy, Betty, Mandy, Matt, KC, Keri, Delaney, Molly, Macy, and Ben from the Armstrong clan and Nancy, Amy, Melissa, and Jessica from the Kotler family. To them, we dedicate this book.

Gary Armstrong
Philip Kotler

Marketing
An Introduction
Global Edition

1

Marketing

Creating and Capturing **Customer Value**

ROAD MAP

Previewing the Concepts

Fasten your seat belt! You're about to begin an exciting journey toward learning about marketing. In this chapter, we start with the question, What *is* marketing? Simply put, marketing is managing profitable customer relationships. The aim of marketing is to create value *for* customers and to capture value *from* customers in return. Next, we discuss the five steps in the marketing process—from understanding customer needs, to designing customer-driven marketing strategies and integrated marketing programs, to building customer relationships and capturing value for the firm. Finally, we discuss the major trends and forces affecting marketing in this age of customer relationships. Understanding these basic concepts, and forming your own ideas about what they really mean to you, will give you a solid foundation for all that follows.

Objective Outline

 Objective 1 Define marketing and outline the steps in the marketing process.
What Is Marketing? **pp 32–34**

 Objective 2 Explain the importance of understanding customers and the marketplace, and identify the five core marketplace concepts.
Understanding the Marketplace and Customer Needs **pp 34–36**

 Objective 3 Identify the key elements of a customer-driven marketing strategy and discuss the marketing management orientations that guide marketing strategy.
Designing a Customer-Driven Marketing Strategy **pp 37–40**
Preparing an Integrated Marketing Plan and Program **pp 40–41**

 Objective 4 Discuss customer relationship management and identify strategies for creating value *for* customers and capturing value *from* customers in return.
Building Customer Relationships **pp 41–48**
Capturing Value from Customers **pp 48–51**

 Objective 5 Describe the major trends and forces that are changing the marketing landscape in this age of relationships.
The Changing Marketing Landscape **pp 52–58**

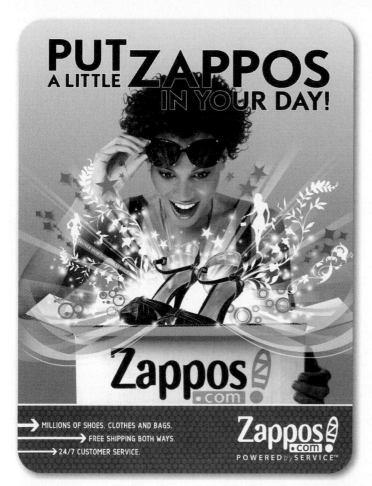

PUT A LITTLE ZAPPOS IN YOUR DAY!

Zappos.com!

MILLIONS OF SHOES, CLOTHES AND BAGS.
FREE SHIPPING BOTH WAYS.
24/7 CUSTOMER SERVICE.

Zappos.com!
POWERED by SERVICE™

▲ At Zappos taking good care of customers starts with a deep-down, customer focused culture. The company is "powered by service."

Let's start with a good story about marketing in action at Zappos, one of the world's fastest-growing Web retailers. The secret to Zappos' success? It's really no secret at all. Zappos is flat out customer obsessed. It has a passion for creating customer value and relationships. In return, customers reward Zappos with their brand loyalty and buying dollars. You'll see this theme of creating customer value in order to capture value in return repeated throughout the first chapter and throughout the text.

First Stop

Zappos: A Passion for Creating Customer Value and Relationships

Imagine a retailer with service so good its customers wish it would take over the Internal Revenue Service or start up an airline. It might sound like a marketing fantasy, but this scenario is reality for 9-year-old Zappos.com. At Zappos, the customer experience really does come first—it's a daily obsession. Says Zappos understated CEO, Tony Hsieh (pronounced *shay*), "Our whole goal at Zappos is for the Zappos brand to be about the very best customer service and customer experience."

Launched in 1999 as a Web site that offered the absolute best selection in shoes—in terms of brands, styles, colors, sizes, and widths—the online retailer now carries many other categories of goods, such as clothing, handbags, and accessories. From the start, the scrappy Web retailer made customer service a cornerstone of its marketing. As a result, Zappos has grown astronomically. It now serves more than 10 million customers annually, and gross merchandise sales now top $1 billion, up from only $1.6 million in 2000. Three percent of the U.S. population now shops at Zappos. And despite the crippling economy, Zappos sales grew more than 20 percent last year.

Interestingly, Zappos doesn't spend a lot of money on media advertising. Instead, it relies on customer service so good that customers not only come back but also tell their friends. More than 75 percent of Zappos' sales come from repeat customers. "We actually take a lot of the money that we would have normally spent on paid advertising and put it back into the customer experience," says CEO Hsieh. "We've always stuck with customer service, even when it was not a sexy thing to do." Adds Aaron Magness, Zappos' director of business development and brand marketing, "We decided if we can put all the money possible into our customer service, word of mouth will work in our favor."

Free delivery, free returns, and a 365-day return policy have been the cornerstone of Zappos' customer-centric approach. It even quietly upgrades the experience, from four-to-five-day shipping to second-day or next-day shipping, to wow customers. Its customer-service center is staffed 24/7 with 500 highly-motivated employees—about a third of the company's payroll—answering 5,000 calls a day. "Those things are all pretty expensive, but we view that as our marketing dollars," says Hsieh. "It's just a lot cheaper to get existing customers to buy from you again than it is to try to convince someone [new]."

Zappos has been steadfast in its focus on customer service even as it's grown. "They've focused on customer service and haven't allowed themselves to be distracted by other things," says an online retailing expert. In a down economy, retailers especially should be focusing on customer service. But as Hsieh points out, it's often the first thing to go. "The payoff for great customer service might be a year or two down the line. And the payoff for having a great company culture might be three or four years down the line."

Web seller Zappos is obsessed with creating the very best customer service and customer experience. In return, customers reward the company with their brand loyalty and buying dollars. The result: Zappos' sales have grown astronomically.

▲ Says CEO Tony Hsieh, "Our whole goal . . . is for the Zappos brand to be about the very best customer service and customer experience."

At Zappos, taking good care of customers starts with a deep-down, customer-focused culture. "We have a saying," proclaims the company at its Web site. "We are a service company that happens to sell [shoes (or handbags, or clothing, or eventually, anything and everything)]." The Zappos culture is built around 10 "Core Values," ranging from "Build open and honest relationships with communication" to "Create fun and a little weirdness." Value number one: "Deliver WOW through service!"

To make sure Zappos' customer obsession permeates the entire organization, each new hire—everyone from the CEO and chief financial officer to the children's footwear buyer—is required to go through four weeks of customer-loyalty training. In fact, in an effort to weed out the half-hearted, Zappos actually bribes people to quit. During the four weeks of customer-service training, it offers employees $2,000 cash, plus payment for the time worked, if they leave the company. The theory goes that those willing to take the money and run aren't right for Zappos' culture anyway.

Hsieh says that originally the incentive was $100, but the amount keeps rising because not enough people take it. On average, only 1 percent take the offer, and Hsieh believes that's too low. Zappos argues that each employee needs to be a great point of contact with customers. "Getting customers excited about the service they had at Zappos has to come naturally," says Magness. "You can't teach it; you have to hire for it."

When dealing with customers, Zappos employees must check their egos and competitiveness at the door. Customer-service reps are trained to look on at least three rival Web sites if a shopper asks for specific shoes that Zappos doesn't have in stock and refer customers accordingly. "My guess is that other companies don't do that," Hsieh says. "For us, we're willing to lose that sale, that transaction in the short term. We're focused on building the lifelong loyalty and relationship with the customer."

Relationships mean everything at Zappos. Hsieh and many other employees stay in direct touch with customers, with each other, and with just about anyone else interested in the company. They use social networking tools such as Facebook, Twitter, and blogs to share information, both good and bad. And the company invites customers to submit frank online reviews. Such openness might worry some retailers, but Zappos embraces it. As Magness points out, "you only need to worry if you have something to hide," and Zappos seems to take even criticism as a free gift of information.

Zappos has set new standards in the industry, leading the way for a new type of consumer-focused company. "There's something about these young Internet companies," says the retailing expert. "I'm not sure exactly why—if it was because they were born in a different era, the leadership has a different worldview, or if they just have amazing access to customer data and see firsthand what customers are thinking," he says. "It seems that Zappos is really the poster child for this new age of consumer companies that truly are customer focused. A lot of companies like to say they are, but none of them is as serious as Zappos."

It's that intense customer focus that has set the stage for Zappos' growth, as the company branches out into new categories such as electronics and home goods. "Hopefully, 10 years from now, people won't even realize we started out selling shoes online. We've actually had customers ask us if we would please start an airline or run the IRS," Hsieh says, adding, "30 years from now I wouldn't rule out a Zappos airline that's all about the very best service."[1]

*t*oday's successful companies have one thing in common: Like Zappos, they are strongly customer-focused and heavily committed to marketing. These companies share a passion for understanding and satisfying customer needs in well-defined target markets. They motivate everyone in the organization to help build lasting customer relationships based on creating value.

Customer relationships and value are especially important in today's tough economic times, when more frugal consumers are cutting back and spending more carefully. "The challenge facing us is not just one of consumers being more-value conscious," says one marketing consultant. "It's how we gain . . . a renewed relationship with consumers who have less inclination to listen to [companies with whom] they do not have strong and valued relationships."[2]

Author Comment ≫
Stop here for a second and think about how you'd answer this question before studying marketing. Then, see how your answer changes as you go through the chapter.

WHAT IS MARKETING? (pp 32–34)

Marketing, more than any other business function, deals with customers. Although we will soon explore more-detailed definitions of marketing, perhaps the simplest definition is this one: *Marketing is managing profitable customer relationships*. The twofold goal of marketing is to attract new customers by promising superior value and to keep and grow current customers by delivering satisfaction.

For example, Wal-Mart has become the world's largest retailer—and the world's second-largest *company*—by delivering on its promise, "Save money. Live better." Nintendo surged ahead in the videogames market with the promise that "Wii would like to play," backed by its wildly popular Wii console and growing list of popular games and accessories for all ages. And Apple fulfills its motto to "Think Different" with dazzling, customer-driven innovation that captures customer imaginations and loyalty. Its incredibly successful iPod grabs more than 70 percent of the music player market; its iTunes music store is now the world's number-two music store—online or offline (Wal-Mart is number one).[3]

Sound marketing is critical to the success of every organization. Large for-profit firms such as Procter & Gamble, Google, Target, Toyota, and Marriott use marketing. But so do not-for-profit organizations such as colleges, hospitals, museums, symphony orchestras, and even churches.

You already know a lot about marketing—it's all around you. Marketing comes to you in the good old traditional forms: You see it in the abundance of products at your nearby shopping mall and in the advertisements that fill your TV screen, spice up your magazines, or stuff your mailbox. But in recent years, marketers have assembled a host of new marketing approaches, everything from imaginative Web sites and online social networks to interactive TV and your cell phone. These new approaches do more than just blast out messages to the masses. They reach you directly and personally. Today's marketers want to become a part of your life and to enrich your experiences with their brands—to help you to *live* their brands.

At home, at school, where you work, and where you play, you see marketing in almost everything you do. Yet, there is much more to marketing than meets the consumer's casual eye. Behind it all is a massive network of people and activities competing for your attention and purchases. This book will give you a complete introduction to the basic concepts and practices of today's marketing. In this chapter, we begin by defining marketing and the marketing process.

Marketing Defined

What *is* marketing? Many people think of marketing only as selling and advertising. And no wonder—every day we are bombarded with TV commercials, direct-mail offers, sales calls, and e-mail pitches. However, selling and advertising are only the tip of the marketing iceberg.

Today, marketing must be understood not in the old sense of making a sale—"telling and selling"—but in the new sense of *satisfying customer needs.* If the marketer understands consumer needs; develops products that provide superior customer value; and prices, distributes, and promotes them effectively, these products will sell easily. In fact, according to management guru Peter Drucker, "The aim of marketing is to make selling unnecessary."[4] Selling and advertising are only part of a larger "marketing mix"—a set of marketing tools that work together to satisfy customer needs and build customer relationships.

Broadly defined, marketing is a social and managerial process by which individuals and organizations obtain what they need and want through creating and exchanging value with others. In a narrower business context, marketing involves building profitable, value-laden exchange relationships with customers. Hence, we define **marketing** as the process by which companies create value for customers and build strong customer relationships in order to capture value from customers in return.[5]

Marketing
The process by which companies create value for customers and build strong customer relationships in order to capture value from customers in return.

The Marketing Process

■ **Figure 1.1** presents a simple five-step model of the marketing process. In the first four steps, companies work to understand consumers, create customer value, and build strong customer relationships. In the final step, companies reap the rewards of creating superior customer value. By creating value *for* consumers, they in turn capture value *from* consumers in the form of sales, profits, and long-term customer equity.

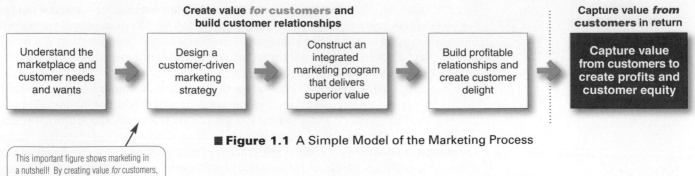

■ **Figure 1.1** A Simple Model of the Marketing Process

This important figure shows marketing in a nutshell! By creating value *for* customers, marketers capture value *from* customers in return. This five-step process forms the marketing framework for the rest of the chapter and the rest of the text.

In this chapter and the next, we will examine the steps of this simple model of marketing. In this chapter, we will review each step but focus more on the customer relationship steps—understanding customers, building customer relationships, and capturing value from customers. In Chapter 2, we'll look more deeply into the second and third steps—designing marketing strategies and constructing marketing programs.

UNDERSTANDING THE MARKETPLACE AND CUSTOMER NEEDS (pp 34–36)

Author Comment ≫
Marketing is all about creating value for customers. So, as the first step in the marketing process, the company must fully understand consumers and the marketplace in which it operates.

As a first step, marketers need to understand customer needs and wants and the marketplace within which they operate. We now examine five core customer and marketplace concepts: (1) *needs, wants, and demands;* (2) *market offerings (products, services, and experiences);* (3) *value and satisfaction;* (4) *exchanges and relationships;* and (5) *markets.*

Customer Needs, Wants, and Demands

Needs
States of felt deprivation.

The most basic concept underlying marketing is that of human needs. Human **needs** are states of felt deprivation. They include basic *physical* needs for food, clothing, warmth, and safety; *social* needs for belonging and affection; and *individual* needs for knowledge and self-expression. These needs were not created by marketers; they are a basic part of the human makeup.

Wants
The form human needs take as shaped by culture and individual personality.

Wants are the form human needs take as they are shaped by culture and individual personality. An American *needs* food but *wants* a Big Mac, french fries, and a soft drink. A person in Papua New Guinea *needs* food but *wants* taro, rice, yams, and pork. Wants are shaped by one's society and are described in terms of objects that will satisfy needs. When backed by buying power, wants become **demands**. Given their wants and resources, people demand products with benefits that add up to the most value and satisfaction.

Demands
Human wants that are backed by buying power.

Outstanding marketing companies go to great lengths to learn about and understand their customers' needs, wants, and demands. They conduct consumer research and analyze mountains of customer data. Their people at all levels—including top management—stay close to customers. For example, Procter & Gamble CEO A. G. Lafley is known for actually going into customers' homes to undertake his own ethnographic research to ensure that customers' needs are well understood. Retailer Cabela's Vice-Chairman James W. Cabela spends hours each morning reading through customer comments and hand-delivering them to each department, circling important customer issues. And at Zappos, CEO Tony Hsieh uses Twitter to build more personal connections with customers and our employees. Some 32,000 people follow Hsieh's Twitter feed.[6]

Market Offerings—Products, Services, and Experiences

Market offerings
Some combination of products, services, information, or experiences offered to a market to satisfy a need or want.

Consumers' needs and wants are fulfilled through **market offerings**—some combination of products, services, information, or experiences offered to a market to satisfy a need or want. Market offerings are not limited to physical *products*. They also include *services*—activities or benefits offered for sale that are essentially intangible and do

▲Market offerings are not limited to physical products. UNCF powerfully markets that idea the "A mind is a terrible thing to waste."

Marketing myopia
The mistake of paying more attention to the specific products a company offers than to the benefits and experiences produced by these products.

Exchange
The act of obtaining a desired object from someone by offering something in return.

not result in the ownership of anything. Examples include banking, airline, hotel, tax preparation, and home repair services.

More broadly, market offerings also include other entities, such as *persons*, *places*, *organizations*, *information*, and *ideas*. ▲For example, UNCF powerfully markets the idea that "A Mind Is a Terrible Thing to Waste." The nation's oldest and most successful African American education assistance organization, UNCF has helped more than 350,000 minority students graduate from college.[7]

Many sellers make the mistake of paying more attention to the specific products they offer than to the benefits and experiences produced by these products. These sellers suffer from **marketing myopia**. They are so taken with their products that they focus only on existing wants and lose sight of underlying customer needs.[8] They forget that a product is only a tool to solve a consumer problem. A manufacturer of quarter-inch drill bits may think that the customer needs a drill bit. But what the customer *really* needs is a quarter-inch hole. These sellers will have trouble if a new product comes along that serves the customer's need better or less expensively. The customer will have the same *need* but will *want* the new product.

Smart marketers look beyond the attributes of the products and services they sell. By orchestrating several services and products, they create *brand experiences* for consumers. For example, you don't just watch a NASCAR race, you immerse yourself in the exhilarating, high-octane NASCAR experience. Similarly, Hewlett-Packard (HP) recognizes that a personal computer is much more than just a collection of wires and electrical components. It's an intensely personal user experience. As noted in a recent HP ad, "There is hardly anything that you own that is *more* personal. Your personal computer is your backup brain. It's your life. . . . It's your astonishing strategy, staggering proposal, dazzling calculation. It's your autobiography, written in a thousand daily words."[9]

Customer Value and Satisfaction

Consumers usually face a broad array of products and services that might satisfy a given need. How do they choose among these many market offerings? Customers form expectations about the value and satisfaction that various market offerings will deliver and buy accordingly. Satisfied customers buy again and tell others about their good experiences. Dissatisfied customers often switch to competitors and disparage the product to others.

Marketers must be careful to set the right level of expectations. If they set expectations too low, they may satisfy those who buy but fail to attract enough buyers. If they raise expectations too high, buyers will be disappointed. Customer value and customer satisfaction are key building blocks for developing and managing customer relationships. We will revisit these core concepts later in the chapter.

Exchanges and Relationships

Marketing occurs when people decide to satisfy needs and wants through exchange relationships. **Exchange** is the act of obtaining a desired object from someone by offering something in return. In the broadest sense, the marketer tries to bring about a response to some market offering. The response may be more than simply buying or trading products and services. A political candidate, for instance, wants votes, a church wants membership, an orchestra wants an audience, and a social action group wants idea acceptance.

Marketing consists of actions taken to build and maintain desirable exchange *relationships* with target audiences involving a product, service, idea, or other object. Beyond simply attracting new customers and creating transactions, the company wants to retain customers and grow their business. Marketers want to build strong relationships by consistently delivering superior customer value. We will expand on the important concept of managing customer relationships later in the chapter.

Markets

Market
The set of all actual and potential buyers of a product or service.

The concepts of exchange and relationships lead to the concept of a market. A **market** is the set of actual and potential buyers of a product. These buyers share a particular need or want that can be satisfied through exchange relationships.

Marketing means managing markets to bring about profitable customer relationships. However, creating these relationships takes work. Sellers must search for buyers, identify their needs, design good market offerings, set prices for them, promote them, and store and deliver them. Activities such as consumer research, product development, communication, distribution, pricing, and service are core marketing activities.

Although we normally think of marketing as being carried on by sellers, buyers also carry on marketing. Consumers do marketing when they search for products and interact with companies and obtain information and make their purchases. In fact, today's digital technologies, from Web sites and online social networks to cell phones, have empowered consumers and made marketing a truly interactive affair. Thus, in addition to customer relationship management, today's marketers must also deal effectively with *customer-managed relationships*. Marketers are no longer asking only "How can we reach our customers?" but also "How should our customers reach us?" and even "How can our customers reach each other?"

■ **Figure 1.2** shows the main elements in a marketing system. Marketing involves serving a market of final consumers in the face of competitors. The company and competitors research the market and interact with consumers to understand their needs. Then they create and send their market offerings and messages to consumers, either directly or through marketing intermediaries. All of the parties in the system are affected by major environmental forces (demographic, economic, physical, technological, political/legal, and social/cultural).

Each party in the system adds value for the next level. All of the arrows represent relationships that must be developed and managed. Thus, a company's success at building profitable relationships depends not only on its own actions but also on how well the entire system serves the needs of final consumers. Wal-Mart cannot fulfill its promise of low prices unless its suppliers provide merchandise at low costs. And Ford cannot deliver a high quality car-ownership experience unless its dealers provide outstanding sales and service.

Arrows represent relationships that must be developed and managed to create customer value and profitable customer relationships.

■ **Figure 1.2** A Modern Marketing System

Each party in the system adds value. Wal-Mart cannot fulfill its promise of low prices unless its suppliers provide low costs. Ford cannot deliver a high quality car-ownership experience unless its dealers provide outstanding service.

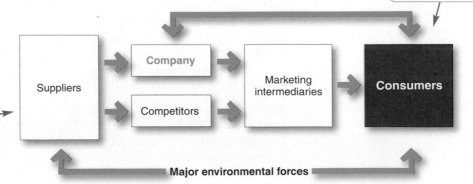

Author Comment ≫
Now that the company fully understands consumers and the marketplace, it must decide which customers it will serve and how it will bring them value.

Marketing management
The art and science of choosing target markets and building profitable relationships with them.

DESIGNING A CUSTOMER-DRIVEN MARKETING STRATEGY (pp 37–40)

Once it fully understands consumers and the marketplace, marketing management can design a customer-driven marketing strategy. We define **marketing management** as the art and science of choosing target markets and building profitable relationships with them. The marketing manager's aim is to find, attract, keep, and grow target customers by creating, delivering, and communicating superior customer value.

To design a winning marketing strategy, the marketing manager must answer two important questions: *What customers will we serve (what's our target market)?* and *How can we serve these customers best (what's our value proposition)?* We will discuss these marketing strategy concepts briefly here, and then look at them in more detail in the next chapter.

Selecting Customers to Serve

The company must first decide *who* it will serve. It does this by dividing the market into segments of customers (*market segmentation*) and selecting which segments it will go after (*target marketing*). Some people think of marketing management as finding as many customers as possible and increasing demand. But marketing managers know that they cannot serve all customers in every way. By trying to serve all customers, they may not serve any customers well. Instead, the company wants to select only customers that it can serve well and profitably. For example, Nordstrom stores profitably target affluent professionals; Family Dollar stores profitably target families with more modest means.

Ultimately, marketing managers must decide which customers they want to target and on the level, timing, and nature of their demand. Simply put, marketing management is *customer management* and *demand management*.

Choosing a Value Proposition

The company must also decide how it will serve targeted customers—how it will *differentiate and position* itself in the marketplace. A brand's *value proposition* is the set of benefits or values it promises to deliver to consumers to satisfy their needs. At AT&T, it's "Your World. Delivered." whereas with T-Mobile, family and friends can "Stick together." ▲The diminutive Smart car suggests that you "Open your mind to the car that challenges the status quo," whereas Infiniti "Makes luxury affordable." And a recent joint advertisement by Kraft and Campbell features a tomato-soup-and-grilled-cheese-sandwich combo that "Warms hearts without stretching budgets."

Such value propositions differentiate one brand from another. They answer the customer's question "Why should I buy your brand rather than a competitor's?" Companies must design strong value propositions that give them the greatest advantage in their target markets. For example, the Kraft/Campbell value proposition positions the companies' brands strongly against spendier eating-out alternatives in today's budget-strapped economy.

▼Value propositions: Smart car suggests that you "Open your mind to the car that challenges the status quo."

Marketing Management Orientations

Marketing management wants to design strategies that will build profitable relationships with target consumers. But what *philosophy* should guide these marketing strategies? What weight should be given to the interests of customers, the organization, and society? Very often, these interests conflict.

There are five alternative concepts under which organizations design and carry out their marketing strategies: the *production, product, selling, marketing,* and *societal marketing concepts.*

The Production Concept

Production concept
The idea that consumers will favor products that are available and highly affordable and that the organization should therefore focus on improving production and distribution efficiency.

The **production concept** holds that consumers will favor products that are available and highly affordable. Therefore, management should focus on improving production and distribution efficiency. This concept is one of the oldest orientations that guides sellers.

The production concept is still a useful philosophy in some situations. For example, computer maker Lenovo dominates the highly competitive, price-sensitive Chinese PC market through low labor costs, high production efficiency, and mass distribution. However, although useful in some situations, the production concept can lead to marketing myopia. Companies adopting this orientation run a major risk of focusing too narrowly on their own operations and losing sight of the real objective—satisfying customer needs and building customer relationships.

The Product Concept

Product concept
The idea that consumers will favor products that offer the most quality, performance, and features and that the organization should therefore devote its energy to making continuous product improvements.

The **product concept** holds that consumers will favor products that offer the most in quality, performance, and innovative features. Under this concept, marketing strategy focuses on making continuous product improvements.

Product quality and improvement are important parts of most marketing strategies. However, focusing *only* on the company's products can also lead to marketing myopia. For example, some manufacturers believe that if they can "build a better mousetrap, the world will beat a path to their door." But they are often rudely shocked. Buyers may be looking for a better solution to a mouse problem, but not necessarily for a better mousetrap. The better solution might be a chemical spray, an exterminating service, a housecat, or something else that works even better than a mousetrap. Furthermore, a better mousetrap will not sell unless the manufacturer designs, packages, and prices it attractively; places it in convenient distribution channels; brings it to the attention of people who need it; and convinces buyers that it is a better product.

The Selling Concept

Selling concept
The idea that consumers will not buy enough of the firm's products unless it undertakes a large-scale selling and promotion effort.

Many companies follow the **selling concept**, which holds that consumers will not buy enough of the firm's products unless it undertakes a large-scale selling and promotion effort. The selling concept is typically practiced with unsought goods—those that buyers do not normally think of buying, such as insurance or blood donations. These industries must be good at tracking down prospects and selling them on product benefits.

Such aggressive selling, however, carries high risks. It focuses on creating sales transactions rather than on building long-term, profitable customer relationships. The aim often is to sell what the company makes rather than making what the market wants. It assumes that customers who are coaxed into buying the product will like it. Or, if they don't like it, they will possibly forget their disappointment and buy it again later. These are usually poor assumptions.

The Marketing Concept

Marketing concept
The marketing management philosophy that holds that achieving organizational goals depends on knowing the needs and wants of target markets and delivering the desired satisfactions better than competitors do.

The **marketing concept** holds that achieving organizational goals depends on knowing the needs and wants of target markets and delivering the desired satisfactions better than competitors do. Under the marketing concept, customer focus and value are the *paths* to sales and profits. Instead of a product-centered "make and sell" philosophy, the marketing concept is a customer-centered "sense and respond" philosophy. The job is not to find the right customers for your product but to find the right products for your customers.

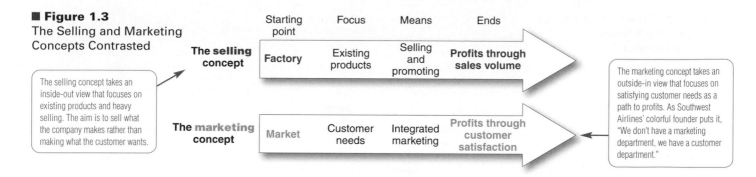

■ **Figure 1.3**
The Selling and Marketing
Concepts Contrasted

The selling concept takes an inside-out view that focuses on existing products and heavy selling. The aim is to sell what the company makes rather than making what the customer wants.

	Starting point	Focus	Means	Ends
The selling concept	Factory	Existing products	Selling and promoting	**Profits through sales volume**
The marketing concept	Market	Customer needs	Integrated marketing	**Profits through customer satisfaction**

The marketing concept takes an outside-in view that focuses on satisfying customer needs as a path to profits. As Southwest Airlines' colorful founder puts it, "We don't have a marketing department, we have a customer department."

■ **Figure 1.3** contrasts the selling concept and the marketing concept. The selling concept takes an *inside-out* perspective. It starts with the factory, focuses on the company's existing products, and calls for heavy selling and promotion to obtain profitable sales. It focuses primarily on customer conquest—getting short-term sales with little concern about who buys or why.

In contrast, the marketing concept takes an *outside-in* perspective. As Herb Kelleher, Southwest Airlines' colorful founder, puts it, "We don't have a marketing department; we have a customer department." The marketing concept starts with a well-defined market, focuses on customer needs, and integrates all the marketing activities that affect customers. In turn, it yields profits by creating lasting relationships with the right customers based on customer value and satisfaction.

Implementing the marketing concept often means more than simply responding to customers' stated desires and obvious needs. *Customer-driven* companies research current customers deeply to learn about their desires, gather new product and service ideas, and test proposed product improvements. Such customer-driven marketing usually works well when a clear need exists and when customers know what they want.

In many cases, however, customers *don't* know what they want or even what is possible. For example, even 20 years ago, how many consumers would have thought to ask for now-commonplace products such as notebook computers, iPhones, digital cameras, 24-hour online buying, and satellite navigation systems in their cars? Such situations call for ▲*customer-driving* marketing—understanding customer needs even better than customers themselves do and creating products and services that meet existing and latent needs, now and in the future. As an executive at 3M puts it, "Our goal is to lead customers where they want to go before *they* know where they want to go."

▲ **Customer-driving marketing: Even 20 years ago, how many consumers would have thought to ask for now-commonplace products such as cell phones, personal digital assistants, notebook computers, iPods, and digital cameras. Marketers must often understand customer needs even better than customers themselves do.**

Societal marketing concept
The idea that a company's marketing decisions should consider consumers' wants, the company's requirements, consumers' long-run interests, and society's long-run interests.

The Societal Marketing Concept

The **societal marketing concept** questions whether the pure marketing concept overlooks possible conflicts between consumer *short-run wants* and consumer *long-run welfare*. Is a firm that satisfies the immediate needs and wants of target markets always doing what's best for consumers in the long run? The societal marketing concept holds that marketing strategy should deliver value to customers in a way that maintains or improves both the consumer's *and society's* well-being. It calls for *sustainable marketing,* socially and environmentally responsible marketing that meets the present needs of consumers and businesses while also preserving or enhancing the ability of future generations to meet their needs.

■ **Figure 1.4** The Considerations Underlying the Societal Marketing Concept

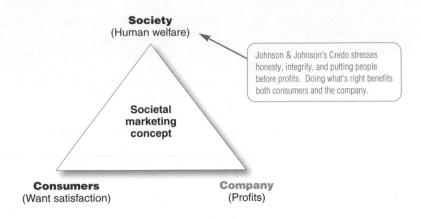

Society
(Human welfare)

Johnson & Johnson's Credo stresses honesty, integrity, and putting people before profits. Doing what's right benefits both consumers and the company.

Societal marketing concept

Consumers
(Want satisfaction)

Company
(Profits)

Our Credo

We believe our first responsibility is to the doctors, nurses and patients, to mothers and fathers and all others who use our products and services. In meeting their needs everything we do must be of high quality. We must constantly strive to reduce our costs in order to maintain reasonable prices. Customers' orders must be serviced promptly and accurately. Our suppliers and distributors must have an opportunity to make a fair profit.

We are responsible to our employees, the men and women who work with us throughout the world. Everyone must be considered as an individual. We must respect their dignity and recognize their merit. They must have a sense of security in their jobs. Compensation must be fair and adequate, and working conditions clean, orderly and safe. We must be mindful of ways to help our employees fulfill their family responsibilities. Employees must feel free to make suggestions and complaints. There must be equal opportunity for employment, development and advancement for those qualified. We must provide competent management, and their actions must be just and ethical.

We are responsible to the communities in which we live and work and to the world community as well. We must be good citizens — support good works and charities and bear our fair share of taxes. We must encourage civic improvements and better health and education. We must maintain in good order the property we are privileged to use, protecting the environment and natural resources.

Our final responsibility is to our stockholders. Business must make a sound profit. We must experiment with new ideas. Research must be carried on, innovative programs developed and mistakes paid for. New equipment must be purchased, new facilities provided and new products launched. Reserves must be created to provide for adverse times. When we operate according to these principles, the stockholders should realize a fair return.

Johnson & Johnson

▲The societal marketing concept: Johnson & Johnson's Credo stresses putting people before profits.

Consider today's flourishing bottled water industry. You may view bottled water companies as offering a convenient, tasty, and healthy product. Its packaging suggests "green" images of pristine lakes and snow-capped mountains. Yet making, filling, and shipping billions of plastic bottles generates huge amounts of carbon dioxide emissions that contribute substantially to global warming. Further, the plastic bottles pose a substantial recycling and solid waste disposal problem. Thus, in satisfying short-term consumer wants, the bottled water industry may be causing environmental problems that run against society's long-run interests.[10]

As ■ **Figure 1.4** shows, companies should balance three considerations in setting their marketing strategies: company profits, consumer wants, *and* society's interests. ▲Johnson & Johnson does this well. Its concern for societal interests is summarized in a company document called "Our Credo," which stresses honesty, integrity, and putting people before profits. Under this credo, Johnson & Johnson would rather take a big loss than ship a bad batch of one of its products.

Johnson & Johnson management has learned that doing what's right benefits both consumers and the company. Says former CEO Ralph Larsen, "The Credo should not be viewed as some kind of social welfare program . . . it's just plain good business. If we keep trying to do what's right, at the end of the day we believe the marketplace will reward us." Thus, over the years, Johnson & Johnson's dedication to consumers and community service has made it one of America's most admired companies *and* one of the most profitable.[11]

Author Comment »
The customer-driven marketing strategy discussed in the previous section outlines which customers the company will serve (the target market) and how it will serve them (the value proposition). Now, the company develops marketing plans and programs—a marketing mix—that will actually deliver the intended customer value.

PREPARING AN INTEGRATED MARKETING PLAN AND PROGRAM (pp 40–41)

The company's marketing strategy outlines which customers the company will serve and how it will create value for these customers. Next, the marketer develops an integrated marketing program that will actually deliver the intended value to target customers. The marketing program builds customer relationships by transforming the marketing strategy into action. It consists of the firm's *marketing mix,* the set of marketing tools the firm uses to implement its marketing strategy.

The major marketing mix tools are classified into four broad groups, called the *four Ps* of marketing: product, price, place, and promotion. To deliver on its value proposition, the firm must first create a need-satisfying market offering (product). It must decide how much it will charge for the offering (price) and how it will make the offering available to target consumers (place). Finally, it must communicate with target customers about the offering and persuade them of its merits (promotion). The firm must blend all of these marketing mix tools into a comprehensive *integrated marketing program* that communicates and delivers the intended value to chosen customers. We will explore marketing programs and the marketing mix in much more detail in later chapters.

Speed Bump: Linking the Concepts

Stop here for a moment and stretch your legs. What have you learned so far about marketing? For the moment, set aside the more formal definitions we've examined and try to develop your own understanding of marketing.

- In *your own words*, what *is* marketing? Write down *your* definition. Does your definition include such key concepts as customer value and relationships?
- What does marketing *mean* to you? How does it affect your life on a daily basis?
- What brand of athletic shoes did you purchase last? Describe your relationship with Nike, Adidas, Converse, New Balance, or whatever brand of shoes you purchased.

BUILDING CUSTOMER RELATIONSHIPS (pp 41–48)

Author Comment >>
Doing a good job with the first three steps in the marketing process sets the stage for step four, building and managing lasting customer relationships.

The first three steps in the marketing process—understanding the marketplace and customer needs, designing a customer-driven marketing strategy, and constructing marketing programs—all lead up to the fourth and most important step: building profitable customer relationships.

Customer Relationship Management

Customer relationship management is perhaps the most important concept of modern marketing. Some marketers define customer relationship management narrowly as a customer data management activity (a practice called *CRM*). By this definition, it involves managing detailed information about individual customers and carefully managing customer "touchpoints" in order to maximize customer loyalty. We will discuss this narrower CRM activity in Chapter 4 when dealing with marketing information.

Customer relationship management
The overall process of building and maintaining profitable customer relationships by delivering superior customer value and satisfaction.

Most marketers, however, give the concept of customer relationship management a broader meaning. In this broader sense, **customer relationship management** is the overall process of building and maintaining profitable customer relationships by delivering superior customer value and satisfaction. It deals with all aspects of acquiring, keeping, and growing customers.

Relationship Building Blocks: Customer Value and Satisfaction
The key to building lasting customer relationships is to create superior customer value and satisfaction. Satisfied customers are more likely to be loyal customers and to give the company a larger share of their business.

Customer-perceived value
The customer's evaluation of the difference between all the benefits and all the costs of a marketing offer relative to those of competing offers.

Customer Value. Attracting and retaining customers can be a difficult task. Customers often face a bewildering array of products and services from which to choose. A customer buys from the firm that offers the highest **customer-perceived value**—the customer's evaluation of the difference between all the benefits and all the costs of a market offering relative to those of competing offers. Importantly, customers often do not judge values and costs "accurately" or "objectively." They act on *perceived* value.

Why add detergent 365 times a year when you could just add it twice?

GE Profile's new frontload washer with the SmartDispense™ pedestal holds up to six months of detergent* and conveniently dispenses the right amount for each load. And now you can reduce wrinkles, refresh fabrics and improve cleaning with the addition of Steam technology to the washer and dryer. Just a few of the many features that will ensure your clothes are well taken care of. To learn more, visit geappliances.com/profilefrontload.

100 years of innovation. And we're just getting started.

GE *Profile*™

▲**Perceived value: To some customers, "value" might mean paying more to get more. For example, are GE's Profile Harmony washers and dryers worth the higher price? To the target segment of style-conscious, affluent buyers, the answer is "yes."**

Customer satisfaction
The extent to which a product's perceived performance matches a buyer's expectations.

To some consumers, "value" might mean sensible products at affordable prices, especially in the aftermath of the recent downward economic spiral. To other consumers, however, value might mean paying more to get more. For example, despite the challenging economic environment, ▲GE recently introduced its new Profile washer-and-dryer set, which retails for more than $2,500. Profile ads feature stylish machines in eye-catching colors such as cherry red. But the ads also focus on down-to-earth practicality. They position the Profile line as a revolutionary new "clothes care system," with technology that allocates the optimal amount of soap and water per load and saves money by being gentle on clothes, extending garment life. As compared to less expensive appliances, are Profile washers and dryers worth the much higher price? It's all a matter of personal value perceptions. To many consumers, the answer is no. But to the target segment of style-conscious, affluent buyers, the answer is yes.[12]

Customer Satisfaction. Customer satisfaction depends on the product's perceived performance relative to a buyer's expectations. If the product's performance falls short of expectations, the customer is dissatisfied. If performance matches expectations, the customer is satisfied. If performance exceeds expectations, the customer is highly satisfied or delighted.

Outstanding marketing companies go out of their way to keep important customers satisfied. Most studies show that higher levels of customer satisfaction lead to greater customer loyalty, which in turn results in better company performance. Smart companies aim to delight customers by promising only what they can deliver, then delivering more than they promise. Delighted customers not only make repeat purchases, they become willing marketing partners and "customer evangelists" who spread the word about their good experiences to others (see Marketing at Work 1.1).[13]

For companies interested in delighting customers, exceptional value and service become part of the overall company culture. For example, year after year, ▲Ritz-Carlton ranks at or near the top of the hospitality industry in terms of customer satisfaction. Its passion for satisfying customers is summed up in the company's credo, which promises that its luxury hotels will deliver a truly memorable experience—one that "enlivens the senses, instills well-being, and fulfills even the unexpressed wishes and needs of our guests."

Check into any Ritz-Carlton hotel around the world, and you'll be amazed by the company's fervent dedication to anticipating and meeting even your slightest need. Without ever asking, they seem to know that you want a king-size bed, a nonallergenic pillow, and breakfast with decaffeinated coffee in your room. Each day, hotel staffers—from those at the front desk to those in maintenance and housekeeping—discreetly observe and record even the smallest guest preferences. Then, every morning, each hotel reviews the files of all new arrivals who have previously stayed at a Ritz-Carlton and prepares a list of suggested extra touches that might delight each guest.

Once they identify a special customer need, the Ritz-Carlton employees go to legendary extremes to meet it. For example, to serve the needs of a guest with food allergies, a Ritz-Carlton chef in Bali located special eggs and milk in a small grocery store in another country and had them delivered to the hotel. In another case, when the hotel's laundry service failed to remove a stain on a guest's suit before the guest departed, the hotel manager traveled to the guest's house and personally delivered a reimbursement check for the cost of the suit. As a result of such customer-service heroics,

Marketing at Work 1.1

iRobot's Roomba: The Power of Customer Delight

When you were a child, you probably didn't like it much when your mother made you vacuum around the house. You probably still don't much like vacuuming—it's a thankless, seemingly never-ending task. But there's one group of people who don't mind vacuuming at all. In fact, they're absolutely delighted about it. They are the folks who own an iRobot Roomba, the cute little robotic vacuum that zips around rooms, avoiding furniture and other obstacles, tirelessly sniffing up dirt, dust, and dog hair.

People love their little Roombas. They name them, talk to them, and even buy a second Roomba so that the first one won't be lonely. Many Roomba owners spend more time watching their little petlike robots than they would spend vacuuming a room themselves. Recognizing the strong attachments that many Roomba owners have to these personable little machines, iRobot does all it can to involve its customers in everything from product development to technical support, turning them into an army of Roomba consumer evangelists and marketing partners.

iRobot began in the 1990s, building devices for the U.S. military—small robots called PackBots now used to diffuse improvised explosive devices (IEDs) in Iraq or explore caves in Afghanistan. Based on this advanced technology, the company introduced its first Roomba in 2002. Made up of more than 100 plastic parts, motors, controllers, sensors, brushes, and a dustbin, the 10-pound Roomba uses a sophisticated algorithm to scoot around a room, even going under tables, chairs, sofas, and beds. When it runs into obstacles, it figures out how to clean around them. And when its rechargeable battery begins to lose its charge, the Roomba finds its way to its home base unit, plugs itself in, and recharges automatically. Owners can even program more expensive models to clean at certain times of the day or days of the week, even when no one is home.

In the summer of 2002, iRobot negotiated distribution deals with key retailers such as Brookstone, and Roomba sales took off. Soon, the company began getting calls from major chains such as Target, Kohl's, and Linens 'n Things. iRobot's factory churned out 50,000 units just to meet that year's holiday demand.

Then the real fun began. As iRobot received Roombas back for servicing, customer-service reps noted that many owners were customizing and humanizing their little robotic assistants. In fact, before consumers sent in their Roombas for repair, they would sometimes etch their names on the machines to be sure of getting their own robots back. "Somehow, they grow attached to the squat, disk-shaped sweepers and worry that a new robot will have a different personality," comments one observer. Rather than selling just a high-tech household appliance, it seems that iRobot had invented a new kind of family pet. Reps reported that owners were often painting their Roombas, dressing them, turning them on to entertain their friends, and referring to them by name and gender. The most popular name was Rosie, after the robotic maid on the classic animated TV series, *The Jetsons*.

▲ Delighting customers: People love their pet-like little Roombas. They name them, talk to them, and even buy a second Roomba so that the first one won't be lonely. Recognizing this, iRobot has turned customers into an army of Roomba consumer evangelists.

Before long, delighted Roomba owners became iRobot's best marketing partners. An independent Web site sprang up, myRoomBud.com, offering RoomBud costumes that transform a Roomba from "just a naked vacuum" into a lovable character such as "Roobit the Frog," "Mooba the Cow," or "RoomBette La French Maid." The site even lets Roomba enthusiasts print out official-looking birth certificates for their newly adopted robotic pets.

Smitten Roomba owners by the hundreds began posting video clips of their Roombas in action on YouTube. One mounted a camera on his Roomba to create a RoombaCam. Other Roomba customers created the Roomba Review Web site featuring news, chats, product reviews, and hacker information.

Noting all of this customer enthusiasm and delight, iRobot developed programs to strengthen and organize the growing sense of community among Roomba owners. For example, it opened its programmatic interface, encouraging owners, amateur robotics enthusiasts, and others to develop their own programs and uses for the Roomba. It also offered an iRobot Create programmable robot for educators, students, and developers to program customized behaviors, sounds, movements and to add their own additional electronics. These actions turned Roomba owners into a community of amateur tinkerers and hobbyists. Customers themselves began to develop improved features that iRobot would later adopt.

(continued)

By monitoring interactions with and among enthusiastic Roomba customers, iRobot was able to discover product problems and additional customer needs. Complaints that animal hair often clogged the machines led the company to introduce the Roomba for Pets model, featuring easy-to-clean brushes that make removing pet hair easier. For customers who wanted a robotic "floor mopper," iRobot introduced the Scooba floor washer, another personable little gizmo that preps, washes, scrubs, and squeegees tile, linoleum, and hardwood floors "so that you don't have to!" For customers who complained about cleaning gutters, iRobot developed the Looj Gutter Cleaning Robot. The Verro Pool Cleaning Robot "gets pools deep-down clean from floor to waterline—just drop it in and let it go!" And the iRobot Dirt Dog, with its high-capacity sweeper bin, cleans up heavy duty messes in workshops, garages, and basements and on patios and decks. Customers are now clamoring for a Roomba lawn mower!

Based on interactions with its customer community, iRobot has also continued to improve the original Roomba. Even smarter Roombas can now free themselves from almost any jam, including rug tassels and power cords, reducing the need to prep a room before unleashing the little sniffer. New models also feature a built-in voice tutorial for new users that explains the Roomba's features right out of the box.

Thus, iRobot has discovered the power of customer delight. More than that, it's working to harness that power by partnering with its satisfied-customer community to improve current products, develop new ones, and help spread the word to new customers. Last year, the company's sales reached nearly $310 million, up almost 63 percent over the previous two years. With the help of its delighted customers, iRobot is filling the vacuum and really cleaning up.

Sources: Based on information found in Paul Gillin, "Cleaning Up with Customer Evangelists," *BtoB*, August 13, 2007, p. 10; Faith Arner, "How the Roomba Was Realized," *BusinessWeek*, October 6, 2003, p. 10; Anita Slomski, "Robots Can Already Perform Surgery and Track Your Meds. Now, New Models Aim to Provide Therapy and Support," *Washington Post*, March 10, 2009, p. F1; "iRobot Corporation," *Hoover's Company Records*, August 1, 2009, p. 132607; and www.myroombud.com, accessed November 2009.

▲ Customer satisfaction: Ritz-Carlton's passion for satisfying customers is summed up in its credo, which promises a truly memorable experience—one that "enlivens the senses, instills well-being, and fulfills even the unexpressed wishes and needs of our guests."

an amazing 95 percent of departing guests report that their stay has been a truly memorable experience. More than 90 percent of Ritz-Carlton's delighted customers return.[14]

However, although a customer-centered firm seeks to deliver high customer satisfaction relative to competitors, it does not attempt to *maximize* customer satisfaction. A company can always increase customer satisfaction by lowering its price or increasing its services. But this may result in lower profits. Thus, the purpose of marketing is to generate customer value profitably. This requires a very delicate balance: The marketer must continue to generate more customer value and satisfaction but not "give away the house."

Customer Relationship Levels and Tools

Companies can build customer relationships at many levels, depending on the nature of the target market. At one extreme, a company with many low-margin customers may seek to develop *basic relationships* with them. For example, Procter & Gamble (P&G) does not phone or call on all of its Tide consumers to get to know them personally. Instead, P&G creates relationships through brand-building advertising, sales promotions, and its Tide Total Care Network Web site (www.Tide.com). At the other extreme, in markets with few customers and high margins, sellers want to create *full partnerships* with key customers. For example, P&G customer teams work closely with Wal-Mart, Safeway, and other large retailers. In between these two extremes, other levels of customer relationships are appropriate.

Beyond offering consistently high value and satisfaction, marketers can use specific marketing tools to develop stronger bonds with consumers. For example, many companies offer *frequency marketing programs* that reward customers who buy frequently or in large amounts. Airlines offer frequent-flyer programs, hotels give room upgrades to their frequent guests, and supermarkets give patronage discounts to "very important customers."

Other companies sponsor *club marketing programs* that offer members special benefits and create member communities. ▲For example, Harley-Davidson spon-

▲ Building customer relationships: Harley-Davidson sponsors the Harley Owners Group (H.O.G.), which gives Harley owners "an organized way to share their passion and show their pride." The worldwide club now numbers more than 1,500 local chapters and 1 million members.

sors the Harley Owners Group (H.O.G.), which gives Harley riders a way to share their common passion of "making the Harley-Davidson dream a way of life." H.O.G. membership benefits include a quarterly *HOG* magazine, the *H.O.G. Touring Handbook,* a roadside assistance program, a specially designed insurance program, theft reward service, a travel center, and a "Fly & Ride" program enabling members to rent Harleys while on vacation. The worldwide club now numbers more than 1,500 local chapters and more than one million members.[15]

The Changing Nature of Customer Relationships

Significant changes are occurring in the ways in which companies are relating to their customers. Yesterday's big companies focused on mass marketing to all customers at arm's length. Today's companies are building deeper, more direct, and lasting relationships with more carefully selected customers. Here are some important trends in the way companies and customers are relating to one another.

Relating with More Carefully Selected Customers

Few firms today still practice true mass marketing—selling in a standardized way to any customer who comes along. Today, most marketers realize that they don't want relationships with every customer. Instead, they target fewer, more profitable customers. "Not all customers are worth your marketing efforts," states one analyst. "Some are more costly to serve than to lose." Adds another marketing expert, "If you can't say who your customers *aren't*, you probably can't say who your customers *are*."[16]

Many companies now use customer profitability analysis to pass up or weed out losing customers and to target winning ones for pampering. One approach is to pre-emptively screen out potentially unprofitable customers. Progressive Insurance does this effectively. It asks prospective customers a series of screening questions to determine if they are right for the firm. If they're not, Progressive will likely tell them, "You might want to go to Allstate." A marketing consultant explains: "They'd rather send business to a competitor than take on unprofitable customers." Screening out unprofitable customers lets Progressive provide even better service to potentially more profitable ones.[17]

▲ Weeding out unprofitable customers: American Express recently sent a letter to some of its members offering them $300 in exchange for paying off their balances and closing out their accounts.

But what should the company do with unprofitable customers that it already has? If it can't turn them into profitable ones, it may even want to dismiss customers that are too unreasonable or that cost more to serve than they are worth. "Like bouncers in glitzy nightspots," says another consultant, "executives will almost certainly have to 'fire' [those] customers." ▲For example, American Express recently sent letters to some of its members offering them $300 in exchange for paying off their balances and closing out their accounts. Reading between the lines, the credit card company was dumping unprofitable customers. Sprint took similar but more abrupt actions:[18]

Sprint recently sent out letters to about 1,000 people to inform them that they had been summarily dismissed—but the recipients were Sprint *customers*, not employees. For about a year, the wireless-service provider had been tracking the number and frequency of support calls made by a group of high-maintenance users. According to a Sprint spokesperson, "in some cases, they were calling customer care hundreds of times a month . . . on the same issues, even after we felt those issues had been resolved." Ultimately, the company determined it could not meet the billing and service needs of this subset of subscribers and, therefore, waved their termination fees and cut off their service. Such "customer divestment" practices were once considered an anomaly. But new segmentation approaches and technologies have made it easier to focus on retaining the right customers and, by extension, to show problem customers the door.

Relating More Deeply and Interactively

Beyond choosing customers more selectively, companies are now relating with chosen customers in deeper, more meaningful ways. Rather than relying only on one-way, mass-media messages, today's marketers are incorporating new, more interactive approaches that help build targeted, two-way customer relationships.

New technologies have profoundly changed the ways in which people relate to one another. New tools for relating include everything from e-mail, Web sites, blogs, cell phones, and video sharing to online communities and social networks such as MySpace, Facebook, YouTube, and Twitter.

This changing communications environment also affects how companies and brands relate to consumers. The new communications approaches let marketers create deeper consumer involvement and a sense of community surrounding a brand—to make the brand a meaningful part of consumers' conversations and lives. "Becoming part of the conversation between consumers is infinitely more powerful than handing down information via traditional advertising," says one marketing expert. Says another, "Brands that engage in two-way conversation with their customers create stronger, more trusting relationships. People today want a voice and a role in their brand experiences. They want co-creation."[19]

However, at the same time that the new technologies create relationship-building opportunities for marketers, they also create challenges. They give consumers greater power and control. Today's consumers have more information about brands than ever before, and they have a wealth of platforms for airing and sharing their brand views with other consumers. Thus, the marketing world is now embracing not just customer relationship management, but also **customer-managed relationships**.

Greater consumer control means that, in building customer relationships, companies can no longer rely on marketing by *intrusion*. Instead, marketers must practice marketing by *attraction*—creating market offerings and messages that involve consumers rather than interrupt them. Hence, most marketers now augment their mass-media marketing efforts with a rich mix of direct marketing approaches that promote brand–consumer interaction.

For example, many brands are creating dialogues with consumers via their own or existing *online social networks*. To supplement their marketing campaigns, companies now routinely post their latest ads and made-for-the-Web videos on video sharing sites. They join social networks. Or they launch their own blogs, online communities, or consumer-generated review systems, all with the aim of engaging customers on a more personal, interactive level.

Take Twitter, for example. Organizations ranging from Dell, JetBlue Airways, Dunkin' Donuts, and Whole Foods to the Chicago Bulls and the L.A. Fire Department have opened Twitter accounts. They use "tweets" to start conversations with Twitter's more than 6 million registered users, address customer service issues, research customer reactions, and drive traffic to relevant articles, Web sites, contests, videos, and other brand activities. For example, Dell monitors Twitter-based discussions and responds quickly to individual problems or questions. ▲Zappos CEO Tony Hsieh, who receives close to 1,000 customer tweets daily, says that Twitter lets him give customers "more depth into what we're like, and my own personality." Another marketer notes that companies can "use Twitter to get the fastest, most honest research any company ever heard—the good, bad, and ugly—and it doesn't cost a cent."[20]

Despite their rapid growth in recent years, most marketers are still learning how to use the social media effectively. The problem is to find unobtrusive ways to enter consumers' social conver-

Customer-managed relationships
Marketing relationships in which customers, empowered by today's new digital technologies, interact with companies and with each other to shape their relationships with brands.

▼**Online social networks: Many brands are creating dialogs via their own or existing networks. Zappos CEO Tony Hsieh uses Twitter to give customers "more depth into what we're like."**

sations with engaging and relevant brand messages. Marketing has "historically been an exposure and intrusion practice—get in someone's face and talk about the attributes of the brand," says a social media analyst. "That approach works less and less effectively all the time, and it is absolutely fatal in the social arena."[21] Moreover, simply posting a humorous video, creating a social network page, or hosting a blog isn't enough. Successful social network marketing means making relevant and genuine contributions to consumer conversations. "Nobody wants to be friends with a brand," says one online marketing executive. "Your job [as a brand] is to be part of other friends' conversations."[22]

As a part of the new customer control and dialogue, consumers themselves are now creating brand conversations and messages on their own. And increasingly, companies are even *inviting* consumers to play a more active role in shaping brand messages and ads. For example, Frito-Lay, Southwest, Visa, Heinz, and many other companies have run contests for consumer-generated commercials that have been aired on national television.[23]

Consumer-generated marketing
Brand exchanges created by consumers themselves—both invited and uninvited—by which consumers are playing an increasing role in shaping their own brand experiences and those of other consumers.

Partner relationship management
Working closely with partners in other company departments and outside the company to jointly bring greater value to customers.

For the 2007 Super Bowl, Frito-Lay's Doritos brand launched a "Crash the Super Bowl" contest in which it invited 30-second ads from consumers and ran the two best during the game. One of the fan-produced ads, which showed a supermarket checkout girl getting frisky with a shopper, was judged in one poll as 67 percent more effective than the average Super Bowl ad. The other selected ad, showing a young driver eating Doritos and flirting with a pretty girl, cost only $12.79 to produce (the cost of four bags of chips) but was judged 45 percent more effective. Doritos has been running the "Crash the Super Bowl" challenge ever since. Last year it offered a cool $1 million to any fan who could generate a Doritos commercial that took the top spot on the *USA Today* Super Bowl Ad Meter. Consumers submitted nearly 2,000 entries. One of the consumer-generated ads—titled "Free Doritos" and featuring a vending-machine-shattering snow globe—claimed No. 1 on the *USA Today* Ad Meter, and Doritos gladly paid out the prize. A second consumer-created ad took the No. 5 spot. It was "the best million dollars the Doritos brand has ever spent," says the brand's marketing vice president.

However, harnessing consumer-generated content can be a time-consuming and costly process, and companies may find it difficult to glean even a little gold from all the garbage. ▲For example, when H.J. Heinz invited consumers to submit homemade ads for its ketchup brand on its YouTube page, it ended up sifting through more than 8,000 entries, of which it posted nearly 4,000. Some of the amateur ads were very good—entertaining and potentially effective. Most, however, are so-so at best, and others were downright dreadful. In one ad, a contestant chugs ketchup straight from the bottle. In another, the would-be filmmaker brushes his teeth, washes his hair, and shaves his face with Heinz's product. **Consumer-generated marketing**, whether invited by marketers or not, has become a significant marketing force. Through a profusion of consumer-generated videos, blogs, and Web sites, consumers are playing an increasing role in shaping their own brand experiences and those of other consumers. Beyond creating brand conversations, on their own or by invitation, customers are having an increasing say about everything from product design, usage, and packaging to pricing and distribution.[24]

▲Harnessing consumer-generated marketing: When H.J. Heinz invited consumers to submit homemade ads for its ketchup brand on YouTube, it received more than 8,000 entries—some very good but most only so-so or even downright dreadful.

Partner Relationship Management

When it comes to creating customer value and building strong customer relationships, today's marketers know that they can't go it alone. They must work closely with a variety of marketing partners. In addition to being good at *customer relationship management,* marketers must also be good at **partner relationship management**. Major changes are occurring in how marketers partner with others inside and outside the company to jointly bring more value to customers.

Partners Inside the Company

Traditionally, marketers have been charged with understanding customers and representing customer needs to different company departments. The old thinking was that marketing is done only by marketing, sales, and customer-support people. However, in today's more connected world, every functional area can interact with customers, especially electronically. The new thinking is that—no matter what your job in a company—you must understand marketing and be customer-focused. David Packard, late cofounder of Hewlett-Packard, wisely said, "Marketing is far too important to be left only to the marketing department."[25]

Today, rather than letting each department go its own way, firms are linking all departments in the cause of creating customer value. Rather than assigning only sales and marketing people to customers, they are forming cross-functional customer teams. For example, Procter & Gamble assigns "customer development teams" to each of its major retailer accounts. These teams—consisting of sales and marketing people, operations specialists, market and financial analysts, and others—coordinate the efforts of many P&G departments toward helping the retailer be more successful.

Marketing Partners Outside the Firm

Changes are also occurring in how marketers connect with their suppliers, channel partners, and even competitors. Most companies today are networked companies, relying heavily on partnerships with other firms.

Marketing channels consist of distributors, retailers, and others who connect the company to its buyers. The *supply chain* describes a longer channel, stretching from raw materials to components to final products that are carried to final buyers. For example, the supply chain for PCs consists of suppliers of computer chips and other components, the computer manufacturer, and the distributors, retailers, and others who sell the computers.

Through *supply chain management*, many companies today are strengthening their connections with partners all along the supply chain. They know that their fortunes rest not just on how well they perform. Success at building customer relationships also rests on how well their entire supply chain performs against competitors' supply chains. These companies don't just treat suppliers as vendors and distributors as customers. They treat both as partners in delivering customer value. On the one hand, for example, Lexus works closely with carefully selected suppliers to improve quality and operations efficiency. On the other hand, it works with its franchise dealers to provide top-grade sales and service support that will bring customers in the door and keep them coming back.

CAPTURING VALUE FROM CUSTOMERS (pp 48–51)

Author Comment »
Check back to Figure 1.1. In the first four steps of the marketing process, the company creates value *for* target customers and builds strong relationships with them. If it does that well, it can capture value *from* customers in return in the form of loyal customers who buy and continue to buy the company's brands.

The first four steps in the marketing process outlined in Figure 1.1 involve building customer relationships by creating and delivering superior customer value. The final step involves capturing value in return in the form of current and future sales, market share, and profits. By creating superior customer value, the firm creates highly satisfied customers who stay loyal and buy more. This, in turn, means greater long-run returns for the firm. Here, we discuss the outcomes of creating customer value: customer loyalty and retention, share of market and share of customer, and customer equity.

Creating Customer Loyalty and Retention

Good customer relationship management creates customer delight. In turn, delighted customers remain loyal and talk favorably to others about the company and its products. Studies show big differences in the loyalty of customers who are less satisfied, somewhat satisfied, and completely satisfied. Even a slight drop from complete satisfaction can create an enormous drop in loyalty. Thus, the aim of customer relationship management is to create not just customer satisfaction, but customer delight.

When the economy tightens, customer loyalty and retention become even more important. There are fewer customers and less spending to go around, so firms must work to hang on to the customers they have. It's five times cheaper to keep an old customer than to acquire a new one. "When wallets tighten up, focusing on [customer] loyalty and retention simply makes sense from an economic standpoint."[26]

The recent economic recession has put strong pressures on customer loyalty. For example, a UK study showed that 88 percent of the British public admit that they are no longer buying their favorite brands. One-third of shoppers are now using cheaper stores to do their weekly shopping and 50 percent are now buying private label products at the supermarket. Even more staggering, 37 percent say that the economic downturn has weakened the trust they have in leading brands.[27] Thus, companies today must shape their value propositions even more carefully and treat their profitable customers well.

Companies are realizing that losing a customer means losing more than a single sale. It means losing the entire stream of purchases that the customer would make over a lifetime of patronage. For example, here is a dramatic illustration of **customer lifetime value**:

Customer lifetime value
The value of the entire stream of purchases that the customer would make over a lifetime of patronage.

▲Customer lifetime value: To keep customers coming back, Stew Leonard's has created the "Disneyland of dairy stores." Rule #1—The customer is always right. Rule #2—If the customer is ever wrong, reread Rule #1.

▲Stew Leonard, who operates a highly profitable four-store supermarket in Connecticut and New York, says that he sees $50,000 flying out of his store every time he sees a sulking customer. Why? Because his average customer spends about $100 a week, shops 50 weeks a year, and remains in the area for about 10 years. If this customer has an unhappy experience and switches to another supermarket, Stew Leonard's has lost $50,000 in revenue. The loss can be much greater if the disappointed customer shares the bad experience with other customers and causes them to defect. To keep customers coming back, Stew Leonard's has created what *The New York Times* has dubbed the "Disneyland of Dairy Stores," complete with costumed characters, scheduled entertainment, a petting zoo, and animatronics throughout the store. From its humble beginnings as a small dairy store in 1969, Stew Leonard's has grown at an amazing pace. It's built 29 additions onto the original store, which now serves more than 300,000 customers each week. This legion of loyal shoppers is largely a result of the store's passionate approach to customer service. Rule #1: At Stew Leonard's—The customer is always right. Rule #2: If the customer is ever wrong, reread rule #1![28]

Stew Leonard is not alone in assessing customer lifetime value. Lexus, for example, estimates that a single satisfied and loyal customer is worth more than $600,000 in lifetime sales.[29] And the estimated lifetime value of a young mobile phone consumer is $26,000. In fact, a company can lose money on a specific transaction but still benefit greatly from a long-term relationship. This means that companies must aim high in building customer relationships. Customer delight creates an emotional relationship with a brand, not just a rational preference. And that relationship keeps customers coming back.

Growing Share of Customer

Share of customer
The portion of the customer's purchasing that a company gets in its product categories.

Beyond simply retaining good customers to capture customer lifetime value, good customer relationship management can help marketers to increase their **share of customer**—the share they get of the customer's purchasing in their product categories. Thus, banks want to increase "share of wallet." Supermarkets and restaurants want to get more "share of stomach." Car companies want to increase "share of garage," and airlines want greater "share of travel."

To increase share of customer, firms can offer greater variety to current customers. Or they can create programs to cross-sell and up-sell in order to market more products and services to existing customers. For example, Amazon.com is highly skilled at leveraging relationships with its 88 million customers to increase its share of each customer's purchases. Originally an online bookseller, Amazon.com now offers customers music, videos, gifts, toys, consumer electronics, office products, home improvement items, lawn and garden products, apparel and accessories, jewelry, tools, and even groceries. In addition, based on each customer's purchase history, previous product searches, and other data, the company recommends related products that might be of interest. This recommendation system influences up to 30 percent of all sales.[30] In these ways, Amazon.com captures a greater share of each customer's spending budget.

Building Customer Equity

We can now see the importance of not just acquiring customers, but of keeping and growing them as well. One marketing consultant puts it this way: "The only value your company will ever create is the value that comes from customers—the ones you have now and the ones you will have in the future. Without customers, you don't have a business."[31] Customer relationship management takes a long-term view. Companies want not only to create profitable customers, but to "own" them for life, earn a greater share of their purchases, and capture their customer lifetime value.

What Is Customer Equity?

Customer equity
The total combined customer lifetime values of all of the company's customers.

The ultimate aim of customer relationship management is to produce high *customer equity*.[32] **Customer equity** is the total combined customer lifetime values of all of the company's current and potential customers. As such, it's a measure of the future value of the company's customer base. Clearly, the more loyal the firm's profitable customers, the higher the firm's customer equity. Customer equity may be a better measure of a firm's performance than current sales or market share. Whereas sales and market share reflect the past, customer equity suggests the future. ▲Consider Cadillac:[33]

▲To increase customer lifetime value and customer equity, Cadillac is cool again. Its ad campaigns target a younger generation of consumers.

In the 1970s and 1980s, Cadillac had some of the most loyal customers in the industry. To an entire generation of car buyers, the name "Cadillac" defined American luxury. Cadillac's share of the luxury car market reached a whopping 51 percent in 1976. Based on market share and sales, the brand's future looked rosy. However, measures of customer equity would have painted a bleaker picture. Cadillac customers were getting older (average age 60) and average customer lifetime value was falling. Many Cadillac buyers were on their last car. Thus, although Cadillac's market share was good, its customer equity was not. Compare this with BMW. Its more youthful and vigorous image didn't win BMW the early market share war. However, it did win BMW younger customers with higher customer lifetime values. The result: In the years that followed, BMW's market share and profits soared while Cadillac's fortunes eroded badly. Thus, market share is not the answer. We should care not just about current sales but also about future sales. Customer lifetime value and customer equity are the name of the game. Recognizing this, in recent years, Cadillac has attempted to make the Caddy cool again by targeting a younger generation of consumers with new high-performance models and more vibrant advertising. The average consumer aspiring to own a Cadillac is now about 36 years old.

Building the Right Relationships with the Right Customers

Companies should manage customer equity carefully. They should view customers as assets that need to be managed and maximized. But not all customers, not even all loyal customers, are good investments. Surprisingly, some loyal customers can be unprofitable, and some disloyal customers can be profitable. Which customers should the company acquire and retain?

The company can classify customers according to their potential profitability and manage its relationships with them accordingly. ■ **Figure 1.5** classifies customers into one of four relationship groups, according to their profitability and projected loyalty.[34] Each group requires a different relationship management strategy. "Strangers" show low potential profitability and little projected loyalty. There is little

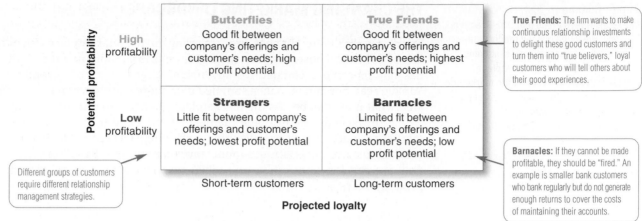

■ **Figure 1.5** Customer Relationship Groups

fit between the company's offerings and their needs. The relationship management strategy for these customers is simple: Don't invest anything in them.

"Butterflies" are potentially profitable but not loyal. There is a good fit between the company's offerings and their needs. However, like real butterflies, we can enjoy them for only a short while and then they're gone. An example is stock market investors who trade shares often and in large amounts but who enjoy hunting out the best deals without building a regular relationship with any single brokerage company. Efforts to convert butterflies into loyal customers are rarely successful. Instead, the company should enjoy the butterflies for the moment. It should create satisfying and profitable transactions with them, capturing as much of their business as possible in the short time during which they buy from the company. Then, it should cease investing in them until the next time around.

"True friends" are both profitable and loyal. There is a strong fit between their needs and the company's offerings. The firm wants to make continuous relationship investments to delight these customers and nurture, retain, and grow them. It wants to turn true friends into "true believers," who come back regularly and tell others about their good experiences with the company.

"Barnacles" are highly loyal but not very profitable. There is a limited fit between their needs and the company's offerings. An example is smaller bank customers who bank regularly but do not generate enough returns to cover the costs of maintaining their accounts. Like barnacles on the hull of a ship, they create drag. Barnacles are perhaps the most problematic customers. The company might be able to improve their profitability by selling them more, raising their fees, or reducing service to them. However, if they cannot be made profitable, they should be "fired."

The point here is an important one: Different types of customers require different relationship management strategies. The goal is to build the *right relationships* with the *right customers*.

Speed Bump Linking the Concepts

We've covered a lot of territory. Again, slow down for a moment and develop *your own* thoughts about marketing.

- In *your own words*, what *is* marketing and what does it seek to accomplish?
- How well does Lexus manage its relationships with customers? What customer relationship management strategy does it use? What relationship management strategy does Wal-Mart use?
- Think of a company for which you are a "true friend." What strategy does this company use to manage its relationship with you?

Author Comment »
Marketing doesn't take place in a vacuum. Now that we've discussed the five steps in the marketing process, let's examine how the ever-changing marketplace affects both consumers and the marketers who serve them. We'll look more deeply into these and other marketing environment factors in Chapter 3.

THE CHANGING MARKETING LANDSCAPE (pp 52–58)

Every day, dramatic changes are occurring in the marketplace. Richard Love of Hewlett-Packard observes, "The pace of change is so rapid that the ability to change has now become a competitive advantage." Yogi Berra, the legendary New York Yankees catcher and manager, summed it up more simply when he said, "The future ain't what it used to be." As the marketplace changes, so must those who serve it.

In this section, we examine the major trends and forces that are changing the marketing landscape and challenging marketing strategy. We look at five major developments: the uncertain economic environment, the digital age, rapid globalization, the call for more ethics and social responsibility, and the growth of not-for-profit marketing.

The Uncertain Economic Environment

Beginning in 2008, the United States and world economies experienced a stunning economic meltdown, unlike anything since the Great Depression of the 1930s. The stock market plunged and trillions of dollars of market value simply evaporated. The financial crisis left shell-shocked consumers short of both money and confidence as they faced losses in income, a severe credit crunch, declining home values, and rising unemployment. "The bad news keeps coming, fast and furious," said one analyst at the time. "Houses are worth less, home-equity lines of credit are being suspended, jobs are at risk, wages aren't keeping up with inflation, and energy prices continue to soar, eating away at Americans' disposable income."[35]

The faltering and uncertain economy caused many consumers to rethink their spending priorities and to cut back on their buying. After a decade of overspending, "frugality has made a comeback," announced one analyst. "A new sense of back-to-basics frugality and common sense has taken hold," said another.[36] In the aftermath of the meltdown, consumers are now spending less and more wisely. More than just a temporary change, the economic downturn will likely affect consumer buying attitudes and spending behavior for many years to come (see Marketing at Work 1.2).

In response, companies in all industries—from discounters such as Target to luxury brands such as Lexus—have tightened their budgets and aligned their marketing strategies with the new economic realities. More than ever, marketers are emphasizing the *value* in their value propositions. They are focusing on value-for-the-money, practicality, and durability in their product offerings and marketing pitches. "Value is the magic word," says a P&G marketing executive. "In these economic times, people are doing the math in their heads, and they're being much more thoughtful before making purchases. Now, we're going to be even more focused on helping consumers see value."[37]

▲ For example, in the past, discount retailer Target focused on the "expect more" side of its "Expect More. Pay Less." value proposition. But that has now changed.[38]

▼ In tough economic times, companies must emphasize the value in their value propositions. Target is now focusing squarely on the "pay less" side of its "Expect More. Pay Less." positioning.

For years, Target's carefully cultivated "upscale-discounter" image successfully differentiated it from Wal-Mart's more hard-nosed "lowest price" position. But in the tougher economy, many consumers believed that Target's trendier assortments and hip marketing also meant steeper prices, and Target's performance slipped relative to Wal-Mart's. So Target has shifted its focus more to the "Pay Less" half of the slogan. It's making certain that its prices are in line with Wal-Mart's and that customers are aware of it. Although still trendy, Target's ads now feature explicit low-price and savings appeals. "We're still trying to define and find the right balance between 'Expect More. Pay Less.'" says Target's CEO. "The current environment means that the focus is squarely on the 'Pay Less' side of it."

Marketing at Work 1.2

An Era of Austerity—The Thrifty Route in Fashion

Recession or not, people still need to look good and feel good. However, a shift in buying behavior has changed the retail landscape. Consumers are stretching every dollar, buying less while making smarter decisions in every purchase. Apparel brands struggle to creatively engage consumers at every conceivable purchase point. So how does a clothing retailer woo shoppers into their stores to make a purchase when these shoppers are resigned to spend less or not spend at all?

Japanese consumers are known to be the most demanding in the world. They have a strong preference for quality and luxury products are a must have. But amid a sharp economic slowdown, price is finally beginning to take priority for many shoppers who are worried about their job. Luxe has lost its luster as more Japanese now take the thrifty route in fashion. Gone are the days of the 1980s and 1990s, when they spent generously on imported branded items.

In early 2009, clothing retailer UNIQLO introduced its blockbuster jeans for 990 yen ($10.70). Frugal and bargain hunting Japanese were enthusiastically acquiring this piece of UNIQLO's eclectic style of affordable fashion. Such frugality is likely to be more than a fad as Japanese are showing good appetites for value-for-money products. The phenomenal growth of UNIQLO is proof that the era of austerity is taking hold.

UNIQLO is a well-storied brand known for its low-cost fleeces and T-shirts. Founded by the Yamaguchi-based company Ogori Shoji in 1949, the store originally sold men's clothing until 1984, when they opened a unisex casual wear store in Hiroshima under the name "Unique Clothing Warehouse." It was at this time that the brand name UNIQLO was born, as a short form for "unique clothing." By 1994, there were over 100 UNIQLO stores operating throughout Japan.

Its first urban store in Tokyo's trendy Harajuku district in 1998 proved such a success that by 2001, more outlets sprouted in major cities in Japan. With over 500 retail outlets in Japan, then UNIQLO expanded overseas and in 2001, opened its first outlet in London, England and then in Shanghai, China. In 2005 more overseas stores opened in the United States of America, Hong Kong and most recently, in 2009, stores have opened in Singapore and Paris, France. In a global marketplace with increasingly pragmatic consumers, UNIQLO has indeed become the favored clothing retailer, serving its value-conscious fans with a stable of 860 stores worldwide.

As a cheap chic brand popular with design-conscious Japanese youths, UNIQLO is now catering to trendsetters outside Japan. Its presence is felt as a flagship store opened in the world's fashion capital, Paris. The company is planning for further expansion including a new store opening in Russia in 2010. UNIQLO has to compete with fast moving contenders such as Esprit, Zara, Mango, and H&M. Will all these brands be able to incite customers to buy fashion items more regularly?

The new era of frugality means that these brands must clearly spell out their value propositions so that customers are willing to part with their hard-earned money. H&M's recession-friendly proposition of fast fashion at affordable prices has helped the brand to weather the economic crisis. It is planning an aggressive expansion into the Asia-Pacific, European, and Russian markets.

On the other hand, Esprit professes to be an international youthful lifestyle brand offering smart, affordable luxury items. Each year, the Esprit attributes are translated into 20,000 products in 12 collections to cater for confident and stylish people. It enjoys 40 years of success with high brand awareness worldwide.

Still, UNIQLO's appeal remains strong. Besides offering discounts on top of already-affordable prices, it attracts a wide consumer base by providing basic, essential garments that are high on quality.

The billionaire owner of UNIQLO, Tadashi Yanai, is proud to claim that his brand offers exceptionally high quality at a relatively low price to his customers. His dream is for UNIQLO to become the biggest maker and retailer of fashion in the world.

He also believes that UNIQLO allows a customer to combine each unit of clothing to express his or her personality. Indeed, the immense popularity of UNIQLO, especially in Japan, is propelled not just by a frugality route in consumption, it is also fueled by a new generation of confident fashionistas who are happy to creatively mix and match and don non-luxury items as a form of self-expression. Most recently, UNIQLO collaborated with the fashion designer Jil Sander. Following a five-year absence from designing, she created a collection for UNIQLO, named "+J," launched globally in 2009 and sold out in most countries in the first week. With this launch brought a whole new demographic of customer as they sought to buy Jil Sander–designed products at UNIQLO prices.

▲ The new consumer frugality: Even the fashion-conscious youth of Japan have been drawn in by "cheap chic" apparel stores such as **UNIQLO.**

(continued)

In a recessionary environment, many consumers are taking pride in being able to discern between buying to fulfill a need and a want and adopting a back-to-basics mentality. Others will constantly search for affordable ways to indulge in an attempt to lessen the stress of worrying about escalating living expenses. Companies and brands stimulate purchases by making it clear to the consumers how their products are totally relevant to the purchasers' needs and that their offerings are worthy of their every cent.

While the shopping mood is one of caution and lower-priced smart wear is the ongoing preference of enlightened trendy shoppers, the UNIQLO chain still enjoys brisk sales in Asia. It is putting top priority in the Asian market as it aims to boost global sales to 5 trillion yen ($ 54 billion) by 2020. UNIQLO is considering making a foray into Asian countries such as Malaysia, Indonesia, Vietnam, and India. It is set to open more outlets in China, Hong Kong, and Korea as these markets are expected to deliver the fastest growth. By 2020, UNIQLO plans to expand the number of global stores to 4,000.

Meanwhile, UNIQLO has inked a deal with mainland China Internet giant Taobao.com to open an online store. It has also entered the Singapore market with great aplomb, needing crowd control measures to ease the flow of human traffic when the stores opened. As many as 7,000 die-hard fans thronged the newest outlet located at ION Orchard in downtown Singapore.

As customers fervently scour UNIQLO outlets for the latest fashion, they are rest assured that the brand offers quality merchandise that is good value for the money. In the new environment, when cheap and chic also means looking and feeling good, UNIQLO has certainly found the best cut in the fabric.

Sources: Based on information from Chauncey Zalkin, "Made in Japan: The Culture Behind the Brand," accessed at www.brandchannel.com; Andrea Graelis, "Japan Clothes Giant Uniqlo Takes on World's Fashion Capital," *Agence France Presse*, September 30, 2009 accessed at www.factiva.com; Kana Inagaki, "Uniqlo Aims 7-Fold Rise in Group Sales to 5 Trillion Yen by 2020," September 2, 2009, *Kyodo News*, accessed at www.factiva.com; Kim Yoon-mi, "Asian Market Is Uniqlo's No. 1 Priority," *The Korea Herald*, September 24, 2009, accessed at www.factiva.com; and Michiyo Nakamoto, "Japanese Shoppers Break with Tradition," *Financial Times* (FT.com), September 9, 2009, accessed at www.factiva.com; www.uniqlo.com, accessed November 2009; www.esprit.com, accessed November 2009; and www.hm.com accessed November 2009.

Even wealthier consumers have joined the trend toward frugality. Conspicuous free spending is no longer fashionable. As a result, even luxury brands are stressing value. For years, Lexus has emphasized status and performance. For example, its pre-Christmas ads typically feature a loving spouse giving his or her significant other a new Lexus wrapped in a big red bow. Lexus is still running those ads, but it's also hedging its bets by running other ads with the tagline "lowest cost of ownership," referring to Lexus' decent fuel economy, durability, and resale value. "It's definitely a time to be more rational," says Lexus' North American marketing chief.[39]

In adjusting to the new economy, companies might be tempted to cut marketing budgets deeply and to slash prices in an effort to coax cash-strapped customers into opening their wallets. However, although cutting costs and offering selected discounts can be important marketing tactics in a down economy, smart marketers understand that making cuts in the wrong places can damage long-term brand images and customer relationships. The challenge is to balance the brand's value proposition with the current times while also enhancing its long-term equity.

"A recession creates winners and losers just like a boom," notes one economist. "When the recession ends, when the road levels off and the world seems full of promise once more, your position in the competitive pack will depend on how skillfully you manage right now."[40] Thus, rather than slashing prices, many marketers are holding the line on prices and instead explaining why their brands are worth it. And rather than cutting their marketing budgets in the difficult times, companies such as Wal-Mart and McDonald's have maintained or actually increased their marketing spending. In fact, a recent survey of more than 650 marketers at companies in a variety of industries found that, despite the down economy, half of the companies surveyed were holding firm on their marketing budgets or planning increases.[41] The goal is to build market share and strengthen customer relationships at the expense of competitors who are cutting back.

A troubled economy can present opportunities as well as threats. For example, the fact that 40 percent of consumers say they are eating out less poses threats for many full-service restaurants. However, it presents opportunities for fast-food marketers. For instance, a Seattle McDonald's franchise operator recently took on

Starbuck's in its hometown with billboards proclaiming "Large is the new grande" and "Four bucks is dumb." Playing on its cheap-eats value proposition, McDonald's worldwide sales grew 7.2 percent in the fourth quarter last year and earnings grew 11 percent, while Starbucks earnings dropped 96 percent.[42]

Similarly, the trend toward saving money by eating at home plays into the hands of name-brand food makers, who are positioning their wares as convenient and—compared with a restaurant meal—inexpensive. Rather than lowering prices, many food makers are instead pointing out the value of their products as compared to eating out. An ad for Francesco Rinaldi pasta sauce asserts, "Now you can feed a family of four for under $10." Kraft's DiGiorno pizza ads employ "DiGiornonomics" showing that the price of a DiGiorno pizza baked at home is half that of a delivery pizza.

The Digital Age

The recent technology boom has created a digital age. The explosive growth in computer, communications, information, and other digital technologies has had a major impact on the ways companies bring value to their customers. Now, more than ever before, we are all connected to each other and to information anywhere in the world. Where it once took days or weeks to receive news about important world events, we now learn about them as they are occurring through live satellite broadcasts and news Web sites. Where it once took weeks to correspond with others in distant places, they are now only moments away by cell phone, e-mail, or Web cam.

The digital age has provided marketers with exciting new ways to learn about and track customers and to create products and services tailored to individual customer needs. It's helping marketers to communicate with customers in large groups or one-to-one. Through Web videoconferencing, marketing researchers at a company's headquarters in New York can look in on focus groups in Chicago or Paris without ever stepping onto a plane. With only a few clicks of a mouse button, a direct marketer can tap into online data services to learn anything from what car you drive to what you read to what flavor of ice cream you prefer. Or, using today's powerful computers, marketers can create their own detailed customer databases and use them to target individual customers with offers designed to meet their specific needs.

Internet
A vast public web of computer networks that connects users of all types all around the world to each other and to an amazingly large information repository.

Digital technology has also brought a new wave of communication, advertising, and relationship building tools—ranging from online advertising, video sharing tools, cell phones, and video games to Web widgets and online social networks. The digital shift means that marketers can no longer expect consumers to always seek them out. Nor can they always control conversations about their brands. The new digital world makes it easy for consumers to take marketing content that once lived only in advertising or on a brand Web site with them wherever they go and to share it with friends. More than just add-ons to traditional marketing channels, the new digital media must be fully integrated into the marketer's customer-relationship-building efforts.

▼**Web 3.0—the third coming of the Web—"will bring you a virtual world you can carry in your pocket."**

The most dramatic digital technology is the **Internet**. The number of Internet users worldwide now stands at more than 1.4 billion and will reach an estimated 3.4 billion by 2015. People now spend twice as much time surfing the Web as they do watching TV—an average of 32.7 hours per week. On a typical day, 58 percent of American adults check their e-mail, 49 percent Google or use another search engine to find information, 36 percent get the news, 19 percent keep in touch with friends on social networking sites such as Facebook and LinkedIn, and 16 percent watch a video on a video-sharing site such as YouTube. And by 2020, many experts believe, the Internet will be accessed primarily via a mobile device operated by voice, touch, and even thought or "mind-controlled human-computer interaction."[43]

Whereas *Web 1.0* connected people with information, the next generation *Web 2.0* has connected people with people, employing a fast-growing set of new Web technologies such as blogs, social-networking sites, and video-sharing sites. ▲*Web 3.0*, starting now, puts all of these information and people connections together in ways that will make our Internet experience more relevant, useful, and enjoyable.[44]

In Web 3.0, small, fast, customizable Internet applications, accessed through multifunction mobile devices, "will bring you a virtual world you can carry in your pocket. We will be carrying our amusements with us—best music collections, video collections, instant news access—all tailored to our preferences and perpetually updatable. And as this cooler stuff [evolves], we won't be connecting to this new Web so much as walking around inside it."[45] The interactive, community-building nature of these new Web technologies makes them ideal for relating with consumers.

Online marketing is now the fastest-growing form of marketing. These days, it's hard to find a company that doesn't use the Web in a significant way. In addition to the "click-only" dot-coms, most traditional "brick-and-mortar" companies have now become "click-and-mortar" companies. They have ventured online to attract new customers and build stronger relationships with existing ones. Today, more than 70 percent of American online users use the Internet to shop.[46] Business-to-business online commerce is also booming. It seems that almost every business has set up shop on the Web.

Thus, the technology boom is providing exciting new opportunities for marketers. We will explore the impact of digital marketing technologies in future chapters, especially Chapter 14.

Rapid Globalization

As they are redefining their customer relationships, marketers are also taking a fresh look at the ways in which they relate with the broader world around them. In an increasingly smaller world, companies are now connected *globally* with their customers and marketing partners.

Today, almost every company, large or small, is touched in some way by global competition. A neighborhood florist buys its flowers from Mexican nurseries, and a large U.S. electronics manufacturer competes in its home markets with giant Korean rivals. A fledgling Internet retailer finds itself receiving orders from all over the world at the same time that an American consumer-goods producer introduces new products into emerging markets abroad.

▼U.S. companies in a wide range of industries have developed truly global operations. Quintessentially American McDonald's captures 66 percent of its revenues from outside of the United States.

American firms have been challenged at home by the skillful marketing of European and Asian multinationals. Companies such as Toyota, Nokia, Nestlé, and Samsung have often outperformed their U.S. competitors in American markets. Similarly, U.S. companies in a wide range of industries have developed truly global operations, making and selling their products worldwide. ▲Quintessentially American McDonald's now serves 52 million customers daily in more than 30,000 local restaurants in 100 countries worldwide—some 66 percent of its corporate revenues come from outside the United States. Similarly, Nike markets in more than 180 countries, with non-U.S. sales accounting for 57 percent of its worldwide sales.[47] Today, companies are not only trying to sell more of their locally produced goods in international markets, they also are buying more supplies and components abroad.

Thus, managers in countries around the world are increasingly taking a global, not just local, view of the company's industry, competitors, and opportunities. They are asking: What is global marketing? How does it differ from domestic marketing? How do global competitors and forces affect our business? To what extent should we "go global"? We will discuss the global marketplace in more detail in Chapter 15.

Sustainable Marketing—The Call for More Social Responsibility

Marketers are reexamining their relationships with social values and responsibilities and with the very Earth that sustains us. As the worldwide consumerism and environmentalism movements mature, today's marketers are being called to develop *sustainable marketing* practices.

Corporate ethics and social responsibility have become hot topics for almost every business. And few companies can ignore the renewed and very demanding environmental movement. Every company action can affect customer relationships:[48]

> There is an unwritten contract today between customers and the brands they buy. First, they expect companies to consistently deliver what they advertise. Second, they expect the companies they do business with to treat them with respect and to be honorable and forthright. . . . Everything a company does affects the brand in the eyes of the customer. For example, Celestial Seasonings incurred customers' wrath by ignoring its advertised corporate image of environmental stewardship when it poisoned prairie dogs on its property. By contrast, Google's decision to use solar energy for its server farms reinforces what Google stands for and strengthens the Google brand.

The social-responsibility and environmental movements will place even stricter demands on companies in the future. Some companies resist these movements, budging only when forced by legislation or organized consumer outcries. More forward-looking companies, however, readily accept their responsibilities to the world around them. They view sustainable marketing as an opportunity to do well by doing good. They seek ways to profit by serving the best long-run interests of their customers and communities.

Some companies—such as Patagonia, Ben & Jerry's, Timberland, and others—are practicing "caring capitalism," setting themselves apart by being civic-minded and responsible. They are building social responsibility and action into their company value and mission statements. For example, when it comes to environmental responsibility, outdoor gear marketer Patagonia is "committed to the core." "Those of us who work here share a strong commitment to protecting undomesticated lands and waters," says the company's Web site. "We believe in using business to inspire solutions to the environmental crisis." Patagonia backs these words with actions. Each year it pledges at least 1 percent of its sales or 10 percent of its profits, whichever is greater, to the protection of the natural environment.[49] We will revisit the topic of sustainable marketing in greater detail in Chapter 16.

The Growth of Not-for-Profit Marketing

In recent years, marketing also has become a major part of the strategies of many not-for-profit organizations, such as colleges, hospitals, museums, zoos, symphony orchestras, and even churches. The nation's not-for-profits face stiff competition for support and membership. Sound marketing can help them to attract membership and support.[50] Consider the marketing efforts of the American Society for the Prevention of Cruelty to Animals:

▼ Not-for-profit marketing: A single two-minute TV commercial—"The Ad"—has attracted 200,000 new donors and raised roughly $30 million for the ASPCA since it started running in early 2007.

The American Society for the Prevention of Cruelty to Animals (ASPCA) gets its funding from more than 1 million active supporters. However, like many not-for-profits, attracting new donors is tricky—that is until singer-songwriter Sarah McLachlan came along and created what many in not-for-profit circles call "The Ad." Produced by a small 12-person Canadian firm, Eagle-Com, ▲the two-minute television commercial features heartbreaking photographs of dogs and cats scrolling across the screen while McLachlan croons the haunting song "Angel" in the background (see the "The Ad" at www.youtube.com/watch?v=Iu_JqNdp2As). McLachlan appears only momentarily to ask viewers to share her support for the ASPCA. The heart-rending commercial has tugged at viewers' heart strings and opened their wallets. This one ad has attracted 200,000 new donors and raised roughly $30 million for the organization since it started running in early 2007. That makes it a landmark in nonprofit fund-raising, where such amounts are virtually unimaginable for a single commercial. The donations from the McLachlan commercial have enabled the ASPCA to buy primetime slots on national networks like CNN, which in turn has generated more income. The ASPCA is now rolling out new McLachlan ads to further bolster its fund-raising efforts.[51]

Government agencies have also shown an increased interest in marketing. For example, the U.S. military has a marketing plan to attract recruits to its different services, and various government agencies are now designing *social marketing campaigns* to encourage energy conservation and concern for the environment or to discourage smoking, excessive drinking, and drug use. Even the once-stodgy U.S. Postal Service has developed innovative marketing to sell commemorative stamps, promote its priority mail services, and lift its image as a contemporary and competitive organization. In all, the U.S. government is the nation's 32nd largest advertiser, with an annual advertising budget of more than $1.2 billion.[52]

Author Comment >>
Remember Figure 1.1 outlining the marketing process? Now, based on everything we've discussed in this chapter, we'll expand that figure to provide a road map for learning marketing throughout the rest of the text.

SO, WHAT IS MARKETING? PULLING IT ALL TOGETHER (pp 58–59)

At the start of this chapter, Figure 1.1 presented a simple model of the marketing process. Now that we've discussed all of the steps in the process, ■ **Figure 1.6** presents an expanded model that will help you pull it all together. What is marketing? Simply put, marketing is the process of building profitable customer relationships by creating value for customers and capturing value in return.

The first four steps of the marketing process focus on creating value for customers. The company first gains a full understanding of the marketplace by researching customer needs and managing marketing information. It then designs a customer-driven marketing strategy based on the answers to two simple questions. The first question is "What consumers will we serve?" (market segmentation and targeting). Good marketing companies know that they cannot serve all customers in every way. Instead, they need to focus their resources on the customers they can serve

This expanded version of Figure 1.1 at the beginning of the chapter provides a good road map for the rest of the text. The underlying concept of the entire text is that marketing creates value *for* customers in order to capture value *from* customers in return.

■ **Figure 1.6** An Expanded Model of the Marketing Process

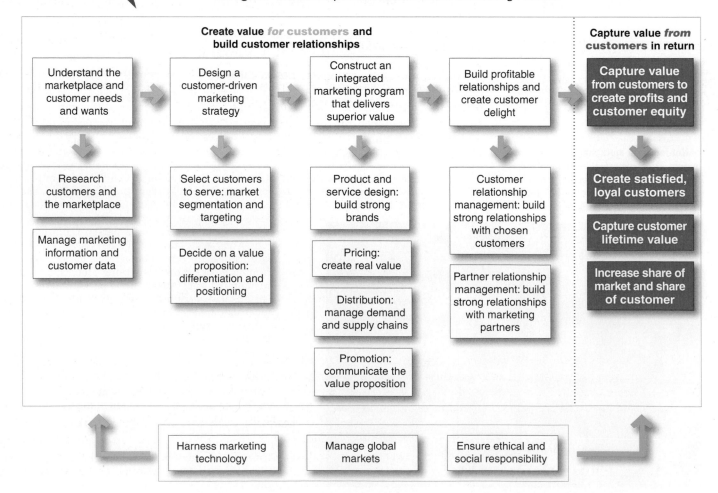

best and most profitably. The second marketing strategy question is "How can we best serve targeted customers?" (differentiation and positioning). Here, the marketer outlines a value proposition that spells out what values the company will deliver in order to win target customers.

With its marketing strategy decided, the company now constructs an integrated marketing program—consisting of a blend of the four marketing mix elements, or the four Ps—that transforms the marketing strategy into real value for customers. The company develops product offers and creates strong brand identities for them. It prices these offers to create real customer value and distributes the offers to make them available to target consumers. Finally, the company designs promotion programs that communicate the value proposition to target consumers and persuade them to act on the market offering.

Perhaps the most important step in the marketing process involves building value-laden, profitable relationships with target customers. Throughout the process, marketers practice customer relationship management to create customer satisfaction and delight. In creating customer value and relationships, however, the company cannot go it alone. It must work closely with marketing partners both inside the company and throughout the marketing system. Thus, beyond practicing good customer relationship management, firms must also practice good partner relationship management.

The first four steps in the marketing process create value *for* customers. In the final step, the company reaps the rewards of its strong customer relationships by capturing value *from* customers. Delivering superior customer value creates highly satisfied customers who will buy more and will buy again. This helps the company to capture customer lifetime value and greater share of customer. The result is increased long-term customer equity for the firm.

Finally, in the face of today's changing marketing landscape, companies must take into account three additional factors. In building customer and partner relationships, they must harness marketing technology, take advantage of global opportunities, and ensure that they act in an ethical and socially responsible way.

Figure 1.6 provides a good road map to future chapters of the text. Chapters 1 and 2 introduce the marketing process, with a focus on building customer relationships and capturing value from customers. Chapters 3, 4, and 5 address the first step of the marketing process—understanding the marketing environment, managing marketing information, and understanding consumer and business buyer behavior. In Chapter 6, we look more deeply into the two major marketing strategy decisions: selecting which customers to serve (segmentation and targeting) and deciding on a value proposition (differentiation and positioning). Chapters 7 through 14 discuss the marketing mix variables, one by one. Then, the final two chapters examine special marketing considerations: global marketing and sustainable marketing.

REST STOP
REVIEWING THE CONCEPTS

Today's successful companies—whether large or small, for-profit or not-for-profit, domestic or global—share a strong customer focus and a heavy commitment to marketing. The goal of marketing is to build and manage customer relationships.

> Objective 1 Define marketing and outline the steps in the marketing process. **(pp 32–34)**

Marketing is the process by which companies create value for customers and build strong customer relationships in order to capture value from customers in return.

The marketing process involves five steps. The first four steps create value *for* customers. First, marketers need to understand the marketplace and customer needs and wants. Next, marketers design a customer-driven marketing strategy with the goal of getting, keeping, and growing target customers. In the third step, marketers construct a marketing program that actually delivers superior value. All of these steps form the basis for the fourth step, building profitable customer relationships and creating customer delight. In the final step, the company reaps the rewards of strong customer relationships by capturing value *from* customers.

> **Objective 2** Explain the importance of understanding customers and the marketplace, and identify the five core marketplace concepts. **(pp 34–36)**

Outstanding marketing companies go to great lengths to learn about and understand their customers' needs, wants, and demands. This understanding helps them to design want-satisfying market offerings and build value-laden customer relationships by which they can capture customer lifetime value and greater share of customer. The result is increased long-term customer equity for the firm.

The core marketplace concepts are needs, wants, and demands; market offerings (products, services, and experiences); value and satisfaction; exchange and relationships; and markets. Wants are the form taken by human needs when shaped by culture and individual personality. When backed by buying power, wants become demands. Companies address needs by putting forth a value proposition, a set of benefits that they promise to consumers to satisfy their needs. The value proposition is fulfilled through a market offering, which delivers customer value and satisfaction, resulting in long-term exchange relationships with customers.

> **Objective 3** Identify the key elements of a customer-driven marketing strategy and discuss the marketing management orientations that guide marketing strategy. **(pp 37–41)**

To design a winning marketing strategy, the company must first decide *who* it will serve. It does this by dividing the market into segments of customers (*market segmentation*) and selecting which segments it will cultivate (*target marketing*). Next, the company must decide *how* it will serve targeted customers (how it will *differentiate and position* itself in the marketplace).

Marketing management can adopt one of five competing market orientations. The *production concept* holds that management's task is to improve production efficiency and bring down prices. The *product concept* holds that consumers favor products that offer the most in quality, performance, and innovative features; thus, little promotional effort is required. The *selling concept* holds that consumers will not buy enough of the organization's products unless it undertakes a large-scale selling and promotion effort. The *marketing concept* holds that achieving organizational goals depends on determining the needs and wants of target markets and delivering the desired satisfactions more effectively and efficiently than competitors do. The *societal marketing concept* calls for generating customer satisfaction *and* long-run societal well-being through sustainable

marketing strategies keyed to both achieving the company's goals and fulfilling its responsibilities.

> **Objective 4** Discuss customer relationship management and identify strategies for creating value *for* customers and capturing value *from* customers in return. **(pp 41–51)**

Broadly defined, *customer relationship management* is the process of building and maintaining profitable customer relationships by delivering superior customer value and satisfaction. The aim of customer relationship management is to produce high *customer equity,* the total combined customer lifetime values of all of the company's customers. The key to building lasting relationships is the creation of superior *customer value* and *satisfaction.*

Companies want not only to acquire profitable customers but also to build relationships that will keep them and grow "share of customer." Different types of customers require different customer relationship management strategies. The marketer's aim is to build the *right relationships* with the *right customers.* In return for creating value *for* targeted customers, the company captures value *from* customers in the form of profits and customer equity.

In building customer relationships, good marketers realize that they cannot go it alone. They must work closely with marketing partners inside and outside the company. In addition to being good at customer relationship management, they must also be good at *partner relationship management.*

> **Objective 5** Describe the major trends and forces that are changing the marketing landscape in this age of relationships. **(pp 52–59)**

Dramatic changes are occurring in the marketing arena. The recent economic meltdown has left many consumers short of both money and confidence, creating a new age of consumer frugality. More than ever, marketers must now emphasize the *value* in their value propositions. The challenge is to balance a brand's value proposition with the current times while also enhancing its long-term equity.

The boom in computer, telecommunications, information, transportation, and other technologies has created exciting new ways to learn about and relate to individual customers. It has also allowed new approaches by which marketers can target consumers more selectively and build closer, two-way customer relationships.

In an increasingly smaller world, many marketers are now connected *globally* with their customers and marketing partners. Today, almost every company, large or small, is touched in some way by global competition. Today's marketers are also reexamining their ethical and societal responsibilities. Marketers are being called upon to take greater responsibility for the social and environmental impact of their actions. Finally, in recent years, marketing also has become a major part of the strategies of many not-for-profit organizations, such as colleges, hospitals, museums, zoos, symphony orchestras, and even churches.

Pulling it all together, as discussed throughout the chapter, the major new developments in marketing can be summed up in a single word: *relationships*. Today, marketers of all kinds are taking advantage of new opportunities for building relationships with their customers, their marketing partners, and the world around them.

Navigating the Key Terms

Objective 1
Marketing (p 33)

Objective 2
Needs (p 34)
Wants (p 34)
Demands (p 34)
Market offering (p 34)
Marketing myopia (p 35)
Exchange (p 35)
Market (p 36)

Objective 3
Marketing management (p 37)
Production concept (p 38)
Product concept (p 38)
Selling concept (p 38)
Marketing concept (p 38)
Societal marketing concept (p 39)

Objective 4
Customer relationship management (p 41)
Customer-perceived value (p 41)
Customer satisfaction (p 42)

Customer-managed relationships (p 46)
Consumer-generated marketing (p 47)
Partner relationship management (p 47)
Customer lifetime value (p 49)
Share of customer (p 49)
Customer equity (p 50)

Objective 5
Internet (p 55)

Travel Log

Discussing the Issues

1. Explain how marketing creates profitable customer relationships. (AASCB: Communication)

2. Marketing has been criticized because it "makes people buy things they don't really need." Refute or support this accusation. (AACSB: Communication; Reflective Thinking)

3. What is a customer-driven marketing strategy and how can a company design one? (AACSB: Communication)

4. Compare and contrast the five different marketing management orientations. Is one orientation "right" and the others "wrong"? Explain. (AACSB: Communication; Reflective Thinking)

5. *Southern Living* magazine has the highest renewal rate in its industry—creating considerable customer equity for this product. What is *customer equity?* Using the customer relationship groups in Figure 1.5, explain which group best describes *Southern Living's* subscribers. Discuss other products or services that *Southern Living* could offer to grow its share of customer. (AACSB: Communication; Reflective Thinking)

6. Discuss trends impacting marketing and the implications of these trends on how marketers deliver value to customers. (AACSB: Communication)

Application Questions

1. Form a small group of three or four students. Have each member of the group talk to five other people, varying in age from young adult to very old, about their automobiles. Ask them what value means to them with regard to an automobile and how the manufacturer and dealer create such value. Discuss your findings with your group and write a brief report of what you learned about customer value. (AACSB: Communication; Reflective Thinking)

2. Research the following brands and try to determine the value proposition offered by each (AACSB: Communication; Reflective Thinking):
   a. Enterprise Rent-A-Car
   b. Lexus automobiles
   c. Gain laundry detergent
   d. iPhone

3. Read Appendix 4 to learn about careers in marketing. Interview someone who works in one of the marketing jobs described in the appendix and ask him or her the following questions:
   a. What does your job entail?
   b. How did you get to this point in your career? Is this what you thought you'd be doing when you grew up? What influenced you to get into this field?
   c. What education is necessary for this job?
   d. What advice can you give to college students?
   e. Add one additional question that you create.

Write a brief report of the responses to your questions and explain why you would or would not be interested in working in this field. (AACSB: Communication; Reflective Thinking)

Under the Hood: Marketing Technology

In only a few short years, *consumer-generated marketing* has increased exponentially. It's also known as *consumer-generated media* and *consumer-generated content*. More than 100 million Web sites contain user-generated content. You may be a contributor yourself if you've ever posted something on a blog, reviewed a product at Amazon.com, uploaded a video on YouTube, or sent a video from your mobile phone to a news Web site, such as CNN.com or FoxNews.com. This force has not gone unnoticed by marketers, and with good reason. Nielsen, the TV ratings giant, found that most consumers trust consumer opinions posted online. As a result, savvy marketers encourage consumers to generate content. For example, Coke has more than 3.5 million fans on Facebook, mothers can share information at Pamper's Village (www.pampers.com), and Dorito's scored a touchdown with consumer-created advertising during the past several Super Bowls. Apple even encourages iPhone users to develop applications for its device. However, consumer-generated marketing is not without problems—just check out the Diet Coke/Mentos videos or just search "I hate (insert company name)" in any search engine!

1. Find two examples (other than those discussed in the chapter) of marketer-supported consumer-generated content, along with two examples of consumer-generated content that is not officially supported by the company whose product is involved. Provide the Web link to each and discuss how the information impacts your attitude toward the companies involved. (AACSB: Communication; Reflective Thinking; Technology)

2. Discuss the advantages and disadvantages of consumer-generated marketing. (AACSB: Communication; Reflective)

Staying on the Road: Marketing Ethics

Did you drive a car today? Use a laptop computer? Buy a product in a store? If so, you emitted carbon dioxide (CO_2) and created a carbon footprint. All of us do that every day. Individuals and companies emit carbon dioxide in everyday activities. Many consumers feel bad about doing this; others expect companies to take action. What's the answer? Reducing carbon emissions is one solution, but another one is to offset your carbon emissions by purchasing carbon offsets and renewable energy certificates (RECs)—forms of "emission trading." Individual consumers do this, and companies are flocking to purchase carbon offsets for themselves or to offer to their customers, resulting in an estimated $100 million annual market. And experts predict exponential growth over the next few years. Airlines routinely offer flyers the option of paying a few extra dollars to offset their carbon emissions. For example, JetBlue Airways introduced its *Jetting to Green* program that allows flyers to make their flight "carbon-neutral" for as little as $2.00. Flyers' donations then support reforestation, wind, and waste management projects.

1. Learn more about carbon offsets and discuss four examples of how businesses are using them. In your opinion, are these companies embracing the societal marketing concept? (AACSB Communication; Reflective Thinking)

2. One criticism of carbon offsetting is that companies are not really helping the environment by changing their own behavior. Instead, they're merely buying "environmental pardons." Recently proposed legislation, referred to as "cap and trade," argues that the marketplace will cause a reduction in pollution. Do you think carbon offsets are a responsible solution to environmental concerns? Write a brief essay debating this issue. (AACSB: Communication; Ethical Reasoning)

Rough Road Ahead: Marketing and the Economy

Hershey

There are still some things that today's consumers just aren't willing to give up—such as chocolate. But as with eating out and clothing purchases, they *are* trading down. That is just fine with Hershey, America's best-known chocolate maker. For years, riding the good times, premium chocolates have grown faster than lower-priced confectionery products. Slow to jump on the premium bandwagon, Hershey lost market share to Mars Inc.'s *Dove* line. But as consumers pinch pennies, sales of premium chocolate brands have gone flat. At the same time, Hershey's sales, profits, and stock price increases as many consumers have passed up the higher-end goods in favor of Hershey's chocolate bars, Reese's Peanut Butter Cups, and Kit Kat wafers. Hershey is responding with tactics such as running new ads that stress the value. It is also cutting costs by paring back the varieties of products like Hershey's Kisses. As supermarkets trim back the shelf space they allot to premium chocolates, Hershey stands poised to cash in as consumers look to affordable Hershey favorites to satisfy their cravings. After all, even on a tight budget, people need to indulge at least a little.

1. Is Hershey's resurgence based on a want or a need?

2. Evaluate the shift in chocolate sales based on the benefits and costs that customers perceive.

3. What other products are harmed or helped by the new consumer frugality?

Travel Budget: Marketing by the Numbers

Not all customers pay their bills on time, while others are considered to be extremely high maintenance. Simply getting rid of customers that fall into these categories is not always the answer. How will valued customers view the policy? It is never easy for a business to try and assess the value of customers, particularly the long-term value of the customer. It is possible to use a fairly simple net present value calculation. To determine a basic customer lifetime value, each stream of profit is discounted back to its present value (PV) and then totaled. The basic equation for calculating net present value (NPV) is as follows:

$$NPV = \sum_{t=0}^{N} \frac{C_t}{(1 + r)^t}$$

Where,

t = time of the cash flow
N = total customer lifetime
r = discount rate

C_t = net cash flow (the profit) at time t (The initial cost of acquiring a customer would be a negative profit at time 0.)

NPV can be calculated easily on most financial calculators or by using one of the calculators available on the Internet, such as the one found at http://www.investopedia.com/calculator/NetPresentValue.aspx. For more discussion of the financial and quantitative implications of marketing decisions, see Appendix 2: Marketing by the Numbers.

1. Assume that a trade customer spends an average of $150 a week and that the retailer earns a five percent margin. Calculate the customer lifetime value if this shopper remains loyal over a 10-year life span, assuming a five percent annual interest rate and no initial cost to acquire the customer.

2. Discuss how a business can increase a customer's lifetime value.

Drive In: Video Case

Harley-Davidson

Few brands engender such intense loyalty as that found in the hearts of Harley-Davidson owners. Why? Because the company's marketers spend a great deal of time thinking about customers. They want to know who customers are, how they think and feel, and why they buy a Harley. That attention to detail has helped build Harley-Davidson into a $5 billion company with more than 900,000 Harley Owners Group (HOG) members, the largest company-sponsored owner's group in the world.

Harley sells much more than motorcycles. The company sells a feeling of independence, individualism, and freedom. These strong emotional connections have made Harley-Davidson ownership much more of a lifestyle than only a product consumption experience. To support that lifestyle, Harley-Davidson recognizes that its most impor-

tant marketing tool is the network of individuals that ride Harleys. For this reason, Harley-Davidson engages its customer base through company-sponsored travel adventures, events, and other things such as clothes and accessories both for riders and for those who simply like to associate with the brand.

After viewing the video featuring Harley-Davidson, answer the following questions about managing profitable customer relationships.

1. How does Harley-Davidson build long-term customer relationships?

2. What is Harley-Davidson's value proposition?

3. Relate the concept of customer equity to Harley-Davidson. How does Harley-Davidson's strategy focus on the right relationships with the right customers?

2

Company and Marketing Strategy
Partnering to Build Customer Relationships

ROAD MAP

Previewing the Concepts

In the first chapter, we explored the marketing process by which companies create value for consumers in order to capture value from them in return. In this leg of the journey, we dig deeper into steps two and three of the marketing process—designing customer-driven marketing strategies and constructing marketing programs. First, we look at the organization's overall strategic planning, which guides marketing strategy and planning. Next, we discuss how, guided by the strategic plan, marketers partner closely with others inside and outside the firm to create value for customers. We then examine marketing strategy and planning— how marketers choose target markets, position their market offerings, develop a marketing mix, and manage their marketing programs. Finally, we look at the important step of measuring and managing return on marketing investment.

Objective Outline

 Objective 1 Explain companywide strategic planning and its four steps.
Companywide Strategic Planning: Defining Marketing's Role **pp 67–70**

 Objective 2 Discuss how to design business portfolios and develop growth strategies.
Designing the Business Portfolio **pp 71–74**

Objective 3 Explain marketing's role in strategic planning and how marketing works with its partners to create and deliver customer value.
Planning Marketing: Partnering to Build Customer Relationships **pp 74–77**

 Objective 4 Describe the elements of a customer-driven marketing strategy and mix and the forces that influence it.
Marketing Strategy and the Marketing Mix **pp 77–82**

 Objective 5 List the marketing management functions, including the elements of a marketing plan, and discuss the importance of measuring and managing return on marketing investment.
Managing the Marketing Effort **pp 82–86**
Measuring and Managing Return on Marketing Investment **pp 86–88**

First, let's look at the Olympic brand. Staging an Olympics is an enormous challenge for any city or country. Not only do venues and accommodations need to be constructed for the Olympians, but also the infrastructure of the Olympic city needs to be transformed. In order to achieve success, the physical issues have to be addressed, along with the ability to market the spectacle to an ever-broadening world audience. None of this is possible unless sponsors are brought onboard at the earliest opportunity, and they are able to see tangible benefits from their involvement.

▲Impossible is nothing: Adidas was one of the main sponsors of the Beijing Olympics in 2008. The company's ad campaign featured medal-hopeful athletes from countries across the globe, reflecting the aspirational nature of Adidas' target markets.

First Stop

The Olympics: Branding on a Global Stage

The Olympic brand is a powerful worldwide symbol representing not only sports, but a celebration of the best in the world and an opportunity for nations to join together and compete for glory. The Beijing Olympics in 2008 was immensely popular worldwide and successful, delivering a quality experience for the athletes, spectators, and millions of viewers around the world. It was also vital in rebranding and repackaging China as a modern nation. China hoped that the Olympics would help it forge business links that would propel the country forward. The massive effort to deliver the games was not without cost; billions were invested, and some of this funding came from sponsors and partners.

The London 2012 Olympic Games promise to be another tremendous spectacle, although the budget is only roughly half of what Beijing's was. Yet sponsors and partners from Visa and Coca Cola to Adidas and British Airways have already signed up. The purpose of the partnerships is not merely financial; it is about building customer relationships, both for the games and for the businesses.

On a slightly less grand level, the Olympics provides smaller businesses with an opportunity to be involved, provide products and services, and promote the fact that they have an association with the 2012 Olympics. In June 2008, before the Beijing Olympics had even got underway, the latest London 2012 "business-engagement" figures were published. Business engagement refers to the numbers of companies registered with the Olympics to provide the event with products and services. Nearly 90 percent of the registered companies (18,000) were small-to-medium sized.

The Olympic Delivery Authority (ODA) and London Organizing Committee (LOCOG) will, in the coming months and years, allocate over $9 billion of work to various businesses. There will be at least 75,000 business opportunities, including the direct contracts and the supply chains used to fulfil those contracts. John Armitt, the ODA chairman, had been involved in numerous discussions

The huge commercial possibilities of being associated with the Olympic brand cannot be underestimated. Businesses that either sponsor the Olympics or those that provide products and services, make full use of their association. This consists of a full partnership approach aimed at securing and building customer relationships.

▲The Olympic logo is one of the world's most powerful brands, attracting sponsorship deals from companies all over the world.

with British businesses and had found that an enormous number were keen to be involved in the London 2012 Games. At this stage it was smaller businesses that were finding opportunities, many being able to establish themselves as key providers with experience in dealing with a project of this size. Armitt believed that this would put them in a prime position to compete with even larger contractors in the future. Armitt recognized it was a challenging project and it needed the best British businesses to keep it on track.

The Organizing Committee's Chief Executive, Paul Deighton, was suitably impressed with the British business response to the London 2012 Business Network. The London 2012 procurement team and business development partners had worked hard to encourage as many businesses as possible to become involved at some level in providing goods and services. The push would go on into 2009, with increasing numbers of U.K. businesses registering on the Compete For system. By registering on this system Deighton was certain that the businesses would not regret getting involved in the Games, as it represented a "lifetime business opportunity."

Tessa Jowell, the Olympics Minister, says "The fact that 70 percent of the 650 companies that have already won work supplying the games are small- and medium-sized firms demonstrates the potential for the business benefits of London 2012 to provide a boost to the whole economy. Since January this year [2008], companies have been signing up at a rate of 500 per week, a clear illustration of the value of the system and the determination of British business to grasp the economic opportunities the games offer. Beyond delivering London 2012 on time and on budget, our ambition is to use the games to raise skills levels, tackle worklessness, and promote longterm growth, leaving a legacy of better trained workers and a more efficient business environment."

Commenting on the fact that being associated with the Olympics is a positive, beyond the value of any contract that a business might be able to secure, Lord Digby Jones, the U.K.'s minister for Trade and Investment notes, "International sporting events offer huge opportunities for U.K. businesses. However size doesn't matter when it comes to British companies winning business in the 2012 London Olympic and Paralympics' Games. Hundreds of small and medium sized businesses have already won contracts with billions of pounds of contracts still to win. Large or small, winning that business for 2012 will provide a springboard for global growth, and an opportunity to promote our capabilities on the international stage."

Clearly, the marketing opportunities are enormous for partner businesses and suppliers to the Olympics. However, one of the key concerns is the use of the Olympic logos by businesses that have nothing to do with the event. According to intellectual property expert Tracey Huxley, "The outstanding success of Team Great Britain in China this summer is likely to encourage companies to use the swell of national pride and the gathering momentum of London 2012 in their marketing, both in the immediate future and throughout the next four years. Adidas, for example, sponsored both the Beijing Games and is a partner with London 2012. The company ran a series of advertisements with medal-winning athletes that feature the phrase: "Impossible is Nothing." The British-orientated advertisements also included the U.K.'s gold-medal winning men's cycling pursuit team with the following tagline: "Awesome away . . . Imagine them at home." Likewise, Lloyds TSB ran a series of advertisements featuring future Olympic hopefuls, and Visa's advertisements proudly announced "The Journey to London 2012 Starts Now."

However, in light of the legislation introduced primarily to stop ambush marketing as seen in previous Olympics, it is extremely easy to fall foul of the restrictions, says Huxley. Ambush marketing tends to come in two different forms—they either falsely imply that the business has an association with the Olympics, or they involve giving away branded products that will be taken into a stadium where they will be seen by viewers if the event is televised. "In fact, the burden of proof in many cases will be reversed, so an infringement will be presumed unless the accused can prove their innocence," Huxley adds. "Brands must therefore be mindful of the restrictions which are already being enforced, or face the consequences. In particular those with licensees or franchisees need to ensure that they, too, are aware of the rules and don't go too far, as this may also draw the brand owner into the infringement."[1]

*l*ike London 2012, outstanding marketing organizations employ strongly customer-driven marketing strategies and programs that create customer value and relationships. These marketing strategies and programs, however, are guided by broader companywide strategic plans, which must also be customer focused. Thus, to understand the role of marketing, we must first understand the organization's overall strategic planning process.

■ **Figure 2.1.** Steps in Strategic Planning

Companywide strategic planning guides marketing strategy and planning.

Author Comment »
Companywide strategic planning guides marketing strategy and planning. Like marketing strategy, the company's broad strategy must also be customer focused.

Strategic planning
The process of developing and maintaining a strategic fit between the organization's goals and capabilities and its changing marketing opportunities.

Mission statement
A statement of the organization's purpose—what it wants to accomplish in the larger environment.

▼Cold Stone Creamery's mission is "to make people happy around the world by selling the highest quality, most creative experience with passion, excellence, and innovation."

COMPANYWIDE STRATEGIC PLANNING: DEFINING MARKETING'S ROLE (pp 67–70)

Each company must find the game plan for long-run survival and growth that makes the most sense given its specific situation, opportunities, objectives, and resources. This is the focus of **strategic planning**—the process of developing and maintaining a strategic fit between the organization's goals and capabilities and its changing marketing opportunities.

Strategic planning sets the stage for the rest of the planning in the firm. Companies usually prepare annual plans, long-range plans, and strategic plans. The annual and long-range plans deal with the company's current businesses and how to keep them going. In contrast, the strategic plan involves adapting the firm to take advantage of opportunities in its constantly changing environment.

At the corporate level, the company starts the strategic planning process by defining its overall purpose and mission (see ■ **Figure 2.1**). This mission is then turned into detailed supporting objectives that guide the whole company. Next, headquarters decides what portfolio of businesses and products is best for the company and how much support to give each one. In turn, each business and product develops detailed marketing and other departmental plans that support the companywide plan. Thus, marketing planning occurs at the business-unit, product, and market levels. It supports company strategic planning with more detailed plans for specific marketing opportunities.

Defining a Market-Oriented Mission

An organization exists to accomplish something, and this purpose should be clearly stated. Forging a sound mission begins with the following questions: What is our business? Who is the customer? What do consumers value? What *should* our business be? These simple-sounding questions are among the most difficult the company will ever have to answer. Successful companies continuously raise these questions and answer them carefully and completely.

Many organizations develop formal mission statements that answer these questions. A **mission statement** is a statement of the organization's purpose—what it wants to accomplish in the larger environment. A clear mission statement acts as an "invisible hand" that guides people in the organization.

Some companies define their missions myopically in product or technology terms ("We make and sell furniture" or "We are a chemical-processing firm"). But mission statements should be *market oriented* and defined in terms of satisfying basic customer needs. Products and technologies eventually become outdated, but basic market needs may last forever. ▲Cold Stone Creamery's mission isn't simply to

■ **Table 2.1** Market-Oriented Business Definitions

Company	Product-Oriented Definition	Market-Oriented Definition
Charles Schwab	We are a brokerage firm.	We are the guardian of our customers' financial dreams.
Home Depot	We sell tools and home repair and improvement items.	We empower consumers to achieve the homes of their dreams.
Hulu	We are an online video service.	We help people find and enjoy the world's premium video content when, where, and how they want it—all for free.
Kraft	We make consumer food and drink products.	We help people around the world eat and live better.
Nike	We sell athletic shoes and apparel.	We bring inspiration and innovation to every athlete* in the world. (*If you have a body, you are an athlete.)
Revlon	We make cosmetics.	We sell lifestyle and self-expression; success and status; memories, hopes, and dreams.
Ritz-Carlton Hotels & Resorts	We rent rooms.	We create the Ritz-Carlton experience—one that enlivens the senses, instills well-being, and fulfills even the unexpressed wishes and needs of our guests.
Wal-Mart	We run discount stores.	We deliver low prices every day and give ordinary folks the chance to buy the same things as rich people. "Save Money. Live Better."

sell ice cream. Its mission is to "make people happy around the world by selling the highest quality, most creative ice cream experience with passion, excellence, and innovation." Likewise, Under Armour's mission isn't just to make performance sports apparel, it's "to make all athletes better through passion, science, and the relentless pursuit of innovation." ■ **Table 2.1** provides several other examples of product-oriented versus market-oriented business definitions.[2]

Mission statements should be meaningful and specific yet motivating. They should emphasize the company's strengths in the marketplace. Too often, mission statements are written for public relations purposes and lack specific, workable guidelines. Says marketing consultant Jack Welch:[3]

> Few leaders actually get the point of forging a mission with real grit and meaning. [Mission statements] have largely devolved into fat-headed jargon. Almost no one can figure out what they mean. [So companies] sort of ignore them or gussy up a vague package deal along the lines of: "our mission is to be the best fill-in-the-blank company in our industry." [Instead, Welch advises, CEOs should] make a choice about how your company will win. Don't mince words! Remember Nike's old mission, "Crush Reebok"? That's directionally correct. And Google's mission statement isn't something namby-pamby like "To be the world's best search engine." It's "To organize the world's information and make it universally accessible and useful." That's simultaneously inspirational, achievable, and completely graspable.

Finally, a company's mission should not be stated as making more sales or profits—profits are only a reward for creating value for customers. Instead, the mission should focus on customers and the customer experience the company seeks to create. Thus, McDonald's mission isn't "to be the world's best and most profitable quick-service restaurant," it's "to be our customers favorite place and way to eat." If McDonald's accomplishes this customer-focused mission, profits will follow (see Marketing at Work 2.1).

Setting Company Objectives and Goals

The company needs to turn its mission into detailed supporting objectives for each level of management. Each manager should have objectives and be responsible for reaching them. For example, Kohler makes and markets familiar kitchen and bathroom

Marketing at Work 2.1

McDonald's: On a Customer-Focused Mission

More than half a century ago, Ray Kroc, a 52-year-old salesman of milk-shake-mixing machines, set out on a mission to transform the way Americans eat. In 1955, Kroc discovered a string of seven restaurants owned by Richard and Maurice McDonald. He saw the McDonald brothers' fast-food concept as a perfect fit for America's increasingly on-the-go, time-squeezed, family-oriented lifestyles. Kroc bought the small chain for $2.7 million and the rest is history.

From the start, Kroc preached a motto of QSCV—quality, service, cleanliness, and value. These goals became mainstays in McDonald's customer-focused mission statement. Applying these values, the company perfected the fast-food concept—delivering convenient, good-quality food at affordable prices.

McDonald's grew quickly to become the world's largest fast-feeder. The fast-food giant's more than 32,000 restaurants worldwide now serve 58 million customers each day, racking up systemwide sales of more than $60 billion annually. The Golden Arches are one of the world's most familiar symbols, and other than Santa Claus, no character in the world is more recognizable than Ronald McDonald.

In the mid-1990s, however, McDonald's fortunes began to turn. The company appeared to fall out of touch with both its mission and its customers. Americans were looking for fresher, better-tasting food and more contemporary atmospheres. They were also seeking healthier eating options. In a new age of health-conscious consumers and $5 lattes at Starbucks, McDonald's seemed a bit out of step with the times. One analyst sums it up this way:

> McDonald's was struggling to find its identity amid a flurry of new competitors and changing consumer tastes. The company careened from one failed idea to another. It tried to keep pace by offering pizza, toasted deli sandwiches, and the Arch Deluxe, a heavily advertised new burger that flopped. It bought into non-burger franchises like Chipotle and Boston Market. It also tinkered with its menu, no longer toasting the buns, switching pickles, and changing the special sauce on Big Macs. None of it worked. All the while, McDonald's continued opening new restaurants at a ferocious pace, as many as 2,000 a year. The new stores helped sales, but customer service and cleanliness declined because the company couldn't hire and train good workers fast enough. Meanwhile, McDonald's increasingly became a target for animal-rights activists, environmentalists, and nutritionists, who accused the chain of contributing to the nation's obesity epidemic with "super size" French fries and sodas as well as Happy Meals that lure kids with the reward of free toys.

While McDonald's remained the world's most visited fast-food chain, the once-shiny Golden Arches lost some of their luster. Sales growth slumped, and its market share fell by more than 3 percent between 1997 and 2003. In 2002, the company posted its first-ever quarterly loss. In the face of changing customer value expectations, the company had lost sight of its fundamental value proposition. "We got distracted from the most important thing: hot, high-quality food at a great value at the

▲McDonald's new mission—"being our customers' favorite place and way to eat"— coupled with its Plan to Win, got the company back to the basics of creating exceptional customer experiences.

speed and convenience of McDonald's," says current CEO Jim Skinner. The company and its mission needed to adapt.

In early 2003, a troubled McDonald's announced a turnaround plan—what it now calls its "Plan to Win." At the heart of this plan was a new mission statement that refocused the company on its customers. According to the analyst:

> The company's mission was changed from "being the world's best quick-service restaurant" to "being our customers' favorite place and way to eat." The Plan to Win lays out where McDonald's wants to be and how it plans to get there, all centered on five basics of an exceptional customer experience: people, products, place, price, and promotion. While the five P's smack of corny corporate speak, company officials maintain that they have profoundly changed McDonald's direction and priorities. The plan, and the seemingly simple shift in mission, forced McDonald's and its employees to focus on quality, service, and the restaurant experience rather than simply providing the cheapest, most convenient option to customers. The Plan to Win—which barely fits on a single sheet of paper—is now treated as sacred inside the company.

Under the Plan to Win, McDonald's got back to the basic business of taking care of customers. It halted rapid expansion, and instead poured money back into improving the food, service, atmosphere, and marketing at existing outlets. McDonald's has redecorated its restaurants with clean, simple, more-modern interiors and amenities such as live plants, wireless Internet access, and flat-screen TVs showing cable news. Play areas in some new restaurants feature video games and even stationary bicycles with video screens. To make the customer experience more convenient, McDonald's stores now open earlier to extend breakfast hours and stay open longer to serve late-night diners—more than a third of McDonald's restaurants are now open 24 hours a day.

A reworked menu now provides more choice and variety, including healthier options such as Chicken McNuggets made with white meat, Chicken Selects whole-breast strips, low-fat "milk jugs," apple slices, and a line of Premium Salads. Within

(*continued*)

only a year of introducing its Premium Salads, McDonald's became the world's largest salad seller. The company also launched a major multifaceted education campaign—themed "it's what i **eat** and what i **do** . . . i'm lovin' it"—that underscores the important interplay between eating right and staying active.

McDonald's rediscovered dedication to customer value sparked a remarkable turnaround. Since announcing its Plan to Win, McDonald's sales have increased by more than 50 percent and profits have more than quadrupled. In 2008, when the stock market lost a third of its value—the worst loss since the Great Depression—McDonald's stock gained nearly 6 percent, making it one of only two companies in the Dow Jones industrial average whose share price rose during that year (the other was Wal-Mart). In the fourth quarter of that year, McDonald's same-store sales increased 5 percent; by comparison, Starbucks' same-store sales decreased 10 percent. Through 2009, as the economy and the restaurant industry as a whole contin-ued to struggle, McDonald's outperformed its competitors by a notable margin.

Thus, McDonald's now appears to have the right mission for the times. Once again, when you think McDonald's you think value—whether it's a college student buying a sandwich for a buck or a working mother at the drive-through grabbing a breakfast latte that's a dollar cheaper than Starbucks. And that has customers and the company alike humming the chain's catchy jingle, "I'm lovin' it."

Sources: Extracts based on information found in Andrew Martin, "At McDonald's, the Happiest Meal Is Hot Profits," *New York Times,* January 11, 2009; and Jeremy Adamy, "McDonald's Seeks Ways to Keep Sizzling," *Wall Street Journal,* March 10, 2009, p. A1. Also see "McDonald's Delivers Another Year of Strong Results in 2008," McDonald's press release, January 26, 2009, accessed at www.McDonald's.com; and other financial information and facts accessed at www.mcdonalds.com/corp/invest.html and http://mcdonalds.com/corp/about/factsheets.html, October 2009.

fixtures—everything from bathtubs and toilets to kitchen sinks. But Kohler also offers a breadth of other products and services, including furniture, tile and stone, and even small engines and backup power systems. It also owns resorts and spas in the United States and Scotland. Kohler ties this diverse product portfolio together under the mission of "contributing to a higher level of gracious living for those who are touched by our products and services."

This broad mission leads to a hierarchy of objectives, including business objectives and marketing objectives. ▲Kohler's overall objective is to build profitable customer relationships by developing efficient yet beautiful products that embrace the "essence of gracious living." It does this by investing heavily in research and design (R&D). Research and design is expensive and requires improved profits to plow back into research programs. So improving profits becomes another major objective for Kohler. Profits can be improved by increasing sales or reducing costs. Sales can be increased by improving the company's share of domestic and international markets. These goals then become the company's current marketing objectives.

Marketing strategies and programs must be developed to support these marketing objectives. To increase its market share, Kohler might increase its products' availability and promotion in existing markets and expand business via acquisitions. For example, Kohler intends to boost its production capacity in Thailand to better serve the Asian market. It is also setting up new facilities in India and China. In addition, Kohler's Hospitality Group opened a Kohler Waters Spa in the Chicago area and the Interiors Group acquired furniture manufacturer Mark David.[4]

These are Kohler's broad marketing strategies. Each broad marketing strategy must then be defined in greater detail. For example, increasing the product's promotion may require more salespeople, advertising, and public relations efforts; if so, both requirements will need to be spelled out. In this way, the firm's mission is translated into a set of objectives for the current period.

▼Kohler's overall objective is to build profitable customer relationships by developing efficient yet beautiful products that embrace the "essence of gracious living."

Designing the Business Portfolio (pp 71–74)

Business portfolio
The collection of businesses and products that make up the company.

Guided by the company's mission statement and objectives, management now must plan its **business portfolio**—the collection of businesses and products that make up the company. The best business portfolio is the one that best fits the company's strengths and weaknesses to opportunities in the environment. Business portfolio planning involves two steps. First, the company must analyze its *current* business portfolio and decide which businesses should receive more, less, or no investment. Second, it must shape the *future* portfolio by developing strategies for growth and downsizing.

Analyzing the Current Business Portfolio

Portfolio analysis
The process by which management evaluates the products and businesses that make up the company.

The major activity in strategic planning is business **portfolio analysis**, whereby management evaluates the products and businesses that make up the company. The company will want to put strong resources into its more profitable businesses and phase down or drop its weaker ones.

Management's first step is to identify the key businesses that make up the company, called *strategic business unit* (SBUs). An SBU can be a company division, a product line within a division, or sometimes a single product or brand. The company next assesses the attractiveness of its various SBUs and decides how much support each deserves. When designing a business portfolio, it's a good idea to add and support products and businesses that fit closely with the firm's core philosophy and competencies.

The purpose of strategic planning is to find ways in which the company can best use its strengths to take advantage of attractive opportunities in the environment. So most standard portfolio analysis methods evaluate SBUs on two important dimensions—the attractiveness of the SBU's market or industry and the strength of the SBU's position in that market or industry. The best-known portfolio-planning method was developed by the Boston Consulting Group, a leading management consulting firm.[5]

Growth-share matrix
A portfolio-planning method that evaluates a company's strategic business units (SBUs) in terms of its market growth rate and relative market share. SBUs are classified as stars, cash cows, question marks, or dogs.

The Boston Consulting Group Approach. Using the now-classic Boston Consulting Group (BCG) approach, a company classifies all its SBUs according to the **growth-share matrix** as shown in ■ **Figure 2.2**. On the vertical axis, *market growth rate* provides a measure of market attractiveness. On the horizontal axis, *relative market share* serves as a measure of company strength in the market. The growth-share matrix defines four types of SBUs:

> *Stars.* Stars are high-growth, high-share businesses or products. They often need heavy investments to finance their rapid growth. Eventually their growth will slow down, and they will turn into cash cows.

■ **Figure 2.2.** The BCG Growth-Share Matrix

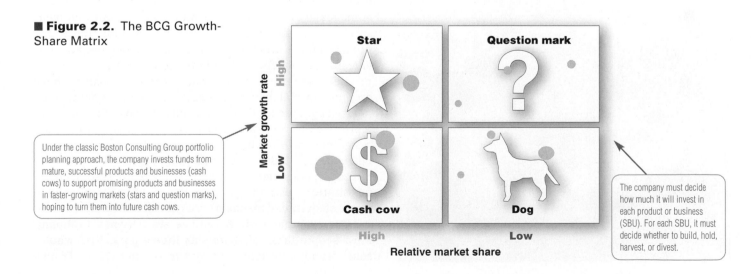

Under the classic Boston Consulting Group portfolio planning approach, the company invests funds from mature, successful products and businesses (cash cows) to support promising products and businesses in faster-growing markets (stars and question marks), hoping to turn them into future cash cows.

The company must decide how much it will invest in each product or business (SBU). For each SBU, it must decide whether to build, hold, harvest, or divest.

Cash Cows. Cash cows are low-growth, high-share businesses or products. These established and successful SBUs need less investment to hold their market share. Thus, they produce a lot of cash that the company uses to pay its bills and to support other SBUs that need investment.

Question Marks. Question marks are low-share business units in high-growth markets. They require a lot of cash to hold their share, let alone increase it. Management has to think hard about which question marks it should try to build into stars and which should be phased out.

Dogs. Dogs are low-growth, low-share businesses and products. They may generate enough cash to maintain themselves but do not promise to be large sources of cash.

The 10 circles in the growth-share matrix represent a company's 10 current SBUs. The company has two stars, two cash cows, three question marks, and three dogs. The areas of the circles are proportional to the SBU's dollar sales. This company is in fair shape, although not in good shape. It wants to invest in the more promising question marks to make them stars and to maintain the stars so that they will become cash cows as their markets mature. Fortunately, it has two good-sized cash cows. Income from these cash cows will help finance the company's question marks, stars, and dogs. The company should take some decisive action concerning its dogs and its question marks.

Once it has classified its SBUs, the company must determine what role each will play in the future. One of four strategies can be pursued for each SBU. The company can invest more in the business unit in order to *build* its share. Or it can invest just enough to *hold* the SBU's share at the current level. It can *harvest* the SBU, milking its short-term cash flow regardless of the long-term effect. Finally, the company can *divest* the SBU by selling it or phasing it out and using the resources elsewhere.

As time passes, SBUs change their positions in the growth-share matrix. Many SBUs start out as question marks and move into the star category if they succeed. They later become cash cows as market growth falls, then finally die off or turn into dogs toward the end of their life cycle. The company needs to add new products and units continuously so that some of them will become stars and, eventually, cash cows that will help finance other SBUs.

Problems with Matrix Approaches. The BCG and other formal methods revolutionized strategic planning. However, such centralized approaches have limitations: They can be difficult, time consuming, and costly to implement. Management may find it difficult to define SBUs and measure market share and growth. In addition, these approaches focus on classifying *current* businesses, but provide little advice for *future* planning.

Because of such problems, many companies have dropped formal matrix methods in favor of more customized approaches that better suit their specific situations. Moreover, unlike former strategic-planning efforts that rested mostly in the hands of senior managers at company headquarters, today's strategic planning has been decentralized. Increasingly, companies are placing responsibility for strategic planning in the hands of cross-functional teams of divisional managers who are close to their markets.

For example, consider ▲The Walt Disney Company. Most people think of Disney as theme parks and wholesome family entertainment. But in the mid-1980s Disney

▼Managing the business portfolio: Most people think of Disney as theme parks and wholesome family entertainment but over the past two decades, it's become a sprawling collection of media and entertainment businesses that requires big doses of the famed "Disney Magic" to manage.

■ Figure 2.3. The
Product/Market Expansion Grid

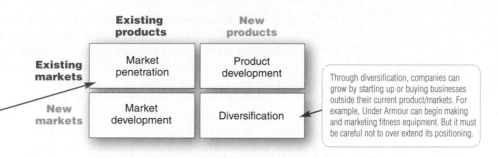

	Existing products	**New products**
Existing markets	Market penetration	Product development
New markets	Market development	Diversification

> Companies can grow by doing a better job of penetrating current markets with current products. For example, Under Armour offers an ever-increasing range of styles and colors in its performance apparel lines, has boosted its promotion spending, and recently added new direct-to-customer distribution channels—its own retail stores, Web site, and toll-free call center.

> Through diversification, companies can grow by starting up or buying businesses outside their current product/markets. For example, Under Armour can begin making and marketing fitness equipment. But it must be careful not to over extend its positioning.

set up a powerful, centralized strategic planning group to guide the company's direction and growth. Over the next two decades, the strategic planning group turned The Walt Disney Company into a huge and diverse collection of media and entertainment businesses. The sprawling Disney grew to include everything from theme resorts and film studios (Walt Disney Pictures, Touchstone Pictures, Hollywood Pictures, and others) to media networks (ABC plus Disney Channel, ESPN, A&E, History Channel, and a half dozen others) to consumer products and a cruise line.

The newly transformed Disney company proved hard to manage and performed unevenly. Recently, Disney disbanded the centralized strategic planning unit, decentralizing its functions to Disney division managers. As a result, Disney reclaimed its position at the head of the world's media conglomerates. And despite recently facing "the weakest economy in our lifetime," Disney's sound strategic management of its broad mix of businesses has helped it fare better than its rival media companies.[6]

Developing Strategies for Growth and Downsizing

Beyond evaluating current businesses, designing the business portfolio involves finding businesses and products the company should consider in the future. Companies need growth if they are to compete more effectively, satisfy their stakeholders, and attract top talent. "Growth is pure oxygen," states one executive. "It creates a vital, enthusiastic corporation where people see genuine opportunity." At the same time, a firm must be careful not to make growth itself an objective. The company's objective must be to manage "profitable growth."[7]

Product/market expansion grid
A portfolio-planning tool for identifying company growth opportunities through market penetration, market development, product development, or diversification.

Market penetration
A strategy for company growth by increasing sales of current products to current market segments without changing the product.

Marketing has the main responsibility for achieving profitable growth for the company. Marketing needs to identify, evaluate, and select market opportunities and lay down strategies for capturing them. One useful device for identifying growth opportunities is the **product/market expansion grid**, shown in **■ Figure 2.3**.[8] We apply it here to performance sports apparel maker ▲Under Armour. Only 13 years ago, Under Armour introduced its innovative line of comfy, moisture-wicking shirts and shorts. Since then, it has grown rapidly in its performance-wear niche. In the five years ending in 2007, Under Armour grew at a blistering 65 percent annual rate. And even as retail sales slumped across the board in last year's down economy, Under Armour's sales grew by nearly 20 percent. Looking forward, the company must look for new ways to keep growing.[9]

▼Growth: Under Armour has grown at a blistering rate under its multipronged growth strategy.

First, Under Armour might consider whether the company can achieve deeper **market penetration**—making more sales without changing its original product. It can spur growth through marketing mix improvements—adjustments to its product design, advertising, pricing, and distribution efforts. For example, Under Armour offers an ever-increasing range of styles and colors in its original apparel lines. And it recently boosted its promotion spending in an effort to drive home its "performance and authenticity" positioning. Following a blockbuster $4.4 million 2008 Super Bowl ad, Under Armour this year launched its largest-ever advertising campaign—themed "Athletes Run." The company

Market development
A strategy for company growth by identifying and developing new market segments for current company products.

Product development
A strategy for company growth by offering modified or new products to current market segments.

Diversification
A strategy for company growth through starting up or acquiring businesses outside the company's current products and markets.

Downsizing
Reducing the business portfolio by eliminating products or business units that are not profitable or that no longer fit the company's overall strategy.

also added direct-to-consumer distribution channels, including its own retail stores, Web site, and toll-free call center. Direct-to-consumer sales grew 47 percent last year and now account for more than 11 percent of total revenues.

Second, Under Armour might consider possibilities for **market development**—identifying and developing new markets for its current products. Under Armour could review new *demographic markets*. For instance, the company recently stepped up its emphasis on women consumers: The "Athletes Run" campaign includes a 30-second "women's only" spot. Under Armour could also pursue new *geographical markets*. For example, the brand has announced its intentions to expand internationally, bringing its products to more athletes throughout the world.

Third, Under Armour could consider **product development**—offering modified or new products to current markets. Last year, in an effort to transform itself from a niche player to mainstream brand, Under Armour entered the $19 billion athletic footwear market with a line of cross-trainer shoes. This year, it introduced high-performance running shoes. Although this puts the company into direct competition with sports heavyweights such as Nike and Adidas, it also offers promise for big growth. In fact, in this year's troubled economy, Under Armour expects that most of its growth will come from its new line of running shoes.

Finally, Under Armour might consider **diversification**—starting up or buying businesses outside of its current products and markets. For example, it could move into nonperformance leisurewear or begin making and marketing Under Armour fitness equipment. When diversifying, companies must be careful not to overextend their brands' positioning.

Companies must not only develop strategies for *growing* their business portfolios, but also strategies for **downsizing** them. There are many reasons that a firm might want to abandon products or markets. The firm may have grown too fast or entered areas where it lacks experience. This can occur when a firm enters too many international markets without the proper research, or when a company introduces new products that do not offer superior customer value. The market environment might change, making some of the company's products or markets less profitable. For example, in difficult economic times, many firms prune out weaker, less-profitable products and markets in order to focus their more limited resources on the strongest ones. Finally, some products or business units simply age and die.

When a firm finds brands or businesses that are unprofitable or that no longer fit its overall strategy, it must carefully prune, harvest, or divest them. Weak businesses usually require a disproportionate amount of management attention. Managers should focus on promising growth opportunities, not fritter away energy trying to salvage fading ones.

Author Comment »
Marketing, alone, can't create superior customer value. Under the companywide strategic plan, marketers must work closely with other departments to form an effective internal company value chain and then must work with other companies in the marketing system to create an overall external value delivery network that jointly serves customers.

PLANNING MARKETING: PARTNERING TO BUILD CUSTOMER RELATIONSHIPS (pp 74–77)

The company's strategic plan establishes what kinds of businesses the company will operate and its objectives for each. Then, within each business unit, more detailed planning takes place. The major functional departments in each unit—marketing, finance, accounting, purchasing, operations, information systems, human resources, and others—must work together to accomplish strategic objectives.

Marketing plays a key role in the company's strategic planning in several ways. First, marketing provides a guiding *philosophy*—the marketing concept—that suggests that company strategy should revolve around building profitable relationships with important consumer groups. Second, marketing provides *inputs* to strategic planners by helping to identify attractive market opportunities and by assessing the firm's potential to take advantage of them. Finally, within individual business units, marketing designs *strategies* for reaching the unit's objectives. Once the unit's objectives are set, marketing's task is to help carry them out profitably.

Customer value is the key ingredient in the marketer's formula for success. However, as we noted in Chapter 1, marketers alone cannot produce superior value for customers. Although marketing plays a leading role, it can be only a partner in attracting, keeping, and growing customers. In addition to *customer relationship management*, marketers must also practice *partner relationship management*. They must work closely with partners in other company departments to form an effective internal *value chain* that serves the customer. Moreover, they must partner effectively with other companies in the marketing system to form a competitively superior external *value delivery network*. We now take a closer look at the concepts of a company value chain and a value delivery network.

Partnering with Other Company Departments

Value chain
The series of internal departments that carry out value-creating activities to design, produce, market, deliver, and support a firm's products.

Each company department can be thought of as a link in the company's internal **value chain**.[10] That is, each department carries out value-creating activities to design, produce, market, deliver, and support the firm's products. The firm's success depends not only on how well each department performs its work, but also on how well the various departments coordinate their activities.

For example, Wal-Mart's goal is to create customer value and satisfaction by providing shoppers with the products they want at the lowest possible prices. Marketers at Wal-Mart play an important role. They learn what customers need and stock the stores' shelves with the desired products at unbeatable low prices. They prepare advertising and merchandising programs and assist shoppers with customer service. Through these and other activities, Wal-Mart's marketers help deliver value to customers.

▲The value chain: Wal-Mart's ability to help you "Save money. Live Better." by offering the right products at lower prices depends on the contributions of people in all of the company's departments.

However, the marketing department needs help from the company's other departments. ▲Wal-Mart's ability to offer the right products at low prices depends on the purchasing department's skill in developing the needed suppliers and buying from them at low cost. Wal-Mart's information technology department must provide fast and accurate information about which products are selling in each store. And its operations people must provide effective, low-cost merchandise handling.

A company's value chain is only as strong as its weakest link. Success depends on how well each department performs its work of adding customer value and on how well the activities of various departments are coordinated. At Wal-Mart, if purchasing can't obtain the lowest prices from suppliers, or if operations can't distribute merchandise at the lowest costs, then marketing can't deliver on its promise of unbeatable low prices.

Ideally then, a company's different functions should work in harmony to produce value for consumers. But, in practice, departmental relations are full of conflicts and misunderstandings. The marketing department takes the consumer's point of view. But when marketing tries to develop customer satisfaction, it can cause other departments to do a poorer job *in their terms*. Marketing department actions can increase purchasing costs, disrupt production schedules, increase inventories, and create budget headaches. Thus, the other departments may resist the marketing department's efforts.

Yet marketers must find ways to get all departments to "think consumer" and to develop a smoothly functioning value chain. Jack Welch, the highly regarded former GE CEO, emphasized that all GE people, regardless of their department, have an impact on customer satisfaction and retention. Another marketing expert puts it this way: "True market orientation does not mean becoming marketing-driven; it means that the entire company obsesses over creating value for the customer and views itself as a bundle of processes that profitably define, create, communicate, and deliver value to its target customers. . . . Everyone must do marketing regardless of function or department."[11] Thus, whether you're an accountant, operations manager, financial analyst, IT specialist, or human resources manager, you need to understand marketing and your role in creating customer value.

Partnering with Others in the Marketing System

In its quest to create customer value, the firm needs to look beyond its own internal value chain and into the value chains of its suppliers, distributors, and, ultimately, its customers. Consider McDonald's. People do not swarm to McDonald's only because they love the chain's hamburgers. Consumers flock to the McDonald's *system*, not just to its food products. Throughout the world, McDonald's finely tuned value delivery system delivers a high standard of QSCV—quality, service, cleanliness, and value. McDonald's is effective only to the extent that it successfully partners with its franchisees, suppliers, and others to jointly create "our customers' favorite place and way to eat."

More companies today are partnering with the other members of the supply chain—suppliers, distributors, and, ultimately, customers—to improve the performance of the customer **value delivery network**. ▲For example, cosmetics maker L'Oréal knows the importance of building close relationships with its extensive network of suppliers, who supply everything from polymers and fats to spray cans and packaging to production equipment and office supplies:

Value delivery network
The network made up of the company, suppliers, distributors, and, ultimately, customers who partner with each other to improve the performance of the entire system.

> L'Oréal is the world's largest cosmetics manufacturer, with 25 brands ranging from Maybelline and Kiehl's to Lancôme and Redken. The company's supplier network is crucial to its success. As a result, L'Oréal treats suppliers as respected partners. On the one hand, it expects a lot from suppliers in terms of design innovation, quality, and socially responsible actions. The company carefully screens new suppliers and regularly assesses the performance of current suppliers. On the other hand, L'Oréal works closely with suppliers to help them meet its exacting standards. Whereas some companies make unreasonable demands of their suppliers and "squeeze" them for short-term gains, L'Oréal builds long-term supplier relationships based on mutual benefit and growth. According to the company's supplier Web site, it treats suppliers with "fundamental respect for their business, their culture, their growth, and the individuals who work there. Each relationship is based on . . . shared efforts aimed at promoting growth and mutual profits that make it possible for suppliers to invest, innovate, and compete." As a result, more than 75 percent of L'Oréal's supplier-partners have been working with the company for 10 years or more, and the majority of them for several decades. Says the company's head of purchasing, "The CEO wants to make L'Oréal a top performer and one of the world's most respected companies. Being respected also means being respected by our suppliers."[12]

▲The value delivery system: L'Oréal builds long-term supplier relationships based on mutual benefit and growth. It "wants to make L'Oréal a top performer and one of the world's most respected companies. Being respected also means being respected by our suppliers."

Increasingly in today's marketplace, competition no longer takes place between individual competitors. Rather, it takes place between the entire value delivery networks created by these competitors. Thus, carmaker Toyota's performance against Ford depends on the quality of Toyota's overall value delivery network versus Ford's. Even if Toyota makes the best cars, it might lose in the marketplace if Ford's dealer network provides more customer-satisfying sales and service.

Speed Bump: Linking the Concepts

Here's a good place to pause for a moment to apply what you've read in the first part of this chapter.

- Why are we talking about companywide strategic planning in a marketing text? What *does* strategic planning have to do with marketing?
- What are McDonald's mission and strategy? What role does marketing play in helping McDonald's accomplish its mission and strategy?
- What roles do other McDonald's departments play, and how can the company's marketers partner with these departments to maximize overall customer value?

Author Comment »
Now that we've set the context in terms of companywide strategy, it's time to talk about customer-driven marketing strategy and programs.

Marketing strategy
The marketing logic by which the company hopes to create customer value and achieve profitable customer relationships.

MARKETING STRATEGY AND THE MARKETING MIX (pp 77–82)

The strategic plan defines the company's overall mission and objectives. Marketing's role and activities are shown in ■ **Figure 2.4**, which summarizes the major activities involved in managing a customer-driven marketing strategy and the marketing mix.

Consumers stand in the center. The goal is to create value for customers and build profitable customer relationships. Next comes **marketing strategy**—the marketing logic by which the company hopes to create this customer value and achieve these profitable relationships. The company decides which customers it will serve (segmentation and targeting) and how (differentiation and positioning). It identifies the total market, then divides it into smaller segments, selects the most promising segments, and focuses on serving and satisfying the customers in these segments.

Guided by marketing strategy, the company designs an integrated *marketing mix* made up of factors under its control—product, price, place, and promotion (the four Ps). To find the best marketing strategy and mix, the company engages in marketing analysis, planning, implementation, and control. Through these activities, the company watches and adapts to the actors and forces in the marketing environment. We will now look briefly at each activity. Then, in later chapters, we will discuss each one in more depth.

■ **Figure 2.4.** Managing Marketing Strategies and the Marketing Mix

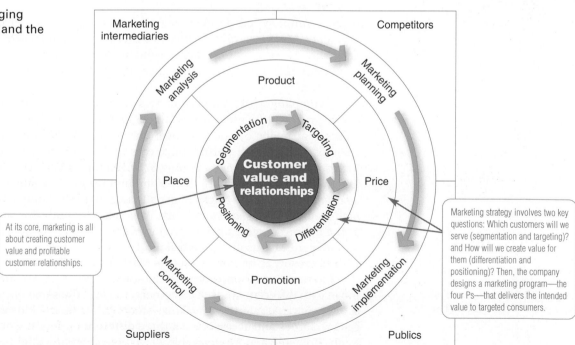

At its core, marketing is all about creating customer value and profitable customer relationships.

Marketing strategy involves two key questions: Which customers will we serve (segmentation and targeting)? and How will we create value for them (differentiation and positioning)? Then, the company designs a marketing program—the four Ps—that delivers the intended value to targeted consumers.

Customer-Driven Marketing Strategy

As we emphasized throughout Chapter 1, to succeed in today's competitive market-place, companies need to be customer centered. They must win customers from competitors, then keep and grow them by delivering greater value. But before it can satisfy customers, a company must first understand their needs and wants. Thus, sound marketing requires careful customer analysis.

Companies know that they cannot profitably serve all consumers in a given market—at least not all consumers in the same way. There are too many different kinds of consumers with too many different kinds of needs. And most companies are in a position to serve some segments better than others. Thus, each company must divide up the total market, choose the best segments, and design strategies for profitably serving chosen segments. This process involves *market segmentation, market targeting, differentiation*, and *positioning*.

Market Segmentation

The market consists of many types of customers, products, and needs. The marketer has to determine which segments offer the best opportunities. Consumers can be grouped and served in various ways based on geographic, demographic, psychographic, and behavioral factors. The process of dividing a market into distinct groups of buyers who have different needs, characteristics, or behaviors, and who might require separate products or marketing programs is called **market segmentation**.

Market segmentation
Dividing a market into distinct groups of buyers who have different needs, characteristics, or behaviors, and who might require separate products or marketing programs.

Market segment
A group of consumers who respond in a similar way to a given set of marketing efforts.

Every market has segments, but not all ways of segmenting a market are equally useful. For example, Tylenol would gain little by distinguishing between low-income and high-income pain reliever users if both respond the same way to marketing efforts. A **market segment** consists of consumers who respond in a similar way to a given set of marketing efforts. In the car market, for example, consumers who want the biggest, most comfortable car regardless of price make up one market segment. Consumers who care mainly about price and operating economy make up another segment. It would be difficult to make one car model that was the first choice of consumers in both segments. Companies are wise to focus their efforts on meeting the distinct needs of individual market segments.

Market Targeting

After a company has defined market segments, it can enter one or many of these segments. **Market targeting** involves evaluating each market segment's attractiveness and selecting one or more segments to enter. A company should target segments in which it can profitably generate the greatest customer value and sustain it over time.

Market targeting
The process of evaluating each market segment's attractiveness and selecting one or more segments to enter.

A company with limited resources might decide to serve only one or a few special segments or "market niches." Such "nichers" specialize in serving customer segments that major competitors overlook or ignore. For example, Ferrari sells only 1,500 of its very high-performance cars in the United States each year, but at very high prices—from an eye-opening $229,500 for its Ferrari F430 F1 Spider convertible to an astonishing more than $2 million for its FXX super sports car, which can be driven only on race tracks (it usually sells 10 in the United States each year). Most nichers aren't quite so exotic. White Wave, maker of Silk Soymilk, has found its niche as the nation's largest soymilk producer. And although Logitech is only a fraction the size of giant Microsoft, through skillful niching, it dominates the PC mouse market, with Microsoft as its runner up (see Marketing at Work 2.2).

Alternatively, a company might choose to serve several related segments—perhaps those with different kinds of customers but with the same basic wants. Abercrombie & Fitch, for example, targets college students, teens, and kids with the same upscale, casual clothes and accessories in three different outlets: the original Abercrombie & Fitch, Hollister, and Abercrombie. Or a large company might decide to offer a complete range of products to serve all market segments.

Marketing at Work 2.2

Nicher Logitech: The Little Mouse That Roars

Among the big tech companies, market leader Microsoft is the king of the jungle. When giant Microsoft looms, even large competitors quake. But when it comes to dominating specific market niches, overall size isn't always the most important thing. For example, in its own corner of the high-tech jungle, Logitech International is the little mouse that roars. In its niches, small but mighty Logitech is the undisputed market leader.

Logitech focuses on what it calls "personal peripherals"—interface devices for PC navigation, Internet communications, home-entertainment systems, and gaming and wireless devices. Logitech's rapidly expanding product portfolio now includes everything from cordless mice and keyboards, gaming controllers, and remote controls to Webcams, PC speakers, headsets, notebook stands, and cooling pads. But it all started with computer mice.

Logitech makes every variation of mouse imaginable. Over the years, it has flooded the world with more 1 billion computer mice of all varieties, mice for left- and right-handed people, wireless mice, travel mice, mini mice, 3-D mice, mice shaped like real mice for children, and even an "air mouse" that uses motion sensors to let you navigate your computer from a distance.

In the PC mouse market, Logitech competes head-on with Microsoft. At first glance it looks like an unfair contest. With more than $60 billion in sales, Microsoft is 25 times bigger than $2.4 billion Logitech. But when it comes to mice and other peripherals, Logitech has a depth of focus and knowledge that no other company in the world—including Microsoft—can match. Whereas mice and other interface devices are pretty much a sideline for software maker Microsoft—almost a distraction—they are the main attraction for Logitech. As a result, each new Logitech device is a true work of both art and science. Logitech's mice, for example, receive raves from designers, expert reviewers, and users alike.

A *BusinessWeek* analyst gives us a behind-the-scenes look at Logitech's deep design and development prowess:

One engineer, given the moniker "Teflon Tim" by amused colleagues, spent three months scouring the Far East to find just the right nonstick coatings and sound-deadening foam. Another spent hours taking apart wind-up toys. Others pored over the contours of luxury BMW motorcycles, searching for designs to crib. They were members of a most unusual team that spent thousands of hours during the past two years on a single goal: to build a better mouse. The result: Logitech's revolutionary MX Revolution, the next-generation mouse that hit consumer electronics shelves about two years ago. It represented the company's most ambitious attempt yet to refashion the lowly computer mouse into a kind of control center for a host of PC applications. The sheer scope of the secret mission—which crammed 420 components, including a tiny motor, into a palmsized device that usually holds about 20—brought together nearly three dozen engineers, designers, and marketers from around the globe.

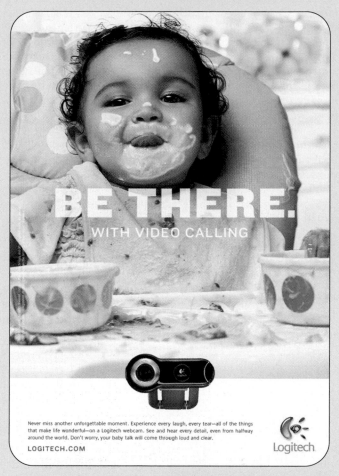

▲ **Nichers: In its own corner of the high-tech jungle, Logitech is a little mouse that roars, with giant Microsoft as its runner-up.**

Part of Logitech's product-development strategy is defensive. Once content to design mice and other peripherals for PC makers to slap their own names on, Logitech over the past half-decade has increasingly focused on selling its branded add-on equipment directly to consumers. Nearly 90 percent of Logitech's annual sales now come from retail. That forces Logitech to deliver regular improvements and new devices to entice new shoppers and purchases.

"We think of mice as pretty simple," says one industry analyst, "but there's a pretty aggressive technology battle going on to prove what the mouse can do." One of Logitech's latest feats of cutting-edge wizardry is its MX Air, which promises to change the very definition of the computer mouse as we know it. More like an airborne remote control than a traditional mouse, you can surf the Web, play games, and control your home theater PC from up to 30 feet away. There's also a cool-factor at play. Wielding the MX Air is like holding a work of art.

And at Logitech, it's not just about mice anymore. Logitech now applies its cool-factor to create sleek, stylish, and functional devices that enhance not only your PC experience, but also help you get the most out of everything from Internet

(*continued*)

navigation to all of the new gadgets in today's digital home. For example, Logitech's family of Harmony advanced universal remote controls helps even technology challenged novices tame the complexities of their home-entertainment systems.

Breeding mice and other peripherals has been very good for nicher Logitech. For example, thanks to its dedication to creating the next best mouse, Logitech has dominated the world mouse market, with giant Microsoft as its runner up. And although Logitech isn't nearly as big as Microsoft, pound for pound it's even more profitable. Over the past six years, despite tough economic times for the PC and consumer electronics industries, Logitech's sales and profits have more than doubled. Looking ahead, as Logitech forges forward in its personal peripherals niche, Logitech is well positioned to weather the recent economic storms and emerge stronger than ever.

"Our business is about the last inch between people and content and technology," explains Logitech CEO Guerrino De Luca.

Nobody spans that last inch better than Logitech. The next time you navigate your PC, watch or listen to downloaded Web audio or video content, or pick up an entertainment-system remote, it's a pretty good bet that you'll have your hand on a Logitech device. It's also a good bet that you'll really like the way it works and feels. "The goal [is] passing the 'ooooh' test," says a Logitech project leader, "creating a visceral experience that communicates both performance and luxury."

Sources: Lisa Johnston and John Laposky, "Logitech Intros Accessories, Ships Billion Mouse," *TWICE,* December 15, 2008, p. 84; Cliff Edwards, "Here Comes Mighty Mouse," *BusinessWeek,* September 4, 2006, p. 76; Cliff Edwards, "The Mouse that Soars," *BusinessWeek,* August 20, 2007, p. 22; "Logitech International S.A.," *Hoover's Company Records,* March 1, 2009, p. 42459; "Haig Simonian, "Logitech Warns of Gloom Ahead," FT.com, January 21, 2009; http://ir.logitech.com/overview.cfm?cl=us,en; and annual reports and other information from http://ir.logitech.com/overview.cfm?cl=us.en and www.logitech.com, accessed October 2009.

Most companies enter a new market by serving a single segment, and if this proves successful, they add more segments. For example, Nike started with innovative running shoes for serious runners. Large companies eventually seek full market coverage. Nike now makes and sells a broad range of sports products for just about anyone and everyone, with the goal of "helping athletes at every level of ability reach their potential."[13] It has different products designed to meet the special needs of each segment it serves.

Market Differentiation and Positioning

Positioning
Arranging for a product to occupy a clear, distinctive, and desirable place relative to competing products in the minds of target consumers.

After a company has decided which market segments to enter, it must decide how it will differentiate its market offering for each targeted segment and what positions it wants to occupy in those segments. A product's *position* is the place the product occupies relative to competitors' products in consumers' minds. Marketers want to develop unique market positions for their products. If a product is perceived to be exactly like others on the market, consumers would have no reason to buy it.

Positioning is arranging for a product to occupy a clear, distinctive, and desirable place relative to competing products in the minds of target consumers. As one positioning expert puts it, positioning is "why a shopper will pay a little more for your brand."[14] Thus, marketers plan positions that distinguish their products from competing brands and give them the greatest advantage in their target markets.

Wal-Mart promises "Save Money. Live Better."; Target says "Expect More. Pay Less." At video site Hulu, you can "Watch Your Favorites. Anytime. Free."; whereas YouTube let's you "Broadcast Yourself." You can "Feel Better" with Tylenol; and with Excedrin, "The Pain Stops. You Don't." And at Burger King, you can "Have it your way," whereas people at McDonald's say "I'm lovin' it." Such deceptively simple statements form the backbone of a product's marketing strategy. ▲For example, Burger King designs its entire worldwide integrated marketing campaign—from television and print commercials to its Web sites—around the "Have it your way" positioning.

▼**Positioning: Burger King builds its entire worldwide marketing campaign around its "Have it your way" positioning.**

In positioning its product, the company first identifies possible customer value differences that provide competitive advantages upon which to build the position. The company can offer greater customer value either by charging lower prices than competitors, or by offering more benefits to justify higher prices. But if the company *promises* greater value, it must then *deliver* that greater value. Thus, effective positioning begins with **differentiation**—actually *differentiating* the company's market offering so that it gives consumers more value. Once the company has chosen a desired position, it must take strong steps to deliver and communicate that position to target consumers. The company's entire marketing program should support the chosen positioning strategy.

Differentiation
Actually differentiating the market offering to create superior customer value.

Developing an Integrated Marketing Mix

After deciding on its overall marketing strategy, the company is ready to begin planning the details of the marketing mix, one of the major concepts in modern marketing. The **marketing mix** is the set of controllable, tactical marketing tools that the firm blends to produce the response it wants in the target market. The marketing mix consists of everything the firm can do to influence the demand for its product. The many possibilities can be collected into four groups of variables known as "the four *P*s": *product*, *price*, *place*, and *promotion*. ■ **Figure 2.5** shows the marketing tools under each *P*.

Marketing mix
The set of controllable tactical marketing tools—product, price, place, and promotion—that the firm blends to produce the response it wants in the target market.

Product means the goods-and-services combination the company offers to the target market. Thus, a Ford Escape consists of nuts and bolts, spark plugs, pistons, headlights, and thousands of other parts. Ford offers several Escape models and dozens of optional features. The car comes fully serviced and with a comprehensive warranty that is as much a part of the product as the tailpipe.

Price is the amount of money customers must pay to obtain the product. Ford calculates suggested retail prices that its dealers might charge for each Escape. But Ford dealers rarely charge the full sticker price. Instead, they negotiate the price with each customer, offering discounts, trade-in allowances, and credit terms. These actions adjust prices for the current competitive and economic situations and bring them into line with the buyer's perception of the car's value.

Place includes company activities that make the product available to target consumers. Ford partners with a large body of independently owned dealerships that sell the company's many different models. Ford selects its dealers carefully and supports them strongly. The dealers keep an inventory of Ford automobiles, demonstrate them to potential buyers, negotiate prices, close sales, and service the cars after the sale.

■ **Figure 2.5.** The Four Ps of the Marketing Mix

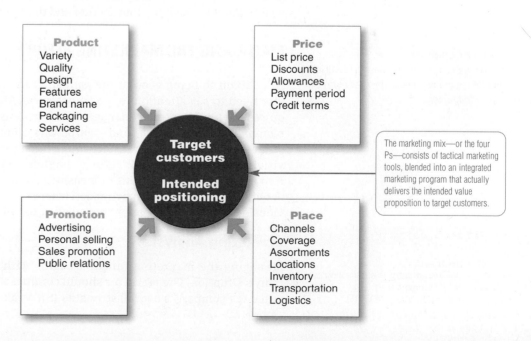

Promotion means activities that communicate the merits of the product and persuade target customers to buy it. Ford Motor Company spends more than $2 billion each year on U.S. advertising to tell consumers about the company and its many products.[15] Dealership salespeople assist potential buyers and persuade them that Ford is the best car for them. Ford and its dealers offer special promotions—sales, cash rebates, low-financing rates—as added purchase incentives.

An effective marketing program blends all of the marketing mix elements into an integrated marketing program designed to achieve the company's marketing objectives by delivering value to consumers. The marketing mix constitutes the company's tactical tool kit for establishing strong positioning in target markets.

Some critics think that the four Ps may omit or underemphasize certain important activities. For example, they ask, "Where are services?" Just because they don't start with a *P* doesn't justify omitting them. The answer is that services, such as banking, airline, and retailing services, are products too. We might call them *service products*. "Where is packaging?" the critics might ask. Marketers would answer that they include packaging as just one of many product decisions. All said, as Figure 2.5 suggests, many marketing activities that might appear to be left out of the marketing mix are subsumed under one of the four Ps. The issue is not whether there should be four, six, or ten Ps so much as what framework is most helpful in designing integrated marketing programs.

There is another concern, however, that is valid. It holds that the four Ps concept takes the seller's view of the market, not the buyer's view. From the buyer's viewpoint, in this age of customer value and relationships, the four Ps might be better described as the four Cs:[16]

4Ps	4Cs
Product	Customer solution
Price	Customer cost
Place	Convenience
Promotion	Communication

Thus, whereas marketers see themselves as selling products, customers see themselves as buying value or solutions to their problems. And customers are interested in more than just the price; they are interested in the total costs of obtaining, using, and disposing of a product. Customers want the product and service to be as conveniently available as possible. Finally, they want two-way communication. Marketers would do well to think through the four Cs first and then build the four Ps on that platform.

Author Comment »
So far we've focused on the *marketing* in marketing management. Now, let's turn to the *management*.

MANAGING THE MARKETING EFFORT (pp 82–86)

In addition to being good at the *marketing* in marketing management, companies also need to pay attention to the *management*. Managing the marketing process requires the four marketing management functions shown in ■ **Figure 2.6**—*analysis, planning, implementation,* and *control*. The company first develops companywide strategic plans and then translates them into marketing and other plans for each division, product, and brand. Through implementation, the company turns the plans into actions. Control consists of measuring and evaluating the results of marketing activities and taking corrective action where needed. Finally, marketing analysis provides information and evaluations needed for all of the other marketing activities.

Marketing Analysis

SWOT analysis
An overall evaluation of the company's strengths (S), weaknesses (W), opportunities (O), and threats (T).

Managing the marketing function begins with a complete analysis of the company's situation. The marketer should conduct a **SWOT analysis**, by which it evaluates the company's overall strengths (S), weaknesses (W), opportunities (O), and

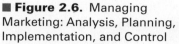

■ **Figure 2.6.** Managing Marketing: Analysis, Planning, Implementation, and Control

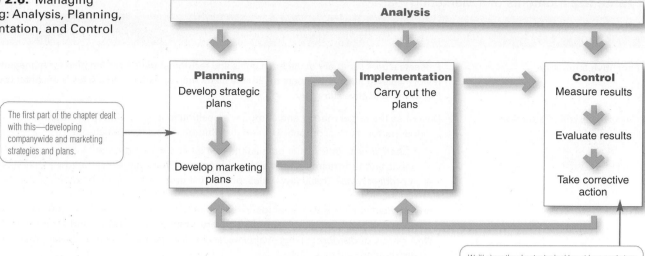

threats (T) (see ■ **Figure 2.7**). Strengths include internal capabilities, resources, and positive situational factors that may help the company to serve its customers and achieve its objectives. Weaknesses include internal limitations and negative situational factors that may interfere with the company's performance. Opportunities are favorable factors or trends in the external environment that the company may be able to exploit to its advantage. And threats are unfavorable external factors or trends that may present challenges to performance.

The company should analyze its markets and marketing environment to find attractive opportunities and identify environmental threats. It should analyze company strengths and weaknesses as well as current and possible marketing actions to determine which opportunities it can best pursue. The goal is to match the company's strengths to attractive opportunities in the environment, while eliminating or overcoming the weaknesses and minimizing the threats. Marketing analysis provides inputs to each of the other marketing management functions. We discuss marketing analysis more fully in Chapter 3.

Marketing Planning

Through strategic planning, the company decides what it wants to do with each business unit. Marketing planning involves deciding on marketing strategies that will help the company attain its overall strategic objectives. A detailed marketing plan is needed for each business, product, or brand. What does a marketing plan look like? Our discussion focuses on product or brand marketing plans.

■ **Table 2.2** outlines the major sections of a typical product or brand marketing plan. (See Appendix 2 for a sample marketing plan.) The plan begins with an

■ **Figure 2.7.** SWOT Analysis: Strengths (S), Weaknesses (W), Opportunities (O), and Threats (T)

■ **Table 2.2** Contents of a Marketing Plan

Section	Purpose
Executive summary	Presents a brief summary of the main goals and recommendations of the plan for management review, helping top management to find the plan's major points quickly. A table of contents should follow the executive summary.
Current marketing situation	Describes the target market and company's position in it, including information about the market, product performance, competition, and distribution. This section includes ● A *market description*, that defines the market and major segments, then reviews customer needs and factors in the marketing environment that may affect customer purchasing. ● A *product review* that shows sales, prices, and gross margins of the major products in the product line. ● A review of *competition* that identifies major competitors and assesses their market positions and strategies for product quality, pricing, distribution, and promotion. ● A review of *distribution* that evaluates recent sales trends and other developments in major distribution channels.
Threats and opportunities analysis	Assesses major threats and opportunities that the product might face, helping management to anticipate important positive or negative developments that might have an impact on the firm and its strategies.
Objectives and issues	States the marketing objectives that the company would like to attain during the plan's term and discusses key issues that will affect their attainment. For example, if the goal is to achieve a 15 percent market share, this section looks at how this goal might be achieved.
Marketing strategy	Outlines the broad marketing logic by which the business unit hopes to create customer value and relationships and the specifics of target markets, positioning, and marketing expenditure levels. How will the company create value for customers in order to capture value from customers in return? This section also outlines specific strategies for each marketing mix element and explains how each responds to the threats, opportunities, and critical issues spelled out earlier in the plan.
Action programs	Spells out how marketing strategies will be turned into specific action programs that answer the following questions: *What* will be done? *When* will it be done? *Who* will do it? *How* much will it cost?
Budgets	Details a supporting marketing budget that is essentially a projected profit-and-loss statement. It shows expected revenues (forecasted number of units sold and the average net price) and expected costs of production, distribution, and marketing. The difference is the projected profit. Once approved by higher management, the budget becomes the basis for materials buying, production scheduling, personnel planning, and marketing operations.
Controls	Outlines the control that will be used to monitor progress and allow higher management to review implementation results and spot products that are not meeting their goals. It includes measures of return on marketing investment.

executive summary that quickly reviews major assessments, goals, and recommendations. The main section of the plan presents a detailed SWOT analysis of the current marketing situation as well as potential threats and opportunities. The plan next states major objectives for the brand and outlines the specifics of a marketing strategy for achieving them.

A *marketing strategy* consists of specific strategies for target markets, positioning, the marketing mix, and marketing expenditure levels. It outlines how the company intends to create value for target customers in order to capture value in return. In this section, the planner explains how each strategy responds to the threats, opportunities, and critical issues spelled out earlier in the plan. Additional sections of the marketing plan lay out an action program for implementing the marketing strategy along with the details of a supporting *marketing budget*. The last section outlines the controls that will be used to monitor progress, measure return on marketing investment, and take corrective action.

Marketing Implementation

Marketing implementation
The process that turns marketing
strategies and plans into marketing
actions in order to accomplish strategic
marketing objectives.

Planning good strategies is only a start toward successful marketing. A brilliant marketing strategy counts for little if the company fails to implement it properly. **Marketing implementation** is the process that turns marketing *plans* into marketing *actions* in order to accomplish strategic marketing objectives. Whereas marketing planning addresses the *what* and *why* of marketing activities, implementation addresses the *who, where, when,* and *how.*

Many managers think that "doing things right" (implementation) is as important as, or even more important than, "doing the right things" (strategy). The fact is that both are critical to success, and companies can gain competitive advantages through effective implementation. One firm can have essentially the same strategy as another, yet win in the marketplace through faster or better execution. Still, implementation is difficult—it is often easier to think up good marketing strategies than it is to carry them out.

In an increasingly connected world, people at all levels of the marketing system must work together to implement marketing strategies and plans. At Black & Decker, for example, marketing implementation for the company's power tools, outdoor equipment, and other products requires day-to-day decisions and actions by thousands of people both inside and outside the organization. Marketing managers make decisions about target segments, branding, packaging, pricing, promoting, and distributing. They talk with engineering about product design, with manufacturing about production and inventory levels, and with finance about funding and cash flows. They also connect with outside people, such as advertising agencies to plan ad campaigns and the news media to obtain publicity support. The sales force urges Home Depot, Lowe's, and other retailers to advertise Black & Decker products, provide ample shelf space, and use company displays.

Marketing Department Organization

The company must design a marketing organization that can carry out marketing strategies and plans. If the company is very small, one person might do all of the research, selling, advertising, customer service, and other marketing work. As the company expands, a marketing department emerges to plan and carry out marketing activities. In large companies, this department contains many specialists. They have product and market managers, sales managers and salespeople, market researchers, advertising experts, and many other specialists.

To head up such large marketing organizations, many companies have now created a *chief marketing officer* (or CMO) position. The CMO heads up the company's entire marketing operation and represents marketing on the company's top management team. The CMO position puts marketing on equal footing with other C-level executives, such as the chief executive officer (CEO) and the chief financial officer (CFO).[17]

Modern marketing departments can be arranged in several ways. The most common form of marketing organization is the *functional organization.* Under this organization, different marketing activities are headed by a functional specialist— a sales manager, advertising manager, marketing research manager, customer-service manager, or new-product manager. A company that sells across the country or internationally often uses a *geographic organization.* Its sales and marketing people are assigned to specific countries, regions, and districts. Geographic organization allows salespeople to settle into a territory, get to know their customers, and work with a minimum of travel time and cost. Companies with many very different products or brands often create a *product management organization.* Using this approach, a product manager develops and implements a complete strategy and marketing program for a specific product or brand.

For companies that sell one product line to many different types of markets and customers that have different needs and preferences, a *market* or *customer management organization* might be best. A market management organization is similar to the product management organization. Market managers are responsible for developing marketing strategies and plans for their specific markets or customers.

▲ **Marketers must continually plan their analysis, implementation, and control activities.**

This system's main advantage is that the company is organized around the needs of specific customer segments. Many companies develop special organizations to manage their relationships with large customers. For example, companies such as Procter & Gamble and Black & Decker have large teams, or even whole divisions, set up to serve large customers such as Wal-Mart, Target, Safeway, or Home Depot.

Large companies that produce many different products flowing into many different geographic and customer markets usually employ some *combination* of the functional, geographic, product, and market organization forms.

Marketing organization has become an increasingly important issue in recent years. More and more, companies are shifting their brand management focus toward *customer management*—moving away from managing just product or brand profitability and toward managing customer profitability and customer equity. They think of themselves not as managing portfolios of brands but as managing portfolios of customers.

Marketing Control

Marketing control
The process of measuring and evaluating the results of marketing strategies and plans and taking corrective action to ensure that objectives are achieved.

Because many surprises occur during the implementation of marketing plans, marketers must practice constant **marketing control**—evaluating the results of marketing strategies and plans and taking corrective action to ensure that objectives are attained. Marketing control involves four steps. Management first sets specific marketing goals. It then measures its performance in the marketplace and evaluates the causes of any differences between expected and actual performance. Finally, management takes corrective action to close the gaps between its goals and its performance. This may require changing the action programs or even changing the goals.

Operating control involves checking ongoing performance against the annual plan and taking corrective action when necessary. Its purpose is to ensure that the company achieves the sales, profits, and other goals set out in its annual plan. It also involves determining the profitability of different products, territories, markets, and channels. *Strategic control* involves looking at whether the company's basic strategies are well matched to its opportunities. Marketing strategies and programs can quickly become outdated, and each company should periodically reassess its overall approach to the marketplace.

Author Comment ≫
Measuring return on marketing investment has become a major marketing emphasis. But it can be difficult. For example, a Super Bowl ad reaches nearly 100 million consumers but may cost as much as $3 million for 30 seconds of airtime alone. How do you measure the specific return on such an investment in terms of sales, profits, and building customer relationships? We'll look into that question again in Chapter 12.

MEASURING AND MANAGING RETURN ON MARKETING INVESTMENT (pp 86–88)

Marketing managers must ensure that their marketing dollars are being well spent. In the past, many marketers spent freely on big, expensive marketing programs, often without thinking carefully about the financial returns on their spending. They believed that marketing produces intangible outcomes, which do not lend themselves readily to measures of productivity or return. But in today's more constrained economy, all that is changing:

> For years, corporate marketers have walked into budget meetings like neighborhood junkies. They couldn't always justify how well they spent past handouts or what difference it all made. They just wanted more money—for flashy TV ads, for big-ticket events, for, you know, getting out the message and building up the brand. But those heady days of blind budget increases are fast being replaced with a new mantra: measurement and accounta-

bility. "Marketers have been pretty unaccountable for many years," notes one expert. "Now they are under big pressure to estimate their impact. Another analyst puts in more bluntly: "Marketing needs to stop fostering 'rock star' behavior and focus on rock-steady results."[18]

According to a recent study, as finances have tightened, marketers see return on marketing investment as the second biggest issue after the economy. "Increasingly, it is important for marketers to be able to justify their expenses," says one marketer. "We need to get smarter as a community as we assess how effective our brand [strategies are]."[19]

In response, marketers are developing better measures of *return on marketing investment*. **Return on marketing investment** (or **marketing ROI**) is the net return from a marketing investment divided by the costs of the marketing investment. It measures the profits generated by investments in marketing activities.

Return on marketing investment (or marketing ROI)
The net return from a marketing investment divided by the costs of the marketing investment.

Marketing returns can be difficult to measure. In measuring financial ROI, both the *R* and the *I* are uniformly measured in dollars. But there is as of yet no consistent definition of marketing ROI. "It's tough to measure, more so than for other business expenses," says one analyst. "You can imagine buying a piece of equipment . . . and then measuring the productivity gains that result from the purchase," he says. "But in marketing, benefits like advertising impact aren't easily put into dollar returns. It takes a leap of faith to come up with a number."[20]

One recent survey found that although two-thirds of companies have implemented return on marketing investment programs in recent years, only one-quarter of companies report making good progress in measuring marketing ROI. Another survey of chief financial officers (CFOs) reported that 93 percent of those surveyed are dissatisfied with their ability to measure return on marketing. The major problem is figuring out what specific measures to use and obtaining good data on these measures.[21]

▲Many companies are assembling marketing dashboards—meaningful sets of marketing performance measures in a single display used to set and adjust their marketing strategies.

A company can assess return on marketing in terms of standard marketing performance measures, such as brand awareness, sales, or market share. Many companies are assembling such measures into ▲*marketing dashboards*—meaningful sets of marketing performance measures in a single display used to monitor strategic marketing performance. Just as automobile dashboards present drivers with details on how their cars are performing, the marketing dashboard gives marketers the detailed measures they need to assess and adjust their marketing strategies.[22]

Increasingly, however, beyond standard performance measures, marketers are using customer-centered measures of marketing impact, such as customer acquisition, customer retention, customer lifetime value, and customer equity. These measures capture not just current marketing performance but also future performance resulting from stronger customer relationships. ■ **Figure 2.8** views marketing expenditures as investments that produce returns in the form of more profitable customer relationships.[23] Marketing investments result in improved customer value and satisfaction, which in turn increases customer attraction and retention. This increases individual customer lifetime values and the firm's overall customer equity. Increased customer equity, in relation to the cost of the marketing investments, determines return on marketing investment.

■ **Figure 2.8.** Return on Marketing Investment

Source: Adapted from Roland T. Rust, Katherine N. Lemon, and Valerie A. Zeithaml, "Return on Marketing: Using Consumer Equity to Focus Marketing Strategy," *Journal of Marketing,* January 2004, p. 112.

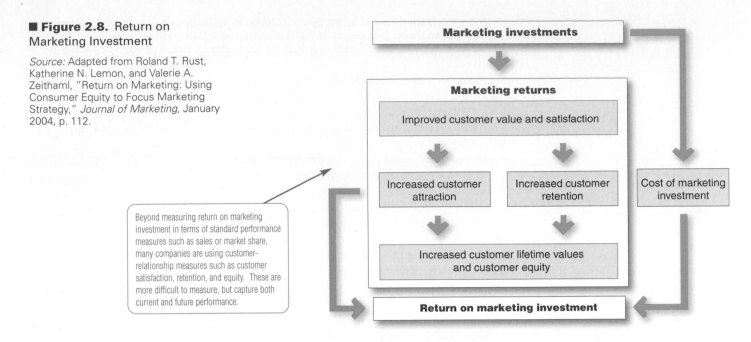

Beyond measuring return on marketing investment in terms of standard performance measures such as sales or market share, many companies are using customer-relationship measures such as customer satisfaction, retention, and equity. These are more difficult to measure, but capture both current and future performance.

Regardless of how it's defined or measured, the return on marketing investment concept is here to stay. "The marketing accountability revolution must continue," says one marketer. In today's demanding business environment, companies must know the impact of their marketing investments." Adds another, "You gotta be accountable."[24]

REST STOP
REVIEWING THE CONCEPTS

In Chapter 1, we defined *marketing* and outlined the steps in the marketing process. In this chapter, we examined companywide strategic planning and marketing's role in the organization. Then, we looked more deeply into marketing strategy and the marketing mix, and reviewed the major marketing management functions. So you've now had a pretty good overview of the fundamentals of modern marketing.

 Objective 1 Explain companywide strategic planning and its four steps. **(pp 67–70)**

Strategic planning sets the stage for the rest of the company's planning. Marketing contributes to strategic planning, and the overall plan defines marketing's role in the company.

Strategic planning involves developing a strategy for long-run survival and growth. It consists of four steps: (1) defining the company's mission, (2) setting objectives and goals, (3) designing a business portfolio, and (4) developing functional plans. The company's mission should be market oriented, realistic, specific, motivating, and consistent with the market environment. The mission is then transformed into detailed *supporting goals and objectives,* which in turn guide decisions about the *business portfolio.* Then each business and product unit must develop *detailed marketing plans* in line with the companywide plan.

Objective 2 Discuss how to design business portfolios and develop growth strategies. **(pp 71–74)**

Guided by the company's mission statement and objectives, management plans its *business portfolio,* or the collection of businesses and products that make up the company. The firm wants to produce a business portfolio that best fits its strengths and weaknesses to opportunities in the environment. To do this, it must analyze and adjust its *current* business portfolio and develop growth and downsizing strategies for adjusting the *future* portfolio. The company might use a formal portfolio-planning method. But many companies are now designing more-customized portfolio-planning approaches that better suit their unique situations.

Objective 3 Explain marketing's role in strategic planning and how marketing works with its partners to create and deliver customer value. **(pp 74–77)**

Under the strategic plan, the major functional departments—marketing, finance, accounting, purchasing, operations, information systems, human resources, and others—must work together to accomplish strategic objectives. Marketing plays a key role in the company's strategic planning by providing a *marketing concept philosophy* and *inputs* regarding attractive market opportunities. Within individual business units, marketing designs *strategies* for reaching the unit's objectives and helps to carry them out profitably.

Marketers alone cannot produce superior value for customers. Marketers must practice partner *relationship management*, working closely with partners in other departments to form an effective *value chain* that serves the customer. And they must partner effectively with other companies in the marketing system to form a competitively superior *value delivery network*.

> **Objective 4** Describe the elements of a customer-driven marketing strategy and mix, and the forces that influence it. **(pp 77–82)**

Consumer value and relationships are at the center of marketing strategy and programs. Through market segmentation, targeting, differentiation, and positioning, the company divides the total market into smaller segments, selects segments it can best serve, and decides how it wants to bring value to target consumers in the selected segments. It then designs an *integrated marketing mix* to produce the response it wants in the target market. The marketing mix consists of product, price, place, and promotion decisions (the four Ps).

> **Objective 5** List the marketing management functions, including the elements of a marketing plan, and discuss the importance of measuring and managing return on marketing investment. **(pp 82–88)**

To find the best strategy and mix and to put them into action, the company engages in marketing analysis, planning, implementation, and control. The main components of a *marketing plan* are the executive summary, current marketing situation, threats and opportunities, objectives and issues, marketing strategies, action programs, budgets, and controls. To plan good strategies is often easier than to carry them out. To be successful, companies must also be effective at *implementation*—turning marketing strategies into marketing actions.

Marketing departments can be organized in one or a combination of ways: *functional marketing organization, geographic organization, product management organization,* or *market management organization*. In this age of customer relationships, more and more companies are now changing their organizational focus from product or territory management to customer relationship management. Marketing organizations carry out *marketing control*, both operating control and strategic control.

Marketing managers must ensure that their marketing dollars are being well spent. In a tighter economy, today's marketers face growing pressures to show that they are adding value in line with their costs. In response, marketers are developing better measures of *return on marketing investment*. Increasingly, they are using customer-centered measures of marketing impact as a key input into their strategic decision making.

Navigating the Key Terms

Travel Log

Discussing the Issues

1. Explain what is meant by a *market-oriented* mission statement and discuss the characteristics of effective mission statements. (AACSB: Communication)

2. Define the four product/market expansion grid strategies and provide an example of each. (AACSB: Communications)

3. Explain why it is important for all departments of an organization—marketing, accounting, finance, operations management, human resources, and so on—to "think consumer." Why is it important that even people who are not in marketing understand it? (AACSB: Communication)

4. Explain how the marketing mix differs from marketing strategy. (AACSB: Communication)

5. Define each of the four Ps. What insights might a firm gain by considering the four Cs rather than the four Ps? (AACSB: Communication; Reflective Thinking)

6. Describe the various ways a company's marketing function can be organized. Which organizational form is best? (AACSB: Communication; Reflective Thinking)

Application Questions

1. In a small group, develop a SWOT analysis for a business in your community. From that analysis, recommend a marketing strategy and marketing mix for this business. (AACSB: Communication; Reflective Thinking)

2. Go to www.pg.com to learn about the brands offered by P&G. Select one product category in which P&G offers multiple brands. What is P&G's positioning for each brand in that product category? Then, visit a store and record the prices of each brand, using a common basis such as price per ounce. Write a brief report on what you learn. Are there meaningful positioning differences between the brands? Are any price differences you find justified? (AACSB: Communication; Reflective Thinking)

3. Explain the role of a chief marketing officer (CMO). Learn more about this C-level executive position and find an article that describes the importance of this position, the characteristics of an effective CMO, or any issues surrounding this position. (AACSB: Communication; Reflective Thinking)

Under the Hood: Marketing Technology

Mobile marketing is touted as the next "big thing," offering the promise of connecting with consumers on the most personal medium—their cell phones. Technological advances are letting marketers send not only text messages to cell phones but also video messages. Although there are still technical roadblocks stifling rapid expansion of this marketing method, some experts claim that marketers had better jump on this bandwagon or risk being left behind.

In Turkey, advertising agency Aerodeon ran a campaign for Pepsi in the first three months of 2008. The purpose of the campaign was to encourage customers to express their emotions using Pepsi "Emoticons." Customers were encouraged to text a unique code found under the Pepsi lids and pull tabs to "Turkcell 3323." They could also enter via the website www.duygularinigoster.com. Prizes were also offered. The first participant per hour would win an iPod Touch. Other prizes included Turkcell credits and airtime, mobile games, and wallpapers. Backing up the campaign were other business-to-business campaigns, promotions in retail outlets, and other venues. The campaign was an enormous success with almost 8.5 million people participating. It has been the most successful mobile campaign to date in Turkey.

1. Visit the Mobile Marketing Association's Web site at www.mmaglobal.com and click on "Resources" and then "MMA Member Case Studies" on the left. Discuss one case study and describe the factors you think made that application of mobile marketing a success.

2. Analysis is an important first step in the marketing management process. The rapid advance in mobile technology poses opportunities as well as threats for marketers. Discuss both the opportunities and threats for marketers.

Staying on the Road: Marketing Ethics

Marketing to children has always been controversial. Indeed, in the 1970s, the Federal Trade Commission (FTC) considered prohibiting all advertising to children. The federal government once again is setting its sights on marketing aimed at children. With the U.S. child obesity rate predicted to exceed 20 percent in just a few years, regulators are pressuring marketers in general, and food marketers in particular, to curb their marketing practices to children. In 2008, the FTC delivered an analysis to Congress of 44 companies' $1.6 billion food and beverage marketing activities targeting children. A provision in the 2009 omnibus spending bill signed into law by President Barack Obama created the Interagency Working Group on Food Marketed to Children. This group will present recommendations to Congress in 2010 regarding marketing to children aged 17 and younger (an expansion of previous under-12 definitions of "children"). With children and teens spending billions of their own dollars and influencing much more of their parents' spending, this is an important market segment to marketers.

1. Studies report that children view more than 20 food ads each day, of which over 90 percent promote high-fat, high-sugar products. The marketing concept focuses on satisfying customers' needs and wants, but are marketers crossing the line when they cater to younger consumers' wants for products that may counter parental wishes or that may be unhealthy? (AACSB: Communication; Ethical Reasoning)

2. What actions are marketers taking to market their products to this market segment more ethically? Discuss industry initiatives that help marketers market to children more responsibly. (AACSB: Communication; Ethical Reasoning)

Rough Road Ahead: Marketing and the Economy

Southwest Airlines

As more and more consumers have cut back on spending, perhaps no industry has been hit harder than the airlines. Even Southwest Airlines, which has posted profits in every one of its 36 years of operation, is now seeing declines in its sales, profits, and stock price. So what's Southwest doing? For starters, Southwest is expanding beyond the 65 cities it now serves. It is also attempting to sweeten the ride by boosting wine and coffee service and experimenting with onboard WiFi, something other carriers have already added. But perhaps more important is what no-frills Southwest *isn't* doing: adding fees. Other airlines are generating millions of dollars in revenues by charging for basics like checking baggage, sitting in aisle seats, or using pillows. But Southwest insists that such fees are no way to grow an airline. Other attempts to jumpstart demand include an ad campaign urging consumers to continue traveling despite the lagging economy and a company-wide fare sale with one-way rates as low as $49. Southwest's hopes that these efforts will bring customers back and curb the revenue slide.

1. Consider every tactic that Southwest is employing to curtail slumping sales. Evaluate the degree to which each is effective at accomplishing Southwest's goal.

2. Are Southwest's efforts enough? Is it possible for Southwest to reverse the effects of the strong industry slump?

Travel Budget: Marketing by the Numbers

Appendix 2: Marketing by the Numbers discusses other marketing profitability metrics in addition to return on marketing investment (marketing ROI) calculations described in this chapter. The following is a profit-and-loss statement for a business. Review Appendix 3 and answer the question below.

1. Calculate the net marketing contribution (NMC) for this company.

2. Calculate both marketing return on sales (or marketing ROS) and marketing return on investment (or marketing ROI) as described in Appendix 3. Is this company doing well?

Net Sales		$640,000,000
Cost of goods sold		$280,000,000
Gross Margin		$360,000,000
Marketing Expenses		
Sales expenses	$50,000,000	
Promotion expenses	$20,000,000	
		$70,000,000
General and Administrative Expenses		
Marketing salaries and expenses	$12,000,000	
Indirect overhead	$40,000,000	$52,000,000
Net profit before income tax		$238,000,000

Drive In: Video Case

Live Nation

Live Nation may not be a household name. But if you've been to a concert in the past few years, chances are you've purchased a Live Nation product. In fact, Live Nation has been the country's largest concert promoter for many years, promoting as many as 29,000 events annually. But through very savvy strategic planning, Live Nation is shaking up the structure of the music industry.

A recent $120 million deal with Madonna illustrates how this concert promoter is diving into other businesses as well. Under this deal, Live Nation will become Madonna's record label, concert promoter, ticket vendor, and merchandise agent. Similar deals have been reached with other performers such as Jay-Z and U2.

But contracting with artists is only part of the picture. Live Nation is partnering with other corporations as well. A venture with Citi will expand its reach to potential customers through a leveraging of database technologies. Joining forces with ticket reseller powerhouses such as StubHub will give Live Nation a position in the thriving business of secondary ticket sales.

After viewing the video featuring Live Nation, answer the following questions about the role of strategic planning:

1. What is Live Nation's mission?

2. Based on the product/market expansion grid, provide support for the strategy that Live Nation is pursuing.

3. How does Live Nation's strategy provide better value for customers?

3

Analyzing the Marketing
Environment

ROAD MAP

Previewing the Concepts

In Part 1 (Chapters 1 and 2), you learned about the basic concepts of marketing and the steps in the marketing process for building profitable relationships with targeted consumers. In Part 2, we'll look deeper into the first step of the marketing process—understanding the marketplace and customer needs and wants. In this chapter, you'll discover that marketing operates in a complex and changing environment. Other *actors* in this environment—suppliers, intermediaries, customers, competitors, publics, and others—may work with or against the company. Major environmental *forces*—demographic, economic, natural, technological, political, and cultural—shape marketing opportunities, pose threats, and affect the company's ability to build customer relationships. To develop effective marketing strategies, you must first understand the environment in which marketing operates.

Objective Outline

Objective 1   Describe the environmental forces that affect the company's ability to serve its customers.
The Company's Microenvironment **pp 95–98**
The Company's Macroenvironment **pp 98–120**

Objective 2   Explain how changes in the demographic and economic environments affect marketing decisions.
Demographic Environment **pp 99–106**
Economic Environment **pp 106–108**

Objective 3   Identify the major trends in the firm's natural and technological environments.
Natural Environment **pp 108–109**
Technological Environment **pp 109–111**

Objective 4   Explain the key changes in the political and cultural environments.
Political and Social Environment **pp 111–116**
Cultural Environment **pp 116–120**

Objective 5   Discuss how companies can react to the marketing environment.
Responding to the Marketing Environment **pp 120–122**

digital growth: 74%

Take a smart printer: Transcontinental Inc. Add relevant data to a catalog run using Xerox digital technology and their client, Reader's Digest Canada, has 74% more sales.
There's a new way to look at it.

Transcontinental Inc. thought a digital print solution could achieve a response breakthrough for Reader's Digest, one of the world's most successful direct marketers. A call to the digital experts from the Xerox 1:1 Lab more than proved them right. Using a Reader's Digest database and Xerox digital printing technology, personalized direct mail was created to test against a traditional direct mail campaign. The result? The 1-to-1 messaging outperformed the traditional by 74%. The more personalized messages simply had more pull. Could you benefit from our digital advantage? Just ask the pros at Reader's Digest and Transcontinental.

xerox.com/printing   1-800-ASK-XEROX

xerox ●

▲ **Xerox has rethought, redefined, and reinvented itself. The company now "connects closely with customers in a content-rich digital marketplace."**

Let's start with a look at an American icon, Xerox. A half-century ago, this venerable old company harnessed changing technology to create a whole new industry—photocopying—and dominated that industry for decades. But did you know that, barely a decade ago, Xerox was on the verge of bankruptcy? Don't worry, the company is once again sound. But Xerox's harrowing experience provides a cautionary tale of what can happen when a company—even a dominant market leader—fails to adapt to its changing marketing environment.

> First Stop

Xerox: Adapting to the Turbulent Marketing Environment

Xerox introduced the first plain-paper office copier nearly 50 years ago. In the decades that followed, the company that invented photocopying flat-out dominated the industry it had created. The name Xerox became almost generic for copying (as in "I'll Xerox this for you"). Through the years, Xerox fought off round after round of rivals to stay atop the fiercely competitive copier industry. In 1998, Xerox's profits were growing at 20 percent a year and its stock price was soaring.

Then, things went terribly wrong for Xerox. The legendary company's stock and fortunes took a stomach-churning dive. In only 18 months, Xerox lost some $38 billion in market value. By mid-2001, its stock price had plunged from almost $70 in 1999 to under $5. The once-dominant market leader found itself on the brink of bankruptcy. What happened? Blame it on change, or—rather—on Xerox's failure to adapt to its rapidly changing marketing environment. The world was quickly going digital but Xerox hadn't kept up.

In the new digital environment, Xerox customers no longer relied on the company's flagship products—stand-alone copiers—to share information and documents. Rather than pumping out and distributing stacks of black-and-white copies, they created digital documents and shared them electronically. Or they popped out copies on their nearby networked printer. On a broader level, while Xerox was busy perfecting copy machines, customers were looking for more sophisticated "document management solutions." They wanted systems that would let them scan documents in Frankfurt, weave them into colorful, customized showpieces in San Francisco, and print them on demand in London—altering for American spelling.

As digital technology changed, so did Xerox's customers and competitors. Instead of selling copiers to equipment purchasing managers, Xerox found itself trying to develop and sell document management systems to high-level information technology managers. And instead of competing head-on with copy machine competitors such as Sharp, Canon, and Ricoh, Xerox was now squaring off against information technology companies such as HP and IBM.

Xerox's large and long-respected sales force—made up of those guys in the toner-stained shirts trained to sell and repair copy machines—simply wasn't equipped to deal effectively in the brave new world of digital document solutions. Xerox, the iconic "copier company," just wasn't cutting it in the new digital environment. Increasingly, Xerox found itself occupying the dusty

> Xerox invented photocopying and for decades flat-out dominated the industry it had created. But Xerox's harrowing experience provides a cautionary tale of what can happen when a company—even a dominant market leader—fails to adapt to its changing marketing environment.

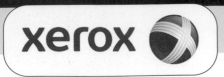

and dying "copy machine" corner of the analog office.

Since those dark days on the brink, however, Xerox has rethought, redefined, and reinvented itself. The company has undergone a remarkable transformation. Xerox no longer defines itself as a "copier company." In fact, it doesn't even make stand-alone copiers anymore. Instead, Xerox bills itself as "the world's leading document-management technology and services enterprise." Xerox's newly minted mission is to help companies and people "be smarter about their documents." Says the company in a recent annual report:

> Documenting any communication used to mean committing it to paper, getting it down in black and white. Now communication is generally scanned, sent, searched, archived, merged, and personalized—often in color. It can move back and forth, many times, from physical to digital. So when we say our mission is to help people be smarter about their documents, it really means giving them a range of tools and techniques to capture, organize, facilitate, and enhance how they communicate. In any form. To an audience of one or many millions.

The Xerox transformation started with a new focus on the customer. Before developing new products, Xerox researchers held seemingly endless customer focus groups. Xerox's Chief Technology Officer, Sophie Vandebroek, calls this "dreaming with the customer." The goal, she argues, is "involving experts who know the technology with customers who know the pain points. . . . Ultimately innovation is about delighting the customer." The new Xerox believes that understanding customers is just as important as understanding technology.

To make certain that happens, top managers at Xerox rotate responsibility to be the Customer Officer of the Day. "When it's your day," says Xerox chairman Anne Mulcahy, "you take any customer calls that might come into headquarters. As you might guess, these are not happy customers. As Customer Officer of the Day, you have three responsibilities: listen to the customer, resolve the problem, and take responsibility for fixing the underlying cause."

As a result of this new thinking, Xerox now offers a broad portfolio of customer-focused products, software, and services that help its customers manage documents and information. Xerox has introduced 100 innovative new products in the last three years. It now offers digital products and systems ranging from network printers and multifunction devices to color printing and publishing systems, digital presses, and "book factories." It also offers an impressive array of consulting and outsourcing services that help businesses develop online document archives, operate in-house print shops or mailrooms, analyze how employees can most efficiently share documents and knowledge, and build Web-based processes for personalizing direct mail, invoices, and brochures.

Xerox currently dominates the managed-print services market, helping big customers to manage their printing operations more efficiently in these difficult economic times. For example Procter & Gamble recently turned over management of its vast fleet of printers and copiers to Xerox in a multiyear contract valued at more than $100 million.

Now that Xerox has transformed its business, it's setting out to transform its image as well. Befitting its new identity, Xerox now has a new brand logo.

> Xerox retired the staid red capital X and block-lettered XEROX that has dominated its logo for 40 years. In its place is "a brand identity that reflects the Xerox of today." The new brand logo consists of a bright red lowercase "xerox" that sits alongside a red sphere sketched with lines that link to form a stylized X. Xerox chose a ball to suggest forward movement and a holistic company, and to reflect the company's connection to customers, partners, industry, and innovation. Xerox settled on lowercase letters because they seemed friendlier, and on a deeper red and a thicker font to stand out better on the Web and on high-definition television. The logo retains the good things that Xerox stands for (dependability and stability), jettisons the not-so-nice (formal, somewhat stodgy), and, most importantly, adds in such attributes as modern, innovative, and flexible.

Xerox chairman Anne Mulcahy sums things up this way: "We have transformed Xerox into a business that connects closely with customers in a content-rich digital marketplace. Our new brand reflects who we are, the markets we serve, and the innovation that differentiates us in our industry. We have expanded into new markets, created new businesses, acquired new capabilities, developed technologies that launched new industries—to ensure we make it easier, faster, and less costly for our customers to share information." A major Xerox customer agrees: "I've watched Xerox transition its business from a copier and printer company to a true partner in helping companies better manage information—whether it's digital, paper, or both. Now the face of Xerox matches the tech savvy, innovative company Xerox is today."

Thus, Xerox isn't an old, fusty copier company anymore. And thanks to a truly remarkable turnaround, Xerox is once again on solid footing. In fact, Xerox was recently ranked by *Fortune* as the world's most admired company in the computer industry. And last year, Xerox received more than 230 outstanding achievement awards from leading industry publications and independent testing and research firms around the world. But the message remains clear. Even the most dominant companies can be vulnerable to the often turbulent and changing marketing environment. Companies that understand and adapt well to their environments can thrive. Those that don't risk their very survival.[1]

Marketing environment
The actors and forces outside marketing that affect marketing management's ability to build and maintain successful relationships with target customers.

company's **marketing environment** consists of the actors and forces outside marketing that affect marketing management's ability to build and maintain successful relationships with target customers. Like Xerox, companies constantly watch and adapt to the changing environment.

Microenvironment
The actors close to the company that affect its ability to serve its customers—the company, suppliers, marketing intermediaries, customer markets, competitors, and publics.

Macroenvironment
The larger societal forces that affect the microenvironment—demographic, economic, natural, technological, political, and cultural forces.

Author Comment »
The microenvironment includes all of the actors close to the company that affect, positively or negatively, its ability to create value for and relationships with its customers.

More than any other group in company, marketers must be the environmental trend trackers and opportunity seekers. Although every manager in an organization needs to observe the outside environment, marketers have two special aptitudes. They have disciplined methods—marketing research and marketing intelligence—for collecting information about the marketing environment. They also spend more time in customer and competitor environments. By carefully studying the environment, marketers can adapt their strategies to meet new marketplace challenges and opportunities.

The marketing environment is made up of a *microenvironment* and a *macroenvironment*. The **microenvironment** consists of the actors close to the company that affect its ability to serve its customers—the company, suppliers, marketing intermediaries, customer markets, competitors, and publics. The **macroenvironment** consists of the larger societal forces that affect the microenvironment—demographic, economic, natural, technological, political, and cultural forces. We look first at the company's microenvironment.

THE COMPANY'S MICROENVIRONMENT (pp 95–98)

Marketing management's job is to build relationships with customers by creating customer value and satisfaction. However, marketing managers cannot do this alone. ■ **Figure 3.1** shows the major actors in the marketer's microenvironment. Marketing success will require building relationships with other company departments, suppliers, marketing intermediaries, customers, competitors, and various publics, which combine to make up the company's value delivery network.

The Company

In designing marketing plans, marketing management takes other company groups into account—groups such as top management, finance, research and development (R&D), purchasing, operations, and accounting. All of these interrelated groups form the internal environment. Top management sets the company's mission, objectives, broad strategies, and policies. Marketing managers make decisions within the strategies and plans made by top management.

As we discussed in Chapter 2, marketing managers must work closely with other company departments. Other departments have an impact on the marketing department's plans and actions. And under the marketing concept, all of these functions must "think consumer." According to Xerox CEO Anne Mulcahy, in order to provide a great customer experience, Xerox must "find out what customers are facing—what their problems and opportunities are. Everyone at Xerox shares this responsibility. That includes people and departments that have not always been customer-facing, like finance, legal, and human resources."[2]

■ **Figure 3.1** Actors in the Microenvironment

In creating value for customers, marketers must partner with other firms in the company's value delivery network. For example, Lexus can't create a high-quality ownership experience for its customers unless its suppliers provide quality parts and its dealers provide high sales and service quality.

Marketers must work in harmony with other company departments to create customer value and relationships. For example, Wal-Mart's marketers can't promise us low prices unless its operations department delivers low costs.

Customers are the most important actors in the company's microenvironment. The aim of the entire value delivery system is to serve target customers and create strong relationships with them.

Suppliers

Suppliers form an important link in the company's overall customer value delivery system. They provide the resources needed by the company to produce its goods and services. Supplier problems can seriously affect marketing. Marketing managers must watch supply availability and costs. Supply shortages or delays, labor strikes, and other events can cost sales in the short run and damage customer satisfaction in the long run. Rising supply costs may force price increases that can harm the company's sales volume.

Most marketers today treat their suppliers as partners in creating and delivering customer value. For example, ▲Toyota knows the importance of building close relationships with its suppliers. In fact, it even includes the phrase "achieve supplier satisfaction" in its mission statement.

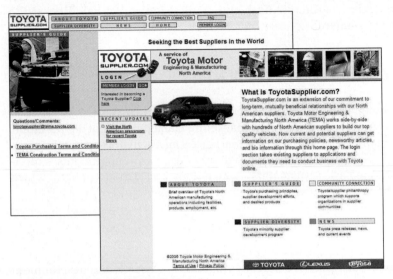

Toyota's competitors often alienate suppliers through self-serving, heavy-handed dealings. According to one supplier, the U.S. automakers "set annual cost-reduction targets [for the parts they buy]. To realize those targets, they'll do anything. [They've unleashed] a reign of terror, and it gets worse every year." By contrast, rather than bullying suppliers, Toyota partners with them and helps them to meet its very high expectations. Toyota learns about their businesses, conducts joint improvement activities, helps train supplier employees, gives daily performance feedback, and actively seeks out supplier concerns. It even recognizes top performers with annual performance awards. High supplier satisfaction means that Toyota can rely on suppliers to help it improve its own quality, reduce costs, and develop new products quickly. In all, creating satisfied suppliers helps Toyota to produce lower-cost, higher-quality cars, which in turn results in more satisfied customers.[3]

▲Toyota partners with its suppliers and helps them meet its very high expectations. Creating satisfied suppliers helps Toyota produce lower-cost, higher quality cars, which in turn results in more satisfied customers.

Marketing intermediaries
Firms that help the company to promote, sell, and distribute its goods to final buyers.

Marketing Intermediaries

Marketing intermediaries help the company to promote, sell, and distribute its products to final buyers. They include resellers, physical distribution firms, marketing services agencies, and financial intermediaries. *Resellers* are distribution channel firms that help the company find customers or make sales to them. These include wholesalers and retailers who buy and resell merchandise. Selecting and partnering with resellers is not easy. No longer do manufacturers have many small, independent resellers from which to choose. They now face large and growing reseller organizations such as Wal-Mart, Target, Home Depot, Costco, and Best Buy. These organizations frequently have enough power to dictate terms or even shut smaller manufacturers out of large markets.

Physical distribution firms help the company to stock and move goods from their points of origin to their destinations. *Marketing services agencies* are the marketing research firms, advertising agencies, media firms, and marketing consulting firms that help the company target and promote its products to the right markets. *Financial intermediaries* include banks, credit companies, insurance companies, and other businesses that help finance transactions or insure against the risks associated with the buying and selling of goods.

Like suppliers, marketing intermediaries form an important component of the company's overall value delivery system. In its quest to create satisfying customer relationships, the company must do more than just optimize its own performance. It must partner effectively with marketing intermediaries to optimize the performance of the entire system.

Thus, today's marketers recognize the importance of working with their intermediaries as partners rather than simply as channels through which they sell their products. For example, when Coca-Cola signs on as the exclusive beverage provider for a fast-food chain, such as McDonald's, Wendy's, or Subway, it provides much more than just soft drinks. It also pledges powerful marketing support.

Coke assigns cross-functional teams dedicated to understanding the finer points of each retail partner's business. It conducts a staggering amount of research on beverage consumers and shares these insights with its partners. It analyzes the demographics of U.S. zip code areas and helps partners to determine which Coke brands are preferred in their areas. Coca-Cola has even studied the design of drive-through menu boards to better understand which layouts, fonts, letter sizes, colors, and visuals induce consumers to order more food and drink. Based on such insights, the Coca-Cola FoodService group develops marketing programs and merchandising tools that help its retail partners to improve their beverage sales and profits. For example, its Ponle Mas Sabor Con Coca-Cola program helps retail partners take full advantage of opportunities in the fast-growing Hispanic market. Coca-Cola FoodService's Web site, www.CokeSolutions.com, provides retailers with a wealth of information, business solutions, and merchandising tips. Such intense partnering efforts have made Coca-Cola a runaway leader in the U.S. fountain soft-drink market.[4]

Competitors

Public
Any group that has an actual or potential interest in or impact on an organization's ability to achieve its objectives.

The marketing concept states that to be successful, a company must provide greater customer value and satisfaction than its competitors do. Thus, marketers must do more than simply adapt to the needs of target consumers. They also must gain strategic advantage by positioning their offerings strongly against competitors' offerings in the minds of consumers.

No single competitive marketing strategy is best for all companies. Each firm should consider its own size and industry position compared to those of its competitors. Large firms with dominant positions in an industry can use certain strategies that smaller firms cannot afford. But being large is not enough. There are winning strategies for large firms, but there are also losing ones. And small firms can develop strategies that give them better rates of return than large firms enjoy.

▼Publics: The Avon Foundation's long-running Walk for Breast Cancer efforts recognize the importance of community publics. The campaign dramatically impacts the lives of millions affected by breast cancer.

Publics

The company's marketing environment also includes various publics. A **public** is any group that has an actual or potential interest in or impact on an organization's ability to achieve its objectives. We can identify seven types of publics:

- *Financial publics.* This group influences the company's ability to obtain funds. Banks, investment houses, and stockholders are the major financial publics.
- *Media publics.* This group carries news, features, and editorial opinion. It includes newspapers, magazines, and radio and television stations.
- *Government publics.* Management must take government developments into account. Marketers must often consult the company's lawyers on issues of product safety, truth in advertising, and other matters.
- *Citizen-action publics.* A company's marketing decisions may be questioned by consumer organizations, environmental groups, minority groups, and others. Its public relations department can help it stay in touch with consumer and citizen groups.
- *Local publics.* This group includes neighborhood residents and community organizations. Large companies usually appoint a community relations officer to deal with the community, attend meetings, answer questions, and contribute to worthwhile causes. For example, ▲the

Avon Foundation's long-running Walk for Breast Cancer efforts recognize the importance of community publics.

● *General public.* A company needs to be concerned about the general public's attitude toward its products and activities. The public's image of the company affects its buying.

● *Internal publics.* This group includes workers, managers, volunteers, and the board of directors. Large companies use newsletters and other means to inform and motivate their internal publics. When employees feel good about their company, this positive attitude spills over to external publics.

A company can prepare marketing plans for these major publics as well as for its customer markets. Suppose the company wants a specific response from a particular public, such as goodwill, favorable word of mouth, or donations of time or money. The company would have to design an offer to this public that is attractive enough to produce the desired response.

Customers

As we've emphasized throughout, customers are the most important actors in the company's microenvironment. The aim of the entire value delivery system is to serve target customers and create strong relationships with them. The company might target any or all of five types of customer markets. *Consumer markets* consist of individuals and households that buy goods and services for personal consumption. *Business markets* buy goods and services for further processing or for use in their production process, whereas *reseller markets* buy goods and services to resell at a profit. *Government markets* are made up of government agencies that buy goods and services to produce public services or transfer the goods and services to others who need them. Finally, *international markets* consist of these buyers in other countries, including consumers, producers, resellers, and governments. Each market type has special characteristics that call for careful study by the seller.

Author Comment »
The macroenvironment consists of broader forces that affect the actors in the microenvironment.

THE COMPANY'S MACROENVIRONMENT (pp 98–120)

The company and all of the other actors operate in a larger macroenvironment of forces that shape opportunities and pose threats to the company. ■ **Figure 3.2** shows the six major forces in the company's macroenvironment. In the remaining sections of this chapter, we examine these forces and show how they affect marketing plans.

■ **Figure 3.2** Major Forces in the Company's Macroenvironment

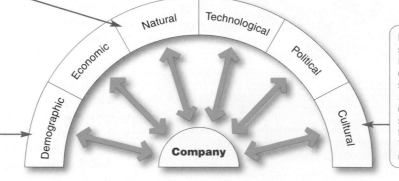

Concern for the natural environment has spawned a so-called green movement in industries ranging from PCs to diesel locomotives. For example, last year HP recovered and recycled 250 million pounds of electronics globally, equivalent to some 800 jumbo jets. The goal of many companies today is **environmental sustainability**—strategies and practices that the planet can support indefinitely.

Changing demographics mean changes in markets, which in turn require changes in marketing strategies. For example, Amerprise Financial now targets aging baby boomers with the promise that it will help them "envision what exactly you want to do in the next phase of your life."

Marketers also want to be socially responsible citizens in their markets and communities. For example, shoe brand TOMS was *founded* on a cause: "No complicated formulas It's simple," says the company's founder. "You buy a pair of TOMS and I give a pair to a child in need on your behalf."

Demography
The study of human populations in terms of size, density, location, age, gender, race, occupation, and other statistics.

▲ Demographics and markets: The growing Chinese "me generation" of only children—the "little emperors"—is affecting markets for everything from children's products to financial services, cell phone services, and luxury goods.

Baby boomers
The 78 million people born during the baby boom following World War II and lasting until 1964.

Demographic Environment

Demography is the study of human populations in terms of size, density, location, age, gender, race, occupation, and other statistics. The demographic environment is of major interest to marketers because it involves people, and people make up markets. The world population is growing at an explosive rate. It now exceeds 6.8 billion people and will grow to more than 8 billion by the year 2030.[5] The world's large and highly diverse population poses both opportunities and challenges.

Changes in the world demographic environment have major implications for business. For example, consider China. Thirty years ago, to curb its skyrocketing population, the Chinese government passed regulations limiting families to one child each. As a result, ▲China's youth born after 1980—called "balinghou" or the "Me generation" by their elders—have been showered with attention and luxuries resulting in what's known as the "little emperor" or "little empress" syndrome. As many as six adults, two parents and four doting grandparents, may be indulging the whims of each only child—all 600 million of them (almost twice the entire U.S. population). Parents with only one child at home now spend about 40 percent of their income on their cherished child.[6]

China's me generation, now ranging in age from newborns to late-20s, is affecting markets for everything from children's products to financial services, cell phone services, and luxury goods. For example, Starbucks is targeting China's me generation, positioning itself as new kind of informal but indulgent meeting place.[7]

> China's one-child rule created a generation who have been pampered by parents and grandparents and have the means to make indulgent purchases. Instead of believing in traditional Chinese collective goals, these young people embrace individuality. "Their view of this world is very different," says the president of Starbucks Greater China. "They have never gone through the hardships of our generation." Starbucks is in sync with that, he says, given its customized drinks, personalized service, and original music compilations.

Thus, marketers keep close track of demographic trends and developments in their markets, both at home and abroad. They track changing age and family structures, geographic population shifts, educational characteristics, and population diversity. Here, we discuss the most important demographic trends in the United States.

Changing Age Structure of the Population

The U.S. population stood at over 305 million by the end of 2008 and may reach almost 364 million by the year 2030.[8] The single most important demographic trend in the United States is the changing age structure of the population. The U.S. population contains several generational groups. Here, we discuss the three largest groups—the baby boomers, Generation X, and the Millennials—and their impact on today's marketing strategies.

The Baby Boomers. The post–World War II baby boom produced 78 million **baby boomers**, born between 1946 and 1964. Over the years, the baby boomers have been one of the most powerful forces shaping the marketing environment. The youngest boomers are now in their mid forties; the oldest are entering their sixties and approaching retirement age. The maturing boomers are rethinking the purpose and value of their work, responsibilities, and relationships.

After years of prosperity, free spending, and saving little, the recent recession hit many baby boomers hard, especially the preretirement boomers. A sharp decline in stock prices and home values has eaten into their nest eggs and retirement prospects. As a result, many boomers are now spending more carefully and planning to work longer. "You have a huge group of preretirement baby boomers, a huge number of people who are asking, 'Can I live off my savings and Social Security for the rest of my life?'" says one economist. "A whopping 70 percent of Americans currently age 45 to 74 plan to work during their retirement years . . . both for enjoyment and because they need the money," notes another.[9]

However, although they might now be feeling the pinch of the weakened economy, the baby boomers are still the wealthiest generation in U.S. history. Today's baby boomers account for about 25 percent of the U.S. population but hold 75 percent of the nation's financial assets and account for about 50 percent of total consumer spending.[10] As they reach their peak earning and spending years, the boomers will continue to constitute a lucrative market for financial services, new housing and home remodeling, travel and entertainment, eating out, health and fitness products, and just about everything else.

It would be a mistake to think of the older boomers as phasing out or slowing down. Today's boomers think young no matter how old they are. Rather than viewing themselves as phasing out, they see themselves as entering new life phases. For example, Toyota recognizes these changing boomer life phases. Ads for its Toyota Highlander show empty-nest boomers and declare "For your newfound freedom." Similarly, Curves fitness centers targets boomer women. Curves' older regulars "want to be strong and fit," says one expert. "They just don't want to go into Gold's Gym and be surrounded by spandex-clad Barbie dolls."[11]

Perhaps no one is targeting the baby boomers more fervently than the financial services industry. Collectively, the baby boomers have earned $3.7 trillion, more than twice as much as members of the prior generation. They'll also be inheriting $7.2 trillion as their parents pass away. Thus, especially in the aftermath of the recession, the boomers will be needing lots of money management help. Ameriprise Financial's entire positioning rests on helping aging baby boomers realize their preretirement and retirement dreams through sound financial planning.[12]

> Based on a large-scale "New Retirement Mindscape" study, Ameriprise Financial developed a *Dream Book* planning guide that helps boomers to explore their retirement dreams and create a life strategy for retirement. The *Dream Book* guide becomes one of the first steps in Ameriprise Financial's Dream > Plan > Track financial planning approach. The company's "Dreams don't retire" advertising campaign promises that the company will help boomers identify new strategies and opportunities for navigating the risks to happy retirement. In one commercial, 1960s icon Dennis Hopper talks plainly about what retirement means in these uncertain economic times. Standing at a crossroads on a major highway, Hopper advises: "So here you are, a little confused. Did you think the road to retirement was an expressway? You can't start this journey without knowing where you're going. You, my friend, need a plan." The solution, of course, is to talk with an Ameriprise Financial advisor. According to the company's CEO, for Ameriprise "it all begins with understanding our client's dreams." And "Dreams don't retire."[13]

Generation X
The 45 million people born between 1965 and 1976 in the "birth dearth" following the baby boom.

Generation X. The baby boom was followed by a "birth dearth," creating another generation of 49 million people born between 1965 and 1976. Author Douglas Coupland calls them **Generation X** because they lie in the shadow of the boomers and lack obvious distinguishing characteristics.

The Generation Xers are defined as much by their shared experiences as by their age. Increasing parental divorce rates and higher employment for their mothers made them the first generation of latchkey kids. Although they seek success, they are less materialistic; they prize experience, not acquisition. For many of the Gen Xers that are parents, family comes first—both children and their aging parents—and career second.[14] From a marketing standpoint, the Gen Xers are a more skeptical bunch. They tend to research products before they consider a purchase, preferring quality over quantity, and they tend to be less receptive to overt marketing pitches.

Once labeled as "the MTV generation" and viewed as body-piercing slackers who whined about "McJobs," the Gen Xers have grown up and are now taking over. They are increasingly displacing the lifestyles, culture, and values of the baby boomers. They are the most educated generation to date and they possess hefty annual purchasing

How can we start a nest egg when we're still saving for the nest?

You'll be surprised what we can help you with.

Too many things to save for to think about investing? Even if you're saving for something short term, like a down payment, Schwab can give you real investment help, plus the research and online resources to help you get ahead. We can also help you roll over your 401(k) and invest in an IRA to help better prepare for your future. It's all about getting your eggs in the right baskets, so to speak.

Talk to a Schwab Investment Professional today.
1-800-4SCHWAB / SCHWAB.COM

TALK TO CHUCK

charles SCHWAB

▲Targeting Gen Xers: Schwab's "Talk to Chuck" campaign speaks directly to Gen Xers and promotes solutions linked with their approach to savings.

Millennials (or Generation Y)
The 83 million children of the baby boomers, born between 1977 and 2000.

power. However, like the baby boomers, the Gen Xers now face growing economic pressures. Like almost everyone else these days, they are spending more carefully.[15]

Still, with so much potential, many companies are focusing on Gen Xers as an important target segment. For example, unlike Ameriprise Financial, which targets baby boomers, ▲Charles Schwab recently launched a campaign targeting Gen Xers.[16]

Most Gen Xers are woefully behind in saving for retirement—and they worry about it. Still, nearly half of Gen Xers say they are so saddled with debt or live on such tight budgets that they can't even think about saving. Recognizing these pressures, Schwab has started offering solutions linked with this generation's approach to savings. For example, it has lowered account minimums to $1,000 and offers a high-yield checking account linked to a brokerage account. "If they can start with a checking account, they can invest easily over time," says a Schwab marketing executive.

To engage Gen Xers, instead of talking about "portfolio diversification" or "free trades," Schwab's "Talk to Chuck" advertising campaign focuses on everyday issues, such as saving for a home or paying down college debt. By speaking to Gen Xers in their language, Schwab makes investing a viable option for these "savers." The campaign avoids the business and finance publications traditionally used by financial services advertisers, instead concentrating on lifestyle publications in the area of parenting, home, fitness, and style. Digital media also concentrate on lifestyle platforms. Schwab places ads on baby shower sites, children's party invitations on Evite.com, mortgage calculators on BankRate.com, and Gen X–oriented entertainment on travel areas of Yahoo! and AOL, along with Wi-Fi sponsorships in airports and sponsorship of MSN's instant messaging platforms. National television ads and a Web site, www.schwabmoneyandmore.com, support the overall communications effort. The result: Six months into the campaign, younger investors new to Schwab increased 118 percent over the previous year.

Millennials. Both the baby boomers and Gen Xers will one day be passing the reins to the **Millennials** (also called Generation Y or the echo boomers). Born between 1977 and 2000, these children of the baby boomers number 83 million, dwarfing the Gen Xers and larger even than the baby boomer segment. This group includes several age cohorts: *tweens* (aged 9–12), *teens* (13–18), and *young adults* (19–32). With total purchasing power of more than $733 billion, the Millennials make up a huge and attractive market.[17]

One thing that all of the Millennials have in common is their utter fluency and comfort with digital technology. They don't just embrace technology, it's a way of life. The Millennials were the first generation to grow up in a world filled with computers, cellphones, satellite TV, iPods, and online social networks. A recent study found that 91 percent of Millennials are on the Web, making up 32 percent of all U.S. Internet users. According to another study, 77 percent of Millennials frequent social networking sites and 71 percent use instant messaging. "All generations are comfortable with technology, but this is the generation that's been formed by technology," says a Yahoo! executive. For them, "it's not something separate. It's just something they do."[18]

Marketers of all kinds now target the Millennials segment, from automakers to political campaigns. However, the Millennials are bombarded with marketing messages coming at them from all directions. And rather than having mass marketing messages pushed at them, they prefer to seek out information and engage in two-way brand conversations. Thus, reaching these message-saturated consumers effectively requires creative marketing approaches. ▲Consider how the Barack Obama presidential campaign succeeded in reaching this group:[19]

"Barack Obama was the first presidential candidate to be marketed like a high-end consumer brand," observed a *Newsweek* reporter. His rising-sun logo echoes the one-world icons of Pepsi, AT&T, and Apple. But what really set the Obama campaign apart was its

▲Reaching Millennials: The Barack Obama presidential campaign's mastery of cutting-edge social media, such as the my.barackobama.com Web site, was optimized for Millennial appeal. Post election, it still is. You can connect with "Obama everywhere."

immense appeal to Millennials, the country's youngest voters. The campaign's mastery of cutting-edge social media, such as the my.barackobama.com Web site, was optimized for Millennial appeal. For this generation, "the new pronoun is me, my," says a marketing expert. "Young people want to be in control of their relationship with a brand. They want to customize and personalize." The Obama campaign site allowed just that, with its use of tagging, discussion boards, photo uploads, and other interactive elements.

In addition, Obama enlisted eight million volunteers using social-networking sites, attracted two million "friends" on Facebook, and drew 90 million viewers to his video presentations on YouTube. On Election Day, the Obama team sent text messages to millions of young supporters. The Obama campaign didn't merely use young volunteers, as most campaigns do. It created a campaign specifically designed by and for today's tech-happy Millennial generation, using the communication tools young people rely on and trust. The result? Young people turned out at the polls in record numbers, with fully 66 percent favoring Obama, turning the tide his way in several key states.

Generational Marketing. Do marketers need to create separate products and marketing programs for each generation? Some experts warn that marketers need to be careful about turning off one generation each time they craft a product or message that appeals effectively to another. Others caution that each generation spans decades of time and many socioeconomic levels. For example, marketers often split the baby boomers into three smaller groups—leading-edge boomers, core boomers, and trailing-edge boomers—each with its own beliefs and behaviors. Similarly, they split the Millennials into tweens, teens, and young adults.

Thus, marketers need to form more precise age-specific segments within each group. More important, defining people by their birth date may be less effective than segmenting them by their lifestyle, life stage, or the common values they seek in the products they buy. We will discuss many other ways to segment markets in Chapter 6.

The Changing American Family

The "traditional household" consists of a husband, wife, and children (and sometimes grandparents). Yet, the once American ideal of the two-child, two-car suburban family has lately been losing some of its luster.

In the United States today, married couples with children make up only 23 percent of the nation's 116 million households; married couples without children make up 29 percent; and single parents comprise another 16 percent. A full 32 percent are nonfamily households—single live-alones or adult live-togethers of one or both sexes.[20] More people are divorcing or separating, choosing not to marry, marrying later, or marrying without intending to have children. Marketers must increasingly consider the special needs of nontraditional households, because they are now growing more rapidly than traditional households. Each group has distinctive needs and buying habits.

The number of working women has also increased greatly, growing from under 40 percent of the U.S. workforce in the late 1950s to 59 percent today. Both husband and wife work in 52 percent of all married-couple families. Meanwhile, more men are staying home with their children, managing the household while their wives go to work. According to the census, the number of stay-at-home dads has risen 18 percent since 1994—some 159,000 fathers now stay at home.[21]

The significant number of women in the workforce has spawned the child day care business and increased consumption of career-oriented women's clothing, financial services, and convenience foods and services. An example is Peapod, the nation's leading Internet grocer. Using Peapod, instead of trekking to the grocery store, battling traffic, and waiting in line, busy working moms and dads can simply buy their groceries online. Peapod offers a virtual selection of more than 8,000 grocery store products and delivers customers' orders to their doorsteps. We "bring a world of food to your door," says Peapod—it's "the solution to today's busy lifestyles." So far, Peapod has filled more than 10 million orders. More important, it figures that it has saved its busy customers more than 10 million hours in trips to the grocery store.[22]

Geographic Shifts in Population

This is a period of great migratory movements between and within countries. Americans, for example, are a mobile people, with about 13 percent of all U.S. residents moving each year. Over the past two decades, the U.S. population has shifted toward the Sunbelt states. The West and South have grown, whereas the Midwest and Northeast states have lost population.[23] Such population shifts interest marketers because people in different regions buy differently. For example, research shows that people in Seattle buy more toothbrushes per capita than people in any other U.S. city; people in Salt Lake City eat more candy bars; and people in Miami drink more prune juice.

Also, for more than a century, Americans have been moving from rural to metropolitan areas. In the 1950s, they made a massive exit from the cities to the suburbs. Today, the migration to the suburbs continues. And more and more Americans are moving to "micropolitan areas," small cities located beyond congested metropolitan areas, such as Bozeman, Montana; Natchez, Mississippi; and Torrington, Connecticut. Drawing refugees from rural and suburban America, these smaller micros offer many of the advantages of metro areas—jobs, restaurants, diversions, community organizations—but without the population crush, traffic jams, high crime rates, and high property taxes often associated with heavily urbanized areas.[24]

The shift in where people live has also caused a shift in where they work. For example, the migration toward micropolitan and suburban areas has resulted in a rapid increase in the number of people who "telecommute"—work at home or in a remote office and conduct their business by phone, fax, modem, or the Internet. This trend, in turn, has created a booming SOHO (small office/ home office) market. An increasing number of people are working from home with the help of electronic conveniences such as PCs, cell phones, fax machines, PDA devices, and fast Internet access. One recent study estimates that 40 percent of American businesses now support some kind of telecommuting program.[25]

Many marketers are actively courting the lucrative telecommuting market. For example, WebEx, the Web-conferencing division of Cisco, helps overcome the isolation that often accompanies telecommuting. ▲With WebEx, people can meet and collaborate online, no matter what their work location. "All you need to run effective online meetings is a browser and a phone," says the company. With WebEx, people working anywhere can interact with other individuals or small groups to make presentations, exchange documents, and share desktops, complete with audio and full-motion video. WebEx's MeetMeNow service can be launched from desktops, Microsoft Outlook and Office, and instant messaging clients such as Yahoo! Messenger and MSN Messenger. MeetMeNow automatically finds and configures users' Webcams and lets meeting hosts switch among

▼Cisco targets the growing telecommuter market with WebEx, which lets people meet and collaborate online, no matter what their work location.

participants' video streams to form a virtual roundtable. More than 2.2 million people participate in WebEx sessions every day.[26]

A Better-Educated, More White-Collar, More Professional Population

The U.S. population is becoming better educated. For example, in 2007, 84 percent of the U.S. population over age 25 had completed high school and 27 percent had completed college, compared with 69 percent and 17 percent in 1980. Moreover, nearly two-thirds of high school graduates now enroll in college within 12 months of graduating.[27] The rising number of educated people will increase the demand for quality products, books, magazines, travel, personal computers, and Internet services.

The workforce also is becoming more white-collar. Between 1983 and 2007, the proportion of managers and professionals in the workforce increased from 23 percent to more than 35 percent. Job growth is now strongest for professional workers and weakest for manufacturing workers. Between 2006 and 2016, the number of professional workers is expected to increase 23 percent, while manufacturing workers are expected to decline more than 10 percent.[28]

Increasing Diversity

Countries vary in their ethnic and racial makeup. At one extreme is Japan, where almost everyone is Japanese. At the other extreme is the United States, with people from virtually all nations. The United States has often been called a melting pot—diverse groups from many nations and cultures have melted into a single, more homogenous whole. Instead, the United States seems to have become more of a "salad bowl" in which various groups have mixed together but have maintained their diversity by retaining and valuing important ethnic and cultural differences.

Marketers now face increasingly diverse markets, both at home and abroad as their operations become more international in scope. The U.S. population is about 65 percent white, with Hispanics at 15 percent and African Americans at a little less than 13 percent. The U.S. Asian American population now totals about 4.5 percent of the population, with the remaining 2.5 percent made up of American Indian, Eskimo, Aleut, or people of two or more races. Moreover, more than 34 million people living in the United States—more than 12 percent of the population—were born in another country. The nation's ethnic populations are expected to explode in coming decades. By 2050, Hispanics will comprise an estimated 24 percent of the population, African Americans will hold steady at about 13 percent, and Asians will almost double to 9 percent.[29]

Most large companies, from Procter & Gamble, Sears, Wal-Mart, Allstate, and Bank of America to Levi Strauss and General Mills, now target specially designed products, ads, and promotions to one or more of these groups. For example, last year Energizer ran an award-winning campaign to introduce Spanish-speaking consumers to its Energizer Bunny. For many Americans, the pink bunny is an advertising icon synonymous with long-lasting batteries. The challenge was to make the Energizer Bunny just as recognizable to Hispanics who didn't grow up in the United States:[30]

> Energizer teamed up with Latin music sensations Elvis Crespo, Camila, and Conjunto Primavera to craft a Latin music campaign dubbed "Musica Que Sigue y Sigue" ("Music That Goes On and On"). The musicians wrote and recorded the longest songs of their careers, tipping their hats to the bunny's reputation for "going and going and going." Energizer then used clips of the songs in television commercials that premiered during the Latin Grammy ceremonies. In the ads, for example, Crespo sang in front of a huge mound of sheet music and Camila's lead singer fought a sore throat from singing so long. The goal of the ads, which aired on the Univision and Telemundo Spanish-language networks, was to drive people to Energizer's Hispanic Web site, www.SigueYSigue.com. The site offered free downloads of Camila's 5-minute, 19-second, written-for-Energizer ballad, called "Amor Eterno" ("Eternal Love"), ring tones, and behind-the-scenes footage that later popped up on YouTube. The site also allowed visitors to upload their own original videos to contribute to the longest song. The campaign was a substantial success. Average visits to the Web site lasted six minutes and artists' video on YouTube generated more than 600,000 views. In just one year, the campaign increased Hispanic brand awareness by 10 percent and purchase consideration by double digits.

Diversity goes beyond ethnic heritage. For example, many major companies have recently begun to explicitly target gay and lesbian consumers. According to PlanetOut Inc., a leading global media and entertainment company that exclusively serves the lesbian, gay, bisexual, and transgender (LGBT) community, the U.S. gay and lesbian segment has buying power of $690 billion. PlanetOut's audience is twice as likely as the general population to have a household income over $250,000. A Simmons Research study of readers of the National Gay Newspaper Guild's 12 publications found that, compared to the average American, respondents are 12 times more likely to be in professional jobs, almost twice as likely to own a vacation home, 8 times more likely to own a notebook computer, and twice as likely to own individual stocks. More than two-thirds have graduated from college and 21 percent hold a master's degree.[31]

As a result of TV shows such as *Ugly Betty, The L Word, The Graham Norton Show*, and *The Ellen DeGeneres Show,* and Oscar-winning movies such as *Brokeback Mountain* and *Milk*, the LGBT community has increasingly emerged into the public eye. A number of media now provide companies with access to this market. For example, PlanetOut Inc. offers several successful magazines (*Out*, the *Advocate, Out Traveler*) and Web sites (Gay.com and PlanetOut.com). In 2005, media giant Viacom's MTV Networks introduced LOGO, a cable television network aimed at gays and lesbians and their friends and family. LOGO is now available in 33 million U.S. households. More than 100 mainstream marketers have advertised on LOGO, including Ameriprise Financial, Anheuser-Busch, Continental Airlines, Dell, Levi Strauss, eBay, Johnson & Johnson, Orbitz, Sears, Sony, and Subaru.

Companies in a wide range of industries are now targeting the LGBT community with gay-specific marketing efforts. For example, American Airlines has a dedicated LGBT sales team, sponsors gay community events, and offers a special gay-oriented Web site (www.aa.com/rainbow) that features travel deals, an e-newsletter, podcasts, and a gay events calendar. The airline's focus on gay consumers has earned it double-digit revenue growth from the LGBT community each year for more than a decade.[32]

Another attractive diversity segment is the estimated 60 million adults with disabilities in the United States—a market larger than African Americans or Hispanics—representing more than $200 billion in annual spending power. Most individuals with disabilities are active consumers. For example, a recent study found that more than two-thirds of adults with disabilities had traveled at least once for business or pleasure during the preceding two years. Thirty-one percent had booked at least one flight, more than half had stayed in hotels, and 20 percent had rented a car. Over 75 percent of people with disabilities dine out at least once a week.[33]

How are companies trying to reach consumers with disabilities? Many marketers now recognize that the worlds of people with disabilities and those without disabilities are one in the same. Marketers such as McDonald's, Verizon Wireless, Sears, Nike, and Honda have featured people with disabilities in their mainstream advertising. For instance, Target features disabled models in sales circulars and Nike signs endorsement deals with Paralympian athletes.

Other companies use specially targeted media to reach this attractive segment. ▲The new Web site Disaboom.com reaches people with disabilities through social networking

▼ **Targeting consumers with disabilities:** Ford highlights its Mobility Motoring Program in ads on Disaboom.com, which reaches people with disabilities with relevant information on everything from medical news to career advice, dating resources, and travel tips.

features akin to Facebook combined with relevant information, everything from medical news to career advice, dating resources, and travel tips. Several large marketers, including Johnson & Johnson, Netflix, Avis, GM, and Ford have already signed on as Disaboom.com marketing partners. Ford uses the site to highlight its Mobility Motoring Program. Among other things, the program provides $1,000 allowances for new car buyers to defray costs of adding adaptive equipment such as wheelchair or scooter lifts, pedal extensions, and steering wheel knobs. Marketing on Disaboom.com has "been a new concept for us and we are pleased with the performance so far," says Ford's mobility motoring manager.[34]

As the population in the United States grows more diverse, successful marketers will continue to diversify their marketing programs to take advantage of opportunities in fast-growing segments.

Speed Bump: Linking the Concepts

Pull over here and think about how deeply these demographic factors impact all of us and, as a result, marketers' strategies.

- Apply these demographic developments to your own life. Think of some specific examples of how the changing demographic factors affect you and your buying behavior.
- Identify a specific company that has done a good job of reacting to the shifting demographic environment—generational segments (baby boomers, GenXers, or Millennials), the changing American family, and increased diversity. Compare this company to one that's done a poor job.

Author Comment »
The economic environment can offer both opportunities and threats. For example, the recent economic downturn took a big bite out of Apple's sales growth and stock performance. Premium products such as iPhones and iPods are often hardest hit in troubled economic times. Said Apple's CEO, "Our stock was being buffeted by factors much larger than ourselves."

Economic environment
Factors that affect consumer buying power and spending patterns.

Economic Environment

Markets require buying power as well as people. The **economic environment** consists of factors that affect consumer purchasing power and spending patterns. Marketers must pay close attention to major trends and consumer spending patterns both across and within their world markets. For example, the recent world economic meltdown had a dramatic impact on consumers spending and buying behavior that will likely be felt for years to come.

Nations vary greatly in their levels and distribution of income. Some countries have *industrial economies*, which constitute rich markets for many different kinds of goods. At the other extreme are *subsistence economies*—they consume most of their own agricultural and industrial output and offer few market opportunities. In between are *developing economies*—which can offer outstanding marketing opportunities for the right kinds of products.

Consider India with its population of 1.1 billion people. In the past, only India's elite could afford to buy a car. In fact, only one in seven Indians now owns one. But recent dramatic changes in India's economy have produced a growing middle class and rapidly rising incomes. Now, to meet the new demand, European, North American, and Asian automakers are introducing smaller, more-affordable vehicles into India. But they'll have to find a way to compete with India's Tata Motors, which has unveiled the least expensive car ever in this market, the ▲Tata Nano. Dubbed "the people's car," the Nano sells for only 100,000 rupees (about US $2,500). It can seat four passengers, gets 50 miles per gallon, and travels at a top speed of 60 miles per hour. The ultralow-cost car is designed to be India's Model T—the car that puts the developing nation on wheels. For starters, Tata hopes to sell one million of these vehicles a year.[35]

Following are some of the major economic trends in the United States.

▲Economic environment: To capture India's growing middle class, Tata Motors introduced the small, affordable Tata Nano, designed to be India's Model T—the car that puts the developing nation on wheels.

Changes in Income and Spending

In recent years, American consumers spent freely, fueled by income growth, a boom in the stock market, rapid increases in housing values, and other economic good fortune. They bought and bought, seemingly without caution, amassing record levels of debt. However, the free spending and high expectations of those days were dashed by the recent worldwide economic crisis. Says one economist, "For a generation that has substituted rising home equity and stock prices for personal savings, the . . . economic meltdown has been psychologically wrenching after a quarter century of unquestioned prosperity."[36]

As a result, people who overconsumed during the past decade have now adopted a back-to-basics frugality in their lifestyles and spending patterns. They are buying less, and they are looking for greater value in the things that they do buy. In turn, *value marketing* has become the watchword for many marketers. Rather than offering high quality at a high price, or lesser quality at very low prices, marketers in all industries are looking for ways to offer today's more financially cautious buyers greater value—just the right combination of product quality and good service at a fair price.

You'd expect value pitches from the makers of everyday products. For example, alongside milk mustache ads featuring glamorous celebrities such as Brooke Shields and Beyonce Knowles, you now see one featuring celebrity financial advisor Suze Orman, telling consumers on how to "Milk your budget." And discounter Kohl's offers "style and savings inspiration." However, these days, even luxury-brand marketers are emphasizing good value. For instance, upscale car brand Infiniti now promises to "make luxury affordable."

Marketers should pay attention to *income distribution* as well as income levels. Over the past several decades, the rich have grown richer, the middle class has shrunk, and the poor have remained poor. The top 1 percent of American earners get 21.2 percent of the country's adjusted gross income, and the top 10 percent of earners capture 46.4 percent of all income. In contrast, the bottom 50 percent of American earners receive just 12.8 percent of total income.[37]

This distribution of income has created a tiered market. Many companies—such as Nordstrom and Neiman Marcus department stores—aggressively target the affluent. Others—such as Dollar General and Family Dollar stores—target those with more modest means. In fact, such dollar stores are now the fastest-growing retailers in the nation. Still other companies tailor their marketing offers across a range of markets, from the affluent to the less affluent. For example, many high-end fashion designers whose designs sell at sky-high prices to those who can afford it now also sell merchandise at prices that the masses can manage.[38]

> Isaac Mizrahi, a high-end fashion designer, pioneered the "fashion for the masses" trend by offering a line of clothing and accessories at Target. Now, other designers such as Nicole Miller and Stella McCartney are offering less expensive lines at JCPenney and H&M, respectively. And Vera Wang, known for her $10,000 wedding gowns found in boutiques and high-end retailers such as Bergdorf Goodman, offers a line called "Simply Vera—Vera Wang" at Kohl's. In one fall collection, a Vera Wang gold brocade skirt that is nearly identical to a skirt that fetches $890 at a high-end department store will sell for $68 at Kohl's.

Changing Consumer Spending Patterns

Food, housing, and transportation use up the most household income. However, consumers at different income levels have different spending patterns. Some of these differences were noted more than a century ago by Ernst Engel, who studied how people shifted their spending as their income rose. He found that as family income rises,

Engel's laws
Differences noted more than a century ago by Ernst Engel in how people shift their spending across food, housing, transportation, health care, and other goods and services categories as family income rises.

Author Comment >>
Today's enlightened companies are developing *environmentally sustainable* strategies in an effort to create a world economy that the planet can support indefinitely.

Natural environment
Natural resources that are needed as inputs by marketers or that are affected by marketing activities.

Environmental sustainability
Developing strategies and practices that create a world economy that the planet can support indefinitely.

the percentage spent on food declines, the percentage spent on housing remains about constant (except for such utilities as gas, electricity, and public services, which decrease), and both the percentage spent on most other categories and that devoted to savings increase. **Engel's laws** generally have been supported by later studies.

Changes in major economic variables such as income, cost of living, interest rates, and savings and borrowing patterns have a large impact on the marketplace. Companies watch these variables by using economic forecasting. Businesses do not have to be wiped out by an economic downturn or caught short in a boom. With adequate warning, they can take advantage of changes in the economic environment.

Natural Environment

The **natural environment** involves the natural resources that are needed as inputs by marketers or that are affected by marketing activities. Environmental concerns have grown steadily during the past three decades. In many cities around the world, air and water pollution have reached dangerous levels. World concern continues to mount about the possibilities of global warming, and many environmentalists fear that we soon will be buried in our own trash.

Marketers should be aware of several trends in the natural environment. The first involves growing *shortages of raw materials*. Air and water may seem to be infinite resources, but some groups see long-run dangers. Air pollution chokes many of the world's large cities, and water shortages are already a big problem in some parts of the United States and the world. By 2030, more than one in three of the world's human beings will not have enough water to drink.[39] Renewable resources, such as forests and food, also have to be used wisely. Nonrenewable resources, such as oil, coal, and various minerals, pose a serious problem. Firms making products that require these scarce resources face large cost increases, even if the materials remain available.

A second environmental trend is *increased pollution*. Industry will almost always damage the quality of the natural environment. Consider the disposal of chemical and nuclear wastes; the dangerous mercury levels in the ocean; the quantity of chemical pollutants in the soil and food supply; and the littering of the environment with nonbiodegradable bottles, plastics, and other packaging materials.

A third trend is *increased government intervention* in natural resource management. The governments of different countries vary in their concern and efforts to promote a clean environment. Some, such as the German government, vigorously pursue environmental quality. Others, especially many poorer nations, do little about pollution, largely because they lack the needed funds or political will. Even the richer nations lack the vast funds and political accord needed to mount a worldwide environmental effort. The general hope is that companies around the world will accept more social responsibility, and that less expensive devices can be found to control and reduce pollution.

In the United States, the Environmental Protection Agency (EPA) was created in 1970 to set and enforce pollution standards and to conduct pollution research. In the future, companies doing business in the United States can expect continued strong controls from government and pressure groups. Instead of opposing regulation, marketers should help develop solutions to the material and energy problems facing the world.

Concern for the natural environment has spawned the so-called green movement. Today, enlightened companies go beyond what government regulations dictate. They are developing strategies and practices that support **environmental sustainability**—an effort to create a world economy that the planet can support indefinitely. They are responding to consumer demands with more environmentally responsible products.

For example, General Electric is using its "ecomagination" to create products for a better world—cleaner aircraft engines, cleaner locomotives, cleaner fuel technologies. Taken together, for instance, all the GE Energy wind turbines in the world could produce enough power for 2.4 million U.S. homes. And in 2005, GE launched its Evolution series locomotives, diesel engines that cut fuel consumption by 5 percent and emissions by 40 percent compared to locomotives built just a year earlier. Up next is a triumph of sheer coolness: a GE hybrid diesel-electric locomotive that, just like a Prius, captures energy from braking and will improve mileage another 10 percent.[40]

Other companies are developing recyclable or biodegradable packaging, recycled materials and components, better pollution controls, and more energy-efficient operations. For example, PepsiCo—which owns businesses ranging from Frito-Lay and Pepsi-Cola to Quaker, Gatorade, and Tropicana—is working to dramatically reduce its environmental footprint.

> PepsiCo markets hundreds of products that are grown, produced, and consumed worldwide. Making and distributing these products requires water, electricity, and fuel. In 2007, the company set as its goal to reduce water consumption by 20 percent, electricity consumption by 20 percent, and fuel consumption by 25 percent per unit of production by 2015. It's already well on its way to meeting these goals. ▲For example, a solar-panel field now generates power for three-quarters of the heat used in Frito-Lay's Modesto, California, SunChips plant. A wind turbine now supplies more than two-thirds of the power at PepsiCo's beverage plant in Mamandur, India. On the packaging front, PepsiCo recently introduced new half-liter bottles of its Lipton iced tea, Tropicana juice, Aquafina FlavorSplash, and Aquafina Alive beverages that contain 20 percent less plastic than the original packaging. Aquafina has trimmed the amount of plastic used in its bottles by 35 percent since 2002, saving 50 million pounds of plastic annually.[41]

▲Environmental sustainability: PepsiCo is working to reduce its environmental footprint. For example, a solar-panel field now generates power for three-quarters of the heat used in Frito-Lay's Modesto, California, SunChips plant. "We're living up to our name."

Companies today are looking to do more than just good deeds. More and more, they are recognizing the link between a healthy ecology and a healthy economy. They are learning that environmentally responsible actions can also be good business.

Technological Environment

The **technological environment** is perhaps the most dramatic force now shaping our destiny. Technology has released such wonders as antibiotics, robotic surgery, miniaturized electronics, laptop computers, and the Internet. It also has released such horrors as nuclear missiles, chemical weapons, and assault rifles. It has released such mixed blessings as the automobile, television, and credit cards.

Our attitude toward technology depends on whether we are more impressed with its wonders or its blunders. For example, what would you think about having tiny little transmitters implanted in all of the products you buy that would allow tracking products from their point of production through use and disposal? On the one hand, it would provide many advantages to both buyers and sellers. On the other hand, it could be a bit scary. Either way, it's already happening:[42]

> Envision a world in which every product contains a tiny transmitter, loaded with information. As you stroll through the supermarket aisles, shelf sensors detect your selections and beam ads to your shopping cart screen, offering special deals on related products. As your cart fills, scanners detect that you might be buying for a dinner party; the screen suggests a wine to go with the meal you've planned. When you leave the store, exit scanners total up your purchases and automatically charge them to your credit card. At home, readers track what goes into and out of your pantry, updating your shopping list when stocks run

Author Comment »
Technological advances are perhaps the most dramatic forces affecting today's marketing strategies. Just think about the tremendous impact of the Web—which emerged only in the mid-1990s—on marketing. You'll see examples of the fast-growing world of online marketing throughout every chapter and we'll discuss it in detail in Chapter 14.

Technological environment
Forces that create new technologies, creating new product and market opportunities.

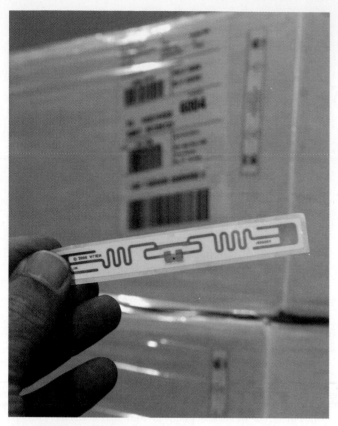

▲**Technological environment: Envision a world in which every product contains a transmitter loaded with information. In fact, that's not so far-fetched, thanks to radio-frequency identification (RFID).**

low. For Sunday dinner, you pop a Butterball turkey into your "smart oven," which follows instructions from an embedded chip and cooks the bird to perfection.

Seem far-fetched? Not really. In fact, it might soon become a reality, thanks to ▲radio-frequency identification (RFID) transmitters that can be embedded in the products you buy. Beyond benefits to consumers, RFID also gives producers and retailers an amazing new way to track their products electronically—anywhere in the world, anytime, automatically—from factories, to warehouses, to retail shelves, to recycling centers. Many large firms are adding fuel to the RFID fire. For example, Wal-Mart requires all suppliers shipping products to its Sam's Club's distribution centers to apply RFID tags to their pallets. If they don't, it charges $2 a pallet to do it for them. Sam's Club plans to use RFID tags on every pallet, case, and item by the fall of 2010. One study found that by using RFID, Wal-Mart can improve its inventory accuracy by 13 percent, saving millions and millions of dollars a year.

The technological environment changes rapidly. Think of all of today's common products that were not available 100 years ago, or even 30 years ago. Abraham Lincoln did not know about automobiles, airplanes, radios, or the electric light. Woodrow Wilson did not know about television, aerosol cans, automatic dishwashers, air conditioners, antibiotics, or computers. Franklin Delano Roosevelt did not know about xerography, synthetic detergents, tape recorders, birth control pills, jet engines, or earth satellites. John F. Kennedy did not know about personal computers, cell phones, the Internet, or googling.

New technologies create new markets and opportunities. However, every new technology replaces an older technology. Transistors hurt the vacuum-tube industry, xerography hurt the carbon-paper business, CDs hurt phonograph records; and digital photography hurt the film business. When old industries fought or ignored new technologies, their businesses declined. Thus, marketers should watch the technological environment closely. Companies that do not keep up will soon find their products outdated. And they will miss new product and market opportunities.

The United States leads the world in research and development (R&D) spending. Total U.S. R&D spending reached an estimated $384 billion last year. The federal government was the largest R&D spender at about $99 billion.[43] Scientists today are researching a wide range of promising new products and services, ranging from practical solar energy, electric cars, paint-on computer and entertainment video displays, and powerful computers that you can wear or fold into your pocket to go-anywhere concentrators that produce drinkable water from the air.

Today's research usually is carried out by research teams rather than by lone inventors such as Thomas Edison, Samuel Morse, or Alexander Graham Bell. Many companies are adding marketing people to R&D teams to try to obtain a stronger marketing orientation. Scientists also speculate on fantasy products, such as flying cars, three-dimensional televisions, and space colonies. The challenge in each case is not only technical but also commercial—to make *practical, affordable* versions of these products.

As products and technology become more complex, the public needs to know that these are safe. Thus, government agencies investigate and ban potentially unsafe products. In the United States, the Food and Drug Administration (FDA) has set up complex regulations for testing new drugs. The Consumer Product Safety Commission sets safety standards for consumer products and penalizes companies that fail to meet them. Such regulations have resulted in much higher research costs and in longer times between new-product ideas and their introduction. Marketers should be aware of these regulations when applying new technologies and developing new products.

Political and Social Environment

Marketing decisions are strongly affected by developments in the political environment. The **political environment** consists of laws, government agencies, and pressure groups that influence or limit various organizations and individuals in a given society.

Legislation Regulating Business

Even the most liberal advocates of free-market economies agree that the system works best with at least some regulation. Well-conceived regulation can encourage competition and ensure fair markets for goods and services. Thus, governments develop *public policy* to guide commerce—sets of laws and regulations that limit business for the good of society as a whole. Almost every marketing activity is subject to a wide range of laws and regulations.

Increasing Legislation. Legislation affecting business around the world has increased steadily over the years. The United States has many laws covering issues such as competition, fair trade practices, environmental protection, product safety, truth in advertising, consumer privacy, packaging and labeling, pricing, and other important areas (see ■ **Table 3.1**). The European Commission has been active in establishing a new framework of laws covering competitive behavior, product standards, product liability, and commercial transactions for the nations of the European Union.

Understanding the public policy implications of a particular marketing activity is not a simple matter. For example, in the United States, there are many laws created at the national, state, and local levels, and these regulations often overlap. Aspirins sold in Dallas are governed both by federal labeling laws and by Texas state advertising laws. Moreover, regulations are constantly changing—what was allowed last year may now be prohibited, and what was prohibited may now be allowed. Marketers must work hard to keep up with changes in regulations and their interpretations.

Business legislation has been enacted for a number of reasons. The first is to *protect companies* from each other. Although business executives may praise competition, they sometimes try to neutralize it when it threatens them. So laws are passed to define and prevent unfair competition. In the United States, such laws are enforced by the Federal Trade Commission and the Antitrust Division of the Attorney General's office.

The second purpose of government regulation is to *protect consumers* from unfair business practices. Some firms, if left alone, would make shoddy products, invade consumer privacy, tell lies in their advertising, and deceive consumers through their packaging and pricing. Unfair business practices have been defined and are enforced by various agencies.

The third purpose of government regulation is to *protect the interests of society* against unrestrained business behavior. Profitable business activity does not always create a better quality of life. Regulation arises to ensure that firms take responsibility for the social costs of their production or products.

Changing Government Agency Enforcement. International marketers will encounter dozens, or even hundreds, of agencies set up to enforce trade policies and regulations. In the United States, Congress has established federal regulatory agencies, such as the Federal Trade Commission, the Food and Drug Administration, the Federal Communications Commission, the Federal Energy Regulatory Commission, the Federal Aviation Administration, the Consumer Product Safety Commission, the Environmental Protection Agency, and hundreds of others. Because such government agencies have some discretion in enforcing the laws, they can have a major impact on a company's marketing performance.

Author Comment »
Even the most liberal free-market advocates agree that the system works best with at least some regulation. But beyond regulation, most companies *want* to be socially responsible. Check almost any company's Web site and you'll find long lists of good deeds and environmentally responsible actions. For example, try the Nike Responsibility page (www.nikebiz.com/responsibility/) or Johnson & Johnson's Community page (www.jnj.com/community/index.htm). We'll dig deeper into marketing and social responsibility in Chapter 16.

Political environment
Laws, government agencies, and pressure groups that influence and limit various organizations and individuals in a given society.

■ **Table 3.1** Major U.S. Legislation Affecting Marketing

Legislation	Purpose
Sherman Antitrust Act (1890)	Prohibits monopolies and activities (price fixing, predatory pricing) that restrain trade or competition in interstate commerce.
Federal Food and Drug Act (1906)	Forbids the manufacture or sale of adulterated or fraudulently labeled foods and drugs. Created the Food and Drug Administration.
Clayton Act (1914)	Supplements the Sherman Act by prohibiting certain types of price discrimination, exclusive dealing, and tying clauses (which require a dealer to take additional products in a seller's line).
Federal Trade Commission Act (1914)	Established the Federal Trade Commission (FTC), which monitors and remedies unfair trade methods.
Robinson-Patman Act (1936)	Amends Clayton Act to define price discrimination as unlawful. Empowers FTC to establish limits on quantity discounts, forbid some brokerage allowances, and prohibit promotional allowances except when made available on proportionately equal terms.
Wheeler-Lea Act (1938)	Makes deceptive, misleading, and unfair practices illegal regardless of injury to competition. Places advertising of food and drugs under FTC jurisdiction.
Lanham Trademark Act (1946)	Protects and regulates distinctive brand names and trademarks.
National Traffic and Safety Act (1958)	Provides for the creation of compulsory safety standards for automobiles and tires.
Fair Packaging and Labeling Act (1966)	Provides for the regulation of packaging and labeling of consumer goods. Requires that manufacturers state what the package contains, who made it, and how much it contains.
Child Protection Act (1966)	Bans sale of hazardous toys and articles. Sets standards for child resistant packaging.
Federal Cigarette Labeling and Advertising Act (1967)	Requires that cigarette packages contain the following statement: "Warning: The Surgeon General Has Determined That Cigarette Smoking Is Dangerous to Your Health."
National Environmental Policy Act (1969)	Establishes a national policy on the environment. The 1970 Reorganization Plan established the Environmental Protection Agency (EPA).
Consumer Product Safety Act (1972)	Establishes the Consumer Product Safety Commission and authorizes it to set safety standards for consumer products as well as exact penalties for failure to uphold those standards.
Magnuson-Moss Warranty Act (1975)	Authorizes the FTC to determine rules and regulations for consumer warranties and provides consumer access to redress, such as the class action suit.
Children's Television Act (1990)	Limits number of commercials aired during children's programs.
Nutrition Labeling and Education Act (1990)	Requires that food product labels provide detailed nutritional information.
Telephone Consumer Protection Act (1991)	Establishes procedures to avoid unwanted telephone solicitations. Limits marketers' use of automatic telephone dialing systems and artificial or prerecorded voices.
Americans with Disabilities Act (1991)	Makes discrimination against people with disabilities illegal in public accommodations, transportation, and telecommunications.
Children's Online Privacy Protection Act (2000)	Prohibits Web sites or online services operators from collecting personal information from children without obtaining consent from a parent and allowing parents to review information collected from their children.
Do-Not-Call Implementation Act (2003)	Authorized the FTC to collect fees from sellers and telemarketers for the implementation and enforcement of a National Do-Not-Call Registry.

New laws and their enforcement will continue to increase. Business executives must watch these developments when planning their products and marketing programs. Marketers need to know about the major laws protecting competition, consumers, and society. They need to understand these laws at the local, state, national, and international levels.

Increased Emphasis on Ethics and Socially Responsible Actions

Written regulations cannot possibly cover all potential marketing abuses, and existing laws are often difficult to enforce. However, beyond written laws and regulations, business is also governed by social codes and rules of professional ethics.

Socially Responsible Behavior. Enlightened companies encourage their managers to look beyond what the regulatory system allows and simply "do the right thing." These socially responsible firms actively seek out ways to protect the long-run interests of their consumers and the environment.

The recent rash of business scandals and increased concerns about the environment have created fresh interest in the issues of ethics and social responsibility. Almost every aspect of marketing involves such issues. Unfortunately, because these issues usually involve conflicting interests, well-meaning people can honestly disagree about the right course of action in a given situation. Thus, many industrial and professional trade associations have suggested codes of ethics. And more companies are now developing policies, guidelines, and other responses to complex social responsibility issues.

The boom in Internet marketing has created a new set of social and ethical issues. Critics worry most about online privacy issues. There has been an explosion in the amount of personal digital data available. Users, themselves, supply some of it. They voluntarily place highly private information on social networking sites such as MySpace or on genealogy sites, which are easily searched by anyone with a PC.

However, much of the information is systematically developed by businesses seeking to learn more about their customers, often without consumers realizing that they are under the microscope. Legitimate businesses plant cookies on consumers' PCs and collect, analyze, and share digital data from every mouse click consumers make at their Web sites. Critics are concerned that companies may now know *too* much, and that some companies might use digital data to take unfair advantage of consumers. Although most companies fully disclose their Internet privacy policies, and most work to use data to benefit their customers, abuses do occur. As a result, consumer advocates and policymakers are taking action to protect consumer privacy.

Throughout the text, we present "Marketing at Work" exhibits that summarize the main public policy and social responsibility issues surrounding major marketing decisions. These exhibits discuss the legal issues that marketers should understand and the common ethical and societal concerns that marketers face. In Chapter 16, we discuss a broad range of societal marketing issues in greater depth.

Cause-Related Marketing. To exercise their social responsibility and build more positive images, many companies are now linking themselves to worthwhile causes. These days, every product seems to be tied to some cause. Buy a pink mixer from KitchenAid and support breast cancer research. Purchase Ethos water from Starbucks and help bring clean water to children around the world. For every Staples Easy Button you buy, the office supplies retailer will donate about $5 to Boys and Girls Clubs of America. Share a "moment of joy" on Lays.com, and PepsiCo's Lays brand will make a donation to the Make-A-Wish foundation. Pay for these purchases with the right charge card and you can support a local cultural arts group or help fight heart disease.

In fact, some companies are founded entirely on cause-related missions. Under the concept of "value-led business" or "caring capitalism," their mission is to use business to make the world a better place. For example, the Masdar Initiative was founded at the government level around a theme of corporate social responsibility. Firms that participate, support the cause of environmental sustainability (see Marketing at Work 3.1).

Marketing at Work 3.1

Spearheading Environmental Responsibility: "Masdar"

If our world with a current population of 6 billion could be shrunk to a village of 100 people, 33 would be children, 28 children would be born every year, one third of the people will not have access to clean water where one third of the land is wasteland. There are clear sustainability issues facing our populations and the future generations. The United Arab Emirates (UAE) is a federation of seven emirates. The average UAE GDP (gross domestic product) per capita is valued at $39,900 (2008 estimate), making it comparable to some of the best European countries. A key contributor to the economy is oil, which is a dwindling resource and also responsible for part of the greenhouse effect. The desert climate and huge dependency of air-conditioning and recent modernization have led to huge consumption of electricity. UAE has ranked fifth in the world in terms of per capita consumption of oil and electricity products. UAE is situated in the desert; its consumption of water is one of the highest in the world. Most of its water is acquired through desalination and groundwater. The increasing population and tourist arrivals make its bottled water consumption the highest per capita in the world (275 liters per year). Its consumption economy generates huge amounts of waste, which are not easily degradable in the desert. Plastics affect the reef and desert life and pollute the shrinking groundwater reserves.

Abu Dhabi is the capital of UAE and has implemented a unique government initiative called the Masdar project. "Masdar" means "the source" in Arabic. It is driven by the Abu Dhabi Future Energy Company (Masdar), a wholly owned subsidiary of the Mubadala Development Company (Mubadala). The objective is to transform UAE into a global leader of sustainable energies by actively pursuing an open engagement to find solutions to environmental concerns. This will help the UAE move from technology consumer to technology producer. Masdar reflects the vision and values of the founder and the former President of the UAE, the late Sheikh Zayed Bin Sultan Al Nahyan, who was a conservationist.

Masdar is facilitating investment, research, and development of technologies in the area of alternative energy. This is done through strategic international acquisitions in order to foster innovation; financing of up-and-coming companies through

▲Architects of Masdar city have planned to build a zero carbon, zero waste city to house 50,000 residents in Abu Dhabi. This ambitious development aims to showcase a sustainable lifestyle to the rest of the world and to future generations'.

venture capital and private equity; and the advancement and exchange of knowledge and expertise in the area of renewable energy in order to generate home-grown distinct patent-protected technologies. There are five key business units: carbon management, industries, science and technology, property development, and utilities and assets. Though this is a government initiative, the focus is to create profitable ventures that not only pursue environmental sustainability both locally and for the world but also contribute to the economic development of the nation.

By focusing on carbon management, Masdar aims to reduce, capture, and store carbon emissions. Though initially the focus is to create a national CO_2 capture network for Abu Dhabi and hence reduce the carbon footprint, this can be extended across the emirates and other oil-producing regions. The captured CO_2 will be transported and injected in oil reservoirs for enhanced oil recovery. One of the key industry projects Masdar is investing in, is Masdar PV. This is one of the world's largest manufacturers of thin-film solar cells. UAE will encourage the use of these new technologies by soon implementing a federal green building code, and encouraging adoption of Estidama (Arabic for "sustainability") and the Pearl Rating System developed in 2007 to provide new buildings in Abu Dhabi with a sustainability rating.

The second factory of Masdar PV will be built in Abu Dhabi, creating an opportunity for employment. Through the Science and Technology business initiative, Masdar will create high-quality training and networking of researchers. The Masdar Institute of Science and Technology is currently being established with the assistance of world-renowned Massachusetts Institute of Technology (MIT). This will increase knowledge capital in the region and contribute to research. Research is a key priority for the UAE. Masdar will contribute back to the people of UAE with employment opportunities. This concept is important for this region as the Middle East has one of the largest youngest populations and currently a low research/innovation output.

In its property development division, Masdar has created the Masdar City, implementing its vision of life in the future: without CO_2 emissions, waste, or environmental damage. It will be on completion, a zero carbon, zero waste city and home to 50,000 residents. This will not only improve quality of life for its citizens but will showcase what can be the future for the people of this world. There will be no cars or exhaust fumes. Solar modules will generate the electricity and concentrated solar energy will ensure cooling. Water will be provided by a desalination plant and green areas will be maintained with processed wastewater.

New technologies are not easily embraced by the consumer and hence because of the low initial profits, new technology ventures find investment financing difficult. To recognize this, Masdar Utilities & Assets is using $15 billion to finance ambitious projects. In addition, the Clean Tech Fund, a private equity fund launched in partnership with Credit Suisse and the Consensus Business Group in 2006, has additional assets of $250 million for investment in global companies with promising technologies in clean energy, water, and waste management solutions. Particular emphasis is placed on technologies that will later be able to cope with Abu Dhabi's climatic conditions and that can make a significant contribution to the goals of the Masdar Initiative. The STAR program (Sustainable Technologies and Advanced Research) invests in near-commercial maturity technologies that are already suitable for demonstration projects. It focuses on cooperative projects in the fields of solar power, photovoltaics, seawater desalination, and biofuels. The Masdar Business Incubator invests in the "early phase" financing to assist entrepreneurs. SMEs are considered to be the growth engine of Middle East economies. For the UAE, SMEs account for 46 percent of the UAE's GDP, while making up between 85 and 95 percent of all businesses in the country. Masdar is encouraging entrepreneurship in collaboration with other large corporations to contribute to the economy and environmental sustainability.

In order to promote this cause-related marketing, Masdar has worked with a network of strong corporate partners like Shell, BP, and General Electric among others. The cost of development of Masdar city is over $22 billion of which Masdar will contribute $4 billion. This is a good example of how a government can take initiative of spearheading a green revolution.

Sources: Based on information from Meadows, D. "State of the Village Report, Sustainability Research," available at www.sustainer.org/; CIA Factbook (2009), "GDP per capita 2008," available at www.cia.gov/; AMEInfo.com (2009), "UAE Ranked Fifth of the World's Energy Consumption," September 3, 2009, available at www.ameinfo.com; Chaudhury, D. M. (2005), "UAE Water Consumption One of the Highest in the World," *Khaleej Times,* July 22, 2005, available at www.khaleejtimes.com; AMEInfo.com (2009), "UAE Tops in Potable Water Consumption," May 13, 2009, available at www .ameinfo.com; www.masdar.ae; Stewart, J. (2009), Exclusive: UAE Federal Green Building Code on Way, Constructionweekonline.com, April 9, 2009, available at www.constructionweekonline.com; International Herald Tribune (2007), "Middle East: Population Poses Huge Challenge for Middle East and North Africa," *The New York Times,* January 18, 2007, available at www .nytimes.com; WTTC (World Travel and Tourism Council). 2007. Executive Summary: Travel and Tourism Navigating the Path Ahead. *World Travel and Tourism Council,* March 8, 2007, available at www.wttc.org. [Accessed January 20, 2009]; ArabianBusiness.com (2008), "Work Starts on Masdar City," ArabianBusiness.com, 01 March 2008, available at www.arabianbusiness.com; BrandCentral Report (2009), "Sustained Brand Positioning to Stimulate Growth of UAE's SME sector," AMEInfo.com, September 14, 2009, available at www.ameinfo.com/.html.

Cause-related marketing has become a primary form of corporate giving. It lets companies "do well by doing good" by linking purchases of the company's products or services with fund-raising for worthwhile causes or charitable organizations. Companies now sponsor dozens of cause-related marketing campaigns each year. Many are backed by large budgets and a full complement of marketing activities. ▲For example, consider P&G's "Pantene Beautiful Lengths" campaign, which last

year received Cause Marketing Forum's Golden Halo Award for the best cause-related health campaign.[44]

The Pantene Beautiful Lengths campaign has involved a broad-based marketing effort, including a campaign Web site, public service TV and prints ads, and promotional items and events. P&G kicked off the Pantene Beautiful Lengths with celebrity spokeswoman Diane Lane having her hair cut for donation on the *Today Show*. Since then the campaign has generated more than 700 million media impressions in major publications, TV shows, and Web sites. To date, the campaign has received more than 24,000 donated ponytails and more than 3,000 free wigs have been distributed through the American Cancer Society's nationwide network of wig banks. Compare that to the 2,000 wigs created over the past 10 years by charity Locks of Love. Pantene Beautiful Lengths has also contributed more than $1 million to the EIF Women's Cancer Research Fund, which raises funds and awareness for millions of women and their families affected by cancer.

Cause-related marketing has stirred some controversy. Critics worry that cause-related marketing is more a strategy for selling than a strategy for giving—that "cause-related" marketing is really "cause-exploitative" marketing. Thus, companies using cause-related marketing might find themselves walking a fine line between increased sales and an improved image, and facing charges of exploitation.

However, if handled well, cause-related marketing can greatly benefit both the company and the cause. The company gains an effective marketing tool while building a more positive public image. The charitable organization or cause gains greater visibility and important new sources of funding and support. Spending on cause-related marketing in the United States skyrocketed from only $120 million in 1990 to more than $1.57 billion by 2009.[45]

▲ **Cause-related marketing: The Pantene Beautiful Lengths campaign encourages people to cut and donate their healthy hair to create free wigs for women who have lost their hair to cancer treatment.**

Cultural Environment

The **cultural environment** is made up of institutions and other forces that affect a society's basic values, perceptions, preferences, and behaviors. People grow up in a particular society that shapes their basic beliefs and values. They absorb a world view that defines their relationships with others. The following cultural characteristics can affect marketing decision making.

Persistence of Cultural Values

People in a given society hold many beliefs and values. Their core beliefs and values have a high degree of persistence. For example, most Americans believe in working, getting married, giving to charity, and being honest. These beliefs shape more specific attitudes and behaviors found in everyday life. *Core* beliefs and values are passed on from parents to children and are reinforced by schools, churches, business, and government.

Secondary beliefs and values are more open to change. Believing in marriage is a core belief; believing that people should get married early in life is a secondary belief. Marketers have some chance of changing secondary values but little chance of changing core values. For example, family-planning marketers could argue more effectively that people should get married later than not getting married at all.

Shifts in Secondary Cultural Values

Although core values are fairly persistent, cultural swings do take place. Consider the impact of popular music groups, movie personalities, and other celebrities on young

Author Comment »
Cultural factors strongly affect how people think and how they consume. So marketers are keenly interested in the cultural environment.

Cultural environment
Institutions and other forces that affect society's basic values, perceptions, preferences, and behaviors.

People's self-views: In its ads, Kenneth Cole targets fashion individualists. "25 years of non-uniform thinking."

people's hairstyling and clothing norms. Marketers want to predict cultural shifts in order to spot new opportunities or threats. Several firms offer "futures" forecasts in this connection. For example, the Yankelovich Monitor has tracked consumer value trends for years. Its annual State of the Consumer report analyzes and interprets the forces that shape consumers' lifestyles and their marketplace interactions. The major cultural values of a society are expressed in people's views of themselves and others, as well as in their views of organizations, society, nature, and the universe.

People's Views of Themselves. People vary in their emphasis on serving themselves versus serving others. Some people seek personal pleasure, wanting fun, change, and escape. Others seek self-realization through religion, recreation, or the avid pursuit of careers or other life goals. Some people see themselves as sharers and joiners; others see themselves as individualists. People use products, brands, and services as a means of self-expression, and they buy products and services that match their views of themselves.

Marketers can target their products and services based on such self-views. For example, TOMS Shoes appeals to people who see themselves as part of the broader world community. ▲In contrast, Kenneth Cole shoes appeal to fashion individualists. In its ads, the company declares, "We all walk in different shoes," asserting that Kenneth Cole represents "25 years of non-uniform thinking."

People's Views of Others. In past decades, observers have noted several shifts in people's attitudes toward others. Recently, for example, many trend trackers have seen a new wave of "cocooning" or "nesting." Due in part to the down economy, people are going out less with others and are staying home more. One observer calls it "Cocooning 2.0," in which people are "newly intent on the simple pleasures of hearth and home." Says another, "The instability of the economy . . . creates uncertainty for consumers, and this uncertainty tends to make them focus more on being home and finding ways to save money. It's a return to more traditional values, like home-cooked meals."[46]

The trend toward more cocooning suggests less demand for theater-going, travel, eating out, and new cars but greater demand for homemade meals, home projects, and home entertainment products. For example, during the past holiday season, sales increased at craft stores such as Michaels, Jo-Ann, and Hobby Lobby, as more people turned to saving money by making homemade holiday gifts. "Across the country, people are crafting more," says a spokesman for the Craft & Hobby Association. "With the [recent] recession, people are looking for ways to save money, and doctors are recommending it as a major form of stress relief."[47]

The faltering economy and increased nesting also gave a boost to home appliances such as high-end coffee makers and big-screen TVs. ▲Consumer electronics chain Best Buy even ran an ad that cast the purchase of a 60-inch flat-screen HDTV not as self-indulgence, but as an act of loving sacrifice and a practical alternative to other forms of entertainment.[48]

In the ad, after a man sells his football season tickets to pay for the wedding, his grateful bride surprises him with a huge set so he can still watch the big game. A kindly salesman sums it up this way: "Another love story at Best Buy with a 60-inch TV in the middle." Says a Samsung marketer, "People still have to live their lives. Even in a tough economy, people may not spring for that 61-inch [TV], but they may get a 42-inch HDTV because they're

▲ Recent economic woes have contributed to a new wave of "cocooning" or "nesting." Best Buy ran an ad selling big-screen TVs as an alternative to more expensive forms of out-of-home entertainment.

home and they're with their families and they'll spend $5 on a movie rental, versus $40 for the theater and $80 for dinner.

People's Views of Organizations. People vary in their attitudes toward corporations, government agencies, trade unions, universities, and other organizations. By and large, people are willing to work for major organizations and expect them, in turn, to carry out society's work.

The past two decades have seen a sharp decrease in confidence in and loyalty toward America's business and political organizations and institutions. In the workplace, there has been an overall decline in organizational loyalty. Waves of company downsizings bred cynicism and distrust. In just the last decade, rounds of layoffs resulting from the recent recession; corporate scandals at Enron, WorldCom, and Tyco; the financial meltdown triggered by Wall Street bankers' greed and incompetence; and other unsettling activities have resulted in a further loss of confidence in big business. Many people today see work not as a source of satisfaction but as a required chore to earn money to enjoy their nonwork hours. This trend suggests that organizations need to find new ways to win consumer and employee confidence.

People's Views of Society. People vary in their attitudes toward their society—patriots defend it, reformers want to change it, malcontents want to leave it. People's orientation to their society influences their consumption patterns and attitudes toward the marketplace. American patriotism has been increasing gradually for the past two decades. It surged, however, following the September 11, 2001, terrorist attacks and the Iraq war. For example, the summer following the start of the Iraq war saw a surge of pumped-up Americans visiting U.S. historic sites, ranging from the Washington, D.C., monuments, Mount Rushmore, the Gettysburg battlefield, and the *USS Constitution* ("Old Ironsides") to Pearl Harbor and the Alamo. Following these peak periods, patriotism in the United States still remains high. A recent global survey on "national pride" found Americans tied for number one among the 17 democracies polled.[49]

Marketers respond with patriotic products and promotions, offering everything from floral bouquets to clothing with patriotic themes. Although most of these marketing efforts are tasteful and well received, waving the red, white, and blue can prove tricky. Except in cases where companies tie product sales to charitable contributions, such flag-waving promotions can be viewed as attempts to cash in on triumph or tragedy. Marketers must take care when responding to such strong national emotions.

People's Views of Nature. People vary in their attitudes toward the natural world—some feel ruled by it, others feel in harmony with it, and still others seek to master it. A long-term trend has been people's growing mastery over nature through technology and the belief that nature is bountiful. More recently, however, people have recognized that nature is finite and fragile, that it can be destroyed or spoiled by human activities.

This renewed love of things natural has created a 63-million-person "lifestyles of health and sustainability" (LOHAS) market, consumers who seek out everything from natural, organic, and nutritional products to fuel-efficient cars and alternative medicine. This segment spends nearly $215 billion annually on such products. In the words of one such consumer,[50]

I am not an early adopter, a fast follower, or a mass-market stampeder. But I am a gas-conscious driver. So that's why I was standing in a Toyota dealership . . . this week, the latest person to check out a hybrid car. Who needs $40 fill-ups? After tooling around in three different hybrid car brands—Toyota, Honda, and a Ford—I thought, How cool could this be? Saving gas money and doing well by the environment. Turns out there's a whole trend-watchers' classification for people who think like that: LOHAS. Lifestyles of Health and Sustainability. Buy a hybrid. Shop at places like Whole Foods. Pick up the Seventh Generation paper towels at Albertsons. No skin off our noses. Conscientious shopping with no sacrifice or hippie stigma.

Many marketers are now tracking and responding to such cultural trends. For example, Wal-Mart recently developed a Live Better Index by which it tracks the attitudes of its more than 200 million annual shoppers. The Live Better Index tracks consumers' decisions regarding eco-friendly products such as compact fluorescent lightbulbs, organic milk, and concentrated liquid laundry detergents in reduced packaging. The index shows that 11 percent of Americans now consider themselves to be converts to more sustainable living and that 43 percent say they will be "extremely green" within the next five years.[51]

Food producers have also found fast-growing markets for natural and organic products. ▲Consider Earthbound Farm, a company that grows and sells organic produce. It started in 1984 as a 2.5-acre raspberry farm in California's Carmel Valley. Founders Drew and Myra Goodman wanted to do the right thing by farming the land organically and producing food they'd feel good about serving to their family, friends, and neighbors. Today, Earthbound Farm has grown to become the world's largest producer of organic vegetables, with 33,000 acres under plow, annual sales of $480 million, and products available in 75 percent of America's supermarkets.[52]

In total, the U.S. organic-food market generated $22.75 billion in sales last year, more than doubling over the past five years. Niche marketers, such as Whole Foods Markets, have sprung up to serve this market, and traditional food chains such as Kroger and Safeway have added separate natural and organic food sections. Even pet owners are joining the movement as they become more aware of what goes into Fido's food. Almost every major pet food brand now offers several types of natural foods.[53]

People's Views of the Universe. Finally, people vary in their beliefs about the origin of the universe and their place in it. Although most Americans practice religion, religious conviction and practice have been dropping off gradually through the years. According to a recent poll, 15 percent of Americans now say they have no religion, almost double the percent of 18 years ago.

However, the fact that people are dropping out of organized religion doesn't mean that they are abandoning their faith. Some futurists have noted a renewed interest in spirituality, perhaps as a part of a broader search for a new inner purpose. People have been moving away from materialism and dog-eat-dog ambition to seek more permanent values—family, community, earth, faith—and a more certain grasp of right and wrong. "We are becoming a nation of spiritually anchored people who are not traditionally religious," says one expert.[54] This changing spiritualism affects consumers in everything from the television shows they watch and the books they read to the products and services they buy.

▼**Riding the trend towards all things natural, Earthbound Farm has grown to become the world's largest producer of organic salads, fruits, and vegetables, with products in 75 percent of America's supermarkets.**

It's green,

even before it's green.

Our organic greens show their true colors long before they begin to peek through the soil. We raise our crops without harmful chemicals, in healthy soil that supports strong, nutrient-rich plants. Sure, organic farming can be more challenging in the short term, but the reward is delicious organic produce and a healthy planet. That's something we can all feel good about.

Earthbound Farm. ORGANIC

Food to live by.

Get our new Pocket Guide to Choosing Organic at www.ebfarm.com.

Speed Bump: Linking the Concepts

Slow down and cool your engine. How are all of the environmental factors you've read about in this chapter linked with each other? With company marketing strategy?

- How are major demographic forces linked with economic changes? With major cultural trends? How are the natural and technological environments linked? Think of an example of a company that has recognized one of these links and turned it into a marketing opportunity.
- Is the marketing environment uncontrollable? Or can companies be proactive in changing environmental factors? Think of a good example that makes your point, then read on.

Author Comment >>
Rather than simply watching and reacting, companies should take proactive steps with respect to the marketing environment.

RESPONDING TO THE MARKETING ENVIRONMENT (pp 120–122)

Someone once observed, "There are three kinds of companies: those who make things happen, those who watch things happen, and those who wonder what's happened."[55] Many companies view the marketing environment as an uncontrollable element to which they must react and adapt. They passively accept the marketing environment and do not try to change it. They analyze the environmental forces and design strategies that will help the company avoid the threats and take advantage of the opportunities the environment provides.

Other companies take a *proactive* stance toward the marketing environment. Rather than simply watching and reacting, these firms take aggressive actions to affect the publics and forces in their marketing environment. Such companies hire lobbyists to influence legislation affecting their industries and stage media events to gain favorable press coverage. They run "advertorials" (ads expressing editorial points of view) to shape public opinion. They press lawsuits and file complaints with regulators to keep competitors in line, and they form contractual agreements to better control their distribution channels.

By taking action, companies can often overcome seemingly uncontrollable environmental events. For example, whereas some companies view the seemingly ceaseless online rumor mill as something over which they have no control, others work proactively to prevent or counter negative word of mouth. Kraft foods did this last year when its Oscar Mayer brand fell victim to a potentially damaging e-mail hoax:[56]

> The bogus e-mail, allegedly penned by a Sgt. Howard C. Wright, claimed that Marines in Iraq had written Oscar Mayer saying how much they liked its hot dogs and requesting that the company send some to the troops there. According to the e-mail, Oscar Mayer refused, saying that it supported neither the war nor anyone in it. The soldier called on all patriotic Americans to forward the e-mail to friends and to boycott Oscar Mayer and its products.
>
> As the e-mail circulated widely, rather than waiting and hoping that consumers would see through the hoax, Kraft responded vigorously with its own e-mails, blog entries, and a "Rumor and Hoaxes" Web page. It explained that Kraft and Oscar Mayer do, in fact, strongly support American troops, both in Iraq and at home. It works with the military to ensure that Kraft products are available wherever in the world troops are stationed. On the home front, Kraft explained, Oscar Mayer Weinermobiles visit about half of all major U.S. military bases each year, about 70 total. The offending e-mail turned out to be a nearly verbatim copy of a 2004 chain e-mail circulated against Starbucks, signed by the same fictitious soldier but with "Oscar Mayer" and "hot dog" substituted for "Starbucks" and "coffee." Kraft's proactive counter campaign quickly squelched the rumor, and Oscar Mayer remains America's favorite hot dog.

Marketing management cannot always control environmental forces. In many cases, it must settle for simply watching and reacting to the environment. For example, a company would have little success trying to influence geographic population shifts, the economic environment, or major cultural values. But whenever possible, smart marketing managers will take a *proactive* rather than *reactive* approach to the marketing environment (see Marketing at Work 3.2).

Marketing at Work 3.2

YourCompanySucks.com

The Internet has been hailed by marketers as the great new relational medium. Companies use the Web to engage customers, gain insights into their needs, and create customer community. In turn, Web-empowered consumers share their brand experiences with companies and with each other. All of this back-and-forth helps both the company and its customers. But sometimes, the dialog can get nasty. Consider the following examples:

MSN Money columnist Scott Burns accuses Home Depot of being a "consistent abuser" of customers' time. Within hours, MSN's servers are caving under the weight of 14,000 blistering e-mails and posts from angry Home Depot customers who storm the MSN comment room, taking the company to task for pretty much everything. It is the biggest response in MSN Money's history.

Blogger Jeff Jarvis posts a series of irate messages to his BuzzMachine blog about the many failings of his Dell computer and his struggles with Dell's customer support. The post quickly draws national attention, and an open letter posted by Jarvis to Dell founder Michael Dell becomes the third most linked-to post on the blogosphere the day after it appears. Jarvis's headline— Dell Hell—becomes shorthand for the ability of a lone blogger to deliver a body blow to an unsuspecting business.

Systems engineer Michael Whitford wakes up one morning to find that his favorite-ever laptop, an Apple Macbook, still under warranty, has "decided not to work." Whitford takes the machine to his local Apple store, where the counter person obligingly sends it off for repairs. However, Whitford later gets a call from an Apple Care representative, who claims that the laptop has "spill damage" not covered by the warranty and says that repairs will cost him $774. "I did not spill anything on my laptop," declares Whitford. "Too bad," says the Apple rep, and the Macbook is returned unrepaired. But that's not the end of the story—far from it. A short time later, Whitford posts a video on YouTube (www.youtube.com/watch?v=hHbrQqrgVgg). In the video, a seemingly rational Whitford calmly selects among a golf club, an ax, and a sword before finally deciding on a sledgeham-

mer as his weapon of choice for bashing his nonfunctioning Macbook to smithereens. More than 475,000 people have viewed the smash-up on YouTube and the video has been passed along on countless blogs and other Web sites.

Extreme events? Not anymore. "Web 2.0" has turned the traditional power relationship between businesses and consumers upside-down. In the good old days, disgruntled consumers could do little more than bellow at a company service rep or shout out their complaints from a street corner. Now, armed with only a PC and a broadband connection, they can take it public, airing their gripes to millions on blogs, chats, online communities, or even hate sites devoted exclusively to their least favorite corporations.

"I hate" and "sucks" sites are becoming almost commonplace. These sites target some highly respected companies with some highly *disrespectful* labels: PayPalSucks.com (aka NoPayPal); WalMart-blows.com; Microsucks.com; NorthWorstAir.org (Northwest Airlines); AmexSux.com (American Express); IHateStarbucks.com; DeltaREALLYsucks.com; and UnitedPackageSmashers.com (UPS), to name only a few.

Some of these sites and other Web attacks air legitimate complaints that should be addressed. Others, however, are little more than anonymous, vindictive slurs that unfairly ransack brands and corporate reputations. Some of the attacks are only a passing nuisance; others can draw serious attention and create real headaches.

How should companies react to Web attacks? The real quandary for targeted companies is figuring out how far they can go to protect their images without fueling the already raging fire. One point upon which all experts seem to agree: Don't try to retaliate in kind. "It's rarely a good idea to lob bombs at the fire starters," says one analyst. "Preemption, engagement, and diplomacy are saner tools."

Some companies have tried to silence the critics through lawsuits but few have succeeded. The courts have tended to regard such criticism as opinion and therefore as protected speech. Given the difficulties of trying to sue consumer online criticisms out of existence, some companies have tried other strategies. For example, most big companies now routinely buy up Web

▲ Today, armed only with a PC and a broadband connection, the little guy can take it public against corporate America. By listening and proactively responding to such seemingly uncontrollable environmental events, companies can prevent the negatives from spiraling out of control or even turn them into positives.

(continued)

addresses for their firm names preceded by the words "I hate" or followed by "sucks.com." But this approach is easily thwarted, as Wal-Mart learned when it registered ihatewalmart.com, only to find that someone else then registered ireallyhatewalmart.com.

In general, attempts to block, counterattack, or shut down consumer attacks may be shortsighted. Such criticisms are often based on real consumer concerns and unresolved anger. Hence, the best strategy might be to proactively monitor these sites and respond to the concerns they express. "The most obvious thing to do is talk to the customer and try to deal with the problem, instead of putting your fingers in your ears," advises one consultant.

For example, Home Depot CEO Francis Blake drew praise when he heeded the criticisms expressed in the MSN Money onslaught and responded positively. Blake posted a heartfelt letter in which he thanked critic Scott Burns, apologized to angry customers, and promised to make things better. And within a month of the YouTube video, Apple fessed up to its misdeeds and replaced Michael Whitford's laptop. "I'm very happy now," says Whitford. "Apple has regained my loyalty. I guess I finally got their attention."

Many companies have now set up teams of specialists that monitor Web conversations and engage disgruntled consumers. In the years since the Dell Hell incident, Dell has set up a 40-member "communities and conversation team," which does outreach on Twitter and communicates with bloggers. Southwest Airlines' social media team "includes a chief Twitter officer who tracks Twitter comments and monitors Facebook groups, an online representative who checks facts and interacts with bloggers, and another person who takes charge of the company's presence on sites such as YouTube, Flickr, and LinkedIn. So if someone posts a complaint in cyberspace, the company can respond in a personal way."

Thus, by listening and proactively responding to seemingly uncontrollable events in the environment, companies can prevent the negatives from spiraling out of control or even turn them into positives. Who knows? With the right responses, WalMart-blows.com might even become WalMart-rules.com. Then again, probably not.

Sources: Quotes, excerpts, and other information from Michelle Conlin, "Web Attack," *BusinessWeek,* April 16, 2007, pp. 54–56; "Top 10 Service Complaint Sites," *Time Out New York,* March 8, 2007, accessed at www.timeout.com; Jena McGregor, "Consumer Vigilantes," *BusinessWeek,* March 3, 2008, p. 38; Christopher L. Marting and Nathan Bennett, "Corporate Reputation; What to Do About Online Attacks," *Wall Street Journal,* March 10, 2008, p. R6; Carolyn Y. Johnson, "Hurry Up, the Customer Has a Complaint," *Boston Globe,* July 7, 2008; and "Corporate Hate Sites," New Media Institute, accessed at www.newmedia.org/categories/Hot-Topics-&-Issues/Corporate-Hate-Sites/, April 2009.

REST STOP
REVIEWING THE CONCEPTS

In this chapter and the next two chapters, you'll examine the environments of marketing and how companies analyze these environments to better understand the marketplace and consumers. Companies must constantly watch and manage the *marketing environment* in order to seek opportunities and ward off threats. The marketing environment consists of all the actors and forces influencing the company's ability to transact business effectively with its target market.

> **Objective 1** Describe the environmental forces that affect the company's ability to serve its customers. **(pp 95–120)**

The company's *microenvironment* consists of other actors close to the company that combine to form the company's value delivery network or that affect its ability to serve its customers. It includes the company's *internal environment*—its several departments and management levels—as it influences marketing decision making. *Marketing channel firms*—suppliers and marketing intermediaries, including resellers, physical distribution firms, marketing services agencies, and financial intermediaries—cooperate to create customer value. Five types of customer *markets* include consumer, business, reseller, government, and international markets. *Competitors* vie with the company in an effort to serve customers better. Finally, various *publics* have an actual or potential interest in or impact on the company's ability to meet its objectives.

The *macroenvironment* consists of larger societal forces that affect the entire microenvironment. The six forces making up the company's macroenvironment include demographic, economic, natural, technological, political, and cultural forces. These forces shape opportunities and pose threats to the company.

> **Objective 2** Explain how changes in the demographic and economic environments affect marketing decisions. **(pp 99–108)**

Demography is the study of the characteristics of human populations. Today's *demographic environment* shows a changing age structure, shifting family profiles, geographic population shifts, a better-educated and more white-collar population, and increasing diversity. The *economic environment* consists of factors that affect buying power and patterns. The economic environment is characterized by more consumer concern for value and shifting consumer spending patterns. Today's squeezed consumers are seeking greater value—just the right combination of good quality and service at a fair price. The distribution of income also is shifting. The rich have grown richer, the middle class has shrunk, and the poor have remained poor, leading to a two-tiered market.

 Objective 3 Identify the major trends in the firm's natural and technological environments. **(pp 108–111)**

The *natural environment* shows three major trends: shortages of certain raw materials, higher pollution levels, and more government intervention in natural resource management. Environmental concerns create marketing opportunities for alert companies. The *technological environment* creates both opportunities and challenges. Companies that fail to keep up with technological change will miss out on new product and marketing opportunities.

 Objective 4 Explain the key changes in the political and cultural environments. **(pp 111–120)**

The *political environment* consists of laws, agencies, and groups that influence or limit marketing actions. The political environment has undergone three changes that affect marketing worldwide: increasing legislation regulating business, strong government agency enforcement, and greater emphasis on ethics and socially responsible actions. The *cultural environment* is made up of institutions and forces that affect a society's values, perceptions, preferences, and behaviors. The environment shows trends toward "cocooning," a lessening trust of institutions, increasing patriotism, greater appreciation for nature, a changing spiritualism, and the search for more meaningful and enduring values.

 Objective 5 Discuss how companies can react to the marketing environment. **(pp 120–122)**

Companies can passively accept the marketing environment as an uncontrollable element to which they must adapt, avoiding threats and taking advantage of opportunities as they arise. Or they can take a *proactive* stance, working to change the environment rather than simply reacting to it. Whenever possible, companies should try to be proactive rather than reactive.

Navigating the Key Terms

Objective 1
Marketing environment (p 94)
Microenvironment (p 95)
Macroenvironment (p 95)
Marketing intermediaries (p 96)
Public (p 97)

Objective 2
Demography (p 99)
Baby boomers (p 99)

Generation X (p 100)
Millennials (Generation Y) (p 101)
Economic environment (p 106)
Engel's laws (p 108)

Objective 3
Natural environment (p 108)
Environmental sustainability (p 108)
Technological environment (p 109)

Objective 4
Political environment (p 111)
Cultural environment (p 116)

Travel Log

Discussing the Issues

1. Compare and contrast a company's microenvironment with a company's macroenvironment. (AACSB: Communication)

2. Describe the various publics that impact a company's marketing environment. (AACSB: Communication)

3. Discuss current trends in the economic environment of which marketers must be aware and provide exam-

ples of companies' responses to each trend. (AACSB: Communication; Reflective Thinking)

4. Discuss trends in the natural environment of which marketers must be aware and provide examples of companies' responses to them. (AACSB: Communication)

5. Discuss the primary reasons why a company would hire a lobbyist in Washington D.C. Would it make sense

for the same company to also hire lobbyists at the state level? Why? (AACSB: Communication; Reflective Thinking)

6. How should marketers respond to the changing environment? (AACSB: Communication)

Application Questions

1. An important macroenvironmental force on companies is the social/cultural environment, particularly in international markets. In a small group, select a country and discuss at least three elements of the cultural environment that differ from the United States and how they impact companies doing business in that culture. (AACSB: Communication; Reflective Thinking; Diversity)

2. Various federal agencies impact marketing activities. Research each agency below, discuss the elements of marketing that are impacted by that agency, and present a recent marketing case or issue on which each agency has focused. (AACSB: Communication; Reflective Thinking)

   a. Federal Trade Commission (www.ftc.gov)
   b. Food and Drug Administration (www.fda.gov)
   c. Consumer Product Safety Commission (www.cpsc.gov)

3. Cause-related marketing has grown considerably over the past ten years. Visit www.causemarketingforum.com to learn about companies that have won Halo Awards for outstanding cause-related marketing programs. Present an award-winning case study to your class. (AACSB: Communication; Use of IT)

Under the Hood: Marketing Technology

If you thought that getting 50 miles per gallon driving a Toyota Prius hybrid was good, how about 230 miles per gallon? Or 367 mpg? Well, you are about to see a new breed of automobiles from big and small automakers touting this level of performance. In 2010, look for GM's Volt and Nissan's Leaf, but there will also be offerings from unknown startups such as V-Vehicle, a California-based electric car company backed by billionaire T. Boone Pickens. These automobiles range from hybrids—a combination of gas and electric—to all-electric vehicles. This level of performance comes at a high price, however. Although consumers will receive an expected $7,500 tax credit for purchasing one of these cars, the Volt's expected $40,000 price tag will still cause sticker shock. Also, the lack of public recharging stations poses a significant challenge, especially for all-electric vehicles such as the Leaf, which needs recharging

approximately every 100 miles. And some might question the efficiency claims, especially since the Environmental Protection Agency is still finalizing the methodology that factors in electricity used when making miles-per-gallon equivalency claims.

1. What factors in the marketing environment present opportunities or threats to automakers? (AACSB: Communication; Reflective Thinking)

2. Will it be possible for a startup automaker such as V-Vehicle to compete with big automakers such as Ford, GM, Chrysler, Toyota, Honda, Nissan, Volvo, Hyundai, BMW, and Mercedes? What factors in the marketing environment will enable or inhibit new competitors? (AACSB: Communication; Reflective Thinking)

Staying on the Road: Marketing Ethics

You've probably heard of heart procedures such as angioplasty and stents that are routinely performed on adults. But such heart procedures, devices, and related medications are not available for infants and children, despite the fact that almost 40,000 children a year are born in the United States with heart defects that oftentimes require repair. This is a life or death situation for many young patients, yet doctors must improvise by using devices designed and tested on adults. For instance, doctors use an adult kidney balloon on an infant's heart because it is the appropriate size for a newborn's aortic valve. However, this device is not approved for the procedure. Why are specific devices and medicines developed for the multibillion-dollar cardiovascular market not also designed for kids? It's a matter of economics—this segment of young con-

sumers is just too small. One leading cardiologist attributed the discrepancy to a "profitability gap" between the children's market and the much more profitable adult market for treating heart disease. While this might make good economic sense for companies, it is little comfort to the parents of these small patients.

1. Discuss the environmental forces acting on medical devices and pharmaceuticals companies that are preventing them from meeting the needs of the infant and child market segment. Is it wrong for these companies to not address the needs of this segment? (AACSB: Communication; Reflective Thinking; Ethical Reasoning)

2. Suggest some solutions to this problem. (AACSB: Communication; Reflective Thinking)

Rough Road Ahead: Marketing and the Economy

Netflix

While the economy has taken its toll on the retail industry as a whole, the stars are shining upon Netflix. Business is so good that Netflix met its most recent new subscriber goal weeks before the deadline. In all, 1.8 million movie watchers joined the Netflix fold in 2008, a 24-percent increase over the previous year. Clearly, all of those new customers are good for company financials. Customers might be signing up for the same reasons they always have. These include the convenience of renting movies without leaving home, a selection of more than 100,000 DVD titles, and low monthly fees. But the company's current good fortunes may also be to the result of consumers looking for less expensive means of entertainment. They may even be the result of consumers escaping the gloom of financial losses and economic bad news. Whatever the case, Netflix appears to have a recession-proof formula.

1. Visit www.netflix.com. After browsing the site and becoming more familiar with the company's offerings, assess the trends of the macroenvironment that have led to Netflix's success in recent years.

2. Which trends do you think have contributed most to Netflix's current growth following the recent economic downturn?

Travel Budget: Marketing by the Numbers

Many marketing decisions boil down to numbers. An important question is this: What is the market sales potential in a given segment? If the sales potential in a market is not large enough to warrant pursing that market, then companies will not offer products and services to that market, even though a need may exist. Consider the market segment of infants and children discussed in the preceding section on Marketing Ethics. Certainly there is a need for medical products to save children's lives. Still, companies are not pursuing this market.

1. Using the chain ratio method described in Appendix 2: Marketing by the Numbers, estimate the market sales potential for heart catheterization products to meet the needs of the infant and child segment. Assume that of the 40,000 children with heart defects each year, 60 percent will benefit from these types of products and that only 50 percent of their families have the financial resources to obtain such treatment. Also assume the average price for a device is $1,000. (AACSB: Communication; Analytical Reasoning)

2. Research the medical devices market and compare the market potential you estimated to the sales of various devices. Are companies justified in not pursuing the infant and child segment? (AACSB: Communication; Reflective Thinking)

Drive In: Video Case

TOMS Shoes

"Get involved: Changing a life begins with a single step." This sounds like a mandate from a nonprofit volunteer organization. But in fact, this is the motto of a for-profit shoe company located in Santa Monica, California. In 2006, Tom Mycoskie founded TOMS Shoes because he wanted to do something different. He wanted to run a company that would make a profit while at the same time helping the needy of the world.

Specifically, for every pair of shoes that TOMS sells, it gives a pair of shoes to a needy child somewhere in the world. So far, the company has given away tens of thousands of pairs of shoes and is on track to give away hundreds of thousands. Can TOMS succeed and thrive based on this idealistic concept? That all depends on how TOMS executes its strategy within the constantly changing marketing environment.

After viewing the video featuring TOMS Shoes, answer the following questions about the marketing environment:

1. What trends in the marketing environment have contributed to the success of TOMS Shoes?

2. Did TOMS Shoes first scan the marketing environment in creating its strategy, or did it create its strategy and fit the strategy to the environment? Does this matter?

3. Is TOMS's strategy more about serving needy children or about creating value for customers? Explain.

4

Managing
Marketing Information
to Gain Customer Insights

ROAD MAP

Previewing the Concepts

In this chapter, we continue our exploration of how marketers gain insights into consumers and the marketplace. We look at how companies develop and manage information about important marketplace elements—customers, competitors, products, and marketing programs. To succeed in today's marketplace, companies must know how to turn mountains of marketing information into fresh customer insights that will help them deliver greater value to customers.

Objective Outline

> **Objective 1**   Explain the importance of information in gaining insights about the marketplace and customers.
> Marketing Information and Customer Insights **pp 129–130**

> **Objective 2**   Define the marketing information system and discuss its parts.
> Assessing Marketing Information Needs **pp 130–131**
> Developing Marketing Information **pp 131–134**

> **Objective 3**   Outline the steps in the marketing research process
> Marketing Research **pp 134–148**

> **Objective 4**   Explain how companies analyze and use marketing information.
> Analyzing and Using Marketing Information
> **pp 148–151**

> **Objective 5**   Discuss the special issues some marketing researchers face, including public policy and ethics issues.
> Other Marketing Information Considerations
> **pp 151–157**

Let's start with a story about marketing research and customer insights in action at PROTRAC, a company which uses all the latest technology to provide marketers with the most accurate and detailed market available. PROTRAC's geo-marketing service is a fantastic tool for marketers to identify and develop their products. They can create the best possible value for consumers by helping to assess market potential and pinpoint market trends. To build meaningful relationships with customers, you first have to understand them and how they connect with your brand. That's where marketing research comes in.

▲Deep immersion tactics: Demographics, district borders, landmarks, street networks, buildings and points of interest all form part of the "helicopter's view" which PROTRAC seeks to achieve when putting together digital maps of potential markets.

First Stop   **PROTRAC:** The Future of Market Research

For the past decade, PROTRAC has been leading the market in providing highly advanced marketing solutions and services in Egypt and the Middle East and North Africa (MENA) region by offering its clients a geo-marketing service through its distinguished data analysts, researchers, geo-professionals and so-phisticated data maps and tools. It was established in 2001, with a registered capital of $5 million. PROTRAC created the first-ever accurate digital maps for Cairo and Alexandria in 2003. PROTRAC is a member of ESOMAR World Research, MRIA (Marketing Research and Intelligence Agency) and GIS development.

Through its geo-marketing service, PROTRAC has successfully managed to provide large international corporations in Egypt with valuable solutions and insights for the most complex market problems. The company provides executives with tools that help prioritize and optimize marketing, capital, and operating costs. PRO-TRAC also provides marketers with essential information that will allow them to develop a detailed marketing research, which will then serve as a base for developing and evaluating strategic business decisions. PROTRAC uses geographical information about consumers, suppliers, and competitors that help marketers make effec-tive decisions. Salespeople find this information useful to approach clients and sustain relationships with existing ones. PROTRAC is used in distribution to identify areas that have high traffic and distribution outlets and offsets areas that are not successful. It helps identify areas where there is tough competition and areas where there is no competition. Finally, PROTRAC is used to build the information databases for companies.

But what is geo-marketing all about? And how does it aid in marketing research? Geo-marketing involves the integration of geographical intelligence into the various marketing elements, especially distribution and sales. Marketers make use of the geo-graphic information in the process of planning and implementing cer-tain marketing activities that have to do with all the elements of the

When it comes to marketing research, PROTRAC provides the necessary geographical-based information that help executives understand the components of a market.

▲ Geo-marketing company PROTRAC doesn't just profile consumers. They'll also gather information on suppliers and competitors to help marketers to see the bigger picture.

marketing mix; that is product, price, place, and promotion. Marketers use geo-marketing to identify better ways to launch new products, improve existing ones and enhance the image of dying products. Further, current market segments can be identified based on their location and potential market segments can be explored.

Geo-marketing aids in marketing research as it helps visualize the customer, market, competition and company data on digital maps. In other words, it helps determine where exactly the customers are on the country, city, and even street level, where the various target groups are located as well as the consumer trends associated with each of these groups. By analyzing the number of people living in a specific area as well as their lifestyle, trends, and buying behavior, a given company can assess whether a specific product will attract people living in this specific area. Moreover, with the help of the highly sophisticated digital maps, PROTRAC provides its customers with a "helicopter's view" on the various markets found in a specific area that will allow companies to identify the location of their competitors and pinpoint market trends or patterns that otherwise pass by unnoticed. "What we can easily see is only a small percentage of what is possible. PROTRAC provides the vision to see what is below the surface and picture what is essential, but invisible to the eye. It is basically mirroring the market on your desk," says Rana Zoheir, Pre-Sales Executive at PROTRAC.

Geo-marketing also helps companies assess market potential and market share and even measure the effectiveness of every single element of the marketing mix by analyzing the demographic and psychographic variables of various locations with the help of the digital maps. These digital maps are comprised of various layers that represent different types of data such as: demographics, district borders, landmarks, street networks, buildings and points of interest. Clients want to see the points of interest, market share, demographic information, streets, competitors, and distribution channels on one plane. It makes things look much easier. Tarek Hassanein, Sales Executive at PROTRAC highlights that: "we are able to produce regional maps with unique administrative boundaries down to a unique block ID. We have the ability to track and identify a single outlet with a unique code in a single block. Block area is approximately 250,000 sq.m." Clients can make specific inquiries from the database. Inquiries can be done by location, which relate to certain streets, subdistricts, or a municipality, district, governorate, or city; or by attribute, such as identifying points of sale that sell certain products, or companies with a certain number of employees.

Other benefits of geo-marketing include: developing channel strategies to maximize profitability, assess untapped opportunities for different sales points, identify concentrations of your target customers, track market share and share of wallet, which helps improve marketing efficiency and increase return on investment (ROI).

So how does PROTRAC build this Geographical Information System (GIS)? PROTRAC employs around 1,000 employees that work on a full-time and part-time basis. This includes: researchers, data analysts, data collectors, surveyors, and geo-professionals who are responsible for gathering information from the market such as street, building, customer, and market information. Zoheir highlights that it takes 18 months to cover the entirety of Egypt. Every 18 months, the entirety of Egypt is fully scanned.

Geo-marketers build the GIS database by "sweeping" as opposed to surveying. Information about product sales at point-of-sale (POS), competitors, sales, and pricing are collected. Information about the average age, income level, number of cars/household, number of air-conditioning units/household, and education level are also collected.

It is interesting to note that PROTRAC is the only company that has created these national digital maps with all required layers in order to provide site selection, distribution trackers, and routing to the diverse Egyptian market. Those who use it realize that it is a valuable tool that helps marketers make precise and successful decisions in the highly competitive, turbulent and dynamic markets we live in today.[1]

a s the PROTRAC story highlights, good products and marketing programs begin with good customer information. Companies also need an abundance of information on competitors, resellers, and other actors and marketplace forces. But more than just gathering information, marketers must *use* the information to gain powerful *customer and market insights*.

MARKETING INFORMATION AND CUSTOMER INSIGHTS (pp 129–130)

To create value for customers and to build meaningful relationships with them, marketers must first gain fresh, deep insights into what customers need and want. Companies use such customer insights to develop competitive advantage. "In today's hypercompetitive world," states a marketing expert, "the race for competitive advantage is really a race for customer and market insights." Such insights come from the good marketing information.[2]

▲Key customer insights, plus a dash of Apple's design and usability magic, have made the iPod a blockbuster. It now captures a more than 75 percent market share.

Consider Apple's phenomenally successful iPod. The iPod wasn't the first digital music player but Apple was the first to get it right. ▲Apple's research uncovered a key insight about how people want to consume digital music—they want to take all their music with them but they want personal music players to be unobtrusive. This insight led to two key design goals—make it as small as a deck of cards and build it to hold 1,000 songs. Add a dash of Apple's design and usability magic to this insight, and you have a recipe for a blockbuster. Apple's expanded iPod line now captures more than 75 percent market share.

Although customer and market insights are important for building customer value and relationships, these insights can be very difficult to obtain. Customer needs and buying motives are often anything but obvious—consumers themselves usually can't tell you exactly what they need and why they buy. To gain good customer insights, marketers must effectively manage marketing information from a wide range of sources.

Today's marketers have ready access to plenty of marketing information. With the recent explosion of information technologies, companies can now generate information in great quantities. In fact, most marketing managers—most people—are overloaded with data and often overwhelmed by it. For example, consider these startling facts about the information environment:[3]

It is estimated that a week's worth of the *New York Times* contains more information than a person was likely to come across in a lifetime in the 18th century. An estimated 4 exabytes (4.0 times 10 to the 19th) of unique information will be generated this year—more than in the previous 5000 years combined. The amount of new technical information is doubling every two years. For students now starting a four year technical degree, this means that half of what they learn in their first year of study will be outdated by their third year of study. Japanese communications giant NTT has successfully tested a fiber-optic cable that pushes 14 trillion bits per second down a single strand of fiber. That's the equivalent of 2660 CDs or 210 million phone calls every second. It is currently tripling that capacity every six months and is expected to do so for the next 20 years.

Despite this data glut, marketers frequently complain that they lack enough information of the right kind. They don't need *more* information, they need *better* information. And they need to make better *use* of the information they already have. Says another marketing information expert, "transforming today's vast, ever-increasing volume of consumer information into actionable marketing insights . . . is the number-one challenge for digital-age marketers."[4]

Thus, the real value of marketing research and marketing information lies in how it is used—in the **customer insights** that it provides. Says a marketing information expert, "Companies that gather, disseminate, and apply deep customer insights obtain powerful, profitable, sustainable competitive advantages for their brands."[5] Based on such thinking, many companies are now restructuring and renaming their marketing research and information functions. They are creating "customer insights teams," headed by a vice president of customer insights and made up of representatives from all of the firm's functional areas. For example, the head of marketing research at Kraft Foods is called the director of consumer insights and strategy.

Customer insights groups collect customer and market information from a wide variety of sources—ranging from traditional marketing research studies to mingling with and observing consumers to monitoring consumer online conversations about the company and its products. Then, they *use* the marketing information to develop

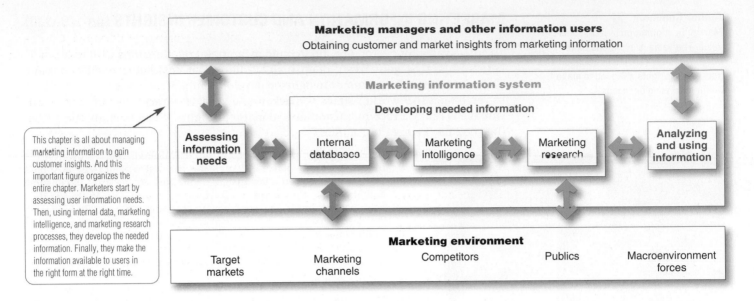

■ **Figure 4.1** The Marketing Information System

important customer insights from which the company can create more value for its customers. For example, Unilever's customer insights group states its mission simply as "getting better at understanding our consumers and meeting their needs."

In gathering and using customer insights, however, companies must be careful not to go too far and become *customer controlled*. The idea is not to give customers everything they request. Rather, it's to understand customers to the core and give them what they need—to create value for customers as a means of capturing value for the firm in return.[6]

Thus, companies must design effective marketing information systems that give managers the right information, in the right form, at the right time and help them to use this information to create customer value and stronger customer relationships. A **marketing information system (MIS)** consists of people and procedures for assessing information needs, developing the needed information, and helping decision makers to use the information to generate and validate actionable customer and market insights.

■ **Figure 4.1** shows that the MIS begins and ends with information users— marketing managers, internal and external partners, and others who need marketing information. First, it interacts with these information users to *assess information needs*. Next, it interacts with the marketing environment to *develop needed information* through internal company databases, marketing intelligence activities, and marketing research. Finally, the MIS helps users to analyze and use the information to develop customer insights, make marketing decisions, and manage customer relationships.

Marketing information system (MIS)
People and procedures for assessing information needs, developing the needed information, and helping decision makers to use the information to generate and validate actionable customer and market insights.

Author Comment >>
The marketing information system begins and ends with users—with assessing their information needs and then delivering information that meets those needs.

ASSESSING MARKETING INFORMATION NEEDS (pp 130–131)

The marketing information system primarily serves the company's marketing and other managers. However, it may also provide information to external partners, such as suppliers, resellers, or marketing services agencies. For example, Wal-Mart's RetailLink system gives key suppliers access to information on customers' buying patterns and store inventory levels. And Dell creates tailored Premier Pages for large customers, giving them access to product design, order status, and product support and service information. In designing an information system, the company must consider the needs of all of these users.

A good MIS balances the information users would *like* to have against what they really *need* and what is *feasible* to offer. The company begins by interviewing managers to find out what information they would like. Some managers will ask for whatever information they can get without thinking carefully about what they really need. Too much information can be as harmful as too little.

Other managers may omit things they ought to know, or they may not know to ask for some types of information they should have. For example, managers might need to know about surges in favorable or unfavorable consumer "word-of-Web" discussions about their brands on blogs or online social networks. Because they do not know about these discussions, they do not think to ask about them. The MIS must monitor the marketing environment in order to provide decision makers with information they should have in order to better understand customers and make key marketing decisions.

Sometimes the company cannot provide the needed information, either because it is not available or because of MIS limitations. For example, a brand manager might want to know how competitors will change their advertising budgets next year and how these changes will affect industry market shares. The information on planned budgets probably is not available. Even if it is, the company's MIS may not be advanced enough to forecast resulting changes in market shares.

Finally, the costs of obtaining, analyzing, storing, and delivering information can mount quickly. The company must decide whether the value of insights gained from additional information is worth the costs of providing it, and both value and cost are often hard to assess. By itself, information has no worth; its value comes from its *use*—from the customer insights it provides and their impact on decision making. Rather, they should weigh carefully the costs of getting more information against the benefits resulting from it.

DEVELOPING MARKETING INFORMATION (pp 131–134)

Marketers can obtain the needed information from *internal data, marketing intelligence,* and *marketing research*.

Internal Data

Many companies build extensive **internal databases**, electronic collections of consumer and market information obtained from data sources within the company network. Marketing managers can readily access and work with information in the database to identify marketing opportunities and problems, plan programs, and evaluate performance. Internal data can provide strong competitive advantage. "Locked within your own records is a huge, largely untapped asset that no [competitor] can hope to match," says one analyst. Companies are "sitting on a gold mine of unrealized potential in their current customer base."[7]

Information in the database can come from many sources. The marketing department furnishes information on customer demographics, psychographics, sales transactions, and Web site visits. The customer service department keeps records of customer satisfaction or service problems. The accounting department prepares financial statements and keeps detailed records of sales, costs, and cash flows. Operations reports on production schedules, shipments, and inventories. The sales force reports on reseller reactions and competitor activities, and marketing channel partners provide data on point-of-sale transactions. Harnessing such information can provide powerful customer insights and competitive advantage.

For example, consider upscale retailer ▲Barneys, which has found a wealth of information contained in online customers' browsing and buying data. According to one business reporter:[8]

A glance in any spam folder is proof positive that most online retailers haven't yet refined their customer tracking. To wit: My spam box currently features Petco.com advertisements for kitty litter (I'm a dog person), a Staples.com ad for Windows software (I'm a

▲**Internal data: Barneys has found a wealth of actionable customer insights by analyzing online customers' browsing and buying behavior at its Web site.**

Mac girl), and four ads for Viagra (enough said). But the e-mails from Barneys.com are different. Barneys knows that I like jewelry and yoga. My most recent Barneys e-mail read, "Love it! Jennifer Meyer Ohm Necklace." I do love it. How does Barneys know? It sorts through the data left by millions of anonymous people clicking around its site and predicts who's likely to buy which products, when, and at what price.

Digging deep into such data provides a wealth of actionable insights into customer buying patterns. Barney's can target customers based on their overall habits, such as "fashionistas" who buy risky new designer products, "bottom feeders" who always buy sale items, or cosmetics zealots. "We even know when you're gonna run out of shampoo, so we might as well send you an e-mail," says Barneys director of Internet marketing. Rather than feeling spied on, customers are thrilled, because the message is relevant.

Better targeting cuts down on wasted marketing efforts. "We used to spend $90,000 on a full-page ad in *The New York Times*," says the marketing director. "Then with the Web site, we would send an e-mail about, say, Lanvin handbags to 100,000 customers. But 90,000 of them probably didn't even know what a Lanvin handbag was." Today, only those people Barneys has identified as handbag fanatics get an e-mail, and Barneys has seen up to a tenfold rise in response rates. Barneys is now considering expanding such analysis to its stores—tracking products as well as customers—to marry its in-store and online marketing efforts.

Internal databases usually can be accessed more quickly and cheaply than other information sources, but they also present some problems. Because internal information was often collected for other purposes, it may be incomplete or in the wrong form for making marketing decisions. For example, sales and cost data used by the accounting department for preparing financial statements must be adapted for use in evaluating the value of a specific customer segment, sales force, or channel performance. Data also ages quickly; keeping the database current requires a major effort. In addition, a large company produces mountains of information, which must be well integrated and readily accessible so that managers can find it easily and use it effectively. Managing that much data requires highly sophisticated equipment and techniques.

Competitive Marketing Intelligence

Competitive marketing intelligence
The systematic collection and analysis of publicly available information about consumers, competitors, and developments in the marketing environment.

Competitive marketing intelligence is the systematic collection and analysis of publicly available information about consumers, competitors, and developments in the marketplace. The goal of competitive marketing intelligence is to improve strategic decision making by understanding the consumer environment, assessing and tracking competitors' actions, and providing early warnings of opportunities and threats.

Marketing intelligence gathering has grown dramatically as more and more companies are now busily eavesdropping on the marketplace and snooping on their competitors. Techniques range from monitoring Internet buzz or observing consumers firsthand to quizzing the company's own employees, benchmarking competitors' products, researching the Internet, lurking around industry trade shows, and even rooting through rivals' trash bins.

Good marketing intelligence can help marketers to gain insights into how consumers talk about and connect with their brands. Many companies send out teams of trained observers to mix and mingle with customers as they use and talk about the company's products. Other companies routinely monitor consumers' online chatter with the help of monitoring services such as Nielsen Online or Radian6. For example, Radian6 helps companies to keep track of almost any relevant online conversation:[9]

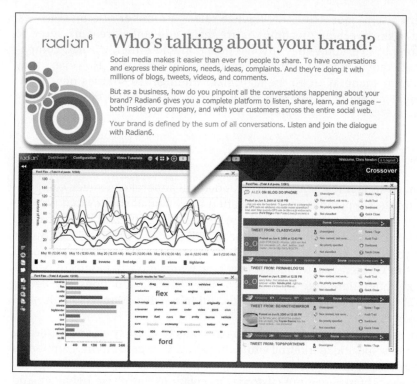

▲Many companies routinely monitor consumers' online conversations with the help of monitoring services and platforms such as Radian6.

Social media make it easier than ever for people to share—to have conversations and express their opinions, needs, ideas, and complaints. And they're doing it with millions of blogs, tweets, videos, and comments daily. Companies face the difficult task of pinpointing all the conversations happening about their brands. Radian6 gives companies a Web-based platform that lets them listen to, share with, learn from, and engage customers across the entire social Web. ▲Radian6's Web dashboard provides for real-time monitoring of consumer mentions of the company, its brands, relevant issues, and competitors on millions of blog posts, viral videos, reviews in forums, sharing of photos, and twitter updates. Dell's Customer Service group uses Radian6 to monitor and respond to what's being said online about its products and any problems after purchase. Lifestyle retailer PacSun uses Radian6 to track important trends and to better respond to customers in the online space.

Companies also need to actively monitor competitors' activities. Firms use competitive marketing intelligence to gain early warnings of competitor moves and strategies, new-product launches, new or changing markets, and potential competitive strengths and weaknesses. Much competitor intelligence can be collected from people inside the company—executives, engineers and scientists, purchasing agents, and the sales force. The company can also obtain important intelligence information from suppliers, resellers, and key customers. Or it can get good information by observing competitors and monitoring their published information.

Competitors often reveal intelligence information through their annual reports, business publications, trade show exhibits, press releases, advertisements, and Web pages. The Web has become an invaluable source of competitive intelligence. Using Internet search engines, marketers can search specific competitor names, events, or trends and see what turns up. And tracking consumer conversations about competing brands is often as revealing as tracking conversations about the company's own brands. Moreover, most competitors now place volumes of information on their Web sites, providing details of interest to customers, partners, suppliers, investors, or franchisees. This can provide a wealth of useful information about competitors' strategies, markets, new products, facilities, and other happenings.

Intelligence seekers can also pore through any of thousands of online databases. Some are free. For example, the U.S. Security and Exchange Commission's database provides a huge stockpile of financial information on public competitors, and the U.S. Patent Office and Trademark database reveals patents competitors have filed. For a fee, companies can also subscribe to any of the more than 3,000 online databases and information search services such as Hoover's, LexisNexis, and Dun & Bradstreet. Today's marketers have an almost overwhelming amount of competitor information only a few keystrokes away.

The intelligence game goes both ways. Facing determined competitive marketing intelligence efforts by competitors, most companies are now taking steps to protect their own information. For example, Unilever trains employees not just how to collect intelligence information but also how to protect company information from competitors. According to a former Unilever staffer, "We were even warned that spies from competitors could be posing as drivers at the minicab company we used." Unilever performs random checks on internal security. Says the former staffer, "At one [internal marketing] conference, we were set up when an actor was employed to infiltrate the group. The idea was to see who spoke to him, how much they told him, and how long it took to realize that no one knew him. He ended up being there for a long time."[10]

The growing use of marketing intelligence raises a number of ethical issues. Although most of the preceding techniques are legal, and some are considered to be shrewdly competitive, some may involve questionable ethics. Clearly, companies should take advantage of publicly available information. However, they should not stoop to snoop. With all the legitimate intelligence sources now available, a company does not need to break the law or accepted codes of ethics to get good intelligence.

MARKETING RESEARCH (pp 134–148)

In addition to marketing intelligence information about general consumer, competitor, and marketplace happenings, marketers often need formal studies that provide customer and market insights for specific marketing situations and decisions. For example, Budweiser wants to know what appeals will be most effective in its Super Bowl advertising. Google wants to know how Web searchers will react to a proposed redesign of its site. Or Samsung wants to know how many and what kinds of people will buy its next-generation large-screen televisions. In such situations, marketing intelligence will not provide the detailed information needed. Managers will need marketing research.

Marketing research is the systematic design, collection, analysis, and reporting of data relevant to a specific marketing situation facing an organization. Companies use marketing research in a wide variety of situations. For example, marketing research gives marketers insights into customer motivations, purchase behavior, and satisfaction. It can help them to assess market potential and market share or to measure the effectiveness of pricing, product, distribution, and promotion activities.

Some large companies have their own research departments that work with marketing managers on marketing research projects. This is how Procter & Gamble, GE, and many other corporate giants handle marketing research. In addition, these companies—like their smaller counterparts—frequently hire outside research specialists to consult with management on specific marketing problems and conduct marketing research studies. Sometimes firms simply purchase data collected by outside firms to aid in their decision making.

The marketing research process has four steps (see ■ **Figure 4.2**): defining the problem and research objectives, developing the research plan, implementing the research plan, and interpreting and reporting the findings.

Defining the Problem and Research Objectives

Marketing managers and researchers must work closely together to define the problem and agree on research objectives. The manager best understands the decision for which information is needed; the researcher best understands marketing research and how to obtain the information. Defining the problem and research objectives is often the hardest step in the research process. The manager may know that something is wrong, without knowing the specific causes.

After the problem has been defined carefully, the manager and researcher must set the research objectives. A marketing research project might have one of three types of objectives. The objective of **exploratory research** is to gather preliminary information that will help define the problem and suggest hypotheses.

Author Comment »
Whereas marketing intelligence involves actively scanning the general marketing environment, marketing research involves more focused studies to gain customer insights relating to specific marketing decisions.

Marketing research
The systematic design, collection, analysis, and reporting of data relevant to a specific marketing situation facing an organization.

Exploratory research
Marketing research to gather preliminary information that will help define problems and suggest hypotheses.

This first step in the marketing research process is probably the most difficult, but is also the most important one. It guides the entire research process. It's pretty frustrating to reach the end of a large and expensive research project only to learn that you were addressing the wrong problem!

■ **Figure 4.2** The Marketing Research Process

| Defining the problem and research objectives | → | Developing the research plan for collecting information | → | Implementing the research plan—collecting and analyzing the data | → | Interpreting and reporting the findings |

Descriptive research
Marketing research to better describe marketing problems, situations, or markets, such as the market potential for a product or the demographics and attitudes of consumers.

Causal research
Marketing research to test hypotheses about cause-and-effect relationships.

The objective of **descriptive research** is to describe things, such as the market potential for a product or the demographics and attitudes of consumers who buy the product. The objective of **causal research** is to test hypotheses about cause-and-effect relationships. For example, would a 10 percent decrease in tuition at a private college result in an enrollment increase sufficient to offset the reduced tuition? Managers often start with exploratory research and later follow with descriptive or causal research.

The statement of the problem and research objectives guides the entire research process. The manager and researcher should put the statement in writing to be certain that they agree on the purpose and expected results of the research.

Developing the Research Plan

Once the research problems and objectives have been defined, researchers must determine the exact information needed, develop a plan for gathering it efficiently, and present the plan to management. The research plan outlines sources of existing data and spells out the specific research approaches, contact methods, sampling plans, and instruments that researchers will use to gather new data.

Research objectives must be translated into specific information needs. ▲For example, suppose that Red Bull wants to conduct research on how consumers would react to a proposed new vitamin-enhanced-water drink in several flavors sold under the Red Bull name. Red Bull currently dominates the worldwide energy drink market. However, in an effort to expand beyond its energy drink niche, the company recently introduced Red Bull Cola ("Why not?" asks the company—it's strong and natural, just like the original Red Bull energy drink). A new line of enhanced waters—akin to Glacéau's VitaminWater—might help Red Bull to leverage its strong brand position even further. The proposed research might call for the following specific information:

▲A decision by Red Bull to add a line of enhanced waters to its already successful mix of energy and cola drinks would call for marketing research that provides lots of specific information.

- The demographic, economic, and lifestyle characteristics of current Red Bull customers. (Do current customers also consume enhanced-water products? Are such products consistent with their lifestyles? Or would Red Bull need to target a new segment of consumers?)

- The characteristics and usage patterns the broader population of enhanced-water users: What do they need and expect from such products, where do they buy them, when and how do they use them, and what existing brands and price points are most popular? (The new Red Bull product would need strong, relevant positioning in the crowded enhanced-water market.)

- Retailer reactions to the proposed new product line: Would they stock and support it? Where would they display it? (Failure to get retailer support would hurt sales of the new drink.)

- Forecasts of sales of both the new and current Red Bull products. (Will the new enhanced-waters create new sales or simply take sales away from current Red Bull products? Will the new product increase Red Bull's overall profits?)

Red Bull's marketers will need these and many other types of information to decide whether and how to introduce the new product.

The research plan should be presented in a *written proposal*. A written proposal is especially important when the research project is large and complex or when an outside firm carries it out. The proposal should cover the management problems addressed and the research objectives, the information to be obtained, and how the results will help management decision making. The proposal also should include research costs.

To meet the manager's information needs, the research plan can call for gathering secondary data, primary data, or both. **Secondary data** consist of information that already exists somewhere, having been collected for another purpose. **Primary data** consist of information collected for the specific purpose at hand.

Secondary data
Information that already exists somewhere, having been collected for another purpose.

Primary data
Information collected for the specific purpose at hand.

Gathering Secondary Data

Researchers usually start by gathering secondary data. The company's internal database provides a good starting point. However, the company can also tap into a wide assortment of external information sources, including commercial data services and government sources (see ■ **Table 4.1**).

Companies can buy secondary data reports from outside suppliers. For example, Nielsen sells buyer data from a consumer panel of more than 250,000 households in 27 countries worldwide, with measures of trial and repeat purchasing, brand loyalty, and buyer demographics. ▲ Experian Consumer Research (Simmons) sells information on more than 8,000 brands in 450 product categories, including detailed consumer profiles that assess everything from the products consumers buy and the brands they prefer to their lifestyles, attitudes, and media preferences. The MONITOR service by Yankelovich sells information on important social and lifestyle trends. These and other firms supply high-quality data to suit a wide variety of marketing information needs.[11]

Commercial online databases
Computerized collections of information available from online commercial sources or via the Internet.

▼ Consumer database services such as Experian Consumer Research sell an incredible wealth of information on everything from the products consumers buy and the brands they prefer to their lifestyles, attitudes, and media preferences. Experian Consumer Research is "The Voice of the American Consumer."

Using **commercial online databases**, marketing researchers can conduct their own searches of secondary data sources. General database services such as Dialog, ProQuest, and LexisNexis put an incredible wealth of information at the keyboards of marketing decision makers. Beyond commercial Web sites offering information for a fee, almost every industry association, government agency, business publication, and news medium offers free information to those tenacious enough to find their Web sites. There are so many Web sites offering data that finding the right ones can become an almost overwhelming task.

Web search engines can also be a big help in locating relevant secondary information sources. However, they can also be very frustrating and inefficient. For example, a Red Bull marketer Googling "enhanced water products" would come up with some 256,000 hits! Still, well-structured, well-designed Web searches can be a good starting point to any marketing research project.

Secondary data can usually be obtained more quickly and at a lower cost than primary data. Also, secondary sources can sometimes provide data an individual company cannot collect on its own—information that either is not directly available or would be too expensive to collect. For example, it would be too expensive for Red Bull's marketers to conduct a continuing retail store audit to find out about the market shares, prices, and displays of competitors' brands. But it can buy the InfoScan service from Information Resources, Inc., which provides this information based on scanner and other data from 34,000 retail stores in markets around the nation.[12]

Secondary data can also present problems. The needed information may not exist—researchers can rarely obtain all the data they need from secondary sources. For example, Red Bull will not find existing information about consumer reactions to a new enhanced-water line that it has not yet placed on the market. Even when data can be found, the information might not be very usable. The

■ **Table 4.1** Selected External Information Sources

For Business Data	For Government Data	For Internet Data
The Nielsen Company (http://nielsen.com) provides point-of-sale scanner data on sales, market share, and retail prices; data on household purchasing; and data on television audiences.	**Securities and Exchange Commission Edgar database** (http://sec.gov/edgar.shtml) provides financial data on U.S. public corporations.	**ClickZ** (http://clickz.com) brings together a wealth of information about the Internet and its users, from consumers to e-commerce.
Experian Consumer Research (Simmons) (http://smrb.com) provides detailed analysis of consumer patterns in 400 product categories in selected markets.	**Small Business Administration** (http://sba.gov) features information and links for small business owners.	**Interactive Advertising Bureau** (http://iab.net) covers statistics about advertising on the Internet.
Information Resources, Inc., (www.infores.com) provides supermarket scanner data for tracking grocery product movement and new product purchasing data.	**Federal Trade Commission** (http://ftc.gov) shows regulations and decisions related to consumer protection and antitrust laws.	**Forrester.com** (www.forrester.com) monitors Web traffic and ranks the most popular sites.
IMS Health (http://imshealth.com) tracks drug sales, monitors performance of pharmaceutical sales representatives, and offers pharmaceutical market forecasts.	**Stat-USA** (http://stat-usa.gov), a Department of Commerce site, highlights statistics on U.S. business and international trade.	
Arbitron (http://arbitron.com) provides local-market and Internet radio audience and advertising expenditure information, among other media and ad spending data.	**U.S. Census** (www.census.gov) provides detailed statistics and trends about the U.S. population.	
J.D. Power and Associates (http://jdpower.com) provides information from independent consumer surveys of product and service quality, customer satisfaction, and buyer behavior.	**U.S. Patent and Trademark Office** (http://uspto.gov) allows searches to determine who has filed for trademarks and patents.	
Dun & Bradstreet (http://dnb.com) maintains a database containing information on more than 50 million individual companies around the globe.		
comScore (http://comscore.com) provides consumer behavior information and geodemographic analysis of Internet and digital media users around the world.		
Thomson Dialog (www.dialog.com) offers access to more than 900 databases containing publications, reports, newsletters, and directories covering dozens of industries.		
LexisNexis (http://lexisnexis.com) features articles from business, consumer, and marketing publications plus tracking of firms, industries, trends, and promotion techniques.		
Factiva (http://factiva.com) specializes in in-depth financial, historical, and operational information on public and private companies.		
Hoover's, Inc., (http://hoovers.com) provides business descriptions, financial overviews, and news about major companies around the world.		
CNN (http://cnn.com) reports U.S. and global news and covers the markets and news-making companies in detail.		
American Demographics (http://adage.com/americandemographics/) reports on demographic trends and their significance for businesses.		

researcher must evaluate secondary information carefully to make certain it is *relevant* (fits research project needs), *accurate* (reliably collected and reported), *current* (up-to-date enough for current decisions), and *impartial* (objectively collected and reported).

Primary Data Collection

Secondary data provide a good starting point for research and often help to define research problems and objectives. In most cases, however, the company must also collect primary data. Just as researchers must carefully evaluate the quality of secondary information, they also must take great care when collecting primary data. They need to make sure that it will be relevant, accurate, current, and unbiased. ■ **Table 4.2** shows that designing a plan for primary data collection calls for a number of decisions on *research approaches, contact methods, sampling plan,* and *research instruments.*

Research Approaches

Research approaches for gathering primary data include observation, surveys, and experiments. Here, we discuss each one in turn.

Observational research
Gathering primary data by observing relevant people, actions, and situations.

Observational Research. Observational research involves gathering primary data by observing relevant people, actions, and situations. For example, a bank might evaluate possible new branch locations by checking traffic patterns, neighborhood conditions, and the location of competing branches.

Researchers often observe consumer behavior to glean customer insights they can't obtain by simply asking customers questions. For instance, Fisher-Price has set up an observation lab in which it can observe the reactions of little tots to new toys. The Fisher-Price Play Lab is a sunny, toy-strewn space where lucky kids get to test Fisher-Price prototypes, under the watchful eyes of designers who hope to learn what will get kids worked up into a new-toy frenzy. Similarly, in its research labs, using high-tech cameras and other equipment, Gillette observes women shaving and uses the insights to design new razors and shaving products.[13]

Kimberly Clark's Huggies brand even had parents wear camera-equipped "glasses" at home so that it could "see what they saw" while changing babies' diapers. Among other things, the Huggies marketers learned that parents change their babies' diapers almost anywhere—on beds, floors, and on top of washing machines—often in awkward positions. The researchers could see they were struggling with wipe containers and lotions requiring two hands. So the company redesigned the wipe package with a push-button one-handed dispenser and designed lotion and shampoo bottles that can be grabbed and dispensed easily with one hand.[14]

Marketers not only observe what consumers do, they also observe what consumers are saying. As discussed earlier, marketers now routinely listen in on consumer conversations on blogs, social networks, and Web sites. Observing such naturally occurring feedback can provide inputs that simply can't be gained through more structure and formal research approaches.[15]

Observational research can obtain information that people are unwilling or unable to provide. In contrast, some things simply cannot be observed, such as feelings,

■ **Table 4.2** Planning Primary Data Collection

Research Approaches	Contact Methods	Sampling Plan	Research Instruments
Observation	Mail	Sampling unit	Questionnaire
Survey	Telephone	Sample size	Mechanical instruments
Experiment	Personal	Sampling procedure	
	Online		

▲Ethnographic research: Teams of Nokia anthropologists "live with the locals" in emerging economies to glean subtle insights into each local culture. Such insights resulted in the robust Nokia 1200 phone, which makes shared use a top priority.

Ethnographic research
A form of observational research that involves sending trained observers to watch and interact with consumers in their "natural habitat."

Survey research
Gathering primary data by asking people questions about their knowledge, attitudes, preferences, and buying behavior.

Experimental research
Gathering primary data by selecting matched groups of subjects, giving them different treatments, controlling related factors, and checking for differences in group responses.

attitudes and motives, or private behavior. Long-term or infrequent behavior is also difficult to observe. Finally, observations can be very difficult to interpret. Because of these limitations, researchers often use observation along with other data collection methods.

A wide range of companies now use **ethnographic research**. Ethnographic research involves sending trained observers to watch and interact with consumers in their "natural habitat." Consider this example:[16]

> Mobile phone maker Nokia wants to add two billion new customers by the end of the decade. To do so, it has invested heavily in ethnographic research, focusing especially on emerging economies. Nokia deploys teams of anthropologists to study deeply the behavior of mobile-phone owners in vast markets such as China, Brazil, and India. By "living with the locals," from the shanty towns of Soweto to the bedrooms of Seoul's painfully tech-savvy teens, Nokia gleans subtle insights into nuances of each local culture. For example, it knows first-hand that 50 percent of the world's women keep their phones in their handbags (and miss 20 percent of their calls) and that most Asian early adopters who watch mobile TV ignore the mobile part and tune in from home.
>
> One of the biggest discoveries came from researchers studying how people in poor rural areas overcome some of the barriers to communication they face in their daily lives. Surprisingly, although usually considered a one-owner item, mobile phones in these areas are often used by entire families or even villages because of the cost. ▲Based on this finding, Nokia designed its 1200 and 1208 phones, which make shared use the top priority. The affordable phones offer many useful and durable features and are robust enough to accommodate many different people using them. For example, they contain a long-life battery and multiple phone books so each member of a family or village can keep his or her own contacts and numbers separately from others.

Observational and ethnographic research often yield the kinds of details that just don't emerge from traditional research questionnaires or focus groups. Whereas traditional quantitative research approaches seek to test known hypotheses and obtain answers to well-defined product or strategy questions, observational research can generate fresh customer and market insights. "The beauty of ethnography," says a research expert, is that it "allows companies to zero in on their customers' unarticulated desires." Agrees another researcher, "Classic market research doesn't go far enough. It can't grasp what people can't imagine or articulate. Think of the Henry Ford quote: 'If I had asked people what they wanted, they would have said faster horses.'"[17]

Survey Research. **Survey research**, the most widely used method for primary data collection, is the approach best suited for gathering *descriptive* information. A company that wants to know about people's knowledge, attitudes, preferences, or buying behavior can often find out by asking them directly.

The major advantage of survey research is its flexibility—it can be used to obtain many different kinds of information in many different situations. Surveys addressing almost any marketing question or decision can be conducted by phone or mail, in person, or on the Web.

However, survey research also presents some problems. Sometimes people are unable to answer survey questions because they cannot remember or have never thought about what they do and why. People may be unwilling to respond to unknown interviewers or about things they consider private. Respondents may answer survey questions even when they do not know the answer in order to appear smarter or more informed. Or they may try to help the interviewer by giving pleasing answers. Finally, busy people may not take the time, or they might resent the intrusion into their privacy.

Experimental Research. Whereas observation is best suited for exploratory research and surveys for descriptive research, **experimental research** is best suited for gathering *causal* information. Experiments involve selecting matched groups of subjects, giving them different treatments, controlling unrelated factors, and checking for differences in group responses. Thus, experimental research tries to explain cause-and-effect relationships.

For example, before adding a new sandwich to its menu, McDonald's might use experiments to test the effects on sales of two different prices it might charge. It could introduce the new sandwich at one price in one city and at another price in another city. If the cities are similar, and if all other marketing efforts for the sandwich are the same, then differences in sales in the two cities could be related to the price charged.

Contact Methods

Information can be collected by mail, telephone, personal interview, or online. ■ **Table 4.3** shows the strengths and weaknesses of each of these contact methods.

Mail, Telephone, and Personal Interviewing. *Mail questionnaires* can be used to collect large amounts of information at a low cost per respondent. Respondents may give more honest answers to more personal questions on a mail questionnaire than to an unknown interviewer in person or over the phone. Also, no interviewer is involved to bias the respondent's answers.

However, mail questionnaires are not very flexible—all respondents answer the same questions in a fixed order. Mail surveys usually take longer to complete, and the response rate—the number of people returning completed questionnaires—is often very low. Finally, the researcher often has little control over the mail questionnaire sample. Even with a good mailing list, it is hard to control *whom* at the mailing address fills out the questionnaire. As a result of the shortcomings, more and more marketers are now shifting to faster, more flexible, and lower cost online surveys.

Telephone interviewing is one of the best methods for gathering information quickly, and it provides greater flexibility than mail questionnaires. Interviewers can explain difficult questions and, depending on the answers they receive, skip some questions or probe on others. Response rates tend to be higher than with mail questionnaires, and interviewers can ask to speak to respondents with the desired characteristics or even by name.

However, with telephone interviewing, the cost per respondent is higher than with mail or online questionnaires. Also, people may not want to discuss personal questions with an interviewer. The method introduces interviewer bias—the way interviewers talk, how they ask questions, and other differences may affect respondents' answers. Finally, in this age of do-not-call lists and promotion-harassed consumers, potential survey respondents are increasingly hanging up on telephone interviewers rather than talking with them.

■ **Table 4.3** Strengths and Weaknesses of Contact Methods

	Mail	Telephone	Personal	Online
Flexibility	Poor	Good	Excellent	Good
Quantity of data that can be collected	Good	Fair	Excellent	Good
Control of interviewer effects	Excellent	Fair	Poor	Fair
Control of sample	Fair	Excellent	Good	Excellent
Speed of data collection	Poor	Excellent	Good	Excellent
Response rate	Poor	Poor	Good	Good
Cost	Good	Fair	Poor	Excellent

Personal interviewing takes two forms—individual and group interviewing. *Individual interviewing* involves talking with people in their homes or offices, on the street, or in shopping malls. Such interviewing is flexible. Trained interviewers can guide interviews, explain difficult questions, and explore issues as the situation requires. They can show subjects actual products, advertisements, or packages and observe reactions and behavior. However, individual personal interviews may cost three to four times as much as telephone interviews.

Group interviewing consists of inviting six to ten people to meet with a trained moderator to talk about a product, service, or organization. Participants normally are paid a small sum for attending. The moderator encourages free and easy discussion, hoping that group interactions will bring out actual feelings and thoughts. At the same time, the moderator "focuses" the discussion—hence the name **focus group interviewing**.

Focus group interviewing
Personal interviewing that involves inviting six to ten people to gather for a few hours with a trained interviewer to talk about a product, service, or organization. The interviewer "focuses" the group discussion on important issues.

Researchers and marketers watch the focus group discussions from behind one-way glass and record comments in writing or on video for later study. Today, focus group researchers can even use videoconferencing and Internet technology to connect marketers in distant locations with live focus group action. Using cameras and two-way sound systems, marketing executives in a far-off boardroom can look in and listen, using remote controls to zoom in on faces and pan the focus group at will.

Along with observational research, focus group interviewing has become one of the major qualitative marketing research tools for gaining fresh insights into consumer thoughts and feelings. However, focus group studies present some challenges. They usually employ small samples to keep time and costs down, and it may be hard to generalize from the results. Moreover, consumers in focus groups are not always open and honest about their real feelings, behavior, and intentions in front of other people.

Thus, although focus groups are still widely used, many researchers are tinkering with focus group design. For example, some companies prefer "immersion groups"—small groups of consumers who interact directly and informally with product designers without a focus group moderator present. Other researchers are combining focus groups with hypnosis in an effort to get deeper, more vivid insights. Consider this example:[18]

Volvo equals safety. In focus group after focus group, participants said the same thing. But to check these findings, Volvo called in a hypnotist. Members of Volvo focus groups were asked to test-drive a car. Immediately afterwards, they were hypnotized and asked their true feelings about the brand. It wasn't pretty: Many revealed that Volvo also equals being middle-aged. That idea "for some people was suffocating," says a Volvo researcher. "Hypnosis helped get past the clichés. We needed the conversation taken to a deeper, more emotional place."

▼New focus group environments: To create a more congenial setting in which women could open up and share personal shaving and moisturizing stories, Schick sponsored "Slow Sip" sessions in local cafés.

Still other researchers are changing the environments in which they conduct focus groups. To help consumers relax and to elicit more authentic responses, they use settings that are more comfortable and more relevant to the products being researched. ▲For example, to get a better understanding of how women shave their legs, Schick Canada created the "Slow Sip" sessions designed to be like a simple get-together with girlfriends.

In these Slow Sip sessions, participants gathered round at a local café to sip coffee or tea and munch on snacks together. The structure was loose, and the congenial setting helped the women to open up and share personal shaving and moisturizing stories on a subject that might have been sensitive in a more formal setting. The Slow Sip sessions produced a number of new customer insights. For example, researchers discovered that the message for their Schick Quattro for Women razor—that Quattro has four-blade technology—was too technical. Women don't care about the engineering behind a razor, they care about shaving results. So Schick Canada repositioned the Quattro as offering a smooth, long-lasting shave. As a side benefit, participants enjoyed the sessions so much that they wanted to stick around for more. They became a kind of ongoing advisory board for Schick's marketers and "brand ambassadors" for Schick's products.[19]

Thus, in recent years, many companies have been moving away from traditional, more formal and numbers-oriented research approaches and contact methods. Instead, more and more, they are employing new ways of listening to consumers that don't involve traditional questionnaire formats. "Long known for crunching numbers and being statistical gatekeepers of the marketing industry," says one marketer, "market researchers need to shift their focus toward listing in developing ideas better on the front and away from 'feeding the metrics monster.'" Beyond conducting surveys and tracking brand metrics, "researchers need to employ softer skills."[20]

Online Marketing Research. The growth of the Internet has had a dramatic impact on the conduct of marketing research. Increasingly, researchers are collecting primary data through **online marketing research**—*Internet surveys, online panels, experiments,* and *online focus groups.* By one estimate, U.S. online research spending reached an estimated $2.1 billion in 2008 and is growing at 15 to 20 percent a year.[21]

Online marketing research
Collecting primary data online through Internet surveys, online focus groups, Web-based experiments, or tracking consumers' online behavior.

Online research can take many forms. A company can use the Web as a survey medium. It can include a questionnaire on its Web site and offer incentives for completing it. It can use e-mail, Web links, or Web pop-ups to invite people to answer questions. It can create online panels that provide regular feedback or conduct live discussions or online focus groups.

Beyond surveys, researchers can conduct experiments on the Web. They can experiment with different prices, headlines, or product features on different Web sites or at different times to learn the relative effectiveness of their offers. Or they can set up virtual shopping environments and use them to test new products and marketing programs. Finally, a company can learn about the behavior of online customers by following their click streams as they visit the Web site and move to other sites.

The Internet is especially well suited to *quantitative* research—conducting marketing surveys and collecting data. Close to three-quarters of all Americans now have access to the Web, making it a fertile channel for reaching a broad cross section of consumers. As response rates for traditional survey approaches decline and costs increase, the Web is quickly replacing mail and the telephone as the dominant data collection methodology. Online research now accounts for about 50 percent of all survey research done in the United States.[22]

Web-based survey research offers some real advantages over traditional phone and mail approaches. The most obvious advantages are speed and low costs. By going online, researchers can quickly and easily distribute Internet surveys to thousands of respondents simultaneously via e-mail or by posting them on selected Web sites. Responses can be almost instantaneous, and because respondents themselves enter the information, researchers can tabulate, review, and share research data as they arrive.

▼ Online research: Thanks to survey services such as Zoomerang, almost any business, large or small, can create, publish, and distribute its own custom surveys in minutes.

Online research usually costs much less than research conducted through mail, phone, or personal interviews. Using the Internet eliminates most of the postage, phone, interviewer, and data-handling costs associated with the other approaches. As a result, Internet surveys typically cost 15 to 20 percent less than mail surveys and 30 percent less than phone surveys. Moreover, sample size has little impact on costs. Once the questionnaire is set up, there's little difference in cost between 10 and 10,000 respondents on the Web.

Thus, online research is well within the reach of almost any business, large or small. In fact, with the Internet, "what was once the domain of the high-cost experts has now become available to practically anybody with a desire to use it," says a marketing research executive.[23] ▲ Even smaller, less sophisticated researchers can use online survey services such as Zoomerang (www.zoomerang.com)

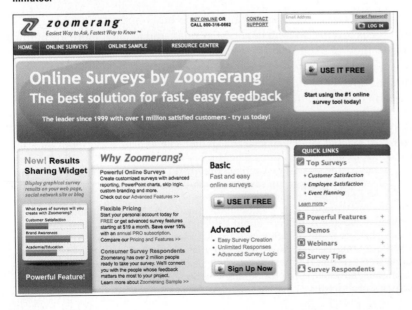

and SurveyMonkey (www.surveymonkey.com) to create, publish, and distribute their own custom surveys in minutes.

Beyond their speed and cost advantages, Web-based surveys also tend to be more interactive and engaging, easier to complete, and less intrusive than traditional phone or mail surveys. As a result, they usually garner higher response rates. The Internet is an excellent medium for reaching the hard-to-reach—the often-elusive teen, single, affluent, and well-educated audiences. It's also good for reaching working mothers and other people who lead busy lives. Such people are well represented online, and they can respond in their own space and at their own convenience.

Just as marketing researchers have rushed to use the Internet for quantitative surveys and data collection, they are now also adopting *qualitative* Web-based research approaches—such as online depth interviews, focus groups, blogs, and social networks. The Internet can provide a fast, low-cost way to gain qualitative customer insights. For example, Anheuser-Busch uses the Web—both formally and informally— as a research "test-lab" for advertising ideas.[24]

> Anheuser-Busch is increasingly using the Web to spread and fine-tune its advertising. The Web allows it to test-drive edgy material that, in years past, would never have seen the light of day for fear of causing offense on TV. Witness the strange life of "Swear Jar," a commercial that portrays an effort to clean up office language by fining staffers 25 cent per profanity. The twist: the cash goes toward buying Bud Light—and the wholesome plan backfires spectacularly. Although the language was too raw for TV, A-B tested it out on the Internet. Someone sent it to YouTube, where it has since gotten more than 3.7 million hits, despite never appearing on television. "The digital space . . . can be an incubator for ideas," says an Anheuser-Busch media executive. Using the Web to gauge fervor for offbeat ads promises broader and quicker insight than the traditional way—peeking through a one-way window as a test group watches new TV commercials. "The Web gives instant credibility or thumbs-down," says the executive.

Online focus groups
Gathering a small group of people online with a trained moderator to chat about a product, service, or organization and gain qualitative insights about consumer attitudes and behavior.

A primary qualitative Web-based research approach is **online focus groups**. Such focus groups offer many advantages over traditional focus groups. Participants can log in from anywhere—all they need is a laptop and a Web connection. Thus, the Internet works well for bringing together people from different parts of the country or world, especially those in higher-income groups who can't spare the time to travel to a central site. Also, researchers can conduct and monitor online focus groups from just about anywhere, eliminating travel, lodging, and facility costs. Finally, although online focus groups require some advance scheduling, results are almost immediate.

Online focus groups can take any of several formats. Most occur in real time, in the form of online chat room discussions in which participants and a moderator sit around a virtual table exchanging comments. Alternatively, researchers might set up an online message board on which respondents interact over the course of several days or a few weeks. Participants log in daily and comment on focus group topics.

Although low in cost and easy to administer, online focus groups can lack the real-world dynamics of more personal approaches. The online world is devoid of the eye contact, body language, and direct personal interactions found in traditional focus group research. And the Internet format—running, typed commentary and online "emoticons" (punctuation marks that express emotion, such as :-) to signify happiness)—greatly restricts respondent expressiveness. The impersonal nature of the Internet can prevent people from interacting with each other in a normal way and getting excited about a concept.

To overcome these shortcomings, some researchers are now adding real-time audio and video to their online focus groups. ▲For example, online research firm Channel M2 "puts the human touch back into online research" by assembling focus group participants in people-friendly "virtual interview rooms."[25]

> Participants are recruited using traditional methods and then sent a Web camera so that both their verbal and nonverbal reactions can be recorded. Participants then receive instructions via e-mail, including a link to the Channel M2 online interviewing room and a toll-free teleconference number to call. At the appointed time, when they click on the link

▲Some researchers have now added real-time audio and video to their online focus groups. For example, Channel M2 "puts the human touch back into online research" by assembling focus group participants in people-friendly "virtual interview rooms."

and phone in, participants sign on and see the Channel M2 interview room, complete with live video of the other participants, text chat, screen or slide sharing, and a whiteboard. Once the focus group is underway, questions and answers occur in "real time" in a remarkably lively setting. Participants comment spontaneously—verbally, via text messaging, or both. Researchers can "sit in" on the focus group from anywhere, seeing and hearing every respondent. Or they can review a recorded version at a later date.

Although the use of online marketing research is growing rapidly, both quantitative and qualitative Web-based research does have some drawbacks. One major problem is controlling who's in the online sample. Without seeing respondents, it's difficult to know who they really are. To overcome such sample and context problems, many online research firms use opt-in communities and respondent panels. For example, Zoomerang offers an online consumer and business panel profiled on more than 500 attributes.[26] Alternatively, many companies are now developing their own custom social networks and using them to gain customer inputs and insights. A primary qualitative Web-based research approach is **online focus groups** (see Marketing at Work 4.1).

Perhaps the most explosive issue facing online researchers concerns consumer privacy. Some critics fear that unethical researchers will use the e-mail addresses and confidential responses gathered through surveys to sell products after the research is completed. They are concerned about the use of technologies that collect personal information online without the respondents' consent. Failure to address such privacy issues could result in angry, less-cooperative consumers and increased government intervention. Despite these concerns, most industry insiders predict healthy growth for online marketing research.[27]

Sampling Plan

Sample
A segment of the population selected for marketing research to represent the population as a whole.

Marketing researchers usually draw conclusions about large groups of consumers by studying a small sample of the total consumer population. A **sample** is a segment of the population selected for marketing research to represent the population as a whole. Ideally, the sample should be representative so that the researcher can make accurate estimates of the thoughts and behaviors of the larger population.

Designing the sample requires three decisions. First, *who* is to be studied (what *sampling unit*)? The answer to this question is not always obvious. For example, to learn about the decision-making process for a family automobile purchase, should the subject be the husband, wife, other family members, dealership salespeople, or all of these? The researcher must determine what information is needed and who is most likely to have it.

Second, *how many* people should be included (what *sample size*)? Large samples give more reliable results than small samples. However, larger samples usually cost more, and it is not necessary to sample the entire target market or even a large portion to get reliable results. If well chosen, samples of less than 1 percent of a population can often give good reliability.

Third, *how* should the people in the sample be *chosen* (what *sampling procedure*)? ■ **Table 4.4** describes different kinds of samples. Using *probability samples*, each population member has a known chance of being included in the sample, and researchers can calculate confidence limits for sampling error. But when probability sampling costs too much or takes too much time, marketing researchers often take *nonprobability samples*, even though their sampling error cannot be measured. These varied ways of drawing samples have different costs and time limitations as well as different accuracy and statistical properties. Which method is best depends on the needs of the research project.

Marketing at Work 4.1

Research at Zay-Dee, Abu Dhabi, United Arab Emirates (UAE)

Zay-Dee for Integrated Engineering Creations is based in Abu Dhabi, the oil rich capital of the United Arab Emirates (UAE), which is situated in the northeastern part of the Arabian Peninsula. The country is made up of seven emirates including Abu Dhabi, Dubai, Sharjah, Ajman, Umm Al Quwain, Fujairah, and Ras Al Khaimah. The population of Abu Dhabi is expected to reach 3 million by 2030. The well-publicized "Plan Abu Dhabi 2030: Urban Structure Framework Plan" has focused on sustainable economic growth, preservation of the environment, and development into a world-class city while preserving and promoting the Emirati way of life and heritage. The plan will ensure that in the contemporary expression of an Arab city, its heritage and culture are maintained. It was the business opportunities that such a city presented to investors that caught the eye of Zay-Dee's young entrepreneurial CEO, Engineer, Asma Jamal Al Dharif. She was particularly interested in providing "Integrated Engineering Creations" that will ensure the contemporary expression to Abu Dhabi's heritage and culture is maintained.

Zay-Dee is a separate business entity of Al-Reyadah International Group (RIG), a family-owned business based in the United Arab Emirates. Al-Reyadah is a service-oriented company founded by Mr. Jamal Al Dharif (Chairman and CEO). At present there are 13 business entities in different industries. Some of these businesses are in facility management, architecture, landscape and interior design, health safety and environment, event organizing, and office furniture supplies, to name a few.

RIG's vision is to be the best service provider in the rapidly growing capital city, Abu Dhabi. Jamal Al Dharif is a qualified chemical engineer from Liverpool University (UK). He previously worked as a general manager at Abu Dhabi National Oil Company (ADNOC) Distribution. He excelled in the field of management and marketing. Under his stewardship the ADNOC business expanded rapidly. It was this experience along with his business and marketing skills and his sharp business acumen that enabled him to establish a successful family business upon his retirement from ADNOC.

The Zay-Dee business unit concentrates on the exterior, interior, and landscaping consultancy business. Zay-Dee provides customized and personalized advanced solutions for its industry. CEO Asma Jamal Al Dharif is Jamal Al Dharif's daughter. She is an interior design engineer by profession. She is also the deputy CEO of the parent group, RIG. She contributes to Zay-Dee with her professional discipline skills and her long experience working closely with the founder of the RIG group.

Zay-Dee's vision is to create a unique local architectural brand that affects global trends. The brand "Zay-Dee" means "my Zayed" referring to the late Shaikh Zayed Bin Sultan Al Nahyan, the founder and former ruler of the UAE.

Since Zay-Dee's inception in 2008, CEO Al Dharif, an Emirati National, along with her dedicated multicultural workforce is focused on understanding the marketplace and customer. She feels knowledge of the target market customer is vital to her business that is competing in the knowledge industry, especially in the

Face the challenge with the right advice !

Zay-Dee • زي دي

▲ Companies such as Zay-Dee have embraced technology by developing tailored web portals, and customized online community chat groups and focus groups. Diverse research methods allow the company to gain consumer insights and to offer them a direct input into the company's services - quickly and cheaply.

rapidly expanding and modernizing cities in the UAE and in the global markets. With regards to the UAE market, she is aware how important knowledge of the local culture is to arrive at the right decision in terms of design, selections, deciding the specifications, future planning, and managing investment. She has used traditional market research and some online market research. The traditional triangular market research methods used so far have been: in-depth interviews, questionnaire surveys, and case studies. What Zay-Dee has found out is the importance of adapting the soul of the UAE heritage with the trends in the marketplace. For example, Zay-Dee has submitted a design for the construction of a heart-shaped Olympic sports village for disabled athletes in which the "social gathering hub" (open plus built form) is in the form of a "heart" in aerial view. The heart shape symbolizes an emotional connection with the disabled participants.

In another example, a local hospital wanted the hospital rooms of royal guests to be refurbished. Modernized version of traditional building elements and Ghaf trees (a tree native to UAE desert) were used to keep with the soul of the heritage to touch the senses of the UAE people. CEO Al Dharif is very keen on adding online research techniques to complement the current traditional research techniques she uses and sees this as an important competitive advantage for Zay-Dee. However, she has used **online community chat groups** within Abu Dhabi and now wants to use other online research techniques such as: **online customer satisfaction and other surveys** on Zay-Dee's website to gather opinions of Zay-Dee services. The response rate can be fast and

(continued)

relatively inexpensive compared with traditional surveys; with **online focus groups** she can bring together current and potential customers who live in several countries to discuss global trends that would have an impact on her business; a new development is to monitor positive or adverse comments on Zay-Dee's business on **social media sites** because if the comments are adverse a quick response can be made to counteract it.

As most of the customers of Zay-Dee are other businesses (B2B), they decided to create an **online web-portal** for one of their projects involving a selected group of specialized professionals from around the globe. Zay-Dee was appointed as the concept designer and cultural advisor. This involved joint effort by the various specialized professionals. This web portal has controlled access to the contents shared by the members that enables control over copyright of the matter published on it. Such web portals enable each member of the team to share their information under various classifications (in Zay-Dee's case, documents, drawings, images, and so on) with due credit given to the contributor, a common task pad, a calendar of events, and notifications. These types of web portals constitute an ideal platform for research and discussion involving cultural surveys, taking into consideration the following: limited access only to the professionals involved, confidentiality of the contents, copyright, ease of access, and cost effectiveness, uniting members across the globe.

Sources: Based on Information from www.upc.gov.ae/en/MasterPlan/PlanAbuDhabi 2030.aspx

Research Instruments

In collecting primary data, marketing researchers have a choice of two main research instruments—the *questionnaire* and *mechanical devices*.

Questionnaires. The *questionnaire* is by far the most common instrument, whether administered in person, by phone, or online. Questionnaires are very flexible—there are many ways to ask questions. *Closed-end questions* include all the possible answers, and subjects make choices among them. Examples include multiple-choice questions and scale questions. *Open-end questions* allow respondents to answer in their own words. In a survey of airline users, Southwest might simply ask, "What is your opinion of Southwest Airlines?" Or it might ask people to complete a sentence: "When I choose an airline, the most important consideration is . . ." These and other kinds of open-end questions often reveal more than closed-end questions because they do not limit respondents' answers.

Open-end questions are especially useful in exploratory research, when the researcher is trying to find out *what* people think but not measuring *how many* people think in a certain way. Closed-end questions, on the other hand, provide answers that are easier to interpret and tabulate.

■ **Table 4.4** Types of Samples

Probability Sample	
Simple random sample	Every member of the population has a known and equal chance of selection.
Stratified random sample	The population is divided into mutually exclusive groups (such as age groups), and random samples are drawn from each group.
Cluster (area) sample	The population is divided into mutually exclusive groups (such as blocks), and the researcher draws a sample of the groups to interview.
Nonprobability Sample	
Convenience sample	The researcher selects the easiest population members from which to obtain information.
Judgment sample	The researcher uses his or her judgment to select population members who are good prospects for accurate information.
Quota sample	The researcher finds and interviews a prescribed number of people in each of several categories.

Researchers should also use care in the *wording* and *ordering* of questions. They should use simple, direct, unbiased wording. Questions should be arranged in a logical order. The first question should create interest if possible, and difficult or personal questions should be asked last so that respondents do not become defensive.

Mechanical Instruments. Although questionnaires are the most common research instrument, researchers also use *mechanical instruments* to monitor consumer behavior. Nielsen Media Research attaches *people meters* to television sets, cable boxes, and satellite systems in selected homes to record who watches which programs. Retailers use *checkout scanners* to record shoppers' purchases.

Other mechanical devices measure subjects' physical responses. For example, advertisers use eye cameras to study viewers' eye movements while watching ads—at what points their eyes focus first and how long they linger on any given ad component. IBM's BlueEyes technology interprets human facial reactions by tracking pupil, eyebrow, and mouth movements. BlueEyes offers a host of potential marketing uses, such as marketing machines that "know how you feel" and react accordingly. An elderly man squints at a bank's ATM screen and the font size doubles almost instantly. A woman at a shopping center kiosk smiles at a travel ad, prompting the device to print out a travel discount coupon.[28]

▲Mechanical measures of consumer response: Some marketers apply neuromarketing—peering into consumers' minds by measuring brain activity to discover how they respond to brands and marketing.

Still other researchers are applying ▲"neuromarketing," measuring brain activity to learn how consumers feel and respond. Marketing scientists using MRI scans have learned that "strong brands trigger activity in parts of the brain associated with self-identification, positive emotions, and rewards." Several high-tech firms—such as EmSense, NeuroFocus, and Sands Research—now help firms peer into the inner workings of their customers' brains and emotions.

According to one observer, it "turns out the Nike's swoosh is more than just a feel-good brand logo. It actually lights up your brain." Similarly, when researchers strapped electrode-loaded caps on the noggins of test subjects during the recent Super Bowl to measure advertising engagement, they learned that brain activity soared for some ads but lagged for others.[29] In fact, Coca-Cola worked with EmSense before the Super Bowl to help it decide which ads would work best:

In the weeks leading up to the game, Coca-Cola produced about a dozen new ads for possible placement and asked EmSense to help it make the right choices. The EmSense device, shaped like a thin plastic headband, reads brain waves and monitors the breathing, heart rate, blinking, and skin temperatures of consumers who preview ads to measure their emotional and cognitive responses. The continuous measures help researchers to decipher consumer feelings and reactions at each moment of any given ad. According to Coca-Cola's North America CMO, the device not only helped whittle down the list of spots, it also aided in editing the two ads chosen to air, shoring up cognitive weak spots. For example, the music in one ad was adjusted in the days leading up to the game to build more of a crescendo than in the original version of the spot. Neuromarketing "provides you with more natural and unedited responses than you get when you force people through the cognitive loop of having to [remember and tell you] how they feel," says the Coca-Cola executive. "It's a great new tool."[30]

Although neuromarketing techniques can measure consumer involvement and emotional responses second by second, such brain responses can be difficult to interpret. Thus, neuromarketing is usually used in combination with other research approaches to gain a more complete picture of what goes on inside consumers' heads.

Implementing the Research Plan

The researcher next puts the marketing research plan into action. This involves collecting, processing, and analyzing the information. Data collection can be carried out by the company's marketing research staff or by outside firms. Researchers should watch closely to make sure that the plan is implemented correctly. They must guard against problems with interacting with respondents, with the quality of participants' response, and with interviewers who make mistakes or take shortcuts.

Researchers must also process and analyze the collected data to isolate important information and insight. They need to check data for accuracy and completeness and code it for analysis. The researchers then tabulate the results and compute statistical measures.

Interpreting and Reporting the Findings

The market researcher must now interpret the findings, draw conclusions, and report them to management. The researcher should not try to overwhelm managers with numbers and fancy statistical techniques. Rather, the researcher should present important findings and insights that are useful in the major decisions faced by management.

However, interpretation should not be left only to the researchers. They are often experts in research design and statistics, but the marketing manager knows more about the problem and the decisions that must be made. The best research means little if the manager blindly accepts faulty interpretations from the researcher. Similarly, managers may be biased—they might tend to accept research results that show what they expected and to reject those that they did not expect or hope for. In many cases, findings can be interpreted in different ways, and discussions between researchers and managers will help point to the best interpretations. Thus, managers and researchers must work together closely when interpreting research results, and both must share responsibility for the research process and resulting decisions.

· ·

◆ **Speed Bump:** Linking the Concepts

Whew! We've covered a lot of territory. Hold up a minute, take a breather, and see if you can apply the marketing research process you've just studied.

- What specific kinds of research can Red Bull's brand managers use to learn more about its customers preferences and buying behaviors? Sketch out a brief research plan for assessing potential reactions to a new Red Bull enhanced-water line.
- Could you use the marketing research process to analyze your career opportunities and job possibilities? (Think of yourself as a "product" and employers as potential "customers.") What would your research plan look like?

· ·

ANALYZING AND USING MARKETING INFORMATION (pp 148–151)

Information gathered in internal databases and through competitive marketing intelligence and marketing research usually requires additional analysis. And managers may need help applying the information to gain customer and market insights that will improve their marketing decisions. This help may include advanced statistical analysis to learn more about the relationships within a set of data. Information analysis might also involve the application of analytical models that will help marketers make better decisions.

Once the information has been processed and analyzed, it must be made available to the right decision makers at the right time. In the following sections, we look deeper into analyzing and using marketing information.

Author Comment 》》
We've talked generally about managing customer relationships throughout the book. But here, "Customer Relationship Management" (CRM) has a much narrower data-management meaning. It refers to capturing and using customer data from all sources to manage customer interactions and build customer relationships.

Customer relationship management (CRM)
Managing detailed information about individual customers and carefully managing customer "touch points" in order to maximize customer loyalty.

Customer Relationship Management (CRM)

The question of how best to analyze and use individual customer data presents special problems. Most companies are awash in information about their customers. In fact, smart companies capture information at every possible customer *touch point*. These touch points include customer purchases, sales force contacts, service and support calls, Web site visits, satisfaction surveys, credit and payment interactions, market research studies—every contact between the customer and the company.

Unfortunately, this information is usually scattered widely across the organization. It is buried deep in the separate databases and records of different company departments. To overcome such problems, many companies are now turning to **customer relationship management (CRM)** to manage detailed information about individual customers and carefully manage customer touch points in order to maximize customer loyalty.

CRM first burst onto the scene in the early 2000s. Many companies rushed in, implementing overly ambitious CRM programs that produced disappointing results and many failures. More recently, however, companies are moving ahead more cautiously and implementing CRM systems that really work. Last year, companies worldwide spent $7.8 billion on CRM systems from companies such as Oracle, Microsoft, Salesforce.com, and SAS, up 14.2 percent from the previous year. By 2012, they will spend an estimated $13.3 billion on CRM systems.[31]

CRM consists of sophisticated software and analytical tools that integrate customer information from all sources, analyze it in depth, and apply the results to build stronger customer relationships. CRM integrates everything that a company's sales, service, and marketing teams know about individual customers to provide a 360-degree view of the customer relationship.

CRM analysts develop *data warehouses* and use sophisticated *data mining* techniques to unearth the riches hidden in customer data. A data warehouse is a companywide electronic database of finely detailed customer information that needs to be sifted through for gems. The purpose of a data warehouse is not just to gather information, but to pull it together into a central, accessible location. Then, once the data warehouse brings the data together, the company uses high-powered data mining techniques to sift through the mounds of data and dig out interesting findings about customers.

These findings often lead to marketing opportunities. For example, Wal-Mart's huge database provides deep insights for marketing decisions. A few years ago, as Hurricane Ivan roared toward the Florida coast, reports one observer, the giant retailer "knew exactly what to rush onto the shelves of stores in the hurricane's path—strawberry Pop Tarts. By mining years of sales data from just prior to other hurricanes, [Wal-Mart] figured out that shoppers would stock up on Pop Tarts—which don't require refrigeration or cooking."[32]

Grocery chain Kroger works with data mining firm Dunnhumby, which it co-owns with successful London-based retailer Tesco, to dig deeply into data obtained from customer loyalty cards. ▲It uses the customer insights gained for a everything from targeting coupons to locating and stocking its stores:

> Lisa Williams has never liked sorting through coupons, and she no longer has to at Kroger grocery stores. Every few weeks, a personalized assortment of coupons arrives from Kroger in Williams' Elizabethtown, Kentucky, mailbox for items she usually loads into her cart: Capri Sun drinks for her two children, Reynolds Wrap foil, Hellmann's mayonnaise. While Kroger is building loyalty—with 95 percent of a recent mailing tailored to specific households—Williams is saving money without searching through dozens of pages of coupons. Although the recent recession revived penny-pinching, Americans are still redeeming only 1 percent to 3 percent of paper coupons. In contrast, Kroger says as many as *half* the coupons it sends regular customers do get used.
>
> Many retailers have loyalty cards and some offer "instant coupons" at checkout based on buyers' habits. But Kroger digs deeper into the reams of information from its more than 55 million shopper cards and uses the resulting insights in more ways than other retailers do. Kroger uses the data mining results, augmented with customer interviews, to guide strategies for tailored promotions, pricing, placement, and even stocking variations from

▲ **Grocery chain Kroger digs deeply into data obtained from customer loyalty cards. It uses the customer insights gained for a everything from targeting coupons to locating and stocking its stores.**

store to store. Kroger says individual treatment builds loyalty by creating more value for customers and making them feel more appreciated. According to an industry analyst, Kroger's ability to turn data into insights creates customer loyalty and drives profitable sales. Adds Kroger's CEO, "This level of personalization is a direct link to our customers that no other U.S. grocery retailer can [match]."[33]

By using CRM to understand customers better, companies can provide higher levels of customer service and develop deeper customer relationships. They can use CRM to pinpoint high-value customers, target them more effectively, cross-sell the company's products, and create offers tailored to specific customer requirements.

CRM benefits don't come without costs or risk, either in collecting the original customer data or in maintaining and mining it. The most common CRM mistake is to view CRM only as a technology and software solution. But technology alone cannot build profitable customer relationships. "CRM is not a technology solution—you can't achieve . . . improved customer relationships by simply slapping in some software," says a CRM expert. Instead, CRM is just one part of an effective overall *customer relationship management strategy.* "Focus on the *R*," advises the expert. "Remember, a relationship is what CRM is all about."[34]

When it works, the benefits of CRM can far outweigh the costs and risks. Based on a study by SAP, customers using its mySAP CRM software reported an average 10 percent increase in customer retention and a 30 percent increase in sales leads. Overall, 90 percent of the companies surveyed increased in value from use of the software and reported an attractive return on investment. The study's conclusion: "CRM pays off."[35]

Distributing and Using Marketing Information

Marketing information has no value until it is used to gain customer insights and make better marketing decisions. Thus, the marketing information system must make the information readily available to the managers and others who need it. In some cases, this means providing managers with regular performance reports, intelligence updates, and reports on the results of research studies.

But marketing managers may also need nonroutine information for special situations and on-the-spot decisions. For example, a sales manager having trouble with a large customer may want a summary of the account's sales and profitability over the past year. Or a retail store manager who has run out of a best-selling product may want to know the current inventory levels in the chain's other stores. These days, therefore, information distribution involves entering information into databases and making it available in a timely, user-friendly way.

Many firms use a company *intranet* to facilitate this process. The intranet provides ready access to research information, reports, shared work documents, contact information for employees and other stakeholders, and more. For example, iGo, a catalog and Web retailer, integrates incoming customer service calls with up-to-date database information about customers' Web purchases and e-mail inquiries. By accessing this information on the intranet while speaking with the customer, iGo's service representatives can get a well-rounded picture of each customer's purchasing history and previous contacts with the company.

In addition, companies are increasingly allowing key customers and value-network members to access account, product, and other data on demand through *extranets.* Suppliers, customers, resellers, and select other network members may access a company's extranet to update their accounts, arrange purchases, and check orders against inventories to improve customer service. For example, Penske Truck Leasing's extranet site, MyFleetAtPenske.com, lets Penske customers access all of the data about their fleets in one spot and provides an array of tools and applications designed to help fleet managers manage their Penske accounts and maximize efficiency. And Target's PartnersOnline extranet lets the retailer's supplier/partners review current sales, inventory, delivery, and forecasting data. Such information sharing helps Target, its suppliers, and its customer by elevating the performance of the supply chain.[36]

Thanks to modern technology, today's marketing managers can gain direct access to the information system at any time and from virtually any location. They can tap into the system while working at a home office, from a hotel room, or from the local Starbucks through a wireless network—anyplace where they can turn on a laptop or BlackBerry. Such systems allow managers to get the information they need directly and quickly and to tailor it to their own needs. From just about anywhere, they can obtain information from company or outside databases, analyze it using statistical software, prepare reports and presentations, and communicate directly with others in the network.

 Speed Bump: Linking the Concepts

Let's stop here for a bit, think back, and be certain that you've got the "big picture" concerning marketing information systems (MIS).

- What's the overall goal of an MIS? How are the individual components linked and what does each contribute? Take another look at Figure 4.1—it provides a good organizing framework for the entire chapter.
- Apply the MIS framework to Converse (a Nike company). How might Converse go about assessing marketing managers' information needs, developing the needed information, and helping managers to analyze and use the information to gain actionable customer and market insights?

Author Comment >>
We'll finish up the chapter by examining three special marketing information topics.

OTHER MARKETING INFORMATION CONSIDERATIONS
(pp 151–157)

This section discusses marketing information in two special contexts: marketing research in small businesses and nonprofit organizations and international marketing research. Finally, we look at public policy and ethics issues in marketing research.

Marketing Research in Small Businesses and Nonprofit Organizations

Just like larger firms, small organizations need market information and the customer and market insights that it can provide. Start-up businesses need information about their potential customers, industries, competitors, unfilled needs, and reactions to new market offers. Existing small businesses must track changes in customer needs and wants, reactions to new products, and changes in the competitive environment.

Managers of small businesses and nonprofit organizations often think that marketing research can be done only by experts in large companies with big research budgets. True, large-scale research studies are beyond the budgets of most small businesses. However, many of the marketing research techniques discussed in this chapter also can be used by smaller organizations in a less formal manner and at little

▲**Before opening Bibbentuckers dry cleaner, owner Robert Byerly conducted research to gain insights into what customers wanted. First on the list: quality.**

or no expense. ▲Consider how one small-business owner conducted market research on a shoestring before even opening his doors:[37]

> After a string of bad experiences with his local dry cleaner, Robert Byerley decided to open his own dry-cleaning business. But before jumping in, he conducted plenty of market research. He needed a key customer insight: How would he make his cleaners stand out? To start, Byerley spent an entire week in the library and online, researching the dry-cleaning industry. To get input from potential customers, using a marketing firm, Byerley held focus groups on the store's name, look, and brochure. He also took clothes to the 15 best competing cleaners in town and had focus group members critique their work. Based on his research, he made a list of features for his new business. First on his list: quality. His business would stand behind everything it did. Not on the list: cheap prices. Creating the perfect dry-cleaning establishment simply didn't fit with a discount operation.
>
> With his research complete, Byerley opened Bibbentuckers, a high-end dry cleaner positioned on high-quality service and convenience. It featured a bank-like drive-through area with curbside delivery. A computerized bar code system read customer cleaning preferences and tracked clothes all the way through the cleaning process. Byerley added other differentiators, such as decorative awnings, TV screens, and refreshments (even "candy for the kids and a doggy treat for your best friend"). "I wanted a place . . . that paired five-star service and quality with an establishment that didn't look like a dry cleaner," he says. The market research yielded results. Today, Bibbentuckers is a thriving three-store operation.

"Too [few] small-business owners have a . . . marketing mind-set," says a small-business consultant. "You have to think like Procter & Gamble. What would they do before launching a new product? They would find out who their customer is and who their competition is."[38]

Thus, small businesses and not-for-profit organizations can obtain good marketing insights through observation or informal surveys using small convenience samples. Also, many associations, local media, and government agencies provide special help to small organizations. For example, the U.S. Small Business Administration offers dozens of free publications and a Web site (www.sba.gov) that give advice on topics ranging from starting, financing, and expanding a small business to ordering business cards. Other excellent Web resources for small businesses include the U.S. Census Bureau (www.census.gov) and the Bureau of Economic Analysis (www.bea.gov). Finally, small businesses can collect a considerable amount of information at very little cost online. They can scour competitor and customer Web sites and use Internet search engines to research specific companies and issues.

In summary, secondary data collection, observation, surveys, and experiments can all be used effectively by small organizations with small budgets. However, although these informal research methods are less complex and less costly, they still must be conducted with care. Managers must think carefully about the objectives of the research, formulate questions in advance, recognize the biases introduced by smaller samples and less skilled researchers, and conduct the research systematically.[39]

International Marketing Research

International marketing research has grown tremendously over the past decade. In 1995, the top 25 global marketing research organizations had total combined revenues of $5.7 billion, with 45 percent of these revenues coming from outside companies' home countries. By 2007, total revenues for these organizations had grown to $17.5 billion, and the out-of-home-country share had grown to more than 57 percent.[40]

International marketing researchers follow the same steps as domestic researchers, from defining the research problem and developing a research plan to interpreting and reporting the results. However, these researchers often face more and different problems. Whereas domestic researchers deal with fairly homogenous markets within a single country, international researchers deal with diverse markets in many different countries. These markets often vary greatly in their levels of economic development, cultures and customs, and buying patterns.

In many foreign markets, the international researcher may have a difficult time finding good secondary data. Whereas U.S. marketing researchers can obtain reliable secondary data from dozens of domestic research services, many countries have almost no research services at all. Some of the largest international research services do operate in many countries. ▲For example, The Nielsen Company (the world's largest marketing research company) has offices in more than 100 countries, from Schaumburg, Illinois, to Hong Kong to Nicosia, Cyprus.[41] However, most research firms operate in only a relative handful of countries. Thus, even when secondary information is available, it usually must be obtained from many different sources on a country-by-country basis, making the information difficult to combine or compare.

▲Some of the largest research services firms have large international organizations. The Nielsen Company has offices in more than 100 countries, here Germany and Japan.

Because of the scarcity of good secondary data, international researchers often must collect their own primary data. For example, they may find it difficult simply to develop good samples. U.S. researchers can use current telephone directories, e-mail lists, census tract data, and any of several sources of socioeconomic data to construct samples. However, such information is largely lacking in many countries.

Once the sample is drawn, the U.S. researcher usually can reach most respondents easily by telephone, by mail, on the Internet, or in person. Reaching respondents is often not so easy in other parts of the world. Researchers in Mexico cannot rely on telephone, Internet, and mail data collection—most data collection is door to door and concentrated in three or four of the largest cities. In some countries, few people have phones or personal computers. For example, whereas there are 73 Internet users per 100 people in the United States, there are only 22 Internet users per 100 people in Mexico. In Kenya, the numbers drop to 8 Internet users per 100 people. In some countries, the postal system is notoriously unreliable. In Brazil, for instance, an estimated 30 percent of the mail is never delivered. In many developing countries, poor roads and transportation systems make certain areas hard to reach, making personal interviews difficult and expensive.[42]

Cultural differences from country to country cause additional problems for international researchers. Language is the most obvious obstacle. For example, questionnaires must be prepared in one language and then translated into the languages of each country researched. Responses then must be translated back into the original language for analysis and interpretation. This adds to research costs and increases the risks of error.

Translating a questionnaire from one language to another is anything but easy. Many idioms, phrases, and statements mean different things in different cultures. For example, a Danish executive noted, "Check this out by having a different translator put back into English what you've translated from English. You'll get the shock of your life. I remember [an example in which] 'out of sight, out of mind' had become 'invisible things are insane.'"[43]

Consumers in different countries also vary in their attitudes toward marketing research. People in one country may be very willing to respond; in other countries, nonresponse can be a major problem. Customs in some countries may prohibit people from talking with strangers. In certain cultures, research questions often are considered too personal. For example, in many Latin American countries, people may feel embarrassed to talk with researchers about their choices of shampoo, deodorant, or other personal care products. Similarly, in many Muslim countries, mixed-gender focus groups are taboo, as is videotaping female-only focus groups. Even when respondents are *willing* to respond, they may not be *able* to because of high functional illiteracy rates.

Despite these problems, as global marketing grows, global companies have little choice but to conduct such international marketing research. Although the costs and problems associated with international research may be high, the costs of not doing it—in terms of missed opportunities and mistakes—might be even higher. Once recognized, many of the problems associated with international marketing research can be overcome or avoided.

Public Policy and Ethics in Marketing Research

Most marketing research benefits both the sponsoring company and its consumers. Through marketing research, companies learn more about consumers' needs, resulting in more satisfying products and services and stronger customer relationships. However, the misuse of marketing research can also harm or annoy consumers. Two major public policy and ethics issues in marketing research are intrusions on consumer privacy and the misuse of research findings.

Intrusions on Consumer Privacy

Many consumers feel positive about marketing research and believe that it serves a useful purpose. Some actually enjoy being interviewed and giving their opinions. However, others strongly resent or even mistrust marketing research. They don't like being interrupted by researchers. They worry that marketers are building huge databases full of personal information about customers. Or they fear that researchers might use sophisticated techniques to probe our deepest feelings, peek over our shoulders as we shop, or eavesdrop on our conversations and then use this knowledge to manipulate our buying.

There are no easy answers when it comes to marketing research and privacy. For example, is it a good or bad thing that marketers track and analyze consumers' Web clicks and target ads to individuals based on their browsing behavior? (See Marketing at Work 4.2.) Should we applaud or resent companies that monitor consumer discussions on YouTube, Facebook, Twitter, or other public social networks in an effort to be more responsive? Remember the Radian6 and Dell example earlier in this chapter?

Last spring, Canadian blogger Carman Pirie questioned Dell's decision to begin selling its computers through Wal-Mart and wrote about it on his blog. Given Dell's previously successful direct-only sales model, Pirie didn't think selling machines through Wal-Mart was a smart strategy and he wasn't shy about sharing his thoughts. What he didn't expect was a reply from a Dell representative in the form of a comment on his blog post, explaining in great detail why Dell was working with Wal-Mart. "Within a couple of hours of posting . . . I got a response from Richard at Dell," said a duly impressed Pirie. "Here's Dell, based in Round Rock, Texas, interacting with a blogger in Halifax, Nova Scotia . . . within a three-hour window," he said.

Dell views tracking and responding to social media conversations as opportunities to engage consumers in helpful two-way conversations. However, some disconcerted consumers might see experiences such as Pirie's as an intrusion of privacy. Although Dell tracks only public forums, it does not inform consumers or obtain their consent. Interestingly, many consumers don't seem to mind. Consumers often moan that companies do not listen to them. Perhaps the monitoring of online discussions can provide an answer to that problem.[44]

Marketing at Work 4.2

Tracking Consumers on the Web: Smart Targeting or a Little Creepy?

On the Internet today, everybody knows who you are. In fact, legions of Internet companies also know your gender, your age, the neighborhood you live in, that you like pickup trucks, and that you spent, say, three hours and 43 seconds on a Web site for pet lovers on a rainy day in January. All that data streams through myriad computer networks, where it's sorted, cataloged, analyzed, and then used to deliver ads aimed squarely at you, potentially anywhere you travel on the Web. It's called *behavioral targeting*—tracking consumers' online browsing behavior and using it to target ads to them.

Information about what consumers do while they're trolling the vast expanse of the Internet—what searches they make, the sites they visit, what they buy—is pure gold to advertisers. And companies such as Google, Yahoo!, Microsoft's MSN, and AOL are busy mining that gold, helping advertisers to target ads based on just about every move you make on the Web. Online advertisers are now deploying a new breed of supersmart, supertargeted display ads geared to individual Web-browsing behavior.

Using electronic markers on people's Web browsers called cookies, marketers have amassed a staggering amount of data about users. All that browsing data, blended with other online user information, can help marketers predict consumer behavior and target their ads more precisely. Say you spent time at Yahoo! Autos sizing up cars based on fuel efficiency, then clicked over to Yahoo!'s Green Center to read about alternative fuels, then looked at cars on eBay (which has a partnership with Yahoo!). Yahoo! can probably predict your next move. In fact, the company claims that it can tell with 75 percent certainty which of the 300,000 monthly visitors to Yahoo! Autos will actually purchase a car within the next three months. And the next time you visit Yahoo! Sports or Finance, you'll likely see ads for hybrid cars.

Also moving quickly into online display advertising are a special breed of behavioral targeting advertising agencies, such as Audience Science (http://audiencescience.com) and BlueLithium (www.bluelithium.com). To get an even broader view of what consumers are thinking and doing online, such agencies track consumer behavior across multiple Web sites. These companies "are, in effect, taking the trail of crumbs people leave behind as they move around the Internet, and then analyzing them to anticipate people's next steps," says an analyst.

This lets them merge audience data from one group of sites with ad placements on another. So if you surf home lawn and garden sites, don't be surprised to see ads for Scotts lawn products the next time you visit Weather.com. Or if you place a cell phone in an Amazon.com shopping cart but don't buy it, expect to see some ads for that very type of phone the next time you visit your favorite ESPN site to catch up on the latest sports scores.

But what about consumer privacy? Yup. As you've no doubt already considered, that's the downside and the biggest danger to the rapidly expanding world of behavioral targeting. As the practice becomes more common, it faces growing consumer backlash. One observer calls it "the dark art of behavioral

▲ Behavioral targeting: Wherever you go on the Internet, marketers are looking over your shoulder, then targeting you with ads based on your Web browsing behavior. Is it smart marketing or just "a little bit creepy"?

ad targeting"—eavesdropping on consumers without their knowledge or consent. "When you start to get into the details, it's scarier than you might suspect," says the director of a consumer privacy rights group. "We're recording preferences, hopes, worries, and fears."

In fact, the government has already stepped in to protect consumers from advertisers going too far. The Federal Trade Commission recently issued recommended voluntary guidelines, urging Web sites that apply behavioral advertising techniques to clearly and concisely spell out what they are doing and to give customers a simple way to opt out. The guidelines also suggested companies put limits on how long they store user information.

Most behavioral targeters have willingly complied with these guidelines. For example, Google labels ads so that people can click to find out more about how it places them. It also provides an online tool called the Ads Preferences Manager, which lets people view, delete, or add interest categories or opt out of ad-targeting cookies altogether. Yahoo! offers similar choices. And to protect consumer privacy further, both companies have agreed to limit the time they hold personally identifiable information to 90 days.

Despite privacy concerns, proponents claim that behavioral ad targeting benefits more than abuses consumers. Such targeting takes information from users' Web browsing behavior and feeds back ads that are more relevant to their needs and interests. Yahoo! calls the practice "interest-matched advertising"; at Google, it's "interest-based advertising." According to Google, people might even welcome more targeted ads. "We believe there is real value in seeing ads about the things that interest you," says a Google executive. "Most users prefer more relevant ads to less relevant ads. If, for example, you love

(continued)

adventure travel and therefore visited venture travel sites, Google could show you more ads for activities like hiking trips to Patagonia or African safaris."

Although the practice may seem sinister to some consumers, advertisers sure like it. According to one estimate, by reaching the right person at the right time with the right ad, dollars spent on behavioral targeting yield a 37 percent return on investment. And behavioral targeting agency BlueLithium claims that 37 of its targeted ads achieve results comparable to 337 nontargeted ones. Still, it won't be easy to maintain consumer trust while at the same time walking the fine line between personalization and privacy. And as more and more companies enter the behavioral targeting ad space, the chances of the tactic getting a bad name grow.

"We have something new and powerful," says an industry executive, "and there are likely to be people who abuse it."

Abusive or beneficial, it'll be a hard sell to consumers. In a recent survey, when asked if they were comfortable with behavioral targeting, only 28 percent of respondents said they were. More than half said they were not. As one analyst observes, following consumers online and stalking them with ads just "feels a little creepy."

Sources. Based on information found in Robert D. Hof, "Behavioral Targeting: Google Pulls out the Stops," *BusinessWeek*, March 12, 2009, accessed at www.businessweek.com; Brian Morissey, "Aim High: Ad Targeting Moves to the Next Level," *Adweek*, January 14, 2008, pp. 49–50; Brian Morissey, "Limits of Search Lead Some to Web Behavior," *Adweek*, March 27, 2006, p. 11; Steve Smith, "Behavioral Targeting Could Change the Game," *EContent,* January–February 2007, p. 22; Louise Story, "To Aim Ads, Web Is Keeping a Closer Eye on You," *New York Times*, March 10, 2008; and Stephanie Clifford, "Many See Privacy on the Web As Big Issue, Survey Says," *New York Times,* March 16, 2009.

Consumers may also have been taken in by previous "research surveys" that actually turned out to be attempts to sell them something. Still other consumers confuse legitimate marketing research studies with promotional efforts and say "no" before the interviewer can even begin. Most, however, simply resent the intrusion. They dislike mail, telephone, or Web surveys that are too long or too personal or that interrupt them at inconvenient times.

Increasing consumer resentment has become a major problem for the marketing research industry, leading to lower survey response rates in recent years. Just as companies face the challenge of unearthing valuable but potentially sensitive consumer data while also maintaining consumer trust, consumers wrestle with the trade-offs between personalization and privacy. Although many consumers willingly exchange personal information for free services, easy credit, discounts, upgrades, and all sorts of rewards, they also worry about the growth in online identity theft. A recent study by TRUSTe, an organization that monitors privacy practices of Web sites, found that more than 90 percent of respondents view online privacy as a "really" or "somewhat" important issue. More than 75 percent agreed with the statement, "The Internet is not well regulated, and naïve users can easily be taken advantage of." So it's no surprise that they are now less than willing to reveal personal information on Web sites.[45]

The marketing research industry is considering several options for responding to this problem. ▲One example is the Marketing Research Association's "Your Opinion Counts" and "Respondent Bill of Rights" initiatives to educate consumers about the benefits of marketing research and to distinguish it from telephone selling and database building. The industry also has considered adopting broad standards, perhaps based on the International Chamber of Commerce's International Code of Marketing and Social Research Practice. This code outlines researchers' responsibilities to respondents and to the general public. For example, it says that researchers should make their names and addresses

▼**Consumer privacy: The Marketing Research Association has developed a "Respondent Bill of Rights" to help promote responsible marketing research.**

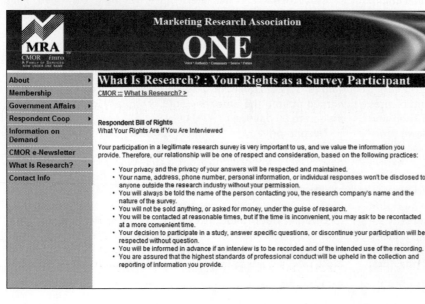

available to participants. It also bans companies from representing activities such as database compilation or sales and promotional pitches as research.[46]

Most major companies—including IBM, Facebook, Citigroup, American Express, and Microsoft—have now appointed a "chief privacy officer (CPO)," whose job is to safeguard the privacy of consumers who do business with the company. IBM's CPO claims that her job requires "multidisciplinary thinking and attitude." She needs to get all company departments, from technology, legal, and accounting to marketing and communications working together to safeguard customer privacy.[47]

American Express, which deals with a considerable volume of consumer information, has long taken privacy issues seriously. The company developed a set of formal privacy principles in 1991, and in 1998 it became one of the first companies to post privacy policies on its Web site. Its online Internet privacy statement tells customers in clear terms what information American Express collects and how it uses it, how it safeguards the information, and how it uses the information to market to its customers (with instructions on how to opt out).[48]

In the end, if researchers provide value in exchange for information, customers will gladly provide it. For example, Amazon.com's customers do not mind if the firm builds a database of products they buy in order to provide future product recommendations. This saves time and provides value. Similarly, Bizrate users gladly complete surveys rating online seller sites because they can view the overall ratings of others when making purchase decisions. The best approach is for researchers to ask only for the information they need, to use it responsibly to provide customer value, and to avoid sharing information without the customer's permission.

Misuse of Research Findings

Research studies can be powerful persuasion tools; companies often use study results as claims in their advertising and promotion. Today, however, many research studies appear to be little more than vehicles for pitching the sponsor's products. In fact, in some cases, the research surveys appear to have been designed just to produce the intended effect. Few advertisers openly rig their research designs or blatantly misrepresent the findings; most abuses tend to be subtle "stretches."

For example, the choice or wording in a survey can greatly affect the conclusions reached. One Black Flag survey asked: "A roach disk . . . poisons a roach slowly. The dying roach returns to the nest and after it dies is eaten by other roaches. In turn these roaches become poisoned and die. How effective do you think this type of product would be in killing roaches?" Not surprisingly, 79 percent said effective.[49]

Recognizing that surveys can be abused, several associations—including the American Marketing Association, Marketing Research Association, and the Council of American Survey Research Organizations (CASRO)—have developed codes of research ethics and standards of conduct. For example, the CASRO Code of Standards and Ethics for Survey Research outlines researcher responsibilities to respondents, including confidentiality, privacy, and avoidance of harassment. It also outlines major responsibilities in reporting results to clients and the public.[50]

In the end, however, unethical or inappropriate actions cannot simply be regulated away. Each company must accept responsibility for policing the conduct and reporting of its own marketing research to protect consumers' best interests and its own.

REST STOP
REVIEWING THE CONCEPTS

To create value for customers and to build meaningful relationships with them, marketers must first gain fresh, deep insights into what customers need and want. Such insights come from good marketing information. As a result of the recent explosion of marketing technology, compa-nies can now obtain great quantities of information, sometimes even too much. The challenge is to transform today's vast volume of consumer information into actionable customer and market insights. A company's marketing research and information system must do more than simply generate lots of information. The real value of marketing research and marketing information lies in how it is used—in the customer insights that it provides.

 Objective 1 Explain the importance of information in gaining insights about the marketplace and customers. **(pp 129–130)**

The marketing process starts with a complete understanding of the marketplace and consumer needs and wants. Thus, the company needs sound information in order to produce superior value and satisfaction for customers. The company also requires information on competitors, resellers, and other actors and forces in the marketplace. Increasingly, marketers are viewing information not only as an input for making better decisions but also as an important strategic asset and marketing tool.

 Objective 2 Define the marketing information system and discuss its parts. **(pp 130–134)**

The *marketing information system (MIS)* consists of people and procedures for assessing information needs, developing the needed information, and helping decision makers to use the information to generate and validate actionable customer and market insights. A well-designed information system begins and ends with users.

The MIS first *assesses information needs*. The MIS primarily serves the company's marketing and other managers, but it may also provide information to external partners. Then, the MIS *develops information* from internal databases, marketing intelligence activities, and marketing research. *Internal databases* provide information on the company's own operations and departments. Such data can be obtained quickly and cheaply but often needs to be adapted for marketing decisions. *Marketing intelligence* activities supply everyday information about developments in the external marketing environment. *Market research* consists of collecting information relevant to a specific marketing problem faced by the company. Lastly, the MIS helps users to analyze and use the information to develop customer insights, make marketing decisions, and manage customer relationships.

Objective 3 Outline the steps in the marketing research process. **(pp 134–148)**

The first step in the marketing research process involves *defining the problem and setting the research objectives,* which may be exploratory, descriptive, or causal research. The second step consists of *developing a research plan* for collecting data from primary and secondary sources. The third step calls for *implementing the marketing research plan* by gathering, processing, and analyzing the information. The fourth step consists of *interpreting and reporting the findings*. Additional information analysis helps marketing managers apply the information and provides them

with sophisticated statistical procedures and models from which to develop more rigorous findings.

Both *internal* and *external* secondary data sources often provide information more quickly and at a lower cost than primary data sources, and they can sometimes yield information that a company cannot collect by itself. However, needed information might not exist in secondary sources. Researchers must also evaluate secondary information to ensure that it is *relevant, accurate, current,* and *impartial*.

Primary research must also be evaluated for these features. Each primary data collection method—*observational, survey,* and *experimental*—has its own advantages and disadvantages. Similarly, each of the various research contact methods—mail, telephone, personal interview, and online—also has its own advantages and drawbacks.

 Objective 4 Explain how companies analyze and use marketing information. **(pp 148–151)**

Information gathered in internal databases and through marketing intelligence and marketing research usually requires more analysis. This may include advanced statistical analysis or the application of analytical models that will help marketers make better decisions. To analyze individual customer data, many companies have now acquired or developed special software and analysis techniques—called *customer relationship management (CRM)*—that integrate, analyze, and apply the mountains of individual customer data contained in their databases.

Marketing information has no value until it is used to make better marketing decisions. Thus, the MIS must make the information available to the managers and others who make marketing decisions or deal with customers. In some cases, this means providing regular reports and updates; in other cases it means making nonroutine information available for special situations and on-the-spot decisions. Many firms use company intranets and extranets to facilitate this process. Thanks to modern technology, today's marketing managers can gain direct access to the MIS at any time and from virtually any location.

Objective 5 Discuss the special issues some marketing researchers face, including public policy and ethics issues. **(pp 151–157)**

Some marketers face special marketing research situations, such as those conducting research in small business, not-for-profit, or international situations. Marketing research can be conducted effectively by small businesses and nonprofit organizations with limited budgets. International marketing researchers follow the same steps as domestic researchers but often face more and different problems. All organizations need to act responsibly to major public policy and ethical issues surrounding marketing research, including issues of intrusions on consumer privacy and misuse of research findings.

Navigating the Key Terms

Travel Log

Discussing the Issues

1. Discuss the real value of marketing research and marketing information and how that value is attained. (AACSB: Communication)

2. Discuss the sources of internal data and the advantages and disadvantages associated with this data. (AACSB: Communication)

3. Briefly describe the four steps in the marketing research process. (AACSB: Communication)

4. Discuss the decisions required when designing a sampling plan. (AACSB: Communication)

5. How does customer relationship management (CRM) help companies develop customer insights and deliver superior customer value? (AACSB: Communication)

6. What are the similarities and differences when conducting research in another country versus the domestic market? (AACSB: Communication)

Application Questions

1. Visit www.zoomerang.com or another free online Web survey site. Using the tools at the site, design a five-question survey on the entertainment opportunities in your area. Send the survey to ten friends and look at the results. What did you think of the online survey method? (AACSB: Communication; Use of IT; Reflective Thinking)

2. Focus groups are commonly used during exploratory research. A focus group interview entails gathering a group of people to discuss a specific topic. In a small group, research how to conduct a focus group interview and then conduct one with six to ten other students to learn what services your university could offer to better meet student needs. Assign one person in your group to be the moderator while the others observe and interpret the responses from the focus group participants. Present a report of what you learned from this research. (AACSB: Communication; Reflective Thinking)

3. Go to SRI Consulting's Web site (http://www.sric-bi.com), click on the VALS survey on the right side of the Web site, and complete the survey. What type of research is being conducted—exploratory, descriptive, or causal? How can marketers use this information? (AACSB: Communication; Use of IT; Reflective Thinking)

Under the Hood: Marketing Technology

Picture yourself with wires hooked up to your head or entering a magnetic tube that can see inside your brain. You must be undergoing some medical test, right? Think again—it's marketing research! Marketing research is becoming more like science fiction with a new field called neuromarketing, which uses technologies such as magnetic resonance imaging (MRIs) to peer into consumers' brains in an attempt to understand cognitive and affective responses to marketing stimuli. One company, Thinkingcraft, uses a methodology called "neurographix" to assist marketers in developing messages that fit the way customers think. Omnicon advertising agency uses "neuroplanning" to determine the appropriate media mix for a client. One study found that consumers preferred Pepsi over Coke in a blind taste test but preferred Coke when they could see names of the brands tasted. Different areas of the brain were activated when they knew the brand compared to when they did not, suggesting that what marketers make us believe is more persuasive than what our own taste buds tell us.

1. Learn more about neuromarketing and discuss another example of its application. (AACSB: Communication; Technology)

2. Critics have raised concerns over the usefulness and ethics of this type of marketing research. Discuss the debate surrounding this methodology. (AACSB: Communication; Reflective Thinking)

Staying on the Road: Marketing Ethics

Marketing information is necessary to develop insights to better meet the needs of customers, and regular competitive intelligence gathering is part of this information. Competitive intelligence (CI) has blossomed into a full-fledged industry, with companies such as Procter & Gamble (P&G), ExxonMobil, and Johnson & Johnson setting up CI units. But not all competitive intelligence gathering is ethical or legal—even at venerable giant, P&G. In 1943, a P&G employee bribed a Lever Brothers (now Unilever) employee to obtain bars of Swan soap, which was then under development, to improve its Ivory brand. Procter & Gamble settled the case by paying Unilever almost $6 million (about $60 million in today's dollars) for patent infringement—a small price to pay given the market success of Ivory. In 2001, P&G once again paid a $10 million settlement to Unilever for a case that involved a contractor rummaging through a trash dumpster outside Unilever's office, an infraction that was actually reported by P&G itself. The U.S. Secret Service estimates that employees commit 75 percent of intellectual property theft. The threat is not just internal, though. The FBI tracks approximately 20 countries actively spying on U.S. companies.

1. Find another example of corporate espionage and write a brief report on the incident. Did the guilty party pay restitution or serve prison time? Discuss what punishments, if any, should be levied in cases of corporate espionage. (AACSB: Communication; Ethical Reasoning)

2. How can businesses to protect themselves from corporate espionage? (AACSB: Communication; Reflective Thinking)

Rough Road Ahead: Marketing and the Economy

Harrah's Entertainment

Over the past decade, Harrah's Entertainment has honed its CRM skills to become bigger and more profitable than any other company in the gaming industry. The foundation of its success is Total Rewards, a loyalty program that collects a mother lode of customer information and mines it to identify important customers and meet their specific needs through a personalized experience. But in recent times, Harrah's has seen its flow of customers slow to a trickle. Not only are customers visiting less often, the normally $50 gamer is now only playing $25. As a result, Harrah's revenues are down 13 percent and profits are down 29 percent. Harrah's isn't alone—the rest of the industry is also suffering as more people save their money or spend it on necessities rather than entertainment.

Harrah's CRM efforts have always focused on delighting every customer. The company claims that customer spending increases 24 percent with a happy experience. But even Harrah's uncanny ability to predict which customers will be motivated by show tickets, room upgrades, or free chips has not made Harrah's immune to the woes of the economic downturn.

1. Is the dip in Harrah's business unavoidable given the recent economic dip or can Harrah's find new ways to connect with customers? What would you recommend?

2. In a time of economic crisis, is it responsible for Harrah's to be trying to get people to spend more money on gambling?

Travel Budget: Marketing by the Numbers

Marketers will frequently use statistics to try and justify claims and to make their products and services appear to be more universally preferred than other brands. The truth is that statistics can appear to mean anything. Rarely do marketers reveal just how many respondents were asked to comment and under what kind of conditions. It is impossible to know that a claim of 70 percent approval was the result of canvassing several hundred people or the first 10 likely candidates. Even a 70 percent approval rate could infer that 30 percent of respondents gave a negative answer. Customer approval based on average ratings are as inaccurate on a scale of 1–3 with 1 being dissatisfied and 3 being very satisfied is weighted toward the center values. Market share claims are particularly problematic to independently measure and assess. How is the market share being calculated? What is the definition of a market? Traditionally market share is calculated in two different ways. It can be calculated as a percentage of the total market, so if a business sells 46 of the 100 units sold, then it has a 43 percent market share. It may also be based on revenue, so if the value of the products sold is $4,600 in a market worth $10,000, then the market share is also 43 percent. For more discussion of the financial and quantitative implications of marketing decisions, see Appendix 2: Marketing by the Numbers.

1. Using census data on health insurance coverage in your country develop statistics, such as percentages, to support the argument that the government should insist on private health insurance. Use any portion of the data you deem important to support your argument.

2. Use the same data to develop different statistics to support the counterargument to the previous question. That is, interpret the data and present it in a way that supports the need for sweeping health care reforms to switch to government-provided health care for all. Again, use any portion of the data you deem important to support your argument.

Drive In: Video Case

Radian6

As more and more consumers converse through digital media, companies are struggling to figure out how to "listen in" on the conversations. Traditional marketing research methods can't sift through the seemingly infinite number of words flying around cyberspace at any given moment. But one company is helping marketers get a handle on "word-of-Web" communication. Radian6 specializes in monitoring social media, tracking Web sites ranging from Facebook to Flickr. Radian6's unique software opens a door to an entirely different kind of research. Instead of using questionnaires, interviews, or focus groups, Radian6 scans online social media for whatever combination of keywords a marketer might specify. This gives companies valuable insights into what consumers are saying about their products and brands.

After viewing the video featuring Radian6, answer the following questions.

1. What benefits does Radian6 provide to marketers over more traditional market research methods? What shortcomings?

2. Classify Radian6's software with respect to research approaches, contact methods, sampling plan, and research instruments.

3. How is Radian6 helping companies develop stronger relationships with customers?

5

Understanding **Consumer** and **Business** Buyer Behavior

ROAD MAP

Previewing the Concepts

In the previous chapter, you studied how marketers obtain, analyze, and use marketing information to gain customer and market insights as a basis for creating customer value and relationships. In this chapter, you'll continue your marketing journey with a closer look at the most important element of the marketplace—customers. The aim of marketing is to affect how customers think about and behave toward the organization and its market offerings. But to affect the *whats, whens,* and *hows* of buying behavior, marketers must first understand the *whys.* We look first at *final consumer* buying influences and processes and then at the buying behavior of *business customers.* You'll see that understanding buying behavior is an essential but very difficult task.

Objective Outline

 Objective 1   Understand the consumer market and the major factors that influence consumer buyer behavior.
Consumer Markets and Consumer Buyer Behavior **pp 164–184**
Model of Consumer Behavior **p 165**
Characteristics Affecting Consumer Behavior **pp 165–179**

 Objective 2   Identify and discuss the stages in the buyer decision process.
The Buyer Decision Process **pp 179–182**

Objective 3   Describe the adoption and diffusion process for new products.
The Buyer Decision Process for New Products **pp 182–184**

 Objective 4   Define the business market and identify the major factors that influence business buyer behavior.
Business Markets and Business Buyer Behavior **pp 184–185**
Business Markets **pp 185–188**
Business Buyer Behavior **pp 188–192**

 Objective 5   List and define the steps in the business buying decision process.
The Business Buying Process **pp 192–195**

▲Apple plays to deep-seated customer buying needs in everything it makes and sells. The company has gained a cult-like following because it somehow manages to breathe new life into every category it touches.

To get a better sense of the importance of understanding consumer behavior, let's look first at Apple. What makes Apple users so fanatically loyal? Just what is it that makes them buy a Mac computer, an iPod, an iPhone, or all of these? Partly, it's the way the equipment works. But at the core, customers buy from Apple because the brand itself is a part of their own self-expression and lifestyle. It's a part of what the loyal Apple customer is.

First Stop | Apple: The Keeper of All Things Cool

Few brands engender such intense loyalty as that found in the hearts of core Apple buyers. Whether they own a Mac computer, an iPod, or an iPhone, Apple devotees are granitelike in their devotion to the brand. At one end are the quietly satisfied Mac users, folks who own a Mac and use it for e-mailing, blogging, browsing, buying, and social networking. At the other extreme, however, are the Mac zealots—the so-called MacHeads or Macolytes. The *Urban Dictionary* defines a Macolyte as "one who is fanatically devoted to Apple products," as in "He's a Macolyte; don't even *think* of mentioning Microsoft within earshot."

The chances are good that you know one of these MacHeads. Maybe you *are* one. They're the diehards who buy all the latest Apple products and accessories to maximize their Mac lives. They virtually live in the local Apple store. Some have even been known to buy two iPhones—one for themselves and the other just to take apart, to see what it looks like on the inside, and maybe, just to marvel at Apple's ingenious ability to cram so much into a tight little elegant package.

There's at least a little MacHead in every Apple customer. Mac enthusiasts see Apple founder Steve Jobs as the Walt Disney of technology. Say the word "Apple" in front of Mac fans and they'll go into rhapsodies about the superiority of the brand. Put two MacHeads together and you'll never shut them up. Some MacHeads even tattoo the Apple logo on their bodies. According to one industry observer, a Mac or iPhone comes "not just as a machine in a box, it [comes] with a whole community" of fellow believers. The fanatically loyal core of Apple users is at the forefront of Apple's recent personal computer resurgence and its burgeoning iPod, iTunes, iPhone empire.

What is it that makes Apple buyers so loyal? Why do they buy a Mac instead of an HP or a Dell, or an iPhone instead of a Nokia or Motorola? Ask the true believers, and they'll tell you simply that Apple's products work better and do more, or that they're simpler to use. But Apple buyer behavior has much deeper roots. Apple puts top priority on understanding its customers and what makes them tick deep down. It knows that, to Apple buyers, a Mac computer or an iPhone is much more than just a piece of electronics equipment. It's a part of buyers' own self-expression and lifestyle—a part of what they are. When you own a Mac, you are anything but mainstream. You're an independent thinker, an innovator, out ahead of the crowd.

Apple plays to these deep-seated customer buying needs and motives in everything it makes and sells. By one account:

> Apple is the epitome of cool—a company that has gained a cult-like following because it somehow manages to breathe new life into every category it touches. From sleek laptops to the even sleeker iPhone, Apple products are imaginative, irreverent, and pleasing to the eye. They're fun to use and have wreaked havoc on competitors. Apple has shown "a marketing and creative genius with a rare ability to get inside the imaginations of consumers and understand what will captivate them," says one analyst. Apple has been "obsessed with the Apple user's experience."

Thanks to Apple's deep understanding of consumer behavior, the Apple brand engenders an intense loyalty in the hearts of core Apple customers. This consumer love affair with Apple has produced stunning sales and profit results.

▲The Urban Dictionary defines a Macolyte as "one who is fanatically devoted to Apple products," as in "He's a Macolyte; don't even think of mentioning Microsoft within earshot."

Apple's obsession with understanding customers and deepening their Apple experience shows in everything the company does. For example, a visit to an Apple retail store is a lot more than a simple shopping trip. Apple stores are very seductive places. The store design is clean, simple, and just oozing with style—much like an Apple iPod or iPhone. The stores invite shoppers to stay a while, use the equipment, and soak up all of the exciting new technology:

> It was 2 o'clock in the morning but in the subterranean retailing mecca in Midtown Manhattan, otherwise known as the Apple store, it might as well have been midafternoon. Late one night shortly before Christmas, parents pushed strollers, and tourists straight off the plane mingled with nocturnal New Yorkers, clicking through iPod playlists, cruising the Internet on MacBooks, and touch-padding their way around iPhones. And through the night, cheerful sales staff stayed busy, ringing up customers at the main checkout counter and on hand-held devices in an uninterrupted stream of brick-and-mortar commerce.

> Not only has the company made many of its stores feel like gathering places, but the bright lights and equally bright acoustics create a buzz that makes customers feel more like they are at an event than a retail store. Apple stores encourage a lot of purchasing, to be sure. But they also encourage lingering, with dozens of fully functioning computers, iPods, and iPhones for visitors to try—for hours on end. The policy

has even given some stores, especially those in urban neighborhoods, the feel of a community center. You don't visit an Apple store, you experience it.

Apple's keen understanding of customers and their needs helped the brand to build a core segment of enthusiastic disciples. The most recent American Consumer Satisfaction Index gave Apple a market-leading customer-satisfaction score of 85—the highest ever recorded for a company in the personal computer industry. Another survey showed that Apple commands the strongest repurchase intent of any personal computer brand—81 percent of households with an Apple as their primary home personal computer plan to repurchase an Apple.

In turn, the consumer love affair with Apple has produced stunning sales and profit results. Despite the 2008 economic meltdown, Apple's sales that year soared to a record $32.5 billion, up 35 percent over the previous year and more than quadruple the sales just four years earlier. In 2009, despite the recession that cripple much of the electronics industry, Apple's iPod and iPhone sales continued to grow at a healthy rate. Last year alone, the company sold almost 12 million iPhones and 55 million iPods. Apple now claims a 14 percent share of the U.S. personal-computer market—third behind HP and Dell—and captures more than 70 percent of the iPod and iTunes markets that it created.

"To say Apple is hot just doesn't do the company justice," concludes one Apple watcher. "Apple is smoking, searing, blisteringly hot, not to mention hip, with a side order of funky. Gadget geeks around the world have crowned Apple the keeper of all things cool." Just ask your Macolyte friends. In fact, don't bother—they've probably already brought it up.[1]

*t*he Apple example shows that factors at many levels affect consumer buying behavior. Buying behavior is never simple, yet understanding it is the essential task of marketing management. First we explore the dynamics of the consumer market and the consumer buyer behavior. We then examine business markets and the business buyer process.

Author Comment »
In some ways, consumer and business markets are similar in their buyer behavior. But in many other ways, they differ a lot. We start by digging into consumer buyer behavior. Later in the chapter, we'll tackle business buyer behavior.

Consumer buyer behavior
The buying behavior of final consumers—individuals and households that buy goods and services for personal consumption.

Consumer market
All the individuals and households that buy or acquire goods and services for personal consumption.

CONSUMER MARKETS AND CONSUMER BUYER BEHAVIOR (pp 164–184)

Consumer buyer behavior refers to the buying behavior of final consumers—individuals and households that buy goods and services for personal consumption. All of these final consumers combine to make up the **consumer market**. The American consumer market consists of more than 300 million people who consume more than $14 trillion worth of goods and services each year, making it one of the most attractive consumer markets in the world. The world consumer market consists of more than 6.8 *billion* people who annually consume an estimated $70 trillion worth of goods and services.[2]

Consumers around the world vary tremendously in age, income, education level, and tastes. They also buy an incredible variety of goods and services. How these diverse consumers relate with each other and with other elements of the world around them impacts their choices among various products, services, and companies. Here we examine the fascinating array of factors that affect consumer behavior.

Author Comment >>
Despite the simple-looking model in Figure 5.1, understanding the *whys* of buying behavior is very difficult. Says one expert, "the mind is a whirling, swirling, jumbled mass of neurons bouncing around. . . ."

Model of Consumer Behavior (p 165)

Consumers make many buying decisions every day, and the buying decision is the focal point of the marketer's effort. Most large companies research consumer buying decisions in great detail to answer questions about what consumers buy, where they buy, how and how much they buy, when they buy, and why they buy. Marketers can study actual consumer purchases to find out what they buy, where, and how much. But learning about the *whys* of consumer buying behavior is not so easy—the answers are often locked deep within the consumer's mind.

Often, consumers themselves don't know exactly what influences their purchases. "The human mind doesn't work in a linear way," says one marketing expert. "The idea that the mind is a computer with storage compartments where brands or logos or recognizable packages are stored in clearly marked folders that can be accessed by cleverly written ads or commercials simply doesn't exist. Instead, the mind is a whirling, swirling, jumbled mass of neurons bouncing around, colliding and continuously creating new concepts and thoughts and relationships inside every single person's brain all over the world."[3]

The central question for marketers is: How do consumers respond to various marketing efforts the company might use? The starting point is the stimulus-response model of buyer behavior shown in ■ **Figure 5.1**. This figure shows that marketing and other stimuli enter the consumer's "black box" and produce certain responses. Marketers must figure out what is in the buyer's black box.

Marketing stimuli consist of the Four Ps: product, price, place, and promotion. Other stimuli include major forces and events in the buyer's environment: economic, technological, political, and cultural. All these inputs enter the buyer's black box, where they are turned into a set of observable buyer responses: the buyer's brand and company relationship behavior and what he or she buys, when, where, and how often.

The marketer wants to understand how the stimuli are changed into responses inside the consumer's black box, which has two parts. First, the buyer's characteristics influence how he or she perceives and reacts to the stimuli. Second, the buyer's decision process itself affects the buyer's behavior. We look first at buyer characteristics as they affect buyer behavior and then discuss the buyer decision process.

Author Comment >>
Many, many levels of factors affect our buying behavior—from broad cultural and social influences to motivations, beliefs, and attitudes lying deep within us. For example, why *did* you buy *that* specific cell phone?

Characteristics Affecting Consumer Behavior (pp 165–179)

Consumer purchases are influenced strongly by cultural, social, personal, and psychological characteristics, shown in ■ **Figure 5.2**. For the most part, marketers cannot control such factors, but they must take them into account.

Cultural Factors

Cultural factors exert a broad and deep influence on consumer behavior. The marketer needs to understand the role played by the buyer's *culture*, *subculture*, and *social class*.

It's very difficult to "see" inside the consumer's head and figure out the *whys* of buying behavior (that's why it's called the black box). Marketers spend a lot of time and dollars trying to figure out what makes customers tick.

■ **Figure 5.1** Model of Buyer Behavior

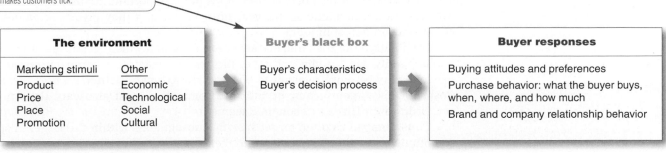

The environment		Buyer's black box	Buyer responses
Marketing stimuli	**Other**	Buyer's characteristics	Buying attitudes and preferences
Product	Economic	Buyer's decision process	Purchase behavior: what the buyer buys, when, where, and how much
Price	Technological		
Place	Social		Brand and company relationship behavior
Promotion	Cultural		

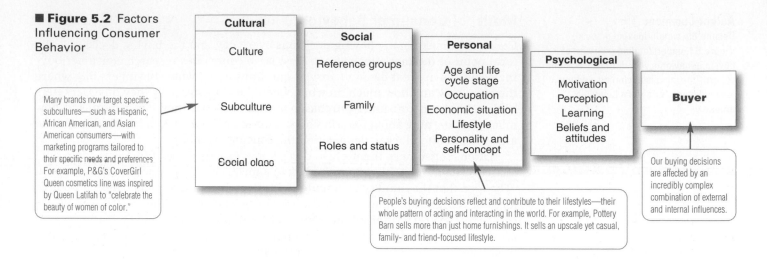

■ Figure 5.2 Factors Influencing Consumer Behavior

Many brands now target specific subcultures—such as Hispanic, African American, and Asian American consumers—with marketing programs tailored to their specific needs and preferences. For example, P&G's CoverGirl Queen cosmetics line was inspired by Queen Latifah to "celebrate the beauty of women of color."

People's buying decisions reflect and contribute to their lifestyles—their whole pattern of acting and interacting in the world. For example, Pottery Barn sells more than just home furnishings. It sells an upscale yet casual, family- and friend-focused lifestyle.

Our buying decisions are affected by an incredibly complex combination of external and internal influences.

Culture

Culture
The set of basic values, perceptions, wants, and behaviors learned by a member of society from family and other important institutions.

Culture. **Culture** is the most basic cause of a person's wants and behavior. Human behavior is largely learned. Growing up in a society, a child learns basic values, perceptions, wants, and behaviors from the family and other important institutions. A child in the United States normally learns or is exposed to the following values: achievement and success, activity and involvement, efficiency and practicality, progress, hard work, material comfort, individualism, freedom, humanitarianism, youthfulness, and fitness and health. Every group or society has a culture, and cultural influences on buying behavior may vary greatly from country to country **(see Marketing at Work 5.1).** Failure to adjust to these differences can result in ineffective marketing or embarrassing mistakes.

Marketers are always trying to spot *cultural shifts* in order to discover new products that might be wanted. For example, the cultural shift toward greater concern about health and fitness has created a huge industry for health-and-fitness services, exercise equipment and clothing, organic foods, and a variety of diets. The shift toward informality has resulted in more demand for casual clothing and simpler home furnishings.

Subculture
A group of people with shared value systems based on common life experiences and situations.

Subculture. Each culture contains smaller **subcultures**, or groups of people with shared value systems based on common life experiences and situations. Subcultures include nationalities, religions, racial groups, and geographic regions. Many subcultures make up important market segments, and marketers often design products and marketing programs tailored to their needs. Examples of four such important subculture groups include Hispanic, African American, Asian American, and mature consumers.

The nation's 46 million Hispanic consumers have an annual buying power of $870 billion, a figure that will grow to an estimated $1.1 trillion by 2012. Although Hispanic consumers share many characteristics and behaviors with the mainstream buying pubic, there are also distinct differences. Hispanic consumers tend to buy more branded, higher-quality products—generics don't sell well to this group. They tend to be deeply family-oriented and make shopping a family affair—children have a big say in what brands they buy. Perhaps more important, Hispanics, particularly first-generation immigrants, are very brand loyal, and they favor companies who show special interest in them.[4]

Even within the Hispanic market, there exist many distinct subsegments based on nationality, age, income, and other factors. For example, a company's product or message may be more relevant to one nationality over another, such as Mexicans, Costa Ricans, Argentineans, or Cubans. Companies must also vary their pitches across different Hispanic economic segments.

Thus, companies often target specific subsegments within the larger Hispanic community with different kinds of marketing efforts. Consider two campaigns cre-

ated by Hispanic agency Conill Advertising of New York for two very different Toyota brands, the full-size Tundra pick-up truck on the one hand and the Lexus on the other.[5]

The Tundra is a high-volume seller among Mexican immigrants in the Southwest who are characterized as *Jefes*, local heroes considered pillars of strength in their communities. To reach that consumer, Conill devised a campaign that catered to *El Jefe's* penchant for the national Mexican sport of *charreadas* (Mexican-style rodeos). The pitch: The Tundra is as tough as the guy who gets behind the wheel.

Conill's campaign for Lexus, couldn't be more different. For Lexus, the agency targeted the luxury market in Miami, reaching out to affluent Hispanics who appreciate refinement, art, and culture with a campaign that centered on art and design. ▲The result was a brightly displayed Lexus print campaign placed in local Hispanic lifestyle magazines that helped move Lexus from the fourth-ranked player in the Miami luxury car market to market leader in only 18 months.

▲Targeting diverse Hispanic subsegments: Toyota's various brands target different Hispanic markets with very different programs and appeals. This ad for Lexus targets the luxury market in Miami, reaching out to affluent Hispanics who appreciate refinement, art, and culture with a campaign that centers on art and design.

With annual buying power of $845 billion, estimated to reach $1.2 trillion by 2013, the nation's 40 million African American consumers also attract much marketing attention. The U.S. black population is growing in affluence and sophistication. Although more price conscious than other segments, blacks are also strongly motivated by quality and selection. Brands are important. So is shopping. Black consumers seem to enjoy shopping more than other groups, even for something as mundane as groceries. Black consumers are also the most fashion conscious of the ethnic groups.[6]

In recent years, many companies have developed special products, appeals, and marketing programs for African American consumers. For example, P&G's roots run deep in this market. Procter & Gamble currently spends six times more on media targeting black consumers than it did just five years ago, and nearly twice as much as the second-place spender. It has a long history of using black spokespeople in its ads, beginning in 1969 with entertainer Bill Cosby endorsing Crest. Today, you'll see Angela Bassett promoting the benefits of Olay body lotion for black skin, Tiger Woods discussing the virtues of Gillette razors, and ▲Queen Latifah in commercials promoting a CoverGirl line for women of color.[7]

In addition to traditional product marketing efforts, P&G also supports a broader "My Black Is Beautiful" movement.[8]

▼Procter & Gamble's roots run deep in targeting African American consumers. For example, its CoverGirl Queen Latifah line is specially formulated "to celebrate the beauty of women of color."

Created by a group of African American women at P&G in 2006, the campaign aims "to ignite and support a sustained national conversation by, for, and about black women." P&G discovered that black women spend on average three times more than the general market on beauty products. Yet, 71 percent of black women feel they're portrayed worse than other women in media and advertising. Supported by brands such as Crest, Pantene Pro-V Relaxed & Natural, CoverGirl Queen Collection, and Olay Definity, the My Black Is Beautiful movement's goals are to make all black girls and women feel beautiful regardless of skin tone or origin and, of course, to forge a closer relationship between P&G brands and African American consumers in the process. What began as just a Web site and a grassroots multi-city road tour has since evolved into a nationwide movement with the launch of a national television series on BET Networks. With P&G as the main sponsor, *My Black Is Beautiful* includes traditional television programming and Webisodes featuring interviews, vignettes, and style tips focusing on African American beauty.[9]

Asian Americans are the most affluent U.S. demographic segment. They now number nearly 15 million and wield more than $453 billion in annual spending power, expected to reach $670 billion in 2012. They are the second-fastest-growing population subsegment after Hispanics. Chinese Americans constitute the largest group, followed by Filipinos, Asian Indians, Vietnamese, Korean Americans, and

▲Targeting Asian Americans: Nationwide Financial targets this segment with humorous Life Comes at You Fast ads like this one, focusing on typical Indian Asian American lifestyle situations.

Japanese Americans. The U.S. Asian American population is expected to more than double by 2050, when it will make up nearly nine percent of the U.S. population.[10]

Asian consumers may be the most tech-savvy segment—more than 90 percent of Asian Americans go online regularly and are most comfortable with Internet technologies such as online banking and instant messaging. As a group, Asian consumers shop frequently and are the most brand conscious of all the ethnic groups. They can be fiercely brand loyal. As a result, many firms are now targeting the Asian American market, from Verizon, Toyota, and Nationwide Financial to Southwest Airlines and Wal-Mart.

For example, as a part of its humorous "Life Comes at You Fast" campaign, Nationwide Financial has tailored a number of advertisements specifically to the South Asian American market.[11]

Consumers with South Asian heritage (from countries such as India and Pakistan) tend to be highly educated and focused on the financial well-being of their families. That makes them an attractive market for Nationwide Financial's investment, retirement planning, and insurance products. The targeted ads focus on typical South Asia lifestyle situations. ▲For example, one ad plays in a humorous way to the segment's educational priorities. The proud parents of a son who has been accepted to an Ivy League college have to sell just about everything they own to keep him there. On graduation day, however, to the utter shock and dismay of his mother and father, the young man proclaims "I'm going to London for my Ph.D." "Life comes at you fast," intones the announcer. "Growing ambitions need an education plan. Get started with Nationwide Financial."

As the U.S. population ages, *mature consumers* are becoming a very attractive market. By 2015, the entire baby boom generation, the largest and wealthiest demographic cohort in the country for more than half a century, will have moved into the 50-plus age bracket. They will control a larger proportion of wealth, income, and consumption than any current or previous generation. Despite some financial setbacks resulting from the recent economic crisis, mature consumers remain an attractive market for companies in all industries, from pharmaceuticals, groceries, beauty products, and clothing to consumer electronics, travel and entertainment, and financial services.[12]

Contrary to popular belief, mature consumers are not "stuck in their ways." To the contrary, a recent AARP study showed that older consumers for products such as stereos, computers, and mobile phones are more willing to shop around and switch brands than their younger Generation X counterparts. For example, notes one expert, "some 25 percent of Apple's iPhones—the epitome of cool, cutting-edge product—have been bought by people over 50."[13]

The growing cadre of mature consumers creates an attractive market for convenient services. For example, Home Depot and Lowe's now target older consumers who are less enthusiastic about do-it-yourself chores than with "do-it-for-me" handyman services. And their desire to look as young as they feel also makes more-mature consumers good candidates for cosmetics and personal care products, health foods, fitness products, and other items that combat the effects of aging. The best strategy is to appeal to their active, multidimensional lives. For example, Dove's Pro.Age hair and skin care product line claims that "Beauty has no age limit." Pro.Age ads feature active and attractive, real women who seem to be benefiting from the product's promise. Says one ad, "Dove created Pro.Age to reflect the unique needs of women in their best years. This isn't anti-age, it's pro-age."[14]

Social class
Relatively permanent and ordered divisions in a society whose members share similar values, interests, and behaviors.

Social Class. Almost every society has some form of social class structure. **Social classes** are society's relatively permanent and ordered divisions whose members share similar values, interests, and behaviors. Social scientists have identified the seven American social classes shown in ■ **Figure 5.3**.

Social class is not determined by a single factor, such as income, but is measured as a combination of occupation, income, education, wealth, and other variables. In

■ Figure 5.3 The Major
American Social Classes

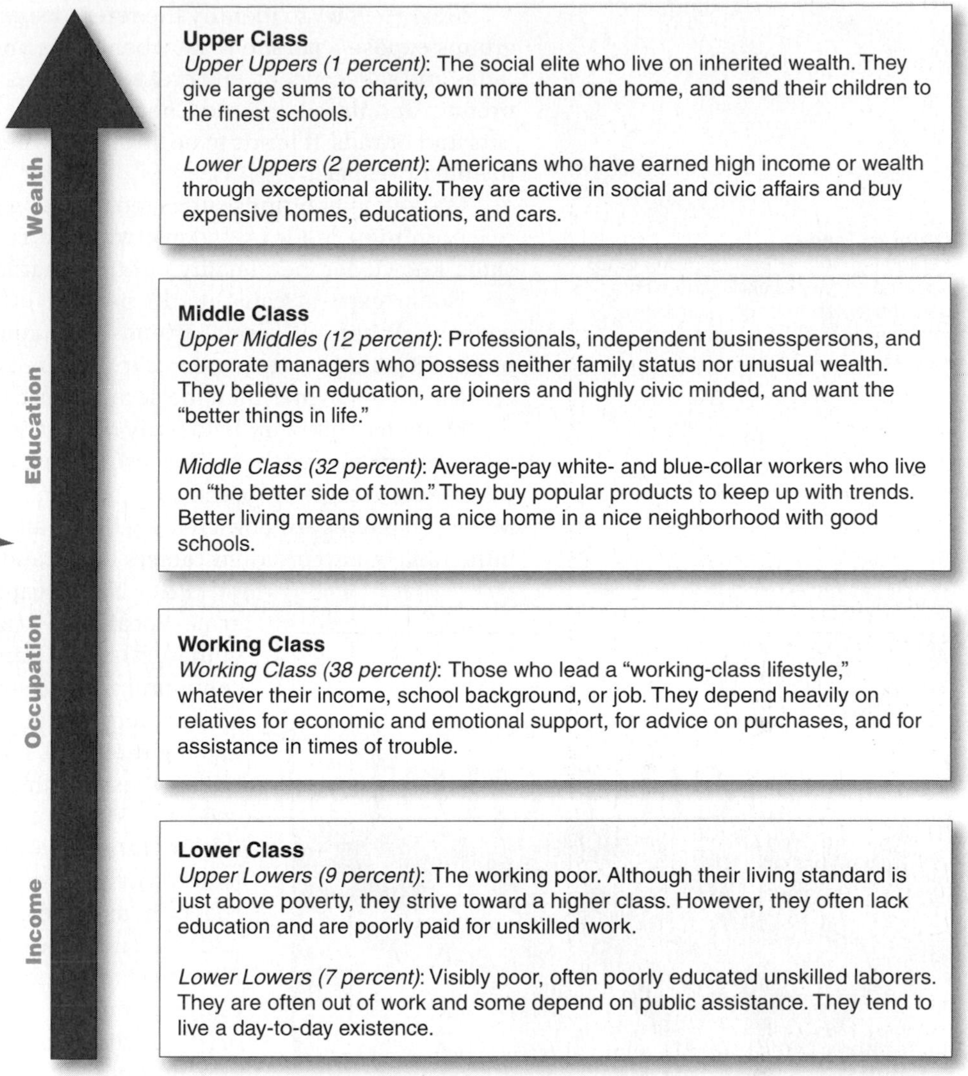

> America's social classes show distinct brand preferences. Social class is not determined by a single factor, but by a combination of all of these factors.

Wealth · Education · Occupation · Income

Upper Class
Upper Uppers (1 percent): The social elite who live on inherited wealth. They give large sums to charity, own more than one home, and send their children to the finest schools.

Lower Uppers (2 percent): Americans who have earned high income or wealth through exceptional ability. They are active in social and civic affairs and buy expensive homes, educations, and cars.

Middle Class
Upper Middles (12 percent): Professionals, independent businesspersons, and corporate managers who possess neither family status nor unusual wealth. They believe in education, are joiners and highly civic minded, and want the "better things in life."

Middle Class (32 percent): Average-pay white- and blue-collar workers who live on "the better side of town." They buy popular products to keep up with trends. Better living means owning a nice home in a nice neighborhood with good schools.

Working Class
Working Class (38 percent): Those who lead a "working-class lifestyle," whatever their income, school background, or job. They depend heavily on relatives for economic and emotional support, for advice on purchases, and for assistance in times of trouble.

Lower Class
Upper Lowers (9 percent): The working poor. Although their living standard is just above poverty, they strive toward a higher class. However, they often lack education and are poorly paid for unskilled work.

Lower Lowers (7 percent): Visibly poor, often poorly educated unskilled laborers. They are often out of work and some depend on public assistance. They tend to live a day-to-day existence.

some social systems, members of different classes are reared for certain roles and cannot change their social positions. In the United States, however, the lines between social classes are not fixed and rigid; people can move to a higher social class or drop into a lower one.

Marketers are interested in social class because people within a given social class tend to exhibit similar buying behavior. Social classes show distinct product and brand preferences in areas such as clothing, home furnishings, leisure activity, and automobiles.

Social Factors

A consumer's behavior also is influenced by social factors, such as the consumer's *small groups, family,* and *social roles* and *status.*

Group
Two or more people who interact to accomplish individual or mutual goals.

Groups and Social Networks. Many small **groups** influence a person's behavior. Groups that have a direct influence and to which a person belongs are called membership groups. In contrast, reference groups serve as direct (face-to-face) or indirect points of comparison or reference in forming a person's attitudes or behavior. People often are influenced by reference groups to which they do not belong. For example, an aspirational group is one to which the individual wishes to belong, as when a young basketball player hopes to someday emulate basketball star Lebron James and play in the NBA.

Marketers try to identify the reference groups of their target markets. Reference groups expose a person to new behaviors and lifestyles, influence the person's attitudes and self-concept, and create pressures to conform that may affect the person's product and brand choices. The importance of group influence varies across products and brands. It tends to be strongest when the product is visible to others whom the buyer respects.

Marketers of brands subjected to strong group influence must figure out how to reach **opinion leaders**—people within a reference group who, because of special skills, knowledge, personality, or other characteristics, exert social influence on others. Some experts call this 10 percent of Americans *the influentials* or *leading adopters*. When influential friends talk, consumers listen. One survey found that nearly 78 percent of respondents trusted "recommendations from consumers," 15 percentage points higher than the second most-credible source, newspapers.[15]

Marketers often try to identify opinion leaders for their products and direct marketing efforts toward them. They use *buzz marketing* by enlisting or even creating opinion leaders to serve as "brand ambassadors" who spread the word about their products. Many companies are now creating brand ambassador programs in an attempt to turn influential but everyday customers into brand evangelists.

Opinion leader
Person within a reference group who, because of special skills, knowledge, personality, or other characteristics, exerts social influence on others.

P&G has created a huge word-of-mouth marketing arm—Vocalpoint—consisting of 350,000 moms. ▲This army of natural-born buzzers uses the power of peer-to-peer communication to spread the word about brands. Vocalpoint recruits "connectors"—people with vast networks of friends and a gift for gab. They create buzz not just for P&G brands but for those of other client companies as well. P&G recently used the Vocalpoint network to help launch its new Pur Flavor Options filters—Pur faucet or pitcher filters that add fruit flavors as they filter water. P&G didn't pay the moms or coach them on what to say. It simply provided free samples and educated Vocalpointers about the product, then asked them to share their "honest opinions with us and with other real women." In turn, the Vocalpoint moms created hundreds of thousands of personal recommendations for the new product.[16]

Over the past few years, a new type of social interaction has exploded onto the scene—online social networking. **Online social networks** are online communities where people socialize or exchange information and opinions. Social networking media range from blogs to social networking Web sites, such as Facebook and YouTube, to entire virtual worlds, such as Second Life and Gaia Online. This new form of high-tech buzz has big implications for marketers.

▲Buzz marketing: The Vocalpoint marketing arm of P&G has enlisted an army of buzzers to create word-of-mouth for brands. "We know that the most powerful form of marketing is a message from a trusted friend."

Online social networks
Online social communities—blogs, social networking Web sites, or even virtual worlds—where people socialize or exchange information and opinions.

Personal connections—forged through words, pictures, video, and audio posted just for the [heck] of it—are the life of the new Web, bringing together the tens of millions of bloggers, more than 175 million active Facebook users, and millions more on single-use social networks where people share one category of stuff, like Flickr (photos), Del.icio.us (links), Digg (news stories), Wikipedia (encyclopedia articles), and YouTube (video). ... It's hard to overstate the impact of these new network technologies on business: They hatch trends and build immense waves of interest in specific products. They serve up giant, targeted audiences to advertisers. They edge out old media with the loving labor of amateurs. They effortlessly provide hyperdetailed data to marketers. The new social networking technologies provide an authentic, peer-to-peer channel of communication that is far more credible than any corporate flackery.[17]

Marketers are working to harness the power of these new social networks to promote their products and build closer customer relationships. Instead of throwing more one-way commercial messages at ad-weary consumers, they hope to use social networks to *interact* with consumers and become a part of their conversations and lives.

Marketing at Work 5.1

Google Is Britain's Top Brand

In July 2008, a research study carried out by The Centre for Brand Analysis (TCBA) on behalf of Superbrands (UK) Ltd, a group of experts in the branding and marketing communication industry, revealed that Google had beaten long-established British and international brand names. Approximately 2,200 consumers were asked to rank the brand names from a list of 750 brands compiled by TCBA following an initial selection process involving a voluntary and independent council of marketing, advertising, and media experts collectively called the Superbrands Council.

Google had come third in the 2007 survey, but in 2008, it pushed Microsoft down into second and Mercedes Benz into third. British supermarkets dropped down in brand image, with Tesco coming in 230th and ASDA (owned by Wal-Mart) coming in 253rd. The only food brand anywhere near the top ten was Marks and Spencer, at 20.

Why did an Internet search engine land at the top of the brand pile? The CEO of TCBA and Chairman of the Superbrands Council, Stephen Cheliotis, explained: "Lifestyle brands, particularly those in the technology sector, have considerably more sway with the public than everyday staples such as the supermarkets, which now seem further than ever from the affections of the British people. As the spectre of rising food costs continues, they are likely to come under further scrutiny. The results are also a further sign that Google is continuing its dominance in the U.K. It is clear that Google is the brand that people value at work and in their personal lives."

Google was also voted the top UK Business Superbrands in 2008, following a poll of the independent business, Superbrands Council and over 1,500 industry professionals—the search engine's first win ever in that poll. The poll surveyed 1,500 industry professionals, who were asked to rank the top 500 brands in Britain. Google ousted the commercial arm of the British Broadcasting Corporation (BBC) from the top position, with Microsoft coming second, followed by British Petroleum (BP). BBC Worldwide dropped to fourth. Stephen Cheliotis said of the significance of this survey: "The top ten positions are dominated by companies who are either British stalwarts such as BA (British Airways) and BP—or like GlaxoSmithKline—can trace their origins to the U.K."

Despite the fact that some of the brands in the poll are up to 90 years old, they still continue to resonate with British consumers. In 2007, TCBA had established that the coolest brand was in fact Aston Martin. In March 2007, Aston Martin was sold back into British hands by the car giant Ford for nearly $750 million. Apple's iPod won second place in the cool brands category, followed by YouTube and the Scandinavian business Bang and Olufsen (the manufacturers of hi-fi equipment).

The 2008 brand image surveys were conducted just as many iconic British brands were moving abroad. There were rumours that the Aston Martin would be moving the production of the Rapide abroad. The production of the iconic confectionary brand Smarties had been moved to Hamburg, Germany. Cadbury also relocated the production of its Curly Wurly and other confectionary brands to Poland. The Burberry brand, which for so many years had been produced in Wales, moved the production of its polo shirts abroad to China.

The shifts in production locations have not taken place without protest. Ray Egan, a retired British police officer, and John Bull, a British impersonator, climbed onto the roof at the HP factory, which had been located in Aston. Other protestors paraded with the Union flag outside Parliament, and inside, a military police officer waved a bottle of the sauce in a heated debate. Executives at Heinz, the company that produces HP, were branded hypocrites because only weeks before they announced the move, they had launched the "Save the Proper British Café" campaign, an effort to help British cafes compete against the rising popularity of the continental-style coffee shop chains. A spokesperson from Heinz confirmed that the brand was as popular as it had ever been and that sales had increased and customer loyalty was still strong. Heinz had looked at all of the options but in the end it had come down to financial considerations. Nestlé, the owner of the Smarties brand, also made a statement about having moved the brand's production to Hamburg: "Smarties aren't going to taste any

▲ Google has become Britain's most recognized brand. It has an elegant, simple, advert-free interface. Results and sponsored links cannot be purchased and integrity is a key factor.

(*continued*)

different." The company was also keen to point out that other brand names would remain in Britain.

How do these moves affect the "Britishness" of the brands? The manufacturers believe that there is no change, and that, on the whole, consumers do not care. Rune Gustafson of Interbrand was firmly of the opinion that customers did know where products were made and that this was important. They did not want to purchase products from dubious sources. Although Britain had declined as a manufacturer since the Second World War, "Britishness" was still important and "Britishness" meant products being made by British people in well run factories.

Perhaps the decline set in much earlier than the aforementioned brands would indicate. For example, Dyson, the vacuum cleaner manufacturer, moved its production from the U.K. to Malaysia in 2002. Is Britain fighting a losing battle to keep its brands? Some believe that it is a battle worth fighting. The British Made For Quality campaign was set up in the same year Dyson moved to Malaysia. A company that wants to be associated with the campaign must manufacture at least 65 percent of its product(s) in Britain. One of the biggest names to sign up for the campaign was Thomas Crapper, the manufacturer of the traditional toilets. That said, the campaign has found it hard to attract members, not necessarily because many products are not 65 percent British, but because manufacturers no longer believe that it matters that much to consumers whether a product is, in fact, British at all. This lukewarm attitude comes at a time when U.K. producers of food are benefiting from the current desire consumers have to purchase more locally grown produce so as to eliminate their transportation and damage it causes to the environment. But in the case of manufacturing, the proof of the pudding seems to be in the buying.

Sources: Quotes and other information from Superbrands Council (www.superbrands.com); British Made for Quality (www.britishmadeforquality.co.uk); "Save the Proper British Café" Campaign (www.brownsauce.org); Beyond the Bean (www.beyondthebean.com); Cadbury (www.cadbury.com); and Heinz (www.heinz.com).

For example, brands ranging from Burger King to the Chicago Bulls are "tweeting" on Twitter. Nike connects with action sports athletes—from snow boarders to surfers to BMX bike racers—through a social community it started on Loop'd (http://nike6.loopd.com). Jeep connects with customers via a community page that links to photos on Flickr, the company's Facebook and MySpace pages, and a list of enthusiast groups. Southwest Airlines employees share stories with each other and customers on the company's "Nuts About Southwest" blog. And Starbucks launched MyStarbucksIdea.com, where customers can submit ideas—"revolutionary or simple"—for what they or others might want from Starbucks. The ideas are voted on by other users and with the best ones to be implemented by the company.[18]

Other companies regularly post ads or custom videos on video-sharing sites such as YouTube. For example, Toyota developed two YouTube channels to market its Corolla. One of these channels, Sketchies 11, hosted a competition offering cash and prizes worth $40,000 for the best user-generated comedy sketches. The most-watched video received some 900,000 views. ▲Similarly, small BlendTec has developed a kind of cult following for its flood of "Will it Blend?" videos, in which the seemingly indestructible Blendtec Total Blender grinds everything from a hockey puck and a golf club to an iPhone into dust. The low-cost, simple idea led to a five-fold increase in BlendTec's sales.[19]

But marketers must be careful when tapping into online social networks. Results are difficult to measure and control. Ultimately, the users control

▼Using online social networks: BlendTec has developed a kind of cult following for its flood of "Will it Blend?" videos on YouTube, resulting in a five-fold increase in BlendTec's sales.

the content, so social network marketing attempts can easily backfire. We will dig deeper into online social networks as a marketing tool in Chapter 14.

Family. Family members can strongly influence buyer behavior. The family is the most important consumer buying organization in society, and it has been researched extensively. Marketers are interested in the roles and influence of the husband, wife, and children on the purchase of different products and services.

Husband-wife involvement varies widely by product category and by stage in the buying process. Buying roles change with evolving consumer lifestyles. In the United States, the wife traditionally has been the main purchasing agent for the family in the areas of food, household products, and clothing. But with 70 percent of women holding jobs outside the home and the willingness of husbands to do more of the family's purchasing, all this is changing. ▲A recent study found that 65 percent of men grocery shop regularly and prepare at least one meal a week for others in the household. At the same time, women now influence 65 percent of all new car purchases, 91 percent of new home purchases, and 92 percent of vacation purchases. In all, women make almost 85 percent of all family purchases, spending two-thirds of the nation's GDP.[20]

Such changes suggest that marketers in industries that have sold their products to only men or only women are now courting the opposite sex. For example, women today account for 50 percent of all technology purchases. So consumer electronics are increasingly designing products that are easier to use and more appealing to female buyers.

▼Family buying: Family buying roles are changing. For example, 65 percent of men grocery shop regularly while women influence 50 percent of all new technology purchases.

As a growing number of women are embracing consumer electronics, engineers and designers are bringing a more feminine sensibility to products historically shaped by masculine tastes, habits, and requirements. Designs are more "feminine and softer," rather than masculine and angular. But many of the new touches are more subtle, like the wider spacing of the keys on a Sony ultraportable computer notebook. It accommodates the longer fingernails that women tend to have. Some of the latest cell phones made by LG Electronics have the cameras' automatic focus calibrated to arms' length. The company observed that young women are fond of taking pictures of themselves with a friend. Men, not so much. Nikon and Olympus recently introduced lines of lighter, more compact and easy-to-use digital single-lens-reflex cameras that were designed with women in mind because they tend to be a family's primary keeper of memories.[21]

Children may also have a strong influence on family buying decisions. The nation's 36 million kids age 8 to 12 wield an estimated $30 billion in disposable income. They also influence an additional $150 billion that their families spend on them in areas such as food, clothing, entertainment, and personal care items. One recent study found that kids significantly influence family decisions about everything from where they take vacations to what cars and cell phones they buy.[22]

As a result, marketers of cars, full-service restaurants, cell phones, and travel destinations are now targeting kids as well as parents. For example, Firefly Mobile targets the family market with mobile phones and calling plans that appeal to both kids and their parents. The phones come in youthful styles, loaded with features that appeal to kids and tweens. At the same time, they include built-in controls that let parents restrict incoming and outgoing calls as well as limit texting at no additional cost. So Firefly phones meet the needs of both the kids who use them and the parents who pay for them.[23]

Roles and Status. A person belongs to many groups—family, clubs, organizations. The person's position in each group can be defined in terms of both role and status. A role consists of the activities people are expected to perform according to the persons around them. Each role carries a status reflecting the general esteem given to it by society.

People usually choose products appropriate to their roles and status. Consider the various roles a working mother plays. In her company, she plays the role of a brand manager; in her family, she plays the role of wife and mother; at her favorite sporting events, she plays the role of avid fan. As a brand manager, she will buy the kind of clothing that reflects her role and status in her company.

Personal Factors

A buyer's decisions also are influenced by personal characteristics such as the buyer's *age and life-cycle stage, occupation, economic situation, lifestyle,* and *personality and self-concept.*

Age and Life-Cycle Stage. People change the goods and services they buy over their lifetimes. Tastes in food, clothes, furniture, and recreation are often age related. Buying is also shaped by the stage of the family life cycle—the stages through which families might pass as they mature over time. Life-stage changes usually result from demographics and life-changing events—marriage, having children, purchasing a home, divorce, children going to college, changes in personal income, moving out of the house, and retirement. Marketers often define their target markets in terms of life-cycle stage and develop appropriate products and marketing plans for each stage.

▲Consumer information giant Acxiom's PersonicX life-stage segmentation system places U.S. households into one of 70 consumer segments and 21 life-stage groups, based on specific consumer behavior and demographic characteristics. PersonicX includes life-stage groups with names such as *Beginnings, Taking Hold, Cash & Careers, Jumbo Families, Transition Blues, Our Turn, Golden Years,* and *Active Elders.* For example, the *Taking Hold* group consists of young, energetic, well-funded couples and young families who are busy with their careers, social lives, and interests, especially fitness and active recreation. *Transition Blues* are blue-collar, less-educated, mid-income consumers who are transitioning to stable lives and talking about marriage and children.

"Consumers experience many life-stage changes during their lifetimes," says Acxiom. "As their life stages change, so do their behavior and purchasing preferences. Marketers who are armed with the data to understand the timing and makeup of life-stage changes among their customers will have a distinct advantage over their competitors."[24]

In line with today's tougher economic times, Acxiom has also developed a set of economic life-stage segments, including groups such as *Squeaking By, Eye on Essentials, Tight with a Purpose, It's My Life, Full Speed Ahead,* and *Potential Rebounders.* The *Potential Rebounders* are those more likely to loosen up on spending sooner. This group appears more likely than other segments to use online research before purchasing electronics, appliances, home decor, and jewelry. Thus, home improvement retailers appealing to this segment should have a strong online presence, providing pricing, features and benefits, and product availability.

Occupation. A person's occupation affects the goods and services bought. Blue-collar workers tend to buy more rugged work clothes, whereas executives buy more business suits. Marketers try to identify the occupational groups that have an above-average interest in their products and services.

▼Life-stage segmentation: The PersonicX 21 life-stage groupings let marketers see customers as they really are and target them precisely. "People aren't just a parent or only a doctor or simply a scuba diver. They are all of these things."

A company can even specialize in making products needed by a given occupational group.

> For example, Spear's Specialty Shoes fills a tiny niche in the shoe world by making high-end shoes for—of all things—clowns (and some team mascots and even store Santas). Founder Gary Spear, a former clown himself, discovered a need for good, comfortable clown shoes with reasonable delivery times. Over the past 25 years his company has built a worldwide reputation. At the company's Web site (www.spearshoes.com), professional clowns can browse different colors and styles and design their own shoes. It's a fun niche but these shoes are no joke. Made for professional clowning around, they are made with lightweight soles and serious padding, at a starting price of $300 a pair.[25]

Economic Situation. A person's economic situation will affect his or her store and product choices. Marketers watch trends in personal income, savings, and interest rates. In the face of the recent recession, most companies are taking steps to redesign, reposition, and reprice their products. For example, at Target, in order to counter the effects of the recession, "cheap has taken over chic." The discount retailer rolled out the "A new day. New ways to save." advertising campaign that focuses on value, with offers such as "the new barber shop—clippers $14.99," and "the new gym—gym ball $11.88." "This is the first time we've featured price points in our broadcast advertising," said a Target marketer at the start of the campaign. "As a whole we've increased our emphasis on value messaging. Our [tagline] is 'Expect more. Pay less.' We're putting more emphasis on the pay less promise."[26]

Lifestyle. People coming from the same subculture, social class, and occupation may have quite different lifestyles. **Lifestyle** is a person's pattern of living as expressed in his or her psychographics. It involves measuring consumers' major AIO dimensions—activities (work, hobbies, shopping, sports, social events), interests (food, fashion, family, recreation), and opinions (about themselves, social issues, business, products). Lifestyle captures something more than the person's social class or personality. It profiles a person's whole pattern of acting and interacting in the world.

When used carefully, the lifestyle concept can help marketers understand changing consumer values and how they affect buying behavior. Consumers don't just buy products, they buy the values and lifestyles those products represent. For example, BMW doesn't just sell convertibles, it sells the convertible lifestyle: "Skies never bluer. Knuckles never whiter." ▲And Merrell sells more than just rugged footwear: it sells a "Let's Get Outside" lifestyle. Says one marketer, "People's product choices are becoming more and more like value choices. It's not, 'I like this water, the way it tastes.' It's 'I feel like this car, or this show, is more reflective of who I am.'"

For example, retailer Anthropologie, with its whimsical, French flea market store atmosphere, sells a bohemian-chic lifestyle to which its young women customers aspire:

> In downtown San Francisco, which is teeming with both high-end and cheap chic outlets, Anthropologie is a mecca. It evokes hole-in-the-wall antique stores, Parisian boutiques, flea markets, and Grandma's kitchen in one fell swoop. It's a lifestyle emporium that you want to move into, or at least have a small piece of, even if it's just a lacquered light switch cover or retro tea towel. When customers enter an Anthropologie, they immediately leave behind the sterile mall or not-so-sterile street

Lifestyle
A person's pattern of living as expressed in his or her activities, interests, and opinions.

▼Lifestyle: Consumers don't just by products, they buy the values and lifestyles those products represent. Merrell sells more than just rugged footwear, it sells a "Let's Get Outside" lifestyle.

and are transported into another lifestyle. As a result, even when retail sales in general have slumped, Anthropologie's sales have continued to grow.[27]

Personality
The unique psychological characteristics that distinguish a person or group.

Personality and Self-Concept. Each person's distinct personality influences his or her buying behavior. **Personality** refers to the unique psychological characteristics that distinguish a person or group. Personality is usually described in terms of traits such as self-confidence, dominance, sociability, autonomy, defensiveness, adaptability, and aggressiveness. Personality can be useful in analyzing consumer behavior for certain product or brand choices.

The idea is that brands also have personalities, and that consumers are likely to choose brands with personalities that match their own. A *brand personality* is the specific mix of human traits that may be attributed to a particular brand. One researcher identified five brand personality traits: *sincerity* (down-to-earth, honest, wholesome, and cheerful); *excitement* (daring, spirited, imaginative, and up-to-date); *competence* (reliable, intelligent, and successful); *sophistication* (upper class and charming); and *ruggedness* (outdoorsy and tough).[28]

Most well-known brands are strongly associated with one particular trait: Jeep with "ruggedness," Apple with "excitement," CNN with "competence," and Dove with "sincerity." Hence, these brands will attract persons who are high on the same personality traits.

Many marketers use a concept related to personality—a person's *self-concept* (also called *self-image*). The idea is that people's possessions contribute to and reflect their identities—that is, "we are what we have." Thus, in order to understand consumer behavior, the marketer must first understand the relationship between consumer self-concept and possessions.

Apple applies these concepts in its long-running "Get a Mac" ad series that characterizes two people as computers—one guy plays the part of an Apple Mac and the other plays a personal computer (PC). The two have very different personalities and self-concepts. "Hello, I'm a Mac," says the guy on the right, who's younger and dressed in jeans. "And I'm a PC," says the one on the left, who's wearing dweeby glasses and a jacket and tie. The two men discuss the relative advantages of Macs versus PCs, with the Mac coming out on top. The ads present the Mac brand personality as young, laid back, and cool. The PC is portrayed as buttoned down, corporate, and a bit dorky. The message? If you see yourself as young and with it, you need a Mac.[29]

Psychological Factors

A person's buying choices are further influenced by four major psychological factors: *motivation, perception, learning,* and *beliefs and attitudes*.

Motive (drive)
A need that is sufficiently pressing to direct the person to seek satisfaction of the need.

Motivation. A person has many needs at any given time. Some are biological, arising from states of tension such as hunger, thirst, or discomfort. Others are psychological, arising from the need for recognition, esteem, or belonging. A need becomes a motive when it is aroused to a sufficient level of intensity. A **motive** (or drive) is a need that is sufficiently pressing to direct the person to seek satisfaction. Psychologists have developed theories of human motivation. Two of the most popular—the theories of Sigmund Freud and Abraham Maslow—have quite different meanings for consumer analysis and marketing.

Sigmund Freud assumed that people are largely unconscious about the real psychological forces shaping their behavior. He saw the person as growing up and repressing many urges. These urges are never eliminated or under perfect control; they emerge in dreams, in slips of the tongue, in neurotic and obsessive behavior, or ultimately in psychoses.

Freud's theory suggests that a person's buying decisions are affected by subconscious motives that even the buyer may not fully understand. ▲Thus, an aging baby boomer who buys a sporty BMW

▼Motivation: An aging baby boomer who buys a sporty convertible might explain that he simply likes the feel of the wind in his thinning hair. At a deeper level, he may be buying the car to feel young and independent again.

330Ci convertible might explain that he simply likes the feel of the wind in his thinning hair. At a deeper level, he may be trying to impress others with his success. At a still deeper level, he may be buying the car to feel young and independent again.

The term *motivation research* refers to qualitative research designed to probe consumers' hidden, subconscious motivations. Consumers often don't know or can't describe just why they act as they do. Thus, motivation researchers use a variety of probing techniques to uncover underlying emotions and attitudes toward brands and buying situations.

Many companies employ teams of psychologists, anthropologists, and other social scientists to carry out motivation research. One ad agency routinely conducts one-on-one, therapy-like interviews to delve into the inner workings of consumers. Another company asks consumers to describe their favorite brands as animals or cars (say, Cadillacs versus Chevrolets) in order to assess the prestige associated with various brands. Still others rely on hypnosis, dream therapy, or soft lights and mood music to plumb the murky depths of consumer psyches.

Such projective techniques seem pretty goofy, and some marketers dismiss such motivation research as mumbo jumbo. But many marketers use such touchy-feely approaches, now sometimes called *interpretive consumer research,* to dig deeper into consumer psyches and develop better marketing strategies.

Abraham Maslow sought to explain why people are driven by particular needs at particular times. Why does one person spend much time and energy on personal safety and another on gaining the esteem of others? Maslow's answer is that human needs are arranged in a hierarchy, as shown in ■ **Figure 5.4**, from the most pressing at the bottom to the least pressing at the top.[30] They include *physiological* needs, *safety* needs, *social* needs, *esteem* needs, and *self-actualization* needs.

A person tries to satisfy the most important need first. When that need is satisfied, it will stop being a motivator and the person will then try to satisfy the next most important need. For example, starving people (physiological need) will not take an interest in the latest happenings in the art world (self-actualization needs), nor in how they are seen or esteemed by others (social or esteem needs), nor even in whether they are breathing clean air (safety needs). But as each important need is satisfied, the next most important need will come into play.

Perception. A motivated person is ready to act. How the person acts is influenced by his or her own perception of the situation. All of us learn by the flow of information through our five senses: sight, hearing, smell, touch, and taste. However, each of us receives, organizes, and interprets this sensory information in an individual way. **Perception** is the process by which people select, organize, and interpret information to form a meaningful picture of the world.

Perception
The process by which people select, organize, and interpret information to form a meaningful picture of the world.

■ **Figure 5.4** Maslow's Hierarchy of Needs

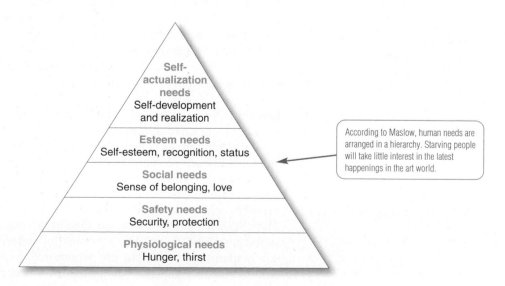

According to Maslow, human needs are arranged in a hierarchy. Starving people will take little interest in the latest happenings in the art world.

▲Selective perception: It's impossible for people to pay attention to the thousands of ads they're exposed to everyday, so they screen most of them out.

People can form different perceptions of the same stimulus because of three perceptual processes: selective attention, selective distortion, and selective retention. People are exposed to a great amount of stimuli every day. ▲For example, people are exposed to an estimated 3,000 to 5,000 ad messages every day. It is impossible for a person to pay attention to all these stimuli. *Selective attention*—the tendency for people to screen out most of the information to which they are exposed—means that marketers must work especially hard to attract the consumer's attention.[31]

Even noticed stimuli do not always come across in the intended way. Each person fits incoming information into an existing mind-set. *Selective distortion* describes the tendency of people to interpret information in a way that will support what they already believe. People also will forget much of what they learn. They tend to retain information that supports their attitudes and beliefs. *Selective retention* means that consumers are likely to remember good points made about a brand they favor and to forget good points made about competing brands. Because of selective attention, distortion, and retention, marketers must work hard to get their messages through.

Interestingly, although most marketers worry about whether their offers will be perceived at all, some consumers worry that they will be affected by marketing messages without even knowing it—through *subliminal advertising*. More than 50 years ago, a researcher announced that he had flashed the phrases "Eat popcorn" and "Drink Coca-Cola" on a screen in a New Jersey movie theater every five seconds for 1/300th of a second. He reported that although viewers did not consciously recognize these messages, they absorbed them subconsciously and bought 58 percent more popcorn and 18 percent more Coke. Suddenly advertisers and consumer-protection groups became intensely interested in subliminal perception. Although the researcher later admitted to making up the data, the issue has not died. Some consumers still fear that they are being manipulated by subliminal messages.

Numerous studies by psychologists and consumer researchers have found little or no link between subliminal messages and consumer behavior. Recent brain wave studies have found that in certain circumstances, our brains may register subliminal messages. However, it appears that subliminal advertising simply doesn't have the power attributed to it by its critics. Scoffs one industry insider, "Just between us, most [advertisers] have difficulty getting a 2 percent increase in sales with the help of $50 million in media and extremely *liminal* images of sex, money, power, and other [motivators] of human emotion. The very idea of [us] as puppeteers, cruelly pulling the strings of consumer marionettes, is almost too much to bear."[32]

Learning
Changes in an individual's behavior arising from experience.

Learning. When people act, they learn. **Learning** describes changes in an individual's behavior arising from experience. Learning theorists say that most human behavior is learned. Learning occurs through the interplay of drives, stimuli, cues, responses, and reinforcement.

A *drive* is a strong internal stimulus that calls for action. A drive becomes a motive when it is directed toward a particular *stimulus object*. For example, a person's drive for self-actualization might motivate him or her to look into buying a camera. The consumer's response to the idea of buying a camera is conditioned by the surrounding cues. *Cues* are minor stimuli that determine when, where, and how the person responds. For example, the person might spot several camera brands in a shop window, hear of a special sale price, or discuss cameras with a friend. These are all cues that might influence a consumer's *response* to his or her interest in buying the product.

Suppose the consumer buys a Nikon camera. If the experience is rewarding, the consumer will probably use the camera more and more, and his or her response will be *reinforced*. Then, the next time the consumer shops for a camera, or for binoculars or some similar product, the probability is greater that he or she will buy a Nikon product. The practical significance of learning theory for marketers is that they can build up demand for a product by associating it with strong drives, using motivating cues, and providing positive reinforcement.

Beliefs and Attitudes. Through doing and learning, people acquire beliefs and attitudes. These, in turn, influence their buying behavior. A **belief** is a descriptive thought that a person has about something. Beliefs may be based on real knowledge, opinion, or faith and may or may not carry an emotional charge. Marketers are interested in the beliefs that people formulate about specific products and services, because these beliefs make up product and brand images that affect buying behavior. If some of the beliefs are wrong and prevent purchase, the marketer will want to launch a campaign to correct them.

People have attitudes regarding religion, politics, clothes, music, food, and almost everything else. **Attitude** describes a person's relatively consistent evaluations, feelings, and tendencies toward an object or idea. Attitudes put people into a frame of mind of liking or disliking things, of moving toward or away from them. Our camera buyer may hold attitudes such as "Buy the best," "The Japanese make the best electronics products in the world," and "Creativity and self-expression are among the most important things in life." If so, the Nikon camera would fit well into the consumer's existing attitudes.

Attitudes are difficult to change. A person's attitudes fit into a pattern, and to change one attitude may require difficult adjustments in many others. Thus, a company should usually try to fit its products into existing attitudes rather than attempt to change attitudes. For example, today's beverage marketers now cater to people's new attitudes about health and well-being with drinks that do a lot more than just taste good or quench your thirst. ▲Coca-Cola's Fuze brand, for example, offers a line of "healthy infusion" beverages packed with vitamins, minerals, and antioxidants but without artificial preservatives, sweeteners, or colors. Fuze promises drinks that are good-tasting (with flavors like Blueberry Raspberry, Strawberry Melon, and Dragonfruit Lime) but also good for you—containing only natural ingredients that "help your metabolism work in your favor." By matching today's attitudes about life and healthful living, the Fuze brand has become a leader in the New Age beverage category.

We can now appreciate the many forces acting on consumer behavior. The consumer's choice results from the complex interplay of cultural, social, personal, and psychological factors.

Belief
A descriptive thought that a person holds about something.

Attitude
A person's consistently favorable or unfavorable evaluations, feelings, and tendencies toward an object or idea.

▲Fuze fits well with people's attitudes about health and well-being: Its "healthy infusion" beverages promise drinks that are "good-tasting but also good for you."

The Buyer Decision Process (pp 179–182)

Now that we have looked at the influences that affect buyers, we are ready to look at how consumers make buying decisions. ■ **Figure 5.5** shows that the buyer decision process consists of five stages: *need recognition, information search, evaluation of alternatives, purchase decision,* and *postpurchase behavior.* Clearly, the buying process starts long before the actual purchase and continues long after. Marketers need to focus on the entire buying process rather than on just the purchase decision.

Author Comment ≫
The actual purchase decision is just part of a much larger buying process—starting with need recognition through how you feel after making the purchase. Marketers want to be involved throughout the entire buyer decision process.

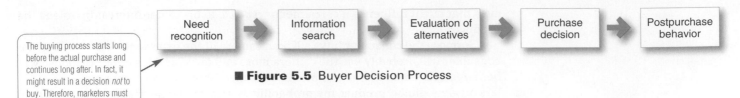

The buying process starts long before the actual purchase and continues long after. In fact, it might result in a decision *not* to buy. Therefore, marketers must focus on the entire buying process, not just the purchase decision.

■ **Figure 5.5** Buyer Decision Process

The figure suggests that consumers pass through all five stages with every purchase. But in more routine purchases, consumers often skip or reverse some of these stages. A woman buying her regular brand of toothpaste would recognize the need and go right to the purchase decision, skipping information search and evaluation. However, we use the model in Figure 5.5 because it shows all the considerations that arise when a consumer faces a new and complex purchase situation.

Need Recognition

The buying process starts with *need recognition*—the buyer recognizes a problem or need. The need can be triggered by *internal stimuli* when one of the person's normal needs—hunger, thirst, sex—rises to a level high enough to become a drive. A need can also be triggered by *external stimuli*. ▲For example, an advertisement or a discussion with a friend might get you thinking about buying a new car. At this stage, the marketer should research consumers to find out what kinds of needs or problems arise, what brought them about, and how they led the consumer to this particular product.

Information Search

An interested consumer may or may not search for more information. If the consumer's drive is strong and a satisfying product is near at hand, the consumer is likely to buy it then. If not, the consumer may store the need in memory or undertake an *information search* related to the need. For example, once you've decided you need a new car, at the least, you will probably pay more attention to car ads, cars owned by friends, and car conversations. Or you may actively search the Web, talk with friends, and gather information in other ways.

▼**Need recognition can be triggered by advertising: Time for a snack?**

Consumers can obtain information from any of several sources. These include *personal sources* (family, friends, neighbors, acquaintances), *commercial sources* (advertising, salespeople, dealer Web sites, packaging, displays), *public sources* (mass media, consumer rating organizations, Internet searches), and *experiential sources* (handling, examining, using the product). The relative influence of these information sources varies with the product and the buyer.

Generally, the consumer receives the most information about a product from commercial sources—those controlled by the marketer. The most effective sources, however, tend to be personal. Commercial sources normally *inform* the buyer, but personal sources *legitimize* or *evaluate* products for the buyer. As one marketer states, "It's rare that an advertising campaign can be as effective as a neighbor leaning over the fence and saying, 'This is a wonderful product.'" Increasingly, that "fence" is a digital one. A recent study revealed that consumers find sources of user-generated content—discussion forums, blogs, online review sites, and social networking sites—three times more influential when making a purchase decision than conventional marketing methods such as TV advertising.[33]

As more information is obtained, the consumer's awareness and knowledge of the available brands and features increase. In your car information search, you may learn about the several brands available. The information might also help you to drop certain brands from consideration. A company must design its marketing mix to make prospects aware of and knowledgeable about its brand. It should carefully identify consumers' sources of information and the importance of each source.

Evaluation of Alternatives

We have seen how the consumer uses information to arrive at a set of final brand choices. How does the consumer choose among the alternative brands? The marketer needs to know about *alternative evaluation*—that is, how the consumer processes information to arrive at brand choices. Unfortunately, consumers do not use a simple and single evaluation process in all buying situations. Instead, several evaluation processes are at work.

The consumer arrives at attitudes toward different brands through some evaluation procedure. How consumers go about evaluating purchase alternatives depends on the individual consumer and the specific buying situation. In some cases, consumers use careful calculations and logical thinking. At other times, the same consumers do little or no evaluating; instead they buy on impulse and rely on intuition. Sometimes consumers make buying decisions on their own; sometimes they turn to friends, online reviews, or salespeople for buying advice.

Suppose you've narrowed your car choices to three brands. And suppose that you are primarily interested in four attributes—styling, operating economy, warranty, and price. By this time, you've probably formed beliefs about how each brand rates on each attribute. Clearly, if one car rated best on all the attributes, we could predict that you would choose it. However, the brands will no doubt vary in appeal. You might base your buying decision on only one attribute, and your choice would be easy to predict. If you wanted styling above everything else, you would buy the car that you think has the best styling. But most buyers consider several attributes, each with different importance. If we knew the importance that you assigned to each of the four attributes, we could predict your car choice more reliably.

Marketers should study buyers to find out how they actually evaluate brand alternatives. If they know what evaluative processes go on, marketers can take steps to influence the buyer's decision.

Purchase Decision

In the evaluation stage, the consumer ranks brands and forms purchase intentions. Generally, the consumer's *purchase decision* will be to buy the most preferred brand, but two factors can come between the purchase *intention* and the purchase *decision*. The first factor is the *attitudes of others*. If someone important to you thinks that you should buy the lowest-priced car, then the chances of you buying a more expensive car are reduced.

The second factor is *unexpected situational factors*. The consumer may form a purchase intention based on factors such as expected income, expected price, and expected product benefits. However, unexpected events may change the purchase intention. For example, the economy might take a turn for the worse, a close competitor might drop its price, or a friend might report being disappointed in your preferred car. Thus, preferences and even purchase intentions do not always result in actual purchase choice.

Postpurchase Behavior

The marketer's job does not end when the product is bought. After purchasing the product, the consumer will be satisfied or dissatisfied and will engage in *postpurchase behavior* of interest to the marketer. What determines whether the buyer is satisfied or dissatisfied with a purchase? The answer lies in the relationship between the *consumer's expectations* and the product's *perceived performance*. If the product falls short of expectations, the consumer is disappointed; if it meets expectations, the consumer is satisfied; if it exceeds expectations, the consumer is delighted. The larger the gap between expectations and performance, the greater the consumer's dissatisfaction. This suggests that sellers should promise only what their brands can deliver so that buyers are satisfied.

Cognitive dissonance
Buyer discomfort caused by postpurchase conflict.

Almost all major purchases, however, result in **cognitive dissonance**, or discomfort caused by postpurchase conflict. After the purchase, consumers are satisfied with the benefits of the chosen brand and are glad to avoid the drawbacks of the brands not bought. However, every purchase involves compromise. So consumers feel uneasy about acquiring the drawbacks of the chosen brand and about losing the benefits of the brands not purchased. Thus, consumers feel at least some postpurchase dissonance for every purchase.[34]

Why is it so important to satisfy the customer? Customer satisfaction is a key to building profitable relationships with consumers—to keeping and growing consumers and reaping their customer lifetime value. Satisfied customers buy a product again, talk favorably to others about the product, pay less attention to competing brands and advertising, and buy other products from the company. Many marketers go beyond merely *meeting* the expectations of customers—they aim to *delight* the customer.

A dissatisfied consumer responds differently. Bad word of mouth often travels farther and faster than good word of mouth. It can quickly damage consumer attitudes about a company and its products. But companies cannot simply rely on dissatisfied customers to volunteer their complaints when they are dissatisfied. Most unhappy customers never tell the company about their problem. Therefore, a company should measure customer satisfaction regularly. It should set up systems that *encourage* customers to complain. In this way, the company can learn how well it is doing and how it can improve.

By studying the overall buyer decision, marketers may be able to find ways to help consumers move through it. For example, if consumers are not buying a new product because they do not perceive a need for it, marketing might launch advertising messages that trigger the need and show how the product solves customers' problems. If customers know about the product but are not buying because they hold unfavorable attitudes toward it, the marketer must find ways either to change the product or change consumer perceptions.

Author Comment >>
Here, we look at some special considerations in *new-product* buying decisions.

The Buyer Decision Process for New Products (pp 182–184)

We have looked at the stages buyers go through in trying to satisfy a need. Buyers may pass quickly or slowly through these stages, and some of the stages may even be reversed. Much depends on the nature of the buyer, the product, and the buying situation.

New product
A good, service, or idea that is perceived by some potential customers as new.

We now look at how buyers approach the purchase of new products. A **new product** is a good, service, or idea that is perceived by some potential customers as new. It may have been around for a while, but our interest is in how consumers learn about products for the first time and make decisions on whether to adopt them. We define the **adoption process** as "the mental process through which an individual passes from first learning about an innovation to final adoption," and *adoption* as the decision by an individual to become a regular user of the product.[35]

Adoption process
The mental process through which an individual passes from first hearing about an innovation to final adoption.

Stages in the Adoption Process
Consumers go through five stages in the process of adopting a new product:

- *Awareness:* The consumer becomes aware of the new product, but lacks information about it.
- *Interest:* The consumer seeks information about the new product.
- *Evaluation:* The consumer considers whether trying the new product makes sense.
- *Trial:* The consumer tries the new product on a small scale to improve his or her estimate of its value.
- *Adoption:* The consumer decides to make full and regular use of the new product.

This model suggests that the new-product marketer should think about how to help consumers move through these stages. For example, as the recent recession set in, Hyundai discovered many potential customers were interested in buy-

▲ The adoption process: To help potential customers past concerns about the uncertain economy, Hyundai offered an assurance program protecting customers against lost jobs and incomes.

ing new cars but refrained from doing so because of the uncertain economy. ▲ To help buyers pass this hurdle, the carmaker offered the Hyundai Assurance Program, promising to let buyers who financed or leased a new Hyundai return their vehicles at no cost and with no harm to their credit rating if they lost their jobs or incomes within a year. Sales of the Hyundai Sonata surged 85 percent in the month following the start of the campaign. Other carmakers soon followed with their own assurance plans.[36]

Individual Differences in Innovativeness

People differ greatly in their readiness to try new products. In each product area, there are "consumption pioneers" and early adopters. Other individuals adopt new products much later. People can be classified into the adopter categories shown in ■ **Figure 5.6**. After a slow start, an increasing number of people adopt the new product. The number of adopters reaches a peak and then drops off as fewer nonadopters remain. Innovators are defined as the first 2.5 percent of the buyers to adopt a new idea (those beyond two standard deviations from mean adoption time); the early adopters are the next 13.5 percent (between one and two standard deviations); and so forth.

The five adopter groups have differing values. *Innovators* are venturesome—they try new ideas at some risk. *Early adopters* are guided by respect—they are opinion leaders in their communities and adopt new ideas early but carefully. The *early majority* are deliberate—although they rarely are leaders, they adopt new ideas before the average person. The *late majority* are skeptical—they adopt an innovation only after a majority of people have tried it. Finally, *laggards* are tradition bound—they are suspicious of changes and adopt the innovation only when it has become something of a tradition itself.

This adopter classification suggests that an innovating firm should research the characteristics of innovators and early adopters in their product categories and should direct marketing efforts toward them.

Influence of Product Characteristics on Rate of Adoption

The characteristics of the new product affect its rate of adoption. Some products catch on almost overnight—for example, the iPod and iPhone, both of which flew off retailers' shelves at an astounding rate from the day they were introduced. Others take a longer time to gain acceptance. For example, the first HDTVs were introduced in the United States in the 1990s, but by 2009 only about 25 percent of U.S. TV households owned a high definition set.[37]

■ **Figure 5.6** Adopter Categorization on the Basis of Relative Time of Adoption of Innovations

Source: Reprinted with permission of the Free Press, a Division of Simon & Schuster, from *Diffusion of Innovations*, Fifth Edition, by Everett M. Rogers. Copyright © 2003 by the Free Press.

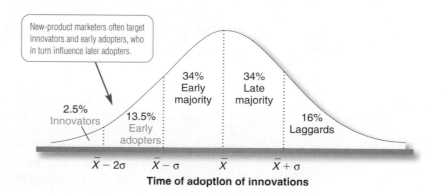

Five characteristics are especially important in influencing an innovation's rate of adoption. For example, consider the characteristics of HDTV in relation to the rate of adoption:

- *Relative advantage:* the degree to which the innovation appears superior to existing products. HDTV offers substantially improved picture quality. This speeded up its rate of adoption.
- *Compatibility:* the degree to which the innovation fits the values and experiences of potential consumers. HDTV, for example, is highly compatible with the lifestyles of the TV-watching public. However, in the early years, HDTV was not yet compatible with programming and broadcasting systems, slowing adoption. Now, as more and more high definition programs and channels have become available, the rate of HDTV adoption has increased. In fact, the number of U.S. HDTV-owning households has more than doubled in just the past two years.
- *Complexity:* the degree to which the innovation is difficult to understand or use. HDTVs are not very complex. Therefore, as more programming has become available and prices have fallen, the rate of HDTV adoption is increasing faster than that of more complex innovations.
- *Divisibility:* the degree to which the innovation may be tried on a limited basis. Early HDTVs and HD cable and satellite systems were very expensive, slowing the rate of adoption. As prices fall, adoption rates are increasing.
- *Communicability:* the degree to which the results of using the innovation can be observed or described to others. Because HDTV lends itself to demonstration and description, its use will spread faster among consumers.

Other characteristics influence the rate of adoption, such as initial and ongoing costs, risk and uncertainty, and social approval. The new-product marketer must research all these factors when developing the new product and its marketing program.

 Speed Bump: Linking the Concepts

Here's a good place to pull over and apply the concepts you've examined in the first part of this chapter.

- Think about a specific major purchase you've made recently. What buying process did you follow? What major factors influenced your decision?
- Pick a company or brand that we've discussed in a previous chapter—Zappos, Nike, McDonald's, P&G's Tide, TOMS shoes, Logitech, or another. How does the company you chose use its understanding of customers and their buying behavior to build better customer relationships?
- Think about a company like Intel, which sells its products to computer makers and other businesses rather than to final consumers. How would Intel's marketing to business customers differ from Starbucks's marketing to final consumers? The second part of the chapter deals with this issue.

Author Comment »
Now that we've looked at consumers markets and buyer behavior, let's dig into business markets and buyer behavior. Thinking ahead, how are they the same? How are they different?

BUSINESS MARKETS AND BUSINESS BUYER BEHAVIOR
(pp 184–185)

In one way or another, most large companies sell to other organizations. Companies such as DuPont, Boeing, IBM, Caterpillar, and countless other firms sell *most* of their products to other businesses. Even large consumer-products companies, which make products used by final consumers, must first sell their products to other businesses. For example, General Mills makes many familiar consumer brands—Big G cereals (Cheerios, Wheaties, Trix, Chex), baking products (Pillsbury, Betty Crocker, Gold Medal flour), snacks (Nature Valley, Pop Secret, Chex Mix), Yoplait yogurt,

Häagen-Dazs ice cream, and others. But to sell these products to consumers, General Mills must first sell them to its wholesaler and retailer customers, who in turn serve the consumer market.

Business buyer behavior refers to the buying behavior of the organizations that buy goods and services for use in the production of other products and services that are sold, rented, or supplied to others. It also includes the behavior of retailing and wholesaling firms that acquire goods to resell or rent them to others at a profit. In the *business buying process*, business buyers determine which products and services their organizations need to purchase and then find, evaluate, and choose among alternative suppliers and brands. *Business-to-business (B-to-B) marketers* must do their best to understand business markets and business buyer behavior. Then, like businesses that sell to final buyers, they must build profitable relationships with business customers by creating superior customer value (see Marketing at Work 5.2).

Business Markets (pp 185–188)

The business market is *huge*. In fact, business markets involve far more dollars and items than do consumer markets. For example, think about the large number of business transactions involved in the production and sale of a single set of Goodyear tires. Various suppliers sell Goodyear the rubber, steel, equipment, and other goods that it needs to produce tires. Goodyear then sells the finished tires to retailers, who in turn sell them to consumers. Thus, many sets of *business* purchases were made for only one set of *consumer* purchases. In addition, Goodyear sells tires as original equipment to manufacturers who install them on new vehicles, and as replacement tires to companies that maintain their own fleets of company cars, trucks, buses, or other vehicles.

In some ways, business markets are similar to consumer markets. Both involve people who assume buying roles and make purchase decisions to satisfy needs. However, business markets differ in many ways from consumer markets. The main differences are in *market structure and demand*, the *nature of the buying unit*, and the *types of decisions and the decision process* involved.

Market Structure and Demand

The business marketer normally deals with *far fewer but far larger buyers* than the consumer marketer does. Even in large business markets, a few buyers often account for most of the purchasing. For example, when Goodyear sells replacement tires to final consumers, its potential market includes the owners of the millions of cars currently in use around the world. But Goodyear's fate in the business market depends on getting orders from one of only a handful of large automakers. Similarly, Black & Decker sells its power tools and outdoor equipment to tens of millions of consumers worldwide. However, it must sell these products through three huge retail customers—Home Depot, Lowe's, and Wal-Mart—which combined account for more than half its sales.

Further, business demand is **derived demand**— it ultimately comes from (derives from) the demand for consumer goods. Hewlett-Packard and Dell buy Intel microprocessor chips because consumers buy personal computers. If consumer demand for computers drops, so will the demand for microprocessors. Therefore, B-to-B marketers sometimes promote their products directly to final consumers to increase business demand. ▲For example, Intel advertises heavily to personal computer buyers, selling them on the virtues of Intel and its microprocessors. Recent ads from Intel position its people as "Sponsors of Tomorrow"—just the folks

Sidebar definitions

Business buyer behavior
The buying behavior of the organizations that buy goods and services for use in the production of other products and services or to resell or rent them to others at a profit.

Author Comment »
Business markets operate "behind-the-scenes" to most consumers. Most of the things you buy involve many sets of business purchases before you ever see them.

Derived demand
Business demand that ultimately comes from (derives from) the demand for consumer goods.

▼**Derived demand: Intel advertises heavily to sell users on the virtues of the company and its microprocessors. "Making microprocessors is tricky business," says this ad. "That's why our workers must wear those silly-looking outfits."**

Marketing at Work 5.2

Tejari.com: Building B-to-B Customer Partnerships

Tejari.com was established in June 2000. *Tejari* is an Arabic word meaning trade or commerce. It is a part of the Dubai World group of companies. Initially when the company was set up its key purpose was to facilitate trading activities, enhance the levels of transparency, and increase efficiency and productivity for the Dubai government departments through a business-to-business e-commerce platform. The e-commerce platform brings buyers and sellers together in a virtual marketplace where members of the community can engage in spot-purchasing and online auctions (or reverse auctions). Since then, Tejari was extended to other quasi-government and private enterprises. Currently, Tejari has a physical presence in 11 countries and has users from more than 40 countries. Tejari's total active membership almost exceeds 1 million across 42 industries. The CEO Sohail Al Banna asserts, "... we are driven to establish Tejari as the preferred e-market place for all trading communities in the Middle East and the Subcontinent within 5 years, by providing powerful yet unsophisticated services that connect Internet-based trading communities. . . ."

Trade contributes 16.4 percent to the GDP (gross domestic product) of the United Arab Emirates (UAE). The second-most sought after product in the electronic purchasing family is e-sourcing, with a global market size of $878 million in 2008 and expected to top $1 billion in 2009. Most of the business in UAE—approximately 85 to 95 percent—is based on small- and medium-sized enterprises, which have the potential to contribute as much as 46 percent to the GDP. In the United States, it is estimated that Internet trading accounts for more than 10 percent of GDP, with the global average at 5 percent, the Middle East at 1.5 percent. The government has been the champion of this venture. UAE tops the region in e-readiness rankings in the Economist Intelligence Unit's survey of 70 countries. E-readiness is a measure of a country's infrastructure investment in connectivity and technology. According to the Global Information Technology Report 2008–2009 on the "Network Readiness Index (NRI)," published by the World Economic Forum and INSEAD, UAE has spearheaded the region's strong performance with its ranking within the top 3 from a list of 134 global economies in the category "importance of ICT to government vision of the future."

Building the market was not easy as the product had a slow adoption. Tejari has invested time, effort, and money to educate the Middle East North Africa business community about the way electronic trading could assist the buyers to procure efficiently and effectively and to help suppliers to promote their products and services to a global audience and grow their business. It meant starting with the top management (CEO or CFO levels) and asking the industry to rethink purchases strategically, with a key assumption being that pricing was dynamic and could be transparent. This was not easy. Since successful adoption of this platform needs understanding of the technology, a change of mindset, and even a redirection of company investment, the Tejari Academy actively educates the marketplace. The eReady program helps the small- to medium-size businesses in the region (and beyond) to understand the benefits of online trade and online sourcing. Tejari trains major buyers on procurement best practices and suppliers on getting an e-readiness certification among other things to optimize usage. Tejari also provides strategic procurement consultancy services advising buyers on ways to enhance transparency, save costs, and improve the overall performance of the procurement departments.

Tejari and Dubai's Department of Economic Development (DED) have made a huge contribution to the UAE e-readiness levels by enabling 16 percent of all Dubai businesses to trade online through MyLinkDubai, an online community of over 77,000 companies. MyLinkDubai serves as a platform to facilitate trade and relationships between businesses based in Dubai and the world. MyLinkDubai focuses on transitioning all business within the DED to a knowedge-based economy where each company is eReady. MyLinkDubai members can upload their company profile on the portal, showcase their products, search for other companies within the community, and above all, have access to a trading floor where they can interact with potential buyers or sellers. DED and Tejari's objective is to have 100 percent of all Dubai businesses eReady by 2012.

These changes have resulted in a massive adoption of Internet-based technologies and other systems' backend of e-procurement systems, which have greatly improved the performance of many organizations in the UAE especially in the government sector. For example, the concept of reverse auction is not new but not very widely adopted. Here finalized suppliers are invited for a final bidding process that lasts a few hours. During that window, the final bidding frenzy leads to major

you'd want making the chip in your computer. "Making microprocessors is a tricky business," says one ad. "This is why our clean rooms are 10,000 times cleaner than a hospital operating room. It's also why our workers must wear those silly-looking outfits." The increased demand for Intel chips boosts demand for the PCs containing them, and both Intel and its business partners win.

Many business markets have *inelastic demand*; that is, total demand for many business products is not affected much by price changes, especially in the short run. A drop in the price of leather will not cause shoe manufacturers to buy much more leather unless it results in lower shoe prices that, in turn, will increase consumer demand for shoes.

savings. The largest local bank in UAE shortlisted 19 from original 24 suppliers submitted, during the reverse auction online negotiations, a total of 77 bids were submitted in 5 hours and 53 minutes leading to a total annual savings of up to 30 percent in some categories such as stationery.

To facilitate sales, sellers can book an online showroom and exhibit their products to over 200,000 members in 15 countries. Tejari.com has also designed products that can deliver a guaranteed number of leads and helps clients find trade matches most suitable for their criteria. They can get the latest information on the electronic marketplace or get rights for bidding. For example, the eReady program trains and advises members to make the most of their online presence. Since there is always apprehension when dealing online, Tejari instituted their own online eVerification service in collaboration with a company based in Hong Kong called Global Authentication and companies receive an online mark of trust as a guarantee to other businesses that indicates that the organization is authentic, credible, and legal. To support a very fluid dynamic market that never goes to sleep, Tejari has toll free numbers, where queries are answered in 4 languages across 11 countries, 24 hours a day, 7 days a week. Buyers using the eBuy Premier package have to integrate their backend e-procurement systems with the Tejari marketplace in order to streamline their sourcing process. Tejari can cut costs by up to 20 percent. This business evolves constantly; products and technology are changed to meet the market demand. Today according to a Forrester research report titled "Holistic View: The ePurchasing Software Market," Tejari.com has been ranked as the eighth largest global electronic sourcing site.

Since 2000, Tejari's total transaction value tops $7.5 billion globally. Its customers are across various industries, including banks, airlines, media, telecommunications, healthcare, construction, and even the government sector. For example, in the governnment-to-business (G2B) sector, Tejari.com helped the Road and Transport Authority (RTA) of the Dubai government to source 2,400 buses for the public transport service. It awarded a contract worth $517 million (AED 1.9 billion) in a single auction. This represents the largest online tender in the Middle East. RTA's purchase department uses Tejari for many of its larger essential transactions, including automobiles, spare parts, electronics items, IT equipment, road maintenance equipment, office supplies, and even food supplies. In the aviation sector, they

▲Teraji.com is one of the companies at the forefront of developing electronic commerce in the United Arab Emirates. Teraji.com has partnered with Dubai's Department of Economic Development (DED) to help achieve the country's target of total e-readiness by 2012.

helped Etihad Airways, a leading player in aviation industry, save up to 20 percent on purchases. Products purchased through the Tejari portal include technology equipment, such as laptops, PCs and servers. Etihad was able to explore options, both in terms of products and pricing, before making a decision.

Sources: Based on information from Tejari.com, www.tejari.com, UAEInteract (2008), "UAE at a Glance 2008," accessed December 27, 2008 at www.uaeinteract.com "The Dubai Police Wins Tejari eLEADER Award," dated April 27, 2009, accessed at www.tejari.com/Tejari/News/NewsListings.aspx?ID=88%20&Type=TIN%20&PID=5; BrandCentral Report (2009), "Sustained Brand Positioning to Stimulate Growth of UAE's SME Sector," AMEInfo.com, dated September 14, 2009, accessed at www.ameinfo.com/209412.html; UAEInteract (2009), "UAE Tops Regional Countries in e-Readiness Rankings," posted on June 18, 2009, accessed at www.uaeinteract.com/docs/UAE_tops_regional_countries_in_e-readiness_rankings_/36354.htm; Morris, M. (2009), "Importance of ICT to UAE Gov't Recognised in New Report," dated June 20, 2009, accessed at www.itp.net/559430-importance-of-ict-to-uae-govt-recognised-in-new-report; and Forrester Research (2009), "Tejari Ranks in the Top Ten eSourcing Vendors Worldwide According to Independent Research Report," dated January 12, 2009, accessed at www.tejari.com/Tejari/News/NewsListings.aspx?ID=85%20&Type=TIN%20&PID=5.

Finally, business markets have more *fluctuating demand*. The demand for many business goods and services tends to change more—and more quickly—than the demand for consumer goods and services does. A small percentage increase in consumer demand can cause large increases in business demand. Sometimes a rise of only 10 percent in consumer demand can cause as much as a 200 percent rise in business demand during the next period.

Nature of the Buying Unit

Compared with consumer purchases, a business purchase usually involves *more decision participants* and a *more professional purchasing effort*. Often, business buying is done by trained purchasing agents who spend their working lives learning how to buy better. The more complex the purchase, the more likely it is that several people will participate in the decision-making process. Buying committees made up of technical experts and top management are common in the buying of major goods. Beyond this, B-to-B marketers now face a new breed of higher-level, better-trained supply managers. Therefore, companies must have well-trained marketers and salespeople to deal with these well-trained buyers.

Types of Decisions and the Decision Process

Business buyers usually face *more complex* buying decisions than do consumer buyers. Business purchases often involve large sums of money, complex technical and economic considerations, and interactions among many people at many levels of the buyer's organization. Because the purchases are more complex, business buyers may take longer to make their decisions. The business buying process also tends to be *more formalized* than the consumer buying process. Large business purchases usually call for detailed product specifications, written purchase orders, careful supplier searches, and formal approval.

Finally, in the business buying process, the buyer and seller are often much *more dependent* on each other. B-to-B marketers may roll up their sleeves and work closely with their customers during all stages of the buying process—from helping customers define problems, to finding solutions, to supporting after-sale operation. They often customize their offerings to individual customer needs. In the short run, sales go to suppliers who meet buyers' immediate product and service needs. In the long run, however, business-to-business marketers keep a customer's sales and create customer value by meeting current needs *and* by partnering with customers to help them solve their problems.

Supplier development
Systematic development of networks of supplier–partners to ensure an appropriate and dependable supply of products and materials for use in making products or reselling them to others

In recent years, relationships between customers and suppliers have been changing from downright adversarial to close and chummy. In fact, many customer companies are now practicing **supplier development**, systematically developing networks of supplier-partners to ensure an appropriate and dependable supply of products and materials that they will use in making their own products or resell to others. For example, Wal-Mart doesn't have a "Purchasing Department," it has a "Supplier Development Department." And giant Swedish furniture retailer IKEA doesn't just buy from its suppliers, it involves them deeply in the customer value-creation process.

> IKEA, the world's largest furniture retailer, is the quintessential global cult brand. Customers from Beijing to Moscow to Middletown, Ohio, flock to the $27 billion Scandinavian retailer's nearly 300 huge stores in 36 countries, drawn by IKEA's trendy but simple and practical furniture at affordable prices. But IKEA's biggest obstacle to growth isn't opening new stores and attracting customers. Rather, it's finding enough of the right kinds of *suppliers* to help design and produce the billions of dollars of affordable goods that those customers will carry out of its stores. IKEA currently relies on about 1,400 suppliers in 54 countries to stock its shelves. IKEA doesn't just rely on spot suppliers who might be available when needed. Instead, it has systematically developed a robust network of supplier-partners that reliably provide the more than 9,500 items it stocks. IKEA's designers start with a basic customer value proposition. Then, they find and work closely with key suppliers to bring that proposition to market. Thus, IKEA does more than just buy from suppliers; it also involves them deeply in the process of designing and making stylish but affordable products to keep IKEA's customers coming back.[38]

Business buying decisions can range from routine to incredibly complex, involving only a few or very many decision makers and buying influences.

Business Buyer Behavior (pp 188–192)

At the most basic level, marketers want to know how business buyers will respond to various marketing stimuli. ■ **Figure 5.7** shows a model of business buyer behavior. In this model, marketing and other stimuli affect the buying organization and produce certain buyer responses. These stimuli enter the organization and are turned into buyer responses. In order to design good marketing strategies, the marketer must understand what happens within the organization to turn stimuli into purchase responses.

■ Figure 5.7 A Model
of Business Buyer Behavior

In some ways, business markets are similar to consumer markets—this model looks a lot like the model of consumer buyer behavior presented in Figure 5.1. But there are some major differences, especially in the nature of the buying unit, the types of decisions made, and the decision process.

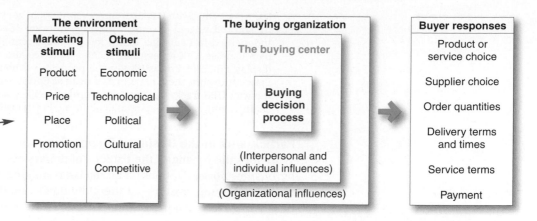

The environment		The buying organization	Buyer responses
Marketing stimuli	**Other stimuli**	*The buying center*	Product or service choice
Product	Economic	**Buying decision process**	Supplier choice
Price	Technological		Order quantities
Place	Political	(Interpersonal and individual influences)	Delivery terms and times
Promotion	Cultural		Service terms
	Competitive	(Organizational influences)	Payment

Within the organization, buying activity consists of two major parts: the buying center, made up of all the people involved in the buying decision, and the buying decision process. The model shows that the buying center and the buying decision process are influenced by internal organizational, interpersonal, and individual factors as well as by external environmental factors.

The model in Figure 5.7 suggests four questions about business buyer behavior: What buying decisions do business buyers make? Who participates in the buying process? What are the major influences on buyers? How do business buyers make their buying decisions?

Major Type of Buying Situations

Straight rebuy
A business buying situation in which the buyer routinely reorders something without any modifications.

Modified rebuy
A business buying situation in which the buyer wants to modify product specifications, prices, terms, or suppliers.

New task
A business buying situation in which the buyer purchases a product or service for the first time.

Systems selling (or solutions selling)
Buying a packaged solution to a problem from a single seller, thus avoiding all the separate decisions involved in a complex buying situation.

There are three major types of buying situations.[39] In a **straight rebuy**, the buyer reorders something without any modifications. It is usually handled on a routine basis by the purchasing department. To keep the business, "in" suppliers try to maintain product and service quality. "Out" suppliers try to find new ways to add value or exploit dissatisfaction so that the buyer will consider them.

In a **modified rebuy**, the buyer wants to modify product specifications, prices, terms, or suppliers. The in suppliers may become nervous and feel pressured to put their best foot forward to protect an account. Out suppliers may see the modified rebuy situation as an opportunity to make a better offer and gain new business.

A company buying a product or service for the first time faces a **new-task** situation. In such cases, the greater the cost or risk, the larger the number of decision participants and the greater their efforts to collect information. The new-task situation is the marketer's greatest opportunity and challenge. The marketer not only tries to reach as many key buying influences as possible but also provides help and information. The buyer makes the fewest decisions in the straight rebuy and the most in the new-task decision.

Many business buyers prefer to buy a complete solution to a problem from a single seller instead of buying separate products and services from several suppliers and putting them together. The sale often goes to the firm that provides the most complete *system* for meeting the customer's needs and solving its problems. Such **systems selling (or solutions selling)** is often a key business marketing strategy for winning and holding accounts.

Thus, UPS does more than just ship packages for its business customers. It develops entire solutions to customers' transportation and logistics problems. For example, UPS bundles a complete system of services that support Nikon's consumer products supply chain—including logistics, transportation, freight, and customs brokerage services—into one smooth-running system.[40]

When Nikon entered the digital camera market, it decided that it needed an entirely new distribution strategy as well. So it asked transportation and logistics giant UPS to design a complete system for moving its entire electronics product line from its Asian factories to retail stores throughout the United States, Latin America, and the Caribbean. Now, products leave Nikon's Asian manufacturing centers and arrive on American retailers' shelves in as few as two days, with UPS handling everything in between. UPS first manages air and ocean freight and related customs brokerage to bring Nikon products from Korea, Japan, and Indonesia to its Louisville, Kentucky, operations center. There, UPS can either "kit" the Nikon merchandise with accessories such as batteries and chargers or repackage it for in-store display. Finally, UPS distributes the products to thousands of retailers across the United States or exports them to Latin American or Caribbean retail outlets and distributors. Along the way, UPS tracks the goods and provides Nikon with a "snapshot" of the entire supply chain, letting Nikon keep retailers informed of delivery times and adjust them as needed.

Participants in the Business Buying Process

Buying center
All the individuals and units that play a role in the purchase decision-making process.

Who does the buying of the trillions of dollars' worth of goods and services needed by business organizations? The decision-making unit of a buying organization is called its **buying center**—all the individuals and units that play a role in the business purchase decision-making process. This group includes the actual users of the product or service, those who make the buying decision, those who influence the buying decision, those who do the actual buying, and those who control buying information.

The buying center is not a fixed and formally identified unit within the buying organization. It is a set of buying roles assumed by different people for different purchases. Within the organization, the size and makeup of the buying center will vary for different products and for different buying situations. For some routine purchases, one person—say, a purchasing agent—may assume all the buying center roles and serve as the only person involved in the buying decision. For more complex purchases, the buying center may include 20 or 30 people from different levels and departments in the organization.

The buying center concept presents a major marketing challenge. The business marketer must learn who participates in the decision, each participant's relative influence, and what evaluation criteria each decision participant uses. This can be difficult.

For instance, the medical products and services group of Cardinal Health sells disposable surgical gowns to hospitals. ▲It identifies the hospital personnel involved in this buying decision as the vice president of purchasing, the operating room administrator, and the surgeons. Each participant plays a different role. The vice president of purchasing analyzes whether the hospital should buy disposable gowns or reusable gowns. If analysis favors disposable gowns, then the operating room administrator compares competing products and prices and makes a choice. This administrator considers the gowns' absorbency, antiseptic quality, design, and cost, and normally buys the brand that meets requirements at the lowest cost. Finally, surgeons affect the decision later by reporting their satisfaction or dissatisfaction with the brand.

▲Buying Center: Cardinal Health deals with a wide range of buying influences, from purchasing executives and hospital administrators to the surgeons who actually use its products.

The buying center usually includes some obvious participants who are involved formally in the buying decision. For example, the decision to buy a corporate jet will probably involve the company's CEO, chief pilot, a purchasing agent, some legal staff, a member of top management, and others formally charged with the buying decision. It may also involve less obvious, informal participants, some of whom may actually make or strongly affect the buying decision. Sometimes, even the people in the buying center are not aware of all the buying participants. For example, the decision about which corporate jet to buy may actually be made by a corporate board member who has an interest in flying and who knows a lot about airplanes. This board member may work behind the scenes to sway the decision. Many business buying decisions result from the complex interactions of ever-changing buying center participants.

▲ Emotions play an important role in business buying: This Peterbilt ad stresses performance factors such as fuel efficiency. But it also stresses more emotional factors, such as the raw beauty of Peterbilt trucks and the pride of owning and driving one—"Class Pays."

Major Influences on Business Buyers

Business buyers are subject to many influences when they make their buying decisions. Some marketers assume that the major influences are economic. They think buyers will favor the supplier who offers the lowest price or the best product or the most service. They concentrate on offering strong economic benefits to buyers. However, business buyers actually respond to both economic and personal factors. Far from being cold, calculating, and impersonal, business buyers are human and social as well. They react to both reason and emotion.

Today, most B-to-B marketers recognize that emotion plays an important role in business buying decisions. For example, you might expect that an advertisement promoting large trucks to corporate fleet buyers or independent owner-operators would stress objective technical, performance, and economic factors. ▲For instance, befitting today's tougher economic times, premium heavy-duty truck maker Peterbilt does stress performance—its dealers and Web site provide plenty of information about factors such as maneuverability, productivity, reliability, comfort, and fuel efficiency. But Peterbilt ads appeal to buyers' emotions as well. They show the raw beauty of the trucks, and the Peterbilt slogan—"Class Pays"—suggests that owning a Peterbilt truck is a matter of pride as well as superior performance. Says the company, "On highways, construction sites, city streets, logging roads—everywhere customers earn their living—Peterbilt's red oval is a familiar symbol of performance, reliability, and pride."

■ **Figure 5.8** lists various groups of influences on business buyers—environmental, organizational, interpersonal, and individual.[41] Business buyers are heavily influenced by *environmental factors*, such as economic, technological, political, competitive, and social and cultural developments. For example, the wake of the recent economic downturn, just like final consumers, business buyers have tightened their budgets and spending. Like final consumers, they are looking for greater value in everything they buy. Now, more than ever, B-to-B marketers must sharpen their value propositions and help customers find effective and efficient solutions. "Anyone who says the economy is not a challenge is totally in denial" says one B-to-B marketing expert. Companies "need to look at the needs of customers. It's customer, customer, and customer now."[42]

Organizational factors are also important. Each buying organization has its own objectives, policies, procedures, structure, and systems, and the business marketer must understand these factors well. Questions such as these arise: How many people are involved in the buying decision? Who are they? What are their evaluative criteria? What are the company's policies and limits on its buyers?

■ **Figure 5.8** Major Influences on Business Buyer Behavior

Like consumer buying decisions in Figure 5.2, business buying decisions are affected by an incredibly complex combination of environmental, interpersonal, and individual influences, but with an extra layer of organizational factors thrown into the mix.

Environmental
Economic developments
Supply conditions
Technological change
Political and regulatory developments
Competitive developments
Culture and customs

Organizational
Objectives
Policies
Procedures
Organizational structure
Systems

Interpersonal
Authority
Status
Empathy
Persuasiveness

Individual
Age
Income
Education
Job position
Personality
Risk attitudes

Buyers

The buying center usually includes many participants who influence each other, so *interpersonal factors* also influence the business buying process. However, it is often difficult to assess such interpersonal factors and group dynamics. Buying center participants do not wear tags that label them as "key decision maker" or "not influential." Nor do buying center participants with the highest rank always have the most influence. Interpersonal factors are often very subtle. Whenever possible, business marketers must try to understand these factors and design strategies that take them into account.

Finally, each participant in the business buying decision process brings in personal motives, perceptions, and preferences. These *individual factors* are affected by personal characteristics such as age, income, education, professional identification, personality, and attitudes toward risk. Also, buyers have different buying styles. Some may be technical types who make in-depth analyses of competitive proposals before choosing a supplier. Other buyers may be intuitive negotiators who are adept at pitting the sellers against one another for the best deal.

▲Problem recognition: Sharp uses ads like this one to alert customers to potential problems and then provide solutions.

Value analysis
Carefully analyzing a product's or service's components to determine if they can be redesigned and made more effectively and efficiently to provide greater value.

The Business Buying Process
■ **Figure 5.9** lists the eight stages of the business buying process.[43] Buyers who face a new-task buying situation usually go through all stages of the buying process. Buyers making modified or straight rebuys may skip some of the stages. We will examine these steps for the typical new-task buying situation.

The buying process begins with *problem recognition*—when someone in the company recognizes a problem or need that can be met by acquiring a specific product or service. Problem recognition can result from internal or external factors. Business marketers use their sales forces or advertising to alert customers to potential problems and then show how their products provide solutions. ▲For example, a Sharp ad notes that a multifunction printer can present data security problems and asks "Is your MFP a portal for identity theft?" The solution? Sharp's data security kits "help prevent sensitive information from falling into the wrong hands."

Having recognized a need, the buyer next prepares a *general need description* that describes the characteristics and quantity of the needed items or solutions. For standard purchases, this process presents few problems. For complex items, however, the buyer may need to work with others—engineers, users, consultants—to define what's needed.

Once the buying organization has defined the need, it develops the item's technical *product specifications*, often with the help of a value analysis engineering team. **Value analysis** is an approach to cost reduction in which the company carefully analyzes a product's or service's components to determine if they can be redesigned and made more effectively and efficiently to provide greater value. The team decides on the best product or service characteristics and specifies them accordingly. Sellers, too, can use value analysis as a tool to help secure new accounts and keep old ones. Especially in a down economy, improving customer value and helping customers find more cost-effective solutions gives the business marketer and important edge in keeping current customers loyal and winning new business.

In the next buying process step, the buyer conducts a *supplier search* to find the best vendors. The buyer can locate qualified suppliers through trade directories, computer searches, or recommendations from others. Today, more and more companies are turning to the Internet to find suppliers. For marketers, this has leveled the playing field—the Internet gives smaller suppliers many of the same advantages as

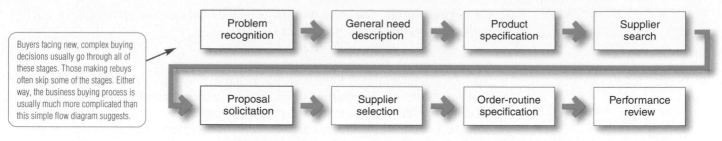

Buyers facing new, complex buying decisions usually go through all of these stages. Those making rebuys often skip some of the stages. Either way, the business buying process is usually much more complicated than this simple flow diagram suggests.

■ **Figure 5.9** Stages of the Business Buying Process

larger competitors. The supplier's task is to understand the search process and make certain that their firm is considered.

In the *proposal solicitation* stage of the business buying process, the buyer invites qualified suppliers to submit proposals. When the purchase is complex or expensive, the buyer will usually require detailed written proposals or formal presentations from each potential supplier. In response, business marketers must be skilled in researching, writing, and presenting proposals. The proposals should be marketing documents, not just technical documents. They should spell out how the seller's solution creates greater value for the customer than competing solutions.

The buyer next reviews the proposals and selects a supplier or suppliers. During *supplier selection*, the buyer will consider many supplier attributes and their relative importance. Such attributes include product and service quality, reputation, on-time delivery, ethical corporate behavior, honest communication, and competitive prices. In the end, they may select a single supplier or a few suppliers. Today's supplier development managers often want to develop a full network of supplier-partners that can help the company bring more value to its customers.

The buyer now prepares an *order-routine specification*. It includes the final order with the chosen supplier or suppliers and lists items such as technical specifications, quantity needed, expected time of delivery, return policies, and warranties. Many large buyers now practice *vendor-managed inventory*, in which they turn over ordering and inventory responsibilities to their suppliers. Under such systems, buyers share sales and inventory information directly with key suppliers. The suppliers then monitor inventories and replenish stock automatically as needed. For example, most major suppliers to large retailers such as Wal-Mart, Target, Home Depot, and Lowe's assume vendor-managed inventory responsibilities.

The final stage of the business buying process is the supplier *performance review*, in which the buyer assesses the supplier's performance and provides feedback. For example, Home Depot has issued a set of supplier guidelines and policies and regularly evaluates each supplier in terms of quality, delivery, and other performance variables. It gives suppliers online performance scorecards that provide ongoing feedback that helps them improve their performance.[44] The supplier performance review may lead the buyer to continue, modify, or drop the arrangement. The seller's job is to monitor the same factors used by the buyer to make sure that the seller is giving the expected satisfaction.

The eight-stage buying-process model provides a simple view of the business buying as it might occur in a new-task buying situation. The actual process is usually much more complex. In the modified rebuy or straight rebuy situation, some of these stages would be compressed or bypassed. Each organization buys in its own way, and each buying situation has unique requirements.

Different buying center participants may be involved at different stages of the process. Although certain buying-process steps usually do occur, buyers do not always follow them in the same order, and they may add other steps. Often, buyers will repeat certain stages of the process. Finally, a customer relationship might involve many different types of purchases ongoing at a given time, all in different stages of the buying process. The seller must manage the total customer relationship, not just individual purchases.

E-Procurement: Buying on the Internet

E-procurement
Purchasing through electronic connections between buyers and sellers—usually online.

Advances in information technology have changed the face of the B-to-B marketing process. Electronic purchasing, often called **e-procurement**, has grown rapidly in recent years. Virtually unknown less than a decade ago, online purchasing is standard procedure for most companies today. E-procurement gives buyers access to new suppliers, lowers purchasing costs, and hastens order processing and delivery. In turn, business marketers can connect with customers online to share marketing information, sell products and services, provide customer support services, and maintain ongoing customer relationships.

Companies can do e-procurement in any of several ways. They can conduct *reverse auctions*, in which they put their purchasing requests online and invite suppliers to bid for the business. Or they can engage in online *trading exchanges,* through which companies work collectively to facilitate the trading process. For example, Exostar is an online trading exchange that connects buyers and sellers in the aerospace and defense industry. The huge exchange has connected more than 300 procurement systems and 40,000 trading partners in 20 countries around the world.

Companies also can conduct e-procurement by setting up their own *company buying sites.* For example, GE operates a company trading site on which it posts its buying needs and invites bids, negotiates terms, and places orders. Or companies can create *extranet links* with key suppliers. For instance, they can create direct procurement accounts with suppliers such as Dell or Office Depot, through which company buyers can purchase equipment, materials, and supplies directly.

B-to-B marketers can help customers who wish to purchase online by creating well-designed, easy-to-use Web sites. For example, *BtoB* magazine rated the site of Cisco Systems—a market leader in Web networking hardware, software, and services—as one of its "10 great B-to-B Web sites":[45]

▼**Online buying: This Cisco Systems site helps customers who want to purchase online by providing deep access to information about thousands of Cisco products and services. The site can also personalize the online experience for users and connect them with appropriate Cisco partner resellers.**

To spur growth, Cisco Systems recently stepped up its focus on the small and midsize business segment (SMB). ▲Its award-winning new SMB-specific Web site is simple, action-oriented, and engaging but gives SMB buyers deep access. At the most basic level, customers can find and download information about thousands of Cisco products and services. Dig deeper, and the site is loaded with useful video content—everything from testimonials to "how to" videos to informational and educational on-demand Webcasts.

Cisco's SMB site gets customers interacting with the company and its partner resellers. For example, its live click-to-chat feature puts users in immediate touch with Cisco product experts. WebEx Web-conferencing software connects potential SMB customers with appropriate Cisco partner resellers, letting them share Web pages, PowerPoints, and other documents in a collaborative online space. Finally, the Cisco SMB site can actually personalize the online experience for users. For example, if it detects that someone from the legal industry is paying attention to wireless content, it might put together relevant pieces of content to create a page for that visitor. Such personalization really pays off. Customers visiting personalized pages stay two times longer than other visitors and go much deeper into the site.

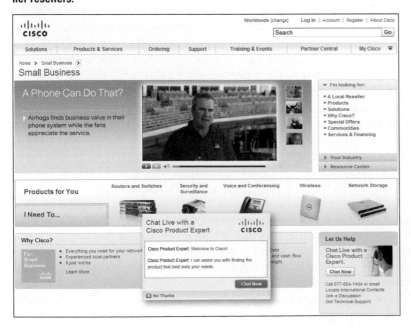

Business-to-business e-procurement yields many benefits. First, it shaves transaction costs and results in more efficient purchasing for both buyers and suppliers. E-procurement reduces the time between order and delivery. And a Web-powered purchasing program eliminates the paperwork associated with traditional requisition and ordering procedures and helps an organization keep better track of all purchases. Finally, beyond the cost and time savings, e-procurement frees purchasing people from a lot of drudgery and paperwork. In turn, it frees them to focus on more-strategic issues, such as finding better supply sources and working with suppliers to reduce costs and develop new products."

To demonstrate these advantages, consider Kodak. When it recently remodeled its headquarters facilities in Rochester, NY, it used only e-procurement. From demolition to restoration, the massive project involved managing more than 1,600 contract bids from 150 contractors. Throughout the project, e-procurement reduced paperwork and speeded up review and award times. In the end, the project was completed on time, and Kodak estimates that using e-procurement saved 15 percent on purchasing-process costs (including $186,000 on photocopying expenses alone).[46]

The rapidly expanding use of e-procurement, however, also presents some problems. For example, at the same time that the Web makes it possible for suppliers and customers to share business data and even collaborate on product design, it can also erode decades-old customer–supplier relationships. Many buyers now use the power of the Web to pit suppliers against one another and to search out better deals, products, and turnaround times on a purchase-by-purchase basis.

REST STOP
REVIEWING THE CONCEPTS

This chapter is the last of three chapters that address understanding the marketplace and consumers. Here, we've looked closely at *consumer* and *business buyer behavior*. The American consumer market consists of more than 300 million people who consume many trillions of dollars' worth of goods and services each year. The business market involves even more dollars and items than the consumer market. Understanding buyer behavior is one of the biggest challenges marketers face.

 Objective 1 Understand the consumer market and the major factors that influence consumer buyer behavior. **(pp 164–179)**

The *consumer market* consists of all the individuals and households who buy or acquire goods and services for personal consumption. A simple model of consumer behavior suggests that marketing stimuli and other major forces enter the consumer's "black box." This black box has two parts: buyer characteristics and the buyer's decision process. Once in the black box, the inputs result in buyer responses, such as buying attitudes and preferences and purchase behavior.

Consumer buyer behavior is influenced by four key sets of buyer characteristics: cultural, social, personal, and psychological. Understanding these factors can help marketers to identify interested buyers and to shape products and appeals to serve consumer needs better. Each factor provides a different perspective for understanding the workings of the buyer's black box.

 Objective 2 Identify and discuss the stages in the buyer decision process. **(pp 179–182)**

When making a purchase, the buyer goes through a decision process consisting of need recognition, information search, evaluation of alternatives, purchase decision, and postpurchase behavior. During *need recognition*, the consumer recognizes a problem or need that could be satisfied by a product or service. Once the need is recognized, the consumer moves into the *information search* stage. With information in hand, the consumer proceeds to *alternative evaluation* and assesses brands in the choice set. From there, the consumer makes a *purchase decision* and actually buys the product. In the final stage of the buyer decision process, *postpurchase behavior*, the consumer takes action based on satisfaction or dissatisfaction. The marketer's job is to understand the buyer's behavior at each stage and the influences that are operating.

Objective 3 Describe the adoption and diffusion process for new products. **(pp 182–184)**

The product *adoption process* is made up of five stages: awareness, interest, evaluation, trial, and adoption. New-product marketers must think about how to help consumers move through these stages. With regard to the *diffusion process* for new products, consumers respond at different rates, depending on consumer and product characteristics. Consumers may be innovators, early adopters, early majority, late majority, or laggards. Each group may require different marketing approaches. Marketers often try to bring their new products to the attention of potential early adopters, especially those who are opinion leaders.

 Objective 4 Define the business market and identify the major factors that influence business buyer behavior. **(pp 184–192)**

The *business market* comprises all organizations that buy goods and services for use in the production of other products and services or for the purpose of reselling or renting them to others at a profit. As compared to consumer markets, business markets usually have fewer, larger buyers who are more geographically concentrated. Business demand is derived demand, and the business buying decision usually involves more, and more professional, buyers.

Business buyers make decisions that vary with the three types of *buying situations:* straight rebuys, modified rebuys, and new tasks. The decision-making unit of a buying organization—the *buying center*— can consist of many different persons playing many different roles. The business marketer needs to know the following: Who are the major buying center participants? In what decisions do they exercise influence and to what degree? What evalua-

tion criteria does each decision participant use? The business marketer also needs to understand the major environmental, organizational, interpersonal, and individual influences on the buying process.

Objective 5 List and define the steps in the business buying decision process. **(pp 192–195)**

The *business buying decision process* itself can be quite involved, with eight basic stages: problem recognition, general need description, product specification, supplier search, proposal solicitation, supplier selection, order-routine specification, and performance review. Buyers who face a new-task buying situation usually go through all stages of the buying process. Buyers making modified or straight rebuys may skip some of the stages. Companies must manage the overall customer relationship, which often includes many different buying decisions in various stages of the buying decision process. Recent advances in information technology have given birth to "e-procurement," by which business buyers are purchasing all kinds of products and services online. Business marketers are increasingly connecting with customers online to share marketing information, sell products and services, provide customer support services, and maintain ongoing customer relationships.

 Navigating the Key Terms

Objective 1
Consumer buyer behavior (p 164)
Consumer market (p 164)

Objective 2
Culture (p 166)
Subculture (p 166)
Social class (p 168)
Group (p 169)
Opinion leader (p 170)
Online social networks (p 170)
Lifestyle (p 175)
Personality (p 176)

Motive (drive) (p 176)
Perception (p 177)
Learning (p 178)
Belief (p 179)
Attitude (p 179)
Cognitive dissonance (p 182)

Objective 3
New product (p 182)
Adoption process (p 182)

Objective 4
Business buyer behavior (p 185)

Derived demand (p 185)
Supplier development (p 188)
Straight rebuy (p 189)
Modified rebuy (p 189)
New task (p 189)
Systems selling (solutions selling) (p 189)
Buying center (p 190)

Objective 5
Value analysis (p 192)
E-procurement (p 194)

Travel Log

Discussing the Issues

1. Discuss the social influences on consumers and provide an example of how one or more of theses factors impacted a product or service purchase you made recently. (AACSB: Communication; Reflective Thinking)

2. Discuss the personal factors influencing consumer buyer behavior. Which of these factors have the greatest influence on your purchasing behavior? (AACSB: Communication; Reflective Thinking)

3. Discuss the stages of the consumer buyer decision process and describe how you or your family used this process to make a purchase. (AACSB: Communication; Reflective Thinking)

4. Describe the five adopter categories for new products. Which group best describes your or your family's behavior with respect to high-definition televisions? (AACSB: Communication; Reflective Thinking)

5. How does the market structure and demand facing business marketers differ from that faced by consumer marketers? (AACSB: Communication)

6. Explain what is meant by the term *buying center* in the business buying process and discuss why it presents a challenge to the business marketer. (AACSB: Communication)

Application Questions

1. Hemopure is a human blood substitute derived from cattle blood. Biopure Corporation still has this product in clinical trials, but the company has received FDA approval for a similar product, Oxyglobin, in the veterinary market. Visit www.biopure.com to learn about Hemopure and explain how the product characteristics of relative advantage, compatibility, complexity, divisibility, and communicability will influence the rate of adoption of this product once FDA approval is attained. (AACSB: Communication; Reflective Thinking)

2. Marketers often target consumers before, during, or after a trigger event—an event in one's life that triggers change. For example, after having a child, new parents have an increased need for baby furniture, clothes, diapers, car seats, and lots of other baby-related goods. Consumers who never paid attention to marketing efforts for certain products may now be focused on ones related to their life change. Discuss other trigger events that may provide opportunities to target the right buyer at the right time. (AACSB: Communication; Reflective Thinking)

3. The North American Industry Classification System (NAICS) code classifies businesses by production processes, providing a common classification system for North America and better compatibility with the International Standard Industrial Classification (ISIC) system. This six-digit number (in some cases, seven or ten digits) is very useful for understanding business markets. Visit www.naics.com and learn what the six digits of the NAICS code represent. What industry is represented by the NAICS code 721110? How many businesses comprise this code? How can marketers use NAICS codes to better deliver customer satisfaction and value? (AACSB: Communication; Reflective Thinking; Use of IT)

Under the Hood: Marketing Technology

Comparison shopping has never been easier. Millions of bytes of information are just a click away. Shopping for a new high-definition television and would like to compare offerings? No problem! Just search "hdtv comparison guide" in an online search engine such as Google and more than a million results return. Google experimented with returning a greater number of results per page and found usage dropped off because it took a fraction of a second longer for results to appear—too long for today's consumers. Of course, buyers cannot go through them all, and it's human nature to start at the top. That spot is valuable real estate for online search results. The top result for TV comparisons was www.ConsumerReports.org. It was the same for most electronic products such as computers and digital cameras, as well as common household appliances such as washing machines and microwave ovens. Con-sumer Reports is not the only game in town, either. There's Shopzilla.com, PriceGrabber.com, bizrate.com, and shopping.com, to name just a few. All of these comparison shopping Web sites assist buyers in selecting the right product and brand to suit their needs and desires.

1. Search for information regarding a product you are interested in purchasing. Using one or more online comparison shopping Web sites, find the brand that is right for you. Discuss how long it took you to make this decision and what influenced your decision. (AACSB: Communication; Use of IT; Reflective Thinking)

2. Discuss the benefits and drawbacks of using comparison-shopping Web sites in making buying decisions. (AACSB: Communication; Reflective Thinking)

Staying on the Road: Marketing Ethics

Companies face many challenges when conducting business abroad. Cultural differences are particularly difficult. In several emerging markets, such as parts of Asia, Africa, the Middle East, the former Soviet Union, Eastern Europe, and South America, bribery is considered "standard operating procedure" in business buying. The World Bank estimates that bribery in international trade amounts to about $1 trillion annually.

The Foreign Corrupt Practices Act (FCPA) has existed in the United States since 1977, but the Securities and Exchange Commission and the U.S. Department of Justice have only recently stepped up enforcement. This law prohibits U.S. companies from giving corrupt payments to obtain favor in business transactions. To get around this law, many companies have used third parties to do their dirty deeds. However, many companies are now confessing their misdeeds rather than remaining silent and hoping to avoid detection. This is because of provisions of the 2002 Sarbanes-Oxley law regarding accounting reporting practices. Under this law, American senior executives can go to prison for violations.

For a long time, the United States was one of few leaders in battling corruption in foreign trade, but now many more countries are joining the fight. In China, bribery is punishable by death, which makes the multimillion dollar penalties levied from FCPA violations seem light. Aside from financial penalties (the largest being over $40 million so far), guilty companies may also be prohibited from do-ing business with the U.S. government or may be denied export licenses.

1. Is it right for U.S. companies to be penalized for going along with cultural norms in other countries? Is it right for the United States and other countries to demand that businesses in other countries follow our laws? (AACSB: Communication; Ethical Reasoning)

2. What are the consequences for U.S. companies of not going along with the cultural factors influencing foreign business customers? (AACSB: Communication; Reflective Thinking)

Rough Road Ahead: Marketing and the Economy

AutoZone

Detroit is suffering and everyone knows it. New car sales were projected to be down as much as 43 percent in 2009. But Detroit's loss is AutoZone's gain. The do-it-yourself car parts retailer's sales and profits have been running counter to those of the retail world as a whole. One reason is that AutoZone's traditional customers have been tackling more complicated do-it-yourself car repair jobs and visiting stores more frequently. But the retail auto parts giant has also seen a notable increase in customers with incomes over $100,000 a year, people who typically never so much as pop the hoods of their own cars.

In the more frugal economy, all types of drivers are now looking to save money by doing their own repairs and maintenance. And as people keep their cars longer, the older cars need more repairs. AutoZone has seen this day coming, long ago scrapping its grungy, industrial-store format for one that's more colorful, brightly lit, and filled with super-friendly sales clerks. Soccer moms are now as comfortable getting "into the Zone" as NASCAR fans. Believing that America's spendthrift habits are now becoming a thing of the past, that's the way AutoZone planned it.

1. Consider the auto parts buyer decision process. How has this process changed for new AutoZone customers. How has the economy influence this change?

2. Visit www.autozone.com. Does it appear that the company is trying to help the newer, less-knowledgeable customer? Based on your observations, what recommendations would you make to AutoZone?

Travel Budget: Marketing by the Numbers

Consumers may often evaluate products and services by making comparisons between the attributes of competing brands. Added to this is a weighting for each of the attributes, which aim to reflect the relative importance of each of the attributes. For a particular brand, the key attributes and their weighting was as follows:

Style	(0.4)
Cost	(0.3)
Delivery time	(0.2)
Warranty	(0.1)

The consumers were asked to rate each of the brands on a sliding scale of 1–7 with 1 rating the product low and 7 extremely high. For brand A the scores were respectively 6, 6, 7, and 2. For brand B they were 5, 3, 4, and 4. For brand C the results were 6, 5, 5, and 5 and for brand D, they were 4, 7, 6, and 3. The score for each brand can be calculated by multiplying the importance weight for each attribute by the brand's score on that attribute. These weighted scores are then summed to determine the score for that brand. The scores given are meant to suggest, as far as the consumer is concerned, that the particular brand performs better in this aspect than the other competing brands. A tied score simply suggests that there is no discernible difference in performance between two or more of the brands in that category. For more discussion of the financial and quantitative implications of marketing decisions, see Appendix 2: Marketing by the Numbers.

1. Determine the scores for brands A, B, C, and D. Which brand would this consumer likely choose?

2. Why might the results be somewhat misleading?

▮▮ ▮ Drive In: Video Case

Radian6

Social networking has had a huge impact on society. And for marketers, online social communications are changing the way that consumers make purchase decisions. Radian6 specializes in monitoring social media. It tracks a wide array of Web sites at which consumers might "chat" about companies, brands, and general market offerings. Companies such as Dell and Microsoft obtain valuable insights about what consumers are saying about their products and about what factors or events are generating the discussions. But more importantly, companies are gaining a stronger understanding of how consumer online conversations are affecting purchase decisions. In this manner, Radian6 is on the cutting edge of getting a grip on the ever-expanding scope of social networking and "word-of-Web" communication.

After viewing the video featuring Radian6, answer the following questions.

1. What cultural factors have led to the explosion of social networking?

2. How has Radian6 changed the way companies understand opinion leaders and buzz marketing?

3. How is Radian6 helping companies gain insights into the buying decision process?

6

Customer-Driven Marketing Strategy
Creating Value for Target Customers

ROAD MAP

Previewing the Concepts

So far, you've learned what marketing is and about the importance of understanding consumers and the marketplace environment. With that as background, you're now ready to delve deeper into marketing strategy and tactics. This chapter looks further into key customer-driven marketing strategy decisions—how to divide up markets into meaningful customer groups (*segmentation*), choose which customer groups to serve (*targeting*), create market offerings that best serve targeted customers (*differentiation*), and position the offerings in the minds of consumers (*positioning*). Then, the chapters that follow explore the tactical marketing tools—the Four Ps—by which marketers bring these strategies to life.

Objective Outline

> **Objective 1**   Define the major steps in designing a customer-driven marketing strategy: market segmentation, targeting, differentiation, and positioning.
> Customer-Driven Marketing Strategy **pp 202–203**

> **Objective 2**   List and discuss the major bases for segmenting consumer and business markets.
> Market Segmentation **pp 203–213**

> **Objective 3**   Explain how companies identify attractive market segments and choose a market-targeting strategy.
> Market Targeting **pp 214–221**

> **Objective 4**   Discuss how companies differentiate and position their products for maximum competitive advantage.
> Differentiation and Positioning **pp 221–230**

To start our discussion of the ins and outs of segmentation, targeting, differentiation, and positioning, let's look at Air Arabia, the first company to position itself as a low budget airline in the Middle East. Air Arabia recognized that there was an untapped market for "no-frills" travel across the Middle Eastern nations. It has segmented its market carefully and concentrates on offering its customers great quality service and excellent value for money.

▲Air Arabia was the first of a string of low budget airlines to launch themselves in the Middle East. The company realized the potential of the 13 million strong expatriate market in a region which had the highest average airfare on the planet.

First Stop

Air Arabia: No-Frills Flying Across the Middle East

The introduction of low-cost carriers (LCCs) to the Middle East airspace has heralded a sea of change in the region's aviation industry. It has altered the industry competitive paradigms, significantly broadened the market, and unearthed new market segments that were previously untouched. By operating from secondary airports, scrapping the class system, in-flights meals and services, and/or VIP lounge services, LCCs are able to cut their operating costs and offer their customers low ticket prices.

Surprisingly, the low-cost carrier segment has been largely overlooked by the region's conventional carriers: the Emirates Airlines, Qatar Airways, Ittihad, and others. These full-service carriers (FSCs) concentrated instead on the frequent and the business traveler, last-minute bookings, and long hauls. This may be partly due to the misconception held by many regarding the region's traditional reputation for opulence. The perception that the air-traveler in these parts of the world is in essence a first-class customer who expects to be offered an all-inclusive product and a certain level of service regardless of the price. Suffice it to say in this respect that the region suffers from the world highest average airfares—most routes cost two and three times more than their equivalent in Europe.

A casual look at the composition of the region's population, however, belies this notion. Statistics show that there are around 13 million expatriates who reside and work in the six GCC countries: Asians, western expatriates, and others. A significant percentage of them, however, are low- and middle-income workers who come mainly from the Indian subcontinent. It is a safe assumption to say that most of these expatriates need low airfares and would settle for less to have them. In view of the high cost of living in the Gulf region, these expatriates leave their families behind in their homeland and travel to see them every one or two years. If the travel cost were somehow reduced, they could choose to visit their families more often. This is the market gap that LCCs have targeted. Having recognized the potential of making travel more affordable to the millions of expatriates who rely mainly on air travel to see their beloved ones, LCCs were quick to grasp the opportunity that presented itself. The Middle East proved to be, after all, a natural ground for low-cost aviation to take roots. The industry price structure changed fundamentally. On most routes LCCs' prices were 30 to 50 percent less than the prices of their FSCs counterparts. For example, a round trip from Kuwait City to Mumbai, India that used to cost $800 on a full-service airliner now costs $240 on a low-cost carrier. Likewise, FSCs charge $540 for a round trip from Dubai to

The remarkable success story of LCCs in the Middle East is attributed to their ability to pinpoint a well-defined target market and cater to its needs with a clear business proposition.

Thiruvanthapuram, India. The same trip from Sharjah on Air Arabia costs $266. Expatriates, who used to travel home only once a year, can now afford to make it four times a year. Rather than bringing their families to the Gulf, frequent travel becomes the preferred solution to their problem.

Low-cost carriers in the Middle East are relatively new compared to their counterparts in Europe and the United States. Nonetheless, the sector has managed to establish itself, within a short period of time, as a growth industry with an immense potential given the region's fast rate of growth and the fact that the low-cost carrier marketing penetration is still small.

The UAE-based Air Arabia was the first low-cost carrier to be launched in the Middle East in 2003. Since then, the number of no-frills airlines in the region has risen to seven. Namely, Air Arabia (Sharjah, UAE), Jazeera Airways (Kuwait), Sama and AlNas Airlines (Saudi Arabia), Bahrain Air (Bahrain), flydubai (Dubai, UAE), and Air Arabia Egypt (UAE, Egypt). Together, these airliners have already captured 5 percent of the region's aviation market. Industry analysts expect this percentage to increase in the near future. One of the notable success examples of the no-frills segment is Air Arabia. It now operates a fleet of 16 new Airbus A320 aircrafts to 46 destinations across the Middle East, North Africa, and South and Central Asia. The company's latest financial results show a 21 percent profit increase in June 2009 compared to the same period in 2008. During the same period, it served approximately 2 million passengers compared to 1.6 million passengers during the first six months of 2008. The average seat load factor—passengers carried as a percentage of available seats—for the first six months of 2009 stood at 80 percent. In 2008, the airline Chief Executive Officer was named low-cost "CEO of the year" and Air Arabia itself voted the "Best Low-cost Airline in the Middle East and Africa." Likewise, in 2007, Jazzera Airways of Kuwait reported a profit increase of 61.2 percent over the previous year. The airline flew 1.2 million passengers by the end of the year, doubling the number of passengers from 2006.

The remarkable success story of LCCs in the Middle East—evident in the examples outlined above—is attributed to their ability to pinpoint a well-defined target market and cater to its needs with a clear business proposition. As the industry matures, and more and more players enter the market, it remains to be seen whether such success is sustainable.[1]

C ompanies today recognize that they cannot appeal to all buyers in the marketplace, or at least not to all buyers in the same way. Buyers are too numerous, too widely scattered, and too varied in their needs and buying practices. Moreover, the companies themselves vary widely in their abilities to serve different segments of the market. Instead, like Air Arabia, a company must identify the parts of the market that it can serve best and most profitably. It must design customer-driven marketing strategies that build the *right* relationships with the *right* customers.

Thus, most companies have moved away from mass marketing and toward *target marketing*—identifying market segments, selecting one or more of them, and developing products and marketing programs tailored to each. Instead of scattering their

■ Figure 6.1 Designing a Customer-Driven Marketing Strategy

In concept, marketing boils down to two questions: (1) Which customers will we serve? and (2) How will we serve them? Of course, the tough part is coming up with good answers to these simple-sounding but difficult questions. The goal is to create more value for the customers we serve than competitors do.

Market segmentation
Dividing a market into smaller segments with distinct needs, characteristics, or behavior that might require separate marketing strategies or mixes.

Market targeting (targeting)
The process of evaluating each market segment's attractiveness and selecting one or more segments to enter.

Author Comment ≫
Market segmentation addresses the first simple-sounding marketing question: What customers will we serve? The answer will be different for each company. For example, The Ritz-Carlton targets the top 5 percent of corporate and leisure travelers. Hampton targets middle Americans traveling on a budget.

Differentiation
Actually differentiating the market offering to create superior customer value.

Positioning
Arranging for a market offering to occupy a clear, distinctive, and desirable place relative to competing products in the minds of target consumers.

Geographic segmentation
Dividing a market into different geographical units such as nations, states, regions, counties, cities, or neighborhoods.

marketing efforts (the "shotgun" approach), firms are focusing on the buyers who have greater interest in the values they create best (the "rifle" approach).

■ **Figure 6.1** shows the four major steps in designing a customer-driven marketing strategy. In the first two steps, the company selects the customers that it will serve. **Market segmentation** involves dividing a market into smaller segments of buyers with distinct needs, characteristics, or behaviors that might require separate marketing strategies or mixes. The company identifies different ways to segment the market and develops profiles of the resulting market segments. **Market targeting (or targeting)** consists of evaluating each market segment's attractiveness and selecting one or more market segments to enter.

In the final two steps, the company decides on a value proposition—on how it will create value for target customers. **Differentiation** involves actually differentiating the firm's market offering to create superior customer value. **Positioning** consists of arranging for a market offering to occupy a clear, distinctive, and desirable place relative to competing products in the minds of target consumers. We discuss each of these steps in turn.

MARKET SEGMENTATION (pp 203–213)

Buyers in any market differ in their wants, resources, locations, buying attitudes, and buying practices. Through market segmentation, companies divide large, heterogeneous markets into smaller segments that can be reached more efficiently and effectively with products and services that match their unique needs. In this section, we discuss four important segmentation topics: segmenting consumer markets, segmenting business markets, segmenting international markets, and requirements for effective segmentation.

Segmenting Consumer Markets

There is no single way to segment a market. A marketer has to try different segmentation variables, alone and in combination, to find the best way to view the market structure. ■ **Table 6.1** outlines the major variables that might be used in segmenting consumer markets. Here we look at the major *geographic, demographic, psychographic,* and *behavioral* variables.

Geographic Segmentation
Geographic segmentation calls for dividing the market into different geographical units such as nations, regions, states, counties, cities, or even neighborhoods. A company may decide to operate in one or a few geographical areas, or to operate in all areas but pay attention to geographical differences in needs and wants.

Many companies today are localizing their products, advertising, promotion, and sales efforts to fit the needs of individual regions, cities, and even neighborhoods. For example, Wal-Mart operates virtually everywhere but has developed special formats tailored to specific types of geographic locations. In strongly Hispanic neighborhoods in Texas and Arizona, Wal-Mart is now testing Hispanic-focused

■ **Table 6.1** Major Segmentation Variables for Consumer Markets

Geographic	
World region or country	North America, Western Europe, Middle East, Pacific Rim, China, India, Canada, Brazil
Country region	Pacific, Mountain, West North Central, West South Central, East North Central, East South Central, South Atlantic, Middle Atlantic, New England
City or metro size	Under 5,000; 5,000–20,000; 20,000–50,000; 50,000–100,000; 100,000–250,000; 250,000–500,000; 500,000–1,000,000; 1,000,000–4,000,000; over 4,000,000
Density	Urban, suburban, exurban, rural
Climate	Northern, southern

Demographic	
Age	Under 6, 6–11, 12–19, 20–34, 35–49, 50–64, 65+
Gender	Male, female
Family size	1–2, 3–4, 5+
Family life cycle	Young, single; married, no children; married with children; single parents; unmarried couples; older, married, no children under 18; older, single; other
Income	Under $20,000; $20,000–$30,000; $30,000–$50,000; $50,000–$100,000; $100,000–$250,000; $250,000 and over
Occupation	Professional and technical; managers, officials, and proprietors; clerical; sales; craftspeople; supervisors; farmers; retired; students; homemakers; unemployed
Education	Primary school or less; some high school; high school graduate; some college; college graduate
Religion	Catholic, Protestant, Jewish, Muslim, Hindu, other
Race	Asian, Hispanic, Black, White
Generation	Baby boomer, Generation X, Millennial
Nationality	North American, South American, British, French, German, Russian, Japanese

Psychographic	
Social class	Lower lowers, upper lowers, working class, middle class, upper middles, lower uppers, upper uppers
Lifestyle	Achievers, strivers, survivors
Personality	Compulsive, outgoing, authoritarian, ambitious

Behavioral	
Occasions	Regular occasion; special occasion; holiday; seasonal
Benefits	Quality, service, economy, convenience, speed
User status	Nonuser, ex-user, potential user, first-time user, regular user
User rates	Light user, medium user, heavy user
Loyalty status	None, medium, strong, absolute
Readiness stage	Unaware, aware, informed, interested, desirous, intending to buy
Attitude toward product	Enthusiastic, positive, indifferent, negative, hostile

Supermercado de Wal-Mart stores, which feature layouts, signage, product assortment, and bilingual staff to make them more relevant to local Hispanic customers. In markets where full-size superstores are impractical, Wal-Mart has opened supermarket-style Marketside grocery stores. Marketside stores are a third the size of Wal-Mart's other small-store format, Neighborhood Market supermarkets, and a 10th the size of one of its supercenters.[2]

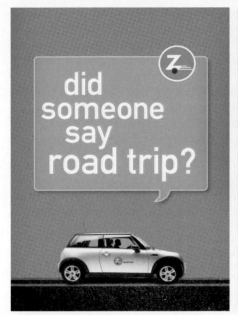

▲Geographic segmentation: Car-sharing service Zipcar focuses only on densely populated metropolitan areas and congested college campuses, positioning itself as a low-cost, low-hassle alternative to owning or driving your own car.

Demographic segmentation
Dividing the market into segments based on variables such as age, gender, family size, family life cycle, income, occupation, education, religion, race, generation, and nationality.

Age and life-cycle segmentation
Dividing a market into different age and life-cycle groups.

Similarly, Citibank offers different mixes of branch banking services depending on neighborhood demographics. And Baskin-Robbins practices what it calls "three-mile marketing," emphasizing local events and promotions close to each local store location. ▲By contrast, car-sharing service Zipcar—which rents out self-service vehicles by the day or hour—focuses only on densely populated metropolitan areas and congested college campuses, positioning itself as a low-cost, low-hassle alternative to owning or driving your own car.[3]

Demographic Segmentation

Demographic segmentation divides the market into segments based on variables such as age, gender, family size, family life cycle, income, occupation, education, religion, race, generation, and nationality. Demographic factors are the most popular bases for segmenting customer groups. One reason is that consumer needs, wants, and usage rates often vary closely with demographic variables. Another is that demographic variables are easier to measure than most other types of variables. Even when marketers first define segments using other bases, such as benefits sought or behavior, they must know segment demographic characteristics in order to assess the size of the target market and to reach it efficiently.

Age and Life-Cycle Stage. Consumer needs and wants change with age. Some companies use **age and life-cycle segmentation**, offering different products or using different marketing approaches for different age and life-cycle groups. For example, for kids, Oscar Mayer offers Lunchables, full of fun, kid-appealing finger food. For older generations, it markets Deli Creations, everything they need to create a "hot and melty fresh-baked sandwich in a microwave minute."

Other companies focus on specific age of life-stage groups. For example, Disney Cruise Lines targets primarily families with kids, large and small. Most of its destinations and shipboard activities are designed with parents and their children in mind. On board, Disney provides trained counselors who help younger kids join in hands-on activities, teen-only spaces for older children, and family-time or individual-time options for parents and other adults. It's difficult to find a Disney Cruise Lines advertisement or Web page that doesn't feature a family full of smiling faces. In contrast, Viking River Cruises, the deluxe smaller-boat cruise line that offers tours along the world's great rivers, primarily targets older adults couples and singles. You won't find a single child in a Viking ad or Web page.

Marketers must be careful to guard against stereotypes when using age and life-cycle segmentation. Although some 80-year-olds fit the doddering stereotypes, others play tennis. Similarly, whereas some 40-year-old couples are sending their children off to college, others are just beginning new families. Thus, age is often a poor predictor of a person's life cycle, health, work or family status, needs, and buying power. Companies marketing to mature consumers usually employ positive images and appeals. For example, one Carnival Cruise Lines ad for its Fun Ships features an older boomer and child riding waterslides, stating "Fun has no age limit."

Gender segmentation
Dividing a market into different segments based on gender.

Gender. **Gender segmentation** has long been used in clothing, cosmetics, toiletries, and magazines. For example, P&G was among the first with Secret, a brand specially formulated for a woman's chemistry, packaged and advertised to reinforce the female image. More recently, many mostly women's cosmetics makers have begun marketing men's lines. Nivea markets Nivea for Men, "an advanced line of enriching skincare and soothing aftershave products specially designed for the active, healthy men's lifestyle," and offers a four-step guide to perfect men's care.

A neglected gender segment can offer new opportunities in markets ranging from consumer electronics to motorcycles. For example, Harley-Davidson has traditionally targeted its product design and marketing to a bread-and-butter market of 35- to 55-year-old males. Women were more often just along for the ride—but no longer:[4]

> Women are now among the fastest growing customer segments in the motorcycle business. The number of female Harley-Davidson owners has tripled in the past 20 years and female buyers now account for 12 percent of new Harley-Davidson purchases. So the company is boosting its efforts to move more women from the back of the bike onto the driver's seat. It started by making its product more accessible to females, modifying motorcycles to fit women's smaller frames, and offering an instructional manual and courses to teach women how to handle their bikes. Ads and other marketing materials aimed at women play to the brand's established strengths but with a softer side.
>
> Rather than indulging in female stereotypes, Harley-Davidson is appealing to "strong, independent women who enjoy taking on a challenge and a feeling of adventure," says the company's women's outreach manager. A recent ad sports the headline: "Not pictured: the weaker sex." A women's Web microsite encourages women to share inspirational riding stories with one another. And to kick off Women Riders Month, Harley-Davidson recently hosted special riding events designed to "celebrate the millions of women who have already grabbed life by the handlebars."
>
> In marketing to women, Harley-Davidson is staying true to its tough, road tested image. "I don't think we're going to see any pink [Harley-Davidson motorcycles] on the road," says an analyst. And "they don't have to add bigger mirrors so women can do their cosmetics. . . . They want to sell Harleys to women, and they want to sell them to women who want to ride a *Harley*."

Income segmentation
Dividing a market into different income segments.

Income. The marketers of products and services such as automobiles, clothing, cosmetics, financial services, and travel have long used **income segmentation**. Many companies target affluent consumers with luxury goods and convenience services. For example, for a price, luxury hotels provide amenities to attract specific groups of affluent travelers, such as families, expectant moms, and even pet owners:[5]

> At the Four Seasons Hotel Chicago, guests can buy the Kids in the City package for $520 a night and, among other things, enjoy a visit in their room from the Ice Cream Man, who arrives with all the fixings to make any concoction they desire. At one spa in Scottsdale, Arizona, expectant parents can purchase the "Bundle of Joy" Babymoon package, which includes a 24-hour Cravings Chef service, a couples massage, and breakfast in bed. ▲The Benjamin Hotel in New York City has the "Dream Dog" program, which provides dog beds in a variety of styles along with doggie bathrobes, canine room service, and DVDs for dogs, as well as access to pet spa treatments and a pet psychic. And if that isn't over the top enough, the Four Seasons Miami offers a Five Diamond package that includes a Graff diamond eternity band (or another diamond piece designed to your specifications) for $45,000, or a stay in the presidential suite with a bottle of 1990 Dom Pérignon Oenothéque champagne, caviar for two, and an 80-minute in-suite couples massage, using a lotion infused with real ground diamonds comes with a price tag: "From $50,000."

▼**Income segmentation: Luxury hotels provide amenities to attract affluent travelers. The Benjamin Hotel in New York City offers a "Dream Dog" program that pampers not just guests, but also their dogs.**

However, not all companies that use income segmentation target the affluent. For example, many retailers—such as the Dollar General, Family Dollar, and Dollar Tree store chains—successfully target low- and middle-income groups. The core market for such stores is families with incomes under $30,000. When Family Dollar real-estate experts scout locations for new stores, they look for lower-middle-class neighborhoods where people wear less-expensive shoes and drive old cars that drip a lot of oil. With their low-income strategies, the dollar stores are now the fastest-growing retailers in the nation.

The recent troubled economy has provided challenges for marketers targeting all income groups. Consumers at all income levels—including affluent consumers—are cutting back on their spending and seeking greater value from their purchases. In many cases, luxury marketers targeting high-income consumers have been hardest hit. Even consumers who can still afford to buy luxuries appear to be pushing the pause button. "It's conspicuous *non*consumption," says one economist. "The wealthy still have the wealth, [but] it's the image you project in a bad economy of driving a nice car when your friends or colleagues may be losing their businesses."[6]

Psychographic Segmentation

Psychographic segmentation divides buyers into different segments based on social class, lifestyle, or personality characteristics. People in the same demographic group can have very different psychographic makeups.

In Chapter 5, we discussed how the products people buy reflect their *lifestyles*. As a result, marketers often segment their markets by consumer lifestyles and base their marketing strategies on lifestyle appeals (See Marketing at Work 6.1). For example, although both Dunkin' Donuts and Starbucks are coffee shops, they offer very different product assortments and store atmospheres. Yet each succeeds because it creates just the right value proposition for its unique mix of customer lifestyles. Starbucks targets more "high-brow" young professionals, whereas Dunkin' Donuts targets the "average Joe."

Marketers also use *personality* variables to segment markets. For example, cruise lines target adventure seekers. Royal Caribbean appeals to high-energy couples and families with hundreds of activities such as rockwall climbing and ice skating. Its commercials urge travelers to "declare your independence and become a citizen of our nation—Royal Caribbean, The Nation of Why Not." By contrast, the Regent Seven Seas Cruise Line targets more serene and cerebral adventurers, mature couples seeking a more elegant ambiance and exotic destinations, such as the Orient. Regent invites them to come along as "luxury goes exploring."[7]

Behavioral Segmentation

Behavioral segmentation divides buyers into segments based on their knowledge, attitudes, uses, or responses to a product. Many marketers believe that behavior variables are the best starting point for building market segments.

Occasions. Buyers can be grouped according to occasions when they get the idea to buy, actually make their purchase, or use the purchased item. **Occasion segmentation** can help firms build up product usage. For example, most consumers drink orange juice in the morning but orange growers have promoted drinking orange juice as a cool, healthful refresher at other times of the day. By contrast, Coca-Cola's "Good Morning" campaign attempts to increase Diet Coke consumption by promoting the soft drink as an early morning pick-me-up.

Some holidays, such as Mother's Day and Father's Day, were originally promoted partly to increase the sale of candy, flowers, cards, and other gifts. And many marketers prepare special offers and ads for holiday occasions. ▲For example, PEEPS creates different shaped sugar-and-fluffy-marshmallow treats for Easter, when it captures

Psychographic segmentation
Dividing a market into different segments based on social class, lifestyle, or personality characteristics.

Behavioral segmentation
Dividing a market into segments based on consumer knowledge, attitudes, uses, or responses to a product.

Occasion segmentation
Dividing the market into segments according to occasions when buyers get the idea to buy, actually make their purchase, or use the purchased item.

▼Occasion segmentation: PEEPS creates different shaped marshmallow treats for special holidays when it captures most of its sales, and advertises that PEEPS are "Always in Season" to increase the demand at other holidays.

Marketing at Work 6.1

Mobinil: Targeting the Mobile Telecommunications Market

On Thursday, May 21, 1998, Egypt witnessed the birth of Mobinil, the first Global System for Mobile Communications operator in the country that changed the way Egyptians communicate forever. Reflected in its name, Mobi*nil*, is the very essence of Egypt, the River Nile. Mobinil is giving Egyptian society the richness and facility of communication as well as the excellence of technology. When the company was first established it faced enormous challenges but with its constant dedication to offer the best service quality to its wide array of customers, the finest working environment to its employees, and ultimate value to all its shareholders, Mobinil has successfully managed to be the largest wireless service provider not only in Egypt but also in the Middle East.

Mobinil's slogan when it first entered the Egyptian market was "Mobile in Every Hand." In 10 years, Mobinil was able to bring in more than 23 million subscribers and remains the leader in the Egyptian mobile telecommunications market. Mobinil have therefore been very successful in a market characterized by relatively low income, around 30 percent of the population are illiterate and the relatively high price of mobile handsets as a percentage of income.

Alex Shalaby, Chairman of Mobinil, highlights that one of the key reasons for Mobinil's success is the company's detailed and segmented marketing strategy. At the beginning of operations in May 1998, Mobinil offered "postpaid" service plans only. Postpaid refers to service plans that have a bill at the end of each month. All customers paid the same monthly fees and price per minute no matter their usage volume.

The Egyptian market is highly polarized says Shalaby. There is a very small segment of high income customers, a large segment of low income customers, and a small middle income segment. Accordingly, Mobinil had to think of ways to target these large customer segments.

Mobinil's philosophy aims to cater to the various needs of its diverse customers with different income levels, age, gender, geographic location, lifestyles, expectations, and requirements and this is reflected in the variety of services it offers. By continuously expanding its services and broadcasting very popular

▲A "Mobile in every hand": By putting their customers' needs first, Mobinil has emerged as one of the leading mobile communications operators in Egypt and across the Middle East.

commercials on both television and radio, Mobinil has succeeded in attracting more and more customers as it highlights their individual importance, emphasizing that the customer comes first and that Mobinil is forever catering to their needs. This is evident in the various options that Mobinil offers its customers.

For example, it is continuously offering new services and different price ranges so that all sectors of the society will be able to afford making calls. Also, during prime times like holidays, feasts, or special occasions, Mobinil is always there with attractive promotion offers that are very tempting and difficult to resist.

Mobinil introduced prepaid services in December 1998 with the brand "Alo." Prepaid services allowed customers to access mobile services by charging their accounts in advance. Alo was a major success for Mobinil. The growth rate for the Alo service was greater than the growth for the postpaid services. It was clear that the Egyptian market has an appetite for prepaid services. Control was a feature that was and is still important for most Egyptians.

Mobinil identified that there was still more room for growth within the prepaid market. Having one standard prepaid service

---

most of its sales, and advertises that PEEPS are "Always in Season" to increase the demand at other holidays such as Valentine's Day, Halloween, and Christmas.

Benefits Sought. A powerful form of segmentation is to group buyers according to the different *benefits* that they seek from the product. **Benefit segmentation** requires finding the major benefits people look for in the product class, the kinds of people who look for each benefit, and the major brands that deliver each benefit.

Champion athletic wear segments its markets according to benefits that different consumers seek from their activewear. For example, "Fit and Polish" consumers seek a balance between function and style—they exercise for results but

Benefit segmentation
Dividing the market into segments according to the different benefits that consumers seek from the product.

plan was not enough to capture a diverse population that is over 80 million. Thus, further segmentation of the prepaid market was adopted. By carefully segmenting its target market into three main categories, Mobinil has managed to create three different services that cater to the specific needs of its customers of different income groups.

Alo is a prepaid service that is divided into four different categories that attract different customers. Alo Magic offers its subscribers a fixed price of 0.4 LE (8 cents) per minute for their calls all day long and everywhere in Egypt. Alo Region is very suitable for people who live or work outside Cairo and Alexandria because it helps them enjoy distinctive prices for calls and messages in the regions outside Cairo and Alexandria. For the Mobinil customers whose lifestyles are fast and dynamic and who use their mobile very frequently, "Alohat" is the ideal plan.

For business professionals, whose activities require that they make numerous phone calls "Alo Business" enables them to enjoy a very low price of 0.3 LE (6 cents) per minute all day long.

"Primo" line combines all the benefits of postpaid and prepaid lines while granting customers full validity in a variety of subscription periods (6 months, 1 year, 2 years) paid in advance at a special price. Primo subscribers are not committed to pay a monthly bill and can control their spending by buying Mobinil scratch cards that vary in price in association with their offered minutes. Prepaid customers account for 97 percent of Mobinil's customer base.

Mobinil "Star" is the personal postpaid Mobinil brand that offers a variety of plans and value added services that suit the lifestyles and sophisticated needs of high income groups. By offering state of the art technology and services, Mobinil Star offers its customers a truly rich mobile experience. It is divided into three categories: Star 100, Star 500, and Star 1000. Star 100 customers enjoy free 100 minutes per month and they can choose up to four other Star customers and call each one of them all day absolutely for free with "Group Service." Star 500 offers its customers 500 free minutes per month, the Group Service, and one additional Mobinil number that they can call for free all day. Star 1000

offers its customers 1000 free minutes per month, Group Service or free number, and also free text messages to any Mobinil number.

Apart from these three main different categories, Mobinil has created loyalty programs, like First Class Gold Loyalty and First Class Platinum, to express its gratitude for the top customers and thank them for their loyalty. These programs offer the top Mobinil customers an exclusive bouquet of gifts and privileges that are tailored to suit the customers' personal preferences. In order to make the other customers more loyal to the company, Mobinil grants them specific privileges like the "Ahsan Nas" service that offers them the opportunity to pick three favorite numbers and call them at a discounted price all day long for free. They also provide them with an exclusive treatment that includes a special call center, special treatment at Mobinil shops, and a more lenient credit policy. In addition, Mobinil offered this exclusive segment a Point Scheme Loyalty program to increase their attachment to Mobinil.

Samir Naguib, Director of Marketing at Mobinil, further highlights that "we developed a micro segmentation approach to the high value postpaid customers." "Twinkle" is an exclusive offer for postpaid customer's kids that includes a postpaid line and a unique mobile phone with features tailored especially for kids. Twinkle granted parents free unlimited calls, two-ways between their current lines, and the new lines in the Twinkle offer. None of the competitors launched a similar proposition.

Privileges like these will not only make customers loyal to Mobinil but will also attract non-Mobinil customers and hence enable Mobinil to expand and reach its main goal as stated in its mission statement to "maintain [its] position as the leading mobile service provider in Egypt."

Sources: Quotes and other information from interview with Samir Maguib, October 21, 2009, Director of Marketing, Mobinil, www.mobinil.com, © Samir Maguib 2010; interview with Alex Shalaby, October 14, 2009, Chairman, Mobinil, www.mobinil.com, © Alex Shalaby 2010; www.mobinil .com

want to look good doing it. "Serious Sports Competitors" exercise heavily and live in and love their activewear—they seek performance and function. By contrast, "Value-Seeking Moms" have low sports interest and low activewear involvement—they buy for the family and seek durability and value. Thus, each segment seeks a different mix of benefits. Champion must target the benefit segment or segments that it can serve best and most profitably, using appeals that match each segment's benefit preferences.

User Status. Markets can be segmented into nonusers, ex-users, potential users, first-time users, and regular users of a product. Marketers want to reinforce and retain regular users, attract targeted nonusers, and reinvigorate relationships with ex-users.

Included in the potential user group are consumers facing life-stage changes—such as newlyweds and new parents—who can be turned into heavy users. For example, upscale kitchen and cookware retailer Williams-Sonoma actively targets newly engaged couples.

Eight-page Williams-Sonoma ad inserts in bridal magazines show a young couple strolling through a park or talking intimately in the kitchen over a glass of wine. The bride-to-be asks, "Now that I've found love, what else do I need?" Pictures of Williams-Sonoma knife sets, toasters, glassware, and pots and pans provide some strong clues. The retailer also offers a bridal registry, of course, but it takes its registry a step further. Through a program called "The Store Is Yours," it opens its stores after hours, by appointment, exclusively for individual couples to visit and make their wish lists. This segment is very important to Williams-Sonoma. About half the people who register are new to the brand—and they'll be buying a lot of kitchen and cookware in the future.[8]

Usage Rate. Markets can also be segmented into light, medium, and heavy product users. Heavy users are often a small percentage of the market but account for a high percentage of total consumption. For example, Burger King targets what it calls "Super Fans," young (age 18 to 34), Whopper-wolfing males and females who make up 18 percent of the chain's customers but account for almost half of all customer visits. They eat at Burger King an average of 16 times a month.[9] Burger King targets these Super Fans openly with ads that exalt monster burgers containing meat, cheese, and more meat and cheese that can turn "innies into outies."[10]

Loyalty Status. A market can also be segmented by consumer loyalty. Consumers can be loyal to brands (Tide), stores (Target), and companies (Toyota). Buyers can be divided into groups according to their degree of loyalty.

Some consumers are completely loyal—they buy one brand all the time. For example, as we discussed in the previous chapter, Apple has an almost cultlike following of loyal users. Other consumers are somewhat loyal—they are loyal to two or three brands of a given product or favor one brand while sometimes buying others. Still other buyers show no loyalty to any brand. They either want something different each time they buy or they buy whatever's on sale.

A company can learn a lot by analyzing loyalty patterns in its market. It should start by studying its own loyal customers. ▲For example, by studying Mac fanatics, Apple can better pinpoint its target market and develop marketing appeals. By studying its less-loyal buyers, the company can detect which brands are most competitive with its own. By looking at customers who are shifting away from its brand, the company can learn about its marketing weaknesses.

Using Multiple Segmentation Bases

Marketers rarely limit their segmentation analysis to only one or a few variables. Rather, they often use multiple segmentation bases in an effort to identify smaller, better-defined target groups. Thus, a bank may not only identify a group of wealthy, retired adults but also, within that group, distinguish several segments based on their current income, assets, savings and risk preferences, housing, and lifestyles.

Several business information services—such as Nielsen Claritas, Acxiom, and Experian—provide multivariable segmentation systems that merge geographic, demographic, lifestyle, and behavioral data to help companies segment their markets down to zip codes, neighborhoods, and even households. One of the leading segmentation systems is the PRIZM NE (New Evolution) system by Nielsen Claritas. PRIZM NE classifies every American household based on a host of demographic factors—such as age, educational level, income, occupa-

▼Customer loyalty: By studying core loyal customers, Apple can pinpoint its target market and build on its marketing strengths. By looking at customers who are shifting away, it can learn about its marketing weaknesses.

Choose Wisely.

Choose Claritas.
Solve your marketing challenges with segmentation solutions from Claritas. Our industry-standard segmentation systems, PRIZM* NE, P$YCLE* and ConneXions* help you know your audience so you can tailor your marketing programs to them. Depth of knowledge gives you leverage for reaching and retaining your most profitable customers and prospects.

And, through our special analytics company, Integras, you can create a segmentation system that is specific to your company—the ultimate in precision marketing!

Choose wisely and call us today!

1-800-234-5973

www.claritas.com

CLARITAS

Adding
Intelligence
to Information

#18
Kids & Cul-de-Sacs

Upscale, suburban, married couples with children—that's the skinny on Kids & Cul-de-Sacs, an enviable lifestyle of large families in recently built subdivisions. With a high rate of Hispanic and Asian Americans, this segment is a refuge for college-educated, white-collar professionals with administrative jobs and upper-middle-class incomes. Their nexus of education, affluence and children translates into large outlays for child centered products and services.

#21
Gray Power

The steady rise of older, healthier Americans over the past decade has produced one important by-product: middle-class, home-owning suburbanites who are aging in place rather than moving to retirement communities. Gray Power reflects this trend, a segment of older, midscale singles and couples who live in quiet comfort.

▲Using Claritas' PRIZM NE system, marketers can paint a surprisingly precise picture of who you are and what you might buy. PRIZM NE segments carry such exotic names as "Kids & Cul-de-Sacs," "Gray Power," "Blue Blood Estates," "Shotguns & Pickups," and "Bright Lites L'il City."

tion, family composition, ethnicity, and housing—and behavioral and lifestyle factors—such as purchases, free-time activities, and media preferences.

PRIZM NE classifies U.S. households into 66 demographically and behaviorally distinct segments, organized into 14 different social groups. PRIZM NE segments carry such exotic names as "Kids & Cul-de-Sacs," "Gray Power," "Blue Blood Estates," "Mayberry-ville," "Shotguns & Pickups," "Old Glories," "Multi-Culti Mosaic," "Big City Blues," and "Bright Lites L'il City." The colorful names help to bring the clusters to life.[11]

▲PRIZM NE and other such systems can help marketers to segment people and locations into marketable groups of like-minded consumers. Each cluster has its own pattern of likes, dislikes, lifestyles, and purchase behaviors. For example, "Winner's Circle" neighborhoods, part of the Elite Suburbs social group, are suburban areas populated by well-off but younger, 25- to 34-year-old couples with large families in new-money neighborhoods. People in this segment are more likely to own a GMC Yukon Denali, go sailing, shop at Neiman Marcus, and read *Working Mother*. In contrast, the "Bedrock America" segment, part of the Rustic Living social group, is populated by young, economically challenged families in small, isolated towns located throughout the nation's heartland. People in this segment are more likely to eat at Little Caesars, buy a used vehicle, watch *Passions* on TV, and read *Parents Magazine*.

Such segmentation provides a powerful tool for marketers of all kinds. It can help companies to identify and better understand key customer segments, target them more efficiently, and tailor market offerings and messages to their specific needs.

Segmenting Business Markets

Consumer and business marketers use many of the same variables to segment their markets. Business buyers can be segmented geographically, demographically (industry, company size), or by benefits sought, user status, usage rate, and loyalty status. Yet, business marketers also use some additional variables, such as customer *operating characteristics*, *purchasing approaches*, *situational factors*, and *personal characteristics*.

Almost every company serves at least some business markets. For example, American Express targets businesses in three segments—merchants, corporations, and small businesses. It has developed distinct marketing programs for each segment. In the merchants segment, American Express focuses on convincing new merchants to accept the card and on managing relationships with those that already do. For larger corporate customers, the company offers a corporate card program, which includes extensive employee expense and travel management services. It also offers this segment a wide range of asset management, retirement planning, and financial education services.

Finally, for small business customers, American Express has created OPEN: The Small Business Network, a system of small business cards and financial services. It includes credit cards and lines of credit, special usage rewards, financial monitoring and spending report features, and 24/7 customized financial support services. "OPEN is how we serve small business," says American Express.[12]

Many companies set up separate systems for dealing with larger or multiple-location customers. For example, Steelcase, a major producer of office furniture, first segments customers into seven industries, including banking, biosciences, healthcare, and higher education. Next, company salespeople work with independent Steelcase dealers to handle smaller, local, or regional Steelcase customers in each segment. But many national, multiple-location customers, such as ExxonMobil or IBM, have special needs that may reach beyond the scope of individual dealers. So Steelcase uses national account managers to help its dealer networks handle its national accounts.

Within a given target industry and customer size, the company can segment by purchase approaches and criteria. As in consumer segmentation, many marketers believe that *buying behavior* and *benefits* provide the best basis for segmenting business markets.

Segmenting International Markets

Few companies have either the resources or the will to operate in all, or even most, of the countries that dot the globe. Although some large companies, such as Coca-Cola or Sony, sell products in more than 200 countries, most international firms focus on a smaller set. Operating in many countries presents new challenges. Different countries, even those that are close together, can vary greatly in their economic, cultural, and political makeup. Thus, just as they do within their domestic markets, international firms need to group their world markets into segments with distinct buying needs and behaviors.

Companies can segment international markets using one or a combination of several variables. They can segment by *geographic location*, grouping countries by regions such as Western Europe, the Pacific Rim, the Middle East, or Africa. Geographic segmentation assumes that nations close to one another will have many common traits and behaviors. Although this is often the case, there are many exceptions. For example, although the United States and Canada have much in common, both differ culturally and economically from neighboring Mexico. Even within a region, consumers can differ widely. For example, some U.S. marketers lump all Central and South American countries together. However, the Dominican Republic is no more like Brazil than Italy is like Sweden. Many Central and South Americans don't even speak Spanish, including 192 million Portuguese-speaking Brazilians and the millions in other countries who speak a variety of Indian dialects.

Intermarket segmentation
Forming segments of consumers who have similar needs and buying behavior even though they are located in different countries.

World markets can also be segmented on the basis of *economic factors*. Countries might be grouped by population income levels or by their overall level of economic development. A country's economic structure shapes its population's product and service needs and, therefore, the marketing opportunities it offers. For example, many companies are now targeting the BRIC countries—Brazil, Russia, India, and China—fast-growing developing economies with rapidly increasing buying power.

Countries can also be segmented by *political and legal factors* such as the type and stability of government, receptivity to foreign firms, monetary regulations, and amount of bureaucracy. *Cultural factors* can also be used, grouping markets according to common languages, religions, values and attitudes, customs, and behavioral patterns.

Segmenting international markets based on geographic, economic, political, cultural, and other factors assumes that segments should consist of clusters of countries. However, as new communications technologies, such as satellite TV and the Internet, connect consumers around the world, marketers can define and reach segments of like-minded consumers no matter where in the world they are. Using **intermarket segmentation** (also called *cross-market segmentation*), they form segments of consumers who have similar needs and buying behaviors even though they are located in different countries. For example, Lexus targets the world's

▼Intermarket segmentation: Swedish furniture giant IKEA targets the aspiring global middle class—it sells good-quality furniture that ordinary people worldwide can afford.

well-to-do—the "global elite" segment—regardless of their country. Coca-Cola creates special programs to target teens, core consumers of its soft drinks the world over. ▲And Swedish furniture giant IKEA targets the aspiring global middle class— it sells good-quality furniture that ordinary people worldwide can afford.

Requirements for Effective Segmentation

Clearly, there are many ways to segment a market, but not all segmentations are effective. For example, buyers of table salt could be divided into blond and brunette customers. But hair color obviously does not affect the purchase of salt. Furthermore, if all salt buyers bought the same amount of salt each month, believed that all salt is the same, and wanted to pay the same price, the company would not benefit from segmenting this market.

To be useful, market segments must be

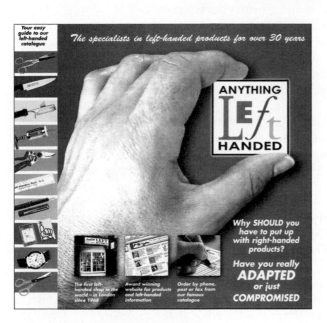

▲The "Leftie" segment can be hard to identify and measure. As a result, few companies tailor their offers to left-handers. However, some nichers such as Anything Left-Handed in the United Kingdom target this segment.

- *Measurable:* The size, purchasing power, and profiles of the segments can be measured. Certain segmentation variables are difficult to measure. ▲For example, there are approximately 30.5 million left-handed people in the United States—almost equaling the entire population of Canada. Yet few products are targeted toward this left-handed segment. The major problem may be that the segment is hard to identify and measure. There are no data on the demographics of lefties, and the U.S. Census Bureau does not keep track of left-handedness in its surveys. Private data companies keep reams of statistics on other demographic segments but not on left-handers.
- *Accessible:* The market segments can be effectively reached and served. Suppose a fragrance company finds that heavy users of its brand are single men and women who stay out late and socialize a lot. Unless this group lives or shops at certain places and is exposed to certain media, its members will be difficult to reach.
- *Substantial:* The market segments are large or profitable enough to serve. A segment should be the largest possible homogenous group worth pursuing with a tailored marketing program. It would not pay, for example, for an automobile manufacturer to develop cars especially for people whose height is greater than seven feet.
- *Differentiable:* The segments are conceptually distinguishable and respond differently to different marketing mix elements and programs. If married and unmarried women respond similarly to a sale on perfume, they do not constitute separate segments.
- *Actionable:* Effective programs can be designed for attracting and serving the segments. For example, although one small airline identified seven market segments, its staff was too small to develop separate marketing programs for each segment.

Speed Bump: Linking the Concepts

Slow down a bit and enjoy the view. How do the companies you do business with employ the segmentation concepts you're reading about here?

- Can you identify specific companies, other than the examples already mentioned, that practice the different types of segmentation just discussed?
- Using the segmentation bases you've just read about, segment the U.S. athletic footwear market. Describe each of the major segments and subsegments. Keep these segments in mind as you read the next section on target market.

Author Comment »
Now that we've divided the market into segments, it's time to answer that first seemingly simple marketing strategy question we raised in Figure 6.1: Which customers will the company serve?

MARKET TARGETING (pp 214–221)

Market segmentation reveals the firm's market segment opportunities. The firm now has to evaluate the various segments and decide how many and which segments it can serve best. We now look at how companies evaluate and select target segments.

Evaluating Market Segments

In evaluating different market segments, a firm must look at three factors: segment size and growth, segment structural attractiveness, and company objectives and resources. The company must first collect and analyze data on current segment sales, growth rates, and expected profitability for various segments. It will be interested in segments that have the right size and growth characteristics.

But "right size and growth" is a relative matter. The largest, fastest-growing segments are not always the most attractive ones for every company. Smaller companies may lack the skills and resources needed to serve the larger segments. Or they may find these segments too competitive. Such companies may target segments that are smaller and less attractive, in an absolute sense, but that are potentially more profitable for them.

The company also needs to examine major structural factors that affect long-run segment attractiveness.[13] For example, a segment is less attractive if it already contains many strong and aggressive *competitors*. The existence of many actual or potential *substitute products* may limit prices and the profits that can be earned in a segment. The relative *power of buyers* also affects segment attractiveness. Buyers with strong bargaining power relative to sellers will try to force prices down, demand more services, and set competitors against one another—all at the expense of seller profitability. Finally, a segment may be less attractive if it contains *powerful suppliers* who can control prices or reduce the quality or quantity of ordered goods and services.

Even if a segment has the right size and growth and is structurally attractive, the company must consider its own objectives and resources. Some attractive segments can be dismissed quickly because they do not mesh with the company's long-run objectives. Or the company may lack the skills and resources needed to succeed in an attractive segment. For example, given current economic conditions, the economy segment of the automobile market is large and growing. But given its objectives and resources, it would make little sense for luxury-performance carmaker BMW to enter this segment. A company should enter only segments in which it can create superior customer value and gain advantages over competitors.

Selecting Target Market Segments

Target market
A set of buyers sharing common needs or characteristics that the company decides to serve.

After evaluating different segments, the company must decide which and how many segments it will target. A **target market** consists of a set of buyers who share common needs or characteristics that the company decides to serve. Market targeting can be carried out at several different levels. ■ **Figure 6.2** shows that companies can target very broadly (undifferentiated marketing), very narrowly (micromarketing), or somewhere in between (differentiated or concentrated marketing).

Undifferentiated Marketing

Undifferentiated (mass) marketing
A market-coverage strategy in which a firm decides to ignore market segment differences and go after the whole market with one offer.

Using an **undifferentiated marketing (or mass-marketing)** strategy, a firm might decide to ignore market segment differences and target the whole market with one offer. This mass-marketing strategy focuses on what is *common* in the needs of consumers rather than on what is *different*. The company designs a product and a marketing program that will appeal to the largest number of buyers.

■ **Figure 6.2** Market Targeting Strategies

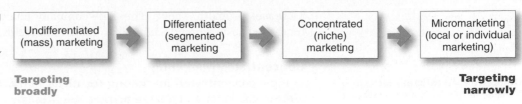

| Undifferentiated (mass) marketing | → | Differentiated (segmented) marketing | → | Concentrated (niche) marketing | → | Micromarketing (local or individual marketing) |

Targeting broadly

Targeting narrowly

This figure covers a pretty broad range of targeting strategies, from mass marketing (virtually no targeting) to individual marketing (customizing products and programs to individual customers). An example of individual marketing: At myMMs.com you can order a batch of M&Ms with your face and personal message printed on each little candy.

As noted earlier in the chapter, most modern marketers have strong doubts about this strategy. Difficulties arise in developing a product or brand that will satisfy all consumers. Moreover, mass marketers often have trouble competing with more-focused firms that do a better job of satisfying the needs of specific segments and niches.

Differentiated Marketing

Using a **differentiated marketing (or segmented marketing)** strategy, a firm decides to target several market segments and designs separate offers for each. Toyota Corporation produces several different brands of cars—from Scion to Toyota to Lexus—each targeting its own segments of car buyers. Procter & Gamble markets six different laundry detergent brands, which compete with each other on supermarket shelves. ▲ And VF Corporation offers a closet full of more than 30 premium lifestyle brands, each of which "taps into consumer aspirations to fashion, status, and well-being" in a well-defined segment.[14]

Differentiated (segmented) marketing
A market-coverage strategy in which a firm decides to target several market segments and designs separate offers for each.

> VF is the nation's number-one jeans maker, with brands such as Lee, Riders, Rustler, and Wrangler. But jeans are not the only focus for VF. The company's brands are carefully separated into five major segments—Jeanswear, Imagewear (workwear), Outdoor, Sportswear, and Contemporary Brands. The North Face, part of the Outdoor unit, offers top-of-the-line gear and apparel for diehard outdoor enthusiasts, especially those who prefer cold weather activities. From the Sportswear unit, Nautica focuses on people who enjoy high-end casual apparel inspired by sailing and the sea. Vans began as a skate shoe maker, and Reef features surf-inspired footwear and apparel. In the Contemporary Brands unit, Lucy features upscale activewear, whereas 7 for All Mankind supplies premium denim and accessories sold in boutiques and high-end department stores such as Saks and Nordstrom. At the other end of the spectrum, Sentinel, part of the Imagewear unit, markets uniforms for security officers.

By offering product and marketing variations to segments, companies hope for higher sales and a stronger position within each market segment. Developing a stronger position within several segments creates more total sales than undifferentiated marketing across all segments. VF Corporation's combined brands give it a much greater, more stable market share than any single brand could. The four Jeanswear brands alone account for a quarter of all jeans sold in the United States. Similarly, P&G's multiple detergent brands capture four times the market share of nearest rival Unilever.

But differentiated marketing also increases the costs of doing business. A firm usually finds it more expensive to develop and produce, say, 10 units of 10 different products than 100 units of one product. Developing separate marketing plans for the separate segments requires extra marketing research, forecasting, sales analysis, promotion planning, and channel management. And trying to reach different market segments with different advertising campaigns

▼ **Differentiated marketing: VF Corporation offers a closet full of over 30 premium lifestyle brands, each of which "taps into consumer aspirations to fashion, status, and well-being" in a well-defined segment.**

increases promotion costs. Thus, the company must weigh increased sales against increased costs when deciding on a differentiated marketing strategy.

Concentrated Marketing

Concentrated (niche) marketing
A market-coverage strategy in which a firm goes after a large share of one or a few segments or niches.

Using a **concentrated marketing (or niche marketing)** strategy, instead of going after a small share of a large market, the firm goes after a large share of one or a few smaller segments or niches. For example, Whole Foods Market has only about 275 stores and $7.9 billion in sales, compared with goliaths such as Kroger (more than 3,600 stores and sales of $70 billion) and Wal-Mart (7,250 stores and sales of $379 billion).[15] Yet the smaller, upscale retailer is growing faster and more profitably than either of its giant rivals. Whole Foods thrives by catering to affluent customers who the Wal-Marts of the world can't serve well, offering them "organic, natural, and gourmet foods, all swaddled in Earth Day politics." In fact, a typical Whole Foods customer is more likely to boycott the local Wal-Mart than to shop at it.

Through concentrated marketing, the firm achieves a strong market position because of its greater knowledge of consumer needs in the niches it serves and the special reputation it acquires. It can market more *effectively* by fine-tuning its products, prices, and programs to the needs of carefully defined segments. It can also market more *efficiently*, targeting its products or services, channels, and communications programs toward only consumers that it can serve best and most profitably.

Whereas segments are fairly large and normally attract several competitors, niches are smaller and may attract only one or a few competitors. Niching lets smaller companies focus their limited resources on serving niches that may be unimportant to or overlooked by larger competitors. Many companies start as nichers to get a foothold against larger, more-resourceful competitors and then grow into broader competitors. For example, Southwest Airlines began by serving intrastate, no-frills commuters in Texas but is now one of the nation's largest airlines. And Enterprise Rent-A-Car began by building a network of neighborhood offices rather competing with Hertz and Avis in airport locations. Enterprise is now the nation's largest car rental company.

In contrast, as markets change, some megamarketers develop niche products to create sales growth. For example, in recent years, as consumers have grown more health conscious, the demand for carbonated soft drinks has declined while the market for energy drinks and juices has grown. Carbonated soft drink sales fell 2.3 percent last year; energy drink sales surged 26 percent. To meet this shifting demand, mainstream cola marketers PepsiCo and Coca-Cola have both developed or acquired their own niche products. PepsiCo developed Amp energy drink and purchased the SoBe and Izze brands of enhanced waters and juices. Similarly, Coca-Cola developed Vault and acquired the Vitaminwater and Odwalla brands. Says Pepsi-Cola North America's chief marketing officer, "The era of the mass brand has been over for a long time."[16]

Today, the low cost of setting up shop on the Internet makes it even more profitable to serve seemingly miniscule niches. Small businesses, in particular, are realizing riches from serving small niches on the Web. ▲Consider Etsy:

▼**Concentrated marketing: Thanks to the reach and power of the Web, online nicher Etsy—sometimes referred to as eBay's funky little sister—is thriving.**

Etsy is "an online marketplace for buying and selling all things handmade"—from hand-knit leg warmers to "Hope on a Rope," hanging shower soap carved in the shape of Barack Obama's head. Sometimes referred to as eBay's funky little sister, the Etsy online crafts fair site was launched four years ago by three New York University students. The site makes money three ways: a 20-cent listing fee for every item, a 3.5 percent sales fee on every transaction, and advertising sold to sellers who want to promote their items. A far cry from the old-fashioned street-corner flea market, thanks to the reach and power of the Web, Etsy now counts 1.8 million members and 2 million listings in 150 countries. Last year alone, Etsy tripled its gross sales to $90 million. As it has grown, Etsy has become as much a community as an e-commerce site. For example, it sponsors actual and virtual meet-ups organized by location (from Syracuse to Saskatchewan and Singapore), medium (papier-mâché, mosaic), and interest area (Chainmailers Guild, Lizards, and Lollipops). Etsy's main goal? According to CEO Maria Thomas, it's "to help people make a living by doing what they love and making things."[17]

Concentrated marketing can be highly profitable. At the same time, it involves higher-than-normal risks. Companies that rely on one or a few segments for all of their business will suffer greatly if the segment turns sour. Or larger competitors may decide to enter the same segment with greater resources. For these reasons, many companies prefer to diversify in several market segments.

Micromarketing

Micromarketing
The practice of tailoring products and marketing programs to the needs and wants of specific individuals and local customer segments—includes *local marketing* and *individual marketing*.

Local marketing
Tailoring brands and promotions to the needs and wants of local customer segments—cities, neighborhoods, and even specific stores.

Differentiated and concentrated marketers tailor their offers and marketing programs to meet the needs of various market segments and niches. At the same time, however, they do not customize their offers to each individual customer. **Micromarketing** is the practice of tailoring products and marketing programs to suit the tastes of specific individuals and locations. Rather than seeing a customer in every individual, micromarketers see the individual in every customer. Micromarketing includes *local marketing* and *individual marketing*.

Local Marketing. **Local marketing** involves tailoring brands and promotions to the needs and wants of local customer groups—cities, neighborhoods, and even specific stores. For example, Wal-Mart customizes its merchandise store by store to meet the needs of local shoppers. The retailer's store designers create each new store's format according to neighborhood characteristics—stores near office parks, for instance, contain prominent islands featuring ready-made meals for busy workers. Then, using a wealth of customer data on daily sales in every store, Wal-Mart tailors individual store merchandise with similar precision. For example, it uses more than 200 finely tuned planograms (shelf plans) to match soup assortments to each store's demand patterns.[18]

Advances in communications technology have given rise to a new high-tech version of location-based marketing. By coupling mobile phone services with GPS devices, many marketers are now targeting customers wherever they are with what they want.[19]

▼**Local marketing: By coupling mobile phone services with GPS devices, marketers like Starbucks are now targeting customers wherever they are with what they want.**

Location. Location. Location. This is the mantra of the real estate business. But it may not be long before marketers quote it, too. "Location-based technology allows [marketers] to reach people when they're mobile, near their stores, looking to make a decision," says one marketing expert. "When customers get information—even advertising information—linked to their location, research shows that's often perceived as value-added information, not as an advertisement." ▲For example, Starbucks recently launched a store locator service for mobile devices, which allows people to use their phones and in-car GPS systems to search for the nearest Starbucks shop. A consumer sends a text message to "MYSBUX" (697289) including his or her zip code. Within 10 seconds, Starbucks replies with up to three nearby store locations. Starbucks plans to expand the service to include a wider range of text-messaging conversations with local customers that will "showcase Starbucks as a brand that truly listens." Such location-based marketing will grow astronomically as the sales of GPS devices skyrocket.

Local marketing has some drawbacks. It can drive up manufacturing and marketing costs by reducing economies of scale. It can also create logistics problems as companies try to meet the varied requirements of different regional and local markets. Further, a brand's overall image might be diluted if the product and message vary too much in different localities.

Still, as companies face increasingly fragmented markets, and as new supporting technologies develop, the advantages of local marketing often outweigh the drawbacks. Local marketing helps a company to market more effectively in the face of pronounced regional and local differences in demographics and lifestyles. It also meets the needs of the company's first-line customers—retailers—who prefer more finely tuned product assortments for their neighborhoods.

Individual marketing
Tailoring products and marketing programs to the needs and preferences of individual customers—also labeled "one-to-one marketing," "customized marketing," and "markets-of-one marketing."

Individual Marketing. In the extreme, micromarketing becomes **individual marketing**—tailoring products and marketing programs to the needs and preferences of individual customers. Individual marketing has also been labeled *one-to-one marketing, mass customization,* and *markets-of-one marketing.*

The widespread use of mass marketing has obscured the fact that for centuries consumers were served as individuals: The tailor custom-made a suit, the cobbler designed shoes for an individual, the cabinetmaker made furniture to order. Today, however, new technologies are permitting many companies to return to customized marketing. More detailed databases, robotic production and flexible manufacturing, and interactive communication media such as cell phones and the Internet—all have combined to foster "mass customization." *Mass customization* is the process through which firms interact one-to-one with masses of customers to design products and services tailor-made to individual needs.

Dell creates custom-configured computers. Hockey-stick maker Branches Hockey lets customers choose from more than two dozen options—including stick length, blade patterns, and blade curve—and turns out a customized stick in five days. Visitors to Nike's NikeID Web site can personalize their sneakers by choosing from hundreds of colors and putting an embroidered word or phrase on the tongue. At www.myMMs.com, you can upload your photo and order a batch of M&Ms with your face and a personal message printed on each little candy. Toyota even lets Scion owners design their own personal "coat of arms" online, "a piece of owner-generated art that is meant to reflect their own job, hobbies, and—um, okay—Karma." Customers can download their designs and have them made into window decals or professionally airbrushed onto their cars.[20]

▼Individual marketing: Video screens in malls and stores can now determine who's watching them and change ads accordingly.

Marketers are also finding new ways to personalize promotional messages. ▲For example, plasma screens placed in shopping malls around the country can now analyze shoppers' faces and place ads based on an individual shopper's gender, age, or ethnicity:[21]

> Watch an advertisement on a video screen in a mall, health club, or grocery store and there's a growing chance that the ad is watching you too. Small cameras can now be embedded in or around the screen, tracking who looks at the screen and for how long. With surprising accuracy, the system can determine the viewer's gender, approximate age range and, in some cases, ethnicity—and change the ads accordingly. That could mean razor ads for men, cosmetics ads for women, and videogame ads for teens. Or a video screen might show a motorcycle ad for a group of men, but switch to a minivan ad when women and children join them. "This is proactive merchandising," says a media executive. "You're targeting people with smart ads."

Business-to-business marketers are also finding new ways to customize their offerings. For example, John Deere manufactures seeding equipment that can be configured in more than two million versions to individual customer specifications. The seeders are produced one at a time, in any sequence, on a single production line. Mass customization provides a way to stand out against competitors.

Unlike mass production, which eliminates the need for human interaction, one-to-one marketing has made relationships with customers more important than ever. Just as mass production was the marketing principle of the past century, interactive marketing is becoming a marketing principle for the twenty-first century. The world appears to be coming full circle—from the good old days when customers were treated as individuals, to mass marketing when nobody knew your name, and back again.

The move toward individual marketing mirrors the trend in consumer *self-marketing*. Increasingly, individual customers are taking more responsibility for shaping both the products they buy and the buying experience. As the trend toward more interactive dialogue and less marketing monologue continues, marketers will need to influence the buying process in new ways. They will need to involve customers more in all phases of the product development and buying processes, increasing opportunities for buyers to practice self-marketing.

Choosing a Targeting Strategy

Companies need to consider many factors when choosing a market-targeting strategy. Which strategy is best depends on *company resources*. When the firm's resources are limited, concentrated marketing makes the most sense. The best strategy also depends on the degree of *product variability*. Undifferentiated marketing is more suited for uniform products such as grapefruit or steel. Products that can vary in design, such as cameras and cars, are more suited to differentiation or concentration. The *product's life-cycle stage* also must be considered. When a firm introduces a new product, it may be practical to launch only one version, and undifferentiated marketing or concentrated marketing may make the most sense. In the mature stage of the product life cycle, however, differentiated marketing often makes more sense.

Another factor is *market variability*. If most buyers have the same tastes, buy the same amounts, and react the same way to marketing efforts, undifferentiated marketing is appropriate. Finally, *competitors' marketing strategies* are important. When competitors use differentiated or concentrated marketing, undifferentiated marketing can be suicidal. Conversely, when competitors use undifferentiated marketing, a firm can gain an advantage by using differentiated or concentrated marketing, focusing on the needs of buyers in specific segments.

Socially Responsible Target Marketing

Smart targeting helps companies to be more efficient and effective by focusing on the segments that they can satisfy best and most profitably. Targeting also benefits consumers—companies serve specific groups of consumers with offers carefully tailored to their needs. However, target marketing sometimes generates controversy and concern. The biggest issues usually involve the targeting of vulnerable or disadvantaged consumers with controversial or potentially harmful products.

For example, over the years, marketers in a wide range of industries—from cereal and toys to fast food and fashion—have been heavily criticized for their marketing efforts directed toward children. Critics worry that premium offers and high-powered advertising appeals presented through the mouths of lovable animated characters will overwhelm children's defenses.

Other problems arise when the marketing of adult products spills over into the kid segment—intentionally or unintentionally. ▲For example, Victoria's Secret targets its Pink line of young, hip, and sexy clothing to young women 18 to 30 years old. In less than five years, Pink has generated more than $1 billion in sales. However, critics charge that Pink is now all the rage among girls as young as 11. Responding to Victoria's Secret's designs and marketing messages, tweens are flocking into stores and buying Pink, with or without their mothers. Other retailers, such as Abercrombie and American Eagle, have also jumped into the

▲Socially responsible targeting: Victoria's Secret targets its Pink line of young, hip, and sexy clothing to young women 18 to 30 years old. However, critics charge that Pink is now all the rage among girls as young as 11.

booming business of loungewear and intimate apparel for young buyers. More broadly, critics worry that marketers of everything from lingerie and cosmetics to Barbie dolls are directly or indirectly targeting young girls with provocative products, promoting a premature focus on sex and appearance.[22]

> Ten-year-old girls can slide their low-cut jeans over "eye-candy" panties. French maid costumes, garter belt included, are available in preteen sizes. Barbie now comes in a "bling-bling" style, replete with halter top and go-go boots. And it's not unusual for girls under 12 to sing, "Don't cha wish your girlfriend was hot like me?" American girls, say experts, are increasingly being fed a cultural catnip of products and images that promote looking and acting sexy. "The message we're telling our girls is a simple one," laments one reporter about the Victoria's Secret Pink line. "You'll have a great life if people find you sexually attractive. Grown women struggle enough with this ridiculous standard. Do we really need to start worrying about it at 11?"

The Federal Trade Commission (FTC) and citizen action groups have accused tobacco and beer companies of targeting underage smokers and drinkers. One study found that more than a third of alcohol radio ads are more likely to be heard by underage listeners than adults on a per capita basis.[23] To encourage responsible advertising, the Children's Advertising Review Unit, the advertising industry's self-regulatory agency, has published extensive children's advertising guidelines that recognize the special needs of child audiences. Still, critics feel that more should been done. Some have even called for a complete ban on advertising to children.

Cigarette, beer, and fast-food marketers have also generated controversy in recent years by their attempts to target inner-city minority consumers. For example, McDonald's and other chains have drawn criticism for pitching their high-fat, salt-laden fare to low-income, urban residents who are much more likely than suburbanites to be heavy consumers. Similarly, R.J. Reynolds took heavy flak in the early 1990s when it announced plans to market Uptown, a menthol cigarette targeted toward low-income blacks. It quickly dropped the brand in the face of a loud public outcry and heavy pressure from African-American leaders.

The growth of the Internet and other carefully targeted direct media has raised fresh concerns about potential targeting abuses. The Internet allows increasing refinement of audiences and, in turn, more precise targeting. This might help makers of questionable products or deceptive advertisers to more readily victimize the most vulnerable audiences. Unscrupulous marketers can now send tailor-made deceptive messages directly to the computers of millions of unsuspecting consumers. For example, the FBI's Internet Crime Complaint Center Web site alone received more than 275,000 complaints last year.[24]

Not all attempts to target children, minorities, or other special segments draw such criticism. In fact, most provide benefits to targeted consumers. For example, Pantene markets Relaxed and Natural hair products to women of color. Samsung markets the Jitterbug phone directly to seniors who need a simpler cell phone that is bigger and has a louder speaker. And Colgate makes a large selection of toothbrush shapes and toothpaste flavors for children—from Colgate Shrek Bubble Fruit toothpaste to Colgate Bratz character toothbrushes. Such products help make tooth brushing more fun and get children to brush longer and more often.

Thus, in target marketing, the issue is not really *who* is targeted but rather *how* and for *what*. Controversies arise when marketers attempt to profit at the expense of targeted segments—when they unfairly target vulnerable segments or target them with questionable products or tactics. Socially responsible marketing calls for segmentation and targeting that serve not just the interests of the company but also the interests of those targeted.

Speed Bump: Linking the Concepts

Time to coast for a bit and take stock.

- At the last speed bump, you segmented the U.S. footwear market. Refer to Figure 6.2 and select two companies that serve this market. Describe their segmentation and targeting strategies. Can you come up with a company that targets many different segments versus another that focuses on only one or a few segments?
- How does each company you chose differentiate its market offering and image? Has each done a good job of establishing this differentiation in the minds of targeted consumers? The final section in this chapter deals with such positioning issues.

<table>
<tr><td valign="top">

Author Comment »

At the same time that it's answering the first simple-sounding question (Which customers will we serve?), the company must be asking the second question (How will we serve them?). For example, Ritz-Carlton serves the top 5 percent of corporate and leisure travelers. Its value proposition is "The Ritz-Carlton Experience"—one that "enlivens the senses, instills a sense of well-being, and fulfills even the unexpressed wishes and needs of our guests."

Product position
The way the product is defined by consumers on important attributes—the place the product occupies in consumers' minds relative to competing products.

</td><td valign="top">

DIFFERENTIATION AND POSITIONING (pp 221–230)

Beyond deciding which segments of the market it will target, the company must decide on a *value proposition*—on how it will create differentiated value for targeted segments and what positions it wants to occupy in those segments. A **product's position** is the way the product is *defined by consumers* on important attributes—the place the product occupies in consumers' minds relative to competing products. "Products are created in the factory, but brands are created in the mind," says a positioning expert.[25]

Tide is positioned as a powerful, all-purpose family detergent; Ivory is positioned as the gentle detergent for fine washables and baby clothes. At IHOP, you "Come hungry. Leave happy."; at Olive Garden, "When You're Here, You're Family"; and Chili's wants you to "Pepper in some fun." In the automobile market, the Nissan Versa and Honda Fit are positioned on economy, Mercedes and Cadillac on luxury, and Porsche and BMW on performance. Volvo positions powerfully on safety. And Toyota positions its fuel-efficient, hybrid Prius as a high-tech solution to the energy shortage: "How far will you go to save the planet?" it asks.

Consumers are overloaded with information about products and services. They cannot reevaluate products every time they make a buying decision. To simplify the buying process, consumers organize products, services, and companies into categories and "position" them in their minds. A product's position is the complex set of perceptions, impressions, and feelings that consumers have for the product compared with competing products.

Consumers position products with or without the help of marketers. But marketers do not want to leave their products' positions to chance. They must *plan* positions that will give their products the greatest advantage in selected target markets, and they must design marketing mixes to create these planned positions.

Positioning Maps

In planning their differentiation and positioning strategies, marketers often prepare *perceptual positioning maps,* which show consumer perceptions of their brands versus competing products on important buying dimensions. ■ **Figure 6.3** shows a positioning map for the U.S. large luxury sport utility vehicle market.[26] The position of each circle on the map indicates the brand's perceived positioning on two dimensions—price and orientation (luxury versus performance). The size of each circle indicates the brand's relative market share.

Thus, customers view the Hummer H2 as a higher-performance vehicle with some luxury thrown in. As the company's Web site puts it: "In a world where SUVs have begun to look like their owners, complete with love handles and mushy seats, the H2 SUV proves that there is still one out there that can drop and give you 20." The market-leading Cadillac Escalade is positioned as a moderately priced large

</td></tr>
</table>

▲ **Toyota's Land Cruiser retains some of its adventure and performance positioning but with luxury added.**

luxury SUV with a balance of luxury and performance. The Escalade is positioned on urban luxury, and in its case, "performance" probably means power and safety performance. You'll find no mention of off-road adventuring in an Escalade ad.

By contrast, Range Rover and Land Cruiser are positioned on luxury with nuances of off-road performance. For example, the Toyota Land Cruiser began in 1951 as a four-wheel drive, Jeep-like vehicle designed to conquer the world's most grueling terrains and climates. ▲In recent years, Land Cruiser has retained this adventure and performance positioning but with luxury added. Its Web site brags of "legendary off-road capability," with off-road technologies such as downhill assist control and kinetic dynamic suspension systems. "In some parts of the world, it's an essential." Despite its ruggedness, however, the company notes that "its available Bluetooth hands-free technology, DVD entertainment, and a sumptuous interior have softened its edges."

Choosing a Differentiation and Positioning Strategy

Some firms find it easy to choose a differentiation and positioning strategy. For example, a firm well known for quality in certain segments will go for this position in a new segment if there are enough buyers seeking quality. But in many cases, two or more firms will go after the same position. Then, each will have to find other ways to set itself apart. Each firm must differentiate its offer by building a unique bundle of benefits that appeals to a substantial group within the segment. Above all else, a brand's positioning must serve the needs and preferences of well-defined target markets.

The differentiation and positioning task consists of three steps: identifying a set of differentiating competitive advantages upon which to build a position, choosing the right competitive advantages, and selecting an overall positioning strategy. The company must then effectively communicate and deliver the chosen position to the market.

Identifying Possible Value Differences and Competitive Advantages

To build profitable relationships with target customers, marketers must understand customer needs better than competitors do and deliver more customer value. To the

■ **Figure 6.3** Positioning Map: Large Luxury SUVs

Source: Based on data provided by Ward's AutoInfoBank and Edmunds.com, 2009.

The location of each circle shows where consumers position a brand on two dimensions: price and luxury-performance orientation. The size of each circle indicates the brand's relative market share in the segment. Thus, Toyota's Land Cruiser is a niche brand that is perceived to be relatively affordable and more performance oriented.

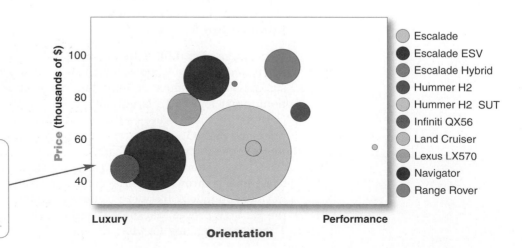

Competitive advantage
An advantage over competitors gained by offering greater customer value, either through lower prices or by providing more benefits that justify higher prices.

extent that a company can differentiate and position itself as providing superior customer value, it gains **competitive advantage**.

But solid positions cannot be built on empty promises. If a company positions its product as *offering* the best quality and service, it must actually differentiate the product so that it *delivers* the promised quality and service. Companies must do much more than simply shout out their positions in ad slogans and taglines. They must first *live* the slogan. ▲For example, when Staples' research revealed that it should differentiate itself on the basis of "an easier shopping experience," the office supply retailer held back its "Staples: That was easy" marketing campaign for more than a year. First, it remade its stores to actually deliver the promised positioning.[27]

Now there's an easy button for your business.

It's called Staples.

Wouldn't it be nice if daily tasks around the office got a little easier? When you shop Staples, it will be as easy as — well — pressing a button. Visit us at **staples.com/easy** to find out what our Easy Button™ can do for you today.

STAPLES
that was easy.®

▲The "Staples: That was easy" marketing campaign has played a major role in repositioning Staples. But marketing promises count for little if they are not backed by the reality of the customer experience.

Only a few years ago, things weren't so easy for Staples—or for its customers. The ratio of customer complaints to compliments was running a dreadful eight to one at Staples stores. Weeks of focus groups produced an answer: Customers wanted an easier shopping experience. That simple revelation has resulted in one of the most successful marketing campaigns in recent history, built around the now-familiar "Staples: That was easy" tagline. But Staples' positioning turnaround took a lot more than simply bombarding customers with a new slogan. Before it could promise customers a simplified shopping experience, Staples had to actually deliver one. First, it had to *live* the slogan.

So, for more than a year, Staples worked to revamp the customer experience. It remodeled its stores, streamlined its inventory, retrained employees, and even simplified customer communications. Only when all of the customer-experience pieces were in place did Staples begin communicating its new positioning to customers. The "Staples: That was easy" repositioning campaign has met with striking success, helping to make Staples the runaway leader in office retail. And the campaign's easy button has become a pop culture icon. No doubt about it, clever marketing helped. But marketing promises count for little if not backed by the reality of the customer experience. "What has happened at the store has done more to drive the Staples brand than all the marketing in the world," says Staples' vice president of marketing.

To find points of differentiation, marketers must think through the customer's entire experience with the company's product or service. An alert company can find ways to differentiate itself at every customer contact point. In what specific ways can a company differentiate itself or its market offer? It can differentiate along the lines of *product, services, channels, people,* or *image*.

Through *product differentiation* brands can be differentiated on features, performance, or style and design. Thus, Bose positions its speakers on their striking design and sound characteristics. By gaining the approval of the American Heart Association as an approach to a healthy lifestyle, Subway differentiates itself as the healthy fast-food choice. And MBT shoes aren't just any shoes: They are fitness aids that "can change your life forever" by reducing stress on joints and toning thigh, stomach, and other muscles.

Beyond differentiating its physical product, a firm can also differentiate the services that accompany the product. Some companies gain *services differentiation* through speedy, convenient, or careful delivery. For example, First Convenience Bank of Texas offers "Real Hours for Real People"—it remains open seven days a week, including evenings. Others differentiate their service based on high-quality customer care. Lexus makes fine cars but is perhaps even better known for the quality service that creates outstanding ownership experiences for Lexus owners.

Firms that practice *channel differentiation* gain competitive advantage through the way they design their channel's coverage, expertise, and performance. Amazon.com and GEICO set themselves apart with their smooth-functioning direct channels. Companies can also gain a strong competitive advantage through *people differentiation*—hiring and training better people than their competitors do. Disney World people are known to be friendly and upbeat. And Singapore Airlines enjoys an excellent reputation, largely because of the grace of its flight attendants. People differentiation requires that a company select its customer-contact people carefully and train them well. For example, Disney trains its theme park people thoroughly to ensure that they are competent, courteous, and friendly—from the hotel check-in agents, to the monorail drivers, to the ride attendants, to the people who sweep Main Street USA. Each employee is carefully trained to understand customers and to "make people happy."

Even when competing offers look the same, buyers may perceive a difference based on company or brand *image differentiation*. A company or brand image should convey the product's distinctive benefits and positioning. Developing a strong and distinctive image calls for creativity and hard work. A company cannot develop an image in the public's mind overnight using only a few advertisements. If Ritz-Carlton means quality, this image must be supported by everything the company says and does.

Symbols—such as the McDonald's golden arches, the red Travelers umbrella, the Nike swoosh, or Google's colorful logo—can provide strong company or brand recognition and image differentiation. The company might build a brand around a famous person, as Nike did with its Air Jordan basketball shoes and Tiger Woods golfing products. Some companies even become associated with colors, such as IBM (blue), UPS (brown), or Coca-Cola (red). The chosen symbols, characters, and other image elements must be communicated through advertising that conveys the company's or brand's personality.

Choosing the Right Competitive Advantages

Suppose a company is fortunate enough to discover several potential differentiations that provide competitive advantages. It now must choose the ones on which it will build its positioning strategy. It must decide *how many* differences to promote and *which ones*.

How Many Differences to Promote. Many marketers think that companies should aggressively promote only one benefit to the target market. Ad man Rosser Reeves, for example, said a company should develop a *unique selling proposition* (USP) for each brand and stick to it. Each brand should pick an attribute and tout itself as "number one" on that attribute. Buyers tend to remember number one better, especially in this overcommunicated society. Thus, Wal-Mart promotes its unbeatable low prices and Burger King promotes personal choice—"have it your way."

Other marketers think that companies should position themselves on more than one differentiator. This may be necessary if two or more firms are claiming to be best on the same attribute. Today, in a time when the mass market is fragmenting into many small segments, companies are trying to broaden their positioning strategies to appeal to more segments.

For example, ▲S.C. Johnson recently introduced a new Pledge multi-surface cleaner. Known mainly as a brand for cleaning and dusting wood furniture, the new Pledge is positioned as a cleaner that works on wood, electronics, glass, marble, stainless steel, and other surfaces. Says its Web site, "No need to keep switching products—this multi-surface cleaner is perfect for a quick and easy cleanup of the whole room!" Clearly, many buyers want these multiple benefits. The challenge was to convince them that one brand can do it all. However, as companies increase the number of claims for their brands, they risk disbelief and a loss of clear positioning.

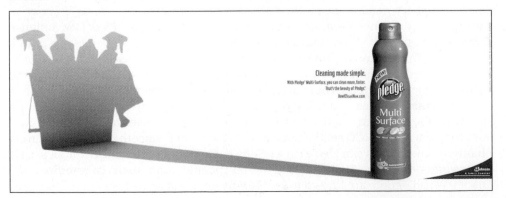

▼**Pledge Multi Surface is positioned on multiple benefits. The challenge is to convince customers that one brand can do it all.**

Which Differences to Promote. Not all brand differences are meaningful or worthwhile; not every difference makes a good differentiator. Each difference has the potential to create company costs as well as customer benefits. A difference is worth establishing to the extent that it satisfies the following criteria:

- *Important:* The difference delivers a highly valued benefit to target buyers.
- *Distinctive:* Competitors do not offer the difference, or the company can offer it in a more distinctive way.
- *Superior:* The difference is superior to other ways that customers might obtain the same benefit.
- *Communicable:* The difference is communicable and visible to buyers.
- *Preemptive:* Competitors cannot easily copy the difference.
- *Affordable:* Buyers can afford to pay for the difference.
- *Profitable:* The company can introduce the difference profitably.

Many companies have introduced differentiations that failed one or more of these tests. When the Westin Stamford Hotel in Singapore once advertised that it is the world's tallest hotel, it was a distinction that was not important to most tourists—in fact, it turned many off. Polaroid's Polarvision, which produced instantly developed home movies, bombed too. Although Polarvision was distinctive and even preemptive, it was inferior to another way of capturing motion, namely, camcorders.

Thus, choosing competitive advantages upon which to position a product or service can be difficult, yet such choices may be crucial to success. Choosing the right differentiators can help a brand to stand out from the pack of competitors. For example, when Raffles Hotel in Singapore made the strategic decision to position itself as "The Grand Old Dame of the East," the hotel knew that its legendary service of excellence would stand up to that claim of "Grandeur." (See Marketing at Work 6.2.)

Selecting an Overall Positioning Strategy

The full positioning of a brand is called the brand's **value proposition**—the full mix of benefits upon which the brand is differentiated and positioned. It is the answer to the customer's question "Why should I buy your brand?" Volvo's value proposition hinges on safety but also includes reliability, roominess, and styling, all for a price that is higher than average but seems fair for this mix of benefits.

■ **Figure 6.4** shows possible value propositions upon which a company might position its products. In the figure, the five green cells represent winning value propositions—differentiation and positioning that gives the company competitive advantage. The red cells, however, represent losing value propositions. The center yellow cell represents at best a marginal proposition. In the following sections, we discuss the five winning value propositions upon which companies can position their products: more for more, more for the same, the same for less, less for much less, and more for less.

Value proposition
The full positioning of a brand—the full mix of benefits upon which it is positioned.

■ **Figure 6.4** Possible Value Propositions

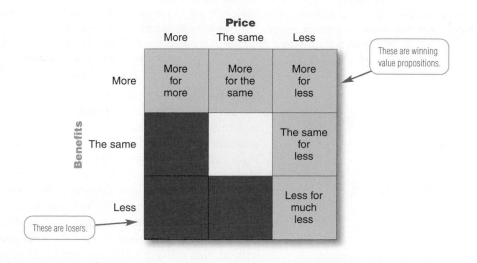

Marketing at Work 6.2

Raffles Hotel in Singapore: The Grand Old Dame of the East

One of the key customer-driven marketing strategy decisions involves dividing up markets into meaningful groups of consumers (segmentation), followed by making a choice on which consumer group to serve (targeting). This then sets the stage for the marketer to create market offerings that best serve that specific chosen consumer group (differentiation). Once the market offerings are created, the marketer proceeds to position them in the mind of these consumers (positioning) through effective communication.

The world-famous and legendary Raffles Hotel in Singapore is a good illustration of how these concepts of segmentation, targeting, differentiation, and positioning, are applied in the real world.

Raffles Hotel opened in 1887 in an old bungalow known as the Beach House. Named after Sir Stamford Raffles, the founder of modern Singapore, it had tropical suites, which came with bentwood tables and rattan chairs. Over the past years, the hotel has evolved into one of the world's most beloved grand hotels and has been residence to innumerable celebrities, writers, and royalty such as Charlie Chaplin, Eva Gardner, Somerset Maugham, Joseph Conrad, George Bush, Elizabeth Taylor, and Michael Jackson.

Declared a National Monument of Singapore in 1987, Raffles Hotel is sometimes known to be more famous than Singapore itself. With its restoration and reopening in 1991, Raffles Hotel today stands as a jewel in the crown of Singapore's hospitality industry, renowned and loved for its inimitable style and unsurpassed excellence in service—a feature that continues to be a part of its successful differentiation and positioning. This, in turn, has led the hotel to be recognized as one of the best hotels in the world, with a list of awards, which includes "Best Luxury Hotel," at the Twentieth Annual TTG Travel Awards and named in the "T+L 500 World's Best Hotels" by Travel + Leisure, both in 2009.

In multicultural Singapore, it is not surprising that the visionary founders of Raffles Hotel were a quartet of enterprising Armenian brothers: Martin, Tigran, Aviet, and Arshak Sarkies.

The hospitality industry provides a wide range of hotel accommodations. These range from very affordable and no-frills backpacker hostels and modest motels, to hotels catering to business travelers, and luxury hotels meeting the needs and wants of the very wealthy. These motels and hotels cater to

▲Targeting consumer life styles: By marketing itself on a premise of old-fashioned luxury and grandeur, the Raffles Hotel in Singapore has attracted high profile clientele such as George Bush and Elizabeth Taylor.

different segments based on their demographics, of which the variable "income" is primary and the focus.

The all-suite Raffles Hotel, which offers 103 tastefully appointed suites complete with Persian and Oriental rugs and silver cutlery, clearly targets the very well-heeled traveler.

It has been reported that at least three-quarters of the residents are leisure guests who are happy to spend their own money to experience a piece of Singapore history. The room rate starts at $550 per night and is amongst the highest in the city.

The two largest suites are known as the Presidential Suites. One is called the Sarkies Suite and the other, the Sir Stamford Raffles Suite. Priced at $5,200 per suite per night, they are distinguished by their premier location in the hotel, their spaciousness and elegant appointments, and the quality of the antiques and artwork displayed. They boast the original 14-foot ceilings and common verandah, and each suite has a parlor, a dining room, two bedrooms, pantry, private balcony, and ever-attentive butlers!

Among hospitality businesses, quality means superior service. It is this very distinctive style of superior service that continually attempts to exceed the expectations of residents at Raffles Hotel, which has served to set it apart from its competitors successfully.

More for More. "More-for-more" positioning involves providing the most upscale product or service and charging a higher price to cover the higher costs. Four Seasons hotels, Mont Blanc writing instruments, Mercedes automobiles, Viking appliances—each claims superior quality, craftsmanship, durability, performance, or style and charges a price to match. Not only is the market offering high in quality, it also gives prestige to the buyer. It symbolizes status and a loftier lifestyle. Often, the price difference exceeds the actual increment in quality.

Sellers offering "only the best" can be found in every product and service category, from hotels, restaurants, food, and fashion to cars and household appliances. Consumers are sometimes surprised, even delighted, when a new competitor enters a category with an unusually high-priced brand. Starbucks coffee entered as a very expensive

The hotel's understanding of the overriding importance of service encounters is its guiding principle. The world-famous Raffles approach to service is referred to as *Rafflessence:*

Rafflessence comprises a collection of the best of the hospitality industry's practices that translate into ultimate quality and comfort for discerning travelers. At the heart of the Rafflessence is not merely a commitment to meet guest and patron expectations, but to exceed them regularly, and by doing so, continually expand and strengthen the Raffles brand.

Since 2007, the 122-year-old hotel has gone on a concerted drive to get its employees to multitask in a bid to raise productivity, efficiency, and better their already much-talked about excellent service.

The butlers in the hotel are multiskilled to work in other departments, such as housekeeping and front desk, while culinary staff are cross-trained to pick up skills needed for different cuisines. Raffles Hotel staff are trained to multitask so that they can effectively attend to the needs and expectations of its discerning residents and patrons, thus leading to enhanced guest satisfaction.

The hotel even goes as far as to ensure its suites feel like home to its residents. Within the hotel suites, they deliberately do not place the hotel's logo on any items. This gives residents the sense that they are not in a commercial accommodation, but in their own home.

With the decidedly strong differentiation on an unparalleled service culture, Raffles Hotel has consistently used its tagline "The Grand Old Dame of the East," giving it a human personality of an elegant, sophisticated, and upper social class lady of impeccable breeding, in all its marketing communications campaigns.

It is a powerful and inimitable tagline because few, if any, other existing hotels in Asia, can pride itself as being more than 100 years old, and still in operation. Such is an example of an excellent positioning strategy as it will be difficult, if not impossible, for another hotel to use a similar stance.

It is a "more for more" positioning, and supports the concept that a difference is worth establishing to the extent that it satisfies the following criteria in the earlier part of this chapter:

- **Important:** The difference delivers a highly valued benefit to target buyers who in this case are discerning and wealthy Raffles Hotel residents who are used to and expect the best service.
- **Distinctive:** Competitors do not offer the difference, or the company can offer it in a more distinctive way. This is

exactly what the competitors of Raffles Hotel cannot offer because it is one of the oldest and still operating hotels in Asia, and offers a service that is unparalleled.

- **Superior:** The difference is superior to other ways that customers might obtain the same benefit. While other hotels have room service staff, Raffles Hotel prides itself on having butlers who are personally in charge of only a few suites and residents.
- **Communicable:** The difference is communicable and visible to buyers. Raffles Hotel's marketing communications efforts focus on their positioning as "The Grand Old Dame of the East," and this is seen in the creative strategy of their advertising campaigns and the legendary and excellent service experienced when residents stay in the hotel.
- **Preemptive:** Competitors cannot easily copy the difference. Raffles Hotel is a beautiful, white, awe-inspiring 122-year old hotel, which has stood the test of time, seen two World Wars, and remains in the same spot on Beach Road as it did more than a century ago.
- **Affordable:** Buyers can afford to pay for the difference. Even though the room rates at Raffles Hotel are very high, its targeted segment, which is a niche market, possesses very high purchasing power and the appreciation of the finer things in life.
- **Profitable:** The company can introduce the difference profitably. Raffles Hotel has always been differentiated by its "more for more" positioning for a long time. As a result of charging more for services that are "more," the hotel has been profitable because of this value proposition.

With such an astute understanding of effective differentiation and a clear positioning strategy that few competitors, if any, can copy, there is little wonder that the very successful Raffles Hotel has become quite possibly more famous than Singapore itself.

Sources: Quotes and other information from www.raffles.com, W. Lazer, R. A. Layton, *Contemporary Hospitality Marketing,* (Lansing, MI: Educational Institution of the American Hotel & Lodging Association, 1999); Wee Beng Geok (ed.), *Hospitality Industry in Asia—Selected Case Studies,* (Singapore: The Asian Business Case Centre, Nanyang Technological University, 2007); W. Lazer, M. Dallas, and C. Riegel, *Hospitality and Tourism Marketing,* (Lansing, MI: Educational Institution of the American Hotel & Lodging Association, 2006); Chris Lazaris, Eleni Mpismpiki, and Mina Moraiti, "Information Systems Management—Case Studies," 2004, accessed at http://e-learning.dmst .aueb.gr/mis/Cases; "Insight: Service That Blows Like a Gentle Breeze," *The Straits Times* (Singapore), Singapore Press Holdings, October 16, 2009, accessed at www.factiva.com.

brand in a largely commodity category. When Apple premiered its iPhone, it offered higher-quality features than a traditional cell phone with a hefty price tag to match.

In general, companies should be on the lookout for opportunities to introduce a "more-for-more" brand in any underdeveloped product or service category. Yet "more-for-more" brands can be vulnerable. They often invite imitators who claim the same quality but at a lower price. For example, Starbucks now faces "gourmet" coffee competitiors ranging from Dunkin' Donuts to McDonald's. Also, luxury goods that sell well during good times may be at risk during economic downturns when buyers become more cautious in their spending. The recent gloomy economy hit premium brands, such as Starbucks, the hardest.

More for the Same. Companies can attack a competitor's more-for-more positioning by introducing a brand offering comparable quality but at a lower price. For example, Toyota introduced its Lexus line with a "more-for-the-same" value proposition versus Mercedes and BMW. Its first ad headline read: "Perhaps the first time in history that trading a $72,000 car for a $36,000 car could be considered trading up." It communicated the high quality of its new Lexus through rave reviews in car magazines and through a widely distributed videotape showing side-by-side comparisons of Lexus and Mercedes automobiles. It published surveys showing that Lexus dealers were providing customers with better sales and service experiences than were Mercedes dealerships. Many Mercedes owners switched to Lexus, and the Lexus repurchase rate has been 60 percent, twice the industry average.

The Same for Less. Offering "the same for less" can be a powerful value proposition—everyone likes a good deal. Discount stores such as Wal-Mart and "category killers" such as Best Buy, Sportmart David's Bridal, and DSW Shoes use this positioning. They don't claim to offer different or better products. Instead, they offer many of the same brands as department stores and specialty stores but at deep discounts based on superior purchasing power and lower-cost operations. Other companies develop imitative but lower-priced brands in an effort to lure customers away from the market leader. For example, AMD makes less-expensive versions of Intel's market-leading microprocessor chips.

Less for Much Less. A market almost always exists for products that offer less and therefore cost less. Few people need, want, or can afford "the very best" in everything they buy. In many cases, consumers will gladly settle for less than optimal performance or give up some of the bells and whistles in exchange for a lower price. For example, many travelers seeking lodgings prefer not to pay for what they consider unnecessary extras, such as a pool, attached restaurant, or mints on the pillow. Hotel chains such as Ramada Limited suspend some of these amenities and charge less accordingly.

"Less-for-much-less" positioning involves meeting consumers' lower performance or quality requirements at a much lower price. For example, Family Dollar and Dollar General stores offer more affordable goods at very low prices. Sam's Club and Costco warehouse stores offer less merchandise selection and consistency and much lower levels of service; as a result, they charge rock-bottom prices. Southwest Airlines, the nation's most consistently profitable air carrier, also practices less-for-much-less positioning.

▼**Less for much less positioning:** Southwest has positioned itself firmly as the no-frills, low-price airline. But no frills doesn't mean drudgery—Southwest's cheerful employees go out of their way to amuse, surprise, or somehow entertain passengers.

From the start, ▲Southwest has positioned itself firmly as *the* no-frills, low-price airline. Southwest's passengers have learned to fly without the amenities. For example, the airline provides no meals—just pretzels. It offers no first-class section, only three-across seating in all of its planes. And there's no such thing as a reserved seat on a Southwest flight. Why, then, do so many passengers love Southwest? Perhaps most importantly, Southwest excels at the basics of getting passengers where they want to go on time, and with their luggage. Beyond the basics, however, Southwest offers shockingly low prices. In fact, prices are so low that when Southwest enters a market, it actually increases total air traffic by attracting customers who might otherwise travel by car or bus. No frills and low prices, however, don't mean drudgery. Southwest's cheerful employees go out of their way to amuse, surprise, or somehow entertain passengers. One analyst sums up Southwest's less-for-much-less positioning this way: "It is not luxurious, but it's cheap and it's fun."

More for Less. Of course, the winning value proposition would be to offer "more for less." Many companies claim to do this. And, in the short run, some companies can actually achieve such lofty positions. For example, when it first opened for business, Home Depot had arguably the best product selection, the best service, *and* the lowest prices compared to local hardware stores and other home improvement chains.

Yet in the long run, companies will find it very difficult to sustain such best-of-both positioning. Offering more usually costs more, making it difficult to deliver on the "for-less" promise. Companies that try to deliver both may lose out to more focused competitors. For example, facing determined competition from Lowe's stores, Home Depot must now decide whether it wants to compete primarily on superior service or on lower prices.

All said, each brand must adopt a positioning strategy designed to serve the needs and wants of its target markets. "More for more" will draw one target market, "less for much less" will draw another, and so on. Thus, in any market, there is usually room for many different companies, each successfully occupying different positions. The important thing is that each company must develop its own winning positioning strategy, one that makes it special to its target consumers.

Developing a Positioning Statement

Positioning statement
A statement that summarizes company or brand positioning—it takes this form: *To (target segment and need) our (brand) is (concept) that (point-of-difference).*

Company and brand positioning should be summed up in a **positioning statement**. The statement should follow the form: *To (target segment and need) our (brand) is (concept) that (point of difference).*[28] For example: "*To busy, mobile professionals who need to always be in the loop, BlackBerry is a wireless connectivity solution that gives you an easier, more reliable way to stay connected to data, people, and resources while on the go.*"

Note that the positioning first states the product's membership in a category (wireless connectivity solution) and then shows its point of difference from other members of the category (easier, more reliable connections to data, people, and resources). Placing a brand in a specific category suggests similarities that it might share with other products in the category. But the case for the brand's superiority is made on its points of difference.

▼**Points of difference: Sometimes marketers put a brand in a surprisingly different category. Kraft positions its DiGiorno pizza in the delivered pizza category. "No calling. No tipping. No kidding. It's not delivery, its DiGiorno!"**

Sometimes marketers put a brand in a surprisingly different category before indicating the points of difference. ▲DiGiorno is a frozen pizza whose crust rises when the pizza is heated. But instead of putting it in the frozen pizza category, the marketers positioned it in the delivered pizza category. DiGiorno ads show delicious pizzas that look like anything but a frozen pizza, proclaiming "No calling. No tipping. No kidding. It's not delivery, its DiGiorno!" Another ad claims that DiGiorno "Makes mouths water. And delivery guys weep." Such positioning helps highlight DiGiorno's fresh quality and superior taste over the normal frozen pizza.

No Calling.

No Tipping.

No Kidding.

DiGIORNO
RISING CRUST PIZZA

It's not delivery. It's DiGiorno.

SUPREME PIZZA

Communicating and Delivering the Chosen Position

Once it has chosen a position, the company must take strong steps to deliver and communicate the desired position to target consumers. All the company's marketing mix efforts must support the positioning strategy.

Positioning the company calls for concrete action, not just talk. If the company decides to build a position on better quality and service, it must first *deliver* that position. Designing the marketing mix—product, price, place, and promotion—involves working out the tactical details of the positioning strategy. Thus, a firm that seizes on a more-for-more position knows that it must produce high-quality products, charge a high price, distribute through high-quality dealers, and advertise in high-quality media. It must hire and train more service people, find retailers who have a good reputation for service, and develop sales and advertising messages that broadcast its superior service. This is the only way to build a consistent and believable more-for-more position.

Companies often find it easier to come up with a good positioning strategy than to implement it. Establishing a position or changing one usually takes a long time. In contrast, positions that have taken years to build can quickly be lost. Once a company has built the desired position, it must take care to maintain the position through consistent performance and communication. It must closely monitor and adapt the position over time to match changes in consumer needs and competitors' strategies. However, the company should avoid abrupt changes that might confuse consumers. Instead, a product's position should evolve gradually as it adapts to the ever-changing marketing environment.

REST STOP
REVIEWING THE CONCEPTS

In this chapter, you've learned about the major elements of a customer-driven marketing strategy: segmentation, targeting, differentiation, and positioning. Marketers know that they cannot appeal to all buyers in their markets, or at least not to all buyers in the same way. Therefore, most companies today practice *target marketing*—identifying market segments, selecting one or more of them, and developing products and marketing mixes tailored to each.

> **Objective 1** Define the major steps in designing a customer-driven marketing strategy: market segmentation, targeting, differentiation, and positioning. **(pp 202–203)**

Customer-driven marketing strategy begins with selecting which customers to serve and deciding on a value proposition that best serves the targeted customers. It consists of four steps. *Market segmentation* is the act of dividing a market into distinct segments of buyers with different needs, characteristics, or behaviors who might require separate products or marketing mixes. Once the groups have been identified, *market targeting* evaluates each market segment's attractiveness and selects one or more segments to serve. Market targeting consists of designing strategies to build the *right relationships* with the *right customers*. *Differentiation* involves actually differentiating the market offering to create superior customer value. *Positioning* consists of positioning the market offering in the minds of target customers.

> **Objective 2** List and discuss the major bases for segmenting consumer and business markets. **(pp 203–213)**

There is no single way to segment a market. Therefore, the marketer tries different variables to see which give the best segmentation opportunities. For consumer marketing, the major segmentation variables are geographic, demographic, psychographic, and behavioral. In *geographic segmentation*, the market is divided into different geographical units such as nations, regions, states, counties, cities, or neighborhoods. In *demographic segmentation*, the market is divided into groups based on demographic variables, including age, gender, family size, family life cycle, income, occupation, education, religion, race, generation, and nationality. In *psychographic segmentation*, the market is divided into different groups based on social class, lifestyle, or personality characteristics. In *behavioral segmentation*, the market is divided into groups based on consumers' knowledge, attitudes, uses, or responses to a product.

Business marketers use many of the same variables to segment their markets. But business markets also can be segmented by business consumer *demographics* (industry, company size), *operating characteristics, purchasing approaches, situational factors*, and *personal characteristics*. The effectiveness of segmentation analysis depends on finding segments that are *measurable, accessible, substantial, differentiable*, and *actionable*.

> **Objective 3** Explain how companies identify attractive market segments and choose a market-targeting strategy. **(pp 214–221)**

To target the best market segments, the company first evaluates each segment's size and growth characteristics, structural attractiveness, and compatibility with company objectives and resources. It then chooses one of four market-targeting strategies—ranging from very broad to very narrow targeting. The seller can ignore segment differences and target broadly using *undifferentiated (or mass) marketing*. This involves mass producing, mass distributing, and mass promoting about the same product in about the same way to all consumers. Or the seller can adopt *differentiated marketing*—developing different market offers for several segments. *Concentrated marketing* (or *niche marketing)* involves focusing on only one or a few market segments. Finally, *micromarketing* is the practice of tailoring products and marketing programs to suit the tastes of specific individuals and locations. Micromarketing includes *local marketing* and *individual marketing*. Which targeting strategy is best depends on company resources, product variability, product life-cycle stage, market variability, and competitive marketing strategies.

Objective 4 Discuss how companies differentiate and position their products for maximum competitive advantage. **(pp 221–230)**

Once a company has decided which segments to enter, it must decide on its *differentiation and positioning strategy*. The differentiation and positioning task consists of three steps: identifying a set of possible differentiations that create competitive advantage, choosing advantages upon which to build a position, and selecting an overall positioning strategy.

The brand's full positioning is called its *value proposition*—the full mix of benefits upon which the brand is positioned. In general, companies can choose from one of five winning value propositions upon which to position their products: more for more, more for the same, the same for less, less for much less, or more for less. Company and brand positioning are summarized in positioning statements that state the target segment and need, positioning concept, and specific points of difference. The company must then effectively communicate and deliver the chosen position to the market.

 ## Navigating the Key Terms

Objective 1
Market segmentation (p 203)
Market targeting (targeting) (p 203)
Differentiation (p 203)
Positioning (p 203)

Objective 2
Geographic segmentation (p 203)
Demographic segmentation (p 205)
Age and life-cycle segmentation
 (p 205)
Gender segmentation (p 205)
Income segmentation (p 206)

Psychographic segmentation
 (p 207)
Behavioral segmentation (p 207)
Occasion segmentation (p 207)
Benefit segmentation (p 208)
Intermarket segmentation (p 212)

Objective 3
Target market (p 214)
Undifferentiated (mass) marketing
 (p 214)
Differentiated (segmented)
 marketing (p 215)

Concentrated (niche) marketing
 (p 216)
Micromarketing (p 217)
Local marketing (p 217)
Individual marketing (p 218)

Objective 4
Product position (p 221)
Competitive advantage (p 223)
Value proposition (p 225)
Positioning statement (p 229)

Travel Log

Discussing the Issues

1. List and briefly describe the four major steps in designing a customer-driven marketing strategy. (AACSB: Communication)

2. Discuss the behavioral variables used to segment buyers and provide an example of each. (AACSB: Communication; Reflective Thinking)

3. Explain how companies segment international markets. (AACSB: Communication)

4. Name and describe the characteristics of useful market segments. (AACSB: Communication)

5. Compare and contrast local marketing and individual marketing. (AACSB: Communication; Reflective Thinking)

6. In the context of marketing, what is a product's "position"? How do marketers know what it is? (AACSB: Communication)

Application Questions

1. The chapter describes psychographic segmentation used by marketers to segment consumer markets. SRI Consulting has developed a typology of consumers based on values and lifestyles, and you completed the survey if you did application question 3 in Chapter 4. If you did not do that application or need to repeat the survey, go to SRI's Web site to complete the survey (www.sric-bi.com). How accurately do your primary and secondary VALS types describe you? How can marketers use this information? Write a brief report of your findings. (AACSB: Communication; Use of IT; Reflective Thinking)

2. Assume you work at a regional state university whose traditional target market—high school students within your region—is shrinking. Projections are that this target segment will decrease approximately 5 percent per year over the next ten years. Recommend other potential target market segments. (AACSB: Communication; Reflective Thinking)

3. Form a small group and create an idea for a new business. Using the steps described in the chapter, develop a customer-driven marketing strategy. Describe your strategy and conclude with a positioning statement for this business. (AACSB: Communication; Reflective Thinking)

Under the Hood: Marketing Technology

When you think of hybrid or electric automobiles, you probably think don't think "sports car." But the Fisker Karma is about to shatter that stereotype. It's been called the hybrid with "sex appeal" and is often compared to a Mercedes-Benz roadster. During the haughty Rolex Monterey Historic Automobile Races, it was seen cruising around Monterey, California, with the likes of Ferraris and Lamborghinis. In the increasingly crowded field of new-generation electric vehicles, Fisker Automotive wants to carve out a niche as a high-performance eco-car with lots of style. The creator, Henrik Fisker, was formerly head of design at Aston Martin. The Fisker Karma goes from 0 to 60 in six seconds, can go 125 miles per hour, and can travel 50 miles on electric power and 300 miles on combined electric and gasoline power. All this performance and style does not come cheaply, however. Prices range from $87,900 to $106,000. The company already has orders from 1,400 buyers. If this is above your means, don't worry—the company is promising a lower-priced, mass-market version for the rest of us in a few years.

1. On what basis is Fisker Automotive segmenting the automobile market? Is the company using a single segmentation approach or a combined approach? Explain. (AACSB: Communication; Reflective Thinking)

2. What market targeting strategy is Fisker pursuing with this automobile? How is the company differentiating its automobile and which value proposition is it using? (AACSB: Communication; Reflective Thinking)

Staying on the Road: Marketing Ethics

In 2009 Anheuser-Busch (A-B) launched the Bud Light "Fan Can," a promotion that included 27 different color combinations of its cans in college team colors. For example, students at Louisiana State University could purchase purple-and-gold cans of Bud Light. Anheuser-Busch timed the campaign, called "Team Pride," to coincide with students returning to campus and with the kickoff of the football season. Several schools, such as Wisconsin, Michigan, Iowa State, University of Colorado, and others, objected strenuously. As a result, A-B halted the program in those markets. The promotion also caught the attention of the Federal Trade Commission (FTC). Both the FTC and college officials are concerned about the high rate of underage and binge drinking on college campuses. Some school officials also were concerned about trademark infringe-ments, and about the appearance that they support Budweiser's activities. As criticism brewed around the country, A-B released a statement claiming that it did not mean to encourage underage drinking—it just wanted to create more fun for sports fans. Although the company halted the promotion in areas where college officials objected, controversy surrounding the promotion appeared in newspapers and on television nationwide.

1. What type of market targeting strategy is Anheuser-Busch using with the Team Pride promotion? (AACSB: Communication; Reflective Thinking)

2. Was this a wise promotion? Explain. (AACSB: Communication; Reflective Thinking; Ethical Reasoning)

Rough Road Ahead: Marketing and the Economy

Vanilla Bikes

Portland-based Vanilla Bicycles sells hand-built bikes with price tags ranging from $4,000 to $12,000. Now, after only nine years in business, owner Sacha White has stopped taking orders—not because business had dried up but because he has a five-year waiting list. White and his crew of three make only 40 to 50 bikes a year. Frames are made from exotic metals, are welded with silver alloy, and weigh as little as 30 ounces. No two Vanilla bikes are the same. Each is custom fitted to the client and features intricate metal carvings and an artisan paint job. Amazingly, almost all of these high-end velocipedes are sold to middle-class customers. Still, orders have not ebbed with the economic downturn. In fact, Vanilla could ramp up production significantly and still sell everything it makes. However, White claims that would compromise the special nature of what customers consider to be works of art. Vanilla bikes are so special that when Portland bike couriers describe something as cool, they routinely say, "That's soooo Vanilla."

1. Based on the segmentation variables discussed in the chapter, construct a profile for Vanilla Bicycle's probable target market.

2. Given that most luxury products suffer in an economic downturn, why has Vanilla still succeeded?

Travel Budget: Marketing by the Numbers

Refer to the information on the Fisker Karma automobile in "Under the Hood: Marketing Technology." The company so far has raised $100 million of capital. But it needs more funding to develop the lower-priced model, so it is vying for a piece of the $25 billion available through the U.S. government's Advanced Technology Vehicles Manufacturing program. If it doesn't receive these funds, Fisker says it will take several more years before it can offer the lower-priced model. The company can use profits from the higher-priced Karma toward this end, but it needs to estimate the market potential for this product before bringing it to market.

1. Discuss variables Fisker Automotive should consider when estimating the potential number of buyers for the high-performance Fisker Karma sports car. (AACSB: Communication; Reflective Thinking)

2. Using the chain ratio method described in Appendix 2, Marketing by the Numbers, estimate the market potential for the Fisker Karma sports car. Search the Internet for reasonable numbers to represent the factors you identified in the previous question. Assume each buyer will only purchase one automobile and that the average price of automobiles in this market is $100,000. (AACSB: Communication; Use of IT; Analytical Reasoning)

Drive In: Video Case

Meredith

The Meredith Corporation has developed an expertise in building customer relationships through segmentation, targeting, and positioning. Amazingly, however, it has done this by focusing on only half of the population—the female half. Meredith has developed the largest database of any U.S. media company and uses that database to meet the specific needs and desires of women.

Meredith is known for leading titles such as *Better Homes and Gardens, Family Circle,* and *Ladies' Home Journal.* But that list has grown to a portfolio of 14 magazines and more than 200 special interest publications. Through these magazines alone, Meredith regularly reaches about 30 million readers. By focusing on core categories of home, family, and personal development, Meredith has developed a prod-uct mix designed to meet various needs of women. This creates multiple touch points as individual women engage with more than one magazine, as well as with specialty books and Web sites.

After viewing the video featuring Meredith, answer the following questions about segmenting, targeting, and positioning:

1. On what main variables has Meredith focused in segmenting its markets?

2. Which target marketing strategy best describes Meredith's efforts? Support your choice.

3. How does Meredith use its variety of products to build relationships with the right customers?

7

Products, Services,
and Brands Building Customer Value

ROAD MAP

Previewing the Concepts

Now that you've had a good look at customer-driven marketing strategy, we'll take a deeper look at the marketing mix—the tactical tools that marketers use to implement their strategies and deliver superior customer value. In this and the next chapter, we'll study how companies develop and manage products and brands. Then, in the chapters that follow, we'll look at pricing, distribution, and marketing communication tools. The product is usually the first and most basic marketing consideration. We'll start with a seemingly simple question: What *is* a product? As it turns out, however, the answer is not so simple.

Objective Outline

> **Objective 1**   Define *product* and the major classifications of products and services.
> What Is a Product? **pp 236–241**

> **Objective 2**   Describe the decisions companies regarding their individual products and services, product lines, and product mixes.
> Product and Service Decisions **pp 242–249**

> **Objective 3**   Identify the four characteristics that affect the marketing of services and the additional marketing considerations that services require.
> Services Marketing **pp 249–255**

> **Objective 4**   Discuss branding strategy—the decisions companies make in building and managing their brands.
> Branding Strategy: Building Strong Brands
> **pp 256–265**

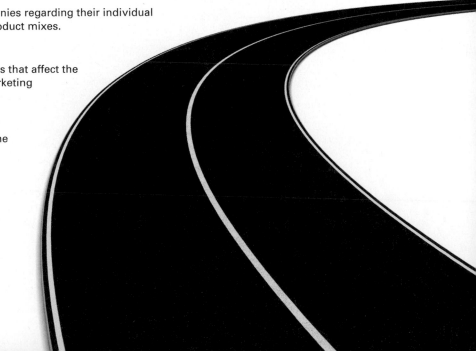

▲ By 2010, Aviva aims to complete the transition set out in its "One Aviva, Twice the Value" vision and become a global brand. This would bring together several of the company's autonomous business units.

Before starting into the chapter, let's look at an interesting brand story. Marketing is all about building brands that connect deeply with customers. So, when you think about top brands, which ones pop up first? Maybe it's megabrands such as Coca-Cola, Nike, or McDonald's. Here's a tale about one strong brand you may not have considered.

First Stop

Aviva: One Name, One Brand

Aviva is an international investment, savings, and insurance group. It was formed in 2000 with the merger of Norwich Union and CGU Insurance. Initially, the group operated under 40 trading brands around the world until the Aviva brand was adopted in 2002.

In terms of gross worldwide premiums for the year ending December 31, 2007, Aviva is the fifth largest insurance group in the world. It focuses on life and pension products, fund management, general insurance, and long-term savings. At the end of 2007, the funds under its management totalled a massive $718 billion, and its total worldwide sales were nearly $98.4 billion.

In April 2008, Aviva announced the final phase of its move towards creating a worldwide brand. The intention was to create the brand in order to ensure continued growth and transform the business so that it could compete more effectively across the world. The group announced that the customer brand for the Aviva Group worldwide would now be Aviva. The group also announced that its Norwich Union, Commercial Union Poland, and Hibernian brands would all be known as Aviva. This was an integral part of "One Aviva, twice the value," Chief Executive Andrew Moss's vision for the transformation of the business. Between 2008 and 2010, it is the group's intention to complete the transition to a global brand, thereby bringing together several autonomous business units.

The company's international savings, investments, and insurance group was already trading as Aviva in over 20 markets across Europe, North America and the Asia Pacific region. Some 40 percent of this group's business is based in Britain, but recent acquisitions will make this market less significant in terms of the company's overall business value. Group Chief Executive Andrew Moss said: "This is an exciting time for us as we build a world-class business with strong growth potential. For Aviva to continue to thrive, we have to compete effectively on the world stage alongside our international peers. Creating a brand that is known across the globe is an important step in being recognized as a worldwide force in financial services and an important milestone in delivering our "One Aviva, twice the value" vision. In today's world, people are becoming more mobile and are targeted by international brands competing for their business across borders through the global media. For our customers, the Aviva name will be recognizable and will represent the same quality, financial strength, and security wherever they do business with us. By integrating our operations more closely, we can take best in breed products and services from around the world and bring innovation to new and existing customers. By investing in a single name, we will amplify the global impact of our advertising and sponsorship spending. Being a well-known international brand also opens doors when [we are] entering new markets and establishing partnerships with other global players, as we already do in bancassurance [the selling of insurance products through banks]."

Moss went on to explain the importance of the brand name: "For our 57,000 staff, it's about bringing them together as one team under a common identity, and enabling us to attract and

Aviva is in the final phases of creating a worldwide brand. The company's executives believe that the creation of a global brand will ensure Aviva's continued growth and transform the business so that it can compete more effectively around the world.

▲ Aviva is the fifth largest insurance group in the world and the largest in Britain.

retain the best. As we've seen in our newer businesses in Asia Pacific and the U.S., people want to work for global companies that stand out on the world stage. I firmly believe that growing and thriving businesses generate the best career opportunities for their people over the long term. For our shareholders, a clear focus on delivering our "One Aviva, twice the value" vision will drive further dividend growth and value. Today Aviva can look to the future with confidence, largely because of its strong heritage with its roots in Norwich Union, Commercial Union, and General Accident. These great companies succeeded because they took decisive action to develop their businesses and helped their customers to thrive and prosper. We will continue to build our global business upon this strong foundation. We will manage this process with care over the next two years, involving all our stakeholders to ensure a smooth transition and that we maximize the opportunities this change will bring."

Aviva maintained that the cost of rebranding would be balanced by the increased effectiveness of its marketing spending. In effect, it would be promoting just one brand instead of several brands.

The move, however, would mean the end of a brand name that had been created in 1797 when the original business was set up in Norwich, Norfolk. Norwich Union has some 28,000 employees in Britain.

Mindful of the challenges surrounding such a rebrand, Aviva has recognized that it is key to manage the migration in a manner that retains all the positive heritage and values associated with the brand, and commit to putting customers at the heart of the process. Aviva's decision is not without risk. Many businesses have tried rebranding and failed miserably. For example, PricewaterhouseCoopers' accountancy business was originally supposed to be renamed Monday, but it was ridiculed by the industry. Mitsubishi launched a new range of cars with the brand name Pajero. However, in Spanish, Pajero has another unfortunate meaning. Similarly, when British Airways decided to drop the Union flag from its tailfins, it attracted the anger of then-British Prime Minister Margaret Thatcher, and the decision was reversed.

Back in 1985, Coca-Cola made perhaps the worse rebranding decision of all time. After realizing that Diet Coke did not taste anything like regular Coke, the company changed its recipe of regular Coke to match it.

Consumers hated the product, and the sales of it plummeted. Coca-Cola was then forced into a humiliating reversal and rebranded the old Coke recipe, *Classic Coke*.

Peter Walshe, the global brands director of the consulting group Millward Brown, warned that Aviva might not necessarily be making the right decision. Whilst he recognized that there were opportunities and potential in creating one brand, it would require Aviva to establish that brand name and make it mean something. In the initial stages the brand name Aviva would mean nothing and would be unknown to the consumer. If Aviva was not careful then Walshe believed it ran the risk of losing the trust, heritage and prestige that it had worked so hard to achieve.[1]

*a*s the Aviva example shows, in their quest to create customer relationships, marketers must build and manage products and brands that connect with customers. This chapter begins with a deceptively simple question: *What is a product?* After addressing this question, we look at ways to classify products in consumer and business markets. Then we discuss the important decisions that marketers make regarding individual products, product lines, and product mixes. Next, we examine the characteristics and marketing requirements of a special form of product—services. Finally, we look into the critically important issue of how marketers build and manage brands.

Author Comment >>
As you'll see, this is a deceptively simple question with a very complex answer. For example, think back to our opening Aviva story. What is the Aviva "product"?

WHAT IS A PRODUCT? (pp 236–241)

We define a **product** as anything that can be offered to a market for attention, acquisition, use, or consumption that might satisfy a want or need. Products include more than just tangible objects, such as cars, computers, or cell phones. Broadly defined, "products" also include services, events, persons, places, organizations, ideas,

Product
Anything that can be offered to a market for attention, acquisition, use, or consumption that might satisfy a want or need.

Service
An activity, benefit, or satisfaction offered for sale that is essentially intangible and does not result in the ownership of anything.

or mixes of these. Throughout this text, we use the term *product* broadly to include any or all of these entities. Thus, an Apple iPhone, a Toyota Camry, and a Caffé Mocha at Starbucks are products. But so are a trip to Las Vegas, Fidelity online investment services, and advice from your family doctor.

Because of their importance in the world economy, we give special attention to services. **Services** are a form of product that consists of activities, benefits, or satisfactions offered for sale that are essentially intangible and do not result in the ownership of anything. Examples are banking, hotel, airline, retail, wireless communication, and home-repair services. We will look at services more closely later in this chapter.

Products, Services, and Experiences

Product is a key element in the overall *market offering.* Marketing-mix planning begins with building an offering that brings value to target customers. This offering becomes the basis upon which the company builds profitable customer relationships.

A company's market offering often includes both tangible goods and services. At one extreme, the offer may consist of a *pure tangible good,* such as soap, toothpaste, or salt—no services accompany the product. At the other extreme are *pure services,* for which the offer consists primarily of a service. Examples include a doctor's exam or financial services. Between these two extremes, however, many goods-and-services combinations are possible.

Today, as products and services become more commoditized, many companies are moving to a new level in creating value for their customers. To differentiate their offers, beyond simply making products and delivering services, they are creating and managing customer *experiences* with their brands or company.

Experiences have always been an important part of marketing for some companies. Disney has long manufactured dreams and memories through its movies and theme parks. And Nike has long declared, "It's not so much the shoes but where they take you." Today, however, all kinds of firms are recasting their traditional goods and services to create experiences. For example, a visit to Umpqua bank involves a lot more than just loans and deposits:[2]

▼Creating experiences: Umpqua Bank's "stores" are designed to make banking a pleasurable experience. "Customers aren't just doing transactions . . . they're paying admission to a club—one that delivers something to satisfy the soul."

Most customers would never describe a bank transaction as soul satisfying, but Oregon-based Umpqua Bank isn't your average bank. Umpqua feels more like a café—think bank crossed with your local Starbucks. ▲Umpqua's "stores" are designed to make banking a pleasurable experience that will cause customers to stick around and maybe buy something. Customers sit at a cozy coffee bar, sip Umpqua-branded coffee, read the morning paper, watch investment news on big-screen TVzs, pay bills online via WiFi access, and don headphones to check out local bands at the bank's online music store. After-hours activities such as movies, knitting, and yoga classes are encouraged just as much as financial events. Turning bank services into a rewarding experience has been good for Umpqua's business. The company has grown from only $140 million in assets in 1994 to more than $8.8 billion. "Customers aren't just . . . doing transactions at Umpqua Bank," says an analyst. "They're paying admission to a club—one that delivers something to satisfy the soul."

Companies that market experiences realize that customers are really buying much more than just products and services. They are buying what those offers will *do* for them. "A brand, product, or service is more than just a physical thing. Humans that connect with the brand add meaning and value to it," says one marketing executive. "Successfully managing the customer experience is the ultimate goal," adds another.[3]

Levels of Product and Services

Product planners need to think about products and services on three levels (see ■ **Figure 7.1**). Each level adds more customer value. The most basic level is the *core customer value,* which addresses the question *What is the buyer really buying?* When

■ **Figure 7.1** Three Levels
of Product

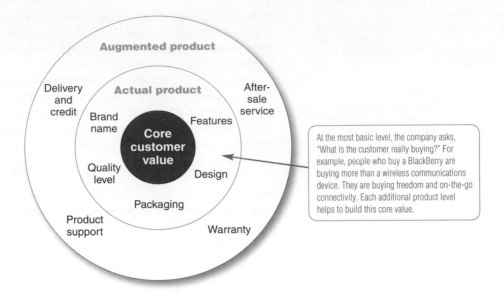

At the most basic level, the company asks, "What is the customer really buying?" For example, people who buy a BlackBerry are buying more than a wireless communications device. They are buying freedom and on-the-go connectivity. Each additional product level helps to build this core value.

▲Core, actual, and augmented product: People who buy a BlackBerry device are buying more than a cell phone, e-mail device, or organizer. They are buying the ability to "Connect to everything you love through the power of the BlackBerry smartphone."

designing products, marketers must first define the core, problem-solving benefits or services that consumers seek. A woman buying lipstick buys more than lip color. Charles Revson of Revlon saw this early: "In the factory, we make cosmetics; in the store, we sell hope." ▲And people who buy a BlackBerry smartphone are buying more than a cell phone, e-mail device, or personal organizer. They are buying freedom and on-the-go connectivity to people and resources.

At the second level, product planners must turn the core benefit into an *actual product*. They need to develop product and service features, design, a quality level, a brand name, and packaging. For example, the BlackBerry is an actual product. Its name, parts, styling, features, packaging, and other attributes have all been combined carefully to deliver the core customer value of staying connected.

Finally, product planners must build an *augmented product* around the core benefit and actual product by offering additional consumer services and benefits. The BlackBerry offers more than just a communications device. It provides consumers with a complete solution to mobile connectivity problems. Thus, when consumers buy a BlackBerry, the company and its dealers also might give buyers a warranty on parts and workmanship, instructions on how to use the device, quick repair services when needed, and a toll-free telephone number and Web site to use if they have problems or questions.

Consumers see products as complex bundles of benefits that satisfy their needs. When developing products, marketers first must identify the *core customer value* that consumers seek from the product. They must then design the *actual* product and find ways to *augment* it in order to create this customer value and the most satisfying customer experience.

Product and Service Classifications

Products and services fall into two broad classes based on the types of consumers that use them—*consumer products* and *industrial products*. Broadly defined, products also include other marketable entities such as experiences, organizations, persons, places, and ideas.

Consumer Products

Consumer product
A product bought by final consumers for personal consumption.

Consumer products are products and services bought by final consumers for personal consumption. Marketers usually classify these products and services further based on how consumers go about buying them. Consumer products include *convenience products, shopping products, specialty products,* and *unsought products.* These products differ in the ways consumers buy them and, therefore, in how they are marketed (see ■ **Table 7.1**).

Convenience product
A consumer product that customers usually buy frequently, immediately, and with a minimum of comparison and buying effort.

Convenience products are consumer products and services that customers usually buy frequently, immediately, and with a minimum of comparison and buying effort. Examples include laundry detergent, candy, magazines, and fast food. Convenience products are usually low priced, and marketers place them in many locations to make them readily available when customers need them.

Shopping product
A consumer product that the customer, in the process of selection and purchase, usually compares on such bases as suitability, quality, price, and style.

Shopping products are less frequently purchased consumer products and services that customers compare carefully on suitability, quality, price, and style. When buying shopping products and services, consumers spend much time and effort in gathering information and making comparisons. Examples include furniture, clothing, used cars, major appliances, and hotel and airline services. Shopping products marketers usually distribute their products through fewer outlets but provide deeper sales support to help customers in their comparison efforts.

Specialty product
A consumer product with unique characteristics or brand identification for which a significant group of buyers is willing to make a special purchase effort.

Specialty products are consumer products and services with unique characteristics or brand identification for which a significant group of buyers is willing to make a special purchase effort. Examples include specific brands of cars, high-priced photographic equipment, designer clothes, and the services of medical or legal specialists. A Lamborghini automobile, for example, is a specialty product because buyers are usually willing to travel great distances to buy one. Buyers normally do not compare specialty products. They invest only the time needed to reach dealers carrying the wanted products.

Unsought product
A consumer product that the consumer either does not know about or knows about but does not normally think of buying.

Unsought products are consumer products that the consumer either does not know about or knows about but does not normally think of buying. Most major new innovations are unsought until the consumer becomes aware of them through advertising. Classic examples of known but unsought products and services are life insurance, preplanned funeral services, and blood donations to the Red Cross. By their very nature, unsought products require a lot of advertising, personal selling, and other marketing efforts.

■ **Table 7.1** Marketing Considerations for Consumer Products

Marketing Considerations	Type of Consumer Product			
	Convenience	**Shopping**	**Specialty**	**Unsought**
Customer buying behavior	Frequent purchase, little planning, little comparison or shopping effort, low customer involvement	Less frequent purchase, much planning and shopping effort, comparison of brands on price, quality, style	Strong brand preference and loyalty, special purchase effort, little comparison of brands, low price sensitivity	Little product awareness, knowledge (or, if aware, little or even negative interest)
Price	Low price	Higher price	High price	Varies
Distribution	Widespread distribution, convenient locations	Selective distribution in fewer outlets	Exclusive distribution in only one or a few outlets per market area	Varies
Promotion	Mass promotion by the producer	Advertising and personal selling by both producer and resellers	More carefully targeted promotion by both producer and resellers	Aggressive advertising and personal selling by producer and resellers
Examples	Toothpaste, magazines, laundry detergent	Major appliances, televisions, furniture, clothing	Luxury goods, such as Rolex watches or fine crystal	Life insurance, Red Cross blood donations

Industrial Products

Industrial products are those purchased for further processing or for use in conducting a business. Thus, the distinction between a consumer product and an industrial product is based on the *purpose* for which the product is bought. If a consumer buys a lawn mower for use around home, the lawn mower is a consumer product. If the same consumer buys the same lawn mower for use in a landscaping business, the lawn mower is an industrial product.

The three groups of industrial products and services include materials and parts, capital items, and supplies and services. *Materials and parts* include raw materials and manufactured materials and parts. Raw materials consist of farm products (wheat, cotton, livestock, fruits, vegetables) and natural products (fish, lumber, crude petroleum, iron ore). Manufactured materials and parts consist of component materials (iron, yarn, cement, wires) and component parts (small motors, tires, castings). Most manufactured materials and parts are sold directly to industrial users. Price and service are the major marketing factors; branding and advertising tend to be less important.

Capital items are industrial products that aid in the buyer's production or operations, including installations and accessory equipment. Installations consist of major purchases such as buildings (factories, offices) and fixed equipment (generators, drill presses, large computer systems, elevators). Accessory equipment includes portable factory equipment and tools (hand tools, lift trucks) and office equipment (computers, fax machines, desks). They have a shorter life than installations and simply aid in the production process.

The final group of industrial products is *supplies and services*. Supplies include operating supplies (lubricants, coal, paper, pencils) and repair and maintenance items (paint, nails, brooms). Supplies are the convenience products of the industrial field because they are usually purchased with a minimum of effort or comparison. Business services include maintenance and repair services (window cleaning, computer repair) and business advisory services (legal, management consulting, advertising). Such services are usually supplied under contract.

▼ Organizational marketing: Cargill markets itself as a company that works closely with business customers—here, fast-food restaurants—to help bring the world better products. "This is how we work with customers: "collaborate > create > succeed."

WE MERELY HAD TO IMPROVE A FOOD THE WHOLE COUNTRY GREW UP LOVING. NO PRESSURE.

Next to the revered hamburger, nothing is more classic to fast food than the french fry. So when a major restaurant chain wanted to create french fries with zero grams trans fat per serving, they knew they couldn't change the taste consumers loved. They called on Cargill, who worked with them to develop a special frying oil. Extensive canola seed research, new processing technologies and an identity preserved supply chain resulted in a cooking oil that performed well for fries, chicken and fish. Consumer tests proved our approach was successful in providing the same great taste. Now our customer serves fries consumers can feel good about, while still enjoying that classic flavor. This is how Cargill works with customers.

collaborate > create > succeed™

www.cargill.com/creates
©2010 Cargill, Incorporated

food, agriculture & risk management solutions

Cargill

Organizations, Persons, Places, and Ideas

In addition to tangible products and services, marketers have broadened the concept of a product to include other market offerings—organizations, persons, places, and ideas.

Organizations often carry out activities to "sell" the organization itself. *Organization marketing* consists of activities undertaken to create, maintain, or change the attitudes and behavior of target consumers toward an organization. Both profit and not-for-profit organizations practice organization marketing. Business firms sponsor public relations or *corporate image advertising* campaigns to market themselves and polish their images. For example, food, agriculture, and industrial products giant Cargill markets itself to the public as a company that works closely with its business customers—from farmers and fisherman to fast-food restaurants and furniture manufacturers—to help bring the world everything from heart-healthy milk and trans fat-free french fries to furniture and bedding foam created from renewable resources. ▲It says in its ads, "This is how Cargill works with customers: "collaborate > create > succeed." Similarly, not-for-profit organizations, such as churches, colleges, charities, museums, and performing arts groups, market their organizations in order to raise funds and attract members or patrons.

People can also be thought of as products. *Person marketing* consists of activities undertaken to create, maintain, or change attitudes or behavior toward particular people. People ranging from presidents, entertainers, and sports figures to professionals such as doctors, lawyers, and architects use person marketing to build their reputations. And businesses, charities, and other organizations use well-known personalities to help sell their products or causes. For example, more than a dozen big-name companies—including Nike, Accenture, EA Sports, American Express, Gillette, Gatorade, and Apple—combine to pay more than $90 million a year to link themselves with golf superstar Tiger Woods.[4]

The skillful use of marketing can turn a person's name into a powerhouse brand. Carefully managed and well-known names such as Oprah Winfrey, Martha Stewart, and businessman Donald Trump now adorn everything from sports apparel, housewares, and magazines to book clubs and casinos. Trump, who describes himself as "the hottest brand on the planet," has skillfully made his life a nonstop media event. Says a friend, "He's a skillful marketer, and what he markets is his name."[5]

Such well-known, well-marketed names hold substantial branding power. Consider Rachael Ray:

> Rachael Ray has become a one-woman marketing phenomenon: In less than a decade, she's zipped from nobody to pop-culture icon. Beginning with her 30-Minute Meals cookbooks, followed later by a Food Network TV show, Ray won her way into the hearts of America by demystifying cooking and dishing out a ton of energy. Thanks to her perky personality, Rachael Ray has moved far beyond quick meals. Bearing her name are more than a dozen best-selling cookbooks (the latest is *Yum-o! The Family Cookbook*), a monthly lifestyle magazine, three Food Network shows, a syndicated daytime talk show, a line of pet foods, and assorted licensing deals that have stamped her name on kitchen essentials from knives to her own "E.V.O.O." (extra virgin olive oil for those not familiar with Rayisms). Ultimately, Ray's brand power derives from all that she has come to represent. Her brands "begin with food and move briskly on to the emotional, social, and cultural benefits that food gives us."[6]

Place marketing involves activities undertaken to create, maintain, or change attitudes or behavior toward particular places. Cities, states, regions, and even entire nations compete to attract tourists, new residents, conventions, and company offices and factories. Texas advertises that "It's like a whole other country" and California urges you to "Find yourself here." The Chinese National Tourist Office (CNTO) invites travelers from around the world to "Discover China now!" The CNTO has 15 overseas tourist offices, including 2 in the United States. Tourism in China has been booming as more and more travelers discover the treasures of China's ancient civilization alongside the towering skylines of modern cities such as Shanghai and Beijing (site of the 2008 Summer Olympics). At its Web site, the CNTO offers information about the country and its attractions, travel tips, lists of tour operators, and much more information that makes it easier to say "yes" to China travel.[7]

Ideas can also be marketed. In one sense, all marketing is the marketing of an idea, whether it is the general idea of brushing your teeth or the specific idea that Crest toothpastes create "healthy, beautiful smiles for life." Here, however, we narrow our focus to the marketing of *social ideas*. This area has been called **social marketing**, defined by the Social Marketing Institute (SMI) as the use of commercial marketing concepts and tools in programs designed to bring about social change.[8]

Social marketing programs include public health campaigns to reduce smoking, drug abuse, and obesity. Other social marketing efforts include environmental campaigns to promote wilderness protection, clean air, and conservation. Still others address issues such as family planning, human rights, and racial equality. The Ad Council of America (*www.adcouncil.org*) has developed dozens of social advertising campaigns, involving issues ranging from preventive health, education, and personal safety to environmental preservation.

But social marketing involves much more than just advertising—the SMI encourages the use of a broad range of marketing tools. "Social marketing goes well beyond the promotional '*P*' of the marketing mix to include every other element to achieve its social change objectives," says the SMI's executive director.[9]

Social marketing
The use of commercial marketing concepts and tools in programs designed to influence individuals' behavior to improve their well-being and that of society.

Author Comment »
Now that we've answered the "What is a product?" question, let's dig into the specific decisions that companies must make when designing and marketing products and services.

PRODUCT AND SERVICE DECISIONS (pp 242–249)

Marketers make product and service decisions at three levels: individual product decisions, product line decisions, and product mix decisions. We discuss each in turn.

Individual Product and Service Decisions

■ **Figure 7.2** shows the important decisions in the development and marketing of individual products and services. We will focus on decisions about *product attributes*, *branding*, *packaging*, *labeling*, and *product support services*.

Product and Service Attributes
Developing a product or service involves defining the benefits that it will offer. These benefits are communicated and delivered by product attributes such as *quality*, *features*, and *style and design*.

Product quality
The characteristics of a product or service that bear on its ability to satisfy stated or implied customer needs.

Product Quality. **Product quality** is one of the marketer's major positioning tools. Quality has a direct impact on product or service performance; thus, it is closely linked to customer value and satisfaction. In the narrowest sense, quality can be defined as "freedom from defects." But most customer-centered companies go beyond this narrow definition. Instead, they define quality in terms of creating customer value and satisfaction. The American Society for Quality defines quality as the characteristics of a product or service that bear on its ability to satisfy stated or implied customer needs. Similarly, Siemens defines quality this way: "Quality is when our customers come back and our products don't."[10]

Total quality management (TQM) is an approach in which all the company's people are involved in constantly improving the quality of products, services, and business processes. For most top companies, customer-driven quality has become a way of doing business. Today, companies are taking a "return on quality" approach, viewing quality as an investment and holding quality efforts accountable for bottom-line results.

Product quality has two dimensions—level and consistency. In developing a product, the marketer must first choose a *quality level* that will support the product's positioning. Here, product quality means *performance quality*—the ability of a product to perform its functions. For example, a Rolls-Royce provides higher performance quality than a Chevrolet: It has a smoother ride, provides more "creature comforts," and lasts longer. Companies rarely try to offer the highest possible performance quality level—few customers want or can afford the high levels of quality offered in products such as a Rolls-Royce automobile, a Viking range, or a Rolex watch. Instead, companies choose a quality level that matches target market needs and the quality levels of competing products.

Beyond quality level, high quality also can mean high levels of quality consistency. Here, product quality means *conformance quality*—freedom from defects and *consistency* in delivering a targeted level of performance. All companies should strive for high levels of conformance quality. In this sense, a Chevrolet can have just as much quality as a Rolls-Royce. Although a Chevy doesn't perform at the same level as a Rolls-Royce, it can deliver as consistently the quality that customers pay for and expect.

Product Features. A product can be offered with varying features. A stripped-down model, one without any extras, is the starting point. The company can create higher-

Don't forget Figure 7.1! The focus of all of these decisions is to create core customer value.

■ **Figure 7.2** Individual Product Decisions

level models by adding more features. Features are a competitive tool for differentiating the company's product from competitors' products. Being the first producer to introduce a valued new feature is one of the most effective ways to compete.

How can a company identify new features and decide which ones to add to its product? The company should periodically survey buyers who have used the product and ask these questions: How do you like the product? Which specific features of the product do you like most? Which features could we add to improve the product? The answers provide the company with a rich list of feature ideas. The company can then assess each feature's *value* to customers versus its *cost* to the company. Features that customers value highly in relation to costs should be added.

Product Style and Design. Another way to add customer value is through distinctive *product style and design*. Design is a larger concept than style. *Style* simply describes the appearance of a product. Styles can be eye-catching or yawn producing. A sensational style may grab attention and produce pleasing aesthetics, but it does not necessarily make the product *perform* better. Unlike style, *design* is more than skin deep—it goes to the very heart of a product. Good design contributes to a product's usefulness as well as to its looks.

▼Product design: OXO focuses on the desired end-user experience, and then translates its pie-cutter-in-the-sky notions into eminently usable gadgets.

Good design doesn't start with brainstorming new ideas and making prototypes. Design begins with observing customers and developing a deep understanding of their needs. More than simply creating product or service attributes, it involves shaping the customer's product-use experience. Product designers should think less about product attributes and technical specifications and more about how customers will use and benefit from the product. ▲Consider OXO's outstanding design philosophy and process:[11]

We've remodeled the most important parts of your kitchen.

We've remodeled the peeler. We've remodeled the garlic press, the can opener and the wooden spoon. And we didn't stop there. Any kitchen tools that weren't comfortable or easy to use were fair game. The idea isn't to make the old tools obsolete, it's to make them better. If we can't make them better, we don't make them at all. Pick up OXO Good Grips® and you'll feel what we mean. They're easy to hold, easy to use and easy to love. In fact, they might just change the way you feel about your kitchen.

OXO GOOD GRIPS
For information call 1-800-545-4411

OXO's uniquely designed kitchen and gardening gadgets look pretty cool. But to OXO, good design means a lot more than good looks. It means that OXO tools work—*really* work—for anyone and everyone. "Oxo is practically the definition of 'good experience,'" notes one observer. For OXO, design means a salad spinner that can be used with one hand; tools with pressure-absorbing, nonslip handles that make them more efficient; or a watering can with a spout that rotates back toward the body, allowing for easier filling and storing. Ever since it came out with its supereffective Good Grips vegetable peeler in 1990, OXO has been known for clever designs that make everyday living easier.

Much of OXO's design inspiration comes directly from users. "Every product that we make starts with . . . watching how people use things," says OXO president Alex Lee. "Those are the gems—when you pull out a latent problem." For example, after watching people struggle with the traditional Pyrex measuring cup, OXO discovered a critical flaw: You can't tell how full it is without lifting it up to eye level. The resulting OXO measuring cups have markings down the *inside* that can be read from above, big enough to read without glasses. Thus, OXO begins with a desired end-user experience and then translates pie-cutter-in-the-sky notions into eminently usable gadgets.

Branding

Brand
A name, term, sign, symbol, design, or a combination of these that identifies the products or services of one seller or group of sellers and differentiates them from those of competitors.

Perhaps the most distinctive skill of professional marketers is their ability to build and manage brands. A **brand** is a name, term, sign, symbol, or design, or a combination of these, that identifies the maker or seller of a product or service. Consumers view a brand as an important part of a product and branding can add value to a product. Customers attach meanings to brands and develop brand relationships. Brands have meaning well beyond a product's physical attributes. For example, consider Coca-Cola:[12]

In one interesting taste test of Coca-Cola versus Pepsi, 67 subjects were hooked up to brain-wave-monitoring machines while they consumed both products. When the soft drinks were unmarked, consumer preferences were split down the middle. But when the brands were identified, subjects choose Coke over Pepsi by a margin of 75 percent to 25 percent. When drinking the identified Coke brand, the brain areas that lit up most were those associated with cognitive control and memory—a place where culture concepts are stored. That didn't happen as much when drinking Pepsi. Why? According to one brand strategist, it's because of Coca-Cola's long-established brand imagery—the almost 100-year-old contour bottle and cursive font, and its association with iconic images ranging from Mean Joe Greene and the Polar Bears to Santa Claus. Pepsi's imagery isn't quite as deeply rooted. Although people might associate Pepsi with a hot celebrity or the "Pepsi generation" appeal, they probably don't link it to the strong and emotional American icons associated with Coke. The conclusion? Plain and simple: consumer preference isn't based on taste alone. Coke's iconic brand appears to make a difference.

Branding has become so strong that today hardly anything goes unbranded. Salt is packaged in branded containers, common nuts and bolts are packaged with a distributor's label, and automobile parts—spark plugs, tires, filters—bear brand names that differ from those of the automakers. Even fruits, vegetables, dairy products, and poultry are branded—Sunkist oranges, Dole Classic iceberg salads, Horizon Organic milk, and Perdue chickens.

Branding helps buyers in many ways. Brand names help consumers identify products that might benefit them. Brands also say something about product quality and consistency—buyers who always buy the same brand know that they will get the same features, benefits, and quality each time they buy. Branding also gives the seller several advantages. The brand name becomes the basis on which a whole story can be built about a product's special qualities. The seller's brand name and trademark provide legal protection for unique product features that otherwise might be copied by competitors. And branding helps the seller to segment markets. For example, Toyota Motor Corporation can offer the major Lexus, Toyota, and Scion brands, each with numerous sub-brands—such as Camry, Corolla, Prius, Matrix, Yaris, Tundra, Land Cruiser, and others—not just one general product for all consumers.

Building and managing brands are perhaps the marketer's most important tasks. We will discuss branding strategy in more detail later in the chapter.

Packaging

Packaging involves designing and producing the container or wrapper for a product. Traditionally, the primary function of the package was to hold and protect the product. In recent times, however, numerous factors have made packaging an important marketing tool as well. Increased competition and clutter on retail store shelves means that packages must now perform many sales tasks—from attracting attention, to describing the product, to making the sale.

Companies are realizing the power of good packaging to create immediate consumer recognition of a brand. For example, an average supermarket stocks 45,000 items; the average Wal-Mart supercenter carries 142,000 items. The typical shopper passes by some 300 items per minute, and more than 70 percent of all purchase decisions are made in stores. In this highly competitive environment, the package may be the seller's last and best chance to influence buyers. Thus, for many companies, the package itself has become an important promotional medium.[13]

Poorly designed packages can cause headaches for consumers and lost sales for the company. Think about all those hard-to-open packages, such as DVD cases sealed with impossibly sticky labels, packaging with finger-splitting wire twist-ties, or sealed plastic clamshell containers that take the equivalent of the fire department's Jaws of Life to open. ▲Such packaging causes what

▼Better packaging: Amazon.com recently launched a multiyear initiatives to create "frustration-free packaging" and eliminate "wrap rage." Its goal is to eventually offer its entire catalog of products in frustration-free packaging.

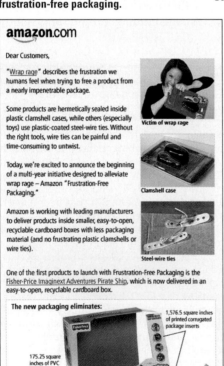

Packaging
The activities of designing and producing the container or wrapper for a product.

Amazon.com calls " 'wrap rage'—the frustration we feel when trying to free a product from a nearly impenetrable package." Amazon.com recently launched a multiyear initiative to alleviate wrap rage. It's working with companies such as Fisher-Price, Mattel, Microsoft, and others to create "frustration-free packaging"—smaller, easy-to-open recyclable packages that use less packaging material and no frustrating plastic clamshells or wire ties. These new packages not only reduce customer frustration, they also cut down on packaging waste and energy usage. "It will take many years," says the company, "but our vision is to offer our entire catalog of products in frustration-free packaging."[14]

Innovative packaging can give a company an advantage over competitors and boost sales. Sometimes even seemingly small packaging improvements can make a big difference. For example, Heinz revolutionized the 170-year-old condiments industry by inverting the good old ketchup bottle, letting customers quickly squeeze out even the last bit of ketchup. At the same time, it adopted a "fridge-door-fit" shape that not only slots into shelves more easily but also has a cap that is simpler for children to open. In the four months following the introduction of the new package, sales jumped 12 percent. What's more, the new package does double duty as a promotional tool. Says a packaging analyst, "When consumers see the Heinz logo on the fridge door every time they open it, it's taking marketing inside homes."[15]

In recent years, product safety has also become a major packaging concern. We have all learned to deal with hard-to-open "childproof" packaging. And after the rash of product tampering scares during the 1980s, most drug producers and food makers now put their products in tamper-resistant packages. In making packaging decisions, the company also must heed growing environmental concerns. Fortunately, many companies have gone "green" by reducing their packaging and using environmentally responsible packaging materials.

Labeling

Labels range from simple tags attached to products to complex graphics that are part of the package. They perform several functions. At the very least, the label *identifies* the product or brand, such as the name Sunkist stamped on oranges. The label might also *describe* several things about the product—who made it, where it was made, when it was made, its contents, how it is to be used, and how to use it safely. Finally, the label might help to *promote* the brand, support its positioning, and connect with customers. For many companies, labels have become an important element in broader marketing campaigns.

Labels and brand logos can support the brand's positioning and add personality to the brand. For example, many companies are now redesigning their brand and company logos to make them more approachable, upbeat, and engaging. "The boxy, monochromatic look is out and soft fonts, lots of colors, and natural imagery is in," says one analyst. For instance, Kraft recently replaced its blocky red, white, and blue hexagon logo with a lower-case, multi-font, multi-color one that includes a colorful starburst and the company's new slogan, "Make today delicious." Similarly, Wal-Mart swapped its blocky, single-color logo for one that has two colors and a sun icon. ▲And Pepsi's recently updated packaging sports a new, more uplifting smiling logo. "It feels like the same Pepsi we know and love," says a brand expert, "but it's more adventurous, more youthful, with a bit more personality to it." It presents a "spirit of optimism and youth," says a Pepsi marketer.[16]

Along with the positives, labeling also raises concerns. There has been a long history of legal concerns about packaging and labels. The Federal Trade Commission Act of 1914 held that false, misleading, or

▼**Labeling and logos can enhance a brand's positioning and personality:** Pepsi's new logo is "more adventurous, more youthful, with a bit more personality to it." It presents a "spirit of optimism and youth."

deceptive labels or packages constitute unfair competition. Labels can mislead customers, fail to describe important ingredients, or fail to include needed safety warnings. As a result, several federal and state laws regulate labeling. The most prominent is the Fair Packaging and Labeling Act of 1966, which set mandatory labeling requirements, encouraged voluntary industry packaging standards, and allowed federal agencies to set packaging regulations in specific industries.

Labeling has been affected in recent times by *unit pricing* (stating the price per unit of standard measure), *open dating* (stating the expected shelf life of the product), and *nutritional labeling* (stating the nutritional values in the product). The Nutritional Labeling and Educational Act of 1990 requires sellers to provide detailed nutritional information on food products, and recent sweeping actions by the Food and Drug Administration regulate the use of health-related terms such as *low fat*, *light*, and *high fiber*. Sellers must ensure that their labels contain all the required information.

Product Support Services

Customer service is another element of product strategy. A company's offer usually includes some support services, which can be a minor or a major part of the total offering. Later in the chapter, we will discuss services as products in themselves. Here, we discuss services that augment actual products.

Support services are an important part of the customer's overall brand experience. For example, Lexus makes outstanding cars. But the company knows that good marketing doesn't stop with making the sale. Keeping customers happy *after* the sale is the key to building lasting relationships. Lexus' goal is to "create the most satisfying ownership experience the world has ever seen." ▲ The Lexus Covenant promises that its dealers will "treat each customer as we would a guest in our own home" and "go to any lengths to serve them better." So Lexus goes to great lengths to provide outstanding after-sale service. Sometimes, that means fulfilling even seemingly outrageous customer requests:[17]

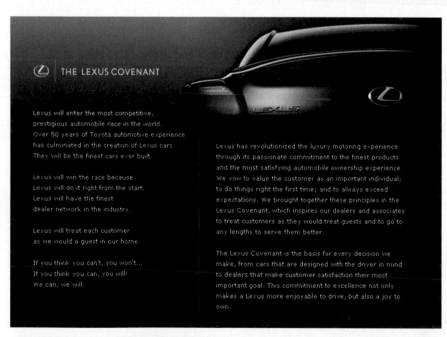

▲ Product support services: To keep customers happy after the sale, the Lexus Covenant promises that Lexus dealers will "treat each customer as we would a guest in our own home" and "go to any lengths to serve them better."

Dave Wilson, owner of several Lexus dealerships in Southern California, tells of a letter he received from an angry Lexus owner who spent $374 to repair her car at his dealership. She'd owned four prior Lexus vehicles without a single problem. She said in her letter that she resented paying to fix her current one. Turns out, she thought they were maintenance free—as in get in and drive . . . and drive and drive. "She didn't think she had to do anything to her Lexus," says Wilson. "She had 60,000 miles on it, and never had the oil changed." Wilson sent back her $374. Losing money on that single transaction meant keeping the customer for life.

The first step in designing support services is to survey customers periodically to assess the value of current services and to obtain ideas for new ones. Once the company has assessed the quality of various support services to customers, it can take steps to fix problems and add new services that will both delight customers and yield profits to the company.

Many companies are now using a sophisticated mix of phone, e-mail, fax, Internet, and interactive voice and data technologies to provide support services that were not possible before. For example, HP offers a complete set of sales and after-sale services. It promises "HP Total Care—expert help for every stage of your computer's life. From choosing it, to configuring it, to protecting it, to tuning it up—all the way to recycling it." Customers can click onto the HP Total Care service portal that offers online resources for HP products and 24/7 tech support, which can be accessed via e-mail, instant online chat, and telephone.[18]

Product Line Decisions

Product line
A group of products that are closely related because they function in a similar manner, are sold to the same customer groups, are marketed through the same types of outlets, or fall within given price ranges.

Beyond decisions about individual products and services, product strategy also calls for building a product line. A **product line** is a group of products that are closely related because they function in a similar manner, are sold to the same customer groups, are marketed through the same types of outlets, or fall within given price ranges. For example, Nike produces several lines of athletic shoes and apparel, and Marriott offers several lines of hotels.

The major product line decision involves *product line length*—the number of items in the product line. The line is too short if the manager can increase profits by adding items; the line is too long if the manager can increase profits by dropping items. Managers need to analyze their product lines periodically to assess each product item's sales and profits and to understand how each item contributes to the line's overall performance.

Product line length is influenced by company objectives and resources. For example, one objective might be to allow for upselling. Thus BMW wants to move customers up from its 3-series models to 5- and 7-series models. Another objective might be to allow cross-selling: Hewlett-Packard sells printers as well as cartridges. Still another objective might be to protect against economic swings: Gap runs several clothing-store chains (Gap, Old Navy, and Banana Republic) covering different price points.

A company can expand its product line in two ways: by *line filling* or by *line stretching*. *Product line filling* involves adding more items within the present range of the line. There are several reasons for product line filling: reaching for extra profits, satisfying dealers, using excess capacity, being the leading full-line company, and plugging holes to keep out competitors. However, line filling is overdone if it results in cannibalization and customer confusion. The company should ensure that new items are noticeably different from existing ones.

Product line stretching occurs when a company lengthens its product line beyond its current range. The company can stretch its line downward, upward, or both ways. Companies located at the upper end of the market can stretch their lines *downward*. A company may stretch downward to plug a market hole that otherwise would attract a new competitor or to respond to a competitor's attack on the upper end. Or it may add low-end products because it finds faster growth taking place in the low-end segments. Honda stretched downward for all of these reasons by adding its thrifty little Honda Fit to its line. The Fit, economical to drive and priced in the $12,000 to $13,000 range, met increasing consumer demands for more frugal cars and preempted competitors in the new-generation minicar segment.

Companies can also stretch their product lines *upward*. Sometimes, companies stretch upward in order to add prestige to their current products. Or they may be attracted by a faster growth rate or higher margins at the higher end. For example, some years ago, each of the leading Japanese auto companies introduced an upmarket automobile: Honda launched Acura; Toyota launched Lexus; and Nissan launched Infiniti. They used entirely new names rather than their own names.

Companies in the middle range of the market may decide to stretch their lines in *both directions*. Marriott did this with its hotel product line. Along with regular Marriott hotels, it added eight new branded hotel lines to serve both the upper and lower ends of the market. For example, Renaissance Hotels & Resorts aims to attract and please top executives; Fairfield Inn by Marriott, vacationers and business travelers on a tight travel budget; and Courtyard by Marriott, salespeople and other "road warriors."[19] The major risk with this strategy is that some travelers will trade down after finding that the lower-price hotels in the Marriott chain give them pretty much everything they want. However, Marriott would rather capture its customers who move downward than lose them to competitors.

Product Mix Decisions

Product mix (or product portfolio)
The set of all product lines and items that a particular seller offers for sale.

An organization with several product lines has a product mix. A **product mix (or product portfolio)** consists of all the product lines and items that a particular seller offers for sale. Some companies manage very complex product portfolios. ▲For example, Sony's diverse portfolio consists of four primary product businesses worldwide: Sony Electronics, Sony Computer Entertainment (games), Sony Pictures Entertainment (movies, TV shows, music, DVDs), and Sony Financial Services (life insurance, banking, and other offerings).

Each major Sony business consists of several product lines. For example, Sony Electronics includes cameras and camcorders, computers, TV and home entertainment products, mobile electronics, and others. In turn, each of these lines contains many individual items. Sony's TV and home entertainment line includes TVs, DVD players, home audio components, digital home products, and more. Altogether, Sony's product mix includes a diverse collection of hundreds and hundreds of products.

A company's product mix has four important dimensions: width, length, depth, and consistency. Product mix *width* refers to the number of different product lines the company carries. Sony markets a wide range of consumer and industrial

▲Product mix decisions: Sony has a large and diverse product portfolio, divided into four primary product businesses, each containing hundreds of products. "Welcome to the world of Sony."

products around the world, from TVs and PlayStation consoles to semiconductors. Product mix *length* refers to the total number of items the company carries within its product lines. Sony typically carries many products within each line. The camera and camcorder line, for instance, includes digital cameras, camcorders, photo printers, memory media, and tons of accessories.

Product mix *depth* refers to the number of versions offered of each product in the line. Sony has a very deep product mix. For example, it makes and markets about any kind of TV you'd ever want to buy—tube, flat panel, rear projection, front projection, HD or low resolution—each in almost any imaginable size. Finally, the *consistency* of the product mix refers to how closely related the various product lines are in end use, production requirements, distribution channels, or some other way. Within each major business, Sony's product lines are fairly consistent in that they perform similar functions for buyers and go through the same distribution channels. Companywide, however, Sony markets a very diverse mix of products. Managing such a broad and diverse product portfolio requires much skill.

These product mix dimensions provide the handles for defining the company's product strategy. The company can increase its business in four ways. It can add new product lines, widening its product mix. In this way, its new lines build on the company's reputation in its other lines. The company can lengthen its existing product lines to become a more full-line company. Or it can add more versions of each product and thus deepen its product mix. Finally, the company can pursue more product line consistency—or less—depending on whether it wants to have a strong reputation in a single field or in several fields.

In the face of recent economic difficulties, many companies have streamlined their product mixes to pare out marginally performing lines and models and sharpen their value propositions. Others have bolstered their product mixes by adding more affordable options. Because of the economy, "consumers are talking about reassessing their favorite brands . . . if they think they can get a better value with the same price," says a marketing consultant. As consumers rethink their brand preferences and priorities, marketers must do the same. They need to align their product mixes with changing customer needs and profitably create better value for customers.[20]

◆ **Speed Bump:** Linking the Concepts

Slow down for a minute. To get a better sense of how large and complex a company's product offering can become, investigate Procter & Gamble's product mix.

- Using P&G's Web site (www.pg.com), its annual report, or other sources, develop a list of all the company's product lines and individual products. What surprises you about this list of products?
- Is P&G's product mix consistent? What overall strategy or logic appears to have guided the development of this product mix?

SERVICES MARKETING (pp 249–255)

Author Comment ≫
As noted at the start of the chapter, services are "products," too—just intangible ones. So all of the product topics we've discussed so far apply to services as well as to physical products. However, in this section, we'll focus in on the special characteristics and marketing needs that set services apart.

Services have grown dramatically in recent years. Services now account for close to 80 percent of U.S. gross domestic product. And the service industry is growing. By 2014, it is estimated that nearly four out of five jobs in the United States will be in service industries. Services are growing even faster in the world economy, making up 64 percent of gross world product.[21]

Service industries vary greatly. *Governments* offer services through courts, employment services, hospitals, military services, police and fire departments, postal service, and schools. *Private not-for-profit organizations* offer services through museums, charities, churches, colleges, foundations, and hospitals. A large number of *business organizations* offer services—airlines, banks, hotels, insurance companies, consulting firms, medical and legal practices, entertainment and telecommunications companies, real-estate firms, retailers, and others.

Nature and Characteristics of a Service

A company must consider four special service characteristics when designing marketing programs: *intangibility*, *inseparability*, *variability*, and *perishability* (see ■ **Figure 7.3**).

Service intangibility
A major characteristic of services—they cannot be seen, tasted, felt, heard, or smelled before they are bought.

Service intangibility means that services cannot be seen, tasted, felt, heard, or smelled before they are bought. For example, people undergoing cosmetic surgery cannot see the result before the purchase. Airline passengers have nothing but a ticket and the promise that they and their luggage will arrive safely at the intended destination, hopefully at the same time. To reduce uncertainty, buyers look for "signals" of service quality. They draw conclusions about quality from the place, people, price, equipment, and communications that they can see.

Therefore, the service provider's task is to make the service tangible in one or more ways and to send the right signals about quality. One analyst calls this

■ **Figure 7.3** Four Service Characteristics

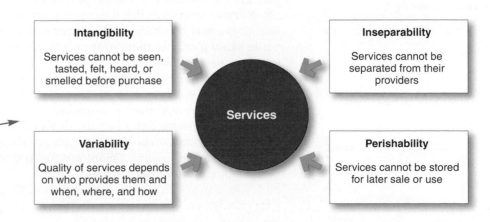

Although services are "products" in a general sense, they have special characteristics and marketing needs. The biggest differences come from the fact that services are essentially intangible and that they are created through direct interactions with customers. Think about your experiences with an airline versus Nike or Apple.

Intangibility
Services cannot be seen, tasted, felt, heard, or smelled before purchase

Inseparability
Services cannot be separated from their providers

Services

Variability
Quality of services depends on who provides them and when, where, and how

Perishability
Services cannot be stored for later sale or use

evidence management, in which the service organization presents its customers with organized, honest evidence of its capabilities. The Mayo Clinic practices good evidence management:[22]

▲ By providing customers with organized, honest evidence of its capabilities, the Mayo Clinic has built one of the most powerful brands in health care. Its Sharing Mayo Clinic blog lets you hear directly from those who have been to the clinic or who work there.

When it comes to hospitals, it's very hard for the average patient to judge the quality of the "product." You can't try it on, you can't return it if you don't like it, and you need an advanced degree to understand it. And so, when we're considering a medical facility, most of us unconsciously turn detective, looking for evidence of competence, caring, and integrity. The Mayo Clinic doesn't leave that evidence to chance. By carefully managing a set of visual and experiential clues, both inside and outside the clinic, Mayo offers patients and their families concrete evidence of its strengths and values.

Inside the clinic, staff are trained to act in a way that clearly signals its patient-first focus. "My doctor calls me at home to check on how I am doing," marvels one patient. "She wants to work with what is best for my schedule." Mayo's physical facilities also send the right signals. They've been carefully designed to offer a place of refuge, convey caring and respect, and signal competence. Looking for external confirmation? Go online and hear directly from those who've been to the clinic or who work there. Mayo now uses social networking—everything from blogs to Facebook and YouTube—to enhance the patient experience. ▲For example, on the Sharing Mayo Clinic blog (http://sharing.mayoclinic.org), patients and their families retell their Mayo experiences and Mayo employees offer behind-the-scenes views. The result? Exceptionally positive word of mouth and abiding customer loyalty have allowed Mayo Clinic to build what is arguably the most powerful brand in health care with very little advertising. "The quality of the [patient] experience is key," says Dr. Thoraf Sundt, a heart surgeon and chair of Mayo's marketing committee.

Service inseparability
A major characteristic of services—they are produced and consumed at the same time and cannot be separated from their providers.

Service variability
A major characteristic of services—their quality may vary greatly, depending on who provides them and when, where, and how.

Service perishability
A major characteristic of services—they cannot be stored for later sale or use.

Physical goods are produced, then stored, later sold, and still later consumed. In contrast, services are first sold, then produced and consumed at the same time. In services marketing, the service provider is the product. **Service inseparability** means that services cannot be separated from their providers, whether the providers are people or machines. If a service employee provides the service, then the employee becomes a part of the service. Because the customer is also present as the service is produced, *provider–customer interaction* is a special feature of services marketing. Both the provider and the customer affect the service outcome.

Service variability means that the quality of services depends on who provides them as well as when, where, and how they are provided. For example, some hotels—say, Marriott—have reputations for providing better service than others. Still, within a given Marriott hotel, one registration-counter employee may be cheerful and efficient, whereas another standing just a few feet away may be unpleasant and slow. Even the quality of a single Marriott employee's service varies according to his or her energy and frame of mind at the time of each customer encounter.

Service perishability means that services cannot be stored for later sale or use. Some doctors charge patients for missed appointments because the service value existed only at that point and disappeared when the patient did not show up. The perishability of services is not a problem when demand is steady. However, when demand fluctuates, service firms often have difficult problems. For example, because of rush-hour demand, public transportation companies have to own much more equipment than they would if demand were even throughout the day. Thus, service firms often design strategies for producing a better match between demand and supply. Hotels and resorts charge lower prices in the off-season to attract more guests. And restaurants hire part-time employees to serve during peak periods.

Marketing Strategies for Service Firms

Just like manufacturing businesses, good service firms use marketing to position themselves strongly in chosen target markets. JetBlue promises "Happy Jetting"; Target says "Expect more, pay less." At Hampton, "We love having you here." And St. Jude Children's Hospital is "Finding cures. Saving children." These and other service firms establish their positions through traditional marketing mix activities. However, because services differ from tangible products, they often require additional marketing approaches.

The Service-Profit Chain

Service-profit chain
The chain that links service firm profits with employee and customer satisfaction.

In a service business, the customer and front-line service employee *interact* to create the service. Effective interaction, in turn, depends on the skills of front-line service employees and on the support processes backing these employees. Thus, successful service companies focus their attention on *both* their customers and their employees. They understand the **service-profit chain**, which links service firm profits with employee and customer satisfaction. This chain consists of five links:[23]

- *Internal service quality:* superior employee selection and training, a quality work environment, and strong support for those dealing with customers, which results in....
- *Satisfied and productive service employees:* more satisfied, loyal, and hard-working employees, which results in....
- *Greater service value:* more effective and efficient customer value creation and service delivery, which results in....
- *Satisfied and loyal customers:* satisfied customers who remain loyal, repeat purchase, and refer other customers, which results in....
- *Healthy service profits and growth:* superior service firm performance.

Therefore, reaching service profits and growth goals begins with taking care of those who take care of customers. Jumeirah Group, a chain legendary for its outstanding customer service, is also legendary for its motivated and satisfied employees (see Marketing at Work 7.1). ▲Similarly, customer-service all-star Zappos, the on-line shoe, clothing, and accessories retailer, knows that happy customers begin with happy, dedicated, and energetic employees:[24]

▼The service-profit chain: Zappos knows that happy customers begin with happy, dedicated, and "perpetually chipper" employees.

Most of Zappos' business is driven by word-of-mouth and customer interactions with company employees. So keeping *customers* happy really does require keeping *employees* happy. Zappos starts by recruiting the right people and training them thoroughly in customer-service basics. Then, the Zappos culture takes over, a culture that emphasizes "a satisfying and fulfilling job . . . and a career you can be proud of. Work hard. Play hard. All the time!" Zappos is a great place to work. The online retailer creates a relaxed, fun-loving, and close-knit family atmosphere, complete with free meals, full benefits, profit sharing, a nap room, and even a full-time life coach. The result is what one observer calls "1,550 perpetually chipper employees." Every year, the company publishes a "culture book," filled with unedited, often gushy testimonials from Zapponians about what it's like to work there. "Oh my gosh," says one employee, "this is my home away from home. . . . It's changed my life. . . . Our culture is the best reason to work here." Says another, "the most surprising thing about coming to work here is that there are no limits. So pretty much anything you are passionate about is possible." And about what are Zapponians most passionate? The company's No. 1 core value: "Creating WOW through service."

Marketing at Work 7.1

Jumeirah Group: Stay Different™

Jumeirah Hotels & Resorts are regarded as among the most luxurious and innovative in the world. The company was founded in 1997 with the aim to become a hospitality industry leader through establishing a world class portfolio of luxury hotels and resorts. Jumeirah has some of the most iconic hotels in its portfolio like the Burj Al Arab, a symbol of Dubai and one of the world's most luxurious hotels. The company's product portfolio extends to managing Jumeirah Living, a luxury brand of service residence; Talise, a spa brand; Jumeirah Restaurant, their restaurant division; Wild Wadi, a water park; Emirates Academy of Hospitality Management; and Jumeirah Retail, a collection of 15 stores and a dedicated online luxury store called JumeirahCollection.com. Building on this success, in 2004 Jumeirah Group became a member of Dubai Holding and its expansion plans to grow its portfolio of luxury hotels and resorts worldwide to 60 by 2012 are underway across the globe.

Jumeirah's core essence to STAY DIFFERENT™ promises guests experiences that are as unique and innovative as the brand itself. Jumeirah's promise is built on the foundation that true luxury is emotional, memorable, and above all personal, and that is what it believes today's sophisticated luxury traveler relates and responds to. Jumeirah has won several awards over the years; it was named the "Best Business Hotel Chain in the Middle East/Africa" for the fifth consecutive year at the Business Traveller UK Awards, and the 'Best Business Hotel Brand in Middle East/Africa' in the Business Traveller Asia Pacific Awards. It is recognized as one of the top four hotel chains in the world alongside Four Seasons, Shangri-La, and Ritz-Carlton.

The foundation of Jumeirah's success lies in its Hallmarks, at the heart of everything that they do. Simply written, these are rules that govern Jumeirah's standards and reinforce an attitude of genuine caring and personal service. The Hallmarks are:

1. I will always smile and greet our guest before they greet me.
2. My first response to a guest will never be no.
3. I will treat all colleagues with respect and integrity.

These Hallmarks look very simple but make a huge difference in the guest experience and the empowerment of employees or "colleagues" as they are known internally. Jumeirah employs over 10,500 people from over 100 different nationalities. All new employees are oriented formally to the Jumeirah culture. These sessions allow interaction with the executive team and include sessions on team building and cultural awareness.

To be different you have to be willing to challenge conventional service norms. Most of what makes Jumeirah different are the small things you cannot see. In Burj Al Arab, the ratio of service staff to guests is 7 to 1. Guests are assigned their personal butler who will go out of the way to indulge them; they are spoiled by the great selection of chocolates, flowers, bath menus, special gifts for couples or children, and a 17-option pillow menu. To be different you need to be bold. For example, a guest had planned a romantic vacation where he planned to propose, but realized he had forgotten the new diamond ring back in the United Kingdom. The team at Burj Al Arab pulled together and the diamond ring was flown to Dubai on that same

▲ The service-profit chain: Just how do hotels like Burj Al Arab in Dubai achieve their iconic status? By treating their staff a cut above the average, happy employees will in turn strive to do their best to make customers satisfied.

day, so the very relieved and grateful guest was able to propose to his girlfriend on the following day.

Understanding regional culture is so important. At Jumeirah Emirates Towers, a considerable increase in the number of female executives traveling alone was noticed and Jumeirah saw an opportunity to create a very attractive and innovative niche. They introduced the Chopard Ladies Floor. The feedback from the guests was extremely positive, indicating that there is a need for such a concept within the Middle East. The Chopard Ladies Floor is located on Level 40 of Jumeirah Emirates Towers and features 10 Tower Rooms and one Apex Suite, designed for the executive woman seeking sophistication, luxury, and exclusivity. This floor is only serviced by female employees and caters to the privacy and comfort of female travelers. Additional amenities designed for the ladies include an in-suite yoga facility and a cosmetics fridge.

Though communication plays a big role in the image, the value of the brand is translated into the superlative service delivered, ensuring that guests come back again and again for more. Jumeirah has a loyalty program called Sirius. Guests can earn Sirius Points each time they stay, dine, relax, or shop at any Jumeirah Hotel & Resort in London, Dubai, and New York. To make it convenient for their customers, Jumeirah launched a new website in February, 2009, where points can be exchanged for rewards like room stays and upgrades with no black-out dates, dining experiences, spa treatments, and luxury shopping from anywhere in the world through the jumeirahcollection.com.

Sources: Based on Information from Jumeirah Group (2009), accessed at www.jumeirah.com/en/Jumeirah-Group/Business Traveller UK Awards 2009, dated September 21, 2009; accessed at www.businesstraveller.com/ awards 2009 Business Traveller Asia-Pacific Awards 2009, dated October 20, 2009; accessed at http://asia.businesstraveller.com/asia-pacific/awards "Jumeirah Wins Prestigious Business Traveller Awards in UK and Asia Pacific," dated September 29, 2009; accessed at www.jumeirah.com; "Jumeirah Group Takes 'Surfing' to a Whole New Level," accessed at www.jumeirah.com.

■ Figure 7.4 Three Types
of Service Marketing

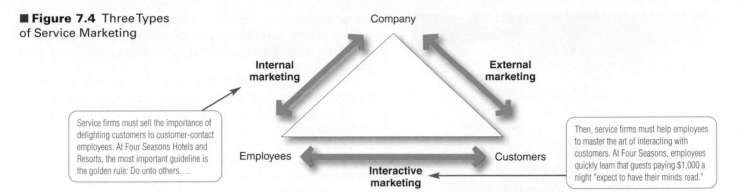

Service firms must sell the importance of delighting customers to customer-contact employees. At Four Seasons Hotels and Resorts, the most important guideline is the golden rule: Do unto others....

Then, service firms must help employees to master the art of interacting with customers. At Four Seasons, employees quickly learn that guests paying $1,000 a night "expect to have their minds read."

Internal marketing
Orienting and motivating customer-contact employees and supporting service people to work as a team to provide customer satisfaction.

Interactive marketing
Training service employees in the fine art of interacting with customers to satisfy their needs.

Thus, service marketing requires more than just traditional external marketing using the Four Ps. **■ Figure 7.4** shows that service marketing also requires *internal marketing* and *interactive marketing*. **Internal marketing** means that the service firm must orient and motivate its customer-contact employees and supporting service people to work as a *team* to provide customer satisfaction. Marketers must get everyone in the organization to be customer centered. In fact, internal marketing must *precede* external marketing. For example, Four Seasons Hotels and Resorts starts by hiring the right people and carefully orienting and inspiring them to give unparalleled customer service.

Interactive marketing means that service quality depends heavily on the quality of the buyer–seller interaction during the service encounter. In product marketing, product quality often depends little on how the product is obtained. But in services marketing, service quality depends on both the service deliverer and the quality of the delivery. Service marketers, therefore, have to master interactive marketing skills. Thus, Four Seasons selects only people with an innate "passion to serve" and instructs them carefully in the fine art of interacting with customers to satisfy their every need. All new hires complete a three-month training regimen, including improvisation exercises to help them improve their customer-interaction skills.

In today's marketplace, companies must know how to deliver interactions that are not only "high-touch" but also "high-tech." For example, customers can log onto the Charles Schwab Web site and access account information, investment research, real-time quotes, after-hours trading, and the Schwab learning center. They can also participate in live online events and chat online with customer-service representatives. Customers seeking more personal interactions can contact service representatives by phone or visit a local Schwab branch office to "talk with Chuck." Thus, Schwab has mastered interactive marketing at all three levels—calls, clicks, *and* personal visits.

Today, as competition and costs increase, and as productivity and quality decrease, more service marketing sophistication is needed. Service companies face three major marketing tasks: They want to increase their *service differentiation*, *service quality*, and *service productivity*.

Managing Service Differentiation

In these days of intense price competition, service marketers often complain about the difficulty of differentiating their services from those of competitors. To the extent that customers view the services of different providers as similar, they care less about the provider than the price.

The solution to price competition is to develop a differentiated offer, delivery, and image. The *offer* can include innovative features that set one company's offer apart from competitors' offers. Some hotels offer no-wait kiosk registration, car-rental, banking, and business-center services in their lobbies and free high-speed Internet connections in their rooms. Some retailers differentiate themselves by offerings that take you well beyond the products they stock. For example, PetSmart

▲ **Service differentiation: PetSmart differentiates itself by offering services that go well beyond the products it stocks. It even offers a PetsHotel with a Doggie Day Camp.**

isn't just your average pet shop. ▲Most locations offer training, grooming salons, veterinarian services, and even a "PetsHotel with a Doggie Day Camp," making it your one-stop shop for all your pet's needs.

Service companies can differentiate their service *delivery* by having more able and reliable customer-contact people, by developing a superior physical environment in which the service product is delivered, or by designing a superior delivery process. For example, many grocery chains now offer online shopping and home delivery as a better way to shop than having to drive, park, wait in line, and tote groceries home. And most banks allow you to access your account information from almost anywhere—from the ATM to your cell phone.

Finally, service companies also can work on differentiating their *images* through symbols and branding. Aflac adopted the duck as its symbol in its advertising, and even as stuffed animals, golf club covers, and free ring tones and screensavers. The well-known Aflac duck, with the familiar voice of comedian Gilbert Gottfried, helped make the big but previously unknown insurance company memorable and approachable. Other well-known service symbols include Merrill Lynch's bull, MGM's lion, McDonald's golden arches, Allstate's "good hands," and The Travelers red umbrella.

Managing Service Quality

A service firm can differentiate itself by delivering consistently higher quality than its competitors provide. Like manufacturers before them, most service industries have now joined the customer-driven quality movement. And like product marketers, service providers need to identify what target customers expect in regards to service quality.

Unfortunately, service quality is harder to define and judge than product quality. For instance, it is harder to agree on the quality of a haircut than on the quality of a hair dryer. Customer retention is perhaps the best measure of quality—a service firm's ability to hang onto its customers depends on how consistently it delivers value to them.

Top service companies set high service-quality standards. They watch service performance closely, both their own and that of competitors. They do not settle for merely good service; they strive for 100 percent defect-free service. A 98 percent performance standard may sound good, but using this standard, UPS would lose or misdirect 310,000 packages each day and U.S. pharmacists would misfill more than 1.4 million prescriptions each week.[25]

Unlike product manufacturers who can adjust their machinery and inputs until everything is perfect, service quality will always vary, depending on the interactions between employees and customers. As hard as they try, even the best companies will have an occasional late delivery, burned steak, or grumpy employee. However, good *service recovery* can turn angry customers into loyal ones. In fact, good recovery can win more customer purchasing and loyalty than if things had gone well in the first place. Consider this example:[26]

Bob Emig was flying home from St. Louis on Southwest Airlines when an all-too-familiar travel nightmare began to unfold. After his airplane backed away from the gate, he and his fellow passengers were told that the plane would need to be de-iced. When the aircraft was ready to fly two and a half hours later, the pilot had reached the hour limit set by the Federal Aviation Administration, and a new pilot was required. By that time, the plane had to be de-iced again. Five hours after the scheduled departure time, Emig's flight was finally ready for takeoff. A customer-service disaster, right? Not to hear Emig tell it. Throughout the wait, the Southwest pilot walked the aisles, answering questions and offering constant updates. Flight attendants, who Emig says "really seemed like they cared,"

▲Service recovery: Southwest created a high-level group—headed by Fred Taylor, "senior manager of proactive customer service communications" (above)—that carefully coordinates responses to major flight disruptions, turning wronged customers into even more loyal ones.

kept up with the news on connecting flights. And within a couple of days of arriving home, Emig received a letter of apology from Southwest that included two free round-trip ticket vouchers.

Unusual? Not at all. It's standard service-recovery procedure for Southwest Airlines. ▲Years ago, Southwest created a high-level group—headed by a "senior manager of proactive customer service communications"—that carefully coordinates information sent to all frontline reps in the event of major flight disruptions. It also sends out letters, and in many cases flight vouchers, to customers caught up in flight delays or cancellations, customer bumping incidents, baggage problems, or other travel messes—even those beyond Southwest's control. Thanks to such caring service recovery, Southwest doesn't just appease wronged customers like Bob Emig, it turns them into even more loyal customers.

Managing Service Productivity

With their costs rising rapidly, service firms are under great pressure to increase service productivity. They can do so in several ways. They can train current employees better or hire new ones who will work harder or more skillfully. Or they can increase the quantity of their service by giving up some quality. The provider can "industrialize the service" by adding equipment and standardizing production, as in McDonald's assembly-line approach to fast-food retailing. Finally, the service provider can harness the power of technology. Although we often think of technology's power to save time and costs in manufacturing companies, it also has great—and often untapped—potential to make service workers more productive.

However, companies must avoid pushing productivity so hard that doing so reduces quality. Attempts to industrialize a service or to cut costs can make a service company more efficient in the short run. But they can also reduce its longer-run ability to innovate, maintain service quality, or respond to consumer needs and desires. For example, some airlines have learned this lesson the hard way as they attempt to economize in the face of rising costs. They stopped offering even the little things for free—such as in-flight snacks—and began charging extra for everything from curbside luggage check-in to aisle seats. The result is a plane full of resentful customers who avoid the airline whenever they can. In their attempts to improve productivity, these airlines mangled customer service.

Thus, in attempting to improve service productivity, companies must be mindful of how they create and deliver customer value. In short, they should be careful not to take the "service" out of service.

. . . .

◆ **Speed Bump:** Linking the Concepts

Let's pause here for a moment. We've said that although services are "products" in a general sense, they have special characteristics and marketing needs. To get a better grasp of this concept, select a traditional product brand, such as Under Armour or Lexus. Next, select a service brand, such as Four Seasons or McDonald's. Then compare the two.

- How are the characteristics and marketing needs of the product and service brands you selected similar?
- How do the characteristics and marketing needs of the two brands differ? How are these differences reflected in each brand's marketing strategy? Keep these differences in mind as we move into the final section of the chapter.

. . . .

BRANDING STRATEGY: BUILDING STRONG BRANDS (pp 256–265)

Author Comment >>
A brand represents everything that a product or service *means* to consumers. As such, brands are valuable assets to a company. For example, when you hear someone say "Coca-Cola," what do you think, feel, or remember? What about "Harley-Davidson"? Or "Google"?

Some analysts see brands as *the* major enduring asset of a company, outlasting the company's specific products and facilities. John Stewart, former CEO of Quaker Oats, once said, "If this business were split up, I would give you the land and bricks and mortar, and I would keep the brands and trademarks, and I would fare better than you." A former CEO of McDonald's declared, "If every asset we own, every building, and every piece of equipment were destroyed in a terrible natural disaster, we would be able to borrow all the money to replace it very quickly because of the value of our brand. . . . The brand is more valuable than the totality of all these assets."[27]

Thus, brands are powerful assets that must be carefully developed and managed. In this section, we examine the key strategies for building and managing product and service brands.

Brand Equity

Brands are more than just names and symbols. They are a key element in the company's relationships with consumers. Brands represent consumers' perceptions and feelings about a product and its performance—everything that the product or service *means* to consumers. In the final analysis, brands exist in the heads of consumers. As one well-respected marketer once said, "Products are created in the factory, but brands are created in the mind."[28]

Brand equity
The differential effect that knowing the brand name has on customer response to the product or its marketing.

A powerful brand has high *brand equity*. **Brand equity** is the differential effect that knowing the brand name has on customer response to the product and its marketing. It's a measure of the brand's ability to capture consumer preference and loyalty. A brand has positive brand equity when consumers react more favorably to it than to a generic or unbranded version of the same product. It has negative brand equity if consumers react less favorably than to an unbranded version.

Brands vary in the amount of power and value they hold in the marketplace. Some brands—such as Coca-Cola, Nike, Disney, GE, McDonald's, Harley-Davidson, and others—become larger-than-life icons that maintain their power in the market for years, even generations. Other brands create fresh consumer excitement and loyalty, brands such as Google, YouTube, Apple, eBay, Twitter, and Wikipedia. These brands win in the marketplace not simply because they deliver unique benefits or reliable service. Rather, they succeed because they forge deep connections with customers.

▼ **Consumers sometimes bond very closely with specific brands. Jokes the bride: "He loves DeWalt nearly as much as he loves me."**

Ad agency Young & Rubicam's Brand Asset Valuator measures brand strength along four consumer perception dimensions: *differentiation* (what makes the brand stand out), *relevance* (how consumers feel it meets their needs), *knowledge* (how much consumers know about the brand), and *esteem* (how highly consumers regard and respect the brand). Brands with strong brand equity rate high on all of these dimensions. A brand must be distinct, or consumers will have no reason to choose it over other brands. But the fact that a brand is highly differentiated doesn't necessarily mean that consumers will buy it. The brand must stand out in ways that are relevant to consumers' needs. But even a differentiated, relevant brand is far from a shoe-in. Before consumers will respond to the brand, they must first know about and understand it. And that familiarity must lead to a strong, positive consumer-brand connection.[29]

Thus, positive brand equity derives from consumer feelings about and connections with a brand. Consumers sometimes bond *very* closely with specific brands. ▲For example, one Michigan couple had such a passion for Black & Decker's DeWalt power tool brand that they designed their entire wedding around it. They wore trademark DeWalt black-and-yellow T-shirts, made their way to a wooden chapel that they'd built with their DeWalt gear, exchanged vows and power tools, and even cut cake with a power saw. Joked the wife about her husband (a carpenter by trade), "He loves DeWalt nearly as much as he loves me."[30]

A brand with high brand equity is a very valuable asset. *Brand valuation* is the process of estimating the total financial value of a brand. Measuring such value is difficult. However, according to one estimate, the brand value of Google is a whopping $100 billion, with Microsoft at $76 billion and Coca-Cola at $67 billion. Other brands rating among the world's most valuable include IBM, McDonald's, Apple, China Mobile, GE, Wal-Mart, and Nokia.[31]

High brand equity provides a company with many competitive advantages. A powerful brand enjoys a high level of consumer brand awareness and loyalty. Because consumers expect stores to carry the brand, the company has more leverage in bargaining with resellers. Because the brand name carries high credibility, the company can more easily launch line and brand extensions. A powerful brand offers the company some defense against fierce price competition.

Above all, however, a powerful brand forms the basis for building strong and profitable customer relationships. The fundamental asset underlying brand equity is *customer equity*—the value of the customer relationships that the brand creates. A powerful brand is important, but what it really represents is a profitable set of loyal customers. The proper focus of marketing is building customer equity, with brand management serving as a major marketing tool. Companies need to think of themselves not as portfolios of products, but as portfolios of customers.

Building Strong Brands

Branding poses challenging decisions to the marketer. ■ **Figure 7.5** shows that the major brand strategy decisions involve brand positioning, brand name selection, brand sponsorship, and brand development.

Brand Positioning

Marketers need to position their brands clearly in target customers' minds. They can position brands at any of three levels.[32] At the lowest level, they can position the brand on *product attributes*. For example, P&G invented the disposable diaper category with its Pampers brand. Early Pampers marketing focused on attributes such as fluid absorption, fit, and disposability. In general, however, attributes are the least desirable level for brand positioning. Competitors can easily copy attributes. More importantly, customers are not interested in attributes as such; they are interested in what the attributes will do for them.

A brand can be better positioned by associating its name with a desirable *benefit*. Thus, Pampers can go beyond technical product attributes and talk about the resulting containment and skin-health benefits from dryness. "There are fewer wet bottoms in the world because of us," says Jim Stengel, P&G's former global marketing officer. Some successful brands positioned on benefits are Volvo (safety), FedEx (guaranteed on-time delivery), Nike (performance), and Lexus (quality).

The strongest brands go beyond attribute or benefit positioning. They are positioned on strong *beliefs and values*. These brands pack an emotional wallop. ▲Brands

Brands are powerful assets that must be carefully developed and managed. As this figure suggests, building strong brands involves many challenging decisions.

Brand positioning	Brand name selection	Brand sponsorship	Brand development
Attributes Benefits Beliefs and values	Selection Protection	Manufacturer's brand Private brand Licensing Co-branding	Line extensions Brand extensions Multibrands New brands

■ **Figure 7.5** Major Brand Strategy Decisions

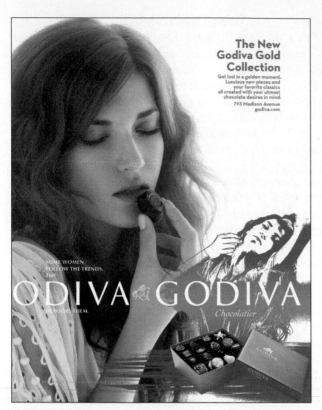

▲ **Brand positioning: The strongest brands go beyond attribute or benefit positioning. Godiva engages customers on a deeper level, touching universal emotions.**

such as Godiva, Starbucks, Apple, and Victoria's Secret rely less on a product's tangible attributes and more on creating surprise, passion, and excitement surrounding a brand. Successful brands engage customers on a deep, emotional level. Thus, P&G knows that, to parents, Pampers mean much more than just containment and dryness. According to Stengel:[33]

> If you go back, we often thought of P&G's brands in terms of functional benefits. But when we began listening very closely to customers, they told us Pampers meant much more to them—Pampers are more about parent–child relationships and total baby care. So we started to say, "We want to be a brand experience; we want to be there to help support parents and babies as they grow and develop." In the initial days people thought we were nuts. How can a diaper help a baby's development? But babies wear diapers 24/7 for almost three years. It actually reorients R&D to ask a question like "How can we help babies sleep better?" Why are we concerned about babies sleeping better? Because sleep is important to brain development. It helps relationship skills. Thinking like that, we're able to help improve life for our consumers. The equity of great brands has to be something that a consumer finds inspirational and the organization finds inspirational. You know, our baby care business didn't start growing aggressively until we changed Pampers from being about dryness to being about helping mom with her baby's development.

When positioning a brand, the marketer should establish a mission for the brand and a vision of what the brand must be and do. A brand is the company's promise to deliver a specific set of features, benefits, services, and experiences consistently to the buyers. The brand promise must be simple and honest. Motel 6, for example, offers clean rooms, low prices, and good service but does not promise expensive furniture or large bathrooms. In contrast, The Ritz-Carlton offers luxurious rooms and a truly memorable experience but does not promise low prices.

Brand Name Selection

A good name can add greatly to a product's success. However, finding the best brand name is a difficult task. It begins with a careful review of the product and its benefits, the target market, and proposed marketing strategies. After that, naming a brand becomes part science, part art, and a measure of instinct.

Desirable qualities for a brand name include the following: (1) It should suggest something about the product's benefits and qualities. Examples: Beautyrest, Acuvue, Breathe Right, Food Saver. (2) It should be easy to pronounce, recognize, and remember: Tide, Jelly Belly, iPod, JetBlue. (3) The brand name should be distinctive: Panera, Uggs. (4) It should be extendable: Amazon.com began as an online bookseller but chose a name that would allow expansion into other categories. (5) The name should translate easily into foreign languages. Before changing its name to Exxon, Standard Oil of New Jersey rejected the name Enco, which it learned meant a stalled engine when pronounced in Japanese. (6) It should be capable of registration and legal protection. A brand name cannot be registered if it infringes on existing brand names.

Choosing a new brand name is hard work. After a decade of choosing quirky names (Yahoo!, Google) or trademark-proof made-up names (Novartis, Aventis, Lycos), today's style is to build brands around names that have real meaning. For example, names like Silk (soy milk), Method (home products), Smartwater (beverages), and Blackboard (school software) are simple and make intuitive sense. But with trademark applications soaring, *available* new names can be hard to find. Try it yourself. Pick a product and see if you can come up with a better name for it. How about Moonshot? Tickle? Vanilla? Treehugger? Simplicity? Google them and you'll find that they're already taken.

Once chosen, the brand name must be protected. Many firms try to build a brand name that will eventually become identified with the product category. Brand names such as Kleenex, Levi's, JELL-O, BAND-AID, Scotch Tape, Formica, and Ziploc have succeeded in this way. However, their very success may threaten the company's rights to the name. Many originally protected brand names—such as cellophane, aspirin, nylon, kerosene, linoleum, yo-yo, trampoline, escalator, thermos, and shredded wheat—are now generic names that any seller can use. To protect their brands, marketers present them carefully using the word "brand" and the registered trademark symbol, as in "BAND-AID® Brand Adhesive Bandages." Even the long-standing "I am stuck on BAND-AID and BAND AID's stuck on me" jingle has now become "I am stuck on BAND AID *brand* and BAND AID's stuck on me."

Brand Sponsorship

A manufacturer has four sponsorship options. The product may be launched as a *national brand* (or *manufacturer's brand*), as when Sony and Kellogg sell their output under their own brand names (Sony Bravia HDTV or Kellogg's Frosted Flakes). Or the manufacturer may sell to resellers who give the product a *private brand* (also called a *store brand* or *distributor brand*). Although most manufacturers create their own brand names, others market *licensed brands*. Finally, two companies can join forces and *co-brand* a product. We discuss each of these options in turn.

Store brand (or private brand)
A brand created and owned by a reseller of a product or service.

National Brands Versus Store Brands. National brands (or manufacturers' brands) have long dominated the retail scene. In recent times, however, an increasing number of retailers and wholesalers have created their own **store brands (or *private brands*)**. Although store brands have been gaining strength for more than a decade, recent tougher economic times have created a store-brand boom. "Bad times are good times for private labels," says a brand expert. "As consumers become more price-conscious, they also become less brand-conscious."[34] (See Marketing at Work 7.2.)

In fact, store brands are growing much faster than national brands. In all, private-label brands now capture some 22 percent of the unit sales of U.S. package-goods (things you'd find in a supermarket or drug store), and more than 17 percent of dollar sales. Private-label apparel, such as Hollister, The Limited, Arizona Jean Company (JCPenney), and Xhilaration (Target), captures a 45 percent share of all U.S. apparel sales. Last year alone, store-brand sales grew 10 percent.[35] Many large retailers skillfully market a deep assortment of store-brand merchandise spanning a broad range of categories. For example, Costco, the world's largest warehouse club, offers a staggering array of goods and services under its Kirkland Signature brand. Costco customers can buy anything from Kirkland Signature rotisserie chickens to Kirkland brand apparel to a $3,439-per-person Kirkland Signature Tahitian cruise package.

In the so-called *battle of the brands* between national and private brands, retailers have many advantages. They control what products they stock, where they go on the shelf, what prices they charge, and which ones they will feature in local circulars. Retailers often price their store brands lower than comparable national brands, thereby appealing to the budget-conscious shopper in all of us. Although store brands can be hard to establish and costly to stock and promote, they also yield higher profit margins for the reseller. And they give resellers exclusive products that cannot be bought from competitors, resulting in greater store traffic and loyalty. Fast-growing retailer Trader Joe's, which carries 80 percent store brands, began creating its own brands so that "we could put our destiny in our own hands," says the company's president.[36]

To compete with store brands, national brands must sharpen their value propositions, especially in these lean economic times. In the long run, however, leading brand marketers must invest in R&D to bring out new brands, new features, and continuous quality improvements. They must design strong advertising programs to maintain high awareness and preference. And they must find ways to "partner" with major distributors in a search for distribution economies and improved joint performance.

Marketing at Work 7.2

Bad Times Are Good Times for Store Brands. But What's a National Brand to Do?

Most things in Michelle Moore's refrigerator, pantry, and laundry room are not name brands—national products with expensive advertising campaigns behind them. They are store-brand products, like Great Value milk from Walmart or Private Selection or Kroger Value products from her local Kroger grocery store. "I'm weird, because I have always, always, with very few exceptions, bought the generic brands even when we are not in a recession," says Moore, a native of Fayetteville, Arkansas. She thinks that store brands are of pretty much the same quality as national brands. And her private-label grocery savings help her two children, 11 and 9, and husband do other things. "It might only be 50 cents, but 50 cents is 50 cents," Moore says. The family saves their change in jars, then uses the money at the end of the month to see a movie or have a restaurant meal.

These days, more and more consumers are joining Moore's way of thinking. Already on the rise over the past decade, "the popularity of store brands has soared recently as the economy tanked, with shoppers looking to stretch their dollars," says one analyst. Notes another, "Bad times are good times for private labels . . . as consumers become more price-conscious, they also become less brand conscious." From trying cheaper laundry detergents to slipping on a more affordable pair of jeans, Americans are changing their spending habits to save money. That often means abandoning brand-name products in favor of store brands.

It seems that almost every retailer now carries its own store brands. Wal-Mart's private brands account for a whopping 40 percent of its sales: brands such as Great Value food products; Sam's Choice beverages; Equate pharmacy, health, and beauty products; White Cloud brand toilet tissue and diapers; Simple Elegance laundry products; and Canopy outdoor home products. Its private label brands alone generate nearly twice the sales of all P&G brands combined, and Great Value is the nation's largest single food brand. At the other end of the spectrum, even upscale retailer Saks Fifth Avenue carries its own clothing line, which features $98 men's ties, $200 halter-tops, and $250 cotton dress shirts.

▲The popularity of store brands has soared recently. Wal-Mart's store brands account for a whopping 40 percent of its sales, and its Great Value brand is the nation's largest single food brand.

Once known as "generic" or "no-name" brands, today's store brands are shedding their image as cheap knockoffs of national brands. Store brands now offer much greater selection and they are rapidly achieving name-brand quality. In fact, retailers such as Target and Trader Joe's are out-innovating many of their national-brand competitors. Rather than simply creating low-end generic brands that offer a low-price alternative to national brands, retailers are now moving toward higher-end private brands that boost both the store's revenues and its image.

As store brand selection and quality have improved, and as the recession put the brakes on spending, consumers have shown an ever-increasing openness to store brands. Some 40 percent of U.S. consumers now identify themselves as frequent store-brand buyers, up from just 12 percent in the early

Licensing. Most manufacturers take years and spend millions to create their own brand names. However, some companies license names or symbols previously created by other manufacturers, names of well-known celebrities, or characters from popular movies and books. For a fee, any of these can provide an instant and proven brand name.

Apparel and accessories sellers pay large royalties to adorn their products—from blouses to ties, and linens to luggage—with the names or initials of well-known fashion innovators such as Calvin Klein, Tommy Hilfiger, Gucci, or Armani. Sellers of children's products attach an almost endless list of character names to clothing, toys, school supplies, linens, dolls, lunch boxes, cereals, and other items. Licensed character names range from classics such as Sesame Street, Disney, Star Wars, the

1990s. And in a recent survey, 68 percent of consumers agreed that store brands "are usually extremely good value for the money." Some retail strategists predict that the slowdown in consumer spending could last for years. That fact, combined with increasingly aggressive, more marketing-savvy retailers, could push the private-label market to dizzying heights. The new consumer frugality could "lead to a 'downturn generation' that learns to scrimp and save permanently, including buying more private-label," says one strategist.

Does the surge in store brands spell doom for name-brand products? That's not likely. But what should national-brand marketers to do to thwart the growing competition from store brands? For starters, they need to sharpen their value propositions in these tougher economic times.

So far, many national brands have been fighting back with a variety of value pitches. Procter & Gamble recently rolled out campaigns for Pantene and Gillette, among others that stress the brand's bang for one's buck. Pantene positions itself as an affordable salon alternative. And Gillette Fusion claims that its pricey razor blades deliver "high-performance" shaves for "as little as a dollar a week." According to one P&G rep, that claim is meant to address an outdated notion about the brand. "Guys have consistently told us that they think our blades are costly, so reframing the true expense for them makes good sense." Faced with tighter-fisted consumers, other national brands have reacted by significantly repositioning themselves. For example, Unilever has integrated a value message into its recent campaign for Ragú. One print ad reads, "With Ragú and a pound of pasta, you can feed a family of four for less than four dollars. The perfect meal when your family is growing and the economy is shrinking."

Although such value pitches might work for now, long-term national-brand success requires continued investment in product innovation and brand marketing. In these lean times and beyond, rather than cheapening their products or lowering their prices, national brands need to distinguish themselves through superior customer value. For example, the Ragú value positioning emphasizes affordable quality rather than low prices. And when asked whether, in a weak economy, consumers aren't more concerned about lower prices (via store brands) than

brand purpose (via national brands), marketing consultant and former P&G global marketing chief Jim Stengel replied:

I don't think it's an either/or. I think great brands have a strong sense of their meaning, their ideals, their mission—and their ideas represent a tremendous value to consumers. [National brands] are very much in touch with consumers, and what's on their minds, and they communicate their value through that message. Those things done well actually create [both short-term value and long-term brand equity]. I think great brands have to tell their stories. They have to do great things . . . [bringing] joy, help, and service to people by making them laugh, giving them an idea, or solving a problem. If they do that, [more than survive in down times, national brands will thrive].

So, even when the economic pendulum swings downward, national brand marketers must remain true to their brand stories. "You can have a value proposition that accentuates good value, but you don't want to walk away from the core proposition of the brand," says one marketing executive. "That's the only thing you have to protect yourself" from private labels in the long run.

Even die-hard store-brand buyers like Melissa Moore would agree. Despite her penchant for private labels and the savings they yield, there are some national brands that she just has to buy. "Cheese is one of the things I have not switched. American cheese, I buy Borden," says Moore. She also buys Sunbeam bread—her family likes the soft texture that she hasn't been able to find in store-brand breads. Despite the tough times, Moore still finds many national brands well worth the higher price.

Sources: Excerpts adapted from Lana A. Flowers, "Consumers Turn to Private Labels in Down Economy," *Morning News (Arkansas),* February 20, 2009, www.nwaonline.net; Elaine Wong, "Foods OK, but Some Can't Stomach More Increases," *Brandweek,* January 5, 2009, p. 7; Elaine Wong, "Stengel: Private Label, Digital Change Game," *Brandweek,* April 13, 2009, pp. 7, 37. Also see Matthew Boyle, "Generics: Making Gains in the Shelf War," *BusinessWeek,* November 10, 2008, p. 62; Sarah Skidmore, "Wal-Mart Revamping Own Brand," *Cincinnati Enquirer,* March 17, 2009, accessed at http://news.cincinnati.com/article/20090317/BIZ/903170336/-1/TODAY; Jack Neff, "Private Label Winning Battle of Brands," *Advertising Age,* February 23, 2009, p. 1; and http://walmartstores.com/Video/?id=1305, November 2009.

Muppets, Scooby Doo, Hello Kitty, and Dr. Seuss characters to the more recent Dora the Explorer; Go, Diego, Go!; Little Einsteins; Hannah Montana; and High School Musical characters. And currently a number of top-selling retail toys are products based on television shows and movies, such as the Hannah Montana Malibu Beach House and the Bob the Builder Interactive Construction Site.

Name and character licensing has grown rapidly in recent years. Annual retail sales of licensed products worldwide have grown from only $4 billion in 1977 to $55 billion in 1987 and more than $187 billion today. Licensing can be a highly profitable business for many companies. ▲For example, Nickelodeon has developed a stable full of hugely popular characters, such as Dora the Explorer; Go, Diego, Go!; and SpongeBob SquarePants. Dora alone has generated more than $5.3 billion in retail

Most fashions only last a season.
These pants never go out of style.

RECORD BREAKING
SpongeBob SquarePants has become an enduring, revolutionary pop icon, inspiring nautical nonsense in millions of people worldwide while generating record-breaking ratings and retail sales.

NICKELODEON
SpongeBob
SQUAREPANTS

▲ **Licensing: Nickelodeon has developed a stable full of hugely popular characters—such as SpongeBob SquarePants—that generate billions of dollars of retail sales each year.**

Co-branding
The practice of using the established brand names of two different companies on the same product.

Line extension
Extending an existing brand name to new forms, colors, sizes, ingredients, or flavors of an existing product category.

sales in under five years. "When it comes to licensing its brands for consumer products, Nickelodeon has proved that it has the Midas touch," states a brand licensing expert.[37]

Co-branding. Although companies have been **co-branding** products for many years, there has been a recent resurgence in co-branding. Co-branding occurs when two established brand names of different companies are used on the same product. For example, financial services firms often partner with other companies to create co-branded credit cards, such as when Chase and United Airlines joined forces to create the Chase United Travel Card. Similarly, Costco teamed with mattress maker Stearns & Foster to market a line of Kirkland Signature by Stearns & Foster mattress sets. And Nike and Apple co-branded the Nike+iPod Sport Kit, which lets runners link their Nike shoes with their iPod Nanos to track and enhance running performance in real time. "Thanks to a unique partnership between Nike and Apple, your iPod Nano [or iPod Touch] becomes your coach. Your personal trainer. Your favorite workout companion."[38]

In most co-branding situations, one company licenses another company's well-known brand to use in combination with its own. Co-branding offers many advantages. Because each brand dominates in a different category, the combined brands create broader consumer appeal and greater brand equity. Co-branding also allows a company to expand its existing brand into a category it might otherwise have difficulty entering alone. For example, the Nike+iPod arrangement gives Apple a presence in the sports and fitness market. At the same time, it helps Nike to bring new value to its customers.

Co-branding also has limitations. Such relationships usually involve complex legal contracts and licenses. Co-branding partners must carefully coordinate their advertising, sales promotion, and other marketing efforts. Finally, when co-branding, each partner must trust that the other will take good care of its brand. For example, consider the marriage between Kmart and the Martha Stewart Everyday housewares brand. When Kmart declared bankruptcy before being acquired by Sears, it cast a shadow on the Martha Stewart brand. In turn, when Martha Stewart was convicted and jailed for illegal financial dealings, it created negative associations for Kmart. Finally, Kmart was further embarrassed when Martha Stewart Living Omnimedia recently struck major licensing agreements with Macy's, Lowe's, and Wal-Mart, announcing that it would separate from Kmart when the current contract ends in 2010. Thus, as one manager puts it, "Giving away your brand is a lot like giving away your child—you want to make sure everything is perfect."[39]

Brand Development

A company has four choices when it comes to developing brands (see ■ **Figure 7.6**). It can introduce *line extensions*, *brand extensions*, *multibrands*, or *new brands*.

Line Extensions. **Line extensions** occur when a company extends existing brand names to new forms, colors, sizes, ingredients, or flavors of an existing product cat-

■ **Figure 7.6** Brand Development Strategies

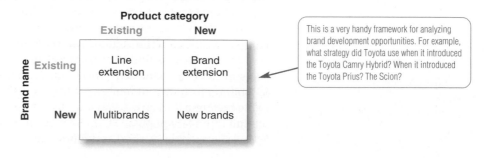

Product category

Brand name		Existing	New
	Existing	Line extension	Brand extension
	New	Multibrands	New brands

This is a very handy framework for analyzing brand development opportunities. For example, what strategy did Toyota use when it introduced the Toyota Camry Hybrid? When it introduced the Toyota Prius? The Scion?

egory. Thus, the Cheerios line of cereals includes Honey Nut, Frosted, Yogurt Burst, MultiGrain, Banana Nut, Yogurt Burst, and several other variations.

A company might introduce line extensions as a low-cost, low-risk way to introduce new products. Or it might want to meet consumer desires for variety, to use excess capacity, or simply to command more shelf space from resellers. However, line extensions involve some risks. An overextended brand name might lose its specific meaning. For example, you can now pick from an array of seven different Jeep SUV models—Commander, Grand Cherokee, Compass, Patriot, Liberty, Wrangler, and Wrangler Unlimited. It's unlikely that many customers will fully appreciate the differences across the many similar models, and such "Jeep creep" can cause consumer confusion or even frustration.

Another risk is that sales of an extension may come at the expense of other items in the line. For example, the original Doritos Tortilla Chips have now morphed into a full line of 20 different types and flavors of chips, including such high-decibel flavors as Blazin' Buffalo Ranch, Black Pepper Jack, and Fiery Habanero. Although the line seems to be doing well, the original Doritos chips seem like just another flavor. A line extension works best when it takes sales away from competing brands, not when it "cannibalizes" the company's other items.

Brand extension
Extending an existing brand name to new product categories.

Brand Extensions. A **brand extension** extends a current brand name to new or modified products in a new category. For example, Campbell Soup extended its V8 juice brand to a line of soups, creating "delicious ways to get your veggies while you please your palate." Victorinox extended its venerable Swiss Army brand from multitool knives to products ranging from cutlery and ballpoint pens to watches, luggage, and apparel. ▲And P&G has leveraged the strength of its Mr. Clean household cleaner brand to launch several new lines: cleaning pads (Magic Eraser), bathroom cleaning tools (Magic Reach), and home auto cleaning kits (Mr. Clean AutoDry). It even launched Mr. Clean-branded car washes.

A brand extension gives a new product instant recognition and faster acceptance. It also saves the high advertising costs usually required to build a new brand name. At the same time, a brand extension strategy involves some risk. Brand extensions such as Cheetos lip balm, Heinz pet food, and Life Savers gum met early deaths. The extension may confuse the image of the main brand. And if a brand extension fails, it may harm consumer attitudes toward the other products carrying the same brand name. Furthermore, a brand name may not be appropriate to a particular new product, even if it is well made and satisfying—would you consider flying on Hooters Air or wearing an Evian water-filled padded bra (both failed).

▲ Brand extensions: P&G has leveraged the strength of its Mr. Clean brand to launch new lines, including Mr. Clean-branded car washes.

Each year, a survey by brand consultancy TippingSprung rates the year's best and worst brand extensions. The most recent poll gave a strong thumbs-up to extensions such as Coppertone sunglasses, Mr. Clean car washes, Zagat physician ratings, and Thin Mint Cookie Blizzard (Girl Scout-inspired treat at Dairy Queen). Among the worst extensions—those that least fit the brand's core values—were Burger King men's apparel, Playboy energy drink, Allstate Green insurance, Kellogg's hip-hop streetwear. "Marketers have come to learn that the potential harm inflicted on the brand can more than offset short-term revenue opportunities," says TippingSprung cofounder Robert Sprung. "But that doesn't seem to stop many from launching extensions that in retrospect seem questionable or even ludicrous." Thus, companies that are tempted to transfer a brand name must research how well the brand's associations fit the new product.[40]

Multibrands. Companies often market many different brands in a given product category. For example, in the United States, P&G sells six brands of laundry detergent (Tide, Cheer, Gain, Era, Dreft, and Ivory), five brands of shampoo (Pantene, Head & Shoulders, Aussie, Herbal Essences, and Infusium 23); and four brands of dishwashing detergent (Dawn, Ivory, Joy, and Cascade). *Multibranding* offers a way to establish different features that appeal to different customer segments, lock up more reseller shelf space, and capture a larger market share. For example, P&G's six brands combined capture a whopping 62 percent of the U.S. laundry detergent market.

A major drawback of multibranding is that each brand might obtain only a small market share, and none may be very profitable. The company may end up spreading its resources over many brands instead of building a few brands to a highly profitable level. These companies should reduce the number of brands they sell in a given category and set up tighter screening procedures for new brands. This happened to GM, which in recent years has cut numerous brands from its portfolio, including Saturn, Oldsmobile, Pontiac, Hummer, and Saab.

New Brands. A company might believe that the power of its existing brand name is waning and a new brand name is needed. Or it may create a new brand name when it enters a new product category for which none of the company's current brand names are appropriate. For example, Toyota created the separate Scion brand, targeted toward Millennial consumers.

As with multibranding, offering too many new brands can result in a company spreading its resources too thin. And in some industries, such as consumer packaged goods, consumers and retailers have become concerned that there are already too many brands, with too few differences between them. Thus, P&G, Frito-Lay, Kraft, and other large consumer-product marketers are now pursuing *megabrand* strategies—weeding out weaker or slower-growing brands and focusing their marketing dollars only on brands that can achieve the number-one or number-two market share positions with good growth prospects in their categories.

Managing Brands

Companies must manage their brands carefully. First, the brand's positioning must be continuously communicated to consumers. Major brand marketers often spend huge amounts on advertising to create brand awareness and to build preference and loyalty. For example, Verizon spends more than $3.7 billion annually to promote its brand. McDonald's spends more than $1.2 billion.[41]

▼Managing brands requires managing "touch points." Says a former Disney executive: "A brand is a living entity, and it is enriched or undermined cumulatively over time, the product of a thousand small gestures."

Such advertising campaigns can help to create name recognition, brand knowledge, and maybe even some brand preference. However, the fact is that brands are not maintained by advertising but by the customers' *brand experiences*. Today, customers come to know a brand through a wide range of contacts and touch points. These include advertising, but also personal experience with the brand, word of mouth, company Web pages, and many others. The company must put as much care into managing these touch points as it does into producing its ads. "Managing each customer's experience is perhaps the most important ingredient in building [brand] loyalty," states one branding expert. "Every memorable interaction . . . must be completed with excellence and . . . must reinforce your brand essence." ▲A former Disney executive agrees: "A brand is a living entity, and it is enriched or undermined cumulatively over time, the product of a thousand small gestures."[42]

The brand's positioning will not take hold fully unless everyone in the company lives the brand. Therefore the company needs to train its people to be customer centered. Even better, the company should carry on internal brand building to help employees understand and be enthusiastic about the

brand promise. Many companies go even further by training and encouraging their distributors and dealers to serve their customers well.

Finally, companies need to periodically audit their brands' strengths and weaknesses.[43] They should ask: Does our brand excel at delivering benefits that consumers truly value? Is the brand properly positioned? Do all of our consumer touch points support the brand's positioning? Do the brand's managers understand what the brand means to consumers? Does the brand receive proper, sustained support? The brand audit may turn up brands that need more support, brands that need to be dropped, or brands that must be rebranded or repositioned because of changing customer preferences or new competitors.

REST STOP
REVIEWING THE CONCEPTS

A product is more than a simple set of tangible features. Each product or service offered to customers can be viewed on three levels. The *core customer value* consists of the core problem-solving benefits that consumers seek when they buy a product. The *actual product* exists around the core and includes the quality level, features, design, brand name, and packaging. The *augmented product* is the actual product plus the various services and benefits offered with it, such as a warranty, free delivery, installation, and maintenance.

> **Objective 1** Define *product* and the major classifications of products and services.
> **(pp 236–241)**

Broadly defined, a *product* is anything that can be offered to a market for attention, acquisition, use, or consumption that might satisfy a want or need. Products include physical objects but also services, events, persons, places, organizations, ideas, or mixes of these entities. *Services* are products that consist of activities, benefits, or satisfactions offered for sale that are essentially intangible, such as banking, hotel, tax preparation, and home-repair services.

Products and services fall into two broad classes based on the types of consumers that use them. *Consumer products*—those bought by final consumers—are usually classified according to consumer shopping habits (convenience products, shopping products, specialty products, and unsought products). *Industrial products*—purchased for further processing or for use in conducting a business—include materials and parts, capital items, and supplies and services. Other marketable entities—such as organizations, persons, places, and ideas—can also be thought of as products.

> **Objective 2** Describe the decisions companies make regarding their individual products and services, product lines, and product mixes. **(pp 242–249)**

Individual product decisions involve product attributes, branding, packaging, labeling, and product support services. *Product attribute* decisions involve product quality, features, and style and design. *Branding* decisions include selecting a brand name and developing a brand strategy. *Packaging* provides many key benefits, such as protection, economy, convenience, and promotion. Package decisions often include designing *labels*, which identify, describe, and possibly promote the product. Companies also develop *product support services* that enhance customer service and satisfaction and safeguard against competitors.

Most companies produce a product line rather than a single product. A *product line* is a group of products that are related in function, customer-purchase needs, or distribution channels. *Line stretching* involves extending a line downward, upward, or in both directions to occupy a gap that might otherwise be filled by a competitor. In contrast, *line filling* involves adding items within the present range of the line. All product lines and items offered to customers by a particular seller make up the *product mix*. The mix can be described by four dimensions: width, length, depth, and consistency. These dimensions are the tools for developing the company's product strategy.

> **Objective 3** Identify the four characteristics that affect the marketing of services and the additional marketing considerations that services require.
> **(pp 249–255)**

Services are characterized by four key characteristics: they are *intangible, inseparable, variable,* and *perishable*. Each characteristic poses problems and marketing requirements. Marketers work to find ways to make the service more tangible, to increase the productivity of providers who are inseparable from their products, to standardize the quality in the face of variability, and to improve demand movements and supply capacities in the face of service perishability.

Good service companies focus attention on *both* customers and employees. They understand the *service-profit chain*, which links service firm profits with employee and customer satisfaction. Services marketing strategy calls not only for external marketing but also for *internal marketing* to motivate employees and *interactive marketing* to create service delivery skills among service providers. To succeed, service marketers must create *competitive differentiation*, offer high *service quality*, and find ways to increase *service productivity*.

> **Objective 4** Discuss branding strategy—the decisions companies make in building and managing their brands. **(pp 256–265)**

Some analysts see brands as *the* major enduring asset of a company. Brands are more than just names and symbols—they embody everything that the product or service *means* to consumers. *Brand equity* is the positive differential effect that knowing the brand name has on customer response to the product or service. A brand with strong brand equity is a very valuable asset.

In building brands, companies need to make decisions about brand positioning, brand name selection, brand sponsorship, and brand development. The most powerful *brand positioning* builds around strong consumer beliefs and values. *Brand name selection* involves finding the best brand name based on a careful review of product benefits, the target market, and proposed marketing strategies. A manufacturer has four *brand sponsorship* options: it can launch a *national brand* (or manufacturer's brand), sell to resellers who use a *private brand*, market *licensed brands*, or join forces with another company to *co-brand* a product. A company also has four choices when it comes to developing brands. It can introduce *line extensions*, *brand extensions*, *multibrands*, or *new brands*.

Companies must build and manage their brands carefully. The brand's positioning must be continuously communicated to consumers. Advertising can help. However, brands are not maintained by advertising but by the customers' *brand experiences*. Customers come to know a brand through a wide range of contacts and interactions. The company must put as much care into managing these touch points as it does into producing its ads. Companies must periodically audit their brands' strengths and weaknesses. In some cases, brands may need to be repositioned because of changing customer preferences or new competitors.

Navigating the Key Terms

Objective 1
Product (p 237)
Service (p 237)
Consumer product (p 238)
Convenience product (p 239)
Shopping product (p 239)
Specialty product (p 239)
Unsought product (p 239)
Industrial product (p 240)
Social marketing (p 241)

Objective 2
Product quality (p 242)
Brand (p 243)
Packaging (p 245)
Product line (p 247)
Product mix (product portfolio) (p 248)

Objective 3
Service intangibility (p 249)
Service inseparability (p 250)
Service variability (p 250)

Service perishability (p 250)
Service-profit chain (p 251)
Internal marketing (p 253)
Interactive marketing (p 253)

Objective 4
Brand equity (p 256)
Store brand (private brand) (p 259)
Co-branding (p 262)
Line extension (p 262)
Brand extension (p 263)

Travel Log

Discussing the Issues

1. Define *product* and the three levels of product. (AACSB: Communication)

2. Name and describe the three groups of industrial products. How do industrial products differ from consumer products? (AACSB: Communication; Reflective Thinking)

3. What is a brand? How does branding help both buyers and sellers? (AACSB: Communication)

4. Discuss the four special characteristics of services. How do the services offered by a doctor's office differ from those offered by a bank in terms of these characteristics? (AACSB: Communication, Reflective Thinking)

5. Why is a brand a powerful asset of an organization? How does a strong brand provide a competitive advantage for a company? (AACSB: Communication)

6. Compare and contrast the four brand sponsorship options available to a manufacturer. Provide an example of each. (AACSB: Communication)

Application Questions

1. The Coca-Cola Company produces concentrate, which is then sold to various licensed Coca-Cola bottlers throughout the world. The bottlers, who hold territorially exclusive contracts with the company, produce the finished product in cans and bottles from the concentrate in combination with filtered water and sweeteners. Visit your national Coca-Cola Web site and examine the list of brands. Name and define the four dimensions of a company's product mix and describe Coca-Cola's product mix on these dimensions. (AACSB: Communication; Reflective Thinking; Use of IT)

2. In a small group, brainstorm five different names for a new brand of energy drink. Evaluate each name using the desirable qualities for a brand name described in the chapter. (AACSB: Communication; Reflective Thinking)

3. Many retailers have their own private-label brands. What does this mean, and are the brands too powerful a force in marketing? (AACSB: Communication; Reflective Thinking)

Under the Hood: Marketing Technology

The home-based telephone is about to undergo a drastic transformation. That's because new *media phones* will change the way we use, or don't use, home telephones. The new media phones are broadband media devices heralded as the 4th screen—the other three screens are the TV, the PC, and mobile handsets. These devices will deliver Internet-based information and entertainment at your fingertips by combining the power of a PC with the functionality of the "always on" home telephone. With a simple touch, you will be able to order a pizza, get the weather forecast, find the perfect recipe, watch a YouTube video, and, oh yeah, make a phone call. That call will be delivered through VoIP technology, which stands for Voice over Internet Protocol. Forecasters predict that 20 to 50 million households will adopt this technology by 2013, depending on whether service providers subsidize the cost of the new media phone devices. There is a substantial business market for media phones as well. They will be found in offices and hotel rooms around the world. Search the Internet or visit www.instat.com/promos/09/media_phone.asp and www.intel.com/embedded/15billion/applications/transforming-the- home-phone.htm to learn more about such devices.

1. What classification of consumer and industrial product best describes the media phone? Explain your choices. (AACSB: Communication; Reflective Thinking)

2. Chapter 5 described the product characteristics influencing the rate of new product adoption. Review these factors and discuss how each factor will influence the rate of adoption of the new media phones. (AACSB: Communication; Reflective Thinking)

Staying on the Road: Marketing Ethics

You may be using a book you purchased or borrowed from another student. People sell or share books all the time, but not if you purchased an e-book! With the growth of electronic readers, such as Amazon.com's Kindle, buying electronic books is easy and growing in popularity, with sales close to $120 million in 2008. But purchasers of e-books don't have the same rights as those purchasing physical books. Some consumers found out that it is just as easy for sellers to take them back as it is for buyers to get them. For instance, Amazon.com realized it did not have the proper rights to sell certain books—such as George Orwell's *1984*—and used its wireless technology to delete them from its customers' Kindle e-readers. While purchases were refunded, some called the company an Orwellian "Big Brother" because the deletion was done without their knowledge. Imagine if you purchased *1984* and tried to read it right before the test only to learn it had disappeared from your Kindle. Owning an e-book is much like licensing software with digital rights management software embedded to prevent sharing and selling. Such digital rights management software also confuses consumers and limits the number of devices that can play a single e-book.

1. How would you classify e-books—a tangible good, an experience, or a service? Explain your choice. (AACSB: Communication; Reflective Thinking)

2. Amazon.com had the legal right to delete e-books from the Kindle, but did the company do it the right way? Also, should consumers be able to do whatever they want with an e-book once they purchase it, just as they can with a tangible book? (AACSB: Communication; Ethical Reasoning)

Rough Road Ahead: Marketing and the Economy

Batteries Plus

A retail store that only sells batteries? That might sound like a surefire product flop in any economy. But weak economic conditions have given a major jolt to Batteries Plus, the nation's first and largest all-battery franchise operation. Its current same-store sales are up a whopping 20 percent from one year ago. What's the secret to this chain's success? Demand for the products and services it sells come from products that maintain high consumption patterns regardless of economic conditions. Specifically, no matter what the economy, people and businesses alike still use their laptops, mp3 players, digital cameras, PDAs, camcorders, and even vehicles. And all these necessary items need battery power. In fact, as people hold onto their devices longer instead of replacing them, that's all the better for Batteries Plus. As older batteries lose their ability to hold a charge, consumers head to Batteries Plus for replacements. This dynamic has made Batteries Plus one of the top franchise opportunities in the United States. People may cut back on luxuries, but demand for batteries is here to stay.

1. Based on derived demand principles—as in the nature of demand for Batteries Plus's market offering—what other businesses should do well in a weak economy?

2. If Batteries Plus does nothing, it still does well in an economic downturn. What recommendations would you make to Batteries Plus to take even better advantage of such conditions?

Travel Budget: Marketing by the Numbers

A business has introduced a new confectionary brand that comes in flavors such as mint chocolate, mocha, chocolate almond, and raspberry-almond with white chocolate. The confections are wrapped in iridescent colors and sold in reclosable cartons. The business also intends to do this with its other, already established brands. The new products carry a higher wholesale price for the company ($0.48 per ounce versus $0.30 per ounce for the original product). They also come with higher variable costs ($0.35 per ounce versus $0.15 per ounce for the original product).

1. What brand development strategy is this business undertaking?

2. Assume the company expects to sell 300 million ounces of the new product within the first year following its introduction. However, half of those sales are expected to come from buyers who would normally purchase the company's original brand. In other words, the new product will cannibalize some of the old product's sales. Assume the company normally sells 1 billion ounces per year of its original product, and it will incur an increase in fixed costs of $5 million during the first year it produces the new brand. Will the new product be profitable for the company? Refer to the discussion of cannibalization in Appendix 2: Marketing by the Numbers for an explanation regarding how to conduct this analysis.

Drive In: Video Case

Swiss Army

It seems appropriate that Swiss Army Brands, maker of multifunction knives, has become a multiproduct brand. The original company dates back to the late 1800s as a small, family-owned cutlery company. After WWII, the fascination that American GIs had with the multifunction pocket knives of their Swiss ally soldiers led to tremendous growth and expansion. Initially, this meant many different variations of the standard Swiss Army Knife that included such applications as fishing, golf, and an accessory for women's purses.

The popularity of the Swiss Army Knife has enabled the company to expand into all manner of consumer goods including watches, luggage, apparel, and other lines. These brand extensions have been based on consumer research to ensure that each fits within the concept that consumers hold for the brand. The success that Swiss Army Brands has achieved through expansion has even allowed it to open its own retail stores.

After viewing the video featuring Swiss Army Brands, answer the following questions about product and branding strategies.

1. What additional products and lines might Swiss Army Brands consider?

2. How do brand extensions affect a company such as Swiss Army Brands, in both positive and neative ways?

3. Why did Swiss Army Brands open retail stores? How do these stores help the company build its brand?

8

Developing
New Products

and Managing the Product Life-Cycle

ROAD MAP

Previewing the Concepts

In the previous chapter, you learned how marketers manage and develop products and brands. In this chapter, we'll look into two additional product topics: developing new products and managing products through their life cycles. New products are the lifeblood of an organization. However, new-product development is risky, and many new products fail. So, the first part of this chapter lays out a process for finding and growing successful new products. Once introduced, marketers want their products to enjoy long and happy lives. In the second part of the chapter, you'll see that every product passes through several life-cycle stages and that each stage poses new challenges requiring different marketing strategies and tactics. Finally, we'll wrap up our product discussion by looking at two additional considerations, social responsibility in product decisions and international product and services marketing.

Objective Outline

 Objective 1   Explain how companies find and develop new-product ideas.
New-Product Development Strategy **pp 272–273**

 Objective 2   List and define the steps in the new-product development process and the major considerations in managing this process.
The New-Product Development Process **pp 273–281**
Managing New-Product Development **pp 281–285**

 Objective 3   Describe the stages of the product life cycle and how marketing strategies change during the product's life cycle.
Product Life-Cycle Strategies **pp 285–292**

 Objective 4   Discuss two additional product issues: socially responsible product decisions and international product and services marketing.
Additional Product and Service Considerations
pp 292–295

▲ Google is spectacularly successful and wildly innovative. Ask the folks who work there and they'll tell you that innovation is more than just a process—it's in the air, in the spirit of the place.

For openers, consider Google, one of the world's most innovative companies. Google seems to come up with an almost unending flow of knock-your-eye-out new technologies and services. If it has to do with finding, refining, or using information, there's probably an innovative Google solution for it. At Google, innovation isn't just a process, it's in the very spirit of the place.

First Stop

Google: Innovation at the Speed of Light

Google is wildly innovative. It recently topped *Fast Company* magazine's list of the world's most innovative companies, and it regularly ranks among everyone else's top two or three innovators. Google is also spectacularly successful. Despite formidable competition from giants such as Microsoft and Yahoo!, Google's share in its core business—online search—has climbed to a decisive 63 percent, twice the combined market share of its two closest competitors. The company also captures more than 70 percent of all U.S. search-related advertising revenues.

But Google has grown to become much more than just an Internet search and advertising company. Google's mission is "to organize the world's information and make it universally accessible and useful." In Google's view, information is a kind of natural resource, one to be mined and refined and universally distributed. That idea unifies what would otherwise appear to be a widely diverse set of Google projects, such as mapping the world, searching the Web on a cell-phone screen, or even providing for early detection of flu epidemics. If it has to do with harnessing and using information, Google's got it covered in some new innovative way.

Google knows how to innovate. At many companies, new-product development is a cautious, step-by-step affair that might take a year or two to unfold. In contrast, Google's freewheeling new-product development process moves at the speed of light. The nimble innovator implements major new services in less time than it takes competitors to refine and approve an initial idea. For example, a Google senior project manager describes the lightning-quick development of iGoogle, Google's customizable home page:

> It was clear to Google that there were two groups [of Google users]: people who loved the site's clean, classic look and people who wanted tons of information there—e-mail, news, local weather. [For those who wanted a fuller home page,] iGoogle started out with me and three engineers. I was 22, and I thought, "This is awesome." Six weeks later, we launched the first version in May. The happiness metrics were good, there was healthy growth, and by September, we had [iGoogle fully operational with] a link on Google.com.

Such fast-paced innovation would boggle the minds of product developers at most other companies, but at Google its standard operating procedure. "That's what we do," says Google's VP for Search Products and User Experience. "The

Google's famously chaotic innovation process has unleashed a seemingly unending flurry of diverse new products. But at Google, innovation is more than a process. It's part of the company's DNA. "Where does innovation happen at Google? It happens everywhere."

1545 CHARLESTON ROAD B47

▲ Google tops almost every list of the world's most innovative companies.

hardest part about indoctrinating people into our culture is when engineers show me a prototype and I'm like, 'Great, let's go!' They'll say, 'Oh, no, it's not ready.' I tell them, 'The Googly thing is to launch it early on Google Labs [a site where users can try out experimental Google applications] and then to iterate, learning what the market wants—and making it great." Adds a Google engineering manager, "We set an operational tempo: When in doubt, do something. If you have two paths and you're not sure which is right, take the fastest path."

According to Google CEO Eric Schmidt, when it comes to new-product development at Google, there are no two-year plans. The company's new-product planning looks ahead only four to five months. Schmidt says that he would rather see projects fail quickly, than see a carefully planned, long drawn-out project fail.

Google's famously chaotic innovation process has unleashed a seemingly unending flurry of diverse products, ranging from an e-mail service (Gmail), a blog search engine (Google Blog Search), an online payment service (Google Checkout), and a photo sharing service (Google Picasa) to a universal platform for mobile-phone applications (Google Android), a cloud-friendly Web browser (Chrome), projects for mapping and exploring the world (Google Maps and Google Earth); and even an early-warning system for flu outbreaks in your area (FluTrends). Google claims that FluTrends has identified outbreaks two weeks sooner than has the U.S. Centers for Disease Control and Prevention.

Google is open to new-product ideas from about any source. What ties it all together is the company's passion for helping people find and use information. Innovation is the responsibility of every Google employee. Google engineers are encouraged to spend 20 percent of their time developing their own new-product ideas. And all new Google ideas are quickly tested in beta form by the ultimate judges—those who will use them. According to one observer:

> Any time you cram some 20,000 of the world's smartest people into one company, you can expect to grow a garden of unrelated ideas. Especially when you give some of those geniuses one workday a week—Google's famous "20 percent time"—to work on whatever projects fan their passions. And especially when you create Google Labs (www.googlelabs.com), a Web site where the public can kick the tires on half-baked Google creations. Some Labs projects go on to become real Google services, and others are quietly snuffed out.

In the end, at Google, innovation is more than a process—it's part of the company's DNA. "Where does innovation happen at Google? It happens everywhere," says a Google research scientist.

> Talk to Googlers at various levels and departments, and one powerful theme emerges: Whether they're designing search engines for the blind or preparing meals for their colleagues, these people feel that their work can change the world. The marvel of Google is its ability to continue to instill a sense of creative fearlessness and ambition in its employees. Prospective hires are often asked, "If you could change the world using Google's resources, what would you build?" But here, this isn't a goofy or even theoretical question: Google wants to know, because thinking—and building—on that scale is what Google does. This, after all, is the company that wants to make available online every page of every book ever published. Smaller-gauge ideas die of disinterest. When it comes to innovation, Google *is* different. But the difference isn't tangible. It's in the air, in the spirit of the place.[1]

*a*s the Google story suggests, companies that excel at developing and managing new products reap big rewards. Every product seems to go through a life cycle—it is born, goes through several phases, and eventually dies as newer products come along that create new or greater value for customers.

This product life cycle presents two major challenges: First, because all products eventually decline, a firm must be good at developing new products to replace aging ones (the challenge of *new-product development*). Second, the firm must be good at adapting its marketing strategies in the face of changing tastes, technologies, and competition as products pass through life-cycle stages (the challenge of *product life-cycle strategies*). We first look at the problem of finding and developing new products and then at the problem of managing them successfully over their life cycles.

Author Comment ≫
New products are the lifeblood of a company. As old products mature and fade away, companies must develop new ones to take their place. For example, only eight years after it unveiled its first iPod, 44 percent of Apple's revenues come from iPods, iPhones, and iTunes.

NEW-PRODUCT DEVELOPMENT STRATEGY (pp 272–273)

A firm can obtain new products in two ways. One is through *acquisition*—by buying a whole company, a patent, or a license to produce someone else's product. The other is through the firm's own **new-product development** efforts. By *new products* we mean original products, product improvements, product modifications, and new brands that the firm develops through its own research-and-development (R&D) efforts. In this chapter, we concentrate on new-product development.

New-product development
The development of original products, product improvements, product modifications, and new brands through the firm's own product-development efforts.

New products are important—to both customers and the marketers who serve them. For customers, they bring new solutions and variety to their lives. For companies, new products are a key source of growth. Even in a down economy, companies must continue to innovate. New products provide new ways to connect with customers as they adapt their buying to the changing economic times. Bad times are "when winners and losers get created," says Xerox CEO Anne Mulcahy. "The ability to reinforce great marketing and great brand is extraordinarily important." John Hayes, CEO of American Express, agrees: "The world will pass you by if you are not constantly innovating."[2]

Yet innovation can be very expensive and very risky. New products face tough odds. According to one estimate, 80 percent of all new products fail or dramatically underperform. Each year, companies lose an estimated $20 billion to $30 billion on failed food products alone.[3]

Why do so many new products fail? There are several reasons. Although an idea may be good, the company may overestimate market size. The actual product may be poorly designed. Or it might be incorrectly positioned, launched at the wrong time, priced too high, or poorly advertised. A high-level executive might push a favorite idea despite poor marketing research findings. Sometimes the costs of product development are higher than expected, and sometimes competitors fight back harder than expected. However, the reasons behind some new-product failures seem pretty obvious. Try the following on for size:[4]

▲The NewProductWorks Showcase highlights both successful new products and abject flops. Each flop represents squandered hopes and dollars. "What were they thinking?"

▲Strolling the aisles of the NewProductWorks collection at GfK Strategic Innovation's Resource Center is like finding yourself in a new-product history museum. Many of the more than 110,000 products on display were quite successful. Others, however, were abject flops. Behind each of these flops are squandered dollars and hopes and the classic question, "What were they thinking?" Some products failed because they simply failed to bring value to customers—for example, Look of Buttermilk Shampoo, Cucumber antiperspirant spray, or Premier smokeless cigarettes. *Smokeless* cigarettes? What were they thinking? Other companies failed because they attached trusted brand names to something totally out of character. Can you imagine swallowing Ben-Gay aspirin? Or how about Gerber Singles food for adults (perhaps the tasty pureed sweet-and-sour pork or chicken Madeira)? Other misbegotten attempts to stretch a good name include Cracker Jack cereal, Exxon fruit punch, Smucker's premium ketchup, Fruit of the Loom laundry detergent, and Harley-Davidson cake-decorating kits. Really, what were they thinking?

Author Comment 》》
Companies can't just hope that they'll stumble across good new products. Instead, they must develop a systematic new-product development process.

THE NEW-PRODUCT DEVELOPMENT PROCESS (pp 273–281)

Companies face a problem—they must develop new products, but the odds weigh heavily against success. In all, to create successful new products, a company must understand its consumers, markets, and competitors and develop products that deliver superior value to customers. It must carry out strong new-product planning and set up a systematic, customer-driven *new-product development process* for finding and growing new products. ■ **Figure 8.1** shows the eight major steps in this process.

Idea Generation

Idea generation
The systematic search for new-product ideas.

New-product development starts with **idea generation**—the systematic search for new-product ideas. A company typically generates hundreds of ideas, even thousands, in order to find a few good ones. Major sources of new-product ideas include internal sources and external sources such as customers, competitors, distributors and suppliers, and others.

Internal Idea Sources

Using *internal sources*, the company can find new ideas through formal research and development. However, in one recent survey, 750 global CEOs reported that only 14 percent of their innovation ideas came from traditional R&D. Instead, 41 percent came from employees and 36 percent from customers.[5]

Thus, companies can pick the brains of employees—from executives to scientists, engineers, and manufacturing staff to salespeople. Using today's new Web 2.0 technology, many companies are making it everybody's business to come up with great ideas. For example, Internet networking company Cisco has set up an internal wiki called Idea Zone or I-Zone, through which any Cisco employee can propose an idea for a new product or comment on or modify someone else's proposed idea. Since its inception, I-Zone has generated hundreds of ideas. Cisco selects ideas that draw the most activity for further development. So far 12 I-Zone ideas have reached the project stage and four new Cisco business units have been formed.[6]

Some companies have developed successful "intrapreneurial" programs that encourage employees to think up and develop new-product ideas. ▲For example, Samsung built a special Value Innovation Program (VIP) Center in Suwon, South Korea, to encourage and support internal new-product innovation.

▲Internal new-product idea sources: Samsung built a special Value Innovation Program Center in which company researchers, engineers, and designers commingle to come up with creative new-product ideas.

The VIP Center is the total opposite of Samsung's typical office facilities—which feature gray computers on gray desks inside gray walls—where workers adhere to strict Confucian traditions and would never dream of questioning a superior or making a wacky suggestion. Instead, the VIP Center features workrooms, dorm rooms, training rooms, a kitchen, and a basement filled with games, a gym, and sauna. Grass sprouts from the ceilings, doors are covered with funhouse mirrors, and walls are covered with chalk drawings of ideas. Inside the center, Samsung researchers, engineers, and designers sport Viking and bumblebee hats, play with Elmo toys and inflatable dolphins, and throw around ideas without regard to rank. Recent ideas sprouting from the VIP Center include a 102-inch plasma HDTV and a process to reduce material costs on a multifunction printer by 30 percent. The center has helped Samsung, once known as the maker of cheap knock-off products, become one of the world's most innovative and profitable consumer electronics companies.[7]

External Idea Sources

Companies can also obtain good new-product ideas from any of a number of external sources. For example, *distributors and suppliers* can contribute ideas. Distributors are close to the market and can pass along information about consumer problems and new-product possibilities. Suppliers can tell the company about new concepts, techniques, and materials that can be used to develop new products.

New-product development starts with good new-product ideas—*lots* of them. For example, a recent IBM online "Innovation Jam" generated 46,000 ideas, of which IBM planned to develop only 10.

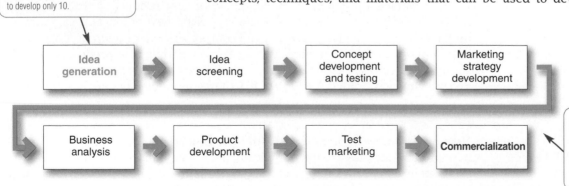

Idea generation → Idea screening → Concept development and testing → Marketing strategy development → Business analysis → Product development → Test marketing → **Commercialization**

Whereas the first step of this process generates a large number of new-product ideas, the remaining steps reduce that number and develop the best ideas into profitable products.

■ **Figure 8.1** Major Stages in New-Product Development

Competitors are another important source. Companies watch competitors' ads to get clues about their new products. They buy competing new products, take them apart to see how they work, analyze their sales, and decide whether they should bring out a new product of their own. Other idea sources include trade magazines, shows, and seminars; government agencies; advertising agencies; marketing research firms; university and commercial laboratories; and inventors.

Some companies seek the help of outside new-product consultancies and design firms, such as ZIBA for new-product ideas and designs. For example, when Cranium needed innovative new ideas for extending its popular family board game, it turned to award-winning design firm. A team of Cranium designers began with the core premise that the games should focus on laughter, togetherness, and creativity rather than competition. For inspiration, the team observed people who exemplified the Cranium characters—Word Worm, Creative Cat, Data Head, and Star Performer—and then tested prototypes in actual game-playing sessions with families. Based on customer insights gained from these observations and interactions, the Cranium team developed four popular new character-based games: Tune Twister (Star Performer), Super Showdown (Data Head), Doodle Tales (Creative Cat), and Wacky Words (Word Worm).[8]

Many companies are also turning to online collaborative communities to help solve new-product problems. For example, collaborative network InnoCentive puts its corporate clients ("seekers") in touch with its global network of more than 100,000 scientists ("solvers"). The seeker companies post "challenges," and solvers can earn up to $100,000 for providing solutions. For example, P&G wanted to create a dishwashing detergent smart enough to reveal when just the right amount of soap has been added to a sink full of dirty dishes. After seeing the problem posted on InnoCentive, an Italian chemist working from her home laboratory, Giorgia Sgargetta, solved the problem by creating a new kind of dye that turns dishwater blue when a certain amount of soap is added. Her reward: $30,000. P&G estimates that more than 50 percent of its new product innovations today have elements that originated outside the company, up from 15 percent in 2000.[9]

Perhaps the most important source of new-product ideas is *customers* themselves. The company can analyze customer questions and complaints to find new products that better solve consumer problems. For example, Staples developed its Easy Rebate program online in response to concerns expressed by small-business customers that lost paper rebates were one of their biggest frustrations.[10] Or a company can actively solicit ideas from customers. For example, Dell's IdeaStorm Web site asks consumers for insights on how to improve the company's product offering. Users post suggestions, the community votes, and the most popular ideas rise to the top. Since its launch in 2007, the site has received over 11,000 ideas and 650,000 votes.[11]

Customers often create new products and uses on their own, and companies can benefit by putting them on the market. For example, for years customers were spreading the word that Avon Skin-So-Soft bath oil and moisturizer was also a terrific bug repellent. Whereas some consumers were content simply to bathe in water scented with the fragrant oil, others carried it in their backpacks to mosquito-infested campsites or kept a bottle on the decks of their beach houses. Avon turned the idea into a complete line of Skin-So-Soft Bug Guard products, including Bug Guard Mosquito Repellant Moisturizing Towelettes and Bug Guard Plus, a combination moisturizer, insect repellent, and sunscreen.[12]

Finally, beyond simply gathering new products *from* customers, companies can work *with* customers to create new products. Through *customer co-creation,* companies involve customers directly in the innovation process in multiple ways at various points. ▲For example, the LEGO Group used customer co-creation to develop its most popular product ever, LEGO MINDSTORMS:[13]

The LEGO MINDSTORMS build-it-yourself robot was initially an internal effort in partnership with MIT. Within three weeks of its introduction, however, more than 1,000 intrigued customers formed their own Web community to outdo each other in making it

▲**Involving customers in the innovation process: The LEGO Group embraced customer co-creation in developing the MINDSTORMS build-it-yourself robot, its most successful product ever.**

Idea screening
Screening new-product ideas in order to spot good ideas and drop poor ones as soon as possible.

better. Rather than fight the idea of co-creation (as Sony did with its Robot Dog), the LEGO Group embraced it. The next generation of LEGO MINDSTORMS featured user-defined parts. Then, the LEGO Group made customer co-creation official by creating the MIND-STORMS Development Program (MDPs), through which it selected the most avid MINDSTORMS fans—100 pioneers, inventors, and innovators from across the globe—to play with LEGO MINDSTORMS and create innovative new features and applications. The MDP's share their ideas with other customers and invite feedback. The MINDSTORMS co-creation experience also spawned the LEGO Factory, where users can design products, create 3-D models on the Web, design packaging (which the LEGO Group will manage), and sell the products on the LEGO site.

Although customer input on new products yields many benefits, companies must be careful not to rely *too* heavily on what customers say. For some products, especially highly technical ones, customers may not know what they need. "You can't ask people what they want if it's around the next corner," says Apple founder and former CEO Steve Jobs. And even when they think they know what they want, adds an innovation management consultant, "Merely giving people what they want isn't always enough. People want to be surprised; they want something that's better than they imagined, something that stretches them in what they like."[14]

Finally, truly innovative companies don't rely only on one source or another for new product ideas. Instead, according to one expert, they create "extensive networks for capturing inspiration from every possible source, from employees at every walk of the company to customers to other innovators and myriad points beyond."[15]

Idea Screening

The purpose of idea generation is to create a large number of ideas. The purpose of the succeeding stages is to *reduce* that number. The first idea-reducing stage is **idea screening**, which helps spot good ideas and drop poor ones as soon as possible. Product development costs rise greatly in later stages, so the company wants to go ahead only with the product ideas that will turn into profitable products.

Many companies require their executives to write up new-product ideas in a standard format that can be reviewed by a new-product committee. The write-up describes the product or service, the proposed customer value proposition, the target market, and the competition. It makes some rough estimates of market size, product price, development time and costs, manufacturing costs, and rate of return. The committee then evaluates the idea against a set of general criteria.

One marketing expert proposes an R-W-W ("real, win, worth it") new-product screening framework that asks three questions. First, *Is it real?* Is there a real need and desire for the product and will customers buy it? Is there a clear product concept and will the product satisfy the market? Second, *Can we win?* Does the product offer a sustainable competitive advantage? Does the company have the resources to make the product a success? Finally, *Is it worth doing?* Does the product fit the company's overall growth strategy? Does it offer sufficient profit potential? The company should be able to answer yes to all three R-W-W questions before developing the new-product idea further.[16]

Concept Development and Testing

Product concept
A detailed version of the new-product idea stated in meaningful consumer terms.

An attractive idea must be developed into a **product concept**. It is important to distinguish between a product idea, a product concept, and a product image. A *product idea* is an idea for a possible product that the company can see itself offering to the market. A *product concept* is a detailed version of the idea stated in meaningful consumer terms. A *product image* is the way consumers perceive an actual or potential product.

▲This is Tesla's initial all-electric road-ster. Later, more-affordable mass-market models will travel more than 300 miles on a single charge, recharge in 45 minutes from a normal 120-volt electrical outlet, and cost about one penny per mile to power.

Concept Development

Suppose that a car manufacturer has developed a practical battery-powered all-electric car. ▲Its ini-tial prototype is a sleek, sporty roadster convert-ible that sells for about $100,000.[17] However, in the near future, it plans to introduce more-affordable, mass-market versions that will complete with to-day's hybrid-powered cars. This 100-percent car will accelerate from 0 to 60 in 5.6 seconds, travel more than 300 miles on a single charge, recharge in 45 minutes from a normal 120-volt electrical outlet, and cost about one penny per mile to power.

Looking ahead, the marketer's task is to develop this new product into alterna-tive product concepts, find out how attractive each concept is to customers, and choose the best one. It might create the following product concepts for the electric car:

- *Concept 1:* An affordably priced midsize car designed as a second family car to be used around town for running errands and visiting friends.
- *Concept 2:* A midpriced sporty compact appealing to young singles and couples.
- *Concept 3:* A "green" car appealing to environmentally conscious people who want practical, low-polluting transportation.
- *Concept 4:* A high-end midsize utility vehicle appealing to those who love the space SUVs provide but lament the poor gas mileage.

Concept Testing

Concept testing

Testing new-product concepts with a group of target consumers to find out if the concepts have strong consumer appeal.

Concept testing calls for testing new-product concepts with groups of target con-sumers. The concepts may be presented to consumers symbolically or physically. Here, in words, is concept 3:

> An efficient, fun-to-drive, battery-powered compact car that seats four. This 100-percent electric wonder provides practical and reliable transportation with no pollution. It goes more than 300 miles on a single charge and costs pennies per mile to operate. It's a sensi-ble, responsible alternative to today's pollution-producing gas-guzzlers. It's priced, fully equipped, at $25,000.

Many firms routinely test new-product concepts with consumers before at-tempting to turn them into actual new products. For some concept tests, a word or picture description might be sufficient. However, a more concrete and physical pres-entation of the concept will increase the reliability of the concept test. After being exposed to the concept, consumers then may be asked to react to it by answering questions such as those in ■ **Table 8.1**.

The answers to such questions will help the company decide which concept has the strongest appeal. For example, the last question asks about the consumer's in-tention to buy. Suppose 2 percent of consumers say they "definitely" would buy, and another 5 percent say "probably." The company could project these figures to the full population in this target group to estimate sales volume. Even then, the estimate is uncertain because people do not always carry out their stated intentions.

Marketing Strategy Development

Marketing strategy development

Designing an initial marketing strategy for a new product based on the product concept.

Suppose the carmaker finds that concept 3 for the fuel-cell-powered electric car tests best. The next step is **marketing strategy development**, designing an initial marketing strategy for introducing this car to the market.

The *marketing strategy statement* consists of three parts. The first part describes the target market; the planned value proposition; and the sales, market share, and profit goals for the first few years. Thus:

> The target market is younger, well-educated, moderate- to high-income individuals, cou-ples, or small families seeking practical, environmentally responsible transportation. The

■ Table 8.1   Questions for Battery-Powered Electric Car Concept Test

1. Do you understand the concept of a battery-powered electric car?
2. Do you believe the claims about the car's performance?
3. What are the major benefits of the battery-powered electric car compared with a conventional car?
4. What are its advantages compared with a gas-electric hybrid car?
5. What improvements in the car's features would you suggest?
6. For what uses would you prefer a battery-powered electric car to a conventional car?
7. What would be a reasonable price to charge for the car?
8. Who would be involved in your decision to buy such a car? Who would drive it?
9. Would you buy such a car (definitely, probably, probably not, definitely not)?

car will be positioned as more fun to drive and less polluting than today's internal combustion engine or hybrid cars. The company will aim to sell 50,000 cars in the first year, at a loss of not more than $15 million. In the second year, the company will aim for sales of 90,000 cars and a profit of $25 million.

The second part of the marketing strategy statement outlines the product's planned price, distribution, and marketing budget for the first year:

The battery-powered electric car will be offered in three colors—red, white, and blue—and will have a full set of accessories as standard features. It will sell at a retail price of $25,000—with 15 percent off the list price to dealers. Dealers who sell more than 10 cars per month will get an additional discount of 5 percent on each car sold that month. A marketing budget of $50 million will be split 50–50 between a national media campaign and local event marketing. Advertising and Web site will emphasize the car's fun spirit and low emissions. During the first year, $100,000 will be spent on marketing research to find out who is buying the car and their satisfaction levels.

The third part of the marketing strategy statement describes the planned long-run sales, profit goals, and marketing mix strategy:

We intend to capture a 3 percent long-run share of the total auto market and realize an after-tax return on investment of 15 percent. To achieve this, product quality will start high and be improved over time. Price will be raised in the second and third years if competition permits. The total marketing budget will be raised each year by about 10 percent. Marketing research will be reduced to $60,000 per year after the first year.

Business Analysis

Business analysis
A review of the sales, costs, and profit projections for a new product to find out whether these factors satisfy the company's objectives.

Once management has decided on its product concept and marketing strategy, it can evaluate the business attractiveness of the proposal. **Business analysis** involves a review of the sales, costs, and profit projections for a new product to find out whether they satisfy the company's objectives. If they do, the product can move to the product development stage.

To estimate sales, the company might look at the sales history of similar products and conduct market surveys. It can then estimate minimum and maximum sales to assess the range of risk. After preparing the sales forecast, management can estimate the expected costs and profits for the product, including marketing, R&D, operations, accounting, and finance costs. The company then uses the sales and costs figures to analyze the new product's financial attractiveness.

Product Development

Product development
Developing the product concept into a physical product in order to ensure that the product idea can be turned into a workable market offering.

So far, for many new-product concepts, the product may have existed only as a word description, a drawing, or perhaps a crude mock-up. If the product concept passes the business test, it moves into **product development**. Here, R&D or engineering develops the product concept into a physical product. The product development step, however, now calls for a large jump in investment. It will show whether the product idea can be turned into a workable product.

The R&D department will develop and test one or more physical versions of the product concept. R&D hopes to design a prototype that will satisfy and excite consumers and that can be produced quickly and at budgeted costs. Developing a successful prototype can take days, weeks, months, or even years depending on the product and prototype methods.

Often, products undergo rigorous tests to make sure that they perform safely and effectively, or that consumers will find value in them. Companies can do their own product testing or outsource testing to other firms that specialize in testing. Here's an example of such product tests:[18]

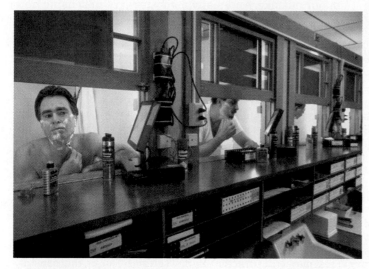

▲ **Product testing: Gillette uses employee-volunteers to test new shaving products— "We bleed so you'll get a good shave at home," says a Gillette employee.**

At Gillette, almost everyone gets involved in new-product testing. ▲Every working day at Gillette, 200 volunteers from various departments come to work unshaven, troop to the second floor of the company's gritty South Boston plant, and enter small booths with a sink and mirror. There they take instructions from technicians on the other side of a small window as to which razor, shaving cream, or aftershave to use. The volunteers evaluate razors for sharpness of blade, smoothness of glide, and ease of handling. In a nearby shower room, women perform the same ritual on their legs, underarms, and what the company delicately refers to as the "bikini area," as high-speed cameras snap thousands of frames per second to study how blades hit their skin for optimal hair removal. "We bleed so you'll get a good shave at home," says one Gillette employee.

A new product must have the required functional features and also convey the intended psychological characteristics. The battery-powered electric car, for example, should strike consumers as being well built, comfortable, and safe. Management must learn what makes consumers decide that a car is well built. To some consumers, this means that the car has "solid-sounding" doors. To others, it means that the car is able to withstand heavy impact in crash tests. Consumer tests are conducted in which consumers test-drive the car and rate its attributes.

Test Marketing

Test marketing
The stage of new-product development in which the product and marketing program are tested in realistic market settings.

If the product passes concept and product tests, the next step is **test marketing**, the stage at which the product and marketing program are introduced into realistic market settings. Test marketing gives the marketer experience with marketing the product before going to the great expense of full introduction. It lets the company test the product and its entire marketing program—targeting and positioning strategy, advertising, distribution, pricing, branding and packaging, and budget levels.

The amount of test marketing needed varies with each new product. Test marketing costs can be high, and it takes time that may allow competitors to gain advantages. When the costs of developing and introducing the product are low, or when management is already confident about the new product, the company may do little or no test marketing. In fact, test marketing by consumer-goods firms has been declining in recent years. Companies often do not test-market simple line extensions or copies of successful competitor products.

However, when introducing a new product requires a big investment, when the risks are high, or when management is not sure of the product or marketing program, a company may do a lot of test marketing. ▲For instance, KFC conducted more than three years of product and market testing before recently rolling out its major new Kentucky Grilled Chicken product. The fast-food chain built its legacy

▲ Test marketing: KFC test marketed its new Kentucky Grilled Chicken product for three years before rolling it out nationally. Says the chain's president, "We had to get it right."

on serving crispy, seasoned fried chicken but hopes that the new product will lure back health-conscious consumers who dropped fried chicken from their diets. "This is transformational for our brand," says KFC's chief food innovation officer. Given the importance of the decision, "You might say, 'what took you so long,'" says the chain's president. "I've asked that question a couple of times myself. The answer is we had to get it right."[19]

Although test-marketing costs can be high, they are often small when compared with the costs of making a major mistake. And many marketers are now using new simulated marketing technologies to reduce the costs of test marketing and to speed up the process. For example, Frito-Lay worked with research firm Decision Insight to create an online virtual convenience store in which to test new products and marketing ideas.[20]

Decision Insight's SimuShop online shopping environment lets Frito-Lay's marketers test shopper reactions to different extensions, shelf placements, pricing, and packaging of its Lay's, Doritos, Cheetos, and Fritos brands in a variety of store setups without investing huge amounts of time and money on actual in-store research in different locations. Recruited shoppers visit the online store, browse realistic virtual shelves featuring Frito-Lay's and competing products, click on individual products to view them in more detail, and select products to put in their carts. When the shopping is done, selected customers are questioned in one-on-one, on-screen interviews about why they chose the products they did. Watching the entire decision process unfold gives Frito-Lay marketers reams of information about what would happen in the real world. With 200-some bags of Frito-Lay products sitting on a typical store shelf, the company doesn't have the luxury of test marketing in actual market settings. "For us, that can only really be done virtually," says a Frito-Lay marketer. The SimuShop tests produce a 90 percent or better correlation to real shopper behavior when compared with later real-world data.

Commercialization

Commercialization
Introducing a new product into the market.

Test marketing gives management the information needed to make a final decision about whether to launch the new product. If the company goes ahead with **commercialization**—introducing the new product into the market—it will face high costs. The company may need to build or rent a manufacturing facility. And, in the case of a major new consumer package good, it may spend hundreds of millions of dollars for advertising, sales promotion, and other marketing efforts in the first year. For example, when Unilever introduced its Sunsilk hair care line, it spent an estimated $200 million in the United States alone, including $30 million for nontraditional media such as MySpace ads and profiles, mall displays that used audio to catch passersby, 3-D ads in tavern bathrooms, and cinema ads.[21]

The company launching a new product must first decide on introduction *timing*. If the carmaker's new battery-powered electric car will eat into the sales of the company's other cars, its introduction may be delayed. If the car can be improved further, or if the economy is down, the company may wait until the following year to launch it. However, if competitors are ready to introduce their own battery-powered models, the company may push to introduce its car sooner.

Next, the company must decide *where* to launch the new product—in a single location, a region, the national market, or the international market. Few companies have the confidence, capital, and capacity to launch new products into full national or international distribution right away. Instead, they develop a planned *market rollout* over time. For example, when Miller introduced Miller Chill, a lighter Mexican-style lager flavored with lime and salt, it started in selected southwestern states, such as Arizona, New Mexico, and Texas, supported by local TV commercials. Based on strong sales in these initial markets, the company then rolled out Miller Chill nationally, supported by $30 million worth of TV commercials, print ads, and a live in-show ad on *Late Night with Conan O'Brien*. Finally, based on the brand's U.S. success, Miller rolled out Miller Chill internationally, starting with Australia.[22]

Some companies, however, may quickly introduce new models into the full national market. Companies with international distribution systems may introduce new products through swift global rollouts. Microsoft did this with its Windows Vista operating system. Microsoft used a mammoth advertising blitz to launch Vista simultaneously in more than 30 markets worldwide.

MANAGING NEW-PRODUCT DEVELOPMENT (pp 281–285)

Author Comment »
Above all else, new-product development must focus on creating customer value. Says P&G's CEO about the company's new-product development: "We've figured out how to keep the consumer at the center of all our decisions. As a result, we don't go far wrong."

The new-product development process shown in Figure 8.1 highlights the important activities needed to find, develop, and introduce new products. However, new-product development involves more than just going through a set of steps. Companies must take a holistic approach to managing this process. Successful new-product development requires a customer-centered, team-based, and systematic effort.

Customer-Centered New-Product Development

Above all else, new-product development must be customer-centered. When looking for and developing new products, companies often rely too heavily on technical research in their R&D labs. But like everything else in marketing, successful new-product development begins with a thorough understanding of what consumers need and value. **Customer-centered new-product development** focuses on finding new ways to solve customer problems and create more customer-satisfying experiences.

Customer-centered new-product development
New-product development that focuses on finding new ways to solve customer problems and create more customer-satisfying experiences.

One study found that the most successful new products are ones that are differentiated, solve major customer problems, and offer a compelling customer value proposition. Another study showed that companies that directly engage their customers in the new-product innovation process had twice the return on assets and triple the growth in operating income of firms that don't.[23]

For example, whereas the consumer package goods industry's new-product success rate is only about 15 to 20 percent, P&G's success rate is over 50 percent. According to P&G CEO A.G. Lafley, the most important factor in this success is understanding what consumers want. In the past, says Lafley, P&G tried to push new products down to consumers rather than first understanding their needs. But now, P&G employs an immersion process it calls "Living It," in which researchers go so far as to live with shoppers for several days at a time to come up with product ideas based directly on consumer needs. P&Gers also hang out in stores for similar insights, a process they call "Working It." "We figured out how to keep the consumer at the center of all our decisions," says Lafley. "As a result, we don't go far wrong."[24]

For products ranging from consumer package goods to financial services, today's innovative companies are getting out of the research lab and mingling with customers in the search for new customer value. For example, when PNC Bank sought new digital services that would connect with high-tech Millennial consumers, it started by observing these consumers in their day-to-day lives:[25]

For three months, researchers and designers followed about 30 young consumers on their daily living paths and quizzed them on how they use their money, where they kept it, what they thought about it, and which mobile and online banking programs did they already use. Next, PNC Bank set up discussion groups made up of both consumers and company employees, who jointly brainstormed hundreds of ideas and then whittled

▲ **Customer-centered new-product development: Based on in-depth customer insights, PNC Bank's Virtual Wallet puts real-time money management at the fingertips of the Millennial generation.**

Team-based new-product development

An approach to developing new products in which various company departments work closely together, overlapping the steps in the product development process to save time and increase effectiveness.

them down to a few core ones. ▲ The result was PNC Bank's successful online real-time money management widget called Virtual Wallet. The digital tool combines three accounts—spend, save, and grow—into one high-definition deal. A Calendar feature provides daily to monthly monitoring of every bill and payment. The Money Bar slider lets young customers move money quickly between their spend and save accounts. The savings component offers a feature called "Punch the Pig," a fun, customizable widget that lets users click to transfer cash instantly into a high-yield savings account. And a "Danger Days" feature automatically warns of potential overspending. In all, based on in-depth consumer insights, PNC Bank's Virtual Wallet puts real-time money management at the fingertips of the Internet generation.

Thus, customer-centered new-product development begins and ends with solving customer problems (see Marketing at Work 8.1 for another great example). Successful innovation boils down to finding fresh ways to meet the needs of customers.

Team-Based New-Product Development

Good new-product development also requires a total-company, cross-functional effort. Some companies organize their new-product development process into the orderly sequence of steps shown in Figure 8.1, starting with idea generation and ending with commercialization. Under this *sequential product development* approach, one company department works individually to complete its stage of the process before passing the new product along to the next department and stage. This orderly, step-by-step process can help bring control to complex and risky projects. But it can also be dangerously slow. In fast-changing, highly competitive markets, such slow-but-sure product development can result in product failures, lost sales and profits, and crumbling market positions.

In order to get their new products to market more quickly, many companies use a **team-based new-product development** approach. Under this approach, company departments work closely together in cross-functional teams, overlapping the steps in the product development process to save time and increase effectiveness. Instead of passing the new product from department to department, the company assembles a team of people from various departments that stays with the new product from start to finish. Such teams usually include people from the marketing, finance, design, manufacturing, and legal departments, and even supplier and customer companies. In the sequential process, a bottleneck at one phase can seriously slow the entire project. In the team-based approach, if one area hits snags, it works to resolve them while the team moves on.

The team-based approach does have some limitations. For example, it sometimes creates more organizational tension and confusion than the more orderly sequential approach. However, in rapidly changing industries facing increasingly shorter product life cycles, the rewards of fast and flexible product development far exceed the risks. Companies that combine a customer-centered approach with team-based new-product development gain a big competitive edge by getting the right new products to market faster.

Systematic New-Product Development

Finally, the new-product development process should be holistic and systematic rather than compartmentalized and haphazard. Otherwise, few new ideas will surface, and many good ideas will sputter and die. To avoid these problems, a company can install an *innovation management system* to collect, review, evaluate, and manage new-product ideas.

Marketing at Work 8.1

BreadTalk's Revolutionary Approach to Selling Bread Meets Customers' Needs

Launched in Singapore in 2000, the bakery brand BreadTalk has come a long way since. As of 2009, BreadTalk boasts a total of 200 stores in 15 territories. What makes this appealing and fast-growing formula so special? It caters to a broad spectrum of tastes and couples great innovation with contemporary design.

The award-winning Singapore-based chain of boutique bakeries is already associated alongside very established icons such as Changi Airport and Singapore Airlines. Its efforts have also put itself on the international retail map at the World Retail Awards, the Oscars of the retail industry.

Starting with the bread, BreadTalk visualizes it as a piece of art. Dr. George Quek, the founder of BreadTalk, depicts that bread can talk to you. Each piece of bread is unique and has a voice that can be seen in the fun and intriguing stories behind it. BreadTalk creates some of the most unusual yet delicious bread varieties in Asia.

Not just any bread does the trick. Good bread makes people happy. And in order to ensure that its confections are just that, fresh bread is made around the clock at BreadTalk. Another key to keeping customers satisfied lies in the wide variety of bread available at the shop. On average, between 100 and 150 products are offered in each shop, comprising about 60 percent bread and 40 percent cakes.

The assortment is also innovative and in keeping with the times. Hiring some of the top master chefs, like legendary Japanese master chef Noriyasu Watanabe, to collaborate with its in-house Research and Development (R&D) team, it seeks new ideas and draws inspiration from different cultures to develop the two ranges. At least twice a year a new product line with eight to ten items is launched. As a counterbalance, the company removes products that do not sell well. Thus, the assortment remains fresh and healthy in economic terms.

The R&D team not only comes up with new bread varieties, but also quirky bread names, which include "Earthquake," "Moshi Mushroom," and "Crouching Tiger, Hidden Bacon," to mention but a few. The bread typically echoes fun, relevance to popular lifestyle and social trends. During U.S. President Barack Obama's inauguration, "Obunma" was created—a pizza bun with cheese reflected Mr. Obama's ability to gel different cultures with the United States together as a melting pot of cultures. On a similar note, they created "Flosss 1" and "Ferraberri," in commemoration of the first 2008 Formula 1 SingTel Singapore Grand Prix race held in the country.

The bread varieties are also creatively used as an expression of its Corporate Social Responsibility. BreadTalk created "Ping Chuan Xiong" 平川熊 (Peace Panda)—a Panda bear-shaped bun with four different expressions symbolizing the terror of the Sichuan's 7.8 magnitude earthquake on 12 May 2008. The proceeds raised went to the Chinese Embassy and Red Cross Society's "China Earthquake Appeal Fund."

All in all, BreadTalk draws on a repertoire of about 600 recipes. Around 80 percent of the assortment is the same regardless of markets; 20 percent is adapted to suit regional preferences. In the Middle East; for example, many products are sweeter and there

▲ Singapore bakery brand BreadTalk achieved success through turning the humble loaf of bread into an art form. Their innovation has allowed the company to expand rapidly and now has outlets in countries ranging from Korea to Dubai, where a fifth of their vast range of product has been adapted to suit regional preferences.

is a bigger choice of cakes. In Korea, to keep customers guessing, BreadTalk puts its baked goods on rotation, serving ideal breakfast bread varieties, like milk toast, in the morning before changing to ideal tea-time pastries, like gratin toast, in the afternoon.

BreadTalk bakeries give customers a great sensory experience. Instead of being placed on typical wooden shelves, the bread is encased in glass boxes much like that of a jewelry gallery. It is like showcasing each piece of bread as a piece of art. This presentation further enhances the artistic flair of the range of bread, bringing bread shopping to a whole new level of experience.

The stores are designed to be distinctive and sleek with clean lines. BreadTalk outlets stand out against the cozy warmth of traditional bakeries with their sophisticated store layouts, and have also sprung up in some of the most fashionable retail malls. The products are displayed in full view of customers in every store. In other words, production and sales are separated by just a few panes of glass. This signature "see through kitchens" allows their chefs to showcase their expertise upfront where customers can view the entire baking process from flour mixing to hot breads being taken out of the ovens. The customers are also treated to the delightful smell of bread and the promise of absolute freshness.

It was quite a revolution in both culinary and visual terms when the company developed the first of its six concepts in Singapore in 2001. This was because Singapore's bakeries were characterized by a very traditional orientation at the beginning of the new millennium. This applied not only to their assortments but also to the shop fittings and design. BreadTalk chose a different approach by entering the market as a "bakery boutique,"

(continued)

drawing its inspiration from modern fashion stores: lots of glass with an open structure so everyone can look inside. Inviting glass shelves mean the entire assortment can be taken in at a glance. The logo is always prominently positioned with white and orange as its signature colors. Additionally, pastel shades on the walls, steel, and glass add a warm touch.

No matter whether it is 800 or 1,600 square feet in size, rectangular, or with a few odd angles in shape, all outlets are decidedly bright and cheerful. And this applies not only to the outlets in Singapore but also to all other national markets, from Indonesia and Malaysia, Dubai and Kuwait, to China and India.

Local bakeries around the world have benefited from BreadTalk's entry into the market. Its revolutionary approach is setting trends and has driven home players to improve. The smaller bakeries were pushed to upgrade themselves to stay competitive and the concept of modern design in BreadTalk's bakery is reflected in many of these upgrades.

With increasing competition, BreadTalk needs to stay ahead of the competition by continuing to innovate and giving consumers a great experience both in culinary and visual terms.

For instance, in mature markets where it has come of age and is now exuding a familiarity with its consumers, BreadTalk wanted to subtly introduce the warmth of close friendships into its stores. The new store concept will exude an understated artistic flair with fascinating wall murals featuring BreadTalk's new inspirational "Happy Chefs" characters portrayed in different nationalities. These serve as a tribute to its chefs the world over for their dedication, creativity, and hard work in kneading out wonderful pieces of delicious artwork.

The new stores, while maintaining their trademark open-concept kitchen, take on a homier feel and recreate the atmosphere of a friend's kitchen. Equipped with new state-of-the-art bakery equipment specially imported from Germany, Spain, and Japan, the taste, aroma, quality, and texture consistency of their bread are further enhanced. New staff uniforms with French and Japanese influences and biodegradable and environmentally friendly packaging for all their products complete the entire new look.

As part of this revamp, over 100 new bread varieties were created by BreadTalk's R&D team in consultation with top chefs and food consultants from France, Japan, Spain, and Taiwan. It has continued to retain the top selling products such as Flosss, together with a new product range, to keep the brand fresh and surprising. In fact, as an innovator and creative force in the bakery business, the R&D team works hard to create new products every six months, always injecting an element of fun and humor into its products.

BreadTalk's innovative lifestyle bakery offers a fresh and healthy experience to the consumers. Coupled with BreadTalk's hot and fresh products and its tasteful ambience, buying bread will never be the same again.

Sources: Based on information from Heike Hucht, "Talking Point: Bread in Asia," *FoodService Europe & Middle East,* July 12, 2008 accessed at www.factiva.com; Jean Oh, "Singapore Bread Rises to Seoul Challenge," *The Korea Herald,* May 31, 2008 accessed at www.factiva.com; Mak Mun San, "Why the Funny Faces?," *The Straits Times,* May 25, 2008 accessed at www.factiva.com; Rachel Sim, "Where Creativity is a Bread and Butter Issue," *The Business Times,* July 11, 2009 accessed at www.factiva.com; Safiya Khan, "BreadTalk Opens Their First Outlet in Bahrain," *Middle East Company News,* April 14, 2009 accessed at www.factiva.com; Tay Suan Chiang, "BreadTalk Thrives on Change," *The Straits Times,* January 6, 2008 accessed at www.factiva.com; www.BreadTalk.com.

The company can appoint a respected senior person to be the company's innovation manager. It can set up Web-based idea management software and encourage all company stakeholders—employees, suppliers, distributors, dealers—to become involved in finding and developing new products. It can assign a cross-functional innovation management committee to evaluate proposed new-product ideas and help bring good ideas to market. It can create recognition programs to reward those who contribute the best ideas.

The innovation management system approach yields two favorable outcomes. First, it helps create an innovation-oriented company culture. It shows that top management supports, encourages, and rewards innovation. Second, it will yield a larger number of new-product ideas, among which will be found some especially good ones. The good new ideas will be more systematically developed, producing more new-product successes. No longer will good ideas wither for the lack of a sounding board or a senior product advocate.

Thus, new-product success requires more than simply thinking up a few good ideas, turning them into products, and finding customers for them. It requires a holistic approach for finding new ways to create valued customer experiences, from generating and screening new-product ideas to creating and rolling out want-satisfying products to customers.

More than this, successful new-product development requires a whole-company commitment. At companies known for their new-product prowess—such as Google, Apple, IDEO, 3M, Procter & Gamble, and General Electric—the entire culture encourages, supports, and rewards innovation.

Speed Bump: Linking the Concepts

Take a break. Think about new products and how companies develop them.

- Suppose that you're on a panel to nominate the "best new products of the year." What products would you nominate and why? See what you can learn about the new-product development process for one of these products.
- Applying the new-product development process you've just studied, develop an idea for an innovative new snack-food product and sketch out a brief plan for bringing it to market. Loosen up and have some fun with this.

Author Comment »
A company's products are born, grow, mature, and then decline, just as living things do. To remain vital, the firm must continually develop new products and manage them effectively through their life cycles.

Product life cycle
The course of a product's sales and profits over its lifetime. It involves five distinct stages: product development, introduction, growth, maturity, and decline.

PRODUCT LIFE-CYCLE STRATEGIES (pp 285–292)

After launching the new product, management wants the product to enjoy a long and happy life. Although it does not expect the product to sell forever, the company wants to earn a decent profit to cover all the effort and risk that went into launching it. Management is aware that each product will have a life cycle, although its exact shape and length is not known in advance.

■ **Figure 8.2** shows a typical **product life cycle** (PLC), the course that a product's sales and profits take over its lifetime. The product life cycle has five distinct stages:

1. *Product development* begins when the company finds and develops a new-product idea. During product development, sales are zero and the company's investment costs mount.
2. *Introduction* is a period of slow sales growth as the product is introduced in the market. Profits are nonexistent in this stage because of the heavy expenses of product introduction.
3. *Growth* is a period of rapid market acceptance and increasing profits.
4. *Maturity* is a period of slowdown in sales growth because the product has achieved acceptance by most potential buyers. Profits level off or decline because of increased marketing outlays to defend the product against competition.
5. *Decline* is the period when sales fall off and profits drop.

Not all products follow this product life cycle. Some products are introduced and die quickly; others stay in the mature stage for a long, long time. Some enter the decline stage and are then cycled back into the growth stage through strong promotion or repositioning. It seems that a well-managed brand could live forever.

■ **Figure 8.2** Sales and Profits Over the Product's Life from Inception to Decline

Some products die quickly; others stay in the mature stage for a long, long time. For example, TABASCO sauce has been around for more than 130 years. Even then, to keep the product young, the company has added a full line of flavors (such as Sweet & Spicy and Chipotle) and a kitchen cabinet full of new TABASCO products (such as spicy beans, a chili mix, and jalapeno nacho slices).

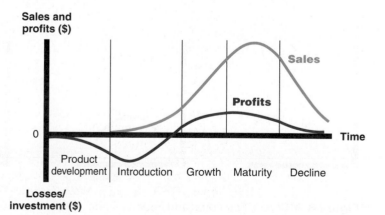

▲Product life cycle: Some products die quickly: others stay in the mature stage for a long, long time. TABASCO® sauce is "over 130 years old and yet still able to totally whup your butt!"

Style
A basic and distinctive mode of expression.

Fashion
A currently accepted or popular style in a given field.

Fad
A temporary period of unusually high sales driven by consumer enthusiasm and immediate product or brand popularity.

▲Such venerable brands as Coca-Cola, Gillette, Budweiser, American Express, Wells Fargo, Kikkoman, and TABASCO®, for instance, are still going strong after more than 100 years.

The PLC concept can describe a *product class* (gasoline-powered automobiles), a *product form* (SUVs), or a *brand* (the Ford Escape). The PLC concept applies differently in each case. Product classes have the longest life cycles—the sales of many product classes stay in the mature stage for a long time. Product forms, in contrast, tend to have the standard PLC shape. Product forms such as "dial telephones" and "VHS tapes" passed through a regular history of introduction, rapid growth, maturity, and decline.

A specific brand's life cycle can change quickly because of changing competitive attacks and responses. For example, although laundry soaps (product class) and powdered detergents (product form) have enjoyed fairly long life cycles, the life cycles of specific brands have tended to be much shorter. Today's leading brands of powdered laundry soap are Tide and Cheer; the leading brands almost 100 years ago were Fels-Naptha, Octagon, and Kirkman.

The PLC concept also can be applied to what are known as styles, fashions, and fads. Their special life cycles are shown in ■ **Figure 8.3**. A **style** is a basic and distinctive mode of expression. For example, styles appear in homes (colonial, ranch, transitional), clothing (formal, casual), and art (realist, surrealist, abstract). Once a style is invented, it may last for generations, passing in and out of vogue. A style has a cycle showing several periods of renewed interest. A **fashion** is a currently accepted or popular style in a given field. For example, the more formal "business attire" look of corporate dress of the 1980s and 1990s gave way to the "business casual" look of today. Fashions tend to grow slowly, remain popular for a while, and then decline slowly.

Fads are temporary periods of unusually high sales driven by consumer enthusiasm and immediate product or brand popularity.[26] A fad may be part of an otherwise normal life cycle, as in the case of recent surges in the sales of poker chips and accessories. Or the fad may comprise a brand's or product's entire life cycle. "Pet rocks" are a classic example. Upon hearing his friends complain about how expensive it was to care for their dogs, advertising copywriter Gary Dahl joked about his pet rock. He soon wrote a spoof of a dog-training manual for it, titled "The Care and Training of Your Pet Rock." Soon Dahl was selling some 1.5 million ordinary beach pebbles at $4 a pop. Yet the fad, which broke one October, had sunk like a stone by the next February. Dahl's advice to those who want to succeed with a fad: "Enjoy it while it lasts." Other examples of such fads include the Rubik's Cube and low-carb diets.[27]

The PLC concept can be applied by marketers as a useful framework for describing how products and markets work. And when used carefully, the PLC concept

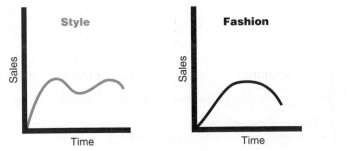

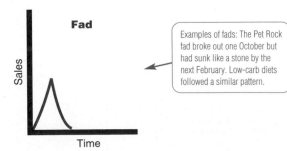

Examples of fads: The Pet Rock fad broke out one October but had sunk like a stone by the next February. Low-carb diets followed a similar pattern.

■ **Figure 8.3** Styles, Fashions, and Fads

can help in developing good marketing strategies for different stages of the product life cycle. But using the PLC concept for forecasting product performance or for developing marketing strategies presents some practical problems. For example, in practice, it is difficult to forecast the sales level at each PLC stage, the length of each stage, and the shape of the PLC curve. Using the PLC concept to develop marketing strategy also can be difficult because strategy is both a cause and a result of the product's life cycle. The product's current PLC position suggests the best marketing strategies, and the resulting marketing strategies affect product performance in later life-cycle stages.

Moreover, marketers should not blindly push products through the traditional stages of the product life cycle. Instead, marketers often defy the "rules" of the life cycle and position or reposition their products in unexpected ways. By doing this, they can rescue mature or declining products and return them to the growth phase of the life cycle. Or they can leapfrog obstacles to slow consumer acceptance and propel new products forward into the growth phase.

The moral of the product life cycle is that companies must continually innovate or they risk extinction. No matter how successful its current product lineup, for future success, a company must skillfully manage the life cycles of existing products. And to grow, it must develop a steady stream of new products that bring new value to customers (see Marketing at Work 8.2).

We looked at the product-development stage of the product life cycle in the first part of the chapter. We now look at strategies for each of the other life-cycle stages.

Introduction Stage

Introduction stage
The product life-cycle stage in which the new product is first distributed and made available for purchase.

The **introduction stage** starts when the new product is first launched. Introduction takes time, and sales growth is apt to be slow. Well-known products such as instant coffee, frozen foods, and HDTVs lingered for many years before they entered a stage of more rapid growth.

In this stage, as compared to other stages, profits are negative or low because of the low sales and high distribution and promotion expenses. Much money is needed to attract distributors and build their inventories. Promotion spending is relatively high to inform consumers of the new product and get them to try it. Because the market is not generally ready for product refinements at this stage, the company and its few competitors produce basic versions of the product. These firms focus their selling on those buyers who are the most ready to buy.

A company, especially the *market pioneer*, must choose a launch strategy that is consistent with the intended product positioning. It should realize that the initial strategy is just the first step in a grander marketing plan for the product's entire life cycle. If the pioneer chooses its launch strategy to make a "killing," it may be sacrificing long-run revenue for the sake of short-run gain. As the pioneer moves through later stages of the life cycle, it must continuously formulate new pricing, promotion, and other marketing strategies. It has the best chance of building and retaining market leadership if it plays its cards correctly from the start.

Growth Stage

Growth stage
The product life-cycle stage in which a product's sales start climbing quickly.

If the new product satisfies the market, it will enter a **growth stage**, in which sales will start climbing quickly. The early adopters will continue to buy, and later buyers will start following their lead, especially if they hear favorable word of mouth. Attracted by the opportunities for profit, new competitors will enter the market. They will introduce new product features, and the market will expand. The increase in competitors leads to an increase in the number of distribution outlets, and sales jump just to build reseller inventories. Prices remain where they are or fall only slightly. Companies keep their promotion spending at the same or a slightly higher level. Educating the market remains a goal, but now the company must also meet the competition.

Marketing at Work 8.2

Kraft: Lots of Good Old Products; Too Few Good New Ones?

Kraft makes and markets an incredible portfolio of known and trusted brands, including half a dozen $1 billion brands and another 50 that top $100 million in sales. Beyond the Kraft label of cheeses, snacks, dips, and dressings, its megabrands include the likes of Oscar Mayer, Post cereals, DiGiorno pizza, Maxwell House coffee, JELL-O, Cool Whip, Kool-Aid, A1 sauce, Velveeta, Planters, Miracle Whip, Light 'n Lively, Grey Poupon, CapriSun, and Nabisco (Oreo, Chips Ahoy!, Triscuit, SnackWells, and a whole lot more). Search America's pantries and you'll find at least one Kraft product in 199 of every 200 households.

However, despite its long list of familiar brands, Kraft hasn't done very well in recent years. Until recently, its sales and profits had stagnated and its stock price had flat-lined. Investors would have made a better return on bank certificates of deposit than on their investments in Kraft stock. The problem? Kraft did a poor job of managing the product life cycle. Although it had a slew of good *old* products, it had far too few good *new* products.

Many of Kraft's venerable old brands—such as Maxwell House, Velveeta, and JELL-O—were showing their age. Other brands were extended about as far as they can go—for instance, Kraft now markets more than 20 varieties of Oreos, from the original sandwich cookies, Oreo Double Stuf, Oreo Double Double Stuf, Chocolate-Covered Oreos, and Double Delight Chocolate Mint 'n Crème Oreos to Oreo Mini Bites, Oreo Snack Cakes, and even Oreo ice cream cones. How much pop would yet one more variety provide?

Over the years, competitors such as P&G have invested dollars and energy in their mature or declining brands, such as Mr. Clean and Old Spice, moving them back into the growth stage of the product life cycle. In contrast, Kraft focused on cost-cutting, leaving its mature brands to wither. Whereas rival P&G developed a constant stream of really new products—even inventing all new product categories, with products such as Swiffer and Febreze—Kraft was slow to innovate. And while P&G was intensely customer-focused, bringing innovative new solutions to its customers, Kraft slowly lost touch with its customers.

▲ **Managing the product life cycle: Despite its long list of familiar old brands, until recently, Kraft developed far too few good *new* products. It's now emphasizing new-product innovation. "Welcome to the new Kraft."**

In 2006, however, under pressure from investors, Kraft installed a brand-new leadership team, including a new CEO, a first-ever chief marketing officer, and a leader of consumer innovation and marketing services. Under the leadership of CEO Irene Rosenfeld, the new leadership team laid out an ambitious turnaround plan to restore Kraft's sales and profit growth.

For starters, the team announced that it would make heavy investments to reconnect with customers and to improve product quality. To better understand what customers think and want, "We're going to connect with the consumer wherever she is," said Rosenfeld. "On the quality side, [we need to] shift from 'good enough' to 'truly delicious,' turning brands that [our] consumers have lived with for years into brands they can't live without." Most importantly, pronounced Rosenfeld, Kraft would invest heavily in innovation and new-product development. Simply put, she said, "We need to rebuild our new-product pipeline."

Rosenfeld and her team began their new-product development efforts not in the test kitchens but by visiting consumers'

Profits increase during the growth stage as promotion costs are spread over a large volume and as unit manufacturing costs fall. The firm uses several strategies to sustain rapid market growth as long as possible. It improves product quality and adds new product features and models. It enters new market segments and new distribution channels. It shifts some advertising from building product awareness to building product conviction and purchase, and it lowers prices at the right time to attract more buyers.

In the growth stage, the firm faces a trade-off between high market share and high current profit. By spending a lot of money on product improvement, promotion, and distribution, the company can capture a dominant position. In doing so,

homes, viewing the world through customers' eyes rather than through a company's lens. "We are about to take this great portfolio of ours in a new direction that's more consistent with the reality of consumers' lives today," she declared. We need "customer-focused innovation!" The team discovered the simple truth that with the way customers live their lives today, they want high-quality but convenient and healthy foods. "Wouldn't it be a whole lot easier if you could have restaurant-quality food at home for a fraction of the cost?" asked Rosenfeld.

The team also realized that Kraft already had all the fixings it needed to complete this mission. It needed only to reframe its offerings in ways that fit customers' changing lifestyles. For example, Kraft developed the highly successful "Deli Creations" brand—a build-your-own premium sandwich kit that includes bread, Oscar Mayer meats, Kraft cheeses, and condiments such as A1 steak sauce and Grey Poupon mustard. Customers can quickly assemble the sandwiches, pop them into the microwave for one minute, and wrap their mouths around a hot, restaurant-style sandwich. In a similar fashion, Kraft rolled out "Fresh Creations" salads, complete with Oscar Mayer meat, Kraft cheese, Good Season's salad dressing, and Planter's nuts, a move that took its product portfolio into a whole new section of the grocery store, the produce section.

In addition to creating new brands and categories, Kraft quickly launched a pantry full of new products under the old familiar brand names. For example, it introduced DiGiorno Ultimate, its best-yet alternative to delivery pizza, featuring premium vine-ripened tomatoes, whole-milk mozzarella cheese, specialty meats, and julienne vegetables. Under previous management, this project had been black-balled because the premium ingredients were considered too hard to get and too expensive. With Rosenfeld's blessing, DiGiorno Ultimate was on the shelves in just 18 months.

Dozens of other new products ranged from higher-quality Oscar Mayer Deli Fresh cold cuts and an entirely rejuvenated line of Kraft salad dressings with no artificial preservatives to Kraft Bagel-Fuls handheld breakfast sandwiches, Cakesters snack cakes, healthy LiveActive products with probiotic cultures and prebiotic fiber, and Oscar Mayer Fast Franks prepackaged microwavable stadium-style hotdogs.

Kraft even invested to reinvigorate some of its old brands. For example, it added four bold new flavors to the Grey Poupon brand, a name that had retained 70 percent consumer awareness even without much investment. The new flavors will be supported by a fresh version of the old and much-liked Grey Poupon "Pardon me" ad campaign. Kraft is also infusing new life into existing brands such as Knudsen and Breakstone by co-marketing them with the LiveActive health brand. And, to get the word out about all its new products, Kraft invested an additional $400 million on a new marketing program designed to better tell the Kraft story. "We [are] telling the consumer that Kraft is back," said Rosenfeld.

And it appears that Kraft *is* back—or at least heading in the right direction. Although profits are still languishing, sales have grown 27 percent over the past two years despite the gloomy economy, and Kraft's brands are market leaders in 80 percent of its categories. Rosenfeld and her team are optimistic. "Our brands are getting stronger every day," she says. "Our insights about consumers are deeper and richer than ever before. And our new product pipeline is flowing with exciting ideas that will accelerate our growth and improve our margins. I'm pleased to tell you, the new Kraft is taking shape."

Kraft has learned that a company can't just sit back, basking in the glory of today's successful brands. Continued success requires skillful management of the product life cycle. But Rosenfeld knows that Kraft still has a long way to go in serving up a tastier investment to shareholders. "It's time to grow. Our investors have told us that, and I would agree with them," she says. "But this is not *Extreme Makeover: Home Edition* that'll get fixed in 60 minutes. We've [still] got some fundamental work to do."

Sources: Quotes and other information from Michael Arndt, "It Just Got Hotter in Kraft's Kitchen," *BusinessWeek*, February 12, 2007; "Kraft Highlights Growth Strategy, Reconfirms 2008 Guidelines and Unveils Product Innovations at CAGNY Conference," *Business Wire*, February 19, 2008; John Schmeltzer, "Foodmaker Whips Up Plan For a Comeback," *Chicago Tribune*, February 21, 2007, p. 1; Emily Bryson York, "Earnings Drop Won't Keep Kraft from Spending," *Advertising Age*, February 4, 2009, accessed at *http://adage.com/print?article_id=134317*; and annual reports and other information from *www.kraft.com*, accessed November 2009.

however, it gives up maximum current profit, which it hopes to make up in the next stage.

Maturity Stage

Maturity stage
The product life-cycle stage in which sales growth slows or levels off.

At some point, a product's sales growth will slow down, and the product will enter a **maturity stage**. This maturity stage normally lasts longer than the previous stages, and it poses strong challenges to marketing management. Most products are in the maturity stage of the life cycle, and therefore most of marketing management deals with the mature product.

The slowdown in sales growth results in many producers with many products to sell. In turn, this overcapacity leads to greater competition. Competitors begin marking down prices, increasing their advertising and sales promotions, and upping their product development budgets to find better versions of the product. These steps lead to a drop in profit. Some of the weaker competitors start dropping out, and the industry eventually contains only well-established competitors.

Although many products in the mature stage appear to remain unchanged for long periods, most successful ones are actually evolving to meet changing consumer needs. Product managers should do more than simply ride along with or defend their mature products—a good offense is the best defense. They should consider modifying the market, product, and marketing mix.

In *modifying the market*, the company tries to increase consumption by finding new users and new market segments for its brands. For example, mature 101-year old card maker American Greetings is now reaching younger consumers through social-networking widgets and instant-messaging channels.[28]

Women buy 80 percent of the greeting cards in the United States, and their median age is 47—not exactly the Facebook crowd. To younger buyers in this digital age, a snail-mail card is as antiquated as getting a $5 birthday check from grandma. ▲So to make its brand more youthful, American Greetings created Kiwee.com, a repository for emoticons, video winks, postcards, graphics, widgets, and glitter text for all the major social-networking sites and instant-messaging services. A 47-year-old housewife may not be interested in the winking-turd emoticon that her 15-year-old son adores, but "we sell emotions," says AG Interactive's (AGI) chief technology officer. "Even younger people need help saying better what they want to say." Kiwee.com content is now being downloaded 1.2 million times per day, signaling American Greetings' adjustment to a segment where paper cards are passé. Young folks may not send paper anymore, but being remembered—that's universal.

▼Modifying the market: 101-year-old card maker American Greetings is reaching out to younger consumers through social-networking widgets and instant-messaging channels.

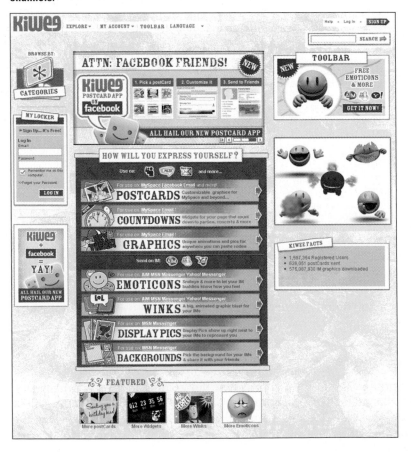

The manager may also look for ways to increase usage among present customers. For example, Glad Products Company helps customers to find new uses for its Press'n Seal wrap, the plastic wrap that creates a Tupperware-like seal. As more and more customers contacted the company about alternative uses for the product, Glad set up a special "1000s of Uses. What's Yours?" Web site (*www.1000uses.com*) at which customers can swap usage tips. "We found out our heavy users use it for a lot more than just covering food," says a Glad brand manager. "And they all became heavy users when they had an 'aha' moment with Press'n Seal." Suggested uses for Press'n Seal range from protecting a computer keyboard from dirt and spills and keeping garden seeds fresh to use by soccer moms sitting on damp benches while watching their tykes play. "We just roll out the Glad Press'n Seal over the long benches," says the mom who shared the tip, "and everyone's bottom stays nice and dry."[29]

The company might also try *modifying the product*—changing characteristics such as quality, features, style, or packaging to attract new users and to inspire more usage. It can improve the product's styling and attractiveness. It might improve the product's quality and performance—its durability, reliability, speed, and taste. Thus, makers of consumer food and household products introduce new flavors, colors, scents, ingredients, or packages to enhance performance and revitalize consumer buying. For example, TABASCO® pepper sauce may have been around for more than 130 years, but to keep the brand young, the company has added a full line of flavors (such as Garlic, Sweet & Spicy, and Chipotle) and a kitchen cabinet full of new products under the TABASCO® name (such as steak sauces, spicy beans, a chili mix, jalapeno nacho slices, and even a TABASCO® lollipop).

Finally, the company can try *modifying the marketing mix*—improving sales by changing one or more marketing mix elements. The company can offer new or improved services to buyers. It can cut prices to attract new users and competitors' customers. It can launch a better advertising campaign or use aggressive sales promotions—trade deals, cents-off, premiums, and contests. In addition to pricing and promotion, the company can also move into new marketing channels to help serve new users.

Decline Stage

The sales of most product forms and brands eventually dip. The decline may be slow, as in the case of oatmeal cereal, or rapid, as in the cases of cassette and VHS tapes. Sales may plunge to zero, or they may drop to a low level where they continue for many years. This is the **decline stage**.

Decline stage
The product life-cycle stage in which a product's sales decline.

Sales decline for many reasons, including technological advances, shifts in consumer tastes, and increased competition. As sales and profits decline, some firms withdraw from the market. Those remaining may prune their product offerings. They may drop smaller market segments and marginal trade channels, or they may cut the promotion budget and reduce their prices further.

Carrying a weak product can be very costly to a firm, and not just in profit terms. There are many hidden costs. A weak product may take up too much of management's time. It often requires frequent price and inventory adjustments. It requires advertising and sales-force attention that might be better used to make "healthy" products more profitable. A product's failing reputation can cause customer concerns about the company and its other products. The biggest cost may well lie in the future. Keeping weak products delays the search for replacements, creates a lopsided product mix, hurts current profits, and weakens the company's foothold on the future.

For these reasons, companies need to pay more attention to their aging products. A firm's first task is to identify those products in the decline stage by regularly reviewing sales, market shares, costs, and profit trends. Then, management must decide whether to maintain, harvest, or drop each of these declining products.

Management may decide to *maintain* its brand without change in the hope that competitors will leave the industry. For example, P&G made good profits by remaining in the declining liquid soap business as others withdrew. Or management may decide to reposition or reinvigorate the brand in hopes of moving it back into the growth stage of the product life cycle. Procter & Gamble has done this with several brands, including Mr. Clean and Old Spice.

Management may decide to *harvest* the product, which means reducing various costs (plant and equipment, maintenance, R&D, advertising, sales force) and hoping that sales hold up. If successful, harvesting will increase the company's profits in the short run. Or management may decide to *drop* the product from the line. It can sell it to another firm or simply liquidate it at salvage value. In recent years, P&G has sold off a number of lesser or declining brands such as Crisco oil, Comet cleanser, Sure deodorant, Duncan Hines cake mixes, and Jif peanut butter. If the company plans to find a buyer, it will not want to run down the product through harvesting.

■ **Table 8.2** summarizes the key characteristics of each stage of the product life cycle. The table also lists the marketing objectives and strategies for each stage.[30]

■ Table 8.2   Summary of Product Life-Cycle Characteristics, Objectives, and Strategies

Characteristics	Introduction	Growth	Maturity	Decline
Sales	Low sales	Rapidly rising sales	Peak sales	Declining sales
Costs	High cost per customer	Average cost per customer	Low cost per customer	Low cost per customer
Profits	Negative	Rising profits	High profits	Declining profits
Customers	Innovators	Early adopters	Middle majority	Laggards
Competitors	Few	Growing number	Stable number beginning to decline	Declining number
Marketing Objectives				
	Create product awareness and trial	Maximize market share	Maximize profit while defending market share	Reduce expenditure and milk the brand
Strategies				
Product	Offer a basic product	Offer product extensions, service, warranty	Diversify brand and models	Phase out weak items
Price	Use cost-plus	Price to penetrate market	Price to match or beat competitors	Cut price
Distribution	Build selective distribution	Build intensive distribution	Build more intensive distribution	Go selective: phase out unprofitable outlets
Advertising	Build product awareness among early adopters and dealers	Build awareness and interest in the mass market	Stress brand differences and benefits	Reduce to level needed to retain hard-core loyals
Sales Promotion	Use heavy sales promotion to entice trial	Reduce to take advantage of heavy consumer demand	Increase to encourage brand switching	Reduce to minimal level

Source: Philip Kotler and Kevin Lane Keller, *Marketing Management*, 13th ed. (Upper Saddle River, NJ: Prentice Hall, 2009), p. 288.

Speed Bump: Linking the Concepts

Pause for a moment and think about some products that have been around for a long time.

- Ask a grandparent or someone else who shaved back then to compare a 1960s or 1970s Gillette razor to the most current model. Is Gillette's latest razor really a new product or just a "retread" of the previous version? What do you conclude about product life cycles?
- Crayola Crayons have been a household staple for more than 100 years. But the brand remains vital. Sixty-five percent of all American children aged two to eight pick up a crayon at least once a day and color for an average of 28 minutes. Nearly 80 percent of the time, they pick up a Crayola crayon. How has the Binney & Smith division of Hallmark protected the Crayola brand from old age and decline (check out *www.crayola.com* and *www.binney-smith.com*)?

Author Comment >>
Let's look at just a few more product topics, including regulatory and social responsibility issues and the special challenges of marketing products internationally.

ADDITIONAL PRODUCT AND SERVICE CONSIDERATIONS (pp 292–295)

Here, we'll wrap up our discussion of products and services with two additional considerations: social responsibility in product decisions and issues of international product and services marketing.

Product Decisions and Social Responsibility

Product decisions have attracted much public attention. Marketers should carefully consider public policy issues and regulations regarding acquiring or dropping products, patent protection, product quality and safety, and product warranties.

Regarding new products, the government may prevent companies from adding products through acquisitions if the effect threatens to lessen competition. Companies dropping products must be aware that they have legal obligations, written or implied, to their suppliers, dealers, and customers who have a stake in the dropped product. Companies must also obey U.S. patent laws when developing new products. A company cannot make its product illegally similar to another company's established product.

Manufacturers must comply with specific laws regarding product quality and safety. The Federal Food, Drug, and Cosmetic Act protects consumers from unsafe and adulterated food, drugs, and cosmetics. Various acts provide for the inspection of sanitary conditions in the meat- and poultry-processing industries. Safety legislation has been passed to regulate fabrics, chemical substances, automobiles, toys, and drugs and poisons. The Consumer Product Safety Act of 1972 established a Consumer Product Safety Commission, which has the authority to ban or seize potentially harmful products and set severe penalties for violation of the law.

If consumers have been injured by a product that has a defective design, they can sue manufacturers or dealers. A recent survey of manufacturing companies found that product liability was the second-largest litigation concern, behind only labor and employment matters. Product liability suits are now occurring in federal courts at the rate of over 20,000 per year. Although manufacturers are found at fault in only 6 percent of all product liability cases, when they are found guilty, the median jury award is $1.5 million and individual awards can run into the tens or even hundreds of millions of dollars. For example, in 2005 a jury ordered Merck to pay $253 million to the widow of a man who died from a heart attack after using the painkiller Vioxx for his arthritis. The judge later reduced the award to a "mere" $26.1 million. However, this was only the first of more than 60,000 Vioxx claims against the company and an eventual proposed settlement of nearly $5 billion that deeply crippled the company.[31]

This litigation phenomenon has resulted in huge increases in product liability insurance premiums, causing big problems in some industries. Some companies pass these higher rates along to consumers by raising prices. Others are forced to discontinue high-risk product lines. Some companies are now appointing "product stewards," whose job is to protect consumers from harm and the company from liability by proactively ferreting out potential product problems.

Many manufacturers offer written product warranties to convince customers of their products' quality. To protect consumers, Congress passed the Magnuson-Moss Warranty Act in 1975. The act requires that full warranties meet certain minimum standards, including repair "within a reasonable time and without charge" or a replacement or full refund if the product does not work "after a reasonable number of attempts" at repair. Otherwise, the company must make it clear that it is offering only a limited warranty. The law has led several manufacturers to switch from full to limited warranties and others to drop warranties altogether.

International Product and Services Marketing

International product and services marketers face special challenges. First, they must figure out what products and services to introduce and in which countries. Then, they must decide how much to standardize or adapt their products and services for world markets.

On the one hand, companies would like to standardize their offerings. Standardization helps a company to develop a consistent worldwide image. It also lowers the product design, manufacturing, and marketing costs of offering a large variety of products.

On the other hand, markets and consumers around the world differ widely. Companies must usually respond to these differences by adapting their product offerings. For example, Nestlé sells a variety of very popular Kit Kat flavors in Japan that might make the average Western chocolate-lover's stomach turn, such as green tea, red bean, and red wine. Beyond taste, Kit Kat's strong following in Japan may also be the result of some unintended cultural factors:

きっと、サクラサクよ。

Nestlé Kit Kat

がんばる受験生へ。 Have a break, have a KitKat.
サイトでも、受験生を応援中 www.breaktown.com

▲Nestlé Kit Kat chocolate bar in Japan benefits from the coincidental similarity between the bar's name and the Japanese phrase *kitto katsu*, which roughly translates to "You will surely win!" The brand's innovative "May cherries blossom" campaign has turned the Kit Kat bar and logo into national good luck charms.

In recent years, Kit Kat—the world's number two chocolate bar behind Snickers—has become very popular in Japan. Some of this popularity, no doubt, derives from the fact that the notoriously sweet-toothed Japanese love the bar's taste. But part of the bar's appeal may also be attributed to the coincidental similarity between its name and the Japanese phrase *kitto katsu*, which roughly translates in Japanese as "You will surely win!" Spotting this opportunity, marketers for Nestlé Japan developed an innovative Juken (college entrance exam) Kit Kat campaign. ▲The multimedia campaign positions the Kit Kat bar and logo as good luck charms during the highly stressful university entrance exam season. Nestlé even developed a cherry flavored Kit Kat bar in packaging containing the message "May cherries blossom," wishing students luck in achieving their dreams. And it partnered with Japan's postal service to create "Kit Kat Mail," a post-card-like product sold at the post office that could be mailed to students as an edible good-luck charm. The campaign has been such a hit in Japan that it has led to a nationwide social movement to cheer up students for Juken. Kit Kat has also become an even broader national good luck charm. For example, a large flag featuring the Kit Kat logo and the phrase "Kitto Katsu!" has been used by fans of professional football team Jubilo IWATA, which is sponsored by Nestlé Japan. Since the Juken campaign began seven years ago, Kit Kat sales in Japan have increased more than 250 percent.[32]

Packaging also presents new challenges for international marketers. Packaging issues can be subtle. For example, names, labels, and colors may not translate easily from one country to another. A firm using yellow flowers in its logo might fare well in the United States but meet with disaster in Mexico, where a yellow flower symbolizes death or disrespect. Similarly, although Nature's Gift might be an appealing name for gourmet mushrooms in America, it would be deadly in Germany, where *gift* means poison. Packaging may also need to be tailored to meet the physical characteristics of consumers in various parts of the world. For instance, soft drinks are sold in smaller cans in Japan to fit the smaller Japanese hand better. Thus, although product and package standardization can produce benefits, companies must usually adapt their offerings to the unique needs of specific international markets.

Service marketers also face special challenges when going global. Some service industries have a long history of international operations. For example, the commercial banking industry was one of the first to grow internationally. Banks had to provide global services in order to meet the foreign exchange and credit needs of their home country clients wanting to sell overseas. In recent years, many banks have become truly global. Germany's Deutsche Bank, for example, serves more than 13 million customers through 1,981 branches in 72 countries. For its clients around the world who wish to grow globally, Deutsche Bank can raise money not only in Frankfurt but also in Zurich, London, Paris, Tokyo, and Moscow.[33]

Professional and business services industries such as accounting, management consulting, and advertising have also globalized. The international growth of these firms followed the globalization of the client companies they serve. For example, as more clients employ worldwide marketing and advertising strategies, advertising agencies have responded by globalizing their own operations. McCann Worldgroup, a large U.S.-based advertising and marketing services agency, operates in more than 130 countries. It serves international clients such as Coca-Cola, General Motors, ExxonMobil, Microsoft, MasterCard, Johnson & Johnson, and Unilever in markets ranging from the United States and Canada to Korea and Kazakhstan. Moreover, McCann Worldgroup is one company in the Interpublic Group of Companies, an immense, worldwide network of advertising and marketing services companies.[34]

Retailers are among the latest service businesses to go global. As their home markets become saturated, American retailers such as Wal-Mart, Office Depot, and Saks Fifth Avenue are expanding into faster-growing markets abroad. For example, since 1995, Wal-Mart has entered 15 countries; its international division's sales grew nearly 18 percent last year, skyrocketing to more than $90.6 billion. Foreign retailers are making similar moves. Asian shoppers can now buy American products in French-owned Carrefour stores. Carrefour, the world's second-largest retailer behind Wal-Mart, now operates more than 15,000 stores in more than 30 countries. It is the leading retailer in Europe, Brazil, and Argentina and the largest foreign retailer in China.[35]

The trend toward growth of global service companies will continue, especially in banking, airlines, telecommunications, and professional services. Today, service firms are no longer simply following their manufacturing customers. Instead, they are taking the lead in international expansion.

REST STOP
REVIEWING THE CONCEPTS

A company's current products face limited lifespans and must be replaced by newer products. But new products can fail—the risks of innovation are as great as the rewards. The key to successful innovation lies in a customer focus, total-company effort, strong planning, and a systematic *new-product development* process.

 Objective 1 Explain how companies find and develop new-product ideas. **(pp 272–273)**

Companies find and develop new-product ideas from a variety of sources. Many new-product ideas stem from *internal sources*. Companies conduct formal research and development, pick the brains of their employees, and brainstorm at executive meetings. Other ideas come from *external sources*. By listening to and working with customers, conducting surveys and focus groups, and analyzing *customer* questions and complaints, companies can generate new-product ideas that will meet specific consumer needs. Companies track *competitors'* offerings and inspect new products, dismantling them, analyzing their performance, and deciding whether to introduce a similar or improved product. *Distributors and suppliers* are close to the market and can pass along information about consumer problems and new-product possibilities.

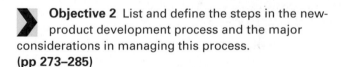 **Objective 2** List and define the steps in the new-product development process and the major considerations in managing this process. **(pp 273–285)**

The new-product development process consists of eight sequential stages. The process starts with *idea generation*. Next comes *idea screening*, which reduces the number of ideas based on the company's own criteria. Ideas that pass the screening stage continue through *product concept development*, in which a detailed version of the new-product idea is stated in meaningful consumer terms. In the next stage, *concept testing*, new-product concepts are tested with a group of target consumers to determine whether the concepts have strong consumer appeal. Strong concepts proceed to *marketing strategy development*, in which an initial marketing strategy for the new product is developed from the product concept. In the *business-analysis* stage, a review of the sales, costs, and profit projections for a new product is conducted to determine whether the new product is likely to satisfy the company's objectives. With positive results here, the ideas become more concrete through *product development* and *test marketing* and finally are launched during *commercialization*.

New-product development involves more than just going through a set of steps. Companies must take a systematic, holistic approach to managing this process. Successful new-product development requires a customer-centered, team-based, systematic effort.

> **Objective 3** Describe the stages of the product life cycle and how marketing strategies change during the product's life cycle. **(pp 285–292)**

Each product has a *life cycle* marked by a changing set of problems and opportunities. The sales of the typical product follow an S-shaped curve made up of five stages. The cycle begins with the *product development stage* in which the company finds and develops a new-product idea. The *introduction stage* is marked by slow growth and low profits as the product is distributed to the market. If successful, the product enters a *growth stage*, which offers rapid sales growth and increasing profits. Next comes a *maturity stage* in which sales growth slows down and profits stabilize. Finally, the product enters a *decline stage* in which sales and profits dwindle. The company's task during this stage is to recognize the decline and to decide whether it should maintain, harvest, or drop the product.

In the *introduction stage*, the company must choose a launch strategy consistent with its intended product positioning. Much money is needed to attract distributors and build their inventories and to inform consumers of the new product and achieve trial. In the *growth stage*, companies continue to educate potential consumers and distributors. In addition, the company works to stay ahead of the competition and sustain rapid market growth by improving product quality, adding new product features and models,

entering new market segments and distribution channels, shifting advertising from building product awareness to building product conviction and purchase, and lowering prices at the right time to attract new buyers.

In the *maturity stage*, companies continue to invest in maturing products and consider modifying the market, the product, and the marketing mix. When *modifying the market*, the company attempts to increase the consumption of the current product. When *modifying the product*, the company changes some of the product's characteristics—such as quality, features, or style—to attract new users or inspire more usage. When *modifying the marketing mix*, the company works to improve sales by changing one or more of the marketing-mix elements. Once the company recognizes that a product has entered the *decline stage*, management must decide whether to *maintain* the brand without change, hoping that competitors will drop out of the market; *harvest* the product, reducing costs and trying to maintain sales; or *drop* the product, selling it to another firm or liquidating it at salvage value.

> **Objective 4** Discuss two additional product issues: socially responsible product decisions and international product and services marketing. **(pp 292–295)**

Marketers must consider two additional product issues. The first is *social responsibility*. This includes public policy issues and regulations involving acquiring or dropping products, patent protection, product quality and safety, and product warranties. The second involves the special challenges facing international product and services marketers. International marketers must decide how much to standardize or adapt their offerings for world markets.

Navigating the Key Terms

Travel Log

Discussing the Issues

1. Discuss the major steps in the new-product development process. (AACSB: Communication)

2. Discuss external sources of new-product ideas. (AACSB: Communication)

3. Compare and contrast the terms *product idea*, *product concept*, and *product image*. (AACSB: Communication)

4. Explain how styles, fashions, and fads differ and discuss an example of each. (AACSB: Communication; Reflective Thinking)

5. Briefly describe the five stages of the product life cycle. Identify a product class, form, or brand that is in each stage. (AACSB: Communication; Reflective Thinking)

6. Discuss the special challenges facing international product and services marketers. (AACSB: Communication)

Application Questions

1. Visit the U.S. Consumer Product Safety Commission's Web site (www.cpsc.gov) to learn about this organization. Search this site for information on product recalls and discuss three recent examples. (AACSB: Communication; Use of IT)

2. Think of a problem that really bugs you or a need you have that is not satisfied by current market offerings. In a small group, brainstorm four ideas for a new product or service that solves this problem or satisfies this need. Test these product concepts with ten students and develop a marketing-strategy statement for the concept that tested best. (AACSB: Communication; Reflective Thinking)

3. Many companies purchase other companies or individual product or brands from other companies to acquire new products. For example, Disney recently agreed to purchase Marvel Entertainment and its portfolio of more than 5,000 characters, such as Spider-Man and Captain America, for $4 billion. Discuss two other recent examples of companies acquiring new products through this means. (AACSB: Communication; Reflective Thinking)

Under the Hood: Marketing Technology

Technology is speeding up new-product develop while at the same time reducing its costs. What used to take months and millions of dollars can now be done in seconds and for pennies. Greater efficiency means a lower cost of failure, so companies can try out new ideas and gain better feedback from customers. Much concept testing these days is done online. Retailers are getting in on it, too, by running experiments—that is, test markets—to see how new concepts influence shoppers. Wal-Mart tests different approaches to signage, displays, and shelf layouts in some stores for only a few days and measures the impact on sales. Because technology is making new-product testing easy and accessible to just about any employee, from the CEO to maintenance personnel, predictions are for a ground-breaking change in corporate cultures surrounding new-product development—much like the Google culture described at the beginning of this chapter. An employee may come up with a great idea and test it—all in a single day. This new environment may present some challenges, however. One is that managers must be prepared to give up control and empower employees. Another is "scaling," which means companies must be able to scale—or implement—new ideas rapidly and more efficiently.

1. What skills would you need to function is this type of work environment? (AACSB: Communication; Reflective Thinking)

2. As describe at the beginning of the chapter, Google is already ahead of this curve. Visit Goggle Labs (www.googlelabs.com) to learn about new products that are still in the testing stage, or "playground stage" as Google likes to say. Briefly discuss two of the experiments and explain why Google hosts a site such as Google Labs. (AACSB: Communication; Reflective Thinking; Use of IT)

Staying on the Road: Marketing Ethics

The Food and Drug Administration's (FDA) original authority did not include tobacco products. Recently, however, the FDA was granted the authority to regulate tobacco as a drug. With this new authority, the FDA is now taking aim at a new tobacco-less product called electronic cigarettes. E-cigarettes look like regular cigarettes but are battery-powered and contain cartridges with nicotine and flavoring, along with other chemicals that create a vapor inhaled by users. On the plus side, these new products are smoke-less, allowing users to "smoke" anywhere and allaying concerns swirling around secondhand smoke risks. However, e-cigarettes still contain dangerous carcinogens and toxic chemicals, such as one that is used in antifreeze. And critics charge that the new products are being targeted to children. Some have bubble gum and fruity flavors added and most are sold at shopping malls and online. The Electronic Cigarette Association, however, denies such allegations, claiming that the $100-$150 cost of the product is prohibitive for kids. E-cigarette marketers, such as Crown7 and Smoking Everywhere, claim they give smokers a safer alternative to tobacco smokes, and some even market them as smoking cessation aides. Unlike regular cigarettes, however, e-cigarettes are marketed without regulation and warning labels.

1. Research this product and the FDA's conclusions and activities regarding marketing this product. Write a brief report of what you learned. (AACSB: Communication; Reflective Thinking)

2. Discuss the pros and cons of selling e-cigarettes. Should marketers be able to sell this product? (AACSB: Communication; Ethical Reasoning)

Rough Road Ahead: Marketing and the Economy

Samsung

Millions of people have dumped their boxy televisions sets in favor of sleek, new flat-panel models with screen sizes of 50 inches or more. Big-screen HDTVs have finally caught on, accounting for two-thirds of all televisions now sold. But like most things these days, as consumers reign in their spending, they are buying fewer TVs. and with big-screen TV prices falling fast, TV-maker revenues are down even more. So what is Samsung—the world's number one television producer—to do? How about convincing consumers that current model flat-panel TVs are no longer good enough? To that end, Samsung is launching a new line of ultraslim TVs, supported by a $50 million media campaign. Samsung and other manufacturers are now making a big-screen TV that's less than one inch thick, far thinner than the current 4-inch standard for big screen TVs. Samsung is betting that many consumers will pay a premium for a unit that's more stylish, lighter and easier to hang, and more energy efficient. In this case, the price premium is about 50 percent, with a 46-inch unit ringing the register at $2,799. And the picture quality? Not *quite* as good as the thicker, cheaper models. That leaves many analysts wondering if this new product can revive a slumping industry during down economic times.

1. Is this a good time for Samsung to be introducing its new, ultrathin TVs? Why or why not? What targeting and positioning strategy would you recommend?

2. With the new TVs, is Samsung practicing customer-centered new-product development? How?

Travel Budget: Marketing by the Numbers

When introducing new products, it's usually not easy to determine at what price it should be offered. At the very least, however, a marketer must understand the costs associated with producing the product and set the price at some level above those costs. For example, suppose that a manufacturer of lawn mowers incurs a cost of $75 for each mower it produces and that it produces a total of 1 million mowers each year. Fixed costs for this company are $5 million. Refer to Appendix 2: Marketing by the Numbers to answer the following questions.

1. What is the unit cost for each mower this company produces? (AACSB: Communication; Analytic Reasoning)

2. If the manufacturer desires a markup of 60 percent on sales, at what price should this product be sold to a reseller such as a wholesaler or distributor? (AACSB: Communication; Analytic Reasoning)

Drive In: Video Case

Electrolux

Since the 1920s, Swedish company Electrolux has been making and selling home appliances worldwide. Decade after decade, the company, originally known for its vacuum cleaners, has been turning out innovative products in a way that seems to magically predict what will work for consumers. The success of Electrolux's new-product development process results from more than just technological and design expertise. More importantly, it is rooted in what the company calls "consumer insight."

The concept of consumer insight is integrated into the Electrolux marketing strategy. It involves starting with the customer and working backward to design the product. Electrolux employs various methods to get deeply into the consumer's mind and to understand consumer needs. It then boils down that information to form concepts and, from concepts, it designs products. Because of its cus-

tomer-centric approach, Electrolux refers to itself as the "thoughtful" design innovator and has for years stood behind the slogan "Thinking of you."

After viewing the video featuring Electrolux, answer the following questions about the company's new product development process:

1. What is consumer insight? What are some ways in which Electrolux develops consumer insight?

2. Describe how Electrolux might go about developing products if it were focused solely on engineering and technology. What might be the result of this product-development process?

3. With household appliances in mind, identify some consumer trends from the video, as well as any others that you can think of. Explain how new products could take advantage of each trend.

9

Pricing
Understanding and Capturing Customer Value

ROAD MAP

Previewing the Concepts

We continue your marketing journey with a look at a second major marketing mix tool—pricing. If effective product development, promotion, and distribution sow the seeds of business success, effective pricing is the harvest. Firms successful at creating customer value with the other marketing mix activities must still capture some of this value in the prices they earn. Yet, despite its importance, many firms do not handle pricing well. In this chapter, we begin with the question: What is a price? Next, we look at three major pricing strategies— customer value-based, cost-based, and competition-based pricing—and at other factors that affect pricing decisions. Finally, we examine strategies for new-product pricing, product mix pricing, price adjustments, and dealing with price changes.

Objective Outline

> **Objective 1**   Identify the three major pricing strategies and discuss the importance of understanding customer-value perceptions, company costs, and competitor strategies when setting prices.
> What Is a Price? **p 303**
> Major Pricing Strategies. **pp 303–308**

> **Objective 2**   Identify and define the other important external and internal factors affecting a firm's pricing decisions.
> Other Internal and External Considerations Affecting Price Decisions **pp 308–313**

> **Objective 3**   Describe the major strategies for pricing new products.
> New-Product Pricing **pp 313–314**

> **Objective 4**   Explain how companies find a set of prices that maximizes the profits from the total product mix.
> Product Mix Pricing **pp 314–318**

> **Objective 5**   Discuss how companies adjust their prices to take into account different types of customers and situations.
> Price-Adjustment Strategies **pp 318–325**

> **Objective 6**   Discuss the key issues related to initiating and responding to price changes.
> Price Changes **pp 325–328**
> Public Policy and Pricing **pp 329–331**

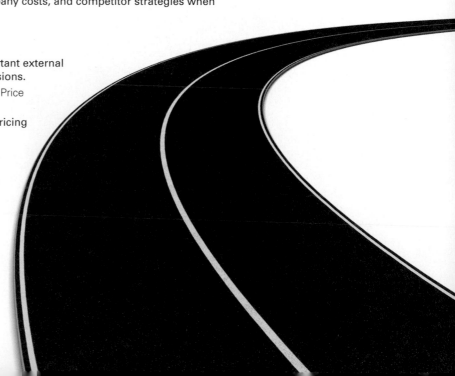

▲ The Harry Potter book series made its debut in 1997. Harry Potter and the Deathly Hallows shattered sales records, selling 11 million copies in the first 24 hours.

The Harry Potter phenomenon has swept the world, but in Britain it has brought a vicious price war between supermarkets and other retailers, with the author and the publisher unable to influence or stop the fighting. Hundreds of thousands of copies of the last of the Harry Potter series were discounted to draw customers in as loss leaders. Among the big hitters in the war was Wal-Mart's and the ASDA supermarket chain.

First Stop

Harry Potter: Sparks Fly During Supermarket Price War

In July 2007, some half a million fans of Harry Potter faced disappointment if they expected to pick up a cut price, hardcover copy of the final episode in the series by J.K. Rowling. That is, if the buyers headed for Wal-Mart-owned ASDA in Britain.

The publisher of the series, Bloomsbury, cancelled the supermarket's order for 500,000 copies in a dispute over money even though tens of thousands of buyers had already ordered copies from ASDA. In response, ASDA accused the publisher of profiteering by pushing up the recommended retail price of the book to £17.99. The dispute also came at a time when smaller bookshops discovered that they would make a better profit and would be able to compete more easily with bigger stores by buying the books from them rather than wholesalers. Tesco and other supermarket giants would be offering the title not at £17.99, but at £7.99. The best price from a wholesaler for a smaller book retailer would be £9.89.

ASDA, among others, noted that progressively, Bloomsbury had increased the price of each successive book in the series. The first book in the series, *Harry Potter and the Philosopher's Stone,* had retailed at £11.99; the sixth book in the series, *Harry Potter and the Half-Blood Prince,* had swelled to £16.99. ASDA claimed that Bloomsbury had cancelled the order because it had intended to sell *Harry Potter and the Deathly Hallows* for £8.87; the publisher claimed the order had been cancelled because ASDA owed them money.

Minna Fry, Bloomsbury's marketing director said of the cancellation, "It's to do with the fact that they owe us money and haven't settled their bills. It has been going on a while, going on for weeks actually, and we always said we wouldn't provide them with the books until that was sorted out. And that's what's happening."

A day later on July 18, the story changed. ASDA climbed down and apologized for claiming that Bloomsbury was profiteering. They withdrew their press release of July 15 and hoped that this would mend the broken bridges with Bloomsbury.

Bloomsbury was quick to grab the olive branch and the mammoth order went through. The Harry Potter price war was on and by July 20 the supermarket chain Morrisons was offering the book for £4.99. It had chosen this price point because it undercut ASDA by 1p. Morrisons would restrict buyers to one copy of the book each and ASDA to two copies per customer. Tesco adopted a different approach by selling the book for £5 to those customers who spent at least £50 on other products, and £10 to all others. Amazon.com's global advanced sales were 2.2 million (some 47 percent higher than the last Harry Potter book).

The eagerly awaited final installment in the globally popular Harry Potter book series sparked off price wars across the globe as retailers vied for customers by slashing prices to draw them in. From the U.K. to Kuala Lumpur, the recommended retail price of each new volume was cut.

▲Although ASDA captured an enormous market share of the Harry Potter books, it was in fact losing money on every copy sold, which amounted to a loss of millions of dollars on its initial order of 500,000 copies of the book.

At its peak in the first week of sales of the new book, Amazon.com was selling a copy every 4 seconds.

Despite the price war, there were sales for everyone. The last installment of the Harry Potter series became the fastest selling book ever. In the first two days it had sold over three million copies. That was one million more than the previous record holder, Harry Potter and the Half-Blood Prince. The early sales figures for everyone were bright. ASDA sold 250,000 copies between midnight on the day the book was released and many more the following morning. By noon, nearly all of its 500,000 copies had sold. Tesco had forecast that it would sell 350,000 in the first twelve hours, but this was a massive underestimate.

Charles Walker, a member of the U.K.'s parliament, had warned of the dangers of this price cut war and its effect on smaller bookshops. He was worried that the smaller bookshops relied on the profits of a handful of blockbusters each year. They simply could not compete with supermarkets, which were using these blockbusters as loss leaders. Whilst he applauded the fact that increased book sales boosted literacy, the result could be that smaller bookshops would be forced to close. The price war made it difficult for smaller bookshops to be viable.

A year later in July 2008, ASDA reignited the Harry Potter price war by placing newspaper advertisements to promote the paperback version of Harry Potter and the Deathly Hallows. The sales price would be £1. ASDA ran the offer from July 10 to July 13. The recommended retail price had been set at £8.99, but the advertisement proudly proclaimed: "£1. Magic Price. ASDA: why pay more?"

ASDA was able to report a 79 percent market share of sales of the Harry Potter and the Deathly Hallows children's edition. It could not have possibly made a profit from the sales; in fact, it was calculated that it lost £150,000. It had sold the book at 89 percent off its recommended retail price.

ASDA was also able to claim that it had captured 53 percent of the sales of the adult edition. According to Nielsen BookScan, the figures from the week ending July 12 meant that overall the book's selling price in all outlets was £1.96 (78 percent of the recommended retail price). In all, retailers had shifted some 46,257 copies in a week.

Meanwhile, in July 2007 in Kuala Lumpur, MPH, Popular, Times, and Harris bookstores decided to withdraw the Harry Potter and the Deathly Hallows novel from their shelves. They were protesting against Tesco and Carrefour's decision to sell the novel at the much cheaper price of RM69.90. The retail price of the book was RM109.90.

Patricia Chen, MPH's chief operating officer, confirmed that the book would not be available and that all of the events that had been planned had been cancelled. She believed it was unfair that hypermarkets were able to retail this vital book even though they were not in the book sector.

All Bloomsbury said about the price wars was, "It's out of our hands."

Bloomsbury, however, saw its revenues and gross profits shrink by 18 percent and 11 percent, respectively, after the end of the Harry Potter series.[1]

Price
The amount of money charged for a product or service, or the sum of the values that customers exchange for the benefits of having or using the product or service.

*C*ompanies today face a fierce and fast-changing pricing environment. Value-seeking customers have put increased pricing pressure on many companies. Thanks to the weakened economy, the pricing power of the Internet, and value-driven retailers such as Wal-Mart, says one analyst. "These days, we're all cheapskates in search of a spend-less strategy." In response, it seems that almost every company is looking for ways to slash prices.[2]

Yet, cutting prices is often not the best answer. Reducing prices unnecessarily can lead to lost profits and damaging price wars. It can cheapen a brand by signaling to customers that the price is more important than the customer value a brand delivers. Instead, no matter what the state of the economy, ▲companies should sell value, not price. In some cases, that means selling lesser products at rock-bottom prices. But in most cases, it means persuading customers that paying a higher price for the company's brand is justified by the greater value they gain.

WHAT IS A PRICE? (p 303)

In the narrowest sense, **price** is the amount of money charged for a product or service. More broadly, price is the sum of all the values that customers give up in order to gain the benefits of having or using a product or service. Historically, price has been the major factor affecting buyer choice. In recent decades, nonprice factors have gained increasing importance. However, price still remains one of the most important elements determining a firm's market share and profitability.

Price is the only element in the marketing mix that produces revenue; all other elements represent costs. Price is also one of the most flexible marketing mix elements. Unlike product features and channel commitments, prices can be changed quickly. At the same time, pricing is the number-one problem facing many marketing executives, and many companies do not handle pricing well. Some managers view pricing as a big headache, preferring instead to focus on the other marketing mix elements. However, smart managers treat pricing as a key strategic tool for creating and capturing customer value. Prices have a direct impact on a firm's bottom line. A small percentage improvement in price can generate a large percentage in profitability. More importantly, as a part of a company's overall value proposition, price plays a key role in creating customer value and building customer relationships. "Instead of running away from pricing," says the expert, "savvy marketers are embracing it."[3]

▲Pricing: No matter what the state of the economy, companies should sell value, not price.

Author Comment »
Setting the right price is one of the marketer's most difficult tasks. A host of factors come into play. But finding and implementing the right price strategy is critical to success.

MAJOR PRICING STRATEGIES (pp 303–308)

The price the company charges will fall somewhere between one that is too high to produce any demand and one that is too low to produce a profit. ■ **Figure 9.1** summarizes the major considerations in setting price. Customer perceptions of the product's value set the ceiling for prices. If customers perceive that the price is greater than the product's value, they will not buy the product. Product costs set the floor for prices. If the company prices the product below its costs, company profits will suffer. In setting its price between these two extremes, the company must consider a number of other internal and external factors, including competitors' strategies and prices, the company's overall marketing strategy and mix, and the nature of the market and demand.

The figure suggests three major pricing strategies: customer value-based pricing, cost-based pricing, and competition-based pricing.

Customer Value-Based Pricing

Author Comment »
Like everything else in marketing, good pricing starts with *customers* and their perceptions of value.

In the end, the customer will decide whether a product's price is right. Pricing decisions, like other marketing mix decisions, must start with customer value. When customers buy a product, they exchange something of value (the price) in order to get something of value (the benefits of having or using the product). Effective, customer-oriented pricing involves understanding how much value consumers place on the benefits they receive from the product and setting a price that captures this value.

■ **Figure 9.1** Considerations in Setting Price

If customers perceive that a product's price is greater than its value, they won't buy it. If the company prices a product below its costs, profits will suffer. Between the two extremes, the "right" pricing strategy is one that delivers both value to the customer and profits to the company.

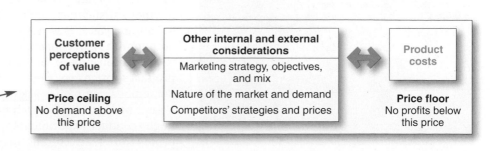

Customer perceptions of value	Other internal and external considerations	Product costs
	Marketing strategy, objectives, and mix	
Price ceiling No demand above this price	Nature of the market and demand Competitors' strategies and prices	**Price floor** No profits below this price

■ **Figure 9.2** Value-Based Pricing Versus Cost-Based Pricing

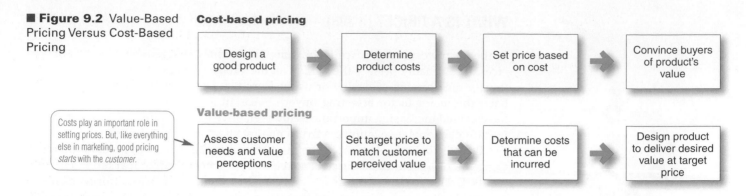

Cost-based pricing

Design a good product ➡ Determine product costs ➡ Set price based on cost ➡ Convince buyers of product's value

Costs play an important role in setting prices. But, like everything else in marketing, good pricing *starts* with the *customer*.

Value-based pricing

Assess customer needs and value perceptions ➡ Set target price to match customer perceived value ➡ Determine costs that can be incurred ➡ Design product to deliver desired value at target price

Customer value-based pricing
Setting price based on buyers' perceptions of value rather than on the seller's cost.

Customer value-based pricing uses buyers' perceptions of value, not the seller's cost, as the key to pricing. Value-based pricing means that the marketer cannot design a product and marketing program and then set the price. Price is considered along with the other marketing mix variables *before* the marketing program is set.

■ **Figure 9.2** compares value-based pricing with cost-based pricing. Although costs are an important consideration in setting prices, cost-based pricing is often product driven. The company designs what it considers to be a good product, adds up the costs of making the product, and sets a price that covers costs plus a target profit. Marketing must then convince buyers that the product's value at that price justifies its purchase. If the price turns out to be too high, the company must settle for lower markups or lower sales, both resulting in disappointing profits.

Value-based pricing reverses this process. The company first assesses customer needs and value perceptions. It then sets its target price based on customer perceptions of value. The targeted value and price drive decisions about what costs can be incurred and the resulting product design. As a result, pricing begins with analyzing consumer needs and value perceptions, and price is set to match consumers' perceived value.

It's important to remember that "good value" is not the same as "low price." ▲For example, a Steinway piano—any Steinway piano—costs a lot. But to those who own one, a Steinway is a great value:[4]

▼**Perceived value: A Steinway piano—any Steinway piano—costs a lot. But to those who own one, a Steinway is a great value. "A Steinway takes you places you've never been."**

A Steinway grand piano typically runs anywhere from $40,000 to $165,000. The most popular model sells for around $72,000. But ask anyone who owns one and they'll tell you that, when it comes to Steinway, price is nothing, the Steinway experience is everything. Steinway makes very high quality pianos—handcrafting each Steinway requires up to one full year. But more important, owners get the Steinway mystique. The Steinway name evokes images of classical concert stages and the celebrities and performers who've owned and played Steinway pianos across more than 155 years.

But Steinways aren't just for world-class pianists and the wealthy. Ninety-nine percent of all Steinway buyers are amateurs who perform only in their dens. To such customers, whatever a Steinway costs, it's a small price to pay for the value of owning one. As one Steinway owner puts it, "My friendship with the Steinway piano is one of the most important and beautiful things in my life." Who can put a price on such feelings?

Companies often find it hard to measure the value customers will attach to its product. For example, calculating the cost of ingredients in a meal at a fancy restaurant is relatively easy. But assigning a value to other satisfactions such as taste, environment, relaxation, conversation, and status is very hard. These values are subjective—they vary both for different consumers and different situations.

Still, consumers will use these perceived values to evaluate a product's price, so the company must work to measure them. Sometimes, companies ask consumers how much they would pay for a basic product and for each benefit added to the offer. Or a company might conduct experiments to test the perceived value of different product offers. According to an old Russian proverb, there are two fools in every market—one who asks too much and one who asks too little. If the seller charges more than the buyers' perceived value, the company's sales will suffer. If the seller charges less, its products sell very well but they produce less revenue than they would if they were priced at the level of perceived value.

We now examine two types of value-based pricing: *good-value pricing* and *value-added pricing*.

Good-Value Pricing Recent economic events have caused a fundamental shift in consumer attitudes toward price and quality. In response, many companies have changed their pricing approaches to bring them into line with changing economic conditions and consumer price perceptions. More and more, marketers have adopted **good-value pricing** strategies—offering just the right combination of quality and good service at a fair price.

Good-value pricing
Offering just the right combination of quality and good service at a fair price.

In many cases, this has involved introducing less-expensive versions of established, brand-name products. To meet the tougher economic times and more frugal consumer spending habits, fast-food restaurants such as Taco Bell and McDonald's offer value meals and dollar menu items. Armani offers the less-expensive, more-casual Armani Exchange fashion line. Alberto-Culver's TRESemmé hair care line promises "A salon look and feel at a fraction of the price." And every car company now offers small, inexpensive models better suited to the strapped consumer's budget.

In other cases, good-value pricing has involved redesigning existing brands to offer more quality for a given price or the same quality for less. Some companies even succeed by offering less value but at rock-bottom prices. For example, passengers flying low-cost European airline Ryanair won't get much in the way of free amenities, but they'll like the airline's unbelievably low prices.[5]

▲Good-value pricing: Ryanair appears to have found a radical new pricing solution, one that customers are sure to love: Make flying free!

▲Ireland's Ryanair, Europe's most profitable airline, appears to have found a radical new pricing solution: Make flying *free*! By the end of the decade, Ryanair promises, more than half of its passengers will pay nothing for their tickets. Remarkably, the airline already offers virtually free fares to a quarter of its customers. What's the secret? Ryanair's frugal cost structure makes even the most cost-conscious competitor look like a reckless spender. In addition, however, the airline charges for virtually everything except the seat itself, from baggage check-in to seat-back advertising space. Once in the air, flight attendants hawk everything from scratch-card games to perfume and digital cameras to their captive audience. Upon arrival at some out-of-the-way airport, Ryanair will sell you a bus or train ticket into town. The airline even gets commissions from sales of Hertz rental cars, hotel rooms, ski packages, and travel insurance. Despite Ryanair's sometimes pushy efforts to extract more revenue from each traveler, customers aren't complaining. Most of the additional purchases are discretionary, and you just can't beat those outrageously low prices.

An important type of good-value pricing at the retail level is *everyday low pricing (EDLP)*. EDLP involves charging a constant, everyday low price with few or no temporary price discounts. Retailers such as Costco and furniture seller Room & Board practice EDLP. The king of EDLP is Wal-Mart, which practically defined the concept. Except for a few sale items every month, Wal-Mart promises everyday low prices on everything it sells. In contrast, *high-low pricing* involves charging higher prices on an everyday basis but running frequent promotions to lower prices temporarily on selected items. Department stores such as Kohl's and Macy's practice high-low pricing by having frequent sales days, early-bird savings, and bonus earnings for store credit-card holders.

Value-added pricing
Attaching value-added features and services to differentiate a company's offers and charging higher prices.

Value-Added Pricing Value-based pricing doesn't mean simply charging what customers want to pay or setting low prices to meet the competition. Instead, many companies adopt **value-added pricing** strategies. Rather than cutting prices to match

▲ **Value-added pricing:** Rather than dropping prices for its venerable Stag umbrella brand to match cheaper imports, Ebrahim Currim & Sons successfully launched umbrellas with funky designs, cool colors, and value-added features and sold them at even higher prices.

competitors, they attach value-added features and services to differentiate their offers and thus support higher prices. ▲ Consider this example:

> The monsoon season in Mumbai, India, is three months of near-nonstop rain. For 147 years, most Mumbaikars protected themselves with a Stag umbrella from venerable Ebrahim Currim & Sons. Like Ford's Model T, the basic Stag was sturdy, affordable, and of any color, as long as it was black. By the end of the twentieth century, however, the Stag was threatened by cheaper imports from China. Stag responded by dropping prices and scrimping on quality. It was a bad move: For the first time since the 1940s, the brand began losing money.
>
> Finally, however, Stag came to its senses. It abandoned the price war and started innovating. It launched designer umbrellas in funky designs and cool colors. Teenagers and young adults lapped them up. It then launched umbrellas with a built-in high-power flashlight for those who walk unlit roads at night, and models with prerecorded tunes for music lovers. For women who walk secluded streets after dark, there's Stag's Bodyguard model, armed with glare lights, emergency blinkers, and an alarm. Customers willingly pay up to a 100 percent premium for the new products. Under the new value-added strategy, the Stag brand has now returned to profitability. Come the monsoon in June, the grand old black Stags still reappear on the streets of Mumbai—but now priced 15 percent higher than the imports.[6]

The Stag example illustrates once again that customers are motivated not by price, but by what they get for what they pay. "If consumers thought the best deal was simply a question of money saved, we'd all be shopping in one big discount store," says one pricing expert. "Customers want value and are willing to pay for it. Savvy marketers price their products accordingly."[7]

Cost-Based Pricing

Whereas customer-value perceptions set the price ceiling, costs set the floor for the price that the company can charge. **Cost-based pricing** involves setting prices based on the costs for producing, distributing, and selling the product plus a fair rate of return for its effort and risk. A company's costs may be an important element in its pricing strategy.

Some companies, such as Ryanair, Wal-Mart, and Dell, work to become the "low-cost producers" in their industries. Companies with lower costs can set lower prices that result in smaller margins but greater sales and profits. Other companies, however, intentionally pay higher costs so that they can claim higher prices and margins. For example, it costs more to make a "handcrafted" Steinway piano than a Yamaha production model. But the higher costs result in higher quality, justifying an eye-popping $75,000 price. The key is to manage the spread between costs and prices—how much the company makes for the customer value it delivers.

Types of Costs

A company's costs take two forms, fixed and variable. **Fixed costs** (also known as **overhead**) are costs that do not vary with production or sales level. For example, a company must pay each month's bills for rent, heat, interest, and executive salaries, whatever the company's output. **Variable costs** vary directly with the level of production. Each PC produced by HP involves a cost of computer chips, wires, plastic, packaging, and other inputs. These costs tend to be the same for each unit produced. They are called variable because their total varies with the number of units produced. **Total costs** are the sum of the fixed and variable costs for any given level of production. Management wants to charge a price that will at least cover the total production costs at a given level of production.

The company must watch its costs carefully. If it costs the company more than competitors to produce and sell a similar product, the company will need to charge a higher price or make less profit, putting it at a competitive disadvantage.

Cost-Plus Pricing

Cost-plus pricing (markup pricing)
Adding a standard markup to the cost of the product.

The simplest pricing method is **cost-plus pricing** (or **markup pricing**)—adding a standard markup to the cost of the product. For example, an electronics retailer might pay a manufacturer $20 for a flash drive and mark it up to sell at $30, a 50 percent markup on cost. The retailer's gross margin is $10. If the store's operating costs amount to $8 per flash drive sold, the retailer's profit margin will be $2. The manufacturer that made the flash drive probably used cost-plus pricing, too. If the manufacturer's standard cost of producing the flash drive was $16, it might have added a 25 percent markup, setting the price to the retailers at $20.

Does using standard markups to set prices make sense? Generally, no. Any pricing method that ignores consumer demand and competitor prices is not likely to lead to the best price. Still, markup pricing remains popular for many reasons. First, sellers are more certain about costs than about demand. By tying the price to cost, sellers simplify pricing. Second, when all firms in the industry use this pricing method, prices tend to be similar, minimizing price competition.

Break-even pricing (target return pricing)
Setting price to break even on the costs of making and marketing a product, or setting price to make a target return.

Another cost-oriented pricing approach is **break-even pricing**, or a variation called **target return pricing**. The firm tries to determine the price at which it will break even or make the target return it is seeking. Target return pricing uses the concept of a *break-even chart*, which shows the total cost and total revenue expected at different sales volume levels. ■ **Figure 9.3** shows a break-even chart for the flash drive manufacturer discussed previously. Fixed costs are $6 million regardless of sales volume, and variable costs are $5 per unit. Variable costs are added to fixed costs to form total costs, which rise with volume. The slope of the total revenue curve reflects the price. Here, the price is $15 (for example, the company's revenue is $12 million on 800,000 units, or $15 per unit).

At the $15 price, the manufacturer must sell at least 600,000 units to *break even* (break-even volume = fixed costs ÷ (price – variable costs) = $6,000,000 ÷ ($15 – $5) = 600,000). That is, at this level, total revenues will equal total costs of $9 million, producing no profit. If the flash drive manufacturer wants a target return of $2 million, it must sell at least 800,000 units to obtain the $12 million of total revenue needed to cover the costs of $10 million plus the $2 million of target profits. In contrast, if the company charges a higher price, say $20, it will not need to sell as many units to break even or to achieve its target profit. In fact, the higher the price, the lower the manufacturer's break-even point will be.

The major problem with this analysis, however, is that it fails to consider customer value and the relationship between price and demand. As the *price* increases, *demand* decreases, and the market may not buy even the lower volume needed to break even at the higher price. For example, suppose the flash drive manufacturer calculates that, given its current fixed and variable costs, it must charge a price of $30 for the product in order to earn its desired target profit. But marketing research

■ **Figure 9.3** Break-Even Chart for Determining Target-Return Price and Break-Even Volume

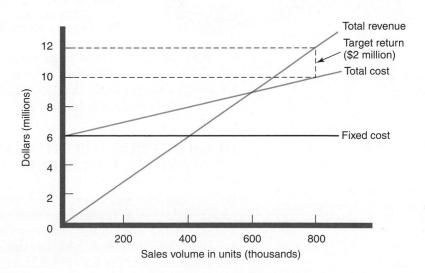

shows that few consumers will pay more than $25. In this case, the company must trim its costs in order to lower the break-even point so that it can charge the lower price consumers expect.

Thus, although break-even analysis and target return pricing can help the company to determine minimum prices needed to cover expected costs and profits, they do not take the price–demand relationship into account. When using this method, the company must also consider the impact of price on sales volume needed to realize target profits and the likelihood that the needed volume will be achieved at each possible price.

Competition-Based Pricing

Author Comment >>
In setting prices, the company must also consider competitors' prices. No matter what price it charges—high, low, or in between—the company must be certain to give customers superior value for that price.

Competition-based pricing
Setting prices based on competitors' strategies, prices, costs, and market offerings.

Competition-based pricing involves setting prices based on competitors' strategies, costs, prices, and market offerings. Consumers will base their judgments of a product's value on the prices that competitors charge for similar products.

In assessing competitors' pricing strategies, the company should ask several questions. First, how does the company's market offering compare with competitors' offerings in terms of customer value? If consumers perceive that the company's product or service provides greater value, the company can charge a higher price. If consumers perceive less value relative to competing products, the company must either charge a lower price or change customer perceptions to justify a higher price.

Next, how strong are current competitors and what are their current pricing strategies? If the company faces a host of smaller competitors charging high prices relative to the value they deliver, it might charge lower prices to drive weaker competitors out of the market. If the market is dominated by larger, low-price competitors, the company may decide to target unserved market niches with value-added products at higher prices.

For example, ▲Annie Bloom's Books, an independent bookseller in Portland, Oregon, isn't likely to win a price war against Amazon.com or Barnes & Noble—it doesn't even try. Instead, the shop relies on its personal approach, cozy atmosphere,

▼Pricing against larger, low-price competitors: Independent bookstore Annie Bloom's Books isn't likely to win a price war against Amazon.com or Barnes & Noble. Instead, it relies on outstanding customer service and a cozy atmosphere to turn booklovers into loyal customers.

and friendly and knowledgeable staff to turn local book lovers into loyal patrons, even if they have to pay a little more. Customers writing on a consumer review Web site recently gave Annie Bloom's straight five-star ratings, supported by the kinds of comments you likely wouldn't see for Barnes & Noble:[8]

> Annie Bloom's is not the biggest bookstore, nor the most convenient to park at, nor are the prices incredibly discounted, nor is the bathroom easy to find. . . . However, it is one of the friendliest bookstores in town. It is just big enough for a solid hour of browsing. And it has a talented, smart, and long-term staff with incredible taste. You'll find common best sellers here, but you'll also find all those cool books you heard about on NPR or in *Vanity Fair* that you never see featured at Barnes & Noble. [It's a] bookstore for the book crowd. Good customer service here! Also, be nice to the cat. PS: [It] has a kid's play area in the back.

What principle should guide decisions about what price to charge relative to those of competitors? The answer is simple in concept but often difficult in practice: No matter what price you charge—high, low, or in between—be certain to give customers superior value for that price.

Author Comment >>
Now that we've looked at the three general pricing approaches—value-, cost-, and competitor-based pricing—let's dig into some of the many other factors that affect pricing decisions.

OTHER INTERNAL AND EXTERNAL CONSIDERATIONS AFFECTING PRICE DECISIONS (pp 308–313)

Beyond customer value perceptions, costs, and competitor strategies, the company must consider several additional internal and external factors. Internal factors affecting pricing include the company's overall marketing strategy, objectives, and marketing mix, as well as other organizational considerations. External factors include the nature of the market and demand and other environmental factors.

Overall Marketing Strategy, Objectives, and Mix

Price is only one element of the company's broader marketing strategy. Thus, before setting price, the company must decide on its overall marketing strategy for the product or service. If the company has selected its target market and positioning carefully, then its marketing mix strategy, including price, will be fairly straightforward. For example, when Honda developed its Acura brand to compete with European luxury-performance cars in the higher-income segment, this required charging a high price. In contrast, when it introduced the Honda Fit model—billed as "a pint-sized fuel miser with feisty giddy up"—this positioning required charging a low price. Thus, pricing strategy is largely determined by decisions on market positioning.

Pricing may play an important role in helping to accomplish company objectives at many levels. A firm can set prices to attract new customers or to profitably retain existing ones. It can set prices low to prevent competition from entering the market or set prices at competitors' levels to stabilize the market. It can price to keep the loyalty and support of resellers or to avoid government intervention. Prices can be reduced temporarily to create excitement for a brand. Or one product may be priced to help the sales of other products in the company's line.

Price is only one of the marketing mix tools that a company uses to achieve its marketing objectives. Price decisions must be coordinated with product design, distribution, and promotion decisions to form a consistent and effective integrated marketing program. Decisions made for other marketing mix variables may affect pricing decisions. For example, a decision to position the product on high-performance quality will mean that the seller must charge a higher price to cover higher costs. And producers whose resellers are expected to support and promote their products may have to build larger reseller margins into their prices.

Companies often position their products on price and then tailor other marketing mix decisions to the prices they want to charge. Here, price is a crucial product-positioning factor that defines the product's market, competition, and design. Many firms support such price-positioning strategies with a technique called **target costing**. Target costing reverses the usual process of first designing a new product, determining its cost, and then asking, "Can we sell it for that?" Instead, it starts with an ideal selling price based on customer-value considerations and then targets costs that will ensure that the price is met. For example, when Honda set out to design the Fit, it began with a $13,950 starting price point and 33-mpg operating efficiency firmly in mind. It then designed a stylish, peppy little car with costs that allowed it to give target customers those values.

Other companies deemphasize price and use other marketing mix tools to create *nonprice* positions. Often, the best strategy is not to charge the lowest price but rather to differentiate the marketing offer to make it worth a higher price. For example, Bang & Olufsen—known for its cutting-edge consumer electronics—builds more value into its products and charges sky-high prices. For example, a B&O 50-inch BeoVision 4 HDTV will cost you $7,500; a 65-inch model runs $13,500. A complete B&O sound system? Well, you don't really want to know. But target customers recognize Bang & Olufsen's very high quality and are willing to pay more to get it.

Some marketers even position their products on *high* prices, featuring high prices as part of their product's allure. For example, Grand Marnier offers a $225 bottle of Cuvée du Cent Cinquantenaire that's marketed with the tagline "Hard to find, impossible to pronounce, and prohibitively expensive." ▲And Titus Cycles, a premium bicycle manufacturer, features its high prices and its advertising. Ads humorously show

Target costing
Pricing that starts with an ideal selling price, then targets costs that will ensure that the price is met.

▼**Positioning on high price:** Titus features its lofty prices in its advertising—"suggested retail price: $7,750.00."

suggested retail: $7750.00

Certain sacrifices have to be made to obtain the 2007 Titus Vuelo.
The Vuelo's patented Isogrid technology is the ultimate fusion of titanium and carbon fiber. Stiff and lively on the climbs, smooth on the rough, stable riding downhill and ever-ready to sprint. Available with a custom fit that makes the Vuelo an extension of your own body. To find out more give us a call at 800.85 TITUS or visit us at titusti.com.

TITUS

people working unusual second jobs to earn the money to afford a Titus. Suggested retail price for a Titus Solera: $7,750.00. But "It's worth a second job," the ads confirm.

Thus, marketers must consider the total marketing strategy and mix when setting prices. But again, even when featuring price, marketers need to remember that customers rarely buy on price alone. Instead, they seek products that give them the best value in terms of benefits received for the prices paid.

Organizational Considerations

Management must decide who within the organization should set prices. Companies handle pricing in a variety of ways. In small companies, prices are often set by top management rather than by the marketing or sales departments. In large companies, pricing is typically handled by divisional or product line managers. In industrial markets, salespeople may be allowed to negotiate with customers within certain price ranges. Even so, top management sets the pricing objectives and policies, and it often approves the prices proposed by lower-level management or salespeople.

In industries in which pricing is a key factor (airlines, aerospace, steel, railroads, oil companies), companies often have pricing departments to set the best prices or to help others in setting them. These departments report to the marketing department or top management. Others who have an influence on pricing include sales managers, production managers, finance managers, and accountants.

The Market and Demand

▼ **Monopolistic competition: Toyota sets its Prius brand apart through strong branding and advertising, reducing the impact of price. The 3rd generation Prius takes you from "zero to sixty in 70% fewer emissions."**

As noted earlier, good pricing starts with an understanding of how customers' perceptions of value affect the prices they are willing to pay. Both consumer and industrial buyers balance the price of a product or service against the benefits of owning it. Thus, before setting prices, the marketer must understand the relationship between price and demand for the company's product. In this section, we take a deeper look at the price–demand relationship and how it varies for different types of markets. We then discuss methods for analyzing the price–demand relationship.

Pricing in Different Types of Markets

The seller's pricing freedom varies with different types of markets. Economists recognize four types of markets, each presenting a different pricing challenge.

Under *pure competition*, the market consists of many buyers and sellers trading in a uniform commodity such as wheat, copper, or financial securities. No single buyer or seller has much effect on the going market price. In a purely competitive market, marketing research, product development, pricing, advertising, and sales promotion play little or no role. Thus, sellers in these markets do not spend much time on marketing strategy.

Under *monopolistic competition*, the market consists of many buyers and sellers who trade over a range of prices rather than a single market price. A range of prices occurs because sellers can differentiate their offers to buyers. Sellers try to develop differentiated offers for different customer segments and, in addition to price, freely use branding, advertising, and personal selling to set their offers apart. Thus, Toyota sets its Prius brand apart through strong branding and advertising,

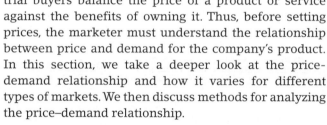

reducing the impact of price. It advertises that the 3rd generation Prius takes you from "zero to sixty in 70% fewer emissions." Because there are many competitors in such markets, each firm is less affected by competitors' pricing strategies than in oligopolistic markets.

Under *oligopolistic competition*, the market consists of a few sellers who are highly sensitive to each other's pricing and marketing strategies. Because there are few sellers, each seller is alert and responsive to competitors' pricing strategies and moves. In a *pure monopoly*, the market consists of one seller. The seller may be a government monopoly (the U.S. Postal Service), a private regulated monopoly (a power company), or a private nonregulated monopoly (DuPont when it introduced nylon). Pricing is handled differently in each case.

Analyzing the Price–Demand Relationship

Each price the company might charge will lead to a different level of demand. The relationship between the price charged and the resulting demand level is shown in the **demand curve** in ■ **Figure 9.4**. The demand curve shows the number of units the market will buy in a given time period at different prices that might be charged. In the normal case, demand and price are inversely related; that is, the higher the price, the lower the demand. Thus, the company would sell less if it raised its price from P_1 to P_2. In short, consumers with limited budgets probably will buy less of something if its price is too high.

Understanding a brand's price–demand curve is crucial to good pricing decisions. ConAgra Foods learned this lesson when pricing its Banquet frozen dinners.[9]

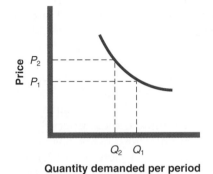

■ **Figure 9.4** Demand Curve

ConAgra found out the hard way about the perils of pushing up the price of a Banquet frozen dinner. When it tried to recoup high commodity costs by hiking the list price last year, many retailers began charging up to $1.25 a meal. The response from shoppers used to paying $1? The cold shoulder. The resulting sales drop forced ConAgra to peddle excess dinners to discounters and contributed to a 40 percent drop in the company's stock price for the year. ▲It turns out that "the key component for Banquet dinners—the key attribute—is you've got to be at $1," says ConAgra's CEO, Gary Rodkin. "Everything else pales in comparison to that." The price is now back to a buck a dinner. To make money at that price, ConAgra is doing a better job of managing costs. It tossed out pricey items such as barbecued chicken and country-fried pork in favor of grilled meat patties and rice and beans. It also shrank portion sizes while swapping in cheaper ingredients, such as mashed potatoes for brownies. Consumers are responding well to the brand's efforts to keep prices down. Where else can you find dinner for 99 cents?

▲The price–demand curve: When ConAgra raised prices on its Banquet frozen dinners, sales fell sharply. "You've got to be at $1," says CEO, Gary Rodkin. "Everything else pales in comparison to that."

Most companies try to measure their demand curves by estimating demand at different prices. The type of market makes a difference. In a monopoly, the demand curve shows the total market demand resulting from different prices. If the company faces competition, its demand at different prices will depend on whether competitors' prices stay constant or change with the company's own prices.

Price Elasticity of Demand

Marketers also need to know **price elasticity**—how responsive demand will be to a change in price. If demand hardly changes with a small change in price, we say demand is *inelastic*. If demand changes greatly, we say the demand is *elastic*.

If demand is elastic rather than inelastic, sellers will consider lowering their prices. A lower price will produce more total revenue. This practice makes sense as long as the extra costs of producing and selling more do not exceed the extra revenue. At the same time, most firms want to avoid pricing that turns their products into commodities. In recent years, forces such as deregulation and the instant price comparisons afforded by the Internet and other technologies have increased consumer price

Demand curve
A curve that shows the number of units the market will buy in a given time period, at different prices that might be charged.

Price elasticity
A measure of the sensitivity of demand to changes in price.

sensitivity, turning products ranging from telephones and computers to new automobiles into commodities in some consumers' eyes.

The Economy

Economic conditions can have a strong impact on the firm's pricing strategies. Economic factors such as a boom or recession, inflation, and interest rates affect pricing decisions because they affect consumer spending, consumer perceptions of the product's price and value, and the company's costs of producing and selling a product.

In the aftermath of the recent recession, consumers have rethought the price–value equation. Many consumers have tightened their belts and become more value conscious. In the new, more-frugal economy, bemoans one marketer, "The frill is gone." As a result, many marketers have increased their emphasis on value-for-the-money pricing strategies. "Value is the magic word," says a P&G marketer. "In these economic times, people are . . . being much more thoughtful before making purchases. . . . Now, we're going to be even more focused on helping consumers see value."[10]

The most obvious response to the new economic realities is to cut prices and offer deep discounts. And thousands of companies have done just that. Lower prices make products more affordable and help spur short-term sales. However, such price cuts can have undesirable long-term consequences. "Tempted to cut prices?" asks one pricing consultant. "You're not alone. With slumping sales, many businesses have been quick to offer discounts. But price cuts raise some tough questions: Will deep discounts cheapen your brand? Once you cut prices, can you raise them again? How do you deal with narrower margins?"[11]

Rather than cutting prices, many companies are instead shifting their marketing focus to more affordable items in their product mixes. ▲For example, whereas its previous promotions emphasized high-end products and pricey concepts such as creating dream kitchens, Home Depot's more recent advertising pushes items like potting soil and hand tools under the tagline: "More saving. More doing. That's the Power of Home Depot." Other companies are holding prices but redefining the "value" in their value propositions. For instance, Unilever has repositioned its higher-end Bertolli frozen meals as an eat-at-home brand that's more affordable than eating out. And Kraft's Velveeta cheese ads tell shoppers to "forget the cheddar, Velveeta is better," claiming that a package of Velveeta is "twice the size of cheddar, for the same price."[12]

Remember, even in tough economic times, consumers do not buy based on prices alone. They balance the price they pay against the value they receive. For example, according to a recent survey, despite selling its shoes for as much as $150 a pair, Nike commands the highest consumer loyalty of any brand in the footwear segment.[13] Customers perceive the value of Nike's products and the Nike ownership experience to be well worth the price. Thus, no matter what price they charge—low or high—companies need to offer great *value for the money*.

Other External Factors

When setting prices, beyond the market and the economy, the company must consider a number of other factors in its external environment. It must know what impact its prices will have on other parties in its environment. How will *resellers* react to various prices? The company should set prices that give resellers a fair profit, encourage their support, and help them to sell the product effectively. The *government* is another important external influence on pricing decisions. Finally, *social concerns* may need to be taken into account. In setting prices, a company's short-term sales, market share, and profit goals may need to be tempered by broader societal considerations. We will examine public policy issues in pricing later in the chapter.

▼Pricing and the economy: Rather than just cutting prices, Home Depot shifted its marketing focus to more affordable items and projects under the tagline: "More saving. More doing."

More saving. More doing.℠

◆ Speed Bump: Linking the Concepts

The concept of customer value is critical to good pricing and to successful marketing in general. Slow down for a minute and be certain that you appreciate what value really means.

- An earlier example states that, although the average Steinway piano costs $75,000, to those who own one, a Steinway is a great value. Does this fit with your idea of value?
- Pick two competing brands from a familiar product category (watches, perfume, consumer electronics, restaurants)—one low priced and the other high priced. Which, if either, offers the greatest value?
- Does "value" mean the same thing as "low price"? How do these concepts differ?

We've now seen that pricing decisions are subject to a complex array of customer, company, competitive, and environmental forces. To make things even more complex, a company sets not a single price but rather a *pricing structure* that covers different items in its line. This pricing structure changes over time as products move through their life cycles. The company adjusts its prices to reflect changes in costs and demand and to account for variations in buyers and situations. As the competitive environment changes, the company considers when to initiate price changes and when to respond to them.

We now examine additional pricing approaches used in special pricing situations or to adjust prices to meet changing situations. We look in turn at *new-product pricing* for products in the introductory stage of the product life cycle, *product mix pricing* for related products in the product mix, *price adjustment tactics* that account for customer differences and changing situations, and strategies for initiating and responding to *price changes*.[14]

NEW-PRODUCT PRICING (pp 313–314)

Pricing strategies usually change as the product passes through its life cycle. The introductory stage is especially challenging. Companies bringing out a new product face the challenge of setting prices for the first time. They can choose between two broad strategies: *market-skimming pricing* and *market-penetration pricing*.

Market-Skimming Pricing

Many companies that invent new products set high initial prices to "skim" revenues layer by layer from the market. Sony frequently uses this strategy, called **market-skimming pricing** (or **price skimming**). When Apple first introduced the iPhone, it charged an initial price of as much as $599 per phone. The phones were purchased only by customers who really wanted the sleek new gadget and could afford to pay a high price for it. Six months later, Apple dropped the price to $399 for an 8GB model and $499 for the 16GB model to attract new buyers. Within a year, it dropped prices again to $199 and $299. In this way, Apple skimmed the maximum amount of revenue from the various segments of the market.[15]

Market skimming makes sense only under certain conditions. First, the product's quality and image must support its higher price and enough buyers must want the product at that price. Second, the costs of producing a smaller volume cannot be so high that they cancel the advantage of charging more. Finally, competitors should not be able to enter the market easily and undercut the high price.

Market-Penetration Pricing

Rather than setting a high initial price to skim off small but profitable market segments, some companies use **market-penetration pricing**. They set a low initial price in order to *penetrate* the market quickly and deeply—to attract a large number

▲Penetration pricing: To lure famously frugal Chinese customers, IKEA slashed its prices. The strategy worked. Weekend crowds at it cavernous Beijing store are so big that employees need to use megaphones to keep them in control.

of buyers quickly and win a large market share. The high sales volume results in falling costs, allowing the companies to cut their prices even further. ▲For example, giant Swedish retailer IKEA used penetration pricing to boost its success in the Chinese market:[16]

> When IKEA first opened stores in China in 2002, people crowded in, but not to buy home furnishings. Instead, they came to take advantage of the freebies—air conditioning, clean toilets, and even decorating ideas. Chinese consumers are famously frugal. When it came time to actually buy, they shopped instead at local stores just down the street that offered knockoffs of IKEA's designs at a fraction of the price. So to lure the finicky Chinese customers, IKEA slashed its prices in China to the lowest in the world, the opposite approach of many Western retailers there. By increasingly stocking its Chinese stores with China-made products, the retailer pushed prices on some items as low as 70 percent below prices in IKEA's outlets outside China. The penetration pricing strategy worked. IKEA now captures a 43 percent market share of China's fast-growing home wares market alone, and the sales of its six mammoth Chinese stores surged 25 percent last year. The cavernous Beijing store draws nearly 6 million visitors annually. Weekend crowds are so big that employees need to use megaphones to keep them in control.

Several conditions must be met for this low-price strategy to work. First, the market must be highly price sensitive so that a low price produces more market growth. Second, production and distribution costs must fall as sales volume increases. Finally, the low price must help keep out the competition, and the penetration pricer must maintain its low-price position—otherwise, the price advantage may be only temporary.

PRODUCT MIX PRICING (pp 314–318)

The strategy for setting a product's price often has to be changed when the product is part of a product mix. In this case, the firm looks for a set of prices that maximizes the profits on the total product mix. Pricing is difficult because the various products have related demand and costs and face different degrees of competition. We now take a closer look at the five product mix pricing situations summarized in ■ **Table 9.1**: *product line pricing, optional-product pricing, captive-product pricing, by-product pricing*, and *product bundle pricing*.

Product Line Pricing

Author Comment ≫
Most individual products are part of a broader product mix and must be priced accordingly. For example, Gillette prices its Fusion razors low. But once you buy the razor, you're a captive customer for its higher-margin replacement cartridges.

Product line pricing
Setting the price steps between various products in a product line based on cost differences between the products, customer evaluations of different features, and competitors' prices.

Companies usually develop product lines rather than single products. For example, Samsonite offers some 20 different collections of bags of all shapes and sizes, at prices that range from under $50 for a Sammie's child's backpack to more than $1,250 for a bag from its Black Label Vintage Collection. In **product line pricing**, manage-

■ **Table 9.1** Product Mix Pricing

Pricing Situation	Description
Product line pricing	Setting prices across an entire product line
Optional-product pricing	Pricing optional or accessory products sold with the main product
Captive-product pricing	Pricing products that must be used with the main product
By-product pricing	Pricing low-value by-products to get rid of them
Product bundle pricing	Pricing bundles of products sold together

ment must decide on the price steps to set between the various products in a line.

The price steps should take into account cost differences between the products in the line. More importantly, they should account for differences in customer perceptions of the value of different features. ▲For example, Quicken offers an entire line of financial management software, including Basic, Deluxe, Premier, and Home & Business versions priced at $29.99, $59.99, $79.99, and $89.99. Although it costs Quicken no more to produce the CD containing the Premier version than the CD containing the Basic version, many buyers happily pay more to obtain additional Premier features, such as financial-planning and investment-monitoring tools. Quicken's task is to establish perceived value differences that support the price differences.

Optional-Product Pricing

Many companies use **optional-product pricing**—offering to sell optional or accessory products along with their main product. For example, a car buyer may choose to order a GPS navigation system and Bluetooth wireless communication. Refrigerators come with optional ice makers. And when you order a new PC, you can select from a bewildering array of hard drives, docking systems, software options, service plans, and carrying cases. Pricing these options is a sticky problem. Companies must decide which items to include in the base price and which to offer as options.

Captive-Product Pricing

Companies that make products that must be used along with a main product are using **captive-product pricing**. Examples of captive products are razor blade cartridges, videogames, and printer cartridges. Producers of the main products (razors, videogame consoles, and printers) often price them low and set high markups on the supplies. For example, when Sony first introduced its PlayStation3 videogame console, priced at $499 and $599 for the regular and premium versions, it lost as much as $306 per unit sold. Sony hoped to recoup the losses through sales of more lucrative PS3 games.[17]

However, companies that use captive-product pricing must be careful. Finding the right balance between the main product and captive product prices can be tricky. For example, despite industry-leading PS3 videogame sales, Sony has yet to earn back its losses on the PS3 console. What's more, consumers trapped into buying expensive captive products may come to resent the brand that ensnared them. This has happened in the printer and cartridges industry (see Marketing at Work 9.1).

In the case of services, this captive-product pricing is called *two-part pricing*. The price of the service is broken into a *fixed fee* plus a *variable usage rate*. ▲Thus, at Six Flags and other amusement parks, you pay a daily ticket or season pass charge plus additional fees for food and other in-park features.

By-Product Pricing

Producing products and services often generates by-products. If the by-products have no value and if getting rid of them is costly, this will affect the pricing of the main product. Using

▲**Product line pricing: Quicken offers an entire line of financial management software, including Basic, Deluxe, Premier, and Home & Business versions priced at $29.99, $59.99, $79.99, and $89.99.**

Optional-product pricing
The pricing of optional or accessory products along with a main product.

Captive-product pricing
Setting a price for products that must be used along with a main product, such as blades for a razor and games for a videogame console.

▼**Captive-product pricing: At Six Flags, you pay a daily ticket or season pass charge plus additional fees for food and other in-park features.**

Marketing at Work 9.1

Kodak: A Whole New Concept in Printer Pricing and Economics

HP, Epson, Canon, and Lexmark have long dominated the $50 billion printer industry with a maddening "razor-and-blades" pricing strategy (as in give away the razor, then make your profits on the blades). They sell printers at little or no profit. But once you own the printer, you're stuck buying their grossly overpriced, high-margin replacement ink cartridges.

For example, you can pick up a nifty little HP multifunction inkjet printer for only $69.99. But the HP tricolor inkjet cartridge that goes with it costs $24.99. And a 100-count pack of HP 4-by-6-inch photo paper costs another $14.49. The price per ounce of inkjet printer ink can exceed the per-ounce price of an expensive perfume, premium champagne, or even caviar. By one estimate, if you bought a gallon of the stuff at those prices, it would cost you a horrifying $4,731.

The big manufacturers seem content with this captive-product pricing strategy. In fact, they pull in four times more revenues from ink cartridges and paper than from the printers themselves. Customers don't like being held hostage and having to pay through the nose for ink and paper—some are outraged by it. But what can they do? Only HP cartridges work with HP printers. Buying another brand isn't the answer, either—all of the manufacturers pursue the same pricing strategy. Besides, it's difficult to compare long-term per-print prices across manufacturers. Few of us know or go to the trouble to figure out in advance how many cartridges we'll use or what future ink prices will be.

Enter Kodak—with a unique solution. Kodak recently introduced its first line of printers—EasyShare All-in-One printers—with a revolutionary pricing strategy that threatens to turn the entire inkjet printer industry upside-down. In a twist on typical industry practice, Kodak sells its printers at premium prices with no discounts, and then sells the ink cartridges for less. EasyShare printers sell for $149.99 to $299.99, depending on features, about $50 higher than comparable printers sold by competitors. However, EasyShare black and color ink cartridges go for just $9.99 and $14.99, respectively, about half the prevailing competitor prices. It's a whole new concept in printer pricing and economics.

To make the strategy work, Kodak first had to create a new kind of inkjet printer. It developed an innovative technology that uses tiny nozzles to squirt pigment ink drops that are just a few

▲ Kodak has the right printer and the right ink prices. Now, all it has to do is to reeducate consumers about the benefits of paying more up front in order to reduce long-run printing costs.

atoms in size. EasyShare printers take about 55 seconds to produce a 4-by-6-inch print, longer than some competitive printers that do it in 32 seconds. But the resulting photos take up to 90 years to fade versus dye-based inks that can begin to fade in as little as a year.

By-product pricing
Setting a price for by-products in order to make the main product's price more competitive.

by-product pricing, the company seeks a market for these by-products to help offset the costs of disposing of them and to help make the price of the main product more competitive. The by-products themselves can even turn out to be profitable—turning trash into cash. For example, papermaker MeadWestvaco created a separate company, Asphalt Innovations, which creates useful chemicals entirely from the by-products of its wood-processing activities, once considered waste. In fact, Asphalt Innovations has grown to become the world's biggest supplier of specialty chemicals for the paving industry.[18]

Moreover, Kodak found a way to contain all of the printing electronics within the EasyShare printer itself, whereas rivals include some of the electronics in the cartridges. This lets Kodak charge less for the cartridges. As a result, according to one independent lab study, Kodak's new printers "whomped" rival's printers in price per printout. The study showed that consumers using an EasyShare printer and buying specially priced packages of photo paper and an ink cartridge can print 4-by-6-inch photos for only 10 cents each, compared with about 29 cents each for typical home printers and 19 cents each at retail store photo services.

Thus, Kodak has the right printer and the right ink prices. Now, all it has to do is to reeducate consumers about printer pricing—about the benefits of paying more up front in order to reduce long-run printing costs. To do this, Kodak launched a "Think Ink" marketing campaign, built around the visual image "ThINK," with the first two letters in black and the last three in gold. The campaign asks the pivotal question: "Is it smarter to save money on a printer or save money on ink? (Hint: You only buy the printer once.)"

The ThINK campaign began with online viral efforts, centered on a series of popular "Inkisit" videos, featuring two dorky guys, Nathan and Max, who love to print photos but who don't like ink's high cost. In the videos, they ask enthusiastically, "Have you ever thought about what life would be like if ink was cheaper?" Kodak posted the videos on YouTube and MySpace and set up an entertaining and informative microsite.

Then came the bread-and-butter "ThINK" media campaign, targeting budget-conscious consumers who want to print at home but have limited this activity because of high ink costs. Kodak's research showed that more than 70 percent of all families restrict their children's printing because of cost concerns. So the campaign targets "enterprising parents" who want to empower their kids' creativity and not have to worry about "silly economics."

The ThINK campaign tackles the very difficult task of shifting consumer value perceptions away from initial printer prices and toward prices per print. "Our strategy," says a Kodak marketing executive, "is to crystallize for consumers that they're not only buying a printer today but also buying into three to four years of ink purchases." The campaign sent shockwaves through the inkjet printer industry and its "razor-and-blades" pricing mentality. Says one analyst, Kodak is "plastering their costs per printed page all over the place. The most recent EasyShare ads even rant about a "$5 billion (ink) stain" on the economy caused by "overpaying" for other brands of inkjet printer ink. No one has ever done that before in this market. [The others] don't want to remind consumers how much it costs." Another analyst agrees:

This was not your usual printer introduction. Kodak completely changes the game . . . and [these printers] will not be welcomed by competition. Competing openly on cost-per-print puts the profits of the printing industry in grave danger. To compete with Kodak, competitors will have to reveal their own printing costs and ultimately lower [their ink] prices. While this is great for consumers, it is bad for printer manufacturers' bottom lines. Kodak's [EasyShare printers] will take the market by storm.

It's still too soon to tell whether Kodak's revolutionary pricing strategy is working, but the early results are promising. The company exceeded its first-year sales forecasts and sold 780,000 EasyShare printers last year. Competitors are now scrambling to introduce their own lower-priced cartridges and longer lasting inks. But Kodak claims that EasyShare printers will still save customers up to 50 percent on everything they print.

As one observer concludes, Kodak "Has its priorities straight: Great-looking photos that last a lifetime," with affordable per-print prices in the bargain. "It makes a world-rocking point about the razor-blades model that's lined the coffers of the inkjet industry for years. If you're mad as hell, you don't have to take it anymore."

Sources: Quotes and other information from: Beth Snyder Bulik, "Kodak Develops New Model: Inexpensive Printer, Cheap Ink," *Advertising Age*, March 12, 2007, p. 4; Clive Akass, "Kodak Inkjets Shake Industry," *Personal Computer World*, April 2007, accessed at www.pcw.co.uk/personal-computer-world/news/2174253/kodak-halves-cost-photo-prints; Stephen H. Wildstrom, "Kodak Moments for Less," *BusinessWeek*, May 14, 2007, p. 24; William M. Bulkeley, "Kodak's Strategy for First Printer—Cheaper Cartridges," *Wall Street Journal*, February 6, 2007, p. B1; "Consumer Launch Campaign of the Year 2008," *PRweek*, March 10, 2008, p. S11; Lonnie Brown, "Database: Why Cartridge Companies Are in the Black," *Ledger* (Lakeland, FL), January 23, 2009, p. C7; Stuart Elliott, "Are You Fed Up? This Ad's for You," *News and Observer* (Raleigh), May 15, 2009, p. 1; and www.kodak.com, accessed November 2009.

Product Bundle Pricing

Product bundle pricing
Combining several products and offering the bundle at a reduced price.

Using **product bundle pricing**, sellers often combine several of their products and offer the bundle at a reduced price. For example, fast-food restaurants bundle a burger, fries, and a soft drink at a "combo" price. Bath & Body Works offers "three-fer" deals on its soaps and lotions (such as 3 antibacterial soaps for $10). And Comcast, Verizon, and other telecommunications companies bundle TV service, phone service, and high-speed Internet connections at a low combined price. Price bundling can promote the sales of products consumers might not otherwise buy, but the combined price must be low enough to get them to buy the bundle.[19]

PRICE ADJUSTMENTS (pp 318–325)

Author Comment >>

Setting the base price for a product is only the start. The company must then adjust the price to account for customer and situational differences. When was the last time you paid the full suggested retail price for something?

Companies usually adjust their basic prices to account for various customer differences and changing situations. Here we examine the seven price adjustment strategies summarized in ■ **Table 9.2**: *discount and allowance pricing, segmented pricing, psychological pricing, promotional pricing, geographical pricing, dynamic pricing,* and *international pricing.*

Discount and Allowance Pricing

Discount
A straight reduction in price on purchases during a stated period of time or of larger quantities.

Most companies adjust their basic price to reward customers for certain responses, such as early payment of bills, volume purchases, and off-season buying. These price adjustments—called *discounts* and *allowances*—can take many forms.

The many forms of **discounts** include a *cash discount,* a price reduction to buyers who pay their bills promptly. A typical example is "2/10, net 30," which means that although payment is due within 30 days, the buyer can deduct 2 percent if the bill is paid within 10 days. A *quantity discount* is a price reduction to buyers who buy large volumes. A *functional discount* (also called a *trade discount*) is offered by the seller to trade-channel members who perform certain functions, such as selling, storing, and record keeping. A *seasonal discount* is a price reduction to buyers who buy merchandise or services out of season.

Allowance
Promotional money paid by manufacturers to retailers in return for an agreement to feature the manufacturer's products in some way.

Allowances are another type of reduction from the list price. For example, *trade-in allowances* are price reductions given for turning in an old item when buying a new one. Trade-in allowances are most common in the automobile industry but are also given for other durable goods. *Promotional allowances* are payments or price reductions to reward dealers for participating in advertising and sales support programs.

Segmented Pricing

Segmented pricing
Selling a product or service at two or more prices, where the difference in prices is not based on differences in costs.

Companies will often adjust their basic prices to allow for differences in customers, products, and locations. In **segmented pricing**, the company sells a product or service at two or more prices, even though the difference in prices is not based on differences in costs.

■ **Table 9.2** Price Adjustments

Strategy	Description
Discount and allowance pricing	Reducing prices to reward customer responses such as paying early or promoting the product
Segmented pricing	Adjusting prices to allow for differences in customers, products, or locations
Psychological pricing	Adjusting prices for psychological effect
Promotional pricing	Temporarily reducing prices to increase short-run sales
Geographical pricing	Adjusting prices to account for the geographic location of customers
Dynamic pricing	Adjusting prices continually to meet the characteristics and needs of individual customers and situations
International pricing	Adjusting prices for international markets

▲Product-form pricing: Evian water in a 1 liter bottle might cost you 5 cents an ounce at your local supermarket, whereas the same water might run $2.28 an ounce when sold in 5-ounce aerosol cans as Evian Brumisateur Mineral Water Spray moisturizer.

Psychological pricing
Pricing that considers the psychology of prices and not simply the economics; the price is used to say something about the product.

Reference prices
Prices that buyers carry in their minds and refer to when they look at a given product.

▼Psychological pricing: What do the prices marked on this tag suggest about the product and buying situation?

Segmented pricing takes several forms. Under *customer-segment* pricing, different customers pay different prices for the same product or service. Museums, for example, may charge a lower admission for students and senior citizens. Under *product-form pricing*, different versions of the product are priced differently but not according to differences in their costs. ▲For instance, a 1-liter bottle (about 34 ounces) of Evian mineral water may cost $1.59 at your local supermarket. But a 5-ounce aerosol can of Evian Brumisateur Mineral Water Spray sells for a suggested retail price of $11.39 at beauty boutiques and spas. The water is all from the same source in the French Alps and the aerosol packaging costs little more than the plastic bottles. Yet you pay about 5 cents an ounce for one form and $2.28 an ounce for the other.

Using *location-based pricing*, a company charges different prices for different locations, even though the cost of offering each location is the same. For instance, theaters vary their seat prices because of audience preferences for certain locations and state universities charge higher tuition for out-of-state students. Finally, using *time-based pricing*, a firm varies its price by the season, the month, the day, and even the hour. Movie theaters charge matinee pricing during the daytime. Resorts give weekend and seasonal discounts.

For segmented pricing to be an effective strategy, certain conditions must exist. The market must be segmentable, and the segments must show different degrees of demand. The costs of segmenting and watching the market cannot exceed the extra revenue obtained from the price difference. Of course, the segmented pricing must also be legal.

Most importantly, segmented prices should reflect real differences in customers' perceived value. Consumers in higher price tiers must feel that they're getting their extra money's worth for the higher prices paid. By the same token, companies must be careful not to treat customers in lower price tiers as second-class citizens. Otherwise, in the long run, the practice will lead to customer resentment and ill will. For example, in recent years, the airlines have incurred the wrath of frustrated customers at both ends of the airplane. Passengers paying full fare for business or first class seats often feel that they are being gouged. At the same time, passengers in lower-priced coach seats feel that they're being ignored or abused. In all, the airlines today face many very difficult pricing issues (see Marketing at Work 9.2).

Psychological Pricing

Price says something about the product. For example, many consumers use price to judge quality. A $100 bottle of perfume may contain only $3 worth of scent, but some people are willing to pay the $100 because this price indicates something special.

In using **psychological pricing**, sellers consider the psychology of prices and not simply the economics. For example, consumers usually perceive higher-priced products as having higher quality. When they can judge the quality of a product by examining it or by calling on past experience with it, they use price less to judge quality. ▲But when they cannot judge quality because they lack the information or skill, price becomes an important quality signal. For example, who's the better lawyer, one who charges $50 per hour or one that charges $500 per hour? You'd have to do a lot of digging into the respective lawyers' credentials to answer this question objectively, and even then, you might not be able to judge accurately. Most of us would simply assume that the higher priced lawyer is better.

Another aspect of psychological pricing is **reference prices**—prices that buyers carry in their minds and refer to when looking at a given product. The reference price might be formed by noting current prices, remembering past prices, or assessing the buying situation. Sellers can influence or use these consumers' reference prices when setting price. For example, a company could display its product next to more expensive ones in order to imply that it belongs in the same class, as when a grocery retailer shelves its store brand of bran flakes and raisins cereal priced at $1.89 next to Kellogg's Raisin Bran priced at $3.20.

Marketing at Work 9.2

Airline Pricing: Balancing the Price–Value Equation

It's the same plane going to the same place at exactly the same time. But these days, not all airline passengers are equal. Nor do they all pay equally. No matter where they sit, however, it seems that all passengers have one thing in common: Almost nobody's very happy with what they get for what they pay.

At the front of the plane, first class or business class passengers—who might pay as much as three to six times the fare paid by economy class passengers at the back of the plane—are wondering whether it's worth it. At the same time, back in coach, tempers are flaring over rising air travel prices coupled with fewer amenities and less attentive customer service. The American Customer Satisfaction Index rates the airline industry second-to-last among 44 industries in customer satisfaction, only a few points ahead of the perennial cellar-dweller, cable and satellite TV services.

Flying in coach has become an increasingly miserable experience. Legroom is practically nonexistent. Passengers are more tightly packed together. Hot meals have been eliminated. Ditto pillows and blankets. And the next time that guy in front of you leans his seat back directly into your face, few of your fellow passengers are likely to blame you if you feel a brief, murderous urge to strike back.

Most of us have had experiences like those of Doug Fesler, an executive at a medical research group in Washington. He wasn't expecting much in the way of amenities on his American Airlines flight to Honolulu in September. In fact, knowing the airline no longer served free meals, he had packed his own lunch for the second leg of his flight from Dallas to Honolulu. But he said he was shocked at the lack of basic services and the overall condition of the cabin. On that flight, the audio for the movie was broken. The light that indicated when the bathroom was occupied was squirrelly, causing confusion and, in some cases, embarrassingly long waits for passengers in need of the lavatory. And though food was available for purchase, it ran out before the flight attendants could serve the entire cabin, leaving some fellow passengers looking longingly at the snack he had packed.

▲ The price–value equation: These days, when it comes to airline pricing, almost nobody's very happy with what they get for what they pay. Back in coach, tempers are flaring over rising prices coupled with cattle-car service [or fewer amenities].

His return flight was just as disappointing. This time the audio for the movie worked—but only in Spanish—and his seat refused to stay in the upright position. "I was just appalled," said Fesler. "You pay $500 or $600 for a seat, and you expect it to be functional." He said he has considered refusing to fly airlines with such poor service, but added that "if you did that with every airline that made you mad, you'd never get anywhere in this country."

The story is much different in the front of the plane—and it's not just things like the four-course meal (served on china, with real utensils, and with a choice of four wines) that American now serves its business-class passengers on overseas flights and the fact that, yes, a pillow and a blanket still await you. Passengers flying business class on United from Washington Dulles to Frankfurt, for example, are now offered "180-degree lie-flat" seats. The seats transform into 6-foot-4-inch

For most purchases, consumers don't have all the skill or information they need to figure out whether they are paying a good price. They don't have the time, ability, or inclination to research different brands or stores, compare prices, and get the best deals. Instead, they may rely on certain cues that signal whether a price is high or low. Interestingly, such pricing cues are often provided by sellers, in the form of sales signs, price-matching guarantees, loss-leader pricing, and other helpful hints.[20]

Even small differences in price can signal product differences. Consider a stereo receiver priced at $300 compared to one priced at $299.99. The actual price difference is only 1 cent, but the psychological difference can be much greater. For example, some consumers will see the $299.99 as a price in the $200 range rather than the $300 range. The $299.99 will more likely be seen as a bargain price, whereas the $300 price suggests more quality. Some psychologists argue that each digit has symbolic

beds and feature larger personal TV screens, iPod adapters, and noise-canceling headphones. American and other airlines are also upgrading their upper-class cabins on international flights with such features as in-flight entertainment and new food options.

What with all these privileges and the impeccable service that comes with them, you'd think that upper-class passengers would be delighted, but that's often not so. Premium passengers *get* more. But, of course, they also *pay* a lot more—some think *too much* more. Many upper-class passengers complain that they're picking up an unfair share of the bill for those who fly cheaply in the back. And they may be right. United says just 8 percent of its customers—the ones paying a premium for first and business class—generate 36 percent of passenger revenue.

But it's the folks back in coach who are grumbling the most. Why, they ask, has the quality of their flying experience degraded so quickly, even as prices have risen? The fact is that airlines, flying so close to full capacity today, have realized that they really don't have to cater to economy passengers—most of whom are booking on price alone and who increasingly have no real airline loyalty. The cost of pampering low-fare passengers would never be worth it in pure bottom-line terms. Thus airlines are increasingly cutting back services in coach or charging passengers for things that used to be free, like meals ($5 for a snack box on United) or drinks ($2 for a 16-fluid-ounce bottle of water on Spirit) or, in the case of Delta, US Airways, Northwest, and Continental, starting to use narrow-body planes more frequently on trans-Atlantic flights, making those long-haul flights more cost-effective, even if it is at the expense of passenger comfort.

It's all simple economics. For example, Northwest claims it saves $2 million a year by cutting pretzels from the economy section of flights. Meanwhile, American estimates that it pares $30 million a year by eliminating free meal service in coach. And wonder why it's almost impossible to get a pillow anymore? Again, it comes down to money. American claims that removing pillows saves it almost $1 million a year. It seems like the airlines are always finding new ways to dig deeper into the pockets of coach passengers—say by charging an extra $5 or $10 for reserving an aisle or window seat or $25 for checking a second bag.

The major airlines insist they want to please all their passengers but concede that it all comes down to the bottom line. "The passenger who is buying a ticket from us based on price sensitivity—we want to make sure they have a comfortable flight," says an executive at American. "But the way we chiefly derive a profit from any given flight is the passenger willing to pay the premium."

In the short run, the restructured pricing scheme might help the airline industry's finances. However, continuing to haul plane loads of increasingly grumpy passengers can't be good for the airlines in the long run. Especially in an economic downdraft, airlines need all the lift it can get from customer goodwill. Any airline that gets pricing right will surely reap the rewards.

The airlines acknowledge that they must do a better job of managing the price–value equation. "We recognize we have missed some opportunities in the last couple of years to do the right thing for the customer experience," says Mark Mitchell, American's managing director of customer experience, a newly created position. Mitchell says he was hired to "work on the broken pieces of our airline," including how American handles delays, the boarding process, cabin cleaning, baggage handling, and flight attendant interactions with customers.

More broadly, perhaps it's just a matter of adjusting passenger expectations. Some passengers seem to feel that the airlines should just acknowledge that the flying experience is no longer a glamorous or, at times, even tolerable one—especially back in coach—and that it's something passengers are going to have to accept. Low-cost carriers such as Southwest and JetBlue have long managed to keep costs down while at the same time keeping customers delighted.

"I actually have more respect for Southwest Airlines in this area," says one experienced traveler, referring to that historically no-frills airline. "They've never pretended to have more than they do."

Sources: Adapted from portions of Michelle Higgins, "Aboard Planes, Class Conflict," *New York Times*, November 25, 2007; with information from Jefferson George, "Want an Aisle Window? Get Ready to Pay for It," *McClatchy-Tribune Business News*, April 17, 2008; Kerry Dougherty, "Opinion: Are You Sick of Poor Customer Service? Get in (a Long) Line," *McClatchy-Tribune Business News*, March 17, 2009; and The American Customer Satisfaction Index, accessed at www.theacsi.org, September 2009.

and visual qualities that should be considered in pricing. Thus, 8 is round and even and creates a soothing effect, whereas 7 is angular and creates a jarring effect.

Promotional Pricing

Promotional pricing
Temporarily pricing products below the list price, and sometimes even below cost, to increase short-run sales.

With **promotional pricing**, companies will temporarily price their products below list price and sometimes even below cost to create buying excitement and urgency. Promotional pricing takes several forms. A seller may simply offer *discounts* from normal prices to increase sales and reduce inventories. Sellers also use *special-event pricing* in certain seasons to draw more customers. Thus, large-screen TVs and other consumer electronics are promotionally priced in November and December to attract Christmas shoppers into stores.

▲Promotional pricing: Companies offer promotional prices to create buying excitement and urgency.

Manufacturers sometimes offer *cash rebates* to consumers who buy the product from dealers within a specified time; the manufacturer sends the rebate directly to the customer. Rebates have been popular with automakers and producers of cell phones and small appliances, but they are also used with consumer packaged goods. Some manufacturers offer *low-interest financing, longer warranties,* or *free maintenance* to reduce the consumer's "price." This practice has become another favorite of the auto industry.

Promotional pricing, however, can have adverse effects. Used too frequently and copied by competitors, price promotions can create "deal-prone" customers who wait until brands go on sale before buying them. Or, constantly reduced prices can erode a brand's value in the eyes of customers. Marketers sometimes become addicted to promotional pricing, especially in difficult economic times. They use price promotions as a quick fix instead of sweating through the difficult process of developing effective longer-term strategies for building their brands. But companies must be careful to balance short-term sales incentives against long-term brand building. One analyst advises:[21]

When times are tough, there's a tendency to panic. One of the first and most prevalent tactics that many companies try is an aggressive price cut. Price trumps all. At least, that's how it feels these days. 20% off. 30% off. 50% off. Buy one, get one free. Whatever it is you're selling, you're offering it at a discount just to get customers in the door. But aggressive pricing strategies can be risky business. Companies should be very wary of risking their brands' perceived quality by resorting to deep and frequent price cuts. Some discounting is unavoidable in a tough economy and consumers have come to expect it. But marketers have to find ways to shore up their brand identity and brand equity during times of discount mayhem.

The point is that promotional pricing can be an effective means of generating sales for some companies in certain circumstances. But it can be damaging for other companies or if taken as a steady diet.

 Speed Bump: Linking the Concepts

Here's a good place to take a brief break. Think about some of the companies and industries you deal with that are "addicted" to promotional pricing.

- Many industries have created "deal-prone" consumers through the heavy use of promotional pricing—fast food, automobiles, cellphones, airlines, tires, furniture, and others. Pick a company in one of these industries and suggest ways that it might deal with this problem.
- How does the concept of value relate to promotional pricing? Does promotional pricing add to or detract from customer value?

Geographical Pricing

A company also must decide how to price its products for customers located in different parts of the country or world. Should the company risk losing the business of more-distant customers by charging them higher prices to cover the higher shipping costs? Or should the company charge all customers the same prices regardless of location? We will look at five *geographical pricing* strategies for the following hypothetical situation:

> The Peerless Paper Company is located in Atlanta, Georgia, and sells paper products to customers all over the United States. The cost of freight is high and affects the companies from whom customers buy their paper. Peerless wants to establish a geographical pricing policy. It is trying to determine how to price a $10,000 order to three specific customers: Customer A (Atlanta), Customer B (Bloomington, Indiana), and Customer C (Compton, California).

One option is for Peerless to ask each customer to pay the shipping cost from the Atlanta factory to the customer's location. All three customers would pay the same factory price of $10,000, with Customer A paying, say, $100 for shipping; Customer B, $150; and Customer C, $250. Called *FOB-origin pricing*, this practice means that the goods are placed *free on board* (hence, *FOB*) a carrier. At that point the title and responsibility pass to the customer, who pays the freight from the factory to the destination. Because each customer picks up its own cost, supporters of FOB pricing feel that this is the fairest way to assess freight charges. The disadvantage, however, is that Peerless will be a high-cost firm to distant customers.

Uniform-delivered pricing is the opposite of FOB pricing. Here, the company charges the same price plus freight to all customers, regardless of their location. The freight charge is set at the average freight cost. Suppose this is $150. Uniform-delivered pricing therefore results in a higher charge to the Atlanta customer (who pays $150 freight instead of $100) and a lower charge to the Compton customer (who pays $150 instead of $250). Although the Atlanta customer would prefer to buy paper from another local paper company that uses FOB-origin pricing, Peerless has a better chance of winning over the California customer.

Zone pricing falls between FOB-origin pricing and uniform-delivered pricing. The company sets up two or more zones. All customers within a given zone pay a single total price; the more distant the zone, the higher the price. For example, Peerless might set up an East Zone and charge $100 freight to all customers in this zone, a Midwest Zone in which it charges $150, and a West Zone in which it charges $250. In this way, the customers within a given price zone receive no price advantage from the company. For example, customers in Atlanta and Boston pay the same total price to Peerless. The complaint, however, is that the Atlanta customer is paying part of the Boston customer's freight cost.

Using *basing-point pricing*, the seller selects a given city as a "basing point" and charges all customers the freight cost from that city to the customer location, regardless of the city from which the goods are actually shipped. For example, Peerless might set Chicago as the basing point and charge all customers $10,000 plus the freight from Chicago to their locations. This means that an Atlanta customer pays the freight cost from Chicago to Atlanta, even though the goods may be shipped from Atlanta. If all sellers used the same basing-point city, delivered prices would be the same for all customers and price competition would be eliminated.

Finally, the seller who is anxious to do business with a certain customer or geographical area might use *freight-absorption pricing*. Using this strategy, the seller absorbs all or part of the actual freight charges in order to get the desired business. The seller might reason that if it can get more business, its average costs will fall and more than compensate for its extra freight cost. Freight-absorption pricing is used for market penetration and to hold on to increasingly competitive markets.

Dynamic Pricing

Throughout most of history, prices were set by negotiation between buyers and sellers. *Fixed price* policies—setting one price for all buyers—is a relatively modern idea that arose with the development of large-scale retailing at the end of the nineteenth century. Today, most prices are set this way. However, some companies are now reversing the fixed pricing trend. They are using **dynamic pricing**—adjusting prices continually to meet the characteristics and needs of individual customers and situations.

Dynamic pricing
Adjusting prices continually to meet the characteristics and needs of individual customers and situations.

▲Dynamic pricing: Alaska Airlines creates unique prices and advertisements for people as they surf the Web.

For example, think about how the Internet has affected pricing. From the mostly fixed pricing practices of the past century, the Web seems now to be taking us back—into a new age of fluid pricing. The flexibility of the Internet allows Web sellers to instantly and constantly adjust prices on a wide range of goods based on demand dynamics (sometimes called *real-time pricing*). In other cases, customers control pricing by bidding on auction sites such as eBay or negotiating on sites such as Priceline. Still other companies customize their offers based on the characteristics and behaviors of specific customers:[22]

It's an offer you can't resist: fly Alaska Airlines to Honolulu for $200 round trip. But what you might not know is that the offer was designed especially for you. ▲Alaska Airlines is introducing a system that creates unique prices and advertisements for people as they surf the Web. The system identifies consumers by their computers, using a small piece of code known as a cookie. It then combines detailed data from several sources to paint a picture of who's sitting on the other side of the screen. When the person clicks on an ad, the system quickly analyzes the data to assess how price-sensitive customers seem to be. Then, in an instant, one customer gets an offer for a flight from Seattle to Portland for $99 and another is quoted $109. Or someone who had visited Alaska Airlines' site frequently but then abruptly stopped visiting might be greeted with the $200 Hawaii offer. "I guarantee you there are a lot of people who will say yes to that," says Marston Gould, director of customer relationship management and online marketing for Alaska Airlines.

Dynamic pricing offers many advantages for marketers. For example, Internet sellers such as Amazon.com can mine their databases to gauge a specific shopper's desires, measure his or her means, instantaneously tailor products to fit that shopper's behavior, and price products accordingly. Catalog retailers such as L.L.Bean or Spiegel can change prices on the fly according to changes in demand or costs, changing prices for specific items on a day-by-day or even hour-by-hour basis. And many direct marketers monitor inventories, costs, and demand at any given moment and adjust prices instantly.

Consumers also benefit from the Web and dynamic pricing. A wealth of price comparison sites—such as Yahoo! Shopping, Bizrate.com, NexTag.com, Epinions .com, PriceGrabber.com, mySimon.com, and PriceScan.com—offer instant product and price comparisons from thousands of vendors. Epinions.com, for instance, lets shoppers browse by category or search for specific products and brands. It then searches the Web and reports back links to sellers offering the best prices along with customer reviews. In addition to simply finding the best product and the vendor with the best price for that product, customers armed with price information can often negotiate lower prices.

In addition, consumers can negotiate prices at online auction sites and exchanges. Suddenly the centuries-old art of haggling is back in vogue. Want to sell that antique pickle jar that's been collecting dust for generations? Post it on eBay, the world's biggest online flea market. Want to name your own price for a hotel room or rental car? Visit Priceline.com or another reverse auction site. Want to bid on a ticket to a Coldplay show? Check out Ticketmaster.com, which now offers an online auction service for concert tickets.

Dynamic pricing makes sense in many contexts—it adjusts prices according to market forces, and it often works to the benefit of the customer. But marketers need to be careful not to use dynamic pricing to take advantage of certain customer groups, damaging important customer relationships.

International Pricing

Companies that market their products internationally must decide what prices to charge in the different countries in which they operate. In some cases, a company can set a uniform worldwide price. For example, Boeing sells its jetliners at about the same price everywhere, whether in the United States, Europe, or a third-world country. However, most companies adjust their prices to reflect local market conditions and cost considerations.

The price that a company should charge in a specific country depends on many factors, including economic conditions, competitive situations, laws and regulations, and development of the wholesaling and retailing system. Consumer perceptions and preferences also may vary from country to country, calling for different prices. Or the company may have different marketing objectives in various world markets, which require changes in pricing strategy. For example, Samsung might introduce a new product into mature markets in highly developed countries with the goal of quickly gaining mass-market share—this would call for a penetration-pricing strategy. In contrast, it might enter a less-developed market by targeting smaller, less price-sensitive segments; in this case, market-skimming pricing makes sense.

Costs play an important role in setting international prices. Travelers abroad are often surprised to find that goods that are relatively inexpensive at home may carry outrageously higher price tags in other countries. A pair of Levi's selling for $30 in the United States might go for $63 in Tokyo and $88 in Paris. A McDonald's Big Mac selling for a modest $3.50 here might cost $7.50 in Reykjavik, Iceland, and an Oral-B toothbrush selling for $2.49 at home may cost $10 in China. Conversely, a Gucci handbag going for only $140 in Milan, Italy, might fetch $240 in the United States. In some cases, such *price escalation* may result from differences in selling strategies or market conditions. In most instances, however, it is simply a result of the higher costs of selling in another country—the additional costs of product modifications, shipping and insurance, import tariffs and taxes, exchange-rate fluctuations, and physical distribution.

Price has become a key element in the international marketing strategies of companies attempting to enter emerging markets, such as China, India, and Brazil. Consider Unilever's pricing strategy for developing countries:

> There used to be one way to sell a product in developing markets, if you bothered to sell there at all: Slap on a local label and market at premium prices to the elite. Unilever—maker of such brands as Dove, Lipton, and Vaseline—changed that. Instead, it built a following among the world's poorest consumers by shrinking packages to set a price even consumers living on $2 a day could afford. The strategy was forged about 25 years ago when Unilever's Indian subsidiary found its products out of reach for millions of Indians. To lower the price while making a profit, Unilever developed single-use packets for everything from shampoo to laundry detergent, costing just pennies a pack. The small, affordable packages put the company's premier brands within reach of the world's poor. Today, Unilever continues to woo cash-strapped customers with great success. For example, its approachable pricing helps explain why Unilever now captures 70 percent of the Brazil detergent market.[23]

Thus, international pricing presents some special problems and complexities. We discuss international pricing issues in more detail in Chapter 15.

Author Comment »
When and how should a company change its price? What if costs rise, putting the squeeze on profits? What if the economy sags and customers become more price-sensitive? Or what if a major competitor raises or drops its prices? As Figure 9.5 suggests, companies face many price-changing options.

PRICE CHANGES (pp 325–328)

After developing their pricing structures and strategies, companies often face situations in which they must initiate price changes or respond to price changes by competitors.

Initiating Price Changes

In some cases, the company may find it desirable to initiate either a price cut or a price increase. In both cases, it must anticipate possible buyer and competitor reactions.

Initiating Price Cuts

Several situations may lead a firm to consider cutting its price. One such circumstance is excess capacity. Another is falling demand in the face of strong price competition or a weakened economy. In such cases, the firm may aggressively cut prices to boost sales and share. But as the airline, fast-food, automobile, and other industries have learned in recent years, cutting prices in an industry loaded with excess capacity may lead to price wars as competitors try to hold on to market share.

A company may also cut prices in a drive to dominate the market through lower costs. Either the company starts with lower costs than its competitors, or it cuts prices in the hope of gaining market share that will further cut costs through larger volume. Bausch & Lomb used an aggressive low-cost, low-price strategy to become an early leader in the competitive soft contact lens market. Costco used this strategy to become the world's largest warehouse retailer.

Initiating Price Increases

A successful price increase can greatly improve profits. For example, if the company's profit margin is 3 percent of sales, a 1 percent price increase will boost profits by 33 percent if sales volume is unaffected. A major factor in price increases is cost inflation. Rising costs squeeze profit margins and lead companies to pass cost increases along to customers. Another factor leading to price increases is overdemand: When a company cannot supply all that its customers need, it may raise its prices, ration products to customers, or both. Consider today's worldwide oil and gas industry.

▲Initiating price increases: When gasoline prices rise rapidly, angry consumers often accuse the major oil companies of enriching themselves by gouging customers.

When raising prices, the company must avoid being perceived as a *price gouger*. ▲For example, when gasoline prices rise rapidly, angry customers often accuse the major oil companies of enriching themselves at the expense of consumers. Customers have long memories, and they will eventually turn away from companies or even whole industries that they perceive as charging excessive prices. In the extreme, claims of price gouging may even bring about increased government regulation.

There are some techniques for avoiding these problems. One is to maintain a sense of fairness surrounding any price increase. Price increases should be supported by company communications telling customers why prices are being raised.

Wherever possible, the company should consider ways to meet higher costs or demand without raising prices. For example, it can consider more cost-effective ways to produce or distribute its products. It can shrink the product or substitute less-expensive ingredients instead of raising the price, as ConAgra did in an effort to hold its Banquet frozen dinner prices at $1. Or it can "unbundle" its market offering, removing features, packaging, or services and separately pricing elements that were formerly part of the offer.

Buyer Reactions to Price Changes

Customers do not always interpret price changes in a straightforward way. A price *increase*, which would normally lower sales, may have some positive meanings for buyers. For example, what would you think if Rolex *raised* the price of its latest watch model? On the one hand, you might think that the watch is even more exclusive or better made. On the other hand, you might think that Rolex is simply being greedy by charging what the traffic will bear.

▲ Price changes: A brand's price and image are often closely linked. Tiffany found this out when it attempted to broaden its appeal by offering a line of more affordable jewelry.

Similarly, consumers may view a price *cut* in several ways. For example, what would you think if Rolex were to suddenly cut its prices? You might think that you are getting a better deal on an exclusive product. More likely, however, you'd think that quality had been reduced, and the brand's luxury image might be tarnished.

A brand's price and image are often closely linked. A price change, especially a drop in price, can adversely affect how consumers view the brand. ▲ Tiffany found this out when it attempted to broaden its appeal by offering a line of more affordable jewelry:[24]

Tiffany is all about luxury and the cachet of its blue boxes. However, in the late 1990s, the high-end jeweler responded to the "affordable luxuries" craze with a new "Return to Tiffany" line of less expensive silver jewelry. The "Return to Tiffany" silver charm bracelet quickly became a must-have item, as teens jammed Tiffany's hushed stores clamoring for the $110 silver bauble. Sales skyrocketed. But despite this early success, the bracelet fad appeared to alienate the firm's older, wealthier, and more conservative clientele, damaging Tiffany's reputation for luxury. So, in 2002, the firm began reemphasizing its pricier jewelry collections. Although high-end jewelry has once again replaced silver as Tiffany's fastest growing business, the company has yet to fully regain its exclusivity. Say's one well-heeled customer: "You used to aspire to be able to buy something at Tiffany, but now it's not that special anymore."

Competitor Reactions to Price Changes

A firm considering a price change must worry about the reactions of its competitors as well as those of its customers. Competitors are most likely to react when the number of firms involved is small, when the product is uniform, and when the buyers are well informed about products and prices.

How can the firm anticipate the likely reactions of its competitors? The problem is complex because, like the customer, the competitor can interpret a company price cut in many ways. It might think the company is trying to grab a larger market share, or that it's doing poorly and trying to boost its sales. Or it might think that the company wants the whole industry to cut prices to increase total demand.

The company must guess each competitor's likely reaction. If all competitors behave alike, this amounts to analyzing only a typical competitor. In contrast, if the competitors do not behave alike—perhaps because of differences in size, market shares, or policies—then separate analyses are necessary. However, if some competitors will match the price change, there is good reason to expect that the rest will also match it.

Responding to Price Changes

Here we reverse the question and ask how a firm should respond to a price change by a competitor. The firm needs to consider several issues: Why did the competitor change the price? Is the price change temporary or permanent? What will happen to the company's market share and profits if it does not respond? Are other competitors going to respond? Besides these issues, the company must also consider its own situation and strategy and possible customer reactions to price changes.

■ **Figure 9.5** shows the ways a company might assess and respond to a competitor's price cut. Suppose the company learns that a competitor has cut its price and decides that this price cut is likely to harm company sales and profits. It might simply decide to hold its current price and profit margin. The company might believe that it will not lose too much market share, or that it would lose too much profit if it reduced its own price. Or it might decide that it should wait and respond when it has more information on the effects of the competitor's price change. However, waiting too long to act might let the competitor get stronger and more confident as its sales increase.

If the company decides that effective action can and should be taken, it might make any of four responses. First, it could *reduce its price* to match the competitor's

■ **Figure 9.5** Assessing and Responding to Competitor Price Changes

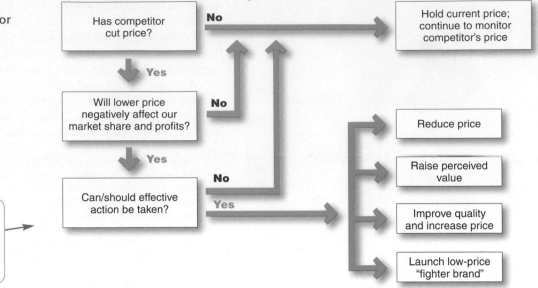

When a competitor cuts prices, a company's first reaction may be to drop its prices as well. But that is often the wrong response. Instead, the firm may want to emphasize the "value" side of the price-value equation.

price. It may decide that the market is price sensitive and that it would lose too much market share to the lower-priced competitor. Cutting the price will reduce the company's profits in the short run. Some companies might also reduce their product quality, services, and marketing communications to retain profit margins, but this will ultimately hurt long-run market share. The company should try to maintain its quality as it cuts prices.

Alternatively, the company might maintain its price but *raise the perceived value* of its offer. It could improve its communications, stressing the relative value of its product over that of the lower-price competitor. The firm may find it cheaper to maintain price and spend money to improve its perceived value than to cut price and operate at a lower margin. Or, the company might *improve quality and increase price*, moving its brand into a higher price–value position. The higher quality creates greater customer value, which justifies the higher price. In turn, the higher price preserves the company's higher margins.

Finally, the company might *launch a low-price "fighter brand"*—adding a lower-price item to the line or creating a separate lower-price brand. This is necessary if the particular market segment being lost is price sensitive and will not respond to arguments of higher quality. Thus, to compete with low-price airlines Southwest and Jet Blue, Virgin Group (an owner of Virgin Atlantic Airways) invested in Virgin America airline, which offers amenities such as Wi-Fi, movies, and food on demand, "all for a radically low fare."[25]

To counter store brands and other low-price entrants, Procter & Gamble turned a number of its brands into fighter brands. Luvs disposable diapers give parents "premium leakage protection for less than pricier brands." And P&G offers popular budget-priced Basic versions of several of its major brands. For example, Charmin Basic is "the quality toilet tissue at a price you'll love." ▲And Bounty Basic is "practical, not pricey." It offers "great strength at a great price—the paper towel that can take care of business without costing a bundle." In all, the Bounty brand claims an astounding 44 percent share of the paper towel market, and Bounty Basic has accounted for much of the brand's recent growth.[26]

▼ **Fighter brands:** P&G offers popular budget-priced Basic versions of several of its major brands. For example, Bounty Basic is "practical, not pricey."

PUBLIC POLICY AND PRICING (pp 329–331)

Price competition is a core element of our free-market economy. In setting prices, companies usually are not free to charge whatever prices they wish. Many federal, state, and even local laws govern the rules of fair play in pricing. In addition, companies must consider broader societal pricing concerns. The most important pieces of legislation affecting pricing are the Sherman, Clayton, and Robinson-Patman acts, initially adopted to curb the formation of monopolies and to regulate business practices that might unfairly restrain trade. Because these federal statutes can be applied only to interstate commerce, some states have adopted similar provisions for companies that operate locally.

■ **Figure 9.6** shows the major public policy issues in pricing. These include potentially damaging pricing practices within a given level of the channel (price-fixing and predatory pricing) and across levels of the channel (retail price maintenance, discriminatory pricing, and deceptive pricing).[27]

Pricing Within Channel Levels

Federal legislation on *price-fixing* states that sellers must set prices without talking to competitors. Otherwise, price collusion is suspected. Price-fixing is illegal per se—that is, the government does not accept any excuses for price-fixing. Companies found guilty of such practices can receive heavy fines. Recently, governments at the state and national levels have been aggressively enforcing price-fixing regulations in industries ranging from gasoline, insurance, and concrete to credit cards, CDs, and computer chips.[28]

Sellers are also prohibited from using *predatory pricing*—selling below cost with the intention of punishing a competitor or gaining higher long-run profits by putting competitors out of business. This protects small sellers from larger ones who might sell items below cost temporarily or in a specific locale to drive them out of business. The biggest problem is determining just what constitutes predatory pricing behavior. Selling below cost to unload excess inventory is not considered predatory; selling below cost to drive out competitors is. Thus, the same action may or may not be predatory depending on intent, and intent can be very difficult to determine or prove.

In recent years, several large and powerful companies have been accused of predatory pricing. For example, Wal-Mart has been sued by dozens of small competitors charging that it lowered prices in their specific geographic areas or on specific products—such as gasoline and generic drugs—to drive them out of business. In fact, the state of New York passed a bill requiring companies to price gas at or above

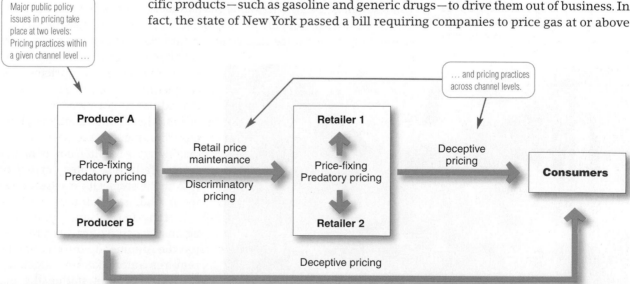

■ **Figure 9.6** Public Policy Issues in Pricing

98 percent of cost to "address the more extreme cases of predatory pricing by big-box stores" such as Wal-Mart and Costco. Yet, in North Dakota, the same gas-pricing proposal was rejected because state representatives did not view the practice as predatory pricing. And in Colorado, a bill was passed that allowed below-cost fuel.[29]

Pricing across Channel Levels

The Robinson-Patman Act seeks to prevent unfair *price discrimination* by ensuring that sellers offer the same price terms to customers at a given level of trade. For example, every retailer is entitled to the same price terms from a given manufacturer, whether the retailer is Sears or your local bicycle shop. However, price discrimination is allowed if the seller can prove that its costs are different when selling to different retailers—for example, that it costs less per unit to sell a large volume of bicycles to Sears than to sell a few bicycles to the local dealer.

The seller can also discriminate in its pricing if the seller manufactures different qualities of the same product for different retailers. The seller has to prove that these differences are proportional. Price differentials may also be used to "match competition" in "good faith," provided the price discrimination is temporary, localized, and defensive rather than offensive.

Laws also prohibit *retail (or resale) price maintenance*—a manufacturer cannot require dealers to charge a specified retail price for its product. Although the seller can propose a manufacturer's *suggested* retail price to dealers, it cannot refuse to sell to a dealer who takes independent pricing action, nor can it punish the dealer by shipping late or denying advertising allowances. For example, the Florida attorney general's office investigated Nike for allegedly fixing the retail price of its shoes and clothing. It was concerned that Nike might be withholding items from retailers who were not selling its most expensive shoes at prices the company considered suitable.

Deceptive pricing occurs when a seller states prices or price savings that mislead consumers or are not actually available to consumers. This might involve bogus reference or comparison prices, as when a retailer sets artificially high "regular" prices then announces "sale" prices close to its previous everyday prices. For example, Overstock.com recently came under scrutiny for inaccurately listing manufacturer's suggested retail prices, often quoting them higher than the actual price. Such comparison pricing is widespread.

Comparison pricing claims are legal if they are truthful. However, the FTC's *Guides Against Deceptive Pricing* warns sellers not to advertise a price reduction unless it is a savings from the usual retail price, not to advertise "factory" or "wholesale" prices unless such prices are what they are claimed to be, and not to advertise comparable value prices on imperfect goods.[30]

▼**Deceptive pricing concerns: The widespread use of checkout scanners has led to increasing complaints of retailers overcharging their customers.**

Other deceptive pricing issues include *scanner fraud* and price confusion. ▲The widespread use of scanner-based computer checkouts has led to increasing complaints of retailers overcharging their customers. Most of these overcharges result from poor management—from a failure to enter current or sale prices into the system. Other cases, however, involve intentional overcharges.

Many federal and state statutes regulate against deceptive pricing practices. For example, the Automobile Information Disclosure Act requires automakers to attach a statement to new-car windows stating the manufacturer's suggested retail price, the prices of optional equipment, and the dealer's transportation charges. However, reputable sellers go beyond what is required by law. Treating customers fairly and making certain that they fully understand prices and pricing terms is an important part of building strong and lasting customer relationships.

REST STOP
REVIEWING THE CONCEPTS

Before you put pricing in the rearview mirror, let's review the important concepts. *Price* can be defined as the sum of all the values that customers give up in order to gain the benefits of having or using a product or service. Pricing decisions are subject to an incredibly complex array of company, environmental, and competitive forces.

> **Objective 1** Identify the three major pricing strategies and discuss the importance of understanding customer-value perceptions, company costs, and competitor strategies when setting prices. **(pp 303–308)**

A price is the sum of all the values that customers give up in order to gain the benefits of having or using a product or service. The three major pricing strategies include customer value-based pricing, cost-based pricing, and competition-based pricing. Good pricing begins with a complete understanding of the value that a product or service creates for customers and setting a price that captures that value. The price the company charges will fall somewhere between one that is too high to produce any demand and one that is too low to produce a profit.

Customer perceptions of the product's value set the ceiling for prices. If customers perceive that the price is greater than the product's value, they will not buy the product. At the other extreme, company and product costs set the floor for prices. If the company prices the product below its costs, its profits will suffer. Between these two extremes, consumers will base their judgments of a product's value on the prices that competitors charge for similar products. Thus, in setting prices, companies need to consider all three factors: customer perceived value, costs, and competitor's pricing strategies.

> **Objective 2** Identify and define the other important external and internal factors affecting a firm's pricing decisions. **(pp 308–313)**

Other *internal* factors that influence pricing decisions include the company's overall marketing strategy, objectives, and marketing mix, as well as organizational considerations. Price is only one element of the company's broader marketing strategy. If the company has selected its target market and positioning carefully, then its marketing mix strategy, including price, will be fairly straightforward. Some companies position their products on price and then tailor other marketing mix decisions to the prices they want to charge. Other companies deemphasize price and use other marketing mix tools to create *nonprice* positions.

Other *external* pricing considerations include the nature of the market and demand and environmental factors such as the economy, reseller needs, and government actions. The seller's pricing freedom varies with different types of markets. Ultimately, the customer decides whether the company has set the right price. The customer weighs the price against the perceived values of using the product—if the price exceeds the sum of the values, consumers will not buy. So the company must understand concepts like demand curves (the price–demand relationship) and price elasticity (consumer sensitivity to prices).

Economic conditions can also have a major impact on pricing decisions. The recent recession caused consumers to rethink the price–value equation. Marketers have responded by increasing their emphasis on value-for-the-money pricing strategies. Even in tough economic times, however, consumers do not buy based on prices alone. Thus, no matter what price they charge—low or high—companies need to offer superior value for the money.

> **Objective 3** Describe the major strategies for pricing new products. **(pp 313–314)**

Pricing is a dynamic process. Companies design a *pricing structure* that covers all their products. They change this structure over time and adjust it to account for different customers and situations. Pricing strategies usually change as a product passes through its life cycle. The company can decide on one of several price–quality strategies for introducing an imitative product, including premium pricing, economy pricing, good value, or overcharging. In pricing innovative new products, it can use *market-skimming pricing* by initially setting high prices to "skim" the maximum amount of revenue from various segments of the market. Or it can use *market-penetrating pricing* by setting a low initial price to penetrate the market deeply and win a large market share.

> **Objective 4** Explain how companies find a set of prices that maximizes the profits from the total product mix. **(pp 314–318)**

When the product is part of a product mix, the firm searches for a set of prices that will maximize the profits from the total mix. In *product line pricing*, the company decides on price steps for the entire set of products it offers. In addition, the company must set prices for *optional products* (optional or accessory products included with the main product), *captive products* (products that are required for use of the main product), *by-products* (waste or residual products produced when making the main product), and *product bundles* (combinations of products at a reduced price).

 Objootivo 5 Discuss how companies adjust their prices to take into account different types of customers and situations. (pp 318–325)

Companies apply a variety of *price adjustment strategies* to account for differences in consumer segments and situations. One is *discount and allowance pricing*, whereby the company establishes cash, quantity, functional, or seasonal discounts, or varying types of allowances. A second strategy is *segmented pricing*, where the company sells a product at two or more prices to accommodate different customers, product forms, locations, or times. Sometimes companies consider more than economics in their pricing decisions, using *psychological pricing* to better communicate a product's intended position. In *promotional pricing*, a company offers discounts or temporarily sells a product below list price as a special event, sometimes even selling below cost as a loss leader. Another approach is *geographical pricing*, whereby the company decides how to price to distant customers, choosing from such alternatives as FOB-origin pricing, uniform-delivered pricing, zone pricing, basing-point pricing, and freight-absorption pricing. Finally, *international pricing* means that the company adjusts its price to meet different conditions and expectations in different world markets.

 Objective 6 Discuss the key issues related to initiating and responding to price changes. (pp 325–331)

When a firm considers initiating a *price change*, it must consider customers' and competitors' reactions. There are different implications to *initiating price cuts* and *initiating price increases*. Buyer reactions to price changes are influenced by the meaning customers see in the price change. Competitors' reactions flow from a set reaction policy or a fresh analysis of each situation.

There are also many factors to consider in responding to a competitor's price changes. The company that faces a price change initiated by a competitor must try to understand the competitor's intent as well as the likely duration and impact of the change. If a swift reaction is desirable, the firm should preplan its reactions to different possible price actions by competitors. When facing a competitor's price change, the company might sit tight, reduce its own price, raise perceived quality, improve quality and raise price, or launch a fighting brand.

Navigating the Key Terms

Objective 1
Price (p 303)
Customer value-based pricing
  (p 304)
Good-value pricing (p 305)
Value-added pricing (p 305)
Cost-based pricing (p 306)
Fixed costs (overhead) (p 306)
Variable costs (p 306)
Total costs (p 306)
Cost-plus pricing (p 307)
Break-even pricing (p 307)
Competition-based pricing (p 308)

Objective 2
Target costing (p 309)
Demand curve (p 311)
Price elasticity (p 311)

Objective 3
Market-skimming pricing (p 313)
Market-penetration pricing (p 313)

Objective 4
Product line pricing (p 314)
Optional-product pricing (p 315)
Captive-product pricing (p 315)

By-product pricing (p 316)
Product bundle pricing (p 317)

Objective 5
Discount (p 318)
Allowance (p 318)
Segmented pricing (p 318)
Psychological pricing (p 319)
Reference prices (p 319)
Promotional pricing (p 321)
Dynamic pricing (p 323)

Travel Log

Discussing the Issues

1. What is price? Discuss factors marketers must consider when setting price. (AACSB: Communication; Reflective Thinking)

2. Describe the types of cost-based pricing and describe the methods of implementing each. (AACSB: Communication)

3. Compare and contrast market-skimming and market-penetration pricing strategies. When would each be appropriate? (AACSB: Communication)

4. Name and briefly describe the types of discounts and allowances. (AACSB: Communication)

5. Why do marketers charge customers different prices for the same product or service? Explain how this type of pricing is implemented and the conditions under which it is effective. (AACSB: Communication)

6. Name and briefly describe the five types of geographical pricing. (AACSB: Communication)

Application Questions

1. Identify three price-comparison shopping Web sites and shop for an MP3 player of your choice. Compare the price ranges given at these three Web sites. (AACSB: Communication; Use of IT)

2. Convert $1.00 U.S. to the currencies of five other countries (you can do this at www.xe.com). What implications do currency exchange rates hold for setting prices in other countries? (AACSB: Communication; Use of IT; Reflective Thinking)

3. In a small group, determine the costs associated with offering an online MBA degree in addition to a traditional MBA degree at a university. Which costs are fixed and which are variable? Determine the tuition (that is, price) to charge for a 3-credit course in this degree program. Which pricing method is your group using to determine the price? (AACSB: Communication; Reflective Thinking)

Under the Hood: Marketing Technology

You know what an auction is, but what about a *reverse auction*? In a typical auction, a seller offers a good or service for sale and buyers bid on it, with the highest bidder winning the auction. In a reverse auction, however, buyer and seller roles are reversed. A buyer wants to purchase a good or service and solicits sellers to make an offer, with the lowest bidder winning the sale. Like traditional auctions that take place on Web sites such as eBay, the Internet is facilitating reverse auctions that drive down a company's procurement costs as much as 25 percent to 50 percent. The key to reverse auctions is that they take place quickly and sellers see the lowest bid, which drives down price for the host buyer. Basically, sellers are bidding for how low they are willing to sell a product or service to the buyer. Reverse auctions became popular in the 1990s, and one researcher estimates that almost half of all corporate expenditures will soon be done through reverse auctions. Reverse auctions aren't just for business-to-business purchases anymore, either. They are now used in the business-to-consumer and consumer-to-consumer marketspace as well. Due to technology, businesses and consumers are now able to set the price they are willing to pay and have sellers compete for their business from anywhere in the world.

1. Search the Internet for reverse auction sites. Learn how these sites operate and explain how they work and the costs associated with conducting a reverse auction. (AACSB: Communication; Use of IT)

2. Search for articles about reverse auctions. What are the advantages and disadvantages of using reverse auctions to purchase products and services for businesses? For consumers? (AACSB: Communication; Reflective Thinking; Use of IT)

Staying on the Road: Marketing Ethics

In airline pricing, $5 here, $10 there—it all starts to add up. It began with charging flyers a fee to call an airline's toll-free number to book a flight, and it's progressed to charging flyers for just about everything else. If you've flown in the past year, you've probably noticed the airlines are nickel and diming flyers right and left, except that there are more zeros after those 5s and 10s! Add-on fees contributed almost $4 billion in airline revenue in just the first six months of 2009—and that's with fewer people flying! Change your flight—that will cost upwards of $150. Check a bag—add another $10 to $25 dollars and maybe $50 for a second bag if traveling overseas. Taking a pet along? That's another $50 to $100. Hungry? $10 or more, please. Southwest Airlines, the low-price carrier that doesn't issue boarding passes, is now offering the privilege to board before the rest of the crowd for $10. These fees are in addition to all the other taxes and fees imposed on flyers. The add-on fees add revenue during the worst downturn in travel since the September 11, 2001, terrorist attacks. The most lucrative fee has been the baggage fee. You can save a little money on that, however, if you pay it online instead of at the airport.

1. Learn about the various taxes and fees imposed on flyers. What would it cost to fly Delta Airlines from Atlanta to Denver for a one week trip next month? What are the

fees if you checked one bag and wanted to eat lunch? Is the fare higher or lower if you booked this flight for next week instead of next month? Do the same for another airline from Atlanta to Denver for the same time period. Are the fares comparable? Which airline imposes the most fees? Are airlines taking unfair advantage of flyers by imposing excessive fees? (AACSB: Communication; Reflective Thinking; Ethical Reasoning)

2. Discuss other ways airlines generate revenues beyond the fares and fees imposed on flyers. (AACSB: Communication; Reflective Thinking)

Rough Road Ahead: Marketing and the Economy

Colgate-Palmolive

As the economy has made people more aware of their spending, many companies have slashed prices on their products and services. Still other companies have been successful at holding prices steady, selling as much or more than they did before the economic bottom fell out. But Colgate-Palmolive is one of the fortunate few that has actually been able to *increase* prices during this more frugal era and reap benefits from doing so. Think about it—how grim would your budget have to get before you'd stop brushing your teeth or taking a shower? Economic conditions have relatively little impact on people's basic personal care habits, and brand preferences are deeply ingrained for these necessities. Based on an accurate evaluation of customer buying habits, Colgate-Palmolive has raised prices by an average of 7.5 percent without experiencing any dip in sales. Higher prices and stable volumes equals—*cha-ching*—higher profits. Indeed, Colgate-Palmolive saw its profits rise by 20 percent over the previous year. It seems as though looking and smelling clean might just be recession-proof concepts.

1. Does the success of Colgate-Palmolive's price increases have anything to do with the economy?

2. In the longer term, what should Colgate-Palmolive anticipate in the wake of its price increases?

Travel Budget: Marketing by the Numbers

When introducing new products, some manufacturers use a price skimming strategy by setting a high initial price and then reducing price later. However, reducing price also reduces contribution margins, which in turn impacts profitability. To be profitable, the reduced price must sufficiently increase sales. For example, a company with a contribution margin of 30 percent on sales of $60 million realizes a total contribution to fixed costs and profits of $18 million ($60 million $\times$ 0.30 = $18 million). If this company decreases price, the contribution margin will also decrease. So to maintain or increase profitability, the price reduction must increase sales considerably.

1. Refer to Appendix 2, Marketing by the Numbers, and calculate the new contribution margin for the company discussed above if it reduces price by 10 percent. Assume that unit variable costs are $70 and the original price was $100. (AACSB: Communication; Analytic Reasoning)

2. What total sales must the company capture at the new price to maintain the same level of total contribution (that is, total contribution = $18 million)? (AACSB: Communication; Analytic Reasoning)

Drive In: Video Case

IKEA

Lots of companies have idealistic missions. But IKEA's vision, "To create a better everyday life for the many people," seems somewhat implausible. How can a company that makes furniture improve everyday life for the masses? Interestingly, the most important part of that strategy is price. For every product that it designs, from leather sofas to plastic mugs, IKEA starts with a target price. The target price is one that's deemed affordable, making the product accessible to the masses."

Only then does IKEA begin the grueling process of creating a high-quality, stylish, and innovative product that can be delivered to the customer for that target price. As IKEA points out, anyone can make high-quality goods for a high price or poor-quality goods for a low price. The real challenge is making high-quality products at a low price. To do so requires a relentless focus on costs combined with a thirst for innovation. That has been IKEA's quest for more than 65 years.

After viewing the video featuring IKEA, answer the following questions about the company's pricing strategy:

1. What is IKEA's promise of value?

2. Referring to the Klippan sofa, illustrate how IKEA delivers its promise of value to consumers.

3. Based on the concepts from the text, does IKEA employ a value-based pricing approach or a cost-based pricing approach? Support your answer.

10

Marketing Channels

Delivering Customer Value

ROAD MAP

Previewing the Concepts

We now arrive at the third marketing mix tool—distribution. Firms rarely work alone in creating value for customers and building profitable customer relationships. Instead, most are only a single link in a larger supply chain and marketing channel. As such, an individual firm's success depends not only on how well *it* performs but also on how well its *entire marketing channel* competes with competitors' channels. To be good at customer relationship management, a company must also be good at partner relationship management. The first part of this chapter explores the nature of marketing channels and the marketer's channel design and management decisions. We then examine physical distribution—or logistics—an area that is growing dramatically in importance and sophistication. In the next chapter, we'll look more closely at two major channel intermediaries—retailers and wholesalers.

Objective Outline

> **Objective 1**   Explain why companies use marketing channels and discuss the functions these channels perform.
> Supply Chains and the Value Delivery Network **pp 338–339**
> The Nature and Importance of Marketing Channels **pp 339–342**

> **Objective 2**   Discuss how channel members interact and how they organize to perform the work of the channel.
> Channel Behavior and Organization **pp 342–349**

> **Objective 3**   Identify the major channel alternatives open to a company.
> Channel Design Decisions **pp 349–353**

> **Objective 4**   Explain how companies select, motivate, and evaluate channel members.
> Channel Management Decisions **pp 353–355**

> **Objective 5**   Discuss the nature and importance of marketing logistics and integrated supply chain management.
> Marketing Logistics and Supply Chain Management **pp 356–364**

▲Al Zaytoun is a non-profit organization working to ensure Palestinian farmers receive a fair price for the olive oil they have harvested.

We'll start with a look at a company that faces tremendous challenges, not because of its product but because of the location of the producers.

First Stop

Zaytoun: The Fairer Way to Trade Olive Oil

Zaytoun is a not-for-profit company based in Britain and Palestine founded in 2004 with the purpose of developing a fair trade market for olive oil and other Palestinian produce in the U.K. It works closely with producer cooperatives, civil society organisations and associated businesses to develop trade opportunities for farmer cooperatives and to enhance the capacity of these coops to meet international export demand. Based in Britain, Zaytoun's goal is to enable Palestinian farmers to receive a fair price for the olive oil they have harvested. Their key objectives are the following:

- To facilitate cooperatives which enable farmers to improve the quality of their oil.
- To increase sales internationally that generate a valuable source of income through growing distribution and wholesale networks.
- To continue the campaign that highlights the impact of the Occupation & the Wall on poverty for farmers in Palestine.

Olive oil is a major crop for the Palestinians and provides work for around 65 percent of the population. It has become far more difficult to grow and harvest the crop due to the continued problems in the region. Historically, due to the lack of access to international markets, around half of the olive oil crop has been wasted. Al Zaytoun is a British-based company that works in partnership with War on Want and other NGOs. Ultimately, the goal is for more producers to gain access to the international market by creating a marketing channel and new supply chain. There have been key advances:

- Supported cooperatives have eradicated the olive fly.
- Oil production increased 40 percent between 2005 and 2008.
- Local committees train farmers in harvest, storage, and production techniques.
- Equipment such as stainless steel tanks have been improved to maintain the oil's quality.

In 2007, Zaytoun managed to sell 70,000 liters of Palestinian olive oil. This compares favorably with the 15,000 liters sold in the first year (2004). Heather Masoud is the co-founder of Zaytoun and she explained the difficulties in securing the supply chain and working with the right kind of partners: "It's absolutely critical to us expanding our market in the U.K., and we have worked on getting the Fairtrade Foundation to come to Palestine and evaluate the supply chain. When Zaytoun's olive oil won the Fairtrade Mark, it became the first in the U.K. Having achieved that, many more wholesalers and supermarkets have begun to stock it, and that kind of support would completely change the

Olive oil is a major crop for Palestinian farmers, providing much needed work. However, historically, due to difficulties in getting their products to the international market, half of the olive oil crop has been wasted, making this supply chain very fragile.

▲ Al Zaytoun must overcome the issue of a fragile supply chain if it is to successfully conquer overseas markets.

scale of what we can commit to buying from the farmers here."

Because the business has to be sustainable, volunteers initially worked for the business for two years without pay, yet support is there for the burgeoning operation. The Manchester-based Olive Co-op, which runs responsible tourism study tours to the West Bank, and the fair trade co-op Equal Exchange have been instrumental in helping the business create a transparent supply chain. Cafédirect's chairman, Martin Meteyard, was among the supporters to underwrite a nearly $40,000 loan taken out by the business to help Palestinian farmers make the necessary investments that come with increasing production to deal with larger orders.

The supply chain is fragile. A container of oil that was meant to arrive in Britain for Christmas 2004 was held up in Italy and did not arrive until February 2005. The business also finds it difficult to explain to Palestinian farmers that British customers (and others) are prepared to pay premium prices for the olive oil when there are cheaper alternatives. The business has also discovered that it is not always wise to use the political situation in the region as a marketing tool. Masoud recalled a situation when a retailer was presented with the first versions of the bottle labels: "We had our labels all printed up with 'Palestinian Olive Oil – Resisting The Occupation.' They liked the oil and wanted to take it, but said very nicely that just 'Produce of Palestine' would do fine for their clientele."

Palestinian olive oil producers face almost insurmountable odds in their production as well as in the transportation of their olives. In some cases Israeli authorities have confiscated or denied access to land, dug up trees, or diverted the water supply.

Some of the olive oil is now officially registered as an organic product. The oil is bottled by the cooperatives and then transported to Britain. The majority of the oil is sold in advance through Zaytoun's network of outlets and customers. There are continued delays by customs and checkpoints, which end up reducing the shelf life of the product. The business knows that this is an obstacle that must be overcome if the product is to have a fighting chance of developing a stronger overseas market.

As Zaytoun admits in its marketing materials, "Distribution is the biggest hurdle facing a grassroots initiative like Zaytoun. We owe our success to the many (extra)ordinary individuals from all walks of life, who have come forward and offered to distribute Palestinian olive oil from their homes, their workplaces, churches, mosques, synagogues, and at community events; plus those who have encouraged their food stores to sell our products. We are keen to maintain our "grassroots" contacts and will continue to supply solidarity and fair trade, distributors."

The project continues to adapt to the environment and the challenges facing it. Step by step the supply chain and the marketing channels are being ironed out. The process may take time to fully develop; however, their own supply chain, as far as local partners are concerned, is now in place: "We source olive oil through all of these suppliers and are developing markets in the U.K. for their other products including: Olive oil soap from Nablus, couscous from Gaza, almonds and za'atar from Jenin, and dates from a cooperative near Jericho. Also, Zaytoun's policy is that as far as possible all value-added activities for these products are kept within the Palestinian economy. To this end the bottling, printing and labelling is done in Palestine. We're also actively working to source all our packaging materials through Palestinian suppliers."[1]

a s the Zaytoun story shows, good distribution strategies can contribute strongly to customer value and create competitive advantage for both a firm and its channel partners. It demonstrates that firms cannot bring value to customers by themselves. Instead, they must work closely with other firms in a larger value delivery network.

Author Comment ≫
These are pretty hefty terms for what's really a simple concept: A company can't go it alone in creating customer value. It must work within an entire network of partners to accomplish this task. Individual companies and brands don't compete; their entire value delivery networks do.

SUPPLY CHAINS AND THE VALUE DELIVERY NETWORK
(pp 338–339)

Producing a product or service and making it available to buyers requires building relationships not just with customers, but also with key suppliers and resellers in the company's *supply chain*. This supply chain consists of "upstream" and "downstream" partners. Upstream from the company is the set of firms that supply the raw materials, components, parts, information, finances, and expertise needed to create a product or service. Marketers, however, have traditionally focused on the "downstream" side of the supply chain—on the *marketing channels* (or *distribution channels*) that look toward the customer. Downstream marketing channel partners, such as wholesalers and retailers, form a vital connection between the firm and its customers.

The term *supply chain* may be too limited—it takes a *make-and-sell* view of the business. It suggests that raw materials, productive inputs, and factory capacity should serve as the starting point for market planning. A better term would be *demand chain* because it suggests a *sense-and-respond* view of the market. Under this view, planning starts with the needs of target customers, to which the company responds by organizing a chain of resources and activities with the goal of creating customer value.

Even a demand chain view of a business may be too limited, because it takes a step-by-step, linear view of purchase-production-consumption activities. With the advent of the Internet and other technologies, however, companies are forming more numerous and complex relationships with other firms. For example, Ford manages numerous supply chains—think about all of the parts it takes to create a vehicle, from radios to catalytic converters to tires. Ford also sponsors or transacts on many B-to-B Web sites and online purchasing exchanges as needs arise. Like Ford, most large companies today are engaged in building and managing a continuously evolving *value delivery network*.

As defined in Chapter 2, a **value delivery network** is made up of the company, suppliers, distributors, and ultimately customers who "partner" with each other to improve the performance of the entire system. For example, in making and marketing its iPod Touch products, Apple manages an entire network of people within Apple plus suppliers and resellers outside the company who work together effectively to give final customers the take-anything-anywhere iPod that's "So much to touch."

This chapter focuses on marketing channels—on the downstream side of the value delivery network. We examine four major questions concerning marketing channels: What is the nature of marketing channels and why are they important? How do channel firms interact and organize to do the work of the channel? What problems do companies face in designing and managing their channels? What role do physical distribution and supply chain management play in attracting and satisfying customers? In Chapter 11, we will look at marketing channel issues from the viewpoint of retailers and wholesalers.

Value delivery network
The network made up of the company, suppliers, distributors, and ultimately customers who "partner" with each other to improve the performance of the entire system in delivering customer value.

Author Comment »
In this section, we look at the "downstream" side of the value delivery network—the marketing channel organizations that connect the company and its customers. To understand their value, imagine life without retailers—say, grocery stores or department stores.

Marketing channel (or distribution channel)
A set of interdependent organizations that help make a product or service available for use or consumption by the consumer or business user.

THE NATURE AND IMPORTANCE OF MARKETING CHANNELS (pp 339–341)

Few producers sell their goods directly to the final users. Instead, most use intermediaries to bring their products to market. They try to forge a **marketing channel** (or **distribution channel**)—a set of interdependent organizations that help make a product or service available for use or consumption by the consumer or business user.

A company's channel decisions directly affect every other marketing decision. Pricing depends on whether the company works with national discount chains, uses high-quality specialty stores, or sells directly to consumers via the Web. The firm's sales force and communications decisions depend on how much persuasion, training, motivation, and support its channel partners need. Whether a company develops or acquires certain new products may depend on how well those products fit the capabilities of its channel members. For example, Kodak initially sold its EasyShare printers only in Best Buy stores to take advantage of the retailer's on-the-floor sales staff and their ability to educate buyers on the economics of paying higher initial prices for the printer but lower long-term ink costs.

Companies often pay too little attention to their distribution channels, sometimes with damaging results. In contrast, many companies have used imaginative distribution systems to *gain* a competitive advantage. ▲FedEx's creative and imposing distribution system made it a leader in express delivery. Enterprise revolutionized the car-rental business by setting up off-airport rental offices. And Apple turned the retail music business on its head by selling music for the iPod via the Internet on iTunes.

▲Innovative marketing channels: FedEx revolutionized express package delivery with its creative and imposing distribution system.

Distribution channel decisions often involve long-term commitments to other firms. For example, companies such as Ford, HP, or McDonald's can easily change their advertising, pricing, or promotion programs. They can scrap old products and introduce new ones as market tastes demand. But when they set up distribution channels through contracts with franchisees, independent dealers, or large retailers, they cannot readily replace these channels with company-owned stores or Web sites if conditions change. Therefore, management must design its channels carefully, with an eye on tomorrow's likely selling environment as well as today's.

How Channel Members Add Value

Why do producers give some of the selling job to channel partners? After all, doing so means giving up some control over how and to whom they sell their products. Producers use intermediaries because they create greater efficiency in making goods available to target markets. Through their contacts, experience, specialization, and scale of operation, intermediaries usually offer the firm more than it can achieve on its own.

■ **Figure 10.1** shows how using intermediaries can provide economies. Figure 10.1A shows three manufacturers, each using direct marketing to reach three customers. This system requires nine different contacts. Figure 10.1B shows the three manufacturers working through one distributor, which contacts the three customers. This system requires only six contacts. In this way, intermediaries reduce the amount of work that must be done by both producers and consumers.

From the economic system's point of view, the role of marketing intermediaries is to transform the assortments of products made by producers into the assortments wanted by consumers. Producers make narrow assortments of products in large quantities, but consumers want broad assortments of products in small quantities. Marketing channel members buy large quantities from many producers and break them down into the smaller quantities and broader assortments wanted by consumers.

For example, Unilever makes millions of bars of Lever 2000 hand soap each day, but you want to buy only a few bars at a time. So big food, drug, and discount retailers, such as Kroger, Walgreens, and Wal-Mart, buy Lever 2000 by the truckload and stock it on their stores' shelves. In turn, you can buy a single bar of Lever 2000, along with a shopping cart full of small quantities of toothpaste, shampoo, and other re-

■ **Figure 10.1** How Adding a Distributor Reduces the Number of Channel Transactions

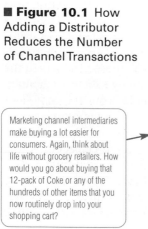

Marketing channel intermediaries make buying a lot easier for consumers. Again, think about life without grocery retailers. How would you go about buying that 12-pack of Coke or any of the hundreds of other items that you now routinely drop into your shopping cart?

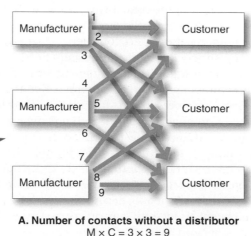

A. Number of contacts without a distributor
$M \times C = 3 \times 3 = 9$

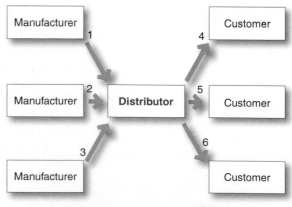

B. Number of contacts with a distributor
$M + C = 3 + 3 = 6$

lated products as you need them. Thus, intermediaries play an important role in matching supply and demand.

In making products and services available to consumers, channel members add value by bridging the major time, place, and possession gaps that separate goods and services from those who would use them. Members of the marketing channel perform many key functions. Some help to complete transactions:

- *Information:* Gathering and distributing marketing research and intelligence information about actors and forces in the marketing environment needed for planning and aiding exchange.
- *Promotion:* Developing and spreading persuasive communications about an offer.
- *Contact:* Finding and communicating with prospective buyers.
- *Matching:* Shaping and fitting the offer to the buyer's needs, including activities such as manufacturing, grading, assembling, and packaging.
- *Negotiation:* Reaching an agreement on price and other terms of the offer so that ownership or possession can be transferred.

Others help to fulfill the completed transactions:

- *Physical distribution:* Transporting and storing goods.
- *Financing:* Acquiring and using funds to cover the costs of the channel work.
- *Risk taking:* Assuming the risks of carrying out the channel work.

The question is not *whether* these functions need to be performed—they must be—but rather *who* will perform them. To the extent that the manufacturer performs these functions, its costs go up and its prices must be higher. When some of these functions are shifted to intermediaries, the producer's costs and prices may be lower, but the intermediaries must charge more to cover the costs of their work. In dividing the work of the channel, the various functions should be assigned to the channel members who can add the most value for the cost.

Number of Channel Levels

Companies can design their distribution channels to make products and services available to customers in different ways. Each layer of marketing intermediaries that performs some work in bringing the product and its ownership closer to the final buyer is a **channel level**. Because the producer and the final consumer both perform some work, they are part of every channel.

The *number of intermediary levels* indicates the *length* of a channel. ■ **Figure 10.2A** shows several consumer distribution channels of different lengths. Channel 1, called a **direct marketing channel**, has no intermediary levels; the company sells directly to consumers. For example, Mary Kay and Amway sell their products door-to-door, through home and office sales parties, and on the Web; GEICO sells insurance direct via the telephone and the Internet. The remaining channels in Figure 10.2A are **indirect marketing channels**, containing one or more intermediaries.

■ **Figure 10.2B** shows some common business distribution channels. The business marketer can use its own sales force to sell directly to business customers. Or it can sell to various types of intermediaries, who in turn sell to these customers. Consumer and business marketing channels with even more levels can sometimes be found, but less often. From the producer's point of view, a greater number of levels means less control and greater channel complexity. Moreover, all of the institutions in the channel are connected by several types of *flows*. These include the *physical flow* of products, the *flow of ownership*, the *payment flow*, the *information flow*, and the *promotion flow*. These flows can make even channels with only one or a few levels very complex.

Channel level
A layer of intermediaries that performs some work in bringing the product and its ownership closer to the final buyer.

Direct marketing channel
A marketing channel that has no intermediary levels.

Indirect marketing channel
Channel containing one or more intermediary levels.

Author Comment >>
Channels are made up of more than just boxes and arrows on paper. They are behavioral systems made up of real companies and people who interact to accomplish their individual and collective goals. Like groups of people, sometimes they work well together and sometimes they don't.

CHANNEL BEHAVIOR AND ORGANIZATION (pp 342–349)

Distribution channels are more than simple collections of firms tied together by various flows. They are complex behavioral systems in which people and companies interact to accomplish individual, company, and channel goals. Some channel systems consist only of informal interactions among loosely organized firms. Others consist of formal interactions guided by strong organizational structures. Moreover, channel systems do not stand still—new types of intermediaries emerge and whole new channel systems evolve. Here we look at channel behavior and at how members organize to do the work of the channel.

Channel Behavior

A marketing channel consists of firms that have partnered for their common good. Each channel member depends on the others. For example, a Honda dealer depends on Honda to design cars that meet consumer needs. In turn, Honda depends on the dealer to attract consumers, persuade them to buy Honda cars, and service cars after the sale. Each Honda dealer also depends on other dealers to provide good sales and service that will uphold the brand's reputation. In fact, the success of individual Honda dealers depends on how well the entire Ford marketing channel competes with the channels of other auto manufacturers.

Each channel member plays a specialized role in the channel. For example, consumer electronics maker Samsung's role is to produce electronics products that consumers will like and to create demand through national advertising. Best Buy's role is to display these Samsung products in convenient locations, to answer buyers' questions, and to complete sales. The channel will be most effective when each member assumes the tasks it can do best.

Ideally, because the success of individual channel members depends on overall channel success, all channel firms should work together smoothly. They should understand and accept their roles, coordinate their activities, and cooperate to attain

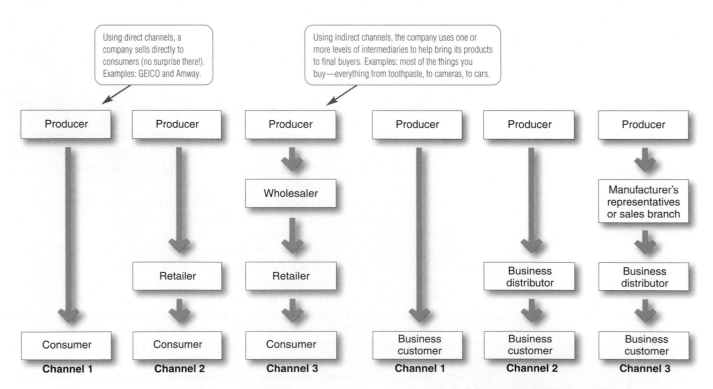

A. Customer marketing channels   **B. Business marketing channels**

■ **Figure 10.2** Consumer and Business Marketing Channels

overall channel goals. However, individual channel members rarely take such a broad view. Cooperating to achieve overall channel goals sometimes means giving up individual company goals. Although channel members depend on one another, they often act alone in their own short-run best interests. They often disagree on who should do what and for what rewards. Such disagreements over goals, roles, and rewards generate **channel conflict**.

Horizontal conflict occurs among firms at the same level of the channel. For instance, some Honda dealers in Chicago might complain that the other dealers in the city steal sales from them by pricing too low or by advertising outside their assigned territories. Or Holiday Inn franchisees might complain about other Holiday Inn operators overcharging guests or giving poor service, hurting the overall Holiday Inn image.

Channel conflict
Disagreement among marketing channel members on goals, roles, and rewards—who should do what and for what rewards.

Vertical conflict, conflicts between different levels of the same channel, is even more common. ▲For example, Goodyear created hard feelings and conflict with its premier independent-dealer channel when it began selling through mass-merchant retailers:[2]

> For more than 60 years, Goodyear sold replacement tires exclusively through its premier network of independent Goodyear dealers. Then, in the 1990s, Goodyear shattered tradition and jolted its dealers by agreeing to sell its tires through mass-merchants such as Sears, Wal-Mart, and Sam's Club, placing dealers in direct competition with the nation's most potent retailers. Goodyear claimed that value-minded tire buyers were increasingly buying from cheaper, multibrand discount outlets and department stores, and that it simply had to put its tires where many consumers were going to buy them.
>
> Not surprisingly, Goodyear's aggressive moves into new channels set off a surge of channel conflict, and dealer relations deteriorated rapidly. Some of Goodyear's best dealers defected to competitors. Other angry dealers struck back by taking on competing brands of cheaper private-label tires. Such dealer actions weakened the Goodyear name, and the company's replacement tire sales—which make up 73 percent of its revenues—went flat, dropping the company into a more than decade-long profit funk. Although Goodyear has since repaired fractured dealer relations, it still has not fully recovered. "We lost sight of the fact that it's in our interest that our dealers succeed," admits a Goodyear executive.

▲Channel conflict: Goodyear created conflict with its premiere independent-dealer channel when it began selling through mass-merchant retailers. Fractured dealer relations weakened the Goodyear name and dropped the company into a more than a decade-long profit funk.

Some conflict in the channel takes the form of healthy competition. Such competition can be good for the channel—without it, the channel could become passive and noninnovative. But severe or prolonged conflict, as in the case of Goodyear, can disrupt channel effectiveness and cause lasting harm to channel relationships. Companies should manage channel conflict to keep it from getting out of hand.

Vertical Marketing Systems

For the channel as a whole to perform well, each channel member's role must be specified and channel conflict must be managed. The channel will perform better if it includes a firm, agency, or mechanism that provides leadership and has the power to assign roles and manage conflict.

Historically, *conventional distribution channels* have lacked such leadership and power, often resulting in damaging conflict and poor performance. One of the biggest channel developments over the years has been the emergence of *vertical marketing systems* that provide channel leadership. ■ **Figure 10.3** contrasts the two types of channel arrangements.

Conventional distribution channel
A channel consisting of one or more independent producers, wholesalers, and retailers, each a separate business seeking to maximize its own profits, even at the expense of profits for the system as a whole.

A **conventional distribution channel** consists of one or more independent producers, wholesalers, and retailers. Each is a separate business seeking to maximize its own profits, perhaps even at the expense of the system as a whole. No channel

■ **Figure 10.3** Comparison of Conventional Distribution Channel with Vertical Marketing System

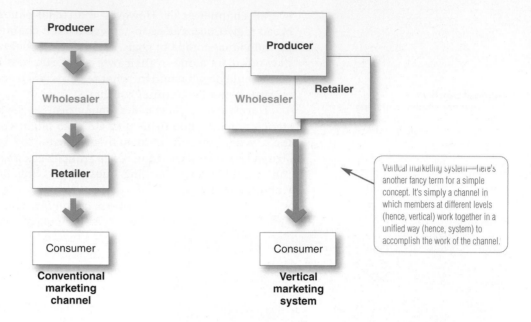

Vertical marketing system—here's another fancy term for a simple concept. It's simply a channel in which members at different levels (hence, vertical) work together in a unified way (hence, system) to accomplish the work of the channel.

Vertical marketing system (VMS)
A distribution channel structure in which producers, wholesalers, and retailers act as a unified system. One channel member owns the others, has contracts with them, or has so much power that they all cooperate.

member has much control over the other members, and no formal means exists for assigning roles and resolving channel conflict.

In contrast, a **vertical marketing system (VMS)** consists of producers, wholesalers, and retailers acting as a unified system. One channel member owns the others, has contracts with them, or wields so much power that they must all cooperate. The VMS can be dominated by the producer, wholesaler, or retailer.

We look now at three major types of VMSs: *corporate, contractual,* and *administered.* Each uses a different means for setting up leadership and power in the channel.

Corporate VMS

Corporate VMS
A vertical marketing system that combines successive stages of production and distribution under single ownership—channel leadership is established through common ownership.

A **corporate VMS** integrates successive stages of production and distribution under single ownership. Coordination and conflict management are attained through regular organizational channels. For example, grocery giant Kroger owns and operates 40 plants—18 dairies, 10 deli and bakery plants, five grocery product plants, three beverage plants, two meat plants, and two cheese plants—that crank out 40 percent of the more than 14,400 private label items found on its store shelves. And little-known Italian eyewear maker Luxottica produces many famous eyewear brands—including its own Ray-Ban brand and licensed brands such as Polo Ralph Lauren, Dolce & Gabbana, Prada, Versace, and Bvlgari. It then sells these brands through two of the world's largest optical chains, LensCrafters and Sunglass Hut, which it also owns.[3] Controlling the entire distribution chain has turned Spanish clothing chain Zara into the world's fastest-growing fashion retailer (see Marketing at Work 10.1).

Contractual VMS

Contractual VMS
A vertical marketing system in which independent firms at different levels of production and distribution join together through contracts to obtain more economies or sales impact than they could achieve alone.

Franchise organization
A contractual vertical marketing system in which a channel member, called a franchisor, links several stages in the production-distribution process.

A **contractual VMS** consists of independent firms at different levels of production and distribution who join together through contracts to obtain more economies or sales impact than each could achieve alone. Channel members coordinate their activities and manage conflict through contractual agreements.

The **franchise organization** is the most common type of contractual relationship—a channel member called a *franchisor* links several stages in the production-distribution process. In the United States alone, some 1,500 franchise businesses and 865,000 franchise outlets account for more than $839 billion of economic output. Industry analysts estimate that a new franchise outlet opens somewhere in the United States every eight minutes and that about one out of every 12 retail business outlets is a franchised business.[4] Almost every kind of business has been franchised—from motels

Zara: Fast Fashions—*Really* Fast

Fashion retailer Zara is on a tear. It sells "cheap chic"—stylish designs that resemble those of big-name fashion houses but at moderate prices. Zara is the prototype for a new breed of "fast-fashion" retailers, companies that recognize and respond to the latest fashion trends quickly and nimbly. While competing retailers are still working out their designs, Zara has already put the latest fashion into its stores and is moving on to the next big thing.

Zara has attracted a near cult-like clientele in recent years. Following the recent economic slide, even upscale shoppers are swarming to buy Zara's stylish but affordable offerings. Thanks to Zara's torrid growth, the sales, profits, and store presence of its parent company, Spain-based Inditex, have more than quadrupled since 2000. Despite the poor economy, Inditex's sales grew 10 percent last year. By comparison, Gap's sales *fell* last year by almost 10 percent. As a result, Inditex sprinted past Gap to become the world's largest clothing retailer. Its 4,264 stores in 71 countries sewed up $14.2 billion in sales. And Inditex plans to open as many as 450 new stores this year, compared with Gap's plans for 50 new stores.

Zara clearly sells the right goods for these times. But its amazing success comes not just from *what* it sells. Perhaps more important, success comes from how and how fast Zara's cutting-edge distribution system *delivers* what it sells to eagerly awaiting customers. Zara delivers fast fashion—*really* fast fashion. Through vertical integration, Zara controls all phases of the fashion process, from design and manufacturing to distribution through its own managed stores. The company's integrated supply system makes Zara faster, more flexible, and more efficient than international competitors such as Gap, Benetton, and H&M. Zara can take a new fashion concept through design, manufacturing, and store-shelf placement in as little as two weeks, whereas competitors often take six months or more. And the resulting low costs let Zara offer the very latest mid-market chic at downmarket prices.

The whole process starts with input about what consumers want. Zara store managers act as trend spotters. They patrol store aisles using handheld computers, reporting in real time what's selling and what's not. They talk with customers to learn what they're looking for but not yet finding. At the same time, Zara trend seekers roam fashion shows in Paris and concerts in Tokyo, looking for young people who might be wearing something new or different. Then, they're on the phone to company headquarters in tiny La Coruña, Spain, reporting on what they've seen and heard. Back home, based on this and other feedback, the company's team of 300 designers conjures up a prolific flow of hot new fashions.

Once the designers have done their work, production begins. But rather than relying on a hodgepodge of slow-moving suppliers in Asia, as most competitors do, Zara makes 40 percent of its own fabrics and produces more than half of its own clothes. Even farmed-out manufacturing goes primarily to local contractors. Almost all clothes sold in Zara's stores worldwide are made quickly and efficiently at or near company headquarters in the remote northwest corner of Spain.

Finished goods then feed into Zara's modern distribution centers, which ship finished products immediately and directly to stores around the world, saving time, eliminating the need

▲ Corporate VMS: Effective vertical integration makes Zara more flexible and more efficient—a virtual blur compared with competitors. It can take a new line from design to production to worldwide distribution in its own stores in less than a month (versus an industry average of nine months).

for warehouses, and keeping inventories low. The highly-automated centers can sort, pack, label, and allocate up to 80,000 items an hour.

Again, the key word describing Zara's distribution system is *fast*. The time between receiving an order at the distribution center to the delivery of goods to a store averages 24 hours for European stores and a maximum of 48 hours for American or Asian stores. Zara stores receive small shipments of new merchandise two to three times each week, compared with competing chains' outlets, which get large shipments seasonally, usually just four to six times per year.

Speedy design and distribution allows Zara to introduce a copious supply of new fashions—some 30,000 items last year, compared with a competitor average of less than 10,000. The combination of a large number of new fashions delivered in frequent small batches gives Zara stores a continually updated merchandise mix that brings customers back more often. Zara customers visit the store an average of 17 times per year, compared to less than 5 customer visits at competing stores. Fast turnover also results in less outdated and discounted merchandise. Because Zara makes what consumers already want or are now wearing, it doesn't have to guess what will be hot six months out.

In all, Zara's carefully integrated design and distribution process gives the fast-moving retailer a tremendous competitive advantage. Its turbocharged system gets out the goods customers what, when they want them—maybe even before:

A couple of summers ago, Zara managed to latch onto one of the season's hottest trends in just four weeks. The process started

(*continued*)

when trend-spotters spread the word back to headquarters: White eyelet—cotton with tiny holes in it—was set to become white-hot. A quick telephone survey of Zara store managers confirmed that the fabric could be a winner, so in-house designers got down to work. They zapped patterns electronically to Zara's factory across the street, and the fabric was cut. Local subcontractors stitched white-eyelet V-neck belted dresses—think Jackie Kennedy, circa 1960—and finished them in less than a week. The $129 dresses were inspected, tagged, and transported through a tunnel under the street to a distribution center. From there, they were quickly dispatched to Zara stores from New York to Tokyo—where they were flying off the racks just two days later.

Sources: Cecilie Rohwedder, "Zara Grows as Retail Rivals Struggle," *Wall Street Journal*, March 26, 2009, p. B1; "Inditex Outperforms with Growth in All Its Markets," *Retail Week*, March 27, 2009, accessed at www.retail-week .com; Kerry Capell, "Fashion Conquistador," *BusinessWeek*, September 4, 2006, pp. 38–39; Cecilie Rohwedder, "Turbocharged Supply Chain May Speed Zara Past Gap as Top Clothing Retailer," *The Globe and Mail*, March 26, 2009, p. B12; and information from the Inditex Press Dossier, accessed at www.inditex.com/en/press/information/press_kit, October 2009.

and fast-food restaurants to dental centers and dating services, from wedding consultants and maid services to fitness centers and funeral homes.

There are three types of franchises. The first type is the *manufacturer-sponsored retailer franchise system*—for example, Honda and its network of independent franchised dealers. The second type is the *manufacturer-sponsored wholesaler franchise system*—Coca-Cola licenses bottlers (wholesalers) in various markets who buy Coca-Cola syrup concentrate and then bottle and sell the finished product to retailers in local markets. The third type is the *service-firm-sponsored retailer franchise system*—for example, Burger King and its nearly 10,000 franchisee-operated restaurants around the world. ▲Other examples can be found in everything from auto rentals (Hertz, Avis), apparel retailers (The Athlete's Foot, Plato's Closet), and motels (Holiday Inn, Ramada Inn) to real estate (Century 21) and personal services (Great Clips, Mr. Handyman, Molly Maid).

▼Franchising systems: Almost every kind of business has been franchised—from motels and fast-food restaurants to dating services and cleaning and handyman companies.

The fact that most consumers cannot tell the difference between contractual and corporate VMSs shows how successfully the contractual organizations compete with corporate chains. Chapter 11 presents a fuller discussion of the various contractual VMSs.

Administered VMS

Administered VMS
A vertical marketing system that coordinates successive stages of production and distribution, not through common ownership or contractual ties, but through the size and power of one of the parties.

In an **administered VMS**, leadership is assumed not through common ownership or contractual ties but through the size and power of one or a few dominant channel members. Manufacturers of a top brand can obtain strong trade cooperation and support from resellers. For example, General Electric, P&G, and Kraft can command unusual cooperation from resellers regarding displays, shelf space, promotions, and price policies. In turn, large retailers such as Wal-Mart, Home Depot, and Barnes & Noble can exert strong influence on the many manufacturers that supply the products they sell.

Horizontal Marketing Systems

Horizontal marketing system
A channel arrangement in which two or more companies at one level join together to follow a new marketing opportunity.

Another channel development is the **horizontal marketing system**, in which two or more companies at one level join together to follow a new marketing opportunity. By working together, companies can combine their financial, production, or marketing resources to accomplish more than any one company could alone.

▲Horizontal marketing channels: McDonald's places "express" versions of its restaurants in Wal-Mart stores. McDonald's benefits from Wal-Mart's heavy store traffic and Wal-Mart keeps hungry shoppers from needing to go elsewhere to eat.

Multichannel distribution system
A distribution system in which a single firm sets up two or more marketing channels to reach one or more customer segments.

Companies might join forces with competitors or noncompetitors. They might work with each other on a temporary or permanent basis, or they may create a separate company. ▲For example, McDonald's now places "express" versions of its restaurants in Wal-Mart stores. McDonald's benefits from Wal-Mart's heavy store traffic, and Wal-Mart keeps hungry shoppers from needing to go elsewhere to eat.

Such channel arrangements also work well globally. For example, McDonald's and KFC recently joined forces with Sinopec, China's largest gasoline retailer, to place drive-through restaurants at Sinopec's more than 29,000 gas stations. The move greatly speeds the expansion of the two fast-food chains in China while at the same time pulling hungry motorists into Sinopec stations. Sinopec has also recently partnered with Grease Monkey car service centers. By working together, Sinopec, McDonald's, KFC, and Grease Monkey create an all-in-one service stop for drivers.[5]

Multichannel Distribution Systems

In the past, many companies used a single channel to sell to a single market or market segment. Today, with the proliferation of customer segments and channel possibilities, more and more companies have adopted **multichannel distribution systems**—often called *hybrid marketing channels*. Such multichannel marketing occurs when a single firm sets up two or more marketing channels to reach one or more customer segments. The use of multichannel systems has increased greatly in recent years.

■ **Figure 10.4** shows a multichannel marketing system. In the figure, the producer sells directly to consumer segment 1 using catalogs, telemarketing, and the Internet and reaches consumer segment 2 through retailers. It sells indirectly to business segment 1 through distributors and dealers and to business segment 2 through its own sales force.

■ **Figure 10.4** Multichannel Distribution System

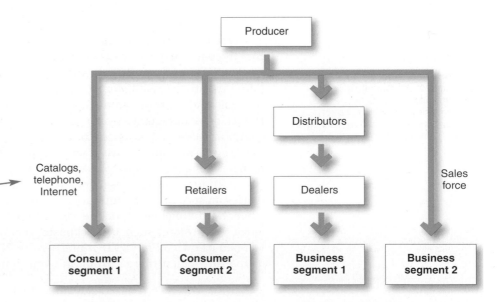

Most large companies distribute through multiple channels. For example, you could buy a familiar green and yellow John Deere lawn tractor from a neighborhood John Deere dealer or from Lowe's. A large farm or forestry business would buy larger John Deere equipment from a premium full-service dealer and its sales force.

▲ **Multichannel distribution: John Deere sells its familiar green and yellow lawn and garden equipment to consumers and commercial users through several channels, including Lowe's home improvement stores and online. It sells its agricultural equipment through the premium John Deere dealer network.**

Disintermediation
The cutting out of marketing channel intermediaries by product or service producers, or the displacement of traditional resellers by radical new types of intermediaries.

These days, almost every large company and many small ones distribute through multiple channels. ▲ For example, John Deere sells its familiar green and yellow lawn and garden tractors, mowers, and outdoor power products to consumers and commercial users through several channels, including John Deere retailers, Lowe's home improvement stores, and online. It sells and services its tractors, combines, planters, and other agricultural equipment through its premium John Deere dealer network. And it sells large construction and forestry equipment through selected large, full-service dealers and their sales forces.

Multichannel distribution systems offer many advantages to companies facing large and complex markets. With each new channel, the company expands its sales and market coverage and gains opportunities to tailor its products and services to the specific needs of diverse customer segments. But such multichannel systems are harder to control, and they generate conflict as more channels compete for customers and sales. For example, when John Deere began selling selected consumer products through Lowe's home improvement stores, many of its dealers complained loudly. To avoid such conflicts in its Internet marketing channels, the company routes all of its Web site sales to John Deere dealers.

Changing Channel Organization

Changes in technology and the explosive growth of direct and online marketing are having a profound impact on the nature and design of marketing channels. One major trend is toward **disintermediation**—a big term with a clear message and important consequences. Disintermediation occurs when product or service producers cut out intermediaries and go directly to final buyers, or when radically new types of channel intermediaries displace traditional ones.

Thus, in many industries, traditional intermediaries are dropping by the wayside. For example, Southwest, JetBlue, and other airlines sell tickets directly to final buyers, cutting travel agents from their marketing channels altogether. In other cases, new forms of resellers are displacing traditional intermediaries. For example, online marketers have taken business from traditional brick-and-mortar retailers. Consumers can buy hotel rooms and airline tickets from Expedia.com and Travelocity.com; electronics from Sonystyle.com; clothes and accessories from Bluefly.com; and books, videos, toys, jewelry, sports, consumer electronics, home and garden items, and almost anything else from Amazon.com; all without ever stepping into a traditional retail store. Online music download services such as iTunes and Amazon.com are threatening the very existence of traditional music-store retailers. In fact, once-dominant music retailers such as Tower Records have declared bankruptcy and closed their doors for good.

Disintermediation presents both opportunities and problems for producers and resellers. Channel innovators who find new ways to add value in the channel can sweep aside traditional resellers and reap the rewards. In turn, traditional intermediaries must continue to innovate in order to avoid being swept aside. ▲ For example, when Netflix pioneered online video rentals, it sent traditional brick-and-mortar video-rental stores such as Blockbuster reeling. To meet the threat, Blockbuster developed its own online DVD-rental service. Now, both Netflix and Blockbuster face disintermediation threats from an even hotter channel—digital video downloads

▲ Netflix faces dramatic changes in how movies and other entertainment content will be distributed. Instead of simply watching the developments, Netflix intends to lead them.

and video on demand. But instead of simply watching digital video distribution developments, Netflix intends to lead them:[6]

> Netflix has already added a "watch instantly" feature to its Web site that allows subscribers to instantly stream near-DVD quality video for a limited but growing list of movie titles and TV programs. "Our intention," says Netflix founder and CEO Reed Hasting, "is to get [our watch instantly] service to every Internet-connected screen, from cellphones to laptops to Wi-Fi-enabled plasma screens." In this way, Netflix plans to disintermediate its own distribution model before others can do it. To Hastings, the key to the future is all in how Netflix defines itself. "If [you] think of Netflix as a DVD rental business, [you're] right to be scared," he says. But "if [you] think of Netflix as an online movie service with multiple different delivery models, then [you're] a lot less scared. We're only now starting to deliver [on] that second vision."

Similarly, to remain competitive, product and service producers must develop new channel opportunities, such as the Internet and other direct channels. However, developing these new channels often brings them into direct competition with their established channels, resulting in conflict.

To ease this problem, companies often look for ways to make going direct a plus for the entire channel. For example, guitar and amp maker Fender knows that many customers would prefer to buy its guitars, amps, and accessories online. But selling directly through its Web site would create conflicts with retail partners, from large chains such as Guitar Center, Sam Ash, and Best Buy to small shops scattered throughout the world, such as the Musician's Junkyard in Windsor, Vermont, or Freddy for Music in Amman, Jordan. So Fender's Web site provides detailed information about the company's products but you can't buy a new Fender Stratocaster or Acoustasonic guitar there. Instead, the Fender Web site refers you to resellers' Web sites and stores. Thus, Fender's direct marketing helps both the company and its channel partners.

 Speed Bump: Linking the Concepts

Stop here for a moment and apply the distribution channel concepts we've discussed so far.

- Compare the Zara and Goodyear channels. Draw a diagram that shows the types of intermediaries in each channel. What kind of channel system does each company use?
- What are the roles and responsibilities of the members in each channel? How well do these channel members work together toward overall channel success?

Author Comment ≫
Like everything else in marketing, good channel design begins with analyzing customer needs. Remember, marketing channels are really *customer-value delivery networks*.

CHANNEL DESIGN DECISIONS (pp 349–353)

We now look at several channel decisions manufacturers face. In designing marketing channels, manufacturers struggle between what is ideal and what is practical. A new firm with limited capital usually starts by selling in a limited market area. Deciding on the best channels might not be a problem: The problem might simply be how to convince one or a few good intermediaries to handle the line.

If successful, the new firm can branch out to new markets through the existing intermediaries. In smaller markets, the firm might sell directly to retailers; in larger markets, it might sell through distributors. In one part of the country, it might grant exclusive franchises; in another, it might sell through all available outlets. Then, it might add a Web store that sells directly to hard-to-reach customers. In this way, channel systems often evolve to meet market opportunities and conditions.

For maximum effectiveness, however, channel analysis and decision making should be more purposeful. **Marketing channel design** calls for analyzing consumer needs, setting channel objectives, identifying major channel alternatives, and evaluating them.

Marketing channel design
Designing effective marketing channels by analyzing consumer needs, setting channel objectives, identifying major channel alternatives, and evaluating them.

Analyzing Consumer Needs

As noted previously, marketing channels are part of the overall *customer-value delivery network*. Each channel member and level adds value for the customer. Thus, designing the marketing channel starts with finding out what target consumers want from the channel. Do consumers want to buy from nearby locations or are they willing to travel to more distant centralized locations? Would they rather buy in person, by phone, or online? Do they value breadth of assortment or do they prefer specialization? Do consumers want many add-on services (delivery, repairs, installation), or will they obtain these elsewhere? The faster the delivery, the greater the assortment provided, and the more add-on services supplied, the greater the channel's service level.

▲ Meeting customers' channel service needs: Your local hardware store probably provides more personalized service, a more convenient location, and less shopping hassle than a huge Home Depot or Lowe's store. But it may also charge higher prices.

Providing the fastest delivery, greatest assortment, and most services may not be possible or practical. The company and its channel members may not have the resources or skills needed to provide all the desired services. Also, providing higher levels of service results in higher costs for the channel and higher prices for consumers. ▲ For example, your local hardware store probably provides more personalized service, a more convenient location, and less shopping hassle than the nearest huge Home Depot or Lowe's store. But it may also charge higher prices. The company must balance consumer needs not only against the feasibility and costs of meeting these needs but also against customer price preferences. The success of discount retailing shows that consumers will often accept lower service levels in exchange for lower prices.

Setting Channel Objectives

Companies should state their marketing channel objectives in terms of targeted levels of customer service. Usually, a company can identify several segments wanting different levels of service. The company should decide which segments to serve and the best channels to use in each case. In each segment, the company wants to minimize the total channel cost of meeting customer-service requirements.

The company's channel objectives are also influenced by the nature of the company, its products, its marketing intermediaries, its competitors, and the environment. For example, the company's size and financial situation determine which marketing functions it can handle itself and which it must give to intermediaries. Companies selling perishable products may require more direct marketing to avoid delays and too much handling.

In some cases, a company may want to compete in or near the same outlets that carry competitors' products. For example, Maytag wants its appliances displayed alongside competing brands to facilitate comparison shopping. In other cases, companies may avoid the channels used by competitors. Mary Kay Cosmetics, for example, sells direct to consumers through its corps of 1.8 million independent beauty consultants in more than 35 markets worldwide rather than going head-to-head with other cosmetics makers for scarce positions in retail stores. And GEICO primarily markets auto and homeowner's insurance directly to consumers via the telephone and Web rather than through agents.

Finally, environmental factors such as economic conditions and legal constraints may affect channel objectives and design. For example, in a depressed economy, producers want to distribute their goods in the most economical way, using shorter channels and dropping unneeded services that add to the final price of the goods.

Identifying Major Alternatives

When the company has defined its channel objectives, it should next identify its major channel alternatives in terms of *types* of intermediaries, the *number* of intermediaries, and the *responsibilities* of each channel member.

Types of Intermediaries

A firm should identify the types of channel members available to carry out its channel work. Most companies face many channel member choices. For example, until recently, Dell sold directly to final consumers and business buyers only through its sophisticated phone and Internet marketing channel. It also sold directly to large corporate, institutional, and government buyers using its direct sales force. However, to reach more consumers and to match competitors such as HP, Dell now sells indirectly through retailers such as Best Buy, Staples, and Wal-Mart. It also sells indirectly through "value-added resellers," independent distributors and dealers who develop computer systems and applications tailored to the special needs of small- and medium-sized business customers.

Using many types of resellers in a channel provides both benefits and drawbacks. For example, by selling through retailers and value-added resellers in addition to its own direct channels, Dell can reach more and different kinds of buyers. However, the new channels will be more difficult to manage and control. And the direct and indirect channels will compete with each other for many of the same customers, causing potential conflict. In fact, Dell is already finding itself "stuck in the middle," with its direct sales reps complaining about new competition from retail stores, while at the same time value-added resellers complain that the direct sales reps are undercutting their business.[7]

▼Exclusive distribution: Rolex sells its watches exclusively through only a handful of authorized dealers in any given market. Such limited distribution enhances the brand's image and generates stronger retailer support.

Number of Marketing Intermediaries

Companies must also determine the number of channel members to use at each level. Three strategies are available: intensive distribution, exclusive distribution, and selective distribution. Producers of convenience products and common raw materials typically seek **intensive distribution**—a strategy in which they stock their products in as many outlets as possible. These products must be available where and when consumers want them. For example, toothpaste, candy, and other similar items are sold in millions of outlets to provide maximum brand exposure and consumer convenience. Kraft, Coca-Cola, Kimberly-Clark, and other consumer-goods companies distribute their products in this way.

By contrast, some producers purposely limit the number of intermediaries handling their products. The extreme form of this practice is **exclusive distribution**, in which the producer gives only a limited number of dealers the exclusive right to distribute its products in their territories. Exclusive distribution is often found in the distribution of luxury brands and brands. ▲For example, exclusive Rolex watches are typically sold by only a handful of authorized dealers in any given market area. By granting exclusive distribution,

Intensive distribution
Stocking the product in as many outlets as possible.

Exclusive distribution
Giving a limited number of dealers the exclusive right to distribute the company's products in their territories.

Selective distribution
The use of more than one, but fewer than all, of the intermediaries who are willing to carry the company's products.

Rolex gains stronger dealer selling support and more control over dealer prices, promotion, and services. Exclusive distribution also enhances the brand's image and allows for higher markups.

Between intensive and exclusive distribution lies **selective distribution**—the use of more than one, but fewer than all, of the intermediaries who are willing to carry a company's products. Most television, furniture, and home appliance brands are distributed in this manner. For example, Whirlpool and General Electric sell their major appliances through dealer networks and selected large retailers. By using selective distribution, they can develop good working relationships with selected channel members and expect a better-than-average selling effort. Selective distribution gives producers good market coverage with more control and less cost than does intensive distribution.

Responsibilities of Channel Members

The producer and intermediaries need to agree on the terms and responsibilities of each channel member. They should agree on price policies, conditions of sale, territory rights, and specific services to be performed by each party. The producer should establish a list price and a fair set of discounts for intermediaries. It must define each channel member's territory, and it should be careful about where it places new resellers.

Mutual services and duties need to be spelled out carefully, especially in franchise and exclusive distribution channels. For example, McDonald's provides franchisees with promotional support, a record-keeping system, training at Hamburger University, and general management assistance. In turn, franchisees must meet company standards for physical facilities and food quality, cooperate with new promotion programs, provide requested information, and buy specified food products.

Evaluating the Major Alternatives

Suppose a company has identified several channel alternatives and wants to select the one that will best satisfy its long-run objectives. Each alternative should be evaluated against economic, control, and adaptability criteria.

Using *economic criteria*, a company compares the likely sales, costs, and profitability of different channel alternatives. What will be the investment required by each channel alternative, and what returns will result? The company must also consider *control issues*. Using intermediaries usually means giving them some control over the marketing of the product, and some intermediaries take more control than others. Other things being equal, the company prefers to keep as much control as possible. Finally, the company must apply *adaptability criteria*. Channels often involve long-term commitments, yet the company wants to keep the channel flexible so that it can adapt to environmental changes. Thus, to be considered, a channel involving long-term commitments should be greatly superior on economic and control grounds.

Designing International Distribution Channels

International marketers face many additional complexities in designing their channels. Each country has its own unique distribution system that has evolved over time and changes very slowly. These channel systems can vary widely from country to country. Thus, global marketers must usually adapt their channel strategies to the existing structures within each country.

In some markets, the distribution system is complex and hard to penetrate, consisting of many layers and large numbers of intermediaries. For example, many Western companies find Japan's distribution system difficult to navigate. It's steeped in tradition and very complex, with many distributors touching one product before it makes it to the store shelf.

At the other extreme, distribution systems in developing countries may be scattered, inefficient, or altogether lacking. For example, China and India are huge markets, each with populations well over one billion people. However, because of inadequate distribution systems, most companies can profitably access only a small portion of the population located in each country's most affluent cities. "China is a very decentralized market," notes a China trade expert. "[It's] made up of two dozen distinct markets sprawling across 2,000 cities. Each has its own culture. . . . It's like operating in an asteroid belt." China's distribution system is so fragmented that logistics costs to wrap, bundle, load, unload, sort, reload, and transport goods amount to more than 22 percent of the nation's GDP, far higher than in most other countries (U.S. logistics costs account for just over 10 percent of the nation's GDP). After years of effort, even Wal-Mart executives admit that they have been unable to assemble an efficient supply chain in China.[8]

▲International channel complexities: When the Chinese government banned door-to-door selling, Avon had to abandon its traditional direct marketing approach and sell through retail shops.

Sometimes customs or government regulation can greatly restrict how a company distributes products in global markets. ▲For example, it wasn't an inefficient distribution structure that caused problems for Avon in China—it was restrictive government regulation. Fearing the growth of multilevel marketing schemes, the Chinese government banned door-to-door selling altogether in 1998, forcing Avon to abandon its traditional direct marketing approach and sell through retail shops. The Chinese government has since given Avon and other direct sellers permission to sell door-to-door again, but that permission is tangled in a web of restrictions. Fortunately for Avon, its earlier focus on store sales is helping it weather the restrictions better than most other direct sellers. In fact, through a combination of direct and retail sales, Avon's sales in China are now booming.[9]

International marketers face a wide range of channel alternatives. Designing efficient and effective channel systems between and within various country markets poses a difficult challenge. We discuss international distribution decisions further in Chapter 15.

Author Comment ≫
Now it's time to implement the chosen channel design and to work with selected channel members to manage and motivate them.

Marketing channel management
Selecting, managing, and motivating individual channel members and evaluating their performance over time.

CHANNEL MANAGEMENT DECISIONS (pp 353–355)

Once the company has reviewed its channel alternatives and decided on the best channel design, it must implement and manage the chosen channel. **Marketing channel management** calls for selecting, managing, and motivating individual channel members and evaluating their performance over time.

Selecting Channel Members

Producers vary in their ability to attract qualified marketing intermediaries. Some producers have no trouble signing up channel members. For example, when Toyota first introduced its Lexus line in the United States, it had no trouble attracting new dealers. In fact, it had to turn down many would-be resellers.

At the other extreme are producers who have to work hard to line up enough qualified intermediaries. For example, when Timex first tried to sell its inexpensive watches through regular jewelry stores, most jewelry stores refused to carry them. The company then managed to get its watches into mass-merchandise outlets. This turned out to be a wise decision because of the rapid growth of mass-merchandising.

When selecting intermediaries, the company should determine what characteristics distinguish the better ones. It will want to evaluate each channel member's years in business, other lines carried, growth and profit record, cooperativeness, and reputation. If the intermediaries are sales agents, the company will want to evaluate the number and character of other lines carried and the size and quality of the sales force. If the intermediary is a retail store that wants exclusive or selective distribution, the company will want to evaluate the store's customers, location, and future growth potential.

Managing and Motivating Channel Members

Once selected, channel members must be continuously managed and motivated to do their best. The company must sell not only *through* the intermediaries but *to* and *with* them. Most companies see their intermediaries as first-line customers and partners. They practice strong *partner relationship management (PRM)* to forge long-term partnerships with channel members. This creates a value delivery system that meets the needs of both the company *and* its marketing partners.

In managing its channels, a company must convince distributors that they can succeed better by working together as a part of a cohesive value delivery system. Thus, P&G works closely with Wal-Mart to create superior value for final consumers. The two jointly plan merchandising goals and strategies, inventory levels, and advertising and promotion programs.

Similarly, heavy-equipment manufacturer Caterpillar and its worldwide network of independent dealers work in close harmony to find better ways to bring value to customers.[10]

Caterpillar produces innovative, high-quality products. Yet the most important reason for Caterpillar's dominance is its distribution network of 181 outstanding independent dealers worldwide. Caterpillar and its dealers work as partners. According to a former Caterpillar CEO: "After the product leaves our door, the dealers take over. They are the ones on the front line. They're the ones who live with the product for its lifetime. They're the ones customers see." ▲When a big piece of Caterpillar equipment breaks down, customers know that they can count on Caterpillar and its outstanding dealer network for support. Dealers play a vital role in almost every aspect of Caterpillar's operations, from product design and delivery to product service and support.

Caterpillar really knows its dealers and cares about their success. It closely monitors each dealership's sales, market position, service capability, and financial situation. When it sees a problem, it jumps in to help. In addition to more formal business ties, Cat forms close personal ties with dealers in a kind of family relationship. Caterpillar and its dealers feel a deep pride in what they are accomplishing together. As the former CEO puts it, "There's a camaraderie among our dealers around the world that really makes it more than just a financial arrangement. They feel that what they're doing is good for the world because they are part of an organization that makes, sells, and tends to the machines that make the world work."

▲Caterpillar works closely with its worldwide network of independent dealers to find better ways to bring value to customers. When a big piece of CAT equipment breaks down, customers know they can count on Caterpillar and its outstanding dealer network for support.

As a result of its partnership with dealers, Caterpillar dominates the world's markets for heavy construction, mining, and logging equipment. Its familiar yellow tractors, crawlers, loaders, bulldozers, and trucks capture some 40 percent of the worldwide heavy-equipment business, twice that of number-two Komatsu.

Many companies are now installing integrated high-tech partner relationship management (PRM) systems to coordinate their whole-channel marketing efforts. Just as they use customer relationship management (CRM) software systems to help manage relationships with important customers, companies can now use PRM and supply chain management (SCM) software to help recruit, train, organize, manage, motivate, and evaluate relationships with channel partners.

Evaluating Channel Members

The company must regularly check channel member performance against standards such as sales quotas, average inventory levels, customer delivery time, treatment of damaged and lost goods, cooperation in company promotion and training programs, and services to the customer. The company should recognize and reward intermediaries who are performing well and adding good value for consumers. Those who are performing poorly should be assisted or, as a last resort, replaced.

Finally, companies need to be sensitive to their channel partners. Those who treat their partners poorly risk not only losing their support but also causing some legal problems. The next section describes various rights and duties pertaining to companies and other channel members.

 Speed Bump: Linking the Concepts

Time for another break. This time, compare the Caterpillar and Goodyear channel systems.

- Diagram the Caterpillar and Goodyear channel systems. How do they compare in terms of channel levels, types of intermediaries, channel member roles and responsibilities, and other characteristics. How well is each system designed?
- Assess how well Caterpillar and Goodyear have managed and supported their channels. With what results?

PUBLIC POLICY AND DISTRIBUTION DECISIONS (pp 355–356)

For the most part, companies are legally free to develop whatever channel arrangements suit them. In fact, the laws affecting channels seek to prevent the exclusionary tactics of some companies that might keep another company from using a desired channel. Most channel law deals with the mutual rights and duties of the channel members once they have formed a relationship.

Many producers and wholesalers like to develop exclusive channels for their products. When the seller allows only certain outlets to carry its products, this strategy is called *exclusive distribution*. When the seller requires that these dealers not handle competitors' products, its strategy is called *exclusive dealing*. Both parties can benefit from exclusive arrangements: The seller obtains more loyal and dependable outlets, and the dealers obtain a steady source of supply and stronger seller support. But exclusive arrangements also exclude other producers from selling to these dealers. This situation brings exclusive dealing contracts under the scope of the Clayton Act of 1914. They are legal as long as they do not substantially lessen competition or tend to create a monopoly and as long as both parties enter into the agreement voluntarily.

Exclusive dealing often includes *exclusive territorial agreements*. The producer may agree not to sell to other dealers in a given area, or the buyer may agree to sell only in its own territory. The first practice is normal under franchise systems as a way to increase dealer enthusiasm and commitment. It is also perfectly legal—a seller has no legal obligation to sell through more outlets than it wishes. The second practice, whereby the producer tries to keep a dealer from selling outside its territory, has become a major legal issue.

Producers of a strong brand sometimes sell it to dealers only if the dealers will take some or all of the rest of the line. This is called full-line forcing. Such *tying agreements* are not necessarily illegal, but they do violate the Clayton Act if they tend to lessen competition substantially. The practice may prevent consumers from freely choosing among competing suppliers of these other brands.

Finally, producers are free to select their dealers, but their right to terminate dealers is somewhat restricted. In general, sellers can drop dealers "for cause." However, they cannot drop dealers if, for example, the dealers refuse to cooperate in a doubtful legal arrangement, such as exclusive dealing or tying agreements.

MARKETING LOGISTICS AND SUPPLY CHAIN MANAGEMENT (pp 356–364)

(pp 356–364)

In today's global marketplace, selling a product is sometimes easier than getting it to customers. Companies must decide on the best way to store, handle, and move their products and services so that they are available to customers in the right assortments, at the right time, and in the right place. Logistics effectiveness has a major impact on both customer satisfaction and company costs. Here we consider the nature and importance of logistics management in the supply chain, goals of the logistics system, major logistics functions, and the need for integrated supply chain management.

Nature and Importance of Marketing Logistics

To some managers, marketing logistics means only trucks and warehouses. But modern logistics is much more than this. **Marketing logistics**—also called **physical distribution**—involves planning, implementing, and controlling the physical flow of goods, services, and related information from points of origin to points of consumption to meet customer requirements at a profit. In short, it involves getting the right product to the right customer in the right place at the right time.

In the past, physical distribution planners typically started with products at the plant and then tried to find low-cost solutions to get them to customers. However, today's marketers prefer *customer-centered* logistics thinking, which starts with the marketplace and works backward to the factory, or even to sources of supply. Marketing logistics involves not only *outbound distribution* (moving products from the factory to resellers and ultimately to customers) but also *inbound distribution* (moving products and materials from suppliers to the factory) and *reverse distribution* (moving broken, unwanted, or excess products returned by consumers or resellers). That is, it involves entire **supply chain management**—managing upstream and downstream value-added flows of materials, final goods, and related information among suppliers, the company, resellers, and final consumers, as shown in ■ **Figure 10.5**.

The logistics manager's task is to coordinate activities of suppliers, purchasing agents, marketers, channel members, and customers. These activities include forecasting, information systems, purchasing, production planning, order processing, inventory, warehousing, and transportation planning.

Companies today are placing greater emphasis on logistics for several reasons. First, companies can gain a powerful competitive advantage by using improved lo-

Author Comment »
Marketers used to call this plain old "physical distribution." But as these titles suggest, the topic has grown in importance, complexity, and sophistication.

Marketing logistics (or physical distribution)
Planning, implementing, and controlling the physical flow of materials, final goods, and related information from points of origin to points of consumption to meet customer requirements at a profit.

Supply chain management
Managing upstream and downstream value-added flows of materials, final goods, and related information among suppliers, the company, resellers, and final consumers.

■ **Figure 10.5** Supply Chain Management

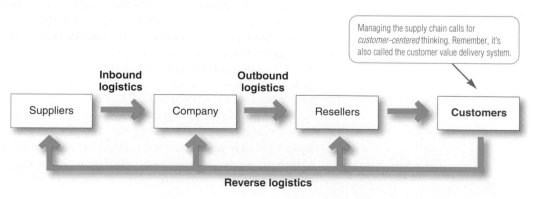

Managing the supply chain calls for *customer-centered* thinking. Remember, it's also called the customer value delivery system.

▲Logistics: American companies spent $1.4 trillion last year—about 10 percent of gross domestic product—to wrap, bundle, load, unload, sort, reload, and transport goods.

gistics to give customers better service or lower prices. Second, improved logistics can yield tremendous cost savings to both the company and its customers. As much as 20 percent of an average product's price is accounted for by shipping and transport alone. This far exceeds the cost of advertising and many other marketing costs. ▲American companies spent $1.4 trillion last year—about 10 percent of gross domestic product—to wrap, bundle, load, unload, sort, reload, and transport goods. That's more than the national GDPs of all but 12 countries worldwide. What's more, as fuel and other costs rise, so do logistics costs. For example, the cost of shipping one 40-foot container from Shanghai to the United States rose from $3,000 in 2000 to more than $8,000 last year.[11] Shaving off even a small fraction of logistics costs can mean substantial savings.

Third, the explosion in product variety has created a need for improved logistics management. For example, in 1911 the typical A&P grocery store carried only 270 items. The store manager could keep track of this inventory on about 10 pages of notebook paper stuffed in a shirt pocket. Today, the average A&P carries a bewildering stock of more than 25,000 items. A Wal-Mart Supercenter store carries more than 100,000 products, 30,000 of which are grocery products.[12] Ordering, shipping, stocking, and controlling such a variety of products presents a sizable logistics challenge.

Improvements in information technology have also created opportunities for major gains in distribution efficiency. Today's companies are using sophisticated supply chain management software, Web-based logistics systems, point-of-sale scanners, RFID tags, satellite tracking, and electronic transfer of order and payment data. Such technology lets them quickly and efficiently manage the flow of goods, information, and finances through the supply chain.

Finally, more than almost any other marketing function, logistics affects the environment and a firm's environmental sustainability efforts. Transportation, warehousing, packaging, and other logistics functions are typically the biggest supply chain contributors to the company's environmental footprint. At the same time, they also provide one of the most fertile areas for cost savings. So developing a *green supply chain* is not only environmentally responsible, it can also be profitable. "Your CO_2 footprint of transportation and your cost of fuel are permanently linked," says one logistics manager. "The good news is if you can reduce logistics costs you can write an environmental story about it."[13] See Marketing at Work 10.2.

Goals of the Logistics System

Some companies state their logistics objective as providing maximum customer service at the least cost. Unfortunately, no logistics system can *both* maximize customer service *and* minimize distribution costs. Maximum customer service implies rapid delivery, large inventories, flexible assortments, liberal returns policies, and other services—all of which raise distribution costs. In contrast, minimum distribution costs imply slower delivery, smaller inventories, and larger shipping lots—which represent a lower level of overall customer service.

The goal of marketing logistics should be to provide a *targeted* level of customer service at the least cost. A company must first research the importance of various distribution services to customers and then set desired service levels for each segment. The objective is to maximize *profits*, not sales. Therefore, the company must weigh the benefits of providing higher levels of service against the costs. Some companies offer less service than their competitors and charge a lower price. Other companies offer more service and charge higher prices to cover higher costs.

Marketing at Work 10.2

Greening the Supply Chain: It's the Right Thing to Do—and It's Profitable Too

You may remember the old song in which Kermit the Frog laments, "it's not easy bein' green." That's often as true for company's supply chains as it is for the Muppet. Greening up a company's channels often takes substantial commitment, ingenuity, and investment. Although challenging, however, today's supply channels are getting ever greener.

Companies have many reasons for reducing the environmental impact of their supply chains. For one thing, in the not too distant future, if companies don't green up voluntarily, a host of "green laws" and sustainability regulations enacted around the world will require them to do so. For another, many large customers—from HP to Wal-Mart to the federal government—are demanding it. "Environmental sustainability is fast becoming a critical element in supplier selection and performance evaluation," says a channels expert. Supply chain managers "need to begin thinking green, and quickly, or they chance risking relationships with prime customers." Perhaps even more important than *having* to do it, designing more environmentally responsible supply chains is simply the *right* thing to do. It's one more way that companies can contribute to saving our world for future generations.

But that's all pretty heady stuff. As it turns out, companies have a more immediate and practical reason for turning their supply chains green. Not only are green channels good for the world, they're also good for the company's bottom line. Companies green their supply chains through greater efficiency, and greater efficiency means lower costs and higher profits. This cost-savings side of environmental responsibility makes good sense. The very logistics activities that create the biggest environmental footprint—such as transportation, warehousing, and packaging—are also the ones that account for a lion's share of logistics costs, especially in an age of scarce resources and soaring energy prices. Although it may require an up-front investment, it doesn't cost more to green up channels. In the long run, it usually costs less.

Here are just a few examples of how creating greener supply chains can benefit both the environment and the company's bottom line:

- Stonyfield Farm, the world's largest yogurt maker, recently set up a small dedicated truck fleet to make regional deliveries in New England and replaced its national less-than-truckload distribution network with a regional multi-stop truckload system. As a result, Stonyfield now moves more product in fewer trucks, cutting in half the number of miles traveled. The changes produced a 40-percent reduction in transportation-related carbon dioxide emissions; they also knocked an eye-popping 8 percent off of Stonyfield's shipping expenses. Says Stonyfield's director of logistics, "We're surprised. We understand that environmental responsibility can be profitable. We expected some savings, but not really in this range."
- Consumer package goods maker SC Johnson made a seemingly simple but smart—and profitable—change in the way it packs its trucks. Under the old system, a load of its Ziploc products filled a truck trailer before reaching the maximum weight limit. In contrast, a load of Windex glass cleaner hit the maximum weight before the trailer was full. By strategically mixing the two products, SC Johnson found it could send the same amount of products with 2,098 fewer shipments, while burning 168,000 fewer gallons of gasoline and eliminating 1,882 tons of greenhouse gasses. Says the company's director of environmental issues, "Loading a truck may seem simple, but making sure that a truck is truly full is a science. Consistently hitting a trailer's maximum weight provided a huge opportunity to

Major Logistics Functions

Given a set of logistics objectives, the company is ready to design a logistics system that will minimize the cost of attaining these objectives. The major logistics functions include *warehousing, inventory management, transportation*, and *logistics information management*.

Warehousing

Production and consumption cycles rarely match, so most companies must store their goods while they wait to be sold. For example, Snapper, Toro, and other lawn mower manufacturers run their factories all year long and store up products for the heavy spring and summer buying seasons. The storage function overcomes differences in needed quantities and timing, ensuring that products are available when customers are ready to buy them.

A company must decide on *how many* and *what types* of warehouses it needs and *where* they will be located. The company might use either *storage warehouses* or

reduce our energy consumption, cut our greenhouse gas emissions, and save money [in the bargain]."

- Con-way, a $5 billion freight transportation company, made the simple decision to lower the maximum speed of its truck fleet from 65 miles per hour to 62. The small three-mile-per-hour change produced a savings of 6 million gallons of fuel per year and emissions reductions equivalent to taking 12,000 to 15,000 cars off the road. Similarly, grocery retailer Safeway switched its fleet of 1,000 trucks to run on cleaner-burning biodiesel fuel. This change will reduce annual CO_2 emissions by 75 million pounds—equivalent to taking another 7,500 cars off the road.

- Wal-Mart is perhaps the world's biggest green-channels champion. Among dozens of other major initiatives (see Marketing at Work 16.1), the giant retailer is now installing more efficient engines and tires, hybrid drive systems, and other technologies in its fleet of 7,000 trucks in an effort to reduce carbon monoxide emissions and increase efficiency 25 percent by 2012. Wal-Mart is also pressuring its throng of suppliers to clean up their environmental acts. For example, it recently set a goal to reduce supplier packaging by 5 percent. Given Wal-Mart's size, even small changes make a substantial impact. For instance, it convinced P&G to produce Charmin toilet paper in more-shippable compact rolls—a 6-pack of Charmin Mega Roll contains as much paper as a regular pack of 24 rolls. This change alone saves 89.5 million cardboard rolls and 360,000 pounds of plastic wrapping a year. Logistics-wise, it also allows Wal-Mart to ship 42 percent more units on its trucks, saving about 54,000 gallons of fuel. More broadly, Wal-Mart estimates that the reduced supplier-packaging

▲ Con-way made the simple decision to lower the maximum speed of its truck fleet, which produced a savings of 6 million gallons of fuel per year and emissions reductions equivalent to taking 12,000 to 15,000 cars off of the road.

initiative will produce savings of $3.4 billion and prevent 667,000 metric tons of carbon dioxide emissions, equivalent to removing 213,000 trucks from the road.

So when it comes to supply chains, Kermit might be right—it's not easy bein' green. But it's now more necessary than ever, and it can pay big returns. It's a challenging area, says one supply chain expert, "but if you look at it from a pure profit-and-loss perspective, it's also a rich one." Another expert concludes, "It's now easier than ever to build a green supply chain without going into the red, while actually saving cash along the way."

Sources: Quotes, examples, and other information from Connie Robbins Gentry, "Green Means Go," *Chain Store Age*, March 2009, p. 47; Daniel P. Bearth, "Finding Profit in Green Logistics," *Transport Topics*, January 21, 2008, p. S4; Dan R. Robinson and Shannon Wilcox, "The Greening of the Supply Chain," *Logistics Management*, October 2008; William Hoffman, "Supplying Sustainability," *Traffic World*, April 7, 2008; "Supply Chain Standard: Going Green without Going into the Red," *Logistics Manager*, March 2009, p. 22; and "Supply Chain Standard: Take the Green Route Out of the Red," *Logistics Manager*, May 2009, p. 28.

Distribution center
A large, highly automated warehouse designed to receive goods from various plants and suppliers, take orders, fill them efficiently, and deliver goods to customers as quickly as possible.

distribution centers. Storage warehouses store goods for moderate to long periods. **Distribution centers** are designed to move goods rather than just store them. They are large and highly automated warehouses designed to receive goods from various plants and suppliers, take orders, fill them efficiently, and deliver goods to customers as quickly as possible.

For example, Wal-Mart operates a network of 147 huge distribution centers. A single center, serving the daily needs of 75 to 100 Wal-Mart stores, typically contains some 1 million square feet of space (about 20 football fields) under a single roof. At a typical center, laser scanners route as many as 190,000 cases of goods per day along 5 miles of conveyer belts, and the center's 500 to 1,000 workers load or unload some 500 trucks daily. Wal-Mart's Monroe, Georgia, distribution center contains a 127,000-square-foot freezer (that's about 2 1/2 football fields) that can hold 10,000 pallets—room enough for 58 million Popsicles.[14]

Like almost everything else these days, warehousing has seen dramatic changes in technology in recent years. Outdated materials-handling methods are steadily being replaced by newer, computer-controlled systems requiring few employees.

▲ **High-tech distribution centers: Staples employs a team of super-retrievers—in day-glo orange—to keep its warehouse humming.**

Computers and scanners read orders and direct lift trucks, electric hoists, or robots to gather goods, move them to loading docks, and issue invoices. ▲For example, office supplies retailer Staples now employs "a team of super-retrievers—in day-glo orange—that keep its warehouse humming":[15]

Imagine a team of employees that works 16 hours a day, seven days a week. They never call in sick or show up late, because they never leave the building. They demand no benefits, require no health insurance, and receive no pay checks. And they never complain. Sounds like a bunch of robots, huh? They are, in fact, robots—and they're dramatically changing the way Staples delivers notepads, pens, and paper clips to its customers. Every day, Staples' huge Chambersburg, Pennsylvania, distribution center receives thousands of customer orders, each containing a wide range of office supply items. Having people run around a warehouse looking for those items is expensive, especially when the company has promised to delight customers by delivering orders the next day.

Enter the robots. On the distribution center floor, the 150 robots most resemble a well-trained breed of working dogs, say, golden retrievers. When orders come in, a centralized computer tells the robots where to find racks with the appropriate items. The robots retrieve the racks and carry them to picking stations, then wait patiently as humans pull the correct products and place them in boxes. When orders are filled, the robots neatly park the racks back among the rest. The robots pretty much take care of themselves. When they run low on power, they head to battery-charging terminals, or, as warehouse personnel say, "They get themselves a drink of water." The robots now run 50 percent of the Chambersburg facility, where average daily output is up 60 percent since they arrived on the scene.

Inventory Management

Inventory management also affects customer satisfaction. Here, managers must maintain the delicate balance between carrying too little inventory and carrying too much. With too little stock, the firm risks not having products when customers want to buy. To remedy this, the firm may need costly emergency shipments or production. Carrying too much inventory results in higher-than-necessary inventory-carrying costs and stock obsolescence. Thus, in managing inventory, firms must balance the costs of carrying larger inventories against resulting sales and profits.

Many companies have greatly reduced their inventories and related costs through *just-in-time* logistics systems. With such systems, producers and retailers carry only small inventories of parts or merchandise, often only enough for a few days of operations. New stock arrives exactly when needed, rather than being stored in inventory until being used. Just-in-time systems require accurate forecasting along with fast, frequent, and flexible delivery so that new supplies will be available when needed. However, these systems result in substantial savings in inventory-carrying and handling costs.

Marketers are always looking for new ways to make inventory management more efficient. In the not-too-distant future, handling inventory might even become fully automated. For example, in Chapter 3 we discussed RFID or "smart tag" technology, by which small transmitter chips are embedded in or placed on products and packaging on everything from flowers and razors to tires. "Smart" products could make the entire supply chain—which accounts for nearly 75 percent of a product's cost—intelligent and automated.

Companies using RFID would know, at any time, exactly where a product is located physically within the supply chain. "Smart shelves" would not only tell them when it's time to reorder, but would also place the order automatically with their suppliers. Such exciting new information technology applications will revolutionize distribution as we know it. Many large and resourceful marketing companies, such as Wal-Mart, P&G, Kraft, IBM, HP, and Best Buy, are investing heavily to make the full use of RFID technology a reality.[16]

Transportation

The choice of transportation carriers affects the pricing of products, delivery performance, and condition of the goods when they arrive—all of which will affect customer satisfaction. In shipping goods to its warehouses, dealers, and customers, the company can choose among five main transportation modes: truck, rail, water, pipeline, and air, along with an alternative mode for digital products—the Internet.

If you rely on it,

wear it,

consume it,

or depend on it,

Trucks Bring It.

Trucks are essential to deliver everything America needs.
Eighty-two percent of U.S. communities depend solely on truck transport for their goods and commodities. Simply put, trucks move America safely, efficiently and on time.

Good stuff.

TRUCKS BRING IT

www.TrucksBringIt.com

▲ **Truck transportation: More than 80 percent of American communities depend solely on the trucking industry for the delivery of their goods. "Good stuff. Trucks bring it."**

Trucks have increased their share of transportation steadily and now account for more than 39 percent of total cargo ton-miles in the United States.[17] Last year in the United States, trucks traveled more than 223 billion miles—more than double the distance traveled 20 years ago—carrying 8.9 billion tons of freight worth more than $8.3 trillion. ▲According to the American Trucking Association, 82 percent of U.S. communities depend solely on trucks for their goods and commodities. Trucks are highly flexible in their routing and time schedules, and they can usually offer faster service than railroads. They are efficient for short hauls of high-value merchandise. Trucking firms have evolved in recent years to become full-service providers of global transportation services. For example, large trucking firms now offer everything from satellite tracking, Web-based shipment management, and logistics planning software to cross-border shipping operations.

Railroads account for 37 percent of total cargo ton-miles moved. They are one of the most cost-effective modes for shipping large amounts of bulk products—coal, sand, minerals, and farm and forest products—over long distances. In recent years, railroads have increased their customer services by designing new equipment to handle special categories of goods, providing flatcars for carrying truck trailers by rail (piggyback), and providing in-transit services such as the diversion of shipped goods to other destinations en route and the processing of goods en route.

Water carriers, which account for about 7 percent of cargo ton-miles, transport large amounts of goods by ships and barges on U.S. coastal and inland waterways. Although the cost of water transportation is very low for shipping bulky, low-value, nonperishable products such as sand, coal, grain, oil, and metallic ores, water transportation is the slowest mode and may be affected by the weather. *Pipelines,* which also account for about 1 percent of cargo ton-miles, are a specialized means of shipping petroleum, natural gas, and chemicals from sources to markets. Most pipelines are used by their owners to ship their own products.

Although *air* carriers transport less than 1 percent of cargo ton-miles of the nation's goods, they are an important transportation mode. Airfreight rates are much higher than rail or truck rates, but airfreight is ideal when speed is needed or distant markets have to be reached. Among the most frequently airfreighted products are perishables (fresh fish, cut flowers) and high-value, low-bulk items (technical instruments, jewelry). Companies find that airfreight also reduces inventory levels, packaging costs, and the number of warehouses needed.

The *Internet* carries digital products from producer to customer via satellite, cable, or phone wire. Software firms, the media, music companies, and education all make use of the Internet to transport digital products. Although these firms primarily use traditional transportation to distribute DVDs, newspapers, and more, the Internet holds the potential for lower product distribution costs. Whereas planes, trucks, and trains move freight and packages, digital technology moves information bits.

Intermodal transportation
Combining two or more modes of transportation.

Shippers also use **intermodal transportation**—combining two or more modes of transportation. Total cargo ton-miles moved via multiple modes is 14 percent. *Piggyback* describes the use of rail and trucks; *fishyback*, water and trucks; *trainship*, water and rail; and *airtruck*, air and trucks. Combining modes provides advantages that no single mode can deliver. Each combination offers advantages to the shipper. For example, not only is piggyback cheaper than trucking alone but it also provides flexibility and convenience.

In choosing a transportation mode for a product, shippers must balance many considerations: speed, dependability, availability, cost, and others. Thus, if a shipper needs speed, air and truck are the prime choices. If the goal is low cost, then water or rail might be best.

Logistics Information Management

Companies manage their supply chains through information. Channel partners often link up to share information and to make better joint logistics decisions. From a logistics perspective, flows of information, such as customer transactions, billing, shipment and inventory levels, and even customer data, are closely linked to channel performance. Companies need simple, accessible, fast, and accurate processes for capturing, processing, and sharing channel information.

Information can be shared and managed in many ways but most sharing takes place through traditional or Internet-based *electronic data interchange (EDI),* the computerized exchange of data between organizations, which primarily is transmitted via the Internet. Wal-Mart, for example, requires EDI links with its more than 90,000 suppliers. If new suppliers don't have EDI capability, Wal-Mart will work with them to find and implement the needed software. "EDI has proven to be the most efficient way of conducting business with our product suppliers," says Wal-Mart. "This system of exchanging information . . . allows us to improve customer service, lower expenses, and increase productivity."[18]

In some cases, suppliers might actually be asked to generate orders and arrange deliveries for their customers. Many large retailers—such as Wal-Mart and Home Depot—work closely with major suppliers such as P&G or Black & Decker to set up *vendor-managed inventory* (VMI) systems or *continuous inventory replenishment* systems. Using VMI, the customer shares real-time data on sales and current inventory levels with the supplier. The supplier then takes full responsibility for managing inventories and deliveries. Some retailers even go so far as to shift inventory and delivery costs to the supplier. Such systems require close cooperation between the buyer and seller.

Integrated Logistics Management

Integrated logistics management
The logistics concept that emphasizes teamwork, both inside the company and among all the marketing channel organizations, to maximize the performance of the entire distribution system.

Today, more and more companies are adopting the concept of **integrated logistics management**. This concept recognizes that providing better customer service and trimming distribution costs require *teamwork*, both inside the company and among all the marketing channel organizations. Inside, the company's various departments must work closely together to maximize the company's own logistics performance. Outside, the company must integrate its logistics system with those of its suppliers and customers to maximize the performance of the entire distribution network.

Cross-Functional Teamwork Inside the Company

Most companies assign responsibility for various logistics activities to many different departments—marketing, sales, finance, operations, and purchasing. Too often, each function tries to optimize its own logistics performance without regard for the activities of the other functions. However, transportation, inventory, warehousing, and information management activities interact, often in an inverse way. Lower inventory levels reduce inventory-carrying costs. But they may also reduce customer service and increase costs from stockouts, back orders, special production runs, and costly fast-freight shipments. Because distribution activities involve strong trade-offs, decisions by different functions must be coordinated to achieve better overall logistics performance.

The goal of integrated supply chain management is to harmonize all of the company's logistics decisions. Close working relationships among departments can be achieved in several ways. Some companies have created permanent logistics committees made up of managers responsible for different physical distribution activities. Companies can also create supply chain manager positions that link the logistics activities of functional areas. For example, P&G has created supply managers, who manage all of the supply chain activities for each of its product categories. Many companies have a vice president of logistics with cross-functional authority.

Finally, companies can employ sophisticated, systemwide supply chain management software, now available from a wide range of software enterprises large and small, from SAP and Oracle to Infor and ▲ Logility. The worldwide market for supply chain management software topped $6.4 billion last year and will reach an estimated $11.6 billion by 2013.[19]

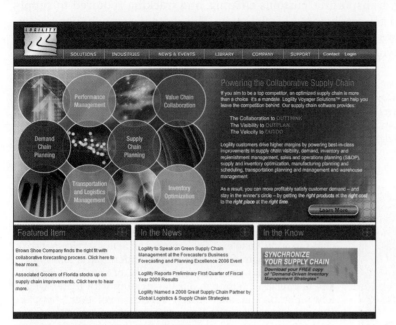

▲ **Integrated logistics management: Many companies now employ sophisticated, systemwide supply chain management software, available from companies such as Logility.**

The important thing is that the company must coordinate its logistics and marketing activities to create high market satisfaction at a reasonable cost.

Building Logistics Partnerships

Companies must do more than improve their own logistics. They must also work with other channel partners to improve whole-channel distribution. The members of a marketing channel are linked closely in creating customer value and building customer relationships. One company's distribution system is another company's supply system. The success of each channel member depends on the performance of the entire supply chain. For example, IKEA can create its stylish but affordable furniture and deliver the "IKEA lifestyle" only if its entire supply chain—consisting of thousands of merchandise designers and suppliers, transport companies, warehouses, and service providers—operates at maximum efficiency and customer-focused effectiveness.

Smart companies coordinate their logistics strategies and forge strong partnerships with suppliers and customers to improve customer service and reduce channel costs. Many companies have created *cross-functional, cross-company teams*. For example, P&G has a team of more than 200 people working in Bentonville, Arkansas, home of Wal-Mart. The P&Gers work jointly with their counterparts at Wal-Mart to find ways to squeeze costs out of their distribution system. Working together benefits not only P&G and Wal-Mart but also their shared, final consumers.

Other companies partner through *shared projects*. For example, many large retailers conduct joint in-store programs with suppliers. Home Depot allows key suppliers to use its stores as a testing ground for new merchandising programs. The suppliers spend time at Home Depot stores watching how their product sells and how customers relate to it. They then create programs specially tailored to Home Depot and its customers. Clearly, both the supplier and the customer benefit from such partnerships. The point is that all supply chain members must work together in the cause of bringing value to final consumers.

Third-Party Logistics

Most big companies love to make and sell their products. But many loathe the associated logistics "grunt work." They detest the bundling, loading, unloading, sorting, storing, reloading, transporting, customs clearing, and tracking required to supply their factories and get products out to customers. They hate it so much that a growing number of firms now outsource some or all of their logistics to **third-party logistics (3PL) providers**. Here's an example:[20]

Third-party logistics (3PL) provider
An independent logistics provider that performs any or all of the functions required to get its client's product to market.

Whirlpool's ultimate goal is to create loyal customers who continue to buy its brands over their lifetimes. One key loyalty factor is good repair service, which in turn depends on fast and reliable parts distribution. Only a few years ago, however, Whirlpool's replacement parts distribution system was fragmented and ineffective, often causing frustrating customer service delays. " ▲ Whirlpool is the world's largest manufacturer and marketer of appliances, but we're not necessarily experts in parts warehousing and distribution," says Whirlpool's national director of parts operations. So to help fix the problem, Whirlpool turned the entire job over to third-party logistics supplier Ryder, which quickly streamlined Whirlpool's service parts distribution system. Ryder now provides order fulfillment and worldwide distribution of Whirlpool's service parts across six continents to hundreds of customers that include, in addition to end-consumers, the Sears service network, authorized repair centers, and independent parts distributors that in turn ship parts out to a network of service companies and technicians. "Through our partnership with Ryder, we are now operating at our highest service level ever," says the Whirlpool executive. "We've . . . dramatically reduced [our parts distribution] costs. Our order cycle time has improved, and our customers are getting their parts more quickly."

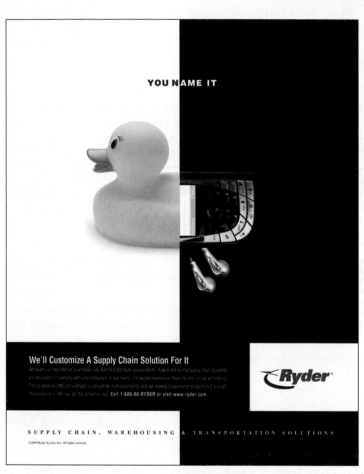

YOU NAME IT

We'll Customize A Supply Chain Solution For It

Ryder

SUPPLY CHAIN, WAREHOUSING & TRANSPORTATION SOLUTIONS

▲**Third-party logistics (3PL): Companies such as Ryder help clients to tighten up sluggish, overstuffed supply chains, slash inventories, and get products to customers more quickly and reliably.**

The "3PLs"—companies such as Ryder, UPS Supply Chain Solutions, Penske Logistics, BAX Global, DHL Logistics, and FedEx Logistics—help clients to tighten up sluggish, overstuffed supply chains, slash inventories, and get products to customers more quickly and reliably. According to a survey of chief logistics executives at *Fortune* 500 companies, 82 percent of these companies use third-party logistics (also called *3PL, outsourced logistics,* or *contract logistics*) services. In just the past 10 years, the revenues for 3PL companies in the United States has more than tripled in size to $128 billion and are expected to reach nearly $650 billion by 2014.[21]

Companies use third-party logistics providers for several reasons. First, because getting the product to market is their main focus, these providers can often do it more efficiently and at lower cost. Outsourcing typically results in 15 percent to 30 percent cost savings. Second, outsourcing logistics frees a company to focus more intensely on its core business. Finally, integrated logistics companies understand increasingly complex logistics environments.

Third-party logistics partners can be especially helpful to companies attempting to expand their global market coverage. For example, companies distributing their products across Europe face a bewildering array of environmental restrictions that affect logistics, including packaging standards, truck size and weight limits, and noise and emissions pollution controls. By outsourcing its logistics, a company can gain a complete pan-European distribution system without incurring the costs, delays, and risks associated with setting up its own system.

REST STOP
REVIEWING THE CONCEPTS

Marketing channel decisions are among the most important decisions that management faces. A company's channel decisions directly affect every other marketing decision. Management must make channel decisions carefully, incorporating today's needs with tomorrow's likely selling environment. Some companies pay too little attention to their distribution channels, but others have used imaginative distribution systems to gain competitive advantage.

 Objective 1 Explain why companies use marketing channels and discuss the functions these channels perform. **(pp 338–341)**

In creating customer value, a company can't go it alone. It must work within an entire network of partners—a value delivery network—to accomplish this task. Individual companies and brands don't compete, their entire value delivery networks do.

Most producers use intermediaries to bring their products to market. They try to forge a *marketing channel* (or *distribution channel*)—a set of interdependent organizations involved in the process of making a product or service available for use or consumption by the consumer or business user. Through their contacts, experience, specialization, and scale of operation, intermediaries usually offer the firm more than it can achieve on its own.

Marketing channels perform many key functions. Some help *complete* transactions by gathering and distributing *information* needed for planning and aiding exchange, by developing and spreading persuasive *communications* about an offer, by performing *contact* work—finding and communicating with prospective buyers, by *matching*—shaping and fitting the offer to the buyer's needs, and by entering into *negotiation* to reach an agreement on price and other terms of the offer so that ownership can be transferred. Other functions help to *fulfill* the completed transactions by offering *physical distribution*—transporting and storing goods, *financing*—acquiring and using funds to cover the costs of the channel work, and *risk taking*—assuming the risks of carrying out the channel work.

Objective 2 Discuss how channel members interact and how they organize to perform the work of the channel. **(pp 342–349)**

The channel will be most effective when each member is assigned the tasks it can do best. Ideally, because the success of individual channel members depends on overall channel success, all channel firms should work together smoothly. They should understand and accept their roles, coordinate their goals and activities, and cooperate to attain overall channel goals. By cooperating, they can more effectively sense, serve, and satisfy the target market.

In a large company, the formal organization structure assigns roles and provides needed leadership. But in a distribution channel made up of independent firms, leadership and power are not formally set. Traditionally, distribution channels have lacked the leadership needed to assign roles and manage conflict. In recent years, however, new types of channel organizations have appeared that provide stronger leadership and improved performance.

Objective 3 Identify the major channel alternatives open to a company. **(pp 349–353)**

Each firm identifies alternative ways to reach its market. Available means vary from direct selling to using one, two, three, or more intermediary *channel levels*. Marketing channels face continuous and sometimes dramatic change. Three of the most important trends are the growth of *vertical*, *horizontal*, and *multichannel marketing systems*. These trends affect channel cooperation, conflict, and competition.

Channel design begins with assessing customer channel service needs and company channel objectives and constraints. The company then identifies the major channel alternatives in terms of the *types* of intermediaries, the *number* of intermediaries, and the *channel responsibilities* of each. Each channel alternative must be evaluated according to economic, control, and adaptive criteria. *Channel management* calls for selecting qualified intermediaries and motivating them. Individual channel members must be evaluated regularly.

Objective 4 Explain how companies select, motivate, and evaluate channel members. **(pp 353–355)**

Producers vary in their ability to attract qualified marketing intermediaries. Some producers have no trouble signing up channel members. Others have to work hard to line up enough qualified intermediaries. When selecting intermediaries, the company should evaluate each channel member's qualifications and select those who best fit its channel objectives.

Once selected, channel members must be continuously motivated to do their best. The company must sell not only *through* the intermediaries but *with* them. It should work to forge strong partnerships with channel members to create a marketing system that meets the needs of both the manufacturer *and* the partners. The company must also regularly check channel member performance against established performance standards, rewarding intermediaries who are performing well and assisting or replacing weaker ones.

> **Objective 5** Discuss the nature and importance of marketing logistics and integrated supply chain management. **(pp 356–364)**

Just as firms are giving the marketing concept increased recognition, more business firms are paying attention to *marketing logistics* (or *physical distribution*). Logistics is an area of potentially high cost savings and improved customer satisfaction. Marketing logistics addresses not only *outbound distribution* but also *inbound distribution* and *reverse distribution*. That is, it involves entire *supply chain management*—managing value-added flows between suppliers, the company, resellers, and final users. No logistics

system can both maximize customer service and minimize distribution costs. Instead, the goal of logistics management is to provide a *targeted* level of service at the least cost. The major logistics functions include *warehousing, inventory management, transportation*, and *logistics information management*.

The *integrated supply chain management concept* recognizes that improved logistics requires teamwork in the form of close working relationships across functional areas inside the company and across various organizations in the supply chain. Companies can achieve logistics harmony among functions by creating cross-functional logistics teams, integrative supply manager positions, and senior-level logistics executives with cross-functional authority. Channel partnerships can take the form of cross-company teams, shared projects, and information-sharing systems. Today, some companies are outsourcing their logistics functions to third-party logistics (3PL) providers to save costs, increase efficiency, and gain faster and more effective access to global markets.

Navigating the Key Terms

Objective 1
Value delivery network (p 339)
Marketing channel (distribution channel) (p 339)
Channel level (p 341)
Direct marketing channel (p 341)
Indirect marketing channel (p 341)

Objective 2
Channel conflict (p 343)
Conventional distribution channel (p 343)
Vertical marketing system (VMS) (p 344)

Corporate VMS (p 344)
Contractual VMS (p 344)
Franchise organization (p 344)
Administered VMS (p 346)
Horizontal marketing system (p 346)
Multichannel distribution system (p 347)
Disintermediation (p 348)

Objective 3
Marketing channel design (p 350)
Intensive distribution (p 352)
Exclusive distribution (p 352)
Selective distribution (p 352)

Objective 4
Marketing channel management (p 353)

Objective 5
Marketing logistics (physical distribution) (p 356)
Supply chain management (p 356)
Distribution center (p 359)
Intermodal transportation (p 362)
Integrated logistics management (p 362)
Third-party logistics (3PL) provider (p 364)

Travel Log

Discussing the Issues

1. Compare and contrast direct marketing channels and indirect marketing channels. Name the various types of resellers in marketing channels. (AACSB: Communication)

2. What is *channel conflict*? Discuss the two main types of channel conflict and give an example of each. (AACSB: Communication; Reflective Thinking)

3. Define *disintermediation*. List three industries for which changes in channel systems have resulted in disintermediation. (AACSB: Communication; Reflective Thinking)

4. Compare and contrast intensive, selective, and exclusive distribution. Give an example of a product or brand that is distributed at each level. (AACSB: Communication; Reflective Thinking)

5. List and briefly describe the major logistics functions. Provide an example of a decision a logistics manager would make for each major function. (AACSB: Communication; Reflective Thinking)

6. Name and describe the main types of transportation modes and discuss when each is appropriate. (AACSB: Communication)

Application Questions

1. Supply chain management is an important issue facing businesses. What is an extended supply chain and what is the impact of globalization on supply chain management? (AACSB: Communication; Reflective Thinking)

2. In a small group, debate whether or not the Internet will result in disintermediation of the following retail stores: (1) video rental stores, (2) music stores, and (3) clothing stores. (AACSB: Communication; Reflective Thinking)

3. Visit http://electronics.howstuffworks.com/rfid.htm# and watch the video "How UPS Smart Labels Work." You can also learn more about RFID technology from this site. What impact will RFID tags have on each of the major logistical functions? What are the biggest current obstacles to adopting this technology? (AACSB: Communication; Use of IT; Reflective Thinking)

Under the Hood: Marketing Technology

Brewing craft beer is both an art and a science, and Sonia Collin, a Belgian researcher, is trying to devise a way for this highly perishable beer to have a longer shelf life. If successful, brewers can ship more for longer distances. Hoping to boost exports of homegrown products, the Belgian government is investing $7 million for research, with $1.7 million of that allocated to Ms. Collins' research. The $250,000 tasting machine in her laboratory identifies the chemical compounds in a sample of beer, which allowed researchers to recommend using organic ingredients, adjusting the oxygen and yeast levels, and reducing the time the beer spends at high temperatures in the brewing process. While pasteurization and bottling methods allow giants like Heineken and Anheuser to export their brews, aficionados prefer the more delicate flavor of craft beers. But craft brews don't travel well—time and sunlight are its worst enemy—so they are limited to local distribution. Most craft beers lose flavor in less than three months.

1. Describe the channel of distribution for a craft beer from Belgium to your city or town. How many channel levels will be involved? (AACSB: Communication; Reflective Thinking)

2. Discuss the options facing Belgian craft brewers wanting to sell their products in the United States if the researchers do not discover a way to sufficiently extend the shelf-life of craft beers. (AACSB: Communication; Reflective Thinking)

Staying on the Road: Marketing Ethics

Parallel imports, *gray products*, and *price diversion* all represent the same activity—diverting imported products meant for one market at lower prices and reselling them at higher profits in other markets. This happens in many industries, from pharmaceuticals, apparel, high-tech electronics, and auto parts to luxury goods, cosmetics, and tobacco. The textbook you're using now might be a gray product if it was intended for an international market but you purchased it from Amazon.com for much less than what you'd pay at your bookstore or the publisher's Web site. And the designer sweater you bought at Marshall's or T.J. Maxx may well have gotten into those stores through gray market trading. Although U.S. Federal law prohibits importing prescription drugs from abroad, the same is not true in other countries. For example, gray traders purchase pharmaceutical drugs in poorer countries, such as Greece and Spain, and resell them in the United Kingdom or Sweden, where higher prices garner profits for the traders. In fact, parallel importing of most products is legal, and some experts claim that it's just the free market working. In some cases, though, counterfeit goods are mixed in with the legitimate brands.

1. Learn more about this phenomenon. Who receives value in such transactions? Who loses value? (AACSB: Communication; Ethical Reasoning)

2. How are manufacturers dealing with this problem? (AACSB: Communication; Reflective Thinking)

Rough Road Ahead: Marketing and the Economy

Expedia

As consumers and businesses alike cut back on travel-related expenses during the economic downturn, the airline, hotel, and car rental industries are all taking hits. It's probably no surprise that online booking agencies like Expedia are also experiencing tough times. Not only must Expedia keep revenues up as travel spending declines, it must also fight to keep customers from buying through an unlikely competitor: the airlines themselves. Historically, Expedia has charged a booking fee of about $10 for every airline ticket. This fee has provided revenue for Expedia, over and above the commissions it earns for ticket sales. But as consumers now count every penny, more of them shop for flights first on Expedia but then book directly through the airlines, avoiding the booking fee. This has led Expedia to eliminate the booking fees for good, forcing other online agencies to follow suit. Expedia's hope is that as more consumers are lured back to its site by the "no fee" promotion, commissions earned from a higher sales volume for airline tickets as well as hotels and car rentals will offset the lost fee revenue.

1. Do you think Expedia's fee elimination will give it more business?

2. As an intermediary, does Expedia have power to spur demand when the travel industries themselves are in such a slump?

Travel Budget: Marketing by the Numbers

One external factor manufacturers must consider when setting prices is reseller margins. Manufacturers do not have the final say concerning the price to consumers—retailers do. So, manufacturers must start with their suggested retail prices and work back, subtracting out the markups required by resellers that sell the product to consumers. Once that is considered, manufacturers know at what price to sell their products to resellers, and they can determine what volume they must sell to break even at that price and cost combination. To answer the following questions, refer to Appendix 2, Marketing by the Numbers.

1. A consumer purchases a flat iron to straighten her hair for $150 from a salon at which she gets her hair cut. If the salon's markup is 40 percent and the wholesaler's markup is 15 percent, both based on their selling prices, for what price does the manufacturer sell the product to the wholesaler? (AACSB: Communication; Analytical Reasoning)

2. If the unit variable costs for each flat iron are $40 and the manufacturer has fixed costs totaling $200,000, how many flat irons must this manufacturer sell to break even? How many must it sell to realize a profit of $800,000? (AACSB: Communication; Analytical Reasoning)

Drive In: Video Case

Progressive

Progressive has attained top-tier status in the insurance industry by focusing on innovation. Progressive was the first company to offer drive-in claims services, installment payment of premiums, and 24/7 customer service. But some of Progressive's most innovative moves involve its channels of distribution. Whereas most insurance companies distribute their products to consumers via intermediary agents or direct-to-consumer methods, Progressive was one of the first companies to recognize the value in doing both. In the late 1980s, it augmented its agency distribution with a direct 800-number channel.

In 1995, Progressive moved into the future by becoming the first major insurer in the world to launch a Web site. In 1997, customers could buy auto insurance policies online in real time. Today, at Progressive's Web site, customers can do everything from managing their own account information to reporting claims directly. Progressive even offers one-stop concierge claim service.

After viewing the Progressive video, answer the following questions about marketing channels:

1. Apply the concept of the supply chain to Progressive.

2. Using the model of consumer and business channels found in the chapter, sketch out as many channels for Progressive as you can. How does each of these channels meet distinct customer needs?

3. Discuss the various ways that Progressive has had an impact on the insurance industry.

11

Retailing and Wholesaling

ROAD MAP

Previewing the Concepts

In the previous chapter, you learned the basics of delivering customer value through good distribution channel design and management. Now, we'll look more deeply into the two major intermediary channel functions, retailing and wholesaling. You already know something about retailing—you're served every day by retailers of all shapes and sizes. However, you probably know much less about the hoard of wholesalers that work behind the scenes. In this chapter, we'll examine the characteristics of different kinds of retailers and wholesalers, the marketing decisions they make, and trends for the future.

Objective Outline

 Objective 1   Explain the role of retailers in the distribution channel and describe the major types of retailers.
Retailing **pp 372–380**

 Objective 2   Describe the major retailer marketing decisions.
Retailer Marketing Decisions **pp 380–387**

 Objective 3   Discuss the major trends and developments in retailing.
Retailing Trends and Developments **pp 387–392**

Objective 4   Explain the major types of wholesalers and their marketing decisions.
Wholesaling **pp 392–398**

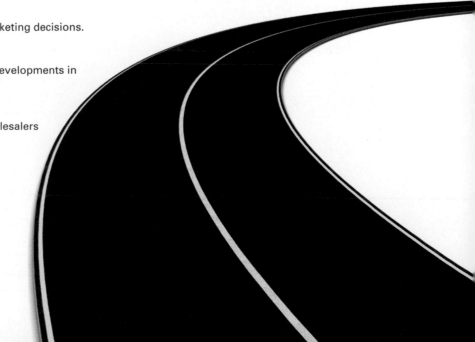

The retail industry in the Middle East is changing fast. The traditional bazaars and local marketplaces that are associated with the region are in decline, whilst hypermarkets, supermarkets and department stores are rapidly transforming the retailing landscape. Here's a story about Ramez Super Discount Store. Despite humble beginnings, the company's lowprice retail strategy has helped it to develop in under ten years into a well known retailing giant and marketing brand throughout the region.

▲ Ramez offers a wide selection of products at discount prices. Shoppers can pick up their soft drinks at the same time as buying furniture for their homes or accessories for their cars.

First Stop

Ramez Super Discount Store:
From Rags to Riches

A silent revolution is under way in the retail sector of the Gulf Cooperation Council (GCC) countries. As a result the retailing landscape in these countries is being transformed beyond recognition. The traditional stand-alone stores, bazaars and local marketplaces (sougs) are gradually being replaced by a modern vibrant retail sector that parallels any in North America, Europe, or Asia. Growing prosperity, a cosmopolitan population, and a hot humid climate have all helped usher in this new age of modern retailing to the Gulf. Today, large-scale retailing formats such as supermarkets, chains, department and specialty stores, hypermarkets, and other discounters have mushroomed in record time throughout the region.

The Kingdom of Saudi Arabia and UAE dominate the industry in terms of investment and retail space, even though other Gulf States are fast catching up with megaretail projects. Saudi Arabia—being the biggest economy in the region and the most populous country—enjoys the most important and dynamic retail market in the area. Its retail sector is forecasted to hit $50 billion in turnover by 2012 and has a retail space of 6 million square meters. Two major players feature heavily in the Saudi retail scene: Savola and Al-Hukair Groups. The Savola Group has 79 retail outlets throughout Saudi Arabia. These include the Panda supermarket chain, which is gradually being developed into a regional hypermarket chain. Al-Hukair Group, a pioneer in international retail franchising in the Kingdom and the region, now owns a network of 11 shopping malls in major Saudi cities; most of these are anchored by the French hypermarket Géant. Prominent retail landmarks in Saudi Arabia include the Kingdom Center, Al-Faisalia Center, and Oruba Plaza in the Capital Riyadh; Al Rashid, Waha, Herra Malls, and the Mall of Arabia in Jeddah City; and the Al-Arab, Delta, and Dhahran Shopping Centres in AlKhubar City.

The UAE retail sector has, likewise, undergone massive expansion in recent years. The country now has over 80 shopping malls and there are more to come. In the City of Dubai alone, retail space has increased by a staggering 19 million square feet (msf) during the last 3 to 4 years. Notable retail landmarks in the country include Ibn Batutta Mall (1.6 msf), Emirates Mall (2.4 msf), Diera City Mall (1.7 msf), Dubai Festival City (2.7 msf), Dubai Mall (3.8 msf), and the Mall of Arabia (5.9 msf) to mention just a few.

The picture does not change much if one looks at other GCC states. Some massive retail projects can be seen everywhere in the region. In the Kingdom of Bahrain, for example, the retail sector has undergone a radical facelift in the last decade. An array of state of the art malls and shopping centers decorate the country's landscape nowadays. Examples here include Al-Seef, Bahrain, Dana, Marina, Riffa Malls, and many others. In 2008 alone, three more shopping centers were added to the list above. Among them is the Bahrain City Center; one of the region's largest. Similar scenarios of the sector's expansion and modernization are also going on in Kuwait, Qatar, and Oman.

A prominent characteristic of the region's retail industry, however, is that more often than not it involves an international anchor

Through sound merchandising, intelligent pricing, customized promotions, and a conducive retail environment, Ramez has managed to come up with a retail format that is both successful and difficult to emulate.

▲ Ramez's promotional strategy targets the back-to-school season, the holy month of Ramadan, Eid Alfitr celebrations and the summer holidays.

an aggressive expansion policy across the Middle East.

One vivid and successful example of these local retailers is the Ramez Super Discount Store chain. From a modest humble beginning of a small store in Saudi Arabia selling everything for under $4 to a retailing empire that employs hundreds of people and generates millions of dollars in annual sales, Ramez epitomizes the successful story of modern retailing in the region at every turn. The history of Ramez started in 1999 in Saudi Arabia, when Ramez "a Yemeni" formed a business partnership with a Saudi entrepreneur, having seen the huge potential of investing in retailing. The first Ramez store was opened in the Saudi city of Al-Dammam on the Gulf coast.

The store was an instant success. It generated a lot of buzz and attracted large crowds of shoppers, especially from neighboring Bahrain, given its geographic proximity to the eastern region of Saudi Arabia. Quickly, Ramez moved into Bahrain itself and opened its first store in Al-Muharraq City, to be followed by two more stores in Isa Town and Manama City, respectively. A grand shopping mall in Riffa City in which Ramez is the anchor store, was the last addition to its expansion in Bahrain. Soon after, Ramez fanned out to build more stores in all GCC countries. As of now, Ramez operates more than fifteen stores and shopping malls in Saudi Arabia, Bahrain, Kuwait, Oman, Qatar, and UAE in addition to two superstores in Libya and Syria.

How did a small, unknown store become in less than ten years a retailing giant and a marketing brand recognized by so many? What factors contributed to such transformation? The answer lies in the strategy and retail mix that Ramez adopts.

Ramez has shrewdly recognized that foot-traffic (the number of people the store attracts) and the time people spend inside the store, (i.e., dwell time) is the key to the success of any retailer.

Armed with a clear customer-focused strategy that targets mainly the working and lower-middle classes, Ramez features an enormous selection of products. To offer its customers the benefits of one-stop shopping, an average

hypermarket; most likely one of the two French retailers: Carrefour and Géant. However, competition in the region is increasing as local retailers are growing in stature by the day as they embark on

Ramez store now carries between 70,000 and 80,000 items on its shelves. These include a wide array of nonfood items such as cooking utensils, toys, electronics, car accessories, furniture, detergents, cosmetics, stationary, antiques, linens, and carpets plus whole sections of foodstuffs. Some of these products carry the Ramez name (i.e., store brands), the rest feature manufacturer or generic brands. The variety of the merchandise offered, the large sizes of Ramez stores, and the carnival-like atmosphere within these stores, have made shopping at Ramez an "experience." As the store faces tough competition from other discounters, Ramez hopes its shopping environment will make a difference and give it an edge over its competitors.

To gain some clout and bargaining over its vendors, Ramez' merchandising policy stresses buying opportunistically and in bulk. China constitutes the main source of supply for most of the store's merchandise where buying offices are located in major Chinese cities. If a product is in demand here, a prototype of it is dispatched to these offices so that it can be ordered quickly from nearby Chinese manufacturers.

To help produce part of its merchandise locally, Ramez is now in the process of establishing two manufacturing facilities in the Gulf.

That said, however, the central theme of Ramez's retail strategy remains its pricing policy: the main traffic generator and attraction. It has contributed immensely to the popularity and success of its stores. Through its well-known slogan, "a scream in the face of inflation," Ramez has managed to project itself as an every day low-prices retailer. A position other discounters find hard to match.

To communicate the components of its retail strategy, Ramez relies mainly on leaflets and free-standing inserts frequently delivered to customers in their homes. These may announce special offers, sale, new product arrivals, raffles, and family entertainment programs. A number of occasions, however, feature heavily in the Ramez promotional strategy; namely, the back-to-school season, the holy month of Ramadan, Eid Alfitr celebrations, and the summer holidays. During these times Ramez initiates special family entertainment programs, raffles to win prizes, and spares no effort to make a shopping trip to Ramez enjoyable.

The successful story of Ramez Discount Stores dwarfs the success stories of other modern retailers in the Gulf region. Through sound merchandising, intelligent pricing, customized promotions, and a conducive retail environment, Ramez has managed to come up with a retail format that is both successful and difficult to emulate.[1]

*t*he story of Ramez Super Discount Store sets the stage for examining the fast-changing world of today's resellers. This chapter looks at *retailing* and *wholesaling*. In the first section, we look at the nature and importance of retailing, major types of store and nonstore retailers, the decisions retailers make, and the future of retailing. In the second section, we discuss these same topics as they relate to wholesalers.

RETAILING (pp 372–380)

What is retailing? We all know that Costco, Home Depot, Macy's, and Target are retailers, but so are Avon representatives, Amazon.com, the local Hampton Inn, and a doctor seeing patients. **Retailing** includes all the activities involved in selling products or

Retailing
All activities involved in selling goods or services directly to final consumers for their personal, nonbusiness use.

Retailer
A business whose sales come *primarily* from retailing.

services directly to final consumers for their personal, nonbusiness use. Many institutions—manufacturers, wholesalers, and retailers—do retailing. But most retailing is done by **retailers**: businesses whose sales come *primarily* from retailing.

Retailing plays a very important role in most marketing channels. Each year, retailers account for more than $4.4 trillion of sales to final consumers. They connect brands to consumers in what marketing agency OgilvyAction calls "the last mile"—the final stop in the consumer's path to purchase. It's the "distance a consumer travels between an attitude and an action," explains OgilvyAction's CEO. At least 40 percent of all consumer decisions are made in or near the store. Thus, retailers "reach consumers at key moments of truth, ultimately [influencing] their actions at the point of purchase."[2]

In fact, many marketers are now embracing the concept of *shopper marketing*, the idea that the retail store itself is an important marketing medium. In fact, point-of-sale marketing inside a large retail store chain can produce the same kinds of numbers as advertising on the hit TV show. For example, whereas 21 million people watch an average episode of *Dancing with the Stars*, even bigger crowds attack the aisles of large retailers. Costco, Walgreens, Safeway, and Kroger attract 20 million, 30 million, 44 million, and 68 million weekly shoppers, respectively. Another 150 million people pass through the automatic doors of Wal-Mart stores across America each week. What's more, unlike TV advertising's remote impact, point-of-sale promotions hit consumers when they are actually making purchase decisions.[3]

Shopper marketing involves focusing the entire marketing process—from product and brand development to logistics, promotion, and merchandising—toward turning shoppers into buyers at the point of sale. Of course, every well-designed marketing effort focuses on customer buying behavior. But the concept of shopper marketing suggests that these efforts should be coordinated around the shopping process itself. Shopper marketing emphasizes the importance of the retail environment on customer buying.

Although most retailing is done in retail stores, in recent years *nonstore retailing* has been growing much faster than has store retailing. Nonstore retailing includes selling to final consumers through the Internet, direct mail, catalogs, the telephone, and other direct-selling approaches. We discuss such direct-marketing approaches in detail in Chapter 14. In this chapter, we focus on store retailing.

Types of Retailers

Retail stores come in all shapes and sizes—from your local hairstyling salon or family-owned restaurant to national specialty chain retailers such as REI or Williams-Sonoma to megadiscounters such as Costco or Wal-Mart. The most important types of retail stores are described in ■ **Table 11.1** and discussed in the following sections. They can be classified in terms of several characteristics, including the *amount of service* they offer, the breadth and depth of their *product lines*, the *relative prices* they charge, and how they are *organized*.

Amount of Service

Different types of customers and products require different amounts of service. To meet these varying service needs, retailers may offer one of three service levels—self-service, limited service, and full service.

Self-service retailers serve customers who are willing to perform their own "locate-compare-select" process to save time or money. Self-service is the basis of all discount operations and is typically used by retailers selling convenience goods (such as supermarkets) and nationally branded, fast-moving shopping goods (such as Wal-Mart or Kohl's). *Limited-service retailers*, such as Sears or JCPenney, provide more sales assistance because they carry more shopping goods about which customers need information. Their increased operating costs result in higher prices.

In *full-service retailers*, such as high-end specialty stores (for example, Tiffany or Williams-Sonoma) and first-class department stores (such as Nordstrom or Neiman Marcus), salespeople assist customers in every phase of the shopping

■ Table 11.1 Major Store Retailer Types

Type	Description	Examples
Specialty stores	Carry a narrow product line with a deep assortment, such as apparel stores, sporting-goods stores, furniture stores, florists, and bookstores. A clothing store would be a *single-line* store, a men's clothing store would be a *limited-line* store, and a men's custom-shirt store would be a *superspecialty* store.	REI, Tiffany, Radio Shack, Williams-Sonoma
Department stores	Carry several product lines—typically clothing, home furnishings, and household goods—with each line operated as a separate department managed by specialist buyers or merchandisers.	Macy's, Sears, Neiman Marcus
Supermarkets	A relatively large, low-cost, low-margin, high-volume, self-service operation designed to serve the consumer's total needs for grocery and household products.	Kroger, Safeway, Supervalu, Publix
Convenience stores	Relatively small stores located near residential areas, open long hours seven days a week, and carrying a limited line of high-turnover convenience products at slightly higher prices.	7-Eleven, Stop-N-Go, Circle K, Sheetz
Discount stores	Carry standard merchandise sold at lower prices with lower margins and higher volumes.	Wal-Mart, Target, Kohl's
Off-price retailers	Sell merchandise bought at less-than-regular wholesale prices and sold at less than retail, often leftover goods, overruns, and irregulars obtained at reduced prices from manufacturers or other retailers. These include *factory outlets* owned and operated by manufacturers; *independent off-price retailers* owned and run by entrepreneurs or by divisions of larger retail corporations; and *warehouse (or wholesale) clubs* selling a limited selection of brand-name groceries, appliances, clothing, and other goods at deep discounts to consumers who pay membership fees.	Mikasa (factory outlet); TJ Maxx (independent off-price retailer); Costco, Sam's Club, BJ's Wholesale Club (warehouse clubs)
Superstores	Very large stores traditionally aimed at meeting consumers' total needs for routinely purchased food and nonfood items. Includes *supercenters,* combined supermarket and discount stores, and *category killers,* which carry a deep assortment in a particular category and have a knowledgeable staff.	Wal-Mart Supercenter, SuperTarget, Meijer (discount stores); Best Buy, PetSmart, Staples, Barnes & Noble (category killers)

process. Full-service stores usually carry more specialty goods for which customers need or want assistance or advice. They provide more services resulting in much higher operating costs, which are passed along to customers as higher prices.

Product Line

Retailers can also be classified by the length and breadth of their product assortments. Some retailers, such as **specialty stores**, carry narrow product lines with deep assortments within those lines. Today, specialty stores are flourishing. The increasing use of market segmentation, market targeting, and product specialization has resulted in a greater need for stores that focus on specific products and segments.

In contrast, **department stores** carry a wide variety of product lines. In recent years, department stores have been squeezed between more focused and flexible

Specialty store
A retail store that carries a narrow product line with a deep assortment within that line.

Department store
A retail organization that carries a wide variety of product lines—each line is operated as a separate department managed by specialist buyers or merchandisers.

specialty stores on the one hand, and more efficient, lower-priced discounters on the other. In response, many have added promotional pricing to meet the discount threat. Others have stepped up the use of store brands and single-brand "designer shops" to compete with specialty stores. Still others are trying catalog, telephone, and Web selling. Service remains the key differentiating factor. Retailers such as Nordstrom, Saks, Neiman Marcus, and other high-end department stores are doing well by emphasizing exclusive merchandise and high-quality service.

Supermarket
A large, low-cost, low-margin, high-volume, self-service store that carries a wide variety of grocery and household products.

Supermarkets are the most frequently shopped type of retail store. Today, however, they are facing slow sales growth because of slower population growth and an increase in competition from discount supercenters (Wal-Mart) on the one hand and upscale specialty food stores (Whole Foods Market, Trader Joe's) on the other. Supermarkets also have been hit hard by the rapid growth of out-of-home eating. In fact, supermarkets' share of the groceries and consumables market plunged from 89 percent in 1989 to less than 50 percent in 2008.[4] Thus, many traditional supermarkets are facing hard times.

In the battle for "share of stomachs," some supermarkets have moved upscale, providing improved store environments and higher-quality food offerings, such as from-scratch bakeries, gourmet deli counters, natural foods, and fresh seafood departments. Others, however, are attempting to compete head-on with food discounters such as Costco and Wal-Mart, the nation's largest grocery seller, by cutting costs, establishing more-efficient operations, and lowering prices. ▲ For example, Kroger, the nation's largest grocery-only retailer has done this successfully:

▲Thanks to customer-focused pricing, despite a sagging economy, Kroger's sales and market share gains have been the best in the industry. Kroger gives you "more value for the way you live."

Despite the recently sagging economy, while other grocery chains have suffered, Kroger's sales and profits have grown steadily. The chain's 6-year-old strategy of cutting costs and lowering prices has put Kroger in the right position for the times. The food seller's price reductions have been just one part of a four-pronged strategy called "Customer First," by which Kroger seeks to continually improve its response to shopper needs through its prices, products, people, and the shopping experience it creates in its stores. The Customer First effort began at a time when most other traditional supermarkets were trying to distinguish themselves from discount food retailers by emphasizing higher-level service, quality, and selection. But instead of trying to maintain higher prices, Kroger recognized lower prices as an important part of the changing food-buying experience. Guided by detailed analysis of customer sales data, it made substantial costs and price cuts, beginning with the most price-sensitive products and categories then expanding to include additional items each year. To help cost-conscious customers further, Kroger also boosted its private-label offerings. It now offers more than 14,400 private-label items, which account for 26 percent of overall sales. Thanks to customer-focused pricing, Kroger's recent sales and market-share gains have been the best in the supermarket industry.[5]

Convenience store
A small store, located near a residential area, that is open long hours seven days a week and carries a limited line of high-turnover convenience goods.

Convenience stores are small stores that carry a limited line of high-turnover convenience goods. After several years of stagnant sales, convenience stores are now experiencing healthy growth. Last year, U.S. convenience stores posted sales of $624.1 billion, an 8 percent increase over the previous year. About 75 percent of overall convenience store revenues come from sales of gasoline; a majority of in-store sales are from tobacco products (33 percent) and beer and other beverages (24 percent).[6]

In recent years, convenience store chains have tried to expand beyond their primary market of young, blue-collar men, redesigning their stores to attract female shoppers. They are shedding the image of a "truck stop" where men go to buy beer, cigarettes, or shriveled hotdogs on a roller grill and are instead offering freshly prepared foods and cleaner, safer, more-upscale environments. For example, consider

▲Convenience stores: Sheetz positions itself as more than just a convenience store. Driven by its Total Customer Focus mission and the motto—"Feel the Love"—Sheetz aims to provide "convenience without compromise."

Sheetz, widely recognized as one of the nation's top convenience stores. ▲Driven by its Total Customer Focus mission and the motto—"Feel the Love"—Sheetz aims to provide "convenience without compromise while being more than just a convenience store. It's our devotion to your satisfaction that makes the difference."[7]

Whether it's for road warriors, construction workers, or soccer moms, Sheetz offers "a mecca for people on the go"—fast, friendly service and quality products in clean and convenient locations. "We really care about our customers," says the company. "If you need to refuel your car or refresh your body, . . . Sheetz has what you need, when you need it. And, we're here 24/7/365." Sheetz certainly isn't your run-of-the-mill convenience store operation. Stores offer up a menu of made-to-order cold and toasted subs, sandwiches, and salads, along with hot fries, onion rings, chicken fingers, and burgers—all ordered through touch-screen terminals. Locations feature Sheetz Bros. Coffeez, a full-service espresso bar staffed by a trained barista. Frozen fruit smoothies round out the menu. To help make paying easier, Sheetz was the first chain in the nation to install system-wide MasterCard PayPass, allowing customers to quickly tap their credit cards and go. Sheetz also partnered with M&T Bank to offer ATM services at any Sheetz without a surcharge. Some analysts say that Sheetz aims to become the Wal-Mart of convenience stores, and it just might get there. The average Sheetz store is nearly twice the size of the average 7-Eleven. And although the privately held company now operates in only six states, it generates sales of more than $4.9 billion. President and CEO Stan Sheetz was recently named by *Chain Store Age* on its list of the top 25 people who have completely changed the way the world does business.

Superstore
A store much larger than a regular supermarket that offers a large assortment of routinely purchased food products, nonfood items, and services.

Superstores are much larger than regular supermarkets and offer a large assortment of routinely purchased food products, nonfood items, and services. Wal-Mart, Target, Meijer, and other discount retailers offer *supercenters*, very large combination food and discount stores. Whereas a traditional grocery store brings in about $333,000 a week in sales, a supercenter brings in about $1.5 million a week. Wal-Mart, which opened its first supercenter in 1988, now has more than 2,400 supercenters worldwide and is opening new ones at a rate of about 140 per year.[8]

Recent years have also seen the explosive growth of superstores that are actually giant specialty stores, the so-called **category killers** (Best Buy, Home Depot, PetSmart). They feature stores the size of airplane hangars that carry a very deep assortment of a particular line with a knowledgeable staff. Category killers are prevalent in a wide range of categories, including books, baby gear, toys, electronics, home-improvement products, linens and towels, party goods, sporting goods, and even pet supplies.

Category killer
A giant specialty store that carries a very deep assortment of a particular line and is staffed by knowledgeable employees.

Service retailer
A retailer whose product line is actually a service, including hotels, airlines, banks, colleges, and many others.

Finally, for many retailers, the product line is actually a service. **Service retailers** include hotels and motels, banks, airlines, colleges, hospitals, movie theaters, tennis clubs, bowling alleys, restaurants, repair services, hair salons, and dry cleaners. Service retailers in the United States are growing faster than product retailers.

Relative Prices

Retailers can also be classified according to the prices they charge (see Table 11.1). Most retailers charge regular prices and offer normal-quality goods and customer service. Others offer higher-quality goods and service at higher prices. The retailers that feature low prices are discount stores and "off-price" retailers.

Discount store
A retail operation that sells standard merchandise at lower prices by accepting lower margins and selling at higher volume.

Discount Stores. A **discount store** (Target, Kmart, Wal-Mart) sells standard merchandise at lower prices by accepting lower margins and selling higher volume. The early discount stores cut expenses by offering few services and operating in warehouse-like facilities in low-rent, heavily traveled districts. Today's discounters have improved their store environments and increased their services, while at the same time keeping prices low through lean, efficient operations. Leading discounters now dominate the retail scene including world-leading retailers such as Carrefour (see Marketing at Work 11.1).

Marketing at Work 11.1

Carrefour Egypt: Buy in Bulk and Save Money

Carrefour, which means "crossroads" in French, is the world's second largest retailer by sales after Wal-Mart Stores Inc. and is regarded as Egypt's most dynamic, fast-moving as well as exciting hypermarket. It is a joint venture company by Majid Al Futtaim and Carrefour France that offers Egyptians the same quality, and variety of products for very reasonable prices that is provided all over the world. The Majid Al Futtaim (MAF) group of companies was founded in 1992 and is regarded as the most dynamic and professional business in the Middle East. It has successfully opened Carrefour in Oman, Qatar, UAE, Saudi Arabia, and Egypt and is still planning to expand in other countries in the region.

Carrefour Egypt started operations in 2003. Today it has 4 hypermarkets in Egypt which are usually crowded with people shopping. Due to the high traffic in Carrefour, many shops prefer to be located next to Carrefour. Carrefour remains to be the largest hypermarket in Egypt compared to other competitors such as Spinneys and Hyper One. Carrefour is located in the outskirts of the 2 main cities in Egypt: Cairo and Alexandria. There are 3 Carrefour stores in Cairo and 1 in Alexandria. Despite the distance to commute to Carrefour, yet many Egyptians are willing to spend the time to commute to Carrefour. As a result various public and private transportation methods are offered for those who want to go to and from Carrefour.

According to the French business newsletter *La Lettre de L'Expansion*, the French-based retail chain Carrefour is intending to open four new hypermarkets in Egypt by 2011—two of which will be located in Alexandria. This news source also revealed that Carrefour plans to open around 17 hypermarkets and 70 supermarkets in Egypt in the next five years. What are the reasons behind Carrefour's tremendous success that make it so unique compared to other hypermarkets in Egypt and the Middle East?

Most hypermarkets offer a diversity of products but Carrefour also provides its customers with the *best* quality of products for the *lowest* price. There are about 55,000 different products offered at Carrefour that have to do with personal care, communication, leisure, entertainment, and household necessities. Moreover, Carrefour also includes specialty departments like bakery, fish, delicatessen, clothing, fresh meat, hardware, and electronics; that is, Carrefour offers simply everything one can think of.

The hypermarket experience is considered to be a new way of shopping in Egypt. Before Carrefour, Egyptians brought their grocery from their small grocery store, electronics from electronics shops, furniture from furniture shops, and clothes from clothes shops. Today with Carrefour, Egyptians have a one-stop-shop for buying grocery, clothing items, furniture, electronics, toys, bakery, and cooked food. Thus, people are spending more time doing shopping. A typical family can spend a weekend evening doing shopping and also spending some good time at Carrefour. Families spend time buying grocery items, kids can

▲ Hypermarket chain Carrefour prides itself on providing its customers with the highest quality of products for the lowest possible price. To achieve this, Carrefour buys in bulk from the wholesaler who, in effect, reduces their charges.

enjoy some entertainment and games, and the family can also having a meal for lunch or dinner. This is something new for Egyptians.

Unlike most of the hypermarkets found in Egypt, Carrefour is frequented by people belonging to different social classes where everyone will find what they need within their budget. That is simply because Carrefour offers all brands of a specific product at different price points but each price level is lower compared to the like product at other hypermarkets located in Egypt, such as UK-based Spinney's and the local Hyper One. It is interesting to visit a place in Egypt that is not only diverse in terms of the products it offers but also with respect to its clientele, which differ in their age, social background, financial status, lifestyle, and buying behavior.

In order to make shopping at Carrefour an extremely pleasant experience the hypermarket grants its customers many privileges that are not offered by other hypermarkets in Egypt. First, free parking and multiple checkouts makes the shopping experience at Carrefour very convenient. Secondly, Carrefour offers gift vouchers that help customers who want to buy a present for family or friends but do not know what they really need. For customers interested in electronics, Carrefour provides a full guarantee on any appliance purchased. Moreover, Carrefour is well known for the numerous promotions it offers its customers, especially during special occasions like mother's day, Ramadan, and the days of Eid.

In 2006, reported sales revealed that Carrefour made a profit of AED 7 billion (around $2 billion). But how does Carrefour generate this huge amount of money with such low prices? And how can such a hypermarket, which employs around 420 personnel, maintain these low prices and generate enough revenue to justify its size? The reason that Carrefour is able to sell products at low prices and still make money is because it buys

(continued)

all its products in huge quantities from the wholesaler who reduces prices for the larger volumes purchased. These reductions in costs of the products allow Carrefour to lower its retail prices, which attract more customers and produces more sales. Moreover, according to MAF MISR's Galal, the general manager of business development and commercial operations, "there is a misunderstanding that providing low costs leads to losing money. MAF Carrefour makes available all kinds of products at competitive prices by reducing the profit margin, and selling 'value for money products,' which makes money." It is Carrefour's emphasis on offering value to its customers that increases their loyalty to this specific hypermarket.

Sources: Based on information from http://online.wsj.com/article/SB10001424052 7487037466045744632117349767 56.html; http://money.cnn.com/magazines/ fortune/fortune_archive/2000/06/26/282982/index.htm; http://weekly.ahram.org.eg/ 2003/623/li1.htm; www.majidalfuttaim.com/maf.php?id_l2=14; www.carrefour .com.eg/aboutus.aspx; and www.datamonitor.com/store/News/carrefour_ announces_plans_to_open_four_new_hypermarkets_in_egypt?productid=821 F44C4-FF1C- 4B20-AD99-05CA58C165CA.

Off-price retailer

A retailer that buys at less-than-regular wholesale prices and sells at less than retail. Examples are factory outlets, independents, and warehouse clubs.

Independent off-price retailer

An off-price retailer that is either independently owned and run or is a division of a larger retail corporation.

Factory outlet

An off-price retailing operation that is owned and operated by a manufacturer and that normally carries the manufacturer's surplus, discontinued, or irregular goods.

Off-Price Retailers. As the major discount stores traded up, a new wave of **off-price retailers** moved in to fill the ultralow-price, high-volume gap. Ordinary discounters buy at regular wholesale prices and accept lower margins to keep prices down. In contrast, off-price retailers buy at less-than-regular wholesale prices and charge consumers less than retail. Off-price retailers can be found in all areas, from food, clothing, and electronics to no-frills banking and discount brokerages.

The three main types of off-price retailers are *independents, factory outlets*, and *warehouse clubs*. **Independent off-price retailers** either are independently owned and run or are divisions of larger retail corporations. Although many off-price operations are run by smaller independents, most large off-price retailer operations are owned by bigger retail chains. Examples include store retailers such as TJ Maxx and Marshalls, owned by TJX Companies, and Web sellers such as Overstock.com.

Factory outlets—manufacturer-owned and operated stores by firms such as J. Crew, Gap, Levi Strauss, and others—sometimes group together in *factory outlet malls* and *value-retail centers*, where dozens of outlet stores offer prices as low as 50 percent below retail on a wide range of mostly surplus, discounted, or irregular goods. Whereas outlet malls consist primarily of manufacturers' outlets, value-retail centers combine manufacturers' outlets with off-price retail stores and department store clearance outlets, such as Nordstrom Rack, Neiman Marcus Last Call Clearance Centers, and Off 5th (Saks Fifth Avenue outlets). Factory outlet malls have become one of the hottest growth areas in retailing.

The malls now are moving upscale—and even dropping "factory" from their descriptions. ▲A growing number of outlet malls now feature luxury brands such as Coach, Polo Ralph Lauren, Dolce & Gabbana, Giorgio Armani, Gucci, and Versace. The combination of highbrow brands and lowbrow prices provides powerful shopper appeal, especially in a tighter economy:[9]

Faced with unprecedented sales declines at full-price stores, a growing group of high-end retailers and luxury brands are building more factory outlets, where sales have fared much better. It is a strategy that would likely have backfired during the 1980s recession when outlets were bare-bones boxes built in the middle of nowhere and designers routinely cut out labels before selling them to off-price retail-

▼**Outlet centers:** The combination of highbrow brands and lowbrow prices provides powerful shopper appeal, especially in a tighter economy.

ers to protect their brand's cachet. "These days, customers are saying they want a brand, customer service, *and* a deal," says the president of Saks's Off 5th outlet division.

What else explains the host of weekday afternoon shoppers recently standing elbow to elbow inside a Coach factory store, as word of an unadvertised sale spread around one outdoor mall? Two clerks directed traffic at the door. Another walked in and out of the stock room armed with fresh handbags and wallets. Three cashiers rang up sales as customers stood in line. Shopper Joan Nichols scored a $458 violet leather satchel from Coach's Parker collection for $145. Her 19-year-old daughter bought a $468 cream Coach logo handbag for $130. Their savings: about 70 percent each. "If [spending's tight]," Nichols said, "it's not apparent here."

Warehouse club
An off-price retailer that sells a limited selection of brand name grocery items, appliances, clothing, and a hodgepodge of other goods at deep discounts to members who pay annual membership fees.

Warehouse clubs (or *wholesale clubs* or *membership warehouses*), such as Costco, Sam's Club, and BJ's, operate in huge, drafty, warehouse-like facilities and offer few frills. Customers themselves must wrestle furniture, heavy appliances, and other large items to the checkout line. Such clubs make no home deliveries and often accept no credit cards. However, they do offer ultralow prices and surprise deals on selected branded merchandise.

Warehouse clubs have grown rapidly in recent years. These retailers appeal not just to low-income consumers seeking bargains on bare-bones products. They appeal to all kinds of customers shopping for a wide range of goods, from necessities to extravagances.

Organizational Approach

Although many retail stores are independently owned, others band together under some form of corporate or contractual organization. The major types of retail organizations—*corporate chains, voluntary chains, retailer cooperatives*, and *franchise organizations* are described in ■ **Table 11.2**.

Chain stores
Two or more outlets that are commonly owned and controlled.

Chain stores are two or more outlets that are commonly owned and controlled. They have many advantages over independents. Their size allows them to buy in large quantities at lower prices and gain promotional economies. They can hire specialists to deal with areas such as pricing, promotion, merchandising, inventory control, and sales forecasting.

The great success of corporate chains caused many independents to band together in one of two forms of contractual associations. One is the *voluntary chain*—a

■ **Table 11.2** Major Types of Retail Organizations

Type	Description	Examples
Corporate chain store	Two or more outlets that are commonly owned and controlled. Corporate chains appear in all types of retailing, but they are strongest in department stores, food stores, drug stores, shoe stores, and women's clothing stores.	Sears, Kroger (grocery stores), CVS (drug stores), Williams-Sonoma (cookware and housewares)
Voluntary chain	Wholesaler-sponsored group of independent retailers engaged in group buying and merchandising.	Independent Grocers Alliance (IGA), Do-It Best hardware, Western Auto, True Value
Retailer cooperative	Group of independent retailers who set up a central buying organization and conduct joint promotion efforts.	Associated Grocers (groceries), Ace (hardware)
Franchise organization	Contractual association between a franchisor (a manufacturer, wholesaler, or service organization) and franchisees (independent businesspeople who buy the right to own and operate one or more units in the franchise system). Franchise organizations are normally based on some unique product or service, on a method of doing business, or on a trade name, goodwill, or patent that the franchisor has developed.	McDonald's, Subway, Pizza Hut, Jiffy Lube, Meineke Mufflers, 7-Eleven

Franchise
A contractual association between a manufacturer, wholesaler, or service organization (a franchisor) and independent businesspeople (franchisees) who buy the right to own and operate one or more units in the franchise system.

wholesaler-sponsored group of independent retailers that engages in group buying and common merchandising—which we discussed in Chapter 10. Examples include Independent Grocers Alliance (IGA), Western Auto, and Do-It Best hardware. The other type of contractual association is the *retailer cooperative*—a group of independent retailers that band together to set up a jointly owned, central wholesale operation and conduct joint merchandising and promotion efforts. Examples are Associated Grocers and Ace Hardware. These organizations give independents the buying and promotion economies they need to meet the prices of corporate chains.

Another form of contractual retail organization is a **franchise**. The main difference between franchise organizations and other contractual systems (voluntary chains and retail cooperatives) is that franchise systems are normally based on some unique product or service; on a method of doing business; or on the trade name, goodwill, or patent that the franchisor has developed. Franchising has been prominent in fast food and restaurants, motels, health and fitness centers, auto sales and service, and real estate.

But franchising covers a lot more than just burger joints and fitness centers. Franchises have sprung up to meet about any need. For example, Mad Science Group franchisees put on science programs for schools, scout troops, and birthday parties. And Mr. Handyman provides repair services for homeowners, while Merry Maids tidies up their houses.

Once considered upstarts among independent businesses, franchises now command 40 percent of all retail sales in the United States. ▲These days, it's nearly impossible to stroll down a city block or drive on a city street without seeing a McDonald's, Subway, Jiffy Lube, or Holiday Inn. One of the best-known and most successful franchisers, McDonald's, now has 32,000 stores in more than 100 countries, including almost 14,000 in the United States. It serves 58 million customers a day and racks up more than $54 billion in annual systemwide sales. Nearly 80 percent of McDonald's restaurants worldwide are owned and operated by franchisees. Gaining fast is Subway, one of the fastest-growing franchises, with more than 30,000 shops in 88 countries, including more than 22,000 in the United States.[10]

▼**Franchising: These days, it's nearly impossible to stroll down a city block or drive on a suburban street without seeing a McDonald's, Jiffy Lube, Subway, or Holiday Inn.**

Speed Bump: Linking the Concepts

Slow down and think about the kinds of retailers you deal with regularly, many of which overlap in the products they carry.

- Pick a familiar product: a camera, microwave oven, lawn tool, or something else. Shop for this product at two different store types, say a discount store on the one hand, and a department store or smaller specialty store on the other. Compare the stores on product assortment, services, and prices. If you were going to buy the product, where would you buy it and why?
- What does your shopping trip suggest about the futures of the competing store formats that you sampled?

Retailer Marketing Decisions (pp 380–387)

Retailers are always searching for new marketing strategies to attract and hold customers. In the past, retailers attracted customers with unique product assortments and more or better services. Today, retail assortments and services are looking more and more alike. Many national-brand manufacturers, in their drive for volume, have placed their brands almost everywhere. You can find most consumer brands not only in department stores but also in mass-merchandise discount stores, off-price dis-

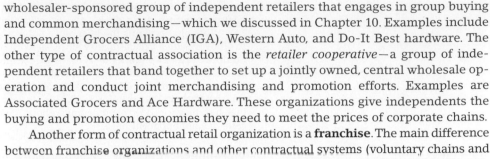

count stores, and on the Web. Thus, it's now more difficult for ar
fer exclusive merchandise.

Service differentiation among retailers has also erode
stores have trimmed their services, whereas discounters h
Customers have become smarter and more price sensitive. They see ...
more for identical brands, especially when service differences are shrinking. ...
these reasons, many retailers today are rethinking their marketing strategies.

As shown in ■ **Figure 11.1**, retailers face major marketing decisions about *segmentation and targeting, store differentiation and positioning,* and the *retail marketing mix.*

Segmentation, Targeting, Differentiation, and Positioning Decisions

Retailers must first segment and define their target markets and then decide how they will differentiate and position themselves in these markets. Should the store focus on upscale, midscale, or downscale shoppers? Do target shoppers want variety, depth of assortment, convenience, or low prices? Until they define and profile their markets, retailers cannot make consistent decisions about product assortment, services, pricing, advertising, store décor, or any of the other decisions that must support their positions.

Too many retailers, even big ones, fail to define their target markets and positions clearly. For example, what market does the clothing chain Gap target? What is its value proposition and positioning? If you're having trouble answering those questions, you're not alone—so is Gap's management.[11]

> Gap was founded in San Francisco in 1969 by Doris and Don Fisher with the intent to "make it easier to find a pair of jeans." By its heyday in the late 1980s and early 1990s, Gap was solidly positioned on the then-fashionable preppy look. But as its core customers aged and moved on, Gap stores didn't. In only the past five years, as the chain has struggled unsuccessfully to define new positioning that works with today's younger shoppers, Gap store sales have slipped more than 22 percent. Says one industry expert, "Gap is in danger of death by a thousand cuts. Abercrombie & Fitch does the authentic preppy look. Uniqlo sells staples such as cashmere [sweaters] and scarves for a penny apiece. Primark, Topshop, and Zara offer access to high-end fashion cheaply, so what is left?" Agrees another expert, "Right now, Gap could be anything. It hasn't got a story." The answer? Gap needs to "define who the brand's core customers are and be exceptional to them; make distinctive and desirable clothes; and be noticed."

In contrast, successful retailers define their target markets well and position themselves strongly. For example, Wal-Mart positions itself strongly on low prices. For decades, it consistently promised "Always low prices. *Always.*" Recently, it successfully extended this positioning to include what those always low prices mean to its customers. It now promises that customers will "Save money. Live better."

■ **Figure 11.1** Retailer Marketing Strategy

If Wal-Mart owns the low-price position, how can other discounters hope to compete? Again, the answer is good targeting and positioning. For example, Whole Foods Market has fewer than 300 stores and less than $8 billion in sales versus Wal-Mart's more than 7,800 stores worldwide and sales of $401 billion. How does this small grocery chain complete with giant Wal-Mart? It doesn't—at least not directly. Whole Foods Market thrives by carefully positioning itself *away* from Wal-Mart. It targets a select group of upscale customers and offers them "organic, natural, and gourmet foods, all swaddled in Earth Day politics." In fact, a devoted Whole Foods customer is more likely to boycott the local Wal-Mart than to shop at it. One analyst sums up the Whole Foods shopping experience this way:[12]

▲Retail targeting and positioning: By positioning itself strongly away from Wal-Mart and other discounters, Whole Foods Market has made itself one of the nation's fastest-growing and most profitable food retailers.

> Counters groan with creamy hunks of artisanal cheese. Medjool dates beckon amid rows of exotic fruit. Savory breads rest near fruit-drenched pastries, and prepared dishes like sesame-encrusted tuna rival what's sold in fine restaurants. In keeping with the company's positioning, most of the store's goods carry labels proclaiming "organic," "100% natural," and "contains no additives." Staff people smile, happy to suggest wines that go with a particular cheese, or pause to debate the virtues of peanut butter malt balls. And it's all done against a backdrop of eye-pleasing earth-toned hues and soft lighting. This is grocery shopping? Well, not as most people know it. Whole Foods Market has cultivated its mystique with shoppers . . . by being anything but a regular supermarket chain. Whole Foods is, well, special.

Whole Foods can't match Wal-Mart's massive economies of scale, incredible volume purchasing power, ultraefficient logistics, wide selection, and hard-to-beat prices. But then again, it doesn't even try. By positioning itself strongly away from Wal-Mart and other discounters, Whole Foods Market has made itself one of the nation's fastest-growing and most profitable food retailers.

Product Assortment and Services Decision

Retailers must decide on three major product variables: product assortment, services mix, and store atmosphere.

The retailer's product assortment should differentiate the retailer while matching target shoppers' expectations. One strategy is to offer merchandise that no other competitor carries, such as store brands or national brands on which it holds exclusives. For example, Saks gets exclusive rights to carry a well-known designer's labels. It also offers its own private-label lines—the Saks Fifth Avenue Signature, Classic, and Sport collections. At JCPenney, private-label brands account for 45 percent of sales.[13]

Another strategy is to feature blockbuster merchandising events—Bloomingdale's is known for running spectacular shows featuring goods from a certain country, such as India or China. Or the retailer can offer surprise merchandise, as when Costco offers surprise assortments of seconds, overstocks, and closeouts. Finally, the retailer can differentiate itself by offering a highly targeted product assortment—Lane Bryant carries plus-size clothing; Brookstone offers an unusual assortment of gadgets in what amounts to an adult toy store, and BatteryDepot.com offers about every imaginable kind of replacement battery.

The *services mix* can also help set one retailer apart from another. For example, some retailers invite customers to ask questions or consult service representatives in person or via phone or keyboard. Home Depot offers a diverse mix of services to do-it-yourselfers, from "how-to" classes to a proprietary credit card. Nordstrom promises to "take care of the customer, no matter what it takes."

The *store's atmosphere* is another important element in the reseller's product arsenal. The retailer wants to create a unique store experience, one that suits the target market and moves customers to buy. Many retailers practice "experiential retailing." None does this better than the Dubai Mall (see Marketing at Work 11.2). Amusements such as a movie complex, ice rink and aquarium create a fun, family orientated atmosphere for shoppers, not to mention a vast and colorful array of stores! More than just a place to go shopping, the Dubai Mall is a place to relax and have fun.

Marketing at Work 11.2

The Dubai Mall: Creating a Sense of "My Space"—A Lifestyle Statement

The Dubai Mall is the world's largest mall based on internal floor area. It is a project developed and operated by Emaar Malls Group, the retail subsidiary of Emaar Properties—the UAE's largest property developer. The Dubai Mall opened its doors on November 4, 2008 with over 600 stores, which was the largest mall opening in the world. When fully complete, The Dubai Mall will feature over 1,200 retail stores including over 165 new or unique brands to the region including anchor department stores Galeries Lafayette and Bloomingdale's. Every week it attracts over 750,000 visitors every week. The competition for share of retail spending is high in the Middle East, especially as the GCC will be home to five of the largest malls in the global top eight by 2012. By 2010, Dubai will have the highest amount of shopping space per capita. Because of the harsh desert weather, a mall culture has evolved. The mall becomes a second home for the people of UAE, a place to hang out and spend weekends and holidays. The challenge for the Mall is to create that space and atmosphere that can accommodate these crowds on a frequent basis while allowing then to browse, interact, shop, explore, dine and be entertained. It's an experiential process where all five senses are involved. According to marketing gurus like Kevin Roberts and Martin Lindstrom, consumers are more likely to buy and be loyal when all five senses are targeted.

The Dubai Mall has a total site area of 12.1 million square feet and offers a total lifestyle experience with retail, dining, and attractions to keep the entire family engaged. The Dubai Mall has surpassed it's projected target over 37 million visitors within the first year of opening, making it a highly sought-after platform for brand recognition on a global scale. Features include The Dubai Fountain, the world's largest performing fountain that runs shows every 20 minutes in the evening; a Guinness World Record-holding indoor aquarium (measuring 50 × 1 × 17 meters); an Olympic-sized skating ice rink; Dubai's largest movie megaplex with 22 theaters; and a two-level, 76,000 square foot indoor theme park—SEGA Republic; and KidZania, an "edu-tainment" role playing concept for children. More importantly there will be over 1,200 retail stores to browse, explore and shop from and 160 food and beverage outlets to keep the customer fueled for the day. To help customers with the wide variety of choice, The Dubai Mall not only updates offers available on their website (www.thedubaimall.com) but also sends e-blasts to their customer database, door drops to neighboring communities (depending on the nature of the promotion or event); places print and/or radio advertising in lifestyle, entertainment, and tourism-focused media; and uses state-of-the art multimedia systems in the mall to promote in-mall events and activities.

UAE ranks fourth in the 2009 AT Kearney Global Retailers List with high market attractiveness. What makes UAE unique is the fact that its population of 6 million residents are largely expatriate urban with an average daily private consumption spending of $26.80. This consumption spending is one of the highest in the Arab world where others spend an average of $3.50 daily on consumer items. Customer may be willing to pay a 50 percent

▲ The Dubai Mall is not just a shopping mall. As well as hundreds of shops tailored to a range of consumers, it also entices customers with a host of attractions including an aquarium, skating rink and even an indoor theme park – all under one roof!

premium for certain high-end British brands. A Global Luxury Brands survey by Neilson of 51 countries found that in the UAE, 43 percent of UAE shoppers think luxury brands provide significantly higher quality than other products and that 3 in 5 (59 percent) of those surveyed said they wear designer brands to project social status. The Dubai Mall has a dedicated luxury precinct—Fashion Avenue, featuring no less than 70 signature stores of the world's leading, haute couture brands such as Louis Vuitton, Armani/Dubai, Chanel, Dior, and Fendi. Fashion Avenue itself creates a personalized ambience, complete with marble flooring, a dedicated VIP entrance with valet parking, a red carpet entrance, and entertainers such as pianists and flutists. The Gold Souk is the world's largest indoor gold souk, with 220 outlets in a themed arabesque/souk-like precinct. Featuring meandering walkways, bronzed statues of camels, stallions, and palm trees, the Gold Souk itself is equally a tourist attraction and a gold and diamond retail paradise.

To ensure that the experience is one of SOSIMO—Sounds, Sights and Motion—The Dubai Mall has invested in cutting edge technology. This helps create an environment of "shoppertainment." Visitors are taken on a visual journey using the multimedia displays. For example Fashion Avenue has a fully retractable LED embedded-catwalk, eight LED columns encircling the stage, and five video rings that lower from above which are all synchronized to a world-class sound system. The world's largest indoor gold souk has a built-in planetarium-like projection system capable of illuminating the 22 meter-wide Treasury Dome with ever-changing displays and images. The Ice rink has a massive 20 × 10 meter display, which doubles up as a scoreboard for sporting matches, or a display for live events. In total, The Dubai Mall features more than 400 high-definition LED displays and over 300 advertising panels. This allows advertisers to capture "moments of exclusivity"—a single image projected across the entire mall that will ensure total visitor attention. The objective to get the "WOW" moment etched in the customer's memory.

(continued)

According to an ACNielsen survey, recreational shopping is becoming more prevalent with 74 percent of global consumers surveyed looking at it more as entertainment. The survey found that shopping during the weekends and at the end of the month was often considered as a family activity. The main enticements customers were looking at were comfort, security, eating establishments, and entertainment facilities. The Dubai Mall provides all of this and more and was designed with the customer in mind. Given the sheer size and scale (across 4 levels) of the mall, retailers are clustered into precincts based on product category. For example, all luxury fashion retailers are found within Fashion Avenue, children's wear and maternity retailers are found on Level 2 near the aquarium and food court, watches and jewelry are on the ground floor (in addition to the Gold Souk), and sportswear/active lifestyle stores are clustered in the "entertainment precinct" near the Dubai Ice Rink. The same strategy applies to the attractions, with SEGA Republic, REEL Cinemas, KidZania, and the Dubai Ice Rink located in the "entertainment walk" precinct of the mall. Visitors are then able to "map" out their experience.

Keeping in mind that the mall traffic increases by almost four times, The Dubai Mall makes sure its facilities are well maintained. There are three primary car parks, with a capacity for 14,000 cars. There are store directories (both static and multimedia/interactive directories) throughout the mall with color-coded floor plans.

They have 20 Guest Services Desks plus "roaming" Guest Services staff at primary entrances/exits and key event areas to assist customers. Guest Services staff are carefully selected and trained, which sets The Dubai Mall apart from competitor malls in the UAE in value-added services for its customers. Mall hours change to accommodate local festivals and needs. For example, during Ramadan (which includes fasting during the day), opening hours are extended to 1:00 a.m. They also have live entertainment and events. This makes the experience of The Dubai Mall a memorable one.

Sources: Based on information from "History of the Mall," *Dubai City* Guide (2009), dated 28 May 2009; accessed at: www.dubaicityguide.com/site/news/news-details.asp?newsid=   24486&newstype=Company%20News; Billing, S. (2008), "UAE's Luxury Brands Shopping List Revealed," dated 21 October, 2008; accessed at: www.arabianbusiness.com/535351-luxury-brands-shopping-list-for-uae- revealed?ln=en; AT Kearney (2009), "Window of Hope for Global Retailers: AT Kearney Global Retail Development Index™"; accessed at: www.atkearney.com/images/global/pdf/2009_Global_Retail_Development_Index .pdf; Dubai Mall (2008), "The Dubai Mall Unveils Retail World's Most Sophisticated Multimedia Systems," dated September 26, 2008; accessed at: www.thedubaimall.com/en/news/media-centre/news-section/the-dubai-mall-unveils-retail-worlds-most-sophisticated-multimedia-systems.html; Indonesia National portal (2008), "Indonesian Tops Regional Survey for Recreational Shopping"; and accessed at: www.indonesia.go.id/en/index.php?option=com_content&task=view&id=7592&Itemid=701.

Today's successful retailers carefully orchestrate virtually every aspect of the consumer store experience. The next time you step into a retail store—whether it sells consumer electronics, hardware, or high fashion—stop and carefully consider your surroundings. Think about the store's layout and displays. Listen to the background sounds. Smell the smells. Chances are good that everything in the store, from the layout and lighting to the music and even the smells, has been carefully orchestrated to help shape the customer's shopping experience—and to open their wallet. ▲At a Sony Style store, for instance, the environment is designed to encourage touch, from the silk wallpaper to the smooth maple wood cabinets, to the etched-glass countertops. Products are displayed like museum pieces and set up to be touched and tried.

▼Next time you shop, stop, look, and listen. Successful retailers like Sony Style orchestrate every aspect of the shopper store experience, down to the music, lighting, and even the smells (a subtle fragrance of vanilla and mandarin orange).

Perhaps the hottest store environment frontier these days is scent—that's right, the way the store smells:[14]

Anyone who's walked into a mall has been enticed by the smell of cinnamon buns or chocolate chip cookies. Now, most large retailers are developing "signature scents" that you smell only in their stores. Luxury shirtmaker Thomas Pink pipes the smell of clean, pressed shirts into its stores—its signature "line-dried linen" scent. Bloomingdale's uses different essences in different departments: baby powder in the baby store; suntan lotion in the bathing suit area; lilacs in lingerie; cinnamon and pine scent during the holiday season. At a Sony Style store, the subtle fragrance of vanilla and mandarin orange—designed exclusively for Sony—wafts down on shoppers, relaxing them and helping them believe that this is a very nice place to be. At Sony's Madison Avenue store in New York, the scent is even pumped onto the street. "From research, we found that scent is closest to the brain and will evoke the most emotion, even faster than the eye," says the Sony retail executive. "Our scent helps us create an environment like no other."

Such "experiential retailing" confirms that retail stores are much more than simply assortments of goods. They are environments to be experienced by the people who shop in them. Store atmospheres offer a powerful tool by which retailers can differentiate their stores from those of competitors.

Price Decision

A retailer's price policy must fit its target market and positioning, product and service assortment, the competition, and economic factors. All retailers would like to charge high markups and achieve high volume, but the two seldom go together. Most retailers seek *either* high markups on lower volume (most specialty stores) *or* low markups on higher volume (mass merchandisers and discount stores).

www.bijan.com

bijan
America on Rodeo
by Appointment
menswear, jewelry, perfume

▲ Bijan's boutique on Rodeo Drive in Beverly Hills sells $1,000 silk tie sets and $75,000 crocodile-skin jackets. Its "by appointment only" policy makes wealthy, high-profile clients comfortable with these prices.

Thus, ▲Bijan's boutique, with locations in New York City and on Rodeo Drive in Beverly Hills, designs and sells "the most expensive menswear in the world" to "men of substance." Its million-dollar wardrobes include $1,000 silk tie sets, each one presented in a matching silk box, numbered and signed, and $75,000 crocodile-skin jackets. Customers must make appointments in advance just to shop at Bijan's. On a typical visit, wealthy, high-profile clients spend in the neighborhood of $100,000 on men's fashions.[15] Since every item is one-of-a-kind and surrounded by personal pampering, Bijan's sells a low volume but reaps a healthy margin on each sale. At the other extreme, T.J. Maxx sells brand-name clothing at discount prices, settling for a lower margin on each sale but selling at a much higher volume.

Retailers must also decide on the extent to which they will use sales and other price promotions. Some retailers use no price promotions at all, competing instead on product and service quality rather than on price. For example, it's difficult to imagine Bijan's holding a two-for-the-price-of-one sale, even in a down economy. In fact, Bijan's actually raises the prices of Bijan designs remaining from previous collections, reflecting their quality and classic look. Retailers—such as Wal-Mart, Costco, Family Dollar, and other mass retailers—practice *everyday low pricing (EDLP)*, charging constant, everyday low prices with few sales or discounts.

Still other retailers practice *"high-low" pricing*—charging higher prices on an everyday basis, coupled with frequent sales and other price promotions to increase store traffic, create a low-price image, or attract customers who will buy other goods at full prices. The recent economic downturn caused a rash of high-low pricing, as retailers poured on price cuts and promotions to coax bargain-hunting customers into their stores. Which pricing strategy is best depends on the retailer's overall marketing strategy, the pricing approaches of competitors, and the economic environment.

Promotion Decision

Retailers use any or all of the promotion tools—advertising, personal selling, sales promotion, public relations, and direct marketing—to reach consumers. They advertise in newspapers, magazines, radio, television, and on the Internet. Advertising may be supported by newspaper inserts, catalogs, and direct mail. Personal selling requires careful training of salespeople in how to greet customers, meet their needs, and handle their complaints. Sales promotions may include in-store demonstrations, displays, contests, and visiting celebrities. Public relations activities, such as press conferences and speeches, store openings, special events, newsletters, magazines, and public service activities, are always available to retailers. Most retailers have also set up Web sites, offering customers information and other features and selling merchandise directly.

Place Decision

Retailers often point to three critical factors in retailing success: *location, location,* and *location!* It's very important that retailers select locations that are accessible to the target market in areas that are consistent with the retailer's positioning. For example, Apple locates its stores in high-end malls and trendy shopping districts—such as the "Miracle Mile" on Chicago's Michigan Avenue or Fifth Avenue in Manhattan—not low-rent strip malls on the edge of town. In contrast, Trader Joe's places its stores in low-rent, out-of-the-way locations to keep costs down and support its "cheap gourmet" positioning. Small retailers may have to settle for whatever locations they can find or afford. Large retailers, however, usually employ specialists who select locations using advanced methods.

Most stores today cluster together to increase their customer pulling power and to give consumers the convenience of one-stop shopping. *Central business districts* were the main form of retail cluster until the 1950s. Every large city and town had a central business district with department stores, specialty stores, banks, and movie theaters. When people began to move to the suburbs, however, these central business districts, with their traffic, parking, and crime problems, began to lose business. Downtown merchants opened branches in suburban shopping centers, and the decline of the central business districts continued. In recent years, many cities have joined with merchants to try to revive downtown shopping areas by building malls and providing underground parking.

A **shopping center** is a group of retail businesses built on a site that is planned, developed, owned, and managed as a unit. A *regional shopping center*, or *regional shopping mall*, the largest and most dramatic shopping center, contains from 50 to more than 100 stores, including 2 or more full-line department stores. It is like a covered mini-downtown and attracts customers from a wide area. A *community shopping center* contains between 15 and 50 retail stores. It normally contains a branch of a department store or variety store, a supermarket, specialty stores, professional offices, and sometimes a bank. Most shopping centers are *neighborhood shopping centers* or *strip malls* that generally contain between 5 and 15 stores. They are close and convenient for consumers. They usually contain a supermarket, perhaps a discount store, and several service stores—dry cleaner, drugstore, video-rental store, barber or beauty shop, hardware store, local restaurant, or other stores.[16]

Combined, the nation's more than 100,000 shopping centers now account for about 52 percent of all U.S. retail activity—$2.3 trillion dollars. Of the 100,000-plus shopping centers, about 48,000 are classified as shopping malls. The average American makes 2.9 trips to the mall a month, shopping for an average of 77 minutes per trip. Many experts suggest that America is now "over-malled." During the 1990s, shopping center space grew at about twice the rate of population growth. As a result, almost 20 percent of America's traditional shopping centers are either dead or dying. In 2009, as many as 3,000 shopping centers went under.[17]

Some developers are still building new "megamalls," such as Xanadu in East Rutherford, NJ, which in addition to shopping features entertainment such as a wave pool and indoor skiing all under one massive roof. However, the current trend is toward the so-called power centers. *Power centers* are huge unenclosed shopping centers consisting of a long strip of retail stores, including large, freestanding anchors such as Wal-Mart, Home Depot, Costco, Best Buy, Michaels, PetSmart, and OfficeMax. Each store has its own entrance with parking directly in front for shoppers who wish to visit only one store. Power centers have increased rapidly during the past few years to challenge traditional indoor malls.

In contrast, ▲*lifestyle centers* are smaller, open-air malls with upscale stores, convenient locations, and nonretail activities such as a play-

Shopping center
A group of retail businesses built on a site that is planned, developed, owned, and managed as a unit.

▼Shopping centers: The current trend is toward large *power centers* on the one hand and smaller *lifestyle centers* on the other—or a hybrid version of the two called a lifestyle–power center. In all, today's centers are more about creating places to be rather than just places to buy.

ground, dining, and a movie theater. They are usually located near affluent residential neighborhoods and cater to the retail needs of consumers in their areas. "Think of lifestyle centers as part Main Street and part Fifth Avenue," comments an industry observer. In fact, the original power center and lifestyle center concepts are now morphing into hybrid lifestyle–power centers. "The idea is to combine the hominess and community of an old-time village square with the cachet of fashionable urban stores; the smell and feel of a neighborhood park with the brute convenience of a strip center." In all, today's centers are more about "creating places to be rather than just places to buy."[18]

Retailing Trends and Developments (pp 387–392)

Retailers operate in a harsh and fast-changing environment, which offers threats as well as opportunities. For example, the industry suffers from chronic overcapacity, resulting in fierce competition for customer dollars, especially in tough economic times. Consumer demographics, lifestyles, and spending patterns are changing rapidly, as are retailing technologies. To be successful, retailers will need to choose target segments carefully and position themselves strongly. They will need to take the following retailing developments into account as they plan and execute their competitive strategies.

New Retail Forms and Shortening Retail Life Cycles

New retail forms continue to emerge to meet new situations and consumer needs, but the life cycle of new retail forms is getting shorter. Department stores took about 100 years to reach the mature stage of the life cycle; more recent forms, such as warehouse stores, reached maturity in about 10 years. In such an environment, seemingly solid retail positions can crumble quickly. Of the top 10 discount retailers in 1962 (the year that Wal-Mart and Kmart began), not one still exists today. Even the most successful retailers can't sit back with a winning formula. To remain successful, they must keep adapting.

Wheel-of-retailing concept
A concept that states that new types of retailers usually begin as low-margin, low-price, low-status operations but later evolve into higher-priced, higher-service operations, eventually becoming like the conventional retailers they replaced.

Many retailing innovations are partially explained by the **wheel-of-retailing concept**. According to this concept, many new types of retailing forms begin as low-margin, low-price, low-status operations. They challenge established retailers that have become "fat" by letting their costs and margins increase. The new retailers' success leads them to upgrade their facilities and offer more services. In turn, their costs increase, forcing them to increase their prices. Eventually, the new retailers become like the conventional retailers they replaced. The cycle begins again when still newer types of retailers evolve with lower costs and prices. The wheel-of-retailing concept seems to explain the initial success and later troubles of department stores, supermarkets, and discount stores and the recent success of off-price retailers.

A Slowed Economy and Tighter Consumer Spending

Following years of good economic times for retailers, the recent recession turned many retailers' fortunes from boom to bust. According to one observer:[19]

> It was great to be in retailing during the past 15 years. Inflated home values, freely available credit, and low interest rates fueled unprecedented levels of consumer spending. Retailers responded by aggressively adding new stores, launching new concepts, building an online presence, and expanding internationally. While the U.S. economy grew 5 percent annually from 1996 to 2006, . . . the retail sector grew at more than double that rate—an eye-popping 12 percent. Revenues rose sharply, profits ballooned, and share prices soared. But that's all gone now. Even before the [recent] financial crisis and recession began, retailers were hitting the wall. Same-store sales . . . have dropped by double digits for many chains, store closures have accelerated, store openings are slowed, and shareholder-value destruction has been massive.

Some retailers actually benefit from a down economy. For example, as consumers cut back and look for ways to spend less on what they buy, big discounters such as Wal-Mart scoop up new business from bargain-hungry shoppers. "Consumers will continue to trade down to the lowest-cost retailer, and Wal-Mart is it," says one analyst.[20] Similarly, lower-priced fast-food retailers, such as McDonald's, have taken business from their pricier eat-out competitors.

For most retailers, however, a faltering economy means tough times. Several large and familiar retailers have recently declared bankruptcy or closed their doors completely—household names such as Linens 'n Things, Circuit City, KB Toys, and Sharper Image, to name just a few. Other retailers, from Macy's and Home Depot to Starbucks, have laid off employees, cut their costs, and offered deep price discounts and promotions aimed at luring cash-strapped customers back into their stores.

Beyond cost-cutting and price promotions, many retailers have also added new value pitches to their positioning. For example, following rapid declines in same-store sales caused by the recent recession, Target, for the first time in its history, introduced TV ads featuring price messages. "Our [tagline] is 'Expect more. Pay less,' says a Target marketer. "We're putting more emphasis on the pay less promise."[21]

Similarly, Home Depot replaced its older "You can do it. We can help" theme with a more thrift-minded one: "More saving. More doing." JCPenney extended its "Every day matters," positioning with phrases such as "Style, quality, and price matter." ▲Even upscale Whole Foods Market has promoted value. It runs regional ads for its private-label brand, 365 Everyday Value, sporting headlines such as "Sticker shock, but in a good way" and "No wallets were harmed in the buying of our 365 Everyday Value products."[22]

When reacting to economic difficulties, retailers must be careful that their short-run actions don't damage their long-run images and positions. Drastic price discounting is "a sign of panic," says a retail strategist. "Anyone can sell product by dropping their prices, but it does not breed loyalty."[23] Instead of relying on cost-cutting and price reductions, retailers should focus on building greater customer value within their long-term store positioning strategies.

▲New value pitches from retailers: Even upscale Whole Foods Market has promoted its private-label brand, 365 Everyday Value, with headlines such as "Sticker shock, but in a good way."

Growth of Nonstore Retailing

Most of us still make most of our purchases the old-fashioned way: We go to the store, find what we want, wait patiently in line to plunk down our cash or credit card, and bring home the goods. However, consumers now have a broad array of alternatives, including mail-order, television, phone, and online shopping. Americans are increasingly avoiding the hassles and crowds at malls by doing more of their shopping by phone or computer. As we'll discuss in Chapter 14, direct and online marketing are now the fastest-growing forms of marketing.

Only a few years ago, prospects for online retailing were soaring. As more and more consumers flocked to the Web, some experts even saw a day when consumers would bypass stodgy "old economy" store retailers and do almost all of their shopping via the Internet. However, the dot-com meltdown of 2000 dashed these overblown expectations. Many once-brash Web sellers crashed and burned and expectations reversed almost overnight. The experts began to predict that online retailing was destined to be little more than a tag-on to in-store retailing.

However, today's online retailing is alive and thriving. With easier-to-use and more-enticing Web sites, improved online service, and the increasing sophistication of search technologies, online business is booming. In fact, although it currently accounts for only 7 percent of total U.S. retail sales, online buying is growing at a much brisker pace than retail buying as a whole. Despite a flagging economy, or perhaps because of it, this year's U.S. online retail sales will reach an estimated $156 billion, an 11 percent leap over the last year's.[24]

Retailer online sites also influence a large amount of in-store buying. Here are some surprising statistics: 80 percent of shoppers research products online before going to a store to make a purchase; 62 percent say that they spend at least 30 min-

▲The Internet has spawned a whole new breed of shoppers—people who just can't buy anything unless they first look it up on-line and get the lowdown.

utes online every week to help them decide whether and what to buy.[25] So it's no longer a matter of customers deciding to shop in the store *or* to shop online. Increasingly, customers are merging store and online outlets into a single shopping process. ▲In fact, the Internet has spawned a whole new breed of shopper and way of shopping:[26]

> Many people just can't buy anything unless they first look it up online and get the lowdown. In a recent survey, 78 percent of shoppers said that ads no longer have enough information they need. So many buyers search online for virtually everything. Window shoppers have become "Windows shoppers." A whopping 92 percent said they had more confidence in information they seek out online than anything coming from a salesclerk or other source. So shoppers are devoting time and energy to ferreting out detailed info before they buy. Whether it's cars, homes, personal computers, or medical care, nearly 4 in 5 shoppers say they gather information on their own from the Web before buying. "Do-it-yourself doctors" (that is, info-seeking patients) show up at their doctor with the Web-derived diagnosis in hand, and a list of the medicines they need prescribed. Customers appear at the car dealership with the wholesale price and the model already picked out. Now this trend is spreading down the product chain. In the survey, 24 percent of shoppers said they are doing online research before buying shampoo. And they have questions: How does this shampoo work on different hair types, thicknesses, and colors? Are the bottles recyclable? Has the product been tested on animals? The Breck Girl is being replaced by a shopping bot.

All types of retailers now employ direct and online channels. The online sales of large brick-and-mortar retailers, such as Sears, Staples, Wal-Mart, and Best Buy, are increasing rapidly. Several large online-only retailers—Amazon.com, online auction site eBay, online travel companies such as Travelocity.com and Expedia.com, and others—are now making it big on the Web. At the other extreme, hordes of niche marketers are using the Web to reach new markets and expand their sales. Today's more-sophisticated search engines (Google, Yahoo!) and comparison-shopping sites (Shopping.com, Buy.com, Shopzilla.com, and others) put almost any online retailer within a mouse click or two's reach of millions of customers.

Still, much of the anticipated growth in online sales will go to multichannel retailers—the click-and-brick marketers who can successfully merge the virtual and physical worlds. In a recent ranking of the top 500 online retail sites, 59 percent were multichannel retailers.[27] For example, Macy's beefed-up Web site complements its more than 800 Macy's stores around the country. While many Macy's customers make purchases online, the site offers a range of features designed to build loyalty to Macy's and to pull customers into stores. Like many retailers, Macy's has discovered that its best customers shop both online and offline. "When our customers shop [both] online and in stores they spend 20 percent more in stores than the average in-store shopper and 60 percent more online than the average online shopper at Macys.com," says the chairman of Macys.com. But the Web site aims to do more than just sell products online. "We see Macys.com as far more than a selling site," says the chairman. "We see it as the online hub of the Macy's brand."[28]

Retail Convergence

Today's retailers are increasingly selling the same products at the same prices to the same consumers in competition with a wider variety of other retailers. For example, you can buy books at outlets ranging from independent local bookstores to warehouse clubs such as Costco, superstores such as Barnes & Noble, or Web sites such as Amazon.com. When it comes to brand-name appliances, department stores, discount stores, home improvement stores, off-price retailers, electronics superstores, and a slew of Web sites all compete for the same customers. So if you can't find the microwave oven you want at Sears, step across the street and find one for a better price at Lowe's or Best Buy—or just order one online from Amazon.com or even RitzCamera.com.

This merging of consumers, products, prices, and retailers is called *retail convergence*. Such convergence means greater competition for retailers and greater difficulty in differentiating offerings. The competition between chain superstores and smaller, independently owned stores has become particularly heated. Because of their bulk-buying power and high sales volume, chains can buy at lower costs and thrive on smaller margins. The arrival of a superstore can quickly force nearby independents out of business. For example, the decision by electronics superstore Best Buy to sell CDs as loss leaders at rock-bottom prices pushed a number of specialty record-store chains into bankruptcy. And with its everyday low prices, Wal-Mart has been accused of destroying independents in countless small towns around the country who sell the same merchandise.

Yet the news is not all bad for smaller companies. Many small, independent retailers are thriving. They are finding that sheer size and marketing muscle are often no match for the personal touch small stores can provide or the specialty merchandise niches that small stores fill for a devoted customer base. Remember Annie Bloom's Books, the cozy independent bookstore we discussed in Chapter 9, whose personal approach turns local book lovers into loyal patrons, even if they have to pay a little more?

The Rise of Megaretailers

The rise of huge mass merchandisers and specialty superstores, the formation of vertical marketing systems, and a rash of retail mergers and acquisitions have created a core of superpower megaretailers. Through their superior information systems and buying power, these giant retailers can offer better merchandise selections, good service, and strong price savings to consumers. As a result, they grow even larger by squeezing out their smaller, weaker competitors.

The megaretailers have shifted the balance of power between retailers and producers. A relative handful of retailers now control access to enormous numbers of consumers, giving them the upper hand in their dealings with manufacturers. For example, in the United States, Home Depot's sales of $77 billion are close to 13 times those of major supplier Black & Decker, and Home Depot generates well over 20 percent of Black & Decker's $6 billion in revenues. Home Depot can, and often does, use this power to wring concessions from Black & Decker and other suppliers.[29]

Growing Importance of Retail Technology

Retail technologies have become critically important as competitive tools. Progressive retailers are using advanced information technology and software systems to produce better forecasts, control inventory costs, interact electronically with suppliers, send information between stores, and even sell to customers within stores. They have adopted sophisticated systems for checkout scanning, RFID inventory tracking, merchandise handling, information sharing, and interacting with customers.

Perhaps the most startling advances in retail technology concern the ways in which retailers are connecting with consumers. Today's customers have gotten used to the speed and convenience of buying online and to the control that the Internet gives them over the buying process. "The Web provides shopping when you like it, where you like it, with access to gobs of research—from a product's attributes to where it's cheapest," says one retail technology expert. "No real-world store can replicate all that."

But increasingly, retailers are attempting to meet these new consumer expectations by bringing Web-style technologies into their stores. Many retailers now routinely use technologies ranging from touch-screen kiosks, handheld shopping assistants, customer-loyalty cards, and self-scanning checkout systems to in-store access to store inventory databases. Consider the following example:[30]

▲ Bloom supermarkets, owned by Food Lion, have poured money into a sophisticated system that allows shoppers to pick up a scanner and grocery bag at the front of the store,

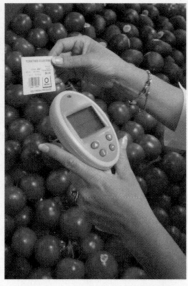

▲ **Retail technology: Bloom supermarket—owned by Southeastern grocery chain Food Lion—is using technology to make shopping easier for its customers.**

keep track of the bill as they shop, download the scanner and grocery bag at the self-service checkout, and pay. Voilà—the weekly food run with fewer hassles, in Internet time. Along the way, a computerized kiosk in the wine section lets shoppers scan a bottle and get serving suggestions. The kiosk, and a second one in the meat section, lets them print recipes off the screen. And if shoppers drop off a prescription, the pharmacy can send a message to the scanner when their order is ready. Visitors to Shopbloom.com can even key in a shopping list before going to the store to get a printout of aisles they need to hit.

Global Expansion of Major Retailers

Retailers with unique formats and strong brand positioning are increasingly moving into other countries. Many are expanding internationally to escape mature and saturated home markets. Over the years, some giant U.S. retailers, such as McDonald's, have become globally prominent as a result of their marketing prowess. Others, such as Wal-Mart, are rapidly establishing a global presence. Wal-Mart, which now operates more than 3,600 stores in 15 countries abroad, sees exciting global potential. Its international division alone last year racked up sales of nearly $100 billion, an increase of 9 percent over the previous year and over 50 percent more than rival Target's *total* sales of $64.9 billion.[31]

However, most U.S retailers are still significantly behind Europe and Asia when it comes to global expansion. Ten of the world's top 20 retailers are U.S. companies; only 3 of these retailers have set up stores outside of North America (Wal-Mart, Home Depot, and Costco). Of the 10 non-U.S. retailers in the world's top 20, 7 have stores in at least 10 countries. Among foreign retailers that have gone global are France's Carrefour and Auchan chains, Germany's Metro and Aldi chains, and Britain's Tesco.[32]

French discount retailer Carrefour, the world's second-largest retailer after Wal-Mart, has embarked on an aggressive mission to extend its role as a leading international retailer:

> The Carrefour Group has an interest in more than 15,000 stores in over 30 countries in Europe, Asia, and the Americas, including over 1,000 hypermarkets (supercenters). It leads Europe in supermarkets and the world in hypermarkets. Carrefour is outpacing Wal-Mart in several emerging markets, including South America, China, and the Pacific Rim. It's the leading retailer in Brazil and Argentina, where it operates almost 1,000 stores, compared to Wal-Mart's 373 units in those two countries. Carrefour is the largest foreign retailer in China, where it operates more than 443 stores versus Wal-Mart's 246. In short, although Wal-Mart has more than three times Carrefour's overall sales, Carrefour is forging ahead of Wal-Mart in most markets outside North America. The only question: Can the French retailer hold its lead? Although no one retailer can safely claim to be in the same league with Wal-Mart as an overall retail presence, Carrefour stands a better chance than most to hold its own in global retailing.[33]

Retail Stores as "Communities"

With the rise in the number of people living alone, working at home, or living in isolated and sprawling suburbs, there has been a resurgence of establishments that, regardless of the product or service they offer, also provide a place for people to get together. These places include coffee shops and cafés, shopping malls, bookstores, children's play spaces, superstores, and urban greenmarkets. For example, today's bookstores have become part bookstore, part library, part living room, and part coffeehouse. On an early evening at your local Barnes & Noble, you'll likely find backpack-toting high school students doing homework with friends in the coffee bar. Nearby, retirees sit in cushy chairs thumbing through travel or gardening books while parents read aloud to their children. Barnes & Noble sells more than just books, it sells comfort, relaxation, and community.

▲ **Retail communities: Scissors and crafting supplies maker Fiskars has created Fiskateers, an online community of more than 5,000 crafting enthusiasts.**

Retailers don't create communities only in their brick-and-mortar stores. Many also build virtual communities on the Internet. ▲For example, Fiskars sells scissors, along with scrapbooking and crafting tools and supplies. A few years ago, Fiskars learned that its image was lackluster. In focus groups, respondents told the company that if Fiskars were a color, it would be beige; if it were a food, it would be saltines. So, to light a fire under the brand, the company created Fiskateers, an exclusive online community of crafters:[34]

Crafting is a very high-involvement product category for the women who love it. As one enthusiast put it: "Crafting isn't a matter of life and death. It's much more important than that." So, to light a fire under the Fiskars brand, the company created Fiskateers, an exclusive community of crafters. You have to be invited to get in. When you join up, you get a box that includes crafting supplies plus unique two-tone scissors available only to members. But, most importantly, you get to connect online at Fiskateers.com to draw ideas and support from fellow crafters. Crafting enthusiasts couldn't wait to join. In just over a year, Fiskars has grown the community to include more than 5,000 members, 25 times its original goal. In that time, mentions of Fiskars in online chatter has surged by a factor of six. Fiskars has found that building relationships with and between the crafting enthusiasts is more important than the week's sales numbers. More than creating sales, the Fiskateers community creates collaboration between the company and important customers. "We are actually listening to them," says the president of Fiskars' School, Office, and Craft Division, "and they are listening to us."

Wholesaling
All activities involved in selling goods and services to those buying for resale or business use.

Wholesaler
A firm engaged *primarily* in wholesaling activities.

WHOLESALING (pp 392–398)

Wholesaling includes all activities involved in selling goods and services to those buying for resale or business use. We call **wholesalers** those firms engaged *primarily* in wholesaling activities.

Wholesalers buy mostly from producers and sell mostly to retailers, industrial consumers, and other wholesalers. As a result, many of the nation's largest and most important wholesalers are largely unknown to final consumers. ▲For example, you may never have heard of Grainger, even though it's very well known and much valued by its more than 1.8 million business and institutional customers across North America, India, China, and Panama.[35]

Grainger may be the biggest market leader you've never heard of. It's a $6.9 billion business that offers more than 900,000 maintenance, repair, and operating (MRO) products to more than 1.8 million customers. Through its branch network, service centers, sales reps, catalog, and Web site, Grainger links customers with the supplies they need to keep their facilities running smoothly—everything from light bulbs, cleaners, and display cases to nuts and bolts, motors, valves, power tools, test equipment, and safety supplies. Grainger's 617 branches, 18 strategically located distribution centers, more than 18,000 employees, and innovative Web site handle more than 115,000 transactions a day. Its customers include organizations ranging from factories, garages, and grocers to schools and military bases. Most American businesses are located within 20 minutes of a Grainger branch. Customers include notables such as Abbott Laboratories, General Motors, Campbell Soup, American Airlines, Chrysler, and the U.S. Postal Service.

Grainger operates on a simple value proposition: to make it easier and less costly for customers to find and buy MRO supplies. It starts by acting as a one-stop shop for products needed to maintain facilities. On a broader level, it builds lasting relationships with customers by helping them find *solutions* to their overall MRO problems. Acting as con-

▲Wholesaling: Many of the nation's largest and most important wholesalers—like Grainger—are largely unknown to final consumers. But they are very well known and much valued by the business customers they serve.

sultants, Grainger sales reps help buyers with everything from improving their supply chain management to reducing inventories and streamlining warehousing operations. So, how come you've never heard of Grainger? Maybe it's because the company operates in the not-so-glamorous world of MRO supplies, which are important to every business but not so important to consumers. More likely, it's because Grainger is a wholesaler. And like most wholesalers, it operates behind the scenes, selling only to other businesses.

Why are wholesalers important to sellers? For example, why would a producer use wholesalers rather than selling directly to retailers or consumers? Simply put, wholesalers add value by performing one or more of the following channel functions:

- *Selling and promoting:* Wholesalers' sales forces help manufacturers reach many small customers at a low cost. The wholesaler has more contacts and is often more trusted by the buyer than the distant manufacturer.
- *Buying and assortment building:* Wholesalers can select items and build assortments needed by their customers, thereby saving the consumers much work.
- *Bulk breaking:* Wholesalers save their customers money by buying in carload lots and breaking bulk (breaking large lots into small quantities).
- *Warehousing:* Wholesalers hold inventories, thereby reducing the inventory costs and risks of suppliers and customers.
- *Transportation:* Wholesalers can provide quicker delivery to buyers because they are closer than the producers.
- *Financing:* Wholesalers finance their customers by giving credit, and they finance their suppliers by ordering early and paying bills on time.
- *Risk bearing:* Wholesalers absorb risk by taking title and bearing the cost of theft, damage, spoilage, and obsolescence.
- *Market information:* Wholesalers give information to suppliers and customers about competitors, new products, and price developments.
- *Management services and advice:* Wholesalers often help retailers train their salesclerks, improve store layouts and displays, and set up accounting and inventory control systems.

Types of Wholesalers

Merchant wholesaler
An independently owned wholesaler business that takes title to the merchandise it handles.

Broker
A wholesaler who does not take title to goods and whose function is to bring buyers and sellers together and assist in negotiation.

Agent
A wholesaler who represents buyers or sellers on a relatively permanent basis, performs only a few functions, and does not take title to goods.

Manufacturers' sales branches and offices
Wholesaling by sellers or buyers themselves rather than through independent wholesalers.

Wholesalers fall into three major groups (see ■ **Table 11.3**): *merchant wholesalers, agents and brokers,* and *manufacturers' sales branches and offices.* **Merchant wholesalers** are the largest single group of wholesalers, accounting for roughly 50 percent of all wholesaling. Merchant wholesalers include two broad types: full-service wholesalers and limited-service wholesalers. *Full-service wholesalers* provide a full set of services, whereas the various *limited-service wholesalers* offer fewer services to their suppliers and customers. The several different types of limited-service wholesalers perform varied specialized functions in the distribution channel.

Brokers and *agents* differ from merchant wholesalers in two ways: They do not take title to goods, and they perform only a few functions. Like merchant wholesalers, they generally specialize by product line or customer type. A **broker** brings buyers and sellers together and assists in negotiation. **Agents** represent buyers or sellers on a more permanent basis. *Manufacturers' agents* (also called manufacturers' representatives) are the most common type of agent wholesaler. The third major type of wholesaling is that done in **manufacturers' sales branches and offices** by sellers or buyers themselves rather than through independent wholesalers.

■ **Table 11.3**   Major Types of Wholesalers

Type	Description
Merchant wholesalers	Independently owned businesses that take title to the merchandise they handle. In different trades they are called *jobbers, distributors,* or *mill supply houses.* They include *full-service wholesalers* and *limited-service wholesalers.*
Full-service wholesalers	Provide a full line of services: carrying stock, maintaining a sales force, offering credit, making deliveries, and providing management assistance. There are two types:
Wholesale merchants	Sell primarily to retailers and provide a full range of services. *General merchandise wholesalers* carry several merchandise lines, whereas *general line wholesalers* carry one or two lines in great depth. *Specialty wholesalers* specialize in carrying only part of a line. Examples: health food wholesalers, seafood wholesalers.
Industrial distributors	Sell to manufacturers rather than to retailers. Provide several services, such as carrying stock, offering credit, and providing delivery. May carry a broad range of merchandise, a general line, or a specialty line.
Limited-service wholesalers	Offer fewer services than full-service wholesalers. Limited-service wholesalers are of several types:
Cash-and-carry wholesalers	Carry a limited line of fast-moving goods and sell to small retailers for cash. Normally do not deliver. Example: A small fish store retailer may drive to a cash-and-carry fish wholesaler, buy fish for cash, and bring the merchandise back to the store.
Truck wholesalers (or truck jobbers)	Perform primarily a selling and delivery function. Carry a limited a line of semiperishable merchandise (such as milk, bread, snack foods), which they sell for cash as they make their rounds to supermarkets, small groceries, hospitals, restaurants, factory cafeterias, and hotels.
Drop shippers	Do not carry inventory or handle the product. On receiving an order, they select a manufacturer, who ships the merchandise directly to the customer. The drop shipper assumes title and risk from the time the order is accepted to its delivery to the customer. They operate in bulk industries, such as coal, lumber, and heavy equipment.
Rack jobbers	Serve grocery and drug retailers, mostly in nonfood items. They send delivery trucks to stores, where the delivery people set up toys, paperbacks, hardware items, health and beauty aids, or other items. They price the goods, keep them fresh, set up point-of-purchase displays, and keep inventory records. Rack jobbers retain title to the goods and bill the retailers only for the goods sold to consumers.
Producers' cooperatives	Are owned by farmer members and assemble farm produce to sell in local markets. The co-op's profits are distributed to members at the end of the year. They often attempt to improve product quality and promote a co-op brand name, such as Sun-Maid raisins, Sunkist oranges, or Diamond walnuts.
Mail-order or Web wholesalers	Send catalogs to or maintain Web sites for retail, industrial, and institutional customers featuring jewelry, cosmetics, specialty foods, and other small items. Maintain no outside sales force. Main customers are businesses in small outlying areas. Orders are filled and sent by mail, truck, or other transportation.

Wholesaler Marketing Decisions

Wholesalers now face growing competitive pressures, more-demanding customers, new technologies, and more direct-buying programs on the part of large industrial, institutional, and retail buyers. As a result, they have taken a fresh look at their marketing strategies. As with retailers, their marketing decisions include choices of segmentation and targeting, differentiation and positioning, and the marketing mix—product and service assortments, price, promotion, and distribution (see ■ **Figure 11.2**).

Segmentation, Targeting, Differentiation, and Positioning Decisions

Like retailers, wholesalers must segment and define their target markets and differentiate and position themselves effectively—they cannot serve everyone. They can choose a target group by size of customer (only large retailers), type of customer

■ **Table 11.3** Continued

Type	Description
Brokers and agents	Do not take title to goods. Main function is to facilitate buying and selling, for which they earn a commission on the selling price. Generally specialize by product line or customer type.
Brokers	Chief function is bringing buyers and sellers together and assisting in negotiation. They are paid by the party who hired them and do not carry inventory, get involved in financing, or assume risk. Examples: food brokers, real estate brokers, insurance brokers, and security brokers.
Agents	Represent either buyers or sellers on a more permanent basis than brokers do. There are several types:
Manufacturers' agents	Represent two or more manufacturers of complementary lines. A formal written agreement with each manufacturer covers pricing, territories, order handling, delivery service and warranties, and commission rates. Often used in such lines as apparel, furniture, and electrical goods. Most manufacturers' agents are small businesses with only a few skilled salespeople as employees. They are hired by small manufacturers who cannot afford their own field sales forces and by large manufacturers who use agents to open new territories or to cover territories that cannot support full-time salespeople.
Selling agents	Have contractual authority to sell a manufacturer's entire output. The manufacturer either is not interested in the selling function or feels unqualified. The selling agent serves as a sales department and has significant influence over prices, terms, and conditions of sale. Found in product areas such as textiles, industrial machinery and equipment, coal and coke, chemicals, and metals.
Purchasing agents	Generally have a long-term relationship with buyers and make purchases for them, often receiving, inspecting, warehousing, and shipping the merchandise to the buyers. They provide helpful market information to clients and help them obtain the best goods and prices available.
Commission merchants	Take physical possession of products and negotiate sales. Normally, they are not employed on a long-term basis. Used most often in agricultural marketing by farmers who do not want to sell their own output and do not belong to producers' cooperatives. The commission merchant takes a truckload of commodities to a central market, sells it for the best price, deducts a commission and expenses, and remits the balance to the producers.
Manufacturers' and retailers' branches and offices	Wholesaling operations conducted by sellers or buyers themselves rather than through independent wholesalers. Separate branches and offices can be dedicated to either sales or purchasing.
Sales branches and offices	Set up by manufacturers to improve inventory control, selling, and promotion. *Sales branches* carry inventory and are found in industries such as lumber and automotive equipment and parts. *Sales offices* do not carry inventory and are most prominent in dry-goods and notions industries.
Purchasing officers	Perform a role similar to that of brokers or agents but are part of the buyer's organization. Many retailers set up purchasing offices in major market centers such as New York and Chicago.

(convenience stores only), need for service (customers who need credit), or other factors. Within the target group, they can identify the more profitable customers, design stronger offers, and build better relationships with them. They can propose automatic reordering systems, set up management-training and advising systems, or even sponsor a voluntary chain. They can discourage less-profitable customers by requiring larger orders or adding service charges to smaller ones.

Marketing Mix Decisions

Like retailers, wholesalers must decide on product and service assortments, prices, promotion, and place. Wholesalers add customer value though the *products and services* they offer. They are often under great pressure to carry a full line and to stock enough for immediate delivery. But this practice can damage profits.

■ **Figure 11.2** Wholesaler Marketing Strategy

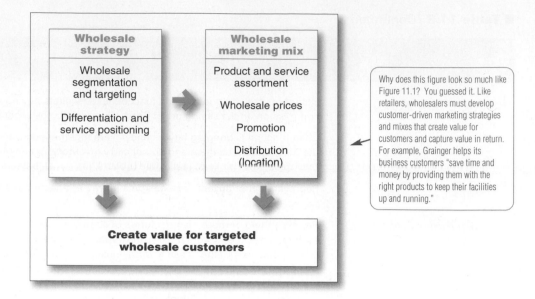

Wholesalers today are cutting down on the number of lines they carry, choosing to carry only the more-profitable ones. They are also rethinking which services count most in building strong customer relationships and which should be dropped or paid for by the customer. The key is to find the mix of services most valued by their target customers.

Price is also an important wholesaler decision. Wholesalers usually mark up the cost of goods by a standard percentage—say, 20 percent. Expenses may run 17 percent of the gross margin, leaving a profit margin of 3 percent. In grocery wholesaling, the average profit margin is often less than 2 percent. Wholesalers are trying new pricing approaches. The recent economic downturn put heavy pressure on wholesalers to cut their costs and prices. As their retail and industrial customers face sales and margin declines, the customers turn to wholesalers looking for lower prices. Wholesalers may cut their margins on some lines in order to keep important customers. They may ask suppliers for special price breaks, when they can turn them into an increase in the supplier's sales.

Although *promotion* can be critical to wholesaler success, most wholesalers are not promotion minded. They use largely scattered and unplanned trade advertising, sales promotion, personal selling, and public relations. Many are behind the times in personal selling—they still see selling as a single salesperson talking to a single customer instead of as a team effort to sell, build, and service major accounts. Wholesalers also need to adopt some of the nonpersonal promotion techniques used by retailers. They need to develop an overall promotion strategy and make greater use of supplier promotion materials and programs.

Finally, *distribution* (location) is important—wholesalers must choose their locations, facilities, and Web locations carefully. There was a time when wholesalers could locate in low-rent, low-tax areas and invest little money in their buildings, equipment, and systems. Today, however, as technology zooms forward, such behavior results in outdated materials-handling, order-processing, and delivery systems.

Instead, today's large and progressive wholesalers have reacted to rising costs by investing in automated warehouses and information technology systems. Orders are fed from the retailer's information system directly into the wholesaler's, and the items are picked up by mechanical devices and automatically taken to a shipping platform where they are assembled. Most large wholesalers are using technology to carry out accounting, billing, inventory control, and forecasting. Modern wholesalers are adapting their services to the needs of target customers and finding cost-reducing methods of doing business. They are also transacting more business online. For example, e-commerce is Grainger's fastest growing sales channel. Online purchasing now accounts for 24 percent of the wholesaler's U.S. sales.[36]

Trends in Wholesaling

Today's wholesalers face considerable challenges. The industry remains vulnerable to one of its most enduring trends—the need for ever greater efficiency. Recent economic conditions have led to demands for even lower prices and the winnowing out of suppliers who are not adding value based on cost and quality. Progressive wholesalers constantly watch for better ways to meet the changing needs of their suppliers and target customers. They recognize that their only reason for existence comes from adding value by increasing the efficiency and effectiveness of the entire marketing channel.

As with other types of marketers, the goal is to build value-adding customer relationships. For example, Grainger succeeds by making life easier and more efficient for the commercial and institutional buyers and sellers it serves:

> Beyond making it easier for customers to find the products they need, Grainger also helps them streamline their acquisition processes. For most companies, acquiring MRO supplies is a very costly process. In fact, 40 percent of the cost of MRO supplies stems from the purchase process, including finding a supplier, negotiating the best deal, placing the order, receiving the order, and paying the invoice. Grainger constantly seeks ways to reduce the costs associated with MRO supplies acquisition, both internally and externally. One company found that working with Grainger cut MRO requisition time by more than 60 percent; lead times went from days to hours. Its supply chain dropped from 12,000 suppliers to 560— significantly reducing expenses. Similarly, a large timber and paper-products company has come to appreciate Grainger's selection and streamlined ordering process. It orders two-thirds of its supplies from Grainger's Web site at an annual acquisition cost of only $300,000. By comparison, for the remainder of its needs, this company deals with more than 1,300 small distributors at an acquisition cost of $2.4 million each year—eight times the cost of dealing with Grainger for half of the volume. The company is now looking for ways to buy all of its MRO supplies from Grainger. As one Grainger branch manager puts it, "If we don't save [customers] time and money every time they come [to us], they won't come back."[37]

▲Pharmaceuticals wholesaler McKesson helps its retail pharmacist customers be more efficient by offering a wide range of online resources. Its retail pharmacy customers can even use the McKesson system to maintain prescription histories and medical profiles on their customers.

▲McKesson, a diversified healthcare services provider and the nation's leading wholesaler of pharmaceuticals, health and beauty care, home health care, and medical supply and equipment products, provides another example of progressive, value-adding wholesaling. To survive, especially in a harsh economic environment, McKesson has to remain more cost effective than manufacturers' sales branches. Thus, the company has built efficient automated warehouses, established direct computer links with drug manufacturers, and set up extensive online supply management and accounts receivable systems for customers. It offers retail pharmacists a wide range of online resources, including supply-management assistance, catalog searches, real-time order tracking, and an account-management system. It has also created solutions such as automated pharmaceutical-dispensing machines that assist pharmacists by reducing costs and improving accuracy. Retailers can even use the McKesson systems to maintain prescription histories and medical profiles on their customers.

McKesson's medical-surgical supply and equipment customers receive a rich assortment of online solutions and supply management tools, including an online order management system and real-time information on products and pricing, inventory availability, and order status. According to McKesson, it adds value in the channel by providing "supply, information, and health care management products and services designed to reduce costs and improve quality across healthcare."[38]

The distinction between large retailers and large wholesalers continues to blur. Many retailers now operate formats such as wholesale clubs and supercenters that perform many wholesale functions. In return, many large wholesalers are setting up their own retailing operations. For example, until recently, SuperValu was classified as a food wholesaler, with a majority of its business derived from supplying grocery products to independent grocery retailers. However, over the past decade, SuperValu has started or acquired several retail food chains of its own—including Albertsons, Jewel-Osco, Save-A-Lot, Cub Foods, Acme, and others—to become the nation's third-largest food retailer (behind Wal-Mart and Kroger). Thus, even though it remains the country's largest food wholesaler, SuperValu is now classified as a retailer because 75 percent of its $44 billion in sales come from retailing.[39]

Wholesalers will continue to increase the services they provide to retailers—retail pricing, cooperative advertising, marketing and management information reports, accounting services, online transactions, and others. The slumping economy on the one hand, and the demand for increased services on the other, will put the squeeze on wholesaler profits. Wholesalers who do not find efficient ways to deliver value to their customers will soon drop by the wayside. However, the increased use of computerized, automated, and Web-based systems will help wholesalers to contain the costs of ordering, shipping, and inventory holding, boosting their productivity.

Finally, facing slow growth in their domestic markets and such developments as the North American Free Trade Agreement, many large wholesalers are now going global. For example, McKesson now derives almost 8 percent of its revenues from Canadian and other international operations. Its Information Solutions group operates widely throughout North America, the United Kingdom, and other European countries.[40]

REST STOP
REVIEWING THE CONCEPTS

Retailing and wholesaling consist of many organizations bringing goods and services from the point of production to the point of use. In this chapter, we first looked at the nature and importance of retailing, major types of retailers, the decisions retailers make, and the future of retailing. We then examined these same topics for wholesalers.

 Objective 1 Explain the role of retailers in the distribution channel and describe the major types of retailers. (pp 372–380)

Retailing includes all activities involved in selling goods or services directly to final consumers for their personal, non-business use. Retail stores come in all shapes and sizes, and new retail types keep emerging. Store retailers can be classified by the *amount of service* they provide (self-service, limited service, or full service), *product line sold* (specialty stores, department stores, supermarkets, convenience stores, superstores, and service businesses), and *relative prices* (discount stores and off-price retailers). Today, many retailers are banding together in corporate and contractual *retail organizations* (corporate chains, voluntary chains, retailer cooperatives, and franchise organizations).

 Objective 2 Describe the major retailer marketing decisions. (pp 380–387)

Retailers are always searching for new marketing strategies to attract and hold customers. They face major market-

ing decisions about segmentation and targeting, store differentiation and positioning, and the retail marketing mix.

Retailers must first segment and define their target markets and then decide how they will differentiate and position themselves in these markets. Those that try to offer "something for everyone" end up satisfying no market well. In contrast, successful retailers define their target markets well and position themselves strongly.

Guided by strong targeting and positioning, retailers must decide on a retail marketing mix—product and services assortment, price, promotion, and place. Retail stores are much more than simply an assortment of goods—beyond the products and services they offer, today's successful retailers carefully orchestrate virtually every aspect of the consumer store experience. A retailer's price policy must fit its target market and positioning, products and services assortment, and competition. Retailers use any or all of the promotion tools—advertising, personal selling, sales promotion, public relations, and direct marketing—to reach consumers. Finally, it's very important that retailers select locations that are accessible to the target market in areas that are consistent with the retailer's positioning.

 Objective 3 Discuss the major trends and developments in retailing. (pp 387–392)

Retailers operate in a harsh and fast-changing environment, which offers threats as well as opportunities. New retail forms continue to emerge to meet new situations and consumer needs, but the life cycle of new retail forms is getting shorter—retailers must pay attention to the wheel-of-retailing concept. Other trends in retailing include the slowed economy and tighter consumer spending, rapid growth of nonstore retailing, retail convergence (the merging of consumers, products, prices, and retailers), the rise of megaretailers, the growing importance of retail technology, the global expansion of major retailers, and the resurgence of retail stores as consumer "communities" or "hangouts."

 Objective 4 Explain the major types of wholesalers and their marketing decisions. **(pp 392–398)**

Wholesaling includes all the activities involved in selling goods or services to those who are buying for the purpose of resale or for business use. Wholesalers fall into three groups. First, *merchant wholesalers* take possession of the goods. They include *full-service wholesalers* (wholesale merchants, industrial distributors) and *limited-service wholesalers* (cash-and-carry wholesalers, truck wholesalers, drop shippers, rack jobbers, producers' cooperatives, and mail-order wholesalers). Second, *brokers* and *agents* do not take possession of the goods but are paid a commission for aiding buying and selling. Finally, *manufacturers' sales branches and offices* are wholesaling operations conducted by nonwholesalers to bypass the wholesalers.

Like retailers, wholesalers must target carefully and position themselves strongly. And, like retailers, wholesalers must decide on product and service assortments, prices, promotion, and place. Progressive wholesalers constantly watch for better ways to meet the changing needs of their suppliers and target customers. They recognize that, in the long run, their only reason for existence comes from adding value by increasing the efficiency and effectiveness of the entire marketing channel. As with other types of marketers, the goal was to build value-adding customer relationships.

Navigating the Key Terms

Objective 1
Retailing (p 373)
Retailer (p 373)
Specialty store (p 374)
Department store (p 374)
Supermarket (p 375)
Convenience store (p 375)
Superstore (p 376)
Category killer (p 376)
Service retailer (p 376)
Discount store (p 376)

Off-price retailer (p 378)
Independent off-price retailer (p 378)
Factory outlet (p 378)
Warehouse club (p 379)
Chain stores (p 379)
Franchise (p 380)

Objective 2
Shopping center (p 386)

Objective 3
Wheel-of-retailing concept (p 387)

Objective 4
Wholesaling (p 392)
Wholesaler (p 392)
Merchant wholesaler (p 393)
Broker (p 393)
Agent (p 393)
Manufacturers' sales branches and offices (p 393)

Travel Log

Discussing the Issues

1. Discuss how retailers and wholesalers add value to the marketing system. Explain why marketers are embracing the concept of *shopper marketing*. (AACSB: Communication; Reflective Thinking)

2. Discuss factors used to classify retail establishments and list the types within each classification. (AACSB: Communication)

3. List and briefly discuss the trends impacting the future of retailing. (AACSB: Communication)

4. What is the wheel-of-retailing concept? Does it apply to online retailing? (AACSB: Communication; Reflective Thinking)

5. What is retail convergence? Has it helped or harmed small retailers? (AACSB: Communication; Reflective Thinking)

6. Explain how wholesalers add value in the channel of distribution. (AACSB: Communication)

Application Questions

1. The atmosphere in a retail store is carefully crafted to influence shoppers. Select a retailer that has both a physical store and an online store. Describe the elements of the physical store's atmosphere such as the colors, lighting, music, scents, and décor. What image is the store's atmosphere projecting? Is it appropriate given the merchandise assortment and target market of the store? Which elements of the physical store's atmosphere are part of the online store's atmosphere? Does the retailer integrate the physical store's atmosphere with its online presence? Explain. (AACSB: Communication; Use of IT; Reflective Thinking)

2. Deciding on a target market and positioning for a retail store are very important marketing decisions. In a small group, develop the concept for a new retail store. Who is the target market for your store? How is your store positioned? What retail atmospherics will enhance this positioning effectively to attract and satisfy your target market? (AACSB: Communication; Reflective Thinking)

3. Visit a local shopping center and classify each retail establishment in terms of the characteristics presented in this chapter. Next, use Table 11.1 to categorize each retailer. (AACSB: Communication; Reflective Thinking)

Under the Hood: Marketing Technology

Amazon.com revolutionized online retailing and reaps $19 billion in sales annually. It wasn't always that way, though. Founded as an online bookstore in 1994, the company did not even make a profit until 2001. Amazon.com's slow-growth strategy paid off. Many of the fast-growth dot-com retailers that rose to meteoric highs in the 1990s burned out just as quickly in the dot-com shakeout in 2000. But Amazon.com now boasts over 600 million visitors, has separate Web sites in several countries, is listed in the S&P 100 Index, and will move into a new 11-building headquarter campus in 2011. Amazon operates the Web sites of several other online retailers such as Sears, bebe Stores, Target, and Lacoste. Maybe you've sold or purchased something through its online marketspace, which hosted over 1.3 million sellers last year. Amazon was also a pioneer in online reviews from customers—allowing the bad with the good—to help shoppers in their purchase decision. Now, Amazon is venturing into private labels, with more than 1,000 products manufactured for sale only through its Web site, including a line of outdoor furniture named Strathwood and home products under the Pinzon name.

1. Search Amazon.com for outdoor furniture. Does Amazon's private label brand, Strathwood, show up on the results list? Do the same for kitchen chopping boards? Does the Pinzon-branded product show up in the results? How do the prices compare to other brands of these products? If you didn't know that these were Amazon's private label brands, could you tell from the Web site? Explain why or why not. (AACSB: Communication; Use of IT; Reflective Thinking)

2. Shop for a product of your choice on Amazon.com. Do the consumer reviews influence your perception of a product/brand offered? Many of the product reviews on Amazon.com are submitted by consumers participating in the Amazon Vine Program. Learn about this program and discuss whether or not a review from a consumer in this program is more useful than one from a consumer not in this program. (AACSB: Communication; Use of IT; Reflective Thinking)

Staying on the Road: Marketing Ethics

Purchase a television, computer, or other electronic device and you are bound to be asked whether you would like to purchase a service contract (or extended warranty). Most large electronics retailers carefully train their salespeople and cashiers to ask this important question. In fact, some retailers urge their salespeople to exert strong sales pressure to sell these contracts. It's no wonder, since service contracts provide extremely high profits for the retailers, several times the profit margins realized from the equipment you are purchasing. But do you know when to say "yes" and when to pass on a contract? Most consumers are confused and will buy the contract because the price seems low in comparison to the price of that new plasma television. Experts suggest that with product reliability and decreasing prices that make replacements more reasonable, such contracts are rarely worth the price. If most consumers do not need them, should retailers continue to offer and promote them?

1. Is it ethical for retailers to offer and strongly promote service contracts?

2. When should you purchase a service contract?

3. Why do retailers continue to offer these contracts, even under criticism from customer advocacy groups?

Rough Road Ahead: Marketing and the Economy

Abercrombie & Fitch

It's no mystery that in a recession, retail sales suffer in general. But since the economy started to slide, teen apparel chain Abercrombie & Fitch has posted some of the worst sales numbers in the entire retailing industry. The purveyor of $50 tank tops and $60 shorts has long nurtured a brand based on quality, aspiration, and in-store experience. As part of that image, it has steered clear of common apparel retailer sales promotions and price-discount strategies. Fearing that caving in to such tactics, even in a weak economy, would damage its premium image, it stuck to its guns on pricing. But as consumer purchases became increasingly driven by price, Abercrombie & Fitch sales plummeted—same-store revenues have fallen by as much as 34 percent. To make matters worse, Abercrombie & Fitch seems to have lost its innovative touch, now peddling goods that aren't notably different from those sold by competitors for lower prices. After almost a year of taking a beating at the registers, Abercrombie & Fitch finally seems to be relenting a bit, announcing that it will offer some more affordable merchandise. However, it remains to be seen just how widely and deeply the retailer will drop prices.

1. Is dropping prices to lure more frugal consumers the best response for Abercrombie & Fitch?

2. How might Abercrombie & Fitch best implement price reductions in a way that will maximize consumer response and minimize damage to the brand?

Travel Budget: Marketing by the Numbers

By breaking down a business into cost and profit centers, budget holders will be expected to effectively bid and argue the case for any capital expenditure that they wish to be allocated to their center. The business will always have a limited amount of funds available to purchase these types of assets and it needs to be assured that any investment in these assets will provide the greatest possible benefits and financial returns to the business. Some capital expenditure costs are unavoidable, perhaps when a fleet of vehicles needs to be replaced or, in order to expand, an adjacent property needs to be purchased.

Each expenditure item is analyzed within the context of the overall activities of the organization. They are assessed to see if they are central to the smooth running of the operation. Not only will the costs and benefits be measured, but also the potential consequences if the capital expenditure is not approved.

1. Why might it be unfair to allocate the full costs of overheads to particular cost and profit centers, purely based on the amount of space that they occupy or the number of employees in that center?

Drive In: Video Case

Zappos

These days, online retailers are a dime a dozen. But in less than 10 years, Zappos has become a billion dollar company. How did it hit the dot-com jackpot? By providing some of the best service available anywhere. Zappos customers are showered with such perks as free shipping both ways, surprise upgrades to overnight service, a 365-day return policy, and a call center that is always open. Customers are also delighted by employees who are empowered to spontaneously hand out rewards based on unique needs. It's no surprise that Zappos has an almost cult-like following of repeat customers.

After viewing the video featuring Zappos, answer the following questions.

1. How has Zappos differentiated itself from other retailers through each element of the retail marketing mix?

2. What is the relationship between how Zappos' treats its employees and how it treats its customers?

3. Why did Amazon buy Zappos, given that it already sells what Zappos sells?

12 Communicating
Customer Value Advertising
and Public Relations

ROAD MAP

Previewing the Concepts

We'll forge ahead now into the last of the marketing mix tools—promotion. Companies must do more than just create customer value. They must also use promotion to clearly and persuasively communicate that value. You'll find that promotion is not a single tool but rather a mix of several tools. Ideally, under the concept of *integrated marketing communications,* the company will carefully coordinate these promotion elements to deliver a clear, consistent, and compelling message about the organization and its products. We'll begin by introducing you to the various promotion mix tools. Next, we'll examine the rapidly changing communications environment and the need for integrated marketing communications. Finally, we'll look more closely at two of the promotion tools—advertising and public relations. In the next chapter, we'll visit two other promotion mix tools—sales promotion and personal selling. Then, in Chapter 14, we'll explore direct and online marketing.

Objective Outline

> **Objective 1**   Define the five promotion mix tools for communicating customer value.

> **Objective 2**   Discuss the changing communications landscape and the need for integrated marketing communications.

> **Objective 3**   Describe and discuss the major decisions involved in developing an advertising program.

> **Objective 4**   Explain how companies use public relations to communicate with their publics.

To start this chapter, let's look at one of the world's biggest marketers—Unilever—and at one of today's biggest marketing communication issues—the impact of the digital revolution on how marketers communicate with customers. More than most other companies, Unilever has mastered the digital marketing space. However, Unilever's marketers will tell you that they don't really do "digital campaigns" as such. Instead, they do *integrated* marketing communications campaigns that include digital.

▲ Suave's TV and other ads pull customers onto a nicely integrated Web site, which creates a "sisterhood" of moms and delivers the brand's "Say yes to beauty" positioning in more detail.

First Stop

Unilever: Crossing the Divide Between Digital and Traditional Media

These days, most advertisers are scrambling to make sense of the Web and other digital media, everything from Web sites and online social networks to Webisodes and viral video. The digital revolution has created a kind of "media divide," pitting traditional media such as television and magazines against the new-age digital media. Consumer goods giant Unilever, however, appears to have mastered the new digital space. In fact, Unilever was recently anointed Digital Marketer of the Year by *Advertising Age*.

But here's the funny thing about Unilever being Digital Marketer of the Year: The company doesn't really do "digital campaigns" as such. For Unilever, it's not an either-or proposition—either traditional media or digital media. Instead, Unilever has made Web and digital tactics just another important part of its mainstream marketing, seamlessly blending the old and the new into fully integrated communications campaigns.

Sure, Unilever does plenty of stand-out digital. It creates innovative Web sites for its bevy of familiar brands, ranging from Dove, Suave, Axe, Lever 2000, and Vaseline to Hellmann's, Knorr, Lipton, Ragú, Slim-Fast, Bertolli, Breyers, and Ben & Jerry's. And Unilever has made headlines for numerous Web and viral video successes. For example, its Dove brand won a cyber Grand Prix award at Cannes for its spectacularly successful "Evolution" viral video. And Suave developed a series of "In the Motherhood" Webisodes—the Web's version of TV soap operas—that drew more than 5.5 million viewers per episode.

It seems that every Unilever brand has something big going digitally. At one extreme, Axe launches an online hair "Crisis Relief Effort," stating that most women think that guys' hair just doesn't cut it and inviting viewers to create ads showing how Axe's new Hair Crisis products will give them "girl-approved hair." At the other extreme, comparatively stodgy Hellmann's produces an online "Real Food Summer School" program, which features recipes and cooking demos by celebrity chefs such as the Food Network's Bobby Flay. During its first season, about a million unique visitors clicked onto the Real Food site, and more than 5,000 visitors signed up to be a part of the Real Food online community. After Hellmann's aired the show, Web searches for "Hellmann's" and related words jumped 50 percent on Yahoo!

Although these and other Unilever digital efforts were highly successful in their own right, none were purely digital campaigns. Instead, each digital effort was carefully integrated with

> **Digital Marketer of the Year** Unilever has mastered the digital marketing space. However, Unilever's marketers will tell you that they don't really do "digital campaigns" as such. Instead, they do complete *integrated marketing communications campaigns.*

▲ One powerful result of Unilever's integration of digital with traditional media is "superdistribution." The spectacularly successful "Evolution" video cost $50,000 to make but created the equivalent of $200 million worth of free media coverage.

other media and marketing tactics, such as TV and print ads and broader public relations initiatives. "Digital is [not] done in isolation," says Rob Master, Unilever's North American media director. "It's part of a broader campaign. In many cases now it's the centerpiece of a broader campaign. I think that's become a real integral part of how we use the Web, moving beyond just promoting Web addresses in TV spots or print ads to really making them a critical part of the storytelling for the brands."

Unilever certainly has not abandoned traditional media in favor of digital—anything but. The world's number two advertiser (behind only Procter & Gamble) still devotes a sizable majority of its huge $5.3 billion global advertising and promotion spending to television and print media. But whereas Unilever is actually cutting back on traditional advertising, such as the 30-second spot, its overall promotion budget is increasing with most of the extra dollars pouring into online and digital. In recent years, spending on digital media has surged from 2 or 3 percent to 15 percent of Unilever's overall marketing budget.

The real secret behind Unilever's digital success is its skillful blending of new media with old to build and extend customer involvement and the brand experience. For example, Suave's "In the Motherhood" Webisodes were only a small part of a much larger integrated communications campaign for the brand. It started with television spots featuring real, funny, frenzied mothers sharing their experiences, including beauty experiences. "Is motherhood messing with your hair?" the commercials asked. "Say yes to beautiful without paying the price."

The TV ads pulled customers onto two related Web sites: www.Suave.com confirmed that "Motherhood Isn't Always Pretty" and let visitors dig more deeply into the lives and trials of mothers featured in the TV ads. And www.inthemotherhood.com presented entertaining and engaging Webisodes created "For Moms. By Moms. About Moms" based on true-life experiences of motherhood. Each site was loaded with links to other Suave-related content.

Public relations has also played a role in the Suave campaign. When "In the Motherhood" was just starting, clips or even whole 5-minute episodes aired on The Ellen DeGeneres Show, whose host called on moms to submit their real-life stories and to vote on the best entries. Thus, the entire Suave campaign—television, digital, and public relations—was all wonderfully integrated to create a "sisterhood" of moms and to deliver the brand's "Say yes to beauty" positioning. The Webisodes became so popular that—much to the dismay of many Web viewers—ABC picked up In the Motherhood as a network TV sitcom, ending the Web series.

The degree to which digital is integrated into the mainstream of Unilever's marketing is clear in how the efforts are managed. "We don't have a digital-media person in the media organization," Master says. "But all of us are very fluent in digital." Unlike many other advertisers today, Unilever doesn't hand its online promotional efforts off to digital shops. Instead, online efforts are handled by Unilever's mainstream advertising agencies, further helping to integrate digital with more traditional promotional tactics.

One powerful result of integrating digital with traditional media is what Unilever calls "superdistribution," the idea of getting Web programs, most often video, picked up by other media—most often for free. One of the best examples is Dove's "Evolution" video created as part of its "Real Beauty" campaign. "Evolution" shows an ordinary young woman being transformed into a beautiful poster model with a lot of help from a make-up artist and photo-editing software. The end line: "It's no wonder our perception of beauty is distorted." "Evolution" has racked up an impressive 20 million views on YouTube and other video sites. But throw in viewership via everything from TV news and talk shows to classrooms and general word-of-Web, and global viewership has exceeded *400* million. To put that in perspective, the video—which cost just $50,000 to make—has created the equivalent of $200 million worth of free media coverage.

But, again, this isn't just about "digital," it's about "communication," says Unilever's global communications planning director. "The right answer for any particular Unilever brand might not be digital. It could be placement in a film or on TV, or some form of content creation, a campaign site or a wiki." But "it so happens that so much of what consumers are doing now is in the digital space." Adds another Unilever marketer: "Our media landscape isn't changing—it's changed. We're in the new world, and there's a new marketing paradigm." Again, we're talking about *integrated* marketing communications.

In all, Unilever—Digital Marketer of the Year and all—understands that the growing shift to digital doesn't really change the fundamentals much. If anything, says Master, it means brand managers have to be more firmly grounded in what their brands are about in order to clearly and consistently define the brands across an exploding array of old and new media. But "almost inherent in what we do, I think, is the importance of storytelling for our brands," he says. "A 30-second ad is a story we pull together for consumers on TV. Digital is an extension of that storytelling in a typically longer format." The richness of the story and the resulting brand experience depend on everything communicating well together.[1]

uilding good customer relationships calls for more than just developing a good product, pricing it attractively, and making it available to target customers. Companies must also *communicate* their value propositions to customers, and what they communicate should not be left to chance. All of their communications must be planned and blended into carefully integrated marketing communications programs. Just as good communication is important in building and maintaining any kind of relationship, it is a crucial element in a company's efforts to build profitable customer relationships.

THE PROMOTION MIX (p 405)

A company's total **promotion mix**—also called its **marketing communications mix**—consists of the specific blend of advertising, public relations, personal selling, sales promotion, and direct-marketing tools that the company uses to persuasively communicate customer value and build customer relationships. Definitions of the five major promotion tools follow:[2]

- **Advertising**: Any paid form of nonpersonal presentation and promotion of ideas, goods, or services by an identified sponsor.
- **Sales promotion**: Short-term incentives to encourage the purchase or sale of a product or service.
- **Personal selling**: Personal presentation by the firm's sales force for the purpose of making sales and building customer relationships.
- **Public relations (PR)**: Building good relations with the company's various publics by obtaining favorable publicity, building up a good corporate image, and handling or heading off unfavorable rumors, stories, and events.
- **Direct marketing**: Direct connections with carefully targeted individual consumers to both obtain an immediate response and cultivate lasting customer relationships.

Each category involves specific promotional tools used to communicate with consumers. For example, advertising includes broadcast, print, Internet, outdoor, and other forms. Sales promotion includes discounts, coupons, displays, and demonstrations. Personal selling includes sales presentations, trade shows, and incentive programs. Public relations includes press releases, sponsorships, special events, and Web pages. And direct marketing includes catalogs, telephone marketing, kiosks, the Internet, mobile, and more.

At the same time, marketing communication goes beyond these specific promotion tools. The product's design, its price, the shape and color of its package, and the stores that sell it *all* communicate something to buyers. Thus, although the promotion mix is the company's primary communication activity, the entire marketing mix—promotion *and* product, price, and place—must be coordinated for greatest communication impact.

INTEGRATED MARKETING COMMUNICATIONS (pp 405–410)

In past decades, marketers perfected the art of mass marketing—selling highly standardized products to masses of customers. In the process, they developed effective mass-media communications techniques to support these strategies. Large companies now routinely invest millions or even billions of dollars in television, magazine, or other mass-media advertising, reaching tens of millions of customers with a single ad. Today, however, marketing managers face some new marketing communications realities. Perhaps no other area of marketing is changing so profoundly as marketing communications, creating both exciting and scary times for marketing communicators.

The New Marketing Communications Landscape

Several major factors are changing the face of today's marketing communications. First, *consumers* are changing. In this digital, wireless age, they are better informed and more communications empowered. Rather than relying on marketer-supplied

---

Author Comment >>
The promotion mix is the marketer's bag of tools for communicating with customers and other stakeholders. All of these tools must be carefully coordinated under the concept of *integrated marketing communications* in order to deliver a clear and compelling message.

Promotion mix (or marketing communications mix)
The specific blend of promotion tools that the company uses to persuasively communicate customer value and build customer relationships.

Advertising
Any paid form of nonpersonal presentation and promotion of ideas, goods, or services by an identified sponsor.

Sales promotion
Short-term incentives to encourage the purchase or sale of a product or service.

Personal selling
Personal presentation by the firm's sales force for the purpose of making sales and building customer relationships.

Public relations (PR)
Building good relations with the company's various publics by obtaining favorable publicity, building up a good corporate image, and handling or heading off unfavorable rumors, stories, and events.

Direct marketing
Direct connections with carefully targeted individual consumers to both obtain an immediate response and cultivate lasting customer relationships.

Author Comment >>
This is a really hot marketing topic these days. Perhaps no other area of marketing is changing so profoundly as marketing communications.

information, they can use the Internet and other technologies to seek out information on their own. More than that, they can more easily connect with other consumers to exchange brand-related information or even to create their own marketing messages.

Second, *marketing strategies* are changing. As mass markets have fragmented, marketers are shifting away from mass marketing. More and more, they are developing focused marketing programs designed to build closer relationships with customers in more narrowly defined micromarkets. Vast improvements in information technology are speeding the movement toward segmented marketing. Today's marketers can amass detailed customer information, keep closer track of customer needs, and tailor their offerings to narrowly defined target groups.

Finally, sweeping changes in *communications technology* are causing remarkable changes in the ways in which companies and customers communicate with each other. The digital age has spawned a host of new information and communication tools—from smart phones and iPods to satellite and cable television systems to the many faces of the Internet (e-mail, social networks, brand Web sites, and so much more). The new communications technologies give companies exciting new media for interacting with targeted consumers. At the same time, they give consumers more control over the nature and timing of messages they choose to send and receive.

The Shifting Marketing Communications Model

The explosive developments in communications technology and changes in marketer and customer communication strategies have had a dramatic impact on marketing communications. Just as mass marketing once gave rise to a new generation of mass-media communications, the new digital media have given birth to a new marketing communications model.

▼The shifting communications model: Although television, magazines, and other mass media remain very important, their dominance is declining. Some advertising industry experts even predict a "chaos scenario," in which the old traditional mass-media model will collapse entirely.

▲Although television, magazines, newspapers, and other mass media remain very important, their dominance is declining. In their place, advertisers are now adding a broad selection of more-specialized and highly targeted media to reach smaller customer segments with more-personalized, interactive messages. The new media range from specialty cable television channels and made-for-the-Web videos to Internet catalogs, e-mail, blogs, cell phone content, and online social networks. In all, companies are doing less *broadcasting* and more *narrowcasting*.

Some advertising industry experts even predict a doom-and-gloom "chaos scenario," in which the old mass-media communications model will collapse entirely. They note that mass media costs are rising, audiences are shrinking, ad clutter is increasing, and viewers are gaining control of message exposure through technologies such as digital video recorders (DVRs) that let them skip past disruptive television commercials. As a result, marketers are rushing to abandon traditional media in favor of new digital technologies. Many skeptics even predict the demise of the old mass-media mainstays—30-second television commercials and glossy magazine advertisements.[3]

In the new marketing communications world, rather than the old approaches that interrupt customers and force-feed them mass messages, the new technologies will let marketers reach smaller groups of consumers in more interactive, engaging ways. For example, just think about what's happening to television viewing these days. Consumers can now watch their favorite programs on just about anything with a screen—on TV but also on laptops, cell phones, or iPods. And they can choose to watch programs whenever and wherever they wish, often with or without commercials.

Moreover, increasingly, some "TV" programs and videos are being produced just for Internet viewing.

Thus, like Unilever in our chapter-opening story, many large advertisers are now shifting their advertising budgets away from network television in favor of more targeted, cost-effective, interactive, and engaging media—especially digital media.

Rather than a "chaos scenario," however, other industry insiders see a more gradual shift to the new marketing communications model. They note that broadcast television and other mass media still capture a lion's share of the promotion budgets of most major marketing firms, a fact that isn't likely to change quickly. For example, Procter & Gamble, a leading proponent of digital media, still spends a lion's share of its huge advertising budget on mass media. Although P&G's digital outlay more than doubled last year, digital still accounts for only about 5 percent of the company's total advertising spending.[4]

At a broader level, although some may question the future of the 30-second spot, it's still very much in use today. Last year, more than 43 percent of U.S. advertising dollars were spent on national and local television commercials versus 7.6 percent on Internet advertising. "So if you think that TV is an aging dinosaur," says one media expert, "maybe you should think again." Another expert agrees: "Does TV work? Of course it does. It's just not the only game in town anymore."[5]

Thus, it seems likely that the new marketing communications model will consist of a shifting mix of both traditional mass media and a wide array of exciting, new, more-targeted, more-personalized media. The challenge for traditional advertisers is to bridge the "media divide" that too often separates traditional approaches from new interactive and digital ones. Many traditional advertising agencies are struggling with this transition, creating a niche in the market for agencies like Ogilvy & Mather who specialize in new media advertising. Though not yet a household name, Ogilvy & Mather boast a range of high profile clients, including Kodak, Yahoo! and IBM (see Marketing at Work 12.1).

In the end, however, regardless of whether it's traditional or digital, the key is to find the mix of media that best communicates the brand message and enhances the customer's brand experience. Says one analyst, "advertisers need to look at old media and new media as just plain media." Says another "The whole landscape has changed. . . . Marketers have to be savvy enough [to understand] what to do with all this stuff."[6]

The Need for *Integrated* Marketing Communications

The shift toward a richer mix of media and communication approaches poses a problem for marketers. Consumers today are bombarded by commercial messages from a broad range of sources. But consumers don't distinguish between message sources the way marketers do. In the consumer's mind, messages from different media and promotional approaches all become part of a single message about the company. Conflicting messages from these different sources can result in confused company images, brand positions, and customer relationships.

All too often, companies fail to integrate their various communications channels. The result is a hodgepodge of communications to consumers. Mass-media advertisements say one thing, while a price promotion sends a different signal, and a product label creates still another message. Company sales literature says something altogether different and the company's Web site seems out of sync with everything else.

The problem is that these communications often come from different parts of the company. Advertising messages are planned and implemented by the advertising department or an advertising agency. Personal selling communications are developed by sales management. Other company specialists are responsible for public relations, sales promotion events, Internet marketing, and other forms of marketing communications. However, whereas these companies have separated their communications

Marketing at Work 12.1

Staying Relevant in a Shifting Advertising Universe: The Old Versus the New

At the mention of Facebook and iPhone, we instantly recognize how the digital age has changed our world completely. Consumers now own multiple devices that they use to communicate with each other, devour content, listen to music, and play games. In particular, today's consumers are embracing new media unabashedly, with a voracious appetite for new content, new gadgets and social networking. Social networking has proliferated at a pace that is unheard of. By the end of 2008 in Asia, Facebook experienced 458 percent growth within the year, led by Taiwan, Malaysia, Singapore, and Hong Kong. In Taiwan alone, Facebook grew 335 percent. In China, more than 100 million Chinese use forums and discussion boards and 41 million are heavy social-media contributors.

A study conducted by Cone's "2009 Cone Consumer New Media Study" revealed that 53 percent of new media users believe that brands should have a presence in new media, interacting with consumers as needed or by request only, while a further 36 percent demand a new media presence with regular interaction. Although brands keep contact with consumers using traditional online and newer channels, 7 in 10 respondents state that they have stronger connections, a more positive impression of, and a greater willingness to engage with, the company if the brand engages them by using new media.

As a sign of the times, luxury brand owners are also beginning to explore digital opportunities. While they still use traditional channels to reach their customers, luxury brands recognize that customers are increasingly using the Internet to help them with purchase decisions. Social media sites that target affluent consumers such as "A Small World" are seeing increasing membership, and luxury brands are experimenting with such similar sites to advertise.

The media is so fragmented and suddenly blogs, social media sites, instant messaging, and search portals are now becoming the new mainstream media. Naturally, in response to this interac-

▲ Social networking sites such as Facebook have transformed the way we communicate with consumers. To keep up the pace, advertising agencies must ride the digital wave and move towards more sophisticated, targeted new media campaigns.

tive and digital phenomenon, the number of interactive and digital agencies have exploded to meet the growth in demand for solutions that will help companies interact with their consumers using new media. With the proliferation of both traditional and new media, identifying the right media to advertise in is increasingly difficult for companies. What happens to traditional media companies who now have to grapple with this change in the way companies communicate with their customers?

Media experts acknowledge the fragmentation of media and the need for traditional agencies to keep up with the pace of change. In response to this paradigm shift, traditional advertising agencies are fast acquiring interactive and digital boutique agencies and going through a time of renewal within their agencies or risk facing the music.

These agencies that have been quick to ride the new digital wave are reaping the rewards. In 2005 Ogilvy & Mather (O&M) launched OgilvyInteractive, a division of OgilvyOne Worldwide.

Integrated marketing communications (IMC)
Carefully integrating and coordinating the company's many communications channels to deliver a clear, consistent, and compelling message about the organization and its products.

tools, customers won't. Mixed communications from these sources will result in blurred consumer brand perceptions.

Today, more companies are adopting the concept of **integrated marketing communications (IMC)**. Under this concept, as illustrated in ■ **Figure 12.1**, the company carefully integrates its many communications channels to deliver a clear, consistent, and compelling message about the organization and its brands.

Integrated marketing communications calls for recognizing all touch points where the customer may encounter the company and its brands. Each *brand contact* will deliver a message, whether good, bad, or indifferent. The company wants to deliver a consistent and positive message with each contact. Integrated marketing communications leads to a total marketing communication strategy aimed at building strong customer relationships by showing how the company and its products can help customers solve their problems.

Integrated marketing communications ties together all of the company's messages and images. The company's television and print advertisements have the same message, look, and feel as its e-mail and personal selling communications. And its public relations materials project the same image as its Web site or social network presence. Often,

Since then, they launched Neo@Ogilvy in 2006, a full-service digital and direct media agency with more than 650 specialists in 39 offices across 32 countries providing a full range of digital and direct media strategy, planning and buying, direct print and TV, e-mail marketing, search marketing, mobile marketing, analytics, and emerging platform services. The agency manages digital media investments for blue-chip clients such as IBM, American Express, Cisco, TD Ameritrade, Kodak, Yahoo!, and others. In July 2009, IBM and Neo@Ogilvy received top honors in the annual Vibrant Awards, recognizing the best in in-text advertising in the United States and Europe.

In August 2009, OgilvyInteractive was cited as a leader in interactive marketing by Forrester Research, Inc. in its independent report, "The Forrester Wave™: US Interactive Agencies—Strategy and Execution," Q3 2009. Its public relations arm, Ogilvy Public Relations, has a division that focuses on public relations in the new media. Ogilvy 360 Degree Digital Influence Practice is O&M's global social media marketing using word of mouth and digital marketing to deliver measurable results to its clients. Some of its clients include Unilever, Intel, Lenovo, Nestle, Ford, and Louis Vuitton.

How did a mammoth of a traditional advertising agency survive this digital phenomenon that has left many trying to keep up to pace? Today it is still one of the top creative agencies in the world, and it has an interactive arm that calls itself the leader in interactive marketing. The O&M Worldwide network includes a collaboration of nine companies, O&M, OgilvyOne Worldwide, OgilvyInteractive, Neo@Ogilvy, OgilvyHealthworld, OgilvyAction, Ogilvy Public Relations, RedWorks, and OgilvyEntertainment. Together, this network of companies offers an integration of services providing the client with a myriad of services that covers all areas of communication with the customer. To further boost the quality of its services to clients, O&M announced in October 2009 that MarketShare Partners, a leading strategic marketing analytics firm, has become O&M's strategic partner for marketing effectiveness solutions and will provide clients with an objective way of allocating their marketing budgets across geographies, segments, marketing tasks, and media.

Ogilvy & Mather subscribes to the twin-rule of "engagement" and "integration." The company believes that advertising is about brands and ideas that make connections and delight consumers. Despite the popularity of social media, one thing remains: Consumers are quick to sense insincerity and new media gurus are quick to add that consumers expect open, honest, collaborative relationships with companies. Advertising on the Internet using banner ads on a site may not be the answer to maximizing the value of having a brand online. Rather, the future of advertising within social media is about creating relationships and connections, much more so than measuring the number of clicks.

Undeniably the Internet has changed the way we communicate with consumers, while some traditional advertising agencies struggle to keep pace with the changing landscape and others have led the pack and successfully integrated the old and the new.

Sources: Based on information from Cover Story: "I Can't See You On Facebook," July 2009, accessed at www.Marketing-Interactive.com; "How Unilever Is Dipping Into Social Media in Asia," posted by Normandy Madden, October 29, 2009, accessed at http://adage.com/globalnews/article?article_id=140028; "Consumers Demand Brand Interaction," October 29, 2009, accessed at www.emarketer.com/Article.aspx?R=1007356; "Well-heeled but Wobbly," July 2009, accessed at www.Marketing-Interactive.com; Patel, K., "Online Ads Not Working for You? Blame the Creative," October 20, 2009, accessed at http"//adage.com/digital/article?article_id=139795; Helm, B., "Struggles of a Mad Man," *Businessweek*, accessed at www.businessweek.com/magazine/content/07_49/b4061044416861.htm; "It's All About Delighting Consumers," October 2009, accessed at www.Marketing-Interactive.com; Study: "College Students: Connecting With the Connected Crowd," accessed at www.emarketer.com/Reports/All/ Emarketer_2000594.aspx; and Ogilvy & Mather website at www.ogilvy.com.

■ **Figure 12.1** Integrated Marketing Communications

▲Integrated marketing communications: Burger King's richly integrated, multipronged Whopper Freakout campaign, which employed a carefully coordinated mix, everything from TV and radio ads to rich media ad banners, YouTube videos, and a Freakout Web site, boosted store traffic and Whopper sales by 29 percent.

different media play unique roles in attracting, informing, and persuading consumers, and these roles must be carefully coordinated under the overall marketing communications plan.

A great example of the power of a well-integrated marketing communications effort is ▲Burger King's now-classic Whopper Freakout campaign:[7]

> To celebrate the 50th anniversary of the iconic Whopper, Burger King launched a campaign to show what would happen if it suddenly removed the sandwich from its menu "forever." It dropped the Whopper in selected restaurants and used hidden cameras to capture the real-time reactions of stricken customers. It then shared the results in a carefully integrated, multipronged promotional campaign. The campaign began with coordinated TV, print, and radio spots announcing that "We stopped selling the Whopper for one day to see what would happen. . . . What happened was, people freaked!" The ads drove consumers to *www.whopperfreakout.com*, which featured a video documentary outlining the entire experiment. The documentary was also uploaded to YouTube. At the Web site, visitors could view Freakout ads showing the disbelieving, often angry reactions of a dozen or more customers. Burger King also promoted the campaign through rich media ad banners on several other popular Web sites. Customers themselves extended the campaign with spoofs and parodies posted on YouTube. The richly integrated Whopper Freakout campaign was a smashing success. The ads became the most recalled campaign in Burger King's history, and the whopperfreakout.com Web site received 4 million views in only the first three months. In all, the IMC campaign drove store traffic and sales of the Whopper up a whopping 29 percent.

In the past, no one person or department was responsible for thinking through the communication roles of the various promotion tools and coordinating the promotion mix. To help implement integrated marketing communications, some companies appoint a marketing communications director who has overall responsibility for the company's communications efforts. This helps to produce better communications consistency and greater sales impact. It places the responsibility in someone's hands—where none existed before—to unify the company's image as it is shaped by thousands of company activities.

SHAPING THE OVERALL PROMOTION MIX (pp 410–413)

The concept of integrated marketing communications suggests that the company must blend the promotion tools carefully into a coordinated *promotion mix*. But how does the company determine what mix of promotion tools it will use? Companies within the same industry differ greatly in the design of their promotion mixes. For example, Mary Kay spends most of its promotion funds on personal selling and direct marketing, whereas competitor CoverGirl spends heavily on consumer advertising. We now look at factors that influence the marketer's choice of promotion tools.

The Nature of Each Promotion Tool

Each promotion tool has unique characteristics and costs. Marketers must understand these characteristics in shaping the promotion mix.

Advertising

Advertising can reach masses of geographically dispersed buyers at a low cost per exposure, and it enables the seller to repeat a message many times. For example, television advertising can reach huge audiences. An estimated 99 million Americans tuned in to watch the most recent Super Bowl, about 36 million people watched at least part of the last Academy Awards broadcast, 30 million fans tuned in to watch the debut episode of the eighth season of *American Idol*. For companies that want to reach a mass audience, TV is the place to be.[8]

Beyond its reach, large-scale advertising says something positive about the seller's size, popularity, and success. Because of advertising's public nature, consumers tend to view advertised products as more legitimate. Advertising is also very expressive—it allows the company to dramatize its products through the artful use of visuals, print, sound, and color. On the one hand, advertising can be used to build up a long-term image for a product (such as Coca-Cola ads). On the other hand, advertising can trigger quick sales (as when Kohl's advertises weekend specials).

Advertising also has some shortcomings. Although it reaches many people quickly, advertising is impersonal and cannot be as directly persuasive as can company salespeople. For the most part, advertising can carry on only a one-way communication with the audience, and the audience does not feel that it has to pay attention or respond. In addition, advertising can be very costly. Although some advertising forms, such as newspaper and radio advertising, can be done on smaller budgets, other forms, such as network TV advertising, require very large budgets.

Personal Selling

Personal selling is the most effective tool at certain stages of the buying process, particularly in building up buyers' preferences, convictions, and actions. It involves personal interaction between two or more people, so each person can observe the other's needs and characteristics and make quick adjustments. Personal selling also allows all kinds of customer relationships to spring up, ranging from matter-of-fact selling relationships to personal friendships. An effective salesperson keeps the customer's interests at heart in order to build a long-term relationship by solving customer problems. ▲Finally, with personal selling, the buyer usually feels a greater need to listen and respond, even if the response is a polite "No thank you."

These unique qualities come at a cost, however. A sales force requires a longer-term commitment than does advertising—advertising can be turned up or down, but sales force size is harder to change. Personal selling is also the company's most expensive promotion tool, costing companies as much as $452 on average per sales call, depending on the industry.[9] U.S. firms spend up to three times as much on personal selling as they do on advertising.

Sales Promotion

Sales promotion includes a wide assortment of tools—coupons, contests, cents-off deals, premiums, and others—all of which have many unique qualities. They attract consumer attention, offer strong incentives to purchase, and can be used to dramatize product offers and to boost sagging sales. Sales promotions invite and reward quick response—whereas advertising says, "Buy our product," sales promotion says, "Buy it now." Sales promotion effects are often short-lived, however, and often are not as effective as advertising or personal selling in building long-run brand preference and customer relationships.

Public Relations

Public relations (PR) is very believable—news stories, features, sponsorships, and events seem more real and believable to readers than ads do. Public relations can also reach many prospects who avoid salespeople and advertisements—the message gets to the buyers as "news" rather than as a sales-directed communication. And, as

■ **Figure 12.3** Major Advertising
Decisions

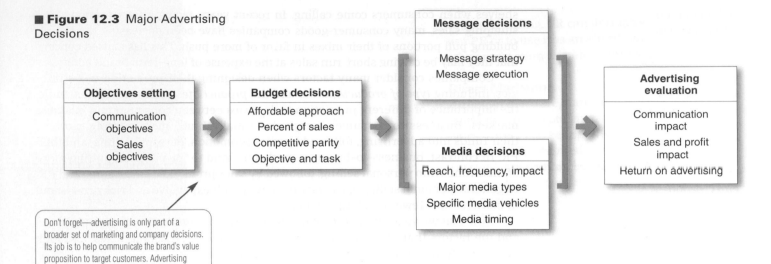

Don't forget—advertising is only part of a
broader set of marketing and company decisions.
Its job is to help communicate the brand's value
proposition to target customers. Advertising
must blend well with other promotion and
marketing mix decisions.

advertising budget, developing advertising strategy (*message decisions* and *media decisions*), and *evaluating advertising campaigns*.

Setting Advertising Objectives

The first step is to set *advertising objectives*. These objectives should be based on past decisions about the target market, positioning, and the marketing mix, which define the job that advertising must do in the total marketing program. The overall advertising objective is to help build customer relationships by communicating customer value. Here, we discuss specific advertising objectives.

Advertising objective
A specific communication *task* to be accomplished with a specific *target* audience during a specific period of *time*. The overall advertising goal is to help build customer relationships by communicating customer value.

An **advertising objective** is a specific communication *task* to be accomplished with a specific *target* audience during a specific period of *time*. Advertising objectives can be classified by primary purpose—whether the aim is to *inform, persuade*, or *remind*. ■ **Table 12.1** lists examples of each of these specific objectives.

Informative advertising is used heavily when introducing a new product category. In this case, the objective is to build primary demand. Thus, early producers of DVD players first had to inform consumers of the image quality and convenience benefits of the new product. *Persuasive advertising* becomes more important as competition increases. Here, the company's objective is to build selective demand. For example, once DVD players became established, Sony began trying to persuade consumers that *its* brand offered the best quality for their money.

Some persuasive advertising has become *comparative advertising* (or *attack advertising*), in which a company directly or indirectly compares its brand with one or more other brands. You see examples of comparative advertising in almost every product category, ranging from sports drinks, coffee, and soup to computers, car rentals, and credit cards. For example, Gatorade recently ran ads comparing the 25 calories in its Propel fitness beverage to the 125 calories found in Glacéau's Vitaminwater, asking "How Fit Is Your Water?" ▲And Dunkin' Donuts ran a TV and Web campaign comparing the chain's coffee to Starbuck's brews. "In a recent national blind taste test," proclaimed the ads, "more Americans preferred the taste of Dunkin' Donuts coffee over Starbucks. It's just more proof it's all about the coffee (not the couches or music)."

Advertisers should use comparative advertising with caution. All too often, such ads invite competitor responses, resulting in an advertising war that neither competitor can win. Or upset competitors might take

▼**Comparative advertising: Dunkin' Donuts ran a TV and Web campaign comparing the chain's coffee to Starbucks brews. "Dunkin' beat Starbucks," says this ad. "It's all about the coffee (not the couches or music)."**

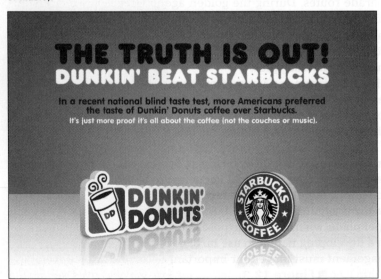

■ **Table 12.1** Possible Advertising Objectives

Informative Advertising	
Communicating customer value	Suggesting new uses for a product
Building a brand and company image	Informing the market of a price change
Telling the market about a new product	Describing available services and support
Explaining how a product works	Correcting false impressions

Persuasive Advertising	
Building brand preference	Persuading customers to purchase now
Encouraging switching to a brand	Persuading customers to receive a sales call
Changing customer's perception of product value	Convincing customers to tell others about the brand

Reminder Advertising	
Maintaining customer relationships	Reminding consumers where to buy the product
Reminding consumers that the product may be needed in the near future	Keeping the brand in customer's mind during off-seasons

more drastic action. For example, Sara Lee recently sued Kraft over ad claims that taste tests showed that Kraft's Oscar Meyer brand hot dogs taste better than Sara Lee's Ball Park Franks. Similarly, PepsiCo sued Coca-Cola, asserting that ads for Coca-Cola's Powerade sports drink made inaccurate claims that Powerade was more "complete" than PepsiCo's Gatorade.[11]

Reminder advertising is important for mature products—it helps to maintain customer relationships and keep consumers thinking about the product. Expensive Coca-Cola television ads primarily build and maintain the Coca-Cola brand relationship rather than inform or persuade customers to buy in the short run.

Advertising's goal is to help move consumers through the buying process. Some advertising is designed to move people to immediate action. For example, a direct-response television ad by Weight Watchers urges consumers to pick up the phone and sign up right away, and a Best Buy newspaper insert for a weekend sale encourages immediate store visits. However, many of the other ads focus on building or strengthening long-term customer relationships. For example, a Nike television ad in which well-known athletes working through extreme challenges in their Nike gear never directly asks for a sale. Instead, the goal is to somehow change the way the customers think or feel about the brand.

Setting the Advertising Budget

Advertising budget
The dollars and other resources allocated to a product or company advertising program.

After determining its advertising objectives, the company next sets its **advertising budget** for each product. Here, we look at four common methods used to set the total budget for advertising: the *affordable method*, the *percentage-of-sales method*, the *competitive-parity method*, and the *objective-and-task method*.[12]

Affordable Method

Affordable method
Setting the promotion budget at the level management thinks the company can afford.

Some companies use the **affordable method**: They set the promotion budget at the level they think the company can afford. Small businesses often use this method, reasoning that the company cannot spend more on advertising than it has. They start with total revenues, deduct operating expenses and capital outlays, and then devote some portion of the remaining funds to advertising.

Unfortunately, this method of setting budgets completely ignores the effects of promotion on sales. It tends to place promotion last among spending priorities, even in situations in which advertising is critical to the firm's success. It leads to an uncertain annual promotion budget, which makes long-range market planning difficult. Although the affordable method can result in overspending on advertising, it more often results in underspending.

Percentage-of-Sales Method

Percentage-of-sales method
Setting the promotion budget at a certain percentage of current or forecasted sales or as a percentage of the unit sales price.

Other companies use the **percentage-of-sales method**, setting their promotion budget at a certain percentage of current or forecasted sales. Or they budget a percentage of the unit sales price. The percentage-of-sales method has advantages. It is simple to use and helps management think about the relationships between promotion spending, selling price, and profit per unit.

Despite these claimed advantages, however, the percentage-of-sales method has little to justify it. It wrongly views sales as the *cause* of promotion rather than as the *result*. Although studies have found a positive correlation between promotional spending and brand strength, this relationship often turns out to be effect and cause, not cause and effect. Stronger brands with higher sales can afford the biggest ad budgets.

Thus, the percentage-of-sales budget is based on availability of funds rather than on opportunities. It may prevent the increased spending sometimes needed to turn around falling sales. Because the budget varies with year-to-year sales, long-range planning is difficult. Finally, the method does not provide any basis for choosing a *specific* percentage, except what has been done in the past or what competitors are doing.

Competitive-Parity Method

Competitive-parity method
Setting the promotion budget to match competitors' outlays.

Still other companies use the **competitive-parity method**, setting their promotion budgets to match competitors' outlays. They monitor competitors' advertising or get industry promotion spending estimates from publications or trade associations, and then set their budgets based on the industry average.

Two arguments support this method. First, competitors' budgets represent the collective wisdom of the industry. Second, spending what competitors spend helps prevent promotion wars. Unfortunately, neither argument is valid. There are no grounds for believing that the competition has a better idea of what a company should be spending on promotion than does the company itself. Companies differ greatly, and each has its own special promotion needs. Finally, there is no evidence that budgets based on competitive parity prevent promotion wars.

Objective-and-Task Method

Objective-and-task method
Developing the promotion budget by (1) defining specific objectives, (2) determining the tasks that must be performed to achieve these objectives, and (3) estimating the costs of performing these tasks. The sum of these costs is the proposed promotion budget.

The most logical budget-setting method is the **objective-and-task method**, whereby the company sets its promotion budget based on what it wants to accomplish with promotion. This budgeting method entails (1) defining specific promotion objectives, (2) determining the tasks needed to achieve these objectives, and (3) estimating the costs of performing these tasks. The sum of these costs is the proposed promotion budget.

The advantage of the objective-and-task method is that it forces management to spell out its assumptions about the relationship between dollars spent and promotion results. But it is also the most difficult method to use. Often, it is hard to figure out which specific tasks will achieve stated objectives. For example, suppose Sony wants 95 percent awareness for its latest Blu-ray player during the six-month introductory period. What specific advertising messages and media schedules should Sony use to attain this objective? How much would these messages and media schedules cost? Sony management must consider such questions, even though they are hard to answer.

No matter what method is used, setting the advertising budget is no easy task. John Wanamaker, the department store magnate, once said, "I know that half of my advertising is wasted, but I don't know which half. I spent $2 million for advertising, and I don't know if that is half enough or twice too much."

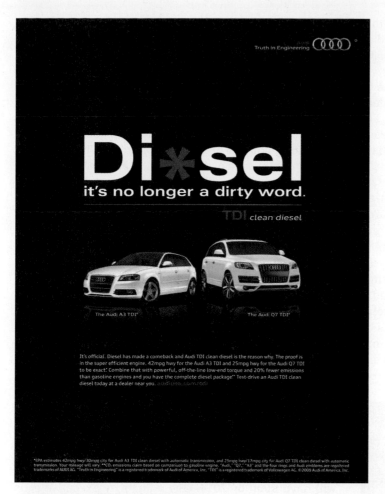

As a result of such thinking, advertising is one of the easiest budget items to cut when economic times get tough. Cuts in brand-building advertising appear to do little short-term harm to sales. For example, in the wake of the recent recession, U.S. advertising expenditures plummeted 12 percent over the previous year. In the long run, however, slashing ad spending risks long-term damage to a brand's image and market share. In fact, companies that can maintain or even increase their advertising spending while competitors are decreasing theirs can gain competitive advantage. ▲Consider car maker Audi:[13]

Although Audi's U.S. sales slipped last year, they fell far less than those of competitors amid a calamitous year for the auto industry. What's more, Audi's brand awareness and buyer consideration reached record levels by the end of the year, with gains outstripping those of BMW, Mercedes, and Lexus. In short: Audi might be the hottest auto brand on the market right now. And it's strongly positioned for the future when the economy recovers. What's Audi's advantage? The brand is spending heavily on advertising and marketing at a time when rivals are retrenching. During the past two years, despite the harsh economy, Audi has increased its ad prescence, including high-profile placements such as the last two Super Bowls, the Academy Awards, the NCAA basketball tournament, and Sunday Night Football. Audi "has kept its foot on the pedal while everyone else is pulling back," says an Audi ad executive. "Why would we go backwards now when the industry is generally locking the brakes and cutting spending?" adds Audi's chief marketing executive. The acceleration has paid off. "In a world of bad news and fear, confidence is contagious," says an industry consultant.

▲ Setting the promotion budget: Promotion spending is one of the easiest items to cut when in tough economic times. But Audi has gained competitive advantage by keeping its foot on the promotion pedal as competitors have retrenched.

Advertising strategy
The strategy by which the company accomplishes its advertising objectives. It consists of two major elements: creating advertising messages and selecting advertising media.

Developing Advertising Strategy

Advertising strategy consists of two major elements: creating advertising *messages* and selecting advertising *media*. In the past, companies often viewed media planning as secondary to the message-creation process. The creative department first created good advertisements, and then the media department selected and purchased the best media for carrying these advertisements to desired target audiences. This often caused friction between creatives and media planners.

Today, however, soaring media costs, more-focused target marketing strategies, and the blizzard of new media have promoted the importance of the media-planning function. The decision about which media to use for an ad campaign—television, magazines, cell phones, a Web site, or e-mail—is now sometimes more critical than the creative elements of the campaign. As a result, more and more, advertisers are orchestrating a closer harmony between their messages and the media that deliver them. In fact, in a really good ad campaign, you often have to ask "Is that a media idea or a creative idea?"[14]

Creating the Advertising Message

No matter how big the budget, advertising can succeed only if advertisements gain attention and communicate well. Good advertising messages are especially important in today's costly and cluttered advertising environment. In 1950, the average U.S. household received just three network television channels and a handful of major national magazines. Today, the average household receives more than 118 channels, and consumers have more than 22,600 magazines from which to choose.[15] Add the countless radio stations and a continuous barrage of catalogs, direct mail, e-mail and online ads, and out-of-home media, and consumers are being bombarded with ads at home, at work, and at all points in between. As a result, consumers are exposed to as many as 3,000 to 5,000 commercial messages every day.[16]

Breaking Through the Clutter. If all this advertising clutter bothers some consumers, it also causes huge headaches for advertisers. Take the situation facing network television advertisers. They pay an average of $381,000 to make a single 30-second commercial. Then, each time they show it, they regularly pay $250,000 or more for 30 seconds of advertising time during a popular prime-time program. They pay even more if it's an especially popular program such as *Sunday Night Football* ($435,000), *Grey's Anatomy* ($327,000), *The Family Guy* ($322,000), *American Idol* (up to $700,000), or a mega-event such as the Super Bowl ($3 million per 30 seconds!).[17]

Then, their ads are sandwiched in with a clutter of other commercials, announcements, and network promotions, totaling nearly 20 minutes of nonprogram material per prime-time hour with commercial breaks coming every 6 minutes on average. Such clutter in television and other ad media has created an increasingly hostile advertising environment. According to recent studies, 63 percent of Americans believe there are too many ads, and 47 percent say ads spoil their viewing enjoyment.[18]

Until recently, television viewers were pretty much a captive audience for advertisers. But today's digital wizardry has given consumers a rich new set of information and entertainment choices. With the growth in cable and satellite TV, the Internet, video on demand (VOD), video downloads, and DVD rentals, today's viewers have many more options.

▲ Digital technology has also armed consumers with an arsenal of weapons for choosing what they watch or don't watch. Increasingly, thanks to the growth of DVR (digital video recorder) systems, consumers are choosing *not* to watch ads. More than 26 percent of American TV households now have DVRs, and an estimated 44 percent will have them by 2014. One ad agency executive calls these DVR systems "electronic weedwhackers." Research shows that 85 percent of DVR owners skip at least three-quarters of all ads. In one study, about 20 percent of brands experienced lower sales in ad-skipping households. At the same time, the number of VOD viewers is expected to quadruple during the next five years. These viewers will be able to watch programming on their own time terms, with or without commercials.[19]

Thus, advertisers can no longer force-feed the same old cookie-cutter ad messages to captive consumers through traditional media. Just to gain and hold attention, today's advertising messages must be better planned, more imaginative, more entertaining, and more emotionally engaging. "Interruption or disruption as the fundamental premise of marketing" no longer works, says one advertising executive. Instead, "you have to create content that is interesting, useful, or entertaining enough to invite [consumers]." According to another, "Everything is about control. If an ad is interesting to you, you'll have a conversation with the brand. If it's not, it's a waste of time."[20]

▲ **Advertising clutter:** Today's consumers, armed with an arsenal of weapons, can choose what they watch and don't watch. Advertising messages must be better planned, more imaginative, more entertaining, and more rewarding to consumers.

Madison & Vine
A term that has come to represent the merging of advertising and entertainment in an effort to break through the clutter and create new avenues for reaching consumers with more engaging messages.

Merging Advertising and Entertainment. To break through the clutter, many marketers are now subscribing to a new merging of advertising and entertainment, dubbed "**Madison & Vine.**" You've probably heard of Madison Avenue. It's the New York City street that houses the headquarters of many of the nation's largest advertising agencies. You may also have heard of Hollywood & Vine, the intersection of Hollywood Avenue and Vine Street in Hollywood, California, long the symbolic heart of the U.S. entertainment industry. Now, Madison Avenue and Hollywood & Vine are coming together to form a new intersection—*Madison & Vine*—that represents the merging of advertising and entertainment in an effort to create new avenues for reaching consumers with more engaging messages.

This merging of advertising and entertainment takes one of two forms: advertainment or branded entertainment. The aim of *advertainment* is to make ads themselves so entertaining, or so useful, that people *want* to watch them. There's no chance that you'd watch ads on purpose, you say? Think again. For example, the Super Bowl has become an annual advertainment showcase. Tens of millions of people tune in to the Super Bowl each year, as much to watch the entertaining ads as to see the game.

In fact, DVR systems can actually *improve* viewership of a really good ad. For example, most Super Bowl ads last year were viewed more in DVR households than non-DVR households. Rather than zipping past the ads, many people were skipping back to watch them again and again. Remember the E-Trade ad with the talking babies? Or how about the Doritos ad in which the two guys use a crystal ball to get free Doritos? If you've got a DVR, chances are you watched these and other ads several times.

Beyond making their regular ads more entertaining, advertisers are also creating new advertising forms that look less like ads and more like short films or shows. For example, Dove's "Evolution" video wasn't technically an ad, but it drew more—and more meaningful—views than many TV ads do, and the views were initiated by consumers. A range of new brand messaging platforms—from Webisodes and blogs to viral videos—are now blurring the line between ads and entertainment.

Branded entertainment (or *brand integrations*) involves making the brand an inseparable part of some other form of entertainment. The most common form of branded entertainment is product placements—imbedding brands as props within other programming. It might be a brief glimpse of the latest LG phone on *Grey's Anatomy* or the men on *How I Met Your Mother* lingering around the Victoria's Secret Fashion Show. The product placement might even be scripted into the theme of the program. For example, in one episode of *30 Rock,* network boss Jack Donaghy blatantly extols the virtues of his Verizon wireless service. Liz Lemon agrees: "Well sure, that Verizon wireless service is just unbeatable." She then turns to the camera and deadpans, "Can we have our money now?"[21]

Originally created with TV in mind, branded entertainment has spread quickly into other sectors of the entertainment industry. It's widely used in movies (remember all those GM vehicles in *Transformers* or the prominence of Purina Puppy Chow in *Marley & Me*?). If you look carefully, you'll also see product placements in video games, comic books, Broadway musicals, and even pop music.

In all, U.S. advertisers shelled out an estimated $10 billion on product placements last year, more than the GDP of Paraguay. In the first three months of last year alone, America's top 11 TV channels produced a massive 117,976 product placements. By itself, Fox's *American Idol* shoehorned in more than 3,000 placements. Old Navy dressed the contestants while Clairol did their hair, Ford supplied the winners with new cars, and Coca-Cola refreshed the judges.[22]

So, Madison & Vine is the new meeting place for the advertising and entertainment industries. The goal is for brand messages to become a part of the entertainment rather than interrupting it. ▲As advertising agency JWT puts it, "We believe advertising needs to stop interrupting what people are interested in and be what people are interested in." However, advertisers must be careful that the new intersection itself doesn't become too congested. With all the new ad formats and product placements, Madison & Vine

▼Madison & Vine: Ad agency JWT suggests that the goal is for brand messages to become a part of the entertainment rather than interrupting it.

AT JWT WE BELIEVE ADVERTISING NEEDS TO STOP INTERRUPTING WHAT PEOPLE ARE INTERESTED IN AND BE WHAT PEOPLE ARE INTERESTED IN.

threatens to create even more of the very clutter that it's designed to break through. At that point, consumers might decide to take yet a different route.

Message Strategy. The first step in creating effective advertising messages is to plan a *message strategy*—to decide what general message will be communicated to consumers. The purpose of advertising is to get consumers to think about or react to the product or company in a certain way. People will react only if they believe that they will benefit from doing so. Thus, developing an effective message strategy begins with identifying customer *benefits* that can be used as advertising appeals.

Ideally, advertising message strategy will follow directly from the company's broader positioning and customer value strategies. Message strategy statements tend to be plain, straightforward outlines of benefits and positioning points that the advertiser wants to stress. The advertiser must next develop a compelling **creative concept**—or *"big idea"*—that will bring the message strategy to life in a distinctive and memorable way. At this stage, simple message ideas become great ad campaigns. Usually, a copywriter and art director will team up to generate many creative concepts, hoping that one of these concepts will turn out to be the big idea. The creative concept may emerge as a visualization, a phrase, or a combination of the two.

The creative concept will guide the choice of specific appeals to be used in an advertising campaign. *Advertising appeals* should have three characteristics. First, they should be *meaningful*, pointing out benefits that make the product more desirable or interesting to consumers. Second, appeals must be *believable*—consumers must believe that the product or service will deliver the promised benefits.

However, the most meaningful and believable benefits may not be the best ones to feature. Appeals should also be *distinctive*—they should tell how the product is better than the competing brands. For example, the most meaningful benefit of owning a wristwatch is that it keeps accurate time, yet few watch ads feature this benefit. Instead, based on the distinctive benefits they offer, watch advertisers might select any of a number of advertising themes. For years, Timex has been the affordable watch. Last Father's Day, for example, Timex ads suggested "Tell Dad more than time this Father's Day. Tell him that you've learned the value of a dollar." Similarly, Rolex ads never talk at all about keeping time. Instead, they talk about the brand's "obsession with perfection" and the fact that "Rolex has been the preeminent symbol of performance and prestige for more than a century."

Message Execution. The advertiser now has to turn the big idea into an actual ad execution that will capture the target market's attention and interest. The creative team must find the best approach, style, tone, words, and format for executing the message. Any message can be presented in different **execution styles**, such as the following:

- *Slice of life:* This style shows one or more "typical" people using the product in a normal setting. For example, a Silk soymilk "Rise and Shine" ad shows a young professional starting the day with a healthier breakfast and high hopes.
- *Lifestyle:* This style shows how a product fits in with a particular lifestyle. For example, an ad for Athleta active wear shows a woman in a complex yoga pose and states "If your body is your temple, build it one piece at a time."
- *Fantasy:* This style creates a fantasy around the product or its use. For example, a recent Travelers Insurance ad features a gentleman carrying a giant red umbrella (the company's brand symbol). The man helps people by using the umbrella to protect them from the rain, sail them across a flooded river, and fly home. The ad closes with "Travelers Insurance. There when you need it."
- *Mood or image:* This style builds a mood or image around the product or service, such as beauty, love, intrigue, or serenity. Few claims are made about the product except through suggestion. For example, ads by India's Ministry of Tourism feature images of inspiring experiences and vibrant local landscapes in "Incredible !ndia."

Creative concept
The compelling "big idea" that will bring the advertising message strategy to life in a distinctive and memorable way.

Execution style
The approach, style, tone, words, and format used for executing an advertising message.

- *Musical:* This style shows people or cartoon characters singing about the product. For example, FreeCreditReport.com tells its story exclusively through a set of popular singing commercials such as "Dreamgirl" and "Pirate." Similarly Oscar Mayer's long-running ads show children singing its now-classic "I wish I were an Oscar Mayer wiener . . ." jingle.
- *Personality symbol:* This style creates a character that represents the product. The character might be *animated* (Mr. Clean, Tony the Tiger, the GEICO Gecko) or *real* (Ol' Lonely the Maytag repairman, the E*TRADE baby, the GEICO cavemen, or the Aflac duck).
- *Technical expertise:* This style shows the company's expertise in making the product. Thus, natural foods maker Kashi shows its buyers carefully selecting ingredients for its products, and Jim Koch of the Boston Beer Company tells about his many years of experience in brewing Samuel Adams beer.
- *Scientific evidence:* This style presents survey or scientific evidence that the brand is better or better liked than one or more other brands. For years, Crest toothpaste has used scientific evidence to convince buyers that Crest is better than other brands at fighting cavities.
- *Testimonial evidence or endorsement:* This style features a highly believable or likable source endorsing the product. It could be ordinary people saying how much they like a given product. For example, Subway uses spokesman Jared, a customer who lost 245 pounds on a diet of Subway heroes. Or it might be a celebrity presenting the product, such as Tiger Woods speaking for Accenture.

The advertiser also must choose a *tone* for the ad. Procter & Gamble always uses a positive tone: Its ads say something very positive about its products. Other advertisers now use edgy humor to break through the commercial clutter. Bud Light commercials are famous for this.

The advertiser must use memorable and attention-getting *words* in the ad. For example, rather than claiming simply that the Toyota Tundra is a "well-designed pickup truck," Toyota uses higher-impact phrasing: It's "The truck that's changing it all. Power and efficiency. Like steak and eggs." Similarly, Flip Video's stylish and innovative little Mino isn't just a "video camcorder." It's "designable, simple, shareable, adaptable, remarkable. Meet the Mino. Now Playing: You."

Finally, ▲*format* elements make a difference in an ad's impact as well as in its cost. A small change in ad design can make a big difference in its effect. In a print ad, the *illustration* is the first thing the reader notices—it must be strong enough to draw attention. Next, the *headline* must effectively entice the right people to read the copy. Finally, the *copy*—the main block of text in the ad—must be simple but strong and convincing. Moreover, these three elements must effectively work *together* to persuasively present customer value.

Consumer-Generated Messages. Taking advantage of today's interactive technologies, many companies are now tapping consumers for message ideas or actual ads. They are searching existing video sites, setting up their own sites, and sponsoring ad-creation contests and other promotions.

Sometimes, marketers capitalize on consumer videos that are already posted on sites hosted by YouTube, MySpace, Yahoo!, and Google. For example, one of the most viewed amateur videos on the Web a couple years ago showed two men in lab coats mixing Diet Coke with Mentos candies to produce shooting fountains of soda. The video

▼**Message format: To attract attention, advertisers can use novelty and contrast, eye-catching pictures and headlines, and distinctive formats, as in this National Aquarium in Baltimore print ad.**

MORE FUN IN EVERY SENSE

NATIONAL AQUARIUM IN BALTIMORE

aqua.org

produced a windfall of free buzz for Coca-Cola. To gain even more mileage, Coca-Cola hired the amateur videographers—a professional juggler and a lawyer—to create another video and to star in a 30-second Coke ad.[23]

Many other brands hold contests or develop brand Web sites of their own that invite consumers to submit ad message ideas and videos. For example, PepsiCo's Doritos brand holds its annual "Crash the Super Bowl Challenge" contest that invites

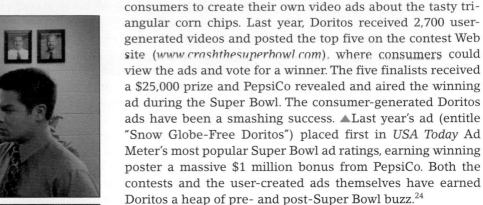

consumers to create their own video ads about the tasty triangular corn chips. Last year, Doritos received 2,700 user-generated videos and posted the top five on the contest Web site (www.crashthesuperbowl.com), where consumers could view the ads and vote for a winner. The five finalists received a $25,000 prize and PepsiCo revealed and aired the winning ad during the Super Bowl. The consumer-generated Doritos ads have been a smashing success. ▲Last year's ad (entitle "Snow Globe-Free Doritos") placed first in *USA Today* Ad Meter's most popular Super Bowl ad ratings, earning winning poster a massive $1 million bonus from PepsiCo. Both the contests and the user-created ads themselves have earned Doritos a heap of pre- and post-Super Bowl buzz.[24]

▲Consumer-generated messages: Last year, the winning ad in Doritos "Crash the Super Bowl" challenge took the top spot on the USA Today Super Bowl Ad Meter.

Not all consumer-generated advertising efforts are so successful. In fact, it can be downright dangerous to give consumers too much creative freedom and control. In one case, when Chevrolet ran a promotion for its Tahoe SUV allowing consumers to write their own text for video clips of the vehicle, it got some unexpected negative results. Many of the user-created ads contained critical gibes about the big SUV's poor gas mileage, high operating costs, and harmful environmental impact. Thus, marketers should be cautious when inviting consumer creative inputs.[25]

If used carefully, however, consumer-generated advertising efforts can produce big benefits. First, for relatively little expense, companies can collect new creative ideas, as well as fresh perspectives on the brand and what it actually means to consumers who experience it. Second, consumer-generated message campaigns can boost consumer involvement and get consumers talking and thinking about a brand and its value to them. Says one marketer, "Engage a satisfied customer in a dialogue about a product—and give them a forum to express their creative aspirations for that product—and you will have a brand advocate who speaks from the heart."[26]

Selecting Advertising Media

Advertising media
The vehicles through which advertising messages are delivered to their intended audiences.

The major steps in **advertising media** selection are (1) deciding on *reach, frequency, and impact*; (2) choosing among major *media types*; (3) selecting specific *media vehicles*; and (4) deciding on *media timing*.

Deciding on Reach, Frequency, and Impact. To select media, the advertiser must decide on the reach and frequency needed to achieve advertising objectives. *Reach* is a measure of the *percentage* of people in the target market who are exposed to the ad campaign during a given period of time. For example, the advertiser might try to reach 70 percent of the target market during the first three months of the campaign. *Frequency* is a measure of how many *times* the average person in the target market is exposed to the message. For example, the advertiser might want an average exposure frequency of three.

But advertisers want to do more than just reach a given number of consumers a specific number of times. The advertiser also must decide on the desired *media impact*—the *qualitative value* of a message exposure through a given medium. For example, the same message in one magazine (say, *Newsweek*) may be more believable than in another (say, the *National Enquirer*). For products that need to be demonstrated, messages on television may have more impact than messages on radio because television uses sight *and* sound. Products for which consumers provide input on design or features might be better promoted at an interactive Web site than in a direct mailing.

More generally, the advertiser wants to choose media that will *engage* consumers rather than simply reach them. For example, for television advertising, how relevant an ad is for its audience is often much more important than how many people it reaches. "This is about 'lean to' TV rather than 'lean back,'" says one expert. According to Unilever's director of global communications, advertising is "moving away from interruption and towards engagement. We have this term: 'penetrate the culture.' It's about getting into what people are interested in, what they are engaged in."[27]

Although Nielsen is beginning to measure levels of television *media engagement*, such measures are hard to come by for most media. "All the measurements we have now are media metrics: ratings, readership, listenership, click-through rates," says an executive of the Advertising Research Foundation, but engagement "happens inside the consumer, not inside the medium. What we need is a way to determine how the targeted prospect connected with, got engaged with, the brand idea. With engagement, you're on your way to a relationship. . . ."[28]

Choosing Among Major Media Types.   The media planner has to know the reach, frequency, and impact of each of the major media types. As summarized in ■ **Table 12.2**, the major media types are television, the Internet, newspapers, direct mail, magazines, radio, and outdoor. Advertisers can also choose from a wide array of new digital media, such as cell phones and other digital devices, which reach consumers directly. Each medium has advantages and limitations. Media planners consider many factors when making their media choices. They want to choose media that will effectively and efficiently present the advertising message to target customers. Thus, they must consider each medium's impact, message effectiveness, and cost.

The mix of media must be reexamined regularly. For a long time, television and magazines dominated in the media mixes of national advertisers, with other media

> Typically, it's not a question of which one medium to use. Rather, the advertiser selects a mix of media and blends them into a fully integrated marketing communications campaign. Each medium plays a specific role.

■ **Table 12.2** Profiles of Major Media Types

Medium	Advantages	Limitations
Television	Good mass-marketing coverage; low cost per exposure; combines sight, sound, and motion; appealing to the senses	High absolute costs; high clutter; fleeting exposure; less audience selectivity
The Internet	High selectivity; low cost; immediacy; interactive capabilities	Relatively low impact; the audience controls exposure
Newspapers	Flexibility; timeliness; good local market coverage; broad acceptability; high believability	Short life; poor reproduction quality; small pass-along audience
Direct mail	High audience selectivity; flexibility; no ad competition within the same medium; allows personalization	Relatively high cost per exposure, "junk mail" image
Magazines	High geographic and demographic selectivity; credibility and prestige; high-quality reproduction; long life and good pass-along readership	Long ad purchase lead time; high cost; no guarantee of position
Radio	Good local acceptance; high geographic and demographic selectivity; low cost	Audio only, fleeting exposure; low attention ("the half-heard" medium); fragmented audiences
Outdoor	Flexibility; high repeat exposure; low cost; low message competition; good positional selectivity	Little audience selectivity; creative limitations

often neglected. However, as discussed previously, the media mix appears to be shifting. As mass-media costs rise, audiences shrink, and exciting new digital media emerge, many advertisers are finding new ways to reach consumers. They are supplementing the traditional mass media with more-specialized and highly targeted media that cost less, target more effectively, and engage consumers more fully.

For example, cable television and satellite television systems are booming. Such systems allow narrow programming formats such as all sports, all news, nutrition, arts, home improvement and gardening, cooking, travel, history, finance, and others that target select groups. Time Warner, Comcast, and other cable operators are even testing systems that will let them target specific types of ads to specific neighborhoods or individually to specific types of customers. For example, ads for a Spanish-language channel would run only in Hispanic neighborhoods, or only pet owners would see ads from pet food companies.

Advertisers can take advantage of such "narrowcasting" to "rifle in" on special market segments rather than use the "shotgun" approach offered by network broadcasting. Cable and satellite television media seem to make good sense. But, increasingly, ads are popping up in far-less-likely places. ▲In their efforts to find less-costly and more-highly targeted ways to reach consumers, advertisers have discovered a dazzling collection of "alternative media." These days, no matter where you go or what you do, you will probably run into some new form of advertising.[29]

▲Marketers have discovered a dazzling collection of "alternative media."

Tiny billboards attached to shopping carts and advertising decals on supermarket floors urge you to buy JELL-O Pudding Pops or Pampers, while ads roll by on the store's checkout conveyor touting your local Volvo dealer. At the local laundromat, you load your laundry through a clever Pepto-Bismol ad plastered on the front of the washing machine. Step outside and there goes a city trash truck sporting an ad for Glad trash bags. You escape to the ballpark, only to find billboard-size video screens running Budweiser ads while a blimp with an electronic message board circles lazily overhead. How about a quiet trip in the country? Sorry—you find an enterprising farmer using his milk cows as four-legged billboards mounted with ads for Ben & Jerry's ice cream.

These days, you're likely to find ads—well, anywhere. Taxi cabs sport electronic messaging signs tied to GPS location sensors that can pitch local stores and restaurants wherever they roam. Ad space is being sold on DVD cases, parking-lot tickets, subway turnstiles, golf scorecards, delivery trucks, pizza boxes, gas pumps, ATMs, municipal garbage cans, police cars, doctors' examining tables, and church bulletins. One agency even leases space on the shaved heads of college students for temporary advertising tattoos ("cranial advertising"). And the group meeting at the office water cooler has a new member—a "coolertising" ad sitting on top of the water cooler jug trying to start up a conversation about the latest episode of *American Idol*.

Such alternative media seem a bit far-fetched, and they sometimes irritate consumers who resent it all as "ad nauseam." But for many marketers, these media can save money and provide a way to hit selected consumers where they live, shop, work, and play. Of course, all this may leave you wondering if there are any commercial-free havens remaining for ad-weary consumers. Public elevators, perhaps, or stalls in a public restroom? Forget it! Each has already been invaded by innovative marketers.

Another important trend affecting media selection is the rapid growth in the number of "media multitaskers," people who absorb more than one medium at a time. One survey found that three-fourths of U.S. TV viewers read the newspaper while they watch TV, and two-thirds of them go online during their TV time. According to another study, Americans aged 8 to 18 are managing to cram an average 8.5 hours of media consumption into 6.5 hours. These days, says one analysts "it's not uncommon to find a teenage boy chasing down photos of Keira Knightly on Google, IMing several friends at once, listening to a mix of music on iTunes, and talking on the cell phone to a friend—all while, in the midst of the multimedia chaos, trying to complete an essay he's got open in a Word file a few layers down on his desktop."[30] Media planners need to take such media interactions into account when selecting the types of media they will use.

Selecting Specific Media Vehicles. The media planner now must choose the best *media vehicles*—specific media within each general media type. For example, television vehicles include *30 Rock* and *ABC World News Tonight*. Magazine vehicles include *Newsweek*, *Vogue*, and *ESPN the Magazine*.

Media planners must compute the cost per 1,000 persons reached by a vehicle. For example, if a full-page, four-color advertisement in the U.S. national edition of *Newsweek* costs $226,590 and *Newsweek's* readership is 2.6 million people, the cost of reaching each group of 1,000 persons is about $87. The same advertisement in *BusinessWeek* may cost only $112,200 but reach only 900,000 persons—at a cost per 1,000 of about $124. The media planner ranks each magazine by cost per 1,000 and favors those magazines with the lower cost per 1,000 for reaching target consumers.[31]

The media planner must also consider the costs of producing ads for different media. Whereas newspaper ads may cost very little to produce, flashy television ads can be very costly. For example, a typical car commercial can cost from $500,000 to $1 million or more to produce. Guinness recently filmed a 90-second commercial titled "Tipping Point" in a tiny town of just 2,000 people high in the mountains of northern Argentina, where you can't even get a pint of the stout. Some billed it as the best beer commercial ever. But the cost to create the ad? An almost unimaginable $20 million.[32]

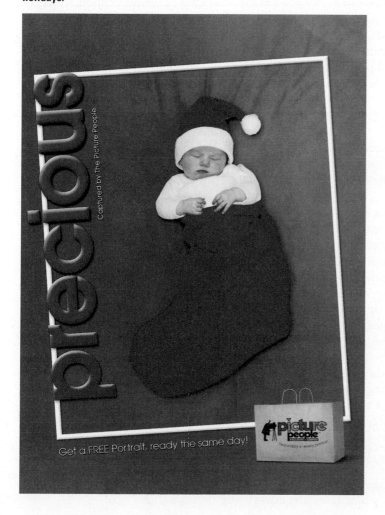

▼**Media timing: The Picture People, the national chain of family portrait studios, advertises more heavily before special holidays.**

In selecting specific media vehicles, the media planner must balance media costs against several media effectiveness factors. First, the planner should evaluate the media vehicle's *audience quality*. For a Huggies disposable diapers advertisement, for example, *Parenting* magazine would have a high exposure value; *Maxim* would have a low-exposure value. Second, the media planner should consider *audience engagement*. Readers of *Vogue*, for example, typically pay more attention to ads than do *Newsweek* readers. Third, the planner should assess the vehicle's *editorial quality*—*Time* and *The Wall Street Journal* are more believable and prestigious than *Star* or the *National Enquirer*.

Deciding on Media Timing. The advertiser must also decide how to schedule the advertising over the course of a year. Suppose sales of a product peak in December and drop in March (for winter sports gear, for instance). The firm can vary its advertising to follow the seasonal pattern, to oppose the seasonal pattern, or to be the same all year. Most firms do some seasonal advertising. ▲For example, The Picture People, the national chain of portraits studios, advertises more heavily before major holidays such as Christmas, Easter, and Valentine's Day. Some marketers do *only* seasonal advertising: For instance, P&G advertises its Vicks NyQuil only during the cold and flu season.

Finally, the advertiser has to choose the pattern of the ads. *Continuity* means scheduling ads evenly within a given period. *Pulsing* means scheduling ads unevenly over a given time period. Thus, 52 ads could either be scheduled at 1 per week during the year or pulsed in several bursts.

The idea behind pulsing is to advertise heavily for a short period to build awareness that carries over to the next advertising period. Those who favor pulsing feel that it can be used to achieve the same impact as a steady schedule but at a much lower cost. However, some media planners believe that although pulsing achieves minimal awareness, it sacrifices depth of advertising communications.

Evaluating Advertising Effectiveness and Return on Advertising Investment

Return on advertising investment
The net return on advertising investment divided by the costs of the advertising investment.

Measuring advertising effectiveness and **return on advertising investment** has become a hot issue for most companies, especially in the tight economic environment. Two separate recent studies show that advertising effectiveness has fallen 40 percent over the past decade and that 37.3 percent of advertising budgets are wasted. This leaves top management and many companies asking their marketing managers, "How do we know that we're spending the right amount on advertising?" and "What return are we getting on our advertising investment?"[33]

Advertisers should regularly evaluate two types of advertising results: the communication effects and the sales and profit effects. Measuring the *communication effects* of an ad or ad campaign tells whether the ads and media are communicating the ad message well. Individual ads can be tested before or after they are run. Before an ad is placed, the advertiser can show it to consumers, ask how they like it, and measure message recall or attitude changes resulting from it. After an ad is run, the advertiser can measure how the ad affected consumer recall or product awareness, knowledge, and preference. Pre- and postevaluations of communication effects can be made for entire advertising campaigns as well.

Advertisers have gotten pretty good at measuring the communication effects of their ads and ad campaigns. However, *sales and profit* effects of advertising are often much harder to measure. For example, what sales and profits are produced by an ad campaign that increases brand awareness by 20 percent and brand preference by 10 percent? Sales and profits are affected by many factors other than advertising—such as product features, price, and availability.

One way to measure the sales and profit effects of advertising is to compare past sales and profits with past advertising expenditures. Another way is through experiments. For example, to test the effects of different advertising spending levels, Coca-Cola could vary the amount it spends on advertising in different market areas and measure the differences in the resulting sales and profit levels. More complex experiments could be designed to include other variables, such as differences in the ads or media used.

However, because so many factors affect advertising effectiveness, some controllable and others not, measuring the results of advertising spending remains an inexact science. For example, it is estimated that governments spend huge amounts of money on tourism annually. Although they sense that the returns are worth the sizable investment, few can actually measure or prove it (see Marketing at Work 12.2). A recent survey of marketing and advertising agency executives concluded that over 80 percent of marketers don't measure return on investment because it's just too difficult to measure.[34] The ANA study cited earlier asked advertising managers if they would be able to "forecast the impact on sales" of a 10 percent cut in advertising spending—63 percent said no.

"Marketers are tracking all kinds of data and they still can't answer basic questions" about advertising accountability, says a marketing analyst, "because they don't have real models and metrics by which to make sense of it." Advertisers are measuring "everything they can, and that ranges from how many people respond to an ad to how many sales are closed and then trying to hook up those two end pieces," says another analyst. "The tough part is, my goodness, we've got so much data. How do we sift through it?"[35] Thus, although the situation is improving as marketers seek more answers, managers often must rely on large doses of judgment along with quantitative analysis when assessing advertising performance.

Marketing at Work 12.2

n7W: Helping in Managing Tourism

Tourism depends on many factors, and some types of communication expenditure that have proven beneficial for tourism have been unconventional types. Movies have historically used places as backdrops and the success of movies has led to increased tourism. Examples can be Lara Croft and Cambodia and more recently Lord of the Rings and New Zealand. Shows like Survivor showcase places too. Olympics have been another substitute vehicle for tourism. The investment for the Sydney Olympics is estimated to be 0.6 percent of Australian GDP and though the event itself lasted 3 weeks, the investment in infrastructure has had mixed results in terms of cost effectiveness. Festivals like WOMAD (music), Cannes (films), and Edinburgh (culture) are other methods to encourage the industry.

Another unconventional advertising medium that has been very successful is the New7Wonders of the World. In 1999, Bernard Weber, a Swiss-Canadian filmmaker wanted to revive the Greek concept of the 7 Wonders of the World. The original list was compiled by a few men, Antipater, Philo, Strabo, Herodotos, and Diodoros, who were all ancient Greek residents. It acted as a guide book for the ancient Hellenic or Greek empire in 200 B.C. The list focused on places around the Mediterranean Rim. Unfortunately, of the original list of these ancient seven wonders, only one survives, the Pyramid of Giza. Bernard recognized that today's modern world is much larger and more easily accessible than that of the Greek empire 2,200 years ago. There was a need for a more updated list.

Bernard Weber created the first website new7wonders.com in 1999. The campaign was officially launched on June 30, 2000. The nonprofit New7Wonders Foundation was established in 2001, headquartered in Switzerland. It was an ambitious project as it was an international campaign focusing on educating and encouraging participation of the global citizens. The New7Wonders of the World were to be selected based on global votes (the first-ever done on this scale) and had to be existing manmade monuments. The winners of this unique vote were announced on July 7, 2007 (i.e., 07.07.07). The process was long. First nominees were solicited. The top 77 elected from a total of 177 popular nominations were shortlisted to 21 finalist candidates, and again based on popular votes, the top seven wonders were chosen. For New7Wonders of the World, the poll took seven years. It gathered enormous pace during the official N7W World Tour, visiting all the finalist monuments in the last year preceding the end of the voting period. While many countries and citizens were enthusiastic, others were not. UNESCO dismissed the campaign as "neither democratic nor scientific." Indignant Egyptian officials said it was a disgrace they had to compete. The Pyramids were the only manmade wonder already on the list.

The fight for the remaining six wonders was fierce. The website was inundated by tens of millions of votes. It is estimated that the Official New7Wonders of the World were elected by millions of citizens from around the world—of all social classes, all ages, all professions. More than 100 million votes were cast, choosing from a list of finalists that included structures from the earliest time that humankind walked the earth through the twentieth century. These votes were cast through the Internet, SMS

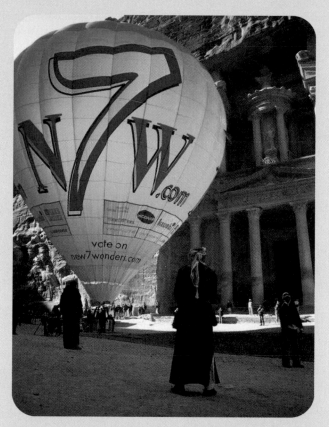

▲Millions of people across the globe voted for the New Seven Wonders of the World over a seven year campaign. The competition had a phenomenal impact on tourism for lesser known sites such as Petra in Jordan, which welcomed a 62 percent increase in visitors as a result.

text messages, and telephone, by all segments of the population on all continents. The heaviest volumes of votes came from China, India, and Latin America. It involved promotion at all levels with some countries and national media getting involved. For example, in Brazil bus tickets were printed urging passengers to vote, and an Indian singer dedicating a song to the Taj Mahal, China's Academy of the Great Wall encouraged Chinese voters to flood the competition website.

Petra, a UNESCO World Heritage Site was one of the 21 finalist candidates in the campaign for choosing the New7Wonders of the World. Petra lies on the edge of the Arabian Desert, nestled away in the mountains south of the Dead Sea, it was the ancient capital of the Nabataean empire of King Aretas IV (9 B.C. to 40 A.D.). Their people were experts of water technology, building their city with hydraulic systems that carried drinking water into the city and reduced the chance of flash floods. The city would have housed 20,000 to 30,000 people during its heyday and even had a Roman amphitheater that could seat an audience of 4,000. It was an important point on the Silk Route and Spice Route. Petra had disappeared from most maps and became a legend until 1812, when the Swiss traveler Johann Burckhardt snuck into the city disguised as a Muslim and shared his story with the world. Due to the active campaigning of a Jordanian family, Petra jumped from the middle of the pack to

(continued)

the top seven in January. In Jordan, "Vote for Petra" signs were placed reminding visitors to vote for Petra. The economic impact of this campaign was large, Petra saw a 62 percent increase in visitors in 2007 that generated $13.4 million in tourism for the country according to *The Jordanian Times*. The national airline registered the highest monthly total for its passengers in its 44-year history. This effect was apparent for all New7Wonders like Machu Picchu, which saw a 70 percent increase in tourism.

The overall worldwide economic impact of New7Wonders is estimated to be in excess of $5 billion worth of tourism, economic, promotional, and national brand value generated. This makes for an interesting comparison with what for some is considered to be the heavy economic burden of participating in the UNESCO World Heritage programme, a burden for each location that can be as high as $640,000 to enter and $230,000 per year, or cumulatively a theoretical cost burden of over $1.5 billion across all 890 UNESCO World Heritage sites over a period of five years.

What is surprising is that the largest group of voters was children. At the first recognition ceremony for the New7Wonders, Bernard Weber acknowledged this fact by stating that children were objective in their voting as they don't have a strong sense of national pride and voted for what they like the most. Though Rome did not actively promote its nomination, being the only wonder representing old Europe and representing ancient Roman civilization, it won enough votes. This could be because it is widely featured in history textbooks and hence it is widely known. In the case of the Alhambra in Spain, a vigorous local campaign was not enough to garner international votes. Another interesting fact about elections emerged in the final phase. Huge amounts of votes came in support of Timbuktu in Mali. There were more votes in a single week than had come from the entire country of Germany. This propelled Timbuktu from the bottom of the list to just below the top seven. The campaign began too late! How

important is the campaign across a global audience? More people voted for the Eiffel Tower from Korea and Japan than did the French. Though children around the world loved the Neuschwanstein Castle (thank you Disney!), the Germans did not. The people of the United States who voted passionately and in large numbers did not vote for their Statue of Liberty. And the first wave of votes came from Turkey in 2000, not the west!

For the current Official New7Wonders of Nature campaign, a billion votes are expected to be cast by the world's population, choosing among participating locations from over 220 countries (more countries than are members of organizations such as the UN, FIFA, or the Olympics), which has overwhelmingly shown its desire for positive dialogue. During the first stage, 441 sites from 222 countries were nominated. On December 31, 2008, the first phase ended and 261 nominees proceeded to the current stage—one national nominee per country, plus all multinational nominees. The race was then on to be in the Top 77, comprised of the top 11 in each of the 7 categories, and on July 21, 2009, the 28 finalist candidates were announced at the New7Wonders foundation headquarters in Zürich.

Sources: Based on information from Chalip, L. (2000), "Leveraging the Sydney Olympics for Tourism," The Centre d'Estudis Olímpics (CEO-UAB); accessed at http://olympicstudies.uab.es/pdf/wp096_eng.pdf; Smith, N. (2007), "World's New Seven Wonders Chosen," Times Online, dated July 8, 2007, accessed at www.timesonline.co.uk/tol/news/world/article2043145.ece#; Weber, B.(2007), "Voting Analysis," available at www.vote7.com/n7w/world/voting-analysis; Visit Jordan (2009), "Petra," accessed at www.visitjordan.com/Default.aspx?Tabid=63; n7W (2008), Economic Impact of the New7Wonders Campaign, available at www.vote7.com/news/economic-impact-new7wonders-campaigns; Official New7Wonders of Nature campaign (2009), accessed at www.vote7.com/n7w/nature/finalists; Announcement during World Travel Market, London, on November 10, 2008, accessed at www.vote7.com/node/13187; and Article in the *London Sunday Times*, December 7, 2008, accessed at www.timesonline.co .uk/tol/news/uk/article5299161.ece.

Other Advertising Considerations

In developing advertising strategies and programs, the company must address two additional questions. First, how will the company organize its advertising function—who will perform which advertising tasks? Second, how will the company adapt its advertising strategies and programs to the complexities of international markets?

Organizing for Advertising

Different companies organize in different ways to handle advertising. In small companies, advertising might be handled by someone in the sales department. Large companies set up advertising departments whose job it is to set the advertising budget, work with the ad agency, and handle other advertising not done by the agency. Most large companies use outside advertising agencies because they offer several advantages.

Advertising agency
A marketing services firm that assists companies in planning, preparing, implementing, and evaluating all or portions of their advertising programs.

How does an **advertising agency** work? Advertising agencies were started in the mid- to late-1800s by salespeople and brokers who worked for the media and received a commission for selling advertising space to companies. As time passed, the salespeople began to help customers prepare their ads. Eventually, they formed agencies and grew closer to the advertisers than to the media.

Today's agencies employ specialists who can often perform advertising tasks better than the company's own staff can. Agencies also bring an outside point of view to solving the company's problems, along with lots of experience from working with different clients and situations. So, today, even companies with strong advertising departments of their own use advertising agencies.

Some ad agencies are huge—the largest U.S. agency, BBDO Worldwide, has annual gross U.S. revenues of more than $635 million. In recent years, many agencies have grown by gobbling up other agencies, thus creating huge agency holding companies. The largest of these agency "megagroups," WPP, includes several large advertising, public relations, and promotion agencies with combined worldwide revenues of $13.6 billion.[36] Most large advertising agencies have the staff and resources to handle all phases of an advertising campaign for their clients, from creating a marketing plan to developing ad campaigns and preparing, placing, and evaluating ads.

International Advertising Decisions

International advertisers face many complexities not encountered by domestic advertisers. The most basic issue concerns the degree to which global advertising should be adapted to the unique characteristics of various country markets. Some large advertisers have attempted to support their global brands with highly standardized worldwide advertising, with campaigns that work as well in Bangkok as they do in Baltimore. For example, McDonald's now unifies its creative elements and brand presentation under the familiar "I'm lovin' it" theme in all of its 100-plus markets worldwide. Coca-Cola pulls advertising together for its flagship brand under the theme, "Open Happiness." And VISA coordinates worldwide advertising for its debit and credit cards under the "more people go with Visa" creative platform, which works as well in Korea as it does in the United States or Brazil.

In recent years, the increased popularity of online social networks and video sharing has boosted the need for advertising standardization for global brands. Most big marketing and advertising campaigns include a large online presence. Connected consumers can now zip easily across borders via the Internet, making it difficult for advertisers to roll out adapted campaigns in a controlled, orderly fashion. As a result, at the very least, most global consumer brands coordinate their Web sites internationally. For example, check out the McDonald's Web sites from Germany to Jordan to China and you'll find the golden arches logo, the "I'm lovin it" logo and jingle, a Big Mac equivalent, and maybe even Ronald McDonald himself.

Standardization produces many benefits—lower advertising costs, greater global advertising coordination, and a more consistent worldwide image. But it also has drawbacks. Most importantly, it ignores the fact that country markets differ greatly in their cultures, demographics, and economic conditions. Thus, most international advertisers "think globally but act locally." They develop global advertising *strategies* that make their worldwide advertising efforts more efficient and consistent. Then they adapt their advertising *programs* to make them more responsive to consumer needs and expectations within local markets. ▲For example, although VISA employs its "more people go with Visa" theme globally, ads in specific locales employ local language and inspiring local imagery that make the theme relevant to the local markets in which they appear.

Global advertisers face several special problems. For instance, advertising media costs and availability

▼Standardized worldwide advertising: Although VISA employs its "more people go with Visa" theme globally, ads in specific locales (here the United States, Brazil, and Asia) employ local language and inspiring local imagery that make the theme relevant to the local markets in which they appear.

differ vastly from country to country. Countries also differ in the extent to which they regulate advertising practices. Many countries have extensive systems of laws restricting how much a company can spend on advertising, the media used, the nature of advertising claims, and other aspects of the advertising program. Such restrictions often require advertisers to adapt their campaigns from country to country.

For example, alcohol products cannot be advertised in India or in Muslim countries. In many countries, Sweden and Canada, for example, junk food ads are banned from kids' TV. To play it safe, McDonald's advertises itself as a family restaurant in Sweden. Comparative ads, although acceptable and even common in the United States and Canada, are less commonly used in the United Kingdom and are illegal in India and Brazil. China bans sending e-mail for advertising purposes to people without their permission and all advertising e-mail that is sent must be titled "advertisement."

China also has restrictive censorship rules for TV and radio advertising; for example, the words *the best* are banned, as are ads that "violate social customs" or present women in "improper ways." McDonald's once avoided government sanctions, thereby publicly apologizing for an ad that crossed cultural norms by showing a customer begging for a discount. Similarly, Coca-Cola's Indian subsidiary was forced to end a promotion that offered prizes, such as a trip to Hollywood, because it violated India's established trade practices by encouraging customers to buy in order to "gamble."

Thus, although advertisers may develop global strategies to guide their overall advertising efforts, specific advertising programs must usually be adapted to meet local cultures and customs, media characteristics, and advertising regulations.

Speed Bump: Linking the Concepts

Think about what goes on behind the scenes for the ads we all tend to take for granted.

- Pick a favorite print or television ad. Why do you like it? Do you think that it's effective? Can you think of an ad that people like that may not be effective?
- Dig a little deeper and learn about the campaign *behind* your ad. What are the campaign's objectives? What is its budget? Assess the campaign's message and media strategies. Looking beyond your own feelings about the ad, is the campaign likely to be effective?

PUBLIC RELATIONS (pp 430–433)

Another major mass-promotion tool is public relations (PR)—building good relations with the company's various publics by obtaining favorable publicity, building up a good corporate image, and handling or heading off unfavorable rumors, stories, and events. Public relations departments may perform any or all of the following functions:[37]

- *Press relations or press agency:* Creating and placing newsworthy information in the news media to attract attention to a person, product, or service.
- *Product publicity:* Publicizing specific products.
- *Public affairs:* Building and maintaining national or local community relations.
- *Lobbying:* Building and maintaining relations with legislators and government officials to influence legislation and regulation.
- *Investor relations:* Maintaining relationships with shareholders and others in the financial community.
- *Development:* Public relations with donors or members of nonprofit organizations to gain financial or volunteer support.

Public relations is used to promote products, people, places, ideas, activities, organizations, and even nations. Companies use PR to build good relations with consumers, investors, the media, and their communities. The state of New York turned its image around when its "I ♥ New York!" publicity and advertising campaign took root, bringing in millions more tourists. Trade associations have used PR to rebuild interest in declining commodities such as eggs, apples, potatoes, and milk. For example, the milk industry's popular "Got Milk?" public relations campaign featuring celebrities with milk mustaches reversed a long-standing decline in milk consumption.[38]

> By 1994, milk consumption had been in decline for 20 years. The general perception was that milk was unhealthy, outdated, just for kids, or good only with cookies and cake. To counter these notions, the National Fluid Milk Processors Education Program (MilkPEP) began a PR campaign featuring milk be-mustached celebrities and the tagline "Got Milk?" The campaign has been wildly popular; it's also been successful—not only did it stop the decline, milk consumption actually increased. The campaign is still running.
>
> Although initially targeted at women in their twenties, the campaign has been expanded to other target markets and has gained cult status with teens, much to their parents' delight. Starting with basic print ads featuring a musician (Kelly Clarkson), actor (Jessica Alba), or sports idol (Tracy McGrady), the campaign has naturally spread to the Internet. One Web site (*www.whymilk.com*) appeals to moms in a search for America's first "Chief Health Officer." Another (*www.bodybymilk.com*) targets young people, who can bid on gear using saved milk UPCs, go behind the scenes of the latest "Got Milk?" photo shoot, or get facts about "everything you ever need to know about milk." There are milk moustache MySpace pages of celebrities such as David Beckham. The milk marketers even created the world's first branded emoticon—the milk moustache :-{).

The Role and Impact of Public Relations

Public relations can have a strong impact on public awareness at a much lower cost than advertising can. The company does not pay for the space or time in the media. Rather, it pays for a staff to develop and circulate information and to manage events. If the company develops an interesting story or event, it could be picked up by several different media, having the same effect as advertising that would cost millions of dollars. And it would have more credibility than advertising.

▲Public relations results can sometimes be spectacular. Starting with preview events like this one, Nintendo's award-winning PR campaign for its new Wii game produced nonstop stock-outs for more than two years.

Public relations results can sometimes be spectacular. ▲Consider the launch of Nintendo's Wii game console:[39]

> By 2006, once-dominant Nintendo had dropped to third place in the video-game industry behind Sony and Microsoft. To get back on top, Nintendo's newest offering, the amazing Wii, needed to soar. The Wii's motion-sensitive controller makes it fun for almost anyone to play. This let Nintendo target the core gaming audience but also "dabblers," "lapsed gamers," and "nongamers," including girls, women, and seniors. But rather than investing millions in media advertising, Nintendo took advantage of Wii's natural appeal to create a results-producing PR campaign. Prelaunch, Nintendo held preview events at which industry analysts and the media spent time with the Wii. The company targeted consumers on MySpace, where the "How Wii Play" profile made more than 60,000 friends. Nintendo also launched an ambassador program that got the game into the hands of gamers, moms, and large intergenerational families, who spread information about the system through blogs and word of mouth.
>
> On launch day, Nintendo midnight events, held in New York and Los Angeles, were attended by thousands of consumers, with coverage by media ranging from AP to MTV and *Good Morning America*. In the end, the Wii PR campaign earned an incredible 10 billion audience impressions over just three months, including 14 *Today Show* appearances and a stint on *South Park*. Despite early surveys showing that only 11 percent of consumers intended to buy it, Wii sales sizzled. Stores experienced two years of nonstop stock-outs, and the Wii outsold the Xbox 360 by two to one and the newly introduced Playstation 3 by three to one. As a result, the Wii PR effort was named *PRWeek's* 2008 Consumer Launch Campaign of the Year.

Despite its potential strengths, public relations is sometimes described as a marketing stepchild because of its often limited and scattered use. The PR department is often located at corporate headquarters or handled by a third-party agency. Its staff is so busy dealing with various publics—stockholders, employees, legislators, the press—that PR programs to support product marketing objectives may be ignored.

Moreover, marketing managers and PR practitioners do not always speak the same language. Whereas many PR practitioners see their jobs as simply communicating, marketing managers tend to be much more interested in how advertising and PR affect brand building, sales and profits, and customer relationships.

This situation is changing, however. Although public relations still captures only a small portion of the overall marketing budgets of most firms, PR can be a powerful brand-building tool. And in this digital age, more and more, the lines between advertising and PR are blurring. For example, are brand Web sites, blogs, and viral brand videos advertising efforts or PR efforts? All are both. The point is advertising and PR should work hand in hand within an integrated marketing communications program to build brands and customer relationships.[40]

Major Public Relations Tools

Public relations uses several tools. One of the major tools is *news*. Public relations professionals find or create favorable news about the company and its products or people. Sometimes news stories occur naturally, and sometimes the PR person can suggest events or activities that would create news. *Speeches* can also create product and company publicity. Increasingly, company executives must field questions from the media or give talks at trade associations or sales meetings, and these events can either build or hurt the company's image. Another common PR tool is *special events*, ranging from news conferences, press tours, grand openings, and fireworks displays to laser shows, hot air balloon releases, multimedia presentations, or educational programs designed to reach and interest target publics.

Public relations people also prepare *written materials* to reach and influence their target markets. These materials include annual reports, brochures, articles, and company newsletters and magazines. *Audiovisual materials*, such as slide-and-sound programs, DVDs, and online videos are being used increasingly as communication tools. *Corporate identity materials* can also help create a corporate identity that the public immediately recognizes. Logos, stationery, brochures, signs, business forms, business cards, buildings, uniforms, and company cars and trucks—all become marketing tools when they are attractive, distinctive, and memorable. Finally, companies can improve public goodwill by contributing money and time to *public service activities*.

As we discussed in Chapter 5, many marketers are now also designing *buzz marketing* campaigns to generate excitement and favorable word of mouth for their brands. Buzz marketing takes advantage of *social networking* processes by getting consumers themselves to spread information about a product or service to others in their communities. ▲For example, Johnson & Johnson Consumer Products Company used buzz marketing to launch its Aveeno Positively Ageless product line:[41]

▼Buzz marketing: Aveeno used social networking processes to get consumers to spread the word about its new product line. This YouTube video has captured close to 1.5 million views.

To build buzz for its new line, Johnson & Johnson Consumer Products employed talented street artist Julian Beever—the "Pavement Picasso"—to create a 3D "Fountain of Youth" chalk drawing on a sidewalk in the heart of New York City. Although the drawing captivated thousands of passersby, Aveeno turned "Fountain of Youth" into an online event via a four-minute, time-lapse video of the artist at work posted on YouTube (*www.youtube.com/watch?v=hfn8Dz_13Ms*). In addition the brand distributed the video to more than 50 blogs, with 21 responding by promoting the YouTube posting. With a soft "Aveeno Presents" slate at the beginning of the video and a closeup of the Fountain of Youth artwork showing the Aveeno logo at the end, the spot was well branded but without appearing to be commercial. The video reverberated through video sites and the blogosphere via strong word of mouth. Within two weeks, on YouTube alone, the video was viewed more than 65,000 times and grew to reach 121,346 views within one month. As of June 2008, the YouTube video had been viewed close to 1.5 million times.

A company's Web site is another important public relations vehicle. Consumers and members of other publics often visit Web sites for information or entertainment. Such sites can be extremely popular. Consider my.barackobama.com, President Barack Obama's community-based, interactive campaign Web site. Created by Obama's campaign committee as a new way to spread the word, by the time the campaign ended successfully, site users had created more than 2 million profiles, planned 200,000 offline events, formed 35,000 groups, posted 400,000 blogs, and raised $30 million on 70,000 personal fund-raising pages.[42]

Web sites can also be ideal for handling crisis situations. For example, when several bottles of Odwalla apple juice sold on the West Coast were found to contain *E. coli* bacteria, Odwalla initiated a massive product recall. Within only three hours, it set up a Web site laden with information about the crisis and Odwalla's response. Company staffers also combed the Internet looking for newsgroups discussing Odwalla and posted links to the site. In all, in this age where "it's easier to disseminate information through e-mail marketing, blogs, and online chat," notes an analyst, "public relations is becoming a valuable part of doing business in a digital world."[43]

As with the other promotion tools, in considering when and how to use product public relations, management should set PR objectives, choose the PR messages and vehicles, implement the PR plan, and evaluate the results. The firm's PR should be blended smoothly with other promotion activities within the company's overall integrated marketing communications effort.

REST STOP
REVIEWING THE CONCEPTS

In this chapter, you've learned how companies use integrated marketing communications (IMC) to communicate customer value. Modern marketing calls for more than just creating customer value by developing a good product, pricing it attractively, and making it available to target customers. Companies also must clearly and persuasively *communicate* that value to current and prospective customers. To do this, they must blend five communication-mix tools, guided by a well-designed and implemented IMC strategy.

 Objective 1 Define the five promotion mix tools for communicating customer value. **(pp 405)**

A company's total *promotion mix*—also called its *marketing communications mix*—consists of the specific blend of *advertising, personal selling, sales promotion, public relations (PR),* and *direct-marketing* tools that the company uses to persuasively communicate customer value and build customer relationships. Advertising includes any paid form of nonpersonal presentation and promotion of ideas, goods, or services by an identified sponsor. In contrast, public relations focuses on building good relations with the company's various publics. Personal selling is any form of personal presentation by the firm's sales force for the purpose of making sales and building customer relationships. Firms use sales promotion to provide short-term incentives to encourage the purchase or sale of a product or service. Finally, firms seeking immediate response from targeted individual customers use direct-marketing tools to communicate with customers and cultivate relationships with them.

 Objective 2 Discuss the changing communications landscape and the need for integrated marketing communications. **(pp 405–410)**

The explosive developments in communications technology and changes in marketer and customer communication strategies have had a dramatic impact on marketing communications. Advertisers are now adding a broad selection of more-specialized and highly targeted media—including digital media—to reach smaller customer segments with more-personalized, interactive messages. As they adopt richer but more fragmented media and promotion mixes to reach their diverse markets, they risk creating a communications hodgepodge for consumers. To prevent this, more companies are adopting the concept of *integrated marketing communications (IMC)*. Guided by an overall IMC strategy, the company works out the roles that the various promotional tools will play and the extent to which each will be used. It carefully coordinates the promotional activities and the timing of when major campaigns take place.

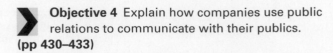

Objective 3 Describe and discuss the major decisions involved in developing an advertising program. (pp 410–430)

Advertising—the use of paid media by a seller to inform, persuade, and remind about its products or organization—is a strong promotion tool that takes many forms and has many uses. *Advertising decision making* involves decisions about the objectives, the budget, the message, the media, and, finally, the evaluation of results. Advertisers should set clear *objectives* as to whether the advertising is supposed to inform, persuade, or remind buyers. The advertising *budget* can be based on what is affordable, on sales, on competitors' spending, or on the objectives and tasks. The *message decision* calls for planning a message strategy and executing it effectively. The *media decision* involves defining reach, frequency, and impact goals; choosing major media types; selecting media vehicles; and deciding on media timing. Message and media decisions must be closely coordinated for maximum campaign effectiveness. Finally, *evaluation* calls for evaluating the communication and sales effects of advertising before, during, and after the advertising is placed and measuring advertising return on investment.

Objective 4 Explain how companies use public relations to communicate with their publics. (pp 430–433)

Public relations (PR) involves building good relations with the company's various publics. Its functions include *press agentry, product publicity, public affairs, lobbying, investor relations,* and *development.* Public relations can have a strong impact on public awareness at a much lower cost than advertising can, and PR results can sometimes be spectacular. Despite its potential strengths, however, PR sometimes sees only limited and scattered use. Public relations tools include *news, speeches, special events, buzz marketing, written materials, audiovisual materials, corporate identity materials,* and *public service activities.* A company's Web site can be a good PR vehicle. In considering when and how to use product PR, management should set PR objectives, choose the PR messages and vehicles, implement the PR plan, and evaluate the results. Public relations should be blended smoothly with other promotion activities within the company's overall IMC effort.

Navigating the Key Terms

Objective 1
Promotion mix (marketing communications mix) (p 405)
Advertising (p 405)
Sales promotion (p 405)
Personal selling (p 405)
Public relations (PR) (p 405)
Direct marketing (p 405)

Objective 2
Integrated marketing communications (IMC) (p 408)

Push strategy (p 412)
Pull strategy (p 412)

Objective 3
Advertising objective (p 414)
Advertising budget (p 415)
Affordable method (p 415)
Percentage-of-sales method (p 416)
Competitive-parity method (p 416)
Objective-and-task method (p 416)
Advertising strategy (p 417)
Madison & Vine (p 418)

Creative concept (p 420)
Execution style (p 420)
Advertising media (p 422)
Return on advertising investment (p 426)
Advertising agency (p 428)

Travel Log

Discussing the Issues

1. Name and define the five promotion mix tools for communicating customer value (AACSB: Communication)

2. Discuss the changing communications landscape and the need for integrated marketing communications. (AACSB: Communication)

3. Compare and contrast pull and push promotion strategies. Which promotion tools are most effective in each? (AACSB: Communication)

4. How do marketers measure the effectiveness of advertising? (AACSB: Communication)

5. Distinguish between *media type* and *media vehicle*. (AACSB: Communication)

6. Describe the role of public relations in an organization and the tools used to carry out that role. (AACSB: Communication)

Application Questions

1. Select two print advertisements (such as magazine ads) and evaluate the appeal used in each ad with respect to the three characteristics advertising appeals should possess. (AACSB: Communication; Reflective Thinking)

2. Brands are now starring in movies, television shows, video games, and books. Select three different television programs and identify the brands shown or mentioned in an episode of the show. What product categories seem to be more prevalent? How were the brands presented? Write a report on what you found. (AACSB: Communication; Reflective Thinking)

3. In a small group, discuss the major public relations tools and develop three public relations items for each of the following: (a) a charity, (b) a high school, (c) a hospital, (d) a bank, and (e) a health club. (AACSB: Communication; Reflective Thinking)

Under the Hood: Marketing Technology

Who better to create your ads than your own customers! Doritos had a smash hit, literally, during the 2009 Super Bowl with a commercial developed by amateurs. Joe and Dave Herbert's ad of a "crystal ball" (snow globe) smashing a vending machine, making the prediction of free Doritos for everyone in the office come true, captured the coveted number-one spot in *USAToday's* Ad Meter. The Ad Meter gives real-time consumer responses to ads during the game. Consumer-generated ads are not new, but now they are tweaking the likes of the professionals on Madison Avenue—New York's advertising Mecca. Doritos is upping the ante for the next Super Bowl—three ads will be selected to air during the game. Doritos wants to dominate the Ad Meter ranking, so it is offering $1 million for a first place finish, $600,000 for second, and another $400,000 for third. To launch the promotion, Doritos handed out free samples and even arranged to have Madison Avenue renamed Doritos Drive for the day. Consumers upload their videos at www.crashthesuperbowl.com, and three of the six finalists selected by online voting will see their ads on the Super Bowl.

1. Which promotion mix tools is Doritos using during this promotion? How does technology facilitate this campaign? (AACSB: Communication; Reflective Thinking)

2. Find other examples on the Internet of ad-creation contests and individual advertisements generated by consumers. (AACSB: Communication; Use of IT)

Staying on the Road: Marketing Ethics

Imagine a young family driving to Disney World. All along the route, the kids see billboards with Mickey, Donald, Kermit the Frog, and other Disney characters. Cinderella, Ariel, and the other princesses are so beautiful. Then come billboards with other beautiful women—only they are scantily clothed and in sexually-suggestive poses. These are ads for businesses such as strip clubs, adult bookstores, and other seedy businesses. "There ought to be a law against that," claims the horrified mother of the two young children in the car. In fact, several states have banned such billboards. But in Missouri, South Carolina, and Kansas, these laws have been overturned by federal courts. Cash-strapped states cannot afford the legal battle and seem to have little chance of winning anyway because of First Amendment protection. The states are losing because they must prove that the purpose of their laws is to prevent "sec-ondary effects," which might include decreased property values or increased crime. Thus, a law recently introduced in Michigan is not attempting to ban the advertising but is instead attempting to restrict the content of the ads to only listing a business's name, location, and hours of operation.

1. Should these types of advertisements have the same protection that individual citizens have under the First Amendment of the Constitution? (AACSB: Communication; Ethical Reasoning)

2. Sex sells, and a lot of advertising uses it even for products or services that are not sexually-oriented. Why are lawmakers more concerned with sexually-explicit ads on billboards than such ads in other media? (AACSB: Communication; Ethical Reasoning)

▚▎▎ Rough Road Ahead: Marketing and the Economy

McDonald's

Despite a down economy—or perhaps because of it—McDonald's has recently been beating competitors badly, in both same-store sales growth and perceptions of value. In fact, the fast-food giant pretty much owns the value menu. But, surprisingly, McDonald's current financial good fortunes are not being driven by its low-price items, but rather by higher-price, higher-margin items. Throughout the economic downturn, McDonald's advertising strategy has focused on its traditional full-priced specialties. One month it pushed Big Macs, the next month Chicken McNuggets, and then Quarter Pounders. McDonald's hasn't forsaken its dollar menu. Instead, it has increased promotional support for its flagship specialties. It's all part of an effort to grab business from diners who are trading down from higher-priced eateries. McDonald's also gambled that people would view the old favorites as comfort food. The promotional strategy worked. McDonald's overall revenues have risen, even as the percentage of revenues generated from lower-price items has fallen from 13 percent to 10 percent. The strategy is attracting new customers, while also encouraging existing value menu customers to trade up. All this has McDonald's executives and franchisees alike singing "I'm lovin' it."

1. What was McDonald's advertising objective with the recent promotion campaign described above?

2. In communicating value during hard times, what elements of McDonald's advertising strategy contributed to its success?

▚▎▎ Travel Budget: Marketing by the Numbers

Donya (http://www.iamediaservice.com) is the first newspaper from Saudi Arabia aimed at Arabian women, including housewives, professionals such as doctors, teachers, office mangers, students, and others.

1. Using the International Advertising LLC (http://www.iamediaservice.com) Web site, determine the cost of placing a full page advertisement in two Egyptian newspapers, one magazine for Oman and UAE and one for Donya. What is the total circulation of the newspapers?

2. Calculate the costs of running these advertisements for 6 issues, taking into account any discounts that may be offered.

Drive In: Video Case

CP+B

Crispin Porter + Bogusky (Crispin) may not be the oldest advertising agency in the world. It isn't the biggest either. But it has been working over time to prove that it is the most innovative firm at integrating marketing promotions. In fact, Crispin relies very little on the king of all advertising channels, broadcast TV. Instead, Crispin has worked miracles for companies such as Virgin Atlantic Airways, BMW's MINI Cooper, and Burger King by employing non-traditional campaigns on limited budgets.

Crispin attributes its success to the fact that it redefined what an advertisement is. Customer appropriate messages, Crispin discovered, could be delivered in many different ways. So its realm of "ad space" includes things as obscure as the side of a mailbox or an oversized phone booth in an airport. By communicating a message in many different ways, Crispin has developed a reputation for truly integrating marketing communications.

After viewing the video featuring Crispin, answer the following questions about advertising and promotions:

1. Alex Bogusky once said, "Anything and everything is an ad." What does this means? How is Crispin demonstrating this mantra?

2. In what ways has Crispin differentiated itself from other advertising agencies?

3. Give some examples as to how Crispin balances strategy with creativity.

Part 1   Defining Marketing and the Marketing Process (Chapters 1, 2)
Part 2   Understanding the Marketplace and Consumers (Chapters 3, 4, 5)
Part 3   Designing a Customer-Driven Strategy and Mix (Chapters 6, 7, 8, 9, 10, 11, 12, 13, 14)
Part 3   Extending Marketing (Chapters 15, 16)

13

Personal Selling
and Sales Promotion

ROAD MAP

Previewing the Concepts

In the previous chapter, you learned about communicating customer value through integrated marketing communications (IMC) and about two elements of the promotion mix—advertising and public relations. In this chapter, we'll look at two more IMC elements—personal selling and sales promotion. Personal selling is the interpersonal arm of marketing communications, in which the sales force interacts with customers and prospects to build relationships and make sales. Sales promotion consists of short-term incentives to encourage purchase or sale of a product or service. As you read on, remember that although this chapter examines personal selling and sales promotion as separate tools, they must be carefully integrated with other elements of the promotion mix.

Objective Outline

> **Objective 1**   Discuss the role of a company's salespeople in creating value for customers and building customer relationships.
> Personal Selling **pp 440–444**

> **Objective 2**   Identify and explain the six major sales force management steps.
> Managing the Sales Force **pp 444–454**

> **Objective 3**   Discuss the personal selling process, distinguishing between transaction-oriented marketing and relationship marketing.
> The Personal Selling Process **pp 454–458**

> **Objective 4**   Explain how sales promotion campaigns are developed and implemented.
> Sales Promotion **pp 459–464**

In a market as potentially large as China, you would be wrong to believe that there are enough sales to go around for everyone. Like any other market, it is a cutthroat business, with international companies vying with local manufacturers, all desperate to retain or to increase their market share as demand rockets. A mix of personal selling, sales promotions, and strategic alliances are all vital.

▲Volkswagen has struggled to compete with local manufacturers in the competitive Asian market. However, the firm's sponsorship of the Beijing Olympics dramatically helped to boost the company's profile in that market.

First Stop

Volkswagen:
Driving Sales in China

In 2000, times were hard for Volkswagen. Volkswagen's chief executive officer, Bernd Pischetrieder, knew that his company was still the biggest carmaker in Europe, but there had been loses in North America and there were production problems in Germany. Volkswagen had also been replaced as the leading car maker in China, a position it had held since 1985. Now it had been overtaken by General Motors. In 2000, Volkswagen had some 50 percent of the passenger car market in China; five years later it was just 15 percent. Winfried Vahland, Volkswagen's man in China, was determined to use the fact that China would be host to the Olympic Games in 2008 as the catalyst to restore the fortunes of the company. Volkswagen saw itself as, and others agreed that it was, a European-centered company.

Volkswagen had 343,000 employees, around 179,000 of which were based in Germany, most in the Wolfsburg main plant. However, since Germany was one of the most expensive places to manufacture cars, Volkswagen needed to cut costs and move production somewhere cheaper; otherwise, its slide in market share would continue.

Volkswagen had opened an office in Beijing in 1985, the first Western car manufacturer to do so. It had a joint venture partnership and near monopoly on government and taxi sales for 20 years.

By targeting government and taxi sales, the company was able to achieve huge economies of scale and sell high volumes. Each time the taxi fleets upgraded, Volkswagen enjoyed a bonanza of sales. Until 2004 it had been law that overseas companies had to enter into joint ventures with local companies in China. Volkswagen worked closely with the Shanghai Automotive International Company (SAIC), which had been founded in 1985, and First Automotive Works (FAW), created in 1987. There was also a range of joint ventures around China to supply parts.

By the beginning of 2000, Volkswagen had captured 53 percent of the passenger car market in China, but soon that market share was tumbling. By 2004 it had slumped to 24 percent and then 15 percent in 2005. In 2006, the total car sales in China reached a staggering 2.25 million; each year had seen double-digit growth in sales. All of the competitors, apart from Volkswagen, were seeing record sales and profits; Volkswagen's profits dropped by 40 percent from 2004.

China had an emerging middle class, a small percentage of the total population, but 60 million strong. Nonetheless, they wanted luxury overseas cars, particularly Italian or German cars. Ultimately it was expected that the middle classes would grow to 300 million, yet customers were price sensitive and it was difficult for them to raise loans due to government restrictions. High taxation on luxury cars was still in place.

A decade ago, after much promise, Volkswagen was floundering in China. With increased competition in all markets, it needed to turn things around. The Beijing Olympics provided a way in which to relaunch the brand and regain market share.

▲ Although Volkswagen is a recognizable brand in Europe, the company has yet to gain a substantial amount of market share in China.

longer available in other parts of the world. This meant that the factories were using out-of-date machinery.

Additionally, Chinese customers wanted the latest versions of the cars. Honda was first to respond by bringing out the new version of the Civic in China, just months after its launch in Western markets. Toyota quickly followed suit with the Prius. While price cuts had the inevitable effect of cutting profits, overcapacity occurred as well. Car manufacturers had invested $13 billion in China to increase production by 300 percent to a target of 10 million cars by 2010. This meant that China would become an exporter of cars instead of an importer.

The Asian car manufacturers were the first to increase their production levels, and it became inevitable that they would overtake Volkswagen and General Motors. By 2006, the Japanese brands of Toyota and Nissan had captured 27.4 percent of the Chinese market and were increasing their investment in production and marketing. The Chinese loved their cars for their reliability and their quality. Another entrant, Hyundai, was also making headway in the market.

Other European car manufacturers were doing well; PSA Peugeot Citroën, which had entered the market in 1992, had a market share of 3.5 percent. BMW had opened a manufacturing plant in 1994 and was appealing to the high end of the market along with Mercedes. Chinese brands were growing, notably Geely, Chery, and Lifan. The most successful Chinese car has been Chery's QQ micro-car; at $4,000 it had seen sales soar by 136 percent in 2006. According to Shanghai consulting business Automotive Resources Asia, "Chinese brands overtook their Japanese counterparts to become the top-selling passenger vehicles in China in January [2006], with total sales of 92,630 units."

To boost demand, competitors introduced price cuts, but there was another problem that could not have been immediately apparent. The car manufacturers were selling outdated models that were no

In October 2005, Volkswagen China announced its "Olympic" program to restructure the group in China. Volkswagen had the following key objectives:

- It wanted to create a stronger differentiation between the two joint ventures to stop Volkswagen from effectively competing against itself.
- It wanted to introduce 10–12 new models specifically for the Chinese market by 2009.
- It wanted to cut costs by centralizing purchasing.
- It aimed to restructure the sales organization and development of more customer-centered sales channels.

Volkswagen Group China, with its two joint ventures Shanghai Volkswagen and FAW-Volkswagen, could claim that its vehicle deliveries to customers in China increased 23.3 percent to 531,612 units in the first half of 2008. In 2007, it had sold 431,160 units in the same period. In all, sales of the Volkswagen brand amounted to 439,218 units (an increase of 15.7 percent), compared to 379,615 units in the first half of 2007.

As a major promotion in July 2008, Volkswagen handed over 5,000 Olympic vehicles to the Beijing Olympic organizing committee (BOCOG). Zhang Suixin, executive vice-president and board member of Volkswagen Group China said, "The 5,000 Olympic official vehicles are now successfully handed over to BOCOG as planned, and that gives full expression to the Olympic spirit of solidarity and dedication. We will do our best to assist BOCOG in transporting athletes, officials, and VIPs and provide quality and satisfactory services during the Games."

The company had already given 1,000 cars for the torch relay and another 30 for the press to use. It would also provide 24-hour service and repair. Pan Qing, director of Volkswagen (China) Olympic marketing added, "After the conclusion of the Games, most of those official vehicles will be sent to our retailers to serve for test drives to let more people feel the Olympics. We hope the Olympic spirit could last for long after the Games."

This was an unprecedented turnaround in fortunes and a priceless promotion to stimulate sales.[1]

*i*n this chapter, we examine two more promotion mix tools—*personal selling* and *sales promotion*. Personal selling consists of interpersonal interactions with customers and prospects to make sales and maintain customer relationships. Sales promotion involves using short-term incentives to encourage customer purchasing, reseller support, and sales force efforts.

Author Comment »
Personal selling is the interpersonal arm of the promotion mix. A company's salespeople create and communicate customer value through personal interactions with customers.

PERSONAL SELLING (pp 440–444)

Robert Louis Stevenson once noted, "everyone lives by selling something." Companies all around the world use sales forces to sell products and services to business customers and final consumers. But sales forces are also found in many other kinds of organizations. For example, colleges use recruiters to attract new students and churches use membership committees to attract new members. Museums and fine arts organizations use fund-raisers to contact donors and raise money. Even governments use sales forces. The U.S. Postal Service, for instance, uses a sales force to sell Express Mail and other services to corporate customers. In the first part of this chapter, we examine personal selling's role in the organization, sales force management decisions, and the personal selling process.

The Nature of Personal Selling

Personal selling
Personal presentation by the firm's sales force for the purpose of making sales and building customer relationships.

Personal selling is one of the oldest professions in the world. The people who do the selling go by many names: salespeople, sales representatives, district managers, account executives, sales consultants, sales engineers, agents, and account development reps to name just a few.

People hold many stereotypes of salespeople—including some unfavorable ones. "Salesman" may bring to mind the image of Arthur Miller's pitiable Willy Loman in *Death of a Salesman* or Dwight Schrute, the opinionated Dunder Mifflin paper salesman from the TV show *The Office*, who lacks both common sense and social skills. And then there are the real-life "yell-and-sell" "pitchmen," who hawk everything from OxiClean, Kaboom, and ShamWow to the Awesome Auger and Samurai Shark sharpener in TV infomercials. However, the majority of salespeople are a far cry from these unfortunate stereotypes.

Most salespeople are well-educated, well-trained professionals who add value for customers and maintain long-term customer relationships. They listen to their customers, assess customer needs, and organize the company's efforts to solve customer problems.[2]

Salesperson
An individual representing a company to customers by performing one or more of the following activities: prospecting, communicating, selling, servicing, information gathering, and relationship building.

Some assumptions about what makes someone a good salesperson are dead wrong. There's this idea that the classic sales personality is overbearing, pushy, and outgoing, the kind of people who walk in and suck all the air out of the room. But the best salespeople are good at one-on-one contact. They create loyalty and customers because people trust them and want to work with them. It's a matter of putting the client's interests first—which is the antithesis of how most people view salespeople. The most successful salespeople are successful for one simple reason: they know how to build relationships. You can go in with a big personality and convince people to do what you want them to do, but that isn't really selling. It's manipulation, and it only works in the short term. A good salesperson can read customer emotions without exploiting them, because the bottom line is that he or she wants what's best for the customer.

▲ Professional selling: It takes more than fast talk and a warm smile to sell high-tech aircraft, where a single big sale can easily run into billions of dollars. Success depends on building solid, long-term relationships with customers.

Consider Boeing, the aerospace giant competing in the rough-and-tumble worldwide commercial aircraft market. ▲It takes more than fast talk and a warm smile to sell expensive high-tech aircraft. A single big sale can easily run into billions of dollars. Boeing salespeople head up an extensive team of company specialists—sales and service technicians, financial analysts, planners, engineers—all dedicated to finding ways to satisfy airline customer needs. The selling process is nerve-rackingly slow—it can take two or three years from the first sales presentation to the day the sale is announced. After getting the order, salespeople then must stay in almost constant touch to make certain the customer stays satisfied. Success depends on building solid, long-term relationships with customers, based on performance and trust.

The term **salesperson** covers a wide range of positions. At one extreme, a salesperson might be largely an *order taker*, such as the department store salesperson standing behind the counter. At the other extreme are *order getters*, whose positions demand *creative selling* and *relationship building* for products and services ranging from appliances, industrial equipment, and airplanes to insurance and information technology services. Here, we focus on the more creative types of selling and on the process of building and managing an effective sales force.

The Role of the Sales Force

Personal selling is the interpersonal arm of the promotion mix. Advertising consists largely of nonpersonal communication with target consumer groups. In contrast, personal selling involves interpersonal interactions between salespeople and individual customers—whether face-to-face, by telephone, via e-mail, through video or Web conferences, or by other means. Personal selling can be more effective than advertising in more complex selling situations. Salespeople can probe customers to learn more about their problems and then adjust the marketing offer and presentation to fit the special needs of each customer.

The role of personal selling varies from company to company. Some firms have no salespeople at all—for example, companies that sell only online or through catalogs, or companies that sell through manufacturer's reps, sales agents, or brokers. In most firms, however, the sales force plays a major role. In companies that sell business products and services, such as IBM, DuPont, or Boeing, the company's salespeople work directly with customers. In consumer product companies such as P&G and Nike, the sales force plays an important behind-the-scenes role. It works with wholesalers and retailers to gain their support and to help them be more effective in selling the company's products.

Linking the Company with Its Customers

The sales force serves as a critical link between a company and its customers. ▲In many cases, salespeople serve both masters—the seller and the buyer. First, they *represent the company to customers*. They find and develop new customers and communicate information about the company's products and services. They sell products by approaching customers, presenting their offerings, answering objections, negotiating prices and terms, and closing sales. In addition, salespeople provide customer service and carry out market research and intelligence work.

▲ **Salespeople link the company with its customers. To many customers, the salesperson *is* the company.**

At the same time, salespeople *represent customers to the company*, acting inside the firm as "champions" of customers' interests and managing the buyer–seller relationship. Salespeople relay customer concerns about company products and actions back inside to those who can handle them. They learn about customer needs and work with other marketing and nonmarketing people in the company to develop greater customer value.

In fact, to many customers, the salesperson *is* the company—the only tangible manifestation of the company that they see. Hence, customers may become loyal to salespeople as well as to the companies and products they represent. This concept of "salesperson-owned loyalty" lends even more importance to the salesperson's customer relationship building abilities. Strong relationships with the salesperson will result in strong relationships with the company and its products. Conversely, poor salesperson relationships will probably result in poor company and product relationships.[3]

Given its role in linking the company with its customers, the sales force must be strongly customer-solutions focused. In fact, such a customer-solutions focus is a must not just for the sales force, but also for the entire organization. Says Anne Mulcahy, successful former CEO and current chairman of Xerox, who started her career in sales, a strong customer-service focus "has to be the center of your universe, the heartland of how you run your company" (see Marketing at Work 13.1).

Marketing at Work 13.1

The Role of the Sales Force—and the Entire Company: Putting Customers First

When someone says "salesperson," what image comes to mind? Perhaps you think about a stereotypical glad-hander who's out to lighten customers' wallets by selling them something they don't really need. Think again. Today, for most companies, personal selling plays an important role in building profitable customer relationships. In turn, those relationships contribute greatly to overall company success.

Just ask Anne Mulcahy, recently retired CEO and current chairman of the board at Xerox. We talked about Mulcahy in Chapter 3. She's the former Xerox CEO who took the reins of the then-nearly-bankrupt copier company in early 2001 and transformed it into a successful modern-day digital technology and services enterprise. Mulcahy has received much praise from analysts, investors, and others as a transformative leader at Xerox. In 2007, *Fortune* magazine named her the second-most-powerful women in business, and *Forbes* ranked her as the 13th-most-powerful woman in the world. In 2008, she became the first female CEO selected by her peers as *Chief Executive* magazine's Chief Executive of the Year.

But the roots of Mulcahy's success go back to the lessons she learned and the skills she honed in sales. The one-time undergraduate English and journalism major began her career in 1976 as a Xerox sales rep in Boston. From there, she worked her way up the sales ladder to become Xerox's vice president of global sales in the late 1990s. Then, 25 years after first knocking on customer doors in New England, she was appointed CEO of Xerox.

As CEO, Mulcahy brought with her a sales and marketing mentality that now permeates the entire Xerox organization. As you may recall from the Chapter 3 Xerox turnaround story, the company's transformation started with a new focus solving customer problems. Mulcahy believes that understanding customers is just as important as understanding technology. "Having spent so much time in sales, . . . I knew you have to keep customers in the forefront." But looking back, Mulcahy recalls, Xerox had had lost touch with its markets. To turn things around at Xerox, the company needed to focus on customers. "In a crisis, that is what really matters."

"Sales helps you understand what drives the business and that customers are a critical part of the business," Mulcahy says. "This will be important in any business function, but you learn it [best] in sales management where it is critical, the jewel in the crown." Implementing this customer-first sales philosophy, one of Mulcahy's first actions as CEO was to put on her old sales hat and hit the road to visit customers. She has stayed in direct touch with customers ever since—she still spends a part of every day responding to customer e-mails.

Mulcahy knows that putting customers first isn't just a sales force responsibility—it's an emphasis for everyone in the com-

▲ Putting the customer first: Says transformative former Xerox CEO and current chairman, Anne Mulcahy, who started her career in sales, that "has to be the center of your universe, the heartland of how you run your company."

pany. To stress that point at all levels, she quickly set up a rotating Customer Officer of the Day program at Xerox, which requires a top executive to answer customer calls that get through to corporate headquarters. As Customer Officer of the Day, the executive has three responsibilities: listen to the customer, resolve the problem, and take responsibility for fixing the underlying cause. That sounds a lot like sales.

So if you're still thinking of salespeople as fast-talking, ever-smiling peddlers who foist their wares off on reluctant customers, you're probably working with an out-of-date stereotype. Good salespeople succeed not by taking customers in, but by helping them out—by assessing customer needs and solving customer problems. At Xerox, salespeople are well-trained professionals who listen to customers and win their business by doing what's right for them. In fact, that isn't just good sales thinking—it applies to the entire organization. According to Mulcahy, that "has to be the center of your universe, the heartland of how you run your company."

Sources: Henry Canaday, "Sales Rep to CEO: Anne Mulcahy and the Xerox Revolution," *Selling Power*, November/December 2008, pp. 53–57; "2008 Chief Executive of the Year," *Chief Executive*, September/October 2008, p. 68; Andrea Deckert, "Mulcahy Describes the Keys to Xerox Turnaround," November 2, 2007, p. 3; "Women CEOs, Xerox," *Financial Times*, December 31, 2008, p. 10; and "Anne Mulcahy to Retire as Xerox CEO," *Wireless News*, May 27, 2009.

Coordinating Marketing and Sales

Ideally, the sales force and the firm's other marketing functions should work together closely to jointly create value for both customers and the company. Unfortunately, however, some companies still treat "marketing" and "sales" as separate functions. When this happens, the separated marketing and sales functions often don't get along well. When things go wrong, the marketers (marketing planners, brand managers, and researchers) blame the sales force for its poor execution of an otherwise splendid strategy. In turn, the sales team blames the marketers for being out of touch with what's really going on with customers. The marketers sometimes feel that salespeople have their "feet stuck in the mud" whereas salespeople feel that the marketers have their "heads stuck in the clouds." Neither group fully values the other's contributions. If not repaired, such disconnects between marketing and sales can damage customer relationships and company performance.

A company can take several actions to help bring its marketing and sales functions closer together. At the most basic level, it can *increase communications* between the two groups by arranging joint meetings and by spelling out when and with whom each group should communicate. The company can create *joint assignments:*[4]

> It's important to create opportunities for marketers and salespeople to work together. This will make them more familiar with each other's ways of thinking and acting. It's useful for marketers, particularly brand managers and researchers, to occasionally go along on sales calls. They should also sit in on important account-planning sessions. Salespeople, in turn, should help to develop marketing plans. They should sit in on product-planning reviews and share their deep knowledge about customers' purchasing habits. They should preview ad and sales-promotion campaigns. Jointly, marketers and salespeople should generate a playbook for expanding business with the top 10 accounts in each market segment. They should also plan events and conferences together.

A company can also create *joint objectives and reward systems* for sales and marketing or appoint *marketing-sales liaisons*—people from marketing who "live with the sales force" and help to coordinate marketing and sales force programs and efforts. Finally, the firm can appoint a *chief revenue officer* (or *chief customer officer*)— a high-level marketing executive who oversees both marketing and sales. Such a person can help infuse marketing and sales with the common goal of creating value for customers in order to capture value in return.

Sales force management
The analysis, planning, implementation, and control of sales force activities. It includes designing sales force strategy and structure and recruiting, selecting, training, supervising, compensating, and evaluating the firm's salespeople.

Author Comment ≫
Here's another definition of sales force management: "Planning, organizing, leading, and controlling personal contact programs designed to achieve profitable customer relationships." Here again, the goal of every marketing activity is to create customer value and build customer relationships.

MANAGING THE SALES FORCE (pp 444–454)

We define **sales force management** as the analysis, planning, implementation, and control of sales force activities. It includes designing sales force strategy and structure and recruiting, selecting, training, compensating, supervising, and evaluating the firm's salespeople. These major sales force management decisions are shown in ■ **Figure 13.1** and are discussed in the following sections.

Designing Sales Force Strategy and Structure

Marketing managers face several sales force strategy and design questions. How should salespeople and their tasks be structured? How big should the sales force be? Should salespeople sell alone or work in teams with other people in the com-

---

■ **Figure 13.1** Major Steps in Sales Force Management

The goal of this process? You guessed it! The company wants to build a skilled and motivated sales team that will help to create customer value and build strong customer relationships.

Designing sales force strategy and structure → Recruiting and selecting salespeople → Training salespeople → Compensating salespeople → Supervising salespeople → Evaluating salespeople

pany? Should they sell in the field or by telephone or on the Web? We address these issues next.

Sales Force Structure

A company can divide sales responsibilities along any of several lines. The structure decision is simple if the company sells only one product line to one industry with customers in many locations. In that case the company would use a *territorial sales force structure*. However, if the company sells many products to many types of customers, it might need either a *product sales force structure*, a *customer sales force structure*, or a combination of the two.

Territorial Sales Force Structure. In the **territorial sales force structure**, each salesperson is assigned to an exclusive geographic area and sells the company's full line of products or services to all customers in that territory. This organization clearly defines each salesperson's job and fixes accountability. It also increases the salesperson's desire to build local customer relationships that, in turn, improve selling effectiveness. Finally, because each salesperson travels within a limited geographic area, travel expenses are relatively small.

A territorial sales organization is often supported by many levels of sales management positions. For example, Black & Decker uses a territorial structure in which each salesperson is responsible for selling all of the company's products—from hand tools to lawn and garden equipment—in assigned territories. Starting at the bottom of the organization are entry-level *territory sales representatives* who report to *territory managers*. Territory sales representatives cover smaller areas, such as Eastern North Carolina, and the territory managers cover larger areas such as the Carolinas and Virginia. Territory managers, in turn, report to *regional managers,* who cover regions such as the Southeast or West Coast. The regional managers, in turn, report to a *director of sales*.

Product Sales Force Structure. Salespeople must know their products—especially when the products are numerous and complex. This need, together with the growth of product management, has led many companies to adopt a **product sales force structure**, in which the sales force sells along product lines. For example, GE employs different sales forces within different product and service divisions of its major businesses. Within GE Infrastructure, for instance, the company has separate sales forces for aviation, energy, transportation, and water processing products and technologies. Within GE Healthcare, it employs different sales forces for diagnostic imaging, life sciences, and integrated IT solutions products and services. In all, a company as large and complex as GE might have dozens of separate sales forces serving its diverse product and service portfolio.

The product structure can lead to problems, however, if a single large customer buys many different company products. For example, several different GE salespeople might end up calling on the same large healthcare customer in a given period. This means that they travel over the same routes and wait to see the same customer's purchasing agents. These extra costs must be compared with the benefits of better product knowledge and attention to individual products.

Customer Sales Force Structure. More and more companies are now using a **customer (or market) sales force structure**, in which they organize the sales force along customer or industry lines. Separate sales forces may be set up for different industries, for serving current customers versus finding new ones, and for major accounts versus regular accounts. Many companies even have special sales forces set up to handle the needs of individual large customers. For example, above its territory structure, Black & Decker has a Home Depot sales organization and a Lowe's sales organization.

Organizing the sales force around customers can help a company to build closer relationships with important customers. ▲Consider Hill-Rom, a leading supplier of

Territorial sales force structure
A sales force organization that assigns each salesperson to an exclusive geographic territory in which that salesperson sells the company's full line.

Product sales force structure
A sales force organization under which salespeople specialize in selling only a portion of the company's products or lines.

Customer (or market) sales force structure
A sales force organization under which salespeople specialize in selling only to certain customers or industries.

▲Leading medical-equipment supplier Hill-Rom recently adopted a customer-based sales force structure, which helped it to focus more intensely on the needs of large key customers. In the two years following the sales force redesign, sales growth doubled.

medical equipment, such as hospital beds, stretchers, and nurse communication systems, which recently restructured its product-based sales force into a customer-based one:[5]

> Hill-Rom has divided its sales force into two customer-based teams. One sales force focuses on "key" customers—large accounts that purchase high-end equipment and demand high levels of sales force collaboration. The second sales force focuses on "prime" customers—smaller accounts that are generally more concerned about getting the features and functions they need for the best possible price. Assigning the separate sales forces helps Hill-Rom to better understand what the different types of customers need. It also lets the company track how much attention the sales force devotes to each customer group.
>
> For example, prior to restructuring the sales force, Hill-Rom had been treating both key and prime customers the same way. As a result, it was trying to sell smaller prime customers a level of service and innovation that they did not value or could not afford. So the cost of sales for prime customers was four to five times higher than for key customers. Now, a single account manager and team focuses intensely on all the areas of each key customer's business, working together to find product and service solutions. Such intensive collaboration would have been difficult under the old product-based sales structure, in which multiple Hill-Rom sales reps serviced the different specialty areas within a single key account. In the two years following the sales force redesign, Hill-Rom's sales growth doubled.

Complex Sales Force Structures. When a company sells a wide variety of products to many types of customers over a broad geographic area, it often combines several types of sales force structures. Salespeople can be specialized by customer and territory, by product and territory, by product and customer, or by territory, product, and customer. For example, Black & Decker specializes its sales force by customer (with different sales forces calling on Home Depot, Lowe's, and smaller independent retailers) *and* by territory for each key customer group (territory representatives, territory managers, regional managers, and so on). No single structure is best for all companies and situations. Each company should select a sales force structure that best serves the needs of its customers and fits its overall marketing strategy.

A good sales structure can mean the difference between success and failure. Over time, sales force structures can grow complex, inefficient, and unresponsive to customers' needs. Companies should periodically review their sales force organizations to be certain that they serve the needs of the company and its customers.

Sales Force Size

Once the company has set its structure, it is ready to consider *sales force size*. Sales forces may range in size from only a few salespeople to tens of thousands. ▲Some sales forces are huge—for example, PepsiCo employs 36,000 salespeople; American Express, 23,400; GE, 16,400; and Xerox, 15,000.[6] Salespeople constitute one of the company's most productive—and most expensive—assets. Therefore, increasing their number will increase both sales and costs.

Many companies use some form of *workload approach* to set sales force size. Using this approach, a company first groups accounts into different classes according to size, account status, or other factors related to the amount of effort re-

▼Some sales forces are huge. For example, GE employs 16,400 salespeople, Xerox 15,000, American Express 23,400, and PepsiCo 36,000.

quired to maintain them. It then determines the number of salespeople needed to call on each class of accounts the desired number of times.

The company might think as follows: Suppose we have 1,000 Type-A accounts and 2,000 Type-B accounts. Type-A accounts require 36 calls a year and Type-B accounts require 12 calls a year. In this case, the sales force's *workload*—the number of calls it must make per year—is 60,000 calls [(1,000 × 36) + (2,000 × 12) = 36,000 + 24,000 = 60,000]. Suppose our average salesperson can make 1,000 calls a year. Thus, we need 60 salespeople (60,000 ÷ 1,000).[7]

Other Sales Force Strategy and Structure Issues

Sales management must also decide who will be involved in the selling effort and how various sales and sales support people will work together.

Outside sales force (or field sales force)
Outside salespeople who travel to call on customers in the field.

Inside sales force
Inside salespeople who conduct business from their offices via telephone, the Internet, or visits from prospective buyers.

Outside and Inside Sales Forces. The company may have an **outside sales force (or field sales force)**, an **inside sales force**, or both. Outside salespeople travel to call on customers in the field. Inside salespeople conduct business from their offices via telephone, the Internet, or visits from buyers.

Some inside salespeople provide support for the outside sales force, freeing them to spend more time selling to major accounts and finding new prospects. For example, *technical sales support people* provide technical information and answers to customers' questions. *Sales assistants* provide administrative backup for outside salespeople. They call ahead and confirm appointments, follow up on deliveries, and answer customers' questions when outside salespeople cannot be reached. Using such combinations of inside and outside salespeople can help to serve important customers better. The inside rep provides daily access and support; the outside rep provides face-to-face collaboration and relationship building.

Other inside salespeople do more than just provide support. *Telemarketers* and *Web sellers* use the phone and Internet to find new leads and qualify prospects or to sell and service accounts directly. Telemarketing and Web selling can be very effective, less costly ways to sell to smaller, harder-to-reach customers. Depending on the complexity of the product and customer, for example, a telemarketer can make from 20 to 33 decision-maker contacts a day, compared to the average of 4 that an outside salesperson can make. And whereas an average business-to-business field sales call costs $329 or more, a routine industrial telemarketing call costs only about $5 and a complex call about $20.[8]

Although the federal government's Do Not Call Registry put a dent in telephone sales to consumers, telemarketing remains a vital tool for many business-to-business marketers. For some smaller companies, telephone and Web selling may be the primary sales approaches. However, larger companies also use these tactics, either to sell directly to small and midsize customers or to help out with larger ones. Especially in the leaner times following the recent recession, many companies are cutting back on in-person customer visits in favor of more telephone, e-mail, and Internet selling.[9]

▼For many types of selling situations, phone or Web selling can be as effective as a personal sales call. Phone reps can build surprisingly strong and personal customer relationships.

▲For many types of products and selling situations, phone or Web selling can be as effective as a personal sales call. Notes a DuPont telemarketer: "I'm more effective on the phone. [When you're in the field], if some guy's not in his office, you lose an hour. On the phone, you lose 15 seconds. . . . Through my phone calls, I'm in the field as much as the rep is." There are other advantages. "Customers can't throw things at you," quips the rep, "and you don't have to outrun dogs."[10]

What's more, although they may seem impersonal, the phone and Internet can be surprisingly personal when it comes to building customer relationships.

Team Selling. As products become more complex, and as customers grow larger and more demanding, a single salesperson simply can't handle all of a large customer's needs. Instead, most companies now use **team selling** to service large, complex accounts. Sales teams can unearth problems, solutions, and sales opportunities that no individual salesperson could. Such teams might include experts from any area or level of the selling firm—sales, marketing, technical and support services, R&D, engineering, operations, finance, and others. In team selling situations, the salesperson shifts from "soloist" to "orchestrator."

Team selling
Using teams of people from sales, marketing, engineering, finance, technical support, and even upper management to service large, complex accounts.

In many cases, the move to team selling mirrors similar changes in customers' buying organizations. "Buyers implementing team-based purchasing decisions have necessitated the equal and opposite creation of team-based selling—a completely new way of doing business for many independent, self-motivated salespeople," says a sales force analyst. "Today, we're calling on teams of buying people, and that requires more firepower on our side," agrees one sales vice president. "One salesperson just can't do it all—can't be an expert in everything we're bringing to the customer. We have strategic account teams, led by customer business managers, who basically are our quarterbacks."[11]

Some companies, such as IBM, Xerox, and P&G, have used teams for a long time. P&G sales reps are organized into "customer business development (CBD) teams." Each CBD team is assigned to a major P&G customer, such as Wal-Mart, Safeway, or CVS Pharmacy. Teams consist of a customer business development manager, several account executives (each responsible for a specific category of P&G products), and specialists in marketing strategy, operations, information systems, logistics, and finance. This organization places the focus on serving the complete needs of each important customer. It lets P&G "grow business by working as a 'strategic partner' with our accounts, not just as a supplier. Our goal: to grow their business, which also results in growing ours."[12]

Team selling does have some pitfalls. For example, salespeople are by nature competitive and have often been trained and rewarded for outstanding individual performance. Salespeople who are used to having customers all to themselves may have trouble learning to work with and trust others on a team. In addition, selling teams can confuse or overwhelm customers who are used to working with only one salesperson. Finally, difficulties in evaluating individual contributions to the team selling effort can create some sticky compensation issues.

Recruiting and Selecting Salespeople

At the heart of any successful sales force operation is the recruitment and selection of good salespeople. The performance difference between an average salesperson and a top salesperson can be substantial. In a typical sales force, the top 30 percent of the salespeople might bring in 60 percent of the sales. Thus, careful salesperson selection can greatly increase overall sales force performance. Beyond the differences in sales performance, poor selection results in costly turnover. When a salesperson quits, the costs of finding and training a new salesperson—plus the costs of lost sales—can be very high. Also, a sales force with many new people is less productive, and turnover disrupts important customer relationships.

What sets great salespeople apart from all the rest? In an effort to profile top sales performers, Gallup Management Consulting Group, a division of the well-known Gallup polling organization, has interviewed hundreds of thousands of salespeople. ▲Its research suggests that the best salespeople possess four key talents: intrinsic motivation, disciplined work style, the ability to close a sale, and perhaps most important, the ability to build relationships with customers.[13]

▲ **Great salespeople: The best salespeople, such as Jennifer Hansen of 3M, possess intrinsic motivation, disciplined work style, the ability to close a sale, and perhaps most important, the ability to build relationships with customers.**

Super salespeople are motivated from within—they have an unrelenting drive to excel. Some salespeople are driven by money, a desire for recognition, or the satisfaction of competing and winning. Others are driven by the desire to provide service and to build relationships. The best salespeople possess some of each of these motivations. They also have a disciplined work style. They lay out detailed, organized plans and then follow through in a timely way.

But motivation and discipline mean little unless they result in closing more sales and building better customer relationships. Super salespeople build the skills and knowledge they need to get the job done. Perhaps most important, top salespeople are excellent customer problem solvers and relationship builders. They understand their customers' needs. Talk to sales executives and they'll describe top performers in these terms: empathetic, patient, caring, responsive, good listeners. Top performers can put themselves on the buyer's side of the desk and see the world through their customers' eyes. They don't want just to be liked, they want to add value for their customers.

When recruiting, a company should analyze the sales job itself and the characteristics of its most successful salespeople to identify the traits needed by a successful salesperson in their industry. Then, it must recruit the right salespeople. The human resources department looks for applicants by getting names from current salespeople, using employment agencies, placing classified ads, searching the Web, and working through college placement services. Another source is to attract top salespeople from other companies. Proven salespeople need less training and can be productive immediately.

Recruiting will attract many applicants from whom the company must select the best. The selection procedure can vary from a single informal interview to lengthy testing and interviewing. Many companies give formal tests to sales applicants. Tests typically measure sales aptitude, analytical and organizational skills, personality traits, and other characteristics. But test scores provide only one piece of information in a set that includes personal characteristics, references, past employment history, and interviewer reactions.

Training Salespeople

New salespeople may spend anywhere from a few weeks or months to a year or more in training. Then, most companies provide continuing sales training via seminars, sales meetings, and Web e-learning throughout the salesperson's career. In all, U.S. companies spend billions of dollars annually on training salespeople, and sales training typical captures the largest share of the training budget. For example, U.S. technology companies invest 29 percent of their training budgets on sales training. Although training can be expensive, it can also yield dramatic returns. For instance, one recent study showed that sales training conducted by administrative services firm ADP resulted in a return on investment of nearly percent in only 90 days.[14]

Training programs have several goals. First, salespeople need to know about customers and how to build relationships with them. So the training program must teach them about different types of customers and their needs, buying motives, and buying habits. And it must teach them how to sell effectively and train them in the basics of the selling process. Salespeople also need to know and identify with the company, its products, and its competitors. So an effective training program teaches them about the company's objectives, organization, chief products and markets, and about the strategies of major competitors.

Today, many companies are adding e-learning to their sales training programs. Online training may range from simple text-based product training to Internet-based sales exercises that build sales skills to sophisticated simulations that re-create the dynamics of real-life sales calls. Training online instead of on-site can cut travel and other training costs, and it takes up less of salespeople's selling time. It also makes on-demand training available to salespeople, letting them train as little or as much as needed, whenever and wherever needed. Most e-learning is Web-based but many companies now offer on-demand training for PDAs, cell phones, and even video iPods.

Many companies are now using imaginative and sophisticated e-learning techniques to make sales training more efficient—and sometimes even more fun. ▲For example, Bayer HealthCare Pharmaceuticals worked with healthcare marketing agency Concentric Rx to create a role-playing simulation video game to train its sales force on a new drug marketing program:[15]

▲E-Training can make sales training more efficient—and more fun. Bayer HealthCare Pharmaceuticals' role-playing video game—Rep Race—helped improve sales rep effectiveness by 20 percent.

You don't usually associate fast-paced rock music and flashy graphics with online sales training tools. But Concentric Rx's innovative role-playing video game—Rep Race: The Battle for Office Supremacy—has all that and a lot more. Rep Race gives Bayer sales reps far more entertainment than the staid old multiple-choice skills tests it replaces. The game was created to help breathe new life into a mature Bayer product—Betaseron, a 17-year-old multiple sclerosis (MS) therapy treatment. The aim was to find a fresh, more active way to help Bayer sales reps apply the in-depth information they learned about Betaseron to actual selling and objections-handling situations. Bayer also wanted to increase rep engagement through interactive learning and feedback through real-time results. Bayer reps liked Rep Race from the start. According to Bayer, when the game was first launched, reps played it as many as 30 times. In addition to its educational and motivational value, Rep Race allowed Bayer to measure sales reps' individual and collective performance. In the end, Bayer calculates that the Rep Race simulation helped improve the Betaseron sales team's effectiveness by 20 percent.

Compensating Salespeople

To attract good salespeople, a company must have an appealing compensation plan. Compensation is made up of several elements—a fixed amount, a variable amount, expenses, and fringe benefits. The fixed amount, usually a salary, gives the salesperson some stable income. The variable amount, which might be commissions or bonuses based on sales performance, rewards the salesperson for greater effort and success.

Management must decide what *mix* of these compensation elements makes the most sense for each sales job. Different combinations of fixed and variable compensation give rise to four basic types of compensation plans—straight salary, straight commission, salary plus bonus, and salary plus commission. A study of sales force compensation showed that the average salesperson's pay consists of about 67 percent salary and 33 percent incentive pay.[16]

The sales force compensation plan can both motivate salespeople and direct their activities. Compensation should direct salespeople toward activities that are consistent with overall sales force and marketing objectives. For example, if the strategy is to acquire new business, grow rapidly, and gain market share, the compensation plan might include a larger commission component, coupled with a new-account bonus to encourage high sales performance and new-account development. In contrast, if the goal is to maximize current account profitability, the compensation plan might contain a larger base-salary component with additional incentives for current account sales or customer satisfaction.

In fact, more and more companies are moving away from high commission plans that may drive salespeople to make short-term grabs for business. They worry that a salesperson who is pushing too hard to close a deal may ruin the customer relationship. Instead, companies are designing compensation plans that reward salespeople for building customer relationships and growing the long-run value of each customer.

Supervising and Motivating Salespeople

New salespeople need more than a territory, compensation, and training—they need supervision and motivation. The goal of *supervision* is to help salespeople "work smart" by doing the right things in the right ways. The goal of *motivation* is to encourage salespeople to "work hard" and energetically toward sales force goals. If salespeople work smart and work hard, they will realize their full potential, to their own and the company's benefit.

Supervising Salespeople

Companies vary in how closely they supervise their salespeople. Many help salespeople to identify target customers and set call norms. Some may also specify how much time the sales force should spend prospecting for new accounts and set other time management priorities. One tool is the weekly, monthly, or annual *call plan* that shows which customers and prospects to call on and which activities to carry out. Another tool is *time-and-duty analysis*. In addition to time spent selling, the salesperson spends time traveling, waiting, taking breaks, and doing administrative chores.

■ **Figure 13.2** shows how salespeople spend their time. On average, active selling time accounts for only 10 percent of total working time! If selling time could be raised from 10 percent to 30 percent, this would triple the time spent selling.[17] Companies always are looking for ways to save time—simplifying administrative duties, developing better sales-call and routing plans, supplying more and better customer information, and using phones, e-mail, or video conferencing instead of traveling. Consider the changes GE made to increase its sales force's face-to-face selling time.[18]

When Jeff Immelt became General Electric's new chairman, he was dismayed to find that members of the sales team were spending far more time on deskbound administrative chores than in face-to-face meetings with customers and prospects. "He said we needed to turn that around," recalls Venki Rao, an IT leader in global sales and marketing at GE Power Systems, a division focused on energy systems and products. "[We need] to spend four days a week in front of the customer and one day for all the admin stuff." GE Power's salespeople spent much of their time at their desks because they had to go to many sources for the information needed to sell multimillion-dollar turbines, turbine parts, and services to energy companies worldwide. To fix the problem, GE created a new sales portal, a kind of "one-stop shop" for just about everything they need. The sales portal connects the vast array of existing GE databases, providing everything from sales tracking and customer data to parts pricing and information on planned outages. GE also added external data,

■ **Figure 13.2** How Salespeople Spend Their Time

Source: Proudfoot Consulting. Data used with permission

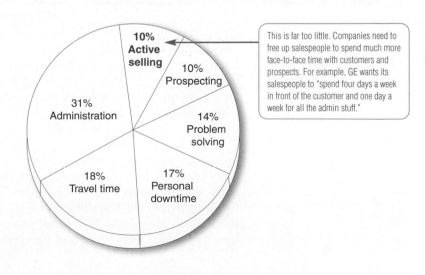

10%
Active selling

This is far too little. Companies need to free up salespeople to spend much more face-to-face time with customers and prospects. For example, GE wants its salespeople to "spend four days a week in front of the customer and one day a week for all the admin stuff."

10%
Prospecting

31%
Administration

14%
Problem solving

18%
Travel time

17%
Personal downtime

such as news feeds. "Before, you were randomly searching for things," says Bill Snook, a GE sales manager. Now, he says, "I have the sales portal as my home page, and I use it as the gateway to all the applications that I have." The sales portal has freed Snook and 2,500 other users around the globe from once time-consuming administrative tasks, greatly increasing their face time with customers.

Many firms have adopted *sales force automation systems*—computerized, digitized sales force operations that let salespeople work more effectively anytime, anywhere. Companies now routinely equip their salespeople with technologies such as laptops, smart phones, wireless Web connections, Webcams for videoconferencing, and customer-contact and relationship management software. Armed with these technologies, salespeople can more effectively and efficiently profile customers and prospects, analyze and forecast sales, schedule sales calls, make presentations, prepare sales and expense reports, and manage account relationships. The result is better time management, improved customer service, lower sales costs, and higher sales performance.[19]

Selling and the Internet

Perhaps the fastest-growing sales technology tool is the Internet. The Internet offers explosive potential for conducting sales operations and for interacting with and serving customers. Sales organizations are now both enhancing their effectiveness and saving time and money by using a host of Internet approaches to train sales reps, hold sales meetings, service accounts, and even conduct live sales meetings with customers.

Some call it **Sales 2.0**, the merging of innovative sales practices with Internet 2.0 technologies to improve sales force effectiveness and efficiency:[20]

Sales 2.0
The merging of innovative sales practices with Internet 2.0 technologies to improve sales force effectiveness and efficiency.

▲Selling and the Internet: Sales 2.0 let's salespeople connect, learn, plan, analyze, engage, collaborate, and conduct business in ways that were not even imaginable a few years ago.

▲Web 2.0 enables a new way of interacting, collaborating, and information sharing. With the Internet as a new business platform, now all stakeholders—prospects, customers, salespeople, and marketers—can't connect, learn, plan, analyze, engage, collaborate, and conduct business in ways that were not even imaginable a few years ago. Such innovations as Wikipedia, online conferencing, i-reports, user ratings, blogs, Twitter, and social networking have elevated the potential for human collaboration to a higher level. In turn, Sales 2.0 brings together customer-focused methodologies and productivity-enhancing technologies that transform selling from an art to an interactive science. Sales 2.0 has forever changed the process by which people buy and companies sell.

Web-based technologies can produce big organizational benefits for sales forces. They help conserve salespeople's valuable time, save travel dollars, and give salespeople a new vehicle for selling and servicing accounts. Over the past decade, customer buying patterns have changed. In today's Web 2.0 world, customers often know almost as much about a company's products as salespeople do. This gives customers more control over the sales process than they had in the days when brochures and pricing were only available from a sales rep. Sales 2.0 recognizes and takes advantage of these buying process changes, creating new avenues for connecting with customers in the Internet age.

For example, sales organizations can now generate lists of prospective customers from online databases and networking sites such as Hoovers and Linked In. They create dialogs when prospective customers visit their Web sites through live chats with the sales team. They can use Web conferencing tools such as WebEx or GoToMeeting to talk live with customers about products and services. Other Sales 2.0 tools allow salespeople to monitor Internet interactions between customers about how they would like to buy, how they feel about a vendor, and what it would take to make a sale. Ultimately, "Sales 2.0 technologies are delivering instant information that builds relationships and enables sale to be more efficient and cost-effective and more productive. . . . Just as the Internet allowed buyers to literally let their fingers do the walking, these new Sales 2.0 technologies are allowing the customer's online behavior to dictate the communication—before sales does the talking."[21]

But the technologies also have some drawbacks. For starters, they're not cheap. And such systems can intimidate low-tech salespeople or clients. What's more, there are some things you just can't present or teach via the Web, things that require personal interactions. For these reasons, some high-tech experts recommend that sales executives use Web technologies to supplement training, sales meetings, and preliminary client sales presentations, but resort to old-fashioned, face-to-face meetings when the time draws near to close the deal.

Motivating Salespeople

Beyond directing salespeople, sales managers must also motivate them. Some salespeople will do their best without any special urging from management. To them, selling may be the most fascinating job in the world. But selling can also be frustrating. Salespeople often work alone and they must sometimes travel away from home. They may face aggressive competing salespeople and difficult customers. Therefore, salespeople often need special encouragement to do their best.

Management can boost sales force morale and performance through its organizational climate, sales quotas, and positive incentives. *Organizational climate* describes the feeling that salespeople have about their opportunities, value, and rewards for a good performance. Some companies treat salespeople as if they are not very important and performance suffers accordingly. Other companies treat their salespeople as valued contributors and allow virtually unlimited opportunity for income and promotion. Not surprisingly, these companies enjoy higher sales force performance and less turnover.

Sales quota
A standard that states the amount a salesperson should sell and how sales should be divided among the company's products.

Many companies motivate their salespeople by setting **sales quotas**—standards stating the amount they should sell and how sales should be divided among the company's products. Compensation is often related to how well salespeople meet their quotas. Companies also use various *positive incentives* to increase sales force effort. *Sales meetings* provide social occasions, breaks from routine, chances to meet and talk with "company brass," and opportunities to air feelings and to identify with a larger group. Companies also sponsor *sales contests* to spur the sales force to make a selling effort above what would normally be expected. Other incentives include honors, merchandise and cash awards, trips, and profit-sharing plans.

Evaluating Salespeople and Sales Force Performance

We have thus far described how management communicates what salespeople should be doing and how it motivates them to do it. This process requires good feedback. And good feedback means getting regular information about salespeople to evaluate their performance.

Management gets information about its salespeople in several ways. The most important source is *sales reports,* including weekly or monthly work plans and longer-term territory marketing plans. Salespeople also write up their completed activities on *call reports* and turn in *expense reports* for which they are partly or wholly repaid. The company can also monitor the sales and profit performance data in the salesperson's territory. Additional information comes from personal observation, customer surveys, and talks with other salespeople.

Using various sales force reports and other information, sales management evaluates members of the sales force. It evaluates salespeople on their ability to "plan their work and work their plan." Formal evaluation forces management to develop and communicate clear standards for judging performance. It also provides salespeople with constructive feedback and motivates them to perform well.

On a broader level, management should evaluate the performance of the sales force as a whole. Is the sales force accomplishing its customer relationship, sales, and profit objectives? Is it working well with other areas of the marketing and company organization? Are sales force costs in line with outcomes? As with other marketing activities, the company wants to measure its *return on sales investment*.

◆ Speed Bump: Linking the Concepts

Take a break and reexamine your thoughts about salespeople and the personal selling process.

- Again, when someone says "salesperson," what image comes to mind? Have your perceptions of salespeople changed after what you've just read? How? Be specific.
- Find and talk with someone employed in professional sales. Ask about and report on how this salesperson's company designs its sales force and recruits, selects, trains, compensates, supervises, and evaluates its salespeople. Would you like to work as a salesperson for this company?

Author Comment 》》
So far, we've examined how sales management develops and implements overall sales force strategies and programs. In this section, we'll look at how individual salespeople and sales teams sell to customers and build relationships with them.

THE PERSONAL SELLING PROCESS (pp 454–458)

We now turn from designing and managing a sales force to the actual personal selling process. The **selling process** consists of several steps that salespeople must master. These steps focus on the goal of getting new customers and obtaining orders from them. However, most salespeople spend much of their time maintaining existing accounts and building long-term customer *relationships*. We discuss the relationship aspect of the personal selling process in a later section.

Steps in the Selling Process

Selling process
The steps that salespeople follow when selling, which include prospecting and qualifying, preapproach, approach, presentation and demonstration, handling objections, closing, and follow-up.

As shown in ■ **Figure 13.3**, the selling process consists of seven steps: prospecting and qualifying, preapproach, approach, presentation and demonstration, handling objections, closing, and follow-up.

Prospecting and Qualifying

Prospecting
The step in the selling process in which the salesperson or company identifies qualified potential customers.

The first step in the selling process is **prospecting**—identifying qualified potential customers. Approaching the right potential customers is crucial to the selling success. As one sales expert puts it, "If the sales force starts chasing anyone who is breathing and seems to have a budget, you risk accumulating a roster of expensive-to-serve, hard-to-satisfy customers who never respond to whatever value proposition you have." He continues, "The solution to this isn't rocket science. [You must] train salespeople to actively scout the right prospects." Another expert concludes, "Increasing your prospecting effectiveness is the fastest single way to boost your sales."[22]

■ **Figure 13.3** Steps in the Selling Process

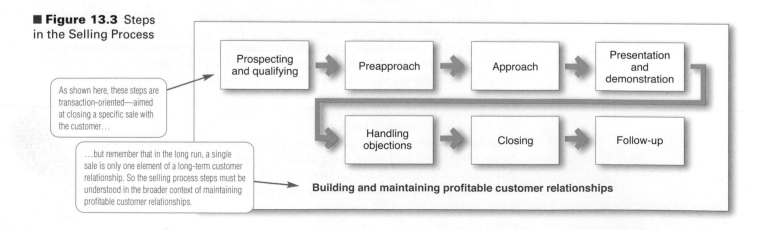

As shown here, these steps are transaction-oriented—aimed at closing a specific sale with the customer…

…but remember that in the long run, a single sale is only one element of a long-term customer relationship. So the selling process steps must be understood in the broader context of maintaining profitable customer relationships.

Building and maintaining profitable customer relationships

The salesperson must often approach many prospects to get just a few sales. Although the company supplies some leads, salespeople need skill in finding their own. The best source is referrals. Salespeople can ask current customers for referrals and cultivate other referral sources, such as suppliers, dealers, noncompeting salespeople, and Web or other social networks. They can also search for prospects in directories or on the Web and track down leads using the telephone and e-mail. Or they can drop in unannounced on various offices (a practice known as "cold calling").

Salespeople also need to know how to *qualify* leads—that is, how to identify the good ones and screen out the poor ones. Prospects can be qualified by looking at their financial ability, volume of business, special needs, location, and possibilities for growth.

Preapproach

Preapproach
The step in the selling process in which the salesperson learns as much as possible about a prospective customer before making a sales call.

Before calling on a prospect, the salesperson should learn as much as possible about the organization (what it needs, who is involved in the buying) and its buyers (their characteristics and buying styles). This step is known as the **preapproach**. "Revving up your sales starts with your preparation," says one sales consultant. "A successful sale begins long before you set foot in the prospect's office." Preapproach begins with good research. The salesperson can consult standard industry and online sources, acquaintances, and others to learn about the company. Then, the salesperson must apply the research to develop a customer strategy. "Being able to recite the prospect's product line in your sleep isn't enough," says the consultant. "You need to translate the data into something useful for your client."[23]

The salesperson should set *call objectives*, which may be to qualify the prospect, to gather information, or to make an immediate sale. Another task is to decide on the best approach, which might be a personal visit, a phone call, or a letter or e-mail. The best timing should be considered carefully because many prospects are busiest at certain times. Finally, the salesperson should give thought to an overall sales strategy for the account.

Approach

▼**Weyerhaeuser created a customer-solutions-focused sales organization called iLevel. It promises customers "a coordinated sales team that gives you access to all the products, logistics, tech services, and software you need [to] quickly resolve issues."**

During the **approach** step, the salesperson should know how to meet and greet the buyer and get the relationship off to a good start. This step involves the salesperson's appearance, opening lines, and the follow-up remarks. The opening lines should be positive to build goodwill from the beginning of the relationship. This opening might be followed by some key questions to learn more about the customer's needs or by showing a display or sample to attract the buyer's attention and curiosity. As in all stages of the selling process, listening to the customer is crucial.

Presentation and Demonstration

During the **presentation** step of the selling process, the salesperson tells the "value story" to the buyer, showing how the company's offer solves the customer's problems. The *customer-solution approach* fits better with today's relationship marketing focus than does a hard-sell or glad-handing approach. Buyers today want answers, not smiles; results, not razzle-dazzle. Moreover, they don't want just products. More than ever in today's economic climate, buyers want to know how those products will add value to their businesses. They want salespeople who listen to their concerns, understand their needs, and respond with the right products and services.

But before salespeople can *present* customer solutions, they must *develop* solutions to present. Many companies now train their salespeople to go beyond "product thinking." ▲Weyerhaeuser, the $8 billion U.S. forest

Approach
The step in the selling process in which the salesperson meets the customer for the first time.

Presentation
The step in the selling process in which the salesperson tells the "value story" to the buyer, showing how the company's offer solves the customer's problems.

products company, reorganized its entire sales force around customer-solutions selling:

> Weyerhaeuser, long a product-driven company, undertook an extreme makeover, creating a customer-solutions-focused sales organization called iLevel. Rather than selling wood products piecemeal, Weyerhaeuser wants to be considered the one-stop location for all of the innovation and products required to construct residential home frames—joists, beams, floors, and all. The new iLevel organization assigns a single salesperson to each major builder or dealer. The sales rep leads a coordinated sales team that serves all of the customer's needs. To implement iLevel, Weyerhaeuser retrained its 250 salespeople to present customers with solutions, not products. "It is a consultative selling approach," says a Weyerhaeuser executive. Never again will salespeople merely sell orders of lumber. "What we want [our sales reps] to do is help our customers find solutions that make them [and us] money."[24]

The solutions approach calls for good listening and problem-solving skills. One study revealed that 74 percent of 200 purchasers surveyed at companies nationwide said they would be much more likely to buy from a salesperson if the seller would simply listen to them. Says one experienced salesperson, "That typecast chatty character may be the kind of person who's most often drawn to sales, but it's not often the one who's most successful at it. Unless you listen to what your customer is saying, you won't understand his deeper wants and needs. And you'll find that the more you listen to others, the more they'll listen to you. As the old saying goes, 'God gave us two ears and only one mouth, to use in that proportion.'"[25]

The qualities that buyers *dislike most* in salespeople include being pushy, late, deceitful, unprepared, or disorganized. The qualities they *value most* include good listening, empathy, honesty, dependability, thoroughness, and follow-through. Great salespeople know how to sell, but more importantly they know how to listen and to build strong customer relationships. Says one professional, "Everything starts with listening. I think the magic of these days is we've got so many more ways to listen."[26]

Finally, salespeople must also plan their presentation methods. Good interpersonal communication skills count when it comes to making effective sales presentations. However, today's media-rich and cluttered communications environment presents many new challenges for sales presenters:[27]

> The goal of a sales presentation is to deliver a clear, concise, and consistent message to your prospects about your product and your brand, as well as why you are better than the competition. Doing that and keeping your audience's attention for longer than 30 minutes is the real challenge. Today's information-overloaded prospects demand a richer presentation experience. And sales presenters must now overcome multiple distractions from cell phones, text messaging, and portable Internet viewers during a presentation. Sales presentations today take creativity, careful planning, and the application of the hottest technologies available. You can't fill your prospects' heads with unnecessary, useless information, and you have to capture their interest fast or risk losing them forever. So you must deliver your message in a more engaging and compelling way than your competition does, and you must deliver more information in less time.

▼ **Presentation technology: Today's media-rich communications environment presents many new opportunities for sales presenters.**

Thus, ▲today's salespeople are employing advanced presentation technologies that allow for full multimedia presentations to only one or a few people. The venerable old flip chart has been replaced by DVDs, online presentation technologies, interactive white boards, and handheld and laptop computers with sophisticated presentation software.

Handling Objections
Customers almost always have objections during the presentation or when asked to place an order. The problem can be either logical or psychologi-

Handling objections
The step in the selling process in which the salesperson seeks out, clarifies, and overcomes customer objections to buying.

cal, and objections are often unspoken. In **handling objections**, the salesperson should use a positive approach, seek out hidden objections, ask the buyer to clarify any objections, take objections as opportunities to provide more information, and turn the objections into reasons for buying. Every salesperson needs training in the skills of handling objections.

Closing

Closing
The step in the selling process in which the salesperson asks the customer for an order.

After handling the prospect's objections, the salesperson now tries to close the sale. Some salespeople do not get around to **closing** or do not handle it well. They may lack confidence, feel guilty about asking for the order, or fail to recognize the right moment to close the sale. Salespeople should know how to recognize closing signals from the buyer, including physical actions, comments, and questions. For example, the customer might sit forward and nod approvingly or ask about prices and credit terms.

Salespeople can use one of several closing techniques. They can ask for the order, review points of agreement, offer to help write up the order, ask whether the buyer wants this model or that one, or note that the buyer will lose out if the order is not placed now. The salesperson may offer the buyer special reasons to close, such as a lower price or an extra quantity at no charge.

Follow-Up

Follow-up
The last step in the selling process in which the salesperson follows up after the sale to ensure customer satisfaction and repeat business.

The last step in the selling process—**follow-up**—is necessary if the salesperson wants to ensure customer satisfaction and repeat business. Right after closing, the salesperson should complete any details on delivery time, purchase terms, and other matters. The salesperson then should schedule a follow-up call when the initial order is received to make sure there is proper installation, instruction, and servicing. This visit would reveal any problems, assure the buyer of the salesperson's interest, and reduce any buyer concerns that might have arisen since the sale.

Personal Selling and Managing Customer Relationships

The steps in the selling process as just described are *transaction oriented*—their aim is to help salespeople close a specific sale with a customer. But in most cases, the company is not simply seeking a sale. Rather, it wants to serve the customer over the long haul in a mutually profitable *relationship*. The sales force usually plays an important role in customer relationship building. Thus, as shown in Figure 13.3, the selling process must be understood in the context of building and maintaining profitable customer relationships.

Today's large customers favor suppliers who can work with them over time to deliver a coordinated set of products and services to many locations. For these customers, the first sale is only the beginning of the relationship. Unfortunately, some companies ignore these relationship realities. They sell their products through separate sales forces, each working independently to close sales. Their technical people may not be willing to lend time to educate a customer. Their engineering, design, and manufacturing people may have the attitude that "it's our job to make good products and the salesperson's to sell them to customers." Their salespeople focus on pushing products toward customers rather than listening to customers and providing solutions.

Olivia Lum started her career by selling products off the back of a motorbike, but is now the CEO of Hyflux, Ltd., a successful global company. The secret to her success? Working hard to build lasting and interactive relationships with customers. In fact, most successful companies want their salespeople to practice value selling—demonstrating and delivering superior customer value and capturing a return on that value that's fair for both the customer and the company (see Marketing at Work 13.2). Value selling requires listening to customers, understanding their needs, and carefully coordinating the whole company's efforts to create lasting relationships based on customer value.

Marketing at Work 13.2

Hyflux: Value Selling—A Corporate Culture of Providing Integrated Solutions

Hyflux Ltd is a Singapore-based global environmental solutions company with operations in China, India, the Middle East, and North Africa, as well as Singapore and Southeast Asia.

What Hyflux sells is not just water treatment products and services but in simple terms, quality integrated solutions with a capital Q—value selling!

Value selling is what Olivia Lum, Hyflux Group's CEO and President, is thoroughly familiar with. Adopted and raised by a poor grandmother in Malaysia, she worked very hard and eventually graduated with Honors in Chemistry from the National University of Singapore in 1986.

After three years working as a chemist, she followed her entrepreneurial instincts and ventured out on her own. Hydrochem (the precursor to Hyflux) was born with a mere capital of just $15,000. In those early days this feisty woman would ride around Singapore on a motorbike selling her company's water filters and treatment chemicals. Within a short span of 14 years, Hyflux was listed on the Singapore Stock Exchange in 2003. By 2007, this young Singaporean company was employing more than 800 people and was worth $700 million.

Selling quality solutions through people who are committed to quality is what Hyflux is all about. This is clearly spelled out in its mantra where the focus of the organization is in providing quality products and services to its valued customers through technology, innovation, quality, and cost effectiveness.

Hyflux sells quality systems solutions in that it develops, designs, and fabricates advanced membrane filtration products and plants for its customers. Through research and development, it applies its proprietary membrane filtration technology for a wide range of uses.

Thus, the company does not just sell water treatment plants and services. It is an integrated solutions provider offering services that cover the whole range of research and development, process design and development, manufacturing and systems assembly, engineering, procurement and construction, and operation and maintenance of a wide range of water treatment and liquid separation projects. In short, it sells much more than just water.

Hyflux has thus far sold and secured projects way beyond the shores of the tiny island nation it hails from. It has sold impressive desalination plants ranging from $70 million to $500 million. Its projects are found in not just its homeland, but in countries like China, other Southeast Asian countries, the Middle East, and Algeria.

For many Singapore companies, it is critical to expand to new overseas markets if they intend to continue to grow their business after a certain stage. While some have difficulty tapping into unfamiliar countries (like Algeria, where Hyflux has secured a $205 million contract), Hyflux's reputation as the leading water-treatment company in the region has certainly helped in bringing in new customers.

One naturally wonders: What makes a relatively new player in this industry become such a phenomenon in such a short span of time? Traditionally, such infrastructure projects have always been dominated by American and European companies.

Well, this Asian upstart has brought about a refreshing change—fresh ideas backed by solid technology and very competitive pricing. In other words, good old common sense value-for-money!

One cannot discount too that Singapore's government leaders are themselves openly and arduously "selling" Singapore as well. Active interactions at the highest diplomatic levels—in the form of frequent visits by these leaders to the regions where Hyflux operates—has certainly helped in terms of boosting Singapore's image of efficiency and credibility.

Hyflux believes in selling through long-term relationships cultivated over time to build trust and respect. By the very nature of these huge projects, Hyflux cannot be in this business unless it is committed to its customers for the long haul. Selling success simply does not come through a hit-and-miss overnight effort.

By engaging in a sustained, market-driven program of research and development, Hyflux continues to be able to sell cutting-edge technology to its clients. In 2004, Hyflux launched its membrane and materials technology center—the largest in Asia outside Japan—to spearhead its development in cutting-edge membrane technology and environmental engineering solutions. It maintains more than ten research laboratories in Singapore just to support its status as a truly leading environmental solutions company.

At one of its corporate functions, Olivia Lum urged her staff to provide good customer service to both internal and external customers and practice the Hyflux values of "boldness," "entrepreneurship," "satisfaction," and "testimony"—values which have made the company what it is today.

Even though it has a staff strength of more than 1,000 now, its roaring success clearly shows that it has remained true to its founder's DNA way back when she was still riding her motorbike, humbly peddling water filters and chemicals.

She was selling solutions then and Hyflux is still in the business of selling integrated and quality solutions today. Solutions always lead to satisfied customers, which is what value selling is all about.

Sources: Based on information from www.hyflux.com/contactus.htm; http://ir.asiaone.com/hyflux/index.html; www.siww.com.sg/sponsors/hyflux.php; and www.channelnewsasia.com/stories/singaporebusinessnews/view/447294/1/.html, accessed October 2009; also from "Hyflux Achieves Record Earnings for Fy2008/09," *Hyflux News* Mar–Apr 2008, Vol 5, Issue 2.

Sales promotion
Short-term incentives to encourage the purchase or sale of a product or service.

SALES PROMOTION (pp 459–464)

Personal selling and advertising often work closely with another promotion tool, sales promotion. **Sales promotion** consists of short-term incentives to encourage purchase or sales of a product or service. Whereas advertising offers reasons to buy a product or service, sales promotion offers reasons to buy *now*.

Examples of sales promotions are found everywhere. A freestanding insert in the Sunday newspaper contains a coupon offering $1 off Pedigree GoodBites treats for your dog. An e-mail from LLBean.com offers free shipping on your next purchase over $100. ▲A Bed Bath & Beyond ad in your favorite magazine offers 20 percent off your next purchase. The end-of-the-aisle display in the local supermarket tempts impulse buyers with a wall of Coke cases. An executive buys a new HP laptop and gets a free carrying case, or a family buys a new Ford Escape and receives a factory rebate of $1,000. A hardware store chain receives a 10 percent discount on selected Black & Decker portable power tools if it agrees to advertise them in local newspapers. Sales promotion includes a wide variety of promotion tools designed to stimulate earlier or stronger market response.

▲Sales promotions are found everywhere. For example, your favorite magazine is loaded with offers like this one that promote a strong and immediate response.

Rapid Growth of Sales Promotion

Sales promotion tools are used by most organizations, including manufacturers, distributors, retailers, and not-for-profit institutions. They are targeted toward final buyers (*consumer promotions*), retailers and wholesalers (*trade promotions*), business customers (*business promotions*), and members of the sales force (*sales force promotions*). Today, in the average consumer packaged-goods company, sales promotion accounts for 74 percent of all marketing expenditures.[28]

Several factors have contributed to the rapid growth of sales promotion, particularly in consumer markets. First, inside the company, product managers face greater pressures to increase their current sales, and promotion is viewed as an effective short-run sales tool. Second, externally, the company faces more competition and competing brands are less differentiated. Increasingly, competitors are using sales promotion to help differentiate their offers. Third, advertising efficiency has declined because of rising costs, media clutter, and legal restraints. Finally, consumers have become more deal oriented. In the current economy, consumers are demanding lower prices and better deals. Sales promotions can help attract today's more frugal consumers.

The growing use of sales promotion has resulted in *promotion clutter*, similar to advertising clutter. A given promotion runs the risk of being lost in a sea of other promotions, weakening its ability to trigger immediate purchase. Manufacturers are now searching for ways to rise above the clutter, such as offering larger coupon values, creating more dramatic point-of-purchase displays, or delivering promotions through new interactive media, such as the Internet or cell phones.

In developing a sales promotion program, a company must first set sales promotion objectives and then select the best tools for accomplishing these objectives.

Sales Promotion Objectives

Sales promotion objectives vary widely. Sellers may use *consumer promotions* to urge short-term customer buying or to enhance customer brand involvement. Objectives for *trade promotions* include getting retailers to carry new items and more inventory, buy ahead, or promote the company's products and give them more shelf space. For the *sales force*, objectives include getting more sales force support for current or new products or getting salespeople to sign up new accounts.

Sales promotions are usually used together with advertising, personal selling, direct marketing, or other promotion mix tools. Consumer promotions must usually be advertised and can add excitement and pulling power to ads. Trade and sales force promotions support the firm's personal selling process.

When the economy sours and sales lag, it's tempting to offer deep promotional discounts to spur consumer spending. In general, however, rather than creating only short-term sales or temporary brand switching, sales promotions should help to reinforce the product's position and build long-term *customer relationships*. If properly designed, every sales promotion tool has the potential to build both short-term excitement and long-term consumer relationships. Marketers should avoid "quick fix," price-only promotions in favor of promotions designed to build brand equity.

Examples include all of the "frequency marketing programs" and loyalty cards that have mushroomed in recent years. Most hotels, supermarkets, and airlines offer frequent-guest/buyer/ flyer programs giving rewards to regular customers to keep them coming back. All kinds of companies now offer rewards programs. Such promotional programs can build loyalty through added value rather than discounted prices.

▲Customer loyalty programs: Rather than offering promotional discounts that might damage its premium positioning, Starbucks ran ads telling customers why its coffee is worth the higher price. Then, to build loyalty, the company promoted the Starbucks Card Rewards program.

For example, Starbucks suffered sales setbacks resulting from the recent economic downturn, coupled with the introduction of cheaper gourmet coffees by a host of fast-food competitors. Starbucks could have lowered its prices or offered promotional discounts. But deep discounts might have damaged the chain's long-term premium positioning. So instead, Starbucks dropped its prices only slightly and ran ads telling customers why its coffee is worth a higher price. With headlines such as "Beware of a cheaper cup of coffee. It comes with a price," the ads laid out what separates Starbucks from the competition, such as its practices of buying fair-trade beans and providing health care for employees who work more than 20 hours a week. ▲At the same time, to build loyalty, Starbucks promoted its Starbucks Card Rewards program:[29]

In 1981, when American Airlines was struggling to differentiate itself in a newly deregulated industry, it invented the frequent flyer mile. Ten years later, American Express responded to its own competitive crisis by introducing what we now know as Membership Rewards. So it shouldn't come as any big surprise that Starbucks, facing its own troubled times, would also turn to a loyalty program, Starbucks Card Rewards. In order to fight off lower-priced competitors such as Dunkin' Donuts and McDonald's and keep its loyal customers, well, loyal, Starbucks unveiled a rewards card. Cardholders benefit from perks such as free in-store refills on coffee, complementary in-store Wi-Fi for up to 2 hours per day, and a free coffee with a purchase of a pound of coffee beans. Such perks increase customer value without big discounts or price reductions. "There is a need for Starbucks to win back customers," says a loyalty marketing consultancy. "The [loyalty] card is a vehicle for doing that."

Major Sales Promotion Tools

Many tools can be used to accomplish sales promotion objectives. Descriptions of the main consumer, trade, and business promotion tools follow.

Consumer Promotions

Consumer promotions include a wide range of tools—from samples, coupons, refunds, premiums, and point-of-purchase displays to contests, sweepstakes, and event sponsorships.

Consumer promotions
Sales promotion tools used to boost short-term customer buying and involvement or to enhance long-term customer relationships.

Samples are offers of a trial amount of a product. Sampling is the most effective—but most expensive—way to introduce a new product or to create new excitement for an existing one. Some samples are free; for others, the company charges a small amount to offset its cost. The sample might be delivered door-to-door, sent by mail, handed out in a store or kiosk, attached to another product, or featured in an ad. Sometimes, samples are combined into sample packs, which can then be used to promote other products and services. Sampling can be a powerful promotional tool.

Coupons are certificates that give buyers a saving when they purchase specified products. Most consumers love coupons. U.S. package-goods companies distributed more than 317 billion coupons last year with an average face value of $1.44. Consumers redeemed more than 2.6 billion of them for a total savings of about $3.7 billion.[30] Coupons can promote early trial of a new brand or stimulate sales of a mature brand. However, as a result of coupon clutter, redemption rates have been declining in recent years. Thus, most major consumer-goods companies are issuing fewer coupons and targeting them more carefully.

Marketers are also cultivating new outlets for distributing coupons, such as supermarket shelf dispensers, electronic point-of-sale coupon printers, e-mail and online media, or even mobile text-messaging systems. Mobile couponing is very popular in Europe, India, and Japan and is now gaining popularity in the United States. For example, consider Cellfire, a mobile couponing company in California:[31]

> Cellfire (*www.cellfire.com*) distributes digital coupons to the cell phones of consumers nationwide who sign up for its free service. Cellfire's growing list of clients ranges from Domino's Pizza, T.G.I. Friday's, Sears, and Hardee's and Carl's Jr. restaurants to Kimberly-Clark, Supercuts, Hollywood Video, 1-800-FLOWERS.COM, and Enterprise Rent-A-Car. Cellfire sends an ever-changing assortment of digital coupons to users' cell phones. To use the coupons, users simply call up the stored coupon list, navigate to the coupon they want, press the "Use Now" button, and show the digital coupon to the store cashier. Domino's even permits consumers holding the mobile coupons to simply click on a link to have their cell phones dial the nearest Domino's store to place an order. To date, Cellfire users have redeemed more than $29 million in coupon savings.
>
> Coupons distributed through Cellfire offer distinct advantages to both consumers and marketers. Consumers don't have to find and clip paper coupons or print out Web coupons and bring them along when they shop. They always have their cell phone coupons with them. For marketers, mobile coupons allow more careful targeting and eliminate the costs of printing and distributing paper coupons. "We don't pay for distribution of digital coupons," says one client. "We pay on redemptions." And the redemption rates can be dazzling. Redemption rates are as high as [20] percent, while the industry average paper response is . . . less than 1 percent.

Cash refunds (or *rebates*) are like coupons except that the price reduction occurs after the purchase rather than at the retail outlet. The consumer sends a "proof of purchase" to the manufacturer, who then refunds part of the purchase price by mail. For example, Toro ran a clever preseason promotion on some of its snowblower models, offering a rebate if the snowfall in the buyer's market area turned out to be below average. Competitors were not able to match this offer on such short notice, and the promotion was very successful.

Price packs (also called *cents-off deals*) offer consumers savings off the regular price of a product. The producer marks the reduced prices directly on the label or package. Price packs can be single packages sold at a reduced price (such as two for the price of one), or two related products banded together (such as a toothbrush and toothpaste). Price packs are very effective—even more so than coupons—in stimulating short-term sales.

Premiums are goods offered either free or at low cost as an incentive to buy a product, ranging from toys included with kids' products to phone cards and DVDs. A premium may come inside the package (in-pack), outside the package (on-pack), or through the mail. For example, over the years, McDonald's has offered a variety of premiums in its Happy Meals—from Teeny Beanie Babies to Speed Racers to *Monsters vs. Aliens* toy characters. Customers can visit *www.happymeal.com*

and play games and watch commercials associated with the current Happy Meal sponsor.[32]

Advertising specialties, also called *promotional products,* are useful articles imprinted with an advertiser's name, logo, or message that are given as gifts to consumers. Typical items include T-shirts and other apparel, pens, coffee mugs, calendars, key rings, mouse pads, matches, tote bags, coolers, golf balls, and caps. U.S. marketers spent over $19 billion on advertising specialties last year. Such items can be very effective. The "best of them stick around for months, subtly burning a brand name into a user's brain," notes a promotional products expert.[33]

Point-of-purchase (POP) promotions include displays and demonstrations that take place at the point of sale. Think of your last visit to the local Safeway, CVS, or Bed Bath & Beyond. Chances are good that you were tripping over aisle displays, promotional signs, "shelf talkers," or demonstrators offering free tastes of featured food products. Unfortunately, many retailers do not like to handle the hundreds of displays, signs, and posters they receive from manufacturers each year. Manufacturers have responded by offering better POP materials, offering to set them up, and tying them in with television, print, or online messages.

▲Contests can create considerable consumer involvement: The "Create Dunkin's Next Donut" contest generated 130,000 online creations.

Contests, sweepstakes, and games give consumers the chance to win something, such as cash, trips, or goods, by luck or through extra effort. A *contest* calls for consumers to submit an entry—a jingle, guess, suggestion—to be judged by a panel that will select the best entries. A *sweepstakes* calls for consumers to submit their names for a drawing. A *game* presents consumers with something—bingo numbers, missing letters—every time they buy, which may or may not help them win a prize. Such promotions can create considerable brand attention and consumer involvement.[34]

Dunkin' Donuts recently launched a new $10 million integrated campaign to remind people of its roots as a doughnut maker and not just a coffee brand. From TV to Internet to in-store displays, "you can't walk in the door without thinking about donuts," says Dunkin's vice president of consumer engagement. ▲At the heart of the "donut domination" campaign is a "Create Dunkin's Next Donut" contest that urges people to visit the contest Web site and design their own doughnuts. "Put on your apron and get creative," the campaign urges. "You kin' do it." At the site, entrants selected from a list of approved ingredients to create the new doughnut, give it a name, and write a 100-word essay about why they think their doughnut creation is the best. Online voting selected from among 12 semifinalists, who cooked up their creations at a bake-off in the company's test kitchens at Dunkin' Donuts University in Braintree, MA. The grand winner received $12,000 and the winning doughnut—Toffee for Your Coffee—was added to the company's everyday value menu. In all, contestants submitted nearly 130,000 creations online. "We were absolutely amazed at the number of entries into our contest," says a Dunkin' marketing executive.

Event marketing
Creating a brand-marketing event or serving as a sole or participating sponsor of events created by others.

Finally, marketers can promote their brands through **event marketing** (or *event sponsorships*). They can create their own brand-marketing events or serve as sole or participating sponsors of events created by others. The events might include anything from mobile brand tours to festivals, reunions, marathons, concerts, or other sponsored gatherings. Event marketing is huge, and it may be the fastest-growing area of promotion, especially in tough economic times. Consumer event-marketing spending in the United States exceeded $19 billion last year, up 12 percent from a year earlier.[35]

Event marketing can provide a less costly alternative to expensive TV commercials. When it comes to event marketing, sports are in a league of their own. Marketers spent more than $7.6 billion last year to associate their brands with sporting events. For example, Sprint is paying $700 million over 10 years to sponsor the NASCAR Sprint Cup Series. Express carrier DHL sponsors its annual DHL All-Star FanFest, associated with Major League Baseball's All-Star Game week. The 2008 FanFest drew more than 150,000 baseball die-hards to New York's Jacob Javits Convention Center, providing substantial positive exposure for the DHL brand and other sponsors. And Pepsi fields a host of promotional efforts at MLB stadiums. For instance, events at Citi Field, the New York Mets stadium, include The Pepsi Party Patrol—brand reps that run contests and give away t-shirts—and the Pepsi Porch, a 1,284-seat area in right field that extends over the playing field, identified by a Pepsi sign above it.[36]

Procter & Gamble creates numerous events for its major brands. Consider this example:

> For the past few years, P&G has sponsored a holiday event promotion for its Charmin brand in New York's Times Square, where it can be very difficult to find a public restroom. P&G sets up 20 free, sparkling clean Charmin-themed mini-bathrooms, each with its own sink and a bountiful supply of Charmin. The event is the ultimate in experiential marketing—touching people in places advertising wouldn't dare to go. Over the past three holiday seasons, more than one million people have gratefully used the facilities.[37]

Trade Promotions

Trade promotions
Sales promotion tools used to persuade resellers to carry a brand, give it shelf space, promote it in advertising, and push it to consumers.

Manufacturers direct more sales promotion dollars toward retailers and wholesalers (81 percent) than to final consumers (19 percent).[38] **Trade promotions** can persuade resellers to carry a brand, give it shelf space, promote it in advertising, and push it to consumers. Shelf space is so scarce these days that manufacturers often have to offer price-offs, allowances, buy-back guarantees, or free goods to retailers and wholesalers to get products on the shelf and, once there, to keep them on it.

Manufacturers use several trade promotion tools. Many of the tools used for consumer promotions—contests, premiums, displays—can also be used as trade promotions. Or the manufacturer may offer a straight *discount* off the list price on each case purchased during a stated period of time (also called a *price-off, off-invoice*, or *off-list*). Manufacturers also may offer an *allowance* (usually so much off per case) in return for the retailer's agreement to feature the manufacturer's products in some way. An advertising allowance compensates retailers for advertising the product. A display allowance compensates them for using special displays.

Manufacturers may offer *free goods*, which are extra cases of merchandise, to resellers who buy a certain quantity or who feature a certain flavor or size. They may offer *push money*—cash or gifts to dealers or their sales forces to "push" the manufacturer's goods. Manufacturers may give retailers free *specialty advertising items* that carry the company's name, such as pens, pencils, calendars, paperweights, matchbooks, memo pads, and yardsticks.

Business Promotions

Business promotions
Sales promotion tools used to generate business leads, stimulate purchases, reward customers, and motivate salespeople.

Companies spend billions of dollars each year on promotion to industrial customers. **Business promotions** are used to generate business leads, stimulate purchases, reward customers, and motivate salespeople. Business promotions include many of the same tools used for consumer or trade promotions. Here, we focus on two additional major business promotion tools—conventions and trade shows, and sales contests.

Many companies and trade associations organize *conventions and trade shows* to promote their products. Firms selling to the industry show their products at the trade show. Vendors receive many benefits, such as opportunities to find new sales leads, contact customers, introduce new products, meet new customers, sell more to present customers, and educate customers with publications and audiovisual materials. Trade shows also help companies reach many prospects not reached through their sales forces.

▲Some trade shows are huge. At this year's International Consumer Electronics Show, 3,000 exhibitors attracted more than 110,000 professional visitors.

Some trade shows are huge. ▲For example, at this year's International Consumer Electronics Show, 3,000 exhibitors attracted more than 110,000 professional visitors. Even more impressive, at the BAUMA mining and construction equipment trade show in Munich, Germany, more than 3,000 exhibitors from 49 countries presented their latest product innovations to more than 500,000 attendees from 191 countries.[39]

A *sales contest* is a contest for salespeople or dealers to motivate them to increase their sales performance over a given period. Sales contests motivate and recognize good company performers, who may receive trips, cash prizes, or other gifts. Some companies award points for performance, which the receiver can turn in for any of a variety of prizes. Sales contests work best when they are tied to measurable and achievable sales objectives (such as finding new accounts, reviving old accounts, or increasing account profitability).

Developing the Sales Promotion Program

Beyond selecting the types of promotions to use, marketers must make several other decisions in designing the full sales promotion program. First, they must decide on the *size of the incentive*. A certain minimum incentive is necessary if the promotion is to succeed; a larger incentive will produce more sales response. The marketer also must set *conditions for participation*. Incentives might be offered to everyone or only to select groups.

Marketers must decide how to *promote and distribute the promotion* program itself. A $2-off coupon could be given out in a package, at the store, via the Internet, or in an advertisement. Each distribution method involves a different level of reach and cost. Increasingly, marketers are blending several media into a total campaign concept. The *length of the promotion* is also important. If the sales promotion period is too short, many prospects (who may not be buying during that time) will miss it. If the promotion runs too long, the deal will lose some of its "act now" force.

Evaluation is also very important. Many companies fail to evaluate their sales promotion programs, and others evaluate them only superficially. Yet marketers should work to measure the returns on their sales promotion investments, just as they should seek to assess the returns on other marketing activities. The most common evaluation method is to compare sales before, during, and after a promotion. Marketers should ask: Did the promotion attract new customers or more purchasing from current customers? Can we hold onto these new customers and purchases? Will the long-run customer relationship and sales gains from the promotion justify its costs?

Clearly, sales promotion plays an important role in the total promotion mix. To use it well, the marketer must define the sales promotion objectives, select the best tools, design the sales promotion program, implement the program, and evaluate the results. Moreover, sales promotion must be coordinated carefully with other promotion mix elements within the overall integrated marketing communications program.

REST STOP
REVIEWING THE CONCEPTS

This chapter is the second of three chapters covering the final marketing mix element—promotion. The previous chapter dealt with overall integrated marketing communications (IMC) and with advertising and public relations (PR). This one investigated personal selling and sales promotion. Personal selling is the interpersonal arm of the communications mix. Sales promotion consists of short-term incentives to encourage the purchase or sale of a product or service.

 Objective 1 Discuss the role of a company's salespeople in creating value for customers and building customer relationships. **(pp 440–444)**

Most companies use salespeople and many companies assign them an important role in the marketing mix. For companies selling business products, the firm's salespeople work directly with customers. Often, the sales force is the customer's only direct contact with the company and therefore may be viewed by customers as representing the company itself. In contrast, for consumer-product companies that sell through intermediaries, consumers usually do not meet salespeople or even know about them. The sales force works behind the scenes, dealing with wholesalers and retailers to obtain their support and helping them become effective in selling the firm's products.

As an element of the promotion mix, the sales force is very effective in achieving certain marketing objectives and carrying out such activities as prospecting, communicating, selling and servicing, and information gathering. But with companies becoming more market oriented, a customer-focused sales force also works to produce both *customer satisfaction* and *company profit*. The sales force plays a key role in developing and managing profitable *customer relationships*.

 Objective 2 Identify and explain the six major sales force management steps. **(pp 444–454)**

High sales force costs necessitate an effective sales management process consisting of six steps: designing sales force strategy and structure, recruiting and selecting, training, compensating, supervising, and evaluating salespeople and sales force performance.

In designing a sales force, sales management must address strategy issues such as what type of sales force structure will work best (territorial, product, customer, or complex structure), how large the sales force should be, who will be involved in the selling effort, and how its various salespeople and sales-support people will work together (inside or outside sales forces and team selling).

To hold down the high costs of hiring the wrong people, salespeople must be recruited and selected carefully. In recruiting salespeople, a company may look to job duties and the characteristics of its most successful salespeople to suggest the traits it wants in its salespeople. It must then look for applicants through recommendations of current salespeople, employment agencies, classified ads, the Internet, and contacting college students. In the selection process, the procedure can vary from a single informal interview to lengthy testing and interviewing. After the selection process is complete, training programs familiarize new salespeople not only with the art of selling but also with the company's history, its products and policies, and the characteristics of its market and competitors.

The sales force compensation system helps to reward, motivate, and direct salespeople. In compensating salespeople, companies try to have an appealing plan, usually close to the going rate for the type of sales job and needed skills. In addition to compensation, all salespeople need supervision, and many need continuous encouragement because they must make many decisions and face many frustrations. Periodically, the company must evaluate their performance to help them do a better job. In evaluating salespeople, the company relies on getting regular information gathered through sales reports, personal observations, customers' letters and complaints, customer surveys, and conversations with other salespeople.

 Objective 3 Discuss the personal selling process, distinguishing between transaction-oriented marketing and relationship marketing. **(pp 454–458)**

The art of selling involves a seven-step selling process: prospecting and qualifying, preapproach, approach, presentation and demonstration, handling objections, closing, and follow-up. These steps help marketers close a specific sale and as such are transaction oriented. However, a seller's dealings with customers should be guided by the larger concept of relationship marketing. The company's sales force should help to orchestrate a whole-company effort to develop profitable long-term relationships with key customers based on superior customer value and satisfaction.

 Objective 4 Explain how sales promotion campaigns are developed and implemented. **(pp 459–464)**

Sales promotion campaigns call for setting sales promotions objectives (in general, sales promotions should be *consumer relationship building*); selecting tools; and developing and implementing the sales promotion program by using *consumer promotion tools* (from coupons, refunds, premiums, and point-of-purchase promotions to contests, sweepstakes, and events), *trade promotion tools* (discounts, allowances, free goods, push money), and *business promotion tools* (conventions, trade shows, sales contests), as well as deciding on such things as the size of the incentive, the conditions for participation, how to promote and distribute the promotion package, and the length of the promotion. After this process is completed, the company evaluates its sales promotion results.

Navigating the Key Terms

Objective 1
Personal selling (p 441)
Salesperson (p 441)

Objective 2
Sales force management (p 444)
Territorial sales force structure (p 445)
Product sales force structure (p 445)
Customer (or market) sales force structure (p 445)

Outside sales force (or field sales force) (p 447)
Inside sales force (p 447)
Team selling (p 448)
Sales 2.0 (p 452)
Sales quota (p 453)

Objective 3
Selling process (p 454)
Prospecting (p 454)
Preapproach (p 455)
Approach (p 456)

Presentation (p 456)
Handling objections (p 457)
Closing (p 457)
Follow-up (p 457)

Objective 4
Sales promotion (p 459)
Consumer promotions (p 460)
Event marketing (p 462)
Trade promotions (p 463)
Business promotions (p 463)

Travel Log

Discussing the Issues

1. Discuss the role of personal selling in the promotion mix. In what situations is it more effective than advertising? (AACSB: Communication; Reflective Thinking)

2. Compare and contrast the three sales force structures outlined in the chapter. Which structure is most effective? (AACSB: Communication; Reflective Thinking)

3. What role does an inside sales force play in an organization? (AACSB: Communication)

4. Discuss the activities involved in sales force management. (AACSB: Communication)

5. Define *sales promotion* and discuss the factors contributing to its rapid growth. (AACSB: Communication)

6. Discuss the different types of trade sales promotions and distinguish these types of promotions from business promotions. (AACSB: Communication)

Application Questions

1. Interview two sales people—one an *order taker* and the other an *order getter*. How much training did each receive to perform their job? Write a report of what you learned. (AACSB: Communication; Reflective Thinking)

2. Select a product or service and role-play a sales call—from the approach to the close—with another student. Have one member of the team act as the salesperson with the other member acting as the customer, raising at least three objections. Select another product or service and perform this exercise again with your roles reversed. (AACSB: Communication; Reflective Thinking)

3. Design a sales promotion campaign for your local animal shelter with the goal of increasing pet adoption. Use at least three types of consumer promotions and explain the decisions regarding this campaign. (AACSB: Communication; Reflective Thinking)

Under the Hood: Marketing Technology

Want to improve your business's operations? Hold a contest and get some of the best and brightest minds in the world working on it! That's what Netflix did. Netflix, the DVD rental company, held a 3-year, $1 million contest with the goal of improving its movie-recommendation system by 10 percent. The company wanted to improve its system for predicting what customers might like to rent based on their ratings of previous movies rented. The contest garnered more than 51,000 contestants from almost 200 countries. The contest attracted entries from scientists, researchers, and engineers, and the winning team consisted of one-time competitors who joined forces to submit the best solution within a few minutes of the contest's deadline. Netflix is not done with contests, though. The sequel—Netflix Prize 2—aims to improve the movie-recommendation system for Netflix customers who do not regularly rate movies on Netflix. Brush up on your math and computer skills and maybe you can be the next winner!

1. Visit http://www.netflixprize.com//index to learn about this contest and evaluate it on the sales promotion design decisions discussed in the chapter. (AACSB: Communication; Use of IT; Reflective Thinking)

2. Discuss drawbacks of contests compared to the similar promotions of sweepstakes and games. (AACSB: Communication; Reflective Thinking)

Staying on the Road: Marketing Ethics

Free samples, gifts, expensive trips, dinners, and entertainment—these tools have been, and sometimes still are, widely used by pharmaceutical companies to influence doctors' prescribing behavior. Physicians control the majority of healthcare expenditures through the prescriptions they write. Although direct-to-consumer advertising has grown exponentially over the past decade, an estimated 90 percent of pharmaceutical marketing dollars are directed at physicians. More than 90,000 pharmaceutical sales representatives in the United States, called "physician detailers," vie for healthcare professionals' attention to pitch their drugs. Research has shown that pharmaceutical company marketing tactics do influence physicians, causing them to prescribe more expensive drugs over less expensive alternatives. Critics claim that such tactics are unethical. However, the pharmaceutical companies claim that their sales representatives keep healthcare professionals well informed in this rapidly changing industry.

1. Is it ethical for pharmaceutical sales representatives to influence physician prescribing behavior using free samples and promotional gifts? (AACSB: Communication; Ethical Reasoning)

2. National and international pharmaceuticals trade associations publish codes of conduct regarding interactions with healthcare professionals. Visit the Web sites of the Pharmaceutical Research and Manufacturers of America (PhRMA) (www.phrma.org) and the International Federation of Pharmaceutical Manufacturers Association (IFPMA) (http://ifpma.org). Examine their codes of ethics regarding sales activities. Write a brief report of what you learn. (AACSB: Communication; Use of IT; Reflective Thinking)

Rough Road Ahead: Marketing and the Economy

Starbucks

After riding high for so many years, Starbucks' steamy-hot growth has gone cold. The coffee house's sales, profits, and stock price have plummeted, resulting in layoffs and store closures. Much of the blame goes to increased consumer frugality brought on by tough economic times. Newly intensified competition hasn't helped Starbucks either, especially from companies now selling premium brews at much lower prices. Starbucks has tried various tactics to convince customers that its products offer high value for the price. It has also tenaciously avoided reducing prices, doing everything possible to maintain its premium image.

Instead, Starbucks is putting efforts into things like its Starbucks Card Rewards, a major sales promotion initiative designed to generate customer loyalty. The rewards program offers incentives such as free add-ins to coffee drinks, free in-store refills on drip coffee, complementary in-store Wi-Fi, and free coffee with the purchase of a pound of coffee beans. The company hopes that such incentives will entice customers to visit more often and to spend more when they visit. Starbucks asserts that, as it gains experience in using the program to gather customer

information and track customer purchases, Starbucks Card Rewards will become more effective in achieving its goals.

1. Does the Starbucks Card Rewards program go far enough in providing incentives to increase customer spending in the wake of the economic downturn? What else could Starbucks do with the program?

2. More generally, are sales promotions sufficient for the Starbucks situation? Why or why not? What other actions would you recommend?

Travel Budget: Marketing by the Numbers

Salespeople do more than just sell products and services—they manage relationships with customers to deliver value to both the customer and their company. Companies must ensure that they have enough salespeople to do the job.

1. Refer to Appendix 2, Marketing by the Numbers, to determine the number of salespeople a company needs if it has 3,000 customers who must be called on 10 times per year. Each sales call lasts approximately 2 1/2 hours, and each sales rep has approximately 1,250 hours per

year to devote to customers. (AACSB: Communication; Analytical Reasoning)

2. If each sales representative earns a salary of $60,000 per year, what sales are necessary to break even on sales force costs if the company has a contribution margin of 40 percent? What effect will adding each additional sales rep have on the break-even sales? (AACSB: Communication; Analytical Reasoning)

Drive In: Video Case

The Principal Financial Group

The Principal Financial Group delivered strong growth in its first six years as a public company. Operating earnings grew from $577 million in 2001 to $1.06 billion in 2007 alone. In that same year, total assets under management soared from $98 billion to $311 billion. The Principal also achieved a 16.4 percent return on equity for 2007, compared to 8.9 percent for 2001. As a result, its stock price increased 236 percent from its opening price at the October 2001 initial public offering (IPO) through its closing price at year-end 2007.

One of the biggest reasons for this success is The Principal Financial Group's strongly customer-centered sales force. The company's varied and complex product line

(from retirement products to insurance) demands the one-on-one attention of a salesperson who understands how to build customer relationships. The company's sales force has helped make The Principal a global player in the financial services industry.

After viewing the video featuring The Principal Financial Group, answer the following questions:

1. How is the sales force at The Principal Financial Group structured?

2. Identify the selling process of the company. Give evidence of each step.

3. How does The Principal build long-term customer relationships through its sales force?

14 Direct and Online Marketing:
Building Direct Customer Relationships

ROAD MAP

Previewing the Concepts

In the previous two chapters, you learned about communicating customer value through integrated marketing communication (IMC) and about four specific elements of the marketing communications mix—advertising, publicity, personal selling, and sales promotion. In this chapter, we'll look at the final IMC element, direct marketing, and at its fastest-growing form, online marketing. Actually, direct marketing can be viewed as more than just a communications tool. In many ways it constitutes an overall marketing approach—a blend of communication and distribution channels all rolled into one. As you read on, remember that although this chapter examines direct marketing as a separate tool, it must be carefully integrated with other elements of the promotion mix.

Objective Outline

> **Objective 1**   Define direct marketing and discuss its benefits to customers and companies.
> The New Direct Marketing Model **p 473**
> Growth and Benefits of Direct Marketing **pp 473–475**
> Customer Databases and Direct Marketing **pp 476–477**

> **Objective 2**   Identify and discuss the major forms of direct marketing.
> Forms of Direct Marketing **pp 477–486**

> **Objective 3**   Explain how companies have responded to the Internet and other powerful new technologies with online marketing strategies.
> Online Marketing **pp 486–491**

> **Objective 4**   Discuss how companies go about conducting online marketing to profitably deliver more value to customers.
> Setting up an Online Marketing Presence
> **pp 491–499**

> **Objective 5**   Overview the public policy and ethical issues presented by direct marketing.
> Public Policy Issues in Direct Marketing
> **pp 499–502**

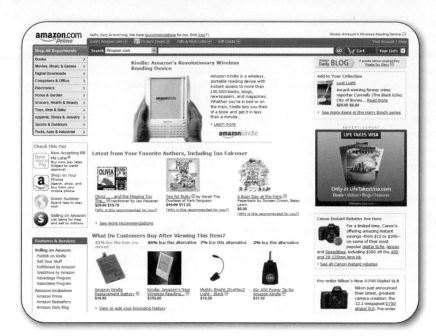

▲ Amazon.com obsesses over making each customer's experience uniquely personal. "If we have 88 million customers, we should have 88 million stores."

For starters, let's look at Amazon.com. In 15 years, Amazon.com has blossomed from an obscure dot-com upstart into one of the best-known names on the Internet. According to one estimate, 52 percent of people who shopped the Internet last year started at Amazon.com. How has Amazon.com become such an incredibly successful direct and online marketer in such a short time? It's all about creating direct, personal, satisfying customer experiences. Few direct marketers do that as well as Amazon.com.

| First Stop | **Amazon.com:**
The Wal-Mart
of the Internet? |

When you think of shopping on the Web, chances are good that you think first of Amazon.com. Amazon.com first opened its virtual doors in 1995, selling books out of founder Jeff Bezos's garage in suburban Seattle. The online pioneer still sells books—*lots and lots* of books. But it now sells just about everything else as well, from music, videos, electronics, tools, housewares, apparel, shoes, groceries, and kids' products to loose diamonds and Maine lobsters. "We have the Earth's Biggest Selection," declares the company's Web site.

In only a decade and a half, Amazon.com has become one of the best-known names on the Web. In perfecting the art of online selling, it has also rewritten the rules of marketing. Many analysts view Amazon.com as *the* model for businesses in the digital age. They predict that it will one day become the Wal-Mart of the Internet.

From the start, Amazon.com has grown explosively. Its annual sales have rocketed from a modest $150 million in 1997 to more than $19 *billion* today. In only the past five years, despite the recent shaky economy, its sales have more than tripled. Although it took Amazon.com eight years to turn its first full-year profit in 2003, profits have since surged more than 18-fold. Last year alone, sales grew 29 percent; profits popped 36 percent. This past holiday season, the online store's more than 88 million active customers purchased 72.9 items per second on its site. One study estimates that 52 percent of all consumers who went to the Internet to shop last year started at Amazon.com. Fifty percent of Amazon.com's sales come from overseas.

What has made Amazon.com one of the world's premier direct marketers? To its core, the company is relentlessly customer driven. "The thing that drives everything is creating genuine value for customers," says founder Jeff Bezos. "If you focus on what customers want and build a relationship, they will allow you to make money." In one promotion in Japan, for example, Bezos donned a delivery driver's uniform and went house to house with packages. His point: Everything at Amazon—from top to bottom—begins and ends with the customer.

Anyone at Amazon.com will tell you that the company wants to do much more than just sell books or DVDs or digital cameras. It wants to deliver a special *experience* to every customer. "The customer experience really matters," says Bezos. "We've focused on just having a better store, where it's easier to shop, where you can learn more about the products, where you have a bigger selection, and where you have the lowest prices. You combine all of that stuff together and people say, 'Hey, these guys really get it.'"

In perfecting the art of online selling, Amazon.com has rewritten the rules of marketing. The Web pioneer excels at creating personal, satisfying direct marketing customer experiences.

471

▲ Says Amazon founder and CEO Jeff Bezos, "We are not great advertisers. So we start with customers, figure out what they want, and figure out how to get it to them."

And customers get it too. Most Amazon.com regulars feel a surprisingly strong relationship with the company, especially given the almost complete lack of actual human interaction. Amazon.com obsesses over making each customer's experience uniquely personal. For example, the Amazon.com Web site greets customers with their very own personalized home pages, and the site's "Recommended for you" feature prepares personalized product recommendations. Amazon.com was first to use "collaborative filtering" technology, which sifts through each customer's past purchases and the purchasing patterns of customers with similar profiles to come up with personalized site content. "We want Amazon.com to be the right store for you as an individual," says Bezos. "If we have 88 million customers, we should have 88 million stores."

Visitors to Amazon.com's Web site receive a unique blend of benefits: huge selection, good value, convenience, and what the company calls "discovery." In books alone, for example, Amazon.com offers an easily searchable virtual selection of more than 3 million titles, 15 times more than in any physical bookstore. Good value comes in the form of reasonable prices, plus free delivery on orders over $25. And at Amazon.com, it's irresistibly convenient to buy. You can log on, find anything and everything you want, and order with a single mouse click, all in less time than it takes to find a parking space at the local mall.

But it's the "discovery" factor that makes the Amazon.com buying experience really special. Once on the Web site, you're compelled to stay for a while—looking, learning, and discovering. Amazon.com has become a kind of online community, in which customers can browse for products, research purchase alternatives, share opinions and reviews with other visitors, and chat online with authors and experts. In this way, Amazon.com does much more than just sell goods on the Web. It creates direct, personalized customer relationships and satisfying online experiences. Year after year, Amazon.com comes in number one or number two on the American Customer Satisfaction Index, regardless of industry.

In fact, Amazon.com has become so good at managing online relationships that many traditional "brick-and-mortar" retailers are turning to Amazon for help in adding more "clicks" to their "bricks." For example, Amazon.com now partners with well-known retailers such as Target and Bebe to help them run their Web interfaces. And to create even greater selection and convenience for customers, Amazon.com allows competing retailers—from mom-and-pop operations to Marks & Spencer—to offer their products on its Web site, creating a virtual shopping mall of incredible proportions. It even encourages customers to sell used items on the site.

Amazon.com is constantly on the lookout for innovative new ways to use the power of the Web and direct marketing to create more shopping selection, value, convenience, and discovery. For example, it started Amazon Prime, a program by which members pay $79 per year and get free two-day shipping on all orders and next-day shipping for $3.99 on any order. Amazon.com now offers music downloading, with the music files not restricted by digital rights management software (DRM), which means that (unlike iTunes) you can freely and conveniently copy the songs. All four major music labels promptly signed on. The Web merchant also launched an Amazon.com application for the iPhone, which allows consumers to shop on the go.

And two years ago, Amazon.com took another bold customer-convenience and personalization step. It introduced the Kindle, a wireless reading device for downloading books, blogs, magazines, newspapers, and other matter. Lighter and thinner than a typical paperback book, the Kindle wireless reader connects like a cell phone, letting customers buy and download content of personal interest—from the *Wall Street Journal* or *Time* magazine to the latest *New York Times* bestsellers—from home or on the go in less than 60 seconds. The Kindle has a paper-like electronic-ink display that's easy to read even in bright daylight. Now available in two models, Kindles are flying off the Web seller's virtual shelves.

So, what do you think? Will Amazon.com become the Wal-Mart of the Web? That remains to be seen. But whatever its fate, the direct and online pioneer has forever changed the face of marketing. Most importantly, Amazon.com has set a very high bar for the online customer experience. "The reason I'm so obsessed with . . . the customer experience is that I believe [that our success] has been driven exclusively by that experience," says Jeff Bezos. "We are not great advertisers. So we start with customers, figure out what they want, and figure out how to get it to them."[1]

*m*any of the marketing and promotion tools that we've examined in previous chapters were developed in the context of *mass marketing*: targeting broad markets with standardized messages and offers distributed through intermediaries. Today, however, with the trend toward more narrowly targeted marketing, many companies are adopting *direct marketing,* either as a primary marketing approach, as in Amazon.com's case, or as a supplement to other approaches. In this section, we explore the exploding world of direct marketing.

Direct marketing
Connecting directly with carefully targeted individual consumers to both obtain an immediate response and cultivate lasting customer relationships.

Direct marketing consists of connecting directly with carefully targeted individual consumers to both obtain an immediate response and cultivate lasting customer relationships. Direct marketers communicate directly with customers, often on a one-to-one, interactive basis. Using detailed databases, they tailor their marketing offers and communications to the needs of narrowly defined segments or even individual buyers.

Beyond brand and relationship building, direct marketers usually seek a direct, immediate, and measurable consumer response. For example, as we learned in the chapter-opening story, Amazon.com interacts directly with customers on its Web site to help them discover and buy almost anything and everything on the Internet, with only a few clicks of the mouse button. Similarly, GEICO interacts directly with customers, by telephone, through its Web site, or even on its Facebook page to give insurance quotes, sell policies, or service customer accounts.

Author Comment »
For most companies, direct marketing is a supplemental channel or medium. But for many other companies today—such as Amazon.com, eBay, or GEICO—direct marketing is a complete way of doing business.

THE NEW DIRECT MARKETING MODEL (p 473)

Early direct marketers—catalog companies, direct mailers, and telemarketers—gathered customer names and sold goods mainly by mail and telephone. Today, however, fired by rapid advances in database technologies and new marketing media—especially the Internet—direct marketing has undergone a dramatic transformation.

In previous chapters, we've discussed direct marketing as direct distribution—as marketing channels that contain no intermediaries. We also include direct marketing as one element of the promotion mix—as an approach for communicating directly with consumers. In actuality, direct marketing is both of these things and more.

▼**The new direct marketing model:** Companies such as GEICO have built their entire approach to the marketplace around direct marketing: Just visit www.geico.com or call 1-800-947-auto.

Most companies still use direct marketing as a supplementary channel or medium. Thus, Lexus markets mostly through mass-media advertising and its high-quality dealer network but also supplements these channels with direct marketing. Its direct marketing includes promotional DVDs and other materials mailed directly to prospective buyers and a Web page (www.lexus.com) that provides consumers with information about various models, competitive comparisons, financing, and dealer locations. Similarly, most department stores such as Sears or Macy's sell the majority of their merchandise off their store shelves but also sell through direct mail and online catalogs.

However, for many companies today, direct marketing is more than just a supplementary channel or advertising medium. For these companies, direct marketing—especially in its most recent transformation, online marketing—constitutes a complete model for doing business. Rather than using direct marketing and the Internet only as supplemental approaches, firms employing this new *direct model* use it as the *only* approach. ▲Companies such as Amazon.com, eBay, and GEICO have built their entire approach to the marketplace around direct marketing. The direct model is rapidly changing the way that companies think about building relationships with customers.

Author Comment »
Direct marketing—especially online marketing—is growing explosively. It's at the heart of the trend toward building closer, more interactive customer relationships.

GROWTH AND BENEFITS OF DIRECT MARKETING (pp 473–475)

Direct marketing has become the fastest-growing form of marketing. According to the Direct Marketing Association (DMA), U.S. companies spent $176.9 billion on direct marketing last year, which is 52 percent of total dollars spent on advertising. In 2008, an investment of $1 in direct marketing advertising expenditures returned, on average, and estimated $11.63 in incremental revenue across all industries. Put another way, these expenditures generated an estimated $2.1 trillion in direct marketing sales, or about 10 percent of total sales in the U.S. economy. The DMA estimates that direct marketing sales will grow 5.3 percent annually through 2013, compared with a projected 4.1 percent annual growth for total U.S. sales.[2]

Direct marketing continues to become more Web-oriented, and Internet marketing is claiming a fast-growing share of direct marketing spending and sales. The Internet now accounts for only about 23 percent of direct marketing-driven sales. However, the DMA predicts that over the next five years, Internet marketing expenditures will grow at a blistering 13 percent a year, about three times faster than expenditures in other direct marketing media. Internet-driven sales will also grow by 13 percent.

Whether employed as a complete business model or as a supplement to a broader integrated marketing mix, direct marketing brings many benefits to both buyers and sellers.

Benefits to Buyers

For buyers, direct marketing is convenient, easy, and private. Direct marketers never close their doors, and customers don't have to battle traffic, find parking spaces, and trek through stores to find products. From the comfort of their homes or offices, they can browse catalogs or company Web sites at any time of the day or night. Business buyers can learn about products and services without tying up time with salespeople.

Direct marketing gives buyers ready access to a wealth of products. Unrestrained by physical boundaries, direct marketers can offer an almost unlimited selection to consumers almost anywhere in the world. Just compare the huge selections offered by many Web merchants to the more meager assortments of their brick-and-mortar counterparts. For instance, log onto Bulbs.com, "the Web's number-one light bulb superstore," and you'll have instant access to every imaginable kind of light bulb or lamp—incandescent bulbs, fluorescent bulbs, projection bulbs, surgical bulbs, automotive bulbs—you name it. Similarly, Web shoes and accessories retailer Zappos.com stocks more than 2.7 million shoes, handbags, clothing items, and accessories from more than 1,300 brands. No physical store could offer handy access to such vast selections.

Direct marketing channels also give buyers access to a wealth of comparative information about companies, products, and competitors. Good catalogs or Web sites often provide more information in more useful forms than even the most helpful retail salesperson can. For example, the Amazon.com site offers more information than most of us can digest, ranging from top-10 product lists, extensive product descriptions, and expert and user product reviews to recommendations based on customers' previous purchases. And Sears catalogs offer a treasure trove of information about the store's merchandise and services. In fact, you probably wouldn't think it strange to see a Sears salesperson referring to a catalog in the store for more detailed information while trying to advise a customer on a specific product or offer.

Finally, direct marketing is interactive and immediate—buyers can interact with sellers by phone or on the seller's Web site to create exactly the configuration of information, products, or services they desire, and then order them on the spot. Moreover, direct marketing gives consumers a greater measure of control. Consumers decide which catalogs they will browse and which Web sites they will visit.

Benefits to Sellers

For sellers, direct marketing is a powerful tool for building customer relationships. Using database marketing, today's marketers can target small groups or individual consumers and promote their offers through personalized communications.

Because of the one-to-one nature of direct marketing, companies can interact with customers by phone or online, learn more about their needs, and tailor products and services to specific customer tastes. In turn, customers can ask questions and volunteer feedback.

Direct marketing also offers sellers a low-cost, efficient, speedy alternative for reaching their markets. Direct marketing has grown rapidly in business-to-business marketing, partly in response to the ever-increasing costs of marketing through the sales force. When personal sales calls cost an average of more than $400 per contact, they should be made only when necessary and to high-potential customers and prospects.[3] Lower-cost-per-contact media—such as business-to-business telemarketing, direct mail, and company Web sites—often prove more cost effective.

Similarly, online direct marketing results in lower costs, improved efficiencies, and speedier handling of channel and logistics functions, such as order processing, inventory handling, and delivery. Direct marketers such as Amazon.com or Netflix also avoid the expense of maintaining a store and the related costs of rent, insurance, and utilities, passing the savings along to customers.

Direct marketing can also offer greater flexibility. It allows marketers to make ongoing adjustments to its prices and programs, or to make immediate, timely, and personal announcements and offers. ▲For example, in its signature folksy manner, Southwest Airlines uses techie direct marketing tools—including a widget and a blog—to inject itself directly into customers' everyday lives, at their invitation:[4]

▲Southwest Airlines uses techie direct marketing tools—including a widget and a blog—to inject itself directly into customers' everyday lives. Its Nuts About Southwest blog builds direct, interactive customer relationships that media advertising simply can't achieve.

The widget—called DING!—is a computer application that consumers can download to their personal computer desktop. Whenever exclusive discount fares are offered, the program emits the familiar in-flight seatbelt-light bell dinging sound. The deep discounts last only 6–12 hours and can only be accessed online by clicking on the application. DING! lets Southwest bypass the reservations system and pass bargain fares directly to interested customers. Eventually, DING! may even allow Southwest to customize fare offers based on each customer's unique characteristics and travel preferences. In its first two years, the DING! application was downloaded by about 2 million consumers and generated more than $150 million in ticket sales.

Based in part on the success of DING!, Southwest launched a "Nuts About Southwest" blog. Written by employees, the blog lets Southwest talk directly with and solicit comments from customers. In turn, it gives customers an inside look at the company and access to 30 cross-department employee bloggers. The blog generates a decisive response from Southwest loyalists. Last year, the blog attracted more than 100,000 total visits and more than 40,000 unique visitors. A blog post by CEO Gary Kelly about the airline's consideration of assigned seating drew more than 600 comments, mainly in support of the current nonassigned seating practice. In all, the low-key blog builds direct, interactive customer relationships that media advertising simply can't achieve.

Finally, direct marketing gives sellers access to buyers that they could not reach through other channels. Smaller firms can mail catalogs to customers outside their local markets and post 1-800 telephone numbers to handle orders and inquiries. Internet marketing is a truly global medium that allows buyers and sellers to click from one country to another in seconds. A Web user from Paris or Istanbul can access an online L.L.Bean catalog as easily as someone living in Freeport, Maine, the direct retailer's hometown. Even small marketers find that they have ready access to global markets.

CUSTOMER DATABASES AND DIRECT MARKETING (pp 476–477)

Effective direct marketing begins with a good customer database. A **customer database** is an organized collection of comprehensive data about individual customers or prospects, including geographic, demographic, psychographic, and behavioral data. A good customer database can be a potent relationship-building tool. The database gives companies a 360-degree view of their customers and how they behave. A company is no better than what it knows about its customers.

In consumer marketing, the customer database might contain a customer's demographics (age, income, family members, birthdays), psychographics (activities, interests, and opinions), and buying behavior (buying preferences and the recency, frequency, and monetary value—RFM—of past purchases). In business-to-business marketing, the customer profile might contain the products and services the customer has bought, past volumes and prices, key contacts (and their ages, birthdays, hobbies, and favorite foods), competing suppliers, status of current contracts, estimated customer spending for the next few years, and assessments of competitive strengths and weaknesses in selling and servicing the account.

Some of these databases are huge. For example, casino operator Harrah's Entertainment has built a customer database containing 700 terabytes worth of customer information, roughly 70 times the amount of the printed collection in the Library of Congress. It uses this data to create special customer experiences. Similarly, Wal-Mart captures data on every item, for every customer, for every store, every day. Its database contains more than 2.5 petabytes of data—that's equivalent to 50 million, 4-door filing cabinets full of text. Google processes an astonishing 20 petabytes of data a day.[5]

Companies use their databases in many ways. They use databases to locate good potential customers and to generate sales leads. They can mine their databases to learn about customers in detail, and then fine-tune their market offerings and communications to the special preferences and behaviors of target segments or individuals. In all, a company's database can be an important tool for building stronger long-term customer relationships.

For example, ▲financial services provider USAA uses its database to find ways to serve the long-term needs of customers, regardless of immediate sales impact, creating an incredibly loyal customer base:

> USAA provides financial services to U.S. military personnel and their families, largely through direct marketing via the telephone and Internet. It maintains a customer database built from customer purchasing histories and from information collected directly from customers. To keep the database fresh, the organization regularly surveys its more than 7 million customers worldwide to learn such things as whether they have children (and if so, how old they are), if they have moved recently, and when they plan to retire. USAA uses the database to tailor direct marketing offers to the specific needs of individual customers. For example, for customers looking toward retirement, it sends information on estate planning. If the family has college-age children, USAA sends those children information on how to manage their credit cards. If the family has younger children, it sends booklets on things such as financing a child's education.
>
> One delighted reporter, a USAA customer, recounts how USAA even helped him teach his 16-year-old daughter to drive. Just before her birthday, but before she received her driver's license, USAA mailed a "package of materials, backed by research, to help me teach my daughter how to drive, help her practice, and help us find ways to agree on what constitutes safe driving later on, when she gets her license." What's more, marvels the reporter, "USAA didn't try to sell me a thing. My take-away: that USAA is investing in me for the long term, that it defines profitability not just by what it sells today." Through such skillful use of its database, USAA serves each customer uniquely, resulting in high levels of customer loyalty and sales growth. The average customer household owns almost five USAA products, and the $13.4 billion company retains 97 per-

▼Customer databases: Financial services provider USAA uses its extensive database to tailor its services to the specific needs of individual customers, creating incredible customer loyalty.

cent of its customers. For four years running, USAA has received the top score of any insurance company in Forrester Research, Inc.'s respected customer advocacy survey. And it ranked number 1 among companies from all industries on last year's MSN Money Customer Service Hall of Fame survey, ahead of such well-regarded companies as Amazon.com, Southwest Airlines, Nordstrom, and Apple.[6]

Like many other marketing tools, database marketing requires a special investment. Companies must invest in computer hardware, database software, analytical programs, communication links, and skilled personnel. The database system must be user-friendly and available to various marketing groups, including those in product and brand management, new-product development, advertising and promotion, direct mail, telemarketing, Web marketing, field sales, order fulfillment, and customer service. However, a well-managed database should lead to sales and customer-relationship gains that will more than cover its costs.

Author Comment »
Direct marketing is rich in tools, from traditional old favorites such as direct mail, catalogs, and telemarketing to the Internet and other new digital approaches.

FORMS OF DIRECT MARKETING (pp 477–486)

The major forms of direct marketing—as shown in ■ **Figure 14.1**—include personal selling, direct-mail marketing, catalog marketing, telephone marketing, direct-response television marketing, kiosk marketing, new digital direct marketing technologies, and online marketing. We examined personal selling in depth in Chapter 13. Here, we examine the other direct-marketing forms.

Direct-Mail Marketing

Direct-mail marketing
Direct marketing by sending an offer, announcement, reminder, or other item to a person at a particular physical or virtual address.

Direct-mail marketing involves sending an offer, announcement, reminder, or other item to a person at a particular physical or virtual address. Using highly selective mailing lists, direct marketers send out millions of mail pieces each year—letters, catalogs, ads, brochures, samples, DVDs, and other "salespeople with wings." Direct mail is by far the largest direct marketing medium. The DMA reports that direct mail (including both catalog and noncatalog mail) accounts for 34 percent of all U.S. direct marketing spending and drives 29 percent of direct marketing sales.[7]

■ **Figure 14.1** Forms of Direct Marketing

What these many diverse marketing tools have in common is that they reach selected customers directly, and often interactively, building close, one-to-one relationships.

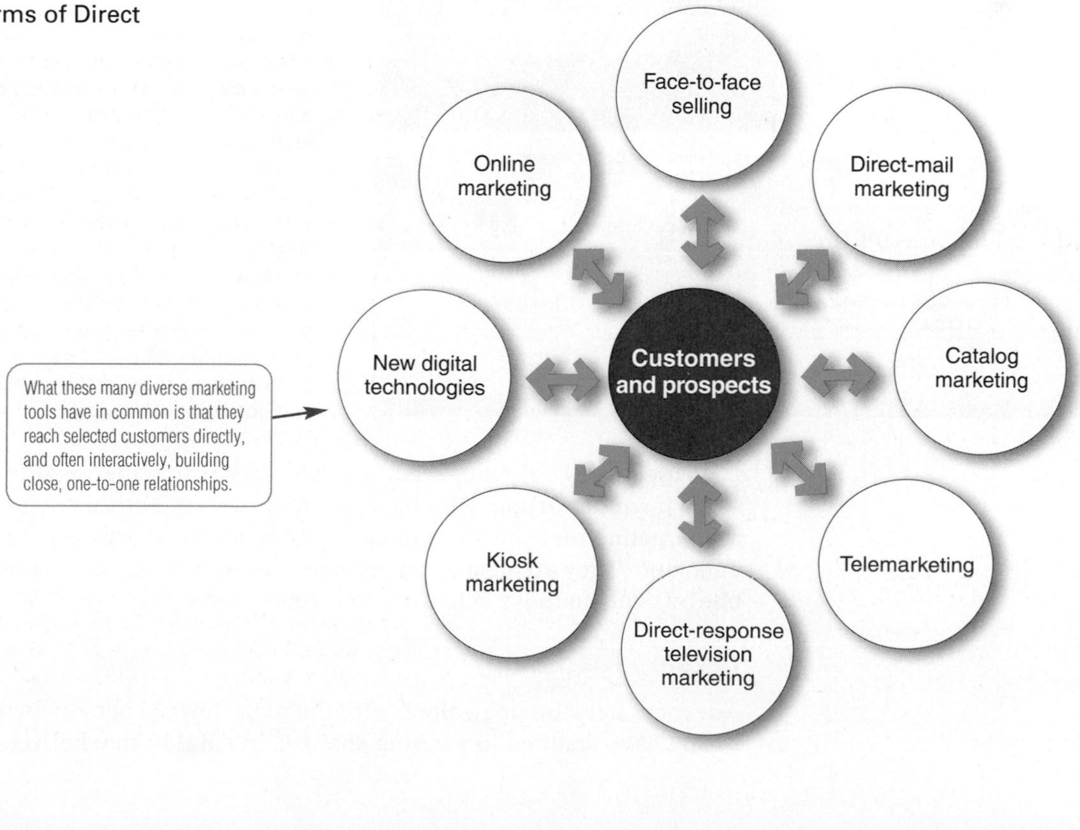

Direct mail is well suited to direct, one-to-one communication. It permits high target-market selectivity, can be personalized, is flexible, and allows easy measurement of results. Although direct mail costs more per thousand people reached than mass media such as television or magazines, the people it reaches are much better prospects. Direct mail has proved successful in promoting all kinds of products, from books, music, DVDs, and magazine subscriptions to insurance, gift items, clothing, gourmet foods, and industrial products. Charities also use direct mail heavily to raise billions of dollars each year.

Some analysts predict a decline in the use of traditional forms of direct mail in coming years, as marketers switch to newer digital forms, such as e-mail and mobile (cell phone) marketing. E-mail, in particular, is booming as a direct marketing tool. Today's new breed of e-mail ads use animation, interactive links, streaming video, and personalized audio messages to reach out and grab attention. E-mail, mobile, and other newer forms of direct mail deliver direct messages at incredible speeds and lower costs compared to the post office's "snail mail" pace. We will discuss e-mail and mobile marketing in more detail later in the chapter.

However, even though the new digital forms of direct mail are gaining popularity, the traditional form is still by far the most widely used. Mail marketing offers some distinct advantages. "Mail advertising provides a tangible piece to hold and keep," says one analyst. "E-mail is trashed too easily." Says another, "Mail is real, tactile, and shows you care more than a blanket e-mail."[8]

Traditional direct mail can be used effectively in combination with other media, such as company Web sites. For example, some marketers now send out direct mail featuring personalized URLs (PURLs)—Web addresses such as www.intel.com/John.Doe—that invite intrigued prospects to individualized Web sites. ▲Consider this example:[9]

▼**Combining direct mail with personalized URLs (PURLs) cost JDA only $50,000 but yielded a high response rate and $13 million in sales.**

For companies that had their heads in the clouds when it came time to upgrade their computers, JDA Software Group decided it was time for some skywriting. It teamed with HP, Intel, and marketing agency The Mahoney Company to send out personalized direct mail pieces that featured a man with his arms spread upward, experiencing an epiphany in the form of fluffy words forming above his head: "Bruce Schwartz, The Moment Has Arrived." In reality, the direct mail piece didn't come from out of the blue. Based on customers' upgrade schedules, JDA targeted carefully selected decision makers who were considering buying $500,000 to $1.5 million software suites. These high-value prospects received personalized direct mailings and e-mails, complete with personalized URLs (PURLs) that led them to individualized Web pages. Once there, prospects learned all about how hardware from HP and Intel would support software from JDA. Customers revealed more information about themselves each time they visited the PURL, which allowed JDA, HP, and Intel to work with them throughout the buying process. The result? The $50,000 campaign yielded a 9.2 percent response rate and $13 million in sales. "Sending specific [information] to specific people does make a huge difference," says Intel's strategic relationships manager.

Direct mail, whether traditional or digital may be resented as "junk mail" or spam if sent to people who have no interest in it. For this reason, smart marketers are targeting their direct mail carefully so as not to waste their money and recipients' time. They are designing permission-based programs, sending e-mail and mobile ads only to those who want to receive them.

Catalog Marketing

Advances in technology, along with the move toward personalized, one-to-one marketing have resulted in exciting changes in **catalog marketing**. *Catalog Age* maga-

Catalog marketing
Direct marketing through print, video, or digital catalogs that are mailed to select customers, made available in stores, or presented online.

zine used to define a *catalog* as "a printed, bound piece of at least eight pages, selling multiple products, and offering a direct ordering mechanism." Today, only a few years later, this definition is sadly out of date.

With the stampede to the Internet, more and more catalogs are going digital. A variety of Web-only catalogers have emerged, and most print catalogers have added Web-based catalogs to their marketing mixes. For example, click on the Shop by Catalog link at www.llbean.com and you can flip through the latest L.L.Bean catalog page by page online. Web-based catalogs eliminate production, printing, and mailing costs. And whereas print-catalog space is limited, online catalogs can offer an almost unlimited amount of merchandise. Finally, online catalogs allow real-time merchandising—products and features can be added or removed as needed and prices can be adjusted instantly to match demand.

However, despite the advantages of Web-based catalogs, as your overstuffed mailbox may suggest, printed catalogs are still thriving. Why aren't companies ditching their old-fashioned paper catalogs in this new digital era? It turns out that printed catalogs are one of the best ways to drive online sales. "Our catalog is itself an advertising vehicle, and it is an effective way to drive traffic to our Web site," says an L.L.Bean marketer. A recent study found that 70 percent of Web purchases are driven by catalogs. Even online-only retailers, such as eBay and UncommonGoods, have started producing catalogs with the hopes of driving online sales. The retailers said that 13 percent of new online customers in one year resulted from catalog mailings, and about 43 percent of catalog customers also buy online.[10]

In addition, paper catalogs can also create emotional connections with customers that Web-based sales spaces simply can't. For example, Sears recently brought back its holiday Wish Book after a 14-year hiatus. According to Sears' chief marketing officer, many customers were nostalgic for the catalog, reminiscing about the days when they would fold over pages and hope that Santa would notice.[11]

▼Catalog marketing—printed and online—has grown explosively during the past 25 years. There are 8,000 to 10,000 unique catalog titles in the United States alone.

In all, ▲catalog marketing—printed and online—has grown explosively during the past 25 years. According to one study, there are 8,000 to 10,000 unique catalog titles in the United States that collectively send out over 19 billion catalogs a year to American consumers, 6 million more than a decade ago. Annual catalog sales amounted to about $155 billion last year and are expected to top $182 billion by 2013.[12]

These days, consumers can buy just about anything from a catalog. Each year Lillian Vernon sends out 17 editions of its 3 catalogs with total circulation of 80 million copies to its 20-million-person database, selling more than 700 products in each catalog, ranging from shoes to decorative lawn birds and monogrammed oven mitts.[13] Specialty department stores, such as Neiman Marcus, Bloomingdale's, and Saks Fifth Avenue, use catalogs to cultivate upper-middle-class markets for high-priced, often exotic, merchandise. Want Jack Nicklaus to design a 3-hole golf course for your backyard? It's featured in the latest Neiman Marcus Christmas catalog for only $1 million (not including construction and site preparation costs).

Telephone Marketing

Telephone marketing
Using the telephone to sell directly to customers.

Telephone marketing involves using the telephone to sell directly to consumers and business customers. Telephone marketing now accounts for more than 17 percent of all direct marketing-driven sales. We're all familiar with telephone marketing directed toward consumers, but business-to-business marketers also use telephone marketing extensively, accounting for more than 56 percent of all telephone marketing sales.[14]

Marketers use *outbound* telephone marketing to sell directly to consumers and businesses. ▲They use *inbound* toll-free 800 numbers to receive orders from television and print ads, direct mail, or catalogs. The use of 800 numbers has taken off in

Careful...you might sprain a taste bud.

Don't wait another day! Call now to place an order or request a catalog. Also, go on line at **www.carolinacookie.com** to place an order, request a catalog or view our entire selection of products.

1-800-447-5797

CAROLINA COOKIE COMPANY · JUST BAKED

▲ Marketers use inbound toll-free 800 numbers to receive orders from television and print ads, direct mail, or catalogs. Here, the Carolina Cookie Company urges, "Don't wait another day. Call now to place an order or request a catalog."

recent years as more and more companies have begun using them, and as current users have added new features such as toll-free fax numbers. To accommodate this rapid growth, new toll-free area codes, such as 888, 877, and 866, have been added.

Properly designed and targeted telemarketing provides many benefits, including purchasing convenience and increased product and service information. However, the explosion in unsolicited outbound telephone marketing over the years annoyed many consumers, who objected to the almost daily "junk phone calls" that pulled them away from the dinner table or filled the answering machine.

In 2003, U.S. lawmakers responded with a National Do Not Call Registry, managed by the Federal Trade Commission. The legislation bans most telemarketing calls to registered phone numbers (although people can still receive calls from nonprofit groups, politicians, and companies with which they have recently done business). Consumers have responded enthusiastically. To date, nearly three-fourths of Americans have registered their phone numbers at www.donotcall.gov or by calling 888-382-1222. Businesses that break do-not-call laws can be fined up to $11,000 per violation. As a result, reports an FTC spokesperson, the program "has been exceptionally successful."[15]

Do-not-call legislation has hurt the telemarketing industry, but not all that much. Two major forms of telemarketing—inbound consumer telemarketing and outbound business-to-business telemarketing—remain strong and growing. Telemarketing also remains a major fund-raising tool for nonprofit and political groups. However, many telemarketers are shifting to alternative methods for capturing new customers and sales, from direct mail, direct-response TV, and live-chat Web technology to sweepstakes that prompt customers to call in.

For example, ServiceMaster's TruGreen lawn-care service used to generate about 90 percent of its sales through telemarketing. It now uses more direct mail, as well as having employees go door-to-door in neighborhoods where it already has customers. The new approach appears to be working even better than the old cold-calling one. The company's sales have grown under the new methods, and less than 50 percent of sales come from telemarketing. "We were nervous, but were thrilled with what we've accomplished," says ServiceMaster's chief executive.[16]

In fact, do-not-call appears to be helping most direct marketers more than it's hurting them. Many of these marketers are shifting their call-center activity from making cold calls on often resentful customers to managing existing customer relationships. They are developing "opt-in" calling systems, in which they provide useful information and offers to customers who have invited the company to contact them by phone or e-mail. These "sales tactics have [produced] results as good—or even better—than telemarketing," declares one analyst. "The opt-in model is proving [more] valuable for marketers [than] the old invasive one." [17]

Meanwhile, marketers who violate do-not-call regulations have themselves increasingly become the targets of crusading consumer activist groups, who return the favor by flooding the violating company's phone system with return calls and messages.[18]

Direct-Response Television Marketing

Direct-response television marketing
Direct marketing via television, including direct-response television advertising (or infomercials) and home shopping channels.

Direct-response television marketing takes one of two major forms. The first is *direct-response television advertising* (DRTV). Direct marketers air television spots, often 60 or 120 seconds long, which persuasively describe a product and give customers a toll-free number or Web site for ordering. Television viewers also often encounter full 30-minute or longer advertising programs, or *infomercials*, for a single product.

Successful direct-response television campaigns can ring up big sales. For example, Bowflex has grossed more than $1.3 billion in infomercial sales. And little-known infomercial maker Guthy-Renker has helped propel Proactiv Solution acne treatment into a power brand that pulls in $850 million in sales annually to 5 million active customers (compare that to annual American drugstore sales of acne products of only about $150 million). Proactiv's incredible success derives from powerful, formulaic infomercials in which celebrities and average Joes gush about how Proactiv cleared their skin. "My skin is now clear and beautiful," says Serena Williams. "Yours can be too!"[19]

▲Direct response TV advertising: Ads for products like the Snuggie have become DRTV classics. However, thanks to the recently weakened economy and stepped-up consumer bargain hunting, marketers of all kinds—from P&G and Coca-Cola to Disney—now use infomercials to sell their wares.

DRTV ads are most often associated with somewhat loud or questionable pitches for cleaners and stain removers, kitchen gadgets, and nifty ways to stay in shape without working very hard at it. For example, over the past few years yell-and-sell TV pitchmen like Anthony Sullivan (Swivel Sweeper, Awesome Auger) and smooth-talking peddlers like Vince Offer (ShamWow chamois cloths) have racked up billions of dollars sales of "as seen on TV" products. Brands like OxiClean, ShamWow, and the ▲Snuggie (a blanket with sleeves), have become DRTV cult classics.[20]

In recent years, however, a number of large companies—from P&G, Dell, Sears, Disney, Bose, and Revlon to Apple, Coca-Cola, Anheuser-Busch, and even AARP and the U.S. Navy—have begun using infomercials to sell their wares, refer customers to retailers, send out product information, recruit members, or attract buyers to their Web sites. For example, Coca-Cola has used DRTV to promote its "My Coke Rewards" program. An estimated 20 percent of all new infomercials now come to you courtesy of *Fortune* 1000 companies.[21]

The recently weakened economy has given DRTV a boost, thanks to stepped-up consumer bargain hunting and lower TV media and production costs. Whereas overall U.S. advertising spending fell last year, DRTV spending increased by more than 9 percent. Moreover, unlike most media campaigns, direct-response ads always include a 1-800 number, Web address, or SMS number (Short Message Service number for mobile phones), making it easier for marketers to track the impact of their pitches. "In a business environment where marketers are obsessed with return on investment," notes one expert, "direct response is tailor-made—[marketers can] track phone calls and Web-site hits generated by the ads. [They can] use DRTV to build brand awareness while simultaneously generating leads and sales."[22]

Home shopping channels, another form of direct-response television marketing, are television programs or entire channels dedicated to selling goods and services. Some home shopping channels, such as the Quality Value Channel (QVC), Home Shopping Network (HSN), and ShopNBC, broadcast 24 hours a day. Program hosts chat with viewers by phone and offer products ranging from jewelry, lamps, collectible dolls, and clothing to power tools and consumer electronics. Viewers call a toll-free number or go online to order goods. With widespread distribution on cable and satellite television, the top three shopping networks combined now reach 248 million homes worldwide.

Despite their lowbrow images, home shopping channels have evolved into highly sophisticated, very successful marketing operations. For example, HSN has upgraded both its products and its pitches, and its TV operations now work hand in hand with sophisticated Web marketing to build close customer relationships.

Want to learn how to whip up chef Wolfgang Puck's soy-steamed salmon fillets with shiitakes and brown rice? Check out the two-minute video on HSN.com, where Puck prepares it using his 5-Cup Rice Cooker. The appliance sells for $24.90 through HSN's round-the-clock TV channel and Web outlet. "You don't have to turn your oven on," coos Puck in the Web demonstration. What is notable on both media is HSN's new, toned-down approach to huckstering. Abandoning the yell-and-sell it helped pioneer 31 years ago, HSN now has hosts not so pushy and goods not so schlocky. HSN has replaced the cheesy baubles and generic electronics once featured on HSN with mainstream brands like Sephora cosmetics and 7 For All Mankind jeans. Celebrities and entrepreneurs, including Puck, interior designer Colin Cowie, and Joy Mangano, inventor of HSN's curiously popular Huggable Hangers, often get as much airtime as HSN's TV and Web hosts. They chitchat with shoppers who call in to rave about products—the effervescent Mangano often refers to callers as "my darling"—more often than they push merchandise. HSN wants to be its female audience's "best girlfriend," says HSN's CEO: "It's not just a transactional relationship. It becomes an emotional relationship."[23]

Kiosk Marketing

As consumers become more and more comfortable with computer and digital technologies, many companies are placing information and ordering machines—called *kiosks* (in contrast to vending machines, which dispense actual products)—in stores, airports, and other locations. Kiosks are popping up everywhere these days, from self-service hotel and airline check-in devices to in-store ordering kiosks that let you order merchandise not carried in the store.

In-store Kodak, Fuji, and HP kiosks let customers transfer pictures from memory sticks, mobile phones, and other digital storage devices, edit them, and make high-quality color prints. Kiosks in Hilton hotel lobbies let guests view their reservations, get room keys, view prearrival messages, check in and out, and even change seat assignments and print boarding passes for flights on any of 18 airlines. At JetBlue's Terminal Five at New York's JFK airport, more than 200 screens throughout the terminal allow travelers to order food and beverages to be delivered to their gate. ▲And Redbox operates more than 15,000 DVD rental kiosks in McDonald's, Wal-Marts, Walgreens drug stores, and other retail outlets. Customers make their selections on a touch screen, then swipe a credit or debit card to rent DVDs at $1 a day. Customers can even prereserve DVDs online to ensure that their trip to the kiosk will not be a wasted one. Thanks to an ailing economy, even as DVD sales slid last year, wallet-friendly Redbox's sales nearly doubled.[24]

Business marketers also use kiosks. For example, Dow Plastics places kiosks at trade shows to collect sales leads and to provide information on its 700 products. The kiosk system reads customer data from encoded registration badges and produces technical data sheets that can be printed at the kiosk or faxed or mailed to the customer. The system has resulted in a 400 percent increase in qualified sales leads.[25]

▲Kiosk marketing: Redbox operates more than 15,000 DVD rental kiosks in supermarkets and fast-food outlets nationwide.

New Digital Direct Marketing Technologies

Today, thanks to a wealth of new digital technologies, direct marketers can reach and interact with consumers just about anywhere, at anytime, about almost anything. Here, we look into several exciting new digital direct marketing technologies: mobile phone marketing, podcasts and vodcasts, and interactive TV (iTV).

Mobile Phone Marketing

With more than 270 million Americans now subscribing to wireless services, many marketers view mobile phones as the next big direct marketing medium. About 87 percent of consumers in the United States use cell phones and about 60 percent of those people also text message. Currently, 20 percent of cell phone subscribers use their phones to access the Web, a number that will rise to 40 percent within the next five years. Some 23 percent of cell phone users have seen advertising on their phones in the last 30 days and about half of them responded to the ads.[26]

A recent study estimated that U.S. mobile ad spending will grow from a current $3.1 billion annually worldwide to $28.8 billion by 2013.[27] Marketers of all kinds—from Pepsi, Nike, Burger King, Toyota, and Nordstrom to the local bank or supermarket—are now integrating mobile phones into their direct marketing. Cell phone promotions include everything from ring-tone giveaways, mobile games, text-in contests, and ad-supported content to retailer announcements of discounts, brand coupons, gift suggestions, and shopper information apps (see Marketing at Work 14.1).

When used properly, mobile marketing can greatly enrich the buyer's experience. For example, ▲Fresh Encounter, a Findlay, Ohio, grocery store, uses text messaging to help customers plan their meals:[28]

▲Mobile marketing: Fresh Encounter uses text messaging to help customers plan their meals. Offer redemptions can exceed 30 percent.

> Like many food retailers, Fresh Encounter tries to help shoppers resolve their daily dilemma: What to have for dinner? But this 32-store chain has come up with a unique strategy: texting suggestions to the cell phones of shoppers who've opted into its Text-N-Save mobile advertising program. Last month, for example, Fresh Encounter sent text messages at 2 p.m. on a Thursday and Friday offering a deal on a whole rotisserie chickens to shoppers who came in after 5 p.m. on those days. "We asked them, 'What's for dinner?' and if they don't know, then how about this for $3.99?" says Fresh Encounter executive Eric Anderson.
>
> Shoppers in the program receive new text offers each Sunday, ranging from free items (such as milk and soft drinks) to 5 percent off a total purchase of $50 or more. The offers can be customized by store. To cash in, shoppers present their cell phone to the cashier, showing a PLU number in the text message. The redemption rates are "unbelievable," Anderson says—20 percent or more. Takers inevitably buy complementary items as well. When Fresh Encounter sends out a more urgent same-day offer, as in the chicken promotion, redemptions can exceed 30 percent.

As with other forms of direct marketing, however, companies must use mobile marketing responsibly or risk angering already ad-weary consumers. "If you were interrupted every two minutes by advertising, not many people want that," says a mobile marketing expert. "The industry needs to work out smart and clever ways to engage people on mobiles." The key is to provide genuinely useful information and offers that will make consumers want to opt in or call in. One study found that 42 percent of cell phone users are open to mobile advertising if it's relevant.[29]

Podcasts and Vodcasts

Podcasting and vodcasting are the latest on-the-go, on-demand technologies. The name *podcast* derives from Apple's now-everywhere iPod. With podcasting, consumers can download audio files (podcasts) or video files (vodcasts) via the Internet to an iPod or any other handheld device and then listen to or view them whenever and wherever they wish. These days, you can download podcasts or vodcasts on an exploding array of topics, everything from your favorite National Public Radio show, a recent sitcom episode, or current sports features to the latest music video or Bud Light commercial.

▼With podcasting, consumers can download files via the Internet to an iPod or other handheld device and listen to or view them whenever and wherever they wish.

One recent study predicts that the U.S. podcast audience will reach 38 million by 2013, up from 6 million in 2005.[30] As a result, this new medium is drawing much attention from marketers. Many are now integrating podcasts and vodcasts into their direct marketing programs in the form of ad-supported podcasts, downloadable ads and informational features, and other promotions.

For example, The Walt Disney World Resort offers weekly podcasts on a mix of topics, including behind-the-scenes tours, interviews, upcoming events, and news about new attractions. New podcasts automatically download to subscribers' computers, where they can transfer them to portable media players to enjoy and share them. And ▲Nestlé Purina publishes "Petcasts" on animal

Marketing at Work 14.1

Mobile Marketing: *Do* Call Me, Please— or I'll Call You!

You're at the local Best Buy checking out portable GPS navigation systems. You've narrowed it down to a Garmin nüvi 350 versus a less-expensive competing model, but you're not certain that Best Buy has the best prices. Also, you'd love to know how other consumers rate the two brands. No problem. Just pull out your iPhone and launch Amazon.com's iPhone application, which lets you browse the brands you're considering, read consumer reviews, and compare prices of portable GPS systems

▲ Mobile marketing: Amazon.com's iPhone application lets consumers browse brands, read consumer reviews, and compare prices on the go. Consumers welcome a firm's mobile marketing if they see real value in it.

sold by Amazon.com and its retail partners. The application even lets you snap a photo of an item using your phone's camera, and Amazon.com employees will try to find similar items for sale on the Web site. If Amazon.com offers a better deal, you can make the purchase directly from the application.

Welcome to the new world of mobile marketing. Today's new smart phones are changing the way we live—including the way we shop. And as they change how we shop, they also change how marketers sell to us.

A growing number of consumers—especially younger ones—are using their cell phones as a "third screen" for text messaging, surfing the wireless Web, watching downloaded videos and shows, and checking e-mail. According to one expert, "the cell phone . . . is morphing into a content device, a kind of digital Swiss Army knife with the capability of filling its owner's every spare minute with games, music, live and on-demand TV, Web browsing, and, oh yes, advertising." Says the president of the Mobile Marketing Association, "It's only a matter of time before mobile is the 'first screen.'" According to another industry insider:

Mobile phones and wireless devices have quietly become the hottest new frontier for marketers, especially those targeting the coveted 18- to 34-year-old set. TV networks are prodding viewers to send text messages to vote for their favorite reality TV character. Wireless Web sites are lacing sports scores and news digests with banner ads for Lexus, Burger King, and Sheraton. A few companies are even customizing 10-second video ads for short, TV-style episodes that are edging their way onto mobile phones. For advertisers, the young audience is just one selling point.

training and behavioral issues. It invites customers to "Take these shows on the road—from serious discussions with veterinarians about pet health to wacky animal videos featuring dogs and cats, Purina has a podcast (or two) for you."[31]

Interactive TV (iTV)

Interactive TV (iTV) lets viewers interact with television programming and advertising using their remote controls. In the past, iTV has been slow to catch on. However, the technology now appears poised to take off as a direct marketing medium. Research shows that the level of viewer engagement with interactive TV is much higher than with 30-second spots. A recent poll indicated that 66 percent of viewers would be "very interested" in interacting with commercials that piqued their interest. And satellite broadcasting systems such as DIRECTV, EchoStar, and Time Warner are now offering iTV capabilities.[32]

Interactive TV gives marketers an opportunity to reach targeted audiences in an interactive, more involving way. For example, shopping channel HSN developed a "Shop by Remote" interactive TV service that allows viewers to immediately purchase any item on HSN using their remote. TiVo and Domino's Pizza partnered to launch a service that lets consumers order pizza directly via their set-top TiVo box—during Domino's commercials, TiVo flashes pop-up ads asking if users want to order

Wireless gadgets are always-on, ever-present accessories. The fact that a phone is tethered to an individual means that ads can be targeted. And users can respond instantly to time-sensitive offers. The mobile phone is very personal and it's always with you.

Marketers large and small are weaving mobile marketing into their direct marketing mixes. Wal-Mart uses text message alerts to spread the news about sales—you can click on links within the messages to go to the retailer's mobile Web site and check on details. Unilever phones out mobile coupons for Ragu pasta sauce, Dove body wash, Breyers ice cream, and its other brands—just hold up your cell phone at the checkout and the cashier will scan the barcode off the screen. Target's "Gift Globe" iPhone app gives you gift recommendations based on the age and gender of recipients—enter the data and shake your phone, and recommended gift items pop up on the screen. You can also use the app to link to Target's Web site to buy the item or find the nearest store.

Beyond helping you buy, other mobile marketing applications provide helpful services, useful information, and even entertainment. Bank of America's mobile banking application lets you check your balance, transfer funds, or even use your phone's GPS to find the nearest ATM. REI's The Snow and Ski Report app gives ski slope information for locations throughout the United States and Canada, such as snow depth, snow conditions, and number of open lifts. The app also links you to "Shop REI," for times "when you decide you can't live without a new set of K2 skis or a two-man Hoo-Doo tent." For entertainment, carmaker Audi offers The Audi A4 Driving Challenge game, which features a tiny A4 that maneuvers its way through different driving courses—to steer, you tilt your phone right or left. Audi claims that the app has been downloaded nearly 3 mil-lion times since it was introduced, resulting in 400,000 visitors to the Audi A4 iPhone Web site.

One of the most effective mobile marketing applications is Kraft's iFood Assistant, which provides easy-to-prepare recipes for food shoppers on the go. It supplies advice on how to prepare some 7,000 simple but satisfying meals—at three meals a day, that's almost 20 years worth of recipes. The iFood Assistant will even give you directions to local stores. Of course, most of the meals call for ingredients that just happened to be Kraft brands. The iFood Assistant app cost Kraft less than $100,000 to create but has engaged millions of shoppers, providing great marketing opportunities for Kraft and its brands.

Most consumers are initially skeptical about receiving mobile ad messages. Their first reaction is likely to be "Don't call me. I'll call you (yeah, right)." But they often change their minds if the ads deliver value in the form of useful brand and shopping information, entertaining content, or discounted prices and coupons for their favorite products and services. Most mobile marketing efforts target only consumers who voluntarily opt in or who download applications. In the increasingly cluttered mobile marketing space, customers just won't do that unless they see real value in it. The challenge for marketers: Develop useful and engaging mobile marketing applications that make customers say "*Do* call me, please. Or, I *will* call you."

Sources: Adapted extract, quotes, and other information from Joseph De Avila, "Please Hold, My Cell Phone Is Buying a Gift," *Wall Street Journal*, December 9, 2008, p. D1; Todd Wasserman, "I'm on the Phone!" *Adweek*, February 23, 2009, pp. 6–7; Alice Z. Cuneo, "Scramble for Content Drives Mobile," *Advertising Age*, October 24, 2005, p. S6; Jen Arnoff, "Wising Up to Smart Phones," *News & Observer* (Raleigh), April 22, 2009, p. 5B; and Carol Angrisani, "Priced to Cell," *Supermarket News*, June 1, 2009, p. 28.

a pizza, then directs them to a Domino's ordering screen.[33] Nike's "Quick Is Deadly" campaign for its Zoom training-shoe line included more than 20 minutes of interactive content accessible to Dish Network subscribers with DVRs.

> The campaign let Dish DVR users click into 30- and 60-second TV spots starring San Diego Chargers running back LaDanian Tomlinson and other fleet-footed Nike athletes. They could then opt to view interview footage of the football star discussing his exhaustive training regimen, footage of Tomlinson's signature spin move in different speeds, a Nike-branded game designed to test viewers' remote-control reflexes, and a three-dimensional demo of the Zoom shoe. Nike made similar interactive content available in ads featuring several other Nike endorsers, including basketball's Steve Nash, runner Lauren Fleshman, Olympic sprinters Asafa Powell and Sanya Richards, and tennis player Rafael Nadal. Using zip-code information in each Dish unit, users could also find stores carrying the shoe at the click of a button. The campaign stopped short of actually letting viewers buy the shoes directly from their sets, although the technology enables that function. "We've gotten to the point where all media needs to be interactive," says a creative director at Nike's advertising agency.

Mobile phone marketing, podcasts and vodcasts, and interactive TV offer exciting direct marketing opportunities. But marketers must be careful to use these new direct marketing approaches wisely. As with other direct marketing forms, marketers who use them risk backlash from consumers who may resent such marketing as an invasion of their privacy. Marketers must target their direct marketing offers carefully, bringing real value to customers rather than making unwanted intrusions into their lives.

Speed Bump: Linking the Concepts

Hold up a moment and think about the impact of direct marketing on your life.

- When was the last time you *bought* something via direct marketing? What did you buy and why did you buy it direct? When was the last time that you *rejected* a direct-marketing offer? Why did you reject it? Based on these experiences, what advice would you give to direct marketers?
- For the next week, keep track of all the direct-marketing offers that come your way via direct mail and catalogs, telephone, direct-response television, and the Internet. Then analyze the offers by type, source, and what you liked or disliked about each offer and the way it was delivered. Which offer best hit its target (you)? Which missed by the widest margin?

ONLINE MARKETING (pp 486–491)

Author Comment »
Online direct marketing spending is growing at a blistering pace—about 16 percent a year. The Web now accounts for about 20 percent of direct marketing-driven sales.

As noted earlier, **online marketing** is the fastest-growing form of direct marketing. Recent technological advances have created a digital age. Widespread use of the Internet is having a dramatic impact on both buyers and the marketers who serve them. In this section, we examine how marketing strategy and practice are changing to take advantage of today's Internet technologies.

Marketing and the Internet

Online marketing
Company efforts to market products and services and build customer relationships over the Internet.

Internet
A vast public web of computer networks that connects users of all types all around the world to each other and to an amazingly large "information repository."

Much of the world's business today is carried out over digital networks that connect people and companies. The **Internet**, a vast public web of computer networks, connects users of all types all around the world to each other and to an amazingly large information repository. The Web has fundamentally changed customers' notions of convenience, speed, price, product information, and service. As a result, it has given marketers a whole new way to create value for customers and build relationships with them.

Internet usage and impact continues to grow steadily. Last year, Internet household penetration in the United States reached 72.5 percent, with more than 221 million people now using the Internet at home or at work. The average U.S. Internet user spends some 61 hours a month surfing the Web at home and at work. Worldwide, more than 1.5 billion people now have Internet access.[34] Moreover, in a recent survey, 33 percent of American consumers chose the Internet as the second-most-essential medium in their lives—close behind TV at 36 percent. However, the Internet came in first as the "most cool and exciting medium."[35]

Click-only companies
The so-called dot-coms, which operate only online without any brick-and-mortar market presence.

All kinds of companies now market online. **Click-only companies** operate only on the Internet. They include a wide array of firms, from *e-tailers* such as Amazon.com and Expedia.com that sell products and services directly to final buyers via the Internet to *search engines and portals* (such as Yahoo!, Google, and MSN), *transaction sites* (eBay), and *content sites* (*New York Times* on the Web, ESPN.com, and Encyclopaedia Britannica Online). After a frenzied and rocky start in the 1990s, many click-only dot-coms are now prospering in today's online marketspace.

Click-and-mortar companies
Traditional brick-and-mortar companies that have added online marketing to their operations.

As the Internet grew, the success of the dot-coms caused existing *brick-and-mortar* manufacturers and retailers to reexamine how they served their markets. Now, almost all of these traditional companies have set up their own online sales and communications channels, becoming **click-and-mortar companies**. It's hard to find a company today that doesn't have a substantial Web presence.

▲Click-and-mortar marketing: No click-only or brick-only seller can match the call, click, or visit convenience and support afforded by Office Depot's "4 easy ways to shop."

In fact, many click-and-mortar companies are now having more online success than their click-only competitors. In a recent ranking of the top 10 online retail sites, only two were click-only retailers. All of the others were multichannel retailers.[36] ▲For example, Office Depot's more than 1,000 office-supply superstores rack up annual sales of $14.5 billion in more than 48 countries. But you might be surprised to learn that Office Depot's fastest recent growth has come not from its traditional "brick-and-mortar" channels, but from the Internet.[37]

Office Depot's online sales have soared in recent years, now accounting for 33 percent of total sales. Selling on the Web lets Office Depot build deeper, more personalized relationships with customers large and small. For example, a large customer such as GE or P&G can create lists of approved office products at discount prices and then let company departments or even individuals do their own online purchasing. This reduces ordering costs, cuts through the red tape, and speeds up the ordering process for customers. At the same time, it encourages companies to use Office Depot as a sole source for office supplies. Even the smallest companies find 24-hour-a-day online ordering easier and more efficient. Importantly, Office Depot's Web operations don't steal from store sales. Instead, the OfficeDepot.com site actually builds store traffic by helping customers find a local store and check stock. In return, the local store promotes the Web site through in-store kiosks. If customers don't find what they need on the shelves, they can quickly order it via the Web from the kiosk. Thus, Office Depot now offers a full range of contact points and delivery modes—online, by phone or fax, and in the store. No click-only or brick-only seller can match the call, click, or visit convenience and support afforded by Office Depot's click-and-mortar model.

Online Marketing Domains

The four major online marketing domains are shown in ■ **Figure 14.2**. They include B2C (business-to-consumer), B2B (business-to-business), C2C (consumer-to-consumer), and C2B (consumer-to-business).

Business-to-Consumer (B2C)

Business-to-consumer (B2C) online marketing
Businesses selling goods and services online to final consumers.

The popular press has paid the most attention to **business-to-consumer (B2C) online marketing**—businesses selling goods and services online to final consumers. Today's consumers can buy almost anything online—from clothing, kitchen gadgets, and airline tickets to computers and cars. Even in the aftermath of the recent recession, online consumer buying continues to grow at a healthy rate. More than half of all U.S. households now regularly shop online. Last year, U.S. consumers generated $141 billion in online retail sales, up 13 percent from the previous year.[38]

Perhaps more importantly, the Internet now influences 35 percent of total retail sales—sales transacted online plus those carried out offline but encouraged by online research. Some 81 percent of Web-goers now use the Internet to research a product

■ **Figure 14.2** Online Marketing Domains

Online marketing can be classified by who initiates it and to whom it's targeted. As consumers, we're most familiar with B2C and C2C, but B2B is also flourishing.

	Targeted to consumers	Targeted to businesses
Initiated by business	B2C (business-to-consumer)	B2B (business-to-business)
Initiated by consumer	C2C (consumer-to-consumer)	C2B (consumer-to-business)

before purchase. By 2010, the Internet will influence a staggering 50 percent of total retail sales.[39] Thus, smart marketers are employing integrated multichannel strategies that use the Web to drive sales to other marketing channels.

Internet buyers differ from traditional offline consumers in their approaches to buying and in their responses to marketing. In the Internet exchange process, customers initiate and control the contact. Traditional marketing targets a somewhat passive audience. In contrast, online marketing targets people who actively select which Web sites they will visit and what marketing information they will receive about which products and under what conditions. Thus, online marketing requires new marketing approaches.

People now go online to order a wide range of goods—clothing from Gap or L.L.Bean, books or electronics or about anything else from Amazon.com, major appliances from Sears, home mortgages from Quicken Loans, or even a will or divorce from Legal Zoom. Where else but the Web could you find a place that specializes in anything and everything bacon?[40]

▼B2C Web sites: People now go online to buy just about anything. Where else but the Web could you find a place that specializes in anything and everything bacon?

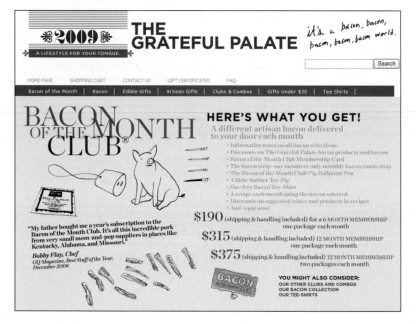

Americans have a guilty relationship with food, and perhaps no food is more guilt-inducing than bacon—forbidden by religions, disdained by dietitians and doctors. Loving bacon is like shoving a middle finger in the face of all that is healthy and holy. There is something comfortingly unambiguous about a thick slab of bacon. It's bad for you. It tastes fantastic. Any questions? As Dan Philips says, "Bacon is the ultimate expression of freedom." Philips is the founder of ▲The Grateful Palate, a company whose products have probably done more for the bacon chic movement than anything else. At The Grateful Palate, bacon enthusiasts can find everything bacon. It offers a bacon of the month club–Iron Chef Bobby Flay's a member—that includes artisnal bacon from farms across North America cured in a variety of delicious ways from applewood smoked to hickory smoked with cinnamon sugar. The Grateful Palate also sells bacon-related gifts for people who can't get enough bacon in their day, such as bacon soap, bacon Christmas tree ornaments, bacon toilet paper, bacon air freshener, and even BLT candles—a set of bacon, lettuce, and tomato votives. Says one fan, "You can light them individually, maybe just tomato and lettuce if your vegetarian friends are visiting."

Business-to-Business (B2B)

Although the popular press has given the most attention to B2C Web sites, **business-to-business (B2B) online marketing** is also flourishing. Business-to-business marketers use B2B Web sites, e-mail, online product catalogs, online trading networks, and other online resources to reach new business customers, serve current customers more effectively, and obtain buying efficiencies and better prices.

Business-to-business (B2B) online marketing
Businesses using B2B Web sites, e-mail, online catalogs, online trading networks, and other online resources to reach new business customers, serve current customers more effectively, and obtain buying efficiencies and better prices.

Most major B2B marketers now offer product information, customer purchasing, and customer-support services online. For example, corporate buyers can visit networking equipment and software maker Cisco Systems' Web site (www.cisco.com), select detailed descriptions of Cisco's products and service solutions, request sales and service information, attend events and training seminars, view videos on a wide range of topics, have live chats with Cisco staff, and place orders. Some major companies conduct almost all of their business on the Web. For example, Cisco Systems takes more than 80 percent of its orders over the Internet.

Beyond simply selling their products and services online, companies can use the Internet to build stronger relationships with important business customers. For example, Dell has set up customized Web sites for more than 113,000 business and institutional customers worldwide. These individualized Premier.Dell.com sites help business customers to more efficiently manage all phases of their Dell computer buying and ownership. Each customer's Premier.Dell.com Web site can include a customized online computer store, purchasing and asset management reports and tools, system-specific technical information, links to useful information throughout Dell's extensive Web site, and more. The site makes all the information a customer needs in order to do business with Dell available in one place, 24 hours a day, 7 days a week.[41]

Consumer-to-Consumer (C2C)

Much **consumer-to-consumer (C2C) online marketing** and communication occurs on the Web between interested parties over a wide range of products and subjects. In some cases, the Internet provides an excellent means by which consumers can buy or exchange goods or information directly with one another. For example, eBay, Overstock.com Auctions, and other auction sites offer popular market spaces for displaying and selling almost anything, from art and antiques, coins and stamps, and jewelry to computers and consumer electronics.

eBay's C2C online trading community of more than 81 million unique monthly visitors worldwide (that's more than the total populations of Britain, Egypt, or Turkey) transacted some $60 billion in trades last year. At any given time, the company's Web site lists more than 113 million items up for auction in more than 50,000 categories. Such C2C sites give people access to much larger audiences than the local flea market or newspaper classifieds (which, by the way, have also gone online at Web sites such as Craigslist.com and eBay's Kijiji.com). Interestingly, based on its huge success in the C2C market, eBay has now attracted more than 500,000 B2C sellers, ranging from small businesses peddling their regular wares to large businesses liquidating excess inventory at auction.[42]

In other cases, C2C involves interchanges of information through Internet forums that appeal to specific special-interest groups. Such activities may be organized for commercial or noncommercial purposes. An example is Web logs, or **blogs**, online journals where people post their thoughts, usually on a narrowly defined topic. Blogs can be about anything, from politics or baseball to haiku, car repair, or the latest television series. Since 2002, 133 million blogs have been "keyed" in 81 different languages. Currently, 47 percent of online consumers read them. Such numbers give blogs—especially those with large and devoted followings—substantial influence.[43]

Many marketers are now tapping into blogs as a medium for reaching carefully targeted consumers. ▲For example, Wal-Mart created the ElevenMoms network (www.elevenmoms.com), a community of influential mommy-bloggers (initially 11, now 24) who were already blogging about money-saving ideas. The blog provides a community in which customers can receive tips and share views on money-saving practices and products. The site also provides a platform for programs by brands such as Kimberly-Clark's Huggies, Unilever's Suave, P&G's Pantene, and others.[44]

Companies can also advertise on existing blogs or influence content there. For example, they might encourage "sponsored conversations" by influential bloggers:[45]

As part of its "Living in High Definition" push, Panasonic wanted to build buzz about its brand at the recent Consumer Electronics Show (CES) in Las Vegas. But rather than relying on the usual tech journalists attending the show, Panasonic recruited five influential bloggers—including popular Internet figures Chris Brogan and Steve Garfield—to travel to CES at its expense. It footed the bill for their travel and passes to the event while also loaning them digital video and still cameras. In return, the bloggers agreed to share their impressions of the show, including Panasonic product previews, with their own powerful distribution networks, in the form of blog posts, Twitter updates, and YouTube videos. The catch: Panasonic had no say on what

Consumer-to-consumer (C2C) online marketing
Online exchanges of goods and information between final consumers.

Blogs
Online journals where people post their thoughts, usually on a narrowly defined topic.

▼**Many companies set up their own blogs, such as Wal-Mart's Check Out blog, on which Wal-Mart buyers and merchandise managers like Alex Cook below speak candidly, even critically, about the products the chain carries.**

their guests posted. To maintain credibility, Panasonic kept its distance and the bloggers fully disclosed the brand's sponsorship. Still, even though Panasonic didn't dictate content—and didn't want to—the "sponsored conversations" allowed the brand to tap into the groundswell of Internet buzz. "When you give [bloggers] equipment and they love it, just like any other consumer they'll evangelize it," says a Panasonic spokesperson. "We're not looking for them to hit message points and in effect shill." Panasonic just wants to be a catalyst for conversations about its brand.

Other companies set up their own blogs. For example, Southwest's Nuts About Southwest blog (www.nutsaboutsouthwest.com) gives visitors a behind-the-scenes look at Southwest and a chance to interact with Southwest insiders. Similarly, at Wal-Mart's Check Out blog (www.checkoutblog.com), with the company's blessing, Wal-Mart buyers and merchandise managers speak candidly, even critically, about the products the chain carries. Says one analyst, the employee-fed blog "has become a forum for [everything from] unfurnished rants about gadgets [and] raves about new video games [to] advice on selecting environmentally sustainable food." The blog also provides a glimpse into the personal lives of posters. According to Wal-Mart, Check Out helps buyers obtain quick feedback on merchandise from consumers, and it shows a softer side of the giant company.[46]

As a marketing tool, blogs offer some advantages. They can offer a fresh, original, personal, and cheap way to enter into consumer Web conversations. However, the blogosphere is cluttered and difficult to control. Blogs journals remain largely a C2C medium. Although companies can sometimes leverage blogs to engage in meaningful customer relationships, consumers remain largely in control.

Whether or not they actively participate in the blogosphere, companies should show up, monitor, and listen to them. For example, Starbucks sponsors its own blog (www.MyStarbucksIdea.com) but also closely follows consumer dialogue on the 30 or more other third-party online sites devoted to the brand. It then uses the customer insights it gains from all of these proprietary and third party blogs to adjust its marketing programs.[47]

In all, C2C means that online buyers don't just consume product information—increasingly, they create it. As a result, "word of Web" is joining "word of mouth" as an important buying influence.

▼C2B marketing: GetSatisfaction.com provides "people-powered customer service" by creating a user-driven customer-service community where customers discuss product and service problems.

Consumer to Business (C2B)

The final online marketing domain is **consumer-to-business (C2B) online marketing**. Thanks to the Internet, today's consumers are finding it easier to communicate with companies. Most companies now invite prospects and customers to send in suggestions and questions via company Web sites. Beyond this, rather than waiting for an invitation, consumers can search out sellers on the Web, learn about their offers, initiate purchases, and give feedback. Using the Web, consumers can even drive transactions with businesses, rather than the other way around. For example, using Priceline.com, would-be buyers can bid for airline tickets, hotel rooms, rental cars, cruises, and vacation packages, leaving the sellers to decide whether to accept their offers.

Consumers can also use Web sites such as GetSatisfaction.com, Complaints.com, and PlanetFeedback.com to ask questions, offer suggestions, lodge complaints, or deliver compliments to companies. ▲GetSatisfaction.com provides "people-powered customer service" by creating a user-driven customer-service community. The site provides forums where customers discuss prob-

Consumer-to-business (C2B) online marketing
Online exchanges in which consumers search out sellers, learn about their offers, and initiate purchases, sometimes even driving transaction terms.

lems they're having with the products and services of 2,500 companies—from Apple to Zappos.com—whether the company participates or not. GetSatisfaction.com also provides tools by which companies can adopt GetSatisfaction.com as an official customer service resource. Since launching in 2007, the site has drawn more than a million unique visitors.[48]

◆ Speed Bump: Linking the Concepts

Pause here and cool your engine for a bit. Think about the relative advantages and disadvantages of *click-only*, *brick-and-mortar only*, and *click-and-mortar* retailers.

- Visit the Amazon.com (www.amazon.com) Web site. Search for a specific book or DVD—perhaps one that's not too well known—and go through the buying process.
- Now visit www.bn.com and shop for the same book or video. Then visit a Barnes & Noble store and shop for the item there.
- What advantages does Amazon.com have over Barnes & Noble? What disadvantages? How does your local independent book store, with its store-only operations, fare against these two competitors?

Setting Up an Online Marketing Presence (pp 491–499)

In one way or another, most companies have now moved online. Companies conduct online marketing in any of the four ways shown in ■ **Figure 14.3**: creating a Web site, placing ads and promotions online, setting up or participating in online social networks, or using e-mail.

Creating a Web Site

For most companies, the first step in conducting online marketing is to create a Web site. However, beyond simply creating a Web site, marketers must design an attractive site and find ways to get consumers to visit the site, stay around, and come back often.

Corporate (or brand) Web site
A Web site designed to build customer goodwill, collect customer feedback, and supplement other sales channels, rather than to sell the company's products directly.

Types of Web Sites. Web sites vary greatly in purpose and content. The most basic type is a **corporate (or brand) Web site**. These sites are designed to build customer goodwill, collect customer feedback, and supplement other sales channels, rather than to sell the company's products directly. They typically offer a rich variety of information and other features in an effort to answer customer questions, build closer customer relationships, and generate excitement about the company or brand.

For example, you can't buy anything at P&G's Old Spice brand site, but you can learn about the different Old Spice products, watch recent ads, enter the latest contest, and post comments on the Old Spice blog. At the other extreme, ▲GE's corporate Web

■ **Figure 14.3** Setting Up for Online Marketing

It's hard to find a company today that doesn't have a substantial Web presence. The first step is one or more Web sites. But most large companies use all of these approaches. Don't forget, they all need to be integrated—with each other and with the rest of the promotion mix.

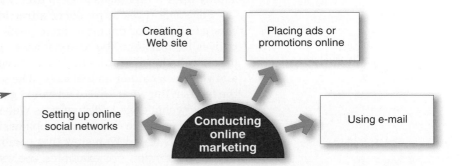

▲ **Corporate Web sites: You can't buy anything at GE's corporate site. Instead, it serves as a public face for the huge company, presenting a massive amount of information to a diverse global audience.**

Marketing Web site
A Web site that engages consumers in interactions that will move them closer to a direct purchase or other marketing outcome.

site serves as a global public face for the huge company. It presents a massive amount of product, service, and company information to a diverse audience of customers, investors, journalists, and employees. It's both a B2B site and a portal for consumers, and it serves as a link to more than 65 other corporate country sites. Whether it's a U.S. consumer researching a microwave, an Indonesian business buyer checking into eco-friendly locomotives, or a German investor looking for shareholder information, "we have to get every different user to their destination," says a GE Web executive. "For such an extensive corporate site, the overall experience is elegantly simple," says a Web site design consultant.[49]

Other companies create a **marketing Web site**. These sites engage consumers in an interaction that will move them closer to a direct purchase or other marketing outcome. For example, visitors to www.SonyStyle.com can search through dozens of categories of Sony products, learn more about specific items, and read expert product reviews. They can check out the latest hot deals and place orders online.

MINI USA operates a marketing Web site at www.MINIUSA.com. Once a potential customer clicks in, the carmaker wastes no time trying to turn the inquiry into a sale, and then into a long-term relationship. The site offers a garage full of useful information and interactive selling features, including detailed and fun descriptions of current MINI models, tools for designing your very own MINI, information on dealer locations and services, and even tools for tracking your new MINI from factory to delivery.

> Before Angela DiFabio bought her MINI Cooper last September, she spent untold hours on the company's Web site, playing with dozens of possibilities before coming up with the perfect combination: a chili-pepper-red exterior, white racing stripes on the hood, and a "custom rally badge bar" on the grill. When DiFabio placed her order with her dealer, the same build-your-own tool—and all the price and product details it provided—left her feeling like she was getting a fair deal. "He even used the site to order my car," she says. While she waited for her MINI to arrive, DiFabio logged on to MINI's Web site every day, this time using its "Where's My Baby?" tracking tool to follow her car, like an expensive FedEx package, from the factory in Britain to its delivery. The Web site does more than just provide information or sell products or services. It makes an impact on the customer experience: It's fun, it's individual, it makes users feel like part of the clan.[50]

Designing Effective Web Sites. Creating a Web site is one thing; getting people to *visit* the site is another. To attract visitors, companies aggressively promote their Web sites in offline print and broadcast advertising and through ads and links on other sites. But today's Web users are quick to abandon any Web site that doesn't measure up. The key is to create enough value and excitement to get consumers who come to the site to stick around and come back again. This means that companies must constantly update their sites to keep them current, fresh, and useful.

For some types of products, attracting visitors is easy. Consumers buying new cars, computers, or financial services will be open to information and marketing initiatives from sellers. Marketers of lower-involvement products, however, may face a difficult challenge in attracting Web site visitors. If you're in the market for a computer and you see a banner ad that says, "The top 10 PCs under $800," you'll likely click on the banner. But what kind of ad would get you to visit a site like dentalfloss.com?

A key challenge is designing a Web site that is attractive on first view and interesting enough to encourage repeat visits. Many marketers create colorful, graphically sophisticated Web sites that combine text, sound, and animation to capture and hold attention (for examples, see www.looneytunes.com or www.nike.com). To

▲Check out the above National Park Service Web site at www.nps.gov. Applying the 7Cs of effective Web site design, is this a good site?

attract new visitors and to encourage revisits, suggests one expert, ▲online marketers should pay close attention to the seven Cs of effective Web site design:[51]

- *Context:* the site's layout and design
- *Content:* the text, pictures, sound, and video that the Web site contains
- *Community:* the ways that the site enables user-to-user communication
- *Customization:* the site's ability to tailor itself to different users or to allow users to personalize the site
- *Communication:* the ways the site enables site-to-user, user-to-site, or two-way communication
- *Connection:* the degree that the site is linked to other sites
- *Commerce:* the site's capabilities to enable commercial transactions

And to keep customers coming back to the site, companies need to embrace yet another "C"—constant change.

At the very least, a Web site should be easy to use, professional looking, and physically attractive. Ultimately, however, Web sites must also be *useful*. When it comes to Web surfing and shopping, most people prefer substance over style and function over flash. Thus, effective Web sites contain deep and useful information, interactive tools that help buyers find and evaluate products of interest, links to other related sites, changing promotional offers, and entertaining features that lend relevant excitement.

Maintaining a top Web site is a complex and ongoing task. For example, The Walt Disney Company recently overhauled its marquee Disney.com site for the second time in only two years:[52]

> The changes to Disney.com will introduce more free videos (including full-length movies like *Finding Nemo*) as well as more games and things for visitors to do with their cell phones. For instance, little girls (or bigger ones) who create fairy avatars in a virtual world called Pixie Hollow will be able to use their cell phones to create pet butterflies for their fairies. With the changes, Disney is trying to position its Web site more as a place that entertains and less of one that exists to promote Disney wares. No longer will the site ask youngsters to navigate through categories like "Movies," "TV," and "Live Events." New options will include "Games," "Videos" and "Characters" and will emphasize how to find immediate entertainment. "It's a repositioning of our digital front door," says a Disney Online executive. The constant changes reflect the whiplash-fast pace at which online is evolving. The previous site overhaul increased unique visitors to Disney.com by about 40 percent to nearly 30 million a month, making it the number-one Web destination for children and family-oriented Web sites. The average user spends 45 minutes per visit. But refreshing the site is an ongoing process.

Placing Ads and Promotions Online

Online advertising
Advertising that appears while consumers are surfing the Web, including display ads, search-related ads, online classifieds, and other forms.

As consumers spend more and more time on the Internet, companies are shifting more of their marketing dollars to **online advertising** to build their brands or to attract visitors to their Web sites. Online advertising has become a major medium. Last year, although overall U.S. advertising spending fell 2.4 percent versus the previous year, online advertising spending increased nearly 11 percent to more than $23 billion, putting it ahead of newspaper, outdoor, and radio advertising. Online ad spending will jump to more than $42 billion by 2011, rivaling or surpassing the amount spent on magazines and even television.[53] Here, we discuss forms of online advertising and promotion and their future.

Forms of Online Advertising. The major forms of online advertising include search-related ads, display ads, and online classifieds. Online display ads might appear anywhere on an Internet user's screen. The most common form is *banners*, banner-shaped ads found at the top, bottom, left, right, or center of a Web page.

▲For instance, while browsing vacation packages on Travelocity.com, you encounter a banner ad offering a free upgrade on a rental car from Enterprise. Or while visiting the Yahoo! Finance site, a flashing E*TRADE banner promises a free BlackBerry smart phone when you open a new account.

Interstitials are online display ads that appear between screen changes on a Web site, especially while a new screen is loading. For example, visit www.marketwatch .com and you'll probably see a 10-second ad for VISA, Verizon, Dell, or another sponsor before the home page loads. *Pop-up*s are online ads that appear suddenly in a new window in front of the window being viewed. Such ads can multiply out of control, creating a major annoyance. As a result, Internet services and Web browser providers have developed applications that let users block most pop-ups. But not to worry. Many advertisers have now developed pop-*unders*, new windows that evade pop-up blockers by appearing behind the page you're viewing.

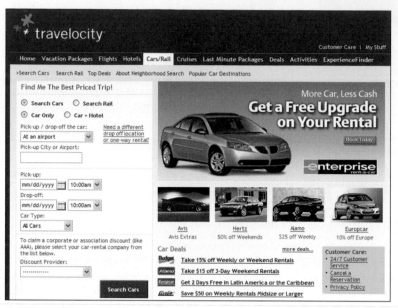

▲Online context-related display ads: While browsing vacation packages on Travelocity.com, you might encounter a display ad offering a free upgrade on a rental car from Enterprise.

With the increase in broadband Internet access in American homes, many companies are developing exciting new *rich media* online display ads, which incorporate animation, video, sound, and interactivity. Rich media ads attract and hold consumer attention better than traditional banner ads. They employ techniques such as float, fly, and snapback—animations that jump out and sail over the Web page before retreating to their original space.

Many rich media ads do more than create a little bit of jumping animation—they also create interactivity. They can provide consumers with product information, local or online buying options, or a brand experience, without taking them away from the site they are viewing. For example, recent Verizon ads touting the LG Versa phone as a gaming device on Yahoo! Games interacted with the site's contents—as the Versa tilted, the site's elements tilted as well. And recent Intel banner ads on information technology sites such as CIO Today, CNET, and Computerworld.com even connected interested users directly into live chats with Intel technology experts.[54]

Another hot growth area for online advertising is *search-related ads* (or *contextual advertising*), in which text-based ads and links appear alongside search engine results on sites such as Google and Yahoo!. For example, search Google for "LCD TVs." At the top and side of the resulting search list, you'll see inconspicuous ads for 10 or more advertisers, ranging from Samsung and Dell to Best Buy, Sears, and Amazon.com, Walmart.com, and Nextag.com. Nearly all of Google's $22 billion in revenues come from ad sales. An advertiser buys search terms from the search site and pays only if consumers click through to its site. Search is an always-on kind of medium. And importantly in today's tight economy, the results are easily measured. Thus, search-related ads account for some 45 percent of all online advertising expenditures, more than any other category of online advertising.[55]

In recent years, search-related advertising has grown increasingly popular with consumer package good firms:[56]

Type "Coke" or "Coca-Cola" or even just "soft drinks" or "rewards" into your Google or Yahoo! search engine and without fail "My Coke Rewards" comes up as one of the top options. Coincidence? Definitely not. Since the popular online loyalty program began, the cola giant has been supporting it largely through search buys. When Coke first launched

My Coke Rewards three years ago, it started with traditional TV and print advertising. But it quickly learned that search was the most effective and efficient way to bring consumers to the www.Mycokerewards.com Web site to register. Now, any of dozens of purchased search terms will return MyCokeRewards.com at or near the top of the search list.

Coca-Cola is not alone—most companies now do search-related advertising. For example, search is the primary driver for ConAgra's recipe site, www.Simpleanddelicious.com. The company has purchased a comprehensive list of search terms, everything from "easy-to-prepare" to "great tasting recipe." ConAgra's interactive marketing director likens search advertising to securing virtual shelf space. "When someone looks for your brand online, what do they see?" he asks. "Do you own those results . . . can you influence those results if other Web sites are coming up and competing against your brand?" Search advertising is 24/7 kind of medium. "That speaks to a dial-tone level of search. Like the electricity in your house, it should always be on."

Other Forms of Online Promotion. Other forms of online promotions include content sponsorships, alliances and affiliate programs, and viral advertising.

Using *content sponsorships,* companies gain name exposure on the Internet by sponsoring special content on various Web sites, such as news or financial information or special-interest topics. For example, Scotts, the lawn-and-garden products company, sponsors the Local Forecast section on WeatherChannel.com, and Marriott sponsors "Summer to the Rescue!" microsite at Travelocity.com. Sponsorships are best placed in carefully targeted sites where they can offer relevant information or service to the audience. Internet companies can also develop *alliances and affiliate programs,* in which they work with other companies, online and offline, to "promote each other." For example, through its Amazon Associates Program, Amazon.com has more than 900,000 affiliates who post Amazon.com banners on their Web sites.

Finally, online marketers use **viral marketing**, the Internet version of word-of-mouth marketing. Viral marketing involves creating a Web site, video, e-mail, cell phone message, advertisement, or other marketing event that is so infectious that customers will want to pass it along to their friends. Because customers pass the message or promotion along to others, viral marketing can be very inexpensive. And when the information comes from a friend, the recipient is much more likely to view or read it.

Sometimes a well-made regular ad can go viral with little help from the company. For example, McDonald's clever "Gimme back the Filet-O-Fish" ad, featuring a mechanized singing fish mounted on a wall, grabbed 780,000 YouTube views and a 5-star rating in little more than 3 months. It also inspired a rash of consumer-generated spots posted on YouTube featuring people singing the song while ordering. However, leaving viral efforts to chance rarely works. "It's one of those things you never really know until it's out there," says a McDonald's marketer.[57]

Although marketers usually have little control over where their viral messages end up, a well-concocted viral campaign can gain vast exposure. ▲Consider Office-Max's wacky ElfYourself.com seasonal viral Web site, which for the past three years has let visitors paste images of their own faces onto dancing elves, along with a personal message.[58]

Viral marketing
The Internet version of word-of-mouth marketing—Web sites, videos, e-mail messages, or other marketing events that are so infectious that customers will want to pass them along to friends.

▼Viral marketing: OfficeMax's ElfYourself .com viral Web site has propelled itself into the digital record books. With no promotion at all, the site logged more than 193 million visits between late November and early January last year. One-third of those visiting the site were influenced to shop at OfficeMax.

OfficeMax's holiday ElfYourself.com viral Web site has propelled itself into the digital record books, all with no hint of promotion. Between late November 2007 and early January 2008, ElfYourself.com logged more than 193 million site visits and a whopping 123 million elves were created, with 53 percent of visitors returning for additional visits. The elves were publicity magnets for OfficeMax, drawing heavy coverage from media ranging from *Good Morning America* to CNN to the *New York Times.* Popular in more than 50 countries, the elves even popped up dancing on the Jumbo Tron overlooking Times Square in New York City. OfficeMax executives joke about the elves replacing Frosty and Rudolph as holiday icons for this generation. More important, one-third of those who visited the ElfYourself.com site were influenced to shop at OfficeMax, and another one-third said the holiday treat improved their perception of the retailer.

However, achieving such success isn't as easy as it might seem. In its first season, ElfYourself.com was just one of 20 holiday-themed viral Web sites developed by OfficeMax, which hoped that at least one would catch fire among bored office workers looking for things to share online over the holidays. (All 20 sites were built at less than the cost of producing just one television commercial—generally about $350,000.) ElfYourself.com was the only one that blossomed. "There's a lot of luck to this stuff," says one of the site's creators. Companies "don't make things viral, consumers do. We were lucky enough to land on something that worked very well."

Creating or Participating in Online Social Networks

Online social networks
Online social communities—blogs, social networking Web sites, or even virtual worlds—where people socialize or exchange information and opinions.

As we discussed in Chapters 1 and 5, the popularity of the Internet has resulted in a rash of **online social networks** or *Web communities*. Countless independent and commercial Web sites have arisen that give consumers online places to congregate, socialize, and exchange views and information. These days, it seems, almost everyone is buddying up on Facebook, checking in with Twitter, tuning into the day's hottest videos at YouTube, or checking out photos on Flickr. And, of course, wherever consumers congregate, marketers will surely follow. More and more marketers are now riding the huge social networking wave.

Marketers can engage in online communities in two ways: They can participate in existing Web communities or they can set up their own. Joining existing networks seems easiest. ▲Thus, many major brands—from Dunkin' Donuts and Harley-Davidson to Volkswagen and Victoria's Secret—have set up YouTube channels. GM and other companies have posted visual content on Flickr. The Apple Students group on Facebook, which offers information and deals on Apple products, has more than 1.3 million members. Coca-Cola's Facebook page has 3.5 million fans, second only to President Barack Obama's page. And Mars recently transformed its Skittles homepage into an online portal that links its core teenage customers—who spend a lot of time using social media—directly to its Twitter feed, Facebook page, and YouTube channel. All of these destinations contain unfiltered consumer-generated conversations and content about the Skittles brand. The new site resulted in a more than 1,300 percent jump in Web traffic for the brand.[59]

▲Online Social Networks: Dunkin' Donuts successfully connects to core customers on its YouTube channel.

Although the large online social networks such as Facebook, YouTube, and Twitter have grabbed most of the headlines, a new breed of more focused niche networks has recently emerged. These more focused networks cater to the needs of smaller communities of like-minded people, making them ideal vehicles for marketers who want to target special interest groups (see Marketing at Work 14.2).

But participating successfully in existing online social networks presents challenges. First, online social networks are new and results are hard to measure. Most companies are still experimenting with how to use them effectively. Second, such Web communities are largely user controlled. The company's goal is to make the brand a part of consumers' conversations and their lives. However, marketers can't simply muscle their way into consumers' online interactions—they need to earn the right to be there. "You're talking about conversations between groups of friends," says one analyst. "And in those conversations a brand has no right to be there, unless the conversation is already about that brand." Rather than intruding, marketers must learn to become a valued part of the online experience. "The only appropriate

Marketing at Work 14.2

Online Social Networks: Targeting Niches of Like-Minded People

Marketers who think bigger is better may want to reconsider, at least when it comes to online social networks. Although giant networks such as Facebook and Twitter get all the attention these days, social networks focused on topics as remote as knitting or bird watching can present marketers with strong targeting opportunities:

When jet-setters began flocking to an exclusive social-networking Web site reserved for the rich, they got the attention of an online community's most valuable ally: advertisers. The invitation-only site, ASmallWorld.net, has 300,000 select members who have become a magnet for companies that make luxury goods and are trying to reach people who can afford them. The site's biggest advertisers include Burberry, Cartier, and Land Rover. Cognac maker Remy Martin last month threw a tasting party for the site's elite members, at which its top-shelf, $1,800-a-bottle liquor flowed freely.

Thousands of social-networking sites have popped up to cater to specific interests, backgrounds, professions, and age groups. Nightclub frequenters can converge at DontStayIn.com. Wine connoisseurs have formed Snooth.com, and people going through divorce can commiserate at Divorce360.com.

More and more, marketers are taking a chance on smaller sites that could be more relevant to their products. AT&T, for example, recently promoted one of its global cell phones on WAYN.com (short for "Where are you now?"), a social network for international travelers. While AT&T advertises on the bigger sites like MySpace to reach a large audience quickly, the wireless

carrier is also turning to niche networks, "where your ads are more meaningful—those are the real gems," says a social networking expert.

There's at least one social network for just about every interest or hobby. Yub.com is for shopaholics, Fuzzster.com is for pet lovers, Ravelry.com sews up the knitting and crocheting community, Jango.com lets music fans find others with similar tastes, and PassportStamp.com is one of several sites for avid travelers. Some cater to the obscure. Passions Network is an "online dating niche social network" with 600,000 members and 110 groups for specific interests, including "Star Trek" fans, truckers, atheists, and people who are shy. The most popular group is a dating site for the overweight. Membership on niche networking sites varies greatly, ranging from a few hundred to a few million. LinkExpats.com, which provides an online haven for U.S. expatriates, launched last month and has about 200 members. Flixster.com has 40 million members who rate movies and gossip about actors.

According to e-marketer, by 2011, half of all adults in the United States and 84 percent of online teens will use social networks. A running tally of emerging social networks, now upward of 7,000 by one estimate, suggests an explosive market. That's both a golden opportunity and a colossal headache for brands trying to nail down the best new network for their campaigns.

Although the niche sites have many fewer members than mega-sites such as MySpace (more than 115 million active profiles) and Facebook (200 million worldwide), they contain dedicated communities of like-minded people. And as on the bigger networks, members can build personalized pages and use them to share information, photos, and news with friends. That makes the niche sites ideal vehicles for marketers who want to target special interest groups.

The niche sites often provide a better marketing message environment. "Because members of niche social networks share common interests and experiences, they tend to spend more time on the site and contribute to the group by chatting and posting comments," notes an online consultant. On bigger sites, "members tend to be less involved . . . and are therefore less appealing to advertisers." Also, "the bigger sites have become so cluttered and overrun with advertisers that members are used to tuning stuff out, even personalized ads. . . . But on networking sites that have a self-selecting demographic, people tend to trust the content, including ads."

Not all niche networks welcome marketers. Sermo.com—a social-networking site at which some 65,000 licensed physicians consult with colleagues specializing in areas ranging from dermatology to psychiatry—allows no marketing. However, for a fee, companies can gain access to Sermo.com data and member discussions. "They can monitor online discussions, with the doctors'

▲ **Niche online social networks: Thousands of social-networking sites have popped up to cater to specific interests, backgrounds, professions, and age groups. Yub.com connects a community of shopaholics.**

(continued)

names omitted, or see a tally of topics being discussed at the site to determine what's rising or falling in popularity," notes a health care industry analyst.

The more focused audiences offered by niche networks are increasingly popular with brands because "relevance," says the consultant, "trumps size." But how brands execute social-networking campaigns is as important as where they do it. Marketers must be careful not to become too commercial or too intrusive. Keeping sites hip and unencumbered by advertising is a balancing act for both the brands and the social networks. The best approach is not to *market* to network members but to *interact* with them on topics of mutual interest. Says one online

marketer, "The real way of getting into social media is you don't advertise, you participate in the community."

Sources: Portions adapted from Betsey Cummings, "Why Marketers Love Small Social Networks," *Brandweek,* April 27, 2008, accessed at www.brandweek.com; with adapted extracts, quotes, and other information from Kim Hart, "Online Networking Goes Small, and Sponsors Follow," *Washington Post,* December 29, 2007, p. D1; and Jessica E. Vascellaro, "Social Networking Goes Professional," *Wall Street Journal,* August 28, 2007, p. D1. Also see Paula Lehman, "Social Networks That Break a Sweat," *BusinessWeek,* February 4, 2008, p. 68; and Tim Parry, "Social Climbing," *Multichannel Merchant,* June 2009, p. 32.

way to insert a brand into social media is to give some kind of benefit to people," says another analyst. "You don't trick people into sharing your brand."[60]

To avoid the mysteries and challenges of building a presence on existing online social networks, many companies are now launching their own targeted Web communities. For example, on Nike's Nike Plus Web site, more than 500,000 runners upload, track, and compare their performances. More than half visit the site at least four times a week, and Nike plans eventually to have 15 percent or more of the world's 100 million runners actively participating in the Nike Plus online community.

Using E-Mail

E-mail is an important and growing online marketing tool. A recent study by the Direct Marketing Association (DMA) found that 79 percent of all direct marketing campaigns employ e-mail. U.S. companies spent about $621 million a year on e-mail marketing, up from just $240 million in 2002. And this spending is estimated to grow by an estimated 18 percent annually through 2013.[61]

To compete effectively in this ever-more-cluttered e-mail environment, marketers are designing "enriched" e-mail messages—animated, interactive, and personalized messages full of streaming audio and video. Then, they are targeting these attention-grabbers more carefully to those who want them and will act upon them.

Spam
Unsolicited, unwanted commercial e-mail messages.

But there's a dark side to the growing use of e-mail marketing. The explosion of **spam**—unsolicited, unwanted commercial e-mail messages that clog up our e-mailboxes—has produced consumer irritation and frustration. According to one research company, spam now accounts for 90 percent of all e-mail sent.[62] E-mail marketers walk a fine line between adding value for consumers and being intrusive.

To address these concerns, most legitimate marketers now practice *permission-based e-mail marketing,* sending e-mail pitches only to customers who "opt in." Financial services firms such as Charles Schwab use configurable e-mail systems that let customers choose what they want to get. Others, such as Yahoo! or Amazon.com, include long lists of opt-in boxes for different categories of marketing material. Amazon.com targets opt-in customers with a limited number of helpful "we thought you'd like to know" messages based on their expressed preferences and previous purchases. Few customers object and many actually welcome such promotional messages.

When used properly, e-mail can be the ultimate direct marketing medium. Blue-chip marketers such as Amazon.com, L.L.Bean, Office Depot, Charles Schwab, and others use it regularly, and with great success. E-mail lets these marketers send highly targeted, tightly personalized, relationship-building messages to consumers who actually *want* to receive them. ▲Consider StubHub:

As a start-up almost a decade ago, online ticket merchant StubHub ran "batch-and-blast" e-mail campaigns focused on building awareness. For years, sheer volume far outweighed e-mail relevancy. But StubHub has now learned the value of carefully targeted, relevant

StubHub! **Ticket** Alert

Get Great Seats in Just a Few Clicks

Hey GERALD.

We noticed Solheim Cup tickets were on your radar.

Great tickets are still available, but act fast. Head back to StubHub.com and use our interactive maps to find your perfect seats. You'll be covered by our FanProtect™ Guarantee, which protects you against fraud and ensures you'll receive authentic tickets on time.

Buy Tickets   Sell Tickets

FanProtect™ ✓

Our guarantee has you covered.

More

Fan Stories

Behind every StubHub experience is a great story!

More

▲ **E-mail marketing: StubHub's highly targeted, personalized e-mail messages produce very high response rates.**

e-mail messages. It now lets customers opt in for e-mail at registration, during purchases, and at sign-up modules throughout the StubHub site. Using opt-in customer data, StubHub targets designated consumer segments with ticket and event information aligned closely with their interests. Incorporating customer data produced immediate and stunning results. E-mail clickthrough rates quickly jumped 30 percent, and the company saw a 79 percent year-over-year increase in ticket sales despite having sent fewer e-mails. The more targeted campaigns have "enabled us to test and deliver the type of high-impact marketing that is needed in these times," says a StubHub marketer. "The results speak for themselves—these [new targeted campaigns] are driving 2,500 percent more revenue per e-mail than [our] average marketing campaigns."[63]

Given its targeting effectiveness and low costs, e-mail can be an outstanding marketing investment. According to the DMA, e-mail marketing produces a return on investment 40 to 50 percent higher than other forms of direct-marketing media.[64]

The Promise and Challenges of Online Marketing

Online marketing continues to offer both great promise and many challenges for the future. Its most ardent apostles still envision a time when the Internet and online marketing will replace magazines, newspapers, and even stores as sources for information and buying. Most marketers, however, hold a more realistic view. To be sure, online marketing has become a successful business model for some companies—Internet firms such as Amazon.com and Google, and direct marketing companies such as GEICO. However, for most companies, online marketing will remain just one important approach to the marketplace that works alongside other approaches in a fully integrated marketing mix.

Despite the many challenges, companies large and small have now integrated online marketing into their marketing strategies and mixes. As it continues to grow, online marketing will prove to be a powerful direct marketing tool for improving sales, communicating company and product information, delivering products and services, and building deeper customer relationships.

Author Comment ≫
Although we mostly benefit from direct marketing, like most other things in life, it has its dark side as well. Marketers and customers alike must guard against irritating or harmful direct marketing practices.

PUBLIC POLICY ISSUES IN DIRECT MARKETING (pp 499–502)

Direct marketers and their customers usually enjoy mutually rewarding relationships. Occasionally, however, a darker side emerges. The aggressive and sometimes shady tactics of a few direct marketers can bother or harm consumers, giving the entire industry a black eye. Abuses range from simple excesses that irritate consumers to instances of unfair practices or even outright deception and fraud. The direct marketing industry has also faced growing invasion-of-privacy concerns, and online marketers must deal with Internet security issues.

Irritation, Unfairness, Deception, and Fraud

Direct marketing excesses sometimes annoy or offend consumers. Most of us dislike direct-response TV commercials that are too loud, too long, and too insistent. Our mailboxes fill up with unwanted junk mail, our e-mailboxes bulge with unwanted spam, and our computer screens flash with unwanted banner or pop-under ads.

Beyond irritating consumers, some direct marketers have been accused of taking unfair advantage of impulsive or less-sophisticated buyers. TV shopping channels and program-long "infomercials" targeting television-addicted shoppers seem to be the worst culprits. They feature smooth-talking hosts, elaborately staged demonstrations, claims of drastic price reductions, "while they last" time limitations, and unequaled ease of purchase to inflame buyers who have low sales resistance. Worse yet, so-called heat merchants design mailers and write copy intended to mislead buyers.

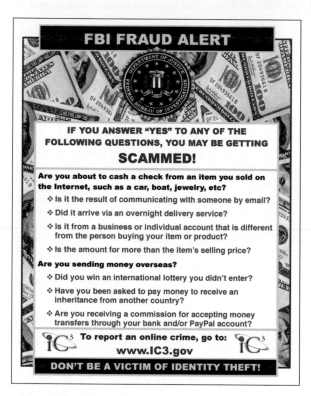

▲Internet fraud has multiplied in recent years. The FBI's Internet Crime Complaint Center provides consumers with a convenient way to alert authorities to suspected violations.

Fraudulent schemes, such as investment scams or phony collections for charity, have also multiplied in recent years. *Internet fraud*, including identity theft and financial scams, has become a serious problem. ▲Last year alone, the Federal Internet Crime Complaint Center (IC3) received about 275,000 complaints related to Internet fraud involving monetary loss, with a total dollar loss of $265 million.[65]

One common form of Internet fraud is *phishing,* a type of identity theft that uses deceptive e-mails and fraudulent Web sites to fool users into divulging their personal data. For example, consumers may receive an e-mail, supposedly from their bank or credit card company, saying that their account's security has been compromised. The sender asks them to log onto a provided Web address and confirm their account number, password, and maybe even their social security number. If they follow the instructions, they are actually turning this sensitive information over to scam artists. Although many consumers are now aware of such schemes, phishing can be extremely costly to those caught in the net. It also damages the brand identities of legitimate online marketers who have worked to build user confidence in Web and e-mail transactions.[66]

Many consumers also worry about *online security*. They fear that unscrupulous snoopers will eavesdrop on their online transactions, picking up personal information or intercepting credit and debit card numbers. Although online shopping has grown rapidly, in a recent survey, 75 percent of participants said they still do not like sending personal or credit card information over the Internet.[67] Internet shoppers are also concerned about contracting annoying or harmful viruses, spyware, and other "malware" (malicious software).

Another Internet marketing concern is that of *access by vulnerable or unauthorized groups*. For example, marketers of adult-oriented materials have found it difficult to restrict access by minors. For example, 13 percent of the respondents in a *Consumer Reports* survey had children in their household registered as MySpace users who were under the online community's official minimum age of 14. The survey also indicated that many parents haven't prepared their children for potential online risks.[68]

Invasion of Privacy

Invasion of privacy is perhaps the toughest public policy issue now confronting the direct marketing industry. Consumers often benefit from database marketing—they receive more offers that are closely matched to their interests. However, many critics worry that marketers may know *too* much about consumers' lives and that they may use this knowledge to take unfair advantage of consumers. At some point, they claim, the extensive use of databases intrudes on consumer privacy.

These days, it seems that almost every time consumers enter a sweepstakes, apply for a credit card, visit a Web site, or order products by mail, telephone, or the Internet, their names enter some company's already bulging database. Using sophisticated computer technologies, direct marketers can use these databases to "microtarget" their selling efforts. *Online privacy* causes special concerns. Most online marketers have become highly skilled at collecting and analyzing detailed consumer information. As Web tracking technology grows in sophistication, digital privacy experts worry that unscrupulous marketers will use such information to take unfair advantage of unknowing customers.

Some consumers and policy makers worry that the ready availability of information may leave consumers open to abuse if companies make unauthorized use of the information in marketing their products or exchanging databases with other companies. For example, they ask, should Web sellers be allowed to plant cookies in the browsers of consumers who visit their sites and use tracking information to target ads and other marketing efforts? Should credit card companies be allowed to make data on their millions of cardholders worldwide available to merchants who accept their cards? Or is it right for states to sell the names and addresses of driver's license holders, along with height, weight, and gender information, allowing apparel retailers to target tall or overweight people with special clothing offers?

A Need for Action

All of this calls for strong actions by marketers to prevent privacy abuses before legislators step in to do it for them. For example, to curb direct marketing excesses, various government agencies are investigating not only do-not-call lists but also "do-not-mail" lists, "do-not-track" lists, and "Can Spam" legislation. And in response to online privacy and security concerns, the federal government has considered numerous legislative actions to regulate how Web operators obtain and use consumer information. For example, Congress is drafting legislation that would give consumers more control over how Web information is used. And the Federal Trade Commission is taking a more active role in policing online privacy. To head off increased government regulation, four advertiser groups—the American Association of Advertising Agencies, the Association of National Advertisers, the Direct Marketing Association, and the Interactive Advertising Bureau—recently issued new guidelines for Web sites. Among other measures, the guidelines call for Web marketers to alert consumers if their activities are being tracked.[69]

Of special concern are the privacy rights of children. In 1998, the Federal Trade Commission surveyed 212 Web sites directed toward children. It found that 89 percent of the sites collected personal information from children. However, 46 percent of them did not include any disclosure of their collection and use of such information. As a result, Congress passed the Children's Online Privacy Protection Act (COPPA), which requires Web site operators targeting children to post privacy policies on their sites. They must also notify parents about the information they're gathering and obtain parental consent before collecting personal information from children under age 13. Under this act, Sony's music division was fined $1 million for collecting and disclosing personal information from 30,000 children under the age of 13 without first notifying parents and obtaining their consent.[70]

Many companies have responded to consumer privacy and security concerns with actions of their own. Still others are taking an industrywide approach. For example, TRUSTe, a nonprofit self-regulatory organization, works with many large corporate sponsors, including Microsoft, AT&T, and Intuit, to audit companies' privacy and security measures and help consumers navigate the Web safely. According to the company's Web site, "TRUSTe believes that an environment of mutual trust and openness will help make and keep the Internet a free, comfortable, and richly diverse community for everyone." To reassure consumers, the company lends its "trustmark" stamp of approval to Web sites that meet its privacy and security standards. [71]

The direct marketing industry as a whole is also addressing public policy issues. For example, in an effort to build consumer confidence in shopping direct, the Direct Marketing Association (DMA)—the largest association for businesses practicing direct, database, and interactive marketing, with more than 4,800 member companies—

launched a "Privacy Promise to American Consumers." The Privacy Promise requires that all DMA members adhere to a carefully developed set of consumer privacy rules. Members must agree to notify customers when any personal information is rented, sold, or exchanged with others. They must also honor consumer requests to "opt out" of receiving further solicitations or having their contact information transferred to other marketers. Finally, they must abide by the DMA's Preference Service by removing the names of consumers who wish not to receive mail, telephone, or e-mail offers.[72]

Direct marketers know that, left untended, such direct marketing abuses will lead to increasingly negative consumer attitudes, lower response rates, and calls for more restrictive state and federal legislation. Most direct marketers want the same things that consumers want: honest and well-designed marketing offers targeted only toward consumers who will appreciate and respond to them. Direct marketing is just too expensive to waste on consumers who don't want it.

REST STOP
REVIEWING THE CONCEPTS

Let's revisit this chapter's key concepts. This chapter is the last of three chapters covering the final marketing mix element—promotion. The previous chapters dealt with advertising, publicity, personal selling, and sales promotion. This one investigates the burgeoning field of direct and online marketing.

> **Objective 1** Define direct marketing and discuss its benefits to customers and companies. (pp 473–477)

Direct marketing consists of direct connections with carefully targeted individual consumers to both obtain an immediate response and cultivate lasting customer relationships. Using detailed databases, direct marketers tailor their offers and communications to the needs of narrowly defined segments or even individual buyers.

For buyers, direct marketing is convenient, easy to use, and private. It gives buyers ready access to a wealth of products and information, at home and around the globe. Direct marketing is also immediate and interactive, allowing buyers to create exactly the configuration of information, products, or services they desire, then order them on the spot. For sellers, direct marketing is a powerful tool for building customer relationships. Using database marketing, today's marketers can target small groups or individual consumers, tailor offers to individual needs, and promote these offers through personalized communications. It also offers them a low-cost, efficient alternative for reaching their markets. As a result of these advantages to both buyers and sellers, direct marketing has become the fastest-growing form of marketing.

> **Objective 2** Identify and discuss the major forms of direct marketing. (pp 477–486)

The main forms of direct marketing include personal selling, direct-mail marketing, catalog marketing, telephone marketing, direct-response television marketing, kiosk marketing, and online marketing. We discussed personal selling in the previous chapter.

Direct-mail marketing, the largest form of direct marketing, consists of the company sending an offer, announcement, reminder, or other item to a person at a specific address. Recently, new forms of "mail delivery" have become popular, such as e-mail and mobile marketing. Some marketers rely on catalog marketing—selling through catalogs mailed to a select list of customers, made available in stores, or accessed on the Web. Telephone marketing consists of using the telephone to sell directly to consumers. Direct-response television marketing has two forms: direct-response advertising (or infomercials) and home shopping channels. Kiosks are information and ordering machines that direct marketers place in stores, airports, and other locations. In recent years, a number of new digital direct marketing technologies have emerged, including mobile marketing, podcasts and vodcasts, and interactive TV. Online marketing involves online channels that digitally link sellers with consumers.

> **Objective 3** Explain how companies have responded to the Internet and other powerful new technologies with online marketing strategies. (pp 486–491)

Online marketing is the fastest-growing form of direct marketing. The Internet enables consumers and companies to access and share huge amounts of information with just a few mouse clicks. In turn, the Internet has given marketers a whole new way to create value for customers and build customer relationships. It's hard to find a company today that doesn't have a substantial Web marketing presence.

Online consumer buying continues to grow at a healthy rate. Most American online users now use the Internet to shop. Perhaps more importantly, the Internet influences offline shopping. Thus, smart marketers are employing integrated multichannel strategies that use the Web to drive sales to other marketing channels.

Objective 4 Discuss how companies go about conducting online marketing to profitably deliver more value to customers. **(pp 491–499)**

Companies of all types are now engaged in online marketing. The Internet gave birth to the *click-only* dot-coms, which operate only online. In addition, many traditional brick-and-mortar companies have now added online marketing operations, transforming themselves into *click-and-mortar* competitors. Many click-and-mortar companies are now having more online success than their click-only competitors.

Companies can conduct online marketing in any of the four ways: creating a Web site, placing ads and promotions online, setting up or participating in Web communities and online social networks, or using e-mail. The first step typically is to set up a Web site. Beyond simply setting up a site, however, companies must make their sites engaging, easy to use, and useful in order to attract visitors, hold them, and bring them back again.

Online marketers can use various forms of online advertising and promotion to build their Internet brands or to attract visitors to their Web sites. Forms of online promotion include online display advertising, search-related advertising, content sponsorships, alliances and affiliate programs, and viral marketing, the Internet version of word-of-mouth marketing. Online marketers can also participate in online social networks and other Web communities, which take advantage of the C2C properties of the Web. Finally, e-mail marketing has become a fast-growing tool for both B2C and B2B marketers. Whatever direct marketing tools they use, marketers must work hard to integrate them into a cohesive marketing effort.

Objective 5 Overview the public policy and ethical issues presented by direct marketing. **(pp 499–502)**

Direct marketers and their customers usually enjoy mutually rewarding relationships. Sometimes, however, direct marketing presents a darker side. The aggressive and sometimes shady tactics of a few direct marketers can bother or harm consumers, giving the entire industry a black eye. Abuses range from simple excesses that irritate consumers to instances of unfair practices or even outright deception and fraud. The direct marketing industry has also faced growing concerns about invasion-of-privacy and Internet security issues. Such concerns call for strong action by marketers and public policy makers to curb direct marketing abuses. In the end, most direct marketers want the same things that consumers want: honest and well-designed marketing offers targeted only toward consumers who will appreciate and respond to them.

Navigating the Key Terms

Objective 1
Direct marketing (p 473)
Customer database (p 476)

Objective 2
Direct-mail marketing (p 477)
Catalog marketing (p 479)
Telephone marketing (p 479)
Direct-response television marketing (p 480)

Objective 3
Online marketing (p 486)
Internet (p 486)
Click-only companies (p 486)
Click-and-mortar companies (p 486)
Business-to-consumer (B2C) online marketing (p 487)
Business-to business (B2B) online marketing (p 488)
Consumer-to-consumer (C2C) online marketing (p 489)

Blogs (p 489)
Consumer-to-business (C2B) online marketing (p 491)

Objective 4
Corporate (brand) Web site (p 491)
Marketing Web site (p 492)
Online advertising (p 493)
Viral marketing (p 495)
Online social networks (p 496)
Spam (p 498)

Travel Log

Discussing the Issues

1. Describe how direct marketing has evolved into a way of doing business for some companies. (AACSB: Communication)

2. List and briefly describe the various forms of direct marketing. (AACSB: Communication)

3. Describe the four major e-marketing domains and provide an example of each. (AACSB: Communication)

4. Compare and contrast a corporate Web site and a marketing Web site. (AACSB: Communication)

5. Describe forms of online promotions other than advertising. (AACSB: Communication)

6. Discuss the public policy issues in direct marketing. What are direct marketers doing to address these issues? (AACSB: Communication; Reflective Thinking)

Application Questions

1. In a small group, design a viral marketing campaign targeted to teens for a brand of soft drink. Discuss the challenges marketers might encounter when implementing this campaign. (AACSB: Communication; Use of IT; Reflective Thinking)

2. Visit Nike's Web site at http://nikeid.nike.com/ and design your own shoe. Print out your shoe design and bring it to class. Do you think the price is appropriate for the value received from being able to customize your shoe? Identify and describe two other Web sites that allow buyers to customize products. (AACSB: Communication; Use of IT; Reflective Thinking)

3. Find articles about two data security breaches in the news. How did the breaches occur and who is potentially affected by them? (AACSB: Communication; Reflective Thinking)

Under the Hood: Marketing Technology

The Internet opened the door for explosive growth in direct marketing, and much of that growth is through applications for mobile devices. For example, for $12.99 per month, Schlage, a lock manufacturer, now offers a wireless, keyless door lock system integrated with cell phones. And Zipcar, a car-sharing service, launched an application for the iPhone enabling customers not only to reserve and locate a car but to even unlock it and drive it away—all without contacting a customer service representative. Honking the virtual horn on an iPhone triggers the horn on the reserved car so the member can locate the car in the Zipcar lot. The application even looks like a key fob, prompting the user to push the button to unlock the door. Once in the car, swiping a membership card allows access to the keys in the car.

1. What key benefits do these forms of direct marketing offer for consumers and for marketers? (AACSB: Communication; Use of IT; Reflective Thinking)

2. Find or conceive of other applications in which the Internet and mobile devices create direct marketing opportunities. (AACSB: Communication; Reflective Thinking)

Staying on the Road: Marketing Ethics

The World Wide Web is often referred to as the "Wild West." Unlike advertising, which openly identifies the sponsor, most of the product and brand information seen on the Internet does not reveal sponsorship. You might read about a product in a blog, see it in a YouTube video, or follow it in Twitter, often unaware that the person was paid or was provided free merchandise or other goodies to say positive things about a product or service. These undercover company shills are difficult to detect. Kmart, Sony Pictures, Hewlett-Packard, and other marketers use companies like IZEA to develop "sponsored conversations" using its network of bloggers. Sponsored conversations generated by IZEA disclose sponsorships, but many others do not. But that is about to change. The Federal Trade Commission recently updated its endorsement guidelines requiring disclosure of sponsorship by bloggers. Violators could be slapped with an $11,000 fine per violation, but with almost 30 million bloggers out there—80 percent of whom occasionally or frequently post product or brand reviews—it will be difficult, if not impossible, to enforce this rule.

1. Find examples of product information posted in blogs. Did the blogger indicate in the post that he or she was paid or provided free products? Should the government enact laws to require bloggers and others on the Internet to disclose sponsorship from marketers? Explain. (AACSB: Communication; Ethical Reasoning)

2. Review the FTC's revised guidelines on sponsored conversations (http://www.ftc.gov/os/2009/10/091005revisedendorsementguides.pdf) and visit the Word of Mouth Marketing Association's Web site (womma.org) and IZEA's Web site (IZEA.com). Write a report on how marketers can effectively use sponsored conversations within the FTC's guidelines. (AACSB: Communication; Reflective Thinking)

Rough Road Ahead: Marketing and the Economy

Dell

Not long ago, Dell was the PC industry darling, turning the industry upside down with its direct marketing approach. At one point, it was the world's leading PC maker. But in recent years, Dell has been hit hard by a combination of factors. One is competition: Hewlett Packard took Dell's "top-seller" status away by providing a better one-stop shop for equipment and services to businesses, where Dell gets three-fourths of its sales. At the same time, Taiwanese competitor Acer took a bite out of Dell's low-cost advantage. By selling cheaper machines, Acer is now in a virtual tie with Dell at the industry's number-two market-share spot. The final blow has come from the sluggish economy, which has made consumers and businesses more reluctant to upgrade to newer, faster models. Dell's PC sales have fallen by as much as 34 percent. The company has cut costs somewhat, and it's also looking to its other businesses to shore up sagging PC sales. But for the most part, Dell appears to be just hanging on while waiting for 2010, when a powerful replacement cycle and a new Windows 7 operating system are expected to reboot the industry.

1. What is wrong with Dell's strategy to increase PC sales?

2. How can Dell overcome this problem, particularly as consumer frugality persists? What would you recommend?

Travel Budget: Marketing by the Numbers

Telemarketing is the new sales force. The practice can cost as little as 10 percent of the costs of dispatching a salesperson, keeping the person on the road, and paying all of his incidental costs. What is more, a telemarketer can speak to more decision makers each day, arguably nine or ten times as many as a conventional salesperson. Of course, businesses are interested in switching over to telemarketers. But are they right to do so in the long run?

1. Use the ROI calculator at this Web site www.marketingtoday.com/tools/roi_calculator.htm and insert the following telemarketing numbers in the "Input Data" section:

   Number of customers being called (use "number of pieces you are mailing or e-mailing"): 1,000 Total cost of program: $30,000

   There will be a 20 percent response rate, and a 5 percent purchase rate

   Average profit per sale: $10,000

   What ROI would a company with these numbers achieve by using telemarketers versus regular salespeople?

2. Research the use of call centers and telemarketing in Latin America. What key trends do you see?

Drive In: Video Case

Zappos

Zappos spends almost no money on advertising—it doesn't have to. Customers are so enamored with the company, they keep coming back. And they keep telling their friends. Instead of mass media advertising, Zappos focuses on strengthening customer relationships through marketing directly to customers. Like its impeccable customer service, the company's unique promotional methods are valued by customers. When Zappos sends out an e-mail or a Tweet, customers listen. Its strength in direct marketing, combined with user-friendly Web design, have made Zappos one of the strongest retailers anywhere.

After viewing the video featuring Zappos, answer the following questions:

1. What benefits has Zappos gained by marketing directly to customers rather than engaging heavily in mass-market advertising?

2. What role does database technology play in Zappos' ability to connect with its customers?

3. Discuss Zappos Web site from the perspective of the seven elements of effective Web design. What are its strengths and weaknesses?

15   The Global Marketplace

ROAD MAP

Previewing the Concepts

You've now learned the fundamentals of how companies develop competitive marketing strategies to create customer value and build lasting customer relationships. In this chapter, we extend these fundamentals to global marketing. We've visited global topics in each previous chapter—it's difficult to find an area of marketing that doesn't contain at least some international applications. Here, however, we'll focus on special considerations that companies face when they market their brands globally. Advances in communication, transportation, and other technologies have made the world a much smaller place. Today, almost every firm, large or small, faces international marketing issues. In this chapter, we will examine six major decisions marketers make in going global.

Objective Outline

 Objective 1   Discuss how the international trade system and the economic, political-legal, and cultural environments affect a company's international marketing decisions.
Global Marketing Today **pp 508–510**
Looking at the Global Marketing Environment **pp 510–517**
Deciding Whether to Go Global **pp 517–518**
Deciding Which Markets to Enter **pp 518–519**

 Objective 2   Describe three key approaches to entering international markets.
Deciding How to Enter the Market **pp 519–522**

 Objective 3   Explain how companies adapt their marketing mixes for international markets.
Deciding on the Global Marketing Program
pp 523–530

 Objective 4   Identify the three major forms of international marketing organization.
Deciding on the Global Marketing Organization
pp 530–531

To start things off, let's look at good old McDonald's. Despite its homegrown American roots, McDonald's is a truly global enterprise. Over the years, the company has learned many important lessons about adapting locally in global markets. Here, we'll examine McDonald's odyssey into Russia, now one of the crown jewels in its global empire.

First Stop

McDonald's: Serving Customers Around the World

▲ Moscow's Pushkin Square location is the busiest McDonald's in the world, and Russia is the crown jewel in McDonald's global empire.

Most Americans think of McDonald's as their very own. The first McDonald's stand popped up in California in 1954, and what could be more American than burger-and-fries fast food? But as it turns out, the quintessentially all-American company now sells more burgers and fries outside the country than within. Nearly 65 percent of McDonald's $23.5 billion of sales last year came from outside the United States, and its international sales grew at close to twice the rate of domestic sales growth.

McDonald's today is a truly global enterprise. Its 32,000 restaurants serve more than 58 million people in more than 100 countries each day. Few firms have more international marketing experience than McDonald's. But going global hasn't always been easy, and McDonald's has learned many important lessons in its journeys overseas. To see how far McDonald's has come, consider its experiences in Russia, a market that's very different culturally, economically, and politically from our own.

McDonald's first set its sights on Russia (then a part of the Soviet Union) in 1976, when George Cohon, head of McDonald's in Canada, took a group of Soviet Olympics officials to a McDonald's while they visited for the Montreal Olympic Games. Cohon was struck by how much the Soviets liked McDonald's hamburgers, fries, and other fare. Over the next 14 years, Cohon flew to Russia more than 100 times, first to get Soviet permission for McDonald's to provide food for the 1980 Moscow Olympics, and later to be allowed to open McDonald's restaurants in the country. He quickly learned that no one in Russia had any idea what a McDonald's was. The Soviets turned Cohon down flat on both requests.

Finally in 1988, as Premier Mikhail Gorbachev began to open the Russian economy, Cohon forged a deal with the city of Moscow to launch the first Russian McDonald's in Moscow's Pushkin Square. But obtaining permission was only the first step. Actually opening the restaurant brought a fresh set of challenges. Thanks to Russia's large and bureaucratic government structure, McDonald's had to obtain some 200 separate signatures just to open the single location. It had difficulty finding reliable suppliers for even such basics as hamburgers and buns. So McDonald's forked over $45 million to build a facility to produce these things itself. It even brought in technical experts from Canada with special strains of disease-resistant seed to teach Russian farmers how to grow Russet Burbank potatoes for french fries, and it built its own pasteurizing plant to ensure a plentiful supply of fresh milk.

When the Moscow McDonald's at Pushkin Square finally opened its doors in January 1990, it quickly won the hearts of Russian consumers. However, the company faced still more hurdles. The Pushkin Square restaurant is huge—26 cash registers (more than you'll find in a typical Wal-Mart supercenter) and 900 seats (compared with 40 to 50 seats in a typical U.S. McDonald's). The logistics of serving customers on such a scale was daunting, made

McDonald's is a truly global enterprise. The quintessentially all-American company now sells more burgers and fries outside the United States than within.

▲The Pushkin Square McDonald's is hugo 26 oaoh rogiotoro and 000 ooato.

even more difficult by the fact that few employees or customers understood the fast-food concept.

Although American consumers were well acquainted with McDonald's, the Russians were clueless. So, in order to meet its high standards for customer satisfaction in this new market, the U.S. fast feeder had to educate employees about the time-tested McDonald's way of doing things. It trained Russian managers at Hamburger University and subjected each of 630 new employees (most of whom didn't know a chicken McNugget from an Egg McMuffin) to 16 to 20 hours of training on such essentials as cooking meat patties, assembling Filet-O-Fish sandwiches, and giving service with a smile. Back in those days, McDonald's even had to train consumers—most Muscovites had never seen a fast-food restaurant. Customers waiting in line were shown videos telling them everything from how to order and pay at the counter, to how to put their coats over the backs of their seats, to how to handle a Big Mac.

However, the new Moscow McDonald's got off to a spectacular start. An incredible 50,000 customers swarmed the restaurant during its first day of business. And in its usual way, McDonald's began immediately to build community involvement. On opening day, it held a kickoff party for 700 Muscovite orphans and then donated all opening-day proceeds to the Moscow Children's Fund.

Today, only 20 years after opening its first restaurant there, McDonald's is thriving in Russia. The Pushkin Square location is now the busiest McDonald's in the world, and Russia is the crown jewel in McDonald's global empire. The company's 240 restaurants in 40 Russian cities each serve an average of 850,000 diners a year—twice the per-store traffic of any of the other 122 countries in which McDonald's operates.

Despite the long lines of customers, McDonald's has been careful about how rapidly it expands in Russia. In recent years, it has reined in its rapid growth strategy and focused instead on improving product and service quality and profitability. The goal is to squeeze more business out of existing restaurants and to grow slowly but profitably. One way to do that is to add new menu items to draw in consumers at different times of the day. So, as it did many years ago in the United States, McDonald's in Russia is now adding breakfast items.

Although only about 5 percent of Russians eat breakfast outside the home, more commuters in the big cities are leaving home earlier to avoid heavy traffic. The company hopes that the new breakfast menu will encourage commuters to stop off at McDonald's on their way to work. However, when the fast-food chain added breakfast items, it stopped offering its traditional hamburger fare during the morning hours. When many customers complained of "hamburger withdrawal," McDonald's introduced the Fresh McMuffin, an English muffin with a sausage patty topped with cheese, lettuce, tomato, and special sauce. The new sandwich became an instant hit.

To reduce the lines inside restaurants and to attract motorists, McDonald's is also introducing Russian consumers to drive-thru windows. At first, many Russians just didn't get the concept. Instead, they treated the drive-thru window as just another line, purchasing their food there, parking, and going inside to eat. Also, Russian cars often don't have cupholders, so drive-thru customers bought fewer drinks. However, as more customers get used to the concept, McDonald's is putting drive-thru and walk-up windows in about half of its new stores.

So, that's a look at McDonald's in Russia. But just as McDonald's has tweaked its formula in Russia, it also adjusts its marketing and operations to meet the special needs of local consumers in other major global markets. To be sure, McDonald's is a global brand. Its restaurants around the world employ a common global strategy—convenient food at affordable prices. And no matter where you go in the world—from Moscow to Montréal or Shanghai to Cheboygan, Michigan—you'll find those good old golden arches and a menu full of Quarter Pounders, Big Macs, fries, milkshakes, and other familiar items. But within that general strategic framework, McDonald's adapts to the subtleties of each local market. Says a McDonald's Europe executive, "Across Europe with 40 different markets, there are 40 sets of tastes. There are also differences within each market. We are a local market but a global brand."[1]

*i*n the past, U.S. companies paid little attention to international trade. If they could pick up some extra sales through exporting, that was fine. But the big market was at home, and it teemed with opportunities. The home market was also much safer. Managers did not need to learn other languages, deal with strange and changing currencies, face political and legal uncertainties, or adapt their products to different customer needs and expectations. Today, however, the situation is much different. Organizations of all kinds, from Coca-Cola, IBM, and Google to MTV and even the NBA, have gone global.

Author Comment ≫
The rapidly changing global environment provides both opportunities and threats. It's difficult to find a marketer today that isn't affected in some way by global developments.

GLOBAL MARKETING TODAY (pp 508–510)

The world is shrinking rapidly with the advent of faster communication, transportation, and financial flows. Products developed in one country—Gucci purses, Sony electronics, McDonald's hamburgers, Japanese sushi, German BMWs—have found enthusiastic acceptance in other countries. We would not be surprised to hear about a German businessman wearing an Italian suit meeting an English friend at a Japanese restaurant who later returns home to drink Russian vodka and watch *American Idol* on TV.

International trade has boomed over the past three decades. Since 1990, the number of multinational corporations in the world has grown from 30,000 to more than 60,000. Some of these multinationals are true giants. In fact, of the largest 150 "economies" in the world, only 81 are countries. The remaining 69 are multinational corporations. Wal-Mart, the world's largest company, has annual revenues greater than the gross domestic product (GDP) of all but the world's 25 largest-GDP countries.[2]

Between 2000 and 2008, total world trade grew more than 7 percent per year, easily outstripping GDP output, which was about 3 percent. Despite a dip in world trade caused by the recent worldwide recession, world trade of products and services last year was valued at over $19.5 trillion about 28 percent of GDP worldwide.[3]

▲Many American companies have now made the world their market.

▲Many U.S. companies have long been successful at international marketing: Coca-Cola, GE, IBM, Colgate, Caterpillar, Ford, Boeing, McDonald's, and dozens of other American firms have made the world their market. And in the United States, names such as Sony, Toyota, BP, IKEA, Nestlé, and Nokia have become household words. Other products and services that appear to be American are in fact produced or owned by foreign companies: Bantam books, Baskin-Robbins ice cream, GE and RCA televisions, Carnation milk, Universal Studios, and Motel 6, to name just a few. Michelin, the oh-so-French tire manufacturer, now does 31 percent of its business in North America; Johnson & Johnson, the maker of quintessentially all-American products such as BAND-AIDs and Johnson's Baby Shampoo, does 49 percent of its business abroad. And America's own Caterpillar belongs more to the wider world, with 61 percent of its sales coming from outside the United States.[4]

But as global trade grows, global competition is also intensifying. Foreign firms are expanding aggressively into new international markets, and home markets are no longer as rich in opportunity. Few industries are now safe from foreign competition. If companies delay taking steps toward internationalizing, they risk being shut out of growing markets in western and eastern Europe, China and the Pacific Rim, Russia, India, and elsewhere. Firms that stay at home to play it safe might not only lose their chances to enter other markets but also risk losing their home markets. Domestic companies that never thought about foreign competitors suddenly find these competitors in their own backyards.

Ironically, although the need for companies to go abroad is greater today than in the past, so are the risks. Companies that go global may face highly unstable governments and currencies, restrictive government policies and regulations, and high trade barriers. The recently dampened global economic environment has also created big global challenges. And corruption is an increasing problem—officials in several countries often award business not to the best bidder but to the highest briber.

Global firm
A firm that, by operating in more than one country, gains R&D, production, marketing, and financial advantages in its costs and reputation that are not available to purely domestic competitors.

A **global firm** is one that, by operating in more than one country, gains marketing, production, R&D, and financial advantages that are not available to purely domestic competitors. The global company sees the world as one market. It minimizes the importance of national boundaries and develops global brands. It raises capital, obtains materials and components, and manufactures and markets its goods wherever it can do the best job. For example, Otis Elevator, the world's largest elevator maker, achieves 81 percent of its sales from outside the United States. It gets its elevators' door systems from France, small geared parts from Spain, electronics from Germany, and special motor drives from Japan. It uses the United States only

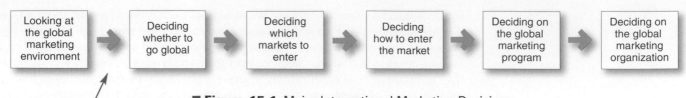

■ **Figure 15.1** Major International Marketing Decisions

It's a big and beautiful but threatening world out there for marketers! Most large American firms have made the world their market. For example, once all-American McDonald's now captures 65 percent of its sales from outside the United States.

for systems integration. "Borders are so 20th century," says one global marketing expert. "Transnationals take 'stateless' to the next level."[5]

This does not mean that small- and medium-size firms must operate in a dozen countries to succeed. These firms can practice global niching. But the world is becoming smaller, and every company operating in a global industry—whether large or small—must assess and establish its place in world markets.

The rapid move toward globalization means that all companies will have to answer some basic questions: What market position should we try to establish in our country, in our economic region, and globally? Who will our global competitors be and what are their strategies and resources? Where should we produce or source our products? What strategic alliances should we form with other firms around the world?

As shown in ■ **Figure 15.1**, a company faces six major decisions in international marketing. We will discuss each decision in detail in this chapter.

Author Comment »

As if operating within a company's own borders wasn't difficult enough, going global adds many layers of complexities. For example, Coca-Cola markets its products in hundreds of countries around the globe. It must understand the varying trade, economic, cultural, and political environments in each market.

LOOKING AT THE GLOBAL MARKETING ENVIRONMENT
(pp 510–517)

Before deciding whether to operate internationally, a company must understand the international marketing environment. That environment has changed a great deal in the past two decades, creating both new opportunities and new problems.

The International Trade System

U.S. companies looking abroad must start by understanding the international *trade system*. When selling to another country, a firm may face restrictions on trade between nations. Governments may charge *tariffs*, taxes on certain imported products designed to raise revenue or to protect domestic firms. Tariffs are often used to force favorable trade behaviors from other nations. ▲For example, the United States recently threatened high tariffs on—of all things—Roquefort cheese in retaliation for a European Union ban on U.S. hormone-treated beef.[6]

▼**Trade barriers: In retaliation for a European Union Ban on U.S. hormone-treated beef, the United States threatened high tariffs on—of all things—Roquefort cheese and other popular European food imports.**

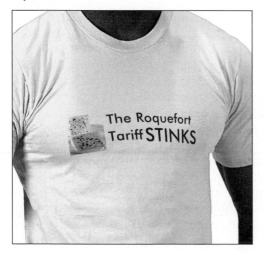

Roquefort cheese and some other popular European food imports could disappear soon from U.S. gourmet shops and fancy food departments. The imports are hostages in a long-running trans-Atlantic food fight over the European Union's French-led refusal to import hormone-treated U.S. beef. By the tit-for-tat logic of playground and trade disputes, if the European Union (EU) doesn't lift its 20-year beef ban, the United States gets to impose punishing World Trade Organization-sanctioned tariffs on selected products that EU members want to sell in the United States. No one's likely to starve as a result, but the pending 300-percent duty on Roquefort would drive its price into the unheard-of, demand-stifling range of $60 a pound. While Roquefort is the most harshly attacked, other 100 percent U.S. tariffs probably would double the retail prices of bottled water from Italy, chestnuts from France, and foie gras, truffles, beef sausage, bone-in hams, canned peaches, and filled chocolates from 26 EU member countries, France prominent among them.

Countries may set *quotas*, limits on the amount of foreign imports that they will accept in certain product categories. The purpose of a quota is to conserve on foreign exchange and to protect local industry and employment. Firms may also face *exchange controls*, which limit the amount of foreign exchange and the exchange rate against other currencies.

A company also may face *nontariff trade barriers,* such as biases against its bids, restrictive product standards, or excessive regulations. The recent global economic meltdown caused an increase in protectionism and the use of increased use of non-tariff trade barriers. For example, the 2009 U.S. American Recovery and Reinvestment Act includes a "Buy American" provision, requiring that economic stimulus funds spent on iron, steel, and manufactured goods go only to U.S. suppliers. The government's goal is to help strengthen the American iron and steel industries. However, the provision can also hurt international steel manufacturers in countries such as Canada, which ships 40 percent of its iron and steel to the United States.[7]

At the same time, certain other forces can *help* trade between nations. Examples include the General Agreement on Tariffs and Trade (GATT) and various regional free trade agreements.

The World Trade Organization and GATT

The General Agreement on Tariffs and Trade (GATT) is a 61-year-old treaty designed to promote world trade by reducing tariffs and other international trade barriers. ▲Since the treaty's inception in 1947, member nations (currently numbering 153) have met in eight rounds of GATT negotiations to reassess trade barriers and set new rules for international trade. The first seven rounds of negotiations reduced the average worldwide tariffs on manufactured goods from 45 percent to just 5 percent.[8]

The most recently completed GATT negotiations, dubbed the Uruguay Round, dragged on for seven long years before concluding in 1994. The benefits of the Uruguay Round will be felt for many years as the accord promotes long-term global trade growth. It reduced the world's remaining merchandise tariffs by 30 percent. The agreement also extended GATT to cover trade in agriculture and a wide range of services, and it toughened international protection of copyrights, patents, trademarks, and other intellectual property. Although the financial impact of such an agreement is difficult to measure, research suggests that cutting agriculture, manufacturing, and services trade barriers by one-third would boost the world economy by $613 billion, the equivalent of adding another Poland to the world economy.[9]

▲**The WTO and GATT:** The General Agreement on Tariffs and Trade (GATT) promotes world trade by reducing tariffs and other international trade barriers. The WTO oversees GATT, imposes trade sanctions, and mediates global disputes.

Beyond reducing trade barriers and setting global standards for trade, the Uruguay Round set up the World Trade Organization (WTO) to enforce GATT rules. In general, the WTO acts as an umbrella organization, overseeing GATT, mediating global disputes, and imposing trade sanctions. The previous GATT organization never possessed such authorities. A new round of GATT negotiations, the Doha round, began in Doha, Qatar, in late 2001 and was set to conclude in 2005, but the discussions continue.[10]

Regional Free Trade Zones

Economic community
A group of nations organized to work toward common goals in the regulation of international trade.

Certain countries have formed *free trade zones* or **economic communities**. These are groups of nations organized to work toward common goals in the regulation of international trade. One such community is the *European Union (EU)*. Formed in 1957, the EU set out to create a single European market by reducing barriers to the free flow of products, services, finances, and labor among member countries and developing policies on trade with nonmember nations. ▲Today, the EU represents one of the world's single largest markets. Currently, it has 27 member countries containing close to half a billion consumers and accounts for more than 20 percent of the world's exports.[11]

European unification offers tremendous trade opportunities for U.S. and other non-European firms. However, it also poses threats. As a result of increased unification, European companies have grown bigger and more competitive. Perhaps an

▲Economic communities: The European Union (EU) represents one of the world's single largest markets. Its current member countries contain more than half a billion consumers and account for 20 percent of the world's exports.

even greater concern, however, is that lower barriers *inside* Europe will create only thicker *outside* walls. Some observers envision a "Fortress Europe" that heaps favors on firms from EU countries but hinders outsiders by imposing obstacles.

Progress toward European unification has been slow—many doubt that complete unification will ever be achieved. In recent years, 16 member nations have taken a significant step toward unification by adopting the euro as a common currency. Many other countries are expected to follow within the next few years. Widespread adoption of the euro will decrease much of the currency risk associated with doing business in Europe, making member countries with previously weak currencies more attractive markets.[12]

However, even with the adoption of the euro, it is unlikely that the EU will ever go against 2,000 years of tradition and become the "United States of Europe." A community with two dozen different languages and cultures will always have difficulty coming together and acting as a single entity. For example, efforts to forge a single European constitution appear to have failed following French and Dutch "no" votes in mid-2005. In 2008, they failed yet again when Irish voters rejected a less-ambitious EU Reform Treaty. Although still a work in progress, unification has made Europe a global force with which to reckon, with a combined annual GDP of more than $18.8 trillion.[13]

In 1994, the *North American Free Trade Agreement (NAFTA)* established a free trade zone among the United States, Mexico, and Canada. The agreement created a single market of 452 million people who produce and consume almost $17 trillion worth of goods and services annually. Over the past 15 years, NAFTA has eliminated trade barriers and investment restrictions among the three countries. According to the International Monetary Fund, total trade among the three countries has more than doubled from $306 billion in 1993 to $830 billion in 2008.[14]

Following the apparent success of NAFTA, in 2005 the Central American Free Trade Agreement (CAFTA-DR) established a free trade zone between the United States and Costa Rica, the Dominican Republic, El Salvador, Guatemala, Honduras, and Nicaragua. And talks have been underway since 1994 to investigate establishing a Free Trade Area of the Americas (FTAA). This mammoth free trade zone would include 34 countries stretching from the Bering Strait to Cape Horn, with a population of more than 800 million and a combined GDP of about $20.3 trillion.[15]

Other free trade areas have formed in Latin America and South America. For example, the Union of South American Nations (UNASUR), modeled after the EU, was formed in 2004 and formalized by treaty in 2008. Composed of 10 countries, UNASUR makes up the largest trading bloc after NAFTA and the EU, with a population of 394 million, a combined economy of more than $3 trillion, and exports worth $561 billion. Similar to NAFTA and the EU, UNASUR aims to eliminate all tariffs between nations by 2019.[16]

Each nation has unique features that must be understood. A nation's readiness for different products and services and its attractiveness as a market to foreign firms depend on its economic, political-legal, and cultural environments.

Economic Environment

The international marketer must study each country's economy. Two economic factors reflect the country's attractiveness as a market: the country's industrial structure and its income distribution.

The country's *industrial structure* shapes its product and service needs, income levels, and employment levels. The four types of industrial structures are as follows:

- *Subsistence economies:* In a subsistence economy, the vast majority of people engage in simple agriculture. They consume most of their output and barter the rest for simple goods and services. They offer few market opportunities.
- *Raw material exporting economies:* These economies are rich in one or more natural resources but poor in other ways. Much of their revenue comes from exporting these resources. Examples are Chile (tin and copper), the Democratic Republic of the Congo (copper, cobalt, and coffee), and Saudi Arabia (oil). These countries are good markets for large equipment, tools and supplies, and trucks. If there are many foreign residents and a wealthy upper class, they are also a market for luxury goods.
- *Emerging economies (industrializing economies):* In an emerging economy, fast growth in manufacturing results in rapid overall economic growth. Examples include the BRIC countries—Brazil, Russia, India, and China. As manufacturing increases, the country needs more imports of raw textile materials, steel, and heavy machinery, and fewer imports of finished textiles, paper products, and automobiles. Industrialization typically creates a new rich class and a small but growing middle class, both demanding new types of imported goods.
- *Industrial economies:* Industrial economies are major exporters of manufactured goods, services, and investment funds. They trade goods among themselves and also export them to other types of economies for raw materials and semifinished goods. The varied manufacturing activities of these industrial nations and their large middle class make them rich markets for all sorts of goods. Examples include the United States, Japan, and Norway.

▼Economic environment: Even poor or emerging economies can be attractive markets. In India, Cadbury sells its premium chocolates to all income levels, including the country's poor. Here, it offers small packets of its Dairy Milk Shots for just two rupees, or about four U.S. cents.

The second economic factor is the country's *income distribution*. Industrialized nations may have low-, medium-, and high-income households. In contrast, countries with subsistence economies may consist mostly of households with very low family incomes. Still other countries may have households with only either very low or very high incomes. Even poor or emerging economies may be attractive markets for all kinds of goods. These days, companies in a wide range of industries—from computers to candy—are increasingly targeting even low-income consumers in emerging economies. ▲For example, in India, Cadbury sells its premium chocolates to all income levels, including the country's poor.[17]

As more Indians begin to treat themselves to little luxuries, Cadbury hopes to capture millions of new customers with chocolates that sell for only a few pennies. The British candy maker has been in India for more than 60 years and dominates the chocolate market there with a 70 percent market share. For years, Cadbury was considered a luxury product purchased only by the elite. Over the past few years, however, the brand has been growing at 20 percent a year in India, spurred by the country's economic growth and its increasingly affluent middle class. Still, India constitutes a vast untapped market—less than half of India's 1.1 billion people have ever tasted chocolate. So Cadbury is now taking aim at India's huge population of lower-income consumers by offering cheaper products. The premium candy maker's latest product for the low end of the Indian market is Cadbury Dairy Milk Shots—pea-sized chocolate balls sold for just two rupees, or about four U.S. cents, for a packet of two. Cadbury also sells other small, low-cost candies, such as Eclair caramels, which cost about two cents each. Last year, emerging markets accounted for 35 percent of Cadbury's sales and around 60 percent of its sales growth. The company estimates that India's chocolate and confectionery market will grow at more than 12 percent a year.

Political-Legal Environment

Nations differ greatly in their political-legal environments. In considering whether to do business in a given country, a company should consider factors such as the country's attitudes toward international buying, government bureaucracy, political stability, and monetary regulations.

Some nations are very receptive to foreign firms; others are less accommodating. For example, India has tended to bother foreign businesses with import quotas, currency restrictions, and other limitations that make operating there a challenge. In contrast, neighboring Asian countries such as Singapore and Thailand court foreign investors and shower them with incentives and favorable operating conditions. Political and regulatory stability is another issue. For example, Venezuela's government is notoriously volatile—due to economic factors such as inflation and steep public spending—increasing the risk of doing business there. Although most international marketers still find the Venezuelan market attractive, the unstable political and regulatory situation will affect how they handle business and financial matters.[18]

Companies must also consider a country's monetary regulations. Sellers want to take their profits in a currency of value to them. Ideally, the buyer can pay in the seller's currency or in other world currencies. Short of this, sellers might accept a blocked currency—one whose removal from the country is restricted by the buyer's government—if they can buy other goods in that country that they need themselves or can sell elsewhere for a needed currency. In addition to currency limits, a changing exchange rate also creates high risks for the seller.

Most international trade involves cash transactions. Yet many nations have too little hard currency to pay for their purchases from other countries. They may want to pay with other items instead of cash. For example, *barter* involves the direct exchange of goods or services: China recently agreed to help the Democratic Republic of Congo develop $6 billion of desperately needed infrastructure—2,400 miles of road, 2,000 miles of railway, 32 hospitals, 145 health centers, and two universities—in exchange for natural resources needed to feed China's booming industries—10 million tons of copper and 400,000 tons of cobalt.[19]

Cultural Environment

Each country has its own folkways, norms, and taboos. When designing global marketing strategies, companies must understand how culture affects consumer reactions in each of its world markets. In turn, they must also understand how their strategies affect local cultures.

The Impact of Culture on Marketing Strategy

The seller must understand the ways that consumers in different countries think about and use certain products before planning a marketing program. There are often surprises. For example, the average French man uses almost twice as many cosmetics and grooming aids as his wife. The Germans and the French eat more packaged, branded spaghetti than do Italians. Some 49 percent of Chinese eat on the way to work. Most American women let down their hair and take off makeup at bedtime, whereas 15 percent of Chinese women style their hair at bedtime and 11 percent put *on* makeup.[20]

Companies that ignore cultural norms and differences can make some very expensive and embarrassing mistakes. Here are examples:

> Nike inadvertently offended Chinese officials when it ran an advertisement featuring LeBron James crushing a number of culturally revered Chinese figures in a kung fu-themed TV spot. ▲ The Chinese government found that the ad violated regulations to uphold na-

▲Overlooking cultural differences can result in embarrassing mistakes. China imposed a nationwide ban on this "blasphemous" kung fu-themed TV spot featuring LeBron James crushing a number of culturally revered Chinese figures.

tional dignity and respect of the "motherland's culture" and yanked the multimillion-dollar campaign. With egg on its face, Nike released a formal apology. Burger King made a similar mistake when it created in-store ads in Spain showing Hindu goddess Lakshmi atop a ham sandwich with the caption "a snack that is sacred." Cultural and religious groups worldwide objected strenuously—Hindus are vegetarian. Burger King apologized and pulled the ads.[21]

Business norms and behavior also vary from country to country. For example, American executives like to get right down to business and engage in fast and tough face-to-face bargaining. However, Japanese and other Asian businesspeople often find this behavior offensive. They prefer to start with polite conversation, and they rarely say no in face-to-face conversations. As another example, South Americans like to sit or stand very close to each other when they talk business—in fact, almost nose-to-nose. The American business executive tends to keep backing away as the South American moves closer. Both may end up being offended. American business executives need to be briefed on these kinds of factors before conducting business in another country.

By the same token, companies that understand cultural nuances can use them to their advantage when positioning products and preparing campaigns internationally. Consider LG Electronics, the $63 billion South Korean electronics, telecommunications, and appliance powerhouse. LG now operates in more than 60 countries and captures 81 percent of its sales from markets outside its home country. LG's global success rests on understanding and catering to the unique characteristics of each local market through in-country research, manufacturing, and marketing.[22]

If you've got kimchi in your fridge, it's hard to keep it a secret. Made from fermented cabbage seasoned with garlic and chili, kimchi is served with most meals in Korea. But when it's stored inside a normal refrigerator, its pungent odor taints nearby foods. That's why, two decades ago, LG introduced the kimchi refrigerator, featuring a dedicated compartment that isolates smelly kimchi from other foods. Kimchi refrigerators now have become a fixture in 65 percent of Korean homes, and LG is the country's top-selling manufacturer.

LG's mission is to make customers happy worldwide by creating products to change their lives, no matter where they live. In India, LG rolled out refrigerators with larger vegetable- and water-storage compartments, surge-resistant power supplies, and brightly colored finishes that reflect local preferences (red in the south, green in Kashmir). Some of LG's Indian microwaves have dark-colored interiors to hide masala stains. In Iran, LG offers a microwave oven with a preset button for reheating shish kebabs—a favorite dish. In the Middle East, the company unveiled a gold-plated 71-inch flat-screen television that sells for $80,000—a tribute to the region's famous affinity for gilded opulence. And in Russia, where many people entertain at home during the country's long winters, LG developed a karaoke phone that can be programmed with the top 100 Russian songs, whose lyrics scroll across the screen when they're played. The phone sold more than 220,000 handsets in the first year.

Thus, understanding cultural traditions, preferences, and behaviors can help companies not only to avoid embarrassing mistakes but also to take advantage of cross-cultural opportunities.

The Impact of Marketing Strategy on Cultures

Whereas marketers worry about the impact of culture on their global marketing strategies, others may worry about the impact of marketing strategies on global cultures. For example, social critics contend that large American multinationals such as McDonald's, Coca-Cola, Starbucks, Nike, Microsoft, Disney, and MTV aren't just "globalizing" their brands, they are "Americanizing" the world's cultures.

Down in the mall, between the fast-food joint and the bagel shop, a group of young people huddle in a flurry of baggy combat pants, skateboards, and slang. They size up a woman teetering past wearing DKNY, carrying *Time* magazine in one hand and a latte in the other. She brushes past a guy in a Yankees baseball cap who is talking on his Motorola cell phone about the Martin Scorsese film he saw last night.

It's a standard American scene—only this isn't America, it's Britain. U.S. culture is so pervasive, the scene could be played out in any one of dozens of cities. Budapest or Berlin, if not Bogota or Bordeaux. Even Manila or Moscow. As the unrivaled global superpower, America exports its culture on an unprecedented scale. . . . Sometimes, U.S. ideals get transmitted—such as individual rights, freedom of speech, and respect for women—and local cultures are enriched. At other times, materialism or worse becomes the message and local traditions get crushed.[23]

"Today, globalization often wears Mickey Mouse ears, eats Big Macs, drinks Coke or Pepsi, and does its computing [with Microsoft] Windows [software]," says Thomas Friedman, in his book *The Lexus and the Olive Tree*.[24] Critics worry that, under such "McDomination," countries around the globe are losing their individual cultural identities. Teens in India watch MTV and ask their parents for more westernized clothes and other symbols of American pop culture and values. Grandmothers in small European villas no longer spend each morning visiting local meat, bread, and produce markets to gather the ingredients for dinner. Instead, they now shop at Wal-Mart Supercenters. Women in Saudi Arabia see American films and question their societal roles. In China, most people never drank coffee before Starbucks entered the market. Now Chinese consumers rush to Starbucks stores "because it's a symbol of a new kind of lifestyle." Similarly, in China, where McDonald's operates more than 80 restaurants in Beijing alone, nearly half of all children identify the chain as a domestic brand.

Such concerns have sometimes led to a backlash against American globalization. Well-known U.S. brands have become the targets of boycotts and protests in some international markets. As symbols of American capitalism, companies such as Coca-Cola, McDonald's, Nike, and KFC have been singled out by antiglobalization protestors in hot spots all around the world, especially when anti-American sentiment peaks.

Despite such problems, defenders of globalization argue that concerns of "Americanization" and the potential damage to American brands are overblown. U.S. brands are doing very well internationally. In the most recent Millward Brown Optimor brand value survey of global consumer brands, 8 of the top 10 brands were American-owned, including megabrands such as Google, Microsoft, Coca-Cola, IBM, McDonald's, Apple, and GE.[25] ▲Many iconic American brands are prospering globally, even in some of the most unlikely places:[26]

▼Many iconic American brands are prospering globally, even in some of the most unlikely places. At this Tehran restaurant, American colas are the drink of choice. Coke and Pepsi have grabbed about half the national soft drink sales in Iran.

It's lunchtime in Tehran's tiny northern suburbs, and around the crowded tables at Nayeb restaurant, elegant Iranian women in Jackie O sunglasses and designer jeans let their table chatter glide effortlessly between French, English, and their native Farsi. The only visual clues that these lunching ladies aren't dining at some smart New York City eatery but in the heart of Washington's Axis of Evil are the expensive Hermès scarves covering their blonde-tipped hair in deference to the mullahs. And the drink of choice? This being revolutionary Iran, where alcohol is banned, the women are making do with Coca-Cola. Yes, Coca-Cola. It's a hard fact for some of Iran's theocrats to swallow. They want Iranians to shun "Great Satan" brands like Coke and Pepsi, and the Iranian government has recently pressured Iranian soft drink companies to clarify their "ties with the Zionist company Coca-Cola." Yet, Coke and Pepsi have grabbed about half the national soft drink sales in Iran, one of the Middle East's biggest drink markets. "I joke with customers not to buy this stuff because it's American," says a Tehran storekeeper, "but they don't care. That only makes them want to buy it more."

More fundamentally, the cultural exchange goes both ways—America gets as well as gives cultural influence. True, Hollywood dominates the global movie market, but British TV gives as much as it gets in dishing out competition to U.S. shows, spawning such hits as *The Office, American Idol,* and *Dancing with the Stars.* Although Chinese and Russian youth are donning NBA superstar jerseys, the increasing popularity of American soccer has deep international roots. Even American childhood has been increasingly influenced by European and Asian cultural imports. Most kids know all about imports such as Hello Kitty, the Bakugan Battle Brawler, or any of a host of Nintendo or Sega game characters. And J. K. Rowling's so-very-British Harry Potter books have shaped the thinking of a generation of American youngsters, not to mention the millions of American oldsters who've fallen under their spell as well. For the moment, English remains the dominant language of the Internet, and having Web access often means that third-world youth have greater exposure to American popular culture. Yet these same technologies let Eastern European students studying in the United States hear Webcast news and music from Poland, Romania, or Belarus.

American companies have also learned that to succeed abroad they must adapt to local cultural values and traditions rather than trying to force their own. Disneyland Paris flopped at first because it failed to take local cultural values and behaviors into account. Once the theme park began adapting to the individual cultures and travel habits of European travelers, business picked up. The movie-themed Walt Disney Studios Park now blends Disney entertainment and attractions with the history and culture of European film. A show celebrating the history of animation features Disney characters speaking six different languages. Rides are narrated by foreign-born stars speaking in their native tongues. Disneyland Paris is now the number-one tourist attraction in Europe.

Thus, globalization is a two-way street. If globalization has Mickey Mouse ears, it is also wearing a French beret, talking on a Nokia cell phone, buying furniture at IKEA, driving a Toyota Camry, and watching a Pioneer big-screen plasma TV.

DECIDING WHETHER TO GO GLOBAL (pp 517–518)

▼Going global: Coca-Cola has emphasized international growth in recent years to offset stagnant or declining U.S. soft drink sales.

Not all companies need to venture into international markets to survive. For example, most local businesses need to market well only in the local marketplace. Operating domestically is easier and safer. Managers don't need to learn another country's language and laws. They don't have to deal with unstable currencies, face political and legal uncertainties, or redesign their products to suit different customer expectations. However, companies that operate in global industries, where their strategic positions in specific markets are affected strongly by their overall global positions, must compete on a regional or worldwide basis to succeed.

Any of several factors might draw a company into the international arena. Global competitors might attack the company's home market by offering better products or lower prices. The company might want to counterattack these competitors in their home markets to tie up their resources. The company's customers might be expanding abroad and require international servicing. Or most likely, international markets might simply provide better opportunities for growth. ▲For example, Coca-Cola has emphasized international growth in recent years to offset stagnant or declining U.S. soft drink sales. "It's been apparent that Coke's signature cola can't grow much on its home turf anymore," states an industry analyst. Today, about 80 percent of Coke's profits come outside North America.[27]

Before going abroad, the company must weigh several risks and answer many questions about its ability to operate globally. Can the company learn to understand the preferences and buyer behavior of consumers in other countries? Can it offer competitively attractive products? Will it be able to adapt to other countries' business cultures and deal effectively with foreign nationals? Do the company's managers have the necessary international experience? Has management considered the impact of regulations and the political environments of other countries?[28]

Because of the difficulties of entering international markets, most companies do not act until some situation or event thrusts them into the global arena. Someone—a domestic exporter, a foreign importer, a foreign government—may ask the company to sell abroad. Or the company may be saddled with overcapacity and need to find additional markets for its goods.

DECIDING WHICH MARKETS TO ENTER (pp 518–519)

Before going abroad, the company should try to define its international *marketing objectives and policies*. It should decide what *volume* of foreign sales it wants. Most companies start small when they go abroad. Some plan to stay small, seeing international sales as a small part of their business. Other companies have bigger plans, seeing international business as equal to or even more important than their domestic business.

The company also needs to choose in *how many* countries it wants to market. Companies must be careful not to spread themselves too thin or to expand beyond their capabilities by operating in too many countries too soon. Next, the company needs to decide on the *types* of countries to enter. A country's attractiveness depends on the product, geographical factors, income and population, political climate, and other factors. The seller may prefer certain country groups or parts of the world. In recent years, many major new markets have emerged, offering both substantial opportunities and daunting challenges.

▼Procter & Gamble's decision to enter the Chinese toothpaste market with Crest is a no-brainer: China is the world's largest toothpaste market. But P&G must still question whether market size alone is reason enough for investing heavily in China.

After listing possible international markets, the company must carefully evaluate each one. It must consider many factors. ▲For example, P&G's decision to enter the Chinese toothpaste market with its Crest is a no-brainer: China's huge population makes it the world's largest toothpaste market. And given that only 20 percent of China's rural dwellers now brush daily, this already huge market can grow even larger. Yet P&G must still question whether market size *alone* is reason enough for investing heavily in China.

Procter & Gamble should ask some important questions: Can Crest compete effectively with dozens of local competitors, Colgate, and a state-owned brand managed by Unilever? Will the Chinese government remain stable and supportive? Does China provide for the needed production and distribution technologies? Can the company master China's vastly different cultural and buying differences? Crest's current success in China suggests that it could answer yes to all of these questions.[29]

"Just 10 years ago, P&G's Crest brand was unknown to China's population, most of whom seldom—if ever—brushed their teeth," says one analyst. "Now

P&G . . . sells more tubes of toothpaste there than it does in America, where Crest has been on store shelves for 52 years." P&G achieved this by sending researchers to get a feel for what urban and rural Chinese were willing to spend and what flavors they preferred. It discovered that urban Chinese are happy to pay more than $1 for tubes of Crest with exotic flavors such as Icy Mountain Spring and Morning Lotus Fragrance. But Chinese living in the countryside prefer the 50-cent Crest Salt White, since many rural Chinese believe that salt whitens the teeth. Armed with such insights, Crest now leads all competitors in China with a 25 percent market share. P&G hopes to find similar success in other emerging markets across its entire product mix. Such markets now account for 30 percent of the company's total sales.

Possible global markets should be ranked on several factors, including market size, market growth, cost of doing business, competitive advantage, and risk level. The goal is to determine the potential of each market, using indicators such as those shown in ■ **Table 15.1**. Then the marketer must decide which markets offer the greatest long-run return on investment.

Author Comment »
A company has many options for entering an international market, from simply exporting its products to working jointly with foreign companies to holding its own foreign-based operations.

DECIDING HOW TO ENTER THE MARKET (pp 519–522)

Once a company has decided to sell in a foreign country, it must determine the best mode of entry. Its choices are *exporting, joint venturing*, and *direct investment*. ■ **Figure 15.2** shows three market entry strategies, along with the options each one offers. As the figure shows, each succeeding strategy involves more commitment and risk, but also more control and potential profits.

■ **Table 15.1** Indicators of Market Potential

Demographic Characteristics	Sociocultural Factors
Education	Consumer lifestyles, beliefs, and values
Population size and growth	Business norms and approaches
Population age composition	Cultural and social norms
	Languages

Geographic Characteristics	Political and Legal Factors
Climate	National priorities
Country size	Political stability
Population density—urban, rural	Government attitudes toward global trade
Transportation structure and market accessibility	Government bureaucracy
	Monetary and trade regulations

Economic Factors
GDP size and growth
Income distribution
Industrial infrastructure
Natural resources
Financial and human resources

■ **Figure 15.2** Market Entry Strategies

> Exporting is the simplest way to enter a foreign market, but it usually offers less control and profit potential.

> Direct investment—owning your own foreign-based operation—affords greater control and profit potential, but it's often riskier.

Exporting

Exporting
Entering a foreign market by selling goods produced in the company's home country, often with little modification.

The simplest way to enter a foreign market is through **exporting**. The company may passively export its surpluses from time to time, or it may make an active commitment to expand exports to a particular market. In either case, the company produces all its goods in its home country. It may or may not modify them for the export market. Exporting involves the least change in the company's product lines, organization, investments, or mission.

Companies typically start with *indirect exporting*, working through independent international marketing intermediaries. Indirect exporting involves less investment because the firm does not require an overseas marketing organization or network. It also involves less risk. International marketing intermediaries bring know-how and services to the relationship, so the seller normally makes fewer mistakes.

Sellers may eventually move into *direct exporting*, whereby they handle their own exports. The investment and risk are somewhat greater in this strategy, but so is the potential return. A company can conduct direct exporting in several ways: It can set up a domestic export department that carries out export activities. It can set up an overseas sales branch that handles sales, distribution, and perhaps promotion. The sales branch gives the seller more presence and program control in the foreign market and often serves as a display center and customer-service center. The company can also send home-based salespeople abroad at certain times in order to find business. Finally, the company can do its exporting either through foreign-based distributors who buy and own the goods or through foreign-based agents who sell the goods on behalf of the company.

Joint Venturing

Joint venturing
Entering foreign markets by joining with foreign companies to produce or market a product or service.

A second method of entering a foreign market is **joint venturing**—joining with foreign companies to produce or market products or services. Joint venturing differs from exporting in that the company joins with a host country partner to sell or market abroad. It differs from direct investment in that an association is formed with someone in the foreign country. There are four types of joint ventures: licensing, contract manufacturing, management contracting, and joint ownership.

Licensing

Licensing
A method of entering a foreign market in which the company enters into an agreement with a licensee in the foreign market.

Licensing is a simple way for a manufacturer to enter international marketing. The company enters into an agreement with a licensee in the foreign market. For a fee or royalty, the licensee buys the right to use the company's manufacturing process, trademark, patent, trade secret, or other item of value. The company thus gains entry into the market at little risk; the licensee gains production expertise or a well-known product or name without having to start from scratch.

In Japan, Budweiser beer flows from Kirin breweries and ▲Sunkist fruit juice, drinks, and dessert items are produced by Moringa Milk Company. British-owned Cadbury licenses Hershey to manufacture its chocolates in the United States. And Coca-Cola markets internationally by licensing bottlers around the

▲Licensing: In Japan, Sunkist fruit juices, drinks, and dessert items are produced by Moringa Milk Company.

Contract manufacturing
A joint venture in which a company contracts with manufacturers in a foreign market to produce the product or provide its service.

Management contracting
A joint venture in which the domestic firm supplies the management know-how to a foreign company that supplies the capital; the domestic firm exports management services rather than products.

Joint ownership
A joint venture in which a company joins investors in a foreign market to create a local business in which the company shares joint ownership and control.

world and supplying them with the syrup needed to produce the product. Its global bottling partners range from the Coca-Cola Bottling Company of Saudi Arabia to huge, Europe-based Coca-Cola Hellenic, which bottles and markets Coca-Cola products to 560 million people in 28 countries, from Italy and Greece to Nigeria and Russia.

Licensing has potential disadvantages, however. The firm has less control over the licensee than it would over its own operations. Furthermore, if the licensee is very successful, the firm has given up these profits, and if and when the contract ends, it may find it has created a competitor.

Contract Manufacturing

Another option is **contract manufacturing**—the company contracts with manufacturers in the foreign market to produce its product or provide its service. Sears used this method in opening up department stores in Mexico and Spain, where it found qualified local manufacturers to produce many of the products it sells. The drawbacks of contract manufacturing are decreased control over the manufacturing process and loss of potential profits on manufacturing. The benefits are the chance to start faster, with less risk, and the later opportunity either to form a partnership with or to buy out the local manufacturer.

Management Contracting

Under **management contracting**, the domestic firm supplies management know-how to a foreign company that supplies the capital. The domestic firm exports management services rather than products. Hilton uses this arrangement in managing hotels around the world. For example, the hotel chain recently signed an agreement by which its new luxury hotel in Pattaya, Thailand will be managed by CPN Pattaya Beach Company, a firm that is well acquainted with the ins and outs of Thai tourism.[30]

Management contracting is a low-risk method of getting into a foreign market, and it yields income from the beginning. The arrangement is even more attractive if the contracting firm has an option to buy some share in the managed company later on. The arrangement is not sensible, however, if the company can put its scarce management talent to better uses or if it can make greater profits by undertaking the whole venture. Management contracting also prevents the company from setting up its own operations for a period of time.

Joint Ownership

Joint ownership ventures consist of one company joining forces with foreign investors to create a local business in which they share joint ownership and control. A company may buy an interest in a local firm, or the two parties may form a new business venture. Joint ownership may be needed for economic or political reasons. The firm may lack the financial, physical, or managerial resources to undertake the venture alone. Or a foreign government may require joint ownership as a condition for entry.

Hershey recently formed a joint venture with Indian-based Godrej Beverages and Foods to make and distribute its chocolates in that country. ▲When it comes to selling chocolate in India, Hershey will need all the help it can get from its new local partner.[31]

"Humans may have first cultivated a taste for chocolate 3,000 years ago," comments one observer, "but India [has] just gotten around to it. Compared to the sweet-toothed Swiss

▲ **Hershey recently formed a joint venture with Indian-based Godrej Beverages and Foods to make and distribute its chocolates in that country.**

and Cadbury-crunching Brits, both of whom devour about 24 pounds of chocolate per capita annually, Indians consume a paltry 5.8 ounces." Indian consumers currently favor a traditional candy known as mithai, and it will take a significant and culturally savvy marketing effort to persuade them to transfer their allegiance to chocolate. To make things even tougher, two global giants—Nestlé and Cadbury—already hold a 90 percent share of Indian chocolate between them. Still, given the sheer size of the Indian population, as discussed earlier in the chapter, if consumers can be persuaded to acquire a taste for chocolate, the rewards for Hershey and Godrej could be substantial. Either company could have decided to go it alone, but both will likely benefit greatly from the joint venture. Godrej gains a highly respected global brand; Hershey reaps the benefits of a local partner that understands the intricacies of the Indian market.

Joint ownership has certain drawbacks. The partners may disagree over investment, marketing, or other policies. Whereas many U.S. firms like to reinvest earnings for growth, local firms often prefer to take out these earnings; and whereas U.S. firms emphasize the role of marketing, local investors may rely on selling.

Direct Investment

Direct investment
Entering a foreign market by developing foreign-based assembly or manufacturing facilities.

The biggest involvement in a foreign market comes through **direct investment**—the development of foreign-based assembly or manufacturing facilities. For example, HP has made direct investments in a number of major markets abroad, including India. It recently opened a second factory near Delhi to make PCs for the local market, along with opening HP-owned retail outlets in 150 Indian cities. Thanks to such commitments, HP has overtaken the favorite local brand, HCL, and now controls more than 21 percent of the market in India.[32]

If a company has gained experience in exporting and if the foreign market is large enough, foreign production facilities offer many advantages. The firm may have lower costs in the form of cheaper labor or raw materials, foreign government investment incentives, and freight savings. The firm may improve its image in the host country because it creates jobs. Generally, a firm develops a deeper relationship with government, customers, local suppliers, and distributors, allowing it to adapt its products to the local market better. Finally, the firm keeps full control over the investment and therefore can develop manufacturing and marketing policies that serve its long-term international objectives.

The main disadvantage of direct investment is that the firm faces many risks, such as restricted or devalued currencies, falling markets, or government changes. In some cases, a firm has no choice but to accept these risks if it wants to operate in the host country.

 Speed Bump: Linking the Concepts

Slow down here and think again about McDonald's global marketing issues.

- To what extent can McDonald's standardize for the Chinese market? What marketing strategy and program elements can be similar to those used in the United States and other parts of the Western world? Which ones must be adapted? Be specific.
- To what extent can McDonald's standardize its products and programs for the Canadian market? What elements can be standardized and which must be adapted?
- To what extent are McDonald's "globalization" efforts contributing to "Americanization" of countries and cultures around the world? What are the positives and negatives of such cultural developments?

Author Comment »
The major global marketing decision usually boils down to this: How much, if at all, should we adapt our marketing strategy and programs to local markets? How would the answer differ for Boeing versus McDonald's?

DECIDING ON THE GLOBAL MARKETING PROGRAM (pp 523–530)

Companies that operate in one or more foreign markets must decide how much, if at all, to adapt their marketing strategies and programs to local conditions. At one extreme are global companies that use **standardized global marketing**, using largely the same marketing strategy approaches and marketing mix worldwide. At the other extreme is **adapted global marketing**. In this case, the producer adjusts the marketing strategy and mix elements to each target market, bearing more costs but hoping for a larger market share and return.

The question of whether to adapt or standardize the marketing strategy and program has been much debated over the years. On the one hand, some global marketers believe that technology is making the world a smaller place and that consumer needs around the world are becoming more similar. This paves the way for "global brands" and standardized global marketing. Global branding and standardization, in turn, result in greater brand power and reduced costs from economies of scale.

On the other hand, the marketing concept holds that marketing programs will be more effective if tailored to the unique needs of each targeted customer group. If this concept applies within a country, it should apply even more across international markets. Despite global convergence, consumers in different countries still have widely varied cultural backgrounds. They still differ significantly in their needs and wants, spending power, product preferences, and shopping patterns. Because these differences are hard to change, most marketers today adapt their products, prices, channels, and promotions to fit consumer desires in each country.

However, global standardization is not an all-or-nothing proposition. It's a matter of degree. Most international marketers suggest that companies should "think globally but act locally" — that they should seek a balance between standardization and adaptation. The company's overall strategy should provide global strategic direction. Then, regional or local units should focus on adapting the strategy to specific local markets.

Collectively, local brands still account for the overwhelming majority of consumers' purchases. "The vast majority of people still lead very local lives," says a global analyst. "By all means go global, but the first thing you have to do is win on the ground. You have to go local." Another analyst agrees: "You need to respect local culture and become part of it." A global brand must "engage with consumers in a way that feels local to them." Simon Clift, head of marketing for global consumer-goods giant Unilever, puts it this way: "We're trying to strike a balance between being mindlessly global and hopelessly local."[33]

McDonald's operates this way: It uses the same basic fast-food look, layout, and operating model in its restaurants around the world but adapts its menu to local tastes. In Japan, it offers up Ebi Filet-O-Shrimp burgers and fancy Salad Macs salad plates. In Korea it sells the Bulgogi Burger, a grilled pork patty on a bun with a garlicky soy sauce. In India, where cows are considered sacred, McDonald's serves McChicken, Filet-O-Fish, McVeggie (a vegetable burger), Pizza McPuffs, McAloo Tikki (a spiced-potato burger), and the Maharaja Mac—two all-chicken patties, special sauce, lettuce, cheese, pickles, onions on a sesame-seed bun.

Similarly, to boost sales of Oreo cookies in China, Kraft Foods has tweaked its recipes and marketing programs to meet the tastes of Chinese consumers. It even developed a brand new Chinese version of the all-American classic (see Marketing at Work 15.1).

Product

Five strategies allow for adapting product and marketing communication strategies to a global market (see ■ **Figure 15.3**).[34] We first discuss the three product strategies and then turn to the two communication strategies.

Straight product extension means marketing a product in a foreign market without any change. Top management tells its marketing people, "Take the product as is and find customers for it." The first step, however, should be to find out whether foreign consumers use that product and what form they prefer.

Standardized global marketing
An international marketing strategy for using basically the same marketing strategy and mix in all the company's international markets.

Adapted global marketing
An international marketing strategy for adjusting the marketing strategy and mix elements to each international target market, bearing more costs but hoping for a larger market share and return.

Straight product extension
Marketing a product in a foreign market without any change.

Marketing at Work 15.1

Oreos and Milk, Chinese Style

Unlike its iconic American version, the most popular Oreo cookie in China is long, thin, four-layered, and coated in chocolate. Still, the two kinds of Oreos, sold half a world apart, have one important thing in common: Both are now best-sellers. But taking the dark chocolate American treasure to China has been no easy journey for Kraft Foods. Although the Oreo has long been the top-selling cookie in the United States, to make Oreos sell well in the world's most populous nation, Kraft had to completely reinvent the popular cookie.

Oreos were first introduced in the United States in 1912, but it wasn't until 1996 that Kraft introduced Oreos to Chinese consumers. It began by selling the same old Oreos in China that it markets in the United States—the ones that Americans love to twist apart to lick the creamy centers or dunk in milk until they're soggy. However, after nine years of trying mostly U.S. marketing themes and programs on Chinese consumers, Oreo sales remained flat. Albert Einstein's definition of insanity—doing the same thing repeatedly and expecting different results—"characterized what we were doing," says Kraft Foods International's vice president of marketing. To make things happen, he concluded, it was time for a major Oreo makeover.

First up: Kraft changed the Oreo management team. Whereas previous decisions about Oreo marketing in China had been made at arm's length by people in Kraft's Northbrook, Illinois, headquarters, the company now handed the task of re-making the brand to an entrepreneurial team of local Chinese managers. The team began with in-depth research on Chinese consumers that yielded some interesting findings. First, the team learned, the Chinese weren't big cookie eaters. Despite China's immense population, the Chinese biscuit and cookie market was one-third the size of the U.S. market. Second, Chinese consumers weren't much enamored with the Oreos

▲ To make Oreo cookies sell well in China, Kraft completely reinvented the popular all-American classic.

that Americans have come to crave. Traditional Oreos were too sweet for Chinese tastes. Also, standard packages of 14 Oreos, priced at 72 cents, were too expensive for most Chinese food budgets, where average annual per capita income is only about $1,900.

So for starters, the company developed 20 prototypes of re-duced-sugar Oreos and tested them with Chinese consumers before arriving at a formula that tasted right. Kraft also intro-duced packages containing fewer Oreos for just 29 cents.

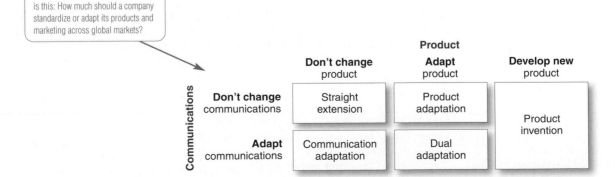

The real question buried in this figure is this: How much should a company standardize or adapt its products and marketing across global markets?

	Product		
Communications	**Don't change** product	**Adapt** product	**Develop new** product
Don't change communications	Straight extension	Product adaptation	Product invention
Adapt communications	Communication adaptation	Dual adaptation	

■ **Figure 15.3** Five Global Product and Communications Strategies

However, some Chinese consumers still found even the reformulated Oreos too sweet. Said one 30-year-old consumer in the eastern part of Beijing, he liked the cookie but "many of my friends think I am a bit weird to stick to Oreo cookies—most think them too sweet to be accepted."

Kraft's research also revealed that Chinese consumers have a growing thirst for milk, which Kraft wasn't fully exploiting. So Kraft began a grassroots marketing campaign to educate Chinese consumers about the American tradition of pairing milk with cookies. The company created Oreo apprentice programs at 30 Chinese universities that drew 6,000 student applications. Three hundred of the applicants were trained to become Oreo brand ambassadors. Some of the students rode around Beijing on bicycles, outfitted with wheel covers resembling Oreos, and handed out cookies to more than 300,000 consumers.

Other ambassadors held Oreo-themed basketball games to reinforce the idea of dunking cookies in milk. Television commercials showed kids twisting apart Oreo cookies, licking the cream center, and dipping the chocolate cookie halves into glasses of milk. Kraft CEO Irene Rosenfeld calls the bicycle campaign "a stroke of genius that only could have come from local managers. [Letting] our local managers deal with local conditions will be a source of competitive advantage for us."

The product and marketing changes made a difference and Oreo sales in China improved. However, Kraft knew that if it was really serious about capturing a bigger share of the Chinese biscuit market, it needed to do more than just tweak its U.S. Oreo recipe and marketing. It needed to remake the Oreo itself.

So in 2006, Kraft introduced a second Oreo in China, one that looked almost nothing like the original. The new Chinese Oreo consisted of four layers of crispy wafer filled with vanilla and chocolate cream, coated in chocolate. The new Oreo was designed not only to satisfy the cravings of China's consumers,

but also stand up to the challenges of selling and distributing across China's vast landscape. Kraft even developed a proprietary handling process to ensure that the chocolate product could withstand the cold climate in the north and the hot, humid weather in the south, yet still be ready to melt in the customer's mouth.

Kraft's efforts to reshape the Oreo brand and its marketing have paid off. Within a year of introduction, Oreo WaferSticks became the best-selling biscuit in China, outpacing HaoChiDian, a biscuit brand made by Chinese company Dali. The new Oreos are also outselling traditional round Oreos in China, and Kraft has begun selling the wafers elsewhere in Asia, as well as in Australia and Canada. Over the past two years, Kraft has doubled its Oreo revenues in China.

What's more, Kraft has learned, its "think globally, act locally" approach applies not just to Oreos and not just in China but to all of its products worldwide. For example, to take advantage of the European preference for dark chocolate, Kraft recently introduced dark chocolate in Germany under its Milka brand. Research in Russia showed that consumers there like premium instant coffee, so Kraft is positioning its Carte Noire freeze-dried coffee as upscale by placing it at film festivals, fashion shows, and operas. And in the Philippines, where iced tea is popular, Kraft last year launched iced-tea-flavored Tang. As a result of such moves, international business now represents 49 percent of Kraft's total sales. Kraft's profit in the European Union last year rose 41.6 percent, and profits in developing countries rose 31.6 percent, far outpacing U.S. profit growth.

Sources: Adapted from portions of Julie Jargon, "Kraft Reformulated Oreo, Scores in China," *Wall Street Journal*, May 1, 2008, p. B1; with information from "Kraft Foods Upbeat on 2009 China Sales," *Reuters*, June 6, 2009, accessed at *www.guardian.co.uk/business/feedarticle/8542629*; and www.kraft.com, accessed December 2009.

Straight extension has been successful in some cases and disastrous in others. Apple iPods, Gillette razors, Heineken beer, and Black & Decker tools are all sold successfully in about the same form around the world. But General Foods introduced its standard powdered JELL-O in the British market only to find that British consumers prefer a solid wafer or cake form. Likewise, Philips began to make a profit in Japan only after it reduced the size of its coffeemakers to fit into smaller Japanese kitchens and its shavers to fit smaller Japanese hands. Straight extension is tempting because it involves no additional product development costs, manufacturing changes, or new promotion. But it can be costly in the long run if products fail to satisfy consumers in specific global markets.

Product adaptation involves changing the product to meet local conditions or wants. For example, Finnish cell phone maker Nokia customizes its cell phones for every major market. Developers build in rudimentary voice recognition for Asia where keyboards are a problem and raise the ring volume so phones can be heard on crowded Asian streets. Nokia is also making a major push to create full-featured

Product adaptation
Adapting a product to meet local conditions or wants in foreign markets.

Objective 4 Identify the three major forms of international marketing organization. **(pp 530–531)**

The company must develop an effective organization for international marketing. Most firms start with an *export department* and graduate to an *international division*. A few become *global organizations*, with worldwide marketing planned and managed by the top officers of the company. Global organizations view the entire world as a single, borderless market.

Navigating the Key Terms

Objective 1
Global firm (p 509)
Economic community (p 511)

Objective 2
Exporting (p 520)
Joint venturing (p 520)
Licensing (p 520)

Contract manufacturing (p 521)
Management contracting (p 521)
Joint ownership (p 521)
Direct investment (p 522)

Objective 3
Standardized global marketing (p 523)

Adapted global marketing (p 523)
Straight product extension (p 523)
Product adaptation (p 525)
Product invention (p 526)
Communication adaptation (p 527)
Whole-channel view (p 529)

Travel Log

Discussing the Issues

1. Explain what is meant by the term *global firm*. (AACSB: Communication)

2. Explain the concept of *economic community* and give examples of economic communities. (AACSB: Communication)

3. Discuss the four types of country industrial structures and the opportunities each offers to international marketers. (AACSB: Communication)

4. What factors do companies consider when deciding on possible global markets to enter? (AACSB: Communication; Reflective Thinking)

5. Discuss the strategies used for adapting product strategies to a global market. Which strategy is best? (AACSB: Communication)

6. Discuss how global distribution channels differ from domestic channels. (AACSB: Communication)

Application Questions

1. A new U.S.-based manufacturer of an electric automobile, called the V-Vehicle, has plans to grow internationally as well as domestically once the car gets into production. In a small group, select a country and write a report explaining how the economic, political-legal, and cultural environments will influence the marketing of this car in that country. The V-Vehicle is expected to be priced at $10,000 in the United States. Suggest a price for this car—in your country's currency—and justify your recommendation. What does your suggested price convert to in U.S. dollars? (AACSB: Communication; Reflective Thinking)

2. The United States restricts trade with Cuba. Visit the U.S. Department of the Treasury at www.ustreas.gov/offices/enforcement/ofac to learn more about economic and trade sanctions. Click on the "Cuba Sanctions" link to learn more about the trade restrictions on Cuba. Are these tariff, quota, or embargo restrictions? To what extent do these trade restrictions allow U.S. businesses to export their products to Cuba? (AACSB: Communication; Use of IT; Reflective Thinking)

3. One way to analyze the cultural differences among countries is to conduct a Hofstede analysis. Visit http://www.geert-hofstede.com/ to learn what this analysis considers. Develop a presentation explaining how three countries of your choice differ from the United States. (AACSB: Communication; Use of IT; Reflective Thinking)

Under the Hood: Marketing Technology

China is the second largest computer market behind the United States, so computer manufacturers want to stay on the Chinese government's good side. That's why many of them are including China's Green Dam Web filtering software, either preinstalled or on a CD-ROM, even though the Chinese government delayed requiring it. China's Ministry of Industry and Information Technology wants the software included to keep children from seeing harmful Internet content. Critics claim, however, that the software violates consumers' rights. Web censorship is spreading throughout much of Southeast Asia—to Saudi Arabia, Iran, Malaysia, Thailand, and Vietnam, for example—but only China and other larger countries have the technology and resources to effectively police the Internet. Even these countries are finding that technology alone cannot stop dissent because people find ways around the technology. As a result, some governments make it a crime to disparage authorities on the Internet.

1. When companies such as Acer, a Taiwan-based computer manufacturer, include Web filtering software on computers sold in China, what global product strategy are they implementing? Explain. (AACSB: Communication; Reflective Thinking)

2. Which element of the global environment does Internet censoring represent? How is the global marketing strategy of computer manufacturers outside China and other Southeast Asia countries impacting those cultures? (AACSB: Communication; Reflective Thinking)

Staying on the Road: Marketing Ethics

Imagine Ford building a passenger van in Turkey, shipping it to the United States, and then ripping out the back windows and seats to convert it into a delivery van. The fabric and foam from the seats are shredded and become landfill cover while the steel and glass are recycled in other ways. Seems like a waste, doesn't it? Well, that's actually cheaper than to pay the 25 percent tariff Ford would have to pay to import its own delivery vans. The windows and seats are there just to get around an on-going trade spat with Europe, known as the "chicken tax." In the 1960s, Europe imposed high tariffs on imported chicken due to increased U.S. poultry sales to West Germany. It retaliation, U.S. President Johnson imposed a tax on imports of foreign-made trucks and commercial vans— specifically targeting German-made Volkswagens. The chicken tax has long pestered automakers. Even U.S. automobile companies like Ford must pay the tariff, which is ironic because U.S. trade rules have protected the U.S. automakers' truck market for years. However, converting the vehicle into a delivery truck after reaching our shores represents costs of 2.5 percent, significantly lower than the 25 percent tariff if the vehicle came into the country that way.

1. Should U.S. companies be penalized for importing their own products from other countries? (AACSB: Communication; Ethical Reasoning)

2. While Ford is complying "to the letter of the law," is what Ford doing right? (AACSB: Communication; Ethical Reasoning)

Rough Road Ahead: Marketing and the Economy

SPAM

For decades, SPAM (the Hormel canned meat product, not the unwanted e-mail) has been the brunt of bad jokes. But it's all in good fun, as consumers all around the world gobble up hundreds of millions of dollars worth of the pork concoction every year. In the United Kingdom, deep-fried SPAM slices, known as "SPAM fritters," adorn menus at fish and chips shops. In Japan, it's an ingredient in a popular stir fry dish. South Koreans eat the meat-on-a-shelf with rice or wrap it up in sushi rolls. In Hawaii, even McDonald's and Burger King sell SPAM specialties.

But here's one of the most interesting things about SPAM: what's been called the "SPAM Index." Over the years, SPAM sales have been so strongly inversely correlated with economic indicators, that some analysts consider the canned meat's revenues themselves as an index of economic conditions. The recent down cycle is no exception. SPAM has experienced double digit increases in sales ever since economists officially announced the beginning of the recent recession. Hormel responded by launching SPAM's first major ad campaign in five years. Radio, TV, and print ads carry a "Break the Monotony" message, showing how SPAM can breath new life into home-cooked meals. The Hormel Web site boasts 350 new SPAM recipes,

including Cheesy Country SPAM Puff, SPAMaroni, and SPAM Lettuce Wraps. A little bit of SPAM goes a long way.

1. Why does SPAM have such universal appeal to global consumers?

2. What recommendations would you make to Hormel to keep SPAM sales high when the economy is strong?

Travel Budget: Marketing by the Numbers

A country's import/export activity is revealed in its balance-of-payments statement. This statement includes three accounts: the current account, the capital account, and the reserves account. The current account is most relevant to marketing because it is a record of all merchandise exported from and imported into a country. The latter two accounts record financial transactions. The U.S. Department of Commerce's Bureau of Economic Analysis provides yearly and monthly figures on the country's trade in goods and services.

1. Visit www.bea.gov and find the U.S. trade in goods and services for 2008. What does that number mean? (AACSB: Communication; Use of IT; Reflective Thinking)

2. Search the Internet for China's balance of trade information for 2008. How does it compare to that of the U.S.? (AACSB: Communication; Use of IT; Reflective Thinking)

Drive In: Video Case

Monster

In 1994, Monster Worldwide pioneered job recruiting on the Internet with Monster.com. Today, it is the only online recruitment provider that can service job seekers and job posters on a truly global basis. With a presence in 50 countries around the world, Monster has unparalleled international reach. And although global economic woes have hindered the growth of corporations everywhere, Monster is investing heavily with plans to become even bigger worldwide. Most recently, Monster's international expansion has included the purchase of ChinaHR.com, giving it a strong presence in the world's largest country. Monster already gets about 45 percent of its annual revenue of $1.3 billion from outside the United States. But it expects to

become even more global in the coming years. To back that geographic expansion, Monster is also investing heavily in search technologies and Web design in order to appeal to clients everywhere.

After viewing the video featuring Monster Worldwide, answer the following questions about the company and the global marketplace:

1. Which of the five strategies for adapting products and promotion for global markets does Monster employ?

2. Which factors in the global marketing environment have challenged Monster's global marketing activities most? How has Monster met those challenges?

16 Sustainable Marketing
Social Responsibility and Ethics

ROAD MAP

Previewing the Concepts

In this final chapter, we'll examine the concepts of sustainable marketing, meeting the needs of consumers, businesses, and society—now and in the future—through socially and environmentally responsible marketing actions. We'll start by defining sustainable marketing and then look at some common criticisms of marketing as it impacts individual consumers and public actions that promote sustainable marketing. Finally, we'll see how companies themselves can benefit from proactively pursuing sustainable marketing practices that bring value not just to individual customers but also to society as a whole. You'll see that sustainable marketing actions are more than just the right thing to do; they're also good for business.

Objective Outline

> **Objective 1**   Define *sustainable marketing* and discuss its importance.
> Sustainable Marketing   **pp 539–540**

> **Objective 2**   Identify the major social criticisms of marketing.
> Social Criticisms of Marketing   **pp 540–549**

> **Objective 3**   Define *consumerism* and *environmentalism* and explain how they affect marketing strategies.
> Consumer Actions to Promote Sustainable Marketing
> **pp 549–558**

> **Objective 4**   Describe the principles of sustainable marketing.
> Business Actions Toward Sustainable Marketing
> **pp 558–563**

> **Objective 5**   Explain the role of ethics in marketing.
> Marketing Ethics   **pp 563–565**
> The Sustainable Company   **pp 565–567**

First, let's look at how businesses in the Middle East are taking corporate social responsibility (CSR) more and more seriously and recognizing that it is an integral part of today's business environment. Numerous initiatives are being set up by businesses and by governments across the Middle East.

First Stop

CSR Middle East: Promoting Corporate Social Responsibility

CSR Middle East is a nonprofit platform that promotes corporate social responsibility in the region and a network of CSR professionals who share CSR solutions and are shaping modern day business.

CSR Middle East also works to collect and disseminate corporate social responsibility and sustainability news, reports, and information in the Middle East. The group has a wide-ranging membership that includes NGOs, agencies, and other organizations.

These members aim to promote corporate citizenship, sustainability, and socially responsible initiatives. In the broadest terms, the group focuses on diversity, philanthropy, socially responsible investment, the environment, human rights, workplace issues, business ethics, community development, and transparent corporate governance. CSR Middle East has had some marked successes, including some key initiatives enacted not only by Middle Eastern businesses, but also multinational corporations operating in the region.

In May 2008 at the World Economic Forum (WEF) held in Egypt's Sharm El Sheikh, Mohammed Alshaya, the executive chairman of the Alshaya retail group, which has some 1,400 stores in the region, made an address entitled "Does Arab Business Care?" It was Alshaya's contention that corporate social responsibility would play an important role in ensuring that the Middle East continues to grow and thrive in economic terms. Alshaya noted that Middle Eastern companies are not adverse to corporate social responsibility projects, but like many businesses around the world they tend to be one-off projects and not an integral part of operations. Many businesses still use CSR as a publicity gimmick, knowing that charitable donations, for example, during well-publicized events will give them useful press coverage.

Alshaya explained, "In the Middle East, CSR is still in its infancy; it is very much associated with 'giving' through charitable donations. There is much more we can do in partnership with governments and NGOs to tackle deeper issues like unemployment, lack of quality education and carbon footprint reduction." Alshaya was not the only speaker at the forum to make it plain that CSR was to the advantage of businesses and the economy of the Middle East. King Abdullah of Jordan pointed out that businesses should make more effort to welcome young people into the workplace environment by becoming involved in active training programs. He highlighted the Egyptian Education Initiative for particular praise in this respect. Sheikh Mohammed bin Rashid Al Maktoum of Dubai had made the major announcement at the previous year's World Economic Forum in Jordan that Dubai was investing $10 billion in its attempts to help bridge the perceived gap in education and knowledge in the Middle East compared to the West.

▲ Leading political and business figures speak at the 2008 World Economic Forum on the Middle East in Sharm El-Sheikh, Egypt.

CSR Middle East is an organization in the region that aims to promote corporate social responsibility. Other initiatives, such as Dubai Cares and company specific projects, aim to create a code of business ethics.

The Dubai Cares project also initiated a drive to encourage Dubai businesses to make charitable donations to the foundation. The foundation aims to educate one million children in poor countries. In his speech, Alshaya noted, "Regional corporations should place more emphasis on their social responsibilities as consumers and governments are becoming increasingly conscious of ethical and environmental issues. Businesses not committing to CSR will not only risk their reputations but also give up the opportunity to contribute to the growth of this region, or successfully expand outside it."

Alshaya's comments were echoed by Neville Isdell, the now former chief executive officer of Coca-Cola: "There has been a societal change; businesses and governments have to be partners not just in business development but in societal development. Unless we do that the legitimacy of our economic model will be jeopardized."

Fadi Ghandour, the chief executive officer of Aramex, a major transportation and logistics company in the Middle East added, "Businesses have to invest in society. Invest being the keyword here; it's not CSR; it's not charity. It's an investment in society."

Alshaya certainly practices what he preaches; his own group has opened a training program for some 1,000 students in Kuwait. Alshaya also made the point that many CSR projects are reactive rather than proactive at present. In other words, a government will announce an initiative and then ask for business support, rather than the businesses taking CSR as a driving force and leading the way.

Another business taking CSR seriously is the Abu Dhabi National Energy Company. It was established in 2005 and is a global energy business that has assets valued at $21 billion with investments all over the world. According to Shayma Majed, the company's manager in charge of CSR, Diversity, and Inclusion, Taqa's CSR objectives are "[To] implement programs of ethical,

environmental, and social benefit to all of the company's stakeholders, which include employees, shareholders, regulators, bondholders, the environment, and the community."

In drafting any CSR policy, according to Majed, it is vital that external experts are included in the conversations and that internal departments of the organization are consulted: "'A company pursues CSR at its peril if it has not consulted widely with external stakeholders such as NGOs, analysts, academics, and, of course, its customers and partners. We need to check periodically that what we have assumed internally will stand up externally."

Transparency is vital for an organization in its efforts to ensure that CSR is working and is effective. Taqa uses external auditing to ensure that progress and tangible benefits are being made. The external auditing is carried out by the ethical trading initiative Forum for The Future and Business in the Community. Each of the groups "regularly have firsthand experiences with Taqa's actions and outputs and challenge us to continually improve our performance."

Taqa has instituted a code of business ethics that incorporates employee conduct both in the organization and with external dealings, specifically when the employee or manager is acting on behalf of the organization.

An integral part of the diversity and inclusion aspect of the CSR policy is that the company has to appreciate that it and its employees and managers operate in some 38 different countries. Majed explained, "Taqa recognizes that our workforce consists of a diverse population of people, and it believes that harnessing these differences helps to create a productive environment where people feel valued, where they feel that their talents are fully utilized, and in which the organizational goals are being met." Since environmental issues are also of concern in the CSR field for the company, Taqa has joined the 3C initiative, a group of business leaders that aims to set global limits for temperature increases and have identified emission reduction targets. As part of this initiative, the company offers its employees an opportunity to buy a hybrid low emissions car. Majed explained why this was so important: "Taqa believes changing individual behavior is the first step towards changing societies and we have begun this journey together with our employees."[1]

*r*esponsible marketers discover what consumers want and respond with market offerings that create value for buyers in order to capture value in return. The *marketing concept* is a philosophy of customer value and mutual gain. Its practice leads the economy by an invisible hand to satisfy the many and changing needs of millions of consumers.

Not all marketers follow the marketing concept, however. In fact, some companies use questionable marketing practices that serve their own rather than consumers' interests. Moreover, even well-intended marketing actions that meet the current needs of some consumers may cause immediate or future harm to other consumers or the larger society. Responsible marketers must consider whether their actions are *sustainable* in the longer run.

Consider the sale of sport-utility vehicles (SUVs). These large vehicles meet the immediate needs of many drivers in terms of capacity, power, and utility. However,

SUV sales involve larger questions of consumer safety and environmental responsibility. For example, in accidents, SUVs are more likely to kill both their own occupants and the occupants of other vehicles. Research shows that SUV occupants are three times more likely to die from their vehicle rolling than are occupants of sedans. Moreover, gas-guzzling SUVs use more than their fair share of the world's energy and other resources and contribute disproportionately to pollution and congestion problems, creating costs that must be borne by both current and future generations.[2]

This chapter examines *sustainable* marketing and the social and environmental effects of private marketing practices. First, we address the question: What is sustainable marketing and why is it important?

Author Comment »
Marketers must think beyond immediate customer satisfaction and business performance toward strategies that preserve the world for future generations.

SUSTAINABLE MARKETING (pp 539–540)

Sustainable marketing
Socially and environmentally responsible marketing that meets the present needs of consumers and businesses while also preserving or enhancing the ability of future generations to meet their needs.

Sustainable marketing calls for socially and environmentally responsible actions that meet the present needs of consumers and businesses while also preserving or enhancing the ability of future generations to meet their needs. ■ **Figure 16.1** compares the sustainable marketing concept with other marketing concepts we studied in earlier chapters.[3]

The *marketing concept* recognizes that organizations thrive from day to day by determining the current needs and wants of target group customers and fulfilling those needs and wants more effectively and efficiently than competitors do. It focuses on meeting the company's short-term sales, growth, and profit needs by giving customers what they want now. However, satisfying consumers' immediate needs and desires doesn't always serve the future best interests of either customers or the business.

For example, McDonald's early decisions to market tasty but fat- and salt-laden fast foods created immediate satisfaction for customers and sales and profits for the company. However, critics assert that McDonald's and other fast-food chains contributed to a longer-term national obesity epidemic, damaging consumer health and burdening the national health system. In turn, many consumers began looking for healthier eating options, causing a slump in fast-food industry sales and profits. Beyond issues of ethical behavior and social welfare, McDonald's was also criticized for the sizable environmental footprint of its vast global operations, everything from wasteful packaging and solid waste creation to inefficient energy use in its stores. Thus, McDonald's strategy was not sustainable in terms of either consumer or company benefit.

Whereas the *societal marketing concept* identified in Figure 16.1 considers the future welfare of consumers and the *strategic planning concept* considers future company needs, the *sustainable marketing concept* considers both. Sustainable marketing calls for socially and environmentally responsible actions that meet both the immediate and future needs of customers and the company.

For example, as we discussed in Chapter 2, in recent years, McDonald's has responded with a more sustainable "Plan to Win" strategy of diversifying into salads, fruits, grilled chicken, low-fat milk, and other healthy fare. Also, after a seven-year search for healthier cooking oil, McDonald's phased out traditional artery-clogging trans fats without compromising the taste of its french fries. And the company launched

■ **Figure 16.1** Sustainable Marketing

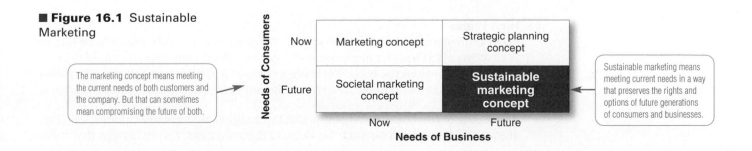

The marketing concept means meeting the current needs of both customers and the company. But that can sometimes mean compromising the future of both.

Sustainable marketing means meeting current needs in a way that preserves the rights and options of future generations of consumers and businesses.

▲Sustainable marketing: McDonald's "Plan to Win" strategy has both created sustainable value for customers and positioned the company for a profitable future.

a major multifaceted education campaign—called "it's what i eat and what i do . . . i'm lovin' it"—to help consumers better understand the keys to living balanced, active lifestyles.

▲The McDonald's "Plan to Win" strategy also addresses environmental issues. For example, it calls for food-supply sustainability, reduced and environmentally sustainable packaging, reuse and recycling, and more responsible store designs. McDonald's has even developed an environmental scorecard that rates its suppliers' performance in areas such as water use, energy use, and solid waste management.

McDonald's more sustainable strategy is benefiting the company as well as its customers. Since announcing its Plan to Win strategy, McDonald's sales have increased by more than 50 percent and profits have more than quadrupled. And for the past four years, the company has been included in the Dow Jones Sustainability Index, recognizing its commitment to sustainable economic, environmental, and social performance. Thus, McDonald's is well positioned for a sustainably profitable future.[4]

Truly sustainable marketing requires a smooth-functioning marketing system in which consumers, companies, public policy makers, and others work together to ensure socially and environmentally responsible marketing actions. Unfortunately, however, the marketing system doesn't always work smoothly. The following sections examine several sustainability questions: What are the most frequent social criticisms of marketing? What steps have private citizens taken to curb marketing ills? What steps have legislators and government agencies taken to promote sustainable marketing? What steps have enlightened companies taken to carry out socially responsible and ethical marketing that creates sustainable value for both individual customers and society as a whole?

Author Comment ≫
In most ways, we all benefit greatly from marketing activities. However, like most other human endeavors, marketing has its flaws. Here, we present both sides of some of the most common criticisms of marketing.

SOCIAL CRITICISMS OF MARKETING (pp 540–549)

Marketing receives much criticism. Some of this criticism is justified; much is not. Social critics claim that certain marketing practices hurt individual consumers, society as a whole, and other business firms.

Marketing's Impact on Individual Consumers

Consumers have many concerns about how well the American marketing system serves their interests. Surveys usually show that consumers hold mixed or even slightly unfavorable attitudes toward marketing practices. Consumer advocates, government agencies, and other critics have accused marketing of harming consumers through high prices, deceptive practices, high-pressure selling, shoddy or unsafe products, planned obsolescence, and poor service to disadvantaged consumers. Such questionable marketing practices are not sustainable in terms of long-term consumer or business welfare.

High Prices

Many critics charge that the American marketing system causes prices to be higher than they would be under more "sensible" systems. Such high prices are hard to swallow, especially when the economy takes a downturn. Critics point to three factors— *high costs of distribution, high advertising and promotion costs*, and *excessive markups*.

High Costs of Distribution. A long-standing charge is that greedy channel intermediaries mark up prices beyond the value of their services. Critics charge that there are too many intermediaries, that intermediaries are inefficient, or that they provide unnecessary or duplicate services. As a result, distribution costs too much, and consumers pay for these excessive costs in the form of higher prices.

How do resellers answer these charges? They argue that intermediaries do work that would otherwise have to be done by manufacturers or consumers. Markups reflect services that consumers themselves want—more convenience, larger stores and assortments, more service, longer store hours, return privileges, and others. In fact, they argue, retail competition is so intense that margins are actually quite low. For example, after taxes, supermarket chains are typically left with barely 1 percent profit on their sales. If some resellers try to charge too much relative to the value they add, other resellers will step in with lower prices. Low-price stores such as Wal-Mart, Costco, and other discounters pressure their competitors to operate efficiently and keep their prices down. In fact, in the wake of the recent recession, only the most efficient retailers have survived profitably.

High Advertising and Promotion Costs. Modern marketing is also accused of pushing up prices to finance heavy advertising and sales promotion. ▲For example, a few dozen tablets of a heavily promoted brand of pain reliever sell for the same price as 100 tablets of less-promoted brands. Differentiated products—cosmetics, detergents, toiletries—include promotion and packaging costs that can amount to 40 percent or more of the manufacturer's price to the retailer. Critics charge that much of the packaging and promotion adds only psychological value to the product rather than functional value.

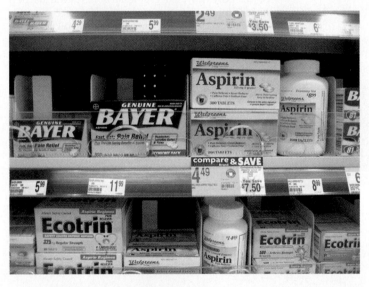

▲A heavily promoted brand of aspirin sells for much more than a virtually identical nonbranded or store-branded product. Critics charge that promotion adds only psychological value to the product rather than functional value.

Marketers respond that advertising does add to product costs, but that it also adds value by informing potential buyers of the availability and merits of a brand. Brand name products may cost more, but branding gives buyers assurances of consistent quality. Moreover, consumers can usually buy functional versions of products at lower prices. However, they *want* and are willing to pay more for products that also provide psychological benefits—that make them feel wealthy, attractive, or special. Also, heavy advertising and promotion may be necessary for a firm to match competitors' efforts—the business would lose "share of mind" if it did not match competitive spending.

At the same time, companies are cost conscious about promotion and try to spend their money wisely. Today's increasingly more frugal consumers are demanding genuine value for the prices they pay. The continuing shift toward buying store brands and generics suggests that when it comes to value, consumers want action, not just talk.

Excessive Markups. Critics also charge that some companies mark up goods excessively. They point to the drug industry, where a pill costing five cents to make may cost the consumer $2 to buy. They point to the pricing tactics of funeral homes that prey on the confused emotions of bereaved relatives and to the high charges for auto repair and other services.

Marketers respond that most businesses try to deal fairly with consumers because they want to build customer relationships and repeat business and that most consumer abuses are unintentional. When shady marketers do take advantage of consumers, they should be reported to Better Business Bureaus and to state and federal agencies. Marketers also respond that consumers often don't understand the reasons for high markups. For example, pharmaceutical markups must cover the costs of purchasing, promoting, and distributing existing medicines plus the high research and development costs of formulating and testing new medicines. As pharmaceuticals company GlaxoSmithKline states in its ads, "Today's medicines finance tomorrow's miracles."

Deceptive Practices

Marketers are sometimes accused of deceptive practices that lead consumers to believe they will get more value than they actually do. Deceptive practices fall into three groups: pricing, promotion, and packaging. *Deceptive pricing* includes practices such as falsely advertising "factory" or "wholesale" prices or a large price reduction from a phony high retail list price. *Deceptive promotion* includes practices such as misrepresenting the product's features or performance or luring the customers to the store for a bargain that is out of stock. *Deceptive packaging* includes exaggerating package contents through subtle design, using misleading labeling, or describing size in misleading terms.

Deceptive practices have led to legislation and other consumer protection actions. For example, in 1938 Congress reacted to such blatant deceptions as Fleischmann's Yeast's claim to straighten crooked teeth by enacting the Wheeler-Lea Act giving the Federal Trade Commission (FTC) power to regulate "unfair or deceptive acts or practices." The FTC has published several guidelines listing deceptive practices. Despite new regulations, some critics argue that deceptive claims are still the norm. Consider the glut of "environmental responsibility" claims marketers are now making:

▲Deceptive practices: Consider all of those "green marketing" claims. A recent TerraChoice study found that 98 percent of products making green claims committed "at least one of the Sins of Greenwashing."

Are you a victim of "greenwashing"? Biodegradable, eco-friendly, recycled, green, carbon neutral, carbon offsets, made from sustainable resources—such phrases are popping up more and more on products worldwide, leading many to question their validity. This year, for example, the FTC has started updating its "Green Guides"—voluntary guidelines that it asks companies to adopt to help them avoid breaking laws against deceptive marketing. "We have seen a surge in environmental claims," says a lawyer at the FTC's Bureau of Consumer Protection. In 2009, TerraChoice Environmental Marketing, which advises companies on green positioning, reviewed claims companies made about 2,219 widely sold goods. ▲Using measures created by government agencies, TerraChoice concluded that 98 percent of the products committed "at least one of the Sins of Greenwashing." "There is a lot going on there that just isn't right," says one environmental trendwatcher. "If truly green products have a hard time differentiating themselves from fake ones, then this whole notion of a green market will fall apart," says a TerraChoice executive.[5]

The toughest problem is defining what is "deceptive." For instance, an advertiser's claim that its powerful laundry detergent "makes your washing machine 10 feet tall," showing a surprised homemaker watching her appliance burst through her laundry room ceiling, isn't intended to be taken literally. Instead, the advertiser might claim, it is "puffery"—innocent exaggeration for effect. One noted marketing thinker, Theodore Levitt, once claimed that advertising puffery and alluring imagery are bound to occur—and that they may even be desirable: "There is hardly a company that would not go down in ruin if it refused to provide fluff, because nobody will buy pure functionality. . . . Worse, it denies . . . people's honest needs and values. Without distortion, embellishment, and elaboration, life would be drab, dull, anguished, and at its existential worst."[6]

However, others claim that puffery and alluring imagery can harm consumers in subtle ways. Think about the popular and long-running MasterCard Priceless commercials that have paint pictures of consumers fulfilling their priceless dreams despite the costs. The ads suggest that your credit card can make it happen. But critics charge that such imagery by credit card companies encouraged a spend-now-pay-later attitude that caused many consumers to *over*use their cards. They point to statistics showing that Americans are carrying record amounts of credit card debt—often more than they can repay—contributing heavily to the nation's financial crisis.[7]

Marketers argue that most companies avoid deceptive practices. Because such practices harm a company's business in the long run, they simply aren't sustainable. Profitable customer relationships are built upon a foundation of value and trust. If consumers do not get what they expect, they will switch to more reliable products. In addition, consumers usually protect themselves from deception. Most consumers recognize a marketer's selling intent and are careful when they buy, sometimes even to the point of not believing completely true product claims.

High-Pressure Selling

Salespeople are sometimes accused of high-pressure selling that persuades people to buy goods they had no thought of buying. It is often said that insurance, real estate, and used cars are *sold*, not *bought*. Salespeople are trained to deliver smooth, canned talks to entice purchase. They sell hard because sales contests promise big prizes to those who sell the most. Similarly, TV infomercial pitchmen use "yell and sell" presentations that create a sense of consumer urgency that only those with the strongest willpower can resist.

But in most cases, marketers have little to gain from high-pressure selling. Such tactics may work in one-time selling situations for short-term gain. However, most selling involves building long-term relationships with valued customers. High-pressure or deceptive selling can do serious damage to such relationships. For example, imagine a P&G account manager trying to pressure a Wal-Mart buyer, or an IBM salesperson trying to browbeat a GE information technology manager. It simply wouldn't work.

Shoddy, Harmful, or Unsafe Products

Another criticism concerns poor product quality or function. One complaint is that, too often, products are not made well and services are not performed well. A second complaint is that many products deliver little benefit, or that they might even be harmful.

For example, think again about the fast-food industry. Many critics blame the plentiful supply of fat-laden, high calorie fast-food fare for the nation's rapidly growing obesity epidemic. Studies show that some 34 percent of American adults and 32 percent of children are obese. The number of people in the United States who are 100 pounds or more overweight quintupled between 2000 and 2005, from 1 adult in 200 to 1 in 40. This weight increase comes despite repeated medical studies showing that excess weight brings increased risks for heart disease, diabetes, and other maladies, even cancer.[8]

The critics are quick to fault what they see as greedy food marketers who are cashing in on vulnerable consumers, turning us into a nation of overeaters. Some food marketers are looking pretty much guilty as charged. ▲Take Hardee's, for example. At a time when other fast-food chains such as McDonald's, Wendy's, and Subway have been pushing healthier meals, Hardee's has launched one artery-clogging burger after another—gifts to consumers fed up with "healthy," low-fat menu items. Its Monster Thickburger contains two-thirds of a pound of Angus beef, four strips of bacon, and three slices of American cheese, all nestled in a buttered sesame-seed bun slathered with mayonnaise. The blockbuster burger weighs in at an eye-popping 1,410 calories and 107 grams of fat, far greater than the government's recommended fat intake for an entire day. Although it appears to be bucking the trends, since introducing the mouth-watering Thickburger line, Hardee's has experienced healthy sales increases and even fatter profits.

Is Hardee's being socially irresponsible by aggressively promoting overindulgence to ill-informed or unwary consumers? Or is it simply practicing good marketing, creating more value for its customers by offering big

▼Harmful products: Is Hardee's being socially irresponsible or simply practicing good marketing by giving customers a big juicy burger that clearly pings their taste buds? Judging by the nutrition calculator at its Web site, the company certainly isn't hiding the nutritional facts.

juicy burgers that ping their taste buds and let them make their own eating choices? Hardee's claims the latter. It says that its target consumers—young men aged 18 to 34—are capable of making their own decisions about health and well-being.

And Hardee's certainly doesn't hide the nutritional facts—they are clearly posted on the company's Web site. The site describes the Monster Thickburger as "a monument to decadence—the only thing that can slay the hunger of a young guy on the move." And the CEO of CKE, Hardee's parent company, notes that the chain does put salads and low-carb burgers on its menus but "we sell very few of them." So, is Hardee's being irresponsible or simply responsive? As in many matters of social responsibility, what's right and wrong may be a matter of opinion.

A third complaint concerns product safety. Product safety has been a problem for several reasons, including company indifference, increased product complexity, and poor quality control. For years, Consumers Union—the nonprofit testing and information organization that publishes the *Consumer Reports* magazine and Web site—has reported various hazards in tested products: electrical dangers in appliances, carbon monoxide poisoning from room heaters, injury risks from lawn mowers, and faulty automobile design, among many others. The organization's testing and other activities have helped consumers make better buying decisions and encouraged businesses to eliminate product flaws.

However, most manufacturers *want* to produce quality goods. The way a company deals with product quality and safety problems can damage or help its reputation. Companies selling poor-quality or unsafe products risk damaging conflicts with consumer groups and regulators. Unsafe products can result in product liability suits and large awards for damages. More fundamentally, consumers who are unhappy with a firm's products may avoid future purchases and talk other consumers into doing the same. Thus, quality missteps are not consistent with sustainable marketing. Today's marketers know that good quality results in customer value and satisfaction, which in turn creates sustainable customer relationships.

Planned Obsolescence

Critics also have charged that some companies practice planned obsolescence, causing their products to become obsolete before they actually should need replacement. They accuse some producers of using materials and components that will break, wear, rust, or rot sooner than they should. One analyst captures the concept this way: "Planned obsolescence, a diabolical manufacturing strategy that took root with the rise of mass production in the 1920s and 1930s, has now escalated from disposable lighters to major appliances. Its evil genius is this: Make the cost of repairs close to the item's replacement price and entice us to buy new." The analyst's 12-year-old stove needed a burner repaired—12 new screws. The price of the repair: $700, which was more than he'd paid for the stove new.[9]

▼Planned obsolescence: Almost everyone, it seems, has a drawer filled with the detritus of yesterday's hottest product, now reduced to the status of fossils.

Other companies are charged with continually changing consumer concepts of acceptable styles to encourage more and earlier buying. An obvious example is constantly changing clothing fashions. Still others are accused of introducing planned streams of new products that make older models obsolete. Critics claim that this occurs in the consumer electronics and computer industries. For example, consider this writer's tale about an aging cell phone:[10]

Today, most people, myself included, are all agog at the wondrous outpouring of new technology, from cell phones to iPods, iPhones, laptops, BlackBerries, and on and on. I have a drawer filled with the detritus of yesterday's hottest product, now reduced to the status of fossils. ▲I have video cameras that use tapes no longer available, laptops with programs incompatible with anything on today's market, portable CD players I no longer use, and more. But what really upsets me is how quickly some still-useful gadgets become obsolete, at least in the eyes of their makers.

I recently embarked on an epic search for a cord to plug into my wife's cell phone to recharge it. We were traveling and the poor phone kept bleating that it was running low and the battery needed recharging. So, we began a search—from big-box technology superstores to smaller suppliers and the cell phone companies themselves—all to no avail. Finally, a salesperson told my wife, "That's an old model, so we don't stock the charger any longer." "But I only bought it last year," she sputtered. "Yeah, like I said, that's an old model," he replied without a hint of irony or sympathy. The proliferation and sheer waste of this type of practice is mind-boggling.

Marketers respond that consumers *like* style changes; they get tired of the old goods and want a new look in fashion. Or they *want* the latest high-tech innovations, even if older models still work. No one has to buy the new product, and if too few people like it, it will simply fail. Finally, most companies do not design their products to break down earlier, because they do not want to lose customers to other brands. Instead, they seek constant improvement to ensure that products will consistently meet or exceed customer expectations. Much of the so-called planned obsolescence is the working of the competitive and technological forces in a free society—forces that lead to ever-improving goods and services.

Poor Service to Disadvantaged Consumers

Finally, the American marketing system has been accused of serving disadvantaged consumers poorly. For example, critics claim that the urban poor often have to shop in smaller stores that carry inferior goods and charge higher prices. The presence of large national chain stores in low-income neighborhoods would help to keep prices down. However, the critics accuse major chain retailers of "redlining," drawing a red line around disadvantaged neighborhoods and avoiding placing stores there.

▲Critics have accused mortgage lenders of "reverse redlining," targeting disadvantaged consumers with subprime mortgages that they couldn't afford.

Similar redlining charges have been leveled at the insurance, consumer lending, banking, and health care industries. ▲Most recently, consumer advocates charged that banks and mortgage lenders have practiced "reverse-redlining." Instead of staying away from people in poor urban areas, they have targeted and exploited them, especially working-class black consumers, by offering them risky subprime mortgages rather than safer mortgages with better terms. These subprime mortgages often featured adjustable interest rates that started out very low but quickly increased. Recently, when the interest rates went up, many owners could no longer afford their mortgage payments. And as housing prices dropped, these owners were trapped in debt and owed more than their houses were worth, leading to bankruptcies, foreclosures, and a subprime mortgage crisis.

Many critics charge that such subprime loans should be treated as bias crimes. A recent report issued by United for a Fair Economy claims that people of color are three times more likely than other groups to have subprime loans. It estimates that the subprime mortgage crisis will drain $213 billion in wealth from black Americans—the "greatest wealth loss in modern U.S. history." In response, the NAACP filed a racial discrimination suit against 18 mortgage providers, including GMAC, Wells Fargo, and HSBC.[11]

Clearly, better marketing systems must be built to service disadvantaged consumers. In fact, many marketers profitably target such consumers with legitimate goods and services that create real value. In cases in which marketers do not step in to fill the void, the government likely will. For example, the FTC has taken action against sellers who advertise false values, wrongfully deny services, or charge disadvantaged customers too much.

◆ **Speed Bump:** Linking the Concepts

Hit the brakes for a moment. Few marketers *want* to abuse or anger consumers—it's simply not good business. Still, some marketing abuses do occur.

- Think back over the past three months or so and list any instances in which you've suffered a marketing abuse such as those discussed. Analyze your list: What kinds of companies were involved? Were the abuses intentional? What did the situations have in common?
- Pick one of the instances you listed and describe it in detail. How might you go about righting this wrong? Write out an action plan and then do something to remedy the abuse. If we all took such actions when wronged, there would be far fewer wrongs to right!

Marketing's Impact on Society as a Whole

The American marketing system has been accused of adding to several "evils" in American society at large. Advertising has been a special target—so much so that the American Association of Advertising Agencies once launched a campaign to defend advertising against what it felt to be common but untrue criticisms.

False Wants and Too Much Materialism

Critics have charged that the marketing system urges too much interest in material possessions, and that Americans' love affair with worldly possessions is not sustainable. Too often, people are judged by what they *own* rather than by who they *are*. The critics do not view this interest in material things as a natural state of mind but rather as a matter of false wants created by marketing. Marketers, they claim, stimulate people's desires for goods and create materialistic models of the good life. Thus, marketers have created an endless cycle of mass consumption based on a distorted interpretation of the "American Dream."

> The Constitution speaks of life, liberty, and the pursuit of happiness, not an automatic chicken in every pot. Average household debt in the United States now equals 130 percent of household income. One sociologist attributes consumer overspending to a growing "aspiration gap"—the gap between what we have and what we want, between the lifestyles we can afford and those to which we aspire. This aspiration gap results at least partly from a barrage of marketing that encourages people to focus on the acquisition and consumption of goods. Credit card offers flood the mail. Advertising encourages consumers to aspire to celebrity lifestyles, to keep up with the Joneses by acquiring more stuff. Even President Bush, following the shock of 9-11-2001, called on Americans to show their patriotism by going out to shop. And now, President Obama is rewarding new home buyers with tax credits to go out and purchase a home and live an "American Dream" they may not be able to afford. Some marketing-frenzied consumers will let nothing stand between them and their acquisitions. Recently, at a Wal-Mart store in New York, a mob of 2,000 eager shoppers broke through a glass door in their rush to get to post-Thanksgiving sales items, trampling a store employee to death in the process.[12]

Thus, marketing is seen as creating false wants that benefit industry more than they benefit consumers. "In the world of consumerism, marketing is there to promote consumption," says one marketing critic. It is "inevitable that marketing will promote overconsumption, and from this, a psychologically, as well as ecologically, unsustainable world." ▲Some critics even take their concerns to the streets.[13]

> For a decade Bill Talen, also known as Reverend Billy, has taken to the streets, exhorting people to resist temptation—the temptation to shop. With the zeal of a street-corner preacher and the schmaltz of a street-corner Santa, Reverend Billy will tell anyone willing to listen that people are walking willingly into the hellfires of consumption. Reverend Billy, leader of the Church of Life After Shopping, believes that shoppers have almost no resis-

▲ **Materialism: With the zeal of a street-corner preacher and the schmaltz of a street-corner Santa, Reverend Billy—founder of the Church of Stop Shopping—will tell anyone who will listen that people are walking willingly into the hellfire of consumption.**

tance to the media messages that encourage them, around the clock, to want things and buy them. He sees a population lost in consumption, the meaning of individual existence vanished in a fog of wanting, buying, and owning too many things, ultimately leading to a "Shopocalypse." Sporting a televangelist's pompadour, a priest's collar, and a white megaphone, Reverend Billy is often accompanied by his gospel choir when he strides into stores he considers objectionable or shows up at protests. When the choir, made up of volunteers, erupts in song, it is hard to ignore: "Stop shopping! Stop shopping! We will never shop again!"

Marketers respond that such criticisms overstate the power of business to create needs. People have strong defenses against advertising and other marketing tools. Marketers are most effective when they appeal to existing wants rather than when they attempt to create new ones. Furthermore, people seek information when making important purchases and often do not rely on single sources. Even minor purchases that may be affected by advertising messages lead to repeat purchases only if the product delivers the promised customer value. Finally, the high failure rate of new products shows that companies are not able to control demand.

On a deeper level, our wants and values are influenced not only by marketers but also by family, peer groups, religion, cultural background, and education. If Americans are highly materialistic, these values arose out of basic socialization processes that go much deeper than business and mass media could produce alone.

Moreover, consumption patterns and attitudes are also subject to larger forces, such as the economy. As discussed in Chapter 1, the recent recession put a damper on materialism and conspicuous spending. In one consumer survey, 75 percent of respondents agreed that "the downturn is encouraging me to evaluate what is really important in life." Many observers predict a new age of consumer thrift. "The American dream is on pause," says one analyst. "The majority of Americans still believe they can achieve the dream in their lifetimes but, for [now], it's all about shoring up the foundations." As a result, far from encouraging today's more frugal consumers to overspend their means, marketers are working to help them find greater value with less. "The glib 'all your dreams will come true' approach to marketing will have to be reevaluated," concludes another analyst.[14]

Too Few Social Goods

Business has been accused of overselling private goods at the expense of public goods. As private goods increase, they require more public services that are usually not forthcoming. For example, an increase in automobile ownership (private good) requires more highways, traffic control, parking spaces, and police services (public goods). The overselling of private goods results in "social costs." For cars, some of the social costs include traffic congestion, gasoline shortages, and air pollution. For example, American travelers lose on average 40 hours a year in traffic jams, costing the United States more than $78 billion a year. In the process, they waste 2.9 billion gallons of fuel and emit millions of tons of greenhouse gases.[15]

A way must be found to restore a balance between private and public goods. One option is to make producers bear the full social costs of their operations. For example, the government is requiring automobile manufacturers to build cars with more efficient engines and better pollution-control systems. Automakers will then raise their prices to cover the extra costs. If buyers find the price of some cars too high, however, the producers of these cars will disappear. Demand will then move to those producers that can support the sum of the private and social costs.

▲Balancing private and public goods: In response to lane-clogging traffic congestion like that above, London now levies a congestion charge. The charge has reduced congestion by 30 percent and raised money to shore up the city's public transportation system.

A second option is to make consumers pay the social costs. ▲For example, many cities around the world are now charging "congestion tolls" in an effort to reduce traffic congestion. To unclog its streets, the city of London levies a congestion charge of £8 per day per car to drive in an eight-square-mile area downtown. The charge has not only reduced traffic congestion within the zone by 21 percent (70,000 fewer vehicles per day) and increased bicycling by 43 percent; it also raises money to shore up London's public transportation system.[16]

Based on London's success, cities such as San Diego, Houston, Seattle, Denver, and Minneapolis have turned some of their HOV (high-occupancy vehicle) lanes into HOT (high-occupancy toll) lanes for drivers carrying too few passengers. Regular drivers can use the HOT lanes, but they must pay tolls ranging from $.50 during off-peak hours to $9 during rush hour. Although congestion tolls might seem a bit "un-American," many states with tight budgets are seriously considering taxing drivers via tolls during peak hours to finance badly needed repairs to their roads and transportation systems.[17]

Cultural Pollution

Critics charge the marketing system with creating *cultural pollution*. Our senses are being constantly assaulted by marketing and advertising. Commercials interrupt serious programs; pages of ads obscure magazines; billboards mar beautiful scenery; spam fills our inboxes. These interruptions continually pollute people's minds with messages of materialism, sex, power, or status. A recent study found that 63 percent of Americans feel constantly bombarded with too many marketing messages, and some critics call for sweeping changes.[18]

Marketers answer the charges of "commercial noise" with these arguments: First, they hope that their ads reach primarily the target audience. But because of mass-communication channels, some ads are bound to reach people who have no interest in the product and are therefore bored or annoyed. People who buy magazines addressed to their interests—such as *Vogue* or *Fortune*—rarely complain about the ads because the magazines advertise products of interest.

Second, ads make much of television and radio free to users and keep down the costs of magazines and newspapers. Many people think commercials are a small price to pay for these benefits. Consumers find many television commercials entertaining and seek them out—for example, ad viewership during the Super Bowl usually equals or exceeds game viewership. Finally, today's consumers have alternatives. For example, they can zip or zap TV commercials on recorded programs or avoid them altogether on many paid cable or satellite channels. Thus, to hold consumer attention, advertisers are making their ads more entertaining and informative.

Marketing's Impact on Other Businesses

Critics also charge that a company's marketing practices can harm other companies and reduce competition. Three problems are involved: acquisitions of competitors, marketing practices that create barriers to entry, and unfair competitive marketing practices.

Critics claim that firms are harmed and competition reduced when companies expand by acquiring competitors rather than by developing their own new products. The large number of acquisitions and the rapid pace of industry consolidation over the past several decades have caused concern that vigorous young competitors will be absorbed and that competition will be reduced. In virtually every major industry—retailing, entertainment, financial services, utilities, transportation, automobiles, telecommunications, health care—the number of major competitors is shrinking.

Acquisition is a complex subject. Acquisitions can sometimes be good for society. The acquiring company may gain economies of scale that lead to lower costs and lower prices. A well-managed company may take over a poorly managed company and improve its efficiency. An industry that was not very competitive might become more competitive after the acquisition. But acquisitions can also be harmful and, therefore, are closely regulated by the government.

Critics have also charged that marketing practices bar new companies from entering an industry. Large marketing companies can use patents and heavy promotion spending or tie up suppliers or dealers to keep out or drive out competitors. Those concerned with antitrust regulation recognize that some barriers are the natural result of the economic advantages of doing business on a large scale. Other barriers could be challenged by existing and new laws. For example, some critics have proposed a progressive tax on advertising spending to reduce the role of selling costs as a major barrier to entry.

Finally, some firms have in fact used unfair competitive marketing practices with the intention of hurting or destroying other firms. They may set their prices below costs, threaten to cut off business with suppliers, or discourage the buying of a competitor's products. Various laws work to prevent such predatory competition. It is difficult, however, to prove that the intent or action was really predatory.

In recent years, Wal-Mart has been accused of using predatory pricing in selected market areas to drive smaller, mom-and-pop retailers out of business. Wal-Mart has become a lightning rod for protests by citizens in dozens of towns who worry that the megaretailer's unfair practices will choke out local businesses. However, whereas critics charge that Wal-Mart's actions are predatory, others assert that its actions are just the healthy competition of a more efficient company against less efficient ones.

For instance, ▲when Wal-Mart began a program to sell generic drugs at $4 a prescription, local pharmacists complained of predatory pricing. They charged that at those low prices, Wal-Mart must be selling under cost to drive them out of business. But Wal-Mart claimed that, given its substantial buying power and efficient operations, it could make a profit at those prices. The $4 pricing program was not aimed at putting competitors out of business. Rather, it was simply a good competitive move that served customers better and brought more of them in the door. Moreover, Wal-Mart's program drove down prescription prices at the pharmacies of other supermarkets and discount stores, such as Kroger and Target. Currently more than 300 prescription drugs are available for $4 at the various chains.[19]

▼Wal-Mart prescription pricing: Is it predatory pricing or is it just good business?

Author Comment ≫
Sustainable marketing isn't the province of only businesses and governments. Through consumerism and environmentalism, consumers themselves can play an important role.

CONSUMER ACTIONS TO PROMOTE SUSTAINABLE MARKETING
(pp 549–558)

Sustainable marketing calls for more responsible actions by both businesses and consumers. Because some people view business as the cause of many economic and social ills, grassroots movements have arisen from time to time to keep business in line. The two major movements have been *consumerism* and *environmentalism*.

Consumerism

American business firms have been the target of organized consumer movements on three occasions. The first consumer movement took place in the early 1900s. It was fueled by rising prices, Upton Sinclair's writings on conditions in the meat industry, and scandals in the drug industry. The second consumer movement, in the mid-1930s, was sparked by an upturn in consumer prices during the Great Depression and another drug scandal.

The third movement began in the 1960s. Consumers had become better educated, products had become more complex and potentially hazardous, and people were unhappy with American institutions. Ralph Nader appeared on the scene to force many issues, and other well-known writers accused big business of wasteful and unethical practices. President John F. Kennedy declared that consumers had the right to safety and to be informed, to choose, and to be heard. Congress investigated certain industries and proposed consumer-protection legislation. Since then, many consumer groups have been organized and several consumer laws have been passed. The consumer movement has spread internationally and has become very strong in Europe.

But what is the consumer movement? **Consumerism** is an organized movement of citizens and government agencies to improve the rights and power of buyers in relation to sellers. Traditional *sellers' rights* include:

Consumerism
An organized movement of citizens and government agencies to improve the rights and power of buyers in relation to sellers.

- The right to introduce any product in any size and style, provided it is not hazardous to personal health or safety; or, if it is, to include proper warnings and controls
- The right to charge any price for the product, provided no discrimination exists among similar kinds of buyers
- The right to spend any amount to promote the product, provided it is not defined as unfair competition
- The right to use any product message, provided it is not misleading or dishonest in content or execution
- The right to use any buying incentive programs, provided they are not unfair or misleading

Traditional *buyers' rights* include:

- The right not to buy a product that is offered for sale
- The right to expect the product to be safe
- The right to expect the product to perform as claimed

Comparing these rights, many believe that the balance of power lies on the seller's side. True, the buyer can refuse to buy. But critics feel that the buyer has too little information, education, and protection to make wise decisions when facing sophisticated sellers. Consumer advocates call for the following additional consumer rights:

- The right to be well informed about important aspects of the product
- The right to be protected against questionable products and marketing practices
- The right to influence products and marketing practices in ways that will improve the "quality of life"
- The right to consume now in a way that will preserve the world for future generations of consumers

Each proposed right has led to more specific proposals by consumerists. ▲The right to be informed includes the right to know the true interest on a loan (truth in lending), the true cost per unit of a brand (unit pricing), the ingredients in a product (ingredient labeling), the nutritional value of foods (nutritional labeling),

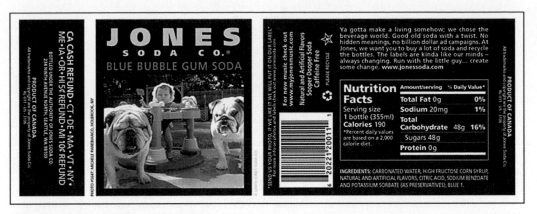

▲Today's labels contain much useful information, from ingredients and nutrition facts to recycling and country of origin information. Jones Soda even puts customer-submitted photos on its labels.

product freshness (open dating), and the true benefits of a product (truth in advertising). Proposals related to consumer protection include strengthening consumer rights in cases of business fraud, requiring greater product safety, ensuring information privacy, and giving more power to government agencies. Proposals relating to quality of life include controlling the ingredients that go into certain products and packaging and reducing the level of advertising "noise." Proposals for preserving the world for future consumption include promoting the use of sustainable ingredients, recycling and reducing solid wastes, and managing energy consumption.

Sustainable marketing is up to consumers as well as to businesses and governments. Consumers have not only the *right* but also the *responsibility* to protect themselves instead of leaving this function to someone else. Consumers who believe they got a bad deal have several remedies available, including contacting the company or the media; contacting federal, state, or local agencies; and going to small-claims courts. Consumers should also make good consumption choices, rewarding companies that act responsibly while punishing those that don't.

Environmentalism

Environmentalism
An organized movement of concerned citizens and government agencies to protect and improve people's current and future living environment.

Whereas consumerists consider whether the marketing system is efficiently serving consumer wants, environmentalists are concerned with marketing's effects on the environment and with the environmental costs of serving consumer needs and wants. **Environmentalism** is an organized movement of concerned citizens, businesses, and government agencies to protect and improve people's current and future living environment.

Environmentalists are not against marketing and consumption; they simply want people and organizations to operate with more care for the environment. The marketing system's goal, they assert, should not be to maximize consumption, consumer choice, or consumer satisfaction, but rather to maximize life quality. And "life quality" means not only the quantity and quality of consumer goods and services, but also the quality of the environment. Environmentalists want current and future environmental costs included in both producer and consumer decision making.

The first wave of modern environmentalism in the United States was driven by environmental groups and concerned consumers in the 1960s and 1970s. They were concerned with damage to the ecosystem caused by strip-mining, forest depletion, acid rain, global warming, toxic and solid wastes, and litter. They were also concerned with the loss of recreational areas and with the increase in health problems caused by bad air, polluted water, and chemically treated food.

The second environmentalism wave was driven by government, which passed laws and regulations during the 1970s and 1980s governing industrial practices impacting the environment. This wave hit some industries hard. Steel companies and utilities had to invest billions of dollars in pollution control equipment and costlier fuels. The auto industry had to introduce expensive emission controls in cars. The packaging industry had to find ways to improve recyclability and reduce solid wastes. These industries and others have often resented and resisted environmental regulations, especially when they have been imposed too rapidly to allow companies to make proper adjustments. Many of these companies claim they have had to absorb large costs that have made them less competitive.

■ **Figure 16.2** The Environmental Sustainability Portfolio

Sources: Stuart L. Hart, "Innovation, Creative Destruction, and Sustainability," *Research Technology Management,* September–October 2005, pp. 21–27.

	Today: Greening	Tomorrow: Beyond Greening
Internal	**Pollution prevention** Eliminating or reducing waste before it is created	**New clean technology** Developing new sets of environmental skills and capabilities
External	**Product stewardship** Minimizing environmental impact throughout the entire product life cycle	**Sustainability vision** Creating a strategic framework for future sustainability

How does "environmental sustainability" relate to "marketing sustainability"? Environmental sustainability involves preserving the natural environment, whereas marketing sustainability is a broader concept that involves both the natural and social environments—pretty much everything in this chapter.

Environmental sustainability
A management approach that involves developing strategies that both sustain the environment and produce profits for the company.

The first two environmentalism waves have now merged into a third and stronger wave in which companies are accepting more responsibility for doing no harm to the environment. They are shifting from protest to prevention, and from regulation to responsibility. More and more companies are adopting policies of **environmental sustainability**. Simply put, environmental sustainability is about generating profits while helping to save the planet. Environmental sustainability is a crucial but difficult societal goal.

Some companies have responded to consumer environmental concerns by doing only what is required to avert new regulations or to keep environmentalists quiet. Enlightened companies, however, are taking action not because someone is forcing them to, or to reap short-run profits, but because it is the right thing to do—for both the company and for the planet's environmental future.

■ **Figure 16.2** shows a grid that companies can use to gauge their progress toward environmental sustainability. In includes both internal and external "greening" activities that will pay off for the firm and environment in the short run and "beyond greening" activities that will pay off in the longer term. At the most basic level, a company can practice *pollution prevention*. This involves more than pollution

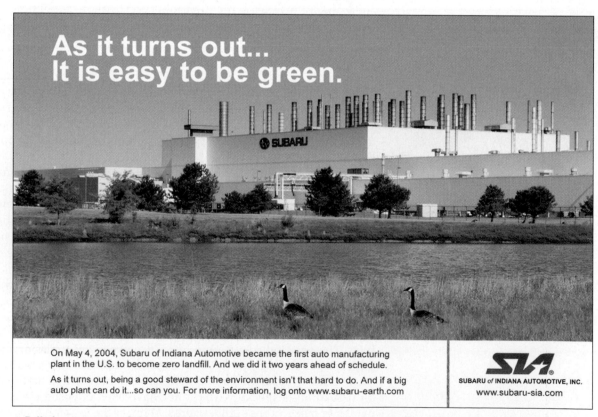

As it turns out... It is easy to be green.

On May 4, 2004, Subaru of Indiana Automotive became the first auto manufacturing plant in the U.S. to become zero landfill. And we did it two years ahead of schedule.

As it turns out, being a good steward of the environment isn't that hard to do. And if a big auto plant can do it...so can you. For more information, log onto www.subaru-earth.com

SIA
SUBARU *of* INDIANA AUTOMOTIVE, INC.
www.subaru-sia.com

▲ Pollution prevention: Subaru of Indiana claims that it now sends less trash to the landfill each year than the average American family.

control—cleaning up waste after it has been created. Pollution prevention means eliminating or minimizing waste before it is created. Companies emphasizing prevention have responded with internal "green marketing" programs—designing and developing ecologically safer products, recyclable and biodegradable packaging, better pollution controls, and more energy-efficient operations.

For example, Nike produces PVC-free shoes, recycles old sneakers, and educates young people about conservation, reuse, and recycling. General Mills shaved 20 percent off the paperboard packaging for Hamburger Helper, resulting in 500 fewer distribution trucks on the road each year. UPS has been developing its "green fleet," which now boasts more than 1,600 low-carbon-emissions vehicles including electric, hybrid-electric, compressed natural gas, liquefied natural gas, and propane trucks. Sun Microsystems created its Open Work program that gives employees the option to work from home, preventing nearly 29,000 tons of CO_2 emissions, while at the same time saving $67.8 million in real-estate costs and increasing worker productivity by 34 percent.[20]

▲Subaru of Indiana, which manufactures all North American Subarus and Toyota Camrys, brags that it now sends less trash to the landfill each year than the average American family.[21]

> In 2000, Subaru of Indiana (SIA) generated 459 pounds of waste for every car built. By the end of 2007, it was down to 251 pounds per unit. Of that, 190 pounds were easily recycled steel. The remaining 61 pounds were pallets, cardboard, and plastic, which were also recycled in various ways. The result: The SIA plant sends zero waste to the landfill. "Whenever we looked at plant efficiency and quality, we also looked to see if we could reduce waste, recycle materials, and cut back gas, water, and energy use," recalls Denise Coogan, Subaru's safety and environmental compliance manager. "Every section manager on the floor had a piece of this and a target. They were held equally accountable for quality, safety, and environmental targets." According to Coogan, while waste reduction was "the right thing to do," it was also "very cost-effective when done right. Every time you throw something away, you've paid to bring it in and you're paying to throw it out. Cut waste and you cut costs." Last year the plant earned $2.4 million on waste reduction.

At the next level, companies can practice *product stewardship*—minimizing not just pollution from production and product design but all environmental impacts throughout the full product life cycle, and all the while reducing costs. Many companies are adopting *design for environment (DFE)* and *cradle-to-cradle* practices. This involves thinking ahead to design products that are easier to recover, reuse, recycle, or safely return to nature after usage, becoming part of the ecological cycle. Design for environment and cradle-to-cradle practices not only help to sustain the environment, they can also be highly profitable for the company.

For example, more than a decade ago, IBM started a business designed to reuse and recycle parts from its mainframe computers returned from lease. Today, IBM takes in 40,000 pieces of used IBM and other equipment per week, strips them down to their chips, and recovers valuable metals. "We find uses for more than 99 percent of what we take in, and have a return-to-landfill rate of [less than 1 percent]," says an IBM spokesperson. What started out as an environmental effort has now grown into a $2 billion IBM business that profitably recycles electronic equipment at 22 sites worldwide.[22]

Today's "greening" activities focus on improving what companies already do to protect the environment. The "beyond greening" activities identified in Figure 16.2 look to the future. First, internally, companies can plan for *new clean technology*. Many organizations that have made good sustainability headway are still limited by existing technologies. To create fully sustainable strategies, they will need to develop innovative new technologies. For example, Coca-Cola is investing heavily in research addressing many sustainability issues:[23]

> From a sustainability viewpoint for Coca-Cola, an aluminum can is an ideal package. Aluminum can be recycled indefinitely. Put a Coke can in a recycling bin, and the aluminum finds its way back to a store shelf in about six weeks. The trouble is, people prefer clear plastic bottles with screw-on tops. Plastic bottles account for nearly 50 percent of

Coke's global volume, three times more than aluminum cans. And they are not currently sustainable. They're made from oil, a finite resource. Most wind up in landfills or, worse, as roadside trash. They can't be recycled indefinitely because the plastic discolors. To attack this waste problem, Coca-Cola will invest about $44 million to build the world's largest state-of-the-art plastic-bottle-to-bottle recycling plant.

As a more permanent solution, Coke is also investing in new clean technologies that address these and other environmental issues. ▲For example, it's researching and testing new bottles made from aluminum, corn, or bioplastics. It's also designing more eco-friendly distribution alternatives. Currently, about ten million or so vending machines and refrigerated coolers gobble up energy and use potent greenhouse gases called HFCs to keep Cokes cold. To eliminate them, the company invested $40 million in research and formed a refrigeration alliance with McDonald's and even competitor PepsiCo. It recently began installing a family of sleek new HFC-free coolers that use 30 to 40 percent less energy. Coca-Cola has also promised to become "water neutral" by researching ways to help its bottlers waste less water and ways to protect or replenish watersheds around the world.

Finally, companies can develop a *sustainability vision*, which serves as a guide to the future. It shows how the company's products and services, processes, and policies must evolve and what new technologies must be developed to get there. This vision of sustainability provides a framework for pollution control, product stewardship, and new environmental technology for the company and others to follow.

Most companies today focus on the upper-left quadrant of the grid in Figure 16.2, investing most heavily in pollution prevention. Some forward-looking companies practice product stewardship and are developing new environmental technologies. Few companies have well-defined sustainability visions. However, emphasizing only

▲ **New clean technologies: Coca-Cola is investing heavily to develop new solutions to environmental issues. To reduce packaging waste problems, it's now testing new contour bottles made from corn, bioplastics, or—here—more easily recycled aluminum.**

one or a few quadrants in the environmental sustainability grid can be shortsighted. Investing only in the left half of the grid puts a company in a good position today but leaves it vulnerable in the future. In contrast, a heavy emphasis on the right half suggests that a company has good environmental vision but lacks the skills needed to implement it. Thus, companies should work at developing all four dimensions of environmental sustainability.

Wal-Mart, for example, is doing just that. Through its own environmental sustainability actions and its impact on the actions of suppliers, Wal-Mart has emerged in recent years as the world's super "eco-nanny." Alcoa, the world's leading producer of aluminum, is also setting a high sustainability standard. For five years running it has been named one of the most sustainable corporations in the annual *Global 100 Most Sustainable Corporations in the World* ranking:

> Alcoa has distinguished itself as a leader through its sophisticated approach to identifying and managing the material sustainability risks that it faces as a company. From pollution prevention via greenhouse gas emissions reduction programs to engaging stakeholders over new environmental technology, such as controversial hydropower projects, Alcoa has the sustainability strategies in place needed to meld its profitability objectives with society's larger environmental protection goals. . . . Importantly, Alcoa's approach to sustainability is firmly rooted in the idea that sustainability programs can indeed add financial value. Perhaps the best evidence is the company's efforts to promote the use of aluminum in transportation, where aluminum—with its excellent strength-to-weight ratio—is making inroads as a material of choice that allows automakers to build low-weight, fuel-efficient vehicles that produce fewer tailpipe emissions. This kind of forward-thinking strategy of supplying the market with the products that will help solve pressing global environmental problems shows a company that sees the future, has plotted a course, and is aligning its business accordingly. Says CEO Alain Belda, "Our values require us to think and act not only on the present challenges, but also with the legacy in mind that we leave for those who will come after us . . . as well as the commitments made by those that came before us."[24]

Environmentalism creates some special challenges for global marketers. As international trade barriers come down and global markets expand, environmental issues are having an ever-greater impact on international trade. Countries in North America, Western Europe, and other developed regions are generating strict environmental standards. In the United States, for example, more than two dozen major pieces of environmental legislation have been enacted since 1970, and recent events suggest that more regulation is on the way. A side accord to the North American Free Trade Agreement (NAFTA) set up the Commission for Environmental Cooperation for resolving environmental matters. The European Union (EU) has recently adopted a climate and energy package and legislation to reduce CO_2 emissions from new cars and transport fuels 20 percent below 1990 levels and to increase the share of renewable energy to 20 percent within one year. And the EU's Eco-Management and Audit Scheme (EMAS) provides guidelines for environmental self-regulation.[25]

However, environmental policies still vary widely from country to country. Countries such as Denmark, Germany, Japan, and the United States have fully developed environmental policies and high public expectations. But major countries such as China, India, Brazil, and Russia are in only the early stages of developing such policies. Moreover, environmental factors that motivate consumers in one country may have no impact on consumers in another. For example, PVC soft-drink bottles cannot be used in Switzerland or Germany. However, they are preferred in France, which has an extensive recycling process for them. Thus, international companies have found it difficult to develop standard environmental practices that work around the world. Instead, they are creating general policies and then translating these policies into tailored programs that meet local regulations and expectations.

Public Actions to Regulate Marketing

Citizen concerns about marketing practices will usually lead to public attention and legislative proposals. New bills will be debated—many will be defeated, others will be modified, and a few will become workable laws (see Marketing at Work 16.1).

Many of the laws that affect marketing are listed in Chapter 3. The task is to translate these laws into the language that marketing executives understand as they make decisions about competitive relations, products, price, promotion, and channels of distribution. ■ **Figure 16.3** illustrates the major legal issues facing marketing management.

■ **Figure 16.3** Major Marketing Decision Areas That May Be Called into Question Under the Law

Selling decisions
Bribing?
Stealing trade secrets?
Disparaging customers?
Misrepresenting?
Disclosure of customer rights?
Unfair discrimination?

Product decisions
Product additions and deletions?
Patent protection?
Product quality and safety?
Product warranty?

Advertising decisions
False advertising?
Deceptive advertising?
Bait-and-switch advertising?
Promotional allowances and services?

Packaging decisions
Fair packaging and labeling?
Excessive cost?
Scarce resources?
Pollution?

Channel decisions
Exclusive dealing?
Exclusive territorial distributorship?
Tying agreements?
Dealer's rights?

Price decisions
Price fixing?
Predatory pricing?
Price discrimination?
Minimum pricing?
Price increases?
Deceptive pricing?

Competitive relations decisions
Anticompetitive acquisition?
Barriers to entry?
Predatory competition?

Marketing at Work 16.1

Fat-Free Promotion

The bulk of brand advertising is intended to affect brand choice. Promotion can affect brand choice without necessarily affecting the overall consumption of a product or service. Why, then, is the finger of guilt being pointed at the advertising and marketing world for the increase in childhood and adult obesity? Branded foods and drinks are not inherently unhealthy. Coca-Cola, for example, contains roughly the same amount of sugar per liter as fruit juice. Therefore, in terms of obesity and calorific intake, simply switching from a branded soft drink to a fruit juice would have no impact whatsoever. In 2003 in Britain, the Hastings Review commissioned by the Food Standards Agency looked at the link between the promotion of food and the eating habits of children. The report concluded that advertising aimed at children had a detrimental impact on children's food preferences and consequently the purchasing behaviors of families and ultimately consumption. In 2004, Dr. David Ashton (Clinical Epidemiology/Cardiac Medicine Department at Imperial College School of Medicine) in an article in the Journal of the *Royal Society of Medicine* argued that the evidence in the Hastings Review did not support the conclusions it made. Ashton saw no value in completely banning advertising, as it would have no appreciable impact on childhood obesity rates.

It was Ashton's contention that the overwhelmingly dominant influence on children's eating habits was their parents. He claimed that this was at least 15 times more important than television advertising. Ashton highlighted the fact that two of the most quoted studies did not find that TV advertising and food promotion were major impacts on the food consumption behaviour of children. The Hastings Review also admitted that the links were not as straightforward and obvious as many believed. However they cautioned that food promotion itself, as an influence on children's dietary habits, could be either a positive or a negative influence.

The Incorporated Society of British Advertisers (ISBA), in response to criticisms leveled at the industry, responded in 2006 by claiming that "It [the views of Ofcom, the regulator] gives far too much weight to the imponderable, and at best, modest influence of food/drink advertising on childhood obesity, given the array of other more powerful factors in play such as parents, friends, school, exercise and lifestyle. It gives far too little weight to the competing interests: for example, the public interest in balance, diversity and quality in programs and the more private interests of broadcasters and advertisers. One of the principle advantages of imposing a lower upper age limit (under 9 or under 12) is that it helps the measures to be precise. An upper age limit of 16 makes it far more difficult for scheduling restrictions to target programs viewed by the protected group. This is because audiences will be much more mixed in terms of age."

The Food Products (Marketing to Children) Bill was blocked in the House of Commons in April 2008. It was to make it an offence to promote "less healthy" foodstuffs to children. The bill also called for no advertising of unhealthy food before 9 p.m. Nigel Griffiths, the Labour Member of Parliament and sponsor

▲More than 90 million units of the George Forman Grill have been sold around the world, making it the best-selling household appliance of all time.

of the bill, believed that the advertising and promotion of junk foods, believed to be worth £800 million each year, undermined any effort made by parents to limit their children's intake of food and sugary drinks. Culture Minister Margaret Hodge spoke about the steps being taken: "If the measures that we have taken so far fail to produce a change in the nature and balance of food promotion to children, we will take action to implement a clearly defined framework for regulating the promotion of food to children. For broadcast advertising we can do that within the existing legislation—so we do not actually need a new bill." Commentators and industry specialists would be forgiven for assuming that obesity is a "first world" disease, as is the prevalence of diabetes. However, both are endemic in the Middle East. In Bahrain, research suggests that close to 83 percent of women are obese or overweight (International Obesity Task Force). In the United Arab Emirates, the percentage stands at 74 percent and in Lebanon is 75 percent. By comparison, in the United States, the number of obese or overweight women stands at 62 percent. Equally, childhood obesity is at record levels in the Middle East and diabetes is spreading.

In the city of Nouakchott in Mauritania, the Pharmacy of Everlasting Beauty sells highly advertised drugs as appetite enhancers. The most expensive is Tres Orix (priced at around $8). The average annual income in Mauritania is $1,800, but sales of the drug are high and sold mainly to women. Marketing and advertising experts, always with an eye open for a potential new market, arranged for the road show of the former boxing champion George Foreman to roll into town in the Middle East in early 2007. Although Foreman's world famous grills have been on sale in some parts of the Gulf since 2004, this was the first time that the man himself had appeared to promote the healthy eating option. Promoting the new G5 grill in the region was Jashanmal Group chief executive Gangu Batra: "We are here to sell grills and we think we can sell literally millions.

When you read everything about obesity in the Middle East, and then you get a product like this, and then you get

(continued)

someone like George Foreman to sell it, you know you have hit the jackpot." Worldwide, Foreman's grills have sold more than 90 million units. The grills are the bestselling household appliance of all time.

Foreman, interviewed at one of the fist promotional events, said, "This is my first time in the Middle East, and I have seen some amazing things and some sad things. I have seen the greatest construction projects anywhere on earth. I have seen the greatest cultural diversity. I have seen the greatest buzz. But sadly, I haven't seen any George Foreman grills." It seems

marketing can pull a success story out of potential disaster every time.

Sources: Quotes and other information taken from Jashanmal National Company (www.jashanmal-uae.com); The Food Products (Marketing to Children) Bill (www.publications.parliament.uk); Department for Culture Media and Sport (www.culture.gov.uk); George Foreman Grills (www.georgeforemangrills.co.uk); The Incorporated Society of British Advertisers (www.isba.org.uk); Food Standards Agency (www.food.gov.uk); and Ofcom quote taken from 'Television Adverting of Food and Drink Products for Children', 21st December 2006 © Ofcom (www.ofcom.org.uk).

Author Comment »
In the end, marketers themselves must take responsibility for sustainable marketing. That means operating in a responsible and ethical way to bring immediate and future value to customers.

BUSINESS ACTIONS TOWARD SUSTAINABLE MARKETING (pp 558–563)

At first, many companies opposed consumerism, environmentalism, and other elements of sustainable marketing. They thought the criticisms were either unfair or unimportant. But by now, most companies have grown to embrace the new consumer rights, at least in principle. They might oppose certain pieces of legislation as inappropriate ways to solve specific consumer problems, but they recognize the consumer's right to information and protection. Many of these companies have responded positively to sustainable marketing as a way to create greater immediate and future customer value and to strengthen customer relationships.

Sustainable Marketing Principles

Under the sustainable marketing concept, a company's marketing should support the best long-run performance of the marketing system. It should be guided by five sustainable marketing principles: *consumer-oriented marketing, customer-value marketing, innovative marketing, sense-of-mission marketing,* and *societal marketing.*

Consumer-Oriented Marketing

Consumer-oriented marketing
The philosophy of sustainable marketing that holds that the company should view and organize its marketing activities from the consumer's point of view.

Consumer-oriented marketing means that the company should view and organize its marketing activities from the consumer's point of view. It should work hard to sense, serve, and satisfy the needs of a defined group of customers, both now and in the future. All of the good marketing companies that we've discussed in this text have had this in common: an all-consuming passion for delivering superior value to carefully chosen customers. Only by seeing the world through its customers' eyes can the company build lasting and profitable customer relationships.

Customer-Value Marketing

Customer-value marketing
A principle of sustainable marketing that holds that a company should put most of its resources into customer-value-building marketing investments.

According to the principle of **customer-value marketing**, the company should put most of its resources into customer-value-building marketing investments. Many things marketers do—one-shot sales promotions, cosmetic packaging changes, direct-response advertising—may raise sales in the short run but add less *value* than would actual improvements in the product's quality, features, or convenience. Enlightened marketing calls for building long-run consumer loyalty and relationships by continually improving the value consumers receive from the firm's market offering. By creating value *for* consumers, the company can capture value *from* consumers in return.

▲ **Innovative marketing: Nintendo's customer-focused innovation not only attracted new gamers and bruised competitors Sony and Microsoft, "it has opened doors of creativity throughout the video-game business."**

Innovative marketing
A principle of sustainable marketing that requires that a company seek real product and marketing improvements.

Sense-of-mission marketing
A principle of sustainable marketing that holds that a company should define its mission in broad social terms rather than narrow product terms.

Innovative Marketing

The principle of **innovative marketing** requires that the company continuously seek real product and marketing improvements. The company that overlooks new and better ways to do things will eventually lose customers to another company that has found a better way. ▲ An excellent example of an innovative marketer is Nintendo:[26]

> After Sony and Microsoft kicked the Mario out of Nintendo's GameCube in the Video Game War of 2001, the smallest of the three game platform makers needed a new plan. "Nintendo took a step back from the technology arms race and chose to focus on [customers and] the fun of playing, rather than cold tech specs," says the president of Nintendo of America. The resulting Wii system, with its intuitive motion-sensitive controller and interactive games, appealed not only to teen boys typically targeted by the game industry but also to their sisters, moms, dads, and even grandparents. The result: the perpetually sold-out Wii system quickly outsold both the PlayStation 3 and Xbox 360. But get this: Unlike its competitors—which lose money on each console and earn it back on software—Nintendo actually turns a profit on its consoles, makes more selling games, then takes in still more in licensing fees. "Not to sound too obvious," says the Nintendo executive, "but it makes good business sense to make a profit on the products you sell." Nintendo's upset is doing more than attracting new gamers and bruising Sony and Microsoft. Says the president of competitor Sega of America, "It has opened doors of creativity throughout the video-game business."

Sense-of-Mission Marketing

Sense-of-mission marketing means that the company should define its mission in broad *social* terms rather than narrow *product* terms. When a company defines a social mission, employees feel better about their work and have a clearer sense of direction. Brands linked with broader missions can serve the best long-run interests of both the brand and consumers. For example, Dove wants to do more than just sell its beauty care products. It's on a mission to discover "real beauty" and to help women be happy just the way they are:[27]

> It all started with a Unilever study that examined the impact on women of images seen in entertainment, in advertising, and on fashion runways. The startling result: Only 2 percent of 3,300 women and girls surveyed in 10 countries around the world considered themselves beautiful. Unilever's conclusion: It's time to redefine beauty. So in 2004, Unilever launched the global Dove Campaign for Real Beauty, with ads that featured candid and confident images of real women of all types (not actresses or models) and headlines that made consumers ponder their perceptions of beauty. Among others, it featured full-bodied women ("Oversized or Outstanding?"), older women ("Gray or Gorgeous?"), and a heavily freckled woman ("Flawed or Flawless?"). The following year, as the campaign's popularity skyrocketed, Dove introduced six new "real beauties" of various proportions, in sizes ranging from 6 to 14. These women appeared in ads wearing nothing but their underwear and big smiles, with headlines proclaiming, "New Dove Firming: As Tested on Real Curves." "In Dove ads," says one advertising expert, "normal is the new beautiful."
>
> The Dove Campaign for Real Beauty quickly went digital, with a www.campaignforreal beauty.com Web site and award-winning viral videos with names such as "Evolution" and "Onslaught" that attacked damaging beauty stereotypes. As the campaign took off, so did sales of Dove products. But the people behind the Dove brand and the Campaign for Real Beauty have noble motives beyond sales and profits. According to a Unilever executive, Dove's bold and compelling mission to redefine beauty and reassure women ranks well above issues of dollars and cents. "You should see the faces of the people working on this brand now," he says. "There is a real love for the brand."

Some companies define their overall corporate missions in broad societal terms. For example, defined in narrow product terms, the mission of Unilever's Ben & Jerry's unit might be "to sell ice cream." However, the Ben & Jerry's brand states its mission more broadly, as one of "linked prosperity," including product, economic, and social missions. From its beginnings, Ben & Jerry's championed a host of social and environmental causes, and it donated a whopping 7.5 percent of pretax profits to support worthy causes each year. By the mid-1990s, Ben & Jerry's had become the nation's number-two superpremium ice cream brand.

However, having a "double bottom line" of values and profits is no easy proposition. Throughout the 1990s, as competitors not shackled by "principles before profits" missions invaded its markets, Ben & Jerry's growth and profits flattened. In 2000, after several years of less-than-stellar financial returns, Ben & Jerry's was acquired by giant food producer Unilever. Looking back, the company appears to have focused too much on social issues at the expense of sound business management. Founder Ben Cohen once commented, "There came a time when I had to admit 'I'm a businessman.' And I had a hard time mouthing those words."[28]

Such experiences taught the socially responsible business movement some hard lessons. The result is a new generation of activist entrepreneurs—not social activists with big hearts who hate capitalism, but well-trained business managers and company builders with a passion for a cause. Founded by businesspeople who are proud of it, the new mission-driven companies are just as dedicated to building a viable, profitable business as to shaping the mission. They know that to "do good," they must first "do well" in terms of successful business operations. Stephen Green, Group Chairman of HSBC, said in the group's Sustainability Report 2008 that HSBC is focused on creating and building sustainable growth opportunities so that customers, employees, and the communities in which the company operates would thrive, flourish, and prosper both now and in the future (see Marketing at Work 16.2).

Societal Marketing

Following the principle of **societal marketing**, a company makes marketing decisions by considering consumers' wants and interests, the company's requirements, and society's long-run interests. The company is aware that neglecting consumer and societal long-run interests is a disservice to consumers and society. Alert companies view societal problems as opportunities.

Sustainable marketing calls for products that are not only pleasing but also beneficial. The difference is shown in ■ **Figure 16.4**. Products can be classified according to their degree of immediate consumer satisfaction and long-run consumer benefit.

Deficient products, such as bad-tasting and ineffective medicine, have neither immediate appeal nor long-run benefits. **Pleasing products** give high immediate satisfaction but may hurt consumers in the long run. Examples include cigarettes and junk food. **Salutary products** have low immediate appeal but may benefit consumers in the long run; for instance, bicycle helmets or some insurance products. **Desirable products** give both high immediate satisfaction and high long-run benefits, such as a tasty *and* nutritious breakfast food.

Examples of desirable products abound. GE's Energy Smart compact fluorescent lightbulb provides good lighting at the same time that it gives long life and energy savings. Toyota's hybrid Prius gives both a quiet ride and fuel efficiency. Maytag's front-loading Neptune washer provides superior cleaning along with water savings and energy efficiency. ▲And Haworth's Zody office chair is not only attractive and functional but also environmentally responsible:

Let's talk about your butt—specifically, what it's sitting on. Chances are, your chair is an unholy medley of polyvinyl chloride and hazardous chemicals that drift into your lungs each time you shift your weight. It was likely produced in a fossil-fuel-swilling factory that in turn spews toxic pollution and effluents. And it's ultimately destined for a landfill or incinerator, where it will emit carcinogenic dioxins and

Societal marketing
A principle of sustainable marketing that holds that a company should make marketing decisions by considering consumers' wants, the company's requirements, consumers' long-run interests, and society's long-run interests.

Deficient products
Products that have neither immediate appeal nor long-run benefits.

Pleasing products
Products that give high immediate satisfaction but may hurt consumers in the long run.

Salutary products
Products that have low appeal but may benefit consumers in the long run.

Desirable products
Products that give both high immediate satisfaction and high long-run benefits.

▼**Desirable products: Haworth's Zody office chair is not only attractive and functional but also environmentally responsible.**

Marketing at Work 16.2

HSBC Holdings plc: Serving Both Profits and Values

HSBC is one of the largest banking and financial services companies in the world. It has 9,500 offices and 325,000 employees located in 86 countries and territories. It believes in developing a sustainable business and has the following priorities: Operating a profitable business in a changing global economy; helping customers affected by the recession; instilling a motivational culture in the company for retaining and developing of top talents; and, investing in the communities. HSBC believes it can serve the double bottom line of both profits and values.

HSBC has committed to invest in the communities in which they operate, especially emerging economies. It has contributed $102.4 million to the community in 2008 and its employees volunteered 406,000 hours of company time. There are three main areas that HSBC invests its time and resources in: education, the environment, and sustainable finance.

In 2006, HSBC launched a five-year global education initiative called "Future First." This is a $10 million program aimed at helping 1 million disadvantaged children to have a brighter future. By the end of 2008, through working with SOS Children's Villages and other charities, it had conducted 141 projects in 39 countries, which benefited more then 130,000 homeless and vulnerable children.

It also partnered Junior Achievement Worldwide (an organization with expertise in teaching finance and entrepreneurship to children) to launch a global business literacy program called "JA More than Money" in 2008. This three-year program has set a target of educating 100,000 children across 25 countries with basic skills and knowledge about earning, spending, sharing, and saving money.

For 2009, it planned to partner Foundation for Environment Education (a Danish-based, nongovernmental organization) to launch an environmental education program called "HSBC Eco-Schools Climate Initiative." The plan is for schools to network across countries to work together to reduce the effects of climate change.

Managing the impact and challenges of climate change in the twenty-first century is an important priority to HSBC. It believes climate change presents new areas of growth, opportunities, and innovation for the company in banking, insurance, investment, trade services, energy efficiency, renewable energy, and carbon management. In 2007, the HSBC Climate Partnership was launched to provide $100 million over a five-year period to work with The Climate Group, Earthwatch, Smithsonian Tropical Research

Institute, and WWF-World Wide Fund for Nature (also known as World Wildlife Fund in North America) to combat climate change.

HSBC chooses to buy carbon offsets materials across technologies because it believes in moving towards a low-carbon world. It has supported numerous renewable energy and energy efficiency projects in many parts of the world. For example, HSBC invested money to build eight small hydrostations in Sichuan province in China to generate electricity from hydropower instead of the burning of coal. This method reduces carbon dioxide emission. Water used to generate electricity is a renewable energy source because it can be recycled.

In addition, HSBC North America was awarded the Leadership in Energy and Environmental Design (LEED) gold certification from the U.S. Green Building Council. The headquarters building in Mettawa, Illinois installed water-efficient equipment that helped the company to achieve more than 30 percent savings compared to existing best practices. There are also other interesting energy-saving designs such as drought-resistant landscaping that reduces irrigation and using rainwater for toilet flushing and irrigation. Renewable sources are used to generate 100 percent of its electricity needs.

Microfinance is a useful method to provide small-scale financial services and development opportunities to people in developing countries who would normally not be able to access such services. HSBC works with many local financial institu-

▲ Over the last few years, HSBC has taken an active role in various sustainability initiatives and education programs. It also invests heavily in carbon offsetting and has pledged to continue its support to combat climate change into 2010 and beyond.

(continued)

tions to provide credit, wholesale lending, cash management, remittances, and foreign exchange handling. HSBC is working with 11 microfinance institutions in India to provide $38 million to about 250,000 people in rural and urban areas. The following is an example of how microfinance helped Shukla's husband, a rickshaw puller from India.

He spent about 30 rupees (approximately $0.64) paying for the rental of his rickshaw every day and earned about 2,200 rupees ($46.60) per month. After learning about Bandhan, a microfinance institution, Shukla obtained a loan of 5,000 rupees ($106) to buy her husband his own hand rickshaw, which eliminated the fee of renting; their income increased significantly within a short period of time.

Shukla was able to repay the loan quickly and borrowed another 6,000 rupees (approximately $127.20) to buy a second rickshaw to rent it out to others. They were able to pay off the loan and then borrowed again to enable her to buy more rickshaws. Eventually they were able to own 5 rickshaws and earned nearly 8,000 rupees ($169.60) per month. Shukla is considering borrowing from Bandhan to realize her dream of opening a traditional Indian costume Sari business.

Through working with HSBC, Bandhan is able to provide loans to customers like Shukla and her husband. This method works well because these loans are not handouts but have to be

paid back. Customers are empowered to take control of their financial situation by being responsible for their own livelihood.

Over the past few years, HSBC has been involved in over 10,000 diverse sustainability initiatives and projects around the world. It has achieved many awards and accolades in 2008 including Most Highly Rated Bank for Climate Change Governance (Awarded by U.S. investor coalition, Ceres) and first in the Hang Seng Index Listed Companies Corporate Social Responsibilities Survey (Oxfam Hong Kong).

For 2009 and beyond, it has also pledged to continue its support for many global environment education programs and to influence public policy on climate change and reduce CO_2 emission. On top of spending money, it is also pushing to train another 400 employees from over 40 countries as HSBC Climate Champions within the business and to include a sustainability module in new global induction course for new employees.

HSBC is a shining example of a global company that is putting "Sense-of-Mission" marketing into practice.

Sources: Based on information from HSBC Holdings plc Sustainability Report 2008, HSBC global homepage, accessed October 28, 2009 at www.hsbc.com/1/2/sustainability.

■ **Figure 16.4** Societal Classification of Products

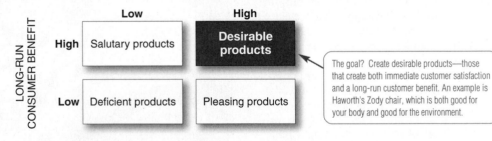

IMMEDIATE SATISFACTION

LONG-RUN CONSUMER BENEFIT

	Low	High
High	Salutary products	**Desirable products**
Low	Deficient products	Pleasing products

The goal? Create desirable products—those that create both immediate customer satisfaction and a long-run customer benefit. An example is Haworth's Zody chair, which is both good for your body and good for the environment.

endocrine-disrupting phthalates, the kind of hormone-mimicking nasties that give male fish female genitalia and small children cancer (or is it the other way around?). Now, envision what you might be sitting on in 2016. Actually, never mind: Office-furniture outfit Haworth already built it. It's called the Zody, and it's made without PVC, CFCs, chrome, or any other toxic fixin's. Ninety-eight percent of it can be recycled; some 50 percent of it already has been. The energy used in the manufacturing process is completely offset by wind-power credits, and when the chair is ready to retire, the company will take it off your hands and reuse its components. And the award-winning Zody's not just good for the environment, it's also good for your body. It was the first chair to be endorsed by the American Physical Therapy Association.[29]

Companies should try to turn all of their products into desirable products. The challenge posed by pleasing products is that they sell very well but may end up hurting the consumer. The product opportunity, therefore, is to add long-run benefits without reducing the product's pleasing qualities. The challenge posed by salutary products is to add some pleasing qualities so that they will become more desirable in consumers' minds.

Marketing Ethics (pp 563–565)

Good ethics are a cornerstone of sustainable marketing. In the long run, unethical marketing harms customers and society as a whole. Further, it eventually damages a company's reputation and effectiveness, jeopardizing the company's very survival. Thus, the sustainable marketing goals of long-term consumer and business welfare can be achieved only through ethical marketing conduct.

Conscientious marketers face many moral dilemmas. The best thing to do is often unclear. Because not all managers have fine moral sensitivity, companies need to develop *corporate marketing ethics policies*—broad guidelines that everyone in the organization must follow. These policies should cover distributor relations, advertising standards, customer service, pricing, product development, and general ethical standards.

The finest guidelines cannot resolve all the difficult ethical situations the marketer faces. ■ **Table 16.1** lists some difficult ethical issues marketers could face during their

■ **Table 16.1** Some Morally Difficult Situations in Marketing

1. Your R&D department has changed one of your products slightly. It is not really "new and improved," but you know that putting this statement on the package and in advertising will increase sales. What would you do?

2. You have been asked to add a stripped-down model to your line that could be advertised to pull customers into the store. The product won't be very good, but salespeople will be able to switch buyers up to higher-priced units. You are asked to give the green light for the stripped-down version. What would you do?

3. You are thinking of hiring a product manager who has just left a competitor's company. She would be more than happy to tell you all the competitor's plans for the coming year. What would you do?

4. One of your top dealers in an important territory recently has had family troubles, and his sales have slipped. It looks like it will take him a while to straighten out his family trouble. Meanwhile you are losing many sales. Legally, on performance grounds, you can terminate the dealer's franchise and replace him. What would you do?

5. You have a chance to win a big account that will mean a lot to you and your company. The purchasing agent hints that a "gift" would influence the decision. Your assistant recommends sending a large-screen television to the buyer's home. What would you do?

6. You have heard that a competitor has a new product feature that will make a big difference in sales. The competitor will demonstrate the feature in a private dealer meeting at the annual trade show. You can easily send a snooper to this meeting to learn about the new feature. What would you do?

7. You work for a cigarette company. Public policy debates over the past many years leave no doubt in your mind that cigarette smoking and cancer are closely linked. Although your company currently runs an "If you don't smoke, don't start" promotion campaign, you believe that other company promotions might encourage young (although legal age) nonsmokers to pick up the habit. What would you do?

8. You have to choose between three ad campaigns outlined by your agency. The first (a) is a soft-sell, honest, straight-information campaign. The second (b) uses sex-loaded emotional appeals and exaggerates the product's benefits. The third (c) involves a noisy, somewhat irritating commercial that is sure to gain audience attention. Pretests show that the campaigns are effective in the following order: c, b, and a. What would you do?

9. You are interviewing a capable female applicant for a job as salesperson. She is better qualified than the men just interviewed. Nevertheless, you know that in your industry some important customers prefer dealing with men, and you will lose some sales if you hire her. What would you do?

careers. If marketers choose immediate sales-producing actions in all these cases, their marketing behavior might well be described as immoral or even amoral. If they refuse to go along with *any* of the actions, they might be ineffective as marketing managers and unhappy because of the constant moral tension. Managers need a set of principles that will help them figure out the moral importance of each situation and decide how far they can go in good conscience.

But *what* principle should guide companies and marketing managers on issues of ethics and social responsibility? One philosophy is that such issues are decided by the free market and legal system. Under this principle, companies and their managers are not responsible for making moral judgments. Companies can in good conscience do whatever the market and legal systems allow.

A second philosophy puts responsibility not on the system but in the hands of individual companies and managers. This more enlightened philosophy suggests that a company should have a "social conscience." Companies and managers should apply high standards of ethics and morality when making corporate decisions, regardless of "what the system allows." History provides an endless list of examples of company actions that were legal but highly irresponsible.

Each company and marketing manager must work out a philosophy of socially responsible and ethical behavior. Under the societal marketing concept, each manager must look beyond what is legal and allowed and develop standards based on personal integrity, corporate conscience, and long-run consumer welfare.

Dealing with issues of ethics and social responsibility in an open and forthright way helps to build strong customer relationships based on honestly and trust. In fact, many companies now routinely include consumers in the social responsibility process. Consider toy maker Mattel:[30]

▲Toy-maker Mattel's recent open and decisive product-recall response, based on input and help from its panel of customer-advisors, helped to maintain customer confidence and create even more trusting customer relationships.

▲In fall 2007, the discovery of lead paint on several of its best-selling products forced Mattel to make worldwide recalls on millions of toys. Threatening as this was, rather hesitating or hiding the incident, the company's brand advisors were up to the challenge. They're quick, decisive response helped to maintain consumer confidence in the Mattel brand, even contributing to a 6 percent sales increase over the same period the year before. Just who were these masterful "brand advisors"? They were the 400 moms with kids aged 3 to 10 comprising The Playground Community, a private online network launched by Mattel's worldwide consumer insights department in June 2007 to "listen to and gain insight from moms' lives and needs." Throughout the crisis, The Playground Community members kept in touch with Mattel regarding the product recalls and the company's forthright response plan, even helping to shape the postrecall promotional strategy for one of the affected product lines. Even in times of crisis, "brands that engage in a two-way conversation with their customers create stronger, more trusting relationships," says a Mattel executive.

As with environmentalism, the issue of ethics presents special challenges for international marketers. Business standards and practices vary a great deal from one country to the next. For example, bribes and kickbacks are illegal for U.S. firms and a variety of treaties against bribery and corruption have been signed and ratified by more than 60 countries. Yet these are still standard business practices in many countries. The World Bank estimates that more than $1 trillion per year worth of bribes are paid out worldwide. One studied showed that the most flagrant bribe-paying firms were from India, Russia, and China. Other countries where corruption is common include Iraq, Myanmar, and Haiti. The least corrupt were companies from Iceland, Finland, New Zealand, and Denmark.[31]

The question arises as to whether a company must lower its ethical standards to compete effectively in countries with lower standards. The answer: No. Companies should make a commitment to a common set of shared standards worldwide. For example, John Hancock Mutual Life Insurance Company operates successfully in Southeast Asia, an area that by Western standards has widespread questionable business and government practices. Despite warnings from locals that Hancock would have to bend its rules to succeed, the company set out strict guidelines. "We told our people that we had the same ethical standards, same procedures, and same policies in these countries that we have in the United States, and we do," said then-CEO Stephen Brown. "We just felt that things like payoffs were wrong—and if we had to do business that way, we'd rather not do business." Hancock employees feel good about the consistent levels of ethics. "There may be countries where you have to do that kind of thing," said Brown. "We haven't found that country yet, and if we do, we won't do business there."[32]

Many industrial and professional associations have suggested codes of ethics, and many companies are now adopting their own codes. For example, the American Marketing Association, an international association of marketing managers and scholars, developed the code of ethics shown in ■ **Table 16.2**. Companies are also developing programs to teach managers about important ethics issues and help them find the proper responses. They hold ethics workshops and seminars and set up ethics committees. Furthermore, most major U.S. companies have appointed high-level ethics officers to champion ethics issues and to help resolve ethics problems and concerns facing employees.

PricewaterhouseCoopers (PwC) is a good example. In 2002, PwC established a global ethics office and comprehensive ethics program, headed by a high-level global ethics officer. The ethics program begins with a code of conduct, called "The Way We Do Business." PwC employees learn about the code of conduct and about how to handle thorny ethics issues in comprehensive ethics training programs, which start when the employee joins the company and continue through the employee's career. The program also includes an ethics help line and regular communications at all levels. "It is obviously not enough to distribute a document," says PwC's global CEO, Samuel DiPiazza. "Ethics is in everything we say and do."[33]

Still, written codes and ethics programs do not ensure ethical behavior. Ethics and social responsibility require a total corporate commitment. They must be a component of the overall corporate culture. According to PwC's DiPiazza, "I see ethics as a mission-critical issue . . . deeply imbedded in who we are and what we do. It's just as important as our product development cycle or our distribution system. . . . It's about creating a culture based on integrity and respect, not a culture based on dealing with the crisis of the day. . . . We ask ourselves every day, 'Are we doing the right things?'"[34]

The Sustainable Company (pp 565–567)

At the foundation of marketing is the belief that companies that fulfill the needs and wants of customers will thrive. Companies that fail to meet customer needs or that intentionally or unintentionally harm customers, others in society, or future generations will decline. Sustainable companies are those that create value for customers through socially, environmentally, and ethically responsible actions.

Sustainable marketing goes beyond caring for the needs and wants of today's customers. It means having concern for tomorrow's customers in assuring the survival and success of the business, shareholders, employees, and the broader world in which they all live. Sustainable marketing provides the context in which companies can build profitable customer relationships by creating value *for* customers in order to capture value *from* customers in return, now and in the future.

■ **Table 16.2** American Marketing Association Code of Ethics

Ethical Norms and Values For Marketers Preamble

The American Marketing Association commits itself to promoting the highest standard of professional ethical norms and values for its members. Norms are established standards of conduct that are expected and maintained by society and/or professional organizations. Values represent the collective conception of what people find desirable, important and morally proper. Values serve as the criteria for evaluating the actions of others. Marketing practitioners must recognize that they not only serve their enterprises but also act as stewards of society in creating, facilitating, and executing the efficient and effective transactions that are part of the greater economy. In this role, marketers should embrace the highest ethical norms of practicing professionals and the ethical values implied by their responsibility toward stakeholders (e.g., customers, employees, investors, channel members, regulators, and the host community).

General Norms

1. Marketers must do no harm. This means doing work for which they are appropriately trained or experienced so that they can actively add value to their organizations and customers. It also means adhering to all applicable laws and regulations and embodying high ethical standards in the choices they make.
2. Marketers must foster trust in the marketing system. This means that products are appropriate for their intended and promoted uses. It requires that marketing communications about goods and services are not intentionally deceptive or misleading. It suggests building relationships that provide for the equitable adjustment and/or redress of customer grievances. It implies striving for good faith and fair dealing so as to contribute toward the efficacy of the exchange process.
3. Marketers must embrace, communicate and practice the fundamental ethical values that will improve consumer confidence in the integrity of the marketing exchange system. These basic values are intentionally aspirational and include honesty, responsibility, fairness, respect, openness, and citizenship.

Ethical Values

Honesty—to be truthful and forthright in our dealings with customers and stakeholders.

- We will tell the truth in all situations and at all times.
- We will offer products of value that do what we claim in our communications.
- We will stand behind our products if they fail to deliver their claimed benefits.
- We will honor our explicit and implicit commitments and promises.

Responsibility—to accept the consequences of our marketing decisions and strategies.

- We will make strenuous efforts to serve the needs of our customers.
- We will avoid using coercion with all stakeholders.
- We will acknowledge the social obligations to stakeholders that come with increased marketing and economic power.
- We will recognize our special commitments to economically vulnerable segments of the market such as children, the elderly, and others who may be substantially disadvantaged.

Fairness—to try to balance justly the needs of the buyer with the interests of the seller.

- We will represent our products in a clear way in selling, advertising, and other forms of communication; this includes the avoidance of false, misleading, and deceptive promotion.
- We will reject manipulations and sales tactics that harm customer trust.
- We will not engage in price fixing, predatory pricing, price gouging or "bait-and-switch" tactics.
- We will not knowingly participate in material conflicts of interest.

Respect—to acknowledge the basic human dignity of all stakeholders.

- We will value individual differences even as we avoid stereotyping customers or depicting demographic groups (e.g., gender, race, sexual orientation) in a negative or dehumanizing way in our promotions.
- We will listen to the needs of our customers and make all reasonable efforts to monitor and improve their satisfaction on an ongoing basis.
- We will make a special effort to understand suppliers, intermediaries, and distributors from other cultures.
- We will appropriately acknowledge the contributions of others, such as consultants, employees, and coworkers, to our marketing endeavors.

■ **Table 16.2** Continued

Openness—to create transparency in our marketing operations.

● We will strive to communicate clearly with all our constituencies.
● We will accept constructive criticism from our customers and other stakeholders.
● We will explain significant product or service risks, component substitutions or other foreseeable eventualities that could affect customers or their perception of the purchase decision.
● We will fully disclose list prices and terms of financing as well as available price deals and adjustments.

Citizenship—to fulfill the economic, legal, philanthropic, and societal responsibilities that serve stakeholders in a strategic manner.

● We will strive to protect the natural environment in the execution of marketing campaigns.
● We will give back to the community through volunteerism and charitable donations.
● We will work to contribute to the overall betterment of marketing and its reputation.
● We will encourage supply chain members to ensure that trade is fair for all participants, including producers in developing countries.

Implementation

Finally, we recognize that every industry sector and marketing subdiscipline (e.g., marketing research, e-commerce, direct selling, direct marketing, advertising) has its own specific ethical issues that require policies and commentary. An array of such codes can be accessed through links on the AMA Web site. We encourage all such groups to develop and/or refine their industry and discipline-specific codes of ethics to supplement these general norms and values.

Source: Reprinted with permission of the American Marketing Association.

REST STOP
REVIEWING THE CONCEPTS

Well—here you are at the end of your introductory marketing journey! In this chapter, we've closed with many important *sustainable marketing* concepts related to marketing's sweeping impact on individual consumers, other businesses, and society as a whole. You learned that sustainable marketing requires socially, environmentally, and ethically responsible actions that bring value not just to present-day consumers and businesses, but also to future generations and to society as a whole. Sustainable companies are those that act responsibly to create value for customers in order to capture value from customers in return, now and in the future.

 Objective 1 Define *sustainable marketing* and discuss its importance. **(pp 539–540)**

Sustainable marketing calls for meeting the present needs of consumers and businesses while still preserving or enhancing the ability of future generations to meet their needs. Whereas the marketing concept recognizes that companies thrive by fulfilling the day-to-day needs of customers, sustainable marketing calls for socially and environmentally responsible actions that meet both the immediate and future needs of customers and the company. Truly sustainable marketing requires a smooth-functioning marketing system in which consumers, companies, public policymakers, and others work together to ensure responsible marketing actions.

 Objective 2 Identify the major social criticisms of marketing. **(pp 540–549)**

Marketing's *impact on individual consumer welfare* has been criticized for its high prices, deceptive practices, high-pressure selling, shoddy or unsafe products, planned obsolescence, and poor service to disadvantaged consumers. Marketing's *impact on society* has been criticized for creating false wants and too much materialism, too few social goods, and cultural pollution. Critics have also criticized marketing's *impact on other businesses* for harming competitors and reducing competition through acquisitions, practices that create barriers to entry, and unfair competitive marketing practices. Some of these concerns are justified; some are not.

Objective 3 Define *consumerism* and *environmentalism* and explain how they affect marketing strategies. **(pp 549–558)**

Concerns about the marketing system have led to *citizen action movements*. *Consumerism* is an organized social movement intended to strengthen the rights and power of consumers relative to sellers. Alert marketers view it as an opportunity to serve consumers better by providing more consumer information, education, and protection. *Environmentalism* is an organized social movement seeking to minimize the harm done to the environment and quality of life by marketing practices. The first wave of modern environmentalism was driven by environmental groups and concerned consumers; whereas the second wave was driven by government, which passed laws and regulations governing industrial practices impacting the environment. The first two environmentalism waves are now merging into a third and stronger wave in which companies are accepting responsibility for doing no environmental harm. Companies now are adopting policies of *environmental sustainability*—developing strategies that both sustain the environment and produce profits for the company. Both consumerism and environmentalism are important components of sustainable marketing.

 Objective 4 Describe the principles of sustainable marketing. **(pp 558–563)**

Many companies originally opposed these social movements and laws, but most of them now recognize a need for positive consumer information, education, and protection. Under the sustainable marketing concept, a company's marketing should support the best long-run performance of the marketing system. It should be guided by five sus-

tainable marketing principles: *consumer-oriented marketing, customer-value marketing, innovative marketing, sense-of-mission marketing,* and *societal marketing.*

 Objective 5 Explain the role of ethics in marketing. **(pp 563–567)**

Increasingly, companies are responding to the need to provide company policies and guidelines to help their managers deal with questions of *marketing ethics*. Of course even the best guidelines cannot resolve all the difficult ethical decisions that individuals and firms must make. But there are some principles that marketers can choose among. One principle states that such issues should be decided by the free market and legal system. A second, and more enlightened principle, puts responsibility not on the system but in the hands of individual companies and managers. Each firm and marketing manager must work out a philosophy of socially responsible and ethical behavior. Under the sustainable marketing concept, managers must look beyond what is legal and allowable and develop standards based on personal integrity, corporate conscience, and long-term consumer welfare.

 Navigating the Key Terms

Objective 1
Sustainable marketing (p 539)

Objective 3
Consumerism (p 550)
Environmentalism (p 551)
Environmental sustainability (p 552)

Objective 4
Consumer-oriented marketing
  (p 558)
Customer-value marketing (p 558)
Innovative marketing (p 559)
Sense-of-mission marketing (p 559)
Societal marketing (p 560)

Deficient products (p 560)
Pleasing products (p 560)
Salutary products (p 560)
Desirable products (p 560)

 Travel Log

Discussing the Issues

1. What is sustainable marketing? Explain how the sustainable marketing concept differs from the marketing concept and the societal marketing concept. (AACSB: Communication)

2. Marketing's impact on society as a whole has been criticized. Discuss the issues relevant to this impact. (AACSB: Communication)

3. Discuss the types of harmful impact that marketing practices can have on competition and the associated problems. (AACSB: Communication)

4. What is consumerism? Describe the rights of sellers and buyers. (AACSB: Communication)

5. Define the five sustainable marketing principles. (AACSB: Communication)

6. Discuss the philosophies that might guide marketers facing ethical issues. (AACSB: Communication)

Application Questions

1. Some cultures are more accepting than others of corrupt practices such as bribery. Corruption is not tolerated in the United States or by U.S. firms operating abroad. However, in some countries, it's the price of entry for many foreign firms. Visit www.transparency .org and look at the Corruption Perception Index (CPI) report. The CPI can range from 0 to 10, where a low index score means a country is perceived as highly corrupt and a higher score means highly ethical. Pick three countries that are rated as least corrupt and three that are highly corrupt. (AACSB: Communication; Use of IT)

2. In a small group, discuss each of the morally difficult situations in marketing presented in Table 16.1. Which ethics philosophy is guiding your decision in each situation? (AACSB: Communication; Ethical Reasoning)

3. Identify three companies that you believe are environmentally responsible. Discuss what they are doing that makes you think that way. (AACSB: Communication; Reflective Thinking)

Under the Hood: Marketing Technology

Does your computer have a floppy disk drive? Do you listen to music on a cassette deck or record movies on a VCR tape? Does your telephone handset have a cord? You probably answered no. All are examples of obsolete products. New products often provide greater value for customers, especially in fast-changing industries such as computers and electronics. But what happens to all the old products? This creates a growing concern over electronic waste, called *e-waste*. Although e-waste represents only 2 percent of the trash in our landfills, according to some analysts, it accounts for 70 percent of overall toxic waste. Recycling programs are increasing and are even required by law in some states. But the waste is often shipped for recycling or disposal to landfills in China, Kenya, India, and other developing countries, which have more lax standards concerning worker and environmental welfare.

1. Who should be responsible for properly disposing of discarded electronic products—consumers or manufacturers? Is it appropriate to ship e-waste to developing countries? Discuss alternative solutions. (AACSB: Communication; Ethical Reasoning; Reflective Thinking)

2. Visit several electronics manufacturers' Web sites to learn if they offer electronic recycling programs. Are manufacturers doing enough? Write a brief report on what you learned. (AACSB: Communication; Ethical Reasoning; Reflective Thinking)

Staying on the Road: Marketing Ethics

K.G.O.Y. stands for "kids getting older younger," and marketers are getting much of the blame. Kids today see all types of messages, especially on the Internet, that they would never have seen in the past. Whereas boys may give up their G.I. Joe's at an earlier age to play war games on their xBox 360s, the greater controversy seems to surround claims of how girls have changed, or rather, how marketers have changed girls. Critics describe clothing designed for young girls aged 8 to 11 as "floozy" and sexual, with department stores selling thongs for youngsters and T-shirts that say "Naughty Girl!" Although Barbie's sexuality has never been subtle, she was originally targeted to girls 9 to 12 years old. Now, Barbie dolls target primarily 3 to 7 year old girls.

1. Are marketers to blame for kids getting older younger? Give some examples other than those listed above. (AACSB: Communication; Ethical Reasoning)

2. Give an example of a company that is countering this trend by offering age-appropriate products for children. (AACSB: Communication; Reflective Thinking)

Rough Road Ahead: Marketing and the Economy

Thrift Stores

It makes sense that as unemployment rates rise and incomes weaken, more middle-class shoppers turn to thrift stores in search of bargains. But in recent times, thrift stores have benefited from more than just a new consumer frugality. The negative stigma of shopping at musty, secondhand shops has diminished. For fashionistas everywhere, the line between "thrift" and "vintage" has grown razor thin. These days, people aren't just buying any old rags at thrift stores. They're finding treasures in some top-name brands. Goodwill Industries is taking advantage of this trend. It promotes its wares to hipster trendsetters through fashion shows and apparel blogs, and by offering store credit for apparel donations.

Goodwill's overall sales have gone up by around 7 percent in the face of a weaker economy. Other thrift stores report increases of up to 35 percent. But the industry's good fortunes present a unique dilemma. The same forces that are driving thrift sales up are driving donations down. People are keeping their own old stuff longer. And rather than donating old apparel, people are selling it elsewhere for cash. As a result, the two-bag donor is now only bringing in one bag. And the goods that do get donated tend to be lower in quality. This unusual dynamic could make it difficult for thrift stores to stock their shelves in the future.

1. In what ways does the thrift store industry present solutions to the common social criticisms of marketing outlined in the text?

2. How might the thrift store industry overcome its supply problems in the current environment of frugal consumers.

Travel Budget: Marketing by the Numbers

Expenditures on prescription drugs in the United States exceeded $200 billion in 2006 and are predicted to increase by more than 100 percent by 2017. A large percentage of those expenditures will fall on state and federal government health programs. From 1995 to 2002—when direct-to-consumer advertising of prescription drugs skyrocketed—pharmaceutical manufacturers were among the nation's most profitable, and the industry has ranked in the top five since that period.

1. Refer to Appendix 2: Marketing by the Numbers to determine the price at which pharmaceutical manufactur-

ers sell the drug to wholesalers if wholesalers earn a 10 percent margin and retailers earn a 20 percent margin, each based on their respective selling prices. Assume the average retail price for a brand name prescription drug is $120. (AACSB: Communication; Analytical Reasoning)

2. What is the pharmaceutical manufacturer's contribution margin if average variable costs equal $10 per prescription drug? Is this contribution margin excessive? Explain why or why not. (AACSB: Communication; Analytical Reasoning; Ethical Reasoning)

Drive In: Video Case

Land Rover

The automotive industry has seen better days. Many auto companies are now facing declining revenues and negative profits. Additionally, because of its primary dependence on products that consume petroleum, the auto industry has a big environmental black eye, especially companies that primarily make gas-guzzling trucks and SUVs.

During the past few years, however, Land Rover has experienced tremendous growth in revenues and profits. It is currently selling more vehicles than ever worldwide. How is this possible for a company that only sells SUVs? One of the biggest reasons is Land Rover's strategic focus on social responsibility and environmentalism. Land Rover believes that it can meet consumer needs for luxury all-terrain vehicles while at the same time providing a vehicle that is kinder to the environment. As a corporation, it is also working feverishly to reduce its carbon emissions, reduce

waste, and reduce water consumption and pollution. With actions like this, Land Rover is successfully repositioning its brand away from the standard perceptions of SUVs as environmental enemies.

After viewing the video featuring Land Rover, answer the following questions about the company's efforts toward social responsibility:

1. Make a list of social criticisms of the automotive industry. Discuss all of the ways that Land Rover is combating those criticisms.

2. By the textbook's definition, does Land Rover practice "sustainable marketing"?

3. Do you believe that Land Rover is sincere in its efforts to be environmentally friendly? Is it even possible for a large SUV to be environmentally friendly? Present support for both sides of these arguments.

Appendix 1 Marketing Plan

THE MARKETING PLAN: AN INTRODUCTION

As a marketer, you'll need a good marketing plan to provide direction and focus for your brand, product, or company. With a detailed plan, any business will be better prepared to launch a new product or build sales for existing products. Nonprofit organizations also use marketing plans to guide their fund-raising and outreach efforts. Even government agencies put together marketing plans for initiatives such as building public awareness of proper nutrition and stimulating area tourism.

The Purpose and Content of a Marketinag Plan

Unlike a business plan, which offers a broad overview of the entire organization's mission, objectives, strategy, and resource allocation, a marketing plan has a more limited scope. It serves to document how the organization's strategic objectives will be achieved through specific marketing strategies and tactics, with the customer as the starting point. It is also linked to the plans of other departments within the organization. Suppose a marketing plan calls for selling 200,000 units annually. The production department must gear up to make that many units, the finance department must arrange funding to cover the expenses, the human resources department must be ready to hire and train staff, and so on. Without the appropriate level of organizational support and resources, no marketing plan can succeed.

Although the exact length and layout will vary from company to company, a marketing plan usually contains the sections described in Chapter 2. Smaller businesses may create shorter or less formal marketing plans, whereas corporations frequently require highly structured marketing plans. To guide implementation effectively, every part of the plan must be described in considerable detail. Sometimes a company will post its marketing plan on an internal Web site, which allows managers and employees in different locations to consult specific sections and collaborate on additions or changes.

The Role of Research

Marketing plans are not created in a vacuum. To develop successful strategies and action programs, marketers need up-to-date information about the environment, the competition, and the market segments to be served. Often, analysis of internal data is the starting point for assessing the current marketing situation, supplemented by marketing intelligence and research investigating the overall market, the competition, key issues, and threats and opportunities. As the plan is put into effect, marketers use a variety of research techniques to measure progress toward objectives and identify areas for improvement if results fall short of projections.

Finally, marketing research helps marketers learn more about their customers' requirements, expectations, perceptions, and satisfaction levels. This deeper understanding provides a foundation for building competitive advantage through well-informed segmenting, targeting, differentiating, and positioning decisions. Thus, the marketing plan should outline what marketing research will be conducted and how the findings will be applied.

The Role of Relationships

The marketing plan shows how the company will establish and maintain profitable customer relationships. In the process, however, it also shapes a number of internal and external relationships. First, it affects how marketing personnel work with each other and with other departments to deliver value and satisfy customers. Second, it affects how the company works with suppliers, distributors, and strategic alliance partners to achieve the objectives listed in the plan. Third, it influences the company's dealings with other stakeholders, including government regulators, the media, and the community at large. All of these relationships are important to the organization's success, so they should be considered when a marketing plan is being developed.

From Marketing Plan to Marketing Action

Companies generally create yearly marketing plans, although some plans cover a longer period. Marketers start planning well in advance of the implementation date to allow time for marketing research, thorough analysis, management review, and coordination between departments. Then, after each action program begins, marketers monitor ongoing results, compare them with projections, analyze any differences, and take corrective steps as needed. Some marketers also prepare contingency plans for implementation if certain conditions emerge. Because of inevitable and sometimes unpredictable environmental changes, marketers must be ready to update and adapt marketing plans at any time.

For effective implementation and control, the marketing plan should define how progress toward objectives will be measured. Managers typically use budgets, schedules, and performance standards for monitoring and evaluating results. With budgets, they can compare planned expenditures with actual expenditures for a given week, month, or other period. Schedules allow management to see when tasks were supposed to be completed—and when they were actually completed. Performance standards track the outcomes of marketing programs to see whether the company is moving toward its objectives. Some examples of performance standards are: market share, sales volume, product profitability, and customer satisfaction.

SAMPLE MARKETING PLAN FOR SONIC

This section takes you inside the sample marketing plan for Sonic, a hypothetical start-up company. The company's first product is the Sonic 1000, a multimedia, cellular/Wi-Fi-enabled smartphone. Sonic will be competing with Apple, Nokia, Research in Motion, Motorola, and other well-established rivals in a crowded, fast-changing marketplace for smartphones that combine communication, entertainment, and storage functionality. The annotations explain more about what each section of the plan should contain and why.

Executive Summary

Executive summary
This section summarizes the main goals, recommendations, and points as an overview for senior managers who will read and approve the marketing plan. Generally a table of contents follows this section, for management convenience.

Sonic is preparing to launch a new multimedia, dual-mode smartphone, the Sonic 1000, in a mature market. Our product offers a competitively unique combination of advanced features and functionality at a value-added price. We are targeting specific segments in the consumer and business markets, taking advantage of opportunities indicated by higher demand for easy-to-use smartphones with expanded communications, entertainment, and storage functionality.

The primary marketing objective is to achieve first-year U.S. sales of 500,000 units. The primary financial objectives are to achieve first-year sales revenues of $75 million, keep first-year losses to less than $8 million, and break even early in the second year.

Current Marketing Situation

Current marketing situation
In this section, marketing managers discuss the overall market, identify the market segments they will target, and provide information about the company's current situation.

Sonic, founded 18 months ago by two entrepreneurs with experience in the PC market, is about to enter the maturing smartphone market. Multifunction cell phones, e-mail devices, and wireless communication devices have become commonplace for both personal and professional use. Research shows that the United States has 262 million wireless phone subscribers, and 85 percent of the population owns a cell phone.

Competition is therefore more intense even as demand flattens, industry consolidation continues, and pricing pressures squeeze profitability. Worldwide, Nokia is the smartphone leader, holding 45 percent of the global market. The runner-up is Research in Motion, maker of the BlackBerry, with 13 percent of the global market. In the U.S. market, BlackBerry is the market leader (with a 42 percent share) and Apple, maker of the iPhone, is the runner-up (with a 20 percent share). To gain market share in this dynamic environment, Sonic must carefully target specific segments with features that deliver benefits valued by each customer group.

Market description
Describing the targeted segments in detail provides context for the marketing strategies and detailed action programs discussed later in the plan.

Market Description   Sonic's market consists of consumers and business users who prefer to use a single device for communication, information storage and exchange, and entertainment on the go. Specific segments being targeted during the first year include

Benefits and product features
Table A1.1 clarifies the benefits that product features will deliver to satisfy the needs of customers in each targeted segment.

professionals, corporations, students, entrepreneurs, and medical users. ■ **Table A1.1** shows how the Sonic 1000 addresses the needs of targeted consumer and business segments.

Buyers can choose between models based on several different operating systems, including systems from Microsoft, Symbian, and BlackBerry, plus Linux variations. Sonic licenses a Linux-based system because it is somewhat less vulnerable to attack by hackers and viruses. Hard drives and removable memory cards are popular smartphone options. Sonic is equipping its first entry with an ultra-fast 20-gigabyte removable memory card for information and entertainment storage. This will allow users to transfer photos and other data from the smartphone to a home or office computer. Technology costs are decreasing even as capabilities are increasing, which makes value-priced models more appealing to consumers and to business users with older devices who want to trade up to new, high-end multifunction units.

Product review
The product review summarizes the main features for all of the company's products, organized by product line, type of customer, market, or order of product introduction.

Product Review   Our first product, the Sonic 1000, offers the following standard features with a Linux OS:

- Built-in dual cell phone/Internet phone functionality and push-to-talk instant calling
- Digital music/video/television recording, wireless downloading, and playback
- Wireless Web and e-mail, text messaging, and instant messaging
- Three-inch color screen for easy viewing
- Organization functions, including calendar, address book, and synchronization
- Global positioning system for directions and maps
- Integrated four-megapixel digital camera
- Ultrafast 20-gigabyte removable memory card with upgrade potential
- Interchangeable case wardrobe of different colors and patterns
- Voice recognition functionality for hands-free operation

■ **Table A1.1** Segment Needs and Corresponding Features/Benefits of Sonic

Targeted Segment	Customer Need	Corresponding Feature/Benefit
Professionals (consumer market)	• Stay in touch conveniently and securely while on the go • Perform many functions hands-free without carrying multiple gadgets	• Built-in cell phone and push-to-talk to communicate anywhere at any time; wireless e-mail/Web access from anywhere; Linux operating system less vulnerable to hackers • Voice-activated applications are convenient; GPS function, camera add value
Students (consumer market)	• Perform many functions hands-free without carrying multiple gadgets • Express style and individuality	• Compatible with numerous applications and peripherals for convenient, cost-effective communication and entertainment • Wardrobe of smartphone cases
Corporate users (business market)	• Security and adaptability for proprietary tasks • Obtain driving directions to business meetings	• Customizable to fit corporate tasks and networks; Linux-based operating system less vulnerable to hackers • Built-in GPS allows voice-activated access to directions and maps
Entrepreneurs (business market)	• Organize and access contacts, schedule details, business and financial files • Get in touch fast	• Hands-free, wireless access to calendar, address book, information files for checking appointments and data, connecting with contacts • Push-to-talk instant calling speeds up communications
Medical users (business market)	• Update, access, and exchange medical records • Photograph medical situations to maintain a visual record	• Removable memory card and hands-free, wireless information recording reduces paperwork and increases productivity • Built-in camera allows fast and easy photography, stores images for later retrieval

First-year sales revenues are projected to be $75 million, based on sales of 500,000 Sonic 1000 units at a wholesale price of $150 each. During the second year, we plan to introduce the Sonic 2000, also with Linux OS, as a higher-end smartphone product offering the following standard features:

● Global phone and messaging compatibility
● Translation capabilities to send English text as Spanish text (other languages to be offered as add-on options)
● Integrated 8-megapixel camera with flash

Competitive review
The purpose of a competitive review is to identify key competitors, describe their market positions, and briefly discuss their strategies.

Competitive Review   The emergence of lower-priced smart phones, including the Apple iPhone, has increased competitive pressure. Competition from specialized devices for text and e-mail messaging, such as BlackBerry devices, is a major factor, as well. Key competitors include the following:

● *Nokia*. The market leader in smartphones, Nokia offers a wide range of products for consumers and professionals. It recently purchased the maker of the Symbian operating system and made it into a separate foundation dedicated to improving and promoting this mobile software platform. Many of Nokia's smartphones offer full keyboards, similar to Research in Motion models, but stripped-down models are available for users who do not require the full keyboard and full multimedia capabilities.
● *Apple*. The stylish, popular iPhone 3G has a 3.5-inch color screen and is well-equipped for music, video, and Web access, as well as having communication, calendar, contact management, and file management functions. Its global positioning system technology can pinpoint a user's location. Also, users can erase data with a remote command if the smartphone is lost or stolen. However, AT&T is the only U.S. network provider. The iPhone is priced at $99 and up, with a two-year service contract.
● *RIM*. Research in Motion makes the lightweight BlackBerry wireless multifunction products that are especially popular among corporate users. RIM's continuous innovation and solid customer-service support clearly strengthen its competitive standing as it introduces smartphones with enhanced features and communication capabilities. RIM's newer smartphones come equipped with the BlackBerry OS.
● *Motorola*. Motorola, a global giant, has been losing U.S. market share to Apple and Research in Motion, in particular, because it has slowed the pace of new product introduction. One of its top smartphone models is the slender, lightweight quad-band Q, which incorporates e-mail and text message functions, photo caller identification, a full keyboard, camera with flash, removable memory, updated multimedia audio/video/image capabilities, dual stereo speakers, and more. After rebate, the Q is priced at $149.99 with a two-year AT&T Wireless contract, although the retail price without a contract is considerably higher.
● *Samsung*. Value, style, function: Samsung is a strong competitor, offering a variety of smartphones for consumer and business segments. Some of its smart phones are available for specific telecommunications carriers and some are "unlocked," ready for any compatible telecommunications network. Its Omnia is a smartphone with features similar to the iPhone. Like the iPhone, service agreements are only available through one provider—Sprint. The Omnia is priced at $189.99 with a two-year contract.
● *Palm*. Although Palm led the PDA (personal digital assistant) market, Palm's smartphone share is well below that of Nokia and other handset marketers. Its new smartphone, the Palm Pre, features high-speed connectivity, Wi-Fi, an integrated GPS, a full keyboard, multimedia capabilities, a Web OS, and Synergy data integration. The Pre is priced at $199 with rebate and a two-year phone contract with its exclusive carrier, Sprint.

Despite this strong competition, Sonic can carve out a definite image and gain recognition among the targeted segments. Our voice-recognition system for completely hands-off operation is a critical point of differentiation for competitive advantage. Also, offering GPS as a standard feature gives us a competitive edge compared with similarly priced smartphones. Moreover, our product is speedier than most and runs the Linux OS, which is an appealing alternative for customers concerned about security. ■ **Table A1.2** shows a sample of competitive products and prices.

■ **Table A1.2** Sample of Competitive Products and Pricing

Competitor	Model	Features	Price
Nokia	E71	Qua-band for worldwide phone, e-mail and Internet access, full keyboard, corporate and personal e-mail integration, 2.36-inch screen, 3.2-megapixel camera, media player, Symbian OS.	$364 without phone contract
Apple	iPhone 3G	Sleek styling, big screen, fast Internet functions, one-touch calling, GPS navigation, integrated personal and corporate e-mail, open and edit Microsoft Office files, 2-megapixel camera, landscape keyboard, Apple Mac operating system.	$99 with two-year phone contract
RIM	BlackBerry Storm	Hi-resolution display, 3.25-inch touch screen navigation, wireless e-mail and Internet access, 3.2-megapixel camera, built-in maps and GPS, camera and video recording, expandable memory, Blackberry OS.	$99 with two-year phone contract
Motorola	Q	Extremely thin and light, 2.4-inch screen, full keyboard, quad-band functionality, e-mail and texting functions, 1.3-megapixel camera, multimedia capabilities, voice-activated dialing, Windows OS.	$225 without phone contract
Samsung	Omnia	High-speed Internet access, embedded GPS, 3.2-inch screen, 5.0-megapixel camera, audio and video capabilities, FM radio, Windows mobile OS.	$189.99 with phone contract
Palm	Pre	Wi-Fi and GPS capable, 3.1-inch touch screen, full keyboard, 3.0-megapixel camera with video playback, music and audio capabilities, e-mail and Internet access, Web OS	$199 with rebate, two-year phone contract

Channels and logistics review
In this section, marketers list the most important channels, provide an overview of each channel arrangement, and identify developing issues in channels and logistics.

Channels and Logistics Review Sonic-branded products will be distributed through a network of retailers in the top 50 U.S. markets. Among the most important channel partners being contacted are:

- *Office supply superstores.* Office Max and Staples will both carry Sonic products in stores, in catalogs, and online.
- *Computer stores.* Independent computer retailers will carry Sonic products.
- *Electronics specialty stores.* Best Buy will feature Sonic products.
- *Online retailers.* Amazon.com will carry Sonic products and, for a promotional fee, will give Sonic prominent placement on its homepage during the introduction.

Initially, our channel strategy will focus on the United States; according to demand, we plan to expand into Canada and beyond, with appropriate logistical support.

Strengths, Weaknesses, Opportunities, and Threat Analysis

Sonic has several powerful strengths on which to build, but our major weakness is lack of brand awareness and image. The major opportunity is demand for multimedia smartphones that deliver a number of valued benefits, eliminating the need for customers to carry more than one device. We also face the threat of ever-higher competition from consumer electronics manufacturers, as well as downward pricing pressure. ■ **Table A1.3** summarizes Sonic's main strengths, weaknesses, opportunities, and threats.

Strengths
Strengths are internal capabilities that can help the company reach its objectives.

Strengths Sonic can build on three important strengths:

1. *Innovative product.* The Sonic 1000 offers a combination of features that would otherwise require customers to carry multiple devices: speedy, hands-free, dual-mode cell/Wi-Fi telecommunications capabilities, GPS functions, and digital video/music/TV program storage/playback.

2. *Security.* Our smartphone uses a Linux-based operating system that is less vulnerable to hackers and other security threats that can result in stolen or corrupted data.

3. *Pricing.* Our product is priced lower than competing multifunction models—none of which offer the same bundle of features—which gives us an edge with price-conscious customers.

■ **Table A1.3** Sonic's Strengths, Weaknesses, Opportunities, and Threats

Strengths	Weaknesses
● Innovative combination of functions in one portable, voice-activated device ● Security due to Linux-based operating system ● Value pricing	● Lack of brand awareness and image ● Heavier and thicker than most competing models

Opportunities	Threats
● Increased demand for multimedia, multifunction smartphones ● Cost-efficient technology	● Intense competition ● Downward pricing pressure ● Compressed product life cycle

Weaknesses
Weaknesses are internal elements that may interfere with the company's ability to achieve its objectives.

Weaknesses   By waiting to enter the smartphone market until some consolidation of competitors has occurred, Sonic has learned from the successes and mistakes of others. Nonetheless, we have two main weaknesses:

1. *Lack of brand awareness.* Sonic has no established brand or image, whereas Apple and others have strong brand recognition. We will address this issue with aggressive promotion.

2. *Physical specifications.* The Sonic 1000 is slightly heavier and thicker than most competing models because it incorporates multiple features, offers sizable storage capacity, and is compatible with numerous peripheral devices. To counteract this weakness, we will emphasize our product's benefits and value-added pricing, two compelling competitive strengths.

Opportunities
Opportunities are external elements that the company may be able to exploit to its advantage.

Opportunities   Sonic can take advantage of two major market opportunities:

1. *Increasing demand for multimedia smartphones with multiple functions.* The market for multimedia, multifunction devices is growing much faster than the market for single-use devices. Growth will accelerate as dual-mode capabilities become mainstream, giving customers the flexibility to make phone calls over cell or Internet connections. Smartphones are already commonplace in public, work, and educational settings, which is boosting primary demand. Also, customers who bought entry-level models are replacing older models with more advanced models.

2. *Cost-efficient technology.* Better technology is now available at a lower cost than ever before. Thus, Sonic can incorporate advanced features at a value-added price that allows for reasonable profits.

Threats
Threats are current or emerging external elements that could potentially challenge the company's performance.

Threats   We face three main threats at the introduction of the Sonic 1000:

1. *Increased competition.* More companies are entering the U.S. market with smartphone models that offer some but not all of the features and benefits provided by Sonic's product. Therefore, Sonic's marketing communications must stress our clear differentiation and value-added pricing.

2. *Downward pressure on pricing.* Increased competition and market-share strategies are pushing smartphone prices down. Still, our objective of seeking a 10 percent profit on second-year sales of the original model is realistic, given the lower margins in this market.

3. *Compressed product life cycle.* Smartphones have reached the maturity stage of their life cycle more quickly than earlier technology products. We have contingency plans to keep sales growing by adding new features, targeting additional segments, and adjusting prices as needed.

Objectives and issues
The company's objectives should be defined in specific terms so management can measure progress and plan corrective action if needed to stay on track. This section describes any major issues that might affect the company's marketing strategy and implementation.

Objectives and Issues

We have set aggressive but achievable objectives for the first and second years of market entry.

First-year Objectives During the Sonic 1000's initial year on the market, we are aiming for unit sales volume of 500,000.

Second-year Objectives Our second-year objectives are to sell a combined total of one million units of our two models and to achieve breakeven early in this period.

Issues In relation to the product launch, our major issue is the ability to establish a well-regarded brand name linked to a meaningful positioning. We will invest heavily in marketing to create a memorable and distinctive brand image projecting innovation, quality, and value. We also must measure awareness and response so we can adjust our marketing efforts as necessary.

Marketing Strategy

Sonic's marketing strategy is based on a positioning of product differentiation. Our primary consumer target is middle- to upper-income professionals who need one portable device to coordinate their busy schedules, communicate with family and colleagues, get driving directions, and be entertained on the go. Our secondary consumer target is high school, college, and graduate students who want a multimedia, dual-mode device. This segment can be described demographically by age (16–30) and education status.

Our primary business target is mid- to large-sized corporations that want to help their managers and employees stay in touch and input or access critical data when out of the office. This segment consists of companies with more than $25 million in annual sales and more than 100 employees. We are also targeting entrepreneurs and small-business owners as well as medical users who want to update or access patients' medical records while reducing paperwork.

Positioning
A positioning built on meaningful differentiation, supported by appropriate strategy and implementation, can help the company build competitive advantage.

Positioning Using product differentiation, we are positioning the Sonic as the most versatile, convenient, value-added model for personal and professional use. Our marketing will focus on the hands-free operation of multiple communication, entertainment, and information capabilities differentiating the Sonic 1000.

Marketing tools
These sections summarize the broad logic that will guide decisions made about the marketing tools to be used during the period covered by the plan.

Product Strategy The Sonic 1000, including all the features described in the earlier Product Review section, will be sold with a one-year warranty. We will introduce a more compact, powerful high-end model (the Sonic 2000) during the following year. Building the Sonic brand is an integral part of our product strategy. The brand and logo (Sonic's distinctive yellow thunderbolt) will be displayed on the product and its packaging and reinforced by its prominence in the introductory marketing campaign.

Pricing Strategy The Sonic 1000 will be introduced at $150 wholesale/$199 estimated retail price per unit. We expect to lower the price of this first model when we expand the product line by launching the Sonic 2000, to be priced at $175 wholesale per unit. These prices reflect a strategy of (1) attracting desirable channel partners and (2) taking share from Nokia, Research in Motion, and other established competitors.

Distribution Strategy Our channel strategy is to use selective distribution, marketing Sonic smartphones through well-known stores and online retailers. During the first year, we will add channel partners until we have coverage in all major U.S. markets and the product is included in the major electronics catalogs and Web sites. We will also investigate distribution through cell-phone outlets maintained by major carriers such as Verizon Wireless. In support of our channel partners, Sonic will provide demonstration products, detailed specification handouts, and full-color photos and displays featuring the product. Finally, we plan to arrange special payment terms for retailers that place volume orders.

Marketing Communications Strategy   By integrating all messages in all media, we will reinforce the brand name and the main points of product differentiation. Research about media consumption patterns will help our advertising agency choose appropriate media and timing to reach prospects before and during product introduction. Thereafter, advertising will appear on a pulsing basis to maintain brand awareness and communicate various differentiation messages. The agency will also coordinate public relations efforts to build the Sonic brand and support the differentiation message. To create buzz, we will host a user-generated video contest on our Web site. To attract, retain, and motivate channel partners for a push strategy, we will use trade sales promotions and personal selling. Until the Sonic brand has been established, our communications will encourage purchases through channel partners rather than from our Web site.

Marketing research
This section shows how marketing research will be used to support development, implementation, and evaluation of strategies and action programs.

Marketing Research   Using research, we are identifying the specific features and benefits that our target market segments value. Feedback from market tests, surveys, and focus groups will help us develop the Sonic 2000. We are also measuring and analyzing customers' attitudes toward competing brands and products. Brand awareness research will help us determine the effectiveness and efficiency of our messages and media. Finally, we will use customer satisfaction studies to gauge market reaction.

Marketing organization
The marketing department may be organized by function, as in this sample, by geography, by product, or by customer (or some combination).

Marketing Organization   Sonic's chief marketing officer, Jane Melody, holds overall responsibility for all of the company's marketing activities. ■ **Figure A1.1** shows the structure of the eight-person marketing organization. Sonic has hired Worldwide Marketing to handle national sales campaigns, trade and consumer sales promotions, and public relations efforts.

Action programs
Action programs should be coordinated with the resources and activities of other departments, including production, finance, and purchasing.

Action Programs

The Sonic 1000 will be introduced in February. Following are summaries of the action programs we will use during the first six months of next year to achieve our stated objectives.

January We will launch a $200,000 trade sales promotion campaign and exhibit at the major industry trade shows to educate dealers and generate channel support for the product launch in February. Also, we will create buzz by providing samples to selected product reviewers, opinion leaders, influential bloggers, and celebrities. Our training staff will work with retail sales personnel at major chains to explain the Sonic 1000's features, benefits, and advantages.

February We will start an integrated print/radio/Internet campaign targeting professionals and consumers. The campaign will show how many functions the Sonic smartphone can perform and emphasize the convenience of a single, powerful handheld

■ **Figure A1.1** Sonic's Marketing Organization

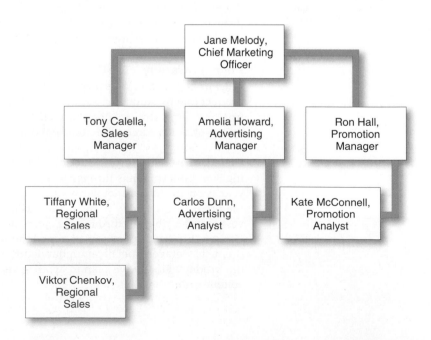

device. This multimedia campaign will be supported by point-of-sale signage as well as online-only ads and video tours.

March As the multimedia advertising campaign continues, we will add consumer sales promotions such as a contest in which consumers post videos to our Web site, showing how they use the Sonic in creative and unusual ways. We will also distribute new point-of-purchase displays to support our retailers.

April We will hold a trade sales contest offering prizes for the salesperson and retail organization that sells the most Sonic smartphones during the four-week period.

May We plan to roll out a new national advertising campaign this month. The radio ads will feature celebrity voices telling their Sonic smartphones to perform functions such as initiating a phone call, sending an e-mail, playing a song or video, and so on. The stylized print and online ads will feature avatars of these celebrities holding their Sonic smartphones.

June Our radio campaign will add a new voice-over tagline promoting the Sonic 1000 as a graduation gift. We will also exhibit at the semiannual electronics trade show and provide channel partners with new competitive comparison handouts as a sales aid. In addition, we will tally and analyze the results of customer satisfaction surveys for use in future promotions and to provide feedback for product and marketing activities.

Budgets

Managers use budgets to project profitability and plan for each marketing program's expenditures, scheduling, and operations.

Budgets

Total first-year sales revenue for the Sonic 1000 is projected at $75 million, with an average wholesale price of $150 per unit and variable cost per unit of $100 for unit sales volume of 500,000. We anticipate a first-year loss of up to $8 million on the Sonic 1000 model. Break-even calculations indicate that the Sonic 1000 will become profitable after the sales volume exceeds 650,000, early in the product's second year. Our break-even analysis of Sonic's first smartphone product assumes per-unit wholesale revenue of $150 per unit, variable cost of $100 per unit, and estimated first-year fixed costs of $32,500,000. Based on these assumptions, the break-even calculation is:

$$\frac{\$32,500,000}{\$150/\text{unit} - \$100/\text{unit}} = 650,000 \text{ units}$$

Controls

Controls help management assess results after the plan is implemented, identify any problems or performance variations, and initiate corrective action.

Controls

We are planning tight control measures to closely monitor quality and customer-service satisfaction. This will enable us to react very quickly in correcting any problems that may occur. Other early warning signals that will be monitored for signs of deviation from the plan include monthly sales (by segment and channel) and monthly expenses. Given the market's volatility, we are developing contingency plans to address fast-moving environmental changes such as new technology and new competition.

MARKETING PLAN TOOLS

Prentice Hall offers two valuable resources to assist you in developing a marketing plan:

- *The Marketing Plan Handbook* by Marian Burk Wood explains the process of creating a marketing plan, complete with detailed checklists and dozens of real-world examples.
- *Marketing Plan Pro* is an award-winning software package that includes sample plans, step-by-step guides, an introductory video, help wizards, and customizable charts for documenting a marketing plan.

Sources: Background information and market data adapted from "Hospital Uses PDA App for Patient Transport," *Health Data Management,* June 2007, p. 14; "Smartphones Get Smarter, Thanks in Part to the iPhone," *InformationWeek,* July 21, 2007; Chris Nutall and others, "Apple Set to Slash iPhone Prices to Lift Sales," *Financial Times,* June 10, 2008, p. 20; Olga Kharif and Roger O. Crockett, "Motorola's Market Share Mess," *BusinessWeek,* July 10, 2008, www.businessweek.com; "Follow the Leader," *Economist,* June 14, 2008, pp. 78–80; Laura M. Holson, "Phone Giants Fight to Keep Subscribers," *New York Times,* July 23, 2008, p. C1; Adam Lashinsky, "Palm Fights Back (Against Apple)," *Fortune,* June 8, 2009, pp 88–92; Moon Ihlwan, "Samsung Smartphones Take on iPhones, Blackberrys," *BusinessWeek Online,* June 23, 2009.

Appendix 2 Marketing by the Numbers

Marketing managers are facing increased accountability for the financial implications of their actions. This appendix provides a basic introduction to measuring marketing financial performance. Such financial analysis guides marketers in making sound marketing decisions and in assessing the outcomes of those decisions.

The appendix is built around a hypothetical manufacturer of consumer electronics products—ConnectPhone. In the past, ConnectPhone has concentrated on making Internet modems. However, the company is now introducing a new type of product—a *media phone* that replaces a household's telephone and provides "always-on" Internet connectivity and wireless phone access through VoIP (Voice over Internet Protocol) technology. In this appendix, we will analyze the various decisions ConnectPhone's marketing managers must make before and after the new-product launch.

The appendix is organized into *three sections*. The *first section* introduces pricing, break-even, and margin analysis assessments that will guide the introduction of ConnectPhone's new product. The *second section* discusses demand estimates, the marketing budget, and marketing performance measures. It begins with a discussion of estimating market potential and company sales. It then introduces the marketing budget, as illustrated through a *pro forma* profit-and-loss statement followed by the actual profit-and-loss statement. Next, we discuss marketing performance measures, with a focus on helping marketing managers to better defend their decisions from a financial perspective. In the *third section,* we analyze the financial implications of various marketing tactics.

Each of the three sections ends with a set of quantitative exercises that provide you with an opportunity to apply the concepts you learned to situations beyond ConnectPhone.

PRICING, BREAK-EVEN, AND MARGIN ANALYSIS

Pricing Considerations

Determining price is one of the most important marketing-mix decisions. The limiting factors are demand and costs. Demand factors, such as buyer-perceived value, set the price ceiling. The company's costs set the price floor. In between these two factors, marketers must consider competitors' prices and other factors such as reseller requirements, government regulations, and company objectives.

Current competing media phone products in this relatively new product category were introduced in 2009 and sell at retail prices between $500 and $1,000. ConnectPhone plans to introduce its new product at a lower price in order to expand the market and to gain market share rapidly. We first consider ConnectPhone's pricing decision from a cost perspective. Then, we consider consumer value, the competitive environment, and reseller requirements.

Determining Costs Recall from Chapter 9 that there are different types of costs. **Fixed costs** do not vary with production or sales level and include costs such as rent, interest, depreciation, and clerical and management salaries. Regardless of the level of output, the company must pay these costs. Whereas total fixed costs remain constant as output increases, the fixed cost per unit (or average fixed cost) will decrease as output increases because the total fixed costs are spread across more units of output. **Variable costs** vary directly with the level of production and include costs related to the direct production of the product (such as costs of goods sold—COGS) and many of the marketing costs associated with selling it. Although these costs tend to be uniform for each unit produced, they are called variable because their total varies with the number of units produced. **Total costs** are the sum of the fixed and variable costs for any given level of production.

ConnectPhone has invested $10 million in refurbishing an existing facility to manufacture the new media phone product. Once production begins, the company estimates that it will incur fixed costs of $20 million per year. The variable cost to produce each device is estimated to be $250 and is expected to remain at that level for the output capacity of the facility.

Fixed costs
Costs that do not vary with production or sales level.

Variable costs
Costs that vary directly with the level of production.

Total costs
The sum of the fixed and variable costs for any given level of production.

Setting Price Based on Costs

Cost-plus pricing (or markup pricing)
A standard markup to the cost of the product.

ConnectPhone starts with the cost-based approach to pricing discussed in Chapter 9. Recall that the simplest method, **cost-plus pricing (or markup pricing)**, simply adds a standard markup to the cost of the product. To use this method, however, ConnectPhone must specify expected unit sales so that total unit costs can be determined. Unit variable costs will remain constant regardless of the output, but *average unit fixed costs* will decrease as output increases.

To illustrate this method, suppose ConnectPhone has fixed costs of $20 million, variable costs of $250 per unit, and expects unit sales of 1 million media phones. Thus, the cost per unit is given by:

$$\text{Unit cost} = \text{variable cost} + \frac{\text{fixed costs}}{\text{unit sales}} = \$250 + \frac{\$20,000,000}{1,000,000} = \$270$$

Relevant costs
Costs that will occur in the future and that will vary across the alternatives being considered.

Note that we do *not* include the initial investment of $10 million in the total fixed cost figure. It is not considered a fixed cost because it is not a *relevant* cost. **Relevant costs** are those that will occur in the future and that will vary across the alternatives being considered. ConnectPhone's investment to refurbish the manufacturing facility was a one-time cost that will not reoccur in the future. Such past costs are *sunk costs* and should not be considered in future analyses.

Break-even price
The price at which total revenue equals total cost and profit is zero.

Also notice that if ConnectPhone sells its product for $270, the price is equal to the total cost per unit. This is the **break-even price**—the price at which unit revenue (price) equals unit cost and profit is zero.

Suppose ConnectPhone does not want to merely break even but rather wants to earn a 25% markup on sales. ConnectPhone's markup price is:[1]

$$\text{Markup price} = \frac{\text{unit cost}}{(1 - \text{desired return on sales})} = \frac{\$270}{1 - .25} = \$360$$

This is the price at which ConnectPhone would sell the product to resellers such as wholesalers or retailers to earn a 25% profit on sales.

Return on investment (ROI) pricing (or target-return pricing)
A cost-based pricing method that determines price based on a specified rate of return on investment.

Another approach ConnectPhone could use is called **return on investment (ROI) pricing (or target-return pricing)**. In this case, the company *would* consider the initial $10 million investment, but only to determine the dollar profit goal. Suppose the company wants a 30% return on its investment. The price necessary to satisfy this requirement can be determined by:

$$\text{ROI price} = \text{unit cost} + \frac{\text{ROI} \times \text{investment}}{\text{unit sales}} = \$270 + \frac{0.3 \times \$10,000,000}{1,000,000} = \$273$$

That is, if ConnectPhone sells its product for $273, it will realize a 30% return on its initial investment of $10 million.

In these pricing calculations, unit cost is a function of the expected sales, which were estimated to be 1 million units. But what if actual sales were lower? Then the unit cost would be higher because the fixed costs would be spread over fewer units, and the realized percentage markup on sales or ROI would be lower. Alternatively, if sales are higher than the estimated 1 million units, unit cost would be lower than $270, so a lower price would produce the desired markup on sales or ROI. It's important to note that these cost-based pricing methods are *internally* focused and do not consider demand, competitors' prices, or reseller requirements. Because ConnectPhone will be selling this product to consumers through wholesalers and retailers offering competing brands, the company must consider markup pricing from this perspective.

Setting Price Based on External Factors

Whereas costs determine the price floor, ConnectPhone also must consider external factors when setting price. ConnectPhone does not have the final say concerning the final price of its media phones to consumers—retailers do. So it must start with its suggested retail price and work back. In doing so, ConnectPhone must consider the markups required by resellers that sell the product to consumers.

Markup
The difference between a company's selling price for a product and its cost to manufacture or purchase it.

In general, a dollar **markup** is the difference between a company's selling price for a product and its cost to manufacture or purchase it. For a retailer, then, the markup is the difference between the price it charges consumers and the cost the retailer must pay for the product. Thus, for any level of reseller:

$$\text{Dollar markup} = \text{selling price} - \text{cost}$$

Markups are usually expressed as a percentage, and there are two different ways to compute markups—on *cost* or on *selling price*:

$$\text{Markup percentage on cost} = \frac{\text{dollar markup}}{\text{cost}}$$

$$\text{Markup percentage on selling price} = \frac{\text{dollar markup}}{\text{selling price}}$$

To apply reseller margin analysis, ConnectPhone must first set the suggested retail price and then work back to the price at which it must sell the product to a wholesaler. Suppose retailers expect a 30% margin and wholesalers want a 20% margin based on their respective selling prices. And suppose that ConnectPhone sets a manufacturer's suggested retail price (MSRP) of $599.99 for its product.

Recall that ConnectPhone wants to expand the market by pricing low and generating market share quickly. ConnectPhone selected the $599.99 MSRP because it is lower than most competitors' prices, which can be as high as $1,000. And the company's research shows that it is below the threshold at which more consumers are willing to purchase the product. By using buyers' perceptions of value and not the seller's cost to determine the MSRP, ConnectPhone is using **value-based pricing**. For simplicity, we will use an MSRP of $600 in further analyses.

Value-based pricing
Offering just the right combination of quality and good service at a fair price.

To determine the price ConnectPhone will charge wholesalers, we must first subtract the retailer's margin from the retail price to determine the retailer's cost ($600 − ($600 × 0.30) = $420). The retailer's cost is the wholesaler's price, so ConnectPhone next subtracts the wholesaler's margin ($420 − ($420 × 0.20) = $336). Thus, the **markup chain** representing the sequence of markups used by firms at each level in a channel for ConnectPhone's new product is:

Markup chain
The sequence of markups used by firms at each level in a channel.

Suggested retail price:	$600
minus retail margin (30%):	− $180
Retailer's cost/wholesaler's price:	$420
minus wholesaler's margin (20%):	− $ 84
Wholesaler's cost/ConnectPhone's price:	$336

By deducting the markups for each level in the markup chain, ConnectPhone arrives at a price for the product to wholesalers of $336.

Break-Even and Margin Analysis

The previous analyses derived a value-based price of $336 for ConnectPhone's product. Although this price is higher than the break-even price of $270 and covers costs, that price assumed a demand of 1 million units. But how many units and what level of dollar sales must ConnectPhone achieve to break even at the $336 price? And what level of sales must be achieved to realize various profit goals? These questions can be answered through break-even and margin analysis.

Determining Break-Even Unit Volume and Dollar Sales Based on an understanding of costs, consumer value, the competitive environment, and reseller requirements, ConnectPhone has decided to set its price to wholesalers at $336. At that price, what sales level will be needed for ConnectPhone to break even or make a profit on its media phones? **Break-even analysis** determines the unit volume and dollar sales needed to be profitable given a particular price and cost structure. At the break-even point, total revenue equals total costs and profit is zero. Above this point, the company

Break-even analysis
Analysis to determine the unit volume and dollar sales needed to be profitable given a particular price and cost structure.

will make a profit; below it, the company will lose money. ConnectPhone can calculate break-even volume using the following formula:

$$\text{Break-even volume} = \frac{\text{fixed costs}}{\text{price} - \text{unit variable cost}}$$

Unit contribution
The amount that each unit contributes to covering fixed costs—the difference between price and variable costs.

The denominator (price – unit variable cost) is called **unit contribution** (sometimes called contribution margin). It represents the amount that each unit contributes to covering fixed costs. Break-even volume represents the level of output at which all (variable and fixed) costs are covered. In ConnectPhone's case, break-even unit volume is:

$$\text{Break-even volume} = \frac{\text{fixed cost}}{\text{price} - \text{variable cost}} = \frac{\$20,000,000}{\$336 - \$250} = 232,558.1 \text{ units}$$

Thus, at the given cost and pricing structure, ConnectPhone will break even at 232,559 units.
To determine the break-even dollar sales, simply multiply unit break-even volume by the selling price:

$$\text{BE}_{\text{sales}} = \text{BE}_{\text{vol}} \times \text{price} = 232,559 \times \$336 = \$78,139,824$$

Contribution margin
The unit contribution divided by the selling price.

Another way to calculate dollar break-even sales is to use the percentage contribution margin (hereafter referred to as **contribution margin**), which is the unit contribution divided by the selling price:

$$\text{Contribution margin} = \frac{\text{price} - \text{variable cost}}{\text{price}} = \frac{\$336 - \$250}{\$336} = 0.256 \text{ or } 25.6\%$$

Then,

$$\text{Break-even sales} = \frac{\text{fixed costs}}{\text{contribution margin}} = \frac{\$20,000,000}{0.256} = \$78,125,000$$

Note that the difference between the two break-even sales calculations is due to rounding.
Such break-even analysis helps ConnectPhone by showing the unit volume needed to cover costs. If production capacity cannot attain this level of output, then the company should not launch this product. However, the unit break-even volume is well within ConnectPhone's capacity. Of course, the bigger question concerns whether ConnectPhone can sell this volume at the $336 price. We'll address that issue a little later.
Understanding contribution margin is useful in other types of analyses as well, particularly if unit prices and unit variable costs are unknown or if a company (say, a retailer) sells many products at different prices and knows the percentage of total sales variable costs represent. Whereas unit contribution is the difference between unit price and unit variable costs, total contribution is the difference between total sales and total variable costs. The overall contribution margin can be calculated by:

$$\text{Contribution margin} = \frac{\text{total sales} - \text{total variable costs}}{\text{total sales}}$$

Regardless of the actual level of sales, if the company knows what percentage of sales is represented by variable costs, it can calculate contribution margin. For example, ConnectPhone's unit variable cost is $250, or 74% of the selling price ($250 ÷ $336 = 0.74). That means for every $1 of sales revenue for ConnectPhone, $0.74 represents variable costs, and the difference ($0.26) represents contribution to fixed costs. But even if the company doesn't know its unit price and unit variable cost, it can calculate the contribution margin from total sales and total variable costs or from knowledge of the total cost structure. It can set total sales equal to 100% regardless of the actual absolute amount and determine the contribution margin:

$$\text{Contribution margin} = \frac{100\% - 74\%}{100\%} = \frac{1 - 0.74}{1} = 1 - 0.74 = 0.26 \text{ or } 26\%$$

Note that this matches the percentage calculated from the unit price and unit variable cost information. This alternative calculation will be very useful later when analyzing various marketing decisions.

Determining "Breakeven" for Profit Goals

Although it is useful to know the break-even point, most companies are more interested in making a profit. Assume ConnectPhone would like to realize a $5 million profit in the first year. How many must it sell at the $336 price to cover fixed costs and produce this profit? To determine this, ConnectPhone can simply add the profit figure to fixed costs and again divide by the unit contribution to determine unit sales:

$$\text{Unit volume} = \frac{\text{fixed cost} - \text{profit goal}}{\text{price} - \text{variable cost}} = \frac{\$20,000,000 + \$5,000,000}{\$336 - \$250} = 290{,}697.7 \text{ units}$$

Thus, to earn a $5 million profit, ConnectPhone must sell 290,698 units. Multiply by price to determine dollar sales needed to achieve a $5 million profit:

$$\text{Dollar sales} = 290{,}698 \text{ units} \times \$336 = \$97{,}674{,}528$$

Or use the contribution margin:

$$\text{Sales} = \frac{\text{fixed cost} + \text{profit goal}}{\text{contribution margin}} = \frac{\$20,000,000 + \$5,000,000}{0.256} = \$97{,}656{,}250$$

Again, note that the difference between the two break-even sales calculations is due to rounding.

As we saw previously, a profit goal can also be stated as a return on investment goal. For example, recall that ConnectPhone wants a 30% return on its $10 million investment. Thus, its absolute profit goal is $3 million ($10,000,000 × 0.30). This profit goal is treated the same way as in the previous example:[2]

$$\text{Unit volume} = \frac{\text{fixed cost} + \text{profit goal}}{\text{price} - \text{variable cost}} = \frac{\$20,000,000 + \$3,000,000}{\$336 - \$250} = 267{,}442 \text{ units}$$

$$\text{Dollar sales} = 267{,}442 \text{ units} \times \$336 = \$89{,}860{,}512$$

Or

$$\text{Dollar sales} = \frac{\text{fixed cost} + \text{profit goal}}{\text{contribution margin}} = \frac{\$20,000,000 + \$3,000,000}{0.256} = \$89{,}843{,}750$$

Finally, ConnectPhone can express its profit goal as a percentage of sales, which we also saw in previous pricing analyses. Assume ConnectPhone desires a 25% return on sales. To determine the unit and sales volume necessary to achieve this goal, the calculation is a little different from the previous two examples. In this case, we incorporate the profit goal into the unit contribution as an additional variable cost. Look at it this way: If 25% of each sale must go toward profits, that leaves only 75% of the selling price to cover fixed costs. Thus, the equation becomes:

$$\text{Unit volume} = \frac{\text{fixed cost}}{\text{price} - \text{variable cost} - (0.25 \times \text{price})} \text{ or } \frac{\text{fixed cost}}{(0.75 \times \text{price}) - \text{variable cost}}$$

So,

$$\text{Unit volume} = \frac{\$20,000,000}{(0.75 \times \$336) - \$250} = 10{,}000{,}000 \text{ units}$$

$$\text{Dollar sales necessary} = 10{,}000{,}000 \text{ units} \times \$336 = \$3{,}360{,}000{,}000$$

Thus, ConnectPhone would need more than $3 billion in sales to realize a 25% return on sales given its current price and cost structure! Could it possibly achieve this level of sales? The major point is this: Although break-even analysis can be useful in determining the level of sales needed to cover costs or to achieve a stated profit goal, it does not tell the company whether it is *possible* to achieve that level of sales at the specified price. To address this issue, ConnectPhone needs to estimate demand for this product.

Before moving on, however, let's stop here and practice applying the concepts covered so far. Now that you have seen pricing and break-even concepts in action as they related to ConnectPhone's new product, here are several exercises for you to apply what you have learned in other contexts.

Marketing by the Numbers Exercise Set One

Now that you've studied pricing, break-even, and margin analysis as they relate to ConnectPhone's new-product launch, use the following exercises to apply these concepts in other contexts.

1.1   Sanborn, a manufacturer of electric roof vents, realizes a cost of $55 for every unit it produces. Its total fixed costs equal $2 million. If the company manufactures 500,000 units, compute the following:

  a. unit cost

  b. markup price if the company desires a 10% return on sales

  c. ROI price if the company desires a 25% return on an investment of $1 million

1.2   An interior decorator purchases items to sell in her store. She purchases a lamp for $125 and sells it for $225. Determine the following:

  a. dollar markup

  b. markup percentage on cost

  c. markup percentage on selling price

1.3   A consumer purchases a toaster from a retailer for $60. The retailer's markup is 20%, and the wholesaler's markup is 15%, both based on selling price. For what price does the manufacturer sell the product to the wholesaler?

1.4   A vacuum manufacturer has a unit cost of $50 and wishes to achieve a margin of 30% based on selling price. If the manufacturer sells directly to a retailer who then adds a set margin of 40% based on selling price, determine the retail price charged to consumers.

1.5   Advanced Electronics manufactures DVDs and sells them directly to retailers who typically sell them for $20. Retailers take a 40% margin based on the retail selling price. Advanced's cost information is as follows:

DVD package and disc	$2.50/DVD
Royalties	$2.25/DVD
Advertising and promotion	$500,000
Overhead	$200,000

  Calculate the following:

  a. contribution per unit and contribution margin

  b. break-even volume in DVD units and dollars

  c. volume in DVD units and dollar sales necessary if Advanced's profit goal is 20% profit on sales

  d. net profit if 5 million DVDs are sold

DEMAND ESTIMATES, THE MARKETING BUDGET, AND MARKETING PERFORMANCE MEASURES

Market Potential and Sales Estimates

ConnectPhone has now calculated the sales needed to break even and to attain various profit goals on its new product. However, the company needs more information regarding demand in order to assess the feasibility of attaining the needed sales levels. This information is also needed for production and other decisions. For example, production schedules need to be developed and marketing tactics need to be planned.

Total market demand
The total volume that would be bought by a defined consumer group in a defined geographic area in a defined time period in a defined marketing environment under a defined level and mix of industry marketing effort.

The **total market demand** for a product or service is the total volume that would be bought by a defined consumer group in a defined geographic area in a defined time period in a defined marketing environment under a defined level and mix of industry marketing effort. Total market demand is not a fixed number but a function of the stated conditions. For example, next year's total market demand for media phones will depend on how much other producers spend on marketing their brands. It also depends on many environmental factors, such as government regulations, economic conditions, and the level of consumer confidence in a given market. The upper limit of market demand is called **market potential**.

Market potential
The upper limit of market demand.

One general but practical method that ConnectPhone might use for estimating total market demand uses three variables: (1) the number of prospective buyers, (2) the quantity purchased by an average buyer per year, and (3) the price of an average unit. Using these numbers, ConnectPhone can estimate total market demand as follows:

$$Q = n \times q \times p$$

Where

Q = total market demand
n = number of buyers in the market
q = quantity purchased by an average buyer per year
p = price of an average unit

Chain ratio method
Estimating market demand by multiplying a base number by a chain of adjusting percentages.

A variation of this approach is the **chain ratio method**. This method involves multiplying a base number by a chain of adjusting percentages. For example, ConnectPhone's product is designed to replace a household's telephone as well as provide "always on" Internet access. Thus, only households with broadband Internet access will be able to use the product. Finally, not all Internet households will be willing and able to purchase the new product. ConnectPhone can estimate U.S. demand using a chain of calculations like the following:

Total number of U.S. households

× The percentage of U.S. households with broadband Internet access
× The percentage of these households willing and able to buy this device

The U.S. Census Bureau estimates that there are approximately 113 million households in the United States.[3] Research also indicates that 50 percent of U.S. households have broadband Internet access.[4] Finally, ConnectPhone's own research indicates that 33.1 percent of households possess the discretionary income needed and are willing to buy a device such as this. Then, the total number of households willing and able to purchase this product is:

113 million households × 0.50 × 0.331 = 18.7 million households

Households will need only one media phone. Assuming the average retail price across all brands is $750 for this product, the estimate of total market demand is as follows:

18.7 million households × 1 device per household × $750 = $14 billion

This simple chain of calculations gives ConnectPhone only a rough estimate of potential demand. However, more detailed chains involving additional segments and other qualifying factors would yield more accurate and refined estimates. Still, these are only *estimates* of market potential. They rely heavily on assumptions regarding adjusting percentages, average quantity, and average price. Thus, ConnectPhone must make certain that its assumptions are reasonable and defendable. As can be seen, the overall market potential in dollar sales can vary widely given the average price used. For this reason, ConnectPhone will use unit sales potential to determine its sales estimate for next year. Market potential in terms of units is 18.7 million (18.7 million households × 1 device per household).

Assuming that ConnectPhone wants to attain 2% market share (comparable to its share of the Internet modem market) in the first year after launching this product, then it can forecast unit sales at 18.7 million units × 0.02 = 374,000 units. At a selling price of $336 per unit, this translates into sales of $125,664,000 (374,000 units × $336 per unit). For simplicity, further analyses will use forecasted sales of $125 million.

This unit volume estimate is well within ConnectPhone's production capacity and exceeds not only the break-even estimate (232,559 units) calculated earlier, but also the volume necessary to realize a $5 million profit (290,698 units) or a 30% return on investment (267,442 units). However, this forecast falls well short of the volume necessary to realize a 25% return on sales (10 million units!) and may require that ConnectPhone revise expectations.

To assess expected profits, we must now look at the budgeted expenses for launching this product. To do this, we will construct a pro forma profit-and-loss statement.

THE PROFIT-AND-LOSS STATEMENT AND MARKETING BUDGET

Pro forma (or projected) profit-and-loss statement (or income statement or operating statement)
A statement that shows projected revenues less budgeted expenses and estimates the projected net profit for an organization, product, or brand during a specific planning period, typically a year.

All marketing managers must account for the profit impact of their marketing strategies. A major tool for projecting such profit impact is a **pro forma** (or projected) **profit-and-loss statement** (also called an **income statement** or **operating statement**). A pro forma statement shows projected revenues less budgeted expenses and estimates the projected net profit for an organization, product, or brand during a specific planning period, typically a year. It includes direct product production costs, marketing expenses budgeted to attain a given sales forecast, and overhead expenses assigned to the organization or product. A profit-and-loss statement typically consists of several major components (see ■ **Table A2.1**):

- *Net sales*—gross sales revenue minus returns and allowances (for example, trade, cash, quantity, and promotion allowances). ConnectPhone's net sales for 2010 are estimated to be $125 million, as determined in the previous analysis.
- *Cost of goods sold*—(sometimes called *cost of sales*)—the actual cost of the merchandise sold by a manufacturer or reseller. It includes the cost of inventory, purchases, and other costs associated with making the goods. ConnectPhone's cost of goods sold is estimated to be 50% of net sales, or $62.5 million.
- *Gross margin (or gross profit)*—the difference between net sales and cost of goods sold. ConnectPhone's gross margin is estimated to be $62.5 million.
- *Operating expenses*—the expenses incurred while doing business. These include all other expenses beyond the cost of goods sold that are necessary to conduct business. Operating expenses can be presented in total or broken down in detail. Here, ConnectPhone's estimated operating expenses include *marketing expenses* and *general and administrative expenses*.

■ **Table A2.1** Pro Forma Profit-and-Loss Statement for the 12-Month Period Ended December 31, 2010

			% of Sales
Net Sales		$125,000,000	100%
Cost of Goods Sold		62,500,000	50%
Gross Margin		$ 62,500,000	50%
Marketing Expenses			
Sales expenses	$17,500,000		
Promotion expenses	15,000,000		
Freight	12,500,000	45,000,000	36%
General and Administrative Expenses			
Managerial salaries and expenses	$2,000,000		
Indirect overhead	3,000,000	5,000,000	4%
Net Profit Before Income Tax		$12,500,000	10%

Marketing expenses include sales expenses, promotion expenses, and distribution expenses. The new product will be sold though ConnectPhone's sales force, so the company budgets $5 million for sales salaries. However, because sales representatives earn a 10% commission on sales, ConnectPhone must also add a variable component to sales expenses of $12.5 million (10% of $125 million net sales), for a total budgeted sales expense of $17.5 million. ConnectPhone sets its advertising and promotion to launch this product at $10 million. However, the company also budgets 4% of sales, or $5 million, for cooperative advertising allowances to retailers who promote ConnectPhone's new product in their advertising. Thus, the total budgeted advertising and promotion expenses are $15 million ($10 million for advertising plus $5 million in co-op allowances). Finally, ConnectPhone budgets 10% of net sales, or $12.5 million, for freight and delivery charges. In all, total marketing expenses are estimated to be $17.5 million + $15 million + $12.5 million = $45 million.

General and administrative expenses are estimated at $5 million, broken down into $2 million for managerial salaries and expenses for the marketing function and $3 million of indirect overhead allocated to this product by the corporate accountants (such as depreciation, interest, maintenance, and insurance). Total expenses for the year, then, are estimated to be $50 million ($45 million marketing expenses + $5 million in general and administrative expenses).

- *Net profit before taxes*—profit earned after all costs are deducted. ConnectPhone's estimated net profit before taxes is $12.5 million.

In all, as Table A2.1 shows, ConnectPhone expects to earn a profit on its new product of $12.5 million in 2010. Also note that the percentage of sales that each component of the profit-and-loss statement represents is given in the right-hand column. These percentages are determined by dividing the cost figure by net sales (that is, marketing expenses represent 36% of net sales determined by $45 million ÷ $125 million). As can be seen, ConnectPhone projects a net profit return on sales of 10% in the first year after launching this product.

MARKETING PERFORMANCE MEASURES

Now let's fast-forward a year. ConnectPhone's product has been on the market for one year and management wants to assess its sales and profit performance. One way to assess this performance is to compute performance ratios derived from ConnectPhone's **profit-and-loss statement** (or **income statement** or **operating statement**).

Whereas the pro forma profit-and-loss statement shows *projected* financial performance, the statement given in ■ **Table A2.2** shows ConnectPhone's *actual* financial performance based on actual sales, cost of goods sold, and expenses during the past year. By

Profit-and-loss statement (or income statement or operating statement)
A statement that shows actual revenues less expenses and net profit for an organization, product, or brand during a specific planning period, typically a year.

■ **Table A2.2** Profit-and-Loss Statement for the 12-Month Period Ended December 31, 2010

			% of Sales
Net Sales		$100,000,000	100%
Cost of Goods Sold		55,000,000	55%
Gross Margin		$ 45,000,000	45%
Marketing Expenses			
Sales expenses	$15,000,000		
Promotion expenses	14,000,000		
Freight	10,000,000	39,000,000	39%
General and Administrative Expenses			
Managerial salaries and expenses	$2,000,000		
Indirect overhead	5,000,000	7,000,000	7%
Net Profit Before Income Tax		($1,000,000)	(1%)

comparing the profit-and-loss statement from one period to the next, ConnectPhone can gauge performance against goals, spot favorable or unfavorable trends, and take appropriate corrective action.

The profit-and-loss statement shows that ConnectPhone lost $1 million rather than making the $12.5 million profit projected in the pro forma statement. Why? One obvious reason is that net sales fell $25 million short of estimated sales. Lower sales translated into lower variable costs associated with marketing the product. However, both fixed costs and the cost of goods sold as a percentage of sales exceeded expectations. Hence, the product's contribution margin was 21% rather than the estimated 26%. That is, variable costs represented 79% of sales (55% for cost of goods sold, 10% for sales commissions, 10% for freight, and 4% for co-op allowances). Recall that contribution margin can be calculated by subtracting that fraction from one $(1 - 0.79 = 0.21)$. Total fixed costs were $22 million, $2 million more than estimated. Thus, the sales that ConnectPhone needed to break even given this cost structure can be calculated as:

$$\text{Break-even sales} = \frac{\text{fixed costs}}{\text{contribution margin}} = \frac{\$22,000,000}{0.21} = \$104,761,905$$

If ConnectPhone had achieved another $5 million in sales, it would have earned a profit.

Although ConnectPhone's sales fell short of the forecasted sales, so did overall industry sales for this product. Overall industry sales were only $2.5 billion. That means that ConnectPhone's **market share** was 4% ($100 million ÷ $2.5 billion = 0.04 = 4%), which was higher than forecasted. Thus, ConnectPhone attained a higher-than-expected market share but the overall market sales were not as high as estimated.

Market share
Company sales divided by market sales.

Analytic Ratios

The profit-and-loss statement provides the figures needed to compute some crucial **operating ratios**—the ratios of selected operating statement items to net sales. These ratios let marketers compare the firm's performance in one year to that in previous years (or with industry standards and competitors' performance in that year). The most commonly used operating ratios are the gross margin percentage, the net profit percentage, and the operating expense percentage. The inventory turnover rate and return on investment (ROI) are often used to measure managerial effectiveness and efficiency.

The **gross margin percentage** indicates the percentage of net sales remaining after cost of goods sold that can contribute to operating expenses and net profit before taxes. The higher this ratio, the more a firm has left to cover expenses and generate profit. ConnectPhone's gross margin ratio was 45%:

Operating ratios
The ratios of selected operating statement items to net sales.

Gross margin percentage
The percentage of net sales remaining after cost of goods sold—calculated by dividing gross margin by net sales.

$$\text{Gross margin percentage} = \frac{\text{gross margin}}{\text{net sales}} = \frac{\$45,000,000}{\$100,000,000} = 0.45 = 45\%$$

Note that this percentage is lower than estimated, and this ratio is seen easily in the percentage of sales column in Table A2.2. Stating items in the profit-and-loss statement as a percent of sales allows managers to quickly spot abnormal changes in costs over time. If there was previous history for this product and this ratio was declining, management should examine it more closely to determine why it has decreased (that is, because of a decrease in sales volume or price, an increase in costs, or a combination of these). In ConnectPhone's case, net sales were $25 million lower than estimated, and cost of goods sold was higher than estimated (55% rather than the estimated 50%).

The **net profit percentage** shows the percentage of each sales dollar going to profit. It is calculated by dividing net profits by net sales:

Net profit percentage
The percentage of each sales dollar going to profit—calculated by dividing net profits by net sales.

$$\text{Net profit percentage} = \frac{\text{net profit}}{\text{net sales}} = \frac{-\$1,000,000}{\$100,000,000} = -0.01 = -1.0\%$$

This ratio is easily seen in the percent of sales column. ConnectPhone's new product generated negative profits in the first year, not a good situation given that before the product launch net profits before taxes were estimated at more than $12 million. Later in this appendix, we will discuss further analyses the marketing manager should conduct to defend the product.

Operating expense percentage
The portion of net sales going to operating expenses—calculated by dividing total expenses by net sales.

The **operating expense percentage** indicates the portion of net sales going to operating expenses. Operating expenses include marketing and other expenses not directly related to marketing the product, such as indirect overhead assigned to this product. It is calculated by:

$$\text{Operating expense percentage} = \frac{\text{total expenses}}{\text{net sales}} = \frac{\$46,000,000}{\$100,000,000} = 0.46 = 46\%$$

This ratio can also be quickly determined from the percent of sales column in the profit-and-loss statement by adding the percentages for marketing expenses and general and administrative expenses (39% + 7%). Thus, 46 cents of every sales dollar went for operations. Although ConnectPhone wants this ratio to be as low as possible, and 46% is not an alarming amount, it is of concern if it is increasing over time or if a loss is realized.

Inventory turnover rate (or stockturn rate)
The number of times an inventory turns over or is sold during a specified time period (often one year)—calculated based on costs, selling price, or units.

Another useful ratio is the **inventory turnover rate** (also called **stockturn rate** for resellers). The inventory turnover rate is the number of times an inventory turns over or is sold during a specified time period (often one year). This rate tells how quickly a business is moving inventory through the organization. Higher rates indicate that lower investments in inventory are made, thus freeing up funds for other investments. It may be computed on a cost, selling price, or unit basis. The formula based on cost is:

$$\text{Inventory turnover rate} = \frac{\text{cost of goods sold}}{\text{average inventory at cost}}$$

Assuming ConnectPhone's beginning and ending inventories were $30 million and $20 million, respectively, the inventory turnover rate is:

$$\text{Inventory turnover rate} = \frac{\$55,000,000}{(\$30,000,000 + \$20,000,000)/2} = \frac{\$55,000,000}{\$25,000,000} = 2.2$$

That is, ConnectPhone's inventory turned over 2.2 times in 2010. Normally, the higher the turnover rate, the higher the management efficiency and company profitability. However, this rate should be compared to industry averages, competitors' rates, and past performance to determine if ConnectPhone is doing well. A competitor with similar sales but a higher inventory turnover rate will have fewer resources tied up in inventory, allowing it to invest in other areas of the business.

Return on investment (ROI)
A measure of managerial effectiveness and efficiency—net profit before taxes divided by total investment.

Companies frequently use **return on investment (ROI)** to measure managerial effectiveness and efficiency. For ConnectPhone, ROI is the ratio of net profits to total investment required to manufacture the new product. This investment includes capital investments in land, buildings, and equipment (here, the initial $10 million to refurbish the manufacturing facility) plus inventory costs (ConnectPhone's average inventory totaled $25 million), for a total of $35 million. Thus, ConnectPhone's ROI for this product is:

$$\text{Return on investment} = \frac{\text{net profit before taxes}}{\text{investment}} = \frac{-\$1,000,000}{\$35,000,000} = -.0286 = -2.86\%$$

ROI is often used to compare alternatives, and a positive ROI is desired. The alternative with the highest ROI is preferred to other alternatives. ConnectPhone needs to be concerned with the ROI realized. One obvious way ConnectPhone can increase ROI is to increase net profit by reducing expenses. Another way is to reduce its investment, perhaps by investing less in inventory and turning it over more frequently.

Marketing Profitability Metrics

Given the above financial results, you may be thinking that ConnectPhone should drop this new product. But what arguments can marketers make for keeping or dropping this product? The obvious arguments for dropping the product are that first-year sales were well below expected levels and the product lost money, resulting in a negative return on investment.

So what would happen if ConnectPhone did drop this product? Surprisingly, if the company drops the product, the profits for the total organization will decrease by $4 million! How can that be? Marketing managers need to look closely at the numbers in the profit-and-loss statement to determine the *net marketing contribution* for this product. In

ConnectPhone's case, the net marketing contribution for the product is $4 million, and if the company drops this product, that contribution will disappear as well. Let's look more closely at this concept to illustrate how marketing managers can better assess and defend their marketing strategies and programs.

Net marketing contribution (NMC)
A measure of marketing profitability that includes only components of profitability controlled by marketing.

Net Marketing Contribution   Net marketing contribution (NMC), along with other marketing metrics derived from it, measures *marketing* profitability. It includes only components of profitability that are controlled by marketing. Whereas the previous calculation of net profit before taxes from the profit-and-loss statement includes operating expenses not under marketing's control, NMC does not. Referring back to ConnectPhone's profit-and-loss statement given in Table A2.2, we can calculate net marketing contribution for the product as:

$$NMC = \text{net sales} - \text{cost of goods sold} - \text{marketing expenses}$$

$$= \$100 \text{ million} - \$55 \text{ million} - \$41 \text{ million} = \$4 \text{ million}$$

The marketing expenses include sales expenses ($15 million), promotion expenses ($14 million), freight expenses ($10 million), and the managerial salaries and expenses of the marketing function ($2 million), which total $41 million.

Thus, the product actually contributed $4 million to ConnectPhone's profits. It was the $5 million of indirect overhead allocated to this product that caused the negative profit. Further, the amount allocated was $2 million more than estimated in the pro forma profit-and-loss statement. Indeed, if only the estimated amount had been allocated, the product would have earned a *profit* of $1 million rather than losing $1 million. If ConnectPhone drops the product, the $5 million in fixed overhead expenses will not disappear—it will simply have to be allocated elsewhere. However, the $4 million in net marketing contribution *will* disappear.

Marketing return on sales (or marketing ROS)
The percent of net sales attributable to the net marketing contribution—calculated by dividing net marketing contribution by net sales.

Marketing Return on Sales and Investment   To get an even deeper understanding of the profit impact of marketing strategy, we'll now examine two measures of marketing efficiency—*marketing return on sales* (marketing ROS) and *marketing return on investment* (marketing ROI).[5]

Marketing return on sales (or marketing ROS) shows the percent of net sales attributable to the net marketing contribution. For our product, ROS is:

$$\text{Marketing ROS} = \frac{\text{net marketing contribution}}{\text{net sales}} = \frac{\$4,000,000}{\$100,000,000} = 0.04 = 4\%$$

Thus, out of every $100 of sales, the product returns $4 to ConnectPhone's bottom line. A high marketing ROS is desirable. But to assess whether this is a good level of performance, ConnectPhone must compare this figure to previous marketing ROS levels for the product, the ROSs of other products in the company's portfolio, and the ROSs of competing products.

Marketing return on investment (or marketing ROI)
A measure of the marketing productivity of a marketing investment—calculated by dividing net marketing contribution by marketing expenses.

Marketing return on investment (or marketing ROI) measures the marketing productivity of a marketing investment. In ConnectPhone's case, the marketing investment is represented by $41 million of the total expenses. Thus, marketing ROI is:

$$\text{Marketing ROI} = \frac{\text{net marketing contribution}}{\text{marketing expenses}} = \frac{\$4,000,000}{\$41,000,000} = 0.0976 - 9.76\%$$

As with marketing ROS, a high value is desirable, but this figure should be compared with previous levels for the given product and with the marketing ROIs of competitors' products. Note from this equation that marketing ROI could be greater than 100%. This can be achieved by attaining a higher net marketing contribution and/or a lower total marketing expense.

In this section, we estimated market potential and sales, developed profit-and-loss statements, and examined financial measures of performance. In the next section, we discuss methods for analyzing the impact of various marketing tactics. However, before moving on to those analyses, here's another set of quantitative exercises to help you apply what you've learned to other situations.

Marketing by the Numbers Exercise Set Two

2.1   Determine the market potential for a product that has 50 million prospective buyers who purchase an average of 3 per year and price averages $25. How many units must a company sell if it desires a 10% share of this market?

2.2   Develop a profit-and-loss statement for the Westgate division of North Industries. This division manufactures light fixtures sold to consumers through home improvement and hardware stores. Cost of goods sold represents 40% of net sales. Marketing expenses include selling expenses, promotion expenses, and freight. Selling expenses include sales salaries totaling $3 million per year and sales commissions (5% of sales). The company spent $3 million on advertising last year, and freight costs were 10% of sales. Other costs include $2 million for managerial salaries and expenses for the marketing function and another $3 million for indirect overhead allocated to the division.

   a. Develop the profit-and-loss statement if net sales were $20 million last year.

   b. Develop the profit-and-loss statement if net sales were $40 million last year.

   c. Calculate Westgate's break-even sales.

2.3   Using the profit-and-loss statement you developed in question 2.2b, and assuming that Westgate's beginning inventory was $11 million, ending inventory was $7 million, and total investment was $20 million including inventory, determine the following:

   a. gross margin percentage

   b. net profit percentage

   c. operating expense percentage

   d. inventory turnover rate

   e. return on investment (ROI)

   f. net marketing contribution

   g. marketing return on sales (marketing ROS)

   h. marketing return on investment (marketing ROI)

   i. Is the Westgate division doing well? Explain your answer.

FINANCIAL ANALYSIS OF MARKETING TACTICS

Although the first-year profit performance for ConnectPhone's new product was less than desired, management feels that this attractive market has excellent growth opportunities. Although the sales of ConnectPhone's product were lower than initially projected, they were not unreasonable given the size of the current market. Thus, ConnectPhone wants to explore new marketing tactics to help grow the market for this product and increase sales for the company.

For example, the company could increase advertising to promote more awareness of the new product and its category. It could add salespeople to secure greater product distribution. ConnectPhone could decrease prices so that more consumers could afford its product. Finally, to expand the market, ConnectPhone could introduce a lower-priced model in addition to the higher-priced original offering. Before pursuing any of these tactics, ConnectPhone must analyze the financial implications of each.

Increase Advertising Expenditures

Although most consumers understand the Internet and telephones, they may not be aware of media phones. Thus, ConnectPhone is considering boosting its advertising to make more people aware of the benefits of this device in general and of its own brand in particular.

What if ConnectPhone's marketers recommend increasing national advertising by 50% to $15 million (assume no change in the variable cooperative component of promotional expenditures)? This represents an increase in fixed costs of $5 million. What increase in sales will be needed to break even on this $5 million increase in fixed costs?

A quick way to answer this question is to divide the increase in fixed cost by the contribution margin, which we found in a previous analysis to be 21%:

$$\text{Increase in sales} = \frac{\text{increase in fixed cost}}{\text{contribution margin}} = \frac{\$5,000,000}{0.21} = \$23,809,524$$

Thus, a 50% increase in advertising expenditures must produce a sales increase of almost $24 million to just break even. That $24 million sales increase translates into an almost 1 percentage point increase in market share (1% of the $2.5 billion overall market equals $25 million). That is, to break even on the increased advertising expenditure, ConnectPhone would have to increase its market share from 4% to 4.95% ($123,809,524 ÷ $2.5 billion = 0.0495 or 4.95% market share). All of this assumes that the total market will not grow, which might or might not be a reasonable assumption.

Increase Distribution Coverage

ConnectPhone also wants to consider hiring more salespeople in order to call on new retailer accounts and increase distribution through more outlets. Even though ConnectPhone sells directly to wholesalers, its sales representatives call on retail accounts to perform other functions in addition to selling, such as training retail salespeople. Currently, ConnectPhone employs 60 sales reps who earn an average of $50,000 in salary plus 10% commission on sales. The product is currently sold to consumers through 1,875 retail outlets. Suppose ConnectPhone wants to increase that number of outlets to 2,500, an increase of 625 retail outlets. How many additional salespeople will ConnectPhone need, and what sales will be necessary to break even on the increased cost?

One method for determining what size sales force ConnectPhone will need is the **workload method**. The workload method uses the following formula to determine the salesforce size:

$$NS = \frac{NC \times FC \times LC}{TA}$$

where

NS = number of salespeople
NC = number of customers
FC = average frequency of customer calls per customer
LC = average length of customer call
TA = time an average salesperson has available for selling per year

ConnectPhone's sales reps typically call on accounts an average of 20 times per year for about 2 hours per call. Although each sales rep works 2,000 hours per year (50 weeks per year × 40 hours per week), they spent about 15 hours per week on nonselling activities such as administrative duties and travel. Thus, the average annual available selling time per sales rep per year is 1,250 hours (50 weeks × 25 hours per week). We can now calculate how many sales reps ConnectPhone will need to cover the anticipated 2,500 retail outlets:

$$NS = \frac{2,500 \times 20 \times 2}{1,250} = 80 \text{ salespeople}$$

Therefore, ConnectPhone will need to hire 20 more salespeople. The cost to hire these reps will be $1 million (20 salespeople × $50,000 salary per sales person).

What increase in sales will be required to break even on this increase in fixed costs? The 10% commission is already accounted for in the contribution margin, so the contribution margin remains unchanged at 21%. Thus, the increase in sales needed to cover this increase in fixed costs can be calculated by:

$$\text{Increase in sales} = \frac{\text{increase in fixed cost}}{\text{contribution margin}} = \frac{\$1,000,000}{0.21} = \$4,761,905$$

That is, ConnectPhone's sales must increase almost $5 million to break even on this tactic. So, how many new retail outlets will the company need to secure to achieve this sales increase? The average revenue generated per current outlet is $53,333 ($100 million in sales divided by 1,875 outlets). To achieve the nearly $5 million sales increase needed to break even, ConnectPhone would need about 90 new outlets ($4,761,905 ÷ $53,333 = 89.3 outlets), or about 4.5 outlets per new rep. Given that current reps cover about 31 outlets apiece (1,875 outlets ÷ 60 reps), this seems very reasonable.

Workload method
An approach to determining sales force size based on the workload required and the time available for selling.

Decrease Price

ConnectPhone is also considering lowering its price to increase sales revenue through increased volume. The company's research has shown that demand for most types of consumer electronics products is elastic—that is, the percentage increase in the quantity demanded is greater than the percentage decrease in price.

What increase in sales would be necessary to break even on a 10% decrease in price? That is, what increase in sales will be needed to maintain the total contribution that ConnectPhone realized at the higher price? The current total contribution can be determined by multiplying the contribution margin by total sales:[6]

$$\text{Current total contribution} = \text{contribution margin} \times \text{sales}$$

$$= .21 \times \$100 \text{ million} = \$21 \text{ million}$$

Price changes result in changes in unit contribution and contribution margin. Recall that the contribution margin of 21% was based on variable costs representing 79% of sales. Therefore, unit variable costs can be determined by multiplying the original price by this percentage: $336 × 0.79 = $265.44 per unit. If price is decreased by 10%, the new price is $302.40. However, variable costs do not change just because price decreased, so the contribution and contribution margin decrease as follows:

	Old	New (reduced 10%)
Price	$336	$302.40
− Unit variable cost	$265.44	$265.44
= Unit contribution	$70.56	$36.96
Contribution margin	$70.56/$336 = 0.21 or 21%	$36.96/$302.40 = 0.12 or 12%

So a 10% reduction in price results in a decrease in the contribution margin from 21% to 12%.[7] To determine the sales level needed to break even on this price reduction, we calculate the level of sales that must be attained at the new contribution margin to achieve the original total contribution of $21 million:

$$\text{New contribution margin} \times \text{new sales level} = \text{original total contribution}$$

So,

$$\text{New sales level} = \frac{\text{original contribution}}{\text{new contribution margin}} = \frac{\$21,000,000}{0.12} = \$175,000,000$$

Thus, sales must increase by $75 million ($175 million − $100 million) just to break even on a 10% price reduction. This means that ConnectPhone must increase market share to 7% ($175 million ÷ $2.5 billion) to achieve the current level of profits (assuming no increase in the total market sales). The marketing manager must assess whether or not this is a reasonable goal.

Extend the Product Line

Cannibalization
The situation in which one product sold by a company takes a portion of its sales from other company products.

As a final option, ConnectPhone is considering extending its product line by offering a lower-priced model. Of course, the new, lower-priced product would steal some sales from the higher-priced model. This is called **cannibalization**—the situation in which one product sold by a company takes a portion of its sales from other company products. If the new product has a lower contribution than the original product, the company's total contribution will decrease on the cannibalized sales. However, if the new product can generate enough new volume, it is worth considering.

To assess cannibalization, ConnectPhone must look at the incremental contribution gained by having both products available. Recall in the previous analysis we determined that unit variable costs were $265.44 and unit contribution was just over $70. Assuming costs remain the same next year, ConnectPhone can expect to realize a contribution per unit of approximately $70 for every unit of the original product sold.

Assume that the first model offered by ConnectPhone is called MP1 and the new, lower-priced model is called MP2. MP2 will retail for $400, and resellers will take the same markup percentages on price as they do with the higher-priced model. Therefore, MP2's price to wholesalers will be $224 as follows:

Retail price:	$400
minus retail margin (30%):	− $120
Retailer's cost/wholesaler's price:	$280
minus wholesaler's margin (20%):	− $ 56
Wholesaler's cost/ConnectPhone's price	$224

If MP2's variable costs are estimated to be $174, then its contribution per unit will equal $50 ($224 − $174 = $50). That means for every unit that MP2 cannibalizes from MP1, ConnectPhone will *lose* $20 in contribution toward fixed costs and profit (that is, contribution$_{MP2}$ − contribution$_{MP1}$ = $50 − $70 = −$20). You might conclude that ConnectPhone should not pursue this tactic because it appears as though the company will be worse off if it introduces the lower-priced model. However, if MP2 captures enough *additional* sales, ConnectPhone will be better off even though some MP1 sales are cannibalized. The company must examine what will happen to *total* contribution, which requires estimates of unit volume for both products.

Originally, ConnectPhone estimated that next year's sales of MP1 would be 600,000 units. However, with the introduction of MP2, it now estimates that 200,000 of those sales will be cannibalized by the new model. If ConnectPhone sells only 200,000 units of the new MP2 model (all cannibalized from MP1), the company would lose $4 million in total contribution (200,000 units × −$20 per cannibalized unit = −$4 million)—not a good outcome. However, ConnectPhone estimates that MP2 will generate the 200,000 of cannibalized sales plus an *additional* 500,000 unit sales. Thus, the contribution on these additional MP2 units will be $25 million (i.e., 500,000 units × $50 per unit = $25 million). The net effect is that ConnectPhone will gain $21 million in total contribution by introducing MP2.

The following table compares ConnectPhone's total contribution with and without the introduction of MP2:

	MP1 only	MP1 and MP2
MP1 contribution	600,000 units × $70 = $42,000,000	400,000 units × $70 = $28,000,000
MP2 contribution	0	700,000 units × $50 = $35,000,000
Total contribution	$42,000,000	$63,000,000

The difference in the total contribution is a net gain of $21 million ($63 million − $42 million). Based on this analysis, ConnectPhone should introduce the MP2 model because it results in a positive incremental contribution. However, if fixed costs will increase by more than $21 million as a result of adding this model, then the net effect will be negative and ConnectPhone should not pursue this tactic.

Now that you have seen these marketing tactic analysis concepts in action as they related to ConnectPhone's new product, here are several exercises for you to apply what you have learned in this section in other contexts.

Marketing by the Numbers Exercise Set Three

3.1 Kingsford, Inc. sells small plumbing components to consumers through retail outlets. Total industry sales for Kingsford's relevant market last year were $80 million, with Kingsford's sales representing 10% of that total. Contribution margin is 25%. Kingsford's sales force calls on retail outlets and each sales rep earns $45,000 per year plus 1% commission on all sales. Retailers receive a 40% margin on selling price and generate average revenue of $10,000 per outlet for Kingsford.

   a. The marketing manager has suggested increasing consumer advertising by $300,000. By how much would dollar sales need to increase to break even on this expenditure? What increase in overall market share does this represent?

b. Another suggestion is to hire three more sales representatives to gain new consumer retail accounts. How many new retail outlets would be necessary to break even on the increased cost of adding three sales reps?

c. A final suggestion is to make a 20% across-the-board price reduction. By how much would dollar sales need to increase to maintain Kingsford's current contribution? (See endnote 13 to calculate the new contribution margin.)

d. Which suggestion do you think Kingsford should implement? Explain your recommendation.

3.2 PepsiCo sells its soft drinks in approximately 400,000 retail establishments, such as supermarkets, discount stores, and convenience stores. Sales representatives call on each retail account weekly, which means each account is called on by a sales rep 52 times per year. The average length of a sales call is 75 minutes (or 1.25 hours). An average salesperson works 2,000 hours per year (50 weeks per year × 40 hours per week), but each spends 10 hours a week on nonselling activities, such as administrative tasks and travel. How many sales people does PepsiCo need?

3.3 Hair Zone manufactures a brand of hair-styling gel. It is considering adding a modified version of the product—a foam that provides stronger hold. Hair Zone's variable costs and prices to wholesalers are:

	Current Hair Gel	New Foam Product
Unit selling price	2.00	2.25
Unit variable costs	.85	1.25

Hair Zone expects to sell 1 million units of the new styling foam in the first year after introduction, but it expects that 60% of those sales will come from buyers who normally purchase Hair Zone's styling gel. Hair Zone estimates that it would sell 1.5 million units of the gel if it did not introduce the foam. If the fixed cost of launching the new foam will be $100,000 during the first year, should Hair Zone add the new product to its line? Why or why not?

References

Chapter 1

1. Portions adapted from Natalie Zmuda, "Zappos: Customer Service First—and a Daily Obsession," *Advertising Age*, October 20, 2008, p. 36; with additional information and quotes from Jeffrey M. O'Brien, "Zappos Knows How to Kick It," February 2, 2009, p. 54; Masha Zager, "Zappos Delivers Service...With Shoes on the Side," *Apparel Magazine*, January 2009, pp. 10–13; and www.youtube.com/users/zappos and www.zappos.com, accessed December 2009.

2. Adam Morgan, "Three Rules for Thriving in 2009," *AdweekMedia*, January 5, 2009, p. 11.

3. See Adam L. Penenberg, "All Eyes on Apple," *Fast Company*, December 2007–January 2008, pp. 83–91; and "Apple Reports First Quarter Results; iPod Sales Set New Record," *PR Newswire*, January 21, 2009.

4. As quoted in John J. Burnett, *Nonprofit Marketing Best Practices* (New York: John Wiley & Sons, 2008), p. 21.

5. The American Marketing Association offers the following definition: "Marketing is an organizational function and a set of processes for creating, communicating, and delivering value to customers and for managing customer relationships in ways that benefit the organization and its stakeholders." Accessed at http://www.marketingpower.com/_layouts/Dictionary.aspx?dLetter=M, November 2009. Also see, Lisa M. Keefe, "Marketing Defined," *Marketing News*, January 15, 2008, pp. 28–29.

6. Jeffrey M. O'Brien, "Zappos Knows How to Kick It," *Fortune*, January 22, 2009, accessed at www.money.cnn.com; Jena McGregor, "Customer Service Champs," *BusinessWeek*, March 5, 2007, pp. 52–57; and Kevin O'Donnell, "Innovation Quest: Catalytic Leaders Set the Pace," *Marketing News*, June 1, 2008, p. 17.

7. Information from Douglas Quentua, "Revising a Name, but Not a Familiar Slogan," *New York Times*, January 17, 2008; and www.adcouncil.org/default.aspx?id=224, November 2009.

8. See Theodore Levitt's classic article, "Marketing Myopia," *Harvard Business Review*, July–August 1960, pp. 45–56. For more recent discussions, see Yves Doz, Jose Santos, and Peter J. Williamson, "Marketing Myopia Re-Visited: Why Every Company Needs to Learn from the World," *Ivey Business Journal*, January–February 2004, p. 1; "What Business Are You In?" *Harvard Business Review*, October 2006, pp. 127–137; and Lance A. Bettencourt, "Debunking Myths about Customer Needs," *Marketing Management*, January/February 2009, pp. 46–51, p. 50.

9. Information from a recent "The Computer Is Personal Again" advertisement and www.hp.com/personal, November 2009.

10. See "The Campaign to Turn on the Tap and Ditch the Bottle," *Canada NewsWire*, December 12, 2008; and "Green PR Campaign," *PR News*, March 2, 2009.

11. See Larry Edwards, et al., "75 Years of Ideas," *Advertising Age*, February 14, 2005, p. 14; Harris Interactive, "The 9th Annual RQ: Reputations of the 60 Most Visible Companies, A Survey of the U.S. General Public," 2008, accessed at http://www.harrisinteractive.com/news/mediaaccess/2008/HI_BSC_REPORT_AnnualRQ_USA Summary07-08.pdf; and www.jnj.com/our_company/our_credo/index.htm, December 2009.

12. See David Kiley, "How to Sell Luxury to Penny-Pinchers," *BusinessWeek*, November 10, 2008, p. 60.

13. For more on how to measure customer satisfaction, see D. Randall Brandt, "For Good Measure," *Marketing Management*, January–February 2007, pp. 21–25.

14. Portions adapted from Julie Barker, "Power to the People," *Incentive*, February 2008, p. 34 and Carmine Gallo, "Employee Motivation the Ritz-Carlton Way," *BusinessWeek*, February 29, 2008, accessed at www.businessweek.com. Also see "The World's Best Hotels—Where Luxury Lives," *Institutional Investor*, November 2007, p. 1; and http://corporate.ritzcarlton.com/en/About/Awards.htm#Hotel, November 2009.

15. Information about the Harley Owners Group accessed at www.harley-davidson.com/wcm/Content/Pages/HOG/HOG.jsp?locale=en_US, November 2009.

16. Elizabeth A. Sullivan, "Just Say No," *Marketing News*, April 15, 2008, p. 17.

17. Sullivan, "Just Say No," p. 17.

18. Josh Hyatt, "Playing Favorites," *CFO Magazine*, January 1, 2009, accessed at www.cfo.com. The Sprint example is adapted from information found in Vikas Mittal, Matthew Sarkees, and Feisal Murshed, "The Right Way to Manage Unprofitable Customers," *Harvard Business Review*, April 2008, pp. 95–102. Also see Christian Homburg, Mathias Droll, and Dirk Totzek, "Customer Prioritization: Does It Pay Off, and How Should It Be Implemented?" *Journal of Marketing*, September 2008, pp. 110–130.

19. Quotes from Andrew Walmsley, "The Year of Consumer Empowerment," *Marketing*, December 20, 2006, p. 9; and Jeff Heilman, "Rules of Engagement: During a Recession, Marketers Need to Have Their Keenest Listening-to-Customers Strategy in Place," *The Magazine of Branded Content*, Winter 2009, p. 7.

20. See Jefferson Graham, "Twitter Took off from Simple to 'Tweet' success," *USA Today*, July 21, 2008, p. B1; Elizabeth A. Sullivan, "We Were Right!" *Marketing News*, December 15, 2008, p. 16; James Rainey, "On the Media: Twitter's Charms Sort of Grow on You," *Los Angeles Times*, February 18, 2009, p. A1; and B. L. Ochman, "Debunking Six Social Media Myths," *BusinessWeek*, February 19, 2009; accessed at www.BusinessWeek.com.

21. David Kenny and Jack Klues, "The Art of Friending: How to Move from Conversation to Conversion in Social Media, the Communications Platform of the Future," *AdWeek.com*, November 18, 2008, accessed at www.Adweek.com.

22. Sullivan, "We Were Right!" p. 17; and Brian Morrissey, "Kraft Gives Facebook Users Reason to Share," *AdWeek.com*, December 30, 2008, accessed at www.Adweek.com.

23. "Frito-Lay, Doritos Fan Trumps Advertising Professionals and Wins $1 Million Super Bowl Advertising Challenge," *Marketing Weekly News*, February 21, 2009, p. 51.

24. For more examples, see Karen E. Klein, "Should Your Customers Make Your Ads?" *BusinessWeek*, January 2, 2008, www.businessweek.com; and Max Chafkin, "The Customer Is the Company," *Inc.*, June 2008, p. 88.

25. Philip Kotler and Kevin Lane Keller, *Marketing Management*, 13th ed. (Upper Saddle River, NJ: Prentice Hall, 2009), p. 11.

26. Michael Bush, "Marketers Put Emphasis on Loyalty," *Advertising Age*, July 9, 2008, accessed at http://adage.com/print?article_id=129501; and Stanley F. Slater, Jakki J. Mohr, and Sanjit Sengupta, "Know Your Customers," *Marketing Management*, February 2009, pp. 37–44.

27. "Customer Loyalty: You Can't Put a Price on True Loyalty," *Precision Marketing*, January 19, 2009, p. 12. Also see Victoria Colliver, "Customer Loyalties Shifting with Prices," *Fort Wayne Journal-Gazette*, January 26, 2009, p. C5.

28. "Stew Leonard's," *Hoover's Company Records*, July 15, 2009, pp. 104–226; and www.stew-leonards.com/html/about.cfm, November 2009.

29. Graham Brown, "MobileYouth Key Statistics," March 28, 2008, www.mobileyouth.org. For interesting discussions on assessing and using customer lifetime value, see Sunil Gupta, et al., "Modeling Customer Lifetime Value," *Journal of Service Research*, November 2006, pp. 139–146; Detlef Schoder, "The Flaw in Customer Lifetime Value," *Harvard Business Review*, December 2007, p. 26; Lynette Ryals, "Determining the Indirect Value of a Customer," *Journal of Marketing Management*, September 2008, p. 847; and Nicolas Glady, Bart Baesens, and Christophe Croux, "Modeling Churn Using Customer Lifetime Value," *European Journal of Operational Research*, August 16, 2009, p. 402.

30. Erick Schonfeld, "Click Here for the Upsell," *Business 2.0*, July 11, 2007, accessed at http://cnnmoney.com; "Getting Shoppers to Crave More," *Fortune Small Business*, August 24, 2007, p. 85; and Heather Green, "How Amazon Aims to Keep You Clicking," *BusinessWeek*, March 2, 2009, pp. 34–40.

31. Don Peppers and Martha Rogers, "Customers Don't Grow on Trees," *Fast Company*, July 2005, pp. 26.

32. See Roland T. Rust, Valerie A. Zeithaml, and Katherine A. Lemon, *Driving Customer Equity* (New York: Free Press 2000); Rust, Lemon, and Zeithaml, "Return on Marketing: Using Customer Equity to

Focus Marketing Strategy," *Journal of Marketing*, January 2004, pp. 109–127; Roland T. Rust, "Seeking Higher ROI? Base Strategy on Customer Equity," *Advertising Age*, September 10, 2007, pp. 26–27; Dominique M. Hanssens, Daniel Thorpe, and Carl Finkbeiner, "Marketing When Customer Equity Matters," *Harvard Business Review*, May 2008, pp 117–124; Verena Vogel, Heiner Evanschitzky, and B. Ramaseshan, "Customer Equity Drivers and Future Sales," *Journal of Marketing*, November 2008, pp. 98–108; and Thorsten Wiesel, Bernd Skieram, and Julián Villanueva, "Customer Equity: An Integral Part of Financial Reporting," *Journal of Marketing*, March 8, 2008, pp. 1–14..

33. This example is adapted from information in Rust, Lemon, and Zeithaml, "Where Should the Next Marketing Dollar Go?" *Marketing Management*, September–October 2001, pp. 24–28. Also see David Welch and David Kiley, "Can Caddy's Driver Make GM Cool?" *BusinessWeek*, September 20, 2004, pp. 105–106; Jean Halliday, "Comeback Kid Cadillac Stalls after Shop Swap," *Advertising Age*, September 24, 2007, p. 1; and "A Caddy Not Just for Granddaddy," *The Review*, February 11, 2009, p. 17.

34. Werner Reinartz and V. Kumar, "The Mismanagement of Customer Loyalty," *Harvard Business Review*, July 2002, pp. 86–94. Also see Stanley F. Slater, Jakki J. Mohr, and Sanjit Sengupta, "Know Your Customer," *Marketing Management*, February 2009, pp. 37–44.

35. Noreen O'Leary, "Riders on the Storm: How Marketers Are Navigating a Downturn that Hit Consumers Hard," *Adweek*, July 28–August 4, 2008, p. 20.

36. Dan Sewell, "New Frugality Emerges," *Washington Times*, December 1, 2008; and Noreen O'Leary, "Squeeze Play," *Adweek*, January 12, 2009, pp. 8–9.

37. Layura Petrecca, "Marketers Try to Promote Value without Cheapening Image," *USA Today*, November 17, 2008, p. B1. Also see Kenneth Hein, "Why Price Isn't Everything," *Brandweek*, March 2, 2009, p. 6.

38. Quote from Natalie Zmuda, "Target to Put More Focus on Value," *Advertising Age*, August 19, 2008, accessed at http://adage.com/print?article_id=130419; and Stuart Elliott, "With Shoppers Pinching Pennies, Some Big Retailers Get the Message," *New York Times*, April 13, 2009.

39. Burt Helm, "How to Sell Luxury to Penny-Pinchers," *BusinessWeek*, November 10, 2008, p. 60.

40. Emily Thornton, "The New Rules," *BusinessWeek*, January 19, 2009, pp. 30–34.

41. CMO Council, "Marketing Outlook 2009: Setting the Course for Marketing Strategy and Spend," accessed at www.cmocouncil.org/resources. Also see John A. Quelch and Katherine E. Jocz, "How to Market in a Downturn," *Harvard Business Review*, April 2009, pp. 52–62.

42. "Let Them Eat Big Macs," *BusinessWeek*, February 9, 2009, p. 8; and O'Leary, "Squeeze Play, p. 9.

43. Internet usage stats from www.internetworldstats.com/stats.htm, accessed March 2009; James Lewin, "People Now Spend Twice as Much Time on the Internet as Watching TV," *Podcasting News*, February 25, 2008, www.podcastingnews.com/2008/02/25/podcasting-statistics-television/; "Pew Internet and the American Life Project: Latest Trends," accessed at www.pewinternet.org/trends.asp, January 2009; and Pew/Internet, "The Future of the Internet III," December 14, 2008, accessed at www.pewinternet.org/PPF/r/270/report_display.asp.

44. "Research and Markets: Semantic Wave Report: Industry Roadmap to Web 3.0 and Multibillion Market Opportunities," *M2 Presswire*, January 20, 2009.

45. Laurie Rowell, "In Search of Web 3.0," *netWorker*, September, 2008, pp. 18–24. Also see "Research and Markets: Web 3.0 Manifesto," *Business Wire*, January 21, 2009; and Jessi Hempel, "Web 2.0 Is So Over. Welcome to Web 3.0," *Fortune*, January 19, 2009, p. 36.

46. "Pew Internet and the American Life Project: Latest Trends," accessed at www.pewinternet.org/trends.asp, January 2009.

47. See Tom Lowry, "The Game's the Thing at MTV Networks," *BusinessWeek*, February 18, 2008, p. 51. Additional information from annual reports and other information found at www.mcdonalds.com, www.viacom.com, and www.nikebiz.com, October 2008.

48. Adapted from information in Don Frischmann, "Nothing Is Insignificant When It Comes to Brand Fulfillment," *Advertising Age*, January 21, 2008, p. 16.

49. Quotes and information found at www.patagonia.com/web/us/contribution/patagonia.go?assetid=2329, September 2009.

50. For examples, and for a good review of nonprofit marketing, see Philip Kotler and Alan R. Andreasen, *Strategic Marketing for Nonprofit Organizations*, 6th ed. (Upper Saddle River, NJ: Prentice Hall, 2003); Philip Kotler and Karen Fox, *Strategic Marketing for Educational Institutions* (Upper Saddle River, NJ: Prentice Hall, 1995); Philip Kotler, John Bowen, and James Makens, *Marketing for Hospitality and Tourism*, 3rd ed. (Upper Saddle River, NJ: Prentice Hall, 2003); and Philip Kotler and Nancy Lee, *Marketing in the Public Sector A Roadmap for Improved Performance* (Philadelphia: Wharton School Publishing, 2007).

51. Adapted from information in Stephanie Strom, "Ad Featuring Singer Proves Bonanza for A.S.P.C.A.," *New York Times*, December 26, 2008, p. 20.

52. "100 Leading National Advertisers," *Advertising Age*, June 23, 2008, accessed at http://adage.com/datacenter/article?article_id=127791. For more on social marketing, see Philip Kotler, Ned Roberto, and Nancy R. Lee, *Social Marketing: Improving the Quality of Life*, 2nd ed. (Thousand Oaks, CA: Sage Publications, 2002).

Chapter 2

1. Quotes and other information from www.london2012.com, www.olympic.org, www.londonolympics2012.com, www.cocacola.com, www.britishairways.com, www.alastinglegacy.co.uk, www.london2012.com, www.culture.gov.uk, and www.berr.gov.uk.

2. Mission statements are from, Cold Stone Creamery, www.coldstonecreamery.com/assets/pdf/secondary/Pyramid1.pdf; and Amazon.com, http://phx.corporate-ir.net/phoenix.zhtml?c=97664&p=irol-faq#14296, accessed September 2009.

3. Jack and Suzy Welch, "State Your Business; Too Many Mission Statements Are Loaded with Fatheaded Jargon. Play It Straight," *BusinessWeek*, January 14, 2008, p. 80. Also see Leia Fransisco, "A Good Mission Statement Can Lead a Business," *McClatchy-Tribune Business News*, November 8, 2008.

4. See "Kohler Mulls Possible Expansion," *Chemical Business Newsbase*, November 30, 2008; "Kohler Waters Spa Opened in Chicago-Area," April 2008,www.destinationkohler.com/pr/presshospitality.html, and "Kohler Acquires Hospitality Furniture Leader Mark David," May 2008, www.kohler.com/corp/pr/news current.html. Also see the Kohler Press Room, "IBS Press Kit," www.us.kohler.com/pr/presskit.jsp?aid=1194383270995, accessed January 2009.

5. The following discussion is based in part on information found at www.bcg.com/publications/files/Experience_Curve_IV_Growth_Share_Matrix_1973.pdf, accessed December 2009.

6. Matthew Garrahan, "Disney Profits Fall as Recession Hits," *Financial Times*, February 4, 2009, p. 25; and Richard Siklos, "Bob Iger Rocks Disney," *Fortune*, January 19, 2009, pp. 80–86.

7. For an interesting discussion on managing growth, see Matthew S. Olson, Derek van Bever, and Seth Verry, "When Growth Stalls," *Harvard Business Review*, March 2008, pp. 51–61.

8. H. Igor Ansoff, "Strategies for Diversification," *Harvard Business Review*, September–October 1957, pp. 113–124.

9. Information about Under Armour in this section is from Stephanie N. Metha, "Under Armour Reboots," *Fortune*, February 2, 2009, pp. 29–34; Elaine Wong, Under Armour Makes Long-Run Calculation," *Brandweek*, January 19, 2009, p. 28; Liz Farmer, "Baltimore-Based Under Armour Says Revenue Will Be Lower," *Daily Record* (Baltimore), January 15, 2009; Farmer, "This Super Bowl Weekend, Baltimore-Based Under Armour Taking Grass Roots Marketing Approach," *Daily Record* (Baltimore), January 30, 2009; "Under Armour Reports 20% Top-Line Growth for the Full Year with 3% Growth for the Fourth Quarter," Under Armour press release, January 29, 2009, accessed at http://investor.underarmour.com; and Under Armour annual reports and other documents accessed at www.underarmour.com, April 2009.

10. See Michael E. Porter, *Competitive Advantage: Creating and Sustaining Superior Performance* (New York: Free Press, 1985); and Michel E. Porter, "What Is Strategy?" *Harvard Business Review*, November–December 1996, pp. 61–78; Also see "The Value Chain," accessed at www.quickmba.com/strategy/value-chain, July 2008; and Philip Kotler and Kevin Lane Keller, *Marketing Management* (Upper Saddle River, NJ: Prentice Hall, 2009), pp. 35–36 and pp. 252–253.

11. Nirmalya Kumar, "The CEO's Marketing Manifesto," *Marketing Management*, November–December 2008, pp. 24–29.

12. Rebecca Ellinor, "Crowd Pleaser," *Supply Management*, December 13, 2007, pp. 26–29; and information from www.loreal.com/_en/_ww/html/suppliers/index.aspx, accessed August 2009.

13. See www.nikebiz.com/company_overview/, accessed April 2009.

14. Jack Trout, "Branding Can't Exist Without Positioning," *Advertising Age*, March 14, 2005, p. 28.

15. "100 Leading National Advertisers," special issue of *Advertising Age*, June 23, 2008, p. 10.

16. The four Ps classification was first suggested by E. Jerome McCarthy, *Basic Marketing: A Managerial Approach* (Homewood, IL: Irwin, 1960). For the 4Cs, other proposed classifications, and more discussion, see Robert Lauterborn, "New Marketing Litany: 4P's Passé C-Words Take Over," *Advertising Age*, October 1, 1990, p. 26; Don E. Schultz, "New Definition of Marketing Reinforces Idea of Integration," *Marketing News*, January 15, 2005, p. 8; Phillip Kotler, "Alphabet Soup," *Marketing Management*, March–April 2006, p. 51; and Nirmalya Kumer, "The CEO's Marketing Manifesto," *Marketing Management*, November/December 2008, pp. 24–29.

17. For more discussion of the CMO position, see Pravin Nath and Vijay Mahajan, "Chief Marketing Officers: A Study of Their Presence in Firms' Top Management Teams," *Journal of Marketing*, January 2008, pp. 65–81; Philip Kotler and Kevin Lane Keller, *Marketing Management* (Upper Saddle River: NJ: Prentice Hall, 2009), pp. 11–12.

18. Adapted from information found in Diane Brady, "Making Marketing Measure Up," *BusinessWeek*, December 13, 2004, pp. 112–113; and Gray Hammond, "You Gotta Be Accountable," *Strategy*, December 2008, p. 48.

19. See Kenneth Hein, "CMOs Pressured to Show ROI," *Brandweek*, December 12, 2008, p. 6; and Hammond, "You Gotta Be Accountable," p. 48. Also see CMO Council, "Marketing Outlook 2009: Setting the Course for Marketing Strategy and Spend," March, 2009, accessed at www.cmocouncil.org/resources.

20. Mark McMaster, "ROI: More Vital than Ever," *Sales & Marketing Management*, January 2002, pp. 51–52. Also see Steven H. Seggie, Erin Cavusgil, and Steven Phelan, "Measurement of Return on Marketing Investment: A Conceptual Framework and the Future of Marketing Metrics," *Industrial Marketing Management*, August 2007, pp. 834–841; and David Armano, "The New Focus Group: The Collective," *BusinessWeek Online*, January 8, 2009, accessed at www.businessweek.com.

21. See Hein, "CMOs Pressured to Show ROI," p. 6; and Hammond, "You Gotta Be Accountable," p. 48.

22. For more discussion, see Bruce H. Clark, Andrew V. Abela, and Tim Ambler, "Behind the Wheel," *Marketing Management*, May–June 2006, pp. 19–23; Christopher Hosford, "Driving Business with Dashboards," *BtoB*, December 11, 2006, p. 18; Allison Enwright, "Measure Up: Create a ROMI Dashboard That Shows Current and Future Value," *Marketing News*, August 15, 2007, pp. 12–13; and Lawrence A. Crosby, Bruce A. Corner, and Cheryl G. Rieger, "Breaking Up Should Be Hard to Do," *Marketing Management*, January/ February 2009, pp. 14–16.

23. For a full discussion of this model and details on customer-centered measures of return on marketing investment, see Roland T. Rust, Katherine N. Lemon, and Valerie A. Zeithaml, "Return on Marketing: Using Customer Equity to Focus Marketing Strategy," *Journal of Marketing*, January 2004, pp. 109–127; Roland T. Rust, Katherine N. Lemon, and Das Narayandas, *Customer Equity Management* (Upper Saddle River, NJ: Prentice Hall, 2005); David Tiltman, "Everything You Know Is Wrong," *Marketing*, June 13, 2007, pp. 28–29; Roland T. Rust, "Seeking Higher ROI? Base Strategy on Customer Equity," *Advertising Age*, September 10, 2007, pp. 26–27; and Thorsen Wiesel, Bernd Skiera, and Julián Villanueva, "Customer Equity: An Integral Part of Financial Reporting," *Journal of Marketing*, March 2008, pp. 1–14.

24. Bob Liodice, "Marketers, Get Serious about Accountability," *Advertising Age*, September 8, 2008, P. 22; and Hammond, "You Gotta Be Accountable," p. 48.

Chapter 3

1. Quotes and other information from or adapted from "Xerox Innovation Shines through Industry Recognition," *Business Wire*, January 26, 2009; Claudia Deutsch, "A Big Red X No Longer Marks the Spot," *New York Times*, January 8, 2008, p. C11; Nanette Byrnes, "Xerox's New Design Team: Customers," *BusinessWeek*, May 7, 2007, p. 72; "Xerox Unveils Biggest Change to Its Brand in Company History," January 7, 2008, Xerox news release, accessed at www.Xerox.com; "Copy This Advice: Xerox's CEO Says 'Let's Get Personal,'" *Marketing News*, October 15, 2008, pp. 18–19; "Xerox Ranked Number One in Computer Industry by Fortune's Most Admired Companies Survey," *Business Wire*, March 2, 2009; William M. Bulkeley, "Xerox Tries to Go Beyond Copiers," *Wall Street Journal*, February 24, 2009, p. B5; and "About Xerox," accessed at www.xerox.com, October 2009.

2. "Copy This Advice: Xerox's CEO Says 'Let's Get Personal,'" *Marketing News*, October 15, 2008, pp. 18–19.

3. Quotes and other information from Jeffery K. Liker and Thomas Y. Choi, "Building Deep Supplier Relationships," *Harvard Business Review*, December 2004, pp. 104–113; Lindsay Chappell, "Toyota Aims to Satisfy Its Suppliers," *Automotive News*, February 21, 2005, p. 10, "Toyota Recognizes Top Suppliers for 2007," *PR Newswire*, March 4, 2008; Nick Zubco, "Tier 1s Say Toyota Is Tops in Supplier Relations," *Industry Week*, October 2008, p. 26; and www.toyotasupplier.com, December 2009.

4. Information from Robert J. Benes, Abbie Jarman, and Ashley Williams, "2007 NRA Sets Records," accessed at www.chefmagazine.com/nra.htm; September 2007; and www.thecoca-colacompany.com/presscenter/presskit_fs.html and www.cokesolutions.com, accessed November 2009.

5. World POPClock, U.S. Census Bureau, accessed online at www.census.gov, September 2009. This Web site provides continuously updated projections of the U.S. and world populations.

6. See Clay Chandler, "Little Emperors," *Fortune*, October 4, 2004, pp. 138–150; "China's 'Little Emperors,'" *Financial Times*, May 5, 2007, p. 1; "Me Generation Finally Focuses on US," *Chinadaily.com.cn*, August 27, 2008; and Melinda Varley, "China: Chasing the Dragon," *Brand Strategy*, October 6, 2008, p. 26; and Clifford Coonan, "New Rules to Enforce Chain's One-Child Policy," *Irish Times*, January 14, 2009, p. 12.

7. Adapted from information in Janet Adamy, "Different Brew: Eyeing a Billion Tea Drinkers, Starbucks Pours It On in China," *Wall Street Journal*, November 29, 2006, p. A1. Also see "Where the Money Is," *Financial Times*, May 12, 2007, p 8; and Melissa Allison, "Starbucks Thrives in China," *McClatchy-Tribune Business News*, January 14, 2009.

8. U.S. Census Bureau projections and POPClock Projection, U.S. Census Bureau, accessed at www.census.gov, September 2009.

9. Noreen O'Leary, "Squeeze Play," *Adweek*, January 12, 2009, pp. 8–9; David Court, "The Downturn's New Rules for Marketers," *The McKinsey Quarterly*, December 2008, accessed at www.mckinseyquarterly.com/the_downturn_new_rules_for_marketers_2262; and Emily Brandon, "Planning to Retire: 10 Things You Didn't Know About Baby Boomers," *USNews.com*, January 15, 2009, accessed at www.usnews.com.

10. Emily Brandon, "Planning to Retire: 10 Things You Didn't Know About Baby Boomers"; Nielsen Wire, "Baby Boomers: a Force to Reckon With," *Adweek*, December 11, 2008, accessed at www.adweek.com; and Richard K. Miller and Kelli Washington, *Consumer Behavior 2009*, chapter 26 (Loganville, GA: Richard K. Miller & Associates, 2009).

11. Dee Depass, "Designed with a Wink, Nod at Boomers," *Minneapolis-St. Paul Star Tribune*, April 1, 2006, p. 1. Also see Linda Stern, "It's Not All Downhill," *Newsweek*, December 1, 2008, www.newsweek.com.

12. Quotes and other information from annual reports and various pages at www.ameriprise.com, accessed September 2009.

13. Quotes and other information from annual reports and various pages at www.ameriprise.com, accessed September 2009.

14. "NAS Insights: Getting to Know Generation X," 2006, www.nasrecruitment.com/TalentTips/NASinsights/GettingtoKnowGenerationX.pdf; and Marshall Lager, "The Slackers' X-cellent Adventure," *CRM Magazine*, November 1, 2008, pp. 30–33.

15. For more discussion, see R. K. Miller and Kelli Washington, *Consumer Behavior 2009*, chapter 27 (Atlanta, GA: Richard K. Miller & Associates, 2009).

16. Extract based on Jennifer Alsever, "For Gen X, It's Time to Grow Up and Get a Broker," www.msnbc.msn.com/id/21083120, November 9, 2007; "Schwab's (Gen) X Files," *Brandweek*, December 17, 2007, p. 18; "Charles Schwab Unveils Gen X Web Site," *Business & Finance Week*, May 5, 2008; and information from Charles Schwab and www.schwabmoneyandmore.com, July 2009.

17. R. K. Miller and Kelli Washington, *Consumer Behavior 2009*, chapter 27 (Atlanta, GA: Richard K. Miller & Associates, 2009); and Piet Levy, "The Quest for Cool," *Marketing News*, February 28, 2009, p. 6.

18. Jessica Tsai, "Who, What, Where, Whey, Y," *Customer Relationship Management*, November 2008, pp. 24–28; and John Austin "Automakers Try to Reach Gen Y: Carmakers Look for New Marketing Approaches, Technological Advances to Attract Millennials," *McClatchy-Tribune Business News*, February 1, 2009.

19. Example adapted from Peter Feld, "What Obama Can Teach You About Millennial Marketing," *Advertising Age*, August 11, 2008, p. 1; Eric Greenberg and Karl Weber, "Why the Youth Vote Is the Big Story—for 2008 and for Decades to Come," *Huffington Post*, January 15, 2009, www.huffingtonpost.com/eric-greenberg-and-karl-weber/why-the-youth-vote-is-the_b_158273.html; Andrew Hampp, "Inauguration Pairing a Watershed Moment," *Advertising Age*, March 30, 2009, p. 12; and www.barackobama.com, accessed May 2009.

20. See "'Families and Living Arrangements: 2007," U.S. Census Bureau, accessed at www.census.gov/population/www/socdemo/hh-fam.html, July 2008.

21. "Families and Living Arrangements: 2007," U.S. Census Bureau, accessed at www.census.gov/population/www/socdemo/hh-fam.html, July 2008; U.S. Census Bureau, "Facts for Features: Father's Day," June 18, 2008, www.census.gov/Press-Release/www/releases/archives/cb08ff-09.pdf; and U.S. Census Bureau, "Facts for Features," March 2009, accessed at www.census.gov/Press-Release/www/releases/archives/facts_for_features_special_editions/013129.html.

22. "Peapod Is in the 'Growth'ery Business: 10 Millionth Order Delivered, 10 Million Hours Saved," *PR Newswire*, February 7, 2007, p. 1; and information from www.peapod.com/corpinfo/GW_index.jhtml; September 2009.

23. U.S. Census Bureau, "Geographical Mobility/Migration," accessed at www.census.gov/population/www/socdemo/migrate.html, April 2009.

24. See U.S. Census Bureau, www.census.gov/population/www/estimates/aboutmetro.html, accessed January 2009; Gordon F. Mulligan and Alexander C. Vias, "Growth and Change in Micropolitan Areas," *The Annals of Regional Science*, June 2006, p. 203; and Madeline Johnson, "Devilish Definitions as Urban Masses Evolve, New Terms and Labels Are Emerging to Try to Describe and Distinguish Them," *Financial Times*, December 29, 2007.

25. Shane Yu, "How to Make Telecommuting Work," *Communication News*, December 2008, pp. 30–32; Nancy Weil, "Afraid of Tele-commuters?" *CIO*, December 1, 2008; Jamie Matlin, "Tele-commuting Benefits Outweigh Negatives," *Oil & Gas Journal*, December 15, 2008, p. S2; and Jennifer Schramm, "Work Turns Flexible," *HRMagazine*, March 2009, p. 88.

26. See Ryan Underwood, "OK, Everybody, Let's Do This!," *Inc.*, July 2008, pp. 40–42; "WebEx Communications, Inc.," *Hoover's Company Records*, March 15, 2009, p. 99024; and "About WebEx," accessed at www.webex.com/companyinfo/company-overview.html, July 2009.

27. "Educational Attainment," U.S. Census Bureau, January 2009, accessed at www.census.gov/population/www/socdemo/educ-attn.html.

28. See U.S. Census Bureau, "*The 2009 Statistical Abstract: Labor Force, Employment, and Earnings*," table 596, accessed at www.census.gov/compendia/statab/cats/labor_force_employment_earnings.html, January 2009; and U.S. Department of Labor, *Occupational Outlook Handbook, 2008–09 Edition*, accessed at www.bls.gov/oco/home.htm.

29. See "U.S. Hispanic Population Surpasses 45 Million," May 1, 2008, www.census.gov/Press-Release/www/releases/archives/population/011910.html; and "Hispanic Fact Pack," supplement to *Advertising Age*," July 28, 2008, pp. 46–47.

30. See Leila Cobo, "Energizer Teams with Latin Acts for Staying Power," *Reuters*, January 4, 2008; Laurel Wentz, "Pop Culture with a Twist," *Advertising Age*, January 21, 2008, p. S11; and "Hispanic Ad Firm Recognized for Energizer Campaign," November 25, 2008, accessed at http://latinobusinessreview.blogspot.com.

31. For these and other statistics, see www.rivendellmedia.com/ngng/executive_summary/NGNG.PPT and www.gaymarket.com/ngng/ngng_reader.html, accessed April 2009; and www.planetoutinc.com/sales/market.html, accessed September 2009.

32. See Brandon Miller, "And the Winner Is . . ." *Out Traveler*, Winter 2008, pp. 64–65"; and www.aa.com/rainbow, accessed April 2009.

33. Andrew Adam Newman, "Web Marketing to a Segment Too Big to Be a Niche," *New York Times*, October 30, 2007, p. 9; and Kenneth Hein, "The Invisible Demographic," *Brandweek*, March 3, 2008, p. 20.

34. See Chris Taylor, "Opening New Worlds: The Disability Boom," *Fortune Small Business*, September 15, 2008, http://money.cnn.com/2008/09/11/smallbusiness/disability_boom.fsb/index.htm; information from Ford, July 2009; and www.disaboom.com, accessed November 2009.

35. Gavin Rabinowitz, "India's Tata Motors Unveils $2,500 Car, Bringing Car Ownership Within Reach of Millions," *Associated Press*, January 10, 2008; Ray Hutton, "Indian Car Firm Plans to Take a Domestic Drive," *Sunday Times* (London), December 28, 2008, p. 6; and Jessica Scanlon, "What Can Tata's Nano Teach Detroit?" *BusinessWeek Online*, March 19, 2009, accessed at www.BusinessWeek.com.

36. Noreen O'Leary, "Squeeze Play," *Adweek*, January 12, 2009, pp. 8–9. Also see Alessandra Stanley, "For Hard Times, Softer Sells," *New York Times*, or February 6, 2009; and Kenneth Hein, "Why Price Isn't Everything," *Brandweek*, March 2, 2009, p. 6.

37. Mark Dolliver, "How the Rise of Inequality Fosters a New Culture of Antagonism," *Adweek*, December 17, 2007, pp. 30–31, 37.

38. Kelly Nolan, "Mass Movement of High Fashion," *Retailing Today*, January 8, 2007, pp. 4–6; Eric Wilson and Michael Barbaro, "Can You Be Too Fashionable?" *New York Times*, June 17, 2007, p. 1; Elizabeth Wellington, "Mirror, Mirror: Discounted to Distraction," *Philadelphia Inquirer*, November 4, 2007, p. M1; and Yelena Moroz, "Mass Fashion in Focus: Cheap Chic Fever Quickly Catching On," *Retailing Today*, February 11 2008, p. 1.

39. Andrew Zolli, "Business 3.0," *Fast Company*, March 2007, pp. 64–70.

40. "GE Transportation's Evolution Hybrid Debuts at RSA Railway Technology Exhibition," *Wireless News*, September 21, 2008; Steve Bronstein, *Fast Company*, November 2007, pp. 90–99; and various pages at www.ge.com, accessed July 2009.

41. Facts from www.pepsico.com/Purpose/Environment.aspx, accessed April 2009.

42. See "Wal-Mart Expands RFID Requirements," *McClatchy-Tribune Business News*, January 30, 2008; David Blanchard, "Wal-Mart Lays Down the Law on RFID," *Industry Week*, May 2008, p. 72; David Blanchard, "The Five Stages of RFID," *Industry Week*, January 2009, p. 50; and information accessed online at www.autoidlabs.org, April 2009.

43. See Lori Vallgra. "US to Spend Less on R&D in 2009," *Science Business*, January 22, 2009, http://bulletin.sciencebusiness.net/ebulletins/showissue.php3?page=/548/art/12638/.

44. See Jack Neff, "Unilever, P&G War Over Which Is Most Ethical," *Advertising Age*, March 3, 2008, p. 1; and information from www.beautifullengths.com, accessed August 2009.

45. See "The Growth of Cause Marketing," accessed at www.causemarketingforum.com/page.asp?ID=188, August 2009.

46. Karen Von Hahn, "Plus ça Change: Get Set for Cocooning 2.0," *Globe and Mail* (Toronto), January 3, 2008, p. L1; and Liza N. Burby, "Tips for Making Your Home a Cozy Nest, or 'Hive,'" *Newsday*, January 23, 2009, www.newsday.com/services/newspaper/printedition/exploreli/ny-hocov6007466jan23,0,2603167.story.

47. Mike Duff, "Consumer Return to the Cocoon Could Help Retailers," *BNET Retail Blog*, December 19, 2008, http://industry.bnet.com/retail/1000343/consumer-return-to-the-cocoon-could-help-retailers/; and Claire Cain Miller, "For Craft Sales, the Recession Is a Help," *New York Times*, December 23, 2008, p. B1.

48. Based on information from Beth Snyder Bulik, "Stay-at-Home Trend Feathers Samsung Nest," *Advertising Age*, November 3, 2008, p. 18; and Alessandra Stanley, "For Hard Times, Softer Sells," *New York Times*, February 6, 2009.

49. Laura Feldmann, "After 9/11 Highs, America's Back to Good Ol' Patriotism," *Christian Science Monitor*, July 5, 2006, p. 1; and "Life-style Statistics: Very Proud of Their Nationality," accessed at www.nationmaster.com, April 2009.

50. L. A. Chung, "New Greetings of Hybrid Fans: Aloha, LOHAS," *Mercury News*, April 29, 2005, accessed at www.mercurynews.com/mld/mercurynews/news/columnists/la_chung/11520890.htm; with information from www.lohas.com, accessed November 2009.

51. See www.livebetterindex.com/sustainability.html, accessed November 2009.

52. "Earthbound Farm Facts," www.earthboundfarm.com, accessed September 2009.

53. See Nigel Hunt and Brad Dorfman, "Organic Food Growth Slows Amid Downturn," *Reuters*, January 28, 2009, accessed at http://uk.reuters.com.

54. Dan Harris, "America Is Becoming Less Christian, Less Religious," *ABC News*, March 9, 2009, accessed at http://abcnews.go.com/print?id=7041036.

55. See Philip Kotler, *Kotler on Marketing* (New York: Free Press, 1999), p. 3; and Kotler, *Marketing Insights from A to Z* (Hoboken, NJ: John Wiley & Sons, 2003), pp. 23–24.

56. Based on information found at www.breakthechain.org/exclusives/oscarmayer.html and www.kraftfoods.com/oscarmayer/hoaxes_rumors, November 2008. Also see David Emery, "Urban Legend: Oscar Meyer Refuses to Send Hotdogs to Marines," *About.com,* accessed at http://urbanlegends.about.com/od/business/a/oscar_mayer.htm, April 2009.

Chapter 4

1. Quotes and other information taken from interview with Rana Zoheir, 15th October 2009, Pre-Sales Executive, PROTRAC, www.protraconline.com © Rana Zoheir 2010; Interview with Terek Hassanein, 15th October 2009, Pre-Sales Executive, PROTRAC, www.protraconline.com © Terek Hassanein 2010; www.protraconline.com; El Bakry, Rehab (2007), Mapping Potential, *Business Monthly*, December 2007, 57; and www.alibaba.com.

2. Unless otherwise noted, quotes in this section are from the excellent discussion of customer insights found in Mohanbir Sawhney, "Insights into Customer Insights," accessed at www.redmond.nl/hro/upload/Insights_into_Customer_Insights.pdf, April 2009. The Apple iPod example is also adapted from this article.

3. Facts obtained from "Did You Know," video presentation, June 2008, accessed at www.flixxy.com/technology-and-education-2008.htm.

4. Michael Fassnacht, "Beyond Spreadsheets," *Advertising Age*, February 19, 2007, p. 15.

5. Robert Scheiffer and Eric Leininger, "Customers at the Core," *Marketing Management,* January/February 2008, pp. 31–37.

6. For more discussion, see Schieffer and Leininger, "Customers at the Core," pp. 31–37.

7. Ian C. MacMillan and Larry Seldon, "The Incumbent's Advantage," *Harvard Business Review*, October 2008, pp. 111–121.

8. Arianne Cohen, "Barneys and Friend," *Fast Company,"* September 11, 2008, accessed at www.fastcompany.com/magazines/125/barneys-and-friend.html.

9. Example based on information from "PacSun to Surf the Social Web with Radian6," Radian6 press release, March 24, 2009, accessed at www.radian6.com; Don Macpherson, "Radian6 Has Ears of Big Business," *Daily Gleaner*, September 25, 2008, p. D1; and www.Radian6.com, accessed November 2009.

10. James Curtis, "Behind Enemy Lines," *Marketing,* May 21, 2001, pp. 28–29. Also see Jim Middlemiss, "Firms Look to Intelligence to Gain a Competitive Edge," *Law Times*, March 5, 2007, accessed at www.lawtimesnews.com; and "Outwards Insights; Competitive Intelligence Drives More Corporate Decisions, New Survey Shows," *Marketing Business Weekly*, October 19, 2008, p. 385.

11. For more on research firms that supply marketing information, see Jack Honomichl, "Honomichl Top 50," special section, *Marketing News,* June 15, 2008, pp. H1–H67. Other information from www.smrb.com; www.nielsen.com; and www.yankelovich.com, August 2009.

12. See http://us.infores.com/page/solutions/market_content/infoscan, accessed April 5, 2008.

13. See Jenn Abelson, "Gillette Sharpens Its Focus on Women," *Boston Globe*, January 4, 2009.

14. See David Kiley, "Shoot the Focus Group," *BusinessWeek*, November 14, 2005, pp. 120–121; Richard G. Starr and Karen V. Fernandez, "The Mindcam Methodology: Perceiving Through the Native's Eye," *Quantitative Market Research*, Spring 2007, pp. 168+; and Todd Wasserman, "Thinking by Design," *Brandweek*, November 3, 2008, pp, 18–21.

15. See Jack Neff, "Marketing Execs: Researchers Could Use a Softer Touch," *Advertising Age*, January 27, 2009, accessed at http://adage.com/article?article_id=134144; and Neff, "The End of Consumer Surveys?" *Advertising Age*, p. 4.

16. Example adapted from information in Rhys Blakely, "You Know When It Feels Like Somebody's Watching You . . ." *Times*, May 14, 2007, p. 46; and Nandini Lakshman, "Nokia: It Takes a Village to Design a Phone for Emerging Markets," *BusinessWeek*, September 10, 2007, p. 12. See also Sara Corbett, "Can the Cellphone Help End Global Poverty?" *New York Times Magazine*, April 13, 2008, p. 34; and Todd Wasserman, "Thinking by Design," *Brandweek*, November 3, 2008, pp, 18–21.

17. Spencer E. Ante, "The Science of Desire," *BusinessWeek,* June 5, 2006, p. 100; Rhys Blakely, "You Know When It Feels Like Somebody's Watching You . . ." *Times*, May 14, 2007, p. 46; and Jack Neff, "Marketing Execs: Researchers Could Use a Softer Touch," *Advertising Age*, January 27, 2009, accessed at http://adage.com/article?article_id=134144.

18. Adapted from information in Kenneth Hein, "Hypnosis Brings Groups into Focus," *Brandweek*, May 23, 2008, p. 4.

19. Emily Spensieri, "A Slow, Soft Touch," *Marketing,* June 5, 2006, pp. 15–16.

20. Jack Neff, "Marketing Execs: Researchers Could Use a Softer Touch," *Advertising Age*, January 27, 2009, accessed at http://adage.com/article?article_id=134144.

21. "E-Rewards Rakes in $60M in New Funding," October 17, 2008, accessed at http://dallas.bizjournals.com/dallas/stories/2008/10/20/story5.html.

22. See "E-Rewards Rakes in $60M in New Funding," p. 1; and Internet penetration statistics found at www.internetworldstats.com/stats14.htm, July 2009.

23. Nikki Hopewell, "Surveys by Design," *Marketing News*, December 15, 2008, p. 12.

24. Based on information found in Jeremiah McWilliams, "A-B Sees Web As Fertile Ground for Advertising Efforts," *St. Louis Post-Dispatch*, December 19, 2007; and www.youtube.com/watch?v=EJJL5dxgVaM, accessed December 2009.

25. Based on information found www.channelm2.com/HowOnlineQualitativeResearch.html; accessed December 2009.

26. See "Company Survey Respondents," www.zoomerang.com, accessed December 2009.

27. For more on Internet privacy, see Jessica E. Vascellaro "They've Got Your Number (and a Lot More)," *Wall Street Journal*, March 13, 2007, pp. D1–D2; "Jim Puzzanghera, "Internet; Tough Cookies for Web Surfers Seeking Privacy," *Los Angeles Times*, April 19, 2008, p. C1; and "What Would You Reveal on the Internet?" *Privacy Journal*, January 2009, p. 1.

28. See "Creating Computers That Know How You Feel," www.almaden.ibm.com/cs/BlueEyes/index.html, accessed November 2009.

29. See Josh Goldstein, "Branding on the Brain," *News & Observer*, December 6, 2006, p. 9E; Jack Neff, "This Is Your Brain on Super Bowl Spots," *Advertising Age*, February 11, 2008, pp. 1, 21; and "Super Bowl Ad Analysis," accessed at www.sandsresearch.com; April 2009.

30. Adapted from Steve McClennan, New Tool Puts Brands in Touch with Feelings," *Adweek*, February 18, 2008, pp. 16–17. Also see Elizabeth A. Sullivan, "Pick Your Brain," *Marketing News*, March 15, 2009, pp. 10–12.

31. See Barney Beal, "Gartner: CRM Spending Looking Up," SearchCRM.com, April 29, 2008, http://searchcrm.techtarget.com/news/article/0,289142,sid11_gci1311658,00.html; and David White, "CRM Magazine Announces Winners of 2009 CRM Service Awards," *Business Wire*, April 1, 2009.

32. Mike Freeman, "Data Company Helps Wal-Mart, Casinos, Airlines Analyze Customers," *San Diego Union Tribune*, February 24, 2006.

33. Example adapted from information found in Dan Sewell, "Kroger User Shopper Data to Target Coupons," *Huffington Post*, January 6, 2009; accessed at www.huffingtonpost.com/2009/01/06/kroger-uses-shopper-data_n_155667.html.

34. Michael Krauss, "At Many Firms, Technology Obscures CRM," *Marketing News,* March 18, 2002, p. 5. Also see William Boulding et al., "A Customer Relationship Management Roadmap: What Is Known, Potential Pitfalls, and Where to Go," *Journal of Marketing*, October 2005, pp. 155–166; "Study: Marketers Stink When It Comes to CRM," *Brandweek*, April 14, 2008, p. 7; and Robert Kane, "Straight Talk: Advice from the Trenches of SaaS CRM," *Customer Relationship Management*, January 2009, p. S3.

35. See "Value Added with mySAP CRM: Benchmarking Study," accessed at www.sap.com/solutions/business-suite/crm/pdf/Misc_CRM_Study.pdf, June 2008.

36. See "Penske Launches Improved Extranet," *Refrigerated Transporter*, March 2009, p. 47; and information found at www.partnersonline.com, September 2009.

37. Adapted from information in Ann Zimmerman, "Small Business; Do the Research," *Wall Street Journal,* May 9, 2005, p. R3; with information from www.bibbentuckers.com, accessed July 2009.

38. Zimmerman, "Small Business; Do the Research," *Wall Street Journal,* p. R3.

39. For some good advice on conducting market research in a small business, see "Marketing Research . . . Basics 101," accessed at www.sba.gov/smallbusinessplanner/index.html, August 2009; and "Researching Your Market," U.S. Small Business Administration, accessed at www.sba.gov/idc/groups/public/documents/sba_homepage/pub_mt8.pdf, November 2009.

40. See Jack Honomichl, "Top Firms Consolidated Grip on Industry," *Marketing News,* August 15, 2008, p. H1.

41. See http://en-us.nielsen.com/main/about/Profile, accessed July 2009.

42. Phone and Internet stats are from http://www.worldbank.org/ July 2009; see also www.iwcp.hpg.ig.com.br/communications.html, accessed February 2009.

43. Subhash C. Jain, *International Marketing Management,* 3rd ed. (Boston: PWS-Kent, 1990), p. 338. For more discussion on international marketing research issues and solutions, Michael Fielding, "Shift the Focus: Ethnography Proves Fruitful in Emerging Economies," *Marketing News,* September 1, 2006, pp. 18, 20; Robert B. Young and Rajshekhar G. Javalgi, "International Marketing Research: A Global Project Management Perspective," *Business Horizons,* March–April 2007, pp. 113–122; and Julia Lin, "By the Numbers: How to Avoid Language Problems in International IT Research," *Quirk's Marketing Research Review,* November 2008, accessed at www.quirks.com.

44. Adapted from David Shipley, "Can Firm Monitor the Word on the Web," *Daily Gleaner,* August 14, 2008, p. D1; Sean McDonald, "Dell and Radian6: It All Starts with Listening," Direct2Dell, August 19, 2008, http://en.community.dell.com/blogs/direct2dell/archive/2008/08/19/dell-and-radian6-it-all-starts-with-listening.aspx.

45. Stephanie Clifford, "Many See Privacy on the Web as Big Issue, Survey Says," *New York Times,* March 16, 2009. Also see, "What Was Privacy?" *Harvard Business Review,* October 2008, p. 123–131.

46. "ICC/ESOMAR International Code of Marketing and Social Research Practice," accessed at www.esomar.org/index.php/codes-guidelines.html, July 2009. Also see "Respondent Bill of Rights," accessed at www.cmor.org/rc/tools.cfm?topic=4, July 2009.

47. Jaikumar Vijayan, "Disclosure Laws Driving Data Privacy Efforts, Says IBM Exec," *Computerworld,* May 8, 2006, p. 26; and "Facebook Chief Privacy Officer—Interview," *Analyst Wire,* February 18, 2009.

48. Information accessed at www10.americanexpress.com/sif/cda/page/0,1641,14271,00.asp, July 2009.

49. Cynthia Crossen, "Studies Galore Support Products and Positions, But Are They Reliable?" *Wall Street Journal,* November 14, 1991, pp. A1, A9. Also see Allan J. Kimmel, "Deception in Marketing Research and Practice: An Introduction," *Psychology and Marketing,* July 2001, pp. 657–661; Jack Neff, "Who's No. 1? Depends on Who's Analyzing the Data," *Advertising Age,* June 12, 2006, p. 8; and Carl Bialik, "In Ads, 1 Out of 5 Stats Is Bogus," *Wall Street Journal,* March 11, 2009.

50. Information accessed at www.casro.org/codeofstandards.cfm#intro, December 2009.

Chapter 5

1. Extracts, quotes, and other information adapted from or found in Peter Burrows, "The World's Most Influential Companies: Apple," *BusinessWeek,* December 22, 2008, p. 46; Katie Hafner, "Inside Apple Stores, a Certain Aura Enchants the Faithful," *New York Times,* December 27, 2007; Terry Semel, "Steve Jobs: Perpetual Innovation Machine," *Time,* April 18, 2005, p. 78; Steve Maich, "Nowhere to Go But Down," *Maclean's,* May 9, 2005, p. 32; Stephen Withers, "Apple Tops for Brand Loyalty: Report," *iTWire,* September 12, 2008, accessed at www.itwire.com/content/view/20603/1151/l; Chris Nuttall, "Credit Crunch Passes Apple by as iPod Popularity Keeps on Growing," *Financial Times* January 22, 2009, p. 15; "Macolyte," *Urban Dictionary,* accessed at www.urban-dictionary.com, May 2009; and financial information found at www.apple.com, accessed May 2009.

2. GDP figures from *The World Fact Book,* April 2, 2009, accessed at www.cia.gov/cia/publications/factbook/. Population figures from the World POPClock, U.S. Census Bureau, www.census.gov, May

2009. This Web site provides continuously updated projections of the U.S. and world populations.

3. Don E. Schultz, "Lines or Circles" *Marketing News,* November 5, 2007, p. 21; and Elizabeth A. Sullivan, "Pick Your Brain," *Marketing News,* March 15, 2009, pp. 10–13.

4. See "Nielsen Reveals Hispanic Consumer Shopping Behavior Insights," *Business Wire,* September 24, 2007; "Hispanic Fact Pack," supplement to *Advertising Age,*" July 28, 2008, pp. 46–47; "Hispanic Economy in Transition," accessed at www.researchandmarkets.com/reports/607870/hispanic_economy_in_transition_chapter_4.pdf, April 2009; and "HispanTelligence Releases the Latest Hispanic Economy in Transition Report," *Hispanic PR Wire,* April 6, 2009, accessed at www.hispanicbusiness.com/hprw/2009/4/6/hispantelligence_releases_the_latest_us_hispanic.htm.

5. Adapted from information found in Della de Lafuente, "The New Weave," *Adweek,* March 3, 2008, pp. 26–28. Also see Della de Lafuente, "A Fluent in Spanish," *Adweek,* July 14, 2008, pp. 20–22; and "Conill Takes Crown at Advertising Age's Hispanic Creative Advertising Awards," *Marketing Business Weekly,* October 5, 2008, p. 143.

6. See Deborah L. Vence, "Scratch the Surface," *Marketing News,* February 2007, pp. 17–18; Elaine Misonzhnik, "American Melting Pot," *Retail Traffic,* November 1, 2008, p. 33; Marissa Miley, "Don't Bypass African-Americans," *Advertising Age,* February 2, 2009; U.S. Census Bureau reports accessed online at www.census.gov, February 2009.

7. "About the Queen Collection," accessed at www.covergirl.com/products/collections/queen/, April 2009. Facts from Cliff Peale, "P&G Showed the Way: Company's Ads Targeted to Blacks Paid Off," *Cincinnati Enquirer,* February 25, 2007, accessed at www.cincinnati.com; and "Top 10 Advertisers across All African American Media," *Adweek,* February 9, 2009, p. 16.

8. Michael Bush, "P&G Unveils 'My Black Is Beautiful,' Campaign," *PRweek,* December 3, 2007; David Holthaus, "P&G, BET Team Up on TV," *Cincinnati Enquirer,* January 22, 2009, and www.cincinnati.com; www.myblackisbeautiful.com, accessed November 2009.

9. Michael Bush, "P&G Unveils 'My Black Is Beautiful,' Campaign," *PRweek,* December 3, 2007; David Holthaus, "P&G, BET Team Up on TV," *Cincinnati Enquirer,* January 22, 2009, and www.cincinnati.com; www.myblackisbeautiful.com, accessed November 2009.

10. See Lynn Russo Whylly, "Marketing to Asian Americans," advertising supplement to *Brandweek,* May 26, 2008, pp. S1–S3; and U.S. Census Bureau reports accessed at www.census.gov, October 2008.

11. Adapted from information found in Stuart Elliott, "When the Celebrity Is the Joke (and Is In on It)," *New York Times,* September 12, 2008, p. C2; and www.nationwide.com/about-us/ads-multicultural.jsp#, accessed April 2009.

12. See Noreen O'Leary, "Squeeze Play," *Adweek,* January 12, 2009, pp. 8–9; and Emily Brandon, "Planning to Retire: 10 Things You Didn't Know About Baby Boomers," USNews.com, January 15, 2009, accessed at www.usnews.com.

13. "Boom Time of America's New Retirees Feel Entitled to Relax—and Intend to Spend," *Financial Times,* December 6, 2007, p. 9.

14. See www.dove.us/#/products/collections/proage.aspx/, accessed November 2009.

15. For a discussion of influencers, see Clive Thompson, "Is the Tipping Point Toast?" *Fast Company,* February 2008, pp. 75–105; and Edward Keller and Jonathan Berry, *The Influentials* (New York: The Free Press, 2003). The study results reported in Holly Shaw, "Buzzing Influencers," *National Post,* March 13, 2009, p. 12.

16. See Rob Walker, "Tap Dance," *New York Times,* January 6, 2009; and facts about Vocalpoint accessed at www.vocalpoint.com, July 2009.

17. Adapted from Anya Kamenetz, "The Network Unbound," *Fast Company,* June 2006, pp. 69–73. Also see Brad Stone, "Social Networking's Next Phase," *New York Times,* March 3, 2007, accessed at www.nytimes.com; Chuck Brymer, "The Birds and the Bees," *Adweek,* January 7, 2008, p. 16; and Facebook statistics, accessed at www.facebook.com/press/info.php?statistics, April 2009.

18. See Aaron Uhrmacher, "35+ Examples of Corporate Social Media in Action," July 23, 2008, http://mashable.com/2008/07/23/corporate-social-media.

19. Beth Krietsch, "YouTube Channel for Congress Builds Dialogue, Transparency," *PR Week,* January 19, 2009, p. 9; "Death of TV Advertising," *Business and Finance,* June 24, 2008; and Samir Balwani, "Presenting: 10 of the Smartest Big Brands in Social Media," *Mashable,* February 6, 2009, http://mashable.com/2009/02/06/social-media-smartest-brands/.

20. See Scott Hidebrink, "Women and the Automotive Aftermarket," *Motor Age*, September 2007, pp. 60+; Andrew Adam Newman, "The Man of the House," *Adweek*, August 11–18, 2008, pp. 16–19; Eleftheria Parpis, "She's in Charge," *Adweek*, October 6–13, 2008, p. 38; and Abigail Posner, "Why Package-Goods Companies Should Market to Men," *Advertising Age*, February 9, 2009, accessed at http://adage.com/print?article_id=134473.

21. Adapted from Michel Marriott, "Gadget Designers Take Aim at Women," *New York Times*, June 7, 2007, p. C7. Also see Dean Takahashi, "Philips Focuses on TVs Women Buyers," *McClatchy-Tribune Business News*, January 6, 2008.

22. R. K. Miller and Kelli Washington, *Consumer Behavior 2009*, Chapter 27 (Atlanta, GA: Richard K. Miller & Associates, 2009).

23. Based on information found at www.fireflymobile.com/, November 2009.

24. For this quote and other information on Acxiom's PersonicX segmentation system, see "Acxiom Study Reveals inside an Evolving Consumer Shopping Behaviors in Trying Economic Times," *Reuters*, January 13, 2009, accessed at www.reuters.com/article/pressRelease/idUS180299+13-Jan-2009+BW20090113 and "Acxiom PersonicX" and "Intelligent Solutions for the Travel Industry: Life-Stage Marketing," accessed at www.acxiom.com, April 2009.

25. Information from www.spearshoes.com, December 2009.

26. Kenneth Hein, "Target Tries Price Point Play," *Adweek.com*, January 15, 2009, www.adweek.com/aw/content_display/creative/news/e3i0b84325122066ed9830db4ccb41e7ecf.

27. Based on Laura Compton, "Seducing Us Softly: Why Women Love Anthropologie," *San Francisco Chronicle*, September 12, 2004, www.sfgate.com/cgi-bin/article.cgi?f=/c/a/2004/09/12/CMG1L890631.DTL; with information from Sohrab Vossoughi, "How to Stand Out? Try Authenticity," *BusinessWeek Online*, May 29, 2008; and information from urbanoutfittersinc.com, accessed November 2009.

28. See Jennifer Aaker, "Dimensions of Measuring Brand Personality," *Journal of Marketing Research*, August 1997, pp. 347–356; and Vanitha Swaminathan, Karen M. Stilley, and Rohini Ahluwalla, "When Brand Personality Matters: The Moderating Role of Attachment Styles," *Journal of Consumer Research*, April 2009, pp. 985–1002.

29. See www.apple.com/getamac/ads/, accessed May 2009.

30. See Abraham. H. Maslow, "A Theory of Human Motivation," *Psychological Review*, 50 (1943), pp. 370–396. Also see Maslow, *Motivation and Personality*, 3rd ed. (New York: HarperCollins Publishers, 1987); and Barbara Marx Hubbard, "Seeking Our Future Potentials," *Futurist*, May 1998, pp. 29–32.

31. See Louise Story, "Anywhere the Eye Can See, It's Now Likely to See an Ad," *New York Times*, January 15, 2007, accessed at www.nytimes.com; Matthew Creamer, "Caught in the Clutter Crossfire: Your Brand," *Advertising Age*, April 1, 2007, p. 35; and Ruth Mortimer, "Consumer Awareness: Getting the Right Attention," *Brand Strategy*, December 10, 2008, p. 55.

32. Bob Garfield, "'Subliminal' Seduction and Other Urban Myths," *Advertising Age*, September 18, 2000, pp. 4, 105; and Lewis Smith, "Subliminal Advertising May Work, but Only If You're Paying Attention," *Times*, March 9, 2007. For more on subliminal advertising, see Alastair Goode, "The Implicit and Explicit Role of Ad Memory in Ad Persuasion: Rethinking the Hidden Persuaders," *International Journal of Marketing Research*, vol. 49, no. 2, 2007, pp. 95–116; Cynthia Crossen, "For a time in the 50s, a Huckster Fanned Fears of an Ad 'Hypnosis,'" *Wall Street Journal*, November 5, 2007, p. B1; and Beth Snyder Bulik, "This Brand Makes You More Creative," *Advertising Age*, March 24, 2008, p. 4.

33. Quotes and information from Yubo Chen and Jinhong Xie, "Online Consumer Review: Word-of-Mouth as a New Element of Marketing Communication Mix," *Management Science*, March 2008, pp. 477–491; Douglas Pruden and Terry G. Vavra, "Controlling the Grapevine," *Marketing Management*, July–August 2004, pp. 25–30; and "Leo J. Shapiro & Associates: User-Generated Content Three Times More Influential Than TV Advertising on Consumer Purchase Decisions," *Marketing Business Weekly*, December 28, 2008, p 34.

34. See Leon Festinger, *A Theory of Cognitive Dissonance* (Stanford, CA: Stanford University Press, 1957); Cynthia Crossen, "'Cognitive Dissonance' Became a Milestone in the 1950s Psychology," *Wall Street Journal*, December 12, 2006, p. B1; and Anupam Bawa and Purva Kansal, "Cognitive Dissonance and the Marketing of Services: Some Issues," *Journal of Services Research*, October 2008–March 2009, p. 31.

35. The following discussion draws from the work of Everett M. Rogers. See his *Diffusion of Innovations*, 5th ed. (New York: Free Press, 2003).

36. Nick Bunkley, "Hyundai, Using a Safety Net, Wins Market Share," *New York Times*, February 5, 2009; and Chris Woodyard and Bruce Horvitz, "GM, Ford Are Latest Offering Help to Those Hit by Job Loss," *USA Today*, April 1, 2009, accessed at www.usatoday.com/money/advertising/2009-03-30-consumers-retail-job-loss_N.htm.

37. See "U.S. HDTV Penetration Nears 25%" *NielsenWire*, December 11, 2008.

38. See Theresa Ooi, "Amazing Key to IKEA Success," *Australian*, September 22, 2008; Kerry Capell, "How the Swedish Retailer Became a Global Cult Brand," *BusinessWeek*, November 14, 2005, p. 103; IKEA, *Hoover's Company Records*, April 1, 2009, p. 42925; "IKEA Group Stores," accessed www.ikea-group.ikea.com/?ID=11, April 2009; and information from www.ikea.com, September 2009.

39. This classic categorization was first introduced in Patrick J. Robinson, Charles W. Faris, and Yoram Wind, *Industrial Buying Behavior and Creative Marketing* (Boston: Allyn & Bacon, 1967). Also see James C. Anderson and James A. Narus, *Business Market Management*, 2nd ed. (Upper Saddle River, NJ: Prentice Hall, 2004), chapter 3; James C. Anderson, James A. Narus, and Wouter van Rossum, "Customer Value Propositions in Business Markets," *Harvard Business Review*, March 2006, pp. 91–99; and Philip Kotler and Kevin Lane Keller, *Marketing Management*, 13th ed. (Upper Saddle River, NJ: Prentice Hall, 2009), chapter 7.

40. Example adapted from information found in "Nikon Focuses on Supply Chain Innovation—and Makes New Product Distribution a Snap," UPS case study, accessed at www.pressroom.ups.com/about/cs_nikon.pdf; July 2009.

41. See Frederick E. Webster, Jr., and Yoram Wind, *Organizational Buying Behavior*, pp. 33–37.

42. Henry Canaday, "What Recession?" *Selling Power*, January–February 2009, pp. 44–49.

43. Robinson, Faris, and Wind, *Industrial Buying Behavior*, p. 14.

44. See https://suppliercenter.homedepot.com/wps/portal, accessed May 2009.

45. For this and other examples, see "10 Great Web Sites," *BtoB Online*, September 15, 2008, accessed at www.btobonline.com. Other information from www.cisco.com/cisco/web/solutions/small_business/index.html, November 2009.

46. See William J. Angelo, "e-Procurement Process Delivers Best Value for Kodak," *Engineering News-Record*, March 17, 2008, p. 22.

Chapter 6

1. Information from www.airarabia.com.

2. See "Less is More," *ProgressiveGrocer.com*, January/February 2009, p. 46; and Jonathan Birchall, "Wal-Mart Looks to Hispanic Market in Expansion Drive," *Financial Times*, March 13, 2009, p. 18.

3. For these and other examples, see Rupal Parekh, "Zipcar Finds a Niche in a Turbulent Economy," *Advertising Age*, January 26, 2009, p. 15; and Philip Kotler and Kevin Lane Keller, *Marketing Management*, 13th ed. (Upper Saddle River, NJ: Prentice Hall, 2009), pp. 210–211.

4. Adapted from information found in Elizabeth A. Sullivan, "H.O.G: Harley-Davidson Shows Brand Strength as It Navigates Down New Roads—and Picks Up More Female Riders Along the Way," November 1, 2008, p. 8; and "Harley-Davidson Hosts Special Rides to Kick Off Women Riders Month," *PR Newswire*, March 23, 2009.

5. Adapted from information found in Laura Koss-Feder, "At Your Service," *Time*, June 11, 2007, p. 1; and "Guide to Hotel Packages," *Travel + Leisure*, www.travelandleisure.com/articles/the-suspicious-package/sidebar/1, accessed February 2009.

6. John Waggoner, "Even the Wealthy Feel Tapped Out," *USA Today*, February 2, 2009, p. B1.

7. Information from www.rssc.com, and www.royalcaribbean.com, accessed September 2009.

8. See Louise Story, "Finding Love and the Right Linens," *New York Times*, December 13, 2006, accessed at www.nytimes.com; and www.williams-sonoma.com/cust/storeevents/index.cfm, accessed September 2009.

9. Janet Adamy, "Man Behind the Burger King Turnaround: Chidsey Says Identifying His Restaurant's Superfan Helped Beef Up Its Offerings," *Wall Street Journal*, April 2, 2008, p. B1; and Blair Chancey, "King, Meet the World," *QSR Magazine*, February 2009,

accessed at www.qsrmagazine.com/articles/interview/112/shaufelberger-3.phtml.

10. Janet Adamy, "Man Behind the Burger King Turnaround: Chidsey Says Identifying His Restaurant's Superfan Helped Beef Up Its Offerings," *Wall Street Journal*, April 2, 2008, p. B1; and Blair Chancey, "King, Meet the World," *QSR Magazine*, February 2009, accessed at www.qsrmagazine.com/articles/interview/112/shaufelberger-3.phtml.

11. For more on the PRIZM NE Lifestyle Segmentation System, see www.claritas.com/claritas/Default.jsp?ci=3&si=4&pn=prizmne_segments and www.claritas.com/MyBestSegments/Default.jsp, accessed October 2009.

12. Information from https://home.americanexpress.com/home/open.shtml, August 2009.

13. See Michael Porter, *Competitive Advantage* (New York: Free Press, 1985), pp. 4–8, 234–236. For more recent discussions, see Stanley Slater and Eric Olson, "A Fresh Look at Industry and Market Analysis," *Business Horizons*, January–February 2002, p. 15–22; Kenneth Sawka and Bill Fiora, "The Four Analytical Techniques Every Analyst Must Know: 2. Porter's Five Forces Analysis," *Competitive Intelligence Magazine*, May–June 2003, p. 57; and Philip Kotler and Kevin Lane Keller, *Marketing Management*, 13th ed. (Upper Saddle River, NJ: Prentice Hall, 2009), pp. 342–343.

14. See Suzanne Kapner, "How Fashion's VF Supercharges Its Brands," *Fortune*, April 14, 2008, pp. 108–110; and www.vfc.com, accessed October 2009.

15. Store information found at www.walmartstores.com, www.wholefoodsmarket.com; and www.kroger.com, accessed February 2009.

16. See Gerry Khermouch, "Call It the Pepsi Blue Generation," *BusinessWeek*, February 3, 2003, p. 96; and Martinne Geller, "U.S. Soft Drink Sales Volume Falls More in '07," *Reuters*, March 12, 2008; and Sarah Theodore, "Energy Drinks: New Concepts Keep Category Charged," *Beverage Industry*, August 2008, pp. 14-16.

17. Adapted from information found in Linda Tischler, "The Fast Company 50 – 2009: Etsy," *Fast Company*, February 11, 2009, accessed at www.fastcompany.com/fast50_09/profile/list/etsy.

18. Examples from in Darell K. Rigby and Vijay Vishwanath, "Localization: The Revolution in Consumer Markets," *Harvard Business Review*, April 2006, pp. 82–92. Also see Jenny McTaggart, "Wal-Mart Unveils New Segmentation Scheme," *Progressive Grocer*, October 1, 2006, pp. 10–11; and Jonathan Birchall, "Wal-Mart Looks to Hispanic Market in Expansion Drive," *Financial Times*, March 13, 2009, p. 18.

19. See Arundhati Parmar, "On the Map," *Marketing News*, February 15, 2008, pp. 13–15; and information from www.mysbuxinteractive.com, accessed July 2009. For more examples see Nitasha Tiku, "We See You: Want a List of Nearby Stores?" *Inc.*, October 2008, p. 55; and Stephen Baker, "The Next Net," *BusinessWeek*, March 9, 2009, p. 42.

20. For these and other examples see Lynnley Browning, "Do-It-Yourself Logos for Proud Scion Owners," *New York Times*, March 24, 2008, accessed at www.nytimes.com; and Mike Beirne, "Mars Gives M&M's a Face," *Brandweek*, May 22, 2008, accessed at www.brandweek.com.

21. Adapted from information found in "When You Watch These Ads, the Ads Check You Out," *New York Times*, January 31, 2009, accessed at www.nytimes.com.

22. Adapted from portions of Fae Goodman, "Lingerie Is Luscious and Lovely," *Chicago Sun-Times*, February 19, 2006, p. B2; and Stacy Weiner, "Goodbye to Girlhood," *Washington Post*, February 20, 2007, p. HE01. Also see Suzanne C. Ryan, "Would Hannah Montana Wear It?" *Boston Globe*, January 10, 2008, www.boston.com; and Betsy Cummings, "Tickled Pink," *Brandweek*, September 8, 2008, pp. MO26–MO28.

23. Katy Bachman, "Study: Radio Alcohol Ads Reaching Young Ears," *Mediaweek*, September 18, 2007, accessed at www.mediaweek.com.

24. See "IC3 2008 Annual Report on Internet Crime Released," March 31, 2009, accessed at www.ic3.gov/media/2009/090331.aspx.

25. Jack Trout, "Branding Can't Exist Without Positioning," *Advertising Age*, March 14, 2005, p. 28.

26. Adapted from a positioning map initially prepared by students Brian May, Josh Payne, Meredith Schakel, and Bryana Sterns, University of North Carolina, April 2003. SUV sales data furnished by www.WardsAuto.com, June 2008. Price data from www.edmunds.com, June 2008.

27. Based on information found in Michael Myser, "Marketing Made Easy," *Business 2.0*, June 2006, pp. 43–44; Steve Smith, "Staples' Sales Rise While Office Depot's Drop," *Twice*, March 10, 2008, p. 62; Alan Wolf, "Staples Sales Rose, Profits Fell in Q3," *Twice*, December 15, 2008, p. 89; and "Staples, Inc." *Hoover's Company Records*, accessed at http://www.premium.hoovers.com/subscribe/co/factsheet.xhtml?ID=14790, April 2009.

28. See Bobby J. Calder and Steven J. Reagan, "Brand Design," in Dawn Iacobucci, ed. *Kellogg on Marketing* (New York: John Wiley & Sons, 2001) p. 61. For more discussion, see Philip Kotler and Kevin Lane Keller, *Marketing Management*, 13th ed. (Upper Saddle River, NJ: Prentice Hall, 2009), pp. 315–316.

Chapter 7

1. All quotes and other information were taken from Aviva (www.aviva.com), Norwich Union (www.norwichunion.com), CGU Insurance Plc (www.norwichunion.com), Commercial Union Poland (www.aviva.com), and Brand Republic (www.brandrepublic.com).

2. Based on information from Philip Kotler and Kevin Lane Keller, *Marketing Management* (Upper Saddle River, NJ: Prentice Hall, 2009), p. 272; Lani Haywood, "A Model of Change," *Bank Systems & Technology*, March 2008, p. 24; and www.umpquabank.com, accessed September 2009.

3. R. K. Krishna Kumar, "Effective Marketing Must Begin with Customer Engagement," *Marketing News*, April 15, 2009, p. 15; and Lawrence A. Crosby and Brian S. Lunde, "The Brand Scorecard," *Marketing Management*, May/June 2008, pp. 12–13.

4. Monte Burke, "The Tao of Boo," *Forbes*, April 13, 2009, pp. 92–95.

5. See Diane Brady, "It's All Donald, All the Time," *BusinessWeek*, January 22, 2007, p. 51; and Liz Wolgemuth, "Build Your Own Brand," *U.S. News & World Report*, December 29, 2008, p. 62.

6. Based on information from Sonia Reyes, "Faster Than a Ray of Light," *Brandweek*, October 9, 2006, pp. M28–M31; "Food Network Orders More Helpings of Rachael Ray," *McClatchy-Tribune Business News*, December 17, 2007; Rachael Ray, "10 Questions," *Time*, April 28, 2008, p. 6; and "'Ray' Hits 500th Show," *TelevisionWeek*, March 30-April 6, 2009, p. 8.

7. Information from www.cnto.org/aboutchina.asp, May 2009. Also see www.TravelTex.com, and www.visitcalifornia.com, October 2009.

8. Accessed online at www.social-marketing.org/aboutus.html, November 2009.

9. See Rob Gould, and Karen Gutierrez, "Social Marketing Has a New Champion," *Marketing News*, February 7, 2000, p. 38. Also see Alan R. Andreasen, *Social Marketing in the 21st Century* (Thousand Oaks, CA: Sage Publications, 2006); Philip Kotler and Nancy Lee, *Social Marketing: Improving the Quality of Life*, 3rd ed. (Thousand Oaks, CA: Sage Publications, 2008); and www.social-marketing.org, October 2009.

10. Quotes and definitions from Philip Kotler, *Kotler on Marketing* (New York: Free Press, 1999), p. 17; and www.asq.org/glossary/q.html, July 2009.

11. Quotes and other information from Regina Schrambling, "Tool Department; The Sharpest Knives in the Drawer," *Los Angeles Times*, March 8, 2006, p. F1; Arricca Elin SanSone, "OXO: Universal Design Innovator," *Cooking Light*, April 2007, p. 118; "Alex Lee at Gel 2008," video and commentary accessed at http://vimeo.com/3200945, June 2009; and www.oxo.com/about.jsp, November 2009.

12. Andy Goldsmith, "Coke vs. Pepsi: The Taste They Don't Want You to Know About," *The 60-Second Marketer*, www.60secondmarketer.com/60SecondArticles/Branding/cokevs.pepsitast.html, accessed May 2009.

13. See "Supermarket facts," accessed at www.fmi.org/facts_figs/?fuseaction=superfact, April 2009; and "Wal-Mart Facts," accessed at www.walmartfacts.com/StateByState/?id=2, April 2009.

14. See "Amazon Frustration-Free packaging," accessed at www.amazon.com/gp/feature.html?ie=UTF8&docId=1000276271, June 2009; and Brennon Slattery, "Amazon Offers Easy-to-Open Packaging," *PC World*, January 2009, p. 36.

15. Sonja Reyes, "Ad Blitz, Bottle Design Fuel Debate over Heinz's Sales," *Brandweek*, February 12, 2007, accessed at www

.brandweek.com/bw/news/recent_display.jsp?vnu_content_id=1003544497.

16. Natalie Zmuda, "What Went into the Updated Pepsi Logo," *Advertising Age*, October 27, 2008, p. 6; Natalie Zmuda, "Pepsi, Coke Tried to Outdo Each Other with Rays of Sunshine," *Advertising Age*, January 19, 2009, p. 6; and Todd Wasserman, "Grim Times Prompt More Upbeat Logos," *Brandweek*, February 23, 2009, p. 9.

17. Example from Steve Finlay, "At Least She Puts Fuel in It," *WARD'S Dealer Business*, August 1, 2003. Other information from www.lexus.com and www.lexus.com/about/corporate/lexus_covenant.html, accessed November 2009.

18. See the HP Total Care site at http://h71036.www7.hp.com/hho/cache/309717-0-0-225-121.html, accessed May 2009.

19. Information accessed online at www.marriott.com/corporateinfo/glance.mi, August 2009.

20. See Stuart Elliott, "A Strategy When Times Are Tough: 'It's New,'" *New York Times*, March 25, 2009; and John A. Quelch and Katherine E. Jocz, "How to Market in a Downturn," *Harvard Business Review*, April 2009, pp. 52–62.

21. See CIA, *The World Factbook*, accessed at www.cia.gov/library/publications/the-world-factbook/geos/xx.html and www.cia.gov/library/publications/the-world-factbook/fields/2012.html, August 2009; and information from the Bureau of Labor Statistics, www.bls.gov, accessed August 2009.

22. Portions adapted from information in Leonard Berry and Neeli Bendapudi, "Clueing in Customers," *Harvard Business Review*, February 2003, pp. 100–106; with additional information and quotes from Jeff Hansel, "Mayo Hits the Blogosphere," *McClatchy-Tribune Business News*, January 22, 2009; and www.mayoclinic.org, August 2009.

23. See James L. Heskett, W. Earl Sasser Jr., and Leonard A. Schlesinger, *The Service Profit Chain: How Leading Companies Link Profit and Growth to Loyalty, Satisfaction, and Value* (New York: Free Press, 1997); Heskett, Sasser, and Schlesinger, *The Value Profit Chain: Treat Employees Like Customers and Customers Like Employees* (New York: Free Press, 2003); John F. Milliman, Jeffrey M. Ferguson, and Andrew J. Czaplewski, "Breaking the Cycle," *Marketing Management*, March–April 2008, pp. 14–17; and Christian Homburg, Jan Wieseke, and Wayne D. Hoyer, "Social Identity and the Service-Profit Chain," *Journal of Marketing*, March 2009, pp. 38–54.

24. Based on quotes and information from Pete Blackshaw, "Zappos Shows How Employees Can Be Brand-Builders," *Advertising Age*, September 2, 2008, accessed at http://adage.com/print?article_id=130646; Jeremy Twitchell, "Fun Counts with Web Retailer," *Fort Wayne Journal-Gazette*, February 16, 2009, p. C5; Jeffrey M. O'Brien, "Zappos Knows How to Kick It," *Fortune*, February 2, 2009, pp. 55–60; and http://about.zappos.com/jobs, accessed August 2009.

25. See Stephanie Saul, "In Sour Economy, Some Scale Back on Medications," *New York Times*, October 21, 2008;" and "UPS Fact Sheet," accessed at http://pressroom.ups.com/mediakits/factsheet/0,2305,866,00.html, June 2009.

26. Portions adapted from Jena McGregor, "Customer Service Champs," *BusinessWeek*, March 5, 2007, pp. 52–64; with information from Daniel B. Honigman, "10 Minutes with . . . Fred Taylor," *Marketing News*, May 1, 2008, pp. 8–27.

27. See "McAtlas Shrugged," *Foreign Policy*, May–June 2001, pp. 26–37; and Philip Kotler and Kevin Lane Keller, *Marketing Management*, 13th ed. (Upper Saddle River, NJ: Prentice Hall, 2009), p. 254.

28. See Jack Trout, "'Branding' Simplified," *Forbes*, April 19, 2007, accessed at www.forbes.com.

29. For more on Young & Rubicam's Brand Asset Valuator, see "Brand Asset Valuator," Value Based Management.net, www.valuebased-management.net/methods_brand_asset_valuator.html, accessed May 2009; W. Ronald Lane, Karen Whitehill King, and J. Thomas Russell, *Kleppner's Advertising Procedure*, 17th ed. (Upper Saddle River, NJ: Prentice Hall, 2008), p. 105; and www.brandassetconsulting.com/, accessed May 2009.

30. Al Ehrbar, "Breakaway Brands," *Fortune*, October 31, 2005, pp. 153–170. Also see "DeWalt Named Breakaway Brand," *Snips*, January 2006, p. 66.

31. See Millward Brown Optimor, "BrandZ Top 100 Most Powerful Brands 2009," accessed at www.millwardbrown.com/Sites/Optimor/Content/KnowledgeCenter/BrandzRanking.aspx.

32. See Scott Davis, *Brand Asset Management*, 2nd ed. (San Francisco: Jossey-Bass, 2002). For more on brand positioning, see Philip Kotler and Kevin Lane Keller, *Marketing Management*, 13th ed. (Upper Saddle River, NJ: Prentice Hall, 2009), chapter 10.

33. Adapted from information found in Geoff Colvin, "Selling P&G," *Fortune*, September 17, 2007, pp. 163–169; "For P&G, Success Lies in More Than Merely a Dryer Diaper," *Advertising Age*, October 15, 2007, p. 20; Jack Neff, "Stengel Discusses Transition at P&G," *Advertising Age*, July 21, 2008, p. 17; and Elaine Wong, "Stengel: Private Label, Digital Change Game," *Brandweek*, March 13, 2009, p. 7.

34. Susan Wong, "Foods OK, but Some Can't Stomach More Ad Increases," *Brandweek*, January 5, 2009, p. 7.

35. See Vanessa L. Facenda, "A Swift Kick to the Privates," *Brandweek*, September 3, 2007, pp. 24+; Jack Neff, "Private Label Winning Battle of Brands," *Advertising Age*, February 23, 2009, p. 1; Chris Burritt and Carol Wolf, "Wal-Mart's Store-Brand Groceries to Get New Emphasis," *Bloomberg.com*, February 19, 2009; and Lana F. Flowers, "Consumers Turn to Private Labels In Down Economy," *Morning News (Arkansas)*, February 20, 2009, www.nwaonline.net.

36. Nirmalya Kumar and Jan-Benedict E. M. Steenkamp, *Private Label Strategy* (Boston, MA: Harvard Business School Press, 2007), p. 5.

37. "Dora the Explorer Takes the Lead as Sales Growth Elevates Property to Megabrand Status as Number-One Toy License in 2006," *PR Newswire*, February 8, 2007; Clint Cantwell, "$187 Billion Global Licensing Industry Comes to Life at Licensing International Expo 2008," *Business Wire*, June 6, 2008; "Nickelodeon Expands Product Offerings and Debuts New Properties for Kids and Teens at Licensing 2008 International Show," June 10, 2008, accessed at http://biz.yahoo.com/prnews/080610/nytu056.html?.v=101; and "SpongeBob SquarePants Swims to the Cricut," *Business Wire*, January 28, 2009.

38. Quote from www.apple.com/ipod/nike, August 2009.

39. Gabrielle Solomon, "Cobranding Alliances: Arranged Marriages Made by Marketers," *Fortune*, October 12, 1998, p. 188; Gene Marcial, "Martha Cozies Up to Wal-Mart," *BusinessWeek*, August 4, 2008, p. 72; "Country Living's Vibrancy Grows with Sears/Kmart Partnership," *Media Industry Newsletter*, April 13, 2009, accessed at www.minonline.com/min/10629.html.

40. The quote and the best/worst examples are from "TippingSprung Publishes Results from Fifth Annual Brand-Extensions Survey," January 6, 2009, accessed at www.tippingsprung.com/index.php?/knowledge/knowledge_article/tippingsprung_publishes_results_from_fifth_annual_brand-extension_survey/.

41. "Leading National Advertisers," *Advertising Age*, June 22, 2009, p. 12.

42. Quotes from Stephen Cole, "Value of the Brand," *CA Magazine*, May 2005, pp. 39–40; and Lawrence A. Crosby and Sheree L. Johnson, "Experience Required," *Marketing Management*, July/August 2007, pp. 21–27.

43. See Kevin Lane Keller, *Strategic Brand Management* (Upper Saddle River, NJ: Prentice Hall, 2008), chapter 10.

Chapter 8

1. Extracts and quotes from or adapted from information found in Chuck Salter, "Google: The Faces and Voices of the World's Most Innovative Company," *Fast Company*, March 2008, pp. 74–88; "The World's Most Innovative Companies," *Fast Company*, March 2009, p. 52; "Google Shines a Light on Innovation," *Computer Weekly*, September 9–September 15, 2008, p. 3; Jessica Guynn, "Internet; Google's Results Defy Downturn," *Los Angeles Times*, October 17, 2008, p. C1; David Pogue, "Geniuses at Play, On the Job," *New York Times*, February 26, 2009, p. B1; and www.google.com and www.googlelabs.com, accessed June 2009.

2. "In a Tough Economy, Innovation Is King," *Marketing News*, April 15, 2009, p. 14.

3. Calvin Hodock, "Winning the New-Products Game," *Advertising Age*, November 12, 2007, p. 35; Neale Martin, "Force of Habit," *Brandweek*, October 13, 2008, pp. 18–20; and "How P&G Plans to Clean up," *BusinessWeek*, April 13, 2009, pp. 44–45.

4. Information and examples from Robert M. McMath and Thom Forbes, *What Were They Thinking? Money-Saving, Time-Saving, Face-Saving Marketing Lessons You Can Learn from Products That Flopped* (New York: Times Business, 1999), various pages; Beatriz

Cholo, "Living with Your 'Ex': A Brand New World," *Brandweek*, December 5, 2005, p. 4; and www.gfkamerica.com/newproduct-works, October 2009.

5. John Peppers and Martha Rogers, "The Buzz on Customer-Driven Innovation," *Sales & Marketing Management*, June 2007, p. 13.

6. See Rik Kirkland, "Cisco's Display of Strength," *Fortune*, November 12, 2007, pp. 90–100; Richard Martin, "Collaboration Cisco Style," *InformationWeek*, January 28, 2008, p. 30; and "Cisco on Cisco: Web 2.0 in the Enterprise," March 2008, accessed at www.cisco.com.

7. Based on material from Anna Fifield, "Samsung Sows for the Future with Its Garden of Delights," *Financial Times*, January 4, 2008, p. 13; and Peter Lewis, "A Perpetual Crisis Machine," *Fortune*, September 19, 2005, pp. 58–67. Also see "Camp Samsung," *BusinessWeek Online*, July 3, 2006, accessed at www.businessweek.com.

8. Example from www.ideo.com/work/item/game-suite, accessed July 2009.

9. Jeff Howe, "Join the Crowd," *Independent (London)*, September 2, 2008, p. 2.

10. Paul Gillin, "Get Customers Involved in Innovations," *BtoB*, March 12, 2007, p. 111. See also Patricia B. Seybold, *Outside Innovation: How Your Customers Will Co-Design Your Company's Future* (New York: Collins, 2006); and Patricia B. Seybold's blog: http://outsideinnovation.blogs.com, accessed April 2007.

11. "Bill Invites Customers to Share Ideas and Original Video via Dell IdeaStorm and StudioDell," February 16, 2007, accessed at www.dell.com; and Jon Fortt, "Michael Dell 'Friends' His Customers," *Fortune*, September 15, 2008, p. 35. Also see www.ideastorm.com, accessed November 2009.

12. Information accessed online at www.avon.com, August 2009. Also see http://ezinearticles.com/?Avons-SSS-Flea-Control—-Plus-Many-Other-Uses-to-Go-Green!&id=1819677, accessed June 2009.

13. Example adapted from information in Kevin O'Donnell, "Where Do the Best Ideas Come From? The Unlikeliest Sources," *Advertising Age*, July 14, 2008, p. 15; and http://mindstorms.lego.com/MeetMDP/default.aspx and http://mindstorms.lego.com/community/default.aspx, accessed June 2009. MINDSTORMS® and LEGO® are registered trademarks of the LEGO Group.

14. Quotes from Robert Gray, "Not Invented Here," *Marketing*, May 6, 2004, pp. 34–37; and Betsy Morris, "What Makes Apple Golden?" *Fortune*, March 17, 2008, pp. 68–74.

15. Kevin O'Donnell, "Where Do the Best Ideas Come From? The Unlikeliest Sources," *Advertising Age*, July 14, 2008, p. 15.

16. See George S. Day, "Is It Real? Can We Win? Is It Worth Doing?" *Harvard Business Review*, December 2007, pp. 110–120.

17. Information for this example obtained from www.teslamotors.com, accessed June 2009.

18. Example adapted from information found in Linda Grant, "Gillette Knows Shaving—and How to Turn Out Hot New Products," *Fortune*, October 14, 1996, pp. 207–210; and Jenn Abelson, "Gillett Sharpens Its Focus on Women," *Boston Globe*, January 4, 2009.

19. "KFC Fires Up Grilled Chicken," March 23, 2008, accessed at www.money.cnn.com; and "KFC Serves Up a Second Secret Recipe: Kentucky Grilled Chicken," *PR Newswire*, April 14, 2009.

20. Example developed from information found in Allison Enright, "Best Practices: Frito-Lay Get Real Results from a Virtual World," *Marketing News*, December 15, 2006, p. 20; and "Decision Insight: Simushop," accessed at www.decisioninsight.com/content/simushop.shtml, September 2009. Also see, Piet Levy, "10 Minutes with . . . Brad Barash, Vice President of Decision Insight, Inc.," *Marketing News*, February 28, 2009, p. 28.

21. See Steve McClellan, "Unilever's Sunsilk Launch Goes Far Beyond the Box," *Adweek*, August 21–28, 2006, p. 9.

22. Jeremy Mullman, "Copying Corona: Miller, Bud Want Their Fun in the Sun," *Advertising Age*, January 29, 2007, p. 1; David Kesmodel, "Miller Gives Lime-and-Salt Beer a Shot at Boosting Sales," *Wall Street Journal*, June 12, 2007, accessed at www.wsj.com; Mike Beirne, "A Distinct Chill Has Been Cast Over the Beer Category," *Brandweek*, September 3, 2007, p. 11; Jeremy Mullman, "Miller Chill Featured on 'Live' Ad on 'Late Night,'" *Advertising Age*, October 1, 2007, p. 6; and David Kesmodel, "Miller to Bring 'Chill' to Australia," *Wall Street Journal*, November 12, 2007, p. B6.

23. Robert G. Cooper, "Formula for Success," *Marketing Management*, March–April 2006, pp. 19–23; and Barry Jaruzelski and Kevin Dehoff, "The Global Innovation of 1000," *Strategy + Business*, Issue 49, fourth quarter, 2007, pp. 68–83.

24. Robert Berner, "How P&G Pampers New Thinking," *BusinessWeek*, April 14, 2008, pp. 73–74; and "How P&G Plans To Clean Up," *BusinessWeek*, April 13, 2009, pp. 44–45.

25. "PNC's Virtual Wallet Takes Online Banking to the Next Level," *PRNewswire*, August 5, 2008; and Todd Wasserman, "Thinking by Design," *Brandweek*, November 3, 2008, pp. 18–21.

26. This definition is based on one found in Bryan Lilly and Tammy R. Nelson, "Fads: Segmenting the Fad-Buyer Market," *Journal of Consumer Marketing*, vol. 20, no. 3, 2003, pp. 252–265.

27. See Katya Kazakina, Robert Johnson, "A Fad's Father Seeks a Sequel," *New York Times*, May 30, 2004, p. 3.2; John Schwartz, "The Joy of Silly," *New York Times*, January 20, 2008, p. 5; and www.crazyfads.com, accessed November 2009.

28. Example adapted from information found in Patrick J. Sauer, "I Just IM'd to say 'I Love You,'" *Fast Company*, May 2008, p. 52. Also see "American Greetings Introduces New 'Ideas' Online," *PR Newswire*, November 28, 2008.

29. See Constantine von Hoffman, "Glad Gives Seal of Approval to Alternate Wrap Uses," *Brandweek*, November 27, 2006, p. 10; and www.1000uses.com, accessed September 2009.

30. For a more comprehensive discussion of marketing strategies over the course of the product life cycle, see Philip Kotler and Kevin Lane Keller, *Marketing Management*, 13th ed. (Upper Saddle River, NJ: Prentice Hall, 2009), pp. 278–290.

31. See "Verdict Warns Drug Makers Not to Suppress Known Risks," *Tampa Tribune*, August 23, 2005, p. 10; "Year-by-Year Analysis Reveals an Overall Compensatory Award of $1,500,000 for Products Liability Cases," *Personal Injury Verdict Reviews*, July 3, 2006; Heather Won Tesoriero, "Merck's Prospects Brighten for Vioxx Settlement," *Wall Street Journal*, January 19, 2008, p. A3; and Sheri Qualters, "U.S. Litigation Filings Up 9% in 2008," *National Law Journal*, January 16, 2009, http://www.nmlegalreform.org/2009-01-16.htm.

32. Example based on information provided by Nestle Japan Ltd., May 2008; with additional information from Laurel Wentz, "Kit Kat Wins Cannes Media Grand Prix for Edible Postcard," *Advertising Age*, accessed at http://adage.com/cannes09/article_id=137520; and http:// en.wikipedia.org/wiki/Kit_Kat and the Japanese Wikipedia discussion of Kit Kat at http://ja.wikipedia.org, accessed November 2009.

33. Information accessed online at www.deutsche-bank.com, July 2009.

34. Information accessed online at www.interpublic.com and www.mccann.com, August 2009.

35. See "2009 Global Powers of Retailing," January 2009, accessed at www.deloitte.com/dtt/article/0,1002,cid%253D242136,00.html; "Wal-Mart International Operations," accessed at www.walmartstores.com, June 2009; and information accessed at www.carrefour.com/english/groupecarrefour/profil.jsp, June 2009.

Chapter 9

1. All quotes and other information were taken from Bloomsbury Publishing (www.bloomsbury.com); ASDA (www.asda.co.uk); This Is Money (www.thisismoney.co.uk), The Book Seller (www.thebookseller.com); Nielsen Book Scan UK (www.nielsenbookscan.co.uk); Borders Books (www.bordersstores.co.uk); and Tesco (www.tesco.com).

2. George Mannes, "The Urge to Unbundle," *Fast Company*, February 27, 2005, pp. 23–24. Also see Stuart Elliott, "Creative Spots, Courtesy of a Stalled Economy," *New York Times*, April 11, 2008; and Elliott, "Nevermind What It Costs. Can I Get 70 Percent Off?" *New York Times*, April 27, 2009.

3. For more on the importance of sound pricing strategy, see Thomas T. Nagle and John Hogan, *The Strategy and Tactics of Pricing: A Guide to Growing More Profitably* (Upper Saddle River, NJ: Prentice Hall, 2007), chapter 1.

4. Based on information from Anne Marie Chaker, "For a Steinway, I Did It My Way," *Wall Street Journal*, May 22, 2008; and www.steinway.com/steinway and www.steinway.com/steinway/quotes.shtml, accessed November 2009.

5. See Kevin Done, "Runway Success—Ryanair," *Financial Times*, March 20, 2009, accessed at www.ft.com; Matthew Maier, "A Radical Fix for

Airlines: Make Flying Free," *Business 2.0*, April 2006, pp. 32–34; Kerry Capell, "Fasten Your Seatbelt, Ryanair," *BusinessWeek*, February 18, 2008, p. 16; and www.ryanair.com, accessed July 2009.

6. Example adapted from Anupam Mukerji, "Monsoon Marketing," *Fast Company*, April 2007, p. 22.

7. Elizabeth A. Sullivan, "Value Pricing: Smart Marketers Know Cost-Plus Can Be Costly," *Marketing News*, January 15, 2008, p. 8. Also see Venkatesh Bala and Jason Green, "Charge What Your Products Are Worth," *Harvard Business Review*, September 2007, p. 22; and Peter J. Williamson and Ming Zeng, "Value-for-the-Money Strategies," *Harvard Business Review*, March 2009, pp. 66–74.

8. Comments from www.yelp.com/biz/annie-blooms-books-portland, accessed June 2009.

9. Adapted from information found in Joseph Weber, "Over a Buck for Dinner? Outrageous," *BusinessWeek*, March 9, 2009, p. 57.

10. Susan Mires, "The New Economy of Frugality: Cost-Seating Skills Going up in Value," *McClatchy-Tribune Business News*, March 19, 2009; Laura Petrecca, "Marketers Try to Promote Value without Cheapening Image," *USA Today*, November 17, 2008, p. B1; and Anne D'Innocenzio, "Butter, Kool-Aid in Limelight in Advertising Shift," April 21, 2009, accessed at www.azcentral.com/business/articles/2009/04/21/20090421biz-NewFrugality0421.html.

11. Ryan McCarthy, "Pricing: How Low Can You Go?" *Inc.*, March 2009, pp. 91–92

12. Petrecca, "Marketers Try to Promote Value without Cheapening Image," *USA Today*, November 17, 2008, p. B1; and D'Innocenzio, "Butter, Kool-Aid in Limelight in Advertising Shift," April 21, 2009, accessed at www.azcentral.com/business/articles/2009/04/21/20090421biz-NewFrugality0421.html.

13. Hein, "Study: Trumps Price among Shoppers," *Brandweek*, March 2, 2009, p. 6.

14. For comprehensive discussions of pricing strategies, see Nagle and Hogan, *The Strategy and Tactics of Pricing*, 4th ed. (Upper Saddle River, NJ: Prentice Hall, 2007).

15. See Brian Chen, "WWDC: Apple Slashes Prices with iPhone 3G, Shipping in July," June 9, 2008, accessed at www.macworld.com/article/133838/2008/06/iphone3g.html; and Olga Kharif, "Can Apple Keep a Shine on the iPhone?" *BusinessWeek (Online)*, March 18, 2009, accessed at www.businessweek.com.

16. Adapted from information found in Mei Fong, "IKEA Hits Home in China; The Swedish Design Giant, Unlike Other Retailers, Slashes Prices for the Chinese," *Wall Street Journal*, March 3, 2006, p. B1; and "IKEA China to Boost Sales by Slashing Prices," *China Knowledge*, March 9, 2009, accessed at www.chinaknowledge.com.

17. Paul Miller, "Sony Losing Mad Loot on Each PS3," *Engadet*, November 16, 2006, www.engadget.com/2006/11/16/sony-losing-mad-loot-on-each-ps3/; and Sam Kennedy, "Sony Has Lost More on the PS3 than It Made on PS2," *1UP News*, August 19, 2008, www.1up.com/do/newsStory?cId=3169439.

18. Information from www.meadwestvaco.com and www.meadwestvaco.com/SpecialtyChemicals/AsphaltAdditives/MWV002106, accessed September 2009.

19. See Nagle and Hogan, *The Strategy and Tactics of Pricing*, 4th ed. (Upper Saddle River, NJ: Prentice Hall, 2007), pp. 244–247; Bram Foubert and Els Gijsbrechts, "Shopper Response to Bundle Promotions for Packaged Goods," *Journal of Marketing Research*, November 2007, pp. 647–662; Roger M. Heeler, et al., "Bundles = Discount? Revisiting Complex Theories of Bundle Effects," *Journal of Product & Brand Management*, vol. 16, no. 7, 2007, pp. 492–500; and Timothy J. Gilbride, et al, "Framing Effects in Mixed Price Bundling," *Marketing Letters*, June 2008, pp. 125–140.

20. Based on information from Eric Anderson and Duncan Simester, "Mind Your Pricing Cues," *Harvard Business Review*, September 2003, pp. 96–103. Also see Monika Kukar-Kinney, et al, "Consumer Responses to Characteristics of Price-Matching Guarantees," *Journal of Retailing*, April 2007, p. 211; and Peter J. Boyle and E. Scott Lathrop, "Are Consumers' Perceptions of Price-Quality Relationships Well Calibrated?" *International Journal of Consumer Studies*, January 2009, p. 58.

21. Adapted from information found in Elizabeth A. Sullivan, "Stay on Course," *Marketing News*, February 15, 2009, pp. 11–13. Also see Stuart Elliott, "Never Mind What It Costs. Can I Get It 70 Percent Off?" *New York Times*, April 27, 2009, accessed at www.nytimes.com.

22. Example adapted from Louise Story, "Online Pitches Made Just for You," *New York Times*, March 6, 2008.

23. Based on information found in "The World's Most Influential Companies: Unilever," *BusinessWeek*, December 22, 2008, p. 47; and www.unilever.com/sustainability/people/consumers/affordability/, accessed June 2009.

24. Example adapted from information found in Ellen Byron, "Fashion Victim: To Refurbish Its Image, Tiffany Risks Profits," *Wall Street Journal*, January 10, 2007, p. A1; and Aliza Rosenbaum and John Christy, "Financial Insight: Tiffany's Boutique Risk; By Breaking Mall Fast, High-End Exclusivity May Gain Touch of Common," *Wall Street Journal*, October 20, 2007, p. B14. Also see Bernadette Morra, "Tiffany Seeks to Break Down Some Barriers," *Toronto Star*, April 23, 2009, p. L3.

25. "Virgin America Launches 'Flydealism' Campaign," *PR Newswire*, March 10, 2009; and www.virginamerica.com/va/vaDifference.do, accessed June 2009.

26. Jack Neff, "Viva Viva! K-C Boosts Brand's marketing," *Advertising Age*, June 11, 2007, p. 4; and Jack Neff, "Bounty," *Advertising Age*, November 17, 2008, p. S-18.

27. For discussions of these issues, see Dhruv Grewal and Larry D. Compeau, "Pricing and Public Policy: A Research Agenda and Overview of Special Issue," *Journal of Public Policy and Marketing*, Spring 1999, pp. 3–10; and Michael V. Marn, Eric V. Roegner, and Craig C. Zawada, *The Price Advantage* (Hoboken, NJ: John Wiley & Sons, 2004), appendix 2.

28. Julie Jargon, "Retailers' Lawsuits Accuse Candy Makers of Fixing Prices," *Wall Street Journal*, April 1, 2008, p. B3; Alia McMullen, "Chocolate Giants Sued for Collusion," *Financial Post*, February 19, 2008, p. FP1; and Pete Shellem, "Judge Rules Chocolate Price-Fixing Suits Can Proceed," *Patriot-News (Pennsylvania)*, March 5, 2009, www.pennlive.com.

29. "Predatory-Pricing Law Passed by New York Governor," *National Petroleum News*, December 2003, p. 7; Charles Ashby, "Senate OKs Bill to Allow Below-Cost Fuel," *Knight Ridder Tribune Business News*, March 14, 2007, p. 1; Martin Sipkoff, "Wal-Mart, Other Discounters Facing Predatory-Pricing Concerns," *Drug Topics*, April 2, 2007, pp. 10–12, and Jack Neff, "Why Wal-Mart's Winning: Gas Prices Pump up Retailer's Sales," *Advertising Age*, December 8, 2008, pp. 1, 2.

30. "FTC Guides Against Deceptive Pricing," accessed at www.ftc.gov/bcp/guides/decptprc.htm, December 2009.

Chapter 10

1. All quotes and other information were taken from Zaytoun Marketing Group (www.zaytoun.org); Cooperative News (www.thenews.coop); Olive Cooperative (www.olivecoop.com); Developments Magazine (www.developments.org.uk); Triodos Awards – Women in Ethical Business (www.activatemoney.com); Fair Trade Foundation (www.fairtrade.org.uk); and Café Direct (www.cafedirect.co.uk).

2. See Kevin Kelleher, "Giving Dealers a Raw Deal," *Business 2.0*, December 2004, pp. 82–84; Jim MacKinnon, "Goodyear Boasts of Bright Future," *McClatchy-Tribune Business News*, April 9, 2008; Andrea Doyle, "Forging Ahead," *Successful Meetings*, May 2009, pp. 36–42; and information accessed at www.goodyear.com, September 2009.

3. Information accessed at www.kroger.com and www.luxottica.com/english/profilo_aziendale/index_keyfacts.html, October 2008.

4. Franchising facts from *2009 Franchise Business Economic Outlook*, January 7, 2009, accessed at www.franchise.org/uploadedFiles/2009%20Economic%20Outlook%20Factsheet.pdf; and www.azfranchises.com/franchisefacts.htm; March 2009.

5. See Melinda Liu, "Just Beware of the White Lightning; Car Culture Is Booming in China," *Newsweek*, November 19, 2007, p. E24; "The First Cooperation of Sinopec, KFC and Grease Monkey Provides One-Stop Services" January 9, 2009, accessed at www.greasemonkeychina.com/eng/news.htm; and http://english.sinopec.com/about_sinopec/our_business/refining_selling/, accessed July 2009.

6. Quotes and other information from Matthew Boyle, "Reed Hastings," *Fortune*, May 28, 2007, p. 30; "Nick Wingfield, "Netflix vs. Naysayers," *Wall Street Journal*, March 27, 2007, p. B1; Michael V. Copeland, "Netflix Lives!" *Fortune*, April 28, 2008, p. 40; and www.netflix.com, accessed June 2009.

7. See Paolo Del Nibletto, "Dell Stuck in the Middle," *Computer Dealer News*, March 21, 2008, p. 12; and Benjamin Sutherland, "Shifting

Gears at Dell," *Newsweek*, November 3, 2008, accessed at www.newsweek.com/id/165381.

8. Quotes and information from Normandy Madden, "Two Chinas," *Advertising Age*, August 16, 2004, pp. 1, 22; Russell Flannery, "China: The Slow Boat," *Forbes*, April 12, 2004, p. 76; Jeff Berman, "U.S. Providers Say Logistics in China on the Right Track," *Logistics Management*, March 2007, p. 22; Jamie Bolton, "China: The Infrastructure Imperative," *Logistics Management*, July 2007, p. 63; and China trade facts from http://cscmp.org/press/fastfacts.asp; March 2009.

9. Nanette Byrnes, "Avon Calls. China Opens the Door," *BusinessWeek Online*, February 28, 2006, p. 19; Mei Fong, "Avon's Calling, but China Opens Door Only a Crack," *Wall Street Journal*, February 26, 2007, p. B1; "Cosmetic Changes in China Market," www.Chinadaily.com.cn, October 11, 2007; and "Avon Products Inc Sees Sales Boom in China," February 10, 2009, accessed at http://news.alibaba.com/article/detail/business-in-china/100049657-1-avon-products-inc-sees-sales.html.

10. Quotes and other information from Alex Taylor III, "Caterpillar," *Fortune*, August 20, 2007, pp. 48–54; Donald V. Fites, "Make Your Dealers Your Partners," *Harvard Business Review*, March–April 1996, pp. 84–95; and information accessed at www.caterpillar.com, August 2009.

11. "U.S. Logistics Costs Top 10% of GDP," *Outsourced Logistics*, June 26, 2008; "GM Shipping Costs Rise with Crude"; Larry Rohter, "Shipping Costs Start to Crimp Globalization," *New York Times*, August 3, 2008, p. A1; and supply chain facts from http://cscmp.org/press/fastfacts.asp; June 2009.

12. Shlomo Maital, "The Last Frontier of Cost Reduction," *Across the Board*, February 1994, pp. 51–52; and information accessed online at www.walmartstores.com, June 2009.

13. William Hoffman, "Supplying Sustainability," *Traffic World*, April 7, 2008.

14. Gail Braccidiferro, "One Town's Rejection Is Another's 'Let's Do Business,'" *New York Times*, June 15, 2003, p. 2; Dan Scheraga, "Wal-Smart," *Chain Store Age*, January 2006 supplement, pp. 16A–21A; and facts from www.walmart.com, June 2009.

15. Example adapted from Evan West, "These Robots Play Fetch," *Fast Company*, July/August 2007, pp. 49–50. See also John Teresko, "Getting Lean with Armless Robots," *Industry Week*, September 2008, p. 26.

16. See "A Worldwide Look at RFID," *Supply Chain Management Review*, April 2007, pp. 48–55; "Wal-Mart Says Use RFID Tags or Pay Up," *Logistics Today*, March 2008, p. 4; and David Blanchard, "The Five Stages of RFID," *Industry Week*, January 1, 2009, p. 50.

17. Transportation percentages and other figures in this section are from Bureau of Transportation Statistics, "Significant Accomplishments Fiscal Year 2008," December 2008, accessed at www.bts.gov/publications; and Bureau of Transportation Statistics, "Pocket Guide to Transportation 2009," February January 2009, accessed at www.bts.gov/publications/pocket_guide_to_transportation/2009.

18. See Wal-Mart's supplier requirements at http://walmartstores.com/Suppliers/248.aspx, accessed June 2009. Also see Sriram Narayanan, Ann S. Marucheck, and Robert B. Handfield, "Electronic Data Interchange: Research Review and Future Directions," *Decision Sciences*, February 2009, p. 121.

19. See Bob Trebilcock, "Top 20 Supply Chain Management Software Suppliers," *Modern Material Handling*, July 1, 2008, www.mmh.com/article/CA6574264.html; and "The 2009 Supply & Demand Chain Executive 100," *Supply & Demand Chain Executive*, June–July 2009, accessed at www.sdcexec.com.

20. "Whirlpool: Outsourcing Its National Service Parts Operation Provides Immediate Benefits," accessed at www.ryder.com/pdf/MCC633_Whirlpool_single.pdf, October 2008.

21. See Alan Field, "Outsourced Logistics Growing," *Journal of Commerce*, March 10, 2009; and Alan Field, "3PL Revenue Drops 6.7 Percent," *Journal of Commerce*, April 3, 2009.

Chapter 11

1. Information gained from students as part of a retailing class assignment. It included store visits, personal interviews with Ramez management and some shoppers. (Dr. Jaafar A.M. Almahy, University of Bahrain)

2. Quotes and other information on OgilvyAction from Katy Bachman, "Suit Your Shelf," *AdweekMedia*, January 19, 2009, pp. 10–12; "OgilvyAction Takes Regional Marketers to the Last Mile," January 23, 2008, accessed at www.entrepreneur.com/tradejournals/article/

173710015.html, and Jack Neff, "Trouble in Store for Shopper Marketing," *Advertising Age*, March 2, 2009, pp. 3–4. Retail sales statistics from "Annual Revision of Monthly Retail and Food Services: Sales and Inventories—January 1992–2008," U.S. Census Bureau, March 2009, p. 3.

3. Store shopping statistics from Bachman, "Suit Your Shelf," p. 10. For more on shopper marketing see Grocery Manufacturers Association and Deloitte Consulting, *Delivering the Promise of Shopper Marketing: Mastering Execution of Competitive Advantage*, 2008, accessed at www.deloitte.com/dtt/article/0,1002,cid%253D226237,00.html; Bob Holston, "Avoid Shopper Marketing Pitfalls," *Advertising Age*, March 31, 2008, pp. 20–21; and Neff, "Trouble in Store for Shopper Marketing," pp. 3–4

4. Jo-Ann Heslin, "Supermarkets—Are They on the Endangered Species List?" *HealthNewsDigest.com*, March 30, 2008, www.healthnewsdigest.com/news/Food_and_Nutrition_690/Supermarkets_—_Are_They_On_The_Endangered_Species_List.shtml.

5. Mark Hamstra, "In Tune," *Supermarket News*, October 13, 2008, p. 14; and www.thekrogerco.com, accessed June 2009.

6. "Convenience Store Industry Sales, Profits Show Gains," April 7, 2009, accessed online at www.nacsonline.com.

7. See "Stan Sheetz Recognized Among Most Influential Retail Leaders in the World," *PR Newswire*, January 29, 2008; "Sheetz, Inc.," *Hoover's Company Records*, April 1, 2009, p. 43078; and www.sheetz.com/main/about/definition.cfm, accessed July 2009.

8. Statistics based on information from "SN Top 75 2008," http://supermarketnews.com/profiles/2008-top-75/, accessed March 2009; Elliot Zwiebach, "Wal-Mart Trims HQ Office Staff," *Supermarket News*, February 16, 2009, p. 4; and "Supermarket Facts," accessed at www.fmi.org/facts_figs/?fuseaction=superfact, March 2009.

9. Adapted from information found in Sandra M. Jones, "Outlets Proved Promising for High-End Retailers: Luxury Goods for Less Attract Shoppers," *McClatchy-Tribune Business News*, April 11, 2009.

10. Company information from www.mcdonalds.com/corp.html and www.subway.com/subwayroot/AboutSubway/index.aspx, June 2009.

11. "Ten Brands, Ten Challenges," *Chain Store Age*, August 2008, p. 6A; and Jeremy Lee, "Gap," *Marketing*, August 27, 2008, p. 19; Marianne Wilson, "Talking Retail," *Chain Store Age*, May 2009, p. 14; and www.gapinc.com/public/Investors/inv_financials.shtml, accessed June 2009.

12. The Whole Foods example is based on quotes and information from Diane Brady, "Eating Too Fast at Whole Foods," *BusinessWeek*, October 24, 2005, pp. 82–84; Kim Wright Wiley, "Think Organic," *Sales & Marketing Management*, January–February 2007, pp. 54–59; "Whole Food Market, Inc.," *Hoover's Company Records*, March 25, 2009, p. 10952, p.1; and www.wholefoods.com, accessed June 2009.

13. JCPenney Annual Report 2008, accessed at www.jcpenney.net.

14. See Ylan Q. Mui, "Dollars and Scents," *Washington Post*, December 19, 2006, p. D01, Denise Power, "Something Is in the Air: Panel Says Scent Sells," *WWD*, March 25, 2008, p. 14; Jonathon Rosenthal, "Led by the Nose," *Economist*, November 19, 2008, accessed at www.economist.com; "Scent Marketing Industry Skyrockets in Crumbling Retail Economy," *Business Wire*, November 18, 2008; and "Brands! Use Some Common Scents," January 2009, accessed at http://binge-thinking.blogspot.com/2009/01/brands-use-some-common-scents.html.

15. Information from www.bijan.com, accessed November 2009.

16. For definitions of these and other types of shopping centers, see "Dictionary," American Marketing Association, accessed at www.marketingpower.com/_layouts/Dictionary.aspx, December 2009.

17. Sasha M. Pardy, "Malls: A Dying Breed? Don't Bet On It," March 25, 2008, www.costar.com/news/Article.aspx?id= 74C268256AB19CFACA1AC5E5947CFC0D; Michael P. Niemira, "U.S. Economic and Industry Outlook: Commercial Real Estate Faces the Credit Crisis and Liquidity Trap," January 14, 2009, www.icsc.org/research/files/ReTel_Jan_14_2009a.pdf; and Sean Gregory, "Postcard: East Rutherford," *Time*, March 30, 2009, p. 9.

18. Dean Starkman, "The Mall, Without the Haul—'Lifestyle Centers' Slip Quietly into Upscale Areas, Mixing Cachet and 'Curb Appeal,'" *Wall Street Journal*, July 25, 2001, p. B1; Paul Grimaldi, "Shopping for a New Look: Lifestyle Centers Are Replacing Enclosed Malls," *Providence Journal (Rhode Island)*, April 29, 2007, p. F10; and Neil Nisperos, "Lifestyle Centers Offer More than Fresh Air," *Inland Valley Daily Bulletin*, January 5, 2009.

19. Ken Favaro, Tim Romberger, and David Meer, "Five Rules for Retailing in a Recession," *Harvard Business Review*, April 2009, pp. 64–72.

20. Elizabeth Ody, "Six Retailers that Are Thriving," February 17, 2009, accessed at http://www.kiplinger.com/printstory.php?pid+15397.

21. Kenneth Hein, "Target Tries First Price Point Driven TV Ads," *Brandweek*, January 14, 2009, accessed at www.brandweek.com.

22. For these and other examples, see Stuart Elliott, "With Shoppers Pinching Pennies, Some Big Retailers Get the Message," *New York Times*, April 13, 2009.

23. Hein, "Target Tries First Price Point Driven TV Ads," p. 1.

24. Helen Leggatt, "Forrester: Growth Forecast for 2009 Online Retail Sales," *BizReport.com*, January 30, 2009, www.bizreport.com/2009/01/forrester_growth_forecast_for_2009_online_retail_sales.html. "".

25. Mark Penn, "New Info Shoppers," *Wall Street Journal*, January 8, 2009, accessed at http://online.wsj.com/article/SB123144483005365353.html.

26. The online shopper statistics and extract example are from or adapted from Mark Penn, "New Info Shoppers," *Wall Street Journal*, January 8, 2009, accessed at http://online.wsj.com/article/SB123144483005365353.html.

27. "Facts About America's Top 500 E-Retailers," *Internet Retailer*, accessed online at www.internetretailer.com/top500/facts.asp, September 2009.

28. See Don Davis, "M Is for Multi-channel," *Internet Retailer*, June 2007, www.internetretailer.com/internet/marketing-conference/30566-m-multi-channel.html; Macy's, Inc., Online Selling Sites Enhance Integration with Bricks-and-Mortar Stores, *Business Wire*, December 8, 2008; and information from www.macys.com, accessed June 2009.

29. See "The Home Depot, Inc.," and "The Black & Decker Corporation," *Hoover's Company Records*, June 1, 2009, www.hoovers.com.

30. See www.shopbloom.com, November 2009.

31. "Wal-Mart International Operations," February 2009, accessed online at http://Wal-Martstores.com/FactsNews/NewsRoom/9012.aspxWal-Mart; and "Target Corporation," *Hoover's Company Records*, April 1, 2009, www.hoovers.com.

32. See "Feeling the Squeeze: Global Powers of Retailing 2009," *Stores*, January 2009, accessed at http://public.deloitte.com/media/0460/2009GlobalPowersofRetail_FINAL2.pdf.

33. "Top 250 Global Retailers," *Stores*, January 2009, pp. G6–G25, accessed at http://public.deloitte.com/media/0460/2009Global PowersofRetail _FINAL2.pdf.; and information from www.walmartstores.com and www.carrefour.com, accessed June 2009.

34. Adapted from information in Josh Bernoff, "Social Networking Needs CMO Lead," *Advertising Age*, April 28, 2008, p. 129; with information from Nancy Nally, "The Genius of Fiskateers: Leveraging Social Media to Promote Fiskars," *Scrapbook Update*, October 2, 2008, www.scrapbookupdate.com/scrapnancy/2008/10/the-genius-of-f.html; and www.fiskars.com, accessed June 2009.

35. Based on 2008 sales data. See the *Grainger 2009 Fact Book* and other information accessed at www.grainger.com.

36. *Grainger 2009 Fact Book*, accessed at www.grainger.com, July 2009.

37. See Dale Buss, "The New Deal," *Sales & Marketing Management*, June 2002, pp. 25–30; Colleen Gourley, "Redefining Distribution," *Warehousing Management*, October 2000, pp. 28–30; Stewart Scharf, "Grainger: Tooled Up for Growth," *BusinessWeek Online*, April 25, 2006, p. 8; and *Grainger 2009 Fact Book*, accessed at www.grainger.com.

38. Information from "About Us" and "Supply Management Online," accessed online at www.mckesson.com, June 2009.

39. Facts accessed at www.supervalu.com, June 2009.

40. See www.mckesson.com/static_files/McKesson.com/CorpIR/PDF_Documents/10K_2009_Final.pdf, p. 115, accessed September 2009.

Chapter 12

1. All quotes and other information were taken from Volkswagen China (www.vw.com.cn); *Business Week* (www.businessweek.com); *China Daily* (www.chinadaily.com); *Chinese Car Times* (www.chinacartimes.com); *Motor Authority* (www.motorauthority.com); *Industry Week* (www.industryweek.com); and *European Business Forum* (www.ebfonline.com).

2. For other definitions, see www.marketingpower.com/_layouts/Dictionary.aspx, accessed December 2009.

3. For more on this "chaos scenario," see Bob Garfield, "The Chaos Scenario," *Advertising Age*, April 4, 2005, pp. 1, 57+; Garfield, "The

Chaos Scenario 2.0: The Post-Advertising Age," *Advertising Age*, March 26, 2007, pp. 1, 12–13; and Garfield, "Future May Be Brighter but It's Apocalypse Now," *Advertising Age*, March 23, 2009, pp. 1, 14.

4. Jack Neff, "'Passion for Digital' Pumps P&G's Spending," *Advertising Age*, June 8, 2009, accessed at http://adage.com/ print?article_id-137134.

5. TV advertising stats accessed at http://adage.com/datacenter/article?article_id=127791, accessed June 2009. Quotes from Mike Shaw, "Direct Your Advertising Dollars Away from TV at Your Own Risk," *Advertising Age*, February 27, 2006, p. 29; Bob Liodice, "TV Make Strides While Marketers Experiment Widely, *Advertising Age*, March 24, 2008, pp. 16–17; and Jack Neff, "Future of Advertising? Print, TV, Online Ads," *Advertising Age*, June 1, 2009, accessed at http://adage.com/datacenter/article?article_ id=136993.

6. Adam Armbruster, "TV Central in Mixology of Multimedia," *TelevisionWeek*, March 3–March 10, 2008, p. 30; Liodice, "TV Make Strides While Marketers Experiment Widely," pp. 16–17; and Ed Castillo, "The Song Remains the Same: Media Platforms Are Exploding, but Human Nature Stays Right Where It's Always Been," *Adweek*, February 16, 2009, p. AM5.

7. "Integrated Campaigns," Advertising Annual 2008, *Communication Arts*, pp. 72–73.

8. See Jonah Bloom, "Turn the Oscars from Boring Twaddle to a Marketing Tool," *Advertising Age*, March 2, 2009, p. 11; Scott Collins, "Take II: Super Bowl Was Most Watched," *Los Angeles Times*, February 4, 2009, p. D8; and Collins, "Viewers Just Weren't That Curious," *Los Angeles Times*, January 15, 2009, p. E13.

9. Garry Duncan, "Every Sales Call Requires an Objective and Decision," *Denver Business Journal*, October 13, 2006, http://denver.bizjournals.com/denver/stories/2006/10/16/smallb8.html.

10. Data on U.S. and global advertising spending obtained at "Leading National Advertisers," *Advertising Age*, June 22, 2009, pp. 12–13; and http://adage.com/datacenter/#top_marketers;_adspend_stats, accessed September 2009.

11. For these and other examples of comparative advertising, see Emily Bryson York, "The Gloves Are Off: More Marketers Opt for Attack Ads," *Advertising Age*, May 25, 2009, accessed at http://adage.com/article?article_id=136841; Bryon York, "Brand vs. Brand: Attack Ads on the Rise," *Advertising Age*, October 27, 2008, p. 1; Kenneth Hein, "Domino's Burns Subway," January 22, 2009, accessed at www.brandweek.com; "Pepsi Suing Coca-Cola Over Powerade Ads," *New York Times*, April 13, 2009, accessed at www.nyt.com.

12. For more on setting promotion budgets, see W. Ronald Lane, Karen Whitehill King, and J. Thomas Russell, *Kleppner's Advertising Procedure*, 17th ed. (Upper Saddle River, NJ: Prentice Hall, 2008), chapter 6.

13. Example adapted from Jean Halliday, "Thinking Big Takes Audi from Obscure to Awesome," *Advertising Age*, February 2, 2009, accessed at http://adage.com/print?article_id=134234. Also see Jack Neff, "Study: Cutting Spending Hurts Brands in Long-Term: Following Boom/Bust Cycle Flirts with Danger," *Advertising Age*, April 6, 2009, accessed at http://adage.com/print?article_id135790; and Joe Mandese, "Nielsen: U.S. Ad Spending Plummets $3.8 Billion," *MediaPost News*, June 8, 2009, accessed at www.mediapost.com.

14. For more discussion, see John Consoli, "Heavy Lifting," *MediaWeek*, March 3, 2008.

15. "Average U.S. Home Now Receives a Record 118.6 TV Channels," June 6, 2008, www.nielsenmedia.com; and "Number of Magazines by Category," accessed at www.magazine.org/editorial/editorial_trends_and_magazine_handbook/1145.cfm, August 2009.

16. Louise Story, "Anywhere the Eye Can See, It's Likely to See an Ad," *New York Times*, January 15, 2007, p. A12, accessed at www.nytimes.com; and Matthew Creamer, "Caught in the Clutter Crossfire: Your Brand," *Advertising Age*, April 1, 2007, pp. 1, 35.

17. See Brian Steinberg, "'Sunday Night Football' Beats 'Grey's Anatomy,'" *Advertising Age*, October 6, 2008, p. 10; Tim Arango, "Broadcast TV Faces Struggle to Stay Viable," *New York Times*, February 28, 2009, p. 1; and Louis Llovio, "Breaking Down the Super Bowl Ads," *McClatchy-Tribune Business News*, February 5, 2009.

18. Ken Krimstein, "Tips for the Ad World," *Forbes*, October 16, 2006, p. 34; and Bob Garfield, "The Chaos Scenario 2.0: The Post-Advertising Age," *Advertising Age*, March 26, 2007, pp. 1, 12–13.

19. Brain Steinberg, "Ad Skipping? Just Wait, It's Going to Get Worse," *Advertising Age*, August 11, 2008, p. 1; Daisy Whitney, "DVR,

Broadband Users Take Control," *Television Week*, October 29, 2007, p. 10; Steinberg, "Ad Nauseum: Repetition of TV Spots Risks Driving Consumers Away," *Advertising Age*, December 1, 2008, p. 1; Anthony Crupi, "Report: Ad Execs Stymied by DVR Ad Skipping," *Mediaweek*, June 29, 2009, accessed at www.mediaweek.com; and Steinberg, "Ad Skippers Beware: Ask.com Going After You with TV Crawl," *Advertising Age*, March 2, 2009, pp. 4–5.

20. See Steve McKee, Advertising: Less Is Much More," *BusinessWeek Online*, May 10, 2006, accessed at www.businessweek.com; Stuart Elliott, "Now, the Clicking Is to Watch the Ads, Not Skip Them," *New York Times*, August 17, 2007, accessed at www.nytimes.com; and Elliott, "Slow Those Fast-Forwarders, Study Says, with Emotion," *New York Times*, March 31, 2009, www.nytimes.com.

21. See Alessandra Stanley, "Commercials You Can't Zap," *New York Times*, June 7, 2009, p. MT1.

22. For more on product placements, see Randee Dawn and Alex Ben Block," Brands Take American Idol Stage," *Adweek*, May 12, 2009, accessed at www.adweek.com; Richard Huff, "Product Placement Outsells Ads," *Daily News*, December 27, 2007, p. 73; Ravi Somaiya, "'Chloe, It's Kac. Who Does Our Phones?" *Guardian*, June 16, 2008, accessed at www.guardian.com; Jeremy Mullman, "How 'Marley' Won Over Purina for Partnership," *Advertising Age*, December 18, 2009, accessed at http://adage.com/print? article_id=133394; and Stanley, "Commercials You Can't Zap," p. MT1.

23. For this and other examples, see Wendy Tanaka, "D.I.Y Ads," *Red Herring*, January 29, 2007, accessed at www.redherring.com/ Home/20955; Lee Gomes, "Tips from Web Greats on Becoming a Legend in Your Spare Time," *Wall Street Journal*, November 14, 2007, p. B1; and Brian Boyko, "Feature: The Diet Coke & Mentos Saga of the EepyBirds," March 18, 2009, accessed at http://www.geeksaresexy.net/2009/03/18/feature-the-diet-coke-mentos-saga-of-the-eepybirds/.

24. "MultiVu Video Feed: Doritos Reveals Final Five Consumer-Created Commercials Vying . . . ," *Reuters.com*, January 23, 2009, www.reuters.com/article/pressRelease/idUS169640+23-Jan-2009 +PRN20090123; www.crashthesuperbowl.com, accessed July 2009; and "*USA Today* 2009 Ad Meter: Best Super Bowl Commercials," accessed at www.usatoday.com/money/advertising/admeter/2009ad-meter.htm, July 2009.

25. See Tanaka, "D.I.Y Ads," accessed at www.redherring.com/Home/ 20955; Laura Petrecca, "Madison Avenue Wants You! (Or at Least Your Videos)," *USA Today*, June 21, 2007, p. 1B; and Michael Learmonth, "Brands Team Up for User-Generated-Ad Contests," *Advertising Age*, March 23, 2009, p. 8.

26. Allision Enright, "Let Them Decide," June 1, 2006, pp. 10–11; and "Who's in Control?" *Advertising Age*, January 28, 2008, p. C1.

27. Woods, "Dragging Unilever into the Digital Age," p. 38.

28. Betsy Cummings, "Marketers Size Up New Metric System," *Brandweek*, April 6, 2008, Accessed at www.brandweek.com; and Castillo, "The Song Remains the Same, p. AM5.

29. For these and other examples and quotes, see Chris Walsh, "Ads on Board," *Rocky Mountain News*, February 27, 2007; Story, "Anywhere the Eye Can See, It's Likely to See an Ad," p. A12; Adam Remson, "School Buses Latest Victim of Ad Creep," *Brandweek*, February 4, 2008, p. 4; and Adam Newman, "The Body Is Billboard: Your Ad Here," *New York Times*, February 18, 2009.

30. See Claudia Wallis, "The Multitasking Generation," *Time*, March 27, 2006, accessed at www.time.com; Tanya Irwin, "Study: Kids Are Master Multitaskers on TV, Web, Mobile," *MediaPost Publications*, March 10, 2008, accessed at www.mediapostpublications.com; and Jon Lafayette, "Integrated Campaigns Worth Overcoming Hurdles," April 29, 2009, accessed at www.tvweek.com.

31. *Newsweek* and *BusinessWeek* cost and circulation data accessed online at http://mediakit.businessweek.com and www.newsweek-mediakit.com, August 2009.

32. See "Pounds 10M Domino Effect Cheers Up Guinness," *Daily Record*, February 15, 2008; and www.youtube.com/watch?v=JinnnukLCbM; and Suzanne Vranica, "Payments Drag Out TV Spots," *Wall Street Journal*, February 23, 2008, p. B6.

33. See Stuart Elliott, "How Effective Is This Ad, in Real Numbers? Beats Me," *New York Times*, July 20, 2005, p. C8; Jack Neff, "Half Your Advertising Isn't Wasted,—Just 37.3 Percent," *Advertising Age*, August 7, 2006, pp. 1, 32; Ben Richards and Faris Yakob, "The New Quid pro Quo," *Adweek*, March 19, 2007, p. 17; Kate Maddox, "ROI Takes Center Stage at CMO Summit," *BtoB*, February 11, 2008, p. 3; and Elizabeth A. Sullivan, "Measure Up," *Marketing News*, May 30, 2009, p. 8.

34. David Tiltman, "Everything You Know Is Wrong," *Marketing*, June 13, 2008, pp. 28+.

35. Elliott, "How Effective Is This Ad, in Real Numbers? Beats Me," p. C8; and "Taking Measure of Which Metrics Matter," *BtoB*, May 5, 2008.

36. Information on advertising agency revenues from "Agency Report 2009," *Advertising Age*, accessed at http://adage.com/datacenter/ article?article_id=136094.

37. Adapted from Scott Cutlip, Allen Center, and Glen Broom, *Effective Public Relations*, 10th ed. (Upper Saddle River, NJ: Prentice Hall, 2009), chapter 1.

38. See Jeff Manning and Kevin Lane Keller, "Got Advertising That Works?" *Marketing Management*, January–February 2004, pp. 16–20; Alice Z. Cuneo, "Now Even Cellphones Have Milk Mustaches," *Advertising Age*, February 26, 2007, p. 8; "Got Milk? Campaign Searches for America's First-Ever 'Chief Health Officer,'" *Business Wire*, May 6, 2008; "Local Man to Tell Got Milk? Ads Story," *McClatchy-Tribune Business News*, May 7, 2009; and information from www.bodybymilk.com and www.whymilk.com, September 2009.

39. "Consumer Launch Campaign of the Year 2008," *PRWeek*, March 6, 2008, accessed at www.prweekus.com/Consumer-Launch-Campaign-of-the-Year-2008/article/100570.

40. See David Robinson. "Public Relations Comes of Age," *Business Horizons*, May–June 2006, pp. 247+; Noelle Weaver, "Why Advertising and PR Can't Be Separated," *Advertising Age*, May 14, 2007, accessed at www.adage.com; and Jennifer Jones, "PR, Marketing Must Blend Together," *PRWeek*, June 30, 2008, p. 8.

41. "Aveeno Case Study," accessed at www.ogilvypr.com/case-studies/ aveeno.cfm, October 2008; And see www.youtube.com/ watch?v=hfn8Dz_13Ms.

42. Ellen McGirt, "How Chris Hughes Helped Launch Facebook and the Barack Obama Campaign," *Fast Company*, March 17, 2009, www.fastcompany.com.

43. Paul Holmes, "Senior Marketers Are Sharply Divided about the Role of PR in the Overall Mix," *Advertising Age*, January 24, 2005, pp. C1–C2.

Chapter 13

1. All quotes and other information were taken from Volkswagen China (www.vw.com.cn); *Business Week* (www.businessweek.com); *China Daily* (www.chinadaily.com); *Chinese Car Times* (www .chinacartimes.com); *Motor Authority* (www.motorauthority.com); *Industry Week* (www.industryweek.com); and *European Business Forum* (www.ebfonline.com).

2. Adapted from information in Kim Wright Wiley, "For the Love of Sales," *Selling Power*, October 2008, pp. 70–73.

3. For more on "salesperson-owned loyalty," see Robert W. Palmatier, et al. "Customer Loyalty to Whom? Managing the Benefits and Risks of Salesperson-Owned Loyalty," *Journal of Marketing Research*, May 2007, pp. 185–199. Also see Norm Brodsky, "It Takes a Company," *Inc.*, August 2008, pp. 63–64.

4. This extract and strategies that follow are based on Philip Kotler, Neil Rackham, and Suj Krishnaswamy, "Ending the War Between Sales and Marketing," *Harvard Business Review*, July–August 2006, pp. 68–78. Also see Timothy Smith, Srinath Gopalakrishna, and Rabikar Chatterjee, "A Three-Stage Model of Integrated Marketing Communications at the Marketing-Sales Interface," *Journal of Marketing Research*, November 2006, pp. 564–579; and Christian Homburg, Ove Jensen, and Harley Krohmer, "Configurations of Marketing and Sales: A Taxonomy," *Journal of Marketing*, March 2008, pp. 133–154.

5. Example based on Ernest Waaser et al., "How You Slice It: Smarter Segmentation for Your Sales Force," *Harvard Business Review*, March 2004, pp. 105–111.

6. "Selling Power 500," accessed at www.sellingpower.com/sp500/ index.asp, October 2009.

7. For more on this and other methods for determining sales force size, see Mark W. Johnston and Greg W. Marshall, *Sales Force Management*, 9th ed. (Boston: McGraw-Hill Irwin, 2009), pp. 152–156.

8. Roy Chitwood, "Making the Most out of Each Outside Sales Call," February 4, 2005, accessed at http://seattle.bizjournals.com/ seattle/stories/2005/02/07/smallb3.html; and "The Cost of the Average Sales Call Today Is More Than $400," *Business Wire*, February 28, 2006.

9. Michael A. Brown, "You Make the Call," *Target Marketing*, October 2008, pp. 81–82.

10. See Martin Everett, "It's Jerry Hale on the Line," *Sales & Marketing Management*, December 1993, pp. 75–79. Also see Irene Cherkassky, "Target Marketing," *BtoB*, October 2006, pp. 22–24.

11. Jennifer J. Salopek, "Bye, Bye, Used Car Guy," *T+D*, April 2007, pp. 22–25; and William F. Kendy, "No More Lone Rangers," *Selling Power*, April 2004, pp. 70–74; Michelle Nichols, "Pull Together—Or Fall Apart," *BusinessWeek* Online, December 2, 2005, accessed at www.businessweek.com; Theodore Kinni, "The Team Solution," *Selling Power*, April 2007, pp. 27–29; and John Boe, "Cross-Selling Takes Teamwork," *American Salesman*, March 2009, pp. 14–16.

12. "Customer Business Development," accessed at www.pg.com/jobs/jobs_us/cac/f_cbd_home.shtml, June 2009.

13. For more information and discussion, see Benson Smith, *Discover Your Strengths: How the World's Greatest Salespeople Develop Winning Careers* (New York: Warner Business Books, 2003); Tom Reilly, "Planning for Success," *Industrial Distribution*, May 2007, p. 25; Dave Kahle, "The Four Characteristics of Successful Salespeople," *Industrial Distribution*, April 2008, p. 54; Wright Wiley, "For the Love of Sales," pp. 70–73; and www.gallup.com/consulting/1477/Sales-Force-Effectiveness.aspx, accessed October 2009.

14. "2008 Corporate Learning Factbook Values U.S. Training at $58.5B," *Business Wire*, January 29, 2008; and "ADP Case Study," Corporate Visions, Inc., www.corporatevisions.com/client_result.html, accessed August 2009.

15. Based on information found in Sara Donnelly, "Staying in the Game," *Pharmaceutical Executive*, May 2008, pp. 158–159; "Improving Sales Force Effectiveness: Bayer's Experiment with New Technology," Bayer Healthcare Pharmaceutical, 2008, www.icmrindia.org/casestudies/catalogue/Marketing/MKTG200.htm; and Tanya Lewis, "Concentric," *Medical Marketing and Media*, July 2008, p. 59.

16. Joseph Kornak, "'07 Compensation Survey: What's It All Worth?" *Sales & Marketing Management*, May 2007, pp. 28–39.

17. See Henry Canady, "How to Increase the Times Reps Spend Selling," *Selling Power*, March 2005, p. 112; David J. Cichelli, "Plugging Sales 'Time Leaks,'" *Sales & Marketing Management*, April 2006, p. 23; and Rebecca Aronauer, "Time Well Spent," *Sales & Marketing Management*, January–February 2007, p. 7.

18. See Gary H. Anthes, "Portal Powers GE Sales," *Computerworld*, June 2, 2003, pp. 31–32. Also see David J. Cichelli, "Plugging Sales 'Time Leaks,'" *Sales & Marketing Management*, April 2006, p. 23; Henry Canaday, "How to Boost Sales Productivity and Save Valuable Time," *Agency Sales*, November 2007, p. 20; and "According to IDC, One-Third of Potential Selling Time Is Wasted Due to Poor Sales Enhancement," *Business Wire*, November 13, 2008.

19. For extensive discussions of sales force automation, see the May 2005 issue of *Industrial Marketing Management*, which is devoted to the subject; Anupam Agarwal, "Bringing Science to Sales," *Customer Relationship Management*, March 2008, p. 16; and, Robert M. Barker, Stephen F. Gohmann, Jian Guan, and David J. Faulds, "Why Is My Sales Force Automation System Failing?" *Harvard Business Review*, May/June 2009, p. 233.

20. Adapted from information found in Pelin Wood Thorogood, "Sales 2.0: How Soon Will It Improve Your Business?" *Selling Power*, November/December 2008, pp. 58–61.

21. See "What Does Sales 2.0 Mean for You?" *Selling Power Sales Management Newsletter*, March 3, 2008; "Why Sales 2.0 Is Fundamentally Different from CRM," *Selling Power Sales Management Newsletter*, November 11, 2008; David Thompson, "Embracing the Future: A Step by Step Overview of Sales 2.0," *Sales and Marketing Management*, July/August 2008, p. 21; and Geoffrey James, "Sales Success through CRM," *Selling Power Source Book*, 2009, pp. 36–38.

22. Quotes from Bob Donath, "Delivering Value Starts with Proper Prospecting," *Marketing News*, November 10, 1997, p. 5; and Bill Brooks, "Power-Packed Prospecting Pointers," *Agency Sales*, March 2004, p. 37. Also see Maureen Hrehocik, "Why Prospecting Gets No Respect," *Sales & Marketing Management*, October 2007, p. 7; and "Referrals," *Partner's Report*, January 2009, p. 8.

23. Quotes in this paragraph from Lain Ehmann, "Prepare to Win," *Selling Power*, April 2008, pp. 27–29.

24. Adapted from Charlotte Huff, "EXTREME Makeover," *Workforce Management*, May 8, 2006, p. 1. Also see "iLevel Performance Home Educates Homebuyers on What to Look for in a Home's Structural Framing," *PR Newswire*, April 29, 2008; and www.ilevel.com, accessed November 2009.

25. Phil Sasso, "Listening in for More Sales," *Professional Distributor*, December 2007, pp. 18–19. Also see Gerhard Gschwandtner, "The Basics of Successful Selling," *Selling Power*, 25th anniversary issue, 2007, pp. 22–26; and Robert L. Bailey, "Story of Two Salespeople," *Rough Notes*, April 2008, p. 142.

26. "For B-to-B, Engagement, Retention Are Key," *Marketing News*, April 15, 2009, p. 9.

27. Adapted from Izabella Iizuka, "Not Your Father's Presentation," *Sales & Marketing Management*, March/April 2008, pp. 33–35.

28. *Shopper-Centric Trade: The Future of Trade Promotion* (Wilton, CT: Cannondale Associates, October 2007), p. 15.

29. Based on information and quotes from Richard H. Levey, "A Slip Between Cup and Lip," *Direct*, May 1, 2008, http://directmag.com/roi/0508-starbucks-loyalty-program/index.html; Ron Lieber, "The Card-Carrying Starbucks Fan," *New York Times*, June 7, 2008, p. C1; and Emily Bryson York, "Starbucks: Don't Be Seduced by Lower Prices," *Advertising Age*, April 30, 2009, accessed at http://adage.com/print?article_id=136389.

30. See "Consumers Turn to Coupons in Tough Economic Times," September 4, 2008, accessed at http://www.pmalink.org/press_releases/default.asp?p=pr_09042008; and "Renewed Consumer Interest Drives Fourth Quarter Surge in Coupon Use," www.couponinfonow.com, February 2009.

31. Quotes and other information from Alan J. Liddle, "Hardee's Connects with Mobile Device Users, Offer Discounts," *Nation's Restaurant News*, May 14, 2007, p. 16; Alice Z. Cuneo, "Package-Goods Giants Roll Out Mobile Coupons," *Advertising Age*, March 10, 2008, p. 3; Alex Palmer, "Cellular Savings," *Incentive*, April 2008, p. 69; and www.cellfire.com, October 2009.

32. See www.happymeal.com, accessed April 2009.

33. See "Promotion Products Fact Sheet," at Promotion Products Association International Web site, www.ppai.org, accessed April 2009.

34. Based on information found in "Dunkin' Donuts Returns to its Roots—Doughnuts—in $10 Million Campaign," *Promo*, March 18, 2009, accessed at http://promomagazine.com/contests/dunkin-donutscampaign/; "Time to Judge the Donuts," *PR Newswire*, May 18, 2009; and Steve Adams, "Dunkin Donuts Contest Finalists Cooked Their Unique Creations in Bake-Off," *Patriot Ledger*, May 29, 2009, accessed at www.patriotledger.com.

35. "Exclusive PQ Media Research: Branded Entertainment Defies Slowing Economy," February 12, 2008, accessed at www.pqmedia.com/about-press-20080212-bemf.html; "Direct Impact," *Promo*, October 1, 2008, http://promomagazine.com/1001-eventmarketing-impact/index.html; and Richard Tedesco, "2009 Promo Event Marketing Survey: Marketers Are Still Staging Events," *Promo*, January 1, 2009, http://promomagazine.com/eventmarketing/0109-marketers-staging-events/.

36. "Pepsi Porch Opens at New York Mets New Home," *Promo*, March 31, 2009, http://promomagazine.com/eventmarketing/news/pepsi-porch-opens-stadium-0331/index.html.

37. "Charmin Restrooms Offers Luxurious Relief to Millions in Times Square on New Year's Eve," *PR Newswire*, January 1, 2009.

38. *Shopper-Centric Trade: The Future of Trade Promotion*, p. 15.

39. See "CES 2009 Attendance Lower than Expected," January 13, 2009, accessed at http://news.softpedia.com; "Economy Does Not Worry Bauma Show Officials," *Roads & Bridges*, February 4, 2009, accessed at www.roadsbridges.com; and the Bauma Web site, www.bauma.de, October 2009.

Chapter 14

1. Quotes and other information from Heather Green, "How Amazon Aims to Keep You Clicking," *BusinessWeek*, March 2, 2009, pp. 34–40; Josh Quittner, "The Charmed Life of Amazon's Jeff Bezos," *CNNMoney.com*, April 15, 2008, accessed at www.cnnmoney.com; Joe Nocera, "Putting Buyers First? What a Concept," *New York Times*, January 5, 2008; Jena McGregor, "Bezos: How Frugality Drives Innovation," *BusinessWeek*, April 28, 2008, p. 64; Jeffrey M. O'Brien, "Amazon's Next Revolution," *Fortune*, June 8, 2009, p. 68; and annual reports and other information found at www.amazon.com, accessed September 2009.

2. For these and other direct marketing statistics in this section, see Direct Marketing Association, *The DMA 2009 Statistical Fact Book, 31th edition*, February 2009; and Direct Marketing Association, *The Power of Direct Marketing: 2008–2009 Edition*, June 2009; "Direct Marketing to Account for 53% of US Ad Spend in 2009," accessed at www.marketingcharts.com, November 24, 2008; and a wealth of other information accessed at www.the-dma.org, November 2009.

3. Roy Chitwood, "Making the Most Out of Each Outside Sales Call," February 4, 2005, accessed at http://seattle.bizjournals.com/seattle/stories/2005/02/07/smallb3.html; and "The Cost of the Average Sales Call Today Is More than $400," *Business Wire*, February 28, 2006.

4. Portions adapted from Mike Beirne, "A Wing—and a Ding," *Brandweek*, October 23, 2006, p. 22; and Jason Voight, "Southwest Keeps Fans from Straying," *Adweek*, August 20, 2007, accessed data at www.adweek.com. Other information from "Southwest Airlines Celebrates Anniversary of DING!" *PR Newswire*, February 28, 2008; Bob Garfield, "What's the Big Deal with Widgets?" *Advertising Age*, December 1, 2008, p. 1; www.blogsouthwest.com and "What Is DING!?" accessed at www.southwest.com/ding, December 2009.

5. Mike Freeman, "Data Company Helps Wal-Mart, Casinos, Airlines Analyze Data," *Knight Ridder Business Tribune News*, February 24, 2006, p. 1; and Eric Lai, "Teradata Creates Elite Club for Petabyte-Plus Data Warehouse Customers," *Computer World*, October 14, 2008, www.computerworld.com/action/article.do?command=viewArticleBasic&articleId=9117159.

6. Quotes from Scott Horstein, "Use Care with That Database," *Sales & Marketing Management*, May 2006, p. 22; with information from Travis E. Poling, "*BusinessWeek* Says USAA Is Best in Nation When It Comes to Customer Service," *Knight Ridder Tribune Business News*, April 9, 2007, p. 1; *Hoover's Company Records*, June 15, 2009, p. 40508 Karen Aho, "10 Companies That Treat You Right," *MSN Money*, June 10, 2009, accessed at http://articles.moneycentral.www.msn.com; and www.usaa.com, October 2009.

7. See DMA, *The Power of Direct Marketing*, June 2009; and "Integrated Marketing Media Mix Study: More Digital with the Stay Traditional," accessed at www.marketingcharts.com, June 2009.

8. Julie Liesse, "When Times Are Hard, Mail Works," *Advertising Age*, March 30, 2009, p. 14. For counterpoints, see Gavin O'Malley, "Direct-Mail Doomed, Long Live E-Mail," *MediaPost News*, May 20, 2009, accessed at www.mediapost.com.

9. Based on information from "JDA, HP, and Intel Team Up with Mahoney to Yield Outstanding Quantifiable Results," The Mahoney Company, www.mahoneyprint.com/caseStudies/jda.pdf; and Heather Fletcher, "PURLs of Wisdom," *Target Marketing*, January 2009, pp. 27–29.

10. Emily Bryson York, "This Isn't the Holiday Catalog You Remember," *Advertising Age*, October 29, 2007; and Jenny Kincaid Boone, "Catalogs Change Roles During Holiday Season," *Roanoke Times*, November 30, 2008, www.roanoke.com.

11. Ylan Q. Mui, "Paging Through the Holidays," *Washington Post*, December 1, 2007, p. D1.

12. See Karen E. Kleing, "Making It with Mail-Order," *BusinessWeek*, January 23, 2006, accessed at www.businessweek.com; Paul Wenske, "Retailers Join Movement to Curb the Cascade of Catalogs," *McClatchy-Tribune Business News*, December 5, 2007; and DMA, *The Power of Direct Marketing*, August 2009.

13. See "About Lillian Vernon," accessed at www.lillianvernon.com, September 2009.

14. DMA, *The Power of Direct Marketing*, August 2009.

15. "Off the Hook," *Marketing Management*, January–February 2008, p. 5; and www.donotcall.gov, accessed October 2009.

16. Ira Teinowitz, "'Do Not Call' Does Not Hurt Direct Marketing," *Advertising Age*, April 11, 2005, pp. 3, 95. See also Brendan B. Read, "Do Not Call, Five Years Later," *Customer Inter@ction Solutions*, October 2008, pp. 34–35.

17. Teinowitz, "'Do Not Call' Does Not Hurt Direct Marketing," p. 3.

18. See Jeffrey A. Fowler, "Peeved at Auto Warranty Calls, a Web Posse Strikes Back," *Wall Street Journal*, May 15, 2009, A1.

19. See Brian Steinberg, "Read This Now!; But Wait! There's More! The Infomercial King Explains," *Wall Street Journal*, March 9, 2005, p. 1; Natasha Singer, "Why Kids Have All the Acne," *New York Times*, October 18, 2007, p. G1; and "Guthy-Renker Celebrates Top Honors at Annual Awards Ceremony," *PR Newswire*, September 26, 2008.

20. Brian O'Keefe, "Secrets of the TV Pitchmen," *Fortune*, April 13, 2009, pp. 82–90; and Andrew Adam Newman, "Snuggie Rode Silly Ads to Stardom Over Rivals," *New York Times*, February 26, 2009.

21. Steve McClellan, "New Clients Embrace DRTV as Sales Soar," *Adweek*, August 25–September 1, 2008, p. 9; and Stephanie Clifford, "As Seen on TV (and Increasingly on Prime Time)," *New York Times*, January 26, 2009, p. B7.

22. "Analysis: Can DRTV Really Build Brands Better than Image Ads?" *Precision Marketing*, February 9, 2007, p. 11; McClellan, "New Clients Embrace DRTV as Sales Soar," p. 9; and O'Keefe, "Secrets of the TV Pitchmen," pp. 82–90.

23. Adapted from Allison Fass, "Extreme Makeover," *Forbes*, September 1, 2008, pp. 64–66. Also see Eric J. Savitz, "Writing on the Wall for HSN and John Malone," *Barron's*, May 25, 2009, p. 32.

24. Beth Snyder Bulik, "Redbox Rakes in Green in Tough Times," *Advertising Age*, February 23, 2009, p. 6; Jessica Mintz, "Redbox's Machines Take on Netflix's Red Envelopes," *USA Today*, June 22, 2009, accessed at www.usatoday.com/tech/news/2009-06-22-redbox_N.htm; and www.redbox.com, accessed August 2009.

25. "Interactive: Ad Age Names Finalists," *Advertising Age*, February 27, 1995, pp. 12–14.

26. Daniel B. Honigman, "On the Verge: Mobile Marketing Will Make Strides," *Marketing News*, January 15, 2008, pp. 18–21; "Nielsen Says Mobile Ads Growing, Consumers Respond," *Reuters*, March 5, 2008, accessed at www.reuters.com; "Mobile Search Ads to Grow 130% by 2013," *TechWeb*, February 25, 2009; and "Wireless Quick Facts," www.ctia.org, accessed July 2009.

27. Cyril Altmeyer, "Smartphones, Social Networks to Boost Mobile Advertising," *Reuters*, June 29, 2009, accessed at www.reuters.com.

28. Adapted from Michael Garry, "Going Mobile," *Supermarket News*, January 12, 2009, p. 65.

29. See Emily Burg, "Acceptance of Mobile Ads on the Rise," *MediaPost Publications*, March 16, 2007, accessed at http://publications.mediapost.com; Steve Miller and Mike Beirne, "The iPhone Effect," *Adweek.com*, April 28, 2008; and Altmeyer, "Smart Phones, Social Networks to Boost Mobile Advertising," June 29, 2009.

30. "Marketing News' Digital Handbook," *Marketing News*, April 3, 2009, pp. 9–18.

31. For these and other examples, see Karyn Strauss and Derek Gale, *Hotels*, March 2006, p. 22; Kate Calder, "Hot Topic Cranks Its Music Biz," *Kidscreen*, May 2007, p. 22; and "Official Disneyland Resort Podcasts," http://disneyland.disney.go.com/disneyland/en_US/podcast/index?name=PodcastListingPage, accessed December 2008.

32. Shahnaz Mahmud, "Survey: Viewers Crave TV Ad Fusion," *Adweek.com*, January 25, 2008; and Andrew Hampp, "Addressable Ads Are Here; Who's Ready?" *Advertising Age*, April 13, 2009, p. 9.

33. See Alice Z. Cuneo, "Nike Setting the Pace in Interactive-TV Race" *Advertising Age*, August 13, 2007, p. 3; and Alana Semuels, "Pizza at the Click of a TiVo Button," *Los Angeles Times*, November 18, 2008, p. C1.

34. For these and other statistics on Internet usage, see "Nielsen Online Reports Topline U.S. Data for February 2009," *Nielsen Online*, March 11, 2009, accessed www.nielsen-online.com/pr/pr_090311.pdf; "Global Index Chart," www.nielsen-online.com/press_fd.jsp?section=pr_netv&nav=3, accessed April 2009; and www.InternetWorldStats.com, accessed July 2009.

35. See Les Luchter, "Study: Internet 2nd Most Essential Medium, but #1 in Coolness," June 27, 2007, accessed at www.publications.mediapost.com; and Gail Schiller, "Ads More Wired, Survey Finds," *Reporter*, December 28, 2007, accessed at http://hollywoodreporter.com.

36. See "America's Top Ten Retail Businesses," accessed at www.internetretailer.com/top500/list.asp, April 2009.

37. See Tom Sullivan, "A Lot More Than Paper Clips," *Barron's*, April 16, 2007, pp. 23–25; and information from www.officedepot.com, September 2009.

38. See Shop.org, Forrester Research Inc., *The State of Retailing Online 2008*, accessed at www.forrester.com/SORO; and Rachel Metz, "Report: Online Retail Could Reach $156B in 2009," *Associated Press*, January 29, 2009, accessed at www.thestandard.com/news/2009/01/29/report-online-retail-could-reach-156b-2009.

39. "JupiterResearch Forecasts Online Retail Spending Will Reach $144 Billion in 2010, a CAGR of 12% from 2005," February 6, 2006, accessed at www.jupitermedia.com/corporate/releases/06.02.06-newjupresearch.html; and Kelly Mooney, "Most Manufacturing

40. Information for this example from Sarah Hepola, "A Divine Cut of Swine," *National Post* (Canada), July 14, 2008, p. AL4; Laura Giovanelli, "Silly Stuff for the Season," *McClatchy-Tribune Business News*, December 11, 2008; and www.gratefulpalate.com, accessed November 2009.

Brands Are Missing the Mark Online," *Advertising Age*, January 5, 2009, accessed at http://adage.com/print?article_id=133547.

41. Information for this example accessed at www.dell.com/html/us/segments/pub/premier/tutorial/users_guide.html, August 2009.

42. See "eBay Inc.," *Hoover's Company Records*, April 19, 2009, p. 56307; and facts from eBay annual reports and other information accessed at www.ebay.com, July 2009.

43. Beth Snyder Bulik, "Who Blogs?" *Advertising Age*, June 4, 2007, p. 20; Nigel Hollis, "Going Global? Better Think Local Instead," *Brandweek*, December 1, 2008 p. 14; and Jeff Vandam, "Blogs Find Favor as Buying Guides," *New York Times*, December 22, 2008, p. B3.

44. Jack Neff, "Owning the Concept of Value Online," *Advertising Age*, March 30, 2009, p. 22; and www.elevenmoms.com, accessed July 2009.

45. Adapted from information found in Brian Morrissey, "Brands Tap into Web Elite for Advertorial 2.0: Well-Connected Bloggers Are Creating Content on Behalf of Sponsors Thirsty for Buzz," *Adweek*, January 12, 2009, p. 9. Also see Josh Bernoff, "Be More Than an Ad, Get in the Conversation," *Marketing News*, March 15, 2009.

46. Michael Barbaro, "Wal-Mart Tastemakers Write Unfiltered Blog," *New York Times*, March 3, 2008, http://www.nytimes.com/2008/03/03/business/03walmart.html?hp; and Jack Neff, "Owning the Concept of Value Online," *Advertising Age*, March 30, 2009, p. 22.

47. See Michael Bush, "Starbucks Gets Web 2.0 Religion, But Can It Convert Nonbelievers?" *Advertising Age*, March 24, 2008, p. 1.

48. Carolyn Kepcher, "Bad Service? Point, Click, Complain," *New York Daily News*, May 12, 2008; and Kermit Pattison, "Does a New Website Hold the Secret to Great Customer Service?" *Fast Company*, April 2008, www.fastcompany.com/articles/2008/04/interview-muller.html.

49. "GE Corporate Website," *Communication Arts Interactive Annual*, 2008, pp. 134–135; and www.ge.com, accessed August 2009.

50. Adapted from Jena McGregor, "High-Tech Achiever: MINI USA," *Fast Company*, October 2004, p. 86, with information from www.miniusa.com, September 2009.

51. Jeffrey F. Rayport and Bernard J. Jaworski, *e-Commerce* (New York: McGraw-Hill, 2001), p. 116. Also see "Looks Are Everything," *Marketing Management*, March/April 2006, p. 7; Benjamin Palmer, "Rethinking the User Experience," *Adweek*, August 25–September 1, 2008, p. 10; and Elizabeth A. Sullivan, "Virtually Satisfied," *Marketing News*, October 15, 2008, p. 26.

52. Adapted from Brooks Barnes, "In Overhaul, Disney.com Seeks a Path to More Fun," *New York Times*, June 25, 2008.

53. Internet Advertising Bureau, *IAB Internet Advertising Revenue Report*, March 8, 2009, accessed at www.iab.net/insights_research/530422/adrevenuereport.

54. Abbey Klaassen, "Breathing New Life into Online Creative," *Advertising Age*, March 30, 2009, p. 6; and Karlene Lukovitz, "Intel Live-Chat Banner Ads Engage End Users," *MediaPost News*, April 2, 2009, accessed at www.mediapost.com.

55. Internet Advertising Bureau, *IAB Internet Advertising Revenue Report*, March 2009.

56. Adapted from information in Elaine Wong, "Coke, ConAgra, Kellogg Cozy Up with Search Buys," *Brandweek*, October 12, 2008, accessed at www.brandweek.com.

57. Leftheria Parpis, "Behind McD's Flashy New Spot: Mounted Musical Mouthpiece Makes a Splash on the Net," *Adweek*, March 10, 2009, accessed at www.adweek.com.

58. Adapted from information found in Jeff Gordon, "Good Cheer: OfficeMax's Viral Campaign Revels in Its Elfin Glory and Returns Happy Results," *Marketing News*, March 15, 2008, pp. 24–28; and Jon Fine, "Bargain-Rate Buzz," *BusinessWeek*, February 9, 2009, p. 65.

59. See Emily Steele, "Skittles Cozies Up to Social Media," *Wall Street Journal*, March 3, 2009, p. B4; and Laura McKay "Skittles: A Rainbow of Social Media Marketing," *Customer Relationship Management*, May 2009, p. 18.

60. Chaddus Bruce, "Big Biz Buddies Up to Gen Y," *Wired*, December 20, 2006, accessed at www.wired.com; and Brian Morrissey, "Kraft Gives Facebook Users Reason to Share," *Adweek*, December 30, 2008, accessed at www.adweek.com.

61. See Heather Fletcher, "DMA Forecasts Continued Growth in Internet, E-mail Marketing," *Target Marketing*, November 5, 2008, www.targetmarketingmag.com/article/dma-forecasts-continued-growth-internet-e-mail-marketing-400373_1.html; DMA, *The Power of Direct Marketing*, June 2009; and "Integrated Marketing Media Mix Study: More Digital with the Stay Traditional," accessed at www.marketingcharts.com, June 2009.

62. Symantec, *The State of Spam: A Monthly Report—June 2009*, accessed at www.symantec.com/business/theme.jsp?themeid=state_of_spam.

63. Jessica Tsai, "How Much Marketing Is Too Much?" *DestinationCRM.com*, October 1, 2008, www.destinationcrm.com/Articles/PrintArticle.aspx?ArticleID=50752; and "StubHub Increases Revenue Per E-mail by Over 2,500 Percent with Responsys Interact and Omniture Recommendations," February 18, 2009, www.responsys.com/company/press/2009_02_18.php.

64. William Hupp, "E-Mail," *Advertising Age*, March 17, 2008, p. 48; and Jessica Tsai, "Email: What's Inside?" *Customer Relationship Management*, January 2009, pp. 32–38.

65. See Internet Crime Complaint Center, "IC3 2008 Annual Report on Internet Crime Released," March 31, 2009, accessed at www.ic3.gov/media/2009/090331.aspx.

66. See "Phishing Attack Trends Report—Second Half 2008," www.antiphishing.org, March 17, 2009; and "Don't Take the Bait When Scam Artists Are Phishing for Your Personal Information," *US Fed News Service*, June 24, 2009.

67. See Greg Sterling, "Pew: Americans Increasingly Shop Online But Still Fear Identity Theft," *SearchEngineLand.com* accessed at http://searchengineland.com/pew-americans-increasingly-shop-online-but-still-fear-identity-theft-13366, February 14, 2008.

68. "Net Threats," *Consumer Reports*, September 2007, p. 28.

69. Emily Steel, "Web Privacy Efforts Targeted—Facing Rules, Ad Firms to Give, Consumers More Control," *Wall Street Journal*, June 26, 2009, B10; and Michael Learmonth, "Since Incoming Regulation, Online Ad Groups Unite," *Advertising Age*, January 13, 2009, accessed at http://adage.com/print?article_id=133730.

70. See Emmanuelle Bartoli, "Children's Data Protection vs Marketing Companies," *International Review of Law, Computers & Technology*, March 2009, p. 35; and Bruce Golding, "$1 Mil for Web Goof," *New York Post*, December 11, 2008, p. 18.

71. Information on TRUSTe accessed at www.truste.com, October 2009.

72. Information on the DMA Privacy Promise obtained at http://www.the-dma.org/cgi/dispissue?article=129, November 2009.

Chapter 15

1. Quotes and other information from Janet Adamy, "Steady Diet: As Burgers Boom in Russia, McDonald's Touts Discipline," *Wall Street Journal*, October 16, 2007, p. A1; Fern Glazer, "NPD: QSR Chains Expanding Globally Must Also Act Locally," *Nation's Restaurant News*, October 22, 2007, p. 18; "McDonald's Eyes Russia with 40 New Stores," *Reuters.com*, February 27, 2009; and information from www.mcdonalds.com/corp, accessed August 2009.

2. Data from Michael V. Copeland, "The Mighty Micro-Multinational," *Business 2.0*, July 28, 2006, accessed at http://cnnmoney.com; "List of Countries by GDP: List by the CIA World Factbook," *Wikipedia*, accessed at http://en.wikipedia.org/wiki/List_of_countries_by_GDP_(nominal); July 2009; and "Fortune 500," *Fortune*, May 4, 2009, pp. F1–F26.

3. "World Trade Volume Contracting," *Prospects for the Global Economy*, World Bank, March 31, 2009, accessed at www.worldbank.org; and "WTO Sees 9% Global Trade Decline in 2009 as Recession Strikes," *World Trade Organization*, March 23, 2009, accessed at www.wto.org.

4. Information from www.michelin.com/corporate, www.jnj.com, and www.caterpillar.com, October 2009.

5. Steve Hamm, "Borders Are So 20th Century," *BusinessWeek*, September 22, 2003, pp. 68–73; Otis Elevator Company," *Hoover's Company Records*, June 15, 2009, p. 56332; and www.otisworldwide.com, accessed August 2009.

6. Adapted from information in Frank Greve, "International Food Fight Could Spell End to Roquefort Dressing," *McClatchy-Tribune Business News*, April 9, 2009.

7. "'Buy American' Rule in Stimulus Bill Sparks Protest," *FoxNews.com*, January 30, 2009, www.foxnews.com/politics/2009/01/30/buy-american-rule-stimulus-sparks-protest/.

8. "What Is the WTO?" accessed at www.wto.org/english/thewto_e/whatis_e.htm, September 2009.

9. See *WTO Annual Report 2005*, accessed at www.wto.org, September 2007; and World Trade Organization, "10 Benefits of the WTO Trading System," accessed at www.wto.org/english/thewto_e/whatis_e/10ben_e/10b00_e.htm, September 2009.

10. "EU Officials Still Hope for Doha Meeting in May," *Journal of Commerce*, April 25, 2008; and Pascal Lamy, "Europe and Recovery: Now Is the Time to Conclude Doha," *Wall Street Journal* (Europe edition), February 11, 2009, p. 13.

11. "The EU at a Glance," accessed online at http://europa.eu/abc/index_en.htm, September 2009.

12. "Economic and Monetary Union (EMU)," accessed at http://europa.eu/abc/12lessons/lesson_7/index_en.htm, September 2009.

13. See David J. Bailey, "Misperceiving Matters: Elite Ideas and the Failure of the European Constitution," *Comparative European Politics*, April 2008, pp. 33+; Quentin Peel, "Blame Game in Full Stride for the Celtic Tiger Losing Its Stripes," *Financial Times*, April 22, 2009, p. 2; and CIA, *The World Factbook*, accessed June 2009 at https://www.cia.gov/library/publications/the-world-factbook.

14. Statistics and other information from CIA, *The World Factbook*, June 2009; "NAFTA Analysis 2007" and "North American FTA," Office of the United States Trade Representative, accessed at www.ustr.gov/Trade_Agreements/Regional/NAFTA/Section_Index.html, July 2009; and John Gallagher, "NAFTA Trade Slowed Last Year," *Journal of Commerce*, March 18, 2009.

15. See Angela Greiling Keane, "Counting on CAFTA," *Traffic World*, August 8, 2005, p. 1; "Integrating the Americas: FTAA and Beyond," *Journal of Common Market Studies*, June 2005, p. 430; Alan M. Field, "Spinning Its Wheels," *Journal of Commerce*, December 3, 2007; CIA, *The World Factbook*, June 2009; "Foreign Trade Statistics," accessed at June 2009 www.census.gov.

16. See CIA, *The World Factbook*, June 2009; and www.comunidadandina.org/ingles/who.htm, accessed May 2009.

17. Adapted from information found in Sonya Misquitta, "Cadbury Redefines Cheap Luxury—Marketing to India's Poor, Candy Makers Sells Small Bites for Pennies," *Wall Street Journal*, June 8, 2009, p. B4.

18. See "Venezuelan Financial Analyst Says Inflation Could Spark Political Instability," *BBC Worldwide Monitoring*, January 24, 2008; and "Venezuela," www.buyusa.gov, accessed May 2009.

19. "$9 Billion Barter Deal," *BarterNews.com*, April 19, 2008, accessed at www.barternews.com/9_billion_dollar_barter_deal.htm.

20. For these and other examples, see Emma Hall, "Do You Know Your Rites? BBDO Does," *Advertising Age*, May 21, 2007, p. 22; and Emily Bryson York and Rupal Parekh, "Burger King's MO: Offend, Earn Media, Apologize, Repeat," *Advertising Age*, July 8, 2009, accessed at http://adage.com/print?article_id=137801.

21. Jamie Bryan, "The Mintz Dynasty," *Fast Company*, April 2006, pp. 56–61; and Viji Sundaram, "Offensive Durga Display Dropped," *India-West*, February 2006, p. A1.

22. See Elizabeth Esfahani, "Thinking Locally, Succeeding Globally," *Business 2.0*, December 2005, pp. 96–98; Evan Ramstas, "LG Electronics' Net Surges 91 Percent as Cell Phone Margins Improve," *Wall Street Journal*, January 25, 2006, p. B2; and www.lge.com, November 2009.

23. Adapted from Mark Rice-Oxley, "In 2,000 Years, Will the World Remember Disney or Plato?" *Christian Science Monitor*, January 15, 2004, p. 16.

24. Thomas L. Friedman, *The Lexus and the Olive Tree: Understanding Globalization* (New York: Anchor Books, 2000).

25. "BrandZ Top 100 Most Valuable Global Brands 2009," Millward Brown Optimor, accessed at www.millwardbrown.com/Sites/Optimor/Content/KnowledgeCenter/BrandzRanking.aspx.

26. Eric Ellis, "Iran's Cola War," *Fortune*, March 5, 2007, pp. 35–38; and "Iran Pressures Firm Over Coca-Cola Links," January 19, 2009, *World News Network*, accessed at http://article.wn.com/view/2009/02/15/Iran_pressures_firm_over_CocaCola_links/.

27. Betsy McKay, "Coke Bets on Russia for Sales Even as Economy Falls Flat," *Wall Street Journal*, January 28, 2009, p. A1.

28. For more discussion of questions to ask before going global, see Marcus Alexander and Harry Korine, "When You Shouldn't Go Global," *Harvard Business Review*, December 2008, pp. 70–74.

29. See Noreen O'Leary, "Bright Lights, Big Challenge," *Adweek*, January 15, 2007, pp. 22–28; Dexter Roberts, "Scrambling to Bring Crest to the Masses," *BusinessWeek*, June 25, 2007, p. 72; and

Jonathan Birchall, P&G Set to Expand in Emerging Markets," *Financial Times*, December 12, 2008, p. 22.

30. "Hilton Signs Management Contract for New Hotel in Pattaya, Thailand," April 4, 2008, accessed at www.asiatraveltips.com/news08/44-HotelinPattaya.shtml.

31. Adapted from information found in the Vicky McCrorie, "Hershey: Hoping to Taste Success in India," *Food Business Review*, April 2007, accessed at www.food-business-review.com; Jennifer Fishbein, "Chocolatiers Look to Asia for Growth," *BusinessWeek*, January 18, 2008, accessed at www.businessweek.com; and "Research and Markets: In 2007, Hershey Entered into a Joint Venture Agreement with Godrej Beverages and Foods," *M2 Presswire*, July 31, 2008.

32. Bruce Einhorn and Nandini Lakshman, "PC Makers Are Racing to India," *BusinessWeek*, October 1, 2007, p. 48; and "HP in Aggressive Move to Expand Market Presence in India," www.Digi-Help.com, June 9, 2008.

33. Quotes from Andrew McMains, "To Compete Globally, Brands Must Adapt," *Adweek*, September 25, 2008, accessed at www.adweek.com; Pankaj Ghemawat, "Regional Strategies for Global Leadership," *Harvard Business Review*, December 2005, pp. 97–108; and Eric Pfanner, "The Myth of the Global Brand," *International Herald Tribune*, January 11, 2009.

34. Warren J. Keegan, *Global Marketing Management*, 7th ed. (Upper Saddle River, NJ: Prentice Hall, 2002), pp. 346–351. Also see Phillip Kotler and Kevin Lane Keller, *Marketing Management*, 13th ed. (Upper Saddle River, NJ: 2009), pp. 596–615.

35. Adapted from Jack Ewing, "First Mover in Mobile: How It's Selling Cell Phones to the Developing World," *BusinessWeek*, May 14, 2007, p. 60.

36. See Douglas McGray, "Translating Sony into English," *Fast Company*, January 2003, p. 38; Tim Jackson, "Micro Computer by Sony Offers 'Bond' Appeal," *Record* (Ontario), July 7, 2007, p. W5; and http://b2b.sony.com/Solutions/subcategory/notebooks/ux-series, accessed June 2009.

37. See McMains, "To Compete Globally, Brands Must Adapt," September 25, 2008.

38. Adapted from Gordon Fairclough and Janet Adamy, "Sex, Skin, Fireworks, Licked Fingers—It's a Quarter Pounder Ad in China," *Wall Street Journal*, September 21, 2006, p. B1.

39. Kate MacArthur, "Coca-Cola Light Employs Local Edge," *Advertising Age*, August 21, 2000, pp. 18–19; "Case Studies: Coke Light Hottest Guy," *Advantage Marketing*, msn India, accessed at http://in.msn.com/, March 15, 2004; and www.youtube.com/watch?v=Tu5dku6YkHA, accessed November 2008.

40. See Alicia Clegg, "One Ad One World?" *Marketing Week*, June 20, 2002, pp. 51–52; Ira Teinowitz, "International Advertising Code Revised," *Advertising Age*, January 23, 2006, p. 3; George E. Belch and Michael A. Belch, *Advertising and Promotion: An Integrated Marketing Communications Perspective*, 7th ed. (New York: McGraw Hill, 2007), chapter 20; and Shintero Okazaki and Charles R. Taylor, "What Is SMS Advertising and Why Do Multinationals Adopt it?" *Journal of Business Research*, January 2008, pp. 4–12.

41. Bill Addison, "Nail Dumping Tariffs Approved," *Home Channel News*, February 11, 2008, pp. 4–5.

42. Adapted from Jack Ewing, "First Mover in Mobile: How It's Selling Cell Phones to the Developing World," *BusinessWeek*, May 14, 2007, p. 60; with information from Anshul Gupta, "Mobile Handsets: Handset Growth to Be Flat in 2009," March 9, 2009, accessed at www.expresscomputeronline.com/20090309/2009anniversary14.shtml.

43. See Leslie Chang, Chad Terhune, and Betsy McKay, "A Global Journal Report; Rural Thing—Coke's Big Gamble in Asia," *Wall Street Journal*, August 11, 2004, p. A1; and "Coca-Cola Rolls Out New Distribution Model with ZAP," www.zapworld.com/zap-coca-cola-truck, January 23, 2008. For some interesting photos of Coca-Cola distribution methods in third-world and emerging markets, see www.flickr.com/photos/73509998@N00/sets/72157594299144032/, accessed November 2009.

Chapter 16

1. All quotes and other information were taken from CSR Middle East (www.csrmiddleeast.org); CSR Summit www.thecsrsummit.com); Business and Human Rights Resource Centre (www.businesshumanrights.org); World Economic Forum (www.weforum.org); Mohammed Alshaya Group (www.alshaya.com); His Highness Sheikh Mohammed Bin Rashid Al Maktoum (www.sheikhmohammed.co.ae); Coca-Cola (www.coca-cola.com);

Aramex (www.aramex.com); and Taqa, the Abu Dhabi National Energy Company (www.taqa.ae).

2. For lots of information on SUV safety and environmental performance, see www.citizen.org/autosafety/suvsafety, accessed September 2009.

3. The figure and the discussion in this section are adapted from Philip Kotler, Gary Armstrong, Veronica Wong, and John Saunders, *Principles of Marketing: European Edition*, 5th ed. (London: Pearson Publishing, 2009), Chapter 2.

4. McDonald's financial information and other facts from www.mcdonalds.com/corp/invest.html and www.mcdonalds.com/corp/about/factsheets.html, accessed September 2009. Also see "Dow Jones Sustainability United States 40 Index," May 2009, accessed at www.sustainability-index.com/07_htmle/publications/factsheets.html.

5. Heather Green, "How Green Is That Gizmo?" *BusinessWeek*, December 31, 2007, p. 36; Tom Wright, "False 'Green' Ads Draw Global Scrutiny," *Wall Street Journal*, January 30, 2008, p. B4; Benjamin Heath, "FTC Updating Green Guides," *www.GlobalClimateLaw.com*, April 7, 2009, www.globalclimatelaw.com/2009/04/articles/environmental/ftc-updating-green-guides-which-govern-environmental-building-claims; and http://sinsofgreenwashing.org, and www.terrachoice.com accessed September 2009.

6. Theodore Levitt, "The Morality (?) of Advertising," *Harvard Business Review*, July–August 1970, pp. 84–92. For counterpoints, see Heckman, "Don't Shoot the Messenger," *Marketing News*, May 24, 1999, pp. 1, 9; and Marc Fetscherin and Mark Toncar, "Visual Puffery in Advertising," *International Journal of Market Research*, Vol. 51, Iss. 2, 2009, pp. 147–148.

7. Jennifer Levitz, "Hi, My Name Is Fred, and I'm Addicted to Credit Cards," *Wall Street Journal*, June 10, 2008, p. A1; and M.J. Stephey, "A Brief History of Credit Cards," *Time*, May 4, 2009, p. 16. For a wealth of credit card statistics see Ben Woolsey and Matt Schulz "Credit Card Statistics, Industry Facts, Debt Statistics," accessed at www.creditcards.com/credit-card-news/credit-card-industry-facts-personal-debt-statistics-1276.php, September 2009.

8. See "Overweight and Obesity," Centers for Disease Control and Prevention, www.cdc.gov/nccdphp/dnpa/obesity/trend/index.htm, accessed July 2009.

9. See Gerri Hirshey, "Time to Buy a New Stove. Again." *New York Times*, December 14, 2008, p. LI 4.

10. Adapted from David Suzuki, "We All Pay for Technology," *Niagara Falls Review*, March 15, 2007, p. A4. For more discussion, see Joseph Guiltinan, "Creative Destruction and Destructive Creations: Environmental Ethics and Planned Obsolescence," *Journal of Business Ethics*, May 2009, pp. 19–28.

11. Harry Alford, "Subprime Scandal—The Largest Hate Crime in History," *New York Beacon*, April 3–9, 2008, p. 12; Edward R. Culvert, "Sub-Prime Loans Should Be Treated as Bias Crimes," *Culvert Chronicles*, March 13–19, 2008, p. 1;" Kenneth R. Harney, "Lawsuit Paints Loan Crisis in Black, White, and Brown," *Washington Post*, November 29, 2008, p. F01; and "NAACP Files Landmark Lawsuit Today Against Wells Fargo and HSBC," March 13, 2009, www.naacp.org/news/press/2009-03-13/index.htm.

12. Adapted from information found in John A. Quelch, "Selling Out the American Dream," *Harvard Business School Working Knowledge*, November 6, 2008, accessed at http://hbswk.hbs.edu/item/6071.html; Leonard Stern, "Aspiration Gap Behind Downward Cycle in U.S.," *Calgary Herald* (Canada), November 9, 2008, p. A11; and Keilo Morris, "Brief: OSHA Cites Wal-Mart in Trampling Death," *McClatchy-Tribune Business News*, May 26, 2009.

13. The quote is from Oliver James, "It's More Than Enough to Make You Sick," *Marketing*, January 23, 2008, pp. 26–28. Portions of the Reverend Billy example adapted from Constance L. Hays, "Preaching to Save Shoppers from 'Evil' of Consumerism," *New York Times*, January 1, 2003, p. C1; and "A Preacher's Plea to Stop the 'Shopocalypse,'" *Knight Ridder Tribune Business News*, December 11, 2006. Also see Trevor Butterworth, "'Stop, Stop Shopping' The Reverend Billy Is No Ordinary Evangelical Preacher," *Financial Times*, December 1, 2007, p. 2; and www.revbilly.com, accessed May 2009.

14. "Consumerism: New Era of Frugality Dawns," *Marketing Week*, December 18, 2008, p. 12; and "The American Dream Has Been Revised Not Reversed," *Business Wire*, March 9, 2009.

15. See "Traffic Congestion and Urban Mobility," Texas Transportation Institute, accessed at http://tti.tamu.edu/infofor/media/topics/congestion_mobility.htm, acc July 2009.

16. See www.tfl.gov.uk/roadusers/congestioncharging/6710.aspx, accessed September 2009.

17. See John D. McKinnon, "Politics & Economics: Bush Plays Traffic Cop in Budget Request," *Wall Street Journal*, February 5, 2007, p. A6; Rich Saskal, "Washington: First HOT Lane Opens Up," *Bond Buyer*, May 9, 2008, p. 9; and Robbie Whelan, "$200M Hole in Transportation Budget Could be Filled with 'Congestion Pricing'," *Daily Record* (Baltimore), March 31, 2009.

18. See Allison Linn, "Ads Inundate Public Places," *MSNBC.com*, January 22, 2007; and Bob Garfield, "The Chaos Scenario 2.0: The Post-Advertising Age," *Advertising Age*, March 26, 2007, pp. 1, 12–13.

19. See Martin Sipkoff, "Four-Dollar Pricing Considered Boom or Bust," *Drug Topics*, August 2008, p. 4S; and Sarah Bruyn Jones, "Economic Survival Guide: Drug Discounts Common Now," *McClatchy-Tribune Business News*, February 23, 2009.

20. For these and other examples, see "Strong Growth in Green Logistics," *World Trade*, December 28, 2008, p. 13; Mark Borden, et al., "50 Ways to Green Your Business," *Fast Company*, November 2007; and Jack Neff, "Green-Marketing Revolution Defies Economic Downturn," *Advertising Age*, April 20, 2009, accessed at http://adage.com/print?article_id=136091.

21. The Subaru example is based on information from Alan S. Brown, "The Many Shades of Green," *Mechanical Engineering*, January 2009, p. 22.

22. See Brown, "The Many Shades of Green," p. 22.

23. Based on information from Marc Gunther, "Coca-Cola's Green Crusader," *Fortune*, April 28, 2008, p. 150; "Cold Test Markets Aluminum Bottles," February 20, 2008, accessed at www.bevnet.com/news/2008/02-20-2008-Coke.asp; Jessie Scanlon, "The Shape of a New Coke," *BusinessWeek*, September 2008, p. 72; and "Coca-Cola to Install 1800 CO2 Coolers in North America," April 30, 2009, accessed at www.r744.com/articles/2009-04-30-coca-cola-to-install-1800-co2-coolers-in-north-america.php.

24. Adapted from "The Top 3 in 2005," *Global 100*, accessed at www.global100.org, July 2005. See also "Alcoa Again Named One of the World's Most Sustainable Companies at Davos," January 29, 2009, accessed at www.alcoa.com; and information from www.global100.org, August 2009. For further information on Alcoa's sustainability program, see Alcoa's Sustainability Report, found at www.alcoa.com.

25. See Geoffrey Garver and Aranka Podhora, "Transboundary Environmental Impact Assessment as Part of the North American Agreement on Environmental Cooperation," *Impact Assessment & Project Appraisal*, December 2008, p. 253–263; http://ec.europa.eu/environment/index_en.htm, accessed May 2009; and "What is EMAS?" accessed at http://ec.europa.eu/environment/emas/index_en.htm, October 2009.

26. Based on information found in Chuck Salter, "Fast 50: The World's Most Innovative Companies," *Fast Company*, March 2008, pp. 73+. Also see Yukari Iwatani Kane and Daisuke Wakabayashi, "Nintendo Looks Outside the Box," *Wall Street Journal*, May 27, 2009, p. B5.

27. See Laurel Wentz, "'Evolution' Win Marks Dawn of New Cannes Era," *Advertising Age*, June 25, 2007, p. 1; Theresa Howard, "Ad Campaign Tells Women to Celebrate How They Are," *USA Today*, August 7, 2005, accessed at www.usatoday.com; "Cause: Conscience Marketing. You Stand for Something. Shouldn't Your Brand?" *Strategy*, June 2007, p. 22; and information found at www.campaignforrealbeauty.com, September 2009. For a thorough case study on the brand, see Jennifer Millard, "Performed Beauty: Dove's 'Real Beauty' Campaign" *Symbolic Interaction*, Spring 2009, pp. 146–168.

28. Information from Mike Hoffman, "Ben Cohen: Ben & Jerry's Homemade, Established in 1978," *Inc.*, April 30, 2001, p. 68; and the Ben & Jerry's Web site at www.benjerrys.com, October 2009.

29. Adapted from Chip Giller and David Roberts, "Resources: The Revolution Begins," *Fast Company*, March 2006, pp. 73–78. Also see Joseph Ogando, "Green Engineering," *Design News*, January 9, 2006, p. 65; and information accessed online at www.haworth.com, October 2009.

30. Adapted from material found in Jeff Heilman, "Rules of Engagement," *The Magazine of Branded Engagement*, Winter 2009, pp. 7–8.

31. See The World Bank, "The Costs of Corruption," April 8, 2004, accessed at www.worldbank.org; Joseph A. McKinney and Carlos W. Moore, "International Bribery: Does a Written Code of Ethics Make a Difference in Perceptions of Business Professionals," *Journal of Business Ethics*, April 2008, pp. 103–111; and *Global Corruption Report 2009*, Transparency International, accessed at www.transparency.org/publications/gcr/download_gcr#download.

32. John F. McGee and P. Tanganath Nayak, "Leaders' Perspectives on Business Ethics," Prizm, first quarter, 1994, pp. 71–72. Also see Adrian Henriques, "Good Decision—Bad Business?" *International Journal of Management & Decision Making*, 2005, p. 273; and Marylyn Carrigan, Svetla Marinova, and Isabelle Szmigin, "Ethics and International Marketing: Research Background and Challenges," *International Marketing Review*, 2005, pp. 481–494.

33. See Samuel A. DiPiazza, "Ethics in Action," *Executive Excellence*, January 2002, pp. 15–16; Samuel A. DiPiazza, Jr., "It's All Down to Personal Values," accessed online at www.pwcglobal.com, August 2003; and "Code of Conduct: The Way We Do Business," accessed at www.pwc.com/ethics, December 2009.

34. DiPiazza, "Ethics in Action," p. 15.

Appendix 2

1. This is derived by rearranging the following equation and solving for price: Percentage markup = (price − cost) ÷ price.
2. Again, using the basic profit equation, we set profit equal to ROI × I: ROI × I = (P × Q) − TFC − (Q × UVC). Solving for Q gives Q = (TFC + (ROI × I)) ÷ (P − UVC).

3. U.S. Census Bureau, available at http://www.census.gov/prod/1/pop/p25-1129.pdf accessed October 26, 2009.
4. "Broadband Internet to Reach 77 Percent of Households by 2012," available at www.tmcnet.com/voip/ip-communications/articles/35393-gartner-broadband-internet-reach-77-percent-households-2012.htm, accessed August 25, 2008.
5. See Roger J. Best, *Market-Based Management*, 4th ed. (Upper Saddle River, NJ: Prentice Hall, 2005).
6. Total contribution can also be determined from the unit contribution and unit volume: Total contribution = unit contribution × unit sales. Total units sold were 297,619 units, which can be determined by dividing total sales by price per unit ($100 million ÷ $336). Total contribution = $70 contribution per unit × 297,619 units = $20,833,330 (difference due to rounding).
7. Recall that the contribution margin of 21% was based on variable costs representing 79% of sales. Therefore, if we do not know price, we can set it equal to $1.00. If price equals $1.00, 79 cents represents variable costs and 21 cents represents unit contribution. If price is decreased by 10%, the new price is $0.90. However, variable costs do not change just because price decreased, so the unit contribution and contribution margin decrease as follows:

	Old	New (reduced 10%)
Price	$1.00	$0.90
− Unit variable cost	$0.79	$0.79
= Unit contribution	$0.21	$0.11
Contribution margin	$0.21/$1.00 = 0.21 or 21%	$0.11/$0.90 = 0.12 or 12%

Glossary

Action programs Action programs should be coordinated with the resources and activities of other departments, including production, finance, and purchasing.

Adapted global marketing An international marketing strategy for adjusting the marketing strategy and mix elements to each international target market, bearing more costs but hoping for a larger market share and return.

Administered VMS A vertical marketing system that coordinates successive stages of production and distribution, not through common ownership or contractual ties, but through the size and power of one of the parties.

Adoption process The mental process through which an individual passes from first hearing about an innovation to final adoption.

Advertising Any paid form of nonpersonal presentation and promotion of ideas, goods, or services by an identified sponsor.

Advertising agency A marketing services firm that assists companies in planning, preparing, implementing, and evaluating all or portions of their advertising programs.

Advertising budget The dollars and other resources allocated to a product or company advertising program.

Advertising media The vehicles through which advertising messages are delivered to their intended audiences.

Advertising objective A specific communication task to be accomplished with a specific target audience during a specific period of time. The overall advertising goal is to help build customer relationships by communicating customer value.

Advertising strategy The strategy by which the company accomplishes its advertising objectives. It consists of two major elements: creating advertising messages and selecting advertising media.

Affordable method Setting the promotion budget at the level management thinks the company can afford.

Age and life-cycle segmentation Dividing a market into different age and life-cycle groups.

Agent A wholesaler who represents buyers or sellers on a relatively permanent basis, performs only a few functions, and does not take title to goods.

Allowance Promotional money paid by manufacturers to retailers in return for an agreement to feature the manufacturer's products in some way.

Approach The step in the selling process in which the salesperson meets the customer for the first time.

Attitude A person's consistently favorable or unfavorable evaluations, feelings, and tendencies toward an object or idea.

Baby boomers The 78 million people born during the baby boom following World War II and lasting until 1964.

Behavioral segmentation Dividing a market into segments based on consumer knowledge, attitudes, uses, or responses to a product.

Belief A descriptive thought that a person holds about something.

Benefit segmentation Dividing the market into segments according to the different benefits that consumers seek from the product.

Benefits and product features Table A1.1 clarifies the benefits that product features will deliver to satisfy the needs of customers in each targeted segment.

Blogs Online journals where people post their thoughts, usually on a narrowly defined topic.

Brand A name, term, sign, symbol, design, or a combination of these that identifies the products or services of one seller or group of sellers and differentiates them from those of competitors.

Brand equity The differential effect that knowing the brand name has on customer response to the product or its marketing.

Brand extension Extending an existing brand name to new product categories.

Break-even analysis Analysis to determine the unit volume and dollar sales needed to be profitable given a particular price and cost structure.

Break-even price The price at which total revenue equals total cost and profit is zero.

Break-even pricing (target return pricing) Setting price to break even on the costs of making and marketing a product, or setting price to make a target return.

Broker A wholesaler who does not take title to goods and whose function is to bring buyers and sellers together and assist in negotiation.

Budgets Managers use budgets to project profitability and plan for each marketing program's expenditures, scheduling, and operations.

Business analysis A review of the sales, costs, and profit projections for a new product to find out whether these factors satisfy the company's objectives.

Business buyer behavior The buying behavior of the organizations that buy goods and services for use in the production of other products and services or to resell or rent them to others at a profit.

Business portfolio The collection of businesses and products that make up the company.

Business promotions Sales promotion tools used to generate business leads, stimulate purchases, reward customers, and motivate salespeople.

Business-to-business (B2B) online marketing Businesses using B2B Web sites, e-mail, online catalogs, online trading networks, and other online resources to reach new business customers, serve current customers more effectively, and obtain buying efficiencies and better prices.

Business-to-consumer (B2C) online marketing Businesses selling goods and services online to final consumers.

Buying center All the individuals and units that play a role in the purchase decision-making process.

By-product pricing Setting a price for by-products in order to make the main product's price more competitive.

Cannibalization The situation in which one product sold by a company takes a portion of its sales from other company products.

Captive-product pricing Setting a price for products that must be used along with a main product, such as blades for a razor and games for a videogame console.

Catalog marketing Direct marketing through print, video, or digital catalogs that are mailed to select customers, made available in stores, or presented online.

Category killer A giant specialty store that carries a very deep assortment of a particular line and is staffed by knowledgeable employees.

Causal research Marketing research to test hypotheses about cause-and-effect relationships.

Chain ratio method Estimating market demand by multiplying a base number by a chain of adjusting percentages.

Chain stores Two or more outlets that are commonly owned and controlled.

Channel conflict Disagreement among marketing channel members on goals, roles, and rewards—who should do what and for what rewards.

Channel level A layer of intermediaries that performs some work in bringing the product and its ownership closer to the final buyer.

Channels and logistics review In this section, marketers list the most important channels, provide an overview of each channel arrangement, and identify developing issues in channels and logistics.

Click-and-mortar companies Traditional brick-and-mortar companies that have added online marketing to their operations.

Click-only companies The so-called dot-coms, which operate only online without any brick-and-mortar market presence.

Closing The step in the selling process in which the salesperson asks the customer for an order.

Co-branding The practice of using the established brand names of two different companies on the same product.

Cognitive dissonance Buyer discomfort caused by postpurchase conflict.

Commercial online databases Computerized collections of information available from online commercial sources or via the Internet.

Commercialization Introducing a new product into the market.

Communication adaptation A global communication strategy of fully adapting advertising messages to local markets.

Competition-based pricing Setting prices based on competitors' strategies, prices, costs, and market offerings.

Competitive advantage An advantage over competitors gained by offering greater customer value, either through lower prices or by providing more benefits that justify higher prices.

Competitive marketing intelligence The systematic collection and analysis of publicly available information about consumers, competitors, and developments in the marketing environment.

Competitive review The purpose of a competitive review is to identify key competitors, describe their market positions, and briefly discuss their strategies.

Competitive-parity method Setting the promotion budget to match competitors' outlays.

Concentrated (niche) marketing A market-coverage strategy in which a firm goes after a large share of one or a few segments or niches.

Concept testing Testing new-product concepts with a group of target consumers to find out if the concepts have strong consumer appeal.

Consumer buyer behavior The buying behavior of final consumers—individuals and households that buy goods and services for personal consumption.

Consumer market All the individuals and households that buy or acquire goods and services for personal consumption.

Consumer product A product bought by final consumer for personal consumption.

Consumer promotions Sales promotion tools used to boost short-term customer buying and involvement or to enhance long-term customer relationships.

Consumer-generated marketing Brand exchanges created by consumers themselves—both invited and uninvited—by which consumers are playing an increasing role in shaping their own brand experiences and those of other consumers.

Consumer-oriented marketing The philosophy of sustainable marketing that holds that the company should view and organize its marketing activities from the consumer's point of view.

Consumer-to-business (C2B) online marketing Online exchanges in which consumers search out sellers, learn about their offers, and initiate purchases, sometimes even driving transaction terms.

Consumer-to-consumer (C2C) online marketing Online exchanges of goods and information between final consumers.

Consumerism An organized movement of citizens and government agencies to improve the rights and power of buyers in relation to sellers.

Contract manufacturing A joint venture in which a company contracts with manufacturers in a foreign market to produce the product or provide its service.

Contractual VMS A vertical marketing system in which independent firms at different levels of production and distribution join together through contracts to obtain more economies or sales impact than they could achieve alone.

Contribution margin The unit contribution divided by the selling price.

Controls Controls help management assess results after the plan is implemented, identify any problems or performance variations, and initiate corrective action.

Convenience product A consumer product that customers usually buy frequently, immediately, and with a minimum of comparison and buying effort.

Convenience store A small store, located near a residential area, that is open long hours seven days a week and carries a limited line of high-turnover convenience goods.

Conventional distribution channel A channel consisting of one or more independent producers, wholesalers, and retailers, each a separate business seeking to maximize its own profits, even at the expense of profits for the system as a whole.

Corporate (or brand) Web site A Web site designed to build customer goodwill, collect customer feedback, and supplement other sales channels, rather than to sell the company's products directly.

Corporate VMS A vertical marketing system that combines successive stages of production and distribution under single ownership—channel leadership is established through common ownership.

Cost-based pricing Setting prices based on the costs for producing, distributing, and selling the product plus a fair rate of return for effort and risk.

Cost-plus pricing (or markup pricing) Adding a standard markup to the cost of the product.

Creative concept The compelling "big idea" that will bring the advertising message strategy to life in a distinctive and memorable way.

Cultural environment Institutions and other forces that affect society's basic values, perceptions, preferences, and behaviors.

Culture The set of basic values, perceptions, wants, and behaviors learned by a member of society from family and other important institutions.

Current marketing situation In this section, marketing managers discuss the overall market, identify the market segments they will target, and provide information about the company's current situation.

Customer database An organized collection of comprehensive data about individual customers or prospects, including geographic, demographic, psychographic, and behavioral data.

Customer equity The total combined customer lifetime values of all of the company's customers.

Customer insights Fresh understandings of customers and the marketplace derived from marketing information that become the basis for creating customer value and relationships.

Customer lifetime value The value of the entire stream of purchases that the customer would make over a lifetime of patronage.

Customer relationship management The overall process of building and maintaining profitable customer relationships by delivering superior customer value and satisfaction.

Customer relationship management (CRM) Managing detailed information about individual customers and carefully managing customer "touch points" in order to maximize customer loyalty.

Customer (or market) sales force structure A sales force organization under which salespeople specialize in selling only to certain customers or industries.

Customer satisfaction The extent to which a product's perceived performance matches a buyer's expectations.

Customer value-based pricing Setting price based on buyers' perceptions of value rather than on the seller's cost.

Customer-centered new-product development New-product development that focuses on finding new ways to solve customer problems and create more customer-satisfying experiences.

Customer-managed relationships Marketing relationships in which customers, empowered by today's new digital technologies, interact with companies and with each other to shape their relationships with brands.

Customer-perceived value The customer's evaluation of the difference between all the benefits and all the costs of a marketing offer relative to those of competing offers.

Customer-value marketing A principle of sustainable marketing that holds that a company should put most of its resources into customer-value-building marketing investments.

Decline stage The product life-cycle stage in which a product's sales decline.

Deficient products Products that have neither immediate appeal nor long-run benefits.

Demand curve A curve that shows the number of units the market will buy in a given time period, at different prices that might be charged.

Demands Human wants that are backed by buying power.

Demographic segmentation Dividing the market into segments based on variables such as age, gender, family size, family life cycle, income, occupation, education, religion, race, generation, and nationality.

Demography The study of human populations in terms of size, density, location, age, gender, race, occupation, and other statistics.

Department store A retail organization that carries a wide variety of product lines—each line is operated as a separate department managed by specialist buyers or merchandisers.

Derived demand Business demand that ultimately comes from (derives from) the demand for consumer goods.

Descriptive research Marketing research to better describe marketing problems, situations, or markets, such as the market potential for a product or the demographics and attitudes of consumers.

Desirable products Products that give both high immediate satisfaction and high long-run benefits.

Differentiated (segmented) marketing A market-coverage strategy in which a firm decides to target several market segments and designs separate offers for each.

Differentiation Actually differentiating the market offering to create superior customer value.

Direct investment Entering a foreign market by developing foreign-based assembly or manufacturing facilities.

Direct marketing Connecting directly with carefully targeted individual consumers to both obtain an immediate response and cultivate lasting customer relationships.

Direct marketing channel A marketing channel that has no intermediary levels.

Direct-mail marketing Direct marketing by sending an offer, announcement, reminder, or other item to a person at a particular physical or virtual address.

Direct-response television marketing Direct marketing via television, including direct-response television advertising (or infomercials) and home shopping channels.

Discount A straight reduction in price on purchases during a stated period of time or of larger quantities.

Discount store A retail operation that sells standard merchandise at lower prices by accepting lower margins and selling at higher volume.

Disintermediation The cutting out of marketing channel intermediaries by product or service producers, or the displacement of traditional resellers by radical new types of intermediaries.

Distribution center A large, highly automated warehouse designed to receive goods from various plants and suppliers, take orders, fill them efficiently, and deliver goods to customers as quickly as possible.

Diversification A strategy for company growth through starting up or acquiring businesses outside the company's current products and markets.

Downsizing Reducing the business portfolio by eliminating products or business units that are not profitable or that no longer fit the company's overall strategy.

Dynamic pricing Adjusting prices continually to meet the characteristics and needs of individual customers and situations.

E-procurement Purchasing through electronic connections between buyers and sellers—usually online.

Economic community A group of nations organized to work toward common goals in the regulation of international trade.

Economic environment Factors that affect consumer buying power and spending patterns.

Engel's laws Differences noted more than a century ago by Ernst Engel in how people shift their spending across food, housing, transportation, health care, and other goods and services categories as family income rises.

Environmental sustainability A management approach that involves developing strategies that both sustain the environment and produce profits for the company.

Environmental sustainability Developing strategies and practices that create a world economy that the planet can support indefinitely.

Environmentalism An organized movement of concerned citizens and government agencies to protect and improve people's current and future living environment.

Ethnographic research A form of observational research that involves sending trained observers to watch and interact with consumers in their "natural habitat."

Event marketing Creating a brand-marketing event or serving as a sole or participating sponsor of events created by others.

Exchange The act of obtaining a desired object from someone by offering something in return.

Exclusive distribution Giving a limited number of dealers the exclusive right to distribute the company's products in their territories.

Execution style The approach, style, tone, words, and format used for executing an advertising message.

Executive summary This section summarizes the main goals, recommendations, and points as an overview for senior managers who will read and approve the marketing plan. Generally a table of contents follows this section for management convenience.

Experimental research Gathering primary data by selecting matched groups of subjects, giving them different treatments, controlling related factors, and checking for differences in group responses.

Exploratory research Marketing research to gather preliminary information that will help define problems and suggest hypotheses.

Exporting Entering a foreign market by selling goods produced in the company's home country, often with little modification.

Factory outlet An off-price retailing operation that is owned and operated by a manufacturer and that normally carries the manufacturer's surplus, discontinued, or irregular goods.

Fad A temporary period of unusually high sales driven by consumer enthusiasm and immediate product or brand popularity.

Fashion A currently accepted or popular style in a given field.

Fixed costs Costs that do not vary with production or sales level.

Focus group interviewing Personal interviewing that involves inviting six to ten people to gather for a few hours with a trained interviewer to talk about a product, service, or organization. The interviewer "focuses" the group discussion on important issues.

Follow-up The last step in the selling process in which the salesperson follows up after the sale to ensure customer satisfaction and repeat business.

Franchise A contractual association between a manufacturer, wholesaler, or service organization (a franchisor) and independent businesspeople (franchisees) who buy the right to own and operate one or more units in the franchise system.

Franchise organization A contractual vertical marketing system in which a channel member, called a franchisor, links several stages in the production-distribution process.

Gender segmentation Dividing a market into different segments based on gender.

Generation X The 45 million people born between 1965 and 1976 in the "birth dearth" following the baby boom.

Geographic segmentation Dividing a market into different geographical units such as nations, states, regions, counties, cities, or neighborhoods.

Global firm A firm that, by operating in more than one country, gains R&D, production, marketing, and financial advantages in its costs and reputation that are not available to purely domestic competitors.

Good-value pricing Offering just the right combination of quality and good service at a fair price.

Gross margin percentage The percentage of net sales remaining after cost of goods sold—calculated by dividing gross margin by net sales.

Group Two or more people who interact to accomplish individual or mutual goals.

Growth stage The product life-cycle stage in which a product's sales start climbing quickly.

Growth-share matrix A portfolio-planning method that evaluates a company's strategic business units (SBUs) in terms of its market growth rate and relative market share. SBUs are classified as stars, cash cows, question marks, or dogs.

Handling objections The step in the selling process in which the salesperson seeks out, clarifies, and overcomes customer objections to buying.

Horizontal marketing system A channel arrangement in which two or more companies at one level join together to follow a new marketing opportunity.

Idea generation The systematic search for new-product ideas.

Idea screening Screening new-product ideas in order to spot good ideas and drop poor ones as soon as possible.

Income segmentation Dividing a market into different income segments.

Independent off-price retailer An off-price retailer that is either independently owned and run or is a division of a larger retail corporation.

Indirect marketing channel Channel containing one or more intermediary levels.

Individual marketing Tailoring products and marketing programs to the needs and preferences of individual customers—also labeled "one-to-one marketing," "customized marketing," and "markets-of-one marketing."

Industrial product A product bought by individuals and organizations for further processing or for use in conducting a business.

Innovative marketing A principle of sustainable marketing that requires that a company seek real product and marketing improvements.

Inside sales force Inside salespeople who conduct business from their offices via telephone, the Internet, or visits from prospective buyers.

Integrated logistics management The logistics concept that emphasizes teamwork, both inside the company and among all the marketing channel organizations, to maximize the performance of the entire distribution system.

Integrated marketing communications (IMC) Carefully integrating and coordinating the company's many communications channels to deliver a clear, consistent, and compelling message about the organization and its products.

Intensive distribution Stocking the product in as many outlets as possible.

Interactive marketing Training service employees in the fine art of interacting with customers to satisfy their needs.

Intermarket segmentation Forming segments of consumers who have similar needs and buying behavior even though they are located in different countries.

Intermodal transportation Combining two or more modes of transportation.

Internal databases Electronic collections of consumer and market information obtained from data sources within the company network.

Internal marketing Orienting and motivating customer-contact employees and supporting service people to work as a team to provide customer satisfaction.

Internet A vast public web of computer networks that connects users of all types all around the world to each other and to an amazingly large "information repository."

Introduction stage The product life-cycle stage in which the new product is first distributed and made available for purchase.

Inventory turnover rate (or stockturn rate) The number of times an inventory turns over or is sold during a specified time period (often one year)—calculated based on costs, selling price, or units.

Joint ownership A joint venture in which a company joins investors in a foreign market to create a local business in which the company shares joint ownership and control.

Joint venturing Entering foreign markets by joining with foreign companies to produce or market a product or service.

Learning Changes in an individual's behavior arising from experience.

Licensing A method of entering a foreign market in which the company enters into an agreement with a licensee in the foreign market.

Lifestyle A person's pattern of living as expressed in his or her activities, interests, and opinions.

Line extension Extending an existing brand name to new forms, colors, sizes, ingredients, or flavors of an existing product category.

Local marketing Tailoring brands and promotions to the needs and wants of local customer segments—cities, neighborhoods, and even specific stores.

Macroenvironment The larger societal forces that affect the microenvironment—demographic, economic, natural, technological, political, and cultural forces.

Madison & Vine A term that has come to represent the merging of advertising and entertainment in an effort to break through the clutter and create new avenues for reaching consumers with more engaging messages.

Management contracting A joint venture in which the domestic firm supplies the management know-how to a foreign company that supplies the capital; the domestic firm exports management services rather than products.

Manufacturers' sales branches and offices Wholesaling by sellers or buyers themselves rather than through independent wholesalers.

Market The set of all actual and potential buyers of a product or service.

Market description Describing the targeted segments in detail provides context for the marketing strategies and detailed action programs discussed later in the plan.

Market development A strategy for company growth by identifying and developing new market segments for current company products.

Market offerings Some combination of products, services, information, or experiences offered to a market to satisfy a need or want.

Market penetration A strategy for company growth by increasing sales of current products to current market segments without changing the product.

Market potential The upper limit of market demand.

Market segment A group of consumers who respond in a similar way to a given set of marketing efforts.

Market segmentation Dividing a market into distinct groups of buyers who have different needs, characteristics, or behaviors, and who might require separate products or marketing programs.

Market share Company sales divided by market sales.

Market targeting (targeting) The process of evaluating each market segment's attractiveness and selecting one or more segments to enter.

Market-penetration pricing Setting a low price for a new product in order to attract a large number of buyers and a large market share.

Market-skimming pricing Setting a high price for a new product to skim maximum revenues layer by layer from the segments willing to pay the high price; the company makes fewer but more profitable sales.

Marketing The process by which companies create value for customers and build strong customer relationships in order to capture value from customers in return.

Marketing channel (or distribution channel) A set of interdependent organizations that help make a product or service available for use or consumption by the consumer or business user.

Marketing channel design Designing effective marketing channels by analyzing consumer needs, setting channel objectives, identifying major channel alternatives, and evaluating them.

Marketing channel management Selecting, managing, and motivating individual channel members and evaluating their performance over time.

Marketing concept The marketing management philosophy that holds that achieving organizational goals depends on knowing the needs and wants of target markets and delivering the desired satisfactions better than competitors do.

Marketing control The process of measuring and evaluating the results of marketing strategies and plans and taking corrective action to ensure that objectives are achieved.

Marketing environment The actors and forces outside marketing that affect marketing management's ability to build and maintain successful relationships with target customers.

Marketing implementation The process that turns marketing strategies and plans into marketing actions in order to accomplish strategic marketing objectives.

Marketing information system (MIS) People and procedures for assessing information needs, developing the needed information, and helping decision makers to use the information to generate and validate actionable customer and market insights.

Marketing intermediaries Firms that help the company to promote, sell, and distribute its goods to final buyers.

Marketing logistics (or physical distribution) Planning, implementing, and controlling the physical flow of materials, final goods, and related information from points of origin to points of consumption to meet customer requirements at a profit.

Marketing management The art and science of choosing target markets and building profitable relationships with them.

Marketing mix The set of controllable tactical marketing tools—product, price, place, and promotion—that the firm blends to produce the response it wants in the target market.

Marketing myopia The mistake of paying more attention to the specific products a company offers than to the benefits and experiences produced by these products.

Marketing organization The marketing department may be organized by function, as in this sample, by geography, by product, or by customer (or some combination).

Marketing research The systematic design, collection, analysis, and reporting of data relevant to a specific marketing situation facing an organization.

Marketing return on investment (or marketing ROI) A measure of the marketing productivity of a marketing investment—calculated by dividing net marketing contribution by marketing expenses.

Marketing return on sales (or marketing ROS) The percent of net sales attributable to the net marketing contribution—calculated by dividing net marketing contribution by net sales.

Marketing strategy The marketing logic by which the company hopes to create customer value and achieve profitable customer relationships.

Marketing strategy development Designing an initial marketing strategy for a new product based on the product concept.

Marketing tools These sections summarize the broad logic that will guide decisions made about the marketing tools to be used during the period covered by the plan.

Marketing Web site A Web site that engages consumers in interactions that will move them closer to a direct purchase or other marketing outcome.

Markup The difference between a company's selling price for a product and its cost to manufacture or purchase it.

Markup chain The sequence of markups used by firms at each level in a channel.

Maturity stage The product life-cycle stage in which sales growth slows or levels off.

Merchant wholesaler An independently owned wholesaler business that takes title to the merchandise it handles.

Microenvironment The actors close to the company that affect its ability to serve its customers—the company, suppliers, marketing intermediaries, customer markets, competitors, and publics.

Micromarketing The practice of tailoring products and marketing programs to the needs and wants of specific individuals and local customer segments—includes local marketing and individual marketing.

Millennials (or Generation Y) The 83 million children of the baby boomers, born between 1977 and 2000.

Mission statement A statement of the organization's purpose—what it wants to accomplish in the larger environment.

Modified rebuy A business buying situation in which the buyer wants to modify product specifications, prices, terms, or suppliers.

Motive (drive) A need that is sufficiently pressing to direct the person to seek satisfaction of the need.

Multichannel distribution system A distribution system in which a single firm sets up two or more marketing channels to reach one or more customer segments.

Natural environment Natural resources that are needed as inputs by marketers or that are affected by marketing activities.

Needs States of felt deprivation.

Net marketing contribution (NMC) A measure of marketing profitability that includes only components of profitability controlled by marketing.

Net profit percentage The percentage of each sales dollar going to profit—calculated by dividing net profits by net sales.

New product A good, service, or idea that is perceived by some potential customers as new.

New task A business buying situation in which the buyer purchases a product or service for the first time.

New-product development The development of original products, product improvements, product modifications, and new brands through the firm's own product-development efforts.

Objective-and-task method Developing the promotion budget by (1) defining specific objectives, (2) determining the tasks that must be performed to achieve these objectives, and (3) estimating the costs of performing these tasks. The sum of these costs is the proposed promotion budget.

Objectives and issues The company's objectives should be defined in specific terms so management can measure progress and plan corrective action if needed to stay on track. This section describes any major issues that might affect the company's marketing strategy and implementation.

Observational research Gathering primary data by observing relevant people, actions, and situations.

Occasion segmentation Dividing the market into segments according to occasions when buyers get the idea to buy, actually make their purchase, or use the purchased item.

Off-price retailer A retailer that buys at less-than-regular wholesale prices and sells at less than retail. Examples are factory outlets, independents, and warehouse clubs.

Online advertising Advertising that appears while consumers are surfing the Web, including display ads, search-related ads, online classifieds, and other forms.

Online focus groups Gathering a small group of people online with a trained moderator to chat about a product, service, or organization and gain qualitative insights about consumer attitudes and behavior.

Online marketing Company efforts to market products and services and build customer relationships over the Internet.

Online marketing research Collecting primary data online through Internet surveys, online focus groups, Web-based experiments, or tracking consumers' online behavior.

Online social networks Online social communities—blogs, social networking Web sites, or even virtual worlds—where people socialize or exchange information and opinions.

Operating expense percentage The portion of net sales going to operating expenses—calculated by dividing total expenses by net sales.

Operating ratios The ratios of selected operating statement items to net sales.

Opinion leader Person within a reference group who, because of special skills, knowledge, personality, or other characteristics, exerts social influence on others.

Opportunities Opportunities are external elements that the company may be able to exploit to its advantage.

Optional-product pricing The pricing of optional or accessory products along with a main product.

Outside sales force (or field sales force) Outside salespeople who travel to call on customers in the field.

Packaging The activities of designing and producing the container or wrapper for a product.

Partner relationship management Working closely with partners in other company departments and outside the company to jointly bring greater value to customers.

Percentage-of-sales method Setting the promotion budget at a certain percentage of current or forecasted sales or as a percentage of the unit sales price.

Perception The process by which people select, organize, and interpret information to form a meaningful picture of the world.

Personal selling Personal presentation by the firm's sales force for the purpose of making sales and building customer relationships.

Personality The unique psychological characteristics that distinguish a person or group.

Pleasing products Products that give high immediate satisfaction but may hurt consumers in the long run.

Political environment Laws, government agencies, and pressure groups that influence and limit various organizations and individuals in a given society.

Portfolio analysis The process by which management evaluates the products and businesses that make up the company.

Positioning Arranging for a market offering to occupy a clear, distinctive, and desirable place relative to competing products in the minds of target consumers.

Positioning statement A statement that summarizes company or brand positioning—it takes this form: To (target segment and need) our (brand) is (concept) that (point-of-difference).

Preapproach The step in the selling process in which the salesperson learns as much as possible about a prospective customer before making a sales call.

Presentation The step in the selling process in which the salesperson tells the "value story" to the buyer, showing how the company's offer solves the customer's problems.

Price The amount of money charged for a product or service, or the sum of the values that customers exchange for the benefits of having or using the product or service.

Price elasticity A measure of the sensitivity of demand to changes in price.

Primary data Information collected for the specific purpose at hand.

Pro forma (or projected) profit-and-loss statement (or income statement or operating statement) A statement that shows projected revenues less budgeted expenses and estimates the projected net profit for an organization, product, or brand during a specific planning period, typically a year.

Product Anything that can be offered to a market for attention, acquisition, use, or consumption that might satisfy a want or need.

Product adaptation Adapting a product to meet local conditions or wants in foreign markets.

Product bundle pricing Combining several products and offering the bundle at a reduced price.

Product concept A detailed version of the new-product idea stated in meaningful consumer terms.

Product concept The idea that consumers will favor products that offer the most quality, performance, and features and that the organization should therefore devote its energy to making continuous product improvements.

Product development A strategy for company growth by offering modified or new products to current market segments.

Product development Developing the product concept into a physical product in order to ensure that the product idea can be turned into a workable market offering.

Product invention Creating new products or services for foreign markets.

Product life cycle The course of a product's sales and profits over its lifetime. It involves five distinct stages: product development, introduction, growth, maturity, and decline.

Product line A group of products that are closely related because they function in a similar manner, are sold to the same customer groups, are marketed through the same types of outlets, or fall within given price ranges.

Product line pricing Setting the price steps between various products in a product line based on cost differences between the products, customer evaluations of different features, and competitors' prices.

Product mix (or product portfolio) The set of all product lines and items that a particular seller offers for sale.

Product position The way the product is defined by consumers on important attributes—the place the product occupies in consumers' minds relative to competing products.

Product quality The characteristics of a product or service that bear on its ability to satisfy stated or implied customer needs.

Product review The product review summarizes the main features for all of the company's products, organized by product line, type of customer, market, or order of product introduction.

Product sales force structure A sales force organization under which salespeople specialize in selling only a portion of the company's products or lines.

Product/market expansion grid A portfolio-planning tool for identifying company growth opportunities through market penetration, market development, product development, or diversification.

Production concept The idea that consumers will favor products that are available and highly affordable and that the organization should therefore focus on improving production and distribution efficiency.

Profit-and-loss statement (or income statement or operating statement) A statement that shows actual revenues less expenses and net profit for an organization, product, or brand during a specific planning period, typically a year.

Promotion mix (or marketing communications mix) The specific blend of promotion tools that the company uses to persuasively communicate customer value and build customer relationships.

Promotional pricing Temporarily pricing products below the list price, and sometimes even below cost, to increase short-run sales.

Prospecting The step in the selling process in which the salesperson or company identifies qualified potential customers.

Psychographic segmentation Dividing a market into different segments based on social class, lifestyle, or personality characteristics.

Psychological pricing Pricing that considers the psychology of prices and not simply the economics; the price is used to say something about the product.

Public Any group that has an actual or potential interest in or impact on an organization's ability to achieve its objectives.

Public relations (PR) Building good relations with the company's various publics by obtaining favorable publicity, building up a good corporate image, and handling or heading off unfavorable rumors, stories, and events.

Pull strategy A promotion strategy that calls for spending a lot on advertising and consumer promotion to induce final consumers to buy the product, creating a demand vacuum that "pulls" the product through the channel.

Push strategy A promotion strategy that calls for using the sales force and trade promotion to push the product through channels. The producer promotes the product to channel members who in turn promote it to final consumers.

Reference prices Prices that buyers carry in their minds and refer to when they look at a given product.

Relevant costs Costs that will occur in the future and that will vary across the alternatives being considered.

Retailer A business whose sales come primarily from retailing.

Retailing All activities involved in selling goods or services directly to final consumers for their personal, nonbusiness use.

Return on advertising investment The net return on advertising investment divided by the costs of the advertising investment.

Return on investment (ROI) A measure of managerial effectiveness and efficiency—net profit before taxes divided by total investment.

Return on investment (ROI) pricing (or target-return pricing) A cost-based pricing method that determines price based on a specified rate of return on investment.

Return on marketing investment (or marketing ROI) The net return from a marketing investment divided by the costs of the marketing investment.

Sales 2.0 The merging of innovative sales practices with Internet 2.0 technologies to improve sales force effectiveness and efficiency.

Sales force management The analysis, planning, implementation, and control of sales force activities. It includes designing sales force strategy and structure and recruiting, selecting, training, supervising, compensating, and evaluating the firm's salespeople.

Sales promotion Short-term incentives to encourage the purchase or sale of a product or service.

Sales quota A standard that states the amount a salesperson should sell and how sales should be divided among the company's products.

Salesperson An individual representing a company to customers by performing one or more of the following activities: prospecting, communicating, selling, servicing, information gathering, and relationship building.

Salutary products Products that have low appeal but may benefit consumers in the long run.

Sample A segment of the population selected for marketing research to represent the population as a whole.

Secondary data Information that already exists somewhere, having been collected for another purpose.

Segmented pricing Selling a product or service at two or more prices, where the difference in prices is not based on differences in costs.

Selective distribution The use of more than one, but fewer than all, of the intermediaries who are willing to carry the company's products.

Selling concept The idea that consumers will not buy enough of the firm's products unless it undertakes a large-scale selling and promotion effort.

Selling process The steps that salespeople follow when selling, which include prospecting and qualifying, preapproach, approach, presentation and demonstration, handling objections, closing, and follow-up.

Sense-of-mission marketing A principle of sustainable marketing that holds that a company should define its mission in broad social terms rather than narrow product terms.

Service An activity, benefit, or satisfaction offered for sale that is essentially intangible and does not result in the ownership of anything.

Service inseparability A major characteristic of services—they are produced and consumed at the same time and cannot be separated from their providers.

Service intangibility A major characteristic of services—they cannot be seen, tasted, felt, heard, or smelled before they are bought.

Service perishability A major characteristic of services—they cannot be stored for later sale or use.

Service retailer A retailer whose product line is actually a service, including hotels, airlines, banks, colleges, and many others.

Service variability A major characteristic of services—their quality may vary greatly, depending on who provides them and when, where, and how.

Service-profit chain The chain that links service firm profits with employee and customer satisfaction.

Share of customer The portion of the customer's purchasing that a company gets in its product categories.

Shopping center A group of retail businesses built on a site that is planned, developed, owned, and managed as a unit.

Shopping product A consumer product that the customer, in the process of selection and purchase, usually compares on such bases as suitability, quality, price, and style.

Social class Relatively permanent and ordered divisions in a society whose members share similar values, interests, and behaviors.

Social marketing The use of commercial marketing concepts and tools in programs designed to influence individuals' behavior to improve their well-being and that of society.

Societal marketing A principle of sustainable marketing that holds that a company should make marketing decisions by considering consumers' wants, the company's requirements, consumers' long-run interests, and society's long-run interests.

Societal marketing concept The idea that a company's marketing decisions should consider consumers' wants, the company's requirements, consumers' long-run interests, and society's long-run interests.

Spam Unsolicited, unwanted commercial e-mail messages.

Specialty product A consumer product with unique characteristics or brand identification for which a significant group of buyers is willing to make a special purchase effort.

Specialty store A retail store that carries a narrow product line with a deep assortment within that line.

Standardized global marketing An international marketing strategy for using basically the same marketing strategy and mix in all the company's international markets.

Store brand (or private brand) A brand created and owned by a reseller of a product or service.

Straight product extension Marketing a product in a foreign market without any change.

Straight rebuy A business buying situation in which the buyer routinely reorders something without any modifications.

Strategic planning The process of developing and maintaining a strategic fit between the organization's goals and capabilities and its changing marketing opportunities.

Strengths Strengths are internal capabilities that can help the company reach its objectives.

Style A basic and distinctive mode of expression.

Subculture A group of people with shared value systems based on common life experiences and situations.

Supermarket A large, low-cost, low-margin, high-volume, self-service store that carries a wide variety of grocery and household products.

Superstore A store much larger than a regular supermarket that offers a large assortment of routinely purchased food products, nonfood items, and services.

Supplier development Systematic development of networks of supplier–partners to ensure an appropriate and dependable supply of products and materials for use in making products or reselling them to others

Supply chain management Managing upstream and downstream value-added flows of materials, final goods, and related information among suppliers, the company, resellers, and final consumers.

Survey research Gathering primary data by asking people questions about their knowledge, attitudes, preferences, and buying behavior.

Sustainable marketing Socially and environmentally responsible marketing that meets the present needs of consumers and businesses while also preserving or enhancing the ability of future generations to meet their needs.

SWOT analysis An overall evaluation of the company's strengths (S), weaknesses (W), opportunities (O), and threats (T).

Systems selling (or solutions selling) Buying a packaged solution to a problem from a single seller, thus avoiding all the separate decisions involved in a complex buying situation.

Target costing Pricing that starts with an ideal selling price, then targets costs that will ensure that the price is met.

Target market A set of buyers sharing common needs or characteristics that the company decides to serve.

Team selling Using teams of people from sales, marketing, engineering, finance, technical support, and even upper management to service large, complex accounts.

Team-based new-product development An approach to developing new products in which various company departments work closely together, overlapping the steps in the product development process to save time and increase effectiveness.

Technological environment Forces that create new technologies, creating new product and market opportunities.

Telephone marketing Using the telephone to sell directly to customers.

Territorial sales force structure A sales force organization that assigns each salesperson to an exclusive geographic territory in which that salesperson sells the company's full line.

Test marketing The stage of new-product development in which the product and marketing program are tested in realistic market settings.

Third-party logistics (3PL) provider An independent logistics provider that performs any or all of the functions required to get its client's product to market.

Threats Threats are current or emerging external elements that could potentially challenge the company's performance.

Total costs The sum of the fixed and variable costs for any given level of production.

Total market demand The total volume that would be bought by a defined consumer group in a defined geographic area in a defined time period in a defined marketing environment under a defined level and mix of industry marketing effort.

Trade promotions Sales promotion tools used to persuade resellers to carry a brand, give it shelf space, promote it in advertising, and push it to consumers.

Undifferentiated (mass) marketing A market-coverage strategy in which a firm decides to ignore market segment differences and go after the whole market with one offer.

Unit contribution The amount that each unit contributes to covering fixed costs—the difference between price and variable costs.

Unsought product A consumer product that the consumer either does not know about or knows about but does not normally think of buying.

Value analysis Carefully analyzing a product's or service's components to determine if they can be redesigned and made more effectively and efficiently to provide greater value.

Value chain The series of internal departments that carry out value-creating activities to design, produce, market, deliver, and support a firm's products.

Value delivery network The network made up of the company, suppliers, distributors, and ultimately customers who "partner" with each other to improve the performance of the entire system in delivering customer value.

Value proposition The full positioning of a brand—the full mix of benefits upon which it is positioned.

Value-added pricing Attaching value-added features and services to differentiate a company's offers and charging higher prices.

Value-based pricing Offering just the right combination of quality and good service at a fair price.

Variable costs Costs that vary directly with the level of production.

Vertical marketing system (VMS) A distribution channel structure in which producers, wholesalers, and retailers act as a unified system. One channel member owns the others, has contracts with them, or has so much power that they all cooperate.

Viral marketing The Internet version of word-of-mouth marketing—Web sites, videos, e-mail messages, or other marketing events that are so infectious that customers will want to pass them along to friends.

Wants The form human needs take as shaped by culture and individual personality.

Warehouse club An off-price retailer that sells a limited selection of brand name grocery items, appliances, clothing, and a hodgepodge of other goods at deep discounts to members who pay annual membership fees.

Weaknesses Weaknesses are internal elements that may interfere with the company's ability to achieve its objectives.

Wheel-of-retailing concept A concept that states that new types of retailers usually begin as low-margin, low-price, low-status operations but later evolve into higher-priced, higher-service operations, eventually becoming like the conventional retailers they replaced.

Whole-channel view Designing international channels that take into account the entire global supply chain and marketing channel, forging an effective global value delivery network.

Wholesaler A firm engaged primarily in wholesaling activities.

Wholesaling All activities involved in selling goods and services to those buying for resale or business use.

Workload method An approach to determining sales force size based on the workload required and the time available for selling.

Credits

Chapter 1

31 © 2009 Zappos.com, Inc. **32** © 2009 Zappos.com, Inc. **35** Ad used with the permission of the UNCF. **37** Courtesy of Daimler. **39** Getty Images, Inc. **40** Courtesy of Johnson & Johnson. Reprinted with permission. **42** Courtesy of General Electric Company. **43** Courtesy of myRoomBud. Used with permission. **45** © Jeff Greenberg/Alamy. **45** Clemson/Flickr.com. **46** Photo: © 2009 Zappos.com, Inc.; Screen: Courtesy of Twitter. **47** © AJ Mast/The New York Times/Redux. **49** Courtesy of Stew Leonard's. Reprinted with permission. **50** Courtesy of Corbis. **52** AP Wide World. **53** © Uniqlo UK Ltd. **55** Getty Images. **56** Richard Jones/Sinopix Photo Agency Limited. **57** Courtesy of the ASPCA, Sarah McLauchlan, and Eagle-Com.

Chapter 2

65 © Lou-Foto/Alamy. **66** © artpartner-images.com/Alamy. **67** Courtesy of Kahala Corp. All rights reserved. **69** AP Wide World. **70** Courtesy of Kohler Co. **72** © Beth A. Keiser/Corbis. **73** © 2008 UNDER ARMOUR INC. **75** Gary Armstrong. **76** Courtesy of Alamy. **79** © 2009 Logitech. All rights reserved. Image used with permission from Logitech. **80** The BURGER KING® trademarks and advertisements are used with permission from Burger King Corporation. **86** Courtesy of Getty. **87** © 2009 MarketingNPV LLC. All rights reserved. Used with permission.

Chapter 3

93 © 2009 Xerox Corporation. All rights reserved. **94** © 2009 Xerox Corporation. All rights reserved. **96** Copyright © 2009 Toyota Motor Engineering & Manufacturing North America, Inc. **97** Courtesy of the Avon Foundation. **99** Mark Ralston Getty Images, Inc. **101** © 2009 Charles Schwab & Co., Inc. All rights reserved. Reprinted with permission. **102** Amanda Kamen. **103** © 2009 Cisco Systems, Inc. **105** Copyright © 2009 Disaboom, Inc. All rights reserved. Reprinted with permission. **107** © Desmond Boylan/Reuters. **109** Courtesy of Frito-Lay, Inc. **110** AP Wide World. **114** © AFP/Getty Images. **116** Courtesy of the Procter & Gamble Company; photo: Digital Vision/Plush Studios. **117** Courtesy of Kenneth Cole. **118** Courtesy of Getty. **119** © 2009 Earthbound Farm. All rights reserved. Used with permission. **121** Courtesy of Michael Whitford. Used with permission.

Chapter 4

127 © Protrac. **128** © Arkady Chubykin-Fotolia.com. **129** AP Wide World. **132** Courtesy of Barney's New York, Inc. **133** Courtesy of Radian6 Technologies Inc. **135** Courtesy of Red Bull North America. **136** Courtesy of Experian Consumer Research. **137** Courtesy of Ken Banks of kiwanja.net. **141** Thinkstock/ Corbis RF. **142** Courtesy of Zoomerang, a MarketTools Company. **144** © 2009 Channel M2, LLC. All rights reserved. Used with permission. **145** © Lauren Burkes/Taxi/Getty Images. **150** Courtesy of The Kroger Co., Elizabeth Johnson Knight, and Keri Miksza. **152** Copyright © 2009 Bibbentuckers. All rights reserved. Reprinted with permission. **153** Copyright © 2009 The Nielsen Company. All rights reserved. Reprinted with permission. **155** Courtesy of Getty Images. **156** Courtesy of the Marketing Research Association.

Chapter 5

163 Getty Images, Inc. **164** Reprinted courtesy of Doug Hardman, www.hardman.org. **167** Copyright © 2008 Lexus. All rights reserved. Used with permission. **167** Product photographer: Olof Wahlund. Beauty photographer: Patrick Demarchelier. Copyright © 2009 The Procter & Gamble Company. All rights reserved. Reprinted with permission. **168** © 2008, Nationwide Mutual Insurance Company. **171** © Alex Segre/Alamy. **170** Copyright © 2008 The Procter & Gamble Company. All rights reserved. Reprinted with permission. Photograph © Kevin Dodge/Corbis. **172** Courtesy of Blendtec. **173** (top) © Randy Faris/CORBIS; (bottom) Jochen Sand/Digital Vision/Getty Images. **174** Courtesy of Acxiom Corporation. **175** Courtesy of Merrell. **176** © Kevin Dodge/Comet/CORBIS. All rights reserved. **178** Courtesy of CORBIS. **179** Amanda Kamen. **180** Courtesy of Campbell Soup Company. **183** Courtesy of Hyundai Motor America. **187** © Celia Peterson/www.photolibrary.com. **185** Courtesy of Intel Corporation. **190** Courtesy of Cardinal Health, Medical Products & Services. **191** © 2009 Peterbilt Motors Company. All rights reserved. Used with permission. **192** Copyright © 2007 Sharp Electronics Company. All rights reserved. Reprinted with permission. Photographer: Carl Zapp. **194** Courtesy of Cisco Systems Inc.

Chapter 6

201 © AirArabia. **202** © PictureArt - Fotolia.com. **205** Courtesy of Zipcar, Inc. **206** Courtesy of The Benjamin Hotel. **207** PEEPS® and the PEEPS® chick shape are registered trademarks and Always in Season™ is a trademark of Just Born, Inc., Bethlehem, PA. www.marshmallowpeeps.com. **208** © fotosearch/www.photolibrary.com. **210** © James Leynse/CORBIS. All Rights Reserved. **211** Courtesy of Claritas. **212** Hans- Jurgen Burkard. **213** Courtesy of Anything Left Handed. All rights reserved. **215** NAUTICA and the sailing symbol are registered trademarks of Nautica Apparel, Inc. All rights reserved. Reef is a registered trademark of South Cone. Riders and Lee are registered trademarks of The H.D. Lee Company, Inc. Wrangler and Rustler are registered trademarks of Wrangler Apparel Corp. Lucy is a registered trademark of lucy activewear inc. 7 For All Mankind is a registered trademark of Seven For All Mankind, LLC. All rights reserved. **216** Courtesy of Etsy, Inc. **217** Amanda Kamen. **218** Courtesy of TruMedia. **220** © Bebeto Matthews/AP Wide World. **222** Courtesy of Toyota Motor Sales. Photographer: Randy Olson. **223** © 2009 Staples Inc. All rights reserved. Used with permission. **226** © Raffles Hotels and Resorts. **224** Courtesy of S.C. Johnson & Son, Inc. **228** Courtesy of Getty. **229** ©2007 Kraft Foods Inc. All rights reserved. Used with permission.

Chapter 7

235 © Vismedia. **236** © Aviva, All rights reserved. **237** Rick Bowmer/AP Wide World Photos. **238** © Jim Craigmyle/CORBIS. All Rights Reserved. **240** Courtesy of Cargill, Inc. **243** © 2009 OXO International Inc. All rights reserved. Used with permission. **244** © 2009 Amazon, Inc. All rights reserved. **245** Courtesy of Pepsi-Cola North America, Inc. **246** Copyright © 2008 Toyota Motor Sales. All rights reserved. Used with permission. **248** © 2009 Sony Electronics Inc. All rights reserved. Used with permission. **250**

Chapter 15

Chapter 16

Indexes

Name, Company, Brand, and Organization

Subject Index